MURPHY ON EVIDENCE

ELEVENTH EDITION

His Honour Judge Peter Murphy

A Circuit Judge on the South-Eastern Circuit

OXFORD

UNIVERSITY PRESS

OXFORD
UNIVERSITY PRESS

Great Clarendon Street, Oxford OX2 6DP

Oxford University Press is a department of the University of Oxford.
It furthers the University's objective of excellence in research, scholarship,
and education by publishing worldwide in

Oxford New York

Auckland Cape Town Dar es Salaam Hong Kong Karachi
Kuala Lumpur Madrid Melbourne Mexico City Nairobi
New Delhi Shanghai Taipei Toronto

With offices in

Argentina Austria Brazil Chile Czech Republic France Greece
Guatemala Hungary Italy Japan Poland Portugal Singapore
South Korea Switzerland Thailand Turkey Ukraine Vietnam

Oxford is a registered trade mark of Oxford University Press
in the UK and in certain other countries

Published in the United States
by Oxford University Press Inc., New York

British Library Cataloguing in Publication Data

Data available

Library of Congress Cataloging in Publication Data

Data available

Typeset by Newgen Imaging Systems Pvt Ltd., Chennai, India
Printed in Great Britain
on acid-free paper by
Ashford Colour Press Ltd., Gosport, Hampshire

ISBN 978–0–19–956112–4

1 3 5 7 9 10 8 6 4 2

CONTENTS SUMMARY

CONTENTS

1 INTRODUCTION TO THE LAW OF EVIDENCE

2 THE LANGUAGE OF THE LAW OF EVIDENCE

5 CHARACTER EVIDENCE I: CHARACTER EVIDENCE GENERALLY; IN CIVIL CASES; EVIDENCE OF GOOD CHARACTER

7 THE RULE AGAINST HEARSAY I: SCOPE AND WORKING OF THE RULE

8 THE RULE AGAINST HEARSAY II: COMMON LAW AND STATUTORY EXCEPTIONS

9 THE RULE AGAINST HEARSAY III: ADMISSIONS AND CONFESSIONS

10 THE RULE AGAINST HEARSAY IV: THE ACCUSED'S DENIALS AND SILENCE

11 OPINION EVIDENCE

12 PREVIOUS JUDGMENTS AS EVIDENCE

PREFACE TO THE ELEVENTH EDITION

Those who have used this book over a period of time will notice a number of structural changes in this new edition. These changes have been based on a careful review of comments made by teachers and students over time and are designed to make the book as helpful as possible to teachers and students alike. They are:

1. For the first time an Online Resource Centre has been established under the supervision of Richard Glover LLB, MSc, Solicitor, and Senior Lecturer in Law at the University of Wolverhampton. Online Resource Centre will have a number of functions. First, important developments in the law during the lifetime of this edition will be noted and made available. Second, the case files in *R v Coke; Littleton* and *Blackstone v Coke*, the fictitious cases which have formed the basis of the teaching in this book have been removed from the book itself and placed in the Online Resource Centre, where it is hoped that they will eventually be supplemented by audio presentations of the 999 call and other materials. For further details, please see the Guide to the Online Resource Centre. At the same time, I have taken the opportunity to rewrite the cases to bring them fully up to date with contemporary practice, to make the issues they raise more precise, and to expand the materials to some extent.

2. Questions for discussion based on the two cases continue to be included at the end of each chapter. In addition, as a further option for teachers, Richard has provided questions of a more general nature to provoke discussion on wider or more academic issues for which reference to the cases may not be required.

3. Richard has also provided some recommended further reading for each chapter, which appears at the end of the chapter.

4. A summary of the main points dealt with in each chapter or part of a chapter has been included at the beginning of the chapter or part.

5. Important parts of the text, such as statutory provisions and significant passages from judgments, are highlighted for ease of access and to draw attention to them.

The introduction of these structural changes was undertaken at the same time as the more traditional task of bringing the book up to date. While there have been no seismic changes since publication of the 10th edition, there are rumblings which suggest the possibility of a coming earthquake. Predictably, evidence of bad character and hearsay have been in the forefront of this activity. The intriguing decision in *Campbell* [2007] 1 WLR 2798, whose true significance may not yet have been fully appreciated, may prove to have nullified the intention of Parliament that evidence of propensity to be untruthful should be generally admissible under gateway (d). The indication in the same case that a failure to follow the JSB specimen direction in relation to bad character may not in future be regarded as a ground of appeal, let alone a reason for allowing an appeal, leaves one wondering what the standards are in that respect.

But even these speculations appear minor when compared to developments in the field of hearsay. The recent decision of the European Court of Human Rights in *Al-Khajawa and Tahery* v *United Kingdom*, 20 January 2009, holding that the admission of hearsay evidence which is the sole or the decisive evidence against the accused violates his right to a fair trial under art. 6 of the Convention, suggests that a substantial number of recent cases in the field must be re-examined, starting with *Cole, Keet* [2008] 1 Cr App R 5, in which the sole or decisive nature of the evidence was held to be no bar in itself to admissibility. The decision by the European Courts of Human Rights comes at a time of intense activity in which we have seen unprecedented (though not unforeseen) use made of the 'interests of justice' rule under s. 114(1)(d) of the Criminal Justice Act 2003. The slippery slope in the field of hearsay generally began with the majority decision of the House of Lords in *Hayter* [2005] 1 WLR 605, a decision dealing with a confession by a co-accused, and criticized in the last edition of this work as effectively undermining the ancient and salutary rule that a confession should be evidence only against the person who makes it. The Court of Appeal has followed a similar and closely related path in such cases as *Y* [2008] 1 WLR 1683 and *L* [2008] 2 Cr App R 18 towards a general principle that any statement can be admitted in the interests of justice under s. 114(1)(d), which is on an equal footing with, and in no way subordinated to, the other three bases of admissibility. It is not to be viewed as a weapon of last resort. As a result, confessions by co-accused, by former co-accused, and by third parties, as well as witness statements, and indeed in theory statements of all kinds, can be admitted under s. 114(1)(d) as evidence in the case generally. The logical consequence of this may be to render s. 114(1)(a), (b), and (c) essentially otiose. The worst consequence, so far brushed aside by the Court, is the possible erosion of the protections afforded to the accused against the improper use of confessions by the simple procedural device of using s. 114(1)(d). It is said that the conditions of admissibility under s. 114(2) provide sufficient protection, but they are hardly apposite where confessions are involved. The trial judge's discretion may now be the last remaining protection available to the accused against the prejudicial admission of hearsay. These cases are discussed critically in this edition.

In the midst of all this excitement some quieter, albeit important developments in other areas have also been noted. Baroness Hale of Richmond may be entitled to claim credit as the judge who has at last clearly articulated a governing principle as to the standard of proof in family and matrimonial cases: see *Re B (Children) (Care Proceedings: Standard of Proof)* [2009] 1 AC 11. And in the continuing saga of *C plc v P* [2008] Ch 1, the Court of Appeal has moderated the reforming zeal of Evans-Lombe J in relation to the privilege against self-incrimination flowing from civil disclosure. An appeal to the House of Lords is awaited. These and many other developments have been noted in their proper places.

I owe a special debt of thanks to Richard Glover for his work in helping to change the face of the book. During the lifetime of this edition the book will have its 30th anniversary. My hope is that Richard will play an ever increasing role in future editions. My thanks to Tom Young at Oxford University Press for shepherding me skilfully through the structural changes, to my editor Dan Leissner; and to Gareth Malna, Joy Ruskin-Tompkins, and Nicholas Wehmeier at Oxford, all of whom have been as efficient as ever in bringing this new edition to life. Any errors that remain are mine alone.

Last but not least, I thank my wife Chris for her love and support through the process of working on this and several previous editions.

I have tried to state the law as at 10 February 2009.

Peter Murphy
London

EXTRACT FROM PREFACE TO THE FIRST EDITION

The law of evidence underlies the whole practice of law in every field capable of leading to litigation. Not only a thorough understanding of the rules of admissibility, but also a mature feel for the weight and tactical significance of evidence should be a part of the foundation of every practice. Cases are probably won and lost more often for reasons of evidential acumen, or the lack of it, than for reasons of any other sort. At the same time, evidential problems have a habit of arising, to quote a celebrated rule to be found in chapter 14 of this book, '*ex improviso*, which no human ingenuity could foresee'. Law and practice can almost always be made the subject of prior research; as often as not, evidence presents problems without warning calling for immediate reaction. Failure to object at the right time, or the making of an unfounded objection may in some cases have serious consequences for the fate of the piece of evidence concerned, or the case as a whole. One's opponent's objections, whether well or ill founded must be dealt with. A colleague at the Bar once said to the author that there was, in his opinion, only one rule of evidence, namely a reaction of instinct on hearing any words spoken in court, which said either, 'Yes, that's all right', or 'No, we can't have that'. That sort of instinct exists and very often works even before the witness speaks at all; it takes time to develop; time, and a thorough knowledge of the rules; but it is of incalculable importance.

Given all this, it is somewhat surprising to survey the textbooks on the subject and to find that they are prone to two distinct tendencies. There are those which treat the subject in a highly academic way, divorced from the realities of practice. There are those which treat the subject as a mass of apparently unrelated minutiae, divorced from any discernible theme. There is also, happily, the matchless but demanding work of Professor Cross, comparisons of which are vain. The present work is intended simply to meet the long-felt need of students for the Bar examinations, now joined by students for the Law Society's examinations, and those on degree courses, for a book soundly based around the considerations of practice in the courts. It is hoped that those concerned professionally with the law of evidence may also find it useful. There are, no doubt, many matters of great interest in academic terms which will not be found here; but equally, the important, recurring issues are dealt with in the context of their practical operation, and of the rules of practice which apply to them.

Islington
1 July 1980

GUIDE TO THE ONLINE RESOURCE CENTRE

For the first time an Online Resource Centre for *Murphy on Evidence* has been established under the supervision of Richard Glover LLB, MSc, Solicitor, and Senior Lecturer in Law at the University of Wolverhampton. The Online Resource Centre will have a number of functions.

Important developments in the law during the lifetime of this edition will be monitored as a supplement to the text. A helpful list of web links will also direct students immediately to useful sources of information.

The case files in *R v. Coke; Littleton* and *Blackstone v. Coke*, the fictitious cases which have formed the basis of the teaching in this book have been removed from the book itself and placed in the online resource centre, where they are supplemented by audio presentations of the 999 call.

This has enabled the materials to be expanded and updated, and makes them easy to access. The cases, while fictitious, are realistic and illustrate how the principles of the law of evidence are applied in practice. Students have the opportunity to study the rules of evidence in the context of issues which arise every day in both civil and criminal cases. At the same time, the questions for discussion at the end of each chapter provide both teachers and students with a way of testing understanding of the legal principles and exploring the issues in depth.

The Online Resource Centre is freely accessible to all and can be found at
www.oxfordtextbooks.co.uk/orc/murphy11e

TABLE OF CASES

TABLE OF STATUTES

*Page references in **bold** indicate that the text is reproduced in full.*

Articles of the European Convention on Human Rights are tabled under Sch 1 of the Human Rights Act 1998.

TABLE OF STATUTORY INSTRUMENTS

1

INTRODUCTION TO THE LAW OF EVIDENCE

SUMMARY OF MAIN POINTS

- The law of evidence is not the same as the science or philosophy of evidence.

- The characteristics of judicial trials demand a particular legal approach to the presentation and use of evidence.

- In most legal systems relevant evidence is admitted and weighed, and conclusions drawn from it; this is the only known method of scientifically reconstructing past events.

- Unlike other legal systems, the common law has developed a law of evidence, i.e. detailed exclusionary rules of evidence, whereby relevant evidence may be excluded for various reasons.

- Among the factors which influenced the development of these rules are the adversarial system of trial (including the use of juries); the accused's procedural disadvantages during the formative periods; and the common law's terror of perjury and fabrication.

- Today the law of evidence is significantly influenced by the fair trial and other provisions of the European Convention on Human Rights.

1.1 WHAT EVIDENCE IS

Most lawyers and students think of evidence as a collection of rules governing what facts may be proved in court, what materials may be placed before the court to prove those facts, and the form in which those materials should be placed before the court. What they have in mind is the law of evidence, but not evidence itself. One of the curiosities of the common law is the emergence of rules of evidence whose purpose is not to enable a party to bring before the court evidence which might help his case, but to prohibit a party from bringing some kinds of evidence if his opponent objects, or even if the court itself refuses to permit it. Because of the demands made by the realities of practice, it is only natural that familiarity with the rules should be emphasized. What is taught and examined in the field of evidence is the law of evidence. Yet there is a whole field of inquiry which relates to evidence itself, rather than the law of evidence. The field is a fascinating mixture of logic, epistemology, sociology, psychology, and the forensic sciences, and is, therefore, wide enough to encompass a vast library of its own. Its concern is the use of evidence as material in the reconstruction of past events.

It is a field which has attracted a distinguished, but relatively small number of investigators, at least as far as lawyers are concerned, and some of its main contributors have been philosophers and psychologists. Some of these contributors, for example, Jeremy Bentham, while deeply interested in the science of evidence, actually disapproved of the whole concept of a law of evidence. Bentham perceived rules of evidence to be nothing more than an artificial restriction on the science of evidence, invented by lawyers for less than honourable purposes.[1] John Henry Wigmore, the dean of American evidence writers, required his students to master the science of evidence before turning to the law (a luxury now foreclosed by the tyranny of practice-based syllabi and examinations) and developed a thorough, though cumbersome system for the methodical analysis of evidence to be presented in court.[2]

Evidence may be defined in general terms as any material which has the potential to change the state of a fact-finder's belief with respect to any factual proposition which is to be decided and which is in dispute. In more formal terms, Achinstein defines evidence as follows: evidence E is potential evidence on hypothesis H if and only if (1) E is true; (2) E does not make H necessary; (3) the probability of H on E is substantial; and (4) the probability of an explanatory connection between H and E is substantial.[3] Although, as we shall see, lawyers do not treat evidence in the courtroom with very much deference to the neat compartmentalization of Achinstein's definition—for example, the question of whether E is true is decided after rather than before E is legally accepted as evidence (see 2.8)—the definition does make clear the logical role of evidence in proving a hypothesis. It is, of course, a logical rather than a legal definition, appropriate to scientific inquiries of any kind. But lawyers have superimposed on it the particular requirements of their own interest in the uses of evidence.

1.2 THE NATURE OF THE JUDICIAL TRIAL

For legal purposes, the nature of evidence can best be understood by reference to the nature of the judicial trial. A trial is an inquiry into past events, the main purpose of which is to establish to an

---

[1] Namely increasing their potential for earning fees, and making it impossible for lay people to penetrate the complexities of the law. Bentham saw the attitudes of lawyers as the most dangerous obstacle to reform. His excoriation of the judiciary and the profession in his monumental treatise on evidence, *The Rationale of Judicial Evidence* (1827) was, however, weakened by its intemperance. There are rules of public policy which support some rules of evidence.

[2] *The Principles of Judicial Proof* (1913). Despite efforts to portray Wigmore's method as a viable practical tool on the part of Twining (*Theories of Evidence, Bentham and Wigmore* (1985), Twining and Anderson, *The Analysis of Evidence*), the pure Wigmorean method involves an unnecessary and impracticable expenditure of time from the point of view of the practitioner. However, it remains of value in showing scientifically how pieces of evidence relate to issues and each other in terms of relevance, and how their weight is affected by various factors. Many of the important primary and secondary sources dealing with the philosophical and scientific aspects of evidence and proof are collected in P. Murphy, *Evidence Proof and Facts: A Book of Sources* (2003).

[3] P. Achinstein, *The Nature of Explanation* (1983).

acceptable degree of probability those past events which it is claimed entitle the court to grant or deny some relief in accordance with law. From a scientific viewpoint, evidence may be defined as any material which would aid the court in establishing the probability of past events into which it must inquire.[4] Historians, journalists, and others also seek to establish the probability of past events, but their inquiries are carried out under quite different circumstances from those under which a court works. The principal characteristics of a judicial trial, which distinguish that process from historical and other inquiries, are as follows:

(a) The parties define for the court what the issues to be inquired into are. Legal proceedings are commenced by a party. The court has no power to bring matters before itself, and must wait to be seised of a case by a party. The parties then further define the issues which the court is to resolve, and once the issues are defined, both the court and the parties must confine their investigation to them.[5] Procedurally, the issues are reflected in the statements of case or indictment. They are narrow and precisely defined, and may exclude much material which a historian would feel bound to consider in exploring the entire history of an event.

(b) Legal disputes must be resolved within a reasonable time and at reasonable expense. The outcome of a judicial trial determines the rights and obligations of the parties, and may result in loss of life or liberty, loss of financial resources, of parental rights over children, or of reputation. There is no possibility of a detached, academic inquiry. Time limits are an integral part of the trial process, and the parties' preparation of the case must be accomplished within the time limits established.

(c) Trials are not objective inquiries into past events, but adversarial contests, in which parties, who have a vital interest in the outcome, not only decide what evidence they wish to present and prevent from being presented, but also present the evidence in as persuasive a manner as possible, a manner calculated to win them the sympathy and support of the court. Each party also seeks to persuade the court, by means of partisan, persuasive argument, to interpret the evidence in a light favourable to his case.

(d) A judicial trial is not a search to ascertain the ultimate truth of the past events inquired into, but to establish that a version of what occurred has an acceptable probability of being correct.[6] It is in the nature of human experience that it is impossible to ascertain the truth of past events with absolute certainty. Nonetheless, a historian or a journalist is entitled to set his own standard of probability which may correspond to truth as closely as he wishes. A court accepts predetermined standards of probability, which depend not on the facts of the individual case, but on the type of case under consideration. The highest standard of proof demanded by a common law court in any circumstances is proof beyond reasonable doubt. This is a high standard (see 4.12) but falls well short of absolute certainty. This standard is demanded only of the prosecution on the issue of guilt in a criminal case; in all other cases, the standard is that of the balance of probability, i.e., that the event is more likely than not

---

[4] This is, of course, quite different from the legal viewpoint, which considers also whether certain kinds of evidence should be excluded, notwithstanding their potential in helping to reconstruct the facts.

[5] Though since the coming into force of the Civil Procedure Rules 1998, the courts have begun to take a more proactive role in defining what issues it is necessary to decide. The Rules require a civil court to undertake the overall management of cases brought before it.

[6] Notwithstanding statements sometimes found to the contrary, e.g., that contained in American Federal Rule of Evidence 102, which states that the purposes of the Rules of Evidence is that: '...the truth shall be ascertained and proceedings justly determined'. The second of these goals is worthy, if imprecise; the first is worthy, but ultimately unattainable.

to have occurred as alleged. In relation to many secondary issues, an even lower standard is employed, namely, that there is some evidence capable of supporting the proponent's version of the event (a *prima facie* case).

(e) To the extent that juries are employed as triers of fact, the above considerations are compounded. Juries consist of lay men and women who have no training in the evaluation of evidence, and who are more likely to be swayed by partisan persuasive argument than those with professional experience of evidence.

1.3 PHILOSOPHICAL BASIS FOR USE OF EVIDENCE

The use of evidence as material in the reconstruction of past events makes a number of important philosophical (specifically epistemological) assumptions. Among these are that past events occur independently of human knowledge of them; that it is possible in principle to attain present knowledge about past events; and that the accumulation of evidence and derivation of rational inferences from that evidence is a correct method of achieving such knowledge.

The last of these assumptions has become virtually axiomatic in modern times. Twining[7] draws attention to the fact that, despite a wide divergence of opinion as to the detail of both the science and the law of evidence, every writer on the subject since it began to be the subject of methodical study in the eighteenth century has agreed, either explicitly or implicitly, on a philosophical basis for evidence which Twining terms optimistic rationalism. The basic tenet of optimistic rationalism is that the drawing of rational inferences from evidence is capable of leading to correct knowledge of past events, and is the only, or the only known, method of arriving at correct knowledge with respect to past events.[8]

While the process of drawing rational inferences from accumulated evidence is the avowed method of modern systems of evidence, and Twining is correct in stating that there has been universal assent to it in modern times, it is also true that it had rivals in earlier times. In the early days of the common law, proof by evidence of the facts given by testifying witnesses, known as 'trial', was only one of several methods of determining cases. Alternatives were 'proof' by ordeal, battle, and compurgators (oath-swearers).[9] While ordeal and battle fell into disuse comparatively early, ordeal because of opposition from the Church, and battle because of its unpopularity with litigants, the use of compurgators continued alongside the growing practice of using witnesses of fact.[10]

Compurgation was a formalistic procedure. A party was required to produce a number of credible persons, the number being fixed by the court, who undertook to swear to the justice of that

---

[7] *Theories of Evidence, Bentham and Wigmore*, p. 13 *et seq.*; *Re-Thinking Evidence; Exploratory Essays* (1990).

[8] Philosophically, optimistic rationalism and utilitarianism are aspirational, i.e., they do not prefer any specific system of evidence law, and do not preclude criticism of an existing system on the ground of inefficiency, or otherwise.

[9] Both ancient Babylonian law (the Code of Hammurabi, c. 1792–1750 BC) and Indian law had forms of ordeal virtually indistinguishable from those prescribed by Anglo-Saxon and Norman English law: see Shraddhakar Suprakar, *The Law of Evidence in Ancient India* (1990). As to the common law practices, see generally Pollock and Maitland, *The History of English Law before Edward I* (1899); Thayer, 'The Older Modes of Trial' (1891) 5 Harv L Rev 45; *A Preliminary Treatise on Evidence*, vol. 1.

[10] Ordeal fell into disuse almost immediately after the Lateran Council of 1215, when the Church forbade clergy to participate in the process. But battle, and particularly compurgation, had a much longer active life, and survived in name for an astonishingly long time after their active life had ended. Battle was abolished by statute as late as 1819 (59 Geo 3, c. 46) and compurgation even later, in 1833 (3 & 4 Will 4, c. 42).

party's case. These persons did not testify, but had to repeat a set form of oath verbatim, any mis-speaking being fatal to the case of the party calling the witness. It is now fashionable to decry compurgation as being a superstitious appeal to the supernatural to resolve the case, and so it was. But there was more to the procedure than meets the eye, some of which is evident from a close reading of Glanvil.[11] In an age when communications were uncertain, it was difficult for the court to investigate the facts of the case. Oath-takers were required to have personal knowledge of the case.[12] The penalties for false swearing were severe, and there is an interesting psychological component of compurgation, namely, that it may not have been an easy matter for a party to procure the necessary number of persons unless there was a general belief that his cause was just. Another interesting facet is that, in Glanvil's time, the procedure of trial using testifying witnesses was well understood, and was used for certain purposes.[13] But it was held to be inferior to compurgation for the trial of serious issues, including capital cases.[14] Even today, when judicial trial depends entirely on the drawing of rational inferences from evidence, there are echoes of compurgation in the practice of taking recognisances for bail or to keep the peace. Witnesses still speak occasionally of going to court to 'swear for' a party.

1.4 NATURE OF JUDICIAL REASONING

Judicial reasoning is a combination of three different kinds of logical process, i.e., inductive (reasoning from an accumulated data base of known instances towards a new first principle); deductive (reasoning from first principles towards a conclusion in a particular instance); and adbuctive (reasoning by way of the comparative analysis of rival hypotheses towards a qualitative preference for one of them over the others). It involves the drawing of logical factual conclusions, known as inferences, from the totality of the available (and admissible) evidence. The inductive element of this process, however, is not the classical experimental induction found in the work of Francis Bacon and John Stuart Mill. Its accumulated data base consists of underlying and often unspoken assumptions which modern writers term 'generalizations'.[15] For example, if it is desired to prove that D killed V, and evidence is available that D expressed a fixed intention of killing V, the court may draw the inference that D killed V. But this inference depends on the underlying generalization that people generally carry out their expressed fixed intentions. The strength of

---

[11] *The Treatise on the Laws and Customs of the Realm of England, Commonly Called Glanvil*, ed. G.D.G. Hall (1965). Ranulph de Glanvil was Justiciar to Henry III (1154–89) and was essentially responsible for the administration of justice in the royal courts. This indicates that the book is well informed, though it is entirely possible that Glanvil did not write it personally. Much of Glanvil is confirmed by Bracton, *Tractatus de Legibus*, written by (or ascribed to) Henry of Bracton or Bratton, a thirteenth-century justiciar, which chronicles the development of the law since Glanvil's time.

[12] There was an exception to this rule in a case where the oath-taker swore that his father had had personal knowledge, and had stated on his deathbed that the party's cause was just and asked the oath-taker to ensure that the case was proved—apparently an early form of dying declaration.

[13] Including issues of title to land by descent and issues of free status or villeinage (Glanvil, op. cit., bk 3, sects 5, 6).

[14] 'Et nemo de capitalibus placitis testimonio convincatur' (No one shall be convicted in capital cases by testimony) (*Leges Henrici*, 31 para. 5).

[15] For a detailed and instructive analysis of generalizations, see T. Anderson (1999) 40 S Tx L Rev 455. Their use in judicial reasoning is implicit in Stephen's definition of relevance (*Digest*, 12th edn, art. 1): '... any two facts are so related to each other that *according to the common course of events*, one taken either by itself or in connection with other facts proves or renders probable the past, present or future existence or non-existence of the other'. (Emphasis added.)

a generalization depends on the consistency with which the court is prepared to assume that it holds true. The generalization could be expressed thus: 'People always/frequently/sometimes/rarely carry out their expressed fixed intentions', and the strength of the generalization, and therefore also of the inference, depends on which of these variables the court is prepared to accept.

Generalizations are assumptions drawn from the accumulated experience of society about the causes and courses of events. Generalizations are acceptable as a basis for inference only to the extent that they correspond to common human experience. But therein lies a danger. Generalizations change, or at any rate, should change with time and developing societal norms. When they lag behind societal development, they may provide a pretext for reactionary or discriminatory reasoning, for example, that members of certain ethnic groups are inherently more likely than others to commit crimes. When a purported generalization is no more than the subjective opinion of a minority group or a single individual, the potential exists for utterly unwarranted inferences. Because generalizations remain an unspoken part of the reasoning process, their influence cannot always be seen directly. The anonymity of a jury verdict or a finding by a bench of magistrates may conceal them, though they can often be detected in judgments and opinions. In the middle ages it was an acceptable assumption that those who consorted with the Devil might acquire certain marks on their bodies. Consequently, in a prosecution for practising witchcraft, evidence that the accused bore such marks was admissible in support of the charge. There was nothing irrational about the inference. It is reliance on the underlying generalization that we would question today. Even today, the rules of character evidence proceed on the underlying generalization that a person who has committed a crime (of whatever kind) is likely to commit a further crime (of whatever kind) in the future, and is unreliable as a witness even in a case in which he has no interest whatsoever.[16]

These generalizations have been seriously impugned by contemporary psychological research, but for the time being continue to be acceptable as the basis for rational inferences about guilt or credibility in judicial trials.[17]

1.4.1 Nature of probability in judicial reasoning

There is a long-running and lively dispute about the nature of probability in relation to judicial inquiries. In essence, opinion divides into two camps, the first consisting of those who consider that probability in a judicial trial is essentially mathematical (the Pascalian school); the second consisting of those who consider that probability in a judicial trial is essentially non-mathematical (the Baconian school).[18] The Pascalians, pointing to the fact that statistical reasoning is commonly used in courts, in connection, for example, with fingerprint and DNA evidence, contend that all proof is inherently mathematical, and in the end can be reduced to functions of a theoretical probability calculus (though there is considerable disagreement as to what calculus should be used). The most important technique for the Pascalian theory is Bayes's Theorem,

---

[16] The rules of character evidence are dealt with in Chapters 5 and 6.

[17] For detailed criticism of such generalizations see P. Murphy (1998) 2 E & P 71.

[18] The literature on this subject is considerable. Among the more important older contributions are J.M. Keynes, *A Treatise on Probability* (1920); L.J. Cohen, *The Probable and the Provable* (1977); and R. Eggleston, *Evidence, Proof and Probability* (1978). The scientific issues are comprehensively reviewed by D. Schum, *Evidential Foundations of Probabilistic Reasoning* (1994). A valuable source for later work is *Bayesianism and Juridical Proof* (1997) a special issue of the *International Journal of Evidence and Proof*, featuring articles by many of the leading thinkers in this field, among them R.J. Allen, R.D. Friedman, and A. Stein, as well as a listing of other important work.

which enables the user to calculate the change produced on an existing probability estimate by the introduction of new evidence, a vital function in judicial reasoning. The Baconians suffered for some time from the criticism that they were unable to offer an objective non-mathematical model of probability, but this criticism was blunted by the work of L. Jonathan Cohen, who in his 1977 book, *The Probable and the Provable*, demonstrated the legal applications of the method of relevant variables, an internally consistent inductive method by which the probability of an event can be analysed by reference to the viability of alternative factual hypotheses.

Mathematical models of theoretical probability (as opposed to well-accepted statistical principles) have not fared well in the courtroom. This may to some extent be due to some lack of sophistication on the part of the lawyers and judges who have tried to grapple with them, rather than any inherent weakness in the models themselves. No better illustration of this could be provided than by the unhappy saga of the *Adams* cases (*Adams* [1996] 2 Cr App R 467 and *Adams (No. 2)* [1998] 1 Cr App R 377), which ended with the Court of Appeal deprecating attempts to have juries perform the kinds of calculation required to apply Bayes's Theorem in order to interpret the evidence. Even the most basic principles of statistical evidence may be misunderstood and abused, as witness the horrific and ultimately tragic consequences of the mistaken application of elementary statistical principles in prosecutions for homicide arising from the deaths of children affected by Sudden Infant Death Syndrome (SIDS).[19] But the mathematical models, particularly Bayes's Theorem, have also encountered significant academic criticism, notably from Cohen (op. cit.) and more recently Stein,[20] from which, in this author's opinion, they are unlikely to recover for some time. One unfortunate feature is that they tend to produce judicially unacceptable results in terms of the civil standard of proof.

To take one well-known example: P organizes a football match, for which he charges an admission fee of £10. One thousand people, including D, attend the match. But instead of collecting £10,000, P finds he has only £4,990, indicating that only 499 spectators paid to see the match, and 501 gained admittance without paying. P sues D to recover £10. In the absence of other evidence, what is the probability that D was a spectator who failed to pay? As the group which failed to pay is more numerous than the group that paid, it is slightly more probable than not that D failed to pay, which satisfies the civil standard of proof on the balance of probabilities. Yet it is inconceivable in reality that any judge would give judgment for P based on this evidence alone.

Mathematical models also tend to examine the probability of each piece of evidence presented individually, and although they consider doubts which arise about each piece, they have so far failed to advance a method of taking into account the transitivity of doubt, i.e., the extent to which a doubt arising about piece of evidence A also taints evidence B, C, and D.

Mathematical models work best in a closed universe, in which there exists a definite and known number of possibilities, e.g., the probability of dealing four consecutive picture cards from a standard pack of playing cards. Legal issues rarely take that form, though they may. An example is *Lowery v R* [1974] AC 85 (dealt with in detail at 6.11.1). In this case, it appeared that one of

---

[19] See *Meadow v General Medical Council* [2007] 1 All ER 1, a case concerned with disciplinary proceedings brought against an expert witness in the wake of decisions of the Court of Appeal exonerating mothers who had been wrongly accused in *Cannings* [2004] 1 WLR 2607 and *Clark* [2000] All ER (D) 1219. See also the disturbing and equally misguided attempt to apply statistical evidence to an issue of visual identification in *People v Collins* 438 P 2d 33 (1968) (Supreme Court of California). Though reference should also be made to a much more satisfactory application of probability theory in the judgment of Murphy J in the Australian case of *TNT Management Pty Ltd v Brooks* (1979) 23 ALR 345.

[20] (1996) 1 E & P 25. See also D. Schum, *The Evidential Foundations of Probabilistic Reasoning* (1994).

two accused, but not both, killed a girl, the only apparent motive being the sadistic pleasure of the killing. If probability is measured on a scale of 0–1, and if $P(A)$ represents the probability that accused A killed the girl, and $P(B)$ the probability that accused B did so, then the probability of A's guilt $= 1 - P(B)$ and the probability of B's guilt $= 1 - P(A)$. By introducing evidence to increase the value of $P(B)$, for example (as occurred in the case), psychological evidence of B's violent nature, A lessens the probability of his own guilt. If we change the given to include the possibility that A and B committed the murder jointly $(P(A \& B))$ the equation changes, but can still be expressed with some degree of confidence. But such situations are exceptional. In most cases, there are numerous intersecting possibilities, and they are complicated by the fact that defences will be raised which cast doubt on the allegations.

1.5 DEVELOPMENT OF RULES OF EVIDENCE

One school of thought is that all rules of evidence are artificial restrictions on the ability of the court to reach a correct decision through judicial reasoning. Jeremy Bentham, probably the most celebrated proponent of this view, ascribed the rules to the tendency of lawyers and judges to promote technicality so as to make themselves indispensable, and to the evils of sentimental liberalism (for example, his celebrated analogy of a criminal trial to a fox hunt—the fox must be given 'fair play'). He believed that the proper approach was the utilitarian one of allowing all rationally helpful evidence to be considered by the tribunal of fact, subject to guidance as to its weight. Correctness of decision was all-important. In his monumental *Rationale of Judicial Evidence*, Bentham developed these themes at great length, and it must be conceded that even today (his writings were influential in producing some reforms) the law is technical in many respects. It must also be borne in mind that exclusionary rules of evidence are primarily associated with common law jurisdictions. In the continental civil law or Romano-Germanic systems prevalent in Europe and other parts of the world, there are relatively few legal rules of evidence. In these systems, the principle is one of 'free proof', meaning that any apparently relevant evidence tends to be admitted, and that factors which in the common law world would lead to the exclusion of some evidence are considered as bearing only on the weight of that evidence. The totality of the available relevant evidence is admitted and considered in an undifferentiated way in evaluating the case as a whole. In this sense, the civil law model is closer to Bentham's utilitarian ideal. But it must be noted that pre-trial and trial procedure in civil law systems is very different from that in common law systems. The procedure is inquisitorial rather than adversarial, with the court taking a proactive lead in supervising the investigation of the case as well as the evaluation of the evidence, and the parties having a more passive role. The trial is conducted by one or more professional judges sitting without a jury as the finders of fact as well as the judges of the law. In this context, exclusionary rules of evidence in the common law sense are generally considered to be unnecessary.[21]

However, most writers have conceded the need for some artificial restrictions on the evidence to be admitted in judicial trials in the common law context. While correctness of decision is the main goal of a judicial trial, there are also other legitimate concurrent goals. These include the

---

[21] Though not entirely so. Rules upholding transcendental legal principles, for example the basic rights of the accused necessary to ensure a fair trial enshrined in the European Convention on Human Rights, and the protection of privileged communications, are recognized. For an alternative view, see P. Murphy, 'Excluding Justice or Facilitating Justice? International Law would Benefit from Rules of Evidence' (2008) 12 E & P 1.

upholding of transcendent rules which guarantee the fairness of the trial, the exclusion of kinds of evidence known by experience to be inherently suspect or unreliable, and the exclusion of kinds of evidence which are known to produce an unacceptable degree of prejudice on the part of the trier of fact. Policy-based exclusionary rules of evidence result from these concurrent goals, not from the goal of correct decision.

The formulation of the common law rules of evidence began to come into its own in the eighteenth century, although some rules predate this period by some time. The theory most favoured in the eighteenth century was the 'Best Evidence Rule', i.e., the rule that a party must produce the best evidence that the nature of the case would allow. In *Omychund v Barker* (1745) 1 Atk 21, 49, Lord Hardwicke LC said that this was the only general rule of evidence. Gilbert's major treatise also contributed to the popularity of this view. But it proved to be inadequate as a general basis for a system of evidence law. Today, it remains only in vestigial form in the rule that, where a document is adduced as substantive evidence of its contents, the original document (as opposed to a copy or other 'secondary' evidence of its contents) is required. The modern working of this rule as regards documents is considered in Chapter 19. The wider implications of the rule are still sometimes canvassed. In *Teper v R* [1952] AC 480, 486, Lord Normand suggested that hearsay was objectionable because it was not the best evidence.[22]

In *Quinn* [1962] 2 QB 245 the accused were charged with keeping a disorderly house. The Court of Criminal Appeal rejected an argument that the trial judge ought to have permitted the showing to the jury of a film depicting striptease acts. The film had been prepared by the defence as a deliberate reconstruction of the acts which the defence contended had taken place in the premises concerned, and which was supported by some evidence indicating its accuracy as such. The easiest way to dispose of the appeal might have been to treat the question as one of relevance, because the film was a deliberate reconstruction, but the Court chose to decide the issue using the best evidence rule. Ashworth J said:

> Indeed, in this case, it was admitted that some of the movements in the film (for instance, that of a snake used in one scene) could not be said with any certainty to be the same movements as were made at the material time. In our judgment, this objection goes not only to weight, as was argued, but to admissibility; it is not the best evidence.

The best evidence theory was superseded by the concept of relevance, which, despite criticisms, remains the basis of our system of judicial reasoning. (For definitions of relevance, see 2.8.) The concept of relevance was developed in the nineteenth century, and refined principally by Sir James Fitzjames Stephen. To make the concept work in relation to policy-based rules of evidence, Stephen was obliged to distinguish logical relevance (the rational, inferential relationship of a piece of evidence to a fact to be proved) from legal relevance (the study of what evidence should be admissible). Stephen's language is still to be seen in the Indian Evidence Act 1872, which he drafted and which is still in effect. But in England, the concept of relevance (a strictly logical analysis of probative value) plus admissibility (a policy decision as to what relevant evidence may be admitted) is now preferred.

The development of specific rules of evidence in England can also be traced to certain definite historical circumstances. Those which had the greatest effect are as follows.

---

[22] And see J. Spencer [1996] Crim LR 29. It has always been recognized that a failure to produce the best available evidence may affect the weight of the evidence in fact produced: see, e.g., *Francis* (1874) LR 2 CCR 128, per Lord Coleridge CJ.

1.5.1 The prevalence of trial by jury

Commenting on the rule against hearsay, Morgan observed that: 'while distrust of the jury had nothing to do with the origin of the hearsay rule, it has exerted a strong influence in preventing or delaying its liberalisation' (*Some Problems of Proof under the Anglo- American System of Litigation*, p. 117). The common law was closely bound up with the peculiar exigencies of jury trial, and because any evidence admitted had to be considered by a body of laymen, the law looked with disfavour on evidence which might expose the jury to evidence that judges considered unreliable, or which might impose on them the need for unreasonable analytical skills. Thus, it was feared that to require juries to weigh up the value of hearsay evidence, or evidence of character, would be to impose too great a burden, and a burden which, if not faithfully borne, might result in an irretrievable prejudice to a party against whom such evidence was tendered. There is, of course, a risk that a jury may, despite careful direction, act upon the wrong principles and it is no doubt necessary to regulate to some extent the material placed before juries. But whether the rules which have developed to keep certain types of evidence from them really operate to prevent them acting misguidedly is open to question. It will become apparent, from the rules discussed later in this book, that juries are habitually called upon to perform considerable feats of analysis, not to say of mental gymnastics. Nonetheless, no major rule of evidence has developed without unmistakeable signs of tailoring to the supposed needs of juries, and without doubt it is the comparative rarity of jury trial in civil cases, in modern practice, which has prompted the willingness to experiment with the inclusionary approach in such cases.[23]

The Civil Evidence Acts 1968, 1972, and 1995 effectively reversed some two centuries of painstaking jurisprudence concerning the circumstances in which hearsay evidence may be adduced, and this has been almost entirely because it has been felt so much safer to trust the trained mind of the judge sitting alone with the task of weighing and sifting such evidence than it ever was to entrust the same task to a jury. The development of the law of evidence in criminal cases has been much more hesitant, and only in recent legislation, the Police and Criminal Evidence Act 1984 and the Criminal Justice Acts 1988 and 2003, has Parliament indicated that juries may now be regarded as capable of evaluating responsibly some significant kinds of hearsay evidence. It is of some interest to note that despite the entrenched constitutional right to jury trial in American Federal courts, and despite the fact that hearsay is always suspect in relation to the conditionally guaranteed right of confrontation, those courts have shown a far greater willingness to admit hearsay than have English courts.

1.5.2 The dread of manufactured evidence

The common law lived in constant fear of perjury, fabrication, and attempts to abuse or pervert the course of justice. The fear had far-reaching consequences, not only in the rejection of specific kinds of evidence which were thought to be particularly prone to abuse (hearsay, again, was a principal offender) but also in the wholesale rejection as witnesses of interested parties and their spouses. The rule that the parties and their spouses were incompetent to give evidence began to

---

[23] It may be more accurate to say that the system of adversarial trial, rather than the particular mode of trial by jury *per se*, was the most important factor in the emergence of rules of admissibility as a feature of the common law, but the two are closely identified, and jury trial has certainly influenced many rules of evidence in highly specific ways: see J. Langbein, *The Origins of Adversary Criminal Trial* (2002) at p. 178.

be relaxed in civil cases as late as 1851, and it was not until the Criminal Evidence Act 1898 that the accused in a criminal case became competent to give evidence in his own defence. As a result, provision had often to be made for the proof of facts without recourse to the evidence of those best able to testify about them. Closely bound up with the fear of fabrication is the rule requiring sworn testimony. The solemnity and sanctity of sworn evidence, and the rule that at common law, evidence might not be given except on oath, has invested the law of competence (including the process of being sworn, which was eventually updated by the Oaths Act 1978) with a number of curious features, in particular with respect to the evidence of children of tender years (see Chapter 15).

1.5.3 The harshness of the criminal law in the late eighteenth and nineteenth centuries

Most of the major common law rules of evidence owe much of their force to judicial attempts, during the formative years of the modern law of evidence, to mitigate some of the harshness of criminal law and procedure towards the accused. Faced with a system in which death was the sentence prescribed for many (at some periods all) felonies, but which denied to the accused the right of representation by counsel in such cases until 1836,[24] and the right to give evidence in his defence until 1898, the judges took seriously their role as the protectors of the accused, and developed many exclusionary rules with a view to redressing the balance. The general exclusion of character evidence, the stringent conditions of admissibility of confessions, the accused's right (until recently) to remain silent without risk of an adverse inference being drawn against him, and the burden and standard of proof in criminal cases, all owe much to that period of legal development. Indeed, they have in most respects remained virtually unchanged, despite the radical changes in the criminal process which have since taken place.

1.6 CLASSIFICATION OF RULES OF EVIDENCE

The artificial restrictions on the process of judicial reasoning known as rules of evidence are not uniform in the policy they seek to implement. They may be classified according to their underlying policy, as follows. Note that they are all attributable to policy considerations, and have nothing to do with their value as links in the rational chain of reasoning. They restrict, rather than promote, access to potentially useful information.

(a) Structural rules (e.g., rules about the burden and standard of proof, authentication of exhibits), which provide a framework for dealing with evidence at trial.
(b) Preferential rules (e.g., the best evidence rule), designed to avoid accepting evidence of inferior quality when evidence of superior quality is available.
(c) Analytic rules (e.g., the rule against hearsay), designed to avoid accepting evidence which experience suggests is likely to be unreliable.

---

[24] The accused was allowed counsel in cases of treason as early as 1695, and appears to have enjoyed the right in the case of misdemeanours from early times. Blackstone, *Commentaries*, vol. IV, ch. 27, 349; 2 Hawk PC 400. Though Blackstone indicates that it was not uncommon for the accused to receive informal assistance from counsel, and the rule was not entirely clear in practice: see A.N. May, *The Bar and the Old Bailey (1750–1850)* (2003), chs 4 and 7.

(d) Prophylactic rules (e.g., the rules generally excluding evidence of previous convictions), designed to avoid accepting evidence which a jury may be incapable of evaluating objectively, or to which the jury may attach undue weight ('prejudicial evidence').

(e) Simplificatory rules (e.g., the rule permitting summaries of voluminous documents), designed to aid the jury in understanding the issues.

(f) Quantitative rules (e.g., rules requiring corroboration) designed either positively to insist upon multiple evidential facts to prove certain facts in issue, or negatively to prevent the needless presentation of cumulative evidence.

(g) Policy-based rules (e.g., privileges), which preclude the acceptance (or compelled revelation) of certain evidential facts, based on extrinsic policy considerations such as upholding confidentiality, protecting state secrets, etc.

(h) Discretionary rules, designed to allow the judge to override the rules of evidence in the interests of justice or expedition; see 3.5 to 3.9.

The proposition that the rules of evidence are not based, or at least not primarily based, on the goal of correctness of decision is clear from the list just given. The goal of correctness of decision would suggest the inclusionary approach of admitting all, or almost all relevant evidence, and leaving the tribunal of fact with the sole responsibility of deciding what view to take of it. Although this utilitarian approach has been advocated by various thinkers, notably Bentham, and although the influence of this approach can be clearly seen in the liberalization of the rules of evidence in recent years, it has never won real acceptance. Rather, the law of evidence is exclusionary in nature, inasmuch as the law excludes, for various policy reasons, much evidence which is undoubtedly relevant and which, if admitted, might have an important or even decisive effect on the outcome of a case. As we have seen, these policies were developed by the judges, and to a lesser extent by Parliament, on a gradual basis from the eighteenth century onwards, under the influence of concerns such as the protection of the rights of the accused, and shielding juries from evidence which (in the opinion of judges and lawyers) they might be incapable of evaluating objectively. Thus, some evidence, for example, hearsay, may be excluded because it is considered unreliable or susceptible to misinterpretation by juries. Character evidence may be excluded because of a fear that it might prejudice the accused in the eyes of the jury to such an extent that they could not judge the case dispassionately. Some evidence is excluded for reasons of public policy or considerations of privilege, in which the interests of the State or a third party sometimes outweigh the right of the parties to make use of the evidence. Some witnesses, such as very young children and some persons under a mental disability, are excluded from giving evidence at all, and witnesses who are not experts are generally prohibited from expressing their opinion on the facts in issue. Some of the policies underlying the rules of evidence are arguably obsolete. The accused no longer labours under the procedural disadvantages imposed in the nineteenth century. Jurors and magistrates are better educated and more sophisticated than they once were. Indeed, studies (to be referred to later) have shown that juries are probably quite capable of taking into account the possible dangers of hearsay evidence. Nonetheless, other policies certainly remain valid. The prejudice arising from disclosure of previous convictions is as real today as it ever was. But, whatever the merits of these arguments, it is salutary to realize that much of what is to be studied in the law of evidence is concerned with deliberate efforts to keep from the tribunal of fact material which would assist greatly in determining the merits of a case.

1.7 IMPACT OF THE EUROPEAN CONVENTION ON HUMAN RIGHTS

More recently, decisions in which provisions of the European Convention on Human Rights[25] have been considered have begun to make their mark on the law of evidence. Several provisions of the Convention have the potential to affect the law. Article 6, which guarantees the right to a fair trial, is wide enough to include almost any issues of fairness or unfairness arising from the nature or operation of domestic rules of evidence, including the court's powers to exclude evidence under s. 78 of the Police and Criminal Evidence Act 1984 (as to which see 3.7 *et seq.*) and the admission of hearsay evidence against the accused (see 7.5). Article 3, which guarantees freedom from torture and inhuman and degrading treatment, may be relevant to the possible exclusion of a confession based on the circumstances in which it is alleged to have been made (see 9.5, 9.7). Article 8, which guarantees the right to respect for private and family life, may be relevant to the possible exclusion of evidence obtained by means of trespass, the interception of communications, or other violations of privacy (see 3.10, 3.11). Article 10, which guarantees the right to freedom of expression, inspired the statutory privilege against disclosure of journalistic sources, and is relevant when balancing the public interests in protecting the confidentiality of communications to journalists, on the one hand, and in allowing parties access to evidence which is needed to protect their own interests, on the other (see 14.19).

1.7.1 Impact before coming into effect of the Act

The Human Rights Act 1998 effectively incorporates the Convention into English law, and requires a court to take account of the provisions of the Convention, and any judgment, decision, declaration, or advisory opinion of the European Court of Human Rights which may affect the issue with which the court is concerned. It also requires the courts, as far as possible, to construe statutory provisions in accordance with the Convention rights. Even before the Act came into effect, the relevant provisions of the Convention had been considered by English courts, and had proved relevant to statutory interpretation, because of the rule of construction that Parliament should not be taken, in the absence of clear indications, to have legislated in a manner contrary to the treaty obligations of the UK (see *Derbyshire County Council* v *Times Newspapers Ltd* [1992] QB 770; *Secretary of State for the Home Department, ex parte Brind* [1991] 1 AC 696).[26] But at this stage

---

[25] The Convention for the Protection of Human Rights and Fundamental Freedoms, signed in 1950 by the members of the Council of Europe, of which the United Kingdom was one, came into effect in 1953. With the coming into effect of the Human Rights Act 1998, the Convention was in effect incorporated into English domestic law. For the full text of the relevant provisions, see *Blackstone's Criminal Practice*, 2009 edn, appendix 6. See generally: Sharpe [1997] Crim LR 848; Ovey [1998] Crim LR 4; Arden [1999] Crim LR 439. The majority of the Act's provisions came into effect on 2 October 2000. In accordance with accepted principles of statutory application, decisions which pre-date the coming into effect of the Act cannot be impugned on the ground that they do not comport with Convention rights: *Lambert* [2002] 2 AC 545; *Wilson* v *First County Trust (No. 2)* [2002] QB 74, 89 per Sir Andrew Morritt V-C.

[26] Moreover, art. 234 of the Treaty establishing the European Community (the Treaty of Rome) enables certain cases to be referred to the European Court of Justice for its ruling on points of European law. For the text of art. 234 (which was formerly numbered 177) and the practice on references by criminal courts to the European Court of Justice, see *Blackstone's Criminal Practice*, 2009 edn, para. D29.3. For references by civil courts see *Blackstone's Civil Practice*, 2009 edn, ch. 75. The European Court of Justice has no power to decide the referred case on the facts, or to rule on the validity of a domestic law.

the Convention failed to make a decisive difference in the outcome of an English case, because the courts held, not surprisingly, that English law provides safeguards at least equal to those of the Convention (see, e.g., the hearsay cases, 7.5) with the result that the cases were resolved simply on the basis of English law. This makes it difficult to assess how much influence the Convention then had on judicial attitudes.

But some indication of both judicial attitudes and the possibilities of enforced changes in domestic law was provided by the cases of *Saunders* [1996] 1 Cr App R 463, and *Staines* [1997] 2 Cr App R 426. Both cases concerned the denial of the privilege against self-incrimination involved in statutory rules which permitted inspectors to require persons interviewed to answer incriminating questions, which might thereafter be used in evidence against them in criminal proceedings. In *Saunders*, the appellant contended that such provisions deprived him of the right to a fair trial guaranteed by art. 6 of the Convention. Lord Taylor of Gosforth CJ said ([1996] 1 Cr App R at 477–8):

> ...English courts can have recourse to the European Convention on Human Rights and decisions thereon by the European Court of Justice only when the law of England is ambiguous or unclear. Saunders has taken his case to Europe on this issue and the European Commission on Human Rights has referred it to the European Court in Strasbourg. Should Saunders succeed there, our treaty obligations will require consideration to be given to the effect of the decision here. But our duty at present is to apply our domestic law which is unambiguous.

Saunders did succeed in Strasbourg (*Saunders* v *United Kingdom* (1997) 23 EHRR 313) on the ground that the complete deprivation of the privilege against self-incrimination did violate the right to a fair trial under art. 6. But any thought that this alone would influence English law was quickly dispelled when the Court of Appeal in *Staines* reached exactly the same result as in *Saunders*, notwithstanding the decision in the European Court of Human Rights. Lord Bingham of Cornhill CJ, referring to the argument that art. 6 as interpreted in *Saunders* v *United Kingdom* now required the trial judge to exclude the evidence in the exercise of his discretion, even though it was technically admissible by statute, said ([1997] 2 Cr App R at 442):

> If the Court were to rule here that this evidence should be excluded, it would be obliged to exclude such evidence in all such cases. That would amount to a repeal, or a substantial repeal, of an English statutory provision which remains in force in deference to a ruling which does not have direct effect and which, as a matter of strict law, is irrelevant.

Lord Bingham conceded that it was unsatisfactory that there should be a direct and inevitable conflict between the English courts and the European Court of Human Rights on this issue (*ibid.* at 443), and in the circumstances of these cases, Parliament recognized that the incorporation of the Convention into domestic law would make the position taken by the Court of Appeal in *Saunders* and *Staines* untenable. Consequently, significant amendments were introduced by the Youth Justice and Criminal Evidence Act 1999 to make the relevant statutes conform to art. 6 as interpreted in *Saunders* v *United Kingdom*. This is dealt with at 14.7.1. But this does not mean that decisions on all questions arising under the Convention will have the same consequences. Compare the approach taken by English courts on the issue of access to legal advice (art. 6; *Murray* v *United Kingdom* (1996) 22 EHRR 29; *Aspinall* [1999] 2 Cr App R 115; see 9.12.5); and the privilege against compelled disclosure of journalistic sources (art. 10; *Camelot Group plc* v *Centaur Communications Ltd* [1999] QB 124; *Goodwin* v *United Kingdom* (1996) 22 EHRR 123; see 14.19).

1.7.2 Impact after coming into effect of the Act

In the light of these cases, it was, to say the least, doubtful whether the coming into effect of the Human Rights Act 1998 would result in a greater impact on the domestic evidence law of England. In fact, the courts have on the whole responded admirably to the challenge. The Convention has been considered and applied in a number of cases, some of which have produced far-reaching effects on the law. These cases are dealt with in their proper places in this book, but as an illustration, it is appropriate here to mention the decision of the House of Lords in *Lambert* [2002] 2 AC 545. In *Lambert*, the House was faced with the issue (a vexed one even under common law principles) of how far a statute which purports to require the accused to bear the legal burden of proof of an affirmative defence may be construed as doing so in the light of the presumption of innocence. At common law, it seemed to have been established that Parliament had the power to require the accused to bear a legal burden of proof of an affirmative defence (though not a burden of disproving an element of the offence). Whether the statute in question had this effect expressly or by necessary implication was to be judged by its language and was essentially a matter of statutory construction. But in *Lambert*, the House held that, subject to a principle of proportionality between the importance of maintaining the presumption of innocence and the social necessity of dealing effectively with offences such as that charged, the Convention may require reading such a statutory provision as if it imposed on the accused no more than an evidential burden of adducing some evidence in support of the defence. Given the number and importance of the statutory provisions which have the same apparent effect as that under consideration in *Lambert*, the ripple effect of the decision will continue for a considerable time to come. Despite some degree of retreat in subsequent cases (see 4.9), it has already had a major impact on the law relating to the burden of proof. It will involve the reconsideration of the principles underlying some cases decided before the coming into effect of the Act, and will necessitate some re-formulation of parliamentary intent in the drafting of criminal statutes.[27] The law in this area and the decision in *Lambert* are considered in more detail at 4.9.

The full extent of the impact of the Convention will not be known for some time to come. If the experience of the United States may be taken as a guide, the impact may be hugely significant. The corresponding provisions of the Fifth and Sixth Amendments to the United States Constitution, which provide basic guarantees of fairness to defendants in criminal cases, have affected almost every area of the law of evidence. But these Amendments operate more directly than the Convention, because the latter cannot directly dictate the content of the domestic law of the States which are party to it, and confines itself to the broad ground of procedural fairness. In *Kostovski* v *Netherlands*,[28] the European Court of Human Rights observed:

> It has to be recalled at the outset that admissibility of evidence is primarily a matter for regulation by national law... Again, as a general rule it is for the national courts to assess the evidence before

---

[27] Thus, the Convention has played an important role in the thinking of the Law Commission in its proposed recommendations for reform of the law of mental disorder defences. The burden of proof as to the present defences of insanity and diminished responsibility may well need to be re-considered, as may proposals for future statutory provisions such as those adopted by the Commission in its report, Draft Criminal Code: Criminal Liability and Mental Disorder, 28 August 2002. See 4.8.1.

[28] (1989) 12 EHRR 434, para. 39; see also *Saidi* v *France* (1993) 17 EHRR 251, para. 43: 'The taking of evidence is governed primarily by the rules of domestic law... it is in principle for the national courts to assess the evidence before them'.

them...In the light of these principles the court sees its task in the present case as not being to express a view as to whether the statements in question were correctly admitted and assessed, but rather to ascertain whether the proceedings considered as a whole, including the way in which the evidence was taken, were fair.

Unlike the United States Supreme Court, the European Court of Human Rights has no power to affect directly the outcome of a case in the domestic courts of a Council of Europe State. The Court will consider whether the framework and basic rules governing the law of evidence is fair, and comports with the standards of fairness required by the Convention. But it will not dictate to a Council State what its detailed rules of evidence should be.

1.7.2.1 *Stare decisis*: precedential value of decisions of European Court of Human Rights

In Kay *and others* v *Lambeth London Borough Council* [2006] 2 AC 465, the House of Lords clarified the precedential value of decisions of the European Court of Human Rights. The House held that while the European Court of Human Rights is authoritative on matters of interpretation of the Convention, and while English courts must give practical recognition to its decisions, they are not strictly bound by those decisions. Consequently, an English court must continue to follow binding decisions of a higher English court in accordance with the usual domestic rules of precedent. The House was prepared to allow a 'partial' exception to this rule in a case in which it is clear that a decision of a higher court rendered before the coming into effect of the Human Rights Act 1998 simply cannot stand in the light of that Act. But such an exception can apply only in an 'extreme' case, where there is no room for doubt: see the opinion of Lord Bingham of Cornhill at [40]–[45].[29]

1.7.3 Relevant Convention provisions

The following articles of the Convention are the most likely to be involved in issues of the admissibility of evidence and the judicial power to exclude evidence as a matter of discretion:

Article 3 (prohibition of torture)
No one shall be subjected to torture or to inhuman or degrading treatment or punishment.

Article 6 (right to a fair trial)
  (1) In the determination of his civil rights and obligations or of any criminal charge against him, everyone is entitled to a fair and public hearing within a reasonable time by an independent and impartial tribunal established by law....
  (2) Everyone charged with a criminal offence shall be presumed innocent until proved guilty according to law.
  (3) Everyone charged with a criminal offence has the following minimum rights:
      (a) to be informed promptly, in a language which he understands and in detail, of the nature and cause of the accusation against him;

---

[29] At para. [45] Lord Bingham provides an example of such an extreme case, involving the decision of the House of Lords in *X (Minors)* v *Bedfordshire County Council* [1995] 2 AC 683, which could not survive the 1998 Act. And see the decision of Evans-Lombe J in *C plc* v *P* [2006] Ch 549 applying the exception in a case involving the privilege against self-incrimination; though this was criticized on appeal by the majority of the Court of Appeal, affirming the result of the case but on much simplified grounds, [2008] Ch 1; see 14.8.

(b) to have adequate time and facilities for the preparation of his defence;

(c) to defend himself in person or through legal assistance of his own choosing or, if he has not sufficient means to pay for legal assistance, to be given it free when the interests of justice so require;

(d) to examine or have examined witnesses against him and to obtain the attendance and examination of witnesses on his behalf under the same conditions as witnesses against him;

(e) to have the free assistance of an interpreter if he cannot understand or speak the language used in court.

Article 8 (right to respect for private and family life)

(1) Everyone has the right to respect for his private and family life, his home and his correspondence.

(2) There shall be no interference by a public authority with the exercise of this right except such as is in accordance with the law and is necessary in a democratic society in the interests of national security, public safety or the economic well-being of the country, for the prevention of disorder and crime, for the protection of health or morals, or for the protection of the rights and freedoms of others.

Article 10 (freedom of expression)

(1) Everyone has the right to freedom of expression. This right shall include freedom to hold opinions and to receive and impart information and ideas without interference by public authority and regardless of frontiers....

(2) The exercise of these freedoms, since it carries with it duties and responsibilities, may be subject to such formalities, conditions, restrictions or penalties as are prescribed by law and are necessary in a democratic society, in the interests of national security, territorial integrity or public safety, for the prevention of disorder or crime, for the protection of health and morals, for the protection of the reputation or rights of others, for preventing the disclosure of information received in confidence, or for maintaining the authority and impartiality of the judiciary.

The Human Rights Act 1998 provides, *inter alia*, with respect to Convention rights:[30]

2—(1) A court or tribunal determining a question which has arisen in connection with a Convention right must take into account any—

(a) judgment, decision, declaration or advisory opinion of the European Court of Human Rights,
[(b), (c), and (d) add opinions or decisions of the Commission and decisions of the Committee of Ministers.]

3—(1) So far as it is possible to do so, primary legislation and subordinate legislation must be read and given effect in a way which is compatible with the Convention rights.

(2) This section—...

(b) does not affect the validity, continuing operation or enforcement of any incompatible primary legislation....

4—(1) Subsection (2) applies in any proceedings in which a court determines whether a provision of primary legislation is compatible with a Convention right.

(2) If the court is satisfied that the provision is incompatible with a Convention right, it may make a declaration of that incompatibility...

---

[30] The term 'Convention rights' is defined by s. 1 of the Act as referring to the rights and freedoms contained in arts 2 to 12 and 14 of the Convention, together with arts 1 to 3 of the First Protocol, and arts 1 and 2 of the Sixth Protocol, as read with arts 16 and 18 of the Convention, subject to any derogation or reservation adopted by the United Kingdom. Only articles having a probable impact on the law of evidence are reproduced in the text.

(6) A declaration under this section ('a declaration of incompatibility')—
    (a) does not affect the validity, continuing operation or enforcement of the provision in respect of which it is given; and
    (b) is not binding on the parties to the proceedings in which it is made....

6—(1) It is unlawful for a public authority to act in a way which is incompatible with a Convention right.
    (2) Subsection (1) does not apply to an act if—
        (a) as the result of one or more provisions of primary legislation, the authority could not have acted differently; or
        (b) in the case of one or more provisions of, or made under, primary legislation which cannot be read or given effect in a way which is compatible with the Convention rights, the authority was acting so as to give effect to or enforce those provisions.
    (3) In this section, 'public authority' includes—
        (a) a court or tribunal, and
        (b) any person certain of whose functions are functions of a public nature, but does not include either House of Parliament, or a person exercising functions in connection with proceedings in Parliament.[31]

These provisions will be referred to further in this book at the appropriate places dealing with issues which have arisen under the Convention.

1.8 RECOMMENDED FURTHER READING

Eggleston, R., *Evidence, Proof and Probability* (2nd edn, London: Weidenfeld & Nicolson, 1983).

Ho, H.L., *A Philosophy of Law: Justice in the Search for Truth* (Oxford: Oxford University Press, 2008).

Laudan, L., *Truth, Error and Criminal Law* (Cambridge: Cambridge University Press, 2008).

Murphy, P., Excluding justice or facilitating justice? International criminal law would benefit from rules of evidence (2008) **12**(1) *International Journal of Evidence and Proof* 1.

Redmayne, M., 'Analysing Evidence Case Law' in Roberts, P. and Redmayne, M., *Innovations in Evidence and Proof* (Oxford: Hart Publishing, 2007) pp. 119–39.

Special issue of *International Journal of Evidence and Proof*, Bayesianism and Juridical Proof, Allen, R.J., Friedman, R.D., Stein, A. et al. (1997).

Stein, A., *Foundations of Evidence Law* (Oxford: Oxford University Press, 2005).

Twining, W., *Rethinking Evidence: Exploratory Essays* (2nd edn, Cambridge: Cambridge University Press, 2006).

1.9 QUESTIONS FOR DISCUSSION

1. Does the term 'contest' accurately describe the nature of a trial in the UK?

2. If a trial is not a search to ascertain the ultimate truth of past events, what is it?

3. Judicial reasoning may be described as a combination of which three kinds of logical process?

4. Is it possible (or desirable) to decide legal cases on the basis of mathematical probability?

---

[31] A jury is not a 'public authority' for the purposes of s. 6(3) and it is, therefore, unnecessary for the jury to satisfy itself of the admissibility of evidence independently of the judge: *Mushtaq* [2005] 1 WLR 1513. See further on this point 3.2.

5. Why do courts exclude evidence?

6. What is meant by the expression 'free proof'? Is this preferable to an exclusionary approach to evidence?

7. What is the 'best evidence' rule and in what form does it apply today?

8. Are decisions of the European Court of Human Rights binding on UK courts?

2

THE LANGUAGE OF THE LAW OF EVIDENCE

SUMMARY OF MAIN POINTS

- The law of evidence has its own terminology, which is important but often used inconsistently.

- Evidence is either direct (consisting of a witness's perception of an event) or circumstantial (requiring an inference to be drawn from what was perceived to reach a conclusion).

- A fact which must be proved to establish an element of a charge, cause of action, or defence is called a fact in issue.

- Evidence is relevant if it makes a fact in issue to any degree more likely or less likely to be true than it would be without the evidence.

- Evidence is admissible if it is relevant and is not excluded by any rule of evidence.

- The term 'weight' refers to the degree of reliability and cogency assigned to admissible evidence by the tribunal of fact.

2.1 INCONSISTENCY OF TERMINOLOGY

Like all legal subjects, the law of evidence has its own characteristic technical terms, which recur throughout any study of the subject and which, therefore, must be clearly understood at the outset. This short chapter will explore these terms. A word of warning is necessary. Some technical terms in the law of evidence have been used in more than one sense by judges and writers, resulting in a sometimes considerable degree of confusion. The term 'direct evidence' and the words 'presumption' and 'presumptive' are good examples of this tendency, and attention is drawn to it in the text below. Sometimes, more than one word is commonly used to mean the same thing. The word 'evidence' itself is often used by judges and lawyers as if it were synonymous with 'legally admissible evidence', as witness the not uncommon admonition given by judges to counsel that 'hearsay is not evidence'; of course, it would be more accurate for the judge to say that hearsay is evidence but that it is not admissible. Every effort will be made in this book to use the technical terms in the sense indicated in this chapter, but it is inevitable that other usages of them will sometimes be encountered in reading cases or other writings on evidence. Frustrating as this can be, the explanation for it is simple enough. As we saw in Chapter 1, the common law of evidence was not developed in a systematic or even in an entirely consistent way. Evidence underlies the whole practice of law in every field of litigation. It is not the product of theory but rather of the need to solve practical problems in trial. One of the most remarkable features of the subject is that even in those countries, such as the United States, which have developed codified rules of evidence to supplement or even replace the common law, those rules reflect rather than alter the common law rules. With the possible exception of Stephen's Indian Evidence Act 1872, which also reflects but does to some extent amend the common law, it is hard even to think of an example of a body of evidence law deliberately constructed from first principles. It is an interesting reflection that until the Civil Evidence Act 1995 came into effect, English law had no statutory definition of a word as basic as 'hearsay', but instead relied on a number of judicial definitions. Given all this, some inconsistency of terminology is only to be expected. In this book, every effort will be made to keep the terminology simple and consistent.

2.2 BASIC TERMINOLOGY OF THE LAW OF EVIDENCE

There are a number of basic terms without which it is almost impossible to construct a sentence in dealing with the law of evidence. These will be considered first.

2.2.1 Parties

A party who seeks to place evidence before the court is said to 'tender' or (more often in the United States) 'offer' the evidence, and is described as the 'proponent' of the evidence. Any party who is adverse to the proponent of the evidence is described as the 'opponent'. When the opponent seeks to persuade the court not to admit the evidence, he is said to make an 'objection' to it.

2.2.2 Admission or exclusion

When the court permits a party to place evidence before it, the court is said to 'admit' (hence the terms 'admissible' and 'inadmissible') or 'receive' the evidence. If there has been an objection, the judge will usually say no more than that he is 'against' the opponent of the evidence, although in the United States it is obligatory for the judge to make a ruling in which he either 'sustains' or 'overrules' the objection. When the proponent actually places the evidence before the court, he is said to 'adduce' or 'introduce' the evidence. If the judge decides not to admit the evidence, he is said to 'exclude' the evidence or simply to 'refuse to admit' it.

2.2.3 Tribunals of law and fact

In a trial on indictment, the judge is responsible for the decision of all matters of law, including the admission of evidence. He is accordingly described as the 'tribunal of law'. The jury, which is responsible for finding the facts of the case, is referred to as the 'tribunal of fact'. In other modes of trial, these terms are applied analogously. Thus, in a summary trial, the magistrates are both the tribunal of law and the tribunal of fact, and the same is true of a judge sitting alone in a civil case. The subject of the judicial function in the law of evidence is dealt with in more detail in Chapter 3.

2.3 TERMINOLOGY OF THE QUALITIES OF EVIDENCE

Evidence may be described as having one of the following qualities.

2.3.1 Direct versus circumstantial evidence

Direct evidence is evidence which requires no mental process on the part of the tribunal of fact in order to draw the conclusion sought by the proponent of the evidence, other than acceptance of the evidence itself. Circumstantial evidence is evidence from which the desired conclusion may be drawn, but which requires the tribunal of fact not only to accept the evidence tendered, but also to draw an inference from it. For example, if D is charged with robbery of a bank, and was seen by W running from the bank clutching a wad of banknotes, W's evidence is direct evidence that D was running away from the bank, and circumstantial evidence that D committed the robbery. To arrive at the latter conclusion, the jury must draw certain inferences from the facts perceived by W, namely that D stole the banknotes from the bank and was running away to avoid being caught. This example also shows that circumstantial evidence is not necessarily inferior to direct evidence, if the inference required is obvious and compelling. Similarly, the production of an incriminating document may be direct evidence of a fact, while evidence that the party potentially embarrassed by it destroyed the document may be equally cogent circumstantial evidence of the same fact.[1]

In *Exall* (1866) 4 F & F 922 Pollock CB, employing the analogy of a rope, said, at 929:

> One strand of the cord might be insufficient to sustain the weight, but three stranded together may be quite of sufficient strength.
>
> Thus, it may be in circumstantial evidence—there may be a combination of circumstances, no one of which would raise a reasonable conviction, or more than a mere suspicion; but the whole, taken together, may create a strong conclusion of guilt, that is, with as much certainty as human affairs can require or admit of.

The most celebrated analysis of circumstantial evidence is that of Wigmore (*The Principles of Judicial Proof* (1913), Part I). Wigmore undertook an exhaustive study of the use of circumstantial

---

[1] From this, it will be apparent that almost all evidence is circumstantial. Direct evidence consists only of matters directly perceived by a witness and objects or documents produced for inspection by the court with a view to assessing their physical qualities. Schum (D. Schum, *The Evidential Foundations of Probabilistic Reasoning* (1994), pp. 18–19, 81–3) contends convincingly that even the direct perception of a witness is ultimately circumstantial. He argues that testimony by a witness, W, of his direct perception of an occurrence (O) is in fact merely potential evidence (E*) of O, and is actual evidence (E) only that W believes that O occurred. Consequently, W's testimony becomes evidence (E) of O only subject to the jury's views as to (1) whether W actually believes that O occurred; (2) whether W's belief was founded on objective sensory evidence; and (3) the quality of that sensory evidence. On the other hand, it could be argued that these are simply factors the jury must take into account in deciding whether to accept W's testimony, which would not do violence to the definition of direct evidence offered in the text.

evidence to prove a wide variety of facts, and in the process amply illustrated the extent to which circumstantial evidence is necessarily employed in every case. The state of a person's mind, such as his intent, knowledge, belief, consciousness, or motive, can be proved only by circumstantial evidence. For example, knowledge or belief is proved by evidence of statements made by or to the person in question. His intent is proved by evidence of acts committed by him. The jury is asked to draw an inference from the evidence of information presented to a person about what that person knew or believed; to draw an inference from evidence of what he did about what he intended to do or what his motive was for what he did; or to draw the inference from his intent or motive that he acted accordingly. As Lord Atkinson put it during argument in *Ball* ([1911] AC 47, 68) it is 'more probable that men are killed by those who have some motive for killing them than by those who have not'. Wigmore presented a systematic analysis of the cases in which circumstantial evidence could be used to prove the physical commission of the act itself, for example evidence of planning and preparation preceding its commission, and evidence of avoidance of detection, such as destruction of evidence, flight from the scene, or other incriminating action taken after its commission. Although now outdated in terms of psychology and forensic science, Wigmore's work remains of interest as a testament both to the universality and utility of circumstantial evidence.

With the exception of the necessary difference implicit in the necessity for the drawing of an inference, there is no reason why the tribunal of fact should treat, or should be directed to treat circumstantial evidence any differently from direct evidence. In *Hodge* (1838) 2 Lewin 227, 228 Baron Alderson said that in a case in which the evidence against the accused consisted entirely of circumstantial evidence, the accused could be found guilty only if the jury were satisfied 'not only that the circumstances were consistent with his having committed the act, but they must also be satisfied that the facts were such as to be inconsistent with any other rational conclusion than that the prisoner was the guilty person'. In *McGreevy* v *DPP* [1973] 1 WLR 276, it was argued to the House of Lords that this dictum required a distinct direction to the jury in such cases in addition to the standard direction about the burden and standard of proof (as to which see 4.12). The appellant had been convicted of murder in a case which turned entirely on circumstantial evidence. He argued that in such a case (though not in a case in which the evidence was a mixture of direct and circumstantial evidence) it was mandatory for the judge to direct the jury, not only that the prosecution must prove the guilt of an accused beyond reasonable doubt, but also that the jury could not convict unless they were sure both that the facts were consistent with the guilt of the accused and that they excluded any reasonable[2] explanation other than the guilt of the accused. The House of Lords declined to adopt any such rule, preferring the view that the standard direction as to the burden and standard of proof was sufficient to cover cases of this kind. Lord Morris of Borth-y-Gest said:

> I think this is consistent with the view that Hodge's Case...was reported not because it laid down a new rule of law, but because it was thought to furnish a helpful example of one way in which a jury could be directed in a case where the evidence was circumstantial...

---

[2] The use of the word 'reasonable' in contradistinction to Baron Alderson's word 'rational' in the appellant's argument and the decision of the House of Lords is interesting, the reason for the departure being unclear. It would seem that Baron Alderson's formulation would have been more favourable to the appellant. Presumably it was felt that 'reasonable' provides a closer relationship to the 'beyond reasonable doubt' standard of proof required of the prosecution.

> I see no advantage in seeking for the purposes of a summing-up to classify evidence into direct and circumstantial, with the result that, if the case for the prosecution depends (as to the commission of the act) entirely on circumstantial evidence (a term which would need to be defined) the judge becomes under an obligation to comply with a special requirement when summing up.

Because the trial judge had directed the jury fully and fairly about the burden and standard of proof, the appeal was dismissed. It is submitted that this view is correct. The report of *Hodge* is very short, and was apparently intended only to record Baron Alderson's approval of the summing-up in the terms given in a case depending on circumstantial evidence, rather than to create a rule of general application. The proposition that the jury should be satisfied that the evidence excludes all reasonable (if not all rational) explanations other than the guilt of the accused is no more than a logical corollary of the general rule that the Prosecution must prove the guilt of the accused beyond reasonable doubt.[3] If the jury find that there is a reasonable explanation of the evidence consistent with the innocence of the accused, it would seem to follow that they should acquit him. For the judge to be obliged to direct the jury as to the meaning of the term circumstantial evidence and then to give an additional direction would seem to be an unnecessary complication.[4] Similarly, there is no requirement that the judge adopt any special approach when dealing with a submission of no case to answer in a case depending wholly or substantially on circumstantial evidence. The test is whether a jury, properly directed in accordance with the principles discussed above, could properly convict: see *P* [2008] 2 Cr App R 6; as to the test generally see 3.4.

2.3.2 Direct or percipient versus hearsay evidence

The term 'direct evidence' is sometimes also used to mean the opposite of hearsay evidence. The alternative term 'percipient evidence' not only avoids any possibility of confusion, but is also more appropriate to describe the opposite of hearsay evidence. Hearsay is a complex subject, occupying in its own right four chapters of this book, and only a brief distinction can be made here. Percipient evidence is evidence of facts which a witness personally perceives using any of his senses. Hearsay evidence is given when a witness recounts a statement made by another person, and where the proponent of the evidence asserts that what the person who made the statement said was true. Thus, the evidence of W that he saw D rob the bank is percipient evidence, whereas the evidence of H (who was not present at the scene of the robbery) that W told H that D robbed the bank is hearsay, if tendered to prove that D robbed the bank.

---

[3] A good example of this principle is *Cannings* [2004] 1 WLR 2607, in which it was held that the conviction of a parent for the murder of her child could not be sustained where it was clear that there existed a reasonable probability of a natural cause of death (Sudden Infant Death Syndrome) and that that probability could not be excluded.

[4] It must be conceded, though, that there is a diversity of opinion on this point among common law jurisdictions. In Canada, it appears to be a 'well-settled', though not invariably followed rule that 'the Rule in Hodge's Case' requires a specific direction in cases which turn on circumstantial evidence: McWilliams, *Canadian Criminal Evidence*, 3rd edn, Release 30 (2003), para. 5:10500. Australia is also sympathetic to the requirement of a specific direction: see *Plump* v *R* (1963) 110 CLR 234. The United States, however, takes the opposite view: *Holland* v *US* 384 US 121 (1954). Interestingly, the Appeals Chamber of the International Criminal Tribunal for the Former Yugoslavia appears to have adopted a *Hodge*-like rule in relation to judicial reasoning in non-jury trials (*Delalic et al.*, Judgment of 20 February 2001, para. 458). It will be interesting to see if this becomes a general rule in international criminal law.

2.3.3 Primary versus secondary evidence

In proving the contents of a document, resort may be had to either primary or secondary evidence. Primary evidence consists of the production of the original document or an admission by the opponent as to what its contents are or were. Secondary evidence consists of a copy of the document, however made, or oral evidence about what its contents are or were. Primary evidence is generally required to prove the contents of a document, but in certain circumstances, secondary evidence is admissible for that purpose.[5]

2.3.4 Presumptive or *prima facie* versus conclusive evidence

Presumptive or *prima facie* evidence is evidence which is declared (usually by statute) to be sufficient evidence of a fact, unless and until an opponent adduces contradictory evidence, in which case the tribunal of fact must weigh all the evidence tendered by all parties, in order to decide whether the fact has been proved. Conclusive evidence, which is rare,[6] is tantamount to a rule of law, because it is evidence which no party is permitted to contradict. Conclusive evidence, therefore, is inaptly named, and it would be preferable to state the fact so proved as a rule of law. An example of conclusive evidence is the rule that a child under the age of 10 years is to be taken as incapable of committing a criminal offence.[7] By way of contrast, the former rule that a child aged between 10 and 14 was presumed to be *doli incapax* was presumptive or *prima facie* evidence, because evidence to contradict the lack of capacity could be introduced by the prosecution.[8]

2.4 TERMINOLOGY OF THE FORM OF EVIDENCE

Evidence which falls substantively into any of the above categories must have, or be put into, a form in which it can be presented to the court. Evidence may be received by a court in the following forms.

2.4.1 Oral evidence

Evidence consisting of what is said by any witness from the witness box in the instant proceedings is known as 'oral evidence'. Oral evidence must, with very few exceptions, be given on oath or affirmation[9] and in court, though if a witness is unable to attend court, his evidence may in some cases be taken out of court on commission or, in criminal cases, by a justice of the peace. There are also some important provisions for evidence to be given on affidavit[10] or witness statement and, in criminal cases, by written statement in a prescribed form or by live television

---

[5] In the case of documents requiring enrolment, there is a further kind of primary evidence. See generally, 19.3. Where a hearsay statement contained in a document is admissible, the strict rules are relaxed, to some extent. See, for example, Civil Evidence Act 1995, s. 8; Criminal Justice Act 2003, s. 133.

[6] For a statutory example, see Civil Evidence Act 1968, s. 13(1).

[7] Children and Young Persons Act 1933, s. 50.

[8] This latter rule has been abolished by the Crime and Disorder Act 1998, s. 34; see *C (A Minor) v DPP* [1996] AC 1.

[9] See 15.15.1, 15.15.2.

[10] An affidavit is a written statement of the evidence of the deponent, made on oath or affirmation. See generally Civil Procedure Rules 1998, r. 32.15–32.17. As to witness statements, see r. 32.4 and 32.5.

link.[11] These instances, where they occur, may be regarded as the equivalent of oral evidence and indeed, evidence so given has in law the same effect as oral evidence given in court. Oral evidence is frequently referred to as 'testimony', and this usage is almost invariable in the United States.

2.4.2 Documentary evidence

This term refers to evidence afforded by any document produced for the inspection of the court, whether as direct or hearsay evidence of its contents. A document may also be produced as a piece of real evidence as defined below. The normal sense of the word 'document' is of some writing or other inscription by which information may be communicated, but modern technology has opened up new possibilities in the form of tape, film, and the like, so that the range of materials which may be so described has expanded somewhat the more traditional understanding of the word.[12]

2.4.3 Real evidence

A term employed to denote any material from which the court may draw conclusions or inferences by using its own senses. It includes material objects produced to the court for its inspection, the presentation of the physical characteristics of any person or animal, the demeanour of witnesses (which may appear quite different to the court than the witness or the party calling him would wish), views of the *locus in quo* or of any object incapable of being brought to court without undue difficulty, and such items as tapes, films, and photographs, the physical appearance or sound of which may be significant over and above the sum total of their contents. These are all considered in Chapter 19. What is of importance in each case is the visual, aural, or other sensory impression which the evidence, by its own characteristics, produces on the court, and on which the court may act to find proved any fact which seems to follow from it.

2.5 TERMINOLOGY OF FACTS TO BE PROVED

Because the purpose of evidence is to establish the probability of the facts upon which the success of a party's case depends in law, evidence must be confined to the proof of those facts which are required for that purpose. The proof of supernumerary or unrelated facts will not assist the court, and may in certain cases prejudice the court against a party, while having no probative value on the issues actually before it. It is by no means always easy to determine what facts are required and what are supernumerary, especially in relation to matters said to form part of the '*res gestae*', or to be relevant to the facts in issue. The facts which a party is permitted to prove are:

(a) facts in issue in the case;
(b) facts constituting part of, or accompanying and explaining, a fact in issue, described as part of the '*res gestae*';
(c) facts relevant to a fact in issue; and
(d) where appropriate, standards of comparison.

---

[11] See, e.g., Criminal Justice Act 1967, s. 9(1); Magistrates' Courts Act 1980, s. 102. Certain evidence may be presented by way of videotaped interview (Youth Justice and Criminal Evidence Act 1999, Part II, Chapter I; see 16.17). Oral evidence is also generally considered to include evidence given in writing or by signs by persons with speech or hearing impediments; see Civil Evidence Act 1995, s. 13.

[12] The meaning of the term is considered further in 19.2. For certain purposes, the word 'document' has been given particular connotations by statute: see, e.g., Civil Evidence Act 1995, s. 13; Criminal Justice Act 2003, ss. 134(1), 140.

2.6 FACTS IN ISSUE

The facts in issue in a case, sometimes called ultimate facts, are the facts which a party to litigation (including the prosecution in a criminal case) must prove in order to succeed in his claim or defence and to show his entitlement to relief (or to obtain a conviction). Such facts are often said to be 'material' to the case. What these facts may be is not really the concern of the law of evidence, but must be derived from the substantive law applicable to the cause of action, charge or defence in each case. In procedural terms, they are to be found in the statements of case, indictment or charge, as the case may be.

In a civil case, any fact is in issue if, having regard to the statements of case and the substantive law, it is a fact necessary to the success of any claim or defence at issue. In respect of the facts that a party must prove in order to establish his claim or defence, the party is said to bear the legal burden of proof.[13] The number of facts in issue will depend entirely on the nature of the case. In a typical action for negligence, the facts in issue are that the defendant owed a duty of care to the claimant, that the defendant was in breach of that duty of care and that such breach caused the claimant loss and damage for which he is entitled in law to recover; together with any further facts raised by an affirmative defence, which goes beyond a mere denial of those pleaded by the claimant, for example such facts as may establish contributory negligence, *volenti non fit injuria*, or Act of God. In a typical action for breach of contract, the facts in issue are that there was a binding and enforceable contract between the claimant and the defendant, the due performance of any conditions precedent, a breach by the defendant of the contract and that such breach caused loss to the claimant for which he is entitled in law to recover; together with any further facts raised by an affirmative defence which goes beyond a mere denial of the claimant's case, such as fraud, illegality, infancy, or accord and satisfaction.

In criminal cases, the facts in issue are ascertained by reference to the essential elements of the offence as charged in the indictment or summons. The position here is rendered somewhat simpler by the fact that a plea of not guilty puts in issue all the facts necessary to establish the commission by the accused of the offence charged, and the prosecution bear the legal burden of proving every such element of the offence.[14] There are, however, exceptional cases where the accused bears the burden of proving some element of his defence, for example insanity within the M'Naghten Rules. In yet other cases the accused has a lesser burden of raising by evidence certain facts which go beyond a mere denial of his guilt, for example provocation, and, if he does so, the prosecution are required to rebut those facts in the discharge of their overall burden of proving his guilt.[15] In such cases, the issues raised by the defence are just as much proper subjects of evidence as those raised by the prosecution. The prosecution's evidence must be directed towards the essential elements of the offence charged in the indictment, taking into account any amendments.[16] In summary trial, no point can be taken on formal defects of the process or any variance of the evidence from the actual wording of a summons.[17] But the evidence in a summary

---

[13] This should be read with Chapter 4, where the legal and evidential burdens of proof are discussed. A fact will be in issue if any party must prove it as a necessary part of his claim or defence.

[14] *Woolmington* v *DPP* [1935] AC 462; *Sims* [1946] KB 531, per Lord Goddard CJ at 539.

[15] As to these cases, see 4.8, 4.8.3. The position in these cases has been greatly affected by the European Convention on Human Rights, art. 6 and the decision of the House of Lords in *Lambert* [2002] 2 AC 545; see 4.9.

[16] Indictments Act 1915, s. 5 as amended.

[17] Magistrates' Courts Act 1980, s. 123.

trial, too, must be directed only to the elements of the offence charged. The facts in issue in a criminal case will be the commission by the accused of the *actus reus*, the presence of any necessary *mens rea*, and any defence, going beyond a mere denial of the prosecution case, which the defence must or may raise.

2.6.1 Secondary facts in issue

Also treated as facts in issue in any case, are facts which must be proved to establish either the credibility of a witness, or the admissibility of any evidence. Such facts are known as 'secondary' or 'collateral' facts in issue. Evidence may be called, for example, tending to show that a witness for the other side is biased or partial; or suffers from some medical condition which renders his evidence unworthy of belief; or to show that a confession is admissible inasmuch as it was made without oppression, or that secondary evidence of the contents of a document may be adduced because the original cannot be found after due search. These are facts which go to the admissibility or weight of evidence called in support of or to prove the 'primary' facts in issue.

2.7 FACTS FORMING PART OF THE *RES GESTAE*

Facts forming part of the '*res gestae*' are facts surrounding an event. It is not always obvious where an event begins and ends. To deal with an event in isolation, without reference to its antecedents in time, place, or surrounding circumstances, may render the event difficult or even impossible to comprehend. Other facts or circumstances may be so closely connected with the event in issue as to be, in reality, part and parcel of the same transaction.[18] Such ancillary facts are described, rather unhappily, as forming part of the *res gestae* of the fact in issue, and may be proved. A witness is permitted to state facts, not in meaningless isolation, but with such reasonable fullness and in such reasonable context as will make them comprehensible and useful. The rule is not confined by any strict limits of time or place. In the Australian case of *O'Leary v R* (1946) 73 CLR 566, a number of men employed at a timber camp went on a drunken orgy lasting several hours, during which a number of serious assaults were committed, and after which one of their number was found dying, having himself been savagely assaulted. On the prosecution of another of them for his murder, it was held that the episode should be looked at as a whole, including the occurrence of the previous assaults. Dixon J said:

> The evidence disclosed that, under the influence of the beer and wine he had drunk and continued to drink, he engaged in repeated acts of violence which might be regarded as amounting to a connected course of conduct. Without evidence of what, during that time, was done by those men who took any significant part in the matter and especially evidence of the behaviour of the prisoner, the transaction of which the alleged murder formed an integral part could not be truly understood and isolated from it, could only be presented as an unreal and not very intelligible event. The prisoner's generally violent and hostile conduct might well serve to explain his mind and attitude and, therefore, to implicate him in the resulting homicide.

One difficulty about the *res gestae* principle is that the kind of evidence necessary to provide the background to the offence charged may well, as it did in *O'Leary*, consist of evidence of other

---

[18] This way of describing evidence admissible under the *res gestae* principle has been held not to be the most accurate when the evidence is hearsay, but remains, it is submitted, a sound statement of the rule for general purposes: *Ratten v R* [1972] AC 378, 389 per Lord Wilberforce.

offences committed by the accused, or evidence of seriously discreditable conduct on his part. While such evidence may have legitimate probative value, it is also highly prejudicial to the accused, but it now seems to be established that evidence admissible as part of the *res gestae* is not inadmissible merely because it includes evidence of other offences or of bad character.[19] More recent cases have expanded the *res gestae* principle considerably, and one or two have used it to justify the adduction of evidence of previous offences or bad character of a kind which seems alarming. The modern rule was clearly stated by Purchas LJ in *Pettman* (2 May 1985, unreported), when he said:

> Where it is necessary to place before the jury evidence of part of a continual background of history relevant to the offence charged in the indictment and without the totality of which the account placed before the jury would be incomplete or incomprehensible, then the fact that the whole account involves including evidence establishing the commission of an offence with which the accused is not charged is not itself a ground for excluding the evidence.

In *Sidhu* (1994) 98 Cr App R 59, the accused was charged with conspiracy to possess explosives in England. It was held that the trial judge had rightly admitted a video-tape which apparently showed the accused leading a group of armed rebels in Pakistan. Although the evidence clearly expanded the jury's view of the extent of the accused's criminal activities, it was justified by the necessity of explaining the background to the accused's activities in England and the motives which lay behind it. In *Sawoniuk* [2000] 2 Cr App R 220, similar reasoning was employed, in a case where the accused was charged with four murders committed in Belarus in 1942, to justify the admission of evidence that during that time period, the accused had been a member of a group of police officers who had carried out an operation to identify and kill Jewish survivors of an earlier massacre. In this case, the necessity that the jury properly understand the circumstances which had prevailed such a long time ago in a foreign country, and the atmosphere surrounding the commission of ethnically based war crimes at that time, required that they be provided with a broadly based background to the incident. As Lord Bingham CJ put it, such an offence 'cannot fairly be judged in a factual vacuum'. In prosecutions for war crimes and crimes against humanity before the International Criminal Tribunal for the Former Yugoslavia, it is usual for the prosecution to adduce substantial evidence from factual and expert witnesses regarding the history of the Balkans conflict and the events leading up to it over the course of many years, and for the Trial Chamber to make detailed findings of fact regarding this background.[20]

This principle, however, is not confined to such unusual cases, but also operates in those of a more routine nature. In *Stevens* [1995] Crim LR 649, evidence of occasions on which the accused had assaulted a woman with whom he was living over a period of time was admitted as background evidence on a charge against the accused of the woman's murder. In *Mackie* (1973) 57 Cr App R 453, where the accused was charged with causing the death of a child, evidence was admitted to show the accused's earlier misconduct towards the child. The evidence was said to explain why the child had run from the accused and fallen to its death, but even the Court of Appeal observed that its prejudicial effect was 'enormous and far outweighed its value'. The accused's

---

[19] As to the relevance and admissibility of evidence of bad character in this context, see further 6.9, 6.16; and generally 6.2 *et seq.*

[20] *Tadic*, Case No. IT-94–1-T, Judgment of the Trial Chamber, 7 May 1997; *Delalic et al.*, Case No. IT-96–21-T, Judgment of the Trial Chamber, 16 November 1998. The same is true of the International Criminal Tribunal for Rwanda and, no doubt, will be true in the International Criminal Court.

conviction was nonetheless upheld. This may, perhaps, be regarded as an instance in which the trial court went too far. A most difficult case was *M (T)* [2000] 1 WLR 421, in which it was held that the trial judge had rightly admitted evidence of a long history of sexual and physical abuse suffered by M and his sister S, including evidence of occasions on which M had been forced to sexually abuse his siblings, with a view to explaining to the jury why S had not turned to members of her family for help with respect to her alleged rape by M. Clearly, the evidence, while adduced as background evidence, had a much more profound effect on the trial than that. It is submitted that the courts should subject such evidence to very close scrutiny, and should be prepared to exercise their discretion to exclude the evidence in a case such as *Mackie*, in which it may be effectively impossible for the jury to view the case against the accused dispassionately even given a scrupulously careful direction by the judge (as to the discretion to exclude, see 3.7 *et seq.*).[21]

The *res gestae* rule also often involves hearsay evidence consisting of statements made by participants in or observers of the relevant events. For example, in *Nye* (1977) 66 Cr App R 252, the Court of Appeal held that a statement made to a police officer by the victim of an assault identifying his assailant, some minutes after the assault, and after the victim had been sitting in his car recovering from the combined effects of the assault and the road traffic accident which preceded it, was admissible under the rule as accompanying and explaining the fact in issue, namely whether the assailant had assaulted the victim. The role of *res gestae* evidence as one of the preserved common law exceptions to the rule against hearsay is dealt with at 8.3 *et seq.*

2.8 FACTS RELEVANT TO FACTS IN ISSUE

In *DPP* v *Kilbourne* [1973] AC 729 at 756 Lord Simon of Glaisdale said:

> Evidence is relevant if it is logically probative or disprobative of some matter which requires proof. It is sufficient to say, even at the risk of etymological tautology, that relevant (i.e., logically probative or disprobative) evidence is evidence which makes the matter which requires proof more or less probable.

This is, perhaps, a simpler and more satisfactory, if less comprehensive definition of relevance, than the classic formulation in Stephen's *Digest*, according to which the word signified that:[22]

> any two facts to which it is applied are so related to each other that according to the common course of events, one either taken by itself or in connection with other facts proves or renders probable the past, present or future existence or non-existence of the other.

Neither attains the appealing simplicity of the American Federal Rule of Evidence 401, whereby the phrase 'relevant evidence'

> means evidence having any tendency to make the existence of any fact that is of consequence to the determination of the action more probable or less probable than it would be without the evidence.

---

[21] This was recognized in *Dolan* [2003] 1 Cr App R 18, in which the Court of Appeal held that it had been wrong to admit as 'background' on a charge of murdering a child, evidence of the accused's violent treatment of inanimate objects while in a 'bad temper'. As to the relevance of evidence of the state of mind or demeanour of a victim of sexual abuse for the purpose of suggesting that the abuse occurred, see *Townsend* [2003] EWCA Crim 3173; *Venn* [2003] EWCA Crim 236; *Keast* [1998] Crim LR 748.

[22] *Digest of the Law of Evidence*, 12th edn, art. 1. The definition was somewhat different in earlier editions, but this seems to be the author's mature view.

Thus, relevant evidence is evidence which has probative value in assisting the court or jury to determine the facts in issue. Relevance is not a legal concept, but a logical one, which describes the relationship between a piece of evidence and a fact in issue to the proof of which the evidence is directed. If the evidence contributes in a logical sense, to any extent, either to the proof or the disproof of the fact in issue, then the evidence is relevant to the fact in issue. If not, it is irrelevant. It is a fundamental rule of the law of evidence that, if not actually material, evidence must be relevant in order to be admissible. The converse, however, is not true, because much relevant evidence is inadmissible under the specific rules of evidence affecting admissibility. In determining the relevance of evidence in the context of a legal trial, certainly a jury trial, a judge must probably work on the assumption that the evidence is true. This is the reverse of the mental process suggested by scientific definitions of evidence (see 1.1) under which evidence cannot properly be described as relevant unless it is true, but in a judicial trial the admission of evidence must precede its factual evaluation. For this purpose, therefore, it seems inevitable that the judge should ask himself how the evidence would relate to the issues and the other evidence in the case on the basis that the jury accept it as true. For the purposes of one particular class of evidence, this assumption has been formalized. In relation to evidence of bad character admissible in criminal cases, s. 109 of the Criminal Justice Act 2003 provides:

> (1) Subject to subsection (2) a reference in this Chapter to the relevance or probative value of evidence is a reference to the relevance or probative value on the assumption that it is true.
>
> (2) In assessing the relevance or probative value of an item of evidence for any purpose of this Chapter, a court need not assume that the evidence is true if it appears, on the basis of any material before the court (including any evidence it decides to hear on the matter) that no court or jury could reasonably find it to be true.

It has been said that relevance is generally determinable by common sense and experience (*Randall* [2004] 1 All ER 67, [20] per Lord Steyn). Nevertheless, relevant facts are easier to identify than to describe in the abstract. A good illustration is provided by what is sometimes called the presumption of continuance. The presumption of continuance is not a legal presumption,[23] but is simply an expression of the natural and logical inference that many facts and circumstances may be taken to continue unchanged, in the absence of evidence that some event intervened to change them. In such circumstances, evidence that a fact existed at a time other than the time in issue is relevant to prove the existence of the same fact at the time in issue. Thus, in *Brown v Wren Brothers* [1895] 1 QB 390, a case in which the continued existence of a partnership was in issue, evidence that the partnership had existed at an earlier time was held to be admissible to support an inference that it had continued to exist. In *Attorney-General v Bradlaugh* (1885) 14 QBD 667, evidence to prove that a person held certain theological views four years before the period of time with which the court was concerned was admitted to support the inference that he continued to hold those views at the relevant time. In *Beresford v St Albans Justices* (1905) 22 TLR 1, on the issue of the speed at which a person was driving at a given time, evidence of the speed at which he had been driving some minutes before was admitted.[24] *Joy v Phillips, Mills & Co. Ltd* [1916] 1 KB 849 was an action concerning the death of a stable-boy, who had been kicked by a horse. Evidence

---

[23] Legal presumptions may be described as inferences which the tribunal of fact is required to draw, as a matter of law, in the absence of rebutting evidence: see 4.4; Chapter 20, part C. A purely factual inference is one which the tribunal of fact is free to draw or decline to draw as it sees fit, though if strong and natural, as in the present instance, it will generally be drawn.

[24] See also *Dalloz* (1908) 1 Cr App R 258.

was admitted to prove that the boy had previously been in the habit of teasing horses, and that, when found, he was holding a halter which he had no occasion to be using at the time. The possession of the halter bore directly on the cause of the boy's death, which was a fact in issue. In this case, the relevant fact was proved by evidence of acts earlier in time than the fact in issue, but it is equally permissible to call evidence proving relevant facts which were contemporaneous with, or subsequent to the fact in issue. In *Woolf* v *Woolf* [1931] P 134, it was held that proof of the fact that a couple, who were not married to each other, occupied the same bedroom was relevant to an allegation that they had committed adultery, and of the existence at that time of an adulterous relationship. On a charge of causing death by dangerous driving, it has been held to be relevant that the accused used cocaine shortly before the accident, without regard to the quantity ingested: *Plevdell* [2006] 1 Cr App R 212.[25]

Another illustration is the rule that evidence of habit or routine practice may be admitted for the purpose of showing that a person or organization behaved on a certain occasion in the same manner in which that person or organization habitually behaved. This rule is conveniently expressed in American Federal Rule of Evidence 406, which provides:

> Evidence of the habit of a person or the routine practice of an organization, whether corroborated or not and regardless of the presence of eyewitnesses, is relevant to prove that the conduct of the person or organization on a particular occasion was in conformity with the habit or routine practice.

For example, if an issue arose as to whether the defendants had cleaned aisle five of their supermarket on the occasion when the claimant fell and was injured there, and there was no other evidence to that effect, evidence that the defendants routinely cleaned aisle five every day at a time earlier than the claimant's accident would be relevant to show that they did so on the occasion in question. The defendants would, of course, have to show a consistent pattern of conduct sufficient to persuade the court that it could safely be regarded as a routine practice. Similarly, evidence that a person arrived for a work at 9 o'clock every weekday morning during the ten-year period of his employment could be regarded as a pattern of habitual conduct on his part sufficient to justify admitting the evidence as relevant to the question of whether he arrived at work at the same time on a particular occasion in respect of which there was no other evidence.

2.8.1 Cases of doubtful relevance

Many of the most difficult judgments about what evidence is and is not relevant occur in the area of acts committed by one of the parties extrinsic to those covered by the pleadings or indictment in the instant case. The most notorious of these cases are those relating to the use of character evidence, for example questions of when, if ever, it can be properly be claimed that the character of the accused in a criminal case is relevant to his guilt of the offence charged, or that the character of a witness is relevant to the credibility of his evidence in the instant case. This is complex issue dealt with at length in Chapters 5 and 6 of this book and discussed succinctly at 5.2. But the relevance of other acts is an issue which causes difficulty in many other kinds of case. In *Holcombe* v *Hewson* (1810) 2 Camp 391, a brewer brought an action against a publican to enforce a covenant to buy beer from the brewer. The publican's defence was that the beer supplied by the brewer was bad. The brewer offered evidence that he had previously supplied good beer to other publicans. The court rejected the evidence as irrelevant. It may be that, in the absence of

---

[25] But contrast cases involving the consumption of alcohol, in which there seems to be a correlation between relevance and the quantity ingested: see, e.g., *Woodward* [1995] 2 Cr App R 388.

evidence that the beer supplied to the defendant came from the same brew as that sold to other publicans, the evidence was irrelevant. But it is not hard to imagine cases in which similar evidence might be at least marginally relevant. In *Hart* v *Lancashire & Yorkshire Railway Co.* (1869) 21 LT 261, it was held to be irrelevant to an action for negligence for the plaintiff to offer evidence that, following the accident allegedly caused by the defendant's negligence, the defendant altered the practice on which the allegation of negligence was based. The argument which prevailed was that negligence must be judged on the basis of the state of the defendant's knowledge at the time before the accident rather than at a subsequent time. On this reasoning, evidence that a defendant engaged in 'subsequent remedial measures' which, if taken previously, might have prevented the accident sustained by the plaintiff, must be excluded on the ground of relevance. If this does represent the law, it is surely highly questionable. Evidence that a defendant corrected a problem may reflect knowledge gained since the accident, but it may also indicate that the problem could equally have been avoided if reasonable steps had been taken in the light of knowledge available at the time of the accident, a question of feasibility and the reasonableness of the defendant's pre-accident conduct, which is surely relevant to the issue of negligence. If the claimant is injured because of a fall on the defendant's premises caused by a defective staircase, evidence that the defendant repaired the staircase the day after the accident may well indicate that the repairs could have been made before the accident, and that it would have been reasonable to expect the defendant to do so. Similar arguments may apply in cases where the defendant re-designs a product after the claimant is injured while using it, or takes steps to restrain his dog after it has bitten the claimant. Such evidence may not go the whole way towards proving negligence, but it is submitted that it is hardly irrelevant. It is of interest that American jurisdictions generally regard such evidence of subsequent remedial measures as inadmissible if tendered on the issue of negligence, but not because it is irrelevant. Rather, the evidence is excluded as a matter of policy because, although relevant, it is thought that its admission may tend to deter defendants from taking such measures and thereby harm public safety. The evidence may be and often is admitted for other purposes, for example to prove ownership or control of the object or premises which caused the injury, if the defendant disputes this: see, e.g., Federal Rule of Evidence 407.

2.8.2 Conditional relevance

It sometimes happens that the relevance of a particular piece of evidence is not immediately clear when it is tendered. This is usually because of the simple truth that evidence must be called in order and by one witness at a time, so that the further facts necessary to demonstrate its relevance may not yet have been elicited. The trial judge is entitled to insist that the relevance of evidence be demonstrated to him, before permitting that evidence to be given. But the practice is to allow proof of the fact '*de bene esse*', which means that it is admitted for the purpose of maintaining the continuity of the trial subject to the condition that it will later be shown to be relevant. This will be done only if the party tendering the evidence undertakes to demonstrate the relevance of the evidence in due course by introducing further evidence. If it does not appear, later, that its relevance has been established, the jury must be directed to ignore it, and in some cases, it may be necessary to discharge them if the fact is highly prejudicial. An illustration is where counsel seeks to put in a document in cross-examination, strict proof of which and the relevance of which to the defence must await the presentation of the defence case. Such evidence is described as 'conditionally relevant', because its actual relevance may stand or fall by reference to other evidence.

2.9 STANDARDS OF COMPARISON

Wherever it is necessary to judge the conduct of a party against an objective standard, it may be proved what such objective standard is, or was at the material time and in the material circumstances. Negligence is a common example. The standard of the reasonable man demands that evidence may be given to show how others might reasonably have behaved in similar circumstances, and this fact, if established, is relevant to the necessary assessment of how the party accused in fact behaved. Where the objective standard is one which involves conduct in a situation outside the everyday experience of the court, the standard may be proved by expert evidence of the conduct in such circumstances, for example, of a reasonable member of a trade or a profession,[26] or of the accepted practice of commercial men.[27] In a common situation of everyday life, it may be a matter of which the judge could take judicial notice, or find proved by the totality of the evidence given in the case.

2.10 TERMINOLOGY OF ADMISSIBILITY AND WEIGHT

2.10.1 Admissibility

Evidence is said to be admissible or receivable if it is relevant and if it is not excluded by the rules of evidence. The rules of evidence are rules of law, and it follows that, unlike relevance, which is determined solely by reference to the logical relationship between the evidence and a fact in issue, admissibility is a matter of law. To be admissible, evidence must be relevant, but relevance is not enough to result in admissibility. While evidence must be relevant to be admissible, the converse proposition is not true. Not all relevant evidence is admissible.[28] Of course, the rules of evidence regarding admissibility are the central feature of the law of evidence, and occupy most of the remaining parts of this book. As a matter of law, questions of admissibility are decided by the court, even when the question involves an investigation of secondary factual issues. This subject is discussed further at 3.2 *et seq*. Questions of admissibility are determined by the *lex fori*, that is, the law of England, even when the question is one of evidence originating abroad, or when the facts in issue arose abroad, or have some foreign aspect.

2.10.1.1 Limited admissibility

Evidence is said to be admissible for one or more purposes. By 'purpose' is meant that the evidence is directed towards the proof of a certain fact. Evidence may, of course, be admissible for more than one purpose, and such evidence causes no problems. However, evidence that is admissible for one purpose, but not for another, referred to as evidence of limited admissibility, causes great difficulty, particularly for juries and other lay tribunals of fact. If evidence is relevant and admissible for one purpose but inadmissible for another purpose, its proponent is entitled to have

---

[26] *Chapman* v *Walton* (1833) 10 Bing 57. The evidence must show what the generally accepted conduct would be, not merely what the witness himself would have done. Such evidence is very common in, e.g., medical and legal negligence cases.

[27] *Noble* v *Kennoway* (1780) 2 Doug KB 510; *Fleet* v *Murton* (1871) LR 7 QB 126.

[28] Cf. American Federal Rule of Evidence 402: 'All relevant evidence is admissible, except as otherwise provided by the Constitution of the United States, by Act of Congress, by these rules, or by other rules prescribed by the Supreme Court pursuant to statutory authority. Evidence which is not relevant is not admissible'.

that evidence admitted. The opponent is, however, entitled to require that the judge direct the jury that they may consider the evidence only for the purpose for which it is admissible, and not for any other purpose: *Bond* [1906] 2 KB 389, 411–12 per Jelf J. The impact of the evidence on the jury usually outweighs even a scrupulously careful direction. Thus, where two accused, A and B, are jointly charged with an offence, the prosecution may adduce evidence of a confession made by A implicating both himself and B. B is entitled to have the jury directed that the confession is evidence against A only, and not against B. But an obvious potential for prejudice remains, especially in the not uncommon situation in which A goes to some lengths to divert the blame to B. It is compounded in criminal cases by the fact that B cannot compel A to give evidence and submit to cross-examination.[29]

2.10.2 Weight

The weight of evidence is a qualitative assessment of the probative value which admissible evidence has in relation to the facts in issue. To say that evidence is relevant and admissible concludes the issue of law, that a party is entitled to bring that evidence before the court. Such evidence then has the potential to persuade the court of the probability of the facts towards which it is directed. But its actual persuasive value in relation to those facts depends upon the view taken by the tribunal of fact of the truthfulness, reliability, and cogency of the evidence. Depending on what that view is, evidence may be of virtually no weight at all, or may rest on one of an infinite number of points on the upwards sliding scale, ending with evidence which is so weighty as almost to conclude the case in itself.[30] Although the weight of evidence is a question of fact, and strictly cannot arise until the evidence is first shown to be relevant and admissible, it is not always possible to segregate these qualities of law and fact altogether. The relevance of evidence is closely bound up with its weight, and to say that evidence is insufficiently relevant to be admitted, necessarily involves some judgment on its weight. And where the judge has a discretion whether to admit or exclude evidence (as to which see 3.6 *et seq.*) it is both usual and legitimate for him to take into account the likely weight of the evidence and to compare this with its likely prejudicial effect.

The assessment of weight depends upon a multiplicity of factors, which would be almost impossible to define, but which may certainly include matters extraneous to the evidence itself, for example other evidence given in the case, or the demeanour of the witness who gives the evidence. In cases where hearsay evidence is admissible by virtue of the provisions of the Civil Evidence Act 1995, Parliament has provided a statement of the matters to be considered in assessing the weight of evidence so admitted.[31] The various factors so enumerated would appear to be those which any reasonable tribunal would in any event take into account, and it is submitted that their elaboration may well be unnecessary.

To say that evidence lacks weight does not mean that such evidence is perjured or dishonestly motivated, or even exaggerated. It is true that evidence having these characteristics will lack weight, but equally, so will evidence which is unreliable because the witness's recollection has

---

[29] Such directions are helpfully referred to in the United States as 'limiting' or 'curative instructions'. Federal Rule of Evidence 105 provides: 'When evidence which is admissible as to one party or for one purpose but not admissible as to another party or for another purpose is admitted, the court, upon request, shall restrict the evidence to its proper scope and instruct the jury accordingly'.

[30] The use of the word 'conclude' to express very weighty evidence should not be confused with its use to describe evidence which as a matter of law may not be contradicted, and so 'concludes' an issue: see 2.3.4.

[31] Civil Evidence Act 1995, s. 4; see 8.34. Similar provisions relating to hearsay admitted in criminal cases made in the Criminal Justice Act 1988 and earlier legislation are not reproduced in the Criminal Justice Act 2003.

failed him, or because he had no adequate opportunity to perceive the facts about which he is called to testify, or because his knowledge of the facts is insufficient, or, in the case of an expert witness, because his expertise or experience or opportunity to investigate is too limited. So, too, will any evidence which is for any reason unable to afford the court the assistance it needs in relation to the facts in issue.

2.11 RECOMMENDED FURTHER READING

Allen, R.J. and Pardo, M.S., 'Facts in law and facts of law' (2003) **7**(3) *International Journal of Evidence and Proof* 153.

Anderson, T., Schum, D., and Twining, W., *Analysis of Evidence* (Cambridge: Cambridge University Press, 2005).

Choo, A.L.-T., 'The notion of relevance and defence evidence' [1993] *Criminal Law Review* 114.

Kirgis, P.F., 'Questions of fact in the practice of law: A response to Allen and Pardo's "Facts in Law and Facts of Law"' (2004) **8**(1) *International Journal of Evidence and Proof* 47.

Ormerod, D., 'Redundant res gestae?' [1998] *Criminal Law Review* 301.

Twining, W., 'Taking Facts Seriously—Again' in Roberts, P. and Redmayne, M., *Innovations in Evidence and Proof* (Oxford: Hart Publishing, 2007) pp. 65–87.

2.12 QUESTIONS FOR DISCUSSION

1. What are tribunals of law and of fact?

2. What are 'facts in issue'?

3. In a criminal case, by reference to what will the 'facts in issue' be determined?

4. What is meant if it is stated that there is *prima facie* evidence that the accused was 'drunk in charge' of her vehicle?

5. How is 'direct evidence' distinguished from 'circumstantial' and also 'hearsay' evidence?

6. Is 'circumstantial evidence' always of little or no value?

7. Define when evidence is 'relevant'?

8. What is meant if evidence is described as being 'weighty' or, alternatively, 'lacking in weight'?

3

THE JUDICIAL FUNCTION IN THE LAW OF EVIDENCE

SUMMARY OF MAIN POINTS (PARTS A AND B)

- A court is composed of a tribunal of law and a tribunal of fact.

- In a jury trial the judge is the tribunal of law, and the jury the tribunal of fact. In a non-jury trial the judge or magistrates perform both functions.

- Questions of the admissibility of evidence are questions of law for the tribunal of law; questions of the weight of the evidence are questions of fact for the tribunal of fact.

- The judge must also decide whether there is a case to answer and, in a jury trial, direct the jury about the uses which may and may not be made of the evidence.

A   DIVISION OF FUNCTIONS

3.1   TRIBUNALS OF LAW AND FACT

Any process of trial must provide for the determination of both issues of law and issues of fact. Broadly speaking, in any case tried by a judge sitting with a jury, questions of law arising in the case fall to be determined by the judge and questions of fact by the jury. Jury trial is now rare in civil cases, and the functions of the jury will be considered principally in relation to criminal trials on indictment, in which they are almost always employed.[1] Where a judge sits alone to consider a civil case, he is himself the tribunal of law and fact and determines all issues of both kinds. In the case of magistrates' courts and tribunals, the court or tribunal is entitled to decide all matters of law and fact canvassed before it, but on matters of law should seek and accept the advice of their clerk.[2]

Questions of law comprise matters of substantive law governing the claim or charge, the admissibility of evidence, any rules of law or practice governing the production or effect of evidence and the question of whether there is sufficient evidence to warrant consideration by the tribunal of fact at all. The judicial function also includes the determination of necessary questions ancillary to the trial itself, such as whether cause has been shown in the challenge of a juror, whether the jury, or a particular member of the jury should be discharged, and matters concerning the administration of the trial, for example bail. It is most important to observe that the judge, as the tribunal of law, is responsible for deciding all questions of the relevance and admissibility of evidence. The jury, or other tribunal of fact, is not concerned with these questions of law. The segregation of the functions of the judge and jury for the purposes of the admissibility of evidence, by virtue of which the jury plays no part in determining questions of admissibility, does not violate the right of the accused to a fair trial under art. 6 of the European Convention on Human Rights. The jury is not a 'public authority' for the purposes of s. 6(3) of the Human Rights Act 1998, and so has no duty or right to satisfy itself of the admissibility of evidence, independently of the judge, for the purposes of determining whether the accused's right to a fair trial under the Convention is being protected: *Mushtaq* [2005] 1 WLR 1513. The practice is not to reveal to the jury the details of the judge's rulings on admissibility, because of the risk that the jury may be tempted to accord additional weight to evidence merely because it has been ruled to be admissible. This is of particular concern in relation to the admissibility of confessions, because the judge may well have made certain findings of fact with respect to the circumstances in which the

---

[1] Juries are employed in civil cases to try actions for defamation, malicious prosecution, false imprisonment, and cases in which fraud is alleged. But their use is not mandatory in such cases, and is not excluded in other cases. See Supreme Court Act 1981, s. 69(1); County Courts Act 1984, s. 66(3); *Blackstone's Civil Practice*, 2009 edn, ch. 58. Under ss. 43 to 50 of the Criminal Justice Act 2003 and ss. 17 and 18 of the Domestic Violence Crime and Victims Act 2004, it is possible for trials on indictment in criminal cases to be conducted by a judge sitting alone in certain limited instances. The detail of these provisions is outside the scope of the present work: reference should be made to *Blackstone's Criminal Practice*, 2009 edn, paras D13.66–13.72.

[2] As to the proper advisory role of the clerk, see *Consolidated Criminal Practice Direction*, para. V.55. Professional magistrates (district judges) are in theory in the same position as lay justices, but the clerk's advice may be less crucial in practice. At courts martial, the tribunal must accept the advice of their judge-advocate on matters of law. Lay magistrates, when sitting with the (legally qualified) judge at the Crown Court, are also judges of the court (see Supreme Court Act 1981, ss. 8, 73) and should participate in all decisions of the court. But they must accept the ruling of the judge on matters of law: *Orpin* [1975] QB 283. Questions of the admissibility of evidence may be questions of mixed law and fact, and the lay magistrates should participate in the factual aspects of the decision.

confession was made. Such findings might pre-dispose the jury to attach greater weight to the confession, even though, in determining admissibility, the judge does not concern himself with the question of whether or not the confession is true: see *Mitchell* v *R* [1998] AC 695; *Thompson* v *R* [1998] AC 811; but see also 9.15.1.

Questions of fact comprise the decision of all matters concerning the truth or probability of all facts in issue as derived from the substantive law, statements of case, indictment or charge (seen in the light of the burden and standard of proof applicable to the issues), and the weight of any evidence admitted for the purpose of proving or disproving the facts in issue. In a criminal trial, a jury also decide, if necessary, whether the accused stands mute of malice or by visitation of God, and the question of fitness to plead; but if the accused is found fit to plead, another jury must be empanelled to try him.[3]

Many issues involve in part a question of law and in part (if the question of law be answered in a way which does not preclude it) a question of fact. Thus, in defamation actions, it is a question of law whether the words complained of are capable of bearing a defamatory meaning, and a question of fact whether they are defamatory of the claimant.

There are cases in which the distinction between matters of law and fact is not at all obvious and in case of doubt, reference must be made to the appropriate substantive law to establish what matters are to be determined by the judge, and what by the jury. For example, in an action for malicious prosecution, it is a question of fact for the jury to determine what steps the defendant took to inform himself of the truth of the charge, and whether the defendant honestly believed in the truth of the charge; it is for the judge to rule as a matter of law whether the defendant had, in the light of the facts found, any reasonable and probable cause. But in other cases, what is reasonable is a question of fact, for example, whether allegedly provocative words or conduct would have led a reasonable man to react as the accused did. Moreover, some questions of substantive fact, for instance the proper interpretation of foreign law, are decided by the judge.[4] The interpretation of ordinary English words, used in their normal sense, is in general a question of fact, but where the words bear some legal significance, their interpretation will be a question of law (see, e.g., *Brutus* v *Cozens* [1973] AC 854, per Lord Reid at 861). In the case of words used as technical terms expert evidence may be admitted to assist the court in determining their proper meaning and usage: *Couzens* [1992] Crim LR 822. Entries in published dictionaries may be admitted to prove the meaning of words generally: see 8.7.2.

B   FUNCTIONS OF THE JUDGE IN LEGAL ISSUES CONCERNING EVIDENCE

The functions of the trial judge in relation to matters involving the law of evidence are concerned with questions of admissibility and the rules governing the production and effect of evidence. A judge sitting alone in a civil case must direct his mind to questions of weight also.

3.2 ADMISSIBILITY

It is as well to put this subject into perspective by noting that most pieces of evidence tendered in most cases are agreed by the parties to be admissible, and are admitted without objection.

---

[3] See the Criminal Procedure (Insanity) Act 1964, s. 4 as substituted by the Criminal Procedure (Insanity and Unfitness to Plead) Act 1991, s. 2.

[4] Questions of foreign law are questions of fact, and should be proved by expert evidence: see 11.7.6.

In such a case, the judge has no role to play until he considers the weight of the evidence (if sitting without a jury) or directs the jury about the evidence. However, where an objection is made to the admissibility of evidence, the judge must rule on the issue in his capacity as the tribunal of law. Where the judge sits with a jury, there is a convenient separation of the tribunals of law and fact, and the procedure for dealing with evidential objections is simple and satisfactory. Where the judge sits alone, or where the magistrates or tribunal are the judges of the law as well as the facts, substantial problems arise. Both situations must be considered.

The parties should inform each other of any questions of admissibility which are to be referred to the judge, and the controverted evidence should not be opened or referred to in the presence of the jury, unless and until it is ruled to be admissible. Questions of admissibility are properly decided at the stage when they naturally arise in the course of the case, but where the prosecution (or in some cases the defence) cannot coherently open or begin to present their case without reference to the controverted evidence, the judge should be invited to rule on it as a preliminary issue. Such a case would be where the only evidence against an accused is a confession, the admissibility of which is disputed.

3.2.1 Procedure in jury trial

We have already seen that, in a trial before a judge and jury, all questions of the relevance and admissibility of evidence fall to be decided by the judge. The jury, whose province is the factual question of the weight of the evidence, are not concerned with admissibility. For obvious reasons, any discussion about the admissibility of evidence, and, *a fortiori*, the presentation of any secondary evidence adduced in support of or in opposition to the disputed evidence, should take place in the absence of the jury. If the jury is exposed to evidence which may be held to be inadmissible, the resulting prejudice to the party affected may require the discharge of the jury and a consequent retrial. At the very least, the judge must take the unsatisfactory course of directing the jury to disregard the evidence, which may have the opposite effect of drawing more attention to it.

The practice, therefore, is for the jury to retire while the judge hears argument and secondary evidence in their absence.[5] Any secondary evidence must itself be admissible under the rules of evidence (*Chadwick* (1934) 24 Cr App R 138; *O'Loughlin* [1988] 3 All ER 431). In most cases, the question can be resolved by legal argument alone, on the basis of agreed or assumed facts. However, in some cases, the question of admissibility will involve a question of mixed fact and law. In such a case, the judge conducts proceedings known as a 'trial within a trial' or proceedings on the '*voir dire*', a name taken from the form of oath prescribed at common law for testimony given on secondary issues. The judge will hear witnesses examined and cross-examined on the secondary issues only, will inspect any relevant documents, and will hear argument from counsel. If the judge decides to admit the evidence, the same witnesses must, of course, give their evidence again when the jury returns to court—which makes the 'trial within a trial' a time-consuming exercise.

Almost always, the procedure on the *voir dire* is employed to determine the admissibility of a confession, in which factual issues about the manner in which the confession was obtained

---

[5] The comparative formality of English courts precludes the useful American device known as a 'side-bar conference', in which counsel address the judge *sotto voce* at the bench on questions of admissibility. This obviously compares favourably in terms of the consumption of time with the retirement of the jury. It is not practicable when secondary evidence is to be given, and some jurisdictions have rules requiring the retirement of the jury in some cases, for example the admissibility of confessions (see, e.g., Federal Rule of Evidence 104(c)). But overall, it serves well to maintain the momentum of the trial.

frequently arise.[6] Indeed, it has been questioned whether the procedure of hearing evidence in the absence of the jury (as opposed to legal argument) is ever necessary or desirable in relation to other questions of admissibility: see *Flemming* (1987) 86 Cr App R 32 (admissibility of evidence of identification). Certainly, its use in determining other issues is, and should be, relatively unusual, as most questions of admissibility are questions of law and the judge should not involve himself with questions of the weight of evidence. However, it is submitted that the procedure has other legitimate applications, for example the determination of the competence of some witnesses,[7] or the existence and extent of a privilege. In *Wright* [2000] Crim LR 851, it was held that the *voir dire* procedure should be used in determining the propriety of proposed cross-examination as to credit based on disputed discreditable conduct not involving previous convictions. In such cases, there may be an absence of concrete evidence to support or refute the charges made in cross-examination, while those charges may be very damaging to the witness, so that the judge may feel obliged to consider the exercise of his discretion to exclude the cross-examination. A *voir dire* hearing would obviously be useful in providing the judge with information relevant to the exercise of his discretion before potentially damaging charges are made in the presence of the jury. There may be other cases to which the same observations apply.

While the procedure on the *voir dire* is useful in avoiding the exposure of the jury to potentially inadmissible evidence, it presents some tactical problems for the defence, inasmuch as the prosecution witnesses concerned (usually police officers proving the obtaining of a confession) enjoy the benefit of learning the line to be taken in cross-examination before they are cross-examined in the presence of the jury. If the confession is excluded, the sacrifice of the element of surprise is justified. If it is not, the officers will have the advantage of a rehearsal, which may greatly enhance their demeanour and thus the weight of their evidence before the jury. For this reason, defence counsel have sometimes elected not to ask for a 'trial within a trial', and have dealt with the confession by attacking its admissibility and weight together in the presence of the jury. The judge might then still exclude the confession in such a case, on a submission being made to him. This involves the calculated risk of permitting the jury to be exposed to a potentially inadmissible confession in return for retaining the element of surprise and the chance of persuading the jury that the confession, even if admitted, should not be relied upon.

This practice was expressly approved by Lord Bridge, delivering the advice of the Privy Council in *Ajodha* v *The State* [1982] AC 204. But it appears that s. 76(2) of the Police and Criminal Evidence Act 1984 has altered it and that a hearing on the *voir dire* is now required whenever the admissibility of a confession is disputed. That subsection provides that where it is represented to the court that the confession was, or may have been obtained in a manner requiring it to be excluded, the court *shall not* allow the confession to be given in evidence unless the prosecution proves that it was not so obtained.[8] It was at one time considered that the judge retained a power to reconsider, at a later stage of the trial, a ruling made on the *voir dire*, if evidence came to light that appeared to justify such a course (*Watson* [1980] 1 WLR 991). An analogous position was

---

[6] As to the substance of these issues, see 9.4 *et seq.*

[7] Including in some cases the competence of an expert witness: see *G* [2004] 2 Cr App R 368. Issues of competence should generally be determined in the absence of the jury: see Youth Justice and Criminal Evidence Act 1999, s. 54(4); 15.3; see also Criminal Justice Act 2003, s. 123(4); 8.26.

[8] See, e.g., *Millard* [1987] Crim LR 196. If the short report of this case is accurate, the result appears both unseemly and unnecessary. It is true that in *Liverpool Juvenile Court, ex parte R* [1988] QB 1, the Divisional Court held that in a summary trial in the magistrates' court a 'trial within a trial' must be held if a s. 76(2) representation is made to the court, but the court disclaimed any intention of laying down rules for trials on indictment in which the circumstances are different.

espoused in relation to summary trial in *Liverpool Juvenile Court, ex parte R* [1988] QB 1. However, more recent cases have held, based on the wording of s. 76 of the Police and Criminal Evidence Act 1984, that an accused who wishes to exclude a confession *must* apply to do so before the confession is adduced in evidence. In *Sat-Bhambra* (1988) 88 Cr App R 55, the Court of Appeal said:

> The words of section 76 are crucial: 'proposes to be given in evidence' and 'shall not allow the confession to be given' are not, in our judgment, appropriate to describe something which has happened in the past. They are directed solely to the situation before the statement goes before the jury. Once the judge has ruled that it should do so, section 76 (and section 78, for the same reasons) ceases to have effect.

It is submitted, however, that the trial judge retains a general discretion to ensure that the accused is given a fair trial, and that there may be cases in which the admission of a confession is later demonstrated to be so plainly wrong that this object can be achieved only by discharging the jury and ordering a new trial. It should also be borne in mind that there is some authority that the defence must request or consent to the jury retiring during the *voir dire*.[9]

3.2.2 Procedure in non-jury trial

The convenient separation of the tribunals of law and fact cannot be duplicated in a trial before a judge sitting alone, a magistrates' court or a tribunal. In very many cases, an effective legal argument can be made using general principle and a generic description of the disputed material, without exposing the court to the detail of the evidence, and this should be done wherever possible. But in some cases, it is necessary that the tribunal of fact hear the disputed evidence and, if it is later excluded, put it out of their minds. While tribunals of fact no doubt make a conscientious effort to perform this difficult mental feat, it is impossible not to sympathize with the opponent of the evidence in such an unenviable situation. In the case of a legally qualified judge sitting alone, the problem is less acute, since the trained judicial mind is at least in theory equipped to adapt to such developments during a case. The most critical problems arise when the admissibility of a confession is disputed in a magistrates' court.

There has been a surprising degree of uncertainty as to the procedure in this situation. There is certainly some force in the proposition that the *voir dire* procedure is of questionable effectiveness in a summary trial, and this has led to some feeling that it is a waste of time. In *F (An Infant) v Chief Constable of Kent* [1982] Crim LR 682, the Divisional Court went so far as to hold that the procedure on the *voir dire* was inappropriate in a magistrates' court, and should not be used. But it has the merit of producing a specific ruling on the issue of admissibility, which may otherwise be lost in a general finding of guilt, and which may be significant not only on appeal, but at trial in making a decision whether or not to call the accused or make a submission of no case to answer. And the court in *F v Chief Constable of Kent* did not offer a workable alternative. A subsequent Divisional Court in *Liverpool Juvenile Court, ex parte R*,[10] directly contradicting the holding in *F v Chief Constable of Kent*, held that a magistrates' court must use the *voir dire* procedure if a

---

[9] *Ajodha* v *The State* [1982] AC 204, 223 per Lord Bridge; *Anderson* (1929) 21 Cr App R 178. *Sed quaere*: the judge surely retains some power to prevent the airing of highly prejudicial and potentially inadmissible evidence in the presence of the jury, even if he may in general defer to the expressed preference of the defence. This seems to be confirmed by *Davis* [1990] Crim LR 860. American jurisdictions generally require the admissibility of confessions to be determined on motion before the trial begins. The Privy Council has held that it is improper for the judge to reveal his ruling on admissibility in a trial within a trial to the jury, because of the danger of prejudice to the accused (*Thompson* v *R* [1998] AC 811; *Mitchell* v *R* [1998] AC 695).

[10] [1988] QB 1. See also *Oxford City Justices, ex parte Berry* [1988] QB 507.

s. 76(2) representation is made to it. The accused is entitled to a ruling on the specific issue of admissibility at or before the end of the prosecution case. Interestingly, the Court added[11] that the defence retain a discretion to withhold a representation and raise the issues of admissibility and weight later in the trial, apparently analogously to the principle stated by Lord Bridge in *Ajodha* v *The State* [1982] AC 204. But whether this is tenable in the light of the Court of Appeal's decision in *Sat-Bhambra* [1988] 88 Cr App R 55 is obviously open to question.

The suggestion that the accused is entitled to a trial within a trial in summary proceedings has sometimes been doubted (see, e.g., *Vel* v *Chief Constable of North Wales* (1987) 151 JP 510). But the balance of convenience surely favours allowing the procedure. Not only does it allow the bench to make a specific finding on the issue of admissibility, but it also permits the accused to give evidence on that issue without prejudicing his right not to give evidence on the main issue. The latter point was acknowledged by the Divisional Court in *Halawa* v *Federation Against Copyright Theft* [1995] 1 Cr App R 21, at least in relation to applications to exclude a confession as a matter of discretion. While the procedure to be followed in a particular case must lie within the discretion of the court, there seems to be little merit in a general prohibition of hearings on the *voir dire*.

Where magistrates hear an application to exclude a confession, particularly when evidence is given as to the substance and circumstances of the making of the confession, it has been suggested that the trial should then proceed before a differently constituted bench: see *DPP* v *Lawrence* [2008] 1 Cr App R 147. But this course, while obviously convenient in some ways, is not free from difficulty. There is some question as to whether it could be proper for two different benches to divide functions in a continuing single case in this way. It is submitted that it could only be proper if the trial begins again *de novo*, and in this case there is no reason other than comity why either party should not insist on having the issue of the confession heard again. It may be best for the magistrates simply to do their best, difficult as it is, to put any excluded evidence out of their minds.

3.2.3 Importance of objections

In the United States, all jurisdictions concur that unless an evidential error is made part of the record of the trial, an appellate court will not consider the point on appeal, unless the error is one of a very few considered to be so fundamental as to require intervention regardless of objection. Although the appellate courts of this country are less strict, and will often consider points not taken below, this will not always be the case, and a specific objection to a ruling for or against the admissibility of evidence should always be made and argued. In *The Tasmania* (1890) 15 App Cas 223, 225,[12] Lord Herschell observed:

> A point not taken at the trial, and presented for the first time in the Court of Appeal...ought to be most jealously scrutinised...A Court of Appeal ought only to decide in favour of an appellant on a

---

[11] [1988] QB 1, 10–11.

[12] More leniency is likely to be shown only if the point not raised below is essentially 'procedural' in nature: see, e.g., *Davis* v *Galmoye* (1888) 39 ChD 322. This should not apply to substantive questions of admissibility of evidence. And even in respect of certain issues which could be described as procedural, the courts have often required a timely objection if this could have resulted in the trial court taking immediate action to resolve the situation, e.g., cases in which it is alleged that a judge or juror was asleep during the trial (*Moringiello* [1997] Crim LR 902; *Tomar* [1997] Crim LR 682; *Edworthy* [1961] Crim LR 325; cf. *Weston-super-Mare Justices, ex parte Taylor* [1981] Crim LR 179).

> ground there put forward for the first time, if it be satisfied beyond doubt, first that it had before it
> all the facts bearing upon the new contention as completely as would have been the case if the con-
> troversy had arisen at the trial; and next, that no satisfactory explanation could have been offered by
> those whose conduct is impugned if an opportunity for explanation had been afforded them in the
> witness box.

The Criminal Division of the Court of Appeal may be more disposed than the Civil Division
to hear an appeal based on a point of evidence not taken below, if there is a risk of injustice. But it
is safer and better not to have to argue that it should do so. An objection should always be made
to what appears to be the wrongful admission or exclusion of evidence.

A somewhat different situation prevails where the error is contained in the summing up. Here,
there is authority that prosecuting counsel (who cannot appeal against a verdict of not guilty) has
a duty to invite the judge to correct any apparent error of law. But the better view is that defence
counsel owes a duty to his client, and has no duty to correct what may be an appealable error:
Cocks (1976) 63 Cr App R 79, 82 per James LJ. In this event, no criticism should attach to counsel appearing below, and the appellate courts should not hesitate to entertain such grounds of
appeal. Although this principle should be, and at present seems to be, well established, it has not
proved to be entirely immune from attack.[13]

3.2.4 Evidential rulings to be made by trial judge

In criminal cases, all decisions relating to the admissibility of evidence are made by the trial
judge, in the case of a trial on indictment, or the magistrates in the case of summary trial. The
magistrates' court has no power to make such orders in relation to a case sent for trial to the
Crown Court, and must leave all evidential decisions to the Crown Court.

It was until recently assumed to be a general principle in civil cases also that evidential rulings
must be made by the trial judge, and not by a judicial officer such as a master or district judge,
who may conduct some essentially procedural interlocutory or preliminary hearings. This rule is
based on strong considerations. The judge making evidential rulings must do so in the context
of the case as a whole, consisting not only of the statements of case, witness statements, and
exhibits, but also the evidence given at trial. Many questions of relevance and admissibility cannot be determined until the course to be taken by the parties at the trial becomes clear, and this
will not have occurred at the time of an interlocutory or preliminary hearing. Only the trial judge
has the advantage of seeing and hearing all the witnesses and hearing the case fully argued. Only
those rulings made or adopted by the trial judge are part of the final judgment in the case, and
final, as opposed to interlocutory orders must form the basis of any appeal brought subsequently
against the verdict or judgment. Where the trial judge personally conducts interlocutory or preliminary hearings, there is obviously no objection to his making such rulings as can be made
based on the information available at the time and the representations of the parties. Indeed,
this is one of the purposes of some such hearings, for example, the preparatory hearings in criminal cases provided for by Part III of the Criminal Procedure and Investigations Act 1996. But
there may be some rulings which cannot be made at that stage. Thus, in *Sullivan* v *West Yorkshire
Passenger Transport Executive* [1985] 2 All ER 134, it was held that, while the master had the interlocutory power to regulate the disclosure, and even, where appropriate, the agreement of expert

---

[13] See, e.g., *Edwards* [1983] Crim LR 484; *Southgate* (1963) 47 Cr App R 252.

reports, he had no power to make any (final) ruling on the admissibility of such evidence. This was a matter for the trial judge alone.

Some doubt has been cast on the position by two provisions of the Civil Procedure Rules 1998. Rule 32.1 empowers to the court to 'control the evidence' by giving directions as to the issues on which it requires evidence, the nature of the evidence and the way in which the evidence is placed before the court. This power extends to the exclusion of evidence which would otherwise be admissible. Rule 2.4 provides that, in the absence of any contrary enactment, rule or direction, any act to be performed by 'the court' may be performed by either a judge, a master or a district judge. The absence of any limitation suggests that a master or district judge could tie the hands of the trial judge by making an order under r. 32.1. But it is submitted that this position should be modified. As was recognized in the authorities in the pre-1998 Rules law, this function is best left to the trial judge. Indeed, it has been suggested, correctly, it is submitted, that questions of admissibility should be decided at trial rather than during a preliminary hearing, because the judge is far better placed to make such decisions when he has a more complete picture of the issues and the evidence as a whole.[14]

3.3 PRODUCTION AND EFFECT OF EVIDENCE

The judge must direct the jury with regard to all matters which arise concerning the production, significance and effect of the evidence given, and the use which they are entitled to make of that evidence. This duty includes the explanation of the burden and standard of proof; the limited use that may be made of evidence of limited admissibility; the operation of any presumptions; the rules regarding the evidential value of confessions; the significance of any character evidence; the position of the accused as a witness in his own defence; and any other such matters of law which may arise. The Judicial Studies Board (JSB) issues judges with specimen directions, which are outlines of the basic requirements of a satisfactory direction on the most important issues, designed to be flexible enough for the judge to adapt to the facts of a particular case (which is always the right approach to directing the jury—it is pointless simply to mouth abstract principles of law divorced from the facts of the case). These specimen directions are considered from time to time by the Court of Appeal and may be amended to accord with a decision of the Court: see, for example, the specimen direction on evidence of bad character, amended in the light of *Campbell* [2007] 1 WLR 2798; 6.10.4. A direction actually given to a jury need not (and should not) slavishly follow the specimen direction as long as it complies substantially with the basic requirements.[15] The judge is entitled to comment on the weight or credibility of any evidence given, provided that he impresses upon the jury that they are the judges of the facts, and it is their view which counts. In some cases, stronger comment is permissible than in others[16] and in certain cases, some observation on the weight of evidence may be essential if the jury are to be properly informed about their task.[17]

---

[14] See *Stroude v Beazer Homes Ltd* [2005] EWCA Civ 265.

[15] The JSB's specimen guidelines are generally available via its website: www.jsboard.co.uk.

[16] See *Blackstone's Criminal Practice*, 2009 edn, para. D25.28.

[17] For example, in identification cases: see *Turnbull* [1977] QB 224, and generally 16.12.2. In general, American judges are not permitted to comment on the facts. Federal judges are permitted to do so, but rarely do because of the strong possibility of reversal on appeal. In some States, the judge gives the jury the charge (sums up) before the closing arguments of counsel, so that counsel argue the case knowing exactly how the jury has been

3.4 WITHDRAWING THE CASE FROM THE JURY

It is the judge's duty to consider whether there is sufficient evidence, at the close of the prosecution's case in a criminal trial, to warrant leaving the case to the jury at all. This is a matter of law, and the judge may decide the question at any time after the close of the prosecution case, and whether or not a submission of no case to answer is made by the defence. The judge should withdraw the case from the jury if either there is no evidence that the accused committed the offence charged, or the evidence to that effect is so tenuous, because of inherent weakness, vagueness, or inconsistency, that a properly directed jury could not properly convict on the basis of it. In all other cases, the judge should leave the case to the jury, whose responsibility it is to act as the judges of the facts: see *Galbraith* [1981] 1 WLR 1039.[18] In addition to this general judicial duty, the Criminal Justice Act 2003 contains limited provisions requiring the judge to stop a criminal case tried on indictment with a jury in favour of the accused in certain specific circumstances. By virtue of s. 107 of the Act, the judge is required to stop the case where evidence of the accused's bad character is admitted, and where, after the close of the case for the prosecution, the judge is satisfied that the evidence is 'contaminated' and that, given the importance of the evidence, a conviction would for that reason be unsafe. Similarly, by virtue of s. 125 of the Act, the judge is required to stop the case where the case against the accused depends wholly or partly on hearsay evidence, and where, after the close of the case for the prosecution, the judge is satisfied that the hearsay evidence is so unconvincing that, given the importance of the evidence, a conviction would for that reason be unsafe. These provisions are dealt with in more detail at 6.21 and 8.24 respectively. The jury may stop the case in favour of the defence of their own motion at any time after the close of the prosecution case, but may convict only after the completion of the summing up. Submissions of no case to answer may also be made in civil cases, whether or not tried with a jury, though other rules then come into play which are outside the scope of the present work, and for which reference should be made to *Blackstone's Civil Practice*, 2009 edn, para. 59.44.

C   FUNCTIONS OF THE JUDGE: JUDICIAL DISCRETION

> **SUMMARY OF MAIN POINTS**
>
> - At common law, the judge has no discretion to admit evidence which is legally inadmissible.
>
> - At common law in civil cases, it is doubtful whether the judge has a discretion to exclude legally admissible evidence; but the judge's case management powers under r. 32.1 of the Civil Procedure Rules 1998 probably amount to the same thing.
>
> - At common law in criminal cases, the judge has a discretion to exclude legally admissible evidence tendered by the prosecution (but not by a co-accused) if its potential for prejudicing the accused in the mind of the jury would be out of proportion to its true evidential value.

directed as to the law. There is a growing practice in England of consultation with counsel as to the content of the summing-up.

[18] Cf. *Young* [1964] 1 WLR 717. The judge must not usurp the function of the jury—weak cases, like strong ones, are to be considered by the jury: see *Barker* (1975) 65 Cr App R 287 n.

- This discretion is now statutory. Police and Criminal Evidence Act 1984, s. 78 provides:

  In any proceedings the court may refuse to allow evidence on which the prosecution proposes to rely to be given if it appears to the court that, having regard to all the circumstances, including the circumstances in which the evidence was obtained, the admission of the evidence would have such an adverse effect on the fairness of the proceedings that the court ought not to admit it.

- This provision is intended to apply at least as broadly as the common law discretion.

The categorization of evidence as either admissible or inadmissible is one well suited to the adversary system of litigation, in the sense that the parties should be free to approach the presentation of their case in the confidence that the rules will be consistently observed. But the question also arises of whether the judge, in addition to deciding questions of admissibility, may by virtue of his function of conducting the trial fairly in the interests of all the parties, superimpose upon the questions of admissibility some discretionary decision, either to admit evidence which is technically inadmissible (inclusionary discretion) or to exclude evidence which is technically admissible (exclusionary discretion) so as to meet the justice of any particular case.

3.5 INCLUSIONARY DISCRETION

There appears to be no common law discretion to admit inadmissible evidence, either in criminal or civil cases. In *Myers* v *DPP* [1965] AC 1001, 1024, Lord Reid said:

> In argument the Solicitor-General maintained that, although the general rule may be against the admission of private records to prove the truth of entries in them, the trial judge has a discretion to admit a record in a particular case if satisfied that it is trustworthy, and that justice requires its admission. That appears to me to be contrary to the whole framework of the existing law. It is true that a judge has a discretion to exclude legally admissible evidence if justice so requires, but it is a very different thing to say that he has a discretion to admit legally inadmissible evidence....No matter how cogent particular evidence may seem to be, unless it comes within a class which is admissible, it is excluded.

In *Sparks* v *R* [1964] AC 964, the appellant was charged with indecently assaulting a young girl. The girl had told her mother that her attacker was 'a coloured boy', whereas the appellant was white. At trial, the girl was not called to give evidence, doubtless because of her young age. It was argued that the description given by the girl should have been admitted because it was 'manifestly unjust' for the jury to be left in ignorance of the fact that the girl had made a statement which tended to exculpate the accused. The statement was, however, hearsay and inadmissible. The Privy Council rejected arguments that the evidence might be admissible as part of the *res gestae* or as evidence of a previous identification. This concluded any possibility of this highly relevant evidence being admitted. Lord Morris of Borth-y-Gest said (*ibid.* at 978):

> It was said that it was 'manifestly unjust for the jury to be left throughout the whole trial with the impression that the child could not give any clue to the identity of her assailant'. The cause of justice is, however, best served by adherence to rules which have long been recognized and settled.

Although the appeal was allowed for other reasons, the obvious relevance and cogency of the excluded evidence suggests that, if any general inclusionary discretion had existed, it would have been employed in *Sparks*. No other authority supports such a discretion (cf. *Blastland* [1986] AC 41). Statute has provided a power to admit hearsay evidence which might alter the result on the facts of *Sparks*, if the judge found the evidence to be reliable. It may be that the evidence would now be admissible under s. 114(1)(d) of the Criminal Justice Act 2003 (see 8.20) but this does not affect the general principle with regard to the question of inclusionary discretion.

3.6 EXCLUSIONARY DISCRETION: CIVIL CASES

At common law, it was unclear whether or not any general exclusionary discretion existed in civil cases. Such judicial authority as there was tended to suggest that the judicial exclusion of evidence in civil cases was a matter of law rather than discretion.[19] But s. 18(5) of the Civil Evidence Act 1968, which provided that nothing in that Act prejudiced any power of a court to exclude evidence in its discretion, appeared to assume that some discretion existed, even if its scope was unclear. In practice, the matter of discretion is of far less importance than in criminal cases, because almost all civil cases are tried by a judge sitting alone; and in civil cases, the function of the judge is to hold the balance between the parties, whereas in a criminal case, the judge has the overriding duty of securing a fair trial for the accused bearing in mind that the jury must weigh the evidence (see 3.7). In civil cases, there is no practical distinction in most instances between the situation in which the judge excludes evidence as a matter of discretion, and the situation in which the judge admits the evidence but assigns no weight to it, a frequent recourse in case of doubt. The presumption in the case of a professional judge is that he is fully capable of distinguishing that evidence on which his judgment should be based from other material which may have been tendered or referred to during the course of the trial, and accordingly there is no rule that a judge may not read such material, for example for the purpose of preparing himself to try the case.[20] Moreover, as Lord Simon of Glaisdale observed in *D v NSPCC* ([1978] AC 171, 239) a judge sitting alone who is the tribunal of fact as well as the tribunal of law enjoys considerable moral authority in suggesting to counsel that he would not find a certain piece of evidence helpful, or that he does not wish a certain line of cross-examination to be pursued. In such circumstances, evidential issues have a way of resolving themselves quite readily because of obvious considerations of forensic judgment on the part of counsel.

The position is now governed by the provisions of r. 32.1 of the Civil Procedure Rules 1998. This rule provides:

> (1) The court may control the evidence by giving directions as to—
>   (a) the issues on which it requires evidence;
>   (b) the nature of the evidence which it requires to decide those issues; and
>   (c) the way in which evidence is to be placed before the court.
> (2) The court may use its power under this rule to exclude evidence that would otherwise be admissible.
> (3) The court may limit cross-examination.

The rule does not use the word discretion; rather it creates a power. But it submitted that such a broad and unfettered power can be exercised only in an essentially discretionary manner. Unlike

---

[19] See, e.g., *D v NSPCC* [1978] AC 171, 239 per Lord Simon of Glaisdale; *ITC Film Distributors Ltd v Video Exchange Ltd* [1982] Ch 431; and the observations of Nourse LJ on the latter case in *Goddard v Nationwide Building Society* [1987] QB 670, 684.

[20] See, e.g., *Barings plc v Coopers and Lybrand* [2001] EWCA Civ 1163.

s. 78 of the Police and Criminal Evidence Act 1984, which applies to criminal cases, and indeed unlike the common law discretion in criminal cases (see 3.7) r. 32.1 does not prescribe any ground on which the judge's decision to exclude evidence should be based. The only general limitation on the court's powers seems to be the basic injunction of r. 1.1 that those powers must be exercised so as to give effect to the overriding objective of the rules, namely to deal with cases justly. It has been said that r. 32.1 provides the court with a case management tool which enables it to prevent the case from getting out of hand.[21] It would certainly seem appropriate for a judge to use the power to exclude in cases in which evidence has been obtained in violation of a provision of the European Convention on Human Rights,[22] as well as for the more prosaic but no less important purposes of protecting litigants of more modest means against better-funded opponents who might seek to deluge them with paper,[23] and restraining excessive cross-examination.[24] However, r. 32.1 does not entitle the court to override the operation of privileges: *General Mediterranean Holdings SA* v *Patel* [2000] 1 WLR 272.

3.7 EXCLUSIONARY DISCRETION: CRIMINAL CASES

3.7.1 Common law

In criminal cases, the judge has both the power and an overriding duty to secure a fair trial for the accused. While this power may be exercised in ways unrelated to the admission of evidence, for example, in restraining oppressive prosecutions or prosecutorial conduct, there is an important exercise of it in respect of the admissibility of evidence tendered by the prosecution. This takes the form of excluding or limiting technically admissible evidence on the ground that its probative value is outweighed by its potential for unfair prejudice to the accused. By 'unfair prejudice' in this context is meant the potential of the evidence to shock or inflame the jury, or to predispose them against the accused for reasons unconnected with the legitimate probative value of the evidence. Examples of common situations in which this power is exercised are given at 3.8. The power may properly be described as discretionary because the judge is not ruling on the admissibility of the evidence as a matter of law; indeed, the admissibility of the evidence as a matter of law is to be assumed if the discretionary power is invoked. The judge should consider the probative value of the evidence, the likely extent of the unfair prejudice, and the circumstances of the trial as a whole, and, in a necessarily subjective manner, do what appears necessary in those circumstances to secure a fair trial.

For this reason, the test for the exercise of the common law discretion is often referred to as a balancing of the admissibility of the evidence and the prosecution's interests in having it admitted, on the one hand, and the overriding duty of the court to secure a fair trial for the accused, on the other. But whether or not it is properly described as a balancing test, the right course seems to be for the judge to ask himself whether, starting with the proposition that relevant and admissible prosecution evidence should in general be admitted, it is nonetheless necessary to exclude

---

[21] *Post Office Counters Ltd* v *Mahida, The Times,* 31 October 2003, per Hale LJ. See also the observations of Lord Phillips in *O'Brien* v *Chief Constable of South Wales Police* [2005] 2 AC 534, [54].

[22] Cf. *Niemietz* v *Germany* (1992) 16 EHRR 97; *Halford* v *United Kingdom* (1997) 24 EHRR 523.

[23] *McPhilemy* v *Times Newspapers Ltd* [1999] 3 All ER 775, 791 per May LJ.

[24] *Rall* v *Hume* [2001] 3 All ER 248; but see also *Watson* v *Chief Constable of Cleveland Police* [2001] EWCA Civ 1547.

it in order to secure a fair trial for the accused.[25] This process has been variously described in a number of leading authorities.

In *Noor Mohamed* v *R* [1949] AC 182,[26] Lord du Parcq, delivering the advice of the Privy Council, said:

> ... in all such cases the judge ought to consider whether the evidence is sufficiently substantial, having regard to the purpose to which it is professedly directed, to make it desirable in the interest of justice that it should be admitted. If, so far as that purpose is concerned, it can in the circumstances have only trifling weight, the judge will be right to exclude it. To say this is not to confuse weight with admissibility. The distinction is plain, but cases must occur in which it would be unjust to admit evidence of a character gravely prejudicial to the accused even though there may be some tenuous ground for holding it technically admissible. The decision must then be left to the discretion and sense of fairness of the judge.

In *List* [1966] 1 WLR 9, 12 Roskill J said:

> A trial judge always has an overriding duty in every case to secure a fair trial, and if in any particular case he comes to the conclusion that, even though certain evidence is strictly admissible, yet its prejudicial effect once admitted is such as to make it virtually impossible for a dispassionate view of the crucial facts of the case to be thereafter taken by the jury, then the trial judge, in my judgment, should exclude that evidence.

In *Sang* [1980] AC 402, 434 Lord Diplock, having considered the authorities, summed up the position by saying:

> So I would hold that there has now developed a general rule of practice whereby in a trial by jury the judge has a discretion to exclude evidence which, though technically admissible, would probably have a prejudicial influence on the minds of the jury, which would be out of proportion to its true evidential value.[27]

The common law discretion is well recognized in other jurisdictions, and has probably attained the status of a general rule of the common law. For example, in the United States, Federal Rule of Evidence 403 provides that: '[A]lthough relevant, evidence may be excluded if its probative value is substantially outweighed by the danger of unfair prejudice, confusion of the issues, or misleading the jury, or by considerations of undue delay, waste of time, or needless presentation of cumulative evidence'.

Because the law expressly confers the discretion on the trial judge and not an appellate court, because the trial judge is better placed than an appellate court to judge the proper application of the discretion, and because discretionary decisions are necessarily subjective, appellate courts have traditionally been extremely reluctant to interfere with the exercise of discretion by the trial judge. Generally, they will do so only where the judge either failed to consider the exercise of discretion, or if there was no evidence or basis on which the judge could properly have arrived at his decision (*Cook* [1959] 2 QB 340; *Selvey* v *DPP* [1970] AC 304, 342 per Lord Dilhorne). The mere fact that the members of the appellate court feel that they might have reached a different conclusion is not sufficient. That said, as we shall see in a number of cases below, there may now be an

---

[25] See *Scott* v *R* [1989] AC 1242, 1256 per Lord Griffiths; *Khan* [1997] AC 558, 578 per Lord Nolan.

[26] At 192. See also *Christie* [1914] AC 545, per Lord Moulton at 559.

[27] In the same case, Lord Scarman observed that magistrates have the same discretion in summary trials, though he added that it should be exercised only in rare cases: *ibid.* at 456.

emerging trend to substitute the collective view of the Court of Appeal that a discretion should have been exercised in favour of the accused, where the interests of justice seem to require it.

3.7.2 Police and Criminal Evidence Act 1984, s. 78

This section provides:

> (1) In any proceedings[28] the court may refuse to allow evidence on which the prosecution proposes to rely to be given if it appears to the court that, having regard to all the circumstances, including the circumstances in which the evidence was obtained, the admission of the evidence would have such an adverse effect on the fairness of the proceedings that the court ought not to admit it.
>
> (2) Nothing in this section shall prejudice any rule of law requiring a court to exclude evidence.

The relationship between s. 78 and the common law discretion has never been defined satisfactorily. It has sometimes been assumed that the section creates a statutory form of the discretion, but that, as the common law discretion is expressly preserved by s. 82(3) of the Act, the two coexist and are more or less interchangeable. But there is also considerable judicial sentiment that s. 78 has expanded the range of discretion from that available at common law. In *Matto v Wolverhampton Crown Court* [1987] RTR 337, Woolf LJ said:

> Whatever is the right interpretation of section 78, I am quite satisfied that it certainly does not reduce the discretion of the court to exclude unfair evidence which existed at common law. Indeed, in my view in any case where the evidence could properly be excluded at common law, it can certainly be excluded under section 78.

In *Khan* [1997] AC 558, 578, Lord Nolan said:

> I turn, then, to the second issue, namely whether the judge should nevertheless have excluded it in the exercise of his common law discretion or under the powers conferred upon him by s. 78. The only element of the common law discretion which is relevant for present purposes is that part of it which authorizes the judge 'to exclude evidence if it is necessary in order to secure a fair trial for the accused', as Lord Griffiths put it in *Scott v R* [1989] AC 1242, 1256. It is therefore unnecessary to consider the common law position separately from that which arises under s. 78. I would respectfully agree with Lord Taylor of Gosforth CJ [in the Court of Appeal in *Khan* [1995] QB 27] that the power conferred by s. 78 to exclude evidence in the interests of a fair trial is at least as wide as that conferred by the common law.

To the same effect see the *dicta* of Lord Griffiths in *Horseferry Road Magistrates' Court, ex parte Bennett* [1994] 1 AC 42. But this seemingly natural view is not free from difficulty. In relation to cases in which it is sought to exclude evidence which has arguably been obtained illegally or unfairly, which comprise a very important group of cases under s. 78,[29] it would seem that, if s. 78 is a statutory version of the common law discretion, it has expanded the common law discretion in one crucial respect. At common law, it is clear after the decision in *Sang* [1980] AC 402 that, with the exception of confessions and other evidence obtained from the accused after the commission of the offence, the judge has no discretion to exclude evidence on the basis of the manner in which it is obtained. Section 78 expressly contemplates that the judge will consider that matter. Moreover, s. 78 creates a specific test, namely, whether or not, having regard to all

---

[28] The section applies only to criminal proceedings, but includes summary trials in magistrates' courts (see s. 82). As to extradition proceedings, see *Governor of Brixton Prison, ex parte Levin* [1997] AC 741.

[29] As to which see 3.11 *et seq.*, where the cases, including *Sang* and *Khan* are dealt with in more detail.

the circumstances including the circumstances in which the evidence was obtained, the admission of the evidence would have such an adverse effect on the fairness of the proceedings that the court ought not to admit it. In *Chalkley* [1998] QB 848, Auld LJ took a very different approach to the section. He said:

> We have put the words 'exercise of discretion' in this context in quotation marks because, as the court said in *Middlebrook* (18 February 1992 unreported), the task of determining (in)admissibility under s. 78 does not strictly involve an exercise of discretion. It is to determine whether the admission of the evidence 'having regard to all the circumstances, including the circumstances in which the evidence was obtained . . . would have such an adverse effect on the fairness of the proceedings that the court ought not to admit it'. If the court is of that view, it cannot logically 'exercise a discretion' to admit the evidence, despite the use of the permissive formula in the opening words of the provision that it 'may refuse' to admit the evidence in that event . . .
>
> At first sight, the words in s. 78 'the circumstances in which the evidence was obtained' might suggest that the means by which evidence was secured, even if they did not affect the fairness of admitting it, could entitle the court to exclude it as a result of a balancing exercise analogous to that when considering a stay for abuse of process. On that approach, the court could, even if it considered that the intrinsic nature of the evidence was not unfair to the accused, exclude it as a mark of disapproval of the way in which it had been obtained. That was certainly not the law before the Act of 1984. And we consider that the inclusion in s. 78 of the words 'the circumstances in which the evidence was obtained' was not intended to widen the common law rule in this respect, as stated by Lord Diplock in *Sang* [1980] AC 402.

A number of criticisms may be made of this reasoning. Firstly, insofar as s. 78 does give the court a discretion, it is not a discretion to admit evidence (which would necessarily refer to evidence which was technically inadmissible) but a discretion to exclude evidence. Secondly, it is not clear in what respect a conclusion that the admission of evidence would cause unfairness in the proceedings is anything other than discretionary, depending as it must on the judge's subjective consideration of essentially the same factors as would suggest the risk of unfairness at common law. Thirdly, the analogy with the test for abuse of process seems inapposite in the context of a reference to *Sang* and s. 78, both of which are concerned specifically with the admission of evidence. Nonetheless, Auld LJ is correct in drawing attention to the fact that the relationship between s. 78 and the common law discretion may not be as simple as has sometimes been assumed. Certainly, in cases in which (as occurred in *Chalkley*) it is alleged that evidence was obtained illegally or unfairly, it is not clear how the two should be reconciled. As Auld LJ rightly stresses throughout his judgment, it is the effect of the evidence on the fairness of the proceedings which is to be considered, and s. 78 certainly makes the circumstances in which the evidence was obtained relevant to that issue.

In *R (Saifi)* v *Governor of Brixton Prison and another* [2001] 1 WLR 1134, it was held that it is not appropriate to speak of any burden of proof in relation to the exercise of discretion under s. 78. The omission of any reference to the burden of proof in s. 78 was deliberate, as the exercise of discretion is a matter for the court to entertain of its own motion. This does not mean that counsel may not suggest the exercise of the discretion to the court, merely that there is no question of the opponent of the evidence having to undertake any proof that its exclusion would be appropriate.

A brief comment should be made as to the application of s. 78 in the case of confessions. Prior to the coming into effect of the Police and Criminal Evidence Act 1984, a trial judge who found that a confession tendered by the prosecution was admissible as a matter of law, but had been obtained by means of a breach of the Judges' Rules, might exercise his discretion to exclude the confession: *May* (1952) 36 Cr App R 91; *Prager* [1972] 1 WLR 260. The judge may similarly take into account breaches of Code of Practice C (which has replaced the Judges' Rules) in considering whether or not the admissibility of a confession would produce an unacceptably adverse effect on the fairness of the proceedings. (See *Samuel* [1988] QB 615; *Absolam* (1988) 88 Cr App R 332; and generally 9.12 *et seq*.) Because the provisions of the Code of Practice are not the ground on which a confession may be excluded, but rather a factor which the judge may take into consideration in exercising his discretion, the discretion applies equally to cases in which the unfairness arises from some other conduct, for example, a subterfuge or deception on the part of the police (*Christou* [1992] QB 979; *Bryce* [1992] 4 All ER 567; 3.10.1, 3.11, 9.12 *et seq*.). For the same reason, the judge may consider whether some breach of the European Convention on Human Rights has occurred. Again, this is not a ground for the exercise of the judge's discretion, but a matter which the judge may take into account in exercising his discretion.

At common law, the test for the admissibility of a confession was whether or not it had been made voluntarily (a test which in some ways was of quite narrow application) and in the absence of oppression. However, s. 76(2) of the Police and Criminal Evidence Act 1984 lays down a different and wider test, which supercedes that of voluntariness and encompasses not only the absence of oppression, but also 'anything said or done which was likely, in the circumstances existing at the time, to render unreliable any confession that might be made in consequence thereof'. It is at least arguable that if a judge finds that a confession may have been obtained in such circumstances, he is also finding, in effect, that its admission would have an unacceptably adverse effect on the fairness of the proceedings. In either case, the judge should exclude the confession. The question arises, therefore, of whether s. 78 really adds anything to s. 76 so far as confessions are concerned. The answer lies in the fact that there may be confessions which are obtained in the absence of any of the circumstances described in s. 76(2) and which, indeed, do appear to be reliable, but the admission of which might have an adverse effect on the fairness of the proceedings. In one such case, *Mason* [1988] 1 WLR 139 (discussed in detail at 9.12.6), the Court of Appeal held that s. 78 applied to confessions in addition to the specific provisions of s. 76.

3.8 APPLICATION OF S. 78

It is submitted that the judge's decision as to whether to exercise his powers under s. 78 involve a question of balancing different factors, as they do at common law, and that this balancing process remains essentially discretionary. It is also clear that, as is the case at common law, this process depends entirely on the facts of each individual case, and that few principles of general application can be laid down, other than the overriding duty to ensure the fairness of the trial. If any principle of general application can be laid down, and if there is any distinction to be made between s. 78 and the common law test, it is surely that the outcome of the balancing test should result in exclusion of the evidence only where the judge is persuaded specifically that the admission of the evidence would have an unacceptably adverse effect on the fairness of the trial. As indicated by Auld LJ in the passage cited at 3.7.2, the purpose of s. 78 is not to allow the judge to mark his disapproval of the manner in which evidence may have been obtained, even if that is a factor to be weighed in the balance. The ultimate question is simply one of the fairness of the trial. Beyond this, the application of s. 78 is quintessentially a matter to be decided on the facts of each case. In *Jelen and Katz* (1990) 90 Cr App R 456, 465, Auld LJ said:

> ...the decision of a judge whether or not to exclude evidence under section 78 of the 1984 Act is made as a result of the exercise by him of a discretion based on the particular circumstances of the case and

upon his assessment of the adverse effect, if any, it would have on the fairness of the proceedings. The circumstances of each case are almost always different, and judges may well take different views in the proper exercise of their discretion, even when the circumstances are similar. This is not an apt field for hard case law and well-founded distinctions between cases.

Citing this passage with approval, a later Court of Appeal in *Shannon* [2001] 1 Cr App R 12, [32] added:

> ...the Court has not laid down, nor has it sought to lay down, save in the most general terms, a touchstone or test for exclusion susceptible of general application. There are two principle reasons why it is both difficult and undesirable to do so. First, the circumstances and situations in which any test may fall to be applied are multifarious. It is therefore important that the broad and unqualified discretion contained in section 78 should not be constrained or standardised.

It is possible to identify certain categories of prosecution evidence to which the discretion under s. 78 is commonly applied. The most common are cases in which it is claimed that prosecution evidence has been obtained illegally or unfairly (these cases are considered in this chapter at 3.11 *et seq.*) and cases involving the admissibility of confessions, which are considered in detail in Chapter 9; 9.12 *et seq.*, with a brief comment in this section, below. In cases decided both at common law and under s. 1(3) of the the Criminal Evidence 1898, it was consistently held that the discretion to exclude might be exercised to prevent evidence of the accused's bad character from being admitted, even when technically admissible, because of the obvious potential of such evidence for rendering the trial unfair.[30] Section 101(3) of the Criminal Justice Act 2003 introduced a new statutory power to exclude evidence of the accused's bad character via gateways (d) and (g) on the same ground as would justify the exercise of the discretion under s. 78. In cases to which the new power does not apply, s. 78 may still be used. This is considered further in Chapter 6 at 6.20 *et seq.* Section 126 of the same Act creates an entirely new discretion to exclude hearsay evidence in criminal cases, on the improbable ground that the case for excluding the evidence, taking into account the danger that admitting it would result in an undue waste of time, substantially outweighs the case for admitting it. As this section is specifically expressed not to preclude the exercise of the discretion under s. 78, its utility seems open to question. It is considered further in Chapter 8; 8.25. But it is important to emphasize that the application of s. 78 is not confined to these or any defined categories of evidence. The discretion may be applied to any prosecution evidence. This is clear not only from the wording of s. 78 but also from the speech of Lord Salmon in *Sang*. Dealing with the common law discretion, Lord Salmon observed ([1980] AC at 445):

> I recognise that there may have been no categories of cases, other than those to which I have referred, in which technically admissible evidence proferred by the Crown has been rejected by the court on the ground that it would make the trial unfair. I cannot, however, accept that a judge's undoubted duty to ensure that the accused has a fair trial is confined to such cases. In my opinion the category of cases is not and never can be closed except by statute.

Moreover, not only may the discretion be exercised so as to exclude legally admissible evidence which falls into certain categories, but it may also be exercised so as to exclude specific

---

[30] *Noor Mohamed* v *R* [1949] AC 182; *Selvey* v *DPP* [1970] AC 304; *Watts* [1983] 3 All ER 101; generally, the 8th edn of this work at 5.20.3, 6.1 *et seq.*; see also *Hacker* [1994] 1 WLR 1659; *Perry* [1984] Crim LR 680 (decided under the Theft Act 1968, s. 27(3)) and *Herron* [1967] 1 QB 107 (decided under the corresponding provisions of the Larceny Act 1916) and the 8th edn of this work at 5.9.3.

pieces of evidence whose individual characteristics create an undue risk of prejudice which outweighs their actual probative value. It would surely be legitimate, for example, for a court to exclude certain particularly gruesome photographs of the deceased in a murder case, where precisely the same evidential value might be obtained by the introduction of more dispassionate forensic evidence. Such attacks upon individual pieces of evidence appear to be much more common in American than in English practice, perhaps because of the greater American affinity for graphic demonstrative evidence. However, even in England it should not be overlooked that it is relatively easy for a jury to be swayed or even inflamed by such evidence, when the jurors have not experienced the hardening effect that frequent exposure to such materials may have on lawyers.

3.9 DISCRETION CONFINED TO PROSECUTION EVIDENCE

It seems clear as a matter of general principle that both the common law discretion and the discretion under s. 78 apply only to evidence tendered by the prosecution and not to evidence tendered by an accused. Section 78(1) expressly limits its application to evidence on which the prosecution proposes to rely. And at common law, it seems well settled that an accused is entitled to have any admissible evidence admitted regardless of the possible prejudice caused to a co-accused. Given the overriding duty of the judge to secure a fair trial for each accused, it seems clear that this principle is not beyond criticism, but in such a case there is no perfect solution from the point of view of protecting the rights of all the accused. In *Thompson* [1995] 2 Cr App R 589, 596–7, Evans LJ pointed out that there is a case for some degree of discretion, because in its absence, it may be necessary in some cases to order separate trials of different accused, an order which may create prejudice in other ways, but may be the only way to secure overall fairness. There is clearly some force in this view, but the creation of a discretion relating to evidence tendered by an accused would require a specific change in the present law. This seems clear from a number of cases. In *Myers* [1998] AC 124, a case involving two accused, A and B, the House of Lords confirmed that B was entitled to make use as evidence of confessions made by A, despite the fact that the prosecution had not even attempted to adduce the confessions as evidence against A because of breaches of the Codes of Practice (as to which see 9.12). There was no discretion to prevent this.[31] The law on this particular point has since been modified by statute, in that s. 128 of the Criminal Justice Act 2003 now prescribes the same test of admissibility of confessions when tendered by a co-accused as applies when tendered by the prosecution (namely, that under s. 76 of the Police and Criminal Evidence Act 1984: see 9.13.2). But this is a test of legal admissibility. The Act does not provide that s. 78 should apply in such a case, so that if the legal test of admissibility is satisfied, it seems that the judge still has no discretion to exclude. Similarly, in cases decided under the Criminal Evidence Act 1898, it was consistently held that although the judge could restrain the prosecution from cross-examining the accused as to his bad character when technically permitted under s. 1(3)(ii) of the Act, there was no corresponding discretion to restrain cross-examination on the same subject by a co-accused when permitted under s. 1(3)(iii) of the Act.[32] This position has been preserved by s. 101(3) of the Criminal Justice Act 2003, which replaces s. 1(3) of the 1898 Act, and by virtue of which the only discretion provided

---

[31] See also *Randall* [2004] 1 All ER 467, [18]; *Lobban v R* [1995] 1 WLR 877; *Rowson* [1986] QB 174.

[32] See, e.g., *Murdoch v Taylor* [1965] AC 574; *Randall* (note 31).

to restrain introduction of evidence of the accused's bad character relates to evidence tendered by the prosecution.

D   FUNCTIONS OF THE JUDGE: ADMISSIBILITY OF EVIDENCE ILLEGALLY OR UNFAIRLY OBTAINED

SUMMARY OF MAIN POINTS

- Evidence obtained by means of torture is never admissible.

- With that exception, the fact that relevant evidence has been obtained illegally or unfairly does not render it inadmissible.

- In criminal cases, the manner in which evidence was obtained (including any illegality or unfairness) may be considered in the exercise of the discretion to exclude under s. 78 of the Police and Criminal Evidence Act 1984; but the ground for the exercise of the discretion is, not the manner in which it was obtained, but the effect of admitting the evidence on the fairness of the proceedings.

3.10 GENERAL PRINCIPLES OF ADMISSIBILITY

Whether the courts should refuse to entertain evidence because it has been obtained by the party tendering it in an illegal or improper manner is a question principally of policy, to which no answer is to be found in the law of evidence as such. Given that the evidence is relevant and does not offend against any of the substantive rules of admissibility, the question resolves itself into whether the courts should admit the evidence as admissible to prove the offence charged, or the claim, and leave the party aggrieved to his civil remedy in respect of any actionable wrong indulged in to obtain it, or whether the courts should act as 'watchdogs' and should decline to allow a party guilty of such wrongdoing to profit by it. A secondary issue is whether, if the evidence so obtained is admissible in law as being relevant and not contrary to the substantive rules, the judge may exclude it in the exercise of some discretion.

In the United States, the constitutionally entrenched rights of the accused in a criminal case require the exclusion of evidence obtained in violation of any of the accused's fundamental constitutional rights. Thus, if evidence is seized during an unlawful search of the person or property contrary to the Fourth Amendment right to be protected against unlawful search and seizure, or if evidence is discovered following a compelled statement contrary to the Fifth Amendment privilege against self-incrimination, or if evidence was obtained by means of depriving the accused of the Sixth Amendment right to counsel, the court must as a matter of law exclude the evidence so obtained. This so-called 'Exclusionary Rule', though subject to periodic attempts to whittle it down, is regarded as one of the pillars of the constitutional protection offered to the accused in a criminal case, and transcends the rules of evidence. American courts have traditionally regarded it as an important part of their constitutional duty to assume the role of watchdog over the conduct of those charged with the investigation of crime, and have been prepared to fulfil this role by excluding from evidence the fruits of wrongful conduct, as well as by offering subsequent civil remedies to those affected by such conduct.

In England, it is quite clear that, with one important exception, evidence is not rendered inadmissible merely by the manner in which it is obtained.[33] Following the decision of the House of Lords in *Sang* [1980] AC 402, it also appeared that the common law recognized no discretion to exclude evidence because of the manner in which it has been obtained. The House confirmed the existence of the discretion discussed above, to exclude in a criminal case evidence whose prejudicial effect might result in a denial of a fair trial to the accused. This, however, is a discretion based upon the prejudicial nature of the evidence, and not upon the manner in which it was obtained. Efforts to include in the Police and Criminal Evidence Act 1984 a provision that illegally or unfairly obtained evidence should be inadmissible or excludable as a matter of discretion failed, but by virtue of s. 78 of the Act, the manner in which prosecution evidence is obtained is one matter which the court may take into account in deciding in the exercise of its discretion whether that evidence should be excluded pursuant to the section. The intractable position of English law on this issue has not been affected by the European Convention on Human Rights,[34] even after the coming into effect of the Human Rights Act 1998. Although the Convention contains rights and freedoms analogous to the Bill of Rights contained in the Fourth, Fifth and Sixth Amendments to the United States Constitution, it is approached very differently. Although breaches of articles of the Convention may be considered on the issue of discretionary exclusion on the ground of unfairness, such a breach does not, in and of itself, render evidence obtained thereby inadmissible, and the fact that there may have been a breach of an article of the Convention does not necessarily mean that the admission of evidence obtained in consequence of that breach will result in unfairness in the trial in breach of art. 6.[35] It appears that the jurisprudence of the European Court of Human Rights supports this position. In *Khan* [1997] AC 558, 583, Lord Nicholls of Birkenhead said:

> ...the discretionary powers of the trial judge to exclude evidence march hand in hand with art. 6(1) of the European Convention on Human Rights and Fundamental Freedoms. Both are concerned to ensure that those facing criminal charges receive a fair hearing. Accordingly, when considering the common law and statutory discretionary powers under English law the jurisprudence on art. 6 can have a valuable role to play. English law relating to the ingredients of a fair trial is highly developed. But every system of law stands to benefit by an awareness of the answers given by other courts and tribunals to similar problems. In the present case the decision of the European Court of Human Rights in *Shenk v Switzerland* (1988) 13 EHRR 242 confirms that the use at a criminal trial of material obtained in breach of the rights of privacy enshrined in art. 8 does not of itself mean that the trial is unfair. Thus the European Court of Human Rights case law on this issue leads to the same conclusion as English law.[36]

One exception to the general rule of great importance was recognized by the House of Lords in *A and others* v *Secretary of State for the Home Department (No. 2)* [2006] 2 AC 221. The question before the House was whether the Special Immigration Appeals Commission (SIAC) was entitled to rely on evidence obtained by agents of a foreign government by means of torture, without

---

[33] See generally Glanville Williams [1955] Crim LR 339; R. Heydon [1973] Crim LR 603, 690. There is, however, a quite distinct principle that where statute requires the strict adherence to a particular procedure in obtaining evidence of certain kinds, e.g., specimens in excess alcohol cases, the court will reject evidence where the statutory procedure is not adhered to: see, e.g., *Scott* v *Baker* [1969] 1 QB 659; *Spicer* v *Holt* [1979] AC 987.

[34] *Khan* [1997] AC 558; *Chalkley* [1998] QB 848.

[35] See, e.g., the observation of Lord Hoffmann in *Montgomery* v *Lord Advocate; Coulter* v *Lord Advocate* [2003] 1 AC 641, 649.

[36] See also Lord Nicholls's observations in *Looseley* [2001] 1 WLR 2060, 2070.

complicity by the British Government,[37] for the purpose of deciding whether or not to issue a certificate that a person is reasonably believed to be a terrorist and a threat to national security under s. 21(1) of the Anti-terrorism, Crime and Security Act 2001. Reversing the decision of the SIAC itself and of the Court of Appeal, the House resoundingly held that evidence obtained by torture is inadmissible in any judicial proceedings.[38] Torture is a criminal offence in England,[39] and is prohibited under a variety of international conventions and agreements, including art. 3 of the European Convention on Human Rights. But given the general rule of English law, it would not have followed from this fact alone that the courts must exclude evidence obtained by means of torture. This would have followed only if unfairness in the trial would result from the admission, in which case the evidence might be excluded under s. 78 of the Police and Criminal Evidence Act 1978, having regard also to art. 6 of the Convention. The appellants contended for a general rule of exclusion based on the existence of an absolute prohibition against torture. The appeal was argued not only on the basis of common law principles, and of arts 3 and 6 of the Convention, but also on the basis of the broader principles of public international law enshrined in successive international conventions and agreements, including the Universal Declaration of Human Rights (10 December 1948), the International Covenant on Civil and Political Rights (19 December 1966), and the International Convention against Torture (26 June 1987).[40] The members of the House were *ad idem* that all these sources of law concur in the general principle that the law can lend no support to torture, and that accordingly, evidence obtained by means of torture may not be admitted in judicial proceedings. Article 15 of the Torture Convention requires the States Parties to ensure that no statement obtained by means of torture shall be admitted in evidence, except in proceedings against the torturer. Although the European Convention contains no directly analogous provision, the jurisprudence of the European Court of Human Rights supports the proposition that no derogation from the absolute prohibition of torture by art. 3 is to be permitted under any circumstances,[41] so that there is no inconsistency in treating that provision differently in terms of the right to a fair trial under art. 6. But the most remarkable aspect of the decision is the unqualified assertion by the House that, irrespective of the concurring principles of European and international law, the exclusion of evidence obtained by means of torture is a principle of the common law. At [51] Lord Bingham noted:

---

[37] The Secretary of State conceded that the admission of such evidence could not be entertained in the case of torture employed by or with the complicity of the British Government (see the opinion of Lord Bingham at [1]). But in the light of the decision of the House, it appears that this is irrelevant. At [45] Lord Bingham observed: 'The House has not been referred to any decision, resolution, agreement or advisory opinion suggesting that a confession or statement obtained by torture is admissible in legal proceedings if the torture was inflicted without the participation of the state in whose jurisdiction the proceedings are held, or that such evidence is admissible in proceedings related to terrorism'.

[38] This, of course, is a question distinct from the question of whether state agencies may take operational actions designed to safeguard the public based in part on information based on torture: see the observations of Lord Nicholls at [67]–[73]. The decisions made by the SIAC are made pursuant to a judicial function, and so are subject to the rule laid down by the House of Lords: *ibid.* at [76].

[39] Criminal Justice Act 1988, s. 134, giving effect to the obligations of the UK under the Torture Convention of 1987 (text below).

[40] It was common ground in the appeal that the prohibition of torture enjoys the status of a *ius cogens*, or peremptory norm of general international law, from which no derogation can be permitted: see the opinion of Lord Bingham at [33]; see also the Vienna Convention on the Law of Treaties, 23 May 1969, art. 53; *Bow Street Stipendiary Magistrate, ex parte Pinochet Ugarte (No. 3)* [2000] 1 AC 147, 197.

[41] Including public emergencies resulting from terrorism (the context of the 2001 Act in the UK): see, e.g., *Chahal v United Kingdom* (1996) 1 BHRC 405, 424, [79].

...the English common law has regarded torture and its fruits with abhorrence for over 500 years, and that abhorrence is now shared by over 140 countries which have acceded to the Torture Convention.

At [51]–[52] he continued:

> It trivialises the issue before the House to treat it as an argument about the law of evidence. The issue is one of constitutional principle, whether evidence obtained by torturing another human being may lawfully be admitted against a party to proceedings in a British court, irrespective of where, or by whom, or on whose authority the torture was inflicted. To that question I would give a very clear negative answer...
>
> The principles of the common law, standing alone, in my opinion compel the exclusion of third party torture evidence as unreliable, unfair, offensive to ordinary standards of humanity and decency and incompatible with the principles which should animate a tribunal seeking to administer justice. But the principles of the common law do not stand alone. Effect must also be given to the European Convention, which itself takes account of the all but universal consensus embodied in the Torture Convention. The answer to the central question posed at the outset of this opinion is to be found not in a governmental policy, which may change, but in law.

Lord Hope, referring to the prohibition on the admission in evidence of evidence obtained by the use of torture contained in art. 15 of the Torture Convention, said:

> This provision has not been incorporated into our domestic law... But I would hold that the formal incorporation of the evidential rule into domestic law was unnecessary, as the same result is reached by an application of common law principles. The rule laid down by Article 15 was accepted by the United Kingdom because it was entirely compatible with our own law... The law will not lend its support to the use of torture for any purpose whatever. [*Ibid.* at [112].]

Lord Carswell said:

> I am satisfied that, whether or not it has ever been affirmatively declared that the common law declines to allow the admission of evidence obtained by the use of torture, it is quite capable now of embracing such a rule. If that is any extension of the existing common law, it is a modest one, a necessary recognition of the conclusions which should be drawn from long-established principles. I accordingly agree with your Lordships that such a rule should be declared to represent the common law. [*Ibid.* at [152].]

Thus, whatever may be the general rule with respect to evidence obtained by other illegal means, evidence obtained by means of torture constitutes an exception, and will never be admitted in judicial proceedings in the courts of this country. This rule applies alike to civil and criminal proceedings.[42] It is, of course, consistent with the jurisprudence of the European Court of Human Rights. In *Jalloh* v *Germany* (2007) 33 EHRR 32, the Court held that a violation of the fair trial provisions of art. 6 of the Convention may be established by means of proof of a violation of the art. 3 prohibition on torture and inhuman or degrading treatment. In a case in which the accused had been forcibly subjected to a dangerous and painful procedure to compel him to regurgitate drugs (to which there was a safer natural alternative) for the purpose of providing

---

[42] There was some disagreement as to whether proceedings before the SIAC were essentially civil or criminal in nature, but the parties agreed that the applicable provisions of the European Convention should be taken as applicable in either case (see *ibid.* at [25]) and there is clearly no basis for making a distinction on this point in the light of the broad principle laid down by the House.

evidence against him, there was a violation of both art. 3 and art. 6; and this despite the rule that the law of evidence is generally within the competence of national jurisdictions (see 1.7.2). The evidence against the accused had been obtained by means of a breach of a 'core right' of the Convention.

3.10.1 Criminal cases

However, with the above exception, the courts have long rejected the concept that evidence should be held to be inadmissible merely on the ground of the manner in which it is obtained. In *Jones* v *Owens* (1870) 34 JP 759, where a constable, in the course of an unlawful search of the accused, found a quantity of young salmon, which became the subject of a charge, Mellor J said that if such evidence could not be used against him, it would be 'a dangerous obstacle to the administration of justice'.[43] And in *Leatham*[44] referring to a letter which had been found only because of inadmissible confessions made by the accused, Crompton J went so far as to say that 'if you steal it even, it would be admissible'.

In more recent times, the rule was restated in the leading case of *Kuruma Son of Kaniu* v *R* [1955] AC 197, 203, in which the accused was charged with the unlawful possession of ammunition during a period of emergency in Kenya. The ammunition was found during an unlawful search, and it was contended on appeal to the Privy Council that the evidence of the finding was inadmissible because of the manner in which it had been obtained. In delivering the advice of the Privy Council, Lord Goddard CJ rejected the argument decisively, saying:

> In their Lordships' opinion the test to be applied in considering whether the evidence is admissible is whether it is relevant to the matters in issue. If it is, it is admissible and the court is not concerned with how the evidence was obtained. While this proposition may not have been stated in so many words in any English case there are decisions which support it, and in their Lordships' opinion it is plainly right in principle.

The rule has been reaffirmed on several occasions since then, and in *Jeffrey* v *Black* [1978] QB 490, the Divisional Court had no doubt that the decision in *Kuruma* was correct.[45]

Consistently with this general rule, it has been held that there is no objection in law to the admissibility of evidence obtained by the police by means of a subterfuge, for example, deliberately leaving attractive goods in a position in which they were vulnerable to theft (*Williams* v *DPP* [1993] 3 All ER 365), operating a sham business purporting to 'fence' stolen goods (*Christou* [1992] QB 979), or obtaining information by 'bugging' a cell in which suspects were being held (*Bailey* [1993] 3 All ER 513; *Roberts* [1997] 1 Cr App R 217). In *Khan*[46] the House of Lords held that the trial judge had not been required to exclude a tape recording which suggested that the

---

[43] The same rule applies in a more modern context to the unlawful obtaining of samples for use in breathalyser cases. See *Fox* [1986] AC 281; cf. *Morris* v *Beardmore* [1981] AC 446. See 3.11.2.

[44] (1861) 8 Cox CC 498. But see also Police and Criminal Evidence Act 1984, s. 76(4), and 9.9.

[45] In *A and others* v *Secretary of State for the Home Department (No. 2)* [2006] 2 AC 221, [87] Lord Hoffmann described the illegal practices in *Leatham* and *Kuruma* as 'fairly technical'. While they are certainly not to be compared to the practice of torture with which Lord Hoffmann was dealing in that case, it is submitted that it would be unfortunate if the impression were to be given that the use of any illegal practice for the purpose of obtaining evidence might be actively condoned by the courts. Although the extent of the illegality may not affect admissibility (with the exception of torture) it may affect the question of discretionary exclusion (text below).

[46] [1997] AC 558; *Khan* v *United Kingdom*, text below; and see *Armstrong* v *United Kingdom* (2003) 36 EHRR 30; *Allan* v *United Kingdom* (2003) 36 EHRR 12; *P* [2002] 1 AC 146, text below; *Preston* [1994] 2 AC 130.

appellant had been involved in importing drugs and which had been obtained by 'bugging' a house visited by the appellant. The House held that the evidence was admissible, even though it had arguably been obtained by conduct which constituted civil trespass, a breach of art. 8 of the European Convention on Human Rights[47] and a violation of the provisions of the Interception of Communications Act 1985. The House also rejected the appellant's argument that the express provision of the 1985 Act rendering information obtained using the powers conferred by the Act inadmissible in evidence, constituted an exception to the general principle laid down in *Sang*.[48]

Lord Nolan said ([1997] AC 558, 577–8):

> In truth, in the light of *Sang*, the argument that the evidence of the taped conversation is inadmissible could only be sustained if two wholly new principles were formulated in our law. The first would be that the appellant enjoyed a right of privacy, in terms similar to those of art. 8 of the Convention, in respect of the taped conversation. The second, which is different though related, is that evidence of the conversation obtained in breach of that right is inadmissible. The objection to the first of these propositions is that there is no such right of privacy in English law. The objection to the second is that, even if there were such a right the decision of your lordships' House in *Sang* and the many decisions which have followed it make it plain that as a matter of English law evidence which is obtained improperly or even unlawfully remains admissible, subject to the power of the trial judge to exclude it in the exercise of his common law discretion or under the provisions of s. 78.

Subsequently, the appellant's case was accepted for hearing by the European Court of Human Rights. For the purposes of this hearing, the appellant abandoned the additional argument that the admission of evidence obtained in contravention of art. 8 amounted to a violation of the art. 6 right to a fair trial. The Court (*Khan* v *United Kingdom* (2001) 31 EHRR 1016) held unanimously that the manner in which the evidence was obtained did amount to a violation of art. 8, but (with some dissent) that because the appellant had the right to contest the admissibility of the evidence both at trial and on appeal, there had been no violation of art. 6.

Khan was followed in *Allan* v *United Kingdom* (2003) 36 EHRR 12, in which it was held that it had been a violation of art. 8 of the Convention for the police to 'bug' the cell in which the accused was being held, and to plant an informant in the cell with a view to obtaining taped incriminating statements from the accused. Nonetheless, the use as evidence of the tapes so obtained did not violate the accused's right to a fair trial under art. 6.[49] Similarly, in *P* [2002] 1 AC 146, the House of Lords held that the use of material obtained by means of telephone intercepts which were authorized by statute and subject to judicial supervision, while constituting an 'interference' with the accused's rights under art. 8 of the Convention, did not infringe the accused's right

---

[47] Article 8(1) guarantees respect for private and family life, home and correspondence—a provision somewhat analogous to the Fourth Amendment to the United States Constitution. There is no exactly corresponding right in English law, though searches and telephone tapping are, to some extent, regulated by law (see the Interception of Communications Act 1985 and the Intelligence Services Act 1994). The appellant did not assert any breach of art. 6 of the Convention, which guarantees the right to a fair trial. For the text of these articles, see 1.7.3. In *Shenk* v *Switzerland* (1988) 13 EHRR 242, a case in which both art. 6 and art. 8 were involved, the European Court held that art. 6 did not purport to establish rules of evidence, which remained 'primarily a matter for regulation under national law'. The House of Lords in *Khan* held that the trial judge is entitled to take any breach of art. 8 into account in considering whether or not to exclude evidence in the exercise of his discretion under s. 78 (3.11 *et seq.*).

[48] A difficulty in the way of this argument was that the Intelligence Services Act 1994 expressly renders admissible evidence obtained by identical means pursuant to the powers conferred by that Act.

[49] Though the court did condemn as a violation of art. 6 the over-aggressive conduct of the informant, on the instructions of the police, in pressing the accused to make statements. As to the general admissibility of evidence obtained in violation of art. 8, see also *Loveridge* [2001] 2 Cr App R 29; *Mason and others* [2002] 2 Cr App R 38.

to a fair trial under art. 6, and so did not require the exclusion of the evidence.[50] This principle applied where the intercepts were made in a member state of the European Union, in accordance with the law of that country. In *Sargent* [2003] 1 AC 347, the House of Lords allowed an appeal against conviction, where tape-recordings of telephone conversations illegally intercepted in violation of the Interception of Communications Act 1985 were used to induce the appellant to make confessions during police interviews, and where both the contents of the intercepts and the resulting confessions were admitted in evidence. By virtue of s. 9(1) of the Act, the intercepts were inadmissible in evidence against the appellant. The trial judge held that this did not mean that the fruits of the use of the intercepts, i.e., the confessions, were rendered inadmissible, and he declined to exclude them in the exercise of his discretion under s. 78. In reliance on the confessions, the jury convicted. The Court of Appeal upheld the conviction. But the House of Lords held that the intercepts should not have been admitted, and that their effect in persuading the jury to act on the evidence of the confessions could not be disregarded. The House emphasized that there was no rule prohibiting the use of illegal intercepts during an interview, and that such use did not without more render evidence obtained as a result, such as the confessions, inadmissible. But the admission of both the intercepts and the confessions in the instant case was fatal to the conviction. However, this decision turns on a specific statutory provision rendering evidence inadmissible, and the appellant's broader arguments that the fruits of evidence illegally obtained should have been held to be inadmissible or excluded in the exercise of the judge's discretion were rejected. Properly understood, therefore, it confirms the general rule stated above with regard to the admissibility of evidence obtained in such circumstances.

3.10.2 Civil cases

The rule in civil cases at common law is the same as that in criminal cases, namely that evidence is admissible regardless of the fact that it may have been obtained illegally or unfairly. Indeed, it was said that the judge had no discretion to exclude such evidence: *Helliwell* v *Piggott-Sims* [1980] FSR 356, 357 per Lord Denning MR.[51] In *ITC Film Distributors Ltd* v *Video Exchange Ltd* [1982] Ch 431, however, Warner J unwittingly caused a certain amount of consternation when he excluded some evidence in the case before him without really making clear the basis on which he was doing do. The evidence consisted of certain documents tendered by the defendant which he had obtained from the plaintiffs by a trick after the plaintiffs and their solicitors had brought them into court for the purposes of the trial. The documents appeared to be relevant and admissible, but on application by the plaintiffs they were excluded because of the manner in which they had been obtained. Warner J appears to have made this decision as a matter of public policy, namely that parties should be free to bring their papers into court without having them filched. He noted that the defendant's conduct probably amounted to a contempt of court. But the learned judge expressly disclaimed any intention of applying the rule in *Lord Ashburton* v *Pape* [1913] 2 Ch 469, whereby a party may be entitled to injunctive relief to secure the return of documents which have come into the hands of an opponent, but which he was entitled to protect against disclosure or inspection, for example because they were privileged. As developed

---

[50] The House also pointed out that art. 8(2) provides a limitation of the right guaranteed by art. 8(1) in the interests of ensuring the detection of crime and the prosecution of criminals, subject to the requirement of a fair trial. As to the judicial oversight of telephone intercepts, see *Malone* v *Metropolitan Police Commissioner* [1979] Ch 344; *Malone* v *United Kingdom* (1984) 7 EHRR 14; *Sunday Times* v *United Kingdom* (1979) 2 EHRR 245; and generally *Morgans* v *DPP* [2001] AC 315; *Preston* [1994] 2 AC 130.

[51] And see *Universal City Studios Inc.* v *Hubbard* [1984] Ch 225.

by later authority, this is an equitable remedy wider than an order to prevent the use of evidence illegally or unfairly obtained, and which does not necessarily require a showing of impropriety.[52] This might well have been an appropriate remedy in the circumstances of the case (see 13.3). As it had not been invoked, however, Warner J's decision could be explained only on one of two bases; either a new rule of law of uncertain scope had been created, according to which a judge might exclude evidence obtained in circumstances contrary to public policy; or the decision could be adequately explained only on the basis of the exercise of discretion. In *Goddard v Nationwide Building Society* [1987] QB 670, 684, Nourse LJ considered the matter and favoured the former theory. He held that Warner J had decided the matter 'on the grounds of public policy' and not as a matter of discretion. This left the law in a rather unsatisfactory condition, because it was not clear in what kinds of case the new rule would apply, whether it would apply only to cases where a contempt of court had been committed, whether it could apply to cases of inadvertent disclosure in which no impropriety was involved, or even whether the decision in *ITC* should be regarded as one confined to its own facts.

This problem has never been resolved as a matter of common law. However, it is submitted that the answer may now be found in the provisions of r. 32.1 of the Civil Procedure Rules 1998, which are set out at 3.6. Under this rule, the judge has ample power to control the admission of evidence, and may exclude evidence on any ground which may seem appropriate to the circumstances, even though it may be legally admissible. Thus, although the common law rule of admissibility survives, the judge may prevent any prejudice or unfairness to a party arising from the illegal or unfair obtaining of evidence by that party's opponent, and he need not rely on any particular considerations of public policy to justify his use of that power. In *Jones v University of Warwick* [2003] 1 WLR 954, inquiry agents acting for the defendant's insurers gained access to the claimant's home by deception and made a video tape of her without her permission. The defendant sought and was granted permission to make use of the tape in evidence notwithstanding the method by which it had been obtained. The Court of Appeal held that, although the method used to obtain the tape had been improper, constituting a trespass and a violation of the claimant's rights under art. 8 of the European Convention on Human Rights, it was not so outrageous as to require extreme measures such as striking out the defence. To exclude the evidence would have been undesirable and artificial and would have had serious implications for the conduct of the litigation, including the necessity of instructing new medical experts. Nonetheless, the Court did not exclude the possibility that on other facts, such a more extreme remedy might be called for. The Court also held that the judge had a discretion in such cases, and must exercise it by considering not only the effect of his order on the instant case, but also its impact on litigation generally. This seems to indicate the existence of a general discretion in civil cases. However, it must be said that the decision on the facts shows a marked preference for the admission of relevant evidence, and it may be read as suggesting that in civil cases the preferred course is to mark the Court's disapproval in other ways. In the instant case, for example, the Court held that the defendant's conduct could be considered in relation to an order for costs, and in a particularly egregious case, no doubt the defence could be struck out. This may represent a pragmatic way of dealing with such conduct which is not available in criminal cases. It should also be noted that,

---

[52] See, e.g., *Guinness Peat Properties Ltd v Fitzroy Robinson Partnership* [1987] 2 All ER 716. The judge's view on this point was, it is submitted, unfortunate, as it was based solely on the mistaken assumption that the plaintiffs would not have been entitled to that relief because they had not filed a separate writ for that purpose, an extremely technical objection effectively demolished by the judgment of Nourse LJ in *Goddard v Nationwide Building Society* [1987] QB 670.

with particular reference to the remedy available under the rule in *Lord Ashburton* v *Pape*, r. 31.20 now provides that, where a party inadvertently allows a privileged document to be inspected, the party who has inspected it may use the document or its contents only with the permission of the court. Whether a document is to be taken as 'inadvertently disclosed' if it is obtained illegally or unfairly by an opponent is an interesting question. This is considered further at 13.3.

3.11 DISCRETIONARY EXCLUSION OF EVIDENCE ILLEGALLY OR UNFAIRLY OBTAINED AT COMMON LAW

Given that evidence illegally or unfairly obtained is not legally inadmissible, the question arises of whether it may be excluded in the exercise of the court's discretion.

3.11.1 *Sang*

In *Sang* [1980] AC 402, the accused was charged with conspiracy to utter counterfeit United States banknotes. He alleged by counsel that he had been induced by an informer, acting on the instructions of the police, to commit an offence that he would not have committed otherwise. As it was then clear law that the existence of entrapment, even if established, would not have been a ground to exclude evidence of the offence as a matter of law, counsel sought to investigate the issue in a trial within a trial, with a view to persuading the trial judge to exclude that evidence in his discretion. The trial judge, taking the view that he had no discretion to exclude admissible prosecution evidence, ruled accordingly after hearing argument on the hypothetical basis that the accused's allegations were true.[53] The Court of Appeal subsequently dismissed an appeal against conviction, and the accused appealed to the House of Lords. The House of Lords held that:

(a) The judge had a general discretion to exclude admissible prosecution evidence on the ground that its prejudicial nature might result in the accused's being denied a fair trial.
(b) With the exception of admissions, confessions and other evidence obtained from the accused after commission of the offence (for example, documentary evidence) the judge had no discretion to exclude evidence obtained by improper or unfair means, the court being concerned with the relevance of the evidence in question, not with its source.

The second of the above holdings merits some elaboration, because it was the cause of some difficulty in subsequent cases. The House of Lords clearly felt that the essence of the discretion to exclude, as applied to confessions or other evidence obtained from the accused after commission of the offence, was the maxim *nemo debet se ipsum prodere*. This maxim would be infringed if such evidence were obtained from the accused by a trick, or oppression, though not necessarily by some other illegal or unfair method, such as an illegal search (see, e.g., the speeches of Lord Diplock [1980] AC 402, 436, and Lord Fraser at 450). Consequently, a distinction could be drawn between evidence obtained from the accused after commission of the offence, and other kinds of evidence. Lord Scarman said, at 456–7:

> The question remains whether evidence obtained from an accused by deception, or a trick, may be excluded at the discretion of the trial judge. Lord Goddard CJ thought it could be: *Kuruma* v *The Queen*

---

[53] The judge's view was supported by some authority, for example, the decision of the Court of Appeal in *Willis* [1976] Crim LR 127, though for the reasons given below in the text, the greater weight of authority supported the existence of the discretion.

[1955] AC 197 at p. 204, Lord Parker CJ and Lord Widgery CJ thought so too: see *Callis* v *Gunn* [1964] 1 QB 495 at p. 502 and *Jeffrey* v *Black* [1978] QB 490. The dicta of three successive Lord Chief Justices are not to be lightly rejected. It is unnecessary for the purposes of this appeal, to express a conclusion upon them. But, always provided that these dicta are treated as relating exclusively to the obtaining of evidence from the accused, I would not necessarily dissent from them. If an accused is misled or tricked into providing evidence (whether it be an admission or the provision of fingerprints or medical evidence or some other evidence), the rule against self-incrimination—*nemo debet se ipsum prodere*—is likely to be infringed. Each case must, of course, depend on its circumstances. All I would say is that the principle of fairness, though concerned exclusively with the use of evidence at trial, is not susceptible to categorization or classification and is wide enough in some circumstances to embrace the way in which, after the crime, evidence has been obtained from the accused.

The decision in *Sang* was in no way dictated by earlier authority. Indeed, as Lord Scarman was constrained to concede in the passage cited above, such authority as there was indicated that the manner in which evidence was obtained was a proper subject for consideration by a judge in deciding whether or not to exercise his general exclusionary discretion. For example, in *Payne* [1963] 1 WLR 637, the accused's conviction for driving while unfit through drink was quashed by the Court of Criminal Appeal, where it appeared that the accused's consent to a medical examination at the police station had been obtained by an express assurance that the doctor would not be asked to testify as to whether the accused was unfit to drive a motor vehicle through drink, and where, in violation of this assurance, the prosecution nonetheless called the doctor at trial for precisely that purpose. The Court of Criminal Appeal held that, while the doctor's evidence was obviously admissible in law, the trial judge should have excluded it in the exercise of his discretion.[54] This was entirely in accord with the earlier view of Lord Goddard CJ in *Kuruma*. Lord Goddard had said ([1955] AC 197, 204):

> No doubt in a criminal case the judge always has a discretion to disallow evidence if the strict rules of admissibility would operate unfairly against an accused. This was emphasized in the case before this Board of *Noor Mohamed* v *R*, and in the recent case in the House of Lords, *Harris* v *DPP* [1952] AC 694. If, for instance, some admission of some piece of evidence, e.g., a document, had been obtained from a defendant by a trick, no doubt the judge might properly rule it out.

Following this pronouncement, the existence of such a discretion had been reaffirmed in a number of cases. In *Callis* v *Gunn* [1964] 1 QB 495, 502, Lord Parker CJ dealing with the question of the admissibility of fingerprint evidence, said:

> In my judgment fingerprint evidence taken in these circumstances is admissible in law subject to this overriding discretion. That discretion, as I understand it, would certainly be exercised by excluding the evidence if there was any suggestion of it having been obtained oppressively, by false representations, by a trick, by threats, by bribes, anything of that sort.

In *Jeffrey* v *Black* [1978] QB 490 the accused was charged with the theft of a sandwich from a public house. Before he was charged, police officers took the accused to his home, stating that they intended to search it. The justices found as a fact that a search of the accused's room was conducted without his consent, and refused to admit evidence of the discovery of cannabis and cannabis resin in the room. On appeal by the prosecutor, the Divisional Court held that, although the justices had erred in exercising their discretion to exclude the evidence merely because of the

---

[54] This decision was distinguished in *Apicella* (1985) 82 Cr App R 295, where a sample of body fluid, taken from the accused with his consent for diagnostic purposes, was later used to provide evidence against him. The distinction was that no deception of the accused was involved.

irregularity of the search, a discretion to exclude did exist. Lord Widgery CJ pointed out that the discretion was not confined to any particular case, but was '...a discretion which every judge has all the time in respect of all the evidence which is tendered by the prosecution'. It appears that Lord Widgery anticipated the statutory position under s. 78 of the Police and Criminal Evidence Act 1984, as his judgment indicates quite clearly both that there exists a general discretion to exclude any evidence tendered by the prosecution, and that one aspect of that discretion is concerned with the manner in which evidence has been obtained. The Lord Chief Justice stressed that the exercise of the discretion would be comparatively rare[55] but added:

> But if the case is exceptional, if the case is such that not only have the police officers entered without authority, but they have been guilty of trickery or they have misled someone, or they have been oppressive or they have been unfair, or in other respects they have behaved in a manner which is morally reprehensible, then it is open to the justices to apply their discretion and decline to allow the particular evidence to be let in as part of the trial.

3.11.2 Cases after *Sang*: the bad faith test

In the wake of *Sang*, various attempts were made to resuscitate the discretion, but with a marked lack of success. These attempts focused mainly on the exception addressed by the House of Lords relating to confessions and other evidence obtained from the accused after commission of the offence. For example, in *Apicella* (1985) 82 Cr App R 295, the appellant was convicted on three counts of rape, after evidence had been adduced that he suffered from a strain of gonorrhoea, from which the three victims also suffered. This evidence had been obtained by means of a body fluid sample taken from the appellant by a doctor while the appellant was on remand in custody. The sample had been taken for diagnostic purposes, not for use as evidence. But the appellant's case was that he had been led by a prison officer to believe that, being a prisoner, he had no right to refuse to provide the specimen. It was argued for the appellant that the specimen was effectively a confession, and should be treated as such, and that the manner in which it had been obtained made its use in evidence unfair. This argument may have been unnecessary, because, on any view, the specimen was evidence obtained from the appellant after commission of the offence. In any event, the Court of Appeal found no unfairness in what had happened, because the appellant had not, in the Court's view, been tricked into providing a specimen.[56]

In *Adams* [1980] QB 575, the Court of Appeal similarly held that the admission of evidence seized from an accused, during a search which was manifestly unlawful, was not unfair, in the absence of any oppressive circumstances.[57]

In *Fox* [1986] AC 281, it was conceded by the prosecution that a specimen of breath provided by the appellant, which formed the basis of his conviction, had been obtained after the appellant had been unlawfully arrested. It was argued that the justices should have exercised their discretion to exclude the evidence. The House of Lords rejected the argument, and in so doing laid

---

[55] Lord Widgery CJ said (*ibid.* at 498): 'I cannot stress the point too strongly that it is a very exceptional situation, and the simple, unvarnished fact that evidence was obtained by police officers who had gone in without bothering to get a search warrant is not enough to justify the magistrates in exercising their discretion to keep the evidence out'. Lord Widgery did not indicate what would be enough. It is possible that the Lord Chief Justice was concerned to avoid any suggestion that the exclusionary discretion should be an object of frequent use in the magistrates' courts in view of the somewhat greater danger that the guidelines might be misunderstood.

[56] See also *Cooke* [1995] 1 Cr App R 318 (sample of hair obtained by assault and used to establish DNA profile—evidence held to be admissible); *Latif* [1996] 1 WLR 104.

[57] And see *McCarthy* [1996] Crim LR 818; *Stewart* [1995] Crim LR 500.

down the test to be applied in such cases, which was based on the earlier authorities cited above, and which has since been referred to generally as the 'bad faith test'. This test was succinctly stated by Lord Fraser of Tullybelton (*ibid.* at 293) in a passage with which the other members of the House concurred:

> Of course, if the appellant had been lured to the police station by some trick or deception, or if the police officers had behaved oppressively towards the appellant, the justices' jurisdiction to exclude otherwise admissible evidence recognised in *Sang* might have come into play. But there is nothing of that sort suggested here. The police officers did no more than make a bona fide mistake as to their powers.

Thus, at common law after *Sang*, it was generally accepted that a showing of bad faith, oppression, or some trick or deception should be made to justify the discretionary exclusion of evidence illegally or unfairly obtained from the accused after commission of the offence.

3.12 EXCLUSION OF EVIDENCE ILLEGALLY OR UNFAIRLY OBTAINED UNDER S. 78

As we saw at 3.7.2, the relationship between the Police and Criminal Evidence Act 1984, s. 78, and the common law discretion (which was expressly preserved by s. 82(3) of the Act) is susceptible of more than one definition. What is clear, however, is that s. 78 changed the common law position as stated by the House of Lords in *Sang* [1980] AC 402, by introducing the specific test of whether an adverse effect would be produced on the fairness of the proceedings by admitting the evidence, and by declaring that the manner in which the evidence was obtained should be considered in relation to that test. Consequently, although the rule of admissibility of evidence illegally or unfairly obtained still obtains, the courts are now free to exclude evidence on the ground that to admit it would produce an unacceptably adverse affect on the fairness of the proceedings. In *Khan* [1997] AC 558, 581–2, Lord Nolan said:

> I am prepared to accept that if evidence has been obtained in circumstances which involve an apparent breach of art. 8 [of the European Convention on Human Rights: see 1.7.3],…that is a matter which may be relevant to the exercise of the s. 78 power. This does not mean that the trial judge is obliged to decide whether or not there has been a breach of the Convention…That is not his function, and it would be inappropriate for him to do so…But if the behaviour of the police in the particular case amounts to an apparent or probable breach of some relevant law or convention, common sense dictates that this is a consideration which may be taken into account for what it is worth. Its significance, however, will normally be determined not so much by its apparent unlawfulness or irregularity as upon its effect, taken as a whole, upon the fairness or unfairness of the proceedings. The fact that the behaviour in question constitutes a breach of the Convention…can plainly be of no greater significance *per se* than if it constituted a breach of English law. Upon the facts of the present case, in agreement with the Court of Appeal, I consider that the judge was fully entitled to hold that the circumstances in which the relevant evidence was obtained, even if they constituted a breach of art. 8, were not such as to require the exclusion of the evidence.

In *Chalkley* [1998] QB 848, 876, Auld LJ said:

> The exercise for the judge under s. 78 is not the marking of his disapproval of the prosecution's breach, if any, of the law in the conduct of the investigation or the proceedings, by a discretionary decision to stay them, but an examination of the question whether it would be unfair to the defendant to admit that evidence.

It must be said, however, that the cases actually decided under s. 78 do not present any consistent picture of the circumstances under which the s. 78 power is to be exercised. The courts seem to be most inclined to exercise it in cases in which the illegality or breach involved in obtaining the evidence is described as 'flagrant, deliberate and cynical' (*Canale* [1990] 2 All ER 187; and see *Samuel* [1988] QB 615) or of a kind which the Court hoped 'would never occur again' (*Mason* [1998] 1 WLR 139) or where police officers acted '*mala fide* and oppressively' (*Matto* v *Wolverhampton Crown Court* [1987] RTR 337; *Alladice* (1988) 87 Cr App R 380). The case of *mala fides* was one which had surfaced in connection with the common law discretion to exclude (*Fox* [1986] AC 281; 3.11.2). But, given that, as Auld LJ put it in *Chalkley*, the court's role is not to mark its disapproval of the prosecution's breach, but to ensure fairness for the accused, it is surely legitimate to ask why it should matter that the state of mind of the police officers was 'cynical', or their conduct 'deliberate' or 'oppressive', as opposed to merely incompetent or mistaken. Moreover, there are cases in which the breaches seem to be extremely serious, for example, the sad parody of an identification parade used to shore up an otherwise almost non-existent case in *Quinn* [1990] Crim LR 581 (see 3.12.1) but the convictions are nonetheless upheld; and cases in which the breaches seem almost inconsequential and accidental, but the convictions are reversed, for example, the natural questions put by an undercover police officer in *Bryce* [1992] 4 All ER 567. And some authority suggests that *mala fides* is not a requirement for the exercise of the s. 78 power in any event (*DPP* v *McGladrigan* [1991] RTR 297, holding that s. 78 gave the court a wider power than the common law discretion under which the *mala fides* argument had arisen in *Fox*).

It may be that this inconsistency results from the unsoundness of the underlying premise that the admission of evidence can actually result in unfairness *in the proceedings* merely because of the manner in which the evidence was obtained, as opposed to unfairness to the accused *in the sense that he has good reason to complain about the course of the investigation*. It may be that the manner in which evidence is obtained is in most cases irrelevant to the issue of whether it would be unfair to admit the evidence at trial. Of course, the manner in which the evidence is obtained is not the only matter which the judge should consider in the course of his analysis under s. 78, but in practice it is the matter which is most often in issue. If the intrinsic nature of the evidence is such that the judge is minded to exclude it regardless of how it is obtained, that decision could equally well be taken relying on the common law discretion to exclude. It may be that, as they have abrogated any responsibility for acting as watchdogs over the investigative process, trial judges and the appellate courts have no logical remedy to afford the accused in such situations. If so, the courts have reduced their role to one of occasional interference when the misconduct of the police reaches a level outrageous enough to irritate them. If so, consistency can hardly be expected in this area, and its absence thus far should occasion no surprise.

3.12.1 Cases involving breaches of Code of Practice

The most important cases in which the exercise of the s. 78 power has been considered because of violations of the Codes of Practice, some of which are mentioned above, are those relating to confessions obtained in breach of Code of Practice C. These cases are considered in Chapter 9, dealing with confessions, at 9.12. But the same principles apply where evidence is obtained in violation of any of the Codes. The test is not the seriousness or otherwise of the breach (though this is certainly relevant) but whether the admission of the evidence produced thereby would have an unacceptably unfair effect on the proceedings. In *Quinn* [1990] Crim LR 581, the prosecution obtained evidence of identification of the accused as the perpetrator of an offence by means of a procedure carried out abroad, which was the antithesis of the properly conducted identification parade which would have been required in England under Code of Practice D. The identifying witness was given virtually no alternative to identifying the accused, and the whole procedure was conducted in a manner calculated to suggest that result. The other evidence against the accused was tenuous in the extreme. Lord Lane CJ said:

> The function of the judge is therefore to protect the fairness of the proceedings, and normally, proceedings are fair if a jury hears all relevant evidence which either side wishes to place before it, but proceedings may become unfair if, for example, one side is allowed to adduce relevant evidence which, for one reason or another, the other side cannot properly challenge or meet, or where there has been an abuse of process, e.g., because evidence has been obtained in deliberate breach of procedures laid down in an official code of practice.

Despite this apparently clear statement, which certainly seems apposite to the facts of the case, the Court of Appeal refused to reverse the conviction because the judge had correctly directed his mind to all the factors which might have borne on the question of fairness or unfairness. It is submitted that the refusal of the Court of Appeal to interfere with the judge's decision in such circumstances is a clear indication that, contrary to the view taken by Auld LJ in *Chalkley* [1998] QB 848 (see 3.7.2), the power to exclude created by s. 78 is in fact essentially a matter for the discretion of the trial judge.

3.12.2 Cases involving entrapment, illegality, and subterfuges

In *Smurthwaite* [1994] 1 All ER 898, an undercover police officer posing as a contract killer recorded conversations with the accused, which the prosecution proposed to adduce in evidence, but which did not fall within the ambit of Code of Practice C. The Court of Appeal held that, even though entrapment might be no defence to a charge, it might be relevant to an application to exclude evidence under s. 78. On the facts of the case, however, the Court of Appeal was not satisfied that the officer was an *agent provocateur* and, as the evidence showed that the officer had played a lesser role in the planning of the offence and had used no persuasion against the accused, it was held that the evidence had been rightly admitted. In *Latif* [1996] 1 WLR 104, the House of Lords reached the same conclusion, even though it was shown that an informer had lured the accused to England in connection with a drug deal, and even though an undercover customs officer had actively participated with the accused in the unlawful importation of heroin into the UK.

Particular difficulties have been caused by such so-called entrapment cases, in which evidence of an offence is obtained by means of the activities of an informer or *agent provocateur* employed by the police. In these cases, the accused is either encouraged in or lured into the commission of an offence for which he is subsequently prosecuted. The question arises of whether or not the trial judge should exclude as a matter of discretion under s. 78 evidence obtained by means of entrapment, even though it is, as we have seen, admissible as a matter of law. Before the decision of the House of Lords in *Looseley* [2001] 1 WLR 2060, the courts had distinguished two different situations; the first in which the *agent provocateur* infiltrates himself into the commission of an offence already underway at the instigation of the accused, for example by posing as a receiver of stolen goods; the second where the *agent* himself initiates the commission of an offence, and where but for his instigation, the accused might not have been disposed to commit the offence. In earlier decisions, the distinction was thought to be relevant to the determination of the offences with which the accused should be charged and to the question of sentence, but was not thought to justify the court in exercising its discretion to exclude the evidence so obtained in either case.[58] Accordingly, the fact that he had been entrapped was of no assistance to the accused in this respect. But in later cases, the Court of Appeal appeared to indicate that it might be prepared to reconsider this position, at least in relation to the second kind of entrapment.[59] Nonetheless, the law remained unclear. In *Looseley*, however, the House of Lords set out to review the law of entrapment in the light of the fair trial provisions of art. 6 of the European Convention on Human Rights. It was held that the existence of 'State-created crime' was not acceptable in English law, especially in the light of art. 6. An accused who is prosecuted for such a crime has two possible remedies, namely a stay of the proceedings against him, and the discretionary exclusion under s. 78 of the evidence obtained as a result of the State's action. Lord Nicholls (at 2068) made the following observations about what amounts to State-created crime, which, it will be observed, corresponds with the distinction between the two kinds of entrapment noted above:

> If the defendant already had the intent to commit a crime of the same or a similar kind, then the police did no more than give him the opportunity to fulfil his existing intent. This is unobjectionable. If the defendant was already presently disposed to commit such a crime, should opportunity arise, that is not entrapment. That is not state-created crime. The matter stands differently if the defendant lacked such a predisposition and the police were responsible for implanting the necessary intent.

But Lord Nicholls went on to hold that this 'traditional analysis' was not adequate to describe the principles of law involved. Instead, his Lordship preferred a more general test (at 2069):

> Ultimately the overall consideration is always whether the conduct of the police or other law enforcement agency was so seriously improper as to bring the administration of justice into disrepute.[60]

In forming a view about this question, the trial judge should have regard to all the circumstances of the case, including the nature (seriousness) of the offence, the reason for the police operation in question, the nature and extent of police participation in the offence, and the accused's criminal record, if any. The point seems to be that even active instigation of an offence by an *agent provocateur* should not be regarded as enough to require the automatic exercise of the s. 78 discretion, though it is clearly a factor to be considered. As Lord Hoffmann pointed out (at 2078) different measures might be justified in different cases, for example where it is necessary to deal firmly with a serious and locally prevalent wave of crime in which the accused's involvement is already suspected, as compared with an opportunistic ploy to entrap in a random way anyone who might be available to be entrapped and where no offence is presently contemplated, a mere fishing expedition in the course of which the accused happens to be caught up in the net. Thus, for Lord Hoffmann, the question of causation of the commission of the offence is not the whole answer, and the distinction between causing crime and providing opportunity is 'important, but not necessarily decisive' (at 2075).

---

[58] See *Mealy* (1974) 60 Cr App R 59; *McEvilly* (1973) 60 Cr App R 150; *Birtles* [1969] 1 WLR 1047; *Macro* [1969] Crim LR 205. Entrapment is not a defence in English law. In the United States, the second but not the first kind of entrapment mentioned in the text is a defence.

[59] *Bryce* [1992] 4 All ER 567; *Jelen* (1989) 90 Cr App R 456; *Gill* [1989] Crim LR 358.

[60] This language mirrors judicial language in other cases in which there is alleged to have been serious police misconduct, for example that of Lord Steyn in *Latif* [1996] 1 WLR 104, 112, 'prosecution which would affront the public conscience'; and of Lord Bingham CJ in *Nottingham City Council v Amin* [2000] 1 WLR 1071, 1076, 'conviction and punishment deeply offensive to ordinary notions of fairness'.

Curiously, although it was canvassed as a reason for this review of the law by the House of Lords, art. 6 of the Convention ultimately played little part in the decision, the House being of the opinion that it adds nothing to English law in this kind of case. And indeed, the jurisprudence of the European Court of Human Rights does make clear that, as a general proposition, as long as the fairness of the trial is not prejudiced and the accused is provided an opportunity to challenge the admissibility of the evidence, the provisions of art. 6 are satisfied. The State is entitled to set its own standards of what is fair and acceptable conduct by the police in the course of the investigation of crime. Nonetheless, on the specific question of entrapment, the authority on which the House relies seems to favour the 'traditional' distinction between accused-created and State-created crime as the basis for a decision of whether or not there has been a violation of art. 6.[61] On this basis, there may be cases in which an accused fails to attract the exercise of discretion under s. 78 under the test propounded in *Looseley*, but would be judged to have been deprived of his right to a fair trial under art. 6 under *Teixera de Castro*. It is submitted that, whatever the merits of the more general test, and of taking into account all the relevant circumstances, it should be only in comparatively rare cases that the courts find justified in terms of art. 6 the instigation by an *agent provocateur* of the commission of a crime which the accused was not otherwise disposed to commit and which might otherwise not have been committed at all. In such cases, there should be a presumption that the discretion to exclude should be exercised.

In *Shannon* [2001] 1 Cr App R 12, it was held that the same principles of admissibility and exercise of discretion apply where the *agent provocateur* is not an agent of the State. In this case, an investigative journalist working for a sensational newspaper posed as a visiting 'sheikh' for the express purpose of entrapping the appellant into offering to supply him with drugs during a meeting at a hotel. When the appellant did so, the resulting tapes were not only published in the newspaper but subsequently handed over to the police, with the result that the appellant was prosecuted for drug-related offences. The appellant applied to the trial judge to exclude the evidence, but the judge saw no ground for so doing. The Court of Appeal agreed. The evidence showed that, although the appellant had been entrapped, he had volunteered to supply drugs with little or no encouragement, had strongly suggested his involvement in the drug scene, and had ignored a clear opportunity to walk away from the situation he was in. It was held that the judge had been correct to rule as he did.[62]

The power to exclude under s. 78 applies also to cases in which the police use a subterfuge to obtain evidence. Such cases include (to return to examples given at 3.10.2) deliberately leaving attractive goods in a position in which they are vulnerable to theft (*Williams* v *DPP* [1993] 3 All ER 365), operating a sham business purporting to 'fence' stolen goods (*Christou* [1992] QB 979)

---

[61] *Teixera de Castro* v *Portugal* (1998) 28 EHRR 101, a case which appears to hold that the incitement of an accused to commit an offence he would not otherwise have committed was a violation of art. 6, and distinguishes *Lüdi* v *Switzerland* (1992) 15 EHRR 173, on the express ground that in the latter case, the initiative for the offence had come from the accused.

[62] The decision has some not altogether satisfactory features. *Texeiro de Castro* was cited to the Court and considered, even though the Human Rights Act 1998 was not yet in effect, but the Court's attempt to distinguish it (even though apparently unnecessary given the judge's finding of fact that the appellant had eagerly volunteered his services) is to say the least unconvincing, and would amount to a retreat from a clear disapproval of *agent*-induced crime. Perhaps the Court found sensational newspaper-sponsored crime to be somewhat more palatable than State-sponsored crime. The European Court of Human Rights subsequently dismissed the appellant's application for relief on the ground that it was 'manifestly unfounded'. The Court found that there was no reason to question the conclusions reached by the trial court or the Court of Appeal on the issue of entrapment, or to believe that the appellant's trial had been in any way unfair: *Shannon* v *United Kingdom* [2005] Crim LR 133.

and obtaining information by 'bugging' a cell in which suspects were being held (*Bailey* [1993] 3 All ER 513; *Roberts* [1997] 1 Cr App R 217). It also applies to cases such as *Khan* [1997] AC 558, *P* [2002] AC 146, and *Chalkley* [1998] QB 848 (3.10.1) in which the conduct indulged in involves arguably illegal searches or surveillances, or other conduct which may constitute a tort such as trespass, or a violation of art. 8 of the European Convention on Human Rights. In all these cases, while the court may take into account the nature and apparent gravity of the breach, the sole issue remains whether the admission of the evidence would produce such an adverse effect on the fairness of the proceedings that the court ought not to admit it.

3.13 RECOMMENDED FURTHER READING

Griew, E., 'Summing up the law' [1989] *Criminal Law Review* 768.

Heydon, R., 'Illegally obtained evidence (1) and (2)' [1973] *Criminal Law Review* 603 and 690.

Ormerod, D. and Birch, D., 'The evolution of the discretionary exclusion of evidence' [2004] *Criminal Law Review* 767.

Squires, D., 'The problem with entrapment' (2006) *Oxford Journal of Legal Studies* 351.

Williams, G., 'Evidence obtained by illegal means' [1955] *Criminal Law Review* 339.

 ## 3.14 QUESTION FOR DISCUSSION BASED ON *R* v *COKE*; *LITTLETON* (for case files go to the Online Resource Centre)

What pieces of evidence, if any, may (1) Coke and (2) Littleton seek to exclude in the exercise of the court's discretion, and with what prospect of success?

3.15 GENERAL QUESTIONS FOR DISCUSSION

1. What is the difference between 'questions of fact' and 'questions of law'?

2. What is the division of responsibilities between the judge and jury in a criminal trial?

3. What is the name of the hearing when a judge hears legal argument in the absence of a jury?

4. In what circumstances may a judge withdraw a case from the jury?

5. May a judge in a civil case exclude evidence that is technically admissible?

6. In terms of a judge's power to exclude evidence, what is the difference between ss. 76 and 78 of the Police and Criminal Evidence Act 1984?

7. If evidence is obtained illegally or unfairly, must it be excluded by the judge in a criminal case? What about in a civil case?

8. In the UK, must evidence obtained by entrapment always be excluded?

4

THE BURDEN AND STANDARD OF PROOF

A THE BURDEN OF PROOF

SUMMARY OF MAIN POINTS

- There are two burdens of proof, the legal burden (to prove the elements of the case or defence to the appropriate standard) and the evidential burden (to adduce sufficient evidence to justify, though not require, a favourable decision).

- At common law in civil cases, the legal burden of proof rests on the party who, on the proper interpretation of the law, asserts the affirmative proposition (usually, but not always, the claimant). The defendant bears the burden of proving a defence going beyond a denial of the claimant's allegations (an affirmative defence).

- At common law in criminal cases the prosecution always bears the burden of proving each element of the offence charged. This rule coincides with the presumption of innocence under art. 6(2) of the European Convention on Human Rights, a fundamental right of the accused. It is not violated in cases where the defence bears an evidential burden of raising facts to contradict the prosecution's allegations which the prosecution must then disprove.

- The fundamental rule does not necessarily prevent the accused being given the legal burden of proving an affirmative defence. But any rule imposing such a reverse burden must be scrutinized closely on fairness and proportionality grounds under art. 6, and if necessary 'read down' so as to impose only an evidential burden on the accused.

- A party who seeks to adduce evidence bears the burden of proving any facts necessary to justify its admission.

4.1 INTRODUCTION

In any case, civil or criminal, there must always be rules as to who must prove what. If, for example, a claimant brings a civil action against a defendant, the court must know whether the claimant must prove his allegations in order to establish liability, or whether, once the allegations are made, the defendant must disprove them to escape liability. It is important to have an answer to this question for several reasons: firstly, in civil cases, it will usually determine who has the right to call evidence first at the trial—which may afford that party a significant advantage;[1] secondly, if the tribunal of fact is conscientiously unable to decide between the parties at the end of the case, the answer will determine who wins and who loses; and thirdly, if the case is appealed, it will enable the appellate court to determine whether or not the judge applied the correct test (in a criminal case, whether the judge correctly directed the jury) in assessing the significance of the evidence. In the language of the law of evidence, a party who must prove something in order to establish or escape liability is said to have the burden of proof.

In *Re B (Children) (Care Proceedings: Standard of Proof) CARCASS Intervening* [2009] 1 AC 11, [2], Lord Hoffmann said:

> If a legal rule requires a fact to be proved (a "fact in issue") a judge or jury must decide whether or not it happened. There is no room for a finding that it might have happened. The law operates a binary system in which the only values are zero and one. The fact either happened or it did not. If the tribunal is in doubt, the doubt is resolved by a rule that one party or the other carries the burden of proof. If the party who bears the burden of proof fails to discharge it, a value of zero is returned and the fact is treated as not having happened. If he does discharge it a value of one is returned and the fact is treated as having happened.

A second question which must be answered is what degree of proof is required of a party who has the burden of proof, in other words to what degree of satisfaction must the tribunal of fact

---

[1] Depending on the elements of the cause of action and the defences thereto, and on the issues in dispute, a defendant may have the burden of proof on the issues the court has to decide, in which case he will have the right to begin: see *Pontifex* v *Jolly* (1839) 9 Car & P 202; *Mercer* v *Whall* (1845) 14 LJ QB 267; *Re Parry* [1977] 1 WLR 93. In criminal cases, the prosecution always has the overall burden of proof and so always begins (see 4.7).

be persuaded, before the burden of proof can be found to have been discharged? This degree of persuasion is referred to as the standard of proof, and is also important in any evaluation by an appellate court of the way in which the trial court dealt with the evidence.

We must consider the burden and standard of proof separately. But it will be observed throughout this chapter that there are fundamental divergences in the law concerning both, as between civil and criminal cases. This is because in a civil case the law maintains a neutrality as between the parties, and tries to keep them on even terms as far as possible. While one party must have the burden of proof, its significance is minimized by a minimal standard of proof, which maintains an even balance and permits the better case to win the day. On the other hand, in a criminal case, the law undertakes to ensure that the accused is not convicted without rigorous safeguards; here, the law does not hold a neutral balance, but imposes on the prosecution the burden of proof and a high standard of proof. These apparently simple propositions have given rise to considerable problems, which we shall examine in due course. Of particular importance in criminal cases is the fundamental impact of art. 6 of the European Convention on Human Rights, and its application to the burden of proof by the House of Lords in *Lambert* [2002] 2 AC 545 (see 4.9).

Every claim, charge or defence has certain essential elements, the proof of which is necessary to the success of the party asserting it. For example, a claimant who asserts a claim for negligence asserts: (1) that the defendant owed the claimant a duty of care; (2) that the defendant, by some act or omission, was in breach of that duty of care; and (3) that as a result of that breach, the claimant suffered injury or damage for which the law permits recovery. These elements derive, not from the law of evidence, but from the substantive law applicable to the claim, in this case, the law of negligence. They are known as 'facts in issue' or 'ultimate facts' (see 2.6). The proof of these facts in issue depends, however, on the detailed facts of the individual case, which are referred to as 'evidential facts'. Thus, for example, in order to prove the fact in issue, negligence, the claimant might set out to prove the evidential facts that the defendant drove while drunk, too fast, on the wrong side of the road, and knocked the claimant down, breaking his leg.

The term 'burden of proof', standing alone, is ambiguous. It may refer to the obligation to prove a fact in issue to the required standard of proof, or to the obligation to adduce enough evidence to support a favourable finding on that issue. It is generally held, therefore, that there are at least two distinct burdens of proof.[2] These are referred to respectively as the 'legal' or 'persuasive' burden, and the 'evidential' burden.[3] The two burdens do not always lie on the same party. For example, although one party may bear the legal burden of proving a fact in issue, some of the evidential facts may be unchallenged, or presumed in his favour. It is, therefore, necessary to consider these burdens separately. This can be done most simply by analysing what happens during a trial, as evidence is presented.

---

[2] Whether the evidential burden is properly called a burden 'of proof' obviously depends on the definition of 'proof'. It certainly does not refer to proof in the same sense as the legal burden, although it does refer to the introduction of evidence sufficient to achieve certain evidential goals: see *Jayasena v R* [1970] AC 618, 624 per Lord Devlin; *Sheldrake v DPP; Attorney-General's Reference (No. 4 of 2002)* [2005] 1 AC 264, [1] per Lord Bingham of Cornhill; and 4.3 below. Some writers contend that there may be other burdens, for example, the so-called 'procedural' burden of properly including all essential matters in the statement of case. However, it is submitted that such a 'burden' is not really a matter of the law of evidence, and is of purely procedural concern.

[3] The legal burden is also known sometimes as the 'ultimate' burden. In the United States, the evidential burden is often known as the 'burden of going forward with evidence', which is helpfully descriptive. The differences are of terminology only. See Denning (1945) 61 LQR 379; Bridge (1949) 12 MLR 273.

4.2 THE LEGAL OR PERSUASIVE BURDEN OF PROOF

The legal or persuasive burden of proof may be defined as the burden of persuading the tribunal of fact, to the required standard of proof and on the whole of the evidence, of the truth or sufficient probability of every essential fact in issue. Assume in our negligence case that the claimant
will bear the legal burden of proving each element of his claim (which, as we shall see below, is
indeed the case). This entitles him to call his evidence first. The claimant and his witnesses will
give evidence and will be cross-examined, and the claimant's case in chief will conclude. Has the
claimant discharged his legal burden of proof? It is too early to say. The legal burden of proof can
only be judged by assessing in the light of the proper standard of proof all the evidence given in
the case, and this cannot be done until the defendant's case has also been presented. Thus, we
will not know whether the claimant has discharged the legal burden until the judge gives judgment at the very end of the case. Failure to discharge the legal burden of proof on the whole of
the evidence is fatal to the case of the party having the burden of proof. This illustrates one of the
reasons why it is important to have a certain rule about the incidence of the burden of proof. If
the court is conscientiously unable to decide between the parties on the whole of the evidence
(an unusual, but by no means unknown occurrence), the result of the case is not a 'draw', but that
the party who has the burden of proof loses.

4.3 THE EVIDENTIAL BURDEN

The conclusion of the claimant's case is nonetheless a critical moment in the case, because it is
the point at which the judge decides whether the claimant has discharged his evidential burden.
Unless the claimant has presented at least some evidence in support of each essential element of
his claim the defendant will be entitled to make a submission of no case to answer, which if successful, entitles the defendant to judgment without being called on to present a case. The case is
fatally defective in law. The defendant could safely refuse to call any evidence, and if the judge
found for the claimant, the judgment would be set aside on appeal. The test on a submission of
no case to answer is whether the claimant has established a *prima facie* case as to each essential
element of the claim. A *prima facie* case is established when there is enough evidence to entitle,
though not compel the tribunal of fact to find in favour of the claimant, if there were to be no
further evidence given. In *Jayasena v R* [1970] AC 618, 624, Lord Devlin described the requirement as being for 'such evidence as, if believed and left uncontradicted and unexplained, could
be accepted by the jury as proof'.

Whether or not the claimant (or the prosecution in a criminal case) has established a *prima facie*
case is a question of law for the judge. The judge should not ask himself what the tribunal of fact
will decide, which would obviously be premature and speculative, but what the tribunal of fact
would be entitled as a matter of law to decide; whether, if the case were to stop at this point, the tribunal of fact *could* find for the claimant without being reversed on appeal for legal insufficiency
of the evidence. The discharge of the evidential burden of proof means, then, that the claimant
has adduced enough evidence of evidential facts to establish a *prima facie* case as to the facts in
issue, and thereby defeat a submission of no case to answer.

4.3.1 The burden of proof diagram

Where the claimant successfully discharges his evidential burden of proof, an interesting phenomenon occurs, which is illustrated by the diagram given below.

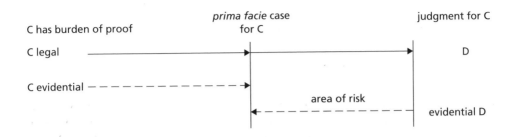

In this diagram, the unbroken line represents the legal burden of proof, and the broken line the evidential burden. It will be seen that the claimant bears the legal burden from first to last, since he must persuade the court at the end of the case, and on the whole of the evidence, that he has proved each essential fact in issue. But at the moment when the claimant establishes his *prima facie* case, he has discharged his evidential burden of proof. At this point, the defendant (who bears no legal burden of proof) nonetheless acquires an evidential burden.[4] This is because, if he does not now adduce some evidence in opposition to the claimant's case, he runs the clear risk that the claimant's uncontradicted case will succeed. It should be noted that, as a matter of law, the defendant is fully entitled to refuse to adduce evidence; because the claimant has the entire legal burden of proof, the judge still has the duty of considering the claimant's case as a whole in the light of the standard of proof. And, in a criminal case, in which the standard required of the prosecution is that beyond reasonable doubt, there may be good tactical reasons for taking this course. But in a civil case, it would be to court disaster. The area in the diagram between the stages of *prima facie* case and judgment for the claimant may, therefore, be described as the defendant's area of risk. Where the defendant, as he may, bears the legal burden of proof of an affirmative defence (see 4.5; 4.6) the same considerations apply, *mutatis mutandis*, to the burdens of proof in respect of that defence.

4.4 THE EFFECT OF PRESUMPTIONS ON THE BURDEN OF PROOF

There are certain rules of law known as presumptions, which have an effect on the normal incidence of the burden of proof.[5]

A presumption is a rule of law which provides that if a party proves a certain fact (known as the primary fact) then another fact (the presumed fact) will also be taken to be proved, unless evidence is adduced by the opponent to 'rebut' the presumption, or, in other words contradict the presumed fact. For example, the presumption of validity of marriage allows a party seeking to prove that H and W are validly married to prove that H and W went through an apparently legitimate ceremony of marriage[6] (which is much easier to prove). Then, unless another party adduces evidence to show that, despite the apparent regularity, the marriage was not valid (for example, because of lack of capacity to marry, or bigamy) the validity of the marriage of H and

---

[4] Some writers speak of the evidential burden 'shifting' to the defendant, and insofar as the evidential burden may usefully be contrasted with the legal burden, which never 'shifts', this is an acceptable concept. However, it is more accurate to say that the claimant has discharged his evidential burden and the defendant has acquired an evidential burden.

[5] There are a number of individual presumptions, which are discussed in detail in Chapter 20. The only matter relevant to the present discussion is the general working of presumptions and their effect on the burden of proof.

[6] Or that the parties have cohabited; see 20.12.

W will be taken as proved without further evidence from the proponent. As regards the fact of the validity of the marriage, it is obvious that the presumption affects the burden of proof, because the proponent now need not adduce further evidence of that fact, at least unless and until another party seeks to rebut the presumption. But it is less easy to identify what precise effect the presumption has. As to this, there are essentially two theories. It is worth observing initially that there has been an important contrast of approach between English and American writers on this subject. English writers have generally started with the proposition that there are different kinds of presumption, which have different effects on the burden of proof.[7] American writers have sought (largely in vain) a principle applicable universally to all presumptions, but have found themselves unable to agree on what principle it should be.[8]

According to the first theory, generally named after Professor Thayer, a leading exponent, proof of the primary fact creates an evidential burden on the opponent with respect to the presumed fact. Therefore, the presumed fact will be taken as proved unless the opponent adduces some evidence to rebut the presumption, though he need not go so far as disproving it. If the opponent does this, the presumption disappears and the normal burden of proof applies as if the presumption had never existed. This sudden disappearance has led to this theory being known also as the 'bursting bubble' theory. Professor Glanville Williams describes presumptions governed by this theory as 'evidential presumptions'.[9]

According to the second theory, named after Professor Morgan, proof of the primary fact operates to shift the legal burden of proof of the presumed fact to the opponent, who must adduce evidence to disprove it to the applicable standard of proof. Professor Glanville Williams describes presumptions governed by this theory as 'persuasive presumptions'.

The distinction is almost certainly of significance only in civil cases, since in criminal cases, the accused cannot be made to bear the legal burden of proof except on certain defined issues (which do not include presumptions as such) and never on the ultimate issue of guilt. To the extent, therefore, that the prosecution could use a presumption against the accused, the accused would acquire at the most an evidential burden of proof as to the presumed fact.[10] This principle has been strongly reinforced by the decision of the House of Lords in *Lambert* [2002] 2 AC 545, in the light of art. 6 of the European Convention on Human Rights (see 4.9).

4.4.1 The presumption diagram

The diagram below is a sequel to the burden of proof diagram, and the broken and unbroken lines mean the same. It illustrates vividly the difference to the defendant's burden as between the Thayer and Morgan theories, and shows how far the presumption assists the proponent of the evidence.

---

[7] Glanville Williams, *Criminal Law (The General Part)*, 2nd edn, p. 887 *et seq.*, cited and criticized by Cross, *Evidence*, 5th edn, pp. 126–7.

[8] J.B. Thayer, *Preliminary Treatise on Evidence*, pp. 314, 336; 9 Wigmore, Evidence, s. 2491(2) (Chadburn Rev 1981); Morgan and Maguire (1937) 50 Harv L Rev 909.

[9] Although much criticized as lending too little weight to presumptions, and rendering them 'slight and evanescent' (Morgan and Maguire, op. cit. note 8 at 913) the Thayer theory has found wide acceptance in the United States. Federal Rule of Evidence 301 provides: 'In all civil actions…a presumption imposes on the party against whom it is directed the burden of going forward with evidence to rebut or meet the presumption, but does not shift to such party the burden of proof in the sense of the risk of non-persuasion, which remains throughout the trial upon the party on whom it was originally cast'.

[10] It is doubtful whether a presumption can ever be employed to prove an essential element of an offence against the accused: see *Dillon* [1982] AC 484; 20.14.1. In the United States there is a constitutional rule against taking an ultimate issue from the jury by presumption or otherwise.

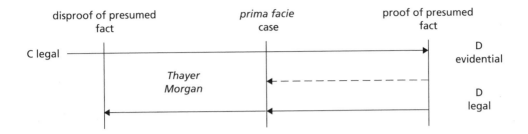

4.5 THE LEGAL BURDEN OF PROOF IN CIVIL CASES

The legal burden of proof as to any fact in issue in a civil case lies upon the party who affirmatively asserts that fact in issue, and to whose claim or defence proof of the fact in issue is essential. This is a sound rule in civil cases, in which the law seeks to hold a neutral balance between the parties, and it has been said judicially (*Joseph Constantine Steamship Line* v *Imperial Smelting Corporation Ltd* [1942] AC 154, 174 per Viscount Maugham) that it is 'an ancient rule founded on considerations of good sense and it should not be departed from without strong reason'. The essential elements of a claim or defence are determined by reference to the substantive law.

If the claimant fails to prove any essential element of his claim, the defendant will be entitled to judgment. The position of the defendant is somewhat different. Since the claimant affirmatively asserts his claim, he bears the burden of proving the claim, and the defendant assumes no legal burden of proof by merely denying the claim. However, if the defendant asserts a defence which goes beyond a mere denial (sometimes referred to as an 'affirmative defence') the defendant must assume the legal burden of proving such defence. An affirmative defence is most easily recognized by the fact that it raises facts in issue which do not form part of the claimant's case. If, for example, the claimant claims that the defendant injured him by a negligent act, the defendant may deny negligence without assuming any legal burden of proof. However, if the defendant goes on to assert that the claimant was injured through his own negligence, he asserts an affirmative defence not raised as a fact in issue by the claimant's case, and must bear the legal burden of proof of that defence.

It is a sound rule, therefore, that every party must prove each necessary element of his claim or defence. There are cases, however, where it is not easy to determine to whose case a fact in issue is essential, and who should be held to fail if the fact in issue is not proved. In such cases, the courts have inclined to require proof of the party to whom the least difficulty or embarrassment will be caused by the burden. This in turn leads to two guidelines which are usually followed: (1) each party should prove facts peculiarly within his own knowledge; and (2) proof of a positive proposition is to be preferred to proof of a negative. In *Joseph Constantine Steamship Line* v *Imperial Smelting Corporation Ltd*[11] charterers claimed damages from the shipowners for breach of charterparty. The defendants claimed that the contract had been frustrated by the destruction of the ship by an explosion, the cause of which was unclear. Such frustration would have concluded the case in favour of the defendants in the absence of any fault on their part. In view of the unsatisfactory state of the evidence, the question of who bore the burden of proving or disproving fault was of crucial importance. The House of Lords held that to require the defendants to prove a negative (the absence of fault) would be unduly onerous. The reality was that the plaintiffs asserted the existence of fault and should be required to prove it. In *Levison v Patent Steam Carpet*

---

[11] [1942] AC 154. See also *Munro Brice & Co.* v *War Risks Association* [1918] 2 KB 78.

Cleaning Ltd [1978] QB 69, the defendants were guilty of the unexplained loss of the plaintiffs' Chinese carpet, which had been delivered to them for cleaning. A clause in the contract signed by the plaintiffs would have exempted the defendants from liability for negligence, but not for any fundamental breach of contract. It was necessary to determine where the burden of proof on the latter issue lay. The Court of Appeal held that the defendants would find the burden far less onerous, the circumstances of the loss being peculiarly within their knowledge, and accordingly they bore the burden of proof. This is in accord with the rule in cases of bailment that it is for the defendant to show that the loss or damage was not caused by want of reasonable care on his part. Similarly, in a case in which conversion is alleged, the burden on proof lies on the bailee to show that he dealt with the goods consigned to him in good faith and without notice of the rights of any person who may transpire to be the owner of the goods: *Marcq v Christie Manson & Woods Ltd (trading as Christie's)* [2002] 4 All ER 1005; and see *Kuwait Airways Corp v Iraqi Airways Co.* [2002] 2 WLR 1353.

4.5.1 Burden is to prove case more probable than not

We have already noted, but it remains important to emphasize, that the incidence of the legal burden of proof will decide the outcome of the case if the tribunal of fact is conscientiously unable to decide on the whole of the evidence which side of the case to prefer. If the claimant bears the burden of proof, and fails to persuade the court that his case has been proved on the balance of probabilities, judgment should be given for the defendant. Moreover, the test is not whether the claimant's case is more probable than the defendant's, but whether the claimant's case is more probably true than not true, i.e., the claimant's case is measured by reference to an objective standard of probability.

An intriguing and vivid example is *Rhesa Shipping Co. SA v Edmunds*.[12] The plaintiff ship-owners sought to recover against underwriters in respect of the loss of their vessel, the *Popi M*. The ship had been lost in the Mediterranean in calm seas and good weather, and the wreck could not be salvaged. The evidence showed that she had sustained a large hole in her side shell-plating, which resulted in flooding which sank the vessel, and it was the cause of this damage on which the case turned. The plaintiffs contended that the *Popi M* had struck a submerged submarine, and argued that this amounted to loss of the ship by the perils of the sea, which was covered by the policy. The defendants asserted that the loss was caused by 'wear and tear', i.e., the poor condition into which the plaintiffs had allowed her to fall. The trial judge ruled out the explanation given by the underwriters, because it did not adequately explain the known damage to the ship. Equally, however, he regarded the plaintiffs' explanation about the submarine, which was wholly unsupported by independent evidence, as extremely improbable. On the basis of these findings, the judge found for the plaintiffs, since the defendants had provided no acceptable explanation to rebut the plaintiffs' claim. This decision was upheld by the Court of Appeal. On appeal to the House of Lords, the underwriters prevailed. The House held that the judge had not been obliged to choose between two competing theories, merely because the underwriters had chosen to put forward an explanation for the loss. The plaintiffs had borne the legal burden of proof on the issue whether the ship had been lost by the perils of the sea, and since the judge had found that the evidence adduced to support the claim was extremely improbable, he ought to have held that the plaintiffs had failed to discharge their burden of proof.

---

[12] [1985] 1 WLR 948. See also *Morris v London Iron and Steel Co. Ltd* [1988] QB 493.

The case throws the importance of the burden of proof into stark relief. An important point is that the burden of proof is the burden to prove that the facts relied on are more probable than not, and not merely that they are more probable than an explanation advanced by the other side. As Lord Brandon pointed out at the beginning of his speech ([1985] 1 WLR at 951):

> In approaching this question it is important that two matters should be borne constantly in mind. The first matter is that the burden of proving, on a balance of probabilities, that the ship was lost by perils of the seas is and remains throughout on the shipowners. Although it is open to the underwriters to suggest and seek to prove some other cause of loss, against which the ship was not insured, there is no obligation on them to do so. Moreover, if they chose to do so, there is no obligation on them to prove, even on a balance of probabilities, the truth of their alternative case.

After reviewing the facts and an earlier authority (*Cia Martiartu v Royal Exchange Assurance Corp.* [1923] 1 KB 650) Lord Brandon said ([1985] 1 WLR at 955–6):

> My Lords, the late Sir Arthur Conan Doyle in his book *The Sign of Four* describes his hero, Mr Sherlock Holmes, as saying to the latter's friend, Dr Watson: 'How often have I said to you that, when you have eliminated the impossible, whatever remains, however improbable, must be the truth?' It is, no doubt, on the basis of this well-known but unjudicial dictum that Bingham J decided to accept the shipowners' submarine theory, even though he regarded it, for seven cogent reasons, as extremely improbable.
>
> In my view, there are three reasons why it is inappropriate to apply the dictum of Mr Sherlock Holmes to which I have just referred to the process of fact-finding which a judge of first instance has to perform at the conclusion of a case of the kind here concerned.
>
> The first reason is one which I have already sought to emphasize as being of great importance, namely that the judge is not bound always to make a finding one way or the other with regard to the facts averred by the parties. He has open to him the third alternative of saying that the party on whom the burden of proof lies in relation to any averment made by him has failed to discharge that burden. No judge likes to decide cases on burden of proof if he can legitimately avoid having to do so. There are cases, however, in which, owing to the unsatisfactory state of the evidence or otherwise, deciding on the burden of proof is the only just course for him to take.
>
> The second reason is that the dictum can only apply when all relevant factors are known, so that all possible explanations, except a single extremely improbable one, can properly be eliminated. That state of affairs does not exist in the present case....
>
> The third reason is that the legal concept of proof of a case on the balance of probabilities must be applied with common sense. It requires a judge of first instance, before he finds that a particular event occurred, to be satisfied on the evidence that it is more likely to have occurred than not. If a judge concludes, on a whole series of cogent grounds, that the occurrence of an event is extremely improbable, a finding by him that it is nevertheless more likely to have occurred than not, does not accord with common sense. This is especially so when it is open to the judge to say simply that the evidence leaves him in doubt whether the event occurred or not, and that the party on whom the burden of proving that the event occurred lies has therefore failed to discharge such burden.

Lord Brandon concluded (*ibid.* at 956):

> In my opinion the only inference which could reasonably be drawn from the primary facts found by Bingham J was that the true reason of the ship's loss was in doubt, and it follows that I consider that neither Bingham J nor the Court of Appeal were justified in drawing the inference that there had been a loss by perils of the seas, whether in the form of collision with a submerged submarine or any other form.[13]

---

[13] It has been suggested that a civil court should resort to the burden of proof as the basis for its decision only in exceptional cases, in which despite its best efforts, the court cannot make a finding on the disputed issues

4.5.2 Identifying burden of proof: examples

Any question of which party relies on a fact in issue as an essential part of his case, or of who
asserts a positive proposition, can in most cases be resolved by reference to the statements of
case. The statements of case should make clear in what way the case or defence is put, and fix the
legal burden accordingly. Ultimately, of course, it is the law, not the pleadings, which establishes
the burden of proof; the pleadings should offer a reliable guide, but they do so only insofar as
they correctly reflect the law: *BHP Billiton Petroleum Ltd* v *Dalmine SpA* [2003] BLR 271. The art of
drafting enables any assertion to be made in more than one way, and care must be taken to look
at the reality and not the language of the statement of case. The mere use of negative language
should not be allowed to obscure the fact that a positive claim or defence is being asserted, and
the substance not the form of the case is the true guide. Thus, an assertion that a tenant has failed
to repair premises pursuant to his covenant is an affirmative allegation, the proof of which lies on
the asserting landlord, even though couched in language in negative form.[14]

   The above rules generally govern the incidence of the legal burden in civil cases. The specific
examples which follow, taken from common kinds of claim, follow from the essential elements
of the cause of action or defence, would be reflected in the statements of case, and are in no way
exceptional.

4.5.2.1 Contract

The claimant bears the burden of proving the contract, the due performance of conditions precedent, breach of contract by the defendant and consequent loss to the claimant. The defendant
bears the burden of proving any facts going beyond a mere denial of the claimant's case, upon
which his defence is founded, such as infancy, fraud, or accord and satisfaction. A party relying
on an exceptive clause in the contract will usually bear the burden of proving that he falls within
its ambit. Thus, where the claimant alleged failure to deliver goods, the defendant bore the burden of proving that he fell within an exceptive clause exempting him where the ship and goods
were lost by the perils of the sea. The claimant would then have to prove any negligence on the
part of the defendant disentitling the defendant to the protection of the clause.[15]

4.5.2.2 Negligence

The claimant bears the burden of proving the duty of care, breach by the defendant of such duty
and consequential loss to the claimant. The defendant bears the burden of proving any facts
going beyond a mere denial of the claimant's case, upon which his defence is founded, such as
Act of God, *volenti non fit injuria*, or contributory negligence.

4.5.2.3 Malicious prosecution

The claimant bears the burden of proving not only the unsuccessful prosecution of him by
the defendant, but also the absence of any reasonable and probable cause for the prosecution,
this being an essential element of the claimant's case, even though expressed as a negative.[16]

based on the evidence presented. In such a case, the court should explain its predicament in detail in the judgment: see *Stephens* v *Cannon* [2005] EWCA Civ 222, (2005) *The Times*, 2 May 2005.

   [14] *Soward* v *Leggatt* (1836) 7 Car & P 613; see also *Osborn* v *Thompson* (1839) 9 Car & P 337 (assertion that horse
unsound, contrary to warranty).

   [15] *The Glendarroch* [1894] P 226.

   [16] *Abrath* v *North Eastern Railway Co.* (CA) (1883) 11 QBD 440; affirmed (HL) (1886) 11 App Cas 247.

By way of contrast, in a claim for false imprisonment, where the claimant proves the fact of restraint, restraint being *prima facie* tortious, it is for the defendant to prove lawful justification for his act.[17]

4.5.2.4 Self-defence

The defendant bears the burden of proving, in response to an allegation of assault, that he acted lawfully and reasonably in self defence.[18]

4.5.2.5 Bailment

Once the claimant proves the fact of the bailment, the burden lies on the defendant to show that the loss of or damage to the goods was not caused by any want of reasonable care on his part.[19]

4.5.2.6 Mitigation of loss and damage

The burden lies on the claimant to prove that he taken any necessary reasonable steps to mitigate the loss and damage caused by any wrongful conduct on the part of the defendant, in respect of which the claimant is claiming damages: *Geest plc* v *Lansiquot* [2002] 1 WLR 3111.

4.5.2.7 Agreement and specific rules

The incidence of the legal burden may in civil cases be varied by agreement between the parties.[20] It may also be provided for expressly by statute, for example the provision that in cases of unfair dismissal, the fact of dismissal being proved, the respondent employer bears the burden of showing that the dismissal was fair, notwithstanding that the applicant relies on the contrary assertion for his cause of action.[21]

4.6 THE EVIDENTIAL BURDEN IN CIVIL CASES

As we have seen, the legal and evidential burdens of proof do not always coincide, or do not always continue to coincide. In a case in which the defendant merely denies the claim and therefore has no legal burden of proof, if the claimant succeeds in establishing a *prima facie* case as to each element of his claim, the defendant acquires an evidential burden of adducing some evidence to contradict the claim. Thus, where the claimant in a claim for unauthorized sub-letting of the premises established a *prima facie* case by showing that a person other than the tenant was in possession, ostensibly in the position of a sub-tenant, an evidential burden lay on the defendant to show that the occupier was there in some other capacity.[22] Where a landlord established a *prima facie* case of title to the premises by proving payment of rent by the tenant, the tenant had an evidential burden to adduce some evidence that the payments had been made, not as rent,

---

[17] *Hicks* v *Faulkner* (1881) 8 QBD 167.

[18] *Ashley* v *Chief Constable of Sussex Police* [2007] 1 WLR 398 (CA). The decision was affirmed by the House of Lords ([2008] 1 AC 962) on substantive legal grounds without referring specifically to the burden of proof, but it seem clear that their Lordships agreed with the Court of Appeal: see, e.g., at [87] per Lord Neuberger.

[19] *Brook's Wharf & Bull Wharf Ltd* v *Goodman Brothers* [1937] 1 KB 534: *Port Swettenham Authority* v *T.W. Wu & Co. (M) Sdn Bhd* [1979] AC 580.

[20] See, e.g., *Levy* v *Assicurazioni Generali* [1940] AC 791.

[21] Employment Rights Act 1996, s. 98(1). For similar examples see Consumer Credit Act 1974, s. 171(7); Disability Discrimination Act 1995, s. 17A(1C).

[22] *Doe d'Hindley* v *Rickarby* (1803) 5 Esp 4.

but by reason of mistake or ignorance of the facts.[23] Where a claimant established a *prima facie* case that the defendant had failed to comply with statutory safety requirements applicable to his mine, the defendant had the evidential burden of adducing some evidence to show that an explosion which had occurred at the mine because of his failure to comply was not due to his lack of care for the safety of those working there.[24] And where it was shown that the defendant had given assurances to a residential housekeeper that she would be permitted to reside in a house at her pleasure, and there was accordingly a *prima facie* case that the housekeeper had remained in the house in reliance on those assurances, the defendant had the evidential burden of adducing some evidence to show that the housekeeper's continued occupation of the house was not in reliance on them.[25]

4.7 THE BURDEN OF PROOF IN CRIMINAL CASES

In criminal cases the rule is that the legal burden of proving every element of the offence charged, and therefore the guilt of the accused, lies from first to last on the prosecution. In *Woolmington v DPP* [1935] AC 462, the accused was charged with the murder of his wife by shooting her. His defence was that the gun had discharged accidentally. The trial judge directed the jury that once the prosecution proved that the deceased was killed by the accused, it was for the accused to show that the killing was not murder. This was held by the House of Lords to be a misdirection. Viscount Sankey LC expressed the rule in striking words which have become justly celebrated (*ibid*. at 481–2):

> Throughout the web of the English criminal law one golden thread is always to be seen, that it is the duty of the prosecution to prove the prisoner's guilt . . . If, at the end of and on the whole of the case, there is a reasonable doubt, created by the evidence given by either the prosecution or the prisoner, as to whether the prisoner killed the deceased with a malicious intention, the prosecution has not made out the case and the prisoner is entitled to an acquittal. No matter what the charge or where the trial, the principle that the prosecution must prove the guilt of the prisoner is part of the common law of England and no attempt to whittle it down can be entertained.[26]

In addition to being a well-established rule of common law, the rule that the prosecution must prove the guilt of the accused, sometimes known as the presumption of innocence, is now regarded as a fundamental attribute of fairness and due process, and it may confidently be asserted that the right of each person charged with a criminal offence to be considered innocent until proved guilty is a fundamental right. In *Lambert* [2002] 2 AC 545, [33], having referred to *Woolmington*, Lord Steyn said:

> In the meantime the human rights movement came into existence. The foundation of it was the Universal Declaration of Human Rights 1948, which has been the starting point of subsequent human rights texts. In article 11(1) it provided: 'Everyone charged with a penal offence has the right to be

---

[23] *Hindle v Hick Brothers Manufacturing Co. Ltd* [1947] 2 All ER 825.

[24] *Britannic Merthyr Coal Co. Ltd v David* [1910] AC 74.

[25] *Greasley v Cooke* [1980] 1 WLR 1306.

[26] See also *Mancini v DPP* [1942] AC 1, per Viscount Simon LC at 11. Despite Viscount Sankey's statement that the principle is 'part of the common law of England', it has been cogently argued that the House of Lords was in fact changing the law, not with respect to the issue of guilt, but with respect to certain affirmative defences: see, e.g., J.C. Smith (1987) 38 NILQ 223, 224 *et seq*. As will be seen below, in the light of *Lambert* [2002] 2 AC 545 and later cases, this argument now has renewed importance (see 4.9).

presumed innocent until proved guilty according to law...' Borrowing this language almost verbatim, article 6(2) of the European Convention for the Protection of Human Rights and Fundamental Freedoms provided: 'Everyone charged with a criminal offence shall be presumed innocent until proved guilty according to law'. Article 14(2) of the International Covenant on Civil and Political Rights 1966, which was signed by the United Kingdom in 1966, is to the same effect. Nevertheless, and despite the right of petition to the European Court of Human Rights created for the United Kingdom in 1961, there was no constraint in our domestic law on legislative incursions on the presumption of innocence. But by the 1998 Act Parliament has provided that, subject to the ultimate constitutional principle of the sovereignty of Parliament, inroads on the presumption of innocence must be compatible with article 6(2) as properly construed.

The presumption of innocence is an element of a fair trial required by art. 6 of the European Convention on Human Rights: *Bernard v France* (2000) 30 EHRR 808, [37], *Salabakiu y France* (1988) 13 EHRR 379. It has also been described, in language of the kind referred to by Lord Steyn, as 'a cardinal principle of international criminal law',[27] and has been incorporated into the Statute of the International Criminal Court and those of the International Criminal Tribunals for the Former Yugoslavia and Rwanda.[28]

The rule applies in general even where part of the case for the prosecution involves a negative, e.g., that the accused in a rape case had sexual intercourse with the victim without her consent. Lack of consent is an integral part of the prosecution's case on a charge of rape, and the burden of proving that element of the offence lies consequently on the prosecution.[29] In *Mandry; Wooster* [1973] 1 WLR 1232, the appellants, who were street traders, were charged with going equipped to cheat and attempting to obtain £1 by deception. They were seen offering bottles of scent for sale to the public for £1. Evidence was given that Mandry said to prospective purshasers: 'you can go down the road and buy it for 2 guineas in the big stores...I'm letting you have it for a dollar'. A police officer gave evidence that he had visited a number of shops, but was unable to find the same perfume on sale. On cross-examination the officer was asked whether he had visited Selfridge's, and he said that he had not. The trial judge directed the jury that the police could not be expected to visit every shop in London, and that, because the question of whether the scent could be bought for 2 guineas in the big stores was one within the knowledge of the accused, it was a matter to be proved by the defence. On appeal, the appellants contended that the prosecution had failed to discharge their burden of proving the falsity of Mandry's statement, and that the judge had misdirected the jury as to the burden of proof. The Court of Appeal held that the direction on the burden of proof 'could have been better put', and emphasized that the prosecution did bear the burden of proving the falsity of the statement, even though it involved proving a negative proposition. But the appeal was dismissed on the basis that the officer's evidence provided legally sufficient evidence of the falsity of the statement, which the jury were free either to accept or reject, the fact that the officer might have visited further shops being a matter which affected only the weight of the evidence. The result of the case seems clearly right, but it must

---

[27] R. May and M. Mierda, *International Criminal Evidence* (2002), p. 289.

[28] Rome Statute of the International Criminal Court, arts 66 67(1)(g) and (i); Statute of the International Criminal Tribunal for the Former Yugoslavia, art. 21(3); Statute of the International Criminal Tribunal for Rwanda, art. 20(3). Article 67(1)(i) of the ICC Statute also includes the right 'not to have imposed on him or her any reversal of the burden of proof or any onus of rebuttal', which is of interest in connection with the extensive discussion of this subject in English law: see 4.8, 4.9 below.

[29] This example must now be read subject to ss. 75 and 76 of the Sexual Offences Act 2003, which create evidential (s. 75) and conclusive (s. 76) presumptions respectively that the victim did not consent to the act in a number of circumstances enumerated in the sections. These presumptions are considered further at 20.10.

be said that the Court of Appeal's criticism of the judge's direction was unduly charitable. With respect, the direction was not simply capable of being 'better put'; it was unequivocally wrong.

4.8 DEFENCE BURDENS OF PROOF BEFORE *LAMBERT*

The question of whether an accused may be called upon to bear the burden of proof on an issue in a criminal case must now be considered primarily in the light of art. 6 of the European Convention on Human Rights and the decision of the House of Lords in *Lambert* [2002] 2 AC 545, which, it is fair to say, have made a sea-change in the law in this area. But, in order to understand the extent of this change, it is necessary first to consider the state of the law before *Lambert*, which continues to be relevant to any discussion of defence burdens of proof. *Woolmington* did not create the rule that the prosecution must prove the guilt of the accused; it merely provides an elegant and succinct statement of a rule which the law had long recognized. But long before *Woolmington*, it was also recognized that there were exceptional cases in which the accused might be called on to bear either the legal burden of proving certain affirmative defences, or the evidential burden of adducing some evidence in support of an issue relevant to the question of guilt. Logically, such cases do not violate the rule in *Woolmington*, because the accused is not called upon to disprove any essential element of the charge; they merely provide that if he raises an affirmative defence or issue of his own, he may be called upon to prove or adduce evidence in support of such defence or issue.[30] If the prosecution fails to establish a *prima facie* case against him, the accused does not need to raise a defence or a new issue, and he is entitled to have the case withdrawn from the jury, so any defence burden can arise only on the assumption that the prosecution has established that the accused has a case to answer. Even if he has a case to answer, the accused cannot be compelled to present a defence or issue. He may simply stand his ground and assert that the prosecution has not proved the case against him beyond reasonable doubt. But, if he wishes to rely on an affirmative defence or issue, he may be required to prove the defence or raise the issue, as the case may be. Three distinct cases, or groups of cases, involving the allocation of some burden of proof to the defence had been identified before *Lambert*.

4.8.1 The defence of insanity

The only case at common law in which the accused is called on to bear the legal burden of proof is the defence of insanity. This rule derives from the celebrated answers given by the judges to questions posed by the House of Lords in the wake of the controversial acquittal on the ground of insanity in *Daniel M'Naghten's Case* (1843) 10 Cl & F 200, 209–10, as found in the following extract.[31]

---

[30] But such 'reverse burden' cases may well now violate the presumption of innocence, judged in the light of art. 6 of the European Convention on Human Rights, insofar as they purport to impose a legal burden: see 4.9. In the United States, although the rule that the prosecution must prove the guilt of the accused has the status of a rule of constitutional law, this is no bar to the accused being required to bear the burden of proving an affirmative defence (though not of disproving an element of the offence): *Patterson* v *New York* 432 US 197 (1977); *Mullaney* v *Wilbur* 421 US 684 (1975).

[31] The questions were posed and answered in connection with the ensuing political debate in the House of Lords, so that any attribution to them of binding authority as a matter of law is obviously questionable. Nonetheless, they have been accorded that status in practice. The answers were drafted by Tindal CJ on behalf of fourteen judges, but with the dissent of Maule J. This rule does not violate the presumption of innocence so as to result in an unfair trial under art. 6 of the European Convention on Human Rights: *H* v *United Kingdom*, *Application No. 15023/89* to European Court of Human Rights (4 April 1990, unreported); see also 4.9.

Question 2: 'What are the proper questions to be submitted to the jury, where a person alleged to be afflicted with insane delusion respecting one or more particular subjects or persons, is charged with the commission of a crime (murder, for example) and insanity is set up as a defence?'

Question 3: 'In what terms ought the question to be left to the jury as to the prisoner's state of mind at the time when the act was committed?'

Answers: (to the second and third questions): 'That the jurors ought to be told in all cases that every man is presumed to be sane and to possess a sufficient degree of reason to be responsible for his crimes, until the contrary be proved to their satisfaction; and that to establish a defence on the grounds of insanity, it must be clearly proved that, at the time of the committing of the act, the party accused was labouring under such a defect of reason from disease of the mind, as not to know the nature and quality of the act he was doing; or, if he did know it, that he did not know he was doing what was wrong.'

The defence of insanity was at one time the only real avenue open to an accused charged with murder who did not have open to him the possibility of a verdict of manslaughter but who wished to avoid the death penalty. It lost much of its importance after the abolition of the death penalty for murder from 1965, and indeed even before that, after the creation of the defence of diminished responsibility by the Homicide Act 1957.[32] Moreover, the formulation of the defence of insanity is anachronistic in terms of modern psychiatric medicine, and it has been much criticized accordingly. Nonetheless, it continues as a case in which the accused bears the burden of proving the defence.[33] In its draft report of 28 August 2002 (*Draft Criminal Code: Criminal Liability and Mental Disorder*), the Law Commission proposes a radical reform of the law with respect to defences based on mental disorder. The Commission would rationalize the present law in the context of the general law relating to mental illness in other areas, for example fitness to plead and the making of hospital orders. A new term, 'mental disorder' would be introduced to replace the older language in the M'Naghten Rules and various statutory provisions, and a new defence would be introduced in place of the present defences of insanity and diminished responsibility, which, if successful, would result in a 'mental disorder verdict' and an appropriate disposal on sentence. But the Commission proposes to retain the rule that the accused must prove the defence on the balance of probabilities (see Part II, paras 2.7, 2.13). It is at least arguable that such a rule would now be held to violate the presumption of innocence under art. 6 of the Convention (see *Lambert* [2002] 2 AC 545, discussed at 4.9). The Commission seems to be aware of this difficulty, and it is understood at the time of writing that it proposes to reconsider this proposal in the light of representations made by various commentators, including the present author. It is submitted that both the existing rules as to burden of proof of the defences of

---

[32] By virtue of s. 2(2) of the Act, the accused also bears the burden of proving diminished responsibility. Ironically, although the popularity of the insanity defence has declined in murder cases, in which the disposal of the accused is fixed by law, it has been suggested that it may enjoy a new lease of life in other cases in which the disposal is discretionary: see Criminal Procedure (Insanity) Act 1964, s. 5, as amended by the Criminal Procedure (Insanity and Unfitness to Plead) Act 1991; and see *DPP v H* [1997] 1 WLR 1406; *Horseferry Road Magistrates' Court, ex parte K* [1997] QB 23.

[33] Though where the prosecution raises insanity in answer to a defence of diminished responsibility (or *vice versa*), it seems the prosecution must then prove its contention beyond reasonable doubt: Criminal Procedure (Insanity) Act 1964, s. 6; *Grant* [1960] Crim LR 424; and on an analogous point, *Podola* [1960] 1 QB 325; *Robertson* [1968] 1 WLR 1767. There is no authority that the prosecution may raise insanity other than in this circumstance, though the Law Commission has tentatively suggested a more general power to do so (*Draft Report: Criminal Liability and Mental Disorder*, 28 August 2002). There is some authority that the judge may raise insanity of his own motion: *Dickie* [1984] 1 WLR 1031. The effect of this on the burden of proof is unclear.

insanity and diminished responsibility should be replaced by a rule that the accused bears only an evidential burden of adducing evidence sufficient to raise a *prima facie* case, and that the same should apply to any new defence introduced by statute to replace the present defences.[34]

4.8.2 Statutory provisions putting legal burden of proof on accused

Various statutes provide, or purport to provide that the accused is to bear the legal burden of proof on some defence or issue.[35] Whether or not a particular statutory provision in fact has that effect is a matter of construction of the wording of the statute, and after the decision of the House of Lords in *Hunt* [1987] AC 352, it was recognized that a provision which did not expressly impose the burden of proof on the accused might nonetheless be construed as doing so 'by necessary implication'. This is considered further in 4.9.1. It would be pointless to attempt to catalogue here the many statutory provisions which operate in this way, but they include provisions relating to serious and frequently charged offences, for example the rule that an accused charged with murder bears the burden of proving the defence of diminished responsibility;[36] the rule that the accused must prove the existence of lawful authority or reasonable excuse for having an offensive weapon with him in a public place;[37] the rule that certain persons in public life who have received money, gifts, or other consideration bear the burden of proving that what they received was not received corruptly as an inducement or reward;[38] and the rule which featured in *Lambert* requiring the accused to prove lack of knowledge or suspicion in various situations in drugs cases.[39] Where the accused bears the burden of proof, the standard of proof is no higher than the civil standard on the balance of probabilities: see *Carr-Briant* [1943] KB 607, and 4.13. This class of case must apparently now be reviewed on a case-by-case basis in the light of art. 6 of the Convention and the decision in *Lambert*. This will be discussed further at 4.9.

4.8.3 Cases in which accused has an evidential burden

Even in cases in which no legal burden is imposed on the accused, he may be required to introduce some evidence in support of an issue which he introduces and which is not an essential element of the offence. In most cases, this rule is a simple matter of practicality, for example where the accused asserts that he has an alibi. Although an alibi is often referred to loosely as a 'defence', it is not an affirmative defence because it is no more than a denial that the accused was present at the scene of the crime and, by the same token, a denial that he committed the *actus reus* of the offence. Because the *actus reus* is necessarily an essential element of the offence,

---

[34] It may seem that this might make it too easy for the accused to succeed in his defence, but this is easily remedied by continuing the present requirement that the evidence in support of the defence of insanity consist of the evidence of two registered medical practitioners, at least one of whom is approved by the Home Secretary as having special expertise in this area: Criminal Procedure (Insanity and Unfitness to Plead) Act 1991, s. 1.

[35] A study by Ashworth and Blake, 'The Presumption of Innocence in English Law' [1996] Crim LR 306 identifies 219 examples, drawn from 540 offences triable in the Crown Court, of cases in which a legal burden of proof or presumption operates against the accused by virtue of statute. In addition, s. 101 of the Magistrates' Courts Act 1980 lays down a general principle that the defendant in summary proceedings bears the burden of proving any 'exception, exemption, proviso, excuse or qualification' on which he may rely; as to this see 4.9.1.

[36] Homicide Act 1957, s. 2(2); and see *Dunbar* [1958] 1 QB 1. But as to cases in which the prosecution seeks to establish diminished responsibility in answer to a defence of insanity, see note 31, above.

[37] Prevention of Crime Act 1953, s. 1(1); *Petrie* [1961] 1 WLR 358. In the same vein, see Criminal Justice Act 1988, s. 139(4); Knives Act 1997, ss. 3 and 4.

[38] Prevention of Corruption Act 1916, s. 2; see *Carr-Briant* [1943] KB 607.

[39] Misuse of Drugs Act 1971, s. 28.

a requirement that the accused prove his alibi would violate the rule in *Woolmington*. But unless the accused takes some steps to establish the alibi, either by cross-examining prosecution witnesses or adducing evidence of his own, the alibi will not become known to the tribunal of fact. Therefore, the accused must adduce some evidence in support of the alibi, and this in turn means that he must bear an evidential burden on the issue of the alibi. This burden is no higher than establishing a *prima facie* case in support of the alibi. As a matter of practicality, unless the accused does this, the prosecution has no obligation to refer to it; indeed, as Hale CJ once aptly expressed it, to do so would be 'like leaping before one come to the stile'.[40] Thus, if the prosecution establishes a *prima facie* case against the accused, he must adduce a *prima facie* case in support of the alibi; if he does so, then the prosecution bears the legal burden of disproving the alibi in order to prove the accused's guilt.[41] Among other issues which the accused must raise if they are to be considered by the tribunal of fact are: non-insane automatism;[42] provocation;[43] self-defence or prevention of crime;[44] drunkenness;[45] duress;[46] mechanical defect in road traffic cases;[47] and reasonable excuse for failing to supply a specimen for a laboratory test in excess alcohol cases.[48] Although these issues are commonly referred to as 'defences', it will be appreciated that it would be preferable to employ some other expression, such as 'explanations involving new issues'. The practice of requiring an accused to raise an issue to the extent of establishing a *prima facie* case is compatible with art. 6 of the Convention (*Attorney-General's Reference (No. 1 of 2004)* [2004] 2 Cr App R 424, [52], guideline [E]).

4.9 DEFENCE BURDENS OF PROOF AFTER *LAMBERT*

Even before *Lambert*, the existence of cases in which an accused may be called upon to bear a legal burden of proof in a criminal case gave rise to great controversy. Many commentators called for a change in the law, to the effect that any burden of proof imposed on the accused should be

---

[40] *Sir Ralph Bovy's Case* (1684) 1 Vent 217. See also Glanville Williams (1978) 128 NLJ 182.

[41] As to the meaning of the term *prima facie* case, see further 4.3. The issue must be raised by admissible evidence, not merely by means of an assertion by counsel: *Parker* v *Smith* [1974] RTR 500. And it is not enough that the issue should be raised by questions in cross-examination of the accused by the prosecution unless the accused adopts the suggestions put to him: *Acott* [1997] 1 WLR 306. But the issue may be raised by defence cross-examination of prosecution witnesses, or of course by evidence adduced by the defence: *Bullard* v *R* [1957] AC 635.

[42] *Hill* v *Baxter* [1958] 1 QB 277; *Bratty* v *Attorney-General for Northern Ireland* [1963] AC 386. The Law Commission (*Draft Report: Criminal Liability and Mental Disorder*) 28 August 2002, has proposed that the accused should bear the legal burden of proof in cases of non-insane automatism, but this is being re-considered in the light of *Lambert* [2002] 2 AC 545, and will, it is to be hoped, be abandoned. It is highly doubtful whether such a rule could survive a challenge based on art. 6 of the Convention (see 4.9).

[43] *Acott* [1997] 1 WLR 306; *Stewart* [1995] 4 All ER 999; *Bullard* v *R* [1957] AC 635; *McPherson* (1957) 41 Cr App R 213.

[44] As to the law, see Criminal Law Act 1967, s. 3; as to the evidentiary burden, see *Abraham* [1973] 1 WLR 1270; *Lobell* [1957] 1 QB 547. Contrast the position in civil cases, see *Ashley* v *Chief Constable of Sussex Police* [2007] 1 WLR 398 (CA); affirmed [2008] 1 AC 962; 4.5.2.4.

[45] *Groark* [1999] Crim LR 669; *Kennedy* v *HM Advocate* 1944 JC 171.

[46] *Gill* [1963] 1 WLR 841. The Law Commission has recommended that the accused should bear the legal burden of proof of the defence of duress (*Legislating the Criminal Code: Offences against the Person and General Principles* (1993) (Law Com No. 218; Cm 2370), paras 33, 34). In *Hasan* [2005] 2 AC 467 at [20] the House of Lords said that this was not a change to be made judicially, and that it must await a decision by Parliament.

[47] *Spurge* [1961] 2 QB 205.

[48] *Clarke* [1969] 1 WLR 1109.

no more than evidential.[49] Nonetheless, in the words of Lord Steyn in *Lambert* ([2002] 2 AC 545, 569), 'It is a fact that the legislature has frequently and in an arbitrary and indiscriminate manner made inroads on the basic presumption of innocence'; and '...the process of enacting legal reverse burden of proof provisions continued apace'. In fairness, it should be said that in very many cases, such provisions have owed more to the principle applied in civil cases that burdens of proof should be assigned in accordance with comparative ease of proof as between the parties (see 4.5) and to the old and highly technical common law pleading rules,[50] than to any systematic attempt to undermine the presumption of innocence. There is nothing inherently unreasonable in the proposition that a defendant charged with driving without a licence should bear the burden of proving that he is the holder of a licence,[51] and particularly with respect to essentially regulatory offences, it is hard to quarrel with the spirit of s. 101 of the Magistrates' Courts Act 1980 (see 4.9.1) which requires the defendant to prove that he is entitled to the benefit of an exception or exemption on which he relies for his defence. At the same time, there is a potential for the rights of the accused to be eroded by means of the statutory redefinition of offences in such a way as to recast what have traditionally been regarded as elements of an offence as matters which must now be disproved by way of 'defence'.[52] As a result, there has always been a strong feeling, now apparently adopted by the House of Lords in *Lambert*, that the existence of legal burdens of proof borne by an accused violates the presumption of innocence. As a matter of theory, this is not as clear as it may appear. For present purposes, the presumption of innocence may be taken to refer to the provision of art. 6(2) of the European Convention on Human Rights: 'Everyone charged with a criminal offence shall be presumed innocent until proved guilty according to law'. This right is part of the right to a fair trial guaranteed by art. 6. At the same time, of course, it must be remembered that English law as expressed in *Woolmington* (see 4.7) recognized the right of the accused to the presumption of innocence long before the enactment of the Convention or of the Human Rights Act 1998. English law saw nothing inconsistent with the presumption of innocence in imposing a legal burden of proof on the accused as to an affirmative offence, provided always that it in no way derogated from the prosecution's burden of proving every element of

[49] See, e.g., the 11th Report of the Criminal Law Revision Committee (Cmnd 4991, 1972) paras 137–42. The Committee was 'strongly' of this opinion, 'both on principle and for the sake of clarity and convenience in practice' (*ibid*. at para. 140). See also Cross, *Evidence*, 5th edn, 107; Glanville Williams [1988] CLJ 261; J.C. Smith (1987) 38 NILQ 223; A. Ashworth and M. Blake [1996] Crim LR 306.

[50] 4.9.1; and see the scholarly analysis of Lawton LJ in *Edwards* [1975] QB 27; A. Zuckerman (1976) 92 LQR 402; *Turner* (1816) 5 M & S 206, 211 per Bayley J. Clearly, ease of proof has never been the only consideration; if it were, it would be arguable that the accused should have to disprove *mens rea*, which is peculiarly within his knowledge.

[51] See, e.g., *John v Humphreys* [1955] 1 WLR 325. In such cases, it is not a question of punishing essentially criminal behaviour subject to an exception, but one of imposing a qualification on essentially lawful behaviour. As J.C. Smith tellingly observed, it is improbable to describe driving as an offence subject to a qualification; 'The supposed offence cannot be stated without the exception' (1987) 38 NILQ at 328; see also *Ewens* [1967] 1 QB 322. The same can be said of very many essentially regulatory offences. In *DPP v Barker* (2006) 168 JP 617, it was held that it was not disproportionate to require the defendant to prove that he was the holder of a valid provisional driving licence, and was driving in accordance with its provisions.

[52] 'After all, it is sometimes simply a matter of which drafting technique is adopted; a true constituent element can be removed from the definition of the crime and cast as a defensive issue, whereas any definition of an offence can be reformulated so as to include all possible defences within it. It is necessary to concentrate not on technicalities and niceties of language but rather on matters of substance': *Lambert* [2002] 2 AC 545, 571 per Lord Steyn. This issue has also been recognized in the United States: *Patterson v New York* 432 US 197 (1977); *Mullaney v Wilbur* 421 US 684 (1975).

the offence charged.[53] It is not clear that this approach is necessarily flawed. Moreover, the jurisprudence of the European Court of Human Rights, while insisting on fundamental fairness in the criminal trial process, does not dictate to the Contracting States the detailed content of their domestic law, and does not require that reverse burdens of proof be outlawed in all cases.[54]

But, even before *Lambert*, the decision in the strangely inconclusive case of *DPP, ex parte Kebilene* [2000] 2 AC 346, suggested that English law was about to change. *Kebilene* was inconclusive in the sense that the House of Lords was unable to reach the burden of proof point because of a more fundamental ground of decision, though it seems clear that the members of the House would have liked to do so. The appeal arose because of a defence challenge by way of judicial review to the decision of the Director of Public Prosecutions to consent to the prosecution of an offence under s. 16(a) of the Prevention of Terrorism (Temporary Provisions) Act 1989. Under this section, the accused can commit an offence by having in his possession an article 'giving rise to a reasonable suspicion that the article is in his possession for a purpose connected with [terrorist activity]'. Section 16(A)(3) and (4) of the Act provide that it shall be a defence for the accused to prove that he had no such purpose, or that he did not know that the article was on his premises. The ground of challenge to the Director's decision was that this reverse legal burden was incompatible with art. 6. But the House held that the decision was not amenable to judicial review because it had been taken before the coming into effect of the Human Rights Act 1998, and because judicial review was not appropriate where the accused had access to the more conventional remedy of taking the point at trial and, if necessary, on appeal. On the part of some members, notably Lord Cooke of Thornton, this conclusion was reached with some reluctance, and notwithstanding that it was sufficient to dispose of the appeal, the members of the House fired a clear warning shot that the compatibility issue was one to be considered seriously in the circumstances of the case, expressly agreeing with the Divisional Court that the point must be regarded open for future decision. Lord Hobhouse referred, clearly with no disapproval, to the following passage from the judgment of Lord Bingham CJ in the Divisional Court (at 345):

> Under s. 16(A) a defendant could be convicted even if the jury entertained a reasonable doubt whether he knew that the items were in his premises, and whether he had the items for a terrorist purpose. Under s. 16(B) a defendant could be convicted even if the jury entertained a reasonable doubt whether the information had been collected or was possessed for any terrorist purpose. In both sections the presumption of innocence is violated.

The House was eventually to have its chance to return to the issue it was unable to decide in *Kebilene*. In the light of the decision of the House in *Lambert* [2002] 2 AC 545, interpreting various pronouncements of the European Court of Human Rights, including those in *Salabaktu v France* (1988) 13 EHRR 388, it is submitted that the imposition of reverse legal burdens of proof is *prima facie* incompatible with art. 6 of the Convention, and must be scrutinized with great care in light of the principle of proportionality. In *Lambert*, the appellant was convicted of possession of a class A controlled drug with intent to supply, contrary to s. 5(3) of the Misuse of Drugs Act

---

[53] This is also the position in the United States, despite the fact that the presumption of innocence has been held to be a constitutional protection to which the accused is entitled in every case: *Martin v Ohio* 480 US 228 (1987); *County Court of Ulster County v Allen* 442 US 140 (1979); *Patterson v New York* (above note 50); *Re Winship* 397 US 358 (1970).

[54] *Salabiaku v France* (1988) 13 EHRR 379 at 388, para. 28; *Kostovski v Netherlands* (1989) 12 EHRR 434, para. 39; *Saidi v France* (1993) 17 EHRR 251, para. 43; and see 1.7.2. For an interesting analysis of the presumption of innocence in the light of the Human Rights Act 1998, see V. Tadros and S. Tierney (2004) 67 MLR 402.

1971. He was found in possession of a bag which contained such a drug, and his defence, under s. 28 of the Act, was that he neither knew nor suspected that the bag contained a drug. Section 28 purports to require the accused to bear the legal burden of proving this defence. He appealed against conviction on the ground that the reverse legal burden of proof provision of s. 28 conflicted with the presumption of innocence guaranteed by art. 6(2) of the Convention. The Court of Appeal dismissed his appeal, and he appealed to the House of Lords. It must be noted initially that the holding of the House on the ground of appeal involving art. 6(2) was probably, strictly speaking, *obiter*. The proceedings in the Court of Appeal (and, therefore, all preceding proceedings) took place before the Human Rights Act 1998 came into effect, although the Court elected to consider the case as if it had been in effect. The majority of the House of Lords (Lords Slynn, Hope, Clyde, and Hutton, Lord Steyn dissenting) held that in general, the relevant provisions of the Human Rights Act were not intended to apply to things happening before their coming into effect, and consequently, decisions of courts before that date could not be impugned on the ground of incompatibility with Convention rights. On that ground alone, the appeal must be dismissed.[55] It has to be said that this view is not free from difficulty. The UK was a signatory of the Convention before the coming into effect of the 1998 Act, and its courts were already bound to observe the fair trial provisions of art. 6. A declaration of incompatibility under the Act (which, it is true, could not be made before it came into effect) would not have been necessary to afford the appellant relief in respect of the serious misdirection of law involved in the judge's erroneous direction to the jury that he bore the burden of proof of his defence. The availability of such relief was a point successfully taken against the accused in *Kebilene*. The decision of the House on the burden of proof issue is so forceful that it ought to be unthinkable that any subsequent court would decline to treat it as binding. But, as we shall see (4.9.2) this has not proved to be the case.

The majority of the House (Lord Hutton dissenting) held (with some differences of reasoning) that the reverse legal burden of proof provision of s. 28 was incompatible with art. 6(2), with the result that s. 28 must be read as if it imposed only an evidential burden on the accused. Thus, the word 'prove' as used in s. 28 must be construed to mean 'give sufficient evidence'.[56] But this does not mean that all such provisions offend against art. 6. Each provision must be considered on its own merits according to the test of proportionality. The question must be asked, whether a sufficient justification exists for reversing the burden of proof in a particular instance, having regard to the seriousness of the offence, the difficulty of obtaining convictions in some cases involving sophisticated criminals who know how to exploit certain defences (including, relevantly to the present case, drug smugglers) and the extent to which it would be possible to combat that difficulty by means other than interfering with the presumption of innocence. Lord Steyn (at [34]) cited with approval a passage, of which the following is part, from the judgment of Sachs J in a case in the Constitutional Court of South Africa, *State* v *Coetzee* [1997] 2 LRC 593, 677–8:

> There is a paradox at the heart of all criminal procedure, in that the more serious the crime and the greater the public interest in securing convictions of the guilty, the more important do constitutional

---

[55] Lords Slynn, Steyn, Hope, and Clyde also held that the evidence against the appellant at trial had been overwhelming, and that, even if the judge had directed the jury consistently with art. 6(2), a conviction would have been inevitable.

[56] Lord Clyde entertained some doubt as to whether s. 28 could properly be read in this way, and doubted whether the difference in reading would make much difference in practice, but in the end, assented to the proposition that the presumption of innocence must prevail. Lord Clyde's reservation could, of course, apply to any statutory provision which uses the word 'prove'; it seems to do some linguistic violence to read it as providing only that some evidence must be adduced. But it seems that this interpretation can be defended, see text below.

protections of the accused become. The starting point of any balancing inquiry where constitutional rights are concerned must be that the public interest in ensuring that innocent people are not convicted and subjected to ignominy and heavy sentences, massively outweighs the public interest in ensuring that a particular criminal is brought to book...Hence the presumption of innocence, which serves not only to protect a particular individual on trial, but to maintain public confidence in the enduring integrity and security of the legal system. Reference to the prevalence and severity of a particular crime therefore does not add anything new or special to the balancing exercise.

Lord Steyn continued:

> The logic of this reasoning is inescapable. It is nevertheless right to say that in a constitutional democracy limited inroads on the presumption of innocence may be justified. The approach to be adopted was stated by the European Court of Human Rights in *Salabiaku* v *France* (1988) 13 EHRR 379 at 388, para. 28:
>
> > 'Presumptions of fact or of law operate in every legal system. Clearly, the Convention does not prohibit such presumptions in principle. It does, however, require the contracting states to remain within certain limits in this respect as regards criminal law...Article 6(2) does not therefore regard presumptions of fact or of law provided for in the criminal law with indifference. It requires states to confine them within reasonable limits which take into account the importance of what is at stake and maintain the rights of the defence.'
>
> This test depends upon the circumstances of the individual case. It follows that a legislative interference with the presumption of innocence requires justification and must not be greater than is necessary. The principle of proportionality must be observed. [*Ibid.*]

Lord Steyn then came to his conclusion with respect to the present case:

It is now necessary to consider the question of justification for the legislative interference with the presumption of innocence. I am satisfied that there is an objective justification for some interference with the burden of proof in prosecutions under section 5 of the 1971 Act. The basis for this justification is that sophisticated drug smugglers, dealers, and couriers typically secrete drugs in some container, thereby enabling the person in possession of the container to say that he was unaware of the contents. Such defences are commonplace and they pose real difficulties for the police and prosecuting authorities...That, is however, not the end of the matter. The burden is on the state to show that the legislative means adopted were not greater than necessary...

The principle of proportionality requires the House to consider whether there was a pressing necessity to impose a legal rather than evidential burden on the accused. The effect of section 28 is that...the accused must prove on the balance of probabilities that he did not know that the package contained controlled drugs. If the jury is in doubt on this issue, they must convict him. This may occur when an accused adduces sufficient evidence to raise a doubt about his guilt but the jury is not convinced on a balance of probabilities that his account is true. *Indeed, it obliges the court to convict if the version of the accused is as likely to be true as not.* This is a far-reaching consequence: a guilty verdict may be returned in respect of an offence punishable by life imprisonment even though the jury may consider that it is reasonably possible that the accused had been duped...In any event, the burden of showing that *only* a reverse legal burden can overcome the difficulties of the prosecution in drugs cases is a heavy one.

A new realism in regard to the problems faced by the prosecution in drugs cases have [sic] significantly reduced their scope. First, the relevant facts are usually peculiarly within the knowledge of the possessor of the container and that possession presumptively suggests, in the absence of exculpatory *evidence*, that the person in possession of it knew what was in the container. This is simply a species of circumstantial evidence. It will usually be a complete answer to a no case submission. It is also a factor which a judge may squarely place before the jury. After all, it is simple common sense that possession of a package containing drugs will generally as a matter of simple common sense demand a full and adequate explanation...

In these circumstances, I am satisfied that the transfer of the legal burden in section 28 does not satisfy the criterion of proportionality. Viewed in its place in the current legal system section 28 of the
1971 Act is a disproportionate reaction to perceived difficulties facing the prosecution in drugs cases. It
would be sufficient to impose an evidential burden on the accused. It follows that section 28 is incompatible with Convention rights. [*Ibid.* at [36], [37], [38], [39], [41], emphasis in original.]

Dealing with the question of whether s. 28 could properly be read down, Lord Steyn agreed with
the view of Lord Hope of Craighead. Lord Hope said that it was his intention to demonstrate that
s. 3(1) of the Human Rights Act 1998, as a 'new approach to the construction of statutes' should
be 'employed consistently with the need (a) to respect the will of the legislature so far as this
remains appropriate and (b) to preserve the integrity of our statute law so far as this is possible'
(*ibid.* at [78]). Despite the provisions of s. 3(1) the function of interpreting legislation:

...belongs, as it has always done, to the judges. But it is not for them to legislate. Section 3(1) preserves
the sovereignty of Parliament. It does not give power to the judges to overrule decisions which the language of the statute shows have been taken on the very point at issue by the legislator...

So far as possible judges should seek to achieve the same attention to detail in their use of language
to express the effect of applying section 3(1) as the parliamentary draftsman would have done if he had
been amending the statute. It ought to be possible for any words that need to be substituted to be fitted
in to the statute as if they had been inserted there by amendment. If this cannot be done without doing
such violence to the statute as to make it unintelligible or unworkable, the use of this technique will not
be possible. It will then be necessary to leave it to Parliament to amend the statute and to resort instead
to the making of a declaration of incompatibility...

But in this case there is no difficulty. As Lord Cooke of Thorndon said in *R v. Director of Public
Prosecutions, ex parte Kebilene* [2000] 2 AC 326, 373:

'for evidence that it is a possible meaning one could hardly ask for more than the opinion of
Professor Glanville Williams in "The Logic of 'Exceptions" [1988] CLJ 261, 265 that "unless the contrary is proved" can be taken, in relation to a defence, to mean "unless sufficient evidence is given to
the contrary"; and the statute may then be satisfied by "evidence that, if believed, and on the most
favourable view, could be taken by a reasonable jury to support the defence".' [*Ibid.* at [79], [80], [84].]

Lord Slynn of Hadley said (*ibid.* at [17]):

The second question in effect asks whether, if the prosecution has proved the three elements to which
I have referred, it is contrary to article 6(2) of the Convention rights for a judge to direct a jury that
'the defendant is guilty as charged unless he discharges a legal, rather than an evidential, burden of
proof to the effect that he neither believed nor suspected nor had reason to suspect that the substance
in question was a controlled drug'. If read in isolation there is obviously much force in the contention
that section 28(2) imposes the legal burden of proof on the accused, in which case serious arguments
arise as to whether this is justified or so disproportionate that there is a violation of article 6(2) of the
Convention rights: see *Salabakiu v. France* (1988) 13 EHRR 379, 388, para. 28. In balancing the interests
of the individual in achieving justice against the needs of society to protect against abuse of drugs this
seems to me a very difficult question but I incline to the view that this burden would not be justified
under article 6(2) of the Convention rights...Even if the most obvious way to read section 28(2) is that
it imposes a legal burden of proof, I have no doubt that it is 'possible', without doing violence to the
language or to the objective of the section, to read the words as imposing only the evidential burden of
proof. Such a reading would in my view be compatible with Convention rights, since, even if this may
create evidential difficulties for the prosecution as I accept, it ensures that the defendant does not have
the legal onus of proving the matters referred to in section 28(2), which, whether they are regarded as
part of the offence or a riposte to the offence prima facie established, are of crucial importance. It is not
enough that the defendant in seeking to establish the evidential burden should merely mouth the words

of the section. The defendant must still establish that the evidential burden has been satisfied. It seems to me that given that that reading is 'possible' courts must give effect to it in cases where Convention rights can be relied on.

Only Lord Hutton differed on the question of whether the reverse legal burden under s. 28 was justified. He said:

> I am, with respect, unable to agree with the view that the problem of obtaining a conviction against a guilty person can be surmounted by imposing an evidential burden on the defendant. All that a defendant would have to do to discharge such a burden would be to adduce some evidence to raise the issue that he did not know that the article in the bag or the tablets on the table were a controlled drug, and the prosecution would then have to destroy that defence in such a manner as to leave in the jury's mind no reasonable doubt that the defendant knew that it was a controlled drug . . .
>
> In my opinion it would be easy for a guilty defendant to raise the defence of lack of knowledge by an assertion in his police statement or by adducing evidence (which could be from a third person), and the Crown would then have to prove beyond a reasonable doubt that the defendant did have knowledge. Therefore, I think that in a drugs case, in practice, there is little difference between the burden of proving knowledge resting throughout on the prosecution and requiring the defendant to raise the issue of knowledge before the burden of proof on that matter reverts to the prosecution. [*Ibid.* at [192].]

There will be (and have already been: see 4.9.2) cases involving offences, for example those involving serious threats to public order or security, in which the test dictates a different result from that in *Lambert*. It is submitted that, after *Lambert*, any statutory provision which purports to impose a reverse burden of proof, must be reviewed in the light of the decision of the House of Lords. It would seem that such a review must involve asking two questions: firstly, whether the provision in question does in fact purport to impose a legal burden of proof on the accused; secondly, if it does so, whether it must nonetheless be read as imposing only an evidential burden. These two questions will now be considered separately.

4.9.1 Construing statutory provisions dealing with defence burdens of proof

At common law, there was much emphasis on the niceties of pleading and statutory interpretation. The burden of proof was inevitably bound up with these mysteries. Some such rules concentrated on the question of whether a defence was set forth in the enacting part of a statute, or in a subsequent proviso. For example, it was recognized as a 'known distinction' that 'what comes by way of proviso in a statute must be insisted upon by way of defence by the party accused; but where exceptions are in the enacting part of a law, it must appear in the charge that the accused does not fall within any of them': *Jarvis* (1754) 1 East 643 n, per Lord Mansfield CJ. Although primarily a rule of pleading, this had the obvious effect of varying the incidence of the burden of proof as between provisos and exceptions. In many cases, such distinctions were difficult to apply, and the law was often unclear.[57] And although such rules may now be regarded as obsolete, they have left their mark on the development of the law. Since the decision of the House of Lords in *Hunt* [1987] AC 352, the rule is that each statute which does not contain an express provision must be construed individually to see whether, 'by necessary implication', it imposes a burden of proof on the accused. But some explanation is necessary to an understanding of this decision.

---

[57] See generally *Jarvis* (1756) 1 East 643 n; *Turner* (1816) 5 M & S 206; *Stone* (1801) 1 East 639; *Oliver* [1944] KB 68; A. Zuckerman (1976) 92 LQR 402; *Edwards* [1975] QB 27, per Lawton LJ.

The distinctions between civil and criminal cases seem, at times, to have been blurred, especially in the case of statutes which provided both civil and criminal remedies.[58] But when Parliament established a new system of summary jurisdiction by the Summary Jurisdiction Act 1848, it was apparently intended to apply to the hearing of informations and complaints under the Act the same principles as then applied in trials on indictment.[59] Section 14 of the Act provided:

> Provided always, that if the information or complaint in any such case shall negative any exemption, exception, proviso or condition in the statute in which the same shall be framed, it shall not be necessary for the prosecutor or complainant in that behalf to prove such negative, but the defendant may prove the affirmative thereof in his defence, if he would have advantage of the same.

It would, of course, lead to absurd results if the rules governing the burden of proof differed according to the procedural question of whether an offence is to be tried summarily or on indictment, especially now that many offences are triable either way. Nonetheless, the matter has from time to time been doubted. Section 14 of the 1848 Act was subsequently re-enacted with different language. The present form of the provision is contained in s. 101 of the Magistrates' Courts Act 1980 (re-enacting without change s. 81 of the Magistrates' Courts Act 1952). This provides:

> Where the defendant to an information or complaint relies for his defence on any exception, exemption, proviso, excuse or qualification, whether or not it accompanies the description of the offence or matter of complaint in the enactment creating the offence or on which the complaint is founded, the burden of proving the exception, exemption, proviso, excuse or qualification shall be on him; and this notwithstanding that the information or complaint contains an allegation negativing the exception, exemption, proviso, excuse or qualification.

In *Edwards* [1975] QB 27, the question arose of whether s. 81 of the 1952 Act represented the rule of common law applicable to cases tried on indictment. The accused was charged on indictment with selling liquor without a licence. The sale of liquor was proved, but the prosecution adduced no evidence to show that the accused was not the holder of a licence. It was argued on his behalf that the prosecution had failed to discharge their burden of proof. The prosecution argued that, even though it would have been comparatively easy for them to prove the matter, the burden lay on the accused because of s. 81. The Court of Appeal upheld the prosecution's contention. After a thorough review of the authorities, the Court held that s. 81 did represent the position at common law, and the ease or otherwise of proof did not affect the issue. The Court was clearly influenced by the fact that the predecessors of s. 81 were thought to represent a general principle of common law, and by the desirability of maintaining the same rule in both summary and indictable cases. It is important to note that the Court regarded itself as dealing only with cases involving offences worded in the manner dealt with by s. 81.

In *Hunt* [1987] AC 352, an effort was made to overturn *Edwards*. It might have been expected that the House of Lords would re-state what had been said in *Edwards*. In fact, however, the House apparently regarded that case as providing a 'guide to construction' rather than a self-contained principle. In *Hunt*, the accused was charged with possessing a controlled drug, namely morphine, contrary to s. 5(2) of the Misuse of Drugs Act 1971. Under para. 3 of Sch. 1 to the Misuse of Drugs

---

[58] For example, the Game Laws. See *Stone* (1801) 1 East 639.
[59] *Hunt* [1987] AC 352 per Lord Griffiths at 372–3; *Edwards* [1975] QB 27 at 36 per Lawton LJ. See also Indictment Rules 1971, r. 6(c).

Regulations 1973, any preparation of morphine containing not more than 0.2 per cent of morphine compounded with other ingredients was exempted from the prohibition under s. 5 of the Act. The prosecution did not adduce any evidence to show that the substance found in the accused's possession contained more than 0.2 per cent of morphine. The accused submitted that there was no case to answer. The trial judge rejected this submission, although for a reason not now pertinent, and later conceded by the prosecution to be wrong. The Court of Appeal heard argument on the burden of proof question, and dismissed the appeal, on the ground that the case was covered by the principle stated in *Edwards*. The accused appealed to the House of Lords. It was held that there was no rule of law that the burden of proving a statutory defence lay on the accused only where a statute so provided expressly. A statute might, equally, place the burden of proving a defence on the accused 'by necessary implication'. The House also held that the occasions on which a statute would be so construed would generally (but not necessarily) be limited to the kinds of case provided for by s. 101 of the 1980 Act. Each case must turn on the construction of the particular statute, but the courts should be extremely slow to infer that a burden of proof was imposed by a statute. On the facts of the case, the House held that the prosecution had failed to prove an essential element of the offence, namely that the accused had possessed a substance whose possession was proscribed by s. 5 of the Act, and quashed the conviction. Hence, the House did not in fact regard this as a case of an affirmative defence. Nonetheless, Lords Griffiths and Ackner explored the depths of the decision in *Edwards*.[60]

Lord Griffiths concluded that *Edwards* did not exhaust the possible cases of implied statutory burdens of proof, because it seemed to him that other examples might be found. For example, in *Nimmo v Alexander Cowan & Sons Ltd* [1968] AC 107,[61] the House of Lords held that it was for the defendants to prove that it was not reasonably practicable for them to provide and maintain a safe working place, as required by s. 29(1) of the Factories Act 1961. The wording of this section was not couched in terms of an exception etc. It provided that such a safe place 'shall, so far as reasonably practicable, be provided and maintained...'. Nonetheless, the statute was construed as imposing a burden of proof on the defendants. For this reason, Lord Griffiths regarded *Edwards* as rightly decided, subject to the qualification that its limitation to exception cases be ignored, and that it should be regarded as a guide to construction, and not as laying down a hard-and-fast rule. Lord Ackner found that the facts of *Hunt* did not fall within the principle of *Edwards*, because the prosecution had failed to prove possession of a proscribed substance. But he agreed that *Edwards* provided a most helpful approach to the necessary statutory construction, while not providing an exhaustive rule.[62]

4.9.2 Determination of compatibility with art. 6; reading down

It was no doubt inevitable that, in the light of *Lambert*, a body of law should emerge dealing with the proper construction of a large number of statutory provisions which purport to impose

[60] And it will take an author braver than this one to describe their Lordships' analysis as *obiter*.

[61] *Nimmo* was a civil case, but since the Act also created a summary criminal offence applying to the same conduct, in which the issue might equally arise, the point is immaterial. Of more interest is that the case produced a sharp division in a strong House of Lords (Lords Guest, Upjohn, and Pearson in the majority, Lords Reid and Wilberforce dissenting).

[62] Lord Ackner pointed out that in *Edwards*, Lawton LJ had himself observed that the court must construe enactments individually whenever the prosecution seeks to avail itself of the exception: [1975] QB 27, 40. The Court of Appeal in *Hunt* shared the view that the case did not fall within the rule in *Edwards*: see [1986] QB 125, 133 per Robert Goff LJ.

a burden of proof of some issue on the accused. After *Lambert*, there is always potentially a question as to whether any particular provision should be taken as imposing the legal burden of proof on an accused, or whether the section must be read down so as to impose only an evidential burden, in the interests of upholding the accused's right to a fair trial in accordance with art. 6. Predictably, a number of decisions emerged from the Court of Appeal, and in one instance (*Johnstone* [2003] 1 WLR 1736) the House of Lords. Equally predictably, these decisions indicated different views of different provisions and, in the light of subsequent developments, it would be pointless to analyse them in detail, though as a general observation it should be said that they all appear to have taken into consideration the factors identified in *Lambert*.[63]

Predictable as this divergence of opinion was, a special five-judge Court of Appeal[64] was convened to hear together *Attorney-General's Reference (No. 1 of 2004)* and appeals in the cases of *Edwards*, *Denton and Jackson*, *Hendley*, and *Crowley* and, furthermore, to consider generally the issues relating to reverse burdens, and to offer guidance to lower courts.[65] The reasons given for the convening of this panel are instructive:

> In the case of reverse burdens[66] there are now a considerable number of authorities from decisions of the European Court of Human Rights at Strasbourg, from courts in other overseas jurisdictions, from this court and from the House of Lords. In this jurisdiction, rulings have to be made by magistrates and Crown Courts up and down the country. This can involve the citation of a very large number of authorities, many of which conflict in the message which they give. The position is illustrated by the fact that five volumes of authorities were appropriately placed before us to help us determine this issue. [[2004] 2 Cr App R at [19].]

It seems clear from the subsequent analysis of the Court that the perceived conflicting message was, not simply the fact that decisions on the issue of reverse defence burdens had been going both ways (which was only to be expected in the light of *Lambert*), but that too many of them had been going in favour of reading down statutory provisions to impose only an evidential

---

[63] At that time, decisions holding that a defence burden provision must be read down so as to impose only an evidential burden included: *Carass* [2002] 1 WLR 1714 (defence of absence of intent to defraud on a charge of concealing the debts of a company in anticipation of its winding-up, Insolvency Act 1986, s. 206(4); this case was said by the later Court of Appeal in *Attorney-General's Reference (No. 1 of 2004)* [2004] 2 Cr App R 424, [84] to have been 'impliedly overruled' by the decision of the House of Lords in *Johnstone* (below) notwithstanding that the latter makes no reference to *Carass* and concerned an entirely different statutory provision); *Sheldrake v DPP* [2004] QB 487 (defence that no likelihood of driving while proportion of alcohol exceeds prescribed limit, Road Traffic Act 1988, s. 5(2)). This decision has since been reversed by the House of Lords (text below). Decisions upholding the imposition of a legal burden include: *L v DPP* [2003] QB 137 (defence of having a good reason or lawful authority for having a lock knife in a public place, Offensive Weapons Act 1996, s. 139(14)); *Drummond* [2002] 2 Cr App R 352 (defence of consuming alcohol after an offence and before providing a specimen, Road Traffic Offenders Act 1988, s. 15(3)(a)(i)); *Johnstone* [2003] 1 WLR 1736 (defence of believing on reasonable grounds that accused was not infringing a trademark, Trade Marks Act 1994, s. 92(5)); *Attorney-General's Reference (No. 4 of 2002)* [2004] 1 All ER 1 (defence that terrorist organization was not proscribed when accused became a member or took part in activities, Terrorism Act 2000, s. 11(2)). This decision has since been reversed in part by the House of Lords (text below).

[64] Lord Woolf CJ, Judge LJ, Gage, Elias, and Stanley Burnton JJ.

[65] [2004] 2 Cr App R 424. The *Attorney-General's Reference* and *Edwards* were concerned with the defence of absence of intent to defraud or conceal the state of the bankrupt's affairs under Insolvency Act 1986, s. 352; *Denton and Jackson* concerned the defence to a charge of unlawful eviction of belief on reasonable grounds that a residential occupier has ceased to reside in premises under Eviction Act 1977, s. 1(2); *Hendley* was concerned with the suicide pact defence to murder under s. 4(2) of the Homicide Act 1957; *Crowley* was concerned with absence of intent to obstruct justice etc., under Criminal Justice and Public Order Act 1994, s. 51(7).

[66] The Court also offered guidance on the quite different subject of when the trial court should hold a preparatory hearing under Part III of the Criminal Procedure and Investigations Act 1996, an issue which had also arisen in each of the cases dealt with except *Crowley*.

burden, a development for which the Court laid the blame squarely on the shoulders of Lord Steyn.[67] The assault on Lord Steyn begins with the observation that his treatment of the subject in *Lambert* (summarized above at 4.9) was *obiter*, a valid but (as will shortly become apparent) hardly compelling point (*ibid.* at [26]). The Court of Appeal preferred the (equally *obiter* and dissenting) view of Lord Hutton, who concluded (consistently with the general approach advocated by Lord Steyn, albeit contrary to the conclusion of each other member of the House about the statutory provision in question) that the evidential burden would make it too difficult to obtain convictions, and that the legal burden of proof was appropriate and did not infringe art. 6 ([2002] AC at [192], 4.9 above). In support of its preference, the Court added:

> As to the difference in approach between Lord Hutton and Lord Steyn on the efficacy of a persuasive burden, it may be of assistance to the Appellate Committee to know that in practice our collective experiences are the same as Lord Hutton's. Some of the later decisions suggest a similar reaction by other members of the constitutions of this court. [[2004] 2 Cr App R at [34].]

The Court then purports to contrast Lord Steyn's approach with that of Lord Nicholls in *Johnstone* [2003] 1 WLR 1736. In that case, the House of Lords had to consider a statutory provision quite different from that in issue in *Lambert*, namely s. 92(5) of the Trade Marks Act 1994, which provides a defence to a prosecution for criminal trade mark infringement if the accused proves that he believed on reasonable grounds that his use of a sign in the manner in which it was used was not an infringement of a registered trade mark. The observations of Lord Nicholls on the subject of reverse burdens were, in fact, just as *obiter* as those of Lord Steyn in *Lambert*. The *ratio decidendi* of the House of Lords in *Johnstone* was unconnected with the issue of burden of proof. But because the reverse burden provision of s. 92(5) had been the subject of inconsistent decisions in the Court of Appeal,[68] the House chose to consider the matter, holding, *per curiam*, that the burden of proof placed on the accused by s. 92(5) was compatible with art. 6.[69] In the course of his brief observations on the subject, Lord Nicholls referred to the principles to be observed in the light of art. 6, and to some earlier authority including *Lambert*, the decision of the European Court of Human Rights in *Salabiaku v France* (1988) 13 EHRR 379, and that of Sachs J in *State v Coetzee* [1997] 2 LRC 593, both of which were dealt with by Lord Steyn in *Lambert* (see 4.9, above). He concluded:

> In evaluating these factors the court's role is one of review. Parliament, not the court, is charged with the primary responsibility for deciding, as a matter of policy, what should be the constituents elements of a criminal offence. I echo the words of Lord Woolf in *A-G of Hong Kong v. Lo Chak-man* [1993] AC 951, 975:
>
> > 'In order to maintain the balance between the individual and the society as a whole, rigid and inflexible standards should not be imposed on the legislature's attempts to resolve the difficult and intransigent problems with which society is faced when seeking to deal with serious crime.'

---

[67] It has to be said that the Court's perception hardly seems justified on a review of the authorities. The Court clearly disapproved of *Carass*, a binding decision which called for reading down in the context of a provision related to, though separate from, those involved in *Attorney-General's Reference* and *Edwards*, but the number of decisions in which provisions had been read down hardly constituted an avalanche.

[68] In *Johnstone*, the Court of Appeal had concluded that the section should be read down in deference to art. 6, and the prosecution did not argue the contrary on that occasion. But in *S v London Borough of Havering* [2003] 1 Cr App R 602, in which the prosecution did argue the contrary view, the Court of Appeal agreed with the prosecution that the legal burden was proper.

[69] 'In the events which have happened this issue does not call for decision in the present case. But the House should not leave the law on this point in its present state, with differing views expressed by the Court of Appeal. *I shall, therefore, state my views as shortly as may be*' [2003] 1 WLR at [46] per Lord Nicholls, emphasis added.

The court will reach a different conclusion from the legislature only when it is apparent the legislature has attached insufficient importance to the fundamental right of an individual to be presumed innocent until proved guilty. [[2003] 1 WLR at [51].]

Following its review of Lord Nicholls' reasoning compared to that of Lord Steyn in *Lambert*, the Court of Appeal concluded:

Lord Steyn and Lord Nicholls of Birkenhead were considering different statutory provisions and it does not follow that they would have used the language which they did if they were considering other statutory reverse burden provisions. Nonetheless, it does appear there is a significant difference in emphasis between their approaches. In practice, a legal burden is much more likely to have to be reduced to an evidential burden on Lord Steyn's approach than it is on Lord Nicholls of Birkenhead's approach ... We suggest that until the position is clarified by a further decision of the House of Lords, lower courts should follow the approach of Lord Nicholls of Birkenhead rather than that of Lord Steyn, if they are in doubt as to what should be the outcome of a challenge to a reverse burden. [[2004] 2 Cr App R at [38].][70]

The Court then laid down the following guidelines for lower courts in resolving reverse burden issues:

(A) Courts should strongly discourage the citation of authority to them other than the decision of the House of Lords in *R v Johnstone* [2003] UKHL 28, [2003] 1 WLR 1736 and this guidance. *Johnstone* is at present the latest word on the subject.

(B) The common law (the golden thread) and the language of Art 6(2) have the same effect. Both permit legal reverse burdens of proof or presumptions in the appropriate circumstances.

(C) Reverse legal burdens are probably justified if the overall burden of proof is on the prosecution i.e. the prosecution has to prove the essential ingredients of the offence, but there is a situation where there are significant reasons why it is fair and reasonable to deny the accused the general protection normally guaranteed by the presumption of innocence.

(D) Where the exception goes no further than is reasonably necessary to achieve the objective of the reverse burden (i.e. it is proportionate), it is sufficient if the exception is reasonably necessary in all the circumstances. The assumption should be that Parliament would not have made an exception without good reason. While the judge must make his own decision as to whether there is a contravention of Art 6, the task of a judge is to 'review' Parliament's approach, as Lord Nicholls of Birkenhead indicates.

(E) If only an evidential burden is placed on the defendant there will be no risk of contravention of Art 6(2).

(F) When ascertaining whether an exception is justified, the court must construe the provision to ascertain what will be the realistic effects of the reverse burden. In doing this the courts should be more concerned with substance than form. If the proper interpretation is that the statutory provision creates an offence plus an exception that will in itself be a strong indication that there is no contravention of Art 6(2).

(G) The easier it is for the accused to discharge the burden the more likely it is that the reverse burden is justified. This will be the case where the facts are within the defendant's own knowledge. How

---

[70] The Court's determination to depart from *Lambert* also resulted in the remarkable statement that the previous decision of the Court of Appeal in *Carass* [2002] 1 WLR 1714 holding that, in the light of *Lambert*, s. 206(4) of the Insolvency Act 1986 must be read down, would have been decided differently if the 'approach' in *Johnstone* had been applied, and must therefore be treated as 'impliedly overruled': [2004] 2 Cr App R at [84]. This is all the more remarkable for the fact that *Carass* was not referred to in the speeches in *Johnstone*, though it is mentioned in the list of authorities, and concerned a statutory provision quite different from that in *Johnstone*.

difficult it would be for the prosecution to establish the facts is also indicative of whether a reverse legal burden is justified.

(H) The ultimate question is: would the exception prevent a fair trial? If it would, it must either be read down if this is possible; otherwise it should be declared incompatible.

(I) Caution must be exercised when considering the seriousness of the offence and the power of punishment. The need for a reverse burden is not necessarily reflected by the gravity of the offence, though, from a defendant's point of view, the more serious the offence, the more important it is that there is no interference with the presumption of innocence.

(J) If guidance is needed as to the approach of the European Court of Human Rights, that is provided by the *Salabiaku* case at para. 28 of the judgment where it is stated that:

> 'Article 6(2) does not therefore regard presumptions of fact or of law provided for in the criminal law with indifference. It requires states to confine them within reasonable limits which take into account the importance of what is at stake and maintains the rights of the defence.'

While these guidelines are generally helpful to lower courts in interpreting statutory provisions concerned with reverse burdens, it is submitted that guideline [A] was erroneous, and cannot be followed in the light of the later decisions of the House of Lords in *Sheldrake v DPP; Attorney-General's Reference (No. 4 of 2002)* [2005] 1 AC 264 (below). It seems contrary to principle for the Court of Appeal to invite lower courts to prefer a decision of its own to a binding authority of the House of Lords (*Lambert* is pointedly omitted). The rationale that *Johnstone* is later and inconsistent authority is, to say the least, tenuous. It is certainly a later decision, but there is no obvious basis for holding that it is inconsistent. The observations of the members of the House in both *Lambert* and *Johnstone* were strictly *obiter*, but the members of the House in *Lambert* gave the question of reverse burdens a much more detailed analysis; Lord Nicholls in *Johnstone* referred to *Lambert* with no obvious intention of disapproving anything said in that case; and, while it is true that the other members of the House in *Lambert* did not expressly endorse Lord Steyn's speech, the only overt disagreement was that of Lord Hutton, dissenting as to the result of the case but not as to the general principles to be applied in reaching such a result. Perhaps most significantly, the two cases were concerned with completely different statutory provisions, and, as the Court of Appeal was constrained to concede in the passage cited above, there is no reason to assume that the outcome would be the same. Indeed, it may be that much of the perceived difficulty in reconciling the various decisions since *Lambert* may be attributable to the misconceived idea that the outcomes ought to have been more uniform. A pattern seems to have arisen of courts distinguishing each other. Thus, in examining the cases listed in note 63 above, we find that *Lambert* was followed in *Sheldrake v DPP* [2004] QB 487; that *Lambert* was distinguished in *L v DPP* [2003] QB 137,[71] and in *Drummond* [2002] 2 Cr App R 352; and that both *Lambert* and *Sheldrake* were distinguished in *Attorney-General's Reference (No. 4 of 2002)* [2004] 1 All ER 1. There are, of course, grounds on which cases in this area can legitimately be distinguished, such as the gravity of the offence and the urgency of the legislature's efforts to curtail it; the consequences to the accused in terms of potential sentence; whether the statutory defence is a legitimate affirmative defence or the absence of an element of the offence; whether the facts underlying the defence are peculiarly within the accused's competence, for example his knowledge or belief; the degree of difficulty that would be caused to the prosecution in obtaining convictions if only an evidential burden were to be imposed on the accused; whether the derogation from the presumption of innocence

---

[71] Which was followed in *Matthews* [2004] QB 690.

is proportionate and reasonable, and so on. But the Court of Appeal seems to have reacted to the fact that some courts appeared to have been more ready than others to read down statutory provisions, without having regard to the crucial fact that in each of these cases, quite different statutory provisions were involved, in relation to which different results might reasonably be anticipated. To a limited extent, the results of the cases considered by the Court reflect this.[72]

The advocacy of the Court of Appeal for its own decision in preference to *Lambert* is rendered all the more curious by the fact that the Court was aware that two other cases which it considered, *Sheldrake v DPP* and *Attorney-General's Reference (No. 4 of 2002)*, were then awaiting a hearing in the House of Lords.[73] These cases were subsequently heard together.[74] It was hardly to be expected that the House would overlook the judgment of the Court of Appeal, and indeed it did not. Lord Bingham delivered a timely reminder of the hierarchy of the courts:

> Both *R v Lambert* and *R v Johnstone* are recent decisions of the House, binding on lower courts for what they decide. [[2005] 1 AC at [30].]

Lord Bingham added (at [32]) that, while the House agreed with the results of the cases decided by the Court of Appeal, the guidelines proposed by the Court were to be read in the light of the decisions of the House of Lords, which must be regarded as the 'primary domestic authority on reverse burdens'.

The decisions reached by the House on the two cases before it were as follows. In *Sheldrake*, it was held that the legal reverse burden of proof in the case of the defence provided by s. 5(2) of the Road Traffic Act 1988, that there was no likelihood of the defendant driving with excess alcohol, was not unreasonable or disproportionate, having regard to the important public policy involved in deterring and punishing drunk driving. Accordingly, no violation of art. 6 was involved. In *Attorney-General's Reference (No. 4 of 2002)*, it was held by a majority (Lords Rodger and Carswell dissenting only as to the result in this case) that, in the case of the defence provided by s. 11(2)(b) of the Terrorism Act 2000, that an organization was not proscribed when the accused last participated in its activities, the legal reverse burden was disproportionate and unreasonable, and must be read down so as to operate as an evidential burden only. The majority held that it might be extremely difficult for an innocent person to prove that he had not participated in the activities of an organization on or between any given dates, and there was, therefore, an appreciable risk that a person innocent of any blameworthy conduct might be convicted of an offence, even if there was a reasonable doubt that he had done so.[75] Despite the strong public interest in dealing with

---

[72] See note 63 above. In relation to the *Attorney-General's Reference* and the appeal in *Edwards*, it was held that the reverse burden under Insolvency Act 1986 s. 352 was justifiable in relation to the offence under s. 353(1) of the Act, but must be read down in relation to the offence under s. 357 which could apply to gifts and disbursements made by the bankrupt up to five years before the bankruptcy, in which case it would be unfair to require the accused to prove the absence of an intent to defraud, a result which required that the appeal in *Edwards* be allowed. With respect to the *Attorney-General's Reference*, it was held that the trial judge's ruling with regard to s. 353(1), which suggested the evidential burden, had been unduly favourable to the accused. In each of the other cases, the reverse legal burden provision was upheld, having regard to the gravity of the offences, the strength of the public interest in suppressing the conduct in question, and the intention of Parliament of enabling that to be done. Accordingly, the appeals in these cases were dismissed.

[73] The Court was unaware of this when the hearing of the appeal was arranged, but became aware of it subsequently, and decided that it should 'nonetheless try to simplify the task of lower courts when faced with reverse burdens': *ibid.* at [10].

[74] *Sheldrake v DPP; Attorney-General's Reference (No. 4 of 2002)* [2005] 1 AC 264 (Lords Bingham of Cornhill, Steyn, Phillips of Worth Matravers, Rodger of Earlsferry, and Carswell). The panel included one member who had also sat in *Lambert* (Lord Steyn) and one who had also sat in *Johnstone* (Lord Rodger).

[75] The burden applicable to the corresponding defence under s. 11(2)(a), of showing that the organization was not proscribed when the accused was last a member of it, was not unreasonable or disproportionate, because in

the dangers of terrorism, the legal burden was inconsistent with art. 6. But the approach taken by the House to the analysis of the issues is more significant than the understandable difference in the outcome of the two cases. This approach was stated in the speech of Lord Bingham, with which the other members of the House (including Lords Rodger and Carswell, except as to the ultimate result in the Attorney-General's Reference) agreed. Lord Bingham noted that in both cases, it was clear that Parliament intended the legal burden of proof to apply. Before the coming into effect of the Human Rights Act 1998, therefore, no issue could have arisen. But now, it was necessary to consider whether or not the legal burden was compatible with the Convention, and, if not, whether the provision could be read down: *ibid* at [1], [7]. The presumption of innocence was an element of a fair trial for the purposes of art. 6 of the Convention.[76] *Salabakiu* (1988) 13 EHRR 379 establishes that any presumption which operates so as to affect the presumption of innocence must be contained within reasonable limits ([12]). It was to be expected that different results might be reached in interpreting different provisions because of the differences of subject-matter. There was nothing in *Johnstone* to suggest that the House intended any departure from *Lambert*. The dissenting opinion of Lord Hutton in *Lambert* was not authoritative, and Lord Steyn had not been a 'lone voice' in that case. The decisive point in Lambert was that, on Lord Hutton's view, an accused might be convicted, even if the jury believed that it was just as likely as not that he had not known that the bag he possessed contained illegal drugs. (See paras [25]–[30].) In conclusion, Lord Bingham observed:

> The task of the court is never to decide whether a reverse burden should be imposed on a defendant, but always to assess whether a burden enacted by Parliament unjustifiably infringes the presumption of innocence. [*ibid.* at [31].]

It is submitted that the House of Lords has now made the position clear, and that the way is open for a case-by-case development of the law on the important question of the presumption of innocence and the relationship of a reverse legal burden in a particular case to the requirements of art. 6 of the Convention.

4.10 THE BURDEN OF PROOF OF SECONDARY FACTS

An evidential burden lies upon a party who asserts a secondary fact, that is to say, a fact which affects the admissibility of evidence or the construction of a document, and consistently with the general rule, the burden so imposed lies on the party who asserts the affirmative proposition.

Thus, a party who asserts that a witness is competent or that secondary evidence is admissible of a lost document, or that the deceased was under a settled, hopeless expectation of death so as to render admissible a statement as a dying declaration, or that the relationship between his opponent and a witness is such as to give rise to bias in the witness's evidence, bears in each case the burden of adducing evidence to support the assertion.[77] The same applies to a party who wishes to adduce parol evidence to complete a written contract, or who asserts a certain interpretation of an ambiguous document.[78] Evidence bearing on secondary facts is adduced, in a criminal case, in the absence of the jury. Two different kinds of case may require the presentation

---

that case it was relatively easy for the accused to prove the necessary facts, and the risk of an innocent person being denied the benefit of the offence was slight.

[76] *Ibid.* at [9]; *Bernard v France* (2000) 30 EHRR 808, [37].

[77] E.g., *Thompson* [1893] 2 QB 12 (confession); *Jenkins* (1869) LR 1 CCR 187 (dying declaration); *Yacoob* (1981) 72 Cr App R 313 (competence); *Shephard* (1991) 93 Cr App R 139 (hearsay statement produced by computer).

[78] *Tucker v Bennett* (1887) 38 ChD 1 (parol evidence); *Falck v Williams* [1900] AC 176 (construction).

of secondary evidence, and although both are spoken of loosely as being questions of 'admissibility', they are analytically quite distinct. These may be referred to respectively as questions of admissibility properly so called, and questions of authenticity and originality.

Questions of admissibility properly so called are those cases in which the judge has to decide whether a proffered piece of evidence is admissible as a matter of law, having regard to the rules of evidence. In order to decide this, the judge may have to receive evidence of secondary facts. For example, the admissibility of the written confession may depend upon the circumstances in which it was made, as the prosecution may have to prove that it was not made under circumstances which were oppressive or which render the confession unreliable. The judge would, therefore, hear evidence about the circumstances in which the confession was made.[79] The admissibility of confessions is dealt with in Chapter 9. Questions of authenticity and originality, on the other hand, are those cases in which there is no question that the evidence tendered is admissible from a legal standpoint, but there is a question whether the piece of evidence tendered is what it purports to be, that it is an original piece of evidence and that it has not been tampered with. These cases concern documents and tangible exhibits, such as photographs and tape-recordings. There is no doubt that such evidence may be admitted, but there must be some foundational showing that the actual exhibit proffered is what it is represented to be. The judge would therefore receive evidence of the secondary facts necessary to demonstrate that the proffered exhibit is authentic and original, that is to say that it was made or found in the manner described by the proponent, and that it has not since been altered or tampered with.[80]

Although the party proffering the evidence has the burden of proof in either case, the distinction between these two kinds of case has, or should have, important consequences in terms of the applicable standard of proof, and as we shall see in 4.14, some courts have created problems in this area by ignoring the distinction. Again, it will be observed that although the form of an assertion may be positive (arguing for admissibility) or negative (arguing for inadmissibility) the burden lies upon the party who in effect asserts the affirmative of the issue.

B   THE STANDARD OF PROOF

SUMMARY OF MAIN POINTS
- In criminal cases, the prosecution must discharge the legal burden of proof to a high standard, usually articulated as proof beyond reasonable doubt, or proof so that the jury (or bench) are sure of guilt. No lesser standard will suffice.

- Where the defence bear the legal burden of proving an affirmative defence, the standard required is the civil standard.

---

[79] The question of the burden and standard of proof on the issue of whether evidence was or may have been procured by means of torture, for the purposes of hearings before the Special Immigration Appeals Commission (SIAC), was the subject of marked disagreement between the members of a divided House of Lords in *A and others v Secretary of State for Home Department (No. 2)* [2006] 2 AC 221. This question, which was held to depend in part on the provisions of the Convention against Torture of 1987, appears to be *sui generis*, and the decision of the majority does not appear to lay down any principle of general application. Moreover, the appeal was argued and decided without resolution of a disputed issue as to whether proceedings before the SIAC were civil or criminal in nature. For these reasons, this question will not be pursued here. As to the facts and substantive holding in this case, see 3.10.

[80] *Robson* [1972] 1 WLR 651; *Stevenson* [1971] 1 WLR 1.

- In civil cases the standard is the balance of probabilities, i.e. the party having the legal burden must satisfy the court that the facts on which he relies are more probably true than not true.

- In certain civil cases having criminal or quasi-criminal attributes, or in which allegations of criminal or quasi-criminal conduct are made, the civil standard (while it does not change) should be applied flexibly, so that stronger evidence may be required to satisfy the standard, according to the gravity of the allegations. In a few such cases, the criminal standard must be applied.

- In family and matrimonial cases the civil standard of proof applies.

- On secondary issues affecting the admissibility of evidence the same standard is to be applied as on the main issue. This rule is not altogether satisfactory.

4.11 INTRODUCTION

The term 'standard of proof' refers to the extent or degree to which the burden of proof must be discharged. It is the measurement of the degree of certainty or probability which the evidence must generate in the mind of the tribunal of fact; the standard to which the tribunal of fact must be convinced by the evidence before the party bearing the burden of proof becomes entitled to succeed in the case, or to have a favourable finding of fact on some issue which he has set out to prove. It is a measurement therefore of the quality and cogency required of evidence tendered with a view to discharging the burden of proof. The standard of proof demanded sometimes varies according to the nature of the issue to be proved, but the fundamental divergence is that between criminal and civil cases.

4.11.1 The standard of proof diagram

In a civil case, the standard of proof required is no more than proof on the balance of probabilities or (in the United States) the preponderance of the evidence, that is to say, sufficient to show that the case of the party having the legal burden of proof is more likely than not to be true.[81] In a criminal case, however, the prosecution must prove the guilt of the accused to a high standard, usually articulated as proof so that the jury are sure of guilt, or proof beyond reasonable doubt.

The following diagram represents the standard of proof in civil and criminal cases, using the analogy of the scales. In a civil case, any tipping of the scales, however slight, in favour of the claimant (or party bearing the legal burden of proof) is sufficient to win. If the scales are tipped the other way, then it is clear that D wins. But what is sometimes overlooked is that if the scales remain evenly balanced (i.e., the tribunal of fact is unable to decide) D must also win because the burden of proof has not been discharged on the balance of probabilities.[82] In a criminal case, the standard of 'beyond reasonable doubt' cannot be precisely measured as a percentage. All that can be said is that the scales must be tipped substantially in favour of the prosecution. If the scales go no further down than the preponderance of probabilities, or remain balanced, D must win.

---

[81] But not just that it is more likely than an account of the facts given by the opponent. See *Rhesa Shipping Co. SA v Edmunds* [1985] 1 WLR 948 and 4.5.1.

[82] *Rhesa Shipping Co. SA v Edmunds* [1985] 1 WLR 948 and 4.5.1.

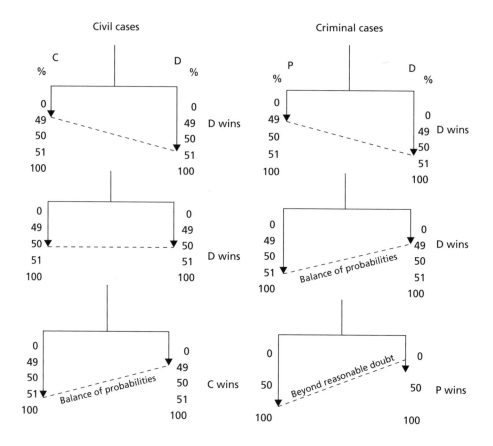

4.12 CRIMINAL CASES: STANDARD OF PROOF REQUIRED OF PROSECUTION

The standard of proof required of the prosecution in the discharge of the legal burden of proving the guilt of the accused is a high one. The judge has a duty in all cases to direct the jury in such a way as to impress upon them, by means of an appropriate formulation, how high the standard is.[83] There are two classic formulations of the standard required.

(a) 'Beyond reasonable doubt'. This formulation has been approved on more than one occasion by the House of Lords[84] and has become a phrase of common usage in the English language. In *Miller v Minister of Pensions* [1947] 2 All ER 372, 373, Denning J elaborated on the nature of proof beyond reasonable doubt in these terms:

> It need not reach certainty, but it must carry a high degree of probability. Proof beyond reasonable doubt does not mean proof beyond the shadow of a doubt. The law would fail to protect the community if it admitted fanciful possibilities to deflect the course of justice. If the evidence is so strong against a man as to leave only a remote possibility in his favour which can be dismissed

---

[83] Failure to give such a direction is a serious error which should be fatal to a conviction unless the prosecution evidence is overwhelming; cf. *Edwards* [1983] Crim LR 484.

[84] *Woolmington v DPP* [1935] AC 462, 481; *Mancini v DPP* [1942] AC 1, 11; see also *McGreevy v DPP* [1973] 1 WLR 276. For a detailed account of the emergence of the criminal standard of proof, see B. Shapiro, *Beyond Reasonable Doubt and Probable Cause: Historical Perspectives on the Anglo-American Law of Evidence* (1991).

> with the sentence 'of course it is possible, but not in the least probable,' the case is proved beyond reasonable doubt, but nothing short of that will suffice.

This formulation fell into some disfavour for a time because of supposed difficulties of explaining to juries the nature of reasonable doubt, if they experienced problems of understanding. Expressions intended to be helpful, but of questionable value, such as, 'a reasonable doubt is one for which you could give reasons if asked' found disfavour in the higher courts and led to some successful appeals against conviction. As a result, a second formulation gained wide favour.

(b) 'Satisfied so that you feel sure' (or more simply 'sure of guilt'). This formulation was advocated by Lord Goddard CJ in *Summers*,[85] when he said:

> If a jury is told that it is their duty to regard the evidence and see that it satisfies them so that they can feel sure when they return a verdict of guilty, that is much better than using the expression 'reasonable doubt' and I hope in future that that will be done.

In modern practice, much more emphasis is placed on the substance of the direction to the jury as a whole than on the adoption of any particular formula. As long as the judge successfully conveys the high degree of probability required, the direction will be proper. In *Hepworth* [1955] 2 QB 600 (CCA), Lord Goddard himself observed that a judge would be 'on safe ground' if he directed a jury that 'You must be satisfied beyond reasonable doubt', and added: 'and one could also say: "You must feel sure of the prisoner's guilt"'. The matter was cogently expressed by Lord Diplock in *Walters* v *R* [1969] 2 AC 26, 30 (PC Jamaica), when he pointed out that the judge has the opportunity of assessing the jury during a trial, and can select whatever formula he feels will best assist that jury, avoiding all gloss upon the formula which he uses, as far as possible. The question is simply whether the judge has succeeded overall in stressing the high standard for which the jury should look. In *Ferguson* v *R*[86] the composite formulation 'satisfied beyond reasonable doubt so that you feel sure of the accused's guilt' was upheld as 'generally safe and sufficient', the Privy Council stressing that there is no set form of words and the test is one of successful communication of the standard in whatever words may be employed. In the ordinary case, of course, use of a time-honoured phrase is wise and above criticism. By way of contrast, the appellate courts have found wanting a number of less emphatic expressions which do not adequately convey the standard, for example: 'satisfied' (standing alone),[87] 'pretty certain',[88] 'reasonably sure'.[89]

In cases where the formula 'beyond reasonable doubt' is used, the use of further comment by way of elucidation still causes problems from time to time. It is submitted that the use of such phrases and analogies should be resorted to only when the jury seem in danger of failing to understand what is required of them, and that the judge must ensure that his language, taken as a whole, does not tend to diminish the standard of proof. In *Ching* (1976) 63 Cr App R 7, 11, the Court of Appeal said: 'We point out and emphasize that if judges stopped trying to define that which is almost impossible to define there would be fewer appeals'. The Court nonetheless recognized that exceptional cases would remain where some further assistance to the jury would be called for. While endorsing earlier criticisms of efforts to define a reasonable doubt as one for

---

[85] [1952] 1 All ER 1059. The passage quoted is taken from the report in 36 Cr App R 14, 15. The All ER report reads a little differently, albeit to the same effect.

[86] [1979] 1 WLR 94. See also *Kritz* [1950] 1 KB 82, per Lord Goddard CJ at 89.

[87] *Hepworth* [1955] 2 QB 600; *Quinn* [1983] Crim LR 474.

[88] *Law* [1961] Crim LR 52.

[89] *Head* (1961) 45 Cr App R 225.

which a reason could be given,[90] the Court upheld the direction given by the trial judge that a reasonable doubt was: 'something to which you can assign a reason. The sort of matter which might influence you if you were to consider some business matter... a matter for example, concerning a mortgage of your house'. The reference to matters related to the personal affairs of the jurors was also approved in *Walters*, but subject to the qualification that the comparison must be with affairs of importance in their lives; and in *Gray* (1973) 58 Cr App R 177, it was held by the Court of Appeal to be a misdirection to compare the standard of proof with the degree of care which the jury might exercise in their 'everyday affairs'.

There may, of course, be problems in the use of any formula, and the strongest safeguard still seems to be that of judicial flexibility to meet the needs of individual juries. Nonetheless, it is submitted that the traditional formula 'beyond reasonable doubt' is to be preferred to that of 'feeling sure of guilt'. The latter may in many cases actually suggest too high a standard, and will sometimes tend to confuse legal with scientific certainty.[91] On the other hand, experience has shown that the phrase 'beyond reasonable doubt' has passed into the language by dint of long usage, is understood by juries and can if necessary be elaborated on without confusion.

Curiously, it cannot be demonstrated with certainty that the requirement that the prosecution's burden of proof be discharged by proof beyond reasonable doubt is an essential attribute of a fair trial under art. 6 of the European Convention on Human Rights. Although the rule regarding the burden of proof, known as the presumption of innocence, is well established as a fundamental right in the most important civil rights instruments, the standard of proof has not been adopted in the same way. Nonetheless, the beyond reasonable doubt standard is now so universally recognized as the correct standard that it has probably attained that status less formally. It is employed throughout the common law world, in most civil law countries, and has been adopted by the International Criminal Court and the International Criminal Tribunals for the Former Yugoslavia and Rwanda.[92]

4.13 STANDARD OF PROOF REQUIRED OF DEFENCE

In the exceptional cases where the defence bear the legal burden of proof on an issue affecting guilt (see 4.8, 4.9) it is not necessary for the issue to be proved beyond reasonable doubt. The standard of proof required of the defence has been defined as 'not higher than the burden which rests upon a plaintiff or an accused in civil proceedings'.[93] The standard required in such cases is always the same, regardless of the issue to be proved. The civil standard of proof is that on the balance of probabilities (see 4.15).

4.14 STANDARD OF PROOF OF SECONDARY FACTS

We have already seen in 4.10 that there are two distinct kinds of case in which proof of secondary facts may be required, that is to say questions of admissibility properly so called, and questions of authenticity and originality. In relation to questions of admissibility, the standard required for the proof of secondary facts is the same as that required as to the facts in issue. Therefore, in

---

[90] See, e.g., *Stafford* [1968] 3 All ER 752.

[91] See, e.g., *Bracewell* (1978) 68 Cr App R 44.

[92] Rome Statute of the International Criminal Court, art. 66(3); Rules of Procedure and Evidence of the International Criminal Tribunal for the Former Yugoslavia, Rule 87(A); Rules of Procedure and Evidence of the International Criminal Tribunal for Rwanda, Rule 87(A). The standard was also previously employed at the International Military Tribunal (Nuremberg).

[93] *Carr-Briant* [1943] KB 607, 610.

a criminal case, where the prosecution must prove secondary facts in order to demonstrate the admissibility of a piece of evidence, the standard required is that beyond reasonable doubt.[94]

Where the question is one of authenticity or originality, it appeared until recently to have been settled (and, it is submitted, should be the law) that the party proffering the evidence should be required to do no more than establish a *prima facie* case of authenticity or originality. The reason for this is simply that authenticity and originality are matters of relevance, which also affect the weight of the evidence. Questions as to its weight, including any questions of whether the evidence is shown to be authentic or original, are matters for the tribunal of fact. A ruling by the judge that evidence has sufficient indicia of authenticity and originality to be admitted does not oblige the jury to reach the ultimate factual conclusion that it is authentic and original.

In *Robson* [1972] 1 WLR 651,[95] the prosecution sought to introduce into evidence certain tape recordings. The defence objected to this course, on the grounds that the recordings had not been shown to be the originals, or at least true copies thereof, and that they were prejudicially unreliable and misleading because of their poor quality. Holding the tape recordings to be admissible, Shaw J considered the contention that the standard to be applied was that beyond reasonable doubt, and continued:

> This is, of course, right if and when the issue does come before the jury as a matter they have to decide as going to weight and cogency. In the first stage, when the question is solely that of admissibility—i.e., is the evidence competent to be considered by the jury at all?—the judge, it seems to me, would be usurping their function if he purported to deal with not merely the primary issue of admissibility but with what is the ultimate issue of cogency. My own view is that in considering that limited question the judge is required to do no more than to satisfy himself that a *prima facie* case of originality has been made out by evidence which defines and describes the provenance and history of the recordings up to the moment of production in court. If that evidence appears to remain intact after cross-examination it is not incumbent on him to hear and weigh other evidence which might controvert the *prima facie* case. To embark on such an enquiry seems to me to trespass on the ultimate function of the jury.

It is noteworthy that Shaw J felt that the judge should not receive evidence from the opponent to controvert the *prima facie* case of authenticity or originality. This is, of course, in marked contrast to the case where evidence is received on an issue of legal admissibility, where there is no risk of trespassing on the function of the jury and where both sides must be allowed the opportunity to adduce evidence of the relevant secondary facts.

More recently, however, there have been indications that the distinction between admissibility properly so called and authenticity and originality is in danger of being overlooked.[96] In *Angeli* [1979] 1 WLR 26, the question was whether disputed writings had rightly been admitted into evidence for the purpose of being compared with samples of the known writings of the appellant. By s. 8 of the Criminal Procedure Act 1865:

> Comparison of the disputed writing with any writing proved to the satisfaction of the judge to be genuine shall be permitted to be made by witnesses, and such writings, and the evidence of witnesses respecting the same, may be submitted to the court and jury as evidence of the genuineness or otherwise of the writing in dispute.

---

[94] See, e.g., *DPP v Ping Lin* [1976] AC 574; *Yacoob* (1981) 72 Cr App R 313. But if the defence make the contention, the standard is the balance of probabilities (*Mattey* [1995] 2 Cr App R 409).

[95] See also *Stevenson* [1971] 1 WLR 1.

[96] The distinction is well recognized and preserved in the United States. For example, Federal Rule of Evidence 901, headed 'Requirement of Authentication or Identification' provides in part: '(1) General Provision. The requirement of authentication or identification as a condition precedent to admissibility is satisfied by evidence sufficient to support a finding that the matter in question is what its proponent claims'. In other words, by a *prima facie* case.

The Court of Appeal held that the words 'proved to the satisfaction of the judge' in the section indicated that Parliament intended the civil standard of proof, on a balance of probabilities, to be applied to proof of the secondary fact of the genuineness of the writing to be used for comparison with the disputed writing. The Court professed itself ready to assume that at common law, the standard of proof in a criminal case on questions of admissibility was that beyond reasonable doubt, but found that the matter was governed by an express statutory provision in the instant case.

In *Ewing* [1983] QB 1039, however, the decision in *Angeli* was expressly disapproved by a differently constituted Court of Appeal, which held that the standard beyond reasonable doubt should have been applied to the same question. In so holding, the Court found that *Angeli* had been decided *per incuriam*, in that the *Angeli* court had not been referred to the decision of the House of Lords in *Blyth* v *Blyth* [1966] AC 643. *Blyth* v *Blyth* was concerned with the very different question of the appropriate standard of proof of a fact in issue, namely whether adultery, relied upon as a ground in a petition for divorce, had been condoned (condonation then being a bar to the grant of a decree of divorce). The relevant statutory provision also contained the word 'satisfied' in the context of condonation, and the issue was what standard this was intended to represent. The House of Lords held that, since divorce was a civil proceeding, the civil standard of proof was appropriate to the issue. This was, however, an application of the general rule of common law that the standard on a secondary issue of admissibility should be the same as that on the facts in issue. The House of Lords held that the word 'satisfied' was not intended to indicate a standard of proof (which was a matter for the common law rule) but only where the burden of proof on the issue should lie.[97]

The Court of Appeal in *Ewing*, purporting to follow or apply *Blyth*, held that the use of the word 'satisfied' in s. 8 of the Criminal Procedure Act 1865, was likewise intended to indicate only the burden of proof, and not the standard. O'Connor LJ said ([1983] 1 QB at 1046–7):

> In our judgment, the words in s. 8 [of the 1865 Act], 'any writing proved to the satisfaction of the judge to be genuine', do not say anything about the standard of proof to be used, but direct that it is the judge, and not the jury, who is to decide, and the standard of proof is governed by common law: see the passage from Lord Pearce's speech in *Blyth* v *Blyth* [1966] AC 643, 672. It follows that when the section is applied in civil cases, the civil standard of proof is used, and when it is applied in criminal cases, the criminal standard should be used. Were it otherwise, the situation created would be unacceptable, where conviction depends on proof that disputed handwriting is that of the accused person and where that proof depends on comparison of the disputed writing with samples alleged to be genuine writings of the accused; we cannot see how this case can be said to be proved beyond reasonable doubt, if the Crown only satisfy the judge, on a balance of probabilities, that the allegedly genuine samples were in fact genuine. The jury may be satisfied beyond a reasonable doubt that the crucial handwriting is by the same hand as the allegedly genuine writings, but if there is a reasonable doubt about the genuineness of such writings, then that must remain a reasonable doubt about the fact that the disputed writing was that of the accused and the case is not proved.

It is submitted that this reasoning is unconvincing. Firstly, *Blyth* v *Blyth* was concerned with a then highly contentious question as to the appropriate standard of proof of facts in issue in divorce cases, at a time when findings of matrimonial offences were thought to carry a stigma of a quasi-criminal nature. It was not concerned with the admissibility of evidence. To describe *Angeli* as having been decided '*per incuriam*' because the Court was not referred to *Blyth* is therefore at least somewhat questionable. Secondly, if the use of the word 'satisfied' in the two very different statutory provisions with which *Blyth* and *Ewing* were concerned was intended to indicate

---

[97] See the speeches of Lord Pearce at 672–3 and Lord Denning at 667. On the same point see *Re H (Minors) (Sexual Abuse: Standard of Proof)* [1996] AC 563, 586 per Lord Nicholls; per Lord Lloyd (dissenting).

only the incidence and not the standard of proof, and that the standard applicable depends on common law principles, it is arguable that both *Ewing* and *Angeli* were wrongly decided.

The question of the genuineness of the samples of handwriting used for comparison with the disputed writing is one of authenticity. Section 8 of the 1865 Act does no more than permit disputed writing to be compared with genuine writing by witnesses, and that evidence submitted to the tribunal of fact. In other words, the section provides for legal admissibility, subject to a foundation of authenticity. The legal admissibility of the writing was not in question. For the reasons set forth by Shaw J in *Robson*, the judge risks usurping the function of the jury by investigating the weight of the evidence. His function, arguably, is the same as in relation to the tape-recordings in *Robson*, namely to be satisfied that a *prima facie* case of authenticity or originality has been established, and then to leave the questions of weight to the jury to be decided by them beyond reasonable doubt. It seems that the courts have for the time being rather lost sight of the distinction between admissibility and authenticity.

4.15 THE STANDARD OF PROOF IN CIVIL CASES

The standard of proof required of any party to civil proceedings for the discharge of the legal burden of proof is proof on the balance of probabilities. This means no more than that the tribunal of fact must be able to say, on the whole of the evidence, that the case for the asserting party has been shown to be more probably true than not true. If the probabilities are equal, i.e., the tribunal of fact is wholly undecided, the party bearing the burden of proof will fail.[98]

4.15.1 Proof of criminal or quasi-criminal conduct

That this standard is clearly lower than that required of the prosecution in a criminal case has given rise to the difficult problem of defining the proper standard where allegations are made in a civil case which amount to conduct by the opponent of a criminal or quasi-criminal nature, or where the successful proof of an allegation may have quasi-criminal consequences. The proof of 'matrimonial offences', which at one time bore a quasi-criminal stigma, caused similar problems which are considered below (this section and 4.16). It now seems clear that the standard of proof where criminal or quasi-criminal conduct is alleged in a civil suit is the normal balance of probabilities.[99] Unfortunately, however, the issue has been clouded more than somewhat by the tendency of judges to stress that the more grave the allegation, the clearer should be the evidence adduced to prove it. There are *dicta* which suggest (wrongly, it is submitted) that there is some sort of sliding scale of standards of proof between the ordinary balance of probabilities, used in cases where no criminal or quasi-criminal stigma attaches to the allegations made, and some higher degree of proof (though falling short of the criminal standard) used in the cases now being considered. Moreover, it has been held in several more recent cases dealing with such matters as anti-social

---

[98] *Miller* v *Minister of Pensions* [1947] 2 All ER 372; *Rhesa Shipping Co. SA* v *Edmunds* [1985] 1 WLR 948.

[99] In the United States, a third standard of proof, defined as proof by a preponderance of the evidence, but also by clear and convincing evidence, has been adopted for use in certain cases, including commitment orders: see *Addington* v *Texas* 441 US 418 (1979). (The 'preponderance of the evidence' standard is the American formulation of the usual civil standard of proof, and for present purposes, may be assumed to be the equivalent of the 'balance of probabilities'.) The third standard solution has been discussed in a number of cases in England, though it has apparently now been firmly rejected. It should be borne in mind that in the United States, it owes its force primarily to the requirements of the 'due process' clause of the Fifth Amendment to the Constitution, which has no direct equivalent in English law, but does have a certain amount in common with the equivalent standard under the European Convention (see text below).

behaviour orders and sex offender orders, which have a direct impact on the liberty of the person against whom the order is made, that any distinction between the civil and criminal standards is essentially illusory in such cases, and that it is simpler to ask magistrates to apply the familiar criminal standard (see 4.15.2). These holdings have, if anything, confused rather than elucidated the law, and appear to be inconsistent with *dicta* in cases relating to the welfare of children (see 4.16). It may be that the overall position has at last been stated with sufficient clarity by the Court of Appeal in *R (N)* v *Mental Health Review Board (Northern Region)* [2006] QB 468. But in order to understand what was said in that case it is necessary to examine earlier pronouncements in some detail.

In *Bater* v *Bater* [1951] P 35, 37, the issue before the Court of Appeal was the proper standard of proof of a matrimonial cause, but in the course of his judgment, Denning LJ said in more general terms:

> As Best CJ and many other great judges have said, 'in proportion as the crime is enormous, so ought the proof to be clear'. So also in civil cases, the case may be proved by a preponderance of probability, but there may be degrees of probability within that standard. The degree depends on the subject-matter. A civil court, when considering a charge of fraud, will naturally require for itself a higher degree of probability than that which it would require when asking if negligence is established. It does not adopt so high a degree as a criminal court, even when it is considering a charge of a criminal nature; but still it does require a degree of probability which is commensurate with the occasion.

This passage was considered by the Court of Appeal (of which Denning LJ was a member) in *Hornal* v *Neuberger Products Ltd* [1957] 1 QB 247, an action for damages for breach of warranty and fraudulent misrepresentation. Hodson LJ pointed out that no responsible counsel or judge would make or consider any serious allegation without admitting that cogent evidence was called for to prove it. There is a necessary distinction between the balance of probabilities and the quantity and cogency of the evidence needed to tilt the balance in favour of the allegation; the latter may legitimately be held to vary with the subject-matter, while the former remains constant. In most cases, the result will be the same, whatever the mental processes involved, and as Denning LJ said in *Bater*, the difference of opinion about standard of proof may be no more than a matter of words. Nonetheless, problems can be avoided by precision of words, and it is submitted that the language of Morris LJ in *Hornal* correctly represents the position ([1957] 1 QB at 266):

> But in truth no real mischief results from an acceptance of the fact that there is some difference of approach in civil actions. Particularly is this so if the words which are used to define that approach are the servants but not the masters of meaning. Though no court and no jury would give less careful attention to issues lacking gravity than to those marked by it, the very elements of gravity become a part of the whole range of circumstances which have to be weighed in the scale when deciding as to the balance of probabilities.

The law was stated with equal clarity by Ungoed-Thomas J in *Re Dellow's Will Trusts*[100] where a wife was the general legatee under the will of her husband. They had died on the same occasion, the wife being deemed the survivor under s. 184 of the Law of Property Act 1925. The question arose whether the wife had feloniously killed the husband. The learned judge, observing that 'there can hardly be a more grave issue than that' went on to hold that he was satisfied that the allegation was

---

[100] [1964] 1 WLR 451, 454–5. And see *Post Office* v *Estuary Radio Ltd* [1968] 2 QB 740, CA (offence against Wireless Telegraphy Act 1949); *S & M Carpets (London) Ltd* v *Cornhill Insurance Co. Ltd* [1981] 1 Lloyd's Rep 667 (arson by plaintiff's manager). Cases involving disciplinary action against persons such as police officers and firemen, which, while not necessarily criminal in nature, may result in loss of employment, have occasioned great uncertainty with respect to the standard of proof. See, e.g., *Hampshire County Council, ex parte Ellerton* [1985] 1 WLR 749, per O'Connor LJ at 754 doubting the *dictum* of McNeill J in *Police Complaints Board, ex parte Madden* [1983] 1 WLR 447, 467.

proved. He said, referring to the passage cited above from the judgment of Morris LJ in *Hornal*:

> It seems to me that in civil cases it is not so much that a different standard of proof is required in different circumstances varying according to the gravity of the issue, but, as Morris LJ says, the gravity of the issue becomes part of the circumstances which the court has to take into consideration in deciding whether or not the burden of proof has been discharged. The more serious the allegation the more cogent is the evidence required to overcome the unlikelihood of what is alleged and thus to prove it.

In *R (N) v Mental Health Review Board (Northern Region)* [2006] QB 468, the Court of Appeal was called on to consider the appropriate standard of proof to be applied by the Mental Health Review Board in deciding whether it was 'satisfied' of the existence of the conditions necessary under s. 70 of the Mental Health Act 1983 to keep in place a hospital order made in respect of the applicant, and to deny his application to have the order discharged. After an exhaustive review of earlier authority, the Court held firmly that English law recognizes only two standards of proof, namely the civil standard on the balance of probabilities, and the criminal standard of proof beyond reasonable doubt. There is no third standard, such as the 'clear and convincing evidence' standard adopted in the United States in commitment cases (*Addington v Texas* 441 US 418 (1979)); nor are there any sub-categories of the two standards. But the civil standard is flexible in its application, and may call for more compelling evidence in cases involving serious allegations or serious consequences for a party, should allegations be proved against him. Addressing what had been said in earlier cases, Richards LJ said:

> Certainly there are differences in the language used and the rationalisations given over time, but the essential point that runs through the authorities is that the civil standard of proof is flexible in its application, and enables proper account to be taken of the seriousness of the allegations to be proved and of the consequences of proving them. [*Ibid.* at [59].]

After rejecting the solution of a third, intermediate, standard, Richards LJ concluded:

> Although there is a single civil standard of proof on the balance of probabilities, it is flexible in its application. In particular, the more serious the allegation or the more serious the consequences if the allegation is proved, the stronger must be the evidence before a court will find the allegation proved on the balance of probabilities. Thus, the flexibility of the standard lies not in any adjustment to the degree of probability required for the allegation to be proved (such that a more serious allegation has to be proved to a higher degree of probability) but in the strength or quality of the evidence that will in practice be required for an allegation to the proved on the balance of probabilities. [*Ibid.* at [62].]

The approach taken by the Court of Appeal in this case has the merit of unifying the approach taken in civil cases generally, but with the apparent exception of cases having specific criminal attributes (see 4.15.2), as to which the judgment shows less of a sure touch. The Court expressed itself as distinguishing *R (McCann) v Crown Court at Manchester* (text below), and apparently felt that the flexibility of the civil standard, enabling the court to require more compelling evidence in more serious cases, would be sufficient to deal even with cases such as *R (N)* itself which involve the liberty of the subject. Although there is authority, some of it pre-Human Rights Act 1998, that the civil standard is appropriate for some cases involving a deprivation of liberty other than imprisonment following conviction of a criminal offence,[101] there is now a heightened European Convention standard in cases such as commitment and forcible imposition of medical treatment.

---

[101] *Secretary of State for Home Department, ex parte Khawaja* [1984] AC 74 (detention as illegal immigrant); *Secretary of State for Home Department v Rehman* [2003] 1 AC 153 (findings of fact relevant to deportation).

This standard has been articulated as a requirement that the necessity for a course of action be 'convincingly shown' or 'reliably shown', and seems to bear some resemblance to the American 'clear and convincing evidence' standard mentioned above. Thus, if a court proposes to impose medical treatment on an incompetent mentally ill patient, it must be convincingly shown that the treatment is necessary: *R (N)* v *Dr. M* [2003] 1 WLR 562. Failure to adhere to this standard may violate the rights of the patient under art. 3 of the European Convention on Human Rights, and it is not clear that the Court's assumption in *R (N)* that a flexible civil standard meets this test (see paras [78]–[83] of the judgment) is correct.

4.15.2 Standard of proof in civil cases having criminal attributes

Certain cases in which a court is asked to make or contemplates the making of specific orders affecting the liberty of the subject, even though essentially civil in nature, have obvious attributes of criminal proceedings. Indeed, though designed and conducted as civil proceedings, they are in reality in the nature of criminal proceedings. Accordingly, they may call for a different approach to the question of the standard of proof. As in the case of civil cases in which allegations of criminal or quasi-criminal conduct are made, there is the question of the consequences of the litigation to the person against whom it is brought. But in the cases now under consideration, those consequences are more direct. The court is called upon to make an order which will seriously affect that person's liberty. In these cases, therefore, an exacting standard of proof is required, and it appears that this standard has effectively been held to be equivalent to the standard of proof required in criminal cases. This will apply in cases involving applications for sex offender orders under s. 2 of the Crime and Disorder Act 1998;[102] applications for football banning orders under s. 14(B) of the Football Spectators Act 1989;[103] and applications for anti-social behaviour orders under s. 1(1) of the Crime and Disorder Act 1998.[104] In *B* v *Chief Constable of Avon and Somerset Constabulary* [2001] 1 WLR 340, the Divisional Court considered the standard of proof to be applied on an appeal against the making of a sex offender order. The magistrates had found that B was a sex offender for the purposes of s. 2(1) of the 1998 Act and that an order was necessary to protect the public from him. Lord Bingham CJ said:

> In a serious case such as the present the difference between the two standards is, in truth, rather illusory. I have no doubt that, in deciding whether the condition in section 2(1)(a) is fulfilled, a magistrates' court should apply a civil standard of proof which will for all practical purposes be indistinguishable from the criminal standard. In deciding whether the condition in section 2(1)(b) is fulfilled, the magistrates' court should apply the civil standard with the strictness appropriate to the seriousness of the matters to be proved and the implications of proving them. [*Ibid.* at [31].]

In *R (McCann)* v *Crown Court at Manchester* [2003] 1 AC 787, the House of Lords considered the standard of proof in relation to anti-social behaviour orders. Lord Steyn said:

> Having concluded that the relevant proceedings are civil, in principle it follows that the standard of proof ordinarily applicable in civil proceedings, namely the balance of probabilities, should apply. However, I agree that, given the seriousness of matters involved, at least some reference to the heightened civil standard would usually be necessary: *In re H (Minors) (Sexual Abuse: Standard of Proof)* [1996] AC 563, 586D–H, per Lord Nicholls of Birkenhead. For essentially practical reasons, the Recorder of Manchester decided to apply the criminal standard. The Court of Appeal said that would usually be the right course to adopt. Lord Bingham of Cornhill has observed that the heightened civil standard and the

---

[102] *B* v *Chief Constable of Avon and Somerset Constabulary* [2001] 1 WLR 340, 354.
[103] *Gough* v *Chief Constable of the Derbyshire Constabulary* [2002] QB 1213.
[104] *R (McCann)* v *Crown Court at Manchester* [2003] 1 AC 787.

criminal standard are virtually indistinguishable. I do not disagree with any of these views. But in my view pragmatism dictates that the task of magistrates should be made more straightforward by ruling that they must in all cases under section 1 apply the criminal standard. [*Ibid.* at [37].]

In *Chief Constable for Merseyside* v *Harrison (Secretary of State for Home Department Intervening)* [2007] QB 79, a Divisional Court distinguished *R (McCann)* in a case involving an application for closure of premises under s. 2 of the Anti-social Behaviour Act 2003, on the grounds that such an order was not directed against the person, was limited by the Act to a relatively short period of time, and generally involved less serious consequences than an anti-social behaviour order. The Court accordingly held that it was appropriate to apply the usual civil standard of proof in such cases (see *ibid.* at [12], [22]).

It is submitted, with respect, that these authorities are not as helpful as might be wished in clarifying the law in this admittedly difficult area. If the criminal standard is appropriate in relation to the making of orders of this kind, then it would be more helpful for Parliament or the courts to say so expressly and to adopt such a rule across the board, rather than to speak of the differences between the civil and criminal standards being illusory, and encouraging the lower courts to adopt the criminal standard in some, though not all, such civil proceedings. It would not be difficult, in the light of art. 6 of the European Convention on Human Rights, to make a case for the proposition that any proceedings which threaten the liberty of the subject are criminal proceedings for the purposes of the standard of proof, whatever the procedural designation attached to them and regardless of the court in which they may be brought. This is the position in relation to contempt of court (below) and it would involve no departure of principle to apply the same principle to orders of the kind now under discussion.[105] An excellent example of the need for a clear rule, it is submitted, is the decision in *Director of Assets Recovery Agency* v *Virtosu* [2008] 3 All ER 637, in which it was held that in proceedings for the recovery of the proceeds of crime under the Proceeds of Crime Act 2002, the court must be satisfied of the facts to 'a standard commensurate with the "gravity"' of the proceedings. Section 6(7) of the Act provides for the civil standard of proof to apply in proceedings under the Act. Because confiscation proceedings are part of the sentencing process and are commenced after conviction, the defendant is no longer a person 'charged with a criminal offence' for the purposes of English criminal law or art. 6(2) of the European Convention on Human Rights. Consequently, there is no requirement for the criminal standard of proof, and it is only in an exceptional case that art. 6 is engaged.[106] But for the express provision of the Act it seems reasonable to think that the criminal standard might have been applied by the courts because of the quasi-criminal nature of the proceedings and the often drastic consequences to the accused. But it is unhelpful to suggest any gloss on the statutory standard of proof, at least without specifying with some precision what it should be.

4.15.3 Contempt of court

Contempt of court is an ancient criminal offence at common law, which is traditionally tried and punished summarily, a practice which gives rise to various procedural difficulties. There is no doubt

---

[105] This is also the clear position in the United States: see *Re Winship* 397 US 358 (1970), in which it was held that the fact that the State of New York designated proceedings taken against a minor for theft as 'delinquency proceedings' did not alter their essentially criminal nature, given that the minor stood to be deprived of his liberty if 'adjudged to be delinquent'. Consequently, the use of the criminal standard was constitutionally required in such proceedings, however they might be described, and an adjudication based on the civil standard was set aside on appeal to the US Supreme Court.

[106] See, e.g., the very unusual facts in *Geering* v *Netherlands* (2007) 46 EHRR 49. As to the application of the rules of evidence to confiscation proceedings generally, see *Silcock* [2004] 2 Cr App R (S) 323.

that contempt in all its forms is essentially a criminal proceeding, because contempt cases involve the imposition of essentially criminal sanctions, including imprisonment and fines. But confusingly, contempt is often classified under two headings as either 'civil' or 'criminal' contempt, these terms being used in this context in a specific and unusual sense.[107] 'Criminal' contempt in this sense refers to acts unlawful in themselves calculated to obstruct or pervert the administration of justice or the working of the courts. In cases of 'criminal' contempt in the face of the court, such as acts of violence or disorder, or acts of intimidation directed against jurors and witnesses, the problems arising from the traditional summary contempt procedure are now often avoided by charging the conduct in question as one or more other offences.[108] If this is done, the criminal standard of proof applies for obvious reasons. But it would seem clear that the criminal standard of proof must apply, even if they are prosecuted at common law as cases of contempt. 'Civil' contempt consists of disobedience to the order of a court, or an undertaking given to a court, and the confusion multiplies because it can be committed against courts having either criminal or civil jurisdiction. It is important to remember that, for the purposes of the standard of proof, 'civil' contempt is a criminal allegation, even in the case of disobedience to the order of a court having purely civil jurisdiction: *Re Bramblevale Ltd* [1970] Ch 128. This is the case despite the fact that for other purposes contempt takes its procedural form from the nature of the case in which it arises, so that in a civil case it is, from a procedural point of view, a civil proceeding.[109] It is submitted that, since the coming into effect of the Human Rights Act 1998, it must be the case that any person subject to any contempt proceedings, whether 'civil' or 'criminal', is entitled to the protection of the fair trial provisions of art. 6 of the European Convention on Human Rights, and that, accordingly, the criminal standard of proof should apply to all cases of contempt as to criminal cases generally.

A different rule applies to proceedings to forfeit a recognizance entered into to keep the peace or to be of good behaviour. These proceedings do not involve prosecution or sentencing for any criminal offence, and are purely civil in nature. Accordingly, the civil standard applies in such cases: *Marlow Justices, ex parte O'Sullivan* [1984] QB 381.

4.16 THE STANDARD OF PROOF IN MATRIMONIAL AND FAMILY CASES

At one time, the standard of proof in family cases was regarded as uncertain because of the stigma which then attached to the commission of the 'matrimonial offences' of adultery, cruelty and desertion. Although divorce cases are undoubtedly civil in nature, the matrimonial offences, proof of which was necessary to obtain a decree of divorce until the coming into effect of the Divorce Reform Act 1969, were thought to have a quasi-criminal character, with the result that there was some feeling in favour of applying the criminal standard of proof beyond reasonable doubt in such cases.[110] In more recent times, however, there was also considerable sentiment to the effect that the civil standard was more appropriate. In *Blyth* v *Blyth* [1966] AC 643,

---

[107] In *Attorney-General* v *Newspaper Publishing plc* [1988] Ch 333, the Court of Appeal suggested that alternative terminology be used to avoid the confusion, but the traditional terms are still in general use.

[108] For example, acts intended to intimidate witnesses or jurors with the intention of obstructing the administration of justice can be prosecuted as discrete offences under s. 51(1) of the Criminal Procedure and Investigations Act 1996. There are a variety of statutory public order offences which can be charged in respect of other conduct which disrupts the workings of the courts.

[109] Thus, the Civil Evidence Act 1968 applied to such proceedings because they are civil proceedings, despite the application of the criminal standard of proof: *Savings and Investment Bank Ltd* v *Gasco Investments (Netherlands) BV (No. 2)* [1988] Ch 422. See also *Dean* v *Dean* [1987] 1 FLR 517.

[110] See, e.g., *Preston-Jones* v *Preston-Jones* [1951] AC 391; *Bater* v *Bater* [1951] P 35; *Ginesi* v *Ginesi* [1948] P 179.

Lord Denning, in a speech with which Lord Pearce concurred, suggested that the grounds for divorce, like any other allegation made in a civil case, might be proved by the ordinary civil standard. The Court of Appeal in *Bastable* v *Bastable* [1968] 1 WLR 1684 reached the same conclusion. But the issue remained somewhat unclear until recently. In *Bastable*, Willmer LJ was driven to say (*ibid.* at 1685):

> If I may say so with all possible respect, sitting in this court I do not find it altogether easy to follow the directions contained in various statements made by members of the House of Lords.

Professor Cross observed that: 'it would be rash to essay a general statement with regard to the standard of proof in matrimonial causes'.[111] Until the decisions of the House of Lords in cases involving care proceedings in *Re H (Minors) (Sexual Abuse: Standard of Proof)* [1996] AC 563, and *Re B (Children) (Care Proceedings: Standard of Proof) CAFCASS Intervening* [2009] 1 AC 11 (dealt with below), there was a puzzling absence of a general statement of principle regarding the whole field of matrimonial and family cases. Nonetheless, it is submitted that it is now clear that the simple civil standard of proof applies, not only to care proceedings but to all family and matrimonial cases. This might perhaps have been inferred earlier from the changed nature of divorce and family proceedings since the Divorce Reform Act 1969, as a result of which the concept of the matrimonial offence disappeared, and the emphasis was redirected towards the making of proper provision for affected members of the family, and ensuring the welfare of children.

In *Re H (Minors) (Sexual Abuse: Standard of Proof)* [1996] AC 563, a local authority applied for a care order in respect of a girl who had alleged that her stepfather had abused her sexually over a considerable period of time. The stepfather had been charged with raping the girl, but had been acquitted at his trial. Pursuant to s. 31(2) of the Children Act 1989, the court had power to make a care order if it was 'satisfied' that the child was 'likely to suffer significant harm'. The issue arose whether, despite the fact that the stepfather had been acquitted, the evidence justified the making of a care order under the terms of this subsection. This issue, in turn, raised the question of the appropriate standard of proof in such a case. The majority of the House of Lords held that the standard of proof should be the ordinary civil standard, but subject to the observation that, the more serious or improbable the allegation of abuse, the stronger should be the evidence adduced to support it. The House referred to a number of earlier decisions in which it had been suggested that a higher standard of proof (albeit falling short of proof beyond reasonable doubt) should be adopted in cases involving alleged child abuse,[112] and held specifically that those suggestions were incorrect. But the House evidently considered itself to be building on the foundation laid down in *Hornal* v *Neuberger Products Ltd* and *Re Dellow's Will Trusts*. Lord Nicholls said ([1996] AC 563 at 586):

> Where the matters in issue are facts the standard of proof required in non-criminal proceedings is the preponderance of probability, usually referred to as the balance of probability. This is the established general principle. There are exceptions such as contempt of court applications, but I can see no reason for thinking that family proceedings are, or should be, an exception.... Despite their special features, family

---

[111] *Evidence*, 4th edn, p. 103. In the 5th edn of his work, however, Cross seemed clearly to prefer the civil standard (*ibid.* at 118) though he continued to regard the law as unsettled.

[112] *Re W (Minors) (Sexual Abuse: Standard of Proof)* [1994] 1 FLR 419 at 429; *Re G (A Minor) (Child Abuse: Standard of Proof)* [1987] 1 WLR 1461, 1466. But see also, *per contra*: *H* v *H (Minors) (Child Abuse: Evidence)* [1990] Fam 86, 94; *Re M (A Minor) (Appeal) (No. 2)* [1994] 1 FLR 59 at 67. Some older pronouncements in favour of a higher standard were made in wardship proceedings, before the enactment of the Children Act 1989, and it seems clear that the House in *Re H (Minors) (Sexual Abuse: Standard of Proof)* was not inclined to regard such pronouncements as in any way definitive.

proceedings remain essentially a form of civil proceedings. Family proceedings often raise very serious issues, but so do other forms of civil proceedings.

The balance of probability standard means that a court is satisfied an event occurred if the court considers that, on the evidence, the occurrence of the event was more likely than not. When assessing the probabilities the court will have in mind as a factor, to whatever extent is appropriate in the particular case, that the more serious the allegation, the less likely it is that the event occurred and, hence, the stronger should be the evidence before the court concludes that the allegation is established on the balance of probability. Fraud is usually less likely than negligence. Deliberate physical injury is usually less likely than accidental physical injury. A stepfather is usually less likely to have repeatedly raped and had non-consensual oral sex with his under age stepdaughter than on some occasion to have lost his temper and slapped her. Built into the preponderance of probability standard is a generous degree of flexibility in respect of the seriousness of the allegation.

Although the result is much the same, this does not mean that where a serious allegation is in issue the standard of proof is higher. It means only that the inherent probability or improbability of an event is itself a matter to be taken into account when weighing the probabilities and deciding whether, on balance, the event occurred. The more improbable the event, the stronger must be the evidence that it did occur before, on the balance of probability, its occurrence will be established.

In the course of argument before the House, all counsel agreed that the formulation proposed by Lord Nicholls was correct. Nonetheless, Lord Lloyd of Berwick dissented on this point, holding that the civil standard should be applied to care cases without any gloss whatsoever. He said (*ibid.* at 577–8):

In my view the standard of proof under that subsection ought to be the simple balance of probability however serious the allegations involved. I have reached that view for a number of reasons, but mainly because s. 31(2) provides only the threshold criteria for making a care order. It by no means follows that an order will be made even if the threshold criteria are satisfied. The court must then go on to consider the statutory checklist in s. 1(3) of the Act. But if the threshold criteria are not met, the local authority can do nothing, however grave the anticipated injury to the child, or however serious the apprehended consequences. This seems to me to be a strong argument in favour of making the threshold lower rather than higher. It would be a bizarre result if the more serious the anticipated injury, whether physical or sexual, the more difficult it became for the local authority to satisfy the initial burden of proof.…

Another indirect pointer may be found in s. 26 of the Family Law Reform Act 1969. At common law the presumption of legitimacy could only be rebutted by proof beyond reasonable doubt…By s. 26 of the Act of 1969 the presumption can now be rebutted on a simple balance of probabilities. Although in *Serio v Serio* (1983) 4 FLR 756 at 763, the Court of Appeal held that the standard of proof should be 'commensurate with the seriousness of the issue involved' (in other words, that it might require more than a mere balance of probabilities), this seems to read words into the statute which are not there. If the legislature has ordained that the presumption of legitimacy can be rebutted on a simple balance of probabilities, I have no great difficulty in concluding that s. 31(2) requires a simple balance of probabilities, and no more, even when there is a serious allegation of sexual abuse.

Nothing in Lord Lloyd's speech indicates that his Lordship would necessarily have rejected the idea of a requirement of clear and convincing evidence in all cases. Indeed, his dissent seems to be based specifically on the application of the principle to the precise issue raised by s. 31(2) of the Children Act, 1989.[113] The majority of the House appear to agree in principle with earlier *dicta*, to the effect that such a requirement does not vary the standard of proof as such, but rather gives guidance as to how the court is to approach the question of whether the standard has been met in the circumstances of any particular case.

---

[113] On this specific issue, see also the later decision of the Court of Appeal in *In re U (A Child); In re B (A Child)* [2005] Fam 134, discussed at 4.16.

The issue of the standard of proof in care proceedings arose again before Bodey J in *In re ET (Serious Injuries: Standard of Proof) (Note)* [2003] 2 FLR 1205. The learned judge held, in the light of authorities subsequent to *Re H*,[114] that the *dictum* of Lord Bingham of Cornhill CJ in *B v Chief Constable of Avon and Somerset Constabulary* [2001] 1 WLR 340, [31], to the effect that the distinction between the civil and criminal standards of proof was now largely 'illusory', applied also in relation to care proceedings. But in *In re U (a Child); In re B (A Child)* [2005] Fam 134, the Court of Appeal rejected this position. Dame Elizabeth Butler-Sloss P said:

> We understand that in many applications for care orders counsel are now submitting that the correct approach to the standard of proof is to treat the distinction between criminal and civil standards as "largely illusory". In our judgment this approach is mistaken. The standard of proof to be applied in Children Act 1989 cases is the balance of probabilities and the approach to these difficult cases was laid down by Lord Nicholls in *In Re H (Minors) (Sexual Abuse: Standard of Proof)* [1996] AC 563. That case has not been varied nor adjusted by the dicta of Lord Bingham of Cornhill CJ or Lord Steyn who were considering applications made under a different statute. There would appear to be no good reason to leap across a division, on the one hand, between crime and preventative measures taken to restrain defendants for the benefit of the community and, on the other hand, wholly different considerations of child protection and welfare nor to apply the reasoning of *McCann's* case [2003] 1 AC 787 to public, or indeed private, law cases concerning children. The strict rules of evidence applicable in a criminal trial which is adversarial in nature is to be contrasted with the partly inquisitorial approach of the court dealing with children cases in which the rules of evidence are considerably relaxed.[115] In our judgment, therefore, Bodey J applied too high a standard of proof in *In Re ET* [2003] 2 FLR 1205, and the principles set out by Lord Nicholls should continue to be followed by the judiciary trying family cases and by magistrates sitting in the family proceedings courts. [*Ibid.* at [13].]

The issue of the standard of proof came before the House of Lords yet again in *In re B (Children) (Care Proceedings: Standard of Proof) CARCASS Intervening* [2009] 1 AC 11. Baroness Hale of Richmond emphasized that the appropriate standard is the simple balance of probabilities. She dealt with the points made in H about the probability of serious acts such as sexual assaults against children occurring as a matter of 'inherent probability' rather than a ground for altering the standard of proof. Such matters should be considered together with other relevant factors in deciding where the truth lies, but do not indicate any need to abandon the usual standard of proof, and are not indicative of a sliding scale. Approving the observations of Dame Elizabeth Butler-Sloss in *U* (above) and rejecting any suggestion that care proceedings required the criminal standard of proof, Baroness Hale said (at [70]):

> My Lords...I would...announce loud and clear that the standard of proof in finding the facts necessary to establish the threshold under s.31(2) or the welfare considerations in s.1 of the 1989 Act is the simple balance of probabilities, neither more nor less. Neither the seriousness of the allegations nor the seriousness of the consequences should make any difference to the standard of proof to be applied in determining the facts. The inherent probabilities are simply something to be taken into account where relevant, in deciding where the truth lies.[116]

[114] In particular *B v Chief Constable of Avon and Somerset Constabulary* [2001] 1 WLR 340 and *R (McCann) v Crown Court at Manchester* [2003] 1 AC 787 (see 4.15.2).

[115] With respect, it is difficult to see what this has to do with preferring one standard of proof to another. The rules of evidence are relaxed in civil cases generally as compared with criminal cases, as witness the admission of hearsay evidence (see 8.30 *et seq.*) and the contemporary flexible judicial control of evidence in civil proceedings (see 3.6), but the difference between the standards of proof is not an illustration of that fact, and indeed pre-dates it by more than 200 years.

[116] The other members of the House agreed with Baroness Hale. Lord Hoffmann specifically endorsed her views on the 'inherent probabilities': *ibid.* at [5].

It is submitted that this decision may finally have settled the vexed question of the standard of proof in family and matrimonial cases generally. Although the precise question in *B* was the narrow one of the standard of proof in proceedings under s. 31(2) of the Children Act 1989, if the civil standard applies to cases in which the court has a statutory duty to safeguard the welfare of children, and to consider the making of care orders, it is difficult to envisage any kind of family proceeding which would call for any higher standard.[117]

4.17 RECOMMENDED FURTHER READING

Ashworth, A., 'Four threats to the presumption of innocence' (2005) **10**(4) *International Journal of Evidence and Proof* 241.

Ashworth, A. and Blake, M., 'The presumption of innocence in English criminal law' [1996] *Criminal Law Review* 306.

Glover, R., 'Regulatory offences and reverse burdens: the "Licensing Approach"' (2007) **71**(3) *Journal of Criminal Law* 259.

Glover, R., 'Codifying the law on evidential burdens' (2008) **72**(4) *Journal of Criminal Law* 305.

Morgan, E.M. and Maguire, J.M., 'Looking backward and forward at evidence' (1937) **50** *Harvard Law Review* 909.

Pattenden, R., 'The proof rules of pre-verdict judicial fact-finding in criminal trials by jury' (2009) **125** *Law Quarterly Review* 79.

Redmayne, M., 'Appeals to reason' (2002) **65** *Modern Law Review* 19.

Smith, J.C., 'The presumption of innocence' (1987) **38** *Northern Ireland Legal Quarterly* 223.

Williams, G., 'The logic of exceptions' (1988) *Cambridge Law Journal* 261.

Zuckerman, A.A.S., 'No third exception to the Woolmington Rule' (1987) **103** *Law Quarterly Review* 170.

Zuckerman, A.A.S., 'The third exception to the Woolmington Rule' (1976) **92** *Law Quarterly Review* 402.

 ## 4.18 QUESTIONS FOR DISCUSSION BASED ON *R* v *COKE; LITTLETON* AND *BLACKSTONE* v *COKE* (for case files go to the Online Resource Centre)

4.18.1 *Coke; Littleton*

1. Where does the legal burden of proof lie on the issue of guilt or innocence?

2. What is the standard of proof required on that issue?

3. Are there any issues in the case as to which either Coke or Littleton bears any legal burden of proof?

4. Are there any issues in the case as to which Coke or Littleton bears any evidential burden?

5. What must the prosecution do in order to establish a *prima facie* case as to the charges against Coke and Littleton respectively? What effect would this have on the further conduct of the defence by each accused?

---

[117] As indicated by Lord Lloyd, dissenting, in *Re H* (quoted at 4.15) and in earlier editions of this work, the provision of s. 26 of the Family Law Reform Act 1969, permitting the presumption of legitimacy to be rebutted on the simple balance of probability, may also be taken as an indication that the tide has turned against any higher standard of proof.

6. Discuss the burden and standard of proof as to any secondary facts bearing upon the admissibility of exhibits GGI and GG4 and the related evidence of Mr Hale.

4.18.2 *Blackstone* v *Coke*

1. Review the statements of case. On what facts in issue do Margaret Blackstone and Coke respectively bear a legal burden of proof?

2. At the outset of the case, who bears the evidential burden of proof as to the underlying evidential facts? How may this change as the case proceeds?

3. Margaret wishes to introduce into evidence the letter written to Coke by his solicitors dated 20 February Yr—0. Coke wishes to exclude this evidence, on the ground that it is a privileged communication. Who bears the burden of proof?

4. Assume that Coke was never charged with an offence against Margaret Blackstone, but that Margaret has brought the present action in the same form, but omitting para. 3 of the particulars of claim. What standard of proof would be required of her in proving her claim?

4.19 GENERAL QUESTIONS FOR DISCUSSION

1. How may the legal burden be distinguished from the evidential burden?

2. How are both burdens discharged?

3. In a criminal case, which party will normally bear the legal burden and why?

4. What is a 'reverse burden'?

5. Does the accused bear the legal burden for non-insane automatism?

6. What was the significance of the decisions in *Edwards* and *Hunt*?

7. What has been the impact of art. 6 of the European Convention on Human Rights on the law relating to burdens of proof?

8. What does it mean to 'read down' a provision?

9. In a civil case, which party bears the burden of proof?

10. If an accused bears an evidential burden, do they discharge it on the balance of probabilities?

11. As in criminal cases there is, technically, not a strict formula for the standard of proof, will it suffice for a judge to direct a jury that they must be 'pretty certain'? What about 'reasonably sure'?

12. Can there be any flexibility in the standard of proof in civil cases?

5

CHARACTER EVIDENCE I: CHARACTER EVIDENCE GENERALLY; IN CIVIL CASES; EVIDENCE OF GOOD CHARACTER

A   USES AND DEVELOPMENT OF CHARACTER EVIDENCE

SUMMARY OF MAIN POINTS

- Character is difficult to define for the purposes of the law of evidence. At common law, evidence of character meant evidence of reputation.

- But with the enactment of the Criminal Evidence Act 1898 the accused's previous convictions and character more generally came into play. The Act rendered the accused a competent witness in his defence and provided him with a shield against cross-examination as to character. The shield could be lost in certain cases.

- At common law there was a separate rule that evidence suggesting some aspect of bad character could be admitted despite that fact, if it was relevant to show guilt of the offence charged, for example to show the identity of the offender, or his intent, or to rebut a defence such as mistake, accident, or innocent association, which might otherwise be open to the accused.

- The relevance of evidence of bad character continues to be problematic and ultimately depends on an abiding faith in recidivism.

- The Criminal Justice Act 2003 replaces the common law rules on bad character with a self-contained code. The Act introduces a definition of 'bad character'. It does not affect evidence of good character, and does not affect the position in civil cases.

5.1 INTRODUCTION

Character evidence is one of the most difficult and controversial areas of the law of evidence. It is primarily of importance in criminal cases. Its application to civil cases is relatively unusual and limited. The law in civil cases remains unaffected by statute and is, therefore, still a creature of common law. It will be considered briefly in this chapter: see 5.3. The application of character evidence to criminal cases, on the other hand, is commonplace, complex, and often decisive of the outcome of a case. In the light of the radical re-structuring of the law by the Criminal Justice Act 2003, separate rules apply to evidence of good character and evidence of bad character. The former is unaffected by the Act and continues to be governed by common law rules. It is dealt with in this chapter, 5.7 *et seq.* The latter is now governed entirely by statute, and occupies the entirety of Chapter 6. The bad character provisions of the Act came into force on 15 December 2004. For the common law and statutory provisions governing character evidence before the 2003 Act, reference should be made to Chapters 5 and 6 of the 8th edition of this work.

As long as there have been criminal trials, the character of the accused has been a significant consideration, whether the accused has in his life to date chosen to model himself on St Francis of Assisi, on Fagin, or on someone with more moderate characteristics. If the accused is a person of previous good character, is that fact to be taken into consideration in his favour on the issue of guilt or innocence, and if so, in what way and to what extent? If he is a person of previous bad character, what use, if any, may the prosecution make of that fact to suggest guilt of the offence now charged?[1] These questions raise fundamental issues both of relevance and admissibility. A separate question, though the boundaries which separate it are still not entirely clear, despite recent developments in the law, is what effect good or bad character has on the credibility of a witness (whether the accused or any other witness) in relation to evidence given by that witness on oath at a trial. This question is of considerable importance in its own right, but if the accused is the witness in question, also has an obvious, albeit less direct effect on the ultimate issue of guilt or innocence.

Any consideration of these issues must begin with the question of what exactly is meant by the word 'character'. This is by no means an easy question. It is clear that character is properly classified as either 'good' or 'bad', but of what does it consist? The answer to that question provided

---

[1] Character, good or bad, is also of great importance in relation to sentencing, if guilt is established, but because its relevance and admissibility for this purpose is uncontroversial, it does not generally present difficulties from the point of view of the law of evidence.

by the common law sounds, in contemporary terms, rather idiosynchratic. At common law, a person's character consisted of his reputation in his community and of nothing else, though the law on this point was probably not finally settled until the landmark case of *Rowton* (1865) Le & Ca 510, and even then with significant dissent. *Rowton* and its present-day application are considered in more detail at 5.7. Reputation consists essentially of the accumulation of hearsay evidence about what a person's character is generally believed to be, but not necessarily what it actually is.[2] It may be based on ephemeral and subjective opinions, on rumour and conjecture, and may be coloured by all manner of prejudice. Today, we would probably regard barometers of a person's actual character, as opposed to his reputed character, for example evidence of his known disposition to behave in certain ways, or evidence of previous convictions of criminal offences, as more reliable forms of character evidence. But at the time of the decision in *Rowton*, there were compelling justifications for the apparently restrictive and anachronistic position it espoused. At that time, the accused was still not a competent witness in his own defence.[3] If he wished to adduce positive evidence of his good character, he could do so only by calling character witnesses. There were few, if any, reliable records of past conduct. On the other hand, it was a time of limited social mobility. People tended to live their whole lives in the same community, or at least within a relatively limited geographical area. The accumulated opinions of people who had known the accused all his life, expressed on their behalf by one of them, was not an unreasonable basis for forming a judgment as to character, and the fact that it was an accumulation of multiple individual opinions at least reduced the risk of prejudiced and subjective views of the accused to some extent. It might validly be viewed as more reliable than speculative or half-remembered evidence of past events in the accused's life, and as less likely to be biased than the individual opinion of the witness, and accordingly *Rowton* excluded these forms of evidence in favour of evidence of reputation as primary evidence of character.[4] Because the judges allowed the accused to adduce evidence of his character, but did not permit the prosecutor to do so except to rebut evidence adduced by the accused (a concession to the enormous procedural disadvantages from which the accused suffered at that time: see 1.5.3) any prejudice arising from the introduction of reputation evidence was likely to enure more to the benefit than to the detriment of the accused.

But within a comparatively short time after the decision in *Rowton* the legal landscape began to change to such an extent that the understanding of the term 'character' was bound to change with it. Increased social mobility and the availability of increasingly reliable records weakened the cogency of the view that reputation was the most reliable form of character evidence. The Criminal Evidence Act 1898 changed the picture overnight. The Act made the accused a competent (though not compellable) witness in his own defence for the first time. This radical change in criminal procedure necessitated some provision to deal with the extent, if any, to which an accused who gave evidence could be cross-examined about his character, whether or not he adduced evidence of it either by calling character witnesses or by the newly available resource of giving evidence about it himself. As amended by later legislation s. 1(2) and (3) of the Act

---

[2] And accordingly requires some relaxation of the rule against hearsay in order to be admissible: see Criminal Justice Act 2003, s. 118(1).

[3] The accused was first rendered competent as a witness by the Criminal Evidence Act 1898, a development which, as we shall see, caused the law of character evidence to undergo radical changes.

[4] However, other matters could be referred to for the purpose of rebutting evidence of character adduced on behalf of the accused. For example, a character witness might be asked whether he was aware of discreditable acts committed by the accused which might reasonably be expected to affect his reputation adversely, including, it seems, other offences commonly attributed to the accused: *Wood* (1841) 5 Jur 225.

provided a complete code, the intent of which was to provide the accused with a limited 'shield' against such cross-examination.

1 ...(2) A person charged in criminal proceedings who is called as a witness in the proceedings may be asked any question in cross-examination notwithstanding that it would tend to criminate him as to any offence with which he is charged in the proceedings.

(3) A person charged in criminal proceedings who is called as a witness in the proceedings shall not be asked, and if asked shall not be required to answer, any question tending to show that he has committed or been convicted of or been charged with any offence other than one with which he is then charged, or is of bad character, unless—

(i) the proof that he has committed or been convicted of such other offences is admissible evidence to show that he is guilty of the offence with which he is then charged; or

(ii) he has personally or by his advocate asked questions of the witnesses for the prosecution with a view to establish his own good character, or the nature or conduct of the defence is such as to involve imputations on the character of the prosecutor or the witnesses for the prosecution or the deceased victim of the alleged crime;[5] or

(iii) he has given evidence against any other person charged in the same proceedings.[6]

The effect of this provision was that, although the accused could be cross-examined freely to show his guilt of any offence charged, he was given a shield against cross-examination about any other offences and about his character, and that shield could be taken away only in the circumstances specified in subsection (3).[7] As might be expected, a considerable jurisprudence developed around the loss of the shield, as to which see the 8th edition of this work, 5.15 *et seq.* Section 1(3) of the 1898 Act was repealed by the Criminal Justice Act 2003, but its effect in expanding the ambit of character evidence has proved to be permanent and the 2003 Act takes for granted the scope of the 1898 Act in that respect. Section 1(3) of the 1898 Act changed and expanded the concept of 'character'. The section was unambiguous in treating previous criminal offences and convictions as a subject of character evidence in their own right, distinct from evidence of 'character' in the *Rowton* sense, and in rendering them a proper subject of cross-examination in cases in which the shield was lost. There was a certain amount of judicial discontent about the fact that the meaning and extent of character evidence differed as between the common law position, which continued to govern the concept of character for general purposes including evidence adduced by the accused to prove his character, and the statutory regime which governed the subject of cross-examination of the accused in cases in which he elected

---

[5] The provision about imputations against the deceased victim did not appear in the section as originally enacted, but was added by s. 31 of the Criminal Justice and Public Order Act 1994, in the light of the fact that such imputations are not an uncommon line of defence. For an unsuccessful attempt to create a judicial solution to the problem see *Biggin* [1920] KB 313.

[6] The phrase 'in the same proceedings' was substituted for the less satisfactory original 'with the same offence' by the Criminal Evidence Act 1979. As to the problems caused by the original wording, see *Hills* [1980] AC 26; *Rockman* (1977) 67 Cr App R 171.

[7] The Act provided a complete code with respect to cross-examination of the accused. The court had no common law power or discretion to permit cross-examination about character in circumstances not covered by the Act: *Weekes* (1983) 77 Cr App R 207. But the judge's discretion to exclude evidence, both at common law and under s. 78 of the Police and Criminal Evidence Act 1984, applied to cross-examination permitted under the Act, and accordingly the judge was entitled to exclude or limit such cross-examination, even where legally permitted, in the interests of ensuring the fairness of the trial: *Noor Mohamed* v R [1949] AC 182; *Selvey* v *DPP* [1970] AC 304; *Watts* [1983] 3 All ER 101; *Britzman* [1983] 1 WLR 350. As to the exercise of discretion generally see 3.7 *et seq.*; 6.20.

to give evidence.[8] But the transition was a sensible and probably necessary one. It is not really possible to cross-examine an accused about his character using only the language of reputation. Effective cross-examination demands that the cross-examiner be free to explore specific acts, including previous convictions. Section 99(1) of the Criminal Justice Act 2003 also abolished the common law rules relating to evidence of bad character, and abrogated any difference between evidence of bad character adduced in cross-examination of the accused and evidence of bad character adduced in other ways, but the Act has no application to evidence of good character, and it is of interest that ss. 99(2) and 118(1) preserve evidence of reputation as a method of proving bad character.

By definition, the provisions of the Criminal Evidence Act 1898 applied only where the accused elected to give evidence, and thereby became liable to cross-examination.[9] But a more or less contemporaneous development in the common law also gradually compelled a broader approach to the concept of character evidence. Implicit in the discussion of the meaning of 'character' up to this point is the idea that a person's previous good or bad character is relevant to the issue of guilt or innocence in the sense that a person of previous good character is assumed to be less likely to have committed any particular offence, while a person of previous bad character is assumed to be more likely to have done so. Under this reasoning, often described as conformity reasoning, i.e., a person can be taken to act in conformity with his known past character, the possession of a certain character is taken to be directly relevant to the issue of guilt or innocence. With respect to this form of reasoning, the common law took an approach which can only be described as fair but illogical. While it permitted the accused to adduce evidence of his good character for the purpose of suggesting that he was not guilty of the offence charged, it did not permit the prosecution to adduce, as part of its own case, evidence of bad character for the purpose of suggesting guilt. On the other hand, if evidence against the accused was relevant to the issue of guilt for other reasons, the fact that it also suggested that he was to some extent of previous bad character would not prevent the evidence from being admitted. This principle applied to any relevant prosecution evidence, and therefore did not depend in any way on whether the accused elected to give evidence and so became available for cross-examination under the Criminal Evidence Act 1898, though it was obviously complemented by s. 1(2) of the Act in cases in which the accused did give evidence. The distinction between mere bad character evidence (inadmissible) and relevant evidence which might also suggest bad character (admissible) gave rise to another important body of jurisprudence, which is likely to continue to be of some importance even under the new statutory rules introduced by the Criminal Justice Act 2003, the language of which clearly owes much to the principles formulated by the courts under the common law rule. (The common law rule as to good character, which is unaffected by the Act, survives, as we shall see later in this chapter.)

The classic statement of this principle of admissibility was that of Lord Herschell in *Makin* v *Attorney-General for New South Wales* [1894] AC 57 at 68:

> It is undoubtedly not competent for the prosecution to adduce evidence tending to show that the accused has been guilty of criminal acts other than those covered by the indictment, for the purpose of leading to the conclusion that the accused is a person likely from his criminal conduct or character

---

[8] See, e.g., *Jones* v *DPP* [1962] AC 635, 699 *et seq.* per Lord Devlin; *Dunkley* [1927] 1 KB 323.

[9] The 1898 Act operated only to permit cross-examination of the accused, which was possible only if he elected to give evidence. It did not entitle the prosecution to adduce evidence of bad character if he did not do so, even in cases in which the shield would have been forfeited, for example where the nature or conduct of the defence involved imputations on the character of prosecution witnesses: *Butterwasser* [1948] 1 KB 1; *De Vere* [1982] QB 75.

to have committed the offence for which he is being tried. On the other hand, the mere fact that the evidence adduced tends to show the commission of other crimes does not render it inadmissible if it be relevant to an issue before the jury, and it may be so relevant if it bears upon the question whether the acts alleged to constitute the crime charged in the indictment were designed or accidental, or to rebut a defence which would otherwise be open to the accused.[10]

Lord Herschell's *dictum* permitted the admissibility of prosecution evidence in a number of factual contexts, which created the appearance of a number of discrete evidential rules, such as the rule permitting the admissibility of 'similar fact evidence', i.e., evidence said to be relevant because of a striking similarity between the crime charged and other uncharged crimes or acts committed by the accused, including those in respect of which he was convicted in other cases. But in reality, and as eventually made clear by the House of Lords in *DPP v P* [1991] 2 AC 447, these rules were no more than examples of the principle of relevance on which Lord Herschell's statement depended. In *P*, Lord Mackay of Clashfern LC said (*ibid.* at 460):

> From all that was said by the House in [*Boardman v DPP* [1975] AC 421] I would deduce the essential feature of evidence which is to be admitted is that its probative force in support of the allegation that an accused person committed a crime is sufficiently great to make it just to admit the evidence, notwithstanding that it is prejudicial to the accused in tending to show that he was guilty of another crime. Such probative force may be derived from striking similarities in the evidence about the manner in which the crime was committed and the authorities provide illustrations of that... But restricting the circumstances in which there is sufficient probative force to overcome prejudice of evidence relating to another crime to cases in which there is some striking similarity between them is to restrict the operation of the principle in a way which gives too much effect to a particular manner of stating it, and is not justified in principle.[11]

Thus, in addition to similar fact evidence, prosecution evidence might be relevant to guilt because it suggested a relevant disposition on the part of the accused to behave in a certain way;[12] or because it was linked to the offence charged by time or circumstances;[13] or because it tended to rebut a defence such as accident, mistake, innocent association, or lack of intent, which might otherwise be available to the accused;[14] or simply because it was relevant background evidence.[15] Although such evidence suggests bad character, it is not really evidence of bad character. It is evidence which suggests that the accused committed the offence charged, as opposed to suggesting that he is the kind of person who might. We shall have occasion to return to each of these examples in discussing the common law rules on good character and the statutory régime on bad character under the Criminal Justice Act 2003, because they are frequently recurring fact patterns in criminal cases and will inevitably arise in connection with the statutory rules.

---

[10] More recent and equally clear expressions of the rule include those of Lord Hailsham in *DPP v Boardman* [1975] AC 421, 449 *et seq.*; and Neill LJ in *Lunt* (1986) 85 Cr App R 241; cf. American Federal Rule of Evidence 404(b): 'Other crimes, wrongs or acts. Evidence of other crimes, wrongs or acts is not admissible to prove the character of a person in order to show action in conformity therewith. It may, however be admissible for other purposes, such as proof of motive, opportunity, intent, preparation, plan, knowledge, identity, or absence of mistake or accident...'

[11] As the use of the word 'prejudice' suggests, the trial judge was always entitled to exclude such evidence in the exercise of his discretion either at common law or under s. 78 of the Police and Criminal Evidence Act 1984: *Noor Mohamed v R* [1949] AC 182; as to the discretion generally, see 3.7.

[12] *DPP v Boardman* [1975] AC 421; cf. *Thompson v R* [1918] AC 221.

[13] *Bond* [1906] 2 KB 389; *Giannetto* [1997] 1 Cr App R 1.

[14] *Harris v DPP* [1952] AC 694; cf. *Sims* [1946] 1 KB 531.

[15] *M* [2000] 1 WLR 421.

The Criminal Justice Act 2003 provides the first ever statutory definition, albeit a partial definition, of 'character'. Section 98 defines the term 'bad character' as follows:

> References in this Chapter to evidence of a person's 'bad character' are to evidence of, or a disposition
> towards, misconduct on his part, other than evidence which—
>   (a) has to do with the alleged facts of the offence with which the defendant is charged, or
>   (b) is evidence of misconduct in connection with the investigation or prosecution of that
>   offence.

Section 112 defines 'misconduct' as 'the commission of an offence or other reprehensible behaviour'. This definition, clearly a broad one going far beyond previous convictions, is considered
further in Chapter 6, 6.3. The Act does not apply to, and does not attempt to define good character. It would seem that bad character can be proved by evidence of specific acts committed by
the person in question, including but not limited to previous convictions, and (presumably in
the case of evidence of disposition) by evidence of reputation, which is specifically preserved as
a method of proof of bad character by ss. 99(2) and 118(1) of the Act. As we shall see in chapter 6, the Act provides for the first time a complete statutory code for the admission of evidence
of bad character in criminal cases, whether it be the bad character of the accused or others such
as witnesses.

5.2 RELEVANCE OF EVIDENCE OF CHARACTER

It is a basic and legitimate question whether evidence of a person's character is relevant to that
person's guilt of an offence now charged against him, or to his credibility as a witness in a case
in which he is now giving evidence. The rules of admissibility have made the assumption that
character evidence is relevant in principle. The Law Commission, broadly speaking, adopted that
view in its Report (*Evidence of Bad Character in Criminal Proceedings* (Law Com No. 273, 2001)), as
has Parliament in the Criminal Justice Act 2003. Thus, no more than a very short description of
the relevance issue is warranted here.[16] But it is of some interest to note the logical foundations
on which the claim of general relevance rests.

   The suggestion that the bad character of a person, including his previous convictions, is relevant to the issue of whether he is guilty of an offence now charged, rests on an abiding faith in
recidivism. Specifically, it rests on the generalization[17] that persons who have previous convictions, or are of bad reputation, are likely or at least more likely than others to commit crimes,
and that such 'bad' persons cannot or do not generally reform their behaviour. The converse
suggestion that persons of previous good character are unlikely or less likely to commit crimes
rests on the opposite generalization that 'good' persons do not generally commit crimes, which
flies in the face of the fact that all offenders commit first offences. The suggestion that persons
of previous bad character, or of bad reputation, are likely or more likely to lie when giving evidence, whereas persons of good character are more likely to tell the truth, similarly rests on the
generalizations that people are either 'good' or 'bad' as defined by their previous character, and do
not reform their behaviour. In essence, this reasoning assumes that society is neatly divided into
classes of 'good' and 'bad' people, an idea which seems more appropriate to the nineteenth century than the twenty-first. Among its defects are that (a) it fails to distinguish between different

---

[16] For a detailed criticism of the law on relevance grounds, see M. Redmayne [2002] CLJ 684; P. Murphy
(1998) 2 E & P 71.
[17] For the meaning of the term 'generalization' and its use in judicial reasoning, see 1.4.

kinds of crime, assuming, e.g., that a previous conviction for shoplifting renders a person more likely to be guilty of a present sexual assault; (b) it fails to recognize that current personal circumstances are at least as likely to be involved in the commission of a crime as the possession of a previous bad character; and (c) it fails to take into account current interests, assuming, e.g., that a person with a conviction for assault in a pub brawl which occurred five years ago is likely to lie when called as a prosecution witness in a fraud case in which he has no personal interest. These generalizations may be described generically as assumptions that a person will act 'in conformity with' his previous character.

The common law rules of admissibility avoided the worst instances of such outdated generalizations, and did not permit the use of evidence of bad character solely to prove that a person acted in conformity with his previous character. The modern trend was towards a more factual form of relevance, i.e., towards evidence which suggests that the accused is the person who committed the offence charged, rather than evidence which suggests that he is the kind of person who might. There is obviously a more solid foundation for relevance where the previous convictions are strikingly similar to acts with which the accused is now charged, or constitute what may properly be called serial crime, or where the prosecution witness's previous conviction is for perjury. In these cases the logic connects the previous acts more directly to those now charged, and the issue is not so much one of character evidence as one of a direct probative link between the previous acts and the acts now charged. As we have seen, at least since the *dictum* of Lord Herschell in *Makin* v *Attorney-General for New South Wales* [1894] AC 57 (see 5.1 above) this kind of distinction between factual relevance and conformity relevance was well understood and insisted on. There is reason to fear, however, that under the regime of the Criminal Justice Act 2003, the scrupulous distinctions as to relevance recognized by the courts in dealing with the common law rules of admissibility and with cross-examination under the Criminal Evidence Act 1898 may be regarded as less significant, if not ignored altogether. As we shall see in Chapter 6, the language of the 2003 Act does not always make the relevance of evidence of bad character clear. By cloaking the rules of admissibility in such phrases as 'important explanatory evidence' (s. 100(1)(a); s. 101(1)(c)) and 'important matter in issue' (s. 100(1)(b); s. 101(1)(d) and (e)) Parliament has rendered the niceties of the use the jury may be expected to make of the evidence obscure and imprecise, and there is a dangerous potential for conformity relevance to play a role one would have hoped to see eliminated from the law by now. The common law would not 'give a dog a bad name and hang it'.[18] The Act may have this effect. If so, it will not be accidental. In the Report referred to above, the Law Commission gave Parliament ample warning of the potential consequences of allowing the indiscriminate admission of evidence of bad character, and advocated a number of safeguards. The warnings were for the most part ignored and the safeguards for the most part rejected. It is to be hoped that judges will be scrupulous in identifying the important issues to which evidence of bad character is said to be directed, and in directing juries to evaluate it fairly. The realities of criminal practice should not be overlooked. Many of the persons who serve on juries and even some who sit as magistrates and judges remain firmly convinced of the validity of conformity relevance. The revelation of the bad character of the accused in a criminal case, whether justified in law or not, produces a devastating and irreversible impact on the course of the trial, and greatly prejudices the accused. Research has shown that not even the most careful directions are effective to repair the damage in most cases.[19]

---

[18] As an American court once put it: 'A very bad man may have a very righteous cause' (*Thompson* v *Church* 1 Root 312 (1791)).

[19] See the research conducted by the London School of Economics and the Oxford University Centre for Socio-Legal Studies, referred to in appendices C and D of the Law Commission's consultation paper No. 141

B   EVIDENCE OF CHARACTER IN CIVIL CASES

SUMMARY OF MAIN POINTS

- Character is not generally relevant in civil cases and is relatively rarely seen.

- In defamation cases, character is a fact in issue, and so is admissible to the extent relevant and material to a cause of action or defence in defamation.

- A defendant may not adduce evidence of his good character in response to allegations in a civil case, even where the acts alleged are intentional. This rule may be the subject of a developing exception in cases in which allegations of criminal or quasi-criminal conduct are made.

- Evidence of bad character is generally inadmissible in civil cases. But where evidence suggestive of bad character is otherwise relevant and has probative value (for example, evidence of similar facts) it may be admitted for that reason along the lines of the former common law rule in criminal cases.

5.3 INTRODUCTION

As we have seen, character evidence is not of great importance in civil cases. It has not been the subject of statutory intervention, and is dealt with in a broad way using general common law principles. Most civil cases are concerned with matters which do not involve intentional or reckless wrongdoing, or even morally reprehensible conduct. In the vast majority of cases, the character of the parties, including the question of whether they may have previous convictions, is either completely irrelevant or so marginally relevant that a judge is unlikely to admit evidence of it. Consequently, such little authority as there is on the subject suggests that relevance is the guiding principle. Unless it can be shown that some aspect of a party's character is relevant to the issues affecting liability, character evidence will not be admitted. To a limited extent, the character of a witness may be relevant to the credibility of his evidence, and the judge may permit some exploration of the subject in cross-examination. But in this case also, given that civil cases are almost always tried by a judge sitting alone, the extent and impact of such evidence will be less than in a criminal case.

5.4 DEFAMATION CASES: CHARACTER A FACT IN ISSUE

Actions for defamation, whether libel or slander, provide the most obvious example of the importance of character evidence in civil cases. Yet defamation is not so much an example of character evidence becoming relevant in a civil case; rather it is a category *sui generis*. In defamation cases, the character of the claimant, or at least some aspect of it, is a fact in issue. The claimant alleges that the defendant has damaged his reputation by making a false statement

---

(1996); see also Cornish and Sealy [1973] Crim LR 208; (1973) 36 MLR 496; Pickel (1995) Law & Hum Behav 407; Tanford and Cox (1988) 12 Law & Hum Behav 477; Wissler and Saks (1985) 9 Law & Hum Behav 37. There was also a good deal of academic commentary in response to the Law Commission's proposals which might have served to sound a note of caution to Parliament: see, e.g., P. Mirfield (2002) 6 E & P 141; J. McEwan [2002] Crim LR 180; M. Redmayne (2002) 6 E & P 71.

about him. The claimant must, therefore, prove what his reputation was before the defendant's statement was made, and the extent to which it has changed as a result of the statement. Therefore, to the extent called into question by the statements of case, the claimant's reputation is a material question of fact to be decided by the tribunal of fact, and evidence relevant to the claimant's reputation must be admitted accordingly. The relevance of the evidence will depend on the allegations and defences as they appear in the statements of case. On the issue of liability, evidence of the claimant's disposition to behave in certain ways, or his conduct on a particular occasion, may be relevant to the issue of his reputation or to a defence relied on by the defendant.[20] But even though the claimant's character is, to some extent, in issue, the usual principles of relevance apply. If the defendant's statement was that the claimant is a habitual crook, who abused his position as a local government official to defraud the town of a large sum of money, wide-ranging evidence of the claimant's financial dealings, as well as his reputation for honesty, will be admitted. But the court will not admit evidence of his sexual behaviour, or his alleged cruelty to animals, which, though aspects of his character, are plainly irrelevant to any issue before the court. On the issue of damages, only evidence of the claimant's reputation is strictly admissible because the award of damages is based exclusively on the extent of the injury to the claimant's reputation.[21]

Although defamation actions constitute a category *sui generis*, so far as character evidence is concerned, it does not follow that the character of a person cannot be a fact in issue for a more limited purpose in other kinds of case. For example, in *Hurst* v *Evans* [1917] 1 KB 352, the defence to an action against an insurance company to recover the sum insured by the policy was that the loss had been sustained because of the dishonesty of the plaintiff's servant. Because the servant's character for honesty was in issue, it was held that evidence was admissible to prove that he was a known associate of burglars and had entered the plaintiff's service on the basis of a forged reference.

5.5 EVIDENCE OF GOOD CHARACTER

In contrast to the position in criminal cases (Part C of this chapter) the defendant in a civil action may not introduce evidence of his good character for the purpose of suggesting that he is not liable, notwithstanding that the allegations in the case may be of intentional blameworthy and possibly criminal conduct. In *Goodright d. Faro* v *Hicks* (1789) Bull NP 296, the defendant to an action to set aside a will on the ground of fraud sought to adduce evidence of his good character to suggest that it was not likely that he had engaged in such a fraud. In similar circumstances on an equivalent criminal charge, the defendant would clearly have been entitled to adduce the evidence. But it was held that, in a civil case, the evidence was inadmissible. The same result was reached in *Attorney-General* v *Bowman* (1791) 2 Bos & P 532 n, in the case of the defendant to a civil action for keeping false weights. And in *Narracott* v *Narracott* (1864) 3 Sw & Tr 408, it was held that the husband in a divorce case could not be permitted to adduce evidence of his 'general humanity' in answer to specific charges of cruelty made against him by the wife. Civil courts have

---

[20] For details, see the current edition of *Gatley on Libel and Slander; Fountain* v *Boodle* (1842) 3 QB 5; *Cornwell* v *Myskow* [1987] 1 WLR 630; *Pamplin* v *Express Newspapers Ltd (No. 2)* [1988] 1 WLR 116.

[21] See *Plato Films Ltd* v *Speidel* [1961] AC 1090. Though Lord Radcliffe suggested that specific instances of conduct might be relevant as part of the picture of general reputation, provided that they were sufficiently notorious to justify the assumption that they must have affected reputation: *ibid.* at 1131. See also *Scott* v *Sampson* (1882) 8 QBD 491, 503 per Cave J.

also generally rejected evidence that the defendant has acted properly or meritoriously on occasions not covered by the pleadings, on the ground that such evidence is irrelevant: as to this see 2.8.1. Where the cause of action is not based on intentional blameworthy conduct, an attempt to introduce evidence of good character would seem particularly inappropriate. Thus in *Hatton* v *Cooper* [2001] RTR 544, an action for negligence arising from a road traffic accident, it was held that evidence of the opinion of the claimant's employer, that the claimant was a calm driver who never took risks, should have been rejected as completely worthless.

5.5.1 Civil cases having criminal or quasi-criminal characteristics

It may be that the above principles are subject to some modification in civil cases in which allegations of a criminal or quasi-criminal nature are made, or in which the consequences of an adverse finding are especially grave. In *Bryant* v *Law Society* [2009] 1 WLR 163, a solicitor was accused of acts of serious dishonesty before a solicitors' disciplinary tribunal. He was found guilty of the acts charged and appealed on the grounds that: (1) the tribunal had wrongly applied a purely objective test for the purpose of determining whether he had acted dishonestly; and (2) the tribunal had erred in excluding positive evidence of his previous good character for honesty. The appeal was allowed on both grounds. In relation to the first ground, the Court held that, having regard to the grave consequences of the findings, the tribunal should have applied the test of dishonesty applicable in criminal cases.[22] Having reached that conclusion, the Court went on to hold, in relation to the second ground, that the evidence of good character was relevant to the issue of dishonesty and should have been considered. It is not easy to reconcile this decision with principle and virtually impossible to reconcile it with older authority. The decision in *R (Campbell)* v *General Medical Council* [2005] 1 WLR 3488 suggests that the tribunal's rejection of the character evidence was correct. Some doubt was cast on this in *Donkin* v *Law Society* [2007] EWHC 414 (Admin), in which it was said that *Campbell* was based on concerns that evidence of good character might be misused for the purpose of downgrading findings of serious professional misconduct. The *Bryant* Court seems to have seized on this to find the way open for a different use of the evidence. Perhaps the members of the Court were influenced by the analogy to criminal cases implicit in their own decision on the first ground of appeal. But *Bryant* raises a number of very difficult questions. The blurring of boundaries between criminal cases and certain classes of civil case is familiar from the law on standards of proof (see 4.15.1 *et seq.*) in which context it has resulted in considerable uncertainty about what principles apply. It is submitted that it would be unfortunate if a similar culture of uncertainty were to arise in the context of evidence of good character. If there is now a class of civil cases in which the defendant is entitled to adduce evidence of good character, of what cases does that class consist? Is it necessary for allegations of criminal conduct to be made, or is the test based on the gravity of the consequences to the defendant? It takes little imagination to foresee the proliferation of civil cases which have potentially grave consequences. It is true that the evidence tendered in *Bryant* was relevant to the allegations of dishonesty, but that may be equally true in the context of many civil cases. These arguments were all considered and rejected in earlier cases. A further question is the purpose or purposes for which the evidence is to be admissible, i.e. is there to be a cloning of the two-limb protocol which applies in criminal cases? What evidence will be admissible in rebuttal of misleading evidence of

---

[22] That is to say, the test in *Ghosh* [1982] QB 1053, which lays down a partly subjective test, an element missing from that applied by the tribunal. As to the *Ghosh* test, see *Blackstone's Criminal Practice*, 2009 edn, para. B4.37.

good character? If a new doctrine is emerging, a doctrine with potentially wide repercussions, it would be as well for its boundaries to be identified as soon as possible.

5.6 EVIDENCE OF BAD CHARACTER

In keeping with the rule stated above, and the equivalent rule in criminal cases, the claimant in a civil case may not adduce evidence of the bad character of the defendant for the purpose of suggesting that he is more likely to be liable because he possesses a bad character. On the other hand, as in criminal cases, if evidence is relevant to the defendant's liability for other reasons, it is not inadmissible merely because it suggests that he may in some manner be of previous bad character. There is older authority that a civil court should be slower than a criminal court to admit such evidence, and should not do so unless it would 'not only afford a reasonable presumption as to the matter in dispute, but would be reasonably conclusive, and would not raise a difficult and doubtful controversy of precisely the same kind as that which the jury would have to determine'.[23] But today, jury trial is rare in civil cases, and the judge has ample power to regulate the admission of evidence, including the power to exclude evidence which will not assist him, and can deal with issues of prejudice in the same way; see 3.6. More modern authority suggests that the position in civil cases is now essentially the same as the common law position in criminal cases, namely that such evidence will be admitted to the extent relevant; indeed it will be more readily admitted in the usual case in which the trial is by a judge sitting alone.[24] Thus, similar factual evidence may be admitted in a civil case if relevant. As might be expected, such evidence will generally be adduced in cases in which the cause of action is based on intentional wrongful conduct, in which case it may be relevant to prove intent, or to rebut a defence of mistake or accident. In *Mood Music Publishing Co. Ltd* v *De Wolfe Ltd* [1976] Ch 119, the plaintiffs sued for copyright infringement in a musical work. The defendants admitted that the works were similar, but claimed that the similarity was coincidental and denied copying. It was held that the plaintiffs were entitled to adduce evidence of other occasions on which the defendants had intentionally reproduced works subject to copyright, one of which had been the product of a 'sting operation' undertaken by the plaintiffs with a view to obtaining evidence against the defendants. In the Court of Appeal Lord Denning MR said (*ibid.* at 127):

> The criminal courts have been very careful not to admit such evidence unless its probative value is so strong that it should be received in the interests of justice: and its admission will not operate unfairly to the accused. In civil cases the courts have followed a similar line but have not been so chary of admitting it. In civil cases the courts will admit evidence of similar facts if it is logically relevant in determining the matter which is in issue: provided that it is not oppressive or unfair to the other side: and also that the other side has fair notice of it and is able to deal with it.[25]

---

[23] *Managers of Metropolitan Asylum District* v *Hill (Appeal No. 1)* (1882) 47 LT 29, 35 per Lord Watson. But see the observations made on this *dictum* in *O'Brien* v *Chief Constable of South Wales Police* (text below). See also *Attorney-General* v *Nottingham Corporation* [1904] 1 Ch 673.

[24] There is authority that, where a civil case is tried with a jury, the judge must be correspondingly more careful in deciding whether to admit the evidence, considering possible prejudice to the defendant: *Thorpe* v *Chief Constable of Greater Manchester Police* [1989] 1 WLR 665, 670 per Dillon LJ. *Sed quaere*: see the comment on this case in the text below, in the light of the decision of the House of Lords in *O'Brien* v *Chief Constable of South Wales Police*.

[25] See also *E.G. Music* v *S.F. (Film) Distributors* [1978] FSR 121; *Berger* v *Raymond & Son Ltd* [1984] 1 WLR 625.

In *O'Brien* v *Chief Constable of South Wales Police* [2005] 2 AC 534, the claimant was convicted of murder and served 11 years of imprisonment before his case was referred to the Court of Appeal, which quashed his conviction. He sued the Chief Constable for malicious prosecution and mis-feasance in public office, alleging misconduct by two senior police officers who, he claimed, had in effect 'framed' him for the murder. He sought to adduce evidence that the same officers had been guilty of similar misconduct in other, unrelated, cases, for the purpose of enhancing the strength of his allegations against them. Both the judge at first instance and the Court of Appeal held that at least some of the proposed evidence should be admitted. The Chief Constable appealed to the House of Lords, which dismissed the appeal. It was argued, relying principally on the *dictum* of Lord Watson in *Managers of Metropolitan Asylum* v *Hill* cited above, that similar fact evidence in civil cases required a showing of enhanced probative value such that it was rea-sonably conclusive of the issues to be decided. The House rejected the argument. Lord Phillips of Worth Matravers pointed out that Lord Watson apparently intended to hold, not that the similar fact evidence should be reasonably conclusive of the facts in issue, but that the evidence tendered to prove the similar facts should be reasonably conclusive of the similar facts (*ibid.* at [46]), and this does indeed appear to be correct. Lord Phillips, in an opinion with which the other members of the House substantially agreed, approved the decision in *Mood Music* (above), and held that evidence of similar facts is admissible in civil cases if it is relevant and probative of the facts in issue, as in the case of other evidence. As with other evidence in civil cases, the judge is entitled to regulate the admission of the evidence, and the quantity of evidence admitted, under r. 32.1 of the Civil Procedure Rules 1998, in the interests of avoiding unjustifiable extensions of the length and complexity of the trial (*ibid.* at [46]–[54]). It would seem, though it is less clear than might have been wished, that the same rule should now apply to all civil cases, whether or not tried with a jury. Lord Phillips pointed out that in *Thorpe* v *Chief Constable of Greater Manchester Police* [1989] 1 WLR 665, the Court of Appeal suggested that the holding of Lord Denning MR in *Mood Music* did not apply to jury trials. This conclusion resulted from the application of the principles laid down for criminal cases by the House of Lords in *Boardman* [1975] AC 421, which the Court thought would exclude the proposed evidence in *Thorpe*. But a later Court of Appeal *in Steel* v *Commissioner of Police for the Metropolis*, unreported, 18 February 1993, applying the more liberal principles of a later House of Lords in *DPP* v *P* [1991] 2 AC 447, reached a different conclusion. The latter case appears to be more consistent with the decision in *O'Brien*, especially in view of the House of Lords' clear approval of the *Mood Music* decision. Given that the law of similar fact evi-dence developed in criminal cases almost exclusively in relation to jury trials, there would seem little point in perpetuating the distinction.[26]

Evidence of a concerted course of action taken by the defendant against the same claimant may be relevant to prove intent or to rebut such defences as mistake, accident, or good faith. In *Barrett* v *Long* (1856) 3 HL Cas 395, a libel action, the plaintiff was permitted to adduce evidence of previous libels of him by the defendant, with a view to showing that the defendant was guilty of actual malice and deliberate publication. In causes of action not based on intentional wrong-doing, evidence of similar facts is likely to be rare, but should not necessarily be excluded. In a negligence case, repeated examples of the same act or omission on the part of the defendant may

---

[26] Though Lord Phillips seems to hint that the prospect of a jury trial might influence the exercise of a discre-tion to exclude or limit evidence under r. 32.1. In *O'Brien*, the claimant had abandoned any intention of request-ing trial by jury by the time of the appeal to the House of Lords: see the opinion of Lord Phillips at [61]. With respect, it is hard to see why this should make any more difference in contemporary practice than it would in a criminal case.

be relevant to show what the defendant knew or ought to have known, for example where the defendant's driver is involved in a succession of accidents by reason of his negligent driving, or where several employees have been injured while using the same machine. In *Osborne* v *Chocqueel* [1896] 2 QB 109, it was held that evidence of the behaviour of a bulldog on occasions other than the occasion in question might be admitted in a case of liability for an animal. And in *Sattin* v *Union Bank* (1978) 122 SJ 367, a plaintiff who brought an action against a bank for losing a diamond which he had deposited with them as security for an overdraft was held to be entitled to adduce evidence of another occasion on which the bank had similarly lost property which had been deposited.

C EVIDENCE OF GOOD CHARACTER IN CRIMINAL CASES

SUMMARY OF MAIN POINTS

- In a criminal case the accused is entitled to adduce evidence of his good character by showing that he has no previous convictions, and by calling character witnesses to give relevant positive evidence of good character.

- Strictly, at common law the positive evidence should be confined to evidence of reputation, but the personal opinion of witnesses is now also permitted. Evidence of prior good or creditworthy conduct is not admissible.

- Evidence of good character is admissible for two purposes: (1) it enhances the credibility of the accused in relation to his evidence (if any) and answers given in interview (if any); and (2) it is some evidence tending to suggest that he is less likely than otherwise might be the case to have committed the offence charged.

- The jury must be fully directed as to both the above 'limbs', with any necessary modifications.

- If the accused tries to mislead the court by false or exaggerated evidence of good character, the prosecution may rebut the evidence.

5.7 ADMISSIBILITY AND METHODS OF PROOF

Out of the conspicuous concern of the common law to offer as much latitude as possible to an accused, in view of the procedural and evidential incapacities from which he suffered before the gradual reforms of the nineteenth century, emerged a rule peculiar to criminal trials, that the accused might in every case prove his general good character.[27] Before the Criminal Evidence Act 1898 rendered the accused a competent witness in his own defence, this could be achieved only by cross-examination of witnesses for the prosecution, or by calling character witnesses for the defence, but the Act also enabled the accused to give evidence about his good character himself.

---

[27] In *Butterwasser* [1948] KB 4, 6, Lord Goddard CJ referred to the antiquity of the rule, noting also that it is permissive in character, as opposed perhaps to a matter of strict entitlement. In similar vein, see the language employed by Lawton LJ in *Redgrave* (1981) Cr App R 10, 15.

5.8 KINDS OF EVIDENCE PERMITTED

There was much discussion at common law about the kinds of evidence which were permitted by the rule. In the end, before the Criminal Evidence Act 1898, it seemed to be settled that it was confined to evidence of general reputation. In *Rowton* (CCR) (1865) Le & Ca 520, the accused was charged with indecent assault on a boy of 14. The accused was a schoolmaster. The question arose of the limits of admissible evidence of character offered by a witness, and it was held that the evidence was confined to that of the general reputation of the accused in the community, and therefore excluded both evidence of specific acts on other occasions, and the witness's own opinion of the accused. *Rowton* itself was the subject of powerful dissent, and the ink was scarcely dry on the judgments before it was doubted. Although the case has never been specifically reversed, the practice in modern times is to allow the accused to state his character more widely.

Whatever the merits of reputation evidence may have been in 1865, it can hardly be regarded as the most reliable form of character evidence available today. Changed social conditions have rendered the basis for it more tenuous, and at the very least demand a somewhat different approach to assessing reputation (for further discussion of this subject, see 11.2) and increasingly reliable records enable character to be established more definitively by means of evidence of specific acts, including previous convictions. Moreover, as we have seen, the Criminal Evidence Act 1898 demanded a wider definition of 'character'. It makes little sense for the accused himself to purport to give evidence of his own reputation, and since the Act it has been viewed as more natural to allow him to deal with the subject of his character in common sense terms when giving evidence. In modern practice, the accused is invariably permitted to give a brief account of his situation in life, and state that he has no previous convictions. There is also no doubt that the accused may now call a character witness to state that witness's individual opinion of the accused. To that extent, the decision in *Rowton* is no longer applied in practice. However, *Rowton* continues to preclude the accused from adducing evidence of prior creditable specific acts. Willes J cited as an example of the reasoning behind this principle, the fact that even a robber might commit acts of generosity; but the contemporary justification for the rule, if any, must rest on questions of relevance.

Whether the accused's evidence of good character may include evidence of his disposition to behave in a certain way is still not absolutely certain after the decision of the Court of Appeal in *Redgrave* (1981) 74 Cr App R 10. The accused was charged with persistently importuning for immoral purposes, by masturbating in a public lavatory while staring at the (male) arresting officers. At the first trial, at which the jury had disagreed, the accused had been permitted to adduce documents which were described as love letters and photographs of himself in the company of women, said to indicate a familiar relationship with the women, in order to show that his sexual tendency was heterosexual rather than homosexual. At his re-trial, the accused sought to adduce a selection of the documents, including letters, Valentine cards and photographs, and to testify about his relationship with the women concerned. The trial judge ruled this evidence to be inadmissible, relying on *Rowton*, and the accused appealed against his conviction on this ground. It was argued that if the prosecution may adduce relevant evidence of the accused's homosexual tendencies it must be open to the accused to adduce evidence of his heterosexual disposition for the purpose of suggesting that it is less likely that he committed such an offence. This argument was somewhat, though not greatly, weakened on the facts of the case by the fact that homosexual intent was not an essential element of the offence charged, but there seems no doubt that the evidence tendered was relevant to rebut the clear suggestion of homosexual intent made by the prosecution. The argument is certainly cogent and sympathetic, but the Court of Appeal held that *Rowton* must be followed, and that such evidence of disposition must be excluded. The Court appears to have based itself in part on the proposition that the prosecution could not have adduced evidence of homosexual disposition as relevant to the offence charged, though there is authority which suggests that this was not necessarily the case.[28]

The invitation given to the Court to refuse to follow *Rowton* was too great a step of faith. That the Court was aware of the seriousness of disallowing relevant defence evidence seems clear, and the Court adverted with some justification to possible difficulties of calling evidence from an accused's sexual partners under subpoena. However, it is submitted that *Redgrave* is an unsatisfactory decision which fails to take into account the realities of modern criminal practice. The Court's dilemma seems evident from a passage near the end of the judgment of Lawton LJ (74 Cr App R at 15), in which the learned Lord Justice said:

> It was brought to our attention by [counsel for the prosecution] that nowadays, as a matter of practice in this class of case, defendants are often allowed to say that they are happily married and having a normal sexual relationship with their wives. We are not seeking to stop defending counsel putting that kind of information before a jury. It has long been the practice for judges to allow some relaxation of the law of evidence on behalf of defendants. Had this young man been a married man, or alternatively, had he confined his relationship to one girl, it might not have been all that objectionable for him to have given evidence in general terms that his relationship with his wife or the girl was satisfactory. That would have been an indulgence on the part of the court. It would not have been his right to have it said. Until such time as Parliament amends the law of evidence, it is the duty of this Court, and of judges, to keep to the rules, and the rules are clear.

If this is the position, it is submitted that the law stands in need of reform. Should the defence in such cases be reduced to depending not only on the indulgence of the court, but also on the fortuitous facts of the accused's marital status or the number of his girlfriends, to be permitted to adduce evidence that is not only apparently relevant but also potentially cogent? If a strict reading of *Rowton* requires such a result, the time may have come to consign the case to history, and it is to be regretted that the House of Lords refused leave to appeal in *Redgrave*.

5.9 REBUTTAL OF EVIDENCE OF GOOD CHARACTER

The prosecution is entitled to rebut evidence of good character adduced on behalf of the accused. This means that the prosecution may adduce evidence of the accused's bad character for the purpose of showing that his claim of good character is false and designed to mislead the jury. Evidence of bad character is now governed by the Criminal Justice Act 2003. Although the Act does not affect the admissibility of evidence of good character, it governs the admissibility of evidence of bad character, and it follows that rebuttal evidence adduced by the prosecution is subject to the applicable statutory rules. Section 99 of the Act abolishes the common law rules governing the admissibility of evidence of bad character, while specifically retaining the rule that evidence of reputation is admissible for the purpose of proving bad character. Section 98 defines 'bad character' as 'evidence of, or of a disposition towards, misconduct' not having to do with the

---

[28] See *King* [1967] 2 QB 338; *Horwood* [1970] 1 QB 133. The prosecution would surely be at liberty to adduce such evidence to rebut evidence of disposition given by the accused (see 5.9 below), so that no prejudice to the prosecution would occur by allowing the accused to do so.

facts of the offence charged and not being misconduct in connection with the investigation or prosecution of that offence. Section 112 defines 'misconduct' as 'the commission of an offence or other reprehensible behaviour'. Evidence of the accused's bad character, as thus defined, is admissible by virtue of s. 101(1)(f) of the Act if: 'it is evidence to correct a false impression given by the defendant'. Evidence of bad character is the subject of Chapter 6 of this book, and, in the interests of consistency, these provisions are considered in more detail at 6.12. Nonetheless, for the sake of completeness, it will be useful to refer here to the position at common law.

At common law, the prosecution could cross-examine any character witness called on behalf of the accused with a view to refuting evidence of the accused's good reputation. The witness could be asked about any matters which might adversely affect the accused's reputation, including rumours as to his participation in offences not covered by the indictment: *Wood* (1841) 5 Jur 225. Because reputation evidence may itself consist of rumour, there can be no objection to inquiring into the full extent of the rumours on which the accused's reputation may be based. In more modern times, once the accused's character was in issue, the prosecution was permitted to adduce evidence of the accused's previous convictions if the defence was not prepared to admit them: *Redd* [1923] 1 KB 104.[29] The prosecution could also cross-examine the character witnesses called on the accused's behalf as to their own credit. After the coming into effect of the Criminal Evidence Act 1898, if the accused elected to give evidence, he could be cross-examined about his character and about offences not covered by the indictment which he had committed, or of which he had been convicted, if:

> ... he has personally or by his advocate asked questions of the witnesses for the prosecution with a view to establish his own good character, or has given evidence of his own good character... [*Ibid.* at s.1(3)(ii).]

For the purposes of evidence rebutting an assertion of good character, the character of the accused was held to be 'indivisible', i.e., if the accused made a partial assertion of his good character in any respect, his evidence could be rebutted by evidence that his character was bad in other respects: *Stirland v DPP* [1944] AC 315, 326 per Lord Simon LC. There was obviously considerable force in this rule in most circumstances; it would not be right to allow the accused to create a false impression by revealing to the jury only selected parts of his character. Nonetheless, there may be cases in which the strict application of such a rule works hardship to the accused. Nokes tellingly suggested that, if a man is charged with forgery, cross-examination about a previous conviction for cruelty to animals 'can have no purpose but prejudice'.[30] In *Winfield* [1939] 4 All ER 164, the accused was charged with indecent assault on a woman. He called a character witness from whom the prosecution elicited in cross-examination that the accused had a previous conviction for an offence of dishonesty. The Court of Appeal held that the cross-examination had been proper. But it is certainly arguable that, in the context of the offence charged, no injustice would have been caused to the prosecution if it had been disallowed in the exercise of the judge's duty to secure a fair trial for the accused (see 3.7). It is now recognized that in some cases, where the accused has previous convictions for offences which are essentially regulatory, or are minor when compared to the offence now charged, or are spent convictions, it may be right to allow him to be treated as a person of previous good character. It seems that the matter is one within the discretion of the judge, who must take into account both the dictates of fairness to the accused and the principle

---

[29] Formerly, the prosecution could also rebut a false assertion of good character given by the accused while exercising his right to make an unsworn statement from the dock, on which he could not be cross-examined (a right eventually abolished by the Criminal Justice Act 1982): *Campbell* (1979) 69 Cr App R 221.

[30] *Introduction to Evidence*, 4th edn, p. 140.

that the jury must not be misled about the accused's character.[31] Whether any of this amounts to 'giving a false impression' for the purposes of s. 101(1)(f) of the Criminal Justice Act 2003 is a matter which will have to be considered in due course.

5.10 EVIDENTIAL VALUE OF EVIDENCE OF GOOD CHARACTER

As we have seen, the original common law rule permitting the accused to adduce evidence of his good character pre-dated the Criminal Evidence Act 1898. This is a significant fact in considering the evidential value of that evidence. There are, in theory, two uses which a jury may make of evidence of good character today. It may be used as evidence which makes it less likely that the accused committed the offence charged. Equally, it may be used as evidence of the accused's credibility as a witness in a case in which he gives evidence. It seems clear enough that, before the 1898 Act rendered the accused a competent witness in his own defence, only the first of these purposes was applicable.[32] Consequently, it would also seem clear that the common law rule is that the accused's evidence of good character is primarily relevant to the issue of guilt or innocence, even though it now also has the secondary use of relevance to his credit as a witness. Moreover, there is clear older authority to that effect.[33] It is, therefore, surprising that in *Falconer-Atlee* (1973) 58 Cr App R 348, the Court of Appeal held that evidence of good character adduced by the accused should be used only as evidence of his credit as a witness. The logical result of *Falconer-Atlee* was that, if the accused chose not to give evidence in his defence, then evidence of good character elicited in cross-examination, or given by character witnesses, would not be relevant for any purpose, and the jury should be directed to disregard it. This consequence arose, and was squarely faced by the trial judge, in *Bryant* [1979] QB 108, 119. The Court of Appeal, while dismissing the appeal against conviction, held that the judge had been wrong to direct the jury that because the accused's credit was not in issue, the evidence of his good character could have no value. This approach was said by the Court of Appeal to be 'too restrictive'. The Court added:

> The possession of a good character is a matter which does go primarily to the issue of credibility. This has been made clear in a number of recent cases. But juries should be directed that it is capable of bearing a more general significance which is best illustrated by what was said by Williams J in *Stannard* [(1837) 7 Car & P 673, 675]: 'I have no doubt...that evidence to character must be considered as evidence in the cause. It is evidence, as my brother Patteson has said, to be submitted to the jury, to induce them to say whether they think it likely that a person with such a character would have committed the offence.'

The principle stated in *Bryant* was confirmed by the House of Lords in *Aziz* [1996] AC 41. Lord Steyn said (*ibid*. at 50) that it had: 'long been recognized that the good character of a defendant is logically relevant to his credibility and to the likelihood that he would commit the offence in question'.

---

[31] *Thompson v R* [1998] AC 811, 844 per Lord Hutton; *Timson* [1993] Crim LR 58; generally 5.11.2. As to spent convictions, *Nye* (1982) 75 Cr App R 247; and 6.4.3.

[32] It can be argued that the accused's good character is relevant to his credibility with respect to any pre-trial statement he may have made or any answers he may have given to questions during the investigation, and today this is regarded as a legitimate use of the evidence (see *Vye* [1993] 1 WLR 471; 5.11). But as statements made by the accused consistent with his defence were not admissible as evidence of the truth of the facts stated at common law when the good character rule developed (see 9.17) this is not an acceptable justification for the theory that the effect of the evidence is limited to credibility.

[33] *Stannard* (1837) 7 C & P 673; *Bellis* [1966] 1 WLR 234.

5.11 DIRECTION TO JURY: GENERALLY; MORE THAN ONE ACCUSED

An accused who wishes the jury to consider his previous good character must raise the issue by evidence, either by cross-examining a witness for the prosecution (typically a police officer), by giving evidence himself, or by calling character witnesses. If no evidence of the accused's good character is introduced, the judge is not required to direct the jury about it (*Thompson* v *R* [1998] AC 811). Indeed, it has been said that it would be 'ill-advised' for the judge to mention the issue of good character unless he is provided with evidence which clearly indicates that it is proper and safe to do so.[34] If the issue is raised, however, the judge must deal with it. But despite the apparent clarity of the decision in *Bryant* considerable uncertainty arose subsequently about the appropriate direction to be given to the jury in cases where the accused is of previous good character.[35] Some of this uncertainty arose from the admittedly difficult situation produced by the joint trial of two or more accused, not all of whom are of previous good character. In such cases, a direction as to the good character of one accused will inevitably have the effect of contrasting that accused favourably with the others.

In *Berrada* (1989) 91 Cr App R 131, the Court of Appeal held that the summing-up should, at a minimum, contain a correct direction as to the relevance of good character to credibility (on the assumption that the accused has given evidence). This direction was described as the 'first limb' of a good character direction. The Court stopped short of laying down a mandatory rule that the jury should also be directed that the accused's good character is one factor which should be taken into account in deciding whether or not it is likely that the accused would have committed the offence charged (the 'second limb') though such a direction was said to be desirable. In some later cases,[36] and in the 4th edition of this work, it was suggested that the second limb, too, should be mandatory—which would obviously be more consistent with *Bryant*.

In *Vye* [1993] 1 WLR 471, the Court of Appeal reviewed the state of the law, and laid down the following guidelines, which, it is submitted, represent a welcome and satisfactory statement of the correct position:

(a) A first-limb direction (as to the effect of good character on credibility) must be given whenever the accused has given evidence, and thereby put his credibility in issue. The same direction must also be given if, even though the accused has not given evidence, he has made any pre-trial statements or given answers to questions, in which case his credit is also an issue. Only if the accused has neither given evidence, nor made any such statements or given any such answers, may this limb be omitted.

(b) A second-limb direction (as to the effect of good character on the likelihood that the accused committed the offence) must also be given, regardless of whether or not the accused has given evidence or made any pre-trial statements or given answers to questions. The judge may, of course, explain to the jury that possession of a hitherto good character is not a defence, but merely one factor to be considered in weighing the issue of guilt or innocence.

(c) In a joint trial, where not all of the accused are of previous good character, the judge must give both the first and second-limb directions with respect to each accused of previous good character. The judge should then use his discretion to ensure that as little prejudice as possible accrues to the

---

[34] By the Privy Council in *Brown* v *The Queen* [2005] 2 WLR 1558.

[35] See, e.g., *Levy* [1987] Crim LR 48; *Gibson* (1991) 93 Cr App R 9; *Wills* (1990) 92 Cr App R 297; *Kabariti* (1990) 92 Cr App R 362.

[36] See, e.g., *Wills* (1990) 92 Cr App R 297; *Anderson* [1990] Crim LR 862.

accused who are not of good character. This may be done by directing the jury not to speculate about the character of the other accused, or by simply not referring to the issue of their character at all. Which course should be followed will depend on the circumstances of the case, including the degree of emphasis placed on the issue of character in the course of the trial, including the speeches of counsel.[37]

In *Aziz* [1996] AC 41, the House of Lords recognized that the line of authority culminating in *Vye* represented a radical change in the approach of the courts to the accused's good character, and suggested that this change was to be welcomed as reflecting the contemporary view that the jury should receive a proper direction on that subject, just as on any other relevant and admissible evidence tendered by the defence. It now seems to be established that an accused who is of previous good character is entitled to a full good character direction consisting of both limbs, subject to the applicable guidelines, and that failure to give an appropriate direction as to good character is likely to result in a conviction being set aside on appeal (see *Fulcher* [1995] 2 Cr App R 251).[38] The direction on both limbs must be full, fair, and specific. The jury cannot be left to infer the implications of one limb for the other. Thus, even if the judge correctly directs the jury that the accused's good character is relevant to the issue of whether or not he committed the offence charged, he cannot assume that the jury will infer from that direction that they should give the accused credit on the issue of his credibility as a witness. That must also be made clear to them specifically: *Jagdeo Singh* v *State of Trinidad and Tobago* [2006] 1 WLR 146.

5.11.1 Direction to jury: accused's conduct compromising previous good character

A difficult situation arises where the accused, though of good character prior to the events which have led to the offence charged, has compromised that good character by some admitted conduct in relation to those events, or by pleading guilty to one or more other offences with which he was also charged. The first of these possibilities occurred in *Aziz* [1996] AC 41, in which two accused admitted, in the course of giving evidence, to having committed acts of dishonesty which were not covered by the indictment. The accused were otherwise of good character, and, in the sense of having no previous convictions, remained of good character, though their good character in the broader sense had obviously been compromised. The issue arose as to whether, in these circumstances, they were entitled to a good character direction. The House of Lords held that the accused continued to be entitled to both limbs of the good character direction, but, because it would be wrong to mislead the jury, the judge should add some qualification by reference to the conduct admitted by the accused. The House added, however, that the judge has a discretion to withhold either or both limbs of the direction where the accused's claim to a good character is 'spurious'. An example of this situation would be where the accused admits, or is clearly shown to be guilty of serious criminal conduct of a nature similar to the offence charged.[39]

---

[37] This discretion must be exercised subject to the rule that, as a matter of law, both the accused of good character and the accused of bad character are entitled to an accurate direction as to the effect of any evidence of character. The situation must not be misrepresented to the jury (*Cain* [1994] 1 WLR 1449). As to the need for clarity in the direction, see Lloyd [2000] 2 Cr App R 355.

[38] Especially in cases in which the accused's credibility is of great importance, or in which he may bear the burden of proof: see *Soukala-Cacace* [1999] All ER (D) 1120; *Scranage* [2001] All ER (D) 185.

[39] Prior to *Aziz* it had been suggested that such a discretion existed, but it was unclear in what circumstances it applied, and whether it covered both limbs or only the second limb of the direction: see *Zoppola-Barraza* [1994]

A similar approach should be taken where the accused has committed some discreditable act short of a criminal offence, such as lying when questioned by the police, or is shown by the evidence to be given to drinking heavily or to have had an extramarital affair. In such a case, the judge may add some slight qualification, commensurate with the nature of the accused's conduct, to a full good character direction.[40]

In cases in which the accused has pleaded guilty to one or more of the offences charged, there is at present no clear rule. In *Teasdale* [1993] 4 All ER 290, an accused charged with causing grievous bodily harm with intent pleaded guilty to assault occasioning actual bodily harm in relation to the same incident. It was held that the accused was entitled to both limbs of the good character direction. But in *Challenger* [1994] Crim LR 202, where the accused pleaded guilty to simple possession of cannabis and was later tried on a concurrent charge of possession with intent to supply, it was held that the judge had a discretion, which he had exercised correctly, to give no good character direction whatsoever. The Court sought to explain away *Teasdale* on the rather tenuous basis that a conviction on the charge of causing grievous bodily harm would require the vacation of the plea of guilty to assault occasioning actual bodily harm. However, the reality is that in both *Teasdale* and *Challenger*, the accused pleaded guilty to criminal conduct concurrent with that charged, and such a technical ground of distinction appears extremely unconvincing. It is submitted that a preferable approach would be for the judge to offer the accused the choice between (a) withholding information about the plea of guilty from the jury (who would ordinarily not be told of it) and receiving no good character direction, or a first-limb direction only, and (b) by way of analogy with the rule laid down in *Aziz*, receiving a full good character direction with information about the plea of guilty added by way of qualification.

5.11.2 Minor offences, offences of different nature

Where the accused has been convicted previously of an offence which is minor compared to the offence now charged, or which is of an entirely different nature, there is some authority that the judge may permit him to be treated as being a person of good character. Clearly, this discretion should be sparingly exercised in the light of the principle that the jury should not be misled about the accused's character. In *Thompson* v R [1998] AC 811, 844, Lord Hutton, delivering the judgment of the Privy Council, said that their lordships were prepared to hold[41] that, in the case of an appellant charged (in Saint Vincent and the Grenadines) with a capital murder alleged to have been committed in 1993, a previous conviction for larceny of about £20 committed in 1980, for which he had reprimanded and discharged by a magistrates' court, might properly have been disregarded as 'immaterial', and the appellant treated as being a person of previous good character. Lord Hutton gave as his reason the fact that the previous offence was 'of such a minor and non-violent nature'. In *Timson* [1993] Crim LR 58, it was held that a previous conviction for drunk

---

Crim LR 833; *Akram* [1995] Crim LR 50. The implication of *Aziz* is clearly that it applies to both limbs, but some uncertainty may remain about the circumstances in which it may be applied. See generally R. Munday [1997] Crim LR 247.

[40] Though, as the Privy Council pointed out in *Shaw* v R [2001] 1 WLR 1519, there may be cases in which such a qualified discretion is less favourable to the accused than simply withholding a good character direction altogether. For similar observations see *Aziz* [1996] AC 41, 53 per Lord Steyn; *Doncaster* (2008) 172 JP 202.

[41] The question was strictly *obiter* because the appellant had not raised the issue of good character at his trial and the Privy Council held that, consequently, the judge had not been required to give a direction on that subject.

driving should have been disregarded where the accused was charged with offences of dishonesty. There is a good argument for saying that offences of an essentially regulatory nature, particularly road traffic offences, should be disregarded in general. A jury would be unlikely to hold such offences against an accused in any event, and an accused may even choose to volunteer them in order to claim credit for frankness. But this would not necessarily apply to more serious offences, such as driving while disqualified. Much must depend on the nature of the current charge, the nature of the previous conviction, and the number of previous convictions. The discretion must be exercised on the facts of each particular case.[42] The lapse of time since the previous conviction is also relevant, particularly where it is a spent conviction (see 6.4.3) though this also is not determinative. It would clearly not be appropriate to treat the accused as being of previous good character where the previous conviction is germane to the general subject-matter of the present case. Thus, in *Rackham* [1997] 2 Cr App R 222, where the accused's sexual preference for young girls was in issue, it was held that his previous conviction for unlawful sexual intercourse with a 13-year-old girl could not be ignored, even though the previous offence had occurred a considerable time before. In *Martin* [2000] 2 Cr App R 42, it was held that where the accused had accumulated two police cautions, which are not convictions but which involve the accused in admitting the offences involved, the judge had a discretion as to what good character direction to give to the jury. Accordingly, the judge could not be criticized for giving a first limb direction only and withholding a second limb direction.[43]

If the judge exercises his discretion to give a good character direction in such cases, it should be a full and fair direction. In *Gray* [2004] 2 Cr App R 30, the accused, who was charged with murder, had previous convictions for driving with excess alcohol and driving without a licence and insurance. It was held that, in the judge's discretion, he could have been put forward as a person of good character. But if this course was taken, the accused was entitled to the benefit of a full character direction. The judge had simply given the jury a perfunctory direction to the effect that it 'might assist' them to know that the accused's bad character was limited to those minor offences. The direction was held to be insufficient.

5.11.3 Convictions by foreign courts

There is no basis either in principle or fairness for regarding a person as being of good character because his only previous conviction happens to be a conviction before a foreign court. Such a conviction cannot be ignored, even where, under the law of the foreign country in question, the conviction may technically not yet be regarded as final pending the outcome of an appeal or other confirmatory procedure: *El Delbi* [2003] EWCA Crim 1767.

5.12 RECOMMENDED FURTHER READING

Lloyd-Bostock, S., 'The effects on lay magistrates of hearing that the defendant is of 'good character', being left to speculate, or hearing that he has a previous conviction' [2006] *Criminal Law Review* 189.

McEwan, J. 'Law Commission dodges the nettles in Consultation Paper No 141' [1997] *Criminal Law Review* 93.

Mirfield, P., 'The Law Commission's character convictions' (2002) 6(2) *International Journal of Evidence and Proof* 141.

---

[42] For an example, see *Sanchez* [2003] EWCA Crim 735.
[43] See also *Maillett* [2005] EWCA Crim 3159.

Murphy, P., 'Character evidence: the search for logic and policy continues' (1998) 2(2) *International Journal of Evidence and Proof* 71.

Redmayne, M., 'The relevance of bad character' (2002) **61**(3) *Cambridge Law Journal* 684.

Roberts, P., 'All the usual suspects: a critical appraisal of Law Commission Consultation Paper No 141' [1997] *Criminal Law Review* 7.

5.13 QUESTIONS FOR DISCUSSION BASED *ON R* v *COKE; LITTLETON* AND *BLACKSTONE* v *COKE* (for case files go to the Online Resource Centre)

5.13.1 *Coke; Littleton*

1. May Littleton establish his good character by way of defence? If so:

    (a) Of what aspects of his character is he entitled to adduce evidence?

    (b) By what means can the evidence be adduced?

    (c) What evidential value does Littleton's good character have, and how should the judge direct the jury about it?

2. How should the fact that Coke is not of good character affect the judge's direction?

3. Would you advise Coke to raise the issue of his character? Explain your reasons.

4. If Coke represented himself to be a person of good character, what steps could the prosecution take? What steps could Littleton take?

5.13.2 *Blackstone* v *Coke*

1. May Margaret Blackstone adduce evidence at trial that she is a young woman of virtuous character (a) to suggest that it is unlikely that she consented to have sexual intercourse with Coke on the occasion in question; or (b) to suggest that she is a credible witness?

2. If she does suggest this, may Coke adduce evidence that Margaret had sexual intercourse with other men for the purpose of showing (a) that it is likely that she did consent; or (b) that she is not a credible witness?

3. May Coke adduce evidence that Margaret had sexual intercourse with Anthony Hennecky (a) to show that Hennecky may be the father of her child; or (b) to suggest that she is promiscuous?

5.14 GENERAL QUESTIONS FOR DISCUSSION

1. What is meant by the term 'character'?

2. Is evidence of good character admissible in civil cases in order to suggest that a party should not be liable? What about in criminal cases?

3. Is evidence of bad character admissible in civil cases?

4. If an accused asserts, incorrectly, that he is of good character, in what circumstances may this be rebutted by the prosecution?

5. What are the two uses that a jury may make of evidence of an accused's good character?

6. How should a jury be directed when an accused asserts his good character? What is the position where there are co-accused, not all of which are of good character?

7. An accused, of previous good character, admits a single punch to the head in an unprovoked attack, but denies inflicting grievous bodily harm. May the jury be directed that he is a person of good character?

8. May an accused be treated as a person of good character if he has only minor previous offences?

6

CHARACTER EVIDENCE II: EVIDENCE OF BAD CHARACTER

A   THE CRIMINAL JUSTICE ACT 2003

SUMMARY OF MAIN POINTS

- Section 99 of the Criminal Justice Act 2003 abolishes the common law rules of evidence of bad character.

- Sections 98 and 112 of the Act provides a definition of bad character as follows:

  - Section 98:

    References in this Chapter to evidence of a person's 'bad character' are to evidence of, or a disposition towards, misconduct on his part, other than evidence which—
    (a) has to do with the alleged facts of the offence with which the defendant is charged, or
    (b) is evidence of misconduct in connection with the investigation or prosecution of that offence.

  - Section 112:

    'misconduct' means 'the commission of an offence or other reprehensible behaviour'.

6.1 INTRODUCTION

This chapter is concerned exclusively with the subject of evidence of bad character in criminal cases. We saw in 5.1 that character evidence developed in a number of separate strands. At common law, the accused was (and is) entitled to adduce evidence of his good character for the purpose of suggesting that he is less likely to have committed the offence charged. Such evidence was originally confined to evidence of reputation. This rule pre-dated the Criminal Evidence Act 1898, which for the first time rendered the accused a competent witness in his own defence. If the accused adduced evidence which amounted to a false assertion of good character, the prosecution was entitled to rebut that evidence with relevant evidence of bad character. But the prosecution was not otherwise entitled to adduce evidence of bad character for the purpose of suggesting that the accused's previous bad character made it more likely that he was guilty of the offence charged. By virtue of the Criminal Evidence Act 1898, the accused became a competent, but not compellable witness, and was gradually permitted to give evidence about his character in a rather broader way, but is still not permitted to give evidence of specific creditable acts or evidence of disposition. If he elected to give evidence, the accused enjoyed a shield against cross-examination about his commission or conviction of offences not covered by the indictment, and about his bad character generally, but the shield could be lost in certain circumstances prescribed by s. 1(3) of the Act (which included an assertion of good character). Finally, we saw that the common law permitted the prosecution to adduce evidence otherwise relevant to the accused's guilt of the offence charged, notwithstanding that it might also suggest that he was of bad character, for example similar fact evidence. This rule operated quite independently of the statutory powers of cross-examination under the 1898 Act. These separate strands were never united and (in common with much of the law of evidence) constituted a difficult patchwork of specific rules which did not work together harmoniously and were often difficult to reconcile.[1]

The tangled state of the law regarding evidence of bad character attracted various proposals for reform. Some fairly radical proposals were made in the Eleventh Report of the Criminal Law Revision Committee in 1972, but because of (largely misplaced) criticism of the Committee's work and because of its advocacy of even more radical changes in other areas of the law of evidence, they were not then implemented.[2] Only considerably later did the continuing dissatisfaction with the state of the law provide sufficient impetus to bring about, not only proposals for reform, but eventually a thorough-going statutory change. The Law Commission's Consultation Paper 141 (*Evidence in Criminal Proceedings: Previous Misconduct of a Defendant*, 1996) and its resulting Report (*Evidence of Bad Character in Criminal Proceedings*, Law Com 273, 2001) not only offered trenchant criticism of the existing law, but considered a wide range of possible changes. They were supplemented by influential criticism from other sources, notably the report of Sir Robin Auld's comprehensive inquiry into the workings of English criminal procedure (*Review of the Criminal Courts of England and Wales*, 2001). It is a measure of the profound disagreement the subject always seems to provoke that the ultimate result of these endeavours, the Criminal Justice Act 2003, departs from many of the recommendations made by the Law Commission, particularly with respect to its proposals for safeguards surrounding the admission of evidence of bad character.[3]

The Act's principal achievements in the field of evidence of bad character are to draw together the various strands of the previous law to form something of a unified field, and to eliminate the friction between the rules governing the admissibility of prosecution evidence and those governing cross-examination of the accused. But the Act also preserves some of the less desirable features of the old law, for example the essentially retributive use of evidence of bad character against an accused who attacks the character of another. The Act's frequent imprecision of language leaves room for the continued blurring of the question of relevance, which was one of the worst features of the Criminal Evidence Act 1898. Without scrupulously careful directions by trial judges, juries

---

[1] In its Report, *Evidence of Bad Character in Criminal Proceedings* (Law Com 273, 2001) the Law Commission found the law defective as consisting of a 'haphazard mixture of statute and common law rules which produce inconsistent and unpredictable results, in crucial respects distort the trial process, make tactical considerations paramount and inhibit the defence in presenting its true case to the fact-finders...' (*ibid.* at para. 1.7). See generally C. Tapper [2004] Crim LR 533; P. Murphy (1998) 2 E & P 71.

[2] Cmnd 4991, 1972. For commentary on the work of the Committee in this report see R. Cross [1973] Crim LR 400.

[3] For commentary on the Law Commission's Report, see the sources mentioned in Chapter 5, note 19.

will encounter significant problems in evaluating evidence of bad character, and it is all too foreseeable that they may be tempted to use that evidence to convict as a substitute for substantive factual evidence, which would amount to a regression to conformity reasoning at its worst. Because the issues which plagued the courts under the old law are destined to arise again, thinly disguised, under the new law, it is inevitable that the courts are once again being called on to define boundaries, and to provide guidelines for trial judges faced with the familiar old problems couched in new and different language. Of greatest concern is that the Act has opened the door to the use of evidence of bad character by the prosecution on a wider scale and in a broader sense than at any previous time. The Home Office's Explanatory Notes[4] (as well as the Act's historical antecedents outlined above) leave no doubt that this was an intentional development. The Notes (see para. 365) indicate, in relation the accused's bad character, that the Act was intended to create an 'inclusionary approach to a defendant's previous convictions and other misconduct or disposition' in contrast to the position under the old law, which rendered it 'generally inadmissible, subject to a number of restricted common law and statutory exceptions'.[5] This was confirmed by the decision of the Court of Appeal in the appeal of *Somanathan* in *Weir and other appeals* [2006] 1 WLR 1885, in which it was argued that the Act had not altered the common law approach to the admission of similar fact evidence. Rejecting this argument, Kennedy LJ said:

> Evidence of bad character is now admissible if it satisfies certain criteria (see s.101(1)) and the approach is no longer one of inadmissibility subject to exceptions...If the evidence of a defendant's bad character is relevant to an important issue between the prosecution and the defence (s.101(1)(d)) then, unless there is an application to exclude the evidence, it is admissible. Leave is not required. So the pre-existing one-stage test which balanced probative value against prejudicial effect is obsolete (see also s. 99(1)). [*Ibid.* at [35], [36].]

The inclusion in the definition of bad character of evidence of misconduct other than the commission of an offence is itself a revolutionary change, which allows the accused's character to be called into question if he has behaved in a way which a judge considers to be 'reprehensible'.[6] Perhaps more than any other Act in recent history, the way in which this Act works depends on the approach of trial judges. When it is applied as broadly as it can be, the balance of power in criminal trials is tilted in favour of the prosecution to a degree unknown since the early nineteenth century. Some provisions of the Act, if applied as broadly as they could be, may present credible grounds for challenge under the fair trial provisions of art. 6 of the European Convention on Human Rights.[7] In *Hanson and other appeals* [2005] 1 WLR 3169 at [4], Rose LJ said:

> The starting point should be for judges and practitioners to bear in mind that Parliament's purpose in the legislation, as we divine it from the terms of the Act, was to assist in the evidence based conviction of the guilty, without putting those who are not guilty at risk of conviction by prejudice. It

---

[4] Because of the obscurity of parts of the Act's language, reference will occasionally be made in this chapter to the Explanatory Notes. Such notes have been held to be 'admissible aids' to the construction of an Act: see *R (Westminster City Council) v National Asylum Support Service* [2002] 1 WLR 2956, [5] per Lord Steyn.

[5] This is in contrast to the view of the Law Commission, which was that: 'All parties to the trial should feel free to present their case on the central facts in issue free from the fear that this will automatically result in previous misconduct being exposed' (Report 273, para. 1.8(1)).

[6] The Law Commission, in Report 273, had proposed that the conduct should be such that it might be 'viewed with disapproval by a reasonable person', a formulation which also appeared in various drafts of the Criminal Justice Bill, but which Parliament apparently ultimately considered to be too vague. It seems open to question whether the wording of the Act successfully meets that particular objection.

[7] A possibility acknowledged generally and without elaboration, *per curiam*, by the Court of Appeal in *Highton and other appeals* [2005] 1 WLR 3472, [13]–[14].

is accordingly to be hoped that prosecution applications to adduce such evidence will not be made routinely, simply because a defendant has previous convictions, but will be based on the particular circumstances of each case.

But it is already clear that, once admitted, evidence of bad character can be used for any relevant purpose, regardless of the gateway through which it is admitted: see *Highton and other appeals* [2005] 1 WLR 3472; 6.6.1, below.

The Act's character evidence provisions, with the exception of s. 113 relating to proceedings in service courts, came into effect for the purposes of any trial or hearing beginning after 15 December 2004: see *Bradley* [2005] EWCA Crim 20, [34].

6.2 BASIC RULE: ADMISSIBILITY OF EVIDENCE OF BAD CHARACTER EXCLUSIVELY STATUTORY

The provisions of the Criminal Justice Act 2003 dealing with evidence of bad character are contained in Chapter 1 of Part 11 of the Act. They are concerned only with issues of admissibility related to the fact that the evidence is evidence of bad character, and do not affect any other rule of evidence which may require its exclusion: see s. 112(3)(c).[8] The subject of admissibility is dealt with under two main headings, the bad character of a non-defendant, which is governed by s. 100, and the bad character of the defendant, which is governed by s. 101, supplemented by ss. 102 to 106. There are also a number of definitional and procedural provisions. The foundation of the new law, however, is to be found in s. 99, which sweeps away the common law rules governing the admissibility of evidence of bad character. The result is that the new statutory rules provide the exclusive basis for the admissibility of such evidence.[9] Section 99 provides:

(1) The common law rules governing the admissibility of bad character in criminal proceedings are abolished.
(2) Subsection (1) is subject to 118(1) in so far as it preserves the rule under which in criminal proceedings a person's reputation is admissible for the purposes of proving his bad character.[10]

At common law, as we have seen, there were two distinct rules of admissibility of evidence of bad character in criminal cases: the rule permitting the prosecution to adduce evidence in rebuttal of evidence of good character adduced by the accused; and the rule permitting the prosecution to adduce any evidence relevant to guilt for reasons other than character, notwithstanding

[8] If the Court concludes that evidence tendered by the prosecution does not amount to evidence of bad character, Chapter 1 of Part 11 does not apply and its admissibility must be assessed with respect to its relevance and any other rules of evidence which may be applicable: see *Weir and other appeals* [2006] 1 WLR 1885 (appeal of *Manister*) at [95]. The fact that the accused, then a man aged 34, had previously entered into a consensual relationship with a 16-year-old girl was not, *per se*, reprehensible, and did not amount to evidence of bad character. But it was admitted as relevant evidence under common law principles on charges of indecent assault on a 13-year-old girl committed when the accused was 39. The relevance was said to be that the evidence showed his interest in young girls. Presumably the Court had in mind the 'background evidence' principle of the *res gestae* rule (see 2.7). But the Court's reliance on this principle, and its dismissal of the possibility of excluding the evidence under s. 78 of the Police and Criminal Evidence Act 1984 (see 3.7), both stated without discussion, are, with respect, unconvincing.
[9] Section 1(3) of the Criminal Evidence Act 1898 is also repealed in consequence of the new provisions: see Sch. 37, Part 5 of the Act.
[10] Section 118 is found in Chapter 2 of Part 11 which deals with hearsay evidence. Section 118(1) preserves the common law exception to the rule against hearsay permitting the admissibility of reputation evidence for this purpose, which would otherwise have been abolished by virtue of s. 114: see 8.1.2 *et seq*.

that it might reveal some aspect of the accused's bad character. Both rules are superseded by the statutory provisions: see s. 101(f) (6.12); and s. 101(d) (6.10). The Act applies only to criminal cases, defined by s. 112 as criminal proceedings in relation to which the strict rules of evidence apply.[11] Thus, the bad character provisions of the Act in general apply both to trials on indictment in the Crown Court and to summary trials in magistrates' courts, though some particular provisions apply only to trials on indictment. Section 113 and Sch. 6 to the Act extend the relevant provisions to proceedings before Service Courts with changes in the wording of some provisions appropriate to court martial proceedings.

6.3 BASIC DEFINITIONS

There are a number of important definitions which apply to the substantive provisions dealing with admissibility. The terms defined are central to an understanding of the rules of admissibility, and it is, therefore, convenient to deal with them here. The most significant definition is that of the expression 'bad character', the first statutory definition of any aspect of character to be enacted for any purpose.

6.3.1 Definition of 'bad character'

Section 98 of the Act provides:

References in this Chapter to evidence of a person's 'bad character' are to evidence of, or a disposition towards, misconduct on his part, other than evidence which—
   (a) has to do with the alleged facts of the offence with which the defendant is charged, or
   (b) is evidence of misconduct in connection with the investigation or prosecution of that offence.
Section 112 supplements this definition by providing that 'misconduct' means 'the commission of an offence or other reprehensible behaviour'.

This is, and is intended to be, a potentially very wide definition.

6.3.2 Evidence of misconduct not having to do with offence charged

Common sense suggests that to adduce evidence tending to prove that the accused committed the offence charged is not to adduce evidence of his 'bad character'. Section 98 recognizes this obvious proposition. Therefore, to qualify as evidence of bad character, evidence of misconduct must not have to do with the facts of the offence charged, or be evidence of misconduct in connection with the investigation or prosecution of that offence. Evidence related to the offence charged because it is part and parcel of the same transaction (including evidence admissible as part of the *res gestae*) is not evidence of bad character at common law, and is admissible on the basis of its relevance: see 2.7. This was also the position under the Criminal Evidence Act 1898. The accused's shield did not protect him against cross-examination directed to showing his guilt of the offence charged (*ibid.* at s. 1(2)). The Criminal Justice Act 2003 takes the same view. Thus, if the accused assaults a police officer in the course of resisting arrest on a charge of robbery for

---

[11] As the Court of Appeal points out in *Bradley* [2005] EWCA Crim 20, [36] this is unnecessarily confusing, as the strict rules of evidence apply to all criminal proceedings. For the admissibility of evidence of bad character in civil cases at common law, see 5.4, 5.6.

which he is later tried, or attempts to destroy evidence connecting him to the crime, or threatens a prosecution witness while awaiting trial, none of these acts would amount to evidence of bad character for the purposes of s. 98 of the Criminal Justice Act 2003. This means that their admissibility would not be governed by the provisions of the Act. It is submitted that they remain admissible by virtue of their obvious relevance as they would have been before the coming into effect of the Act. On the other hand, evidence that the accused committed a similar robbery a week before the crime for which he is being tried would amount to evidence of bad character, and would be admissible, if at all, only by virtue of the provisions of the Act. Whether or not evidence 'has to do with' the offence charged is a question of fact and degree. In *Tirnaveanu*[12] the Court of Appeal held that, for evidence to have to do with the facts of the instant case, there must be a nexus in time between the instant case and the evidence. The accused had posed as a solicitor for the purpose of facilitating the illegal entry of a number of persons into the UK. The asserted evidence of bad character consisted of similar previous acts. Despite the Court's assertion that in some cases there may be a 'possible overlap',[13] there was surely little room for doubt that the evidence in this case, which consisted of separate albeit similar offences, did not have to do with the facts of the instant offence and was evidence of bad character. If an overlap is a possible area of concern, is submitted that it might be more useful to look for a nexus in terms of common facts in addition to a nexus in time; the latter alone may perhaps be misleading in some cases. In most cases the matter should cause no real difficulty.

6.3.3 Commission of offence

That the commission of an offence[14] is to be regarded as misconduct is uncontroversial, and reflects the position at common law. The commission of the offence suffices: there is no requirement that the offence be one of which the subject has been convicted, or even one with which he has been charged. If the accused has been convicted of the offence, then by statute, the fact that he has been convicted may be proved, and on proof of the conviction, he is taken to have committed the offence in question unless he proves the contrary.[15] If there is no conviction, then admissible evidence must be adduced to show that he committed the offence. This was the practice at common law in cases where evidence of offences not covered by the indictment was admitted. The fact that the accused might dispute that he committed the other offences did not render the evidence inadmissible,[16] and the prosecution would adduce evidence with a view to showing that he committed them. At common law, it was further held by the House of Lords in *Z* [2000] 2 AC 483 that even the fact that the accused had previously been charged with and acquitted of

---

[12] [2007] 1 WLR 3049 Cf. *Machado* [2006] EWCA Crim 837; *Watson* [2006] EWCA Crim 2308.

[13] Acknowledging a clearly valid point made by Professor J. Spencer in his monograph *Evidence of Bad Character* (2006) at 2.23.

[14] Section 112 defines 'offence' as including a service offence. The Act is silent as to offences against foreign law, but it has now been held that a foreign conviction can be used as evidence of bad character: see *Kordansinski* [2007] 1 Cr App R 238; a decision consistent with the law on rebuttal of good character: see *El Delbi* [2003] EWCA Crim 1767; 5.11.3. As to the proof of foreign convictions, see Evidence Act 1851, s. 7; *Blackstone's Criminal Practice*, 2009 edn, para. F8.11.

[15] Police and Criminal Evidence Act 1984, s. 74(3); 12.10 *et seq.*; see also Criminal Procedure Act 1865, s. 6; 17.9. There was some limited common law authority suggesting that the prosecution was not entitled to prove the fact of conviction, but merely the commission of the acts relied on: *Shepherd* (1980) 71 Cr App R 120. But this seems to fly in the face of common sense. It also conflicted with the language of s. 1 of the Criminal Evidence Act 1898 under which the conviction was a proper subject of cross-examination. The matter was surely resolved by s. 74(3) of the 1984 Act.

[16] See, e.g., *Rance* (1975) 62 Cr App R 118.

the other offences did not preclude the prosecution from seeking to adduce evidence adduced in the earlier case, even though the effect of doing so was to try to prove that he committed the offences of which the accused had been acquitted. Given that the statutory test is simply that the accused committed the other offences, there is no reason to suppose that the same rule could be not be applied in cases falling under the Criminal Justice Act 2003, and indeed it has been held that this is the proper approach in closely analogous circumstances. In the appeal of *Smith* in *Edwards and other appeals* [2006] 1 WLR 1524, it was held that the principle stated in *Z* was applicable in a case where the accused had been assured that he would not be prosecuted in respect of the conduct later used against him as evidence of bad character.[17] But it is submitted that the decision in *Z* is open to question. The accused was charged with rape. He had previously been charged with and tried for four other rapes, and had been convicted of one and acquitted of three of them. Lord Hutton, with whom the other members of the House agreed, held that the prosecution was entitled to call the complainants in the previous cases for the purpose of establishing that the accused's conduct was similar to his conduct in relation to the offence now charged. The probative value of such evidence lies in the accused's conduct rather than in the question of whether or not he may have been convicted of an offence, and it must be conceded that it may be logically possible in some cases to separate the accused's conduct from the outcome of the previous cases (which may have turned on other matters). For example, if the previous jury had a reasonable doubt as to whether the complainant had consented, it may have been necessary to acquit the accused, but his *modus operandi* in relation to performing a certain sexual act may be relevant to a later case, and may not even have been in dispute in the previous case. There is, therefore, room for some distinction. But it is difficult to avoid the conclusion that the decision of the House of Lords for all practical purposes authorizes trial judges to ignore or overturn the verdict of a jury in a previous case.[18] This seems both undesirable and unfair, and, it is submitted, ought to raise concerns under art. 6 of the European Convention on Human Rights. The House granted that the trial judge should keep his discretion to exclude in mind in such cases, but this is hardly a satisfactory way of dealing with such an important question.[19] In the appeal of *S* in *Edwards and Rowlands and other appeals* [2006] 3 All ER 882, [76]–[85], it was similarly held proper to admit as evidence of bad character evidence of similar acts of sexual assault, notwithstanding that these acts were the subject of counts in the indictment which had been stayed on the ground of abuse of process, and in respect of which the accused had previously been told that he would not be prosecuted.

6.3.4 Reprehensible behaviour

In contrast to the case of other offences, the inclusion of 'other reprehensible behaviour' in the definition of misconduct raises some difficult questions. It seems clear that what is to be regarded

---

[17] See also *Nguyen* [2008] EWCA Crim 585. The Home Office Notes explaining s. 98 state specifically that this was intended: *ibid.* at para. 354; cf. the interesting decision in *McAllister* [2009] 1 Cr App R 10.

[18] The decision may have destroyed by a side-wind the rule against contradiction of previous verdicts, and the House overruled one of the leading cases on that rule, *G (An Infant) v Coltart* [1967] 1 QB 432, while distinguishing another, *Sambasivam v Public Prosecutor, Federation of Malaya* [1950] AC 458, on not altogether satisfactory grounds (see 12.2.1). The accused also argued unsuccessfully that the admission of the evidence violated the rule against double jeopardy, but as there was no question of the accused being re-tried for the offences of which he had been acquitted, this argument was plainly unsound.

[19] See further 12.2.1. *Z* was applied in *Terry* [2005] QB 996, in which it was held that, while it may be proper for the jury to be made aware that the accused was acquitted of the offence in an earlier trial, the acquittal is not conclusive evidence of innocence except to the extent that 'innocence' means 'not guilty of the offence charged', nor does it indicate that all relevant issues were resolved in favour of the accused. Thus, the question is simply whether the evidence in question is relevant to and should be admitted in the instant case.

as reprehensible and what is not is a question for the judge. The judge has the duty of deciding questions of the admissibility of evidence of bad character, which includes the question of
whether or not an item of evidence amounts to evidence of a person's bad character. Indeed, such
a ruling is declared to be a 'relevant ruling' for which the judge is required to give reasons under
s. 110(1) of the Act: see s. 110(2)(a). The basis on which the judge should make such a ruling,
however, is less clear, and the Act provides no further guidance about it.[20]

Perhaps the clearest case is that of conduct which is akin to an offence, but does not amount
to one technically, or is unlikely to be prosecuted as one because of the circumstances in which
the act was committed. In *Marsh* [1994] Crim LR 52, a case decided under the Criminal Evidence
Act 1898, the accused had asserted his previous good character. Although he had no previous
convictions, it appeared that the accused had a considerable disciplinary record arising from a
pattern of violent conduct on the rugby field. It was held that the prosecution was entitled to
cross-examine about this record because it indicated that the accused had, to that extent, a bad
character and was, therefore, relevant to rebut his assertion of good character. Similarly, a person
who has committed a number of acts of sexual harassment in the workplace may have been dismissed from his employment without criminal proceedings being commenced against him, even
though the acts might have been prosecuted as offences of sexual assault. It is submitted that such
acts would amount to reprehensible behaviour for the purposes of s. 98. Evidence of behaviour
which results in the making of an anti-social behaviour order against the subject would no doubt
be admissible, even though such an order is not a conviction, and proceedings for anti-social
behaviour orders are technically civil proceedings.

Beyond these and analogous cases lies a vast grey area. One can only sympathize with the task
of trial judges in having to assess whether or not any given behaviour is reprehensible in a case
in which its moral quality is ambiguous. On the other hand, it may be that judges are simply
in much the same dilemma as they were under s. 1(3)(ii) of the Criminal Evidence Act 1898.
That subsection provided that the accused should lose his shield against cross-examination as to
character if he made 'imputations' against the character of the prosecutor, the witnesses for the
prosecution, or the deceased victim of the alleged crime. The term 'imputation on character' was
similarly not defined by the Act, and it was left to the judges to determine what it meant in the
light of their view of current societal *mores*. The imputation of a crime was clearly covered, but
that provides no assistance under s. 98 because it is independently accounted for. The authorities
appear to hold that any seriously morally discreditable conduct could amount to an imputation.
In the notorious case of *Bishop*,[21] the accused was charged with burglary. He sought to explain
away evidence that his fingerprints were found in a room by alleging that he had had a homosexual affair with the occupier of the room. The evidence was offered, not as an attack on the occupier's character, but to rebut the allegation that the accused had been a trespasser in the room, an
essential element of the offence of burglary. But it was held that he had made an imputation on
the character of the occupier, a prosecution witness, and that his shield was lost. If the occupier
had been a woman, the accused's allegation might not have amounted to an imputation on her
character in 1975, though it probably would have amounted to an imputation in 1948. It is to be
hoped that the question would be decided differently today in either case. In *McLean* [1978] Crim
LR 430, it was held that the judge should not have forfeited the accused's shield simply because

---

[20] Section 106, which deals with attacks on another person's character, provides no clarification. Indeed, as it
relies on a similar definition of 'character' it re-creates the same problem in another context.
[21] [1975] QB 274. And see *Selvey* v *DPP* [1970] AC 304.

it was suggested in cross-examination to a prosecution witness, who admitted to having been drunk, that he had used abusive language. But what if the suggestion had been that the witness had been intoxicated because of his consumption of cannabis or cocaine?

It is inevitable that such decisions will reflect a measure of subjectivity, but it is to be hoped that judges will make a reasonable effort to decide the matter objectively and by reference to current *mores*. But they may have to look even further. Having regard to arts 8 and 10 of the European Convention on Human Rights, it is submitted that judges must now be careful about describing behaviour as reprehensible merely because it does not reflect the values of the majority of society. Society today is composed of persons with diverse cultural and religious backgrounds and practices, and this must surely be considered in evaluating behaviour which a particular judge may personally find to be undesirable or even offensive. It may well be that *Bishop* would have to be decided differently today for that reason alone. Such considerations alone might not prevent behaviour from being viewed as reprehensible, any more than they prevent some acts, such as 'honour killings' or female genital mutilation from amounting to offences. But a judge faced with an accused who had, say, pressured his daughter into an arranged marriage might find himself in some difficulties if he sought to describe that behaviour as reprehensible. In *Saleem* [2007] EWCA Crim 1766, it appears to have been held that the writing of violent rap lyrics could be regarded as 'reprehensible', a view which to some may represent the thin edge of the wedge. While such conduct may in some cases amount to the commission of an offence, for example speech promoting racial hatred, it is submitted that such findings as to non-criminal conduct must be considered with the utmost care; they may infringe on the right of freedom of expression. It is particularly important that they not simply reflect the views of an individual judge (or, for that matter, the Court of Appeal).

6.3.5 Disposition towards misconduct

The subject's disposition towards committing either an offence or other reprehensible behaviour may also amount to bad character. The difference lies in the area of the kind of evidence likely to be adduced. Circumstantial evidence suggesting that a person has the propensity towards certain kinds of behaviour may be adduced in addition to, or instead of evidence that he has behaved in the manner in question. It is submitted that it is of great importance to ensure that the evidence does in fact reflect disposition towards misconduct. At common law, the danger of admitting evidence of disposition indiscriminately was one of the more persistent issues in the law of character evidence. The classic example was the question of the extent to which the accused's sexual propensities were relevant evidence, if he was charged with a sexual offence. This was a hotly debated question, and arguably one which was never finally resolved.[22] In many older cases, and some more recent ones, the accused's disposition towards homosexuality was simply equated without further analysis with a propensity to commit sexual offences against males.[23] But it is submitted that the true rule was laid down in *DPP v Boardman* [1975] AC 221, in which it was held, disapproving *Thompson* and *Sims* (note 23) that sexual cases should be regarded in

---

[22] See, e.g., *King* [1967] 2 QB 338; *Horwood* [1970] 1 QB 133; both cases concerned with the propriety of evidence having the effect simply of suggesting that the accused was homosexual.

[23] *Thompson v R* [1918] AC 221: 'Persons, however, who commit the offences now under consideration seek the habitual gratification of a particular perverted lust, which not only takes them out of the class of ordinary men gone wrong, but stamps them with the hallmark of a specialised and extraordinary class as much as if they carried on their bodies some physical peculiarity', *ibid.* at 235 per Lord Sumner. See also *Sims* [1946] KB 531, 540.

exactly the same way as any other case, the test of admissibility being that of relevance.[24] Leaving aside consideration of arts 8 and 10 of the European Convention, which, by analogy with the point made above, would probably now require the approach taken in *Boardman* and other more recent cases to be followed, it is clear that under s. 98, evidence of disposition must be specifically of disposition towards misconduct, i.e., towards the commission of an offence or other reprehensible behaviour. For example, evidence suggesting a disposition towards sexual involvement with children, such as possession of child pornography, would amount to evidence of bad character, whereas evidence suggesting only sexual propensity towards adults of either sex would not. Similarly, evidence of a pattern of racist speech and actions would be evidence of disposition towards reprehensible behaviour, if not towards racially motivated offences, and thus would also be evidence of bad character.

6.4 PROOF OF BAD CHARACTER

It seems clear from ss. 98 and 99 that the evidence to be permitted as proof of bad character must include evidence that the subject was guilty of acts or omissions which amount to misconduct, i.e., the commission of an offence or other reprehensible behaviour. In addition, circumstantial evidence of his disposition towards misconduct as thus defined is admissible, for example evidence of acts or statements suggestive of past or future misconduct, or possession of articles commonly used on connection with such misconduct. Section 99(2) also clearly contemplates the use of evidence of reputation evidence, though what this might be is not altogether clear. Section 99(2) relies on the preservation of reputation evidence by s. 118(1), but it is important to understand the context of the latter rule. The only effect of s. 118(1) is to preserve certain common law exceptions to the rule against hearsay, which would otherwise have been abolished by virtue of the new statutory régime for hearsay in criminal cases under s. 114. Thus, s. 118(1) has no effect on the substantive working of the reputation rule in relation to character evidence. It preserves (*inter alia*):

> Any rule of law under which in criminal proceedings evidence of a person's reputation is admissible for the purpose of proving his good or bad character.
>
> *Note*
> The rule is preserved only in so far as it allows the court to treat such evidence as proving the matter concerned.[25]

In fact, it is difficult to identify the extent of any common law rule permitting the use of reputation evidence to prove bad character (as opposed to good character). The prosecution is no doubt entitled to use such evidence to rebut a false assertion of good character, but in practice it is rarely, if ever done. As we saw in Chapter 5, reputation evidence is no longer regarded as the most reliable form of character evidence. The use of evidence of previous convictions and other discreditable acts is a far more effective method of rebutting false evidence of good character, and a prosecutor who has no such evidence is likely to leave the subject alone. Because s. 98 clearly

---

[24] See also *DPP v P* [1991] 2 AC 447; *Scarrott* [1978] QB 1016.

[25] This reproduces language to the same effect in s. 7(3) of the Civil Evidence Act 1995. Its effect is obscure; for what other purpose would the evidence be adduced? Section 7(3) of the 1995 Act adds that reputation is to be 'treated as a fact and not as a statement or multiplicity of statements about the matter in question'. This seems to have the effect of reclassifying reputation as something other than hearsay. As the 1995 Act effectively abolishes the rule against hearsay in civil cases for the purpose of admissibility, it is strange that the 1995 Act has this wording while the 2003 Act does not. See 11.2.

permits the use of specific evidence of the commission of offences and reprehensible behaviour, it seems unlikely that reputation evidence will play a significant role in establishing bad character. It may be that it will occasionally be useful in establishing a person's disposition, but even in this context specific evidence of acts or statements or possession of relevant articles would be likely to be far more effective.

One welcome feature of the Act is that there is no longer any distinction between evidence admissible in chief as part of the prosecution's case and matters which can be put to the accused in cross-examination if he elects to give evidence. The admissibility of evidence now depends entirely on the provisions of the Act, which does not distinguish between those two methods of adducing it. Therefore, when admissible, the evidence can be adduced as part of the prosecution's case and used for the purposes of cross-examination if the accused gives evidence. As a practical matter, however, the gateways for admissibility of the accused's bad character under some of the provisions of s. 101(1) may not arise until it becomes clear how the accused intends to present his case. If the gateway for admissibility does not arise until after the close of the prosecution's case, no doubt the prosecution can apply to adduce evidence of bad character in rebuttal.

6.4.1 Proof of previous convictions

By virtue of ss. 73 and 74 of the Police and Criminal Evidence Act 1984, if it is admissible to prove in any proceedings that a person has been convicted or acquitted of an offence, a certificate of conviction or acquittal from the court of trial is admissible for that purpose; and a person who has been convicted of an offence shall be taken to have committed that offence unless he proves the contrary. These provisions, which abrogated the common law rule (the rule in *Hollington v Hewthorn*) according to which a judgment was inadmissible in later proceedings for or against strangers to the judgment as evidence of the facts on which the judgment was based, are considered in greater detail at 12.7 *et seq.*

6.4.2 Exclusion of juvenile convictions

Section 108(2) of the Act precludes the admission in some cases of evidence of juvenile convictions. It provides:

> In proceedings for an offence committed or alleged to have been committed by the defendant when aged 21 or over, evidence of his conviction for an offence when under the age of 14 is not admissible unless—
> (a) both of the offences are triable only on indictment; and
> (b) the court is satisfied that the interests of justice require the evidence to be admissible.

Both the heading of s. 108 ('offences committed by defendant when a child') and the Home Office's Note to the section apparently make it clear that the intent of this provision is to exclude evidence of offences *committed* by the defendant while under the age of 14. The wording of the subsection itself, however, appears ambiguous, and could be read as excluding only offences of which he was also *convicted* while under that age. It would seem more logical to adopt the intent expressed in the heading, given that the concern is to offer protection against the revelation of juvenile crimes (i.e., crimes committed by juveniles) as a concession to the defendant's presumed immaturity at the time when he committed the offence.[26] The date of conviction is arbitrary,

---

[26] The date of commission of an offence, rather than the date of conviction, is in general the significant date for all purposes under the Act: see, e.g., the appeal of *Gilmore* in *Hanson and other appeals* [2005] 1 WLR 3169, [11], [38].

and whether the accused was convicted before or after his fourteenth birthday may depend on matters which have no obvious relevance to the issue of whether or not he should be protected against revelation of the offence. On the other hand, s. 108 repeals and replaces s. 16(2) of the Children and Young Persons Act 1963, which unambiguously provided for the exclusion of evidence of 'any offence of which he was found guilty while under the age of fourteen'. It appears that some clarification may be needed. The 1963 Act excluded evidence of such juvenile convictions in all cases for all purposes connected with the present discussion.[27] The 2003 Act offers more limited protection, and allows the judge to admit them in some cases. The test under s. 2(a) is whether both offences are 'triable' only on indictment; thus, it is submitted, the fact that the juvenile offence would have been tried by summary procedure in a youth court is irrelevant. It is the seriousness of the offence that matters. The test under s. 2(b) ought to predispose judges to exclude juvenile convictions in most cases. It is a far more stringent test than the process of balancing probative value against the prejudice to the accused. It is submitted that a juvenile conviction should be admitted only where it is for a very serious offence, and where it is clearly relevant and has a particularly compelling probative value with respect to the issues before the court. There is a strong public policy interest in offering juvenile offenders the opportunity to put their past behind them. As both s. 108(2) and (3) make clear, the section applies only where the juvenile conviction is that of a defendant in the present case and his bad character is admissible under s. 101. It has no application to the bad character of non-defendants admissible under s. 100.

6.4.3 Spent convictions

The Criminal Justice Act 2003 does not affect the practice with respect to spent convictions under the Rehabilitation of Offenders Act 1974. A conviction becomes spent with age. Section 4(1) of the Act provides that, where a conviction is spent, the offender shall be treated as if he had not committed, or been charged with, or been convicted of or sentenced for that offence. Section 7(2)(a) of the Act provides that s. 4(1) does not apply for the purposes of criminal proceedings.[28] Thus, as a matter of strict law the Act does not prevent reference to spent convictions when they are otherwise admissible under the rules governing the admissibility of evidence of bad character. However, an important Practice Direction was issued by the Lord Chief Justice on 30 June 1975, now replaced in the same terms by the Consolidated Criminal Practice Direction. Paragraph 1.6.4 of the Direction provides that no reference should be made to a spent conviction 'when such reference can reasonably be avoided'. Paragraph 1.6.6 provides that no such reference should be made in open court without the authority of the judge, 'which authority should not be given unless the interests of justice so require'. In *Nye* (1982) 75 Cr App R 247, it was held to be wrong in principle for the prosecution to cross-examine an accused about convictions which are minor or remote in time. Indeed, as we have seen (5.11) an accused may, with leave of the court, be presented to the jury as a person of good character if he has only spent convictions, provided that the jury are not misled. However, in *Corelli* [2001] Crim LR 913, it was held that the Practice Direction could not be used to deprive a co-accused of his statutory right to cross-examine the accused under s. 1(3)(iii) of the Criminal Evidence Act 1898, where the accused lost his shield

---

[27] An amendment allowed reference to such convictions for certain purposes in connection with mandatory minimum and maximum sentences under the Powers of Criminal Courts (Sentencing) Act 2000, which are not germane to the present subject.

[28] In civil proceedings, s. 4(1) applies, although s. 7(3) permits reference to a spent conviction if justice cannot otherwise be done, a strong test which requires exclusion unless the circumstances are exceptional: see *Thomas* v *Commissioner of Police of the Metropolis* [1997] QB 813; cf. *Clifford* v *Clifford* [1961] 1 WLR 1274.

because he gave evidence against the co-accused. This decision was in accordance with the general rule that, while the judge had a discretion to restrain cross-examination by the prosecution under the 1898 Act, there was no such discretion to restrain cross-examination by a co-accused.[29] The Practice Direction is more akin to a discretionary practice, which cannot prevail over the specific provisions of the 1974 Act. How, if at all, the Practice Direction will be applied in relation to the statutory regime under the Criminal Justice Act 2003 remains to be seen. It may be that it will be taken as having been superseded by the specific requirements for leave and the other safeguards which have now been enacted. But it is submitted that, in the interests of fairness, there would be much to be said for continuing the practice which prevailed before the Act.

6.4.4 Proof of the details of previous convictions and reprehensible behaviour

In very many cases, particularly when the evidence is tendered under gateway (c) or (d), it is not sufficient for the prosecution to prove the fact of conviction. If the judge is to consider under gateway (c) whether it would be impossible or difficult for the jury to understand the evidence in the case without reference to the bad character, or, under gateway (d) whether the evidence shows a propensity to commit offences of the kind charged, he must be provided with as much detail as is necessary for that purpose of the previous conviction or the reprehensible behaviour, as the case may be. If the necessary detail is not admitted by the accused, the prosecution must stand ready to prove it. In *Humphris* [2005] EWCA Crim 2030, the Court of Appeal held that the prosecution must anticipate the evidence that will be required and must be in a position to prove the previous conduct in as much detail as necessary.[30] Where the accused has been convicted of an offence, proof of the details may be relatively straightforward. One course is to admit as hearsay evidence under s. 114(1)(d) of the Criminal Justice Act 2003 (see 8.20) relevant statements made by the accused during a police interview pertaining to the offence,[31] or a relevant extract from the police report pertaining to the offence. But these methods of proof cannot be taken for granted. The latter course may present particular difficulties. The report may consist of multiple hearsay, which is subject to special conditions of admissibility (see 7.6.3). Moreover, the judge must consider a variety of important matters under s. 114(2) before concluding that it would be proper to admit hearsay under s. 114(1)(d) (see 8.20.1), and there will be many cases where the accused disputes the detail of the offence, where it would be unfair to do so. In such a case, and where either the accused is alleged to have committed an offence of which he has not been convicted, or the evidence consists of reprehensible behaviour rather than the commission of an offence, it may be necessary to call witnesses to prove the accused's previous conduct. This shows that the prosecution must anticipate any difficulties sufficiently in advance of trial to allow provision to be made for them.

6.5 OTHER DEFINITIONS

Section 112(1) and (2) of the Act provide a number of definitions important to the working of the statutory scheme. These are as follows:

> (1) In this Chapter—
> 'bad character' is to be read in accordance with section 98;

---

[29] See *Murdoch v Taylor* [1965] AC 574; see generally 3.9.
[30] See also *Colliard* [2008] EWCA Crim 1175.
[31] See *Steen* [2008] 2 Cr App R 26.

'criminal proceedings' means criminal proceedings in relation to which the strict rules of evidence apply;

'defendant', in relation to criminal proceedings, means a person charged with an offence in those proceedings; and 'co-defendant', in relation to a defendant, means a person charged with an offence in the same proceedings;

'important matter' means a matter of substantial importance in the context of the case as a whole;

'misconduct' means the commission of an offence or other reprehensible behaviour;

'offence' includes a service offence;

'probative value', and 'relevant' (in relation to an item of evidence), are to be read in accordance with section 109;

'prosecution evidence' means evidence which is to be (or has been) adduced by the prosecution, or which a witness is to be invited to give (or has given) in cross-examination by the prosecution;

'service offence' means an offence under the Army Act 1955 (3 & 4 Eliz. 2 c. 18), the Air Force Act 1955 (3 & 4 Eliz. 2 c. 19) or the Naval Discipline Act 1957 (c. 53);

'written charge' has the same meaning as in section 29 and also includes an information.

(2) Where a defendant is charged with two or more offences in the same criminal proceedings, this Chapter (except section 101(3)) has effect as if each offence were charged in separate proceedings; and references to the offence with which the defendant is charged are to be read accordingly.

In relation to the definition of 'probative value' and 'relevant', s. 109 provides:

(1) Subject to subsection (2) a reference in this Chapter to the relevance or probative value of evidence is a reference to the relevance or probative value on the assumption that it is true.

(2) In assessing the relevance or probative value of an item of evidence for any purpose of this Chapter, a court need not assume that the evidence is true if it appears, on the basis of any material before the court (including any evidence it decides to hear on the matter) that no court or jury could reasonably find it to be true.

To some extent, subsection (1) seems to state the obvious. In legal proceedings, it is probably necessary for a judge to assume the truth of evidence for the purpose of assessing its relevance and probative value (see 2.8). If the state of the evidence is such as to lead the judge to the conclusion in subsection (2), while it might be possible to conclude that the evidence has some relevance and some minimal probative value, it would seem to make it almost impossible for the judge then to make a positive finding in terms of admissibility.

B   SECTION 101: EVIDENCE OF BAD CHARACTER OF ACCUSED

SUMMARY OF MAIN POINTS

- Evidence of the bad character of the accused is governed exclusively by s. 101 of the Criminal Justice At 2003.

- Under that section it is admissible only through any one of the seven 'gateways' provided, namely:

    (a) all parties to the proceedings agree to the evidence being admissible,

    (b) the evidence is adduced by the defendant himself or is given in answer to a question asked by him in cross-examination and intended to elicit it,

> (c) it is important explanatory evidence,
>
> (d) it is relevant to an important matter in issue between the defendant and the prosecution,
>
> (e) it has substantial probative value in relation to an important matter in issue between the defendant and a co-defendant,
>
> (f) it is evidence to correct a false impression given by the defendant, or
>
> (g) the defendant has made an attack on another person's character.

6.6 EVIDENCE OF ACCUSED'S BAD CHARACTER IN GENERAL

The admissibility of the bad character of the accused in criminal proceedings is now governed exclusively by s. 101 of the Criminal Justice Act 2003, which provides:

> (1) In criminal proceedings evidence of the defendant's bad character is admissible if, but only if—
>
> (a) all parties to the proceedings agree to the evidence being admissible,
>
> (b) the evidence is adduced by the defendant himself or is given in answer to a question asked by him in cross-examination and intended to elicit it,
>
> (c) it is important explanatory evidence,
>
> (d) it is relevant to an important matter in issue between the defendant and the prosecution,
>
> (e) it has substantial probative value in relation to an important matter in issue between the defendant and a co-defendant,
>
> (f) it is evidence to correct a false impression given by the defendant, or
>
> (g) the defendant has made an attack on another person's character.
>
> (2) Sections 102 to 106 contain provision supplementing subsection (1).
>
> (3) The court must not admit evidence under subsection (1)(d) or (g) if, on an application by the defendant to exclude it, it appears to the court that the admission of the evidence would have such an adverse effect on the fairness of the proceedings that the court ought not to admit it.
>
> (4) On an application to exclude evidence under subsection (3) the court must have regard, in particular, to the length of time between the matters to which that evidence relates and the matters which form the subject of the offence charged.

Section 101(1) makes it clear that the section is the only basis on which the accused's bad character can now be admitted in criminal proceedings. The subsection provides seven separate grounds for admission, which are generally referred to as 'gateways', any one of which will render evidence of bad character admissible. Gateways (a), (b), (f), and (g) are in a sense related; in each of these cases the accused himself brings up the question of his character, or assents to its being brought up, or conducts his case in such a way that it will be brought up. In the case of gateways (a) and (b) the accused expressly brings up, or assents to the bringing up of his bad character. In the case of gateway (f) he makes an assertion of his good character, in such a way as to create a false impression about his character; in gateway (g) he does not raise the issue of his character himself, but is deemed to put it in issue by making an attack on the character of another. Gateways (c) and (d) are cases in which the prosecution takes the initiative in adducing evidence of the accused's bad character as part of its case, because it is relevant to the issue of guilt or the accused's credibility; accordingly, these gateways do not depend upon any assertion of character, good or bad, made by the accused, or upon his assent to the subject being brought up. Finally, gateway (e) deals with cases in which a question arises as to which of two or more co-accused may be guilty, or which of them has the greater credibility, and one accused adduces evidence of the bad character of his co-accused because it is relevant to one of these issues. Each gateway except (a) and (b) is supplemented by further provisions contained in ss. 102 to 106. Gateways (d) and (g) are subject to a new exclusionary rule dealt with by s. 101(3) and (4), which will be considered later in the chapter under the heading of safeguards (see 6.20).

The judge often rules on the admissibility of evidence of bad character at the outset of the trial. But there is no requirement that he do so at that stage. It may be that it is unclear whether a particular gateway will be open, for example under gateway (d) it may not yet be clear whether the factual basis of the previous offences is relevant to the offence charged; under gateway (g) it may not be clear whether the accused will make an attack on the character of another person. Unless it would result in unfairness to the accused, for example because he may be unsure of the extent of the prosecution case he has to meet, the judge has a discretion to delay his ruling until the position becomes clearer.[32] The judge must, of course, rule before the close of the prosecution case. It is not unusual for additional gateways to open during a trial. For example, where the judge admits evidence under gateway (d) or delays a ruling under that gateway, the accused may open gateway (f) by giving a false impression; gateway (g) by attacking the character of another; or (at the instance of a co-accused) gateway (e) by undermining that co-accused's defence. Where this occurs, it is essential for the judge to give reasons in support of his decision to admit the evidence with reference to each applicable gateway separately, so that it is clear for the purposes of the trial and of any appeal which gateways are in play.[33]

6.6.1 Relevance and use of evidence; direction to jury

The gateways govern the admissibility of evidence of bad character under the Act, but they do not limit the use which may be made of the evidence, once admitted. This is a function of the relevance of the evidence to the issues before the jury.[34] In *Highton and other appeals* [2005] 1 WLR 3472, Highton was charged with kidnapping and theft. Because, as part of his defence, he had accused the victims of the offences of lying, the prosecution were permitted to adduce evidence of Highton's previous convictions for assault and affray under gateway (g) (see 6.13), but the prosecution did not contend that the evidence of bad character might have been admissible separately under gateway (d) as showing the accused's propensity to commit offences of the kind charged. The judge nonetheless directed the jury that they were entitled to make use of the evidence for the latter purpose also, and Highton was convicted. He appealed on the ground that the jury should have been directed that the evidence was admissible only for the purposes of assesssing his credibility in relation to his attack on the credibility of the victims. This would have been the position under the corresponding provisions of the Criminal Evidence Act 1898 (see the 8th edition of this work at 5.19). But the Court of Appeal held that the direction was proper. Lord Woolf CJ said:

> ...s.101(1) itself states that it is dealing with the question of admissibility and makes no reference to the effect that admissible evidence as to bad character is to have. We also consider that the width of the definition in s.98 of what is evidence as to bad character suggests that, wherever such evidence is admitted, it can be admitted for any purpose for which it is relevant in the case in which it is being

---

[32] See, e.g., *Gyima* [2007] EWCA Crim 429.

[33] As to the duty to give reasons, see s. 110 of the Act: 6.22.3.

[34] If the evidence is not relevant to any issue before the jury, then in accordance with general principles, it should not be admitted: see the appeal of *Van Nguyen* in *Highton and other appeals* [2005] 1 WLR 3472, [39].

admitted. We therefore conclude that a distinction must be drawn between the *admissibility* of evidence of bad character, which depends on it getting through one of the gateways, and the *use* to which it may be put once it is admitted. It is true that the reasoning that leads to the admission of evidence under gateway (d) may also determine the matters to which the evidence is relevant or primarily relevant once admitted. That is not true, however, of all the gateways. In the case of gateway (g), for example, admissibility depends on the defendant having made an attack on another person's character, but once the evidence is admitted, it may, depending on the particular facts, be relevant not only to credibility but also to propensity to commit offences of the kind with which the defendant is charged. [*Ibid.* at [9]–[10], emphasis in original.][35]

The departure from the practice under the Criminal Justice Act 1898 is a radical one. It has the merit that the jury need no longer attempt to make a very fine distinction in their minds when considering the evidence, as between the substantive issue of guilt and the credibility of the accused. As the two are often inseparably linked, it was a distinction which was often less than compelling, and one which attracted significant criticism (see the 8th edition of this work, loc. cit.) Nonetheless, the potential for prejudice to the accused is very real, especially as the accused may have no choice but to conduct his defence in such a way that his bad character becomes admissible.

The Court of Appeal has on several occasions emphasized that the judge must direct the jury in the clearest terms as to the relevance and use of evidence of bad character. The direction must emphasize that the possession of a bad character is not in itself evidence of guilt of the offence now charged, or, for that matter, that the accused is necessarily untruthful. The minds of the jury must be focused clearly on the relevance of the evidence and, as far as possible, diverted from any purely prejudicial effect it may tend to produce. In *Hanson and other appeals* [2005] 1 WLR 3169, Rose LJ said:

Our final general observation is that, in any case in which evidence of bad character is admitted to show propensity, whether to commit offences or to be untruthful, the judge in summing-up should warn the jury clearly against placing undue reliance on previous convictions. Evidence of bad character cannot be used simply to bolster a weak case, or to prejudice the minds of the jury against a defendant. In particular, the jury should be directed; that they should not conclude that the defendant is guilty or untruthful merely because he has these convictions; that, although the convictions may show a propensity, this does not mean that he has committed this offence or been untruthful in this case; that whether they in fact show a propensity is for them to decide; that they must take into account what the defendant has said about his previous convictions; and that, although they are entitled, if they find propensity as shown, to take this into account when determining guilt, propensity is only one relevant factor and they must assess its significance in the light of all the other evidence in the case. [*Ibid.* at [18].]

In *Edwards and other appeals* [2006] 1 WLR 1524, Rose LJ observed further:[36]

What the summing up must contain is a clear warning to the jury against placing undue reliance on previous convictions, which cannot, by themselves, prove guilt. It should be explained why the jury has heard the evidence and the ways in which it is relevant to and may help their decision. Bearing in mind

---

[35] See also the appeal of *Somanathan* in *Weir and other appeals* [2006] 1 WLR 1885 at [45].

[36] Both statements of principle by Rose LJ (in *Hanson* and *Edwards*) were cited with approval by Lord Woolf CJ in *Highton and other appeals* [2005] 1 WLR 3472 at [11].

that relevance will depend primarily, though not always exclusively, on the gateway in s.101(1) of the Criminal Justice Act 2003, through which the evidence has been admitted. [*Ibid.* at [3].]

But in *Campbell* [2007] 1 WLR 2798, the Court sent out a rather different signal, indicating (rightly) that each summing-up must be tailored to the facts of the individual case rather than mouthing the language of the statute; but also (more controversially) that the judge's failure to give the Judicial Studies Board's specimen direction (which itself had to be revised as a result of this case: see 6.10.4) would not necessarily be fatal to a conviction. Lord Phillips CJ, giving the judgment of the Court, observed (at [23]) that the failure to give the specimen direction or a direction in substantially the same form had in the past been treated as a reason to allow an appeal, 'without considering whether the jury would have reached the same conclusion by the application of common sense to the evidence, whether or not the specimen direction was given'. Lord Phillips continued:

> Failure to give a direction that is no more than assistance in applying common sense to the evidence should not automatically be treated as a ground of appeal, let alone as a reason to allow the appeal.

With respect, to dismiss the application of the rules of character evidence as a mere question of 'common sense' is unsatisfactory in the light of the Court's previous decisions, particularly those referred to above. It is submitted that when evidence as prejudicial to the accused as evidence of bad character is admitted, it is not a sufficient safeguard against the inevitable tendency of juries to give it too much weight and perhaps even regard it as decisive evidence in the case, to rely on the jury's common sense in evaluating the evidence. The specimen direction, far from being a mere matter of 'assistance in applying common sense', is in fact designed to fulfil two vital functions. Firstly, it is designed to ensure that the jury keep the evidence in perspective, understand that they are not entitled to convict because the accused has a bad character, and in particular do not regard the evidence as proof or at least compelling evidence of the accused's guilt of the offence charged. Secondly, it is designed to ensure that the minds of the jury remain focused on the issues to which the evidence is relevant, an important adjunct to the first goal. Despite the efforts of Parliament in drafting the Criminal Justice Act 2003 and those of the Court of Appeal in seeking to simplify the approach to be taken to the law, it is submitted that this area of the law, fraught as it is with danger to the fairness of the trial, remains quite technical and rightly so. It is submitted that the precision of the direction to the jury in these cases remains a necessary attribute of a fair trial in any case in which the accused's bad character has been adduced. While it is of course artificial to insist on the exact words of a specimen direction, and the Court was right to emphasize the need to tailor directions to the facts of each individual case, it is submitted that the specimen direction should nonetheless be followed in substance. It is to be hoped that the *dicta* on this subject in *Campbell* will be reconsidered when the opportunity arises.

6.7 GATEWAY (A): ALL PARTIES AGREE TO EVIDENCE BEING ADMISSIBLE

Little comment is needed about this gateway. Almost any evidence is admissible if all parties agree that it should be admitted. In this situation, the accused's character should presented to the jury in writing by way of a formal admission (see Part A of Chapter 20). The agreement to admit the evidence need not be in any particular form, but a written formal admission, which can be given to the jury, is the most satisfactory course and suffices in itself as proof of the agreement. But it is submitted that the agreement must be an express agreement to admit the evidence tendered by the prosecution, and that in case of doubt, the judge should inquire into the matter in the absence of the jury before admitting it. If the agreement is to admit the fact of a previous conviction but not the details of the offence, the agreement may be insufficient for the prosecution's purposes. It has sometimes been suggested that the accused's failure to object to the admission of the evidence is in itself sufficient to make it admissible under this gateway as an implied admission. An analogy may be drawn to *Williams v VOSA* [2008] EWHC 849 (Admin), a case on the admissibility of hearsay evidence by agreement under s. 114(1)(c) of the Act (see 8.9). But it is submitted that this proposition should be treated with care: evidence of bad character is qualitatively different from hearsay, and a failure to object may not always amount to an agreement to admit. It would seem prudent for the judge to inquire as the intentions of the defence in every case, and where the accused is unrepresented it is submitted that it is essential to do so before admitting the evidence.

6.8 GATEWAY (B): THE EVIDENCE IS ADDUCED BY THE DEFENDANT HIMSELF OR IS GIVEN IN ANSWER TO A QUESTION ASKED BY HIM IN CROSS-EXAMINATION AND INTENDED TO ELICIT IT

Although it is a relatively unusual course to take, there was no objection at common law to an accused adducing evidence of his own bad character. As in the case of good character, he may do so by cross-examining a prosecution witness to elicit the facts, for example where he questions a police officer about his previous convictions, by giving evidence himself, or (improbably in this case) calling character witnesses. The Criminal Evidence Act 1898 likewise did not prevent the accused from adducing evidence of his previous convictions; the shield provided that if asked, he should not be compelled to answer questions on the subject, but there was no prohibition on the accused bringing the subject up. Gateway (b) preserves this position. There is sometimes a valid reason for the accused to put his bad character before the jury. Where his previous convictions are relatively minor, or are for offences quite different in nature from the offence with which he is now charged, it may do no harm, and may even be advantageous to show the jury that the accused has no history of character related to the kind of offence charged. If the accused remains silent about his character, there is always the risk that the jury may speculate about it, and by bringing the subject up, the accused may even gain some credit for frankness. An accused charged with sexual assault on a child may well decide to let the jury know that he has two previous convictions for shoplifting, but has never been in any kind of trouble for sexual misconduct. An accused could even decide to let the jury know that he has previous convictions, but has always pleaded guilty in the past, with a view to suggesting that his plea of not guilty this time is significant. As we have seen (5.9) the rule in relation to evidence of good character at common law is that the accused's character is indivisible, i.e., that the accused may not introduce part of his character only and seek to exclude other parts. To some extent, the same principle may apply to the present case.[37] However, if an attempt to withhold part of the accused's character creates a false or misleading impression, evidence of his bad character then becomes admissible separately under gateway (f), and the rules governing that gateway then apply: see 6.12.

The rule makes it clear that any introduction of bad character under gateway (b) must be intended by the accused. Where the evidence is adduced by means of the evidence in chief of

---

[37] The Law Commission was prepared to depart from this rule, on the ground that the interests of justice might be best served by revelation only of that part of his character relevant to the issues in the case: Report 273, para. 1.8(6).

the accused, there can hardly be room for doubt on that matter. But it is possible for the accused to be trapped into making statements about his bad character during hostile questioning in cross-examination after he has remained silent on the subject of his character in his evidence in chief. In the analogous situation under s. 1(3)(ii) of the Criminal Evidence Act 1898, the general practice of trial judges was to hold that the accused had not lost his shield and need not answer further questions about his character, provided that his answer was a reasonable response to a hostile question designed to trap him into an admission of his bad character. It can also happen, either through malice or inadvertence, that a witness, especially a prosecution witness, mentions some aspect of the accused's bad character when to do so is not a legitimate response to the question asked. In these cases, it is submitted, gateway (b) does not apply because the question was not intended to elicit it. At common law, any reference to the bad character of the accused other than when permitted by the rules of evidence was a serious irregularity, which usually required the discharge of the jury.[38] In *Arthurton v R* [2004] 1 WLR 949 (a case decided on common law principles), the Privy Council held that the trial judge should have taken that course when a prosecution witness revealed that the accused, who had no previous convictions, had once been arrested on suspicion of an offence of the same kind as that with which he was now charged. The fact that the judge, on being asked to do so, gave the jury a good character direction was not enough to overcome the prejudice that had been caused to the accused.[39] It is submitted that the same principle should apply under the new statutory regime.

6.9 GATEWAY (C): IT IS IMPORTANT EXPLANATORY EVIDENCE

Gateway (c) is supplemented by s. 102, although it is arguable that that section does not really take the matter very much further. Judges will probably find common sense to be the most reliable guide in applying this gateway. Section 102 provides:

> For the purposes of section 101(1)(c) evidence is important explanatory evidence if—
>   (a) without it, the court or jury would find it impossible or difficult properly to understand other evidence in the case, and
>   (b) its value for understanding the case as a whole is substantial.

In the absence of any limitation, it appears that evidence is admissible under gateway (c) if tendered by a co-accused as well as by the prosecution. The evidence adduced under gateway (c) need not have direct probative value on the issue of guilt or innocence. Its purpose is to explain, clarify, or put into context other evidence which has direct probative value on that issue. For this purpose, of course, the evidence of the previous conduct must be presented in sufficient detail to provide the necessary background. The mere fact of a previous conviction will not be sufficient.

---

[38] Unintended disclosure can occur through inadvertence as well as malice: see, e.g., *Lamb* (1980) 71 Cr App R 198, where the prosecution produced Criminal Record Office photographs of the accused, even though he had cooperated in an identification parade and had done nothing at trial to render their production necessary. The Court of Appeal, allowing an appeal against conviction, held that this was equivalent to leading evidence of the fact that the accused had a criminal record.

[39] In an exceptional case, where some oblique reference is made to character in the course of a long trial, and is ignored by all concerned, it may be acceptable for the judge to assume that it has had no effect on the outcome of the case: see *Coughlan* (1976) 63 Cr App R 33. The judge must assess the matter realistically. But it is submitted that in almost every case, the only safe and fair course is to assume that he jury has understood and has been affected by the information.

There are cases in which some aspect of the accused's bad character inevitably forms part of the backdrop to the offence charged. For example, it would hardly be possible to prosecute an accused who is an inmate of a prison on a charge of murdering another prisoner without telling the jury where and in what circumstances the offence was committed.[40] But contextual evidence can be wider in scope that such immediate backdrop evidence. Perhaps the best example is that of evidence admissible under the *res gestae* principle on the ground that it enables the court or jury to view the relevant events in their full context rather than in a factual vacuum. Such evidence may be described as passive background evidence. Examples of this kind of evidence were given in Chapter 2 at 2.7, to which reference should be made. There may also be more active background evidence. In many cases, evidence of offences outside the scope of the indictment, or evidence of other misconduct may be directly linked to the offence charged by time or circumstances. Evidence of this kind is often not only relevant as background evidence, but also has probative value in relation to the offence charged. Examples would be where the accused commits a number of similar offences of theft in quick succession;[41] threatens a girl with violence if she complains to her mother about his raping her;[42] steals a car to be used as the 'getaway' vehicle in a later robbery; forges blank cheque forms for use in a later fraud; commits arson of his house with a view to making a fraudulent insurance claim; kills a bystander by dangerous driving while fleeing from the scene of a crime; or offers a police officer a bribe to give him bail when arrested for an offence. In *Bond*,[43] Kennedy J said:

> The general rule [of exclusion of evidence of bad character] cannot be applied where the facts which constitute distinct offences are at the same time part of the transaction which is the subject of the indictment. Evidence is necessarily admissible as to acts which are so closely and inextricably mixed up with the history of the guilty act itself as to form part of one chain of relevant circumstances, and so could not be excluded in the presentment of the case before the jury without the evidence being thereby rendered unintelligible.

One example envisaged by Kennedy J in *Bond* was the admission, on a charge of murder, of prior acts or threats by the accused against the deceased, which would prove a pattern of hostile intent and conduct. In *Giannetto* [1997] 1 Cr App R 1, the accused was charged with the murder of his wife. He denied any involvement in her death, but was convicted after the prosecution adduced evidence of the contents of diaries kept by the victim, and affidavits to which she had sworn for the purposes of custody proceedings, which detailed a pattern of abuse, violence, and intimidation towards her by her husband, and his determination to gain custody of their child. The Court of Appeal upheld the admission of this evidence as evidence of motive, despite the fact that the evidence was clearly prejudicial to the accused. The evidence effectively proved the accused's willingness to resort to more extreme measures to gain custody of the child when lesser measures had failed. The Court specifically approved the following statement made by the trial judge in his ruling:

> The exclusion of any description of the continuing relationship between the parties would tend to give an unreal picture to the jury. It is not so much any particular remark at any particular moment, but it is

---

[40] Though the extent of the evidence could be limited. There is no reason why the jury should be told what offence the accused had committed to be sentenced to his term of imprisonment, unless that fact is relevant for some other purpose.

[41] *Ellis* (1826) 6 B & C 145. See also the cases dealt with at 2.7, falling under the *res gestae* rule.

[42] *Rearden* (1864) 4 F & F 76.

[43] [1906] 2 KB 389, 400; and see the observations of Lord Atkinson in *Ball* [1911] AC 47, 68.

the continuing bitterness, even hatred, which apparently subsisted between them, the possible interpretation of continuing determination of the defendant to get custody of his child, to take him to Sicily come what may, by hook or by crook, that is material.

In *M* [2000] 1 WLR 421, it was held to be proper for the prosecution to adduce evidence of a long period of sustained sexual abuse of a victim by members of her family, even though much of the evidence amounted to offences not charged in the indictment. The accused were charged with a number of offences of the same kind. The evidence was said to be relevant as 'background' evidence, and for the purpose of showing that the victim was too intimidated to report the offences at the time they were committed.

It is important for judges to apply gateway (c) with awareness of the highly prejudicial effect which such evidence may have, and it is submitted that, as at common law, they should not hesitate to exclude it if unfairness to the accused may result from its admission. Although the new duty to exclude evidence under s. 101(3), on the ground that its admission would have such an adverse effect on the fairness of the proceedings that the court ought not to admit it, does not apply to gateway (c) (see 6.20) it is submitted that the general exclusionary discretion under s. 78 of the Police and Criminal Evidence Act 1978 does apply, and should always be considered (see generally 6.20; 3.7 *et seq.*). If read literally, gateway (c) could be construed as admitting some evidence of the accused's bad character almost automatically in every case, on the theory that its value for understanding the case as a whole is substantial. There is no basis for assuming that such was Parliament's intent, and it is submitted that any impulse to admit evidence on such an undiscriminating basis must be resisted. There must come a point at which the issue of fairness under art. 6 of the European Convention on Human Rights would come into play if such a view of gateway (c) were to be taken. This point was forcefully made in *Davis* [2008] EWCA 1156. The accused was charged with the murder of his partner. His defence was the partial defence of provocation. He asserted that the deceased had told him she was having an affair and intended to leave him with the children. The prosecution tendered evidence that, some 20 years before, he had accused another partner of having an affair; and that this former partner described the accused as 'jealous and controlling'. The judge was persuaded to admit this evidence under gateway (c). The Court of Appeal allowed the accused's appeal against conviction. The evidence did not fit gateway (c). It could not properly be said that the jury would find the evidence impossible or even difficult to understand without the evidence. The evidence was adduced simply to bolster the prosecution's case by casting doubt on the assertion of provocation. Because the issue of provocation was an important issue between the accused and the prosecution, the appropriate gateway would have been gateway (d). It was not proper for the prosecution to seek to admit evidence under gateway (c), relying on an apparently more flexible approach to admission, in order to avoid the detailed considerations of propensity and the potential duty to exclude under s. 101(3) which apply to gateway (d). In the present case, the prosecution might well have had considerable difficulty in persuading the judge that the evidence was relevant to propensity, and (having regard to its age and fairly general nature) that it was compelling enough not to be excluded on fairness grounds under s. 101(3): see 6.10.2 *et seq.*; 6.20). By admitting the evidence under gateway (c) the judge had circumvented these issues and deprived the accused of the protection applicable to gateway (d). This case establishes, rightly, it is submitted, that gateway (c) must be confined to its proper role as background evidence essential to put the evidence in context.

6.10 GATEWAY (D): IT IS RELEVANT TO AN IMPORTANT MATTER IN ISSUE BETWEEN THE DEFENDANT AND THE PROSECUTION

The term 'important matter' is defined by s. 112 (6.5). Gateway (d) is supplemented by s. 103, which provides:

(1) For the purposes of section 101(1)(d) the matters in issue between the defendant and the prosecution include—

(a) the question whether the defendant has a propensity to commit offences of the kind with which he is charged, except where his having such a propensity makes it no more likely that he is guilty of the offence;

(b) the question whether the defendant has a propensity to be untruthful, except where it is not suggested that the defendant's case is untruthful in any respect.

(2) Where subsection (1)(a) applies, a defendant's propensity to commit offences of the kind with which he is charged may (without prejudice to any other way of doing so) be established by evidence that he has been convicted of—

(a) an offence of the same description as the one with which he is charged, or

(b) an offence of the same category as the one with which he is charged.

(3) Subsection (2) does not apply in the case of a particular defendant if the court is satisfied, by reason of the length of time since the conviction or for any other reason, that it would be unjust for it to apply in his case.

(4) For the purposes of subsection (2)—

(a) two offences are of the same description as each other if the statement of the offence in a written charge or indictment would, in each case, be in the same terms;

(b) two offences are of the same category as each other if they belong to the same category of offences prescribed for the purposes of this section by an order made by the Secretary of State.

(5) A category prescribed by an order under subsection (4)(b) must consist of offences of the same type.

(6) Only prosecution evidence is admissible under section 101(1)(d).

This gateway is the widest and most important of all the gateways for the admission of bad character provided by s. 101. Only the prosecution may adduce evidence by virtue of gateway (d): s. 103(6). In some ways, the provisions of s. 103 are perplexing. Section 103(1) provides that the matters in issue between the defendant and the prosecution include questions of propensity.[44] The use of the word 'include' suggests that, as one would expect, there can be other important matters in issue between the defendant and the prosecution, but evidently it has not been thought necessary to provide guidance about them. Gateway (d) is subject to the duty to exclude evidence of bad character if its admission would have such an adverse effect of the fairness of the trial that the court ought not to admit it: see s. 101(3); 6.20.

6.10.1 Propensity

Section 103(1) establishes two distinct ways in which evidence of propensity may be admissible. Under s. 103(1)(a) it may be admissible to establish the accused's guilt of the offence charged

---

[44] As we have seen (6.6.1) evidence of bad character may be used as evidence of propensity not only when admitted specifically under gateway (d), but also if admitted under another gateway, for example gateway (g) in response to an attack by the accused on the character of another person.

directly, where the propensity is said to make it more likely that he is guilty of that offence. Under s. 103(1)(b) evidence of propensity towards untruthfulness is admissible in any case where the truthfulness of the defendant's case is in issue; in this instance, the evidence is relevant primarily to the issue of credit, but indirectly it has probative value of the ultimate issue of guilt. Section 103(1)(a) is essentially no more than the statutory adoption of a principle which was already well established at common law, although s. 103 approaches the admissibility of such evidence of propensity in a rather different way. Section 103(1)(b), on the other hand, is an entirely new basis for admissibility, and is in some ways deeply disturbing.

6.10.2 Section 103(1)(a): propensity to commit offence of kind charged

The determination of whether or not evidence of bad character proves a propensity to commit offences of the kind charged is made in two stages. Firstly, the judge's function is to determine whether the evidence sought to be adduced is relevant to the question of whether the accused has a propensity to commit offences of the kind charged. If it is relevant, then after considering whether it should be excluded because of considerations of the fairness of the proceedings: (see 6.20) the judge will allow the evidence to go to the jury. Whether or not the evidence in fact establishes such a propensity is then a question of fact for the jury, and they must be directed accordingly. For the purpose of establishing propensity to commit offences of the kind charged in connection with gateway (d), it is usually, though not invariably, necessary for the prosecution to be ready to prove, not only the fact of conviction, but also the detailed facts of the previous offences to the extent necessary to demonstrate the relevance of the evidence.[45] Although s. 99 of the Criminal Justice Act 2003 supercedes the common law, and it has been said that it is unhelpful to look back to common law authority,[46] the questions of relevance which confront the courts tend to change remarkably little and recur in substantially the same form as at common law. The basis for the admissibility of evidence of disposition (or propensity) and the related kinds of evidence mentioned below can be traced back to the seminal *dictum* of Lord Herschell in *Makin v Attorney-General for New South Wales* [1894] AC 57, 68:

> It is undoubtedly not competent for the prosecution to adduce evidence tending to show that the accused has been guilty of criminal acts other than those covered by the indictment, for the purpose of leading to the conclusion that the accused is a person likely from his criminal conduct or character to have committed the offence for which he is being tried. On the other hand, the mere fact that the evidence adduced tends to show the commission of other crimes does not render it inadmissible if it be relevant to an issue before the jury, and it may be so relevant if it bears upon the question whether the acts alleged to constitute the crime charged in the indictment were designed or accidental, or to rebut a defence which would otherwise be open to the accused.

Under the new law, as under the old, evidence of bad character is likely to be relevant to propensity if either: (1) the previous offences are so factually similar to the offence charged to warrant the conclusion that taken together they amount to a series of offences likely to have been committed by the same individual; or (2) the previous offences are relevant to suggest a state of mind such as intent, knowledge, or belief; or (3) the previous offences tend to refute an offence such as accident or innocent association. In other words, it is important to consider the nature of the

---

[45] As to the proof of previous convictions and bad character, see *Humphris* [2005] EWCA Crim 2030; 6.4.

[46] See, e.g., *Chopra* [2007] 1 Cr App R 225, holding that the Criminal Justice Act 2003 represents a 'sea change' in the law rendering reference to previous authority unnecessary.

offence charged; the previous offences; and the nature of the issue the jury has to decide (this often being especially important in determining the relevance of the evidence). In relation to the refutation of defences, in contemporary practice, the nature of the defence is usually known to the prosecution in advance of trial as a result of the accused's pre-trial statements to the police or disclosure of his defence, so that the need for relevant evidence of bad character can be anticipated at least in general terms.[47]

In *Hanson and other appeals* [2005] 1 WLR 3169 the Court of Appeal broached the subject of whether a single previous conviction or act may be enough to justify a finding of propensity. The Court clearly thought that it would be a relatively unusual case in which a single instance would suffice, but did not exclude the possibility. It appears that the test is one of the probative value of the single instance, akin to the common law test for the admissibility of evidence of similar facts.[48] Rose LJ said:

> There is no minimum number of events necessary to demonstrate such a propensity. The fewer the number of convictions, the weaker is likely to be the evidence of propensity. A single previous conviction for an offence of the same description or category will often not show propensity. But it may do so where, for example, it shows a tendency to unusual behaviour or where its circumstances demonstrate probative force in relation to the offence charged (compare *Director of Public Prosecutions* v P [1991] 2 AC 447 at 460E to 461A). Child sexual abuse or fire setting are comparatively clear examples of such unusual behaviour but we attempt no exhaustive list. Circumstances demonstrating probative force are not confined to those sharing striking similarity. So, a single conviction for shoplifting will not, without more, be admissible to show propensity to steal. But if the modus operandi has significant features shared by the offence charged it may show propensity. [*Ibid.* at [9].]

DPP v P [1991] 2 AC 447 in many ways represented the culmination of the common law's treatment of similar fact evidence. The most important feature of the case is the recognition by the House of Lords that striking similarity between the offence charged and the previous offences was not in itself the ground of admissibility. Rather, striking similarity was an example of the relevance necessary to justify the admission of such evidence. Lord Mackay of Clashfern LC said:

> From all that was said by the House in [*DPP* v *Boardman* [1975] AC 421] I would deduce the essential feature of evidence which is to be admitted is that its probative force in support of the allegation that an accused person committed a crime is sufficiently great to make it just to admit the evidence, notwithstanding that it is prejudicial to the accused in tending to show that he was guilty of another crime. Such probative force may be derived from striking similarities in the evidence about the manner in which the crime was committed and the authorities provide illustrations of that ... But restricting the circumstances in which there is sufficient probative force to overcome prejudice of evidence relating to another crime to cases in which there is some striking similarity between them is to restrict the operation of the principle in a way which gives too much effect to a particular manner of stating it, and is not justified in principle. [*Ibid.* at 460.]

Whether one starts from *Hanson* or *DPP* v P would seem to make little difference. The test now is whether the evidence shows a propensity to commit offences of the kind charged. If the accused is charged with an offence of assault and he has previous convictions for shoplifting, the

---

[47] The accused's right of silence has been modified, so that adverse inferences may be drawn against him if he seeks to rely at trial on any fact that he did not mention when being questioned about or charged with an offence: Criminal Justice and Public Order Act 1994, ss. 34 to 38; 10.5 *et seq.* A similar result may follow if the accused fails to comply with his disclosure obligations under s. 5 of the Criminal Procedure and Investigations Act 1996.

[48] As to which see 6.10.5.

latter are simply not relevant to propensity to commit assault. If the previous convictions are for robbery (theft accompanied by the use or threat of force) the facts of the cases may or may not provide some relevance. If he has a number of previous convictions for assault, the sheer number of such convictions might perhaps be enough in itself to suggest a propensity to commit such offences, especially if they are all relatively recent. If there is a single previous conviction for assault, or a small number of convictions of some age, that may not be enough in itself. The judge would then have to look for some similarity between the various offences which supplies in the detail what is lacking in the number of convictions. For example, in *Campbell* [2007] 1 WLR 2798 the accused was charged with false imprisonment and assault occasioning actual bodily harm against his girl friend, the latter consisting of dragging her by her hair, banging her head against a wall and attempting to strangle her. The prosecution was rightly permitted to adduce evidence of the accused's previous conviction for a very similar assault on a former girl friend, to which he had pleaded guilty.[49] Conversely, in *Urushadze* [2008] EWCA Crim 2498, the defendant was charged with robbery from the person as a joint enterprise. It was held that evidence of his six previous convictions for theft by shoplifting were not relevant for the purpose of proving propensity to commit an offence of the kind charged. Even though the theft convictions were offences of the same category as the robbery (see 6.10.3) they were simply not relevant factually to suggest that the accused had a propensity to commit robbery. If he had been charged with shoplifting the result would no doubt have been different (subject to any argument about the fairness of the proceedings in relation to a relatively minor offence). In *Leaver* [2006] EWCA Crim 2988, where the accused was charged with rape, it being alleged that he had forcibly continued with sexual intercourse after the complainant had withdrawn her consent, it was held to be wrong to admit the accused's previous conviction for exposure, again an offence of the same category, but one which could have no relevance in showing a propensity to commit rape in the circumstances of the instant case.

The issue to be presented to the jury is always of great importance. If the defence is one of lack of knowledge, even a single previous conviction, for example, for writing worthless cheques, possessing dangerous drugs, or handling stolen goods, may have considerable value in proving propensity: see *Koc* [2008] EWCA Crim 77 (previous conviction for possession of heroin admissible where the defence to a charge of conspiracy to distribute heroin was that the accused believed he was dealing with goods of a perfectly innocent nature).[50] In *Bullen* [2008] 2 Cr App R 25, the accused was charged with murder. It was anticipated that he would raise the defence of self-defence, and in anticipation of this defence the prosecution proposed to adduce evidence of his several previous convictions for offences of violence. In this context, the previous convictions would have been relevant to suggest a propensity to commit offences of violence and so help to refute the defence of self-defence. But the accused changed his defence to admit manslaughter and defend against the murder charge solely on the basis of lack of intent caused by intoxication. It was held that the previous convictions had minimal, if any, relevance to the issues raised by the defence actually placed before the jury, and should have been excluded.

Cases involving a complete denial or an assertion of alibi must be treated with considerable care.[51] Although there may be cases in which a showing of propensity to commit offences of the

---

[49] See also *Tully* [2006] EWCA Crim 2270.

[50] See also to similar effect *Colliard* [2008] EWCA Crim 1175.

[51] At common law, there was some divergence of opinion as to whether similar fact evidence could be relevant if the defence was a complete denial, but the better view seems to be that it could be: see *DPP v Boardman* [1975] AC 421, per Lord Hailsham at 452, per Lord Cross at 458; *Flack* [1969] 2 All ER 784; *Chandor* [1959] 1 QB 545.

kind charged is relevant where the accused denies any involvement, it is obviously less compelling than a case where the accused admits his presence but alleges a defence such as self-defence or innocent association. An example of potentially high probative value would be a case of rape or sexual assault where the *modus operandi* is so individual as to suggest the hallmark of a particular offender, calling to mind the celebrated example suggested by Lord Hailsham in *DPP* v *Boardman* [1975] AC 421, 449 *et seq.* of the offender who always wears a particular form of head dress while committing offences. Such distinctive evidence may suggest propensity so strongly that it casts doubt on the accused's denial by rendering improbable an assertion that anyone other than the accused would have committed the offence. Evidence of serial crime in the true sense is the strongest example of such evidence, but need not be viewed as the only example. It may be conjectured, however, that only compelling bad character evidence is really helpful in rebutting a defence of alibi or complete denial. Additional circumstances may assist with the relevance of the evidence. In *Eastlake* [2007] EWCA 603, two brothers were charged with an offence of violence. The defence was mistaken identification. It was held that evidence that they had a propensity to commit similar offences, both individually and together, was relevant and had been rightly admitted to support the evidence of identification. This conclusion was strengthened by the fact that the accused admitted that they had been in each other's company on the evening in question. In *Brima* [2007] 1 Cr App R 316, the accused was charged with a murder committed with a knife. He asserted that he had been wrongly identified, and that another individual, X, had committed the offence. The forensic evidence was ultimately ambivalent as to whether the accused or X had committed the offence. It was held proper to admit the accused's previous convictions for assaults, during which he had used a knife, for the purpose of showing his propensity to commit such offences, albeit that those offences did not involve serious injury. It is submitted that the decision is probably correct. But it was strictly unnecessary to decide the point. The accused's bad character would in any event have been admissible under gateway (g) as he had made the clearest possible attack on the character of X, and once admitted, the jury were free to use it for any relevant purpose.[52]

6.10.3 Cross-admissibility

At common law it was well established that, if the accused is charged with more than one count, evidence admitted in relation to one count may be admissible on any other count, subject to the principles of relevance discussed above. Such evidence is said to be cross-admissible. Because the evidence on any one count does not 'have to do with' the facts of any other for the purposes of s. 98 of the Criminal Justice Act 2003 (see 6.3.2) it is evidence of bad character with respect to the other counts, and therefore can be admitted as evidence on the other counts only pursuant to one of the gateways. In *DPP* v *Boardman* [1975] AC 421, 460, Lord Cross of Chelsea said the point was:

> ...whether it would be unlikely that two youths who were saying untruly that the appellant had made homosexual advances to them would have put such a suggestion into his mouth.

In other words, cross-admissible evidence is relevant as helping to refute a defence of accident, mistake, or innocent association, because the suggestion that a number of individuals have independently made the same suggestion of criminal conduct against an innocent person becomes

---

[52] See also *Wilkinson* [2006] EWCA Crim 1332.

more improbable in proportion to the number of complainants and the number of alleged offences. It must be said at once that the admissibility of evidence on this basis is immediately vitiated if it is in any manner contaminated by collusion between the complainants (in which case their complaints are no longer independent). Where it appears that this has occurred, the judge has a specific duty to stop the case under s. 107 of the Criminal Justice Act 2003, which is dealt with fully at 6.21. What follows here assumes that there is no problem of contamination. Where evidence of propensity relevant to any one count of the indictment is relevant also to other counts, the jury may consider it in relation to any of the counts to which it is relevant. It is not necessary that the jury first reach a conclusion of guilt on the count in relation to which it is first tendered. Thus, the evidence is perfectly cross-admissible, subject to relevance; and mutual support as between various counts is itself a basis for relevance. In *Chopra* [2007] 1 Cr App R 225, the accused was a dentist who was charged with sexual assaults against three young female patients, the conduct alleged being that he improperly touched their breasts during dental treatment. Adopting the reasoning summarized above, the Court of Appeal held that the evidence of each patient was admissible both in relation to the count involving her and in relation to each of the other counts. It was open to the jury to find it highly improbable that three patients would, independently of each other, all have made the same highly specific allegations against the same dentist. This in turn suggested a propensity on the accused's part to commit such offences, and undermined any defence of innocent or accidental non-sexual touching.[53]

6.10.4 Offences of same description; offences of same category

Section 103(2) of the Criminal Justice Act 2003 provides that an accused's propensity to commit offences of the kind with which he is charged may be established by means of evidence that he has been convicted of offences either (a) of the same description or (b) of the same category as the offence charged. These terms are defined by s. 103(4). By virtue of s. 103(4)(a) an offence is 'of the same description' as the offence charged if it is a previous conviction for exactly the same offence in law, for example where both the offence now charged and the previous offence are offences of rape contrary to s. 1 of the Sexual Offences Act 2003, or where both are common law offences of assault. By virtue of s. 103(4)(b) an offence is an offence 'of the same category' as the offence charged if both offences are included in the same category prescribed for this purpose by the Secretary of State, which must contain offences of the same 'type' (s. 103(4)). At the time of writing, the Secretary of State has prescribed two such categories;[54] the theft category, comprising the most common offences under the Theft Act 1968;[55] and the sexual offences (persons under 16) category, comprising a large number of sexual offences under the Sexual Offences Acts 1956 and 2003, and one or two other statutes, but only when committed against persons under the age of 16.

The purpose of these provisions is to identify a particular form of relevance based on the generic similarities of some groups of offences. This, it is thought, may serve to reduce the number of possible inconsistencies involved in allowing the proper use of certain previous convictions in relation to certain offences charged to develop naturally through judicial pronouncement. In *O'Neil* 22 February 2005, Preston Crown Court, Mitting J held, sitting on circuit, that where

---

[53] For similar examples, see *Wallace* [2008] 1 WLR 572; *Freeman; Crawford* [2009] 1 Cr App R 11.

[54] S.I. 2004 No. 3346, the Criminal Justice Act 2003 (Categories of Offences) Order 2004.

[55] Theft, burglary, taking conveyances without authority, handling stolen goods, going equipped for stealing, and making off without payment; and related inchoate offences.

previous offences on which the prosecution proposed to rely under s. 101(d) were conceded to be neither of the same description within the meaning of s. 103(2)(a), nor of the same category within the meaning of s. 103(2)(b), because they did not fall within either of the two categories thus far prescribed, evidence of the offences was inadmissible in the absence of further evidence that they were relevant to show propensity. Section 103(2) provides that its provisions are without prejudice to other ways of proving propensity. But it was held that there is no category of offences of the same type beyond that described by s. 103(2)(b). Therefore, as the prosecution were unable to demonstrate any facts relating to the previous offences, other than their type, which might have suggested their particular relevance to propensity, there was no basis for admitting the evidence. But this decision must be now be read in the light of that in *Weir* (below).

Section 103(3) gives the judge a power to disallow the use of a particular conviction for this purpose if it would be unjust to permit it, having regard to the length of time which has elapsed since the conviction, or to any other reason.

Section 103(2) makes clear that the use of previous convictions of the same description or the same category is not the only method of proving disposition for the purpose of s. 103(1)(a). This point was emphasized by the Court of Appeal in *Weir and other appeals* [2006] 1 WLR 1885, [5]–[9], in which the Court clearly viewed the approach taken by Mitting J in *O'Neil* as too restrictive. The Court held in the appeal of *Weir*, on a charge of indecent assault on a girl under the age of 13, that propensity to commit an offence of the kind charged could be proved by evidence that the accused had previously been cautioned for taking an indecent photograph of a child, even though a caution is not a conviction, and even though the two offences were not offences either of the same description or in the same category under the 2004 Order. The test is simply one of relevance and probative value. The Court also pointed out that evidence of propensity might similarly be found in offences which an accused has previously asked to have taken into consideration, even though he is not technically convicted of such offences (*ibid.* at [7]). Other methods of proof might include evidence of other misconduct, or evidence of possession of incriminating items such as a collection of child pornography. But the evidence must show a propensity to commit offences, and offences of the kind charged. In the case of *Weir*, it would appear that this was a legitimate conclusion, because the offence for which the accused was cautioned suggested a prurient interest in children consistent with the offence charged. But the subject must be approached with care. It is submitted, for example, that evidence which shows only that the accused is a homosexual, and does not suggest that he has any propensity to commit sexual offences or any improper sexual interest, is certainly not admissible under gateway (d), and that the cases at common law which suggested the contrary no longer represent the law.[56]

Whether the idea of categories of offences is of much value is open to question. In *Hanson and other appeals* [2005] 1 WLR 3169 at [8], the Court of Appeal rightly held that the fact that a previous conviction is of the same description or is in the same category as that charged is not necessarily sufficient in itself to show propensity. Where offences are connected only by virtue of the generic similarity of groups of offences reflected in the categories, there is often a low probability of real probative value as to propensity as between different offences, certainly as the categories are presently defined. For example, robbery and making off without payment are offences in the same category, but it would take some fairly unusual facts to suggest that one would show a propensity for the other. This general proposition is confirmed by a number of cases, including

---

[56] See, e.g., *King* [1967] 2 QB 338; *Horwood* [1970] 1 QB 133. It is submitted that the admission of such evidence purportedly as evidence of propensity to commit an offence may well violate the accused's rights, not only under art. 6, but also under arts 8 and 10 of the European Convention on Human Rights.

Urushadze [2008] EWCA Crim 2498 and *Leaver* [2006] EWCA Crim 2988, which were discussed at 6.10.2, in both of which it was held that the fact that offences were in the same category was plainly insuffucient to show propensity. The same does not hold true with respect to offences of the same description. In this case it is inherently more likely that probative value on the issue of propensity will be found, though in this case too it is by no means automatic. Much may still depend on the facts of the individual cases. Moreover, s. 103(1)(a) itself provides that evidence of propensity to commit offences of the kind charged is not admissible if the propensity makes it no more likely that he is guilty of the offence charged. This will not often be the case. The Home Office Notes accompanying the Act (para. 372) suggest as an example cases in which the facts are not in dispute, but there is a dispute as to whether the admitted facts constitute the offence, and offer the instance of a dispute in a homicide case as to whether the accused's actions caused the deceased's death.

6.10.5 Section 103(1)(b): propensity to be untruthful

This provision must now be read in the light of the decision of the Court of Appeal in *Campbell* [2007] 1 WLR 2798. Section 103(1)(b), considered without any gloss, is a radical departure from the common law. As we have seen, any assertion of good character by the accused could be rebutted by the prosecution (5.9), a rule preserved by s. 101(1)(f): see 6.12. Moreover, the accused could be cross-examined about his character if he lost his shield under any of the provisions of s. 1(3) of the Criminal Evidence Act 1898. But never before has evidence of the accused's propensity for untruthfulness been generally admissible as part of the prosecution's case. Clearly the subsection as enacted is not intended to be confined to cases in which untruthfulness is an element of the offence charged, for example perjury or even offences of more general dishonesty: for these purposes, it would be unnecessary and would be subsumed by s. 103(1)(a) as the evidence would then show propensity to commit offences of the kind charged. It is perfectly apt to apply to any case in which the accused has given evidence, or given answers during an interview, or in any other manner ventured a statement about the facts of the case. In all these cases, the jury must consider his credibility, and evidence of a propensity for untruthfulness may be relevant to that issue. Section 103(b) exempts cases in which it is not suggested that the accused's case is untruthful in any respect, but this is a small and rarely encountered category of case. While the evidence may be directly relevant only to the accused's credit, it obviously has an indirect but nonetheless serious probative value in relation to the ultimate issue of guilt, and there is no restriction on the use to be made of the evidence by the jury. In accordance with the general rule propounded in *Highton* (see 6.6.1), once admitted on the issue of credit, the evidence may in any case be used for any relevant purpose.

   Surprisingly, and in marked contrast to the elaborate treatment of the issue of propensity to commit offences of the kind charged under s. 103(1)(a), the Act offers no guidance whatsoever about the nature of the evidence to be admitted for the purpose of proving propensity for untruthfulness. The Home Office Notes (para. 374) explain:

> This is intended to enable the admission of a limited range of evidence such as convictions for perjury or other offences involving deception (for example, obtaining property by deception) as opposed to the wider range of evidence that will be admissible where the defendant puts his character in issue by, for example, attacking the character of another person.[57]

---

[57] A reference to s. 101(1)(g): see 6.13. For comment on the confusion surrounding these issues, see P. Mirfield, 'Character and Credibility' [2009] Crim LR 135.

Whatever the intention may have been, s. 103(1)(b) contains no indication that the range of evidence is to be so limited and, with the exception of the two most obvious examples imaginable, the Note gives no real guidance as to what kinds of offence should be considered to be appropriate evidence of propensity for untruthfulness. What about theft, bribery, bigamy, and so on? This would have been an excellent purpose for which to enact a category of offences. Would it be permissible to adduce evidence, not only of a previous conviction, but of the fact that the accused gave evidence in his defence at his previous trial, giving rise to the clear implication that the jury in the previous case did not believe him? The answers to these and similar questions remain obscure. The Court of Appeal ventured a few tentative observations on the subject in *Hanson and other appeals* [2005] 1 WLR 3169, [13] as follows:

> As to propensity to untruthfulness, this, as it seems to us, is not the same as propensity to dishonesty. It is to be assumed, bearing in mind the frequency with which the words honest and dishonest appear in the criminal law, that Parliament deliberately chose the word 'untruthful' to convey a different meaning, reflecting a defendant's account of his behaviour, or lies told when committing an offence. Previous convictions, whether for offences of dishonesty or otherwise, are therefore only likely to be capable of showing a propensity to be untruthful where, in the present case, truthfulness is an issue and, in the earlier case, either there was a plea of not guilty and the defendant gave an account, on arrest, in interview, or in evidence, which the jury must have disbelieved, or the way in which the offence was committed shows a propensity for untruthfulness, for example, by the making of false representations.[58]

It can hardly be said that these *dicta* lay down any kind of comprehensive principle to remedy the deficiencies of definition in the statutory provisions. Worse yet, the subsection suggests that it is open to the prosecution to adduce other evidence of bad character, for example evidence of reprehensible behaviour, which may amount to no more than evidence of lies told on some social occasion, or evidence of reputation for untruthfulness, all of which may be vague and unreliable. While it may be true that the credibility of the accused is an important matter in issue between him and the prosecution, and while there will be legitimate cases for allowing evidence of bad character on that issue, for example for the purpose of exposing an obviously fraudulent defence, s. 103(1)(b) has an enormous potential for unfairness.

But these assumptions may have changed in the light of *Campbell* [2007] 1 WLR 2798. In this case, the accused was charged with false imprisonment and assault occasioning actual bodily harm against his girlfriend, the latter consisting of dragging her by her hair, banging her head against a wall and attempting to strangle her. The prosecution were permitted to adduce evidence of the accused's previous conviction for assault on a former girlfriend, to which he had pleaded guilty, and the facts of which were similar to those of the offence charged. There was no difficulty in admitting this evidence under s. 103(1)(a) as tending to show a propensity to commit offences of the kind charged (see 6.10.2). But in accordance with the principle in *Highton* (see 6.6.1), the JSB's specimen direction provided for the jury to be directed that the jury might use the evidence both for the purpose of considering propensity to commit offences of the kind charged and for the purpose of considering his credibility as a witness. The accused was convicted and appealed. The Court of Appeal expressed itself as following *Highton* in holding that, once admitted under any gateway, evidence of bad character may be used for any relevant purpose (*ibid.* at [26]).

---

[58] See also the appeal of *Fysh* in *Edwards and other appeals* [2006] 1 WLR 1524, [33] hinting at a distinction for this purpose between theft and benefit fraud; cf. *S* [2007] 1 WLR 63; 6.17.

But the Court then began to chart a rather different course. This course begins with a seemingly innocuous passage which in many ways seems to be simply a matter of common sense. At para. [28] Lord Phillips CJ, giving the judgment of the Court, said:

> In considering the inference to be drawn from bad character the courts have in the past drawn a distinction between propensity to offend and credibility. The distinction is usually unrealistic. If the jury hears that a defendant has shown a propensity to commit criminal acts they may well at one and the same time conclude that it is more likely that he is guilty and that he is less likely to be telling the truth when he says he is not.

As we have already seen (6.6.1) the purported distinction between evidence going directly to the accused's guilt of the offence charged and evidence going to his credibility is one which had attracted a great deal of criticism under the old law, and which is undoubtedly artificial and difficult for juries to understand. After *Highton*, it had probably been assumed that the distinction was no longer of any great importance because the jury are entitled to use evidence of bad character, under whatever gateway admitted, for any relevant purpose. As the Court in *Campbell* points out, both roads are likely to lead the jury to the same destination. But the Court followed this thought with one which leads in a rather different direction:

> The question of whether a defendant has a propensity for being untruthful will not normally be capable of being described as an *important* matter in issue between the defendant and the prosecution. A propensity for untruthfulness will not of itself go very far to establishing the commission of a criminal offence. To suggest that a propensity for untruthfulness makes it more likely that a defendant has lied to the jury is not likely to help them. If they apply common sense they will conclude that a defendant who has committed a criminal offence may well be prepared to lie about it, even if he has not shown a propensity for lying, whereas a defendant who has not committed the offence charged will be likely to tell the truth, even if he has shown a propensity for telling lies. In short, whether or not a defendant is telling the truth to a jury is likely to depend simply on whether or not he committed the offence charged. The jury should focus on the latter question rather on whether or not he has a propensity for telling lies. [*Ibid.* at [30], emphasis in original.]

In this passage the Court seems almost to discourage the use of s. 103(1)(b) as a discrete basis for admitting evidence of bad character. In terms of fairness, and indeed logic, there is much to commend the Court's approach. The jury should be directed to focus on the accused's guilt, and any evidence of bad character is merely ancillary to that question. The potential for unfairness in the application of the subsection has been stated above and need not be repeated. Nonetheless, in enacting s. 103(1)(b) Parliament evinced the intention that such evidence should be admitted when available and relevant. Thus far, the Court's judgment could be read simply as insisting that the relevance of such evidence be properly understood. But more was to come:

> For these reasons the only circumstances in which there is likely to be an *important* issue as to whether a defendant has a propensity to tell lies is where telling lies is an element of the offence charged. Even then, the propensity to tell lies is only likely to be significant if the lying is in the context of committing criminal offences, in which case the evidence is likely to be admissible under s.103(1)(a). [*Ibid.* at [31], emphasis in original.]

If this passage is taken to its logical conclusion, it has the effect of nullifying s. 103(1)(b) almost competely as an independent rule of evidence. If an issue between the defence and the prosecution is not an important one, it cannot be the subject of evidence of bad character under gateway (d). It is hard to imagine that the Court was not aware of this, and it must be conceded that it is a courageous decision. It is also one which presents a direct challenge to the will of Parliament, and it remains to be seen whether the last word has been spoken on this issue. For now, the JSB standard direction has been amended accordingly, and the current practice is not to direct the jury to consider evidence of bad character for its effect on the accused's credibility except in the limited kinds of case referred to in para. [31] of the judgment in *Campbell*.

6.10.6 Other evidence of important matters in issue between defendant and prosecution

Propensity is not the only important matter in issue between the accused and the prosecution. The use of the word 'include' in s. 103(1) of the Criminal Justice Act 2003 suggests that evidence relevant to other issues is also admissible under gateway (d). In the absence of guidance in s. 103, it is submitted that, consistently with the position at common law, the test of admissibility is whether or not the evidence is relevant to the issue of guilt or innocence, which is of course the ultimate matter in issue between the accused and the prosecution.

There is as yet a paucity of authority under the Act outside the sphere of propensity. But a still compelling example taken from the old law is *Jones v DPP*.[59] The accused was convicted of the murder of a young girl guide in October 1960. He had previously been convicted of raping another girl guide during September 1960. Although the earlier conviction would have been relevant to the offence charged, in that both involved attacks on girl guides, the prosecution did not lead evidence of it because of a desire to spare the victim of the earlier crime the ordeal of giving evidence again. In statements to the police about the murder charged, the accused gave a false alibi. Subsequently, he admitted that this alibi was false and put forward a second alibi. The second alibi was almost identical to an alibi which he had advanced at his trial on the earlier rape charge. The similarity extended to details of conversations that the accused alleged he had had with his wife, which were almost word-for-word the same. At trial, the accused sought to explain his giving of the first, false alibi by giving evidence that he had been 'in trouble' with the police. He was cross-examined about the suspicious similarity of his second alibi for the murder to his alibi on what was referred to as 'another occasion'—no details of the previous conviction being revealed to the jury. The accused appealed on the ground that the cross-examination should not have been permitted.

The House of Lords unanimously dismissed the appeal. The members of the House were not unanimous as to their reasons, though all those advanced appear very sound. Viscount Simonds and Lords Reid and Morris of Borth-y-Gest based their decision on the wording of s. 1(3) of the Criminal Evidence Act 1898, with which we are no longer concerned. Lords Denning and Devlin, more simply, viewed the issue as one of relevance, and it is submitted that their view would remain correct if the same facts were to recur today. Lord Devlin explained the purpose of the cross-examination as follows ([1962] AC 635, 690):

> My Lords, I would dismiss this appeal on the short ground that the questions objected to were relevant to an issue in the case on which the appellant had testified in chief. It is not disputed that the issue to which the questions related was a relevant one. It concerned the identification of the appellant as being at the material time at the scene of the crime. He testified that at the material time he was with a prostitute in the West End and he supported this alibi by giving evidence of a conversation which he had had with his wife about it a day or two later. The purpose of the questions objected to was to obtain from the appellant an admission (which was given) that when he was being questioned about his movements in relation to another incident some weeks earlier, he had set up the same alibi and had supported it with

---

[59] [1962] AC 635; see also *Anderson* [1988] QB 678; *McAllister* [2009] 1 Cr App R 10.

an account of a conversation with his wife in almost identical terms; the prosecution suggested that these similarities showed the whole story of the alibi to be an invented one.

Note that the prosecution did not introduce any details of the 'other occasion'; this would have been irrelevant to the attack on the veracity of the second alibi. Today, it may well be that the evidence would also be admissible (subject to the observations in *Campbell*: 6.10.4) as evidence of a propensity to be untruthful.

6.11 GATEWAY (E): EVIDENCE HAVING SUBSTANTIAL PROBATIVE VALUE IN RELATION TO IMPORTANT MATTER IN ISSUE BETWEEN DEFENDANT AND CO-DEFENDANT

'Important matter' is defined by s. 112(1): see 6.5. The term 'co-defendant' is also defined by s. 112(1) as meaning: 'in relation to a defendant...a person charged with an offence in the same proceedings'. There is no requirement that the two or more accused be jointly charged with any offence; as long as they are being tried together in the same proceedings, they each become 'co-defendants' with respect to each other for all purposes in connection with rules as to evidence of bad character.

This gateway is supplemented by s. 104 of the Act, which provides:

> (1) Evidence which is relevant to the question whether the defendant has a propensity to be untruthful is admissible on that basis under section 101(1)(e) only if the nature or conduct of his defence is such as to undermine the co-defendant's defence.
> (2) Only evidence—
> (a) which is to be (or has been) adduced by the co-defendant, or
> (b) which a witness is to be invited to give (or has given) in cross-examination by the co-defendant,
> is admissible under section 101(1)(e).

As in the case of gateway (d) the important matter in issue may relate either to the substantive question of guilt or innocence, or to the question of credibility. In the case of gateway (e), however, the question is not only whether one defendant is guilty as opposed to not guilty, but also how the guilt or innocence of one defendant relates to that of the co-defendants. In some cases, the evidence is consistent only with the possible guilt of all of those charged or none of them; in other cases, it is consistent with the guilt of some of those charged and the innocence of others; in yet other cases, the guilt of one defendant may logically require the innocence of the others. There are, accordingly, a number of ways in which the bad character of one defendant may be relevant. It is, of course, commonplace that one defendant will seek to place the blame on another, and this may result in a 'cut-throat' defence, in which the issue is, not whether the offence was committed, but which of the defendants committed it. The bad character of a defendant may be relevant in general terms either because it suggests that he has a propensity to commit offences of the kind charged, while the co-defendant lacks that propensity; or because it suggests that, with respect to matters in dispute between the two of them, the co-defendant commands the greater credibility. We must consider both possibilities.

At the outset, it should be noted that only a co-defendant may seek to adduce evidence under s. 101(1)(3). Section 104(2) makes this clear. The prosecution may not take advantage of the fact that there is an important matter in issue between two or more co-defendants to seek to adduce evidence of the bad character or any of them. Any evidence of this kind adduced by the prosecution must be adduced using other gateways without reference to any matters in issue between the defendants. Moreover, the duty to exclude under s. 101(3) does not apply to gateway (e): see 6.20.[60] In contrast to gateway (d), it does not suffice that the evidence tendered is relevant to the important matter in issue. Under gateway (e) it must further have 'substantial' probative value. In effect, if not in name, this gives the judge some discretion to exclude if he feels that the probative value of the evidence is relatively low. In this case, admitting the evidence may not appear to be justified, having regard to the inevitable prejudice that it would cause to the accused against whom it is admitted. The judge must be satisfied that the evidence would have a sufficient impact on the case to merit its admission even at the risk of that obviously considerable prejudice.

6.11.1 Evidence relevant to propensity to commit offence

Before the coming into effect of the Criminal Justice Act 2003, there was a growing recognition that at common law, evidence might be admissible for the purpose of showing that, as between two or more accused, it was more likely that one of them committed an offence. In *Lowery* [1974] AC 85, two accused, A and B, were charged with the murder of a girl in unusual circumstances which suggested that one of them must have been guilty of the offence, and that it was relatively unlikely that both were. There was no apparent motive for the killing except the sadistic pleasure of committing it. A applied for and was granted leave to adduce expert psychiatric evidence to the effect that B had a disposition towards violence of the kind which could have motivated the attack on the girl. B appealed against conviction on the ground that the evidence had been wrongly admitted, but the Privy Council dismissed the appeal. The evidence was relevant to a specific matter in issue between A and B, namely which of them committed the offence. It followed that the evidence of B's propensity for violence had probative value in assisting the jury in deciding that crucial issue. Even though it inevitably prejudiced B, and to some extent invaded the province of the jury in expressing a view about the relative credibility of A and B, the compelling relevance and probative value of the evidence justified its admission. This decision was followed by the Court of Appeal in *Bracewell* (1978) 68 Cr App R 44. In *Randall* [2004] 1 WLR 56, the House of Lords considered it further. A and B were charged with murder, and presented a cut-throat defence, each blaming the other for the crime. While A had only one or two minor previous convictions, B had a very bad record for offences of burglary committed with the use and threat of violence and, at the time of the alleged murder, was on the run from the police in connection with an armed robbery. Because of the nature of the defence, both A and B had lost their shields under s. 1(3)(iii) of the Criminal Evidence Act 1898 and had become liable to be cross-examined by the other about their previous convictions. The judge directed the jury to consider the evidence of the previous convictions only in relation to their credibility as witnesses and not as relevant to the issue of which of them had committed the offence, a direction which would seem to have been correct in terms of evidence elicited in cross-examination under s. 1(3)(iii)

---

[60] This is in accordance with the common law rule and the rule under s. 78 of the Police and Criminal Evidence Act 1984 that the exclusionary discretion applies only to evidence tendered by the prosecution and not to evidence tendered by a co-accused: see *Randall* [2004] 1 WLR 56, [18]; *Myers* [1998] AC 124; and generally 3.9. But it has been held that the judge may exclude evidence tendered under gateway (e) where there has been a deliberate failure to comply with the rules by not giving notice; the evidence is tenuous; and prejudice may be caused to the accused against whom it is tendered: see *Musone* [2007] 1 WLR 2467; *Jarvis* [2008] EWCA Crim 488; 6.22.4.

of the Criminal Evidence Act 1898.[61] The jury convicted A of manslaughter, but acquitted B. A appealed successfully against his conviction. Both the Court of Appeal and the House of Lords held that the judge's direction should have gone further, because the evidence of B's propensity was relevant to the issue of whether A or B had committed the offence, and was, therefore, independently admissible regardless of its evidential value under the 1898 Act. The question certified for appeal to the House of Lords was:

> Where two accused are jointly charged with a crime, and each blames the other for its commission, may one accused rely on the criminal propensity of the other?

Lord Steyn, with whose opinion the other members of the House agreed, answered the question in the affirmative. Referring to *Lowery*, he held that the language of the Privy Council was too narrow insofar as it appeared to link the evidence to the question of credibility rather than 'criminal tendencies', and insofar as it placed too much emphasis on the question of whether the accused against whom the evidence was admitted had put his character in issue. Neither of these matters should determine the issue (*ibid.* at [29]). Lord Steyn said (at [22]):

> Postulate a joint trial involving two accused arising from an assault committed in a pub. Assume it to be clear that one of the two men committed the assault. The one man has a long list of previous convictions involving assaults in pubs. It shows him to be prone to fighting when he had consumed alcohol. The other man has an unblemished record. Relying on experience and common sense one may rhetorically ask why the propensity to violence of one man should not be deployed by the other man as part of his defence that he did not commit the assault... To rule that the jury may use the convictions in regard to his credibility but that convictions revealing his propensity to violence must otherwise be ignored is to ask the jury to put to one side their common sense and experience. It would be curious if the law compelled such an unrealistic result.

Section 101(1)(e) of the Criminal Justice Act 2003 reflects this view. Under gateway (e) it is no longer relevant whether an accused has put his character in issue or not,[62] and there is no basis for restricting evidence of bad character to the issue of credibility. The reasoning applied by Lord Steyn in *Randall*, it is submitted, can now be applied to any case in which evidence of bad character is relevant to an important matter between two or more defendants. It is not confined to cases involving cut-throat defences, though this will continue to be an important example. And, as we have seen, gateway (e) does not confine the principle to cases in which defendants are jointly charged with the same offence, though where they are not jointly charged, it may be more difficult to establish the relevance of the evidence, or that the evidence has a substantial probative value.

There will be cases in which evidence of the bad character of a defendant will be irrelevant when tendered by a co-defendant. In *Neale* (1977) 65 Cr App R 304, A tendered evidence of B's propensity to commit arson, for the purpose of suggesting that B had committed the offence of arson with which both A and B were charged. However, A's defence to the charge was to offer an alibi. This rendered the evidence of B's propensity irrelevant to A's defence, and it was held that the evidence should be excluded. If both A and B had been present at the scene, and the jury had had to decide which of them had started the fire, presumably the result would have been different. Similarly, in *B (C)* [2004] 2 Cr App R 34, A and B were charged in the same proceedings with separate offences of sexual assault against the same children, B being the father of the victims,

---

[61] *Murdoch v Taylor* [1965] AC 574, 584, 593.

[62] Or, of course, whether the evidence is elicited in cross-examination or adduced in any other way (see 6.4).

and A being the mother's later partner. A and B were not jointly charged with any offence, and there was no allegation that the offences were in any way connected except insofar as the same children were the victims. It was held that it was not permissible to allow A to adduce evidence that B had a previous conviction for incest, whereas A had previous convictions only for non-sexual offences. Because the jury did not have to decide between A and B, and it was open to them to convict both A and B of the separate offences with which they were charged, the evidence of B's propensity was not relevant when tendered by A. There would appear to be no reason why these cases should not be decided in the same way if they fell to be decided under the Criminal Justice Act 2003.[63]

6.11.2 Evidence relevant to credibility

As we have seen (5.1), when the Criminal Evidence Act 1898 made the accused a competent witness in his own defence for the first time, it was necessary also to create rules to deal with the cross-examination of the accused about his bad character. He was invested with a shield against such cross-examination, which might be lost in certain circumstances. By virtue of s. 1(3)(iii) of the Act, if an accused had 'given evidence against any other person charged in the same proceedings', the co-accused against whom he gave evidence was entitled to cross-examine him about his previous convictions and bad character. The evidence so adduced was admissible only on the issue of the accused's credibility as a witness against the co-accused, and it was necessary for the jury to be directed that the evidence was evidence only for that purpose, and was not evidence of the accused's guilt of the offence charged.[64] The relative credibility of two or more defendants continues to be a proper subject of evidence of bad character under the Criminal Justice Act 2003, but under the provisions of the 2003 Act it seems that such evidence may be adduced whenever the relative credibility of the accused is relevant and the evidence has substantial probative value for the purpose of resolving the issue. Moreover, there is probably no longer any need for the jury to receive a confusing direction to the effect that they must regard the evidence as evidence going to credit only, and not to guilt. If the bad character of A and its adverse effect on A's credibility makes it more likely that A is guilty, at least in relation to B, there would seem to be no reason why the jury should not regard it as evidence of A's guilt.

Section 104(1) does, however, impose an important restriction. Where the evidence is relevant to the question of whether A has a propensity to be untruthful, it is admissible only where 'the nature or conduct of [A's] defence is such as to undermine [B's] defence'. This provision essentially corresponds to cases in which A would have been held to have given 'evidence against' B for the purposes of s. 1(3)(iii) of the Criminal Evidence Act 1898. The cases decided under that subsection established that A would be held to have given evidence against B if his evidence either supported the prosecution case against B in a material respect, or undermined B's defence. In either case, A's evidence made it more likely that B would be convicted.[65] It is no longer necessary that A achieve this effect by giving evidence, and B's remedy is no longer confined to cross-examination. The court must now look at the conduct of A's defence in all its aspects, including his cross-examination of prosecution witnesses, and of B. But the effect of A's case must be to undermine

---

[63] However, there would seem to be no reason why B's previous conviction could not be admitted if tendered by the prosecution under gateway (d).

[64] *Murdoch* v *Taylor* [1965] AC 574, 584, 593.

[65] *Murdoch* v *Taylor* [1965] AC 574; *Varley* [1982] 2 All ER 519; contrast *Bruce* [1975] 1 WLR 1252; *Kirkpatrick* [1998] Crim LR 63.

B's case to some extent. In providing that either the 'nature' or the 'conduct' of A's defence may have this effect, s. 104(1) reproduces language in s. 1(3)(ii) of the Criminal Evidence Act 1898 which, in the context of the making of imputations against prosecution witnesses, was held to mean that A need not attack B's case out of malice; indeed, it may be necessary and inevitable for the purposes of his own case to do so.[66] The shield was lost regardless of A's reasons for making the attack, and no doubt the same rule will apply under s. 104(1). The same rule had been applied to s. 1(3)(iii); the phrase 'has given evidence against' implied no malicious intent. In *Murdoch* v *Taylor* [1965] AC 574, 584, Lord Morris of Borth-y-Gest said that it was irrelevant whether A's evidence against B was 'the product of pained reluctance or of malevolent eagerness'.

In *Lawson* [2007] 1 Cr App R 11, A and B were jointly charged with manslaughter, and gave different accounts in evidence about what had happened. Unexpectedly and without giving notice, counsel for A cross-examined B about a previous conviction for assault. After argument, the judge held that this conviction was not relevant to propensity to commit an offence of the kind charged, but admitted the evidence on the ground that it was relevant to propensity for untruthfulness. The Court of Appeal upheld the admission of the evidence and dismissed B's appeal against conviction. Hughes LJ said:

> A defendant who is defending himself against the evidence of a person whose history of criminal behaviour or other misconduct is such as to be capable of showing him to be unscrupulous and/or otherwise unreliable should be enabled to present that history before the jury for its evaluation of the evidence of the witness. Such suggested unreliability may be capable of being shown by conduct which does not involve an offence of untruthfulness; it may be capable of being shown by widely differing conduct, ranging from large-scale drug—or people—trafficking via housebreaking to criminal violence. Whether in a particular case it is in fact capable of having substantial probative value in relation to the witness's reliability is for the trial judge to determine on all the facts of the case.

It is submitted that this decision was incorrect. The unfortunate conduct of counsel for A had placed the trial judge in a difficult position, but it is submitted that he should have rejected the argument as to propensity for untruthfulness and refused to admit the evidence. In the circumstances, as the judge no doubt realized, this would surely also have meant discharging the jury so as to avoid prejudice to B, an inconvenient but necessary course. The previous conviction for assault had nothing to do with truthfulness, and its admission on that basis was contrary to *dicta* of the Court of Appeal in *Hanson and other appeals* [2005] 1 WLR 3169 at [13] and other cases (see 6.10.4). The Court of Appeal, in upholding the conviction, professed to be following the decision in the appeal of *Osborne* in *Renda and other appeals* [2006] 2 All ER 553, [58]–[60], but on the facts of that case, the previous conviction of a defence witness was highly relevant to the credibility of his evidence contradicting the testimony of the complainant; the case was very different from *Lawson*.[67] The Court's statement that it is for the judge to determine whether the previous offences have substantial probative value is, with respect, unhelpful in the light of the range of examples given, which would in most cases seem to have no probative value whatsoever, much less substantial probative value. While there will always be differences of approach when evidence of bad character is tendered by a co-accused rather than the prosecution, those differences are now glaring. *Lawson* also seems to take an approach inconsistent in itself. On the one

---

[66] *Selvey* v *DPP* [1970] AC 304; *Bishop* [1975] QB 274.

[67] A better comparison would have been with *M* [2006] EWCA Crim 1126, in which, on similar facts, the lack of relevance of the conviction to propensity for untruthfulness was conceded, and not even contested before the Court of Appeal.

hand, there seems to be an almost wholesale abandonment of ordinary principles of relevance, an invitation to judges to allow attacks on one another by co-accused to become unregulated gladitorial contests. On the other hand, the judges are still to insist on the fundamental basis of gateway (e), that the evidence must have substantial probative value in relation to the important issue between the accused and the co-accused. Nonetheless, *Lawson* remains the leading authority in this area. This was confirmed by a later Court in *Rosato* [2008] EWCA Crim 1243,[68] a decision which did at least involve previous convictions for offences of dishonesty, if not untruthfulness. The Court criticized as too narrow the judge's direction to the jury that they should take account of the previous convictions only if they thought that they showed a propensity to be untruthful. They were to be regarded as evidence of unreliability generally, there being, in the Court's view, no workable distinction between, on the one hand, conduct showing that the accused has a propensity for lying, and, on the other, generic criminal conduct from which a jury might be tempted to infer that the accused is a person likely to lie. But this is a distinction made very clear and treated as important in several other contexts by the Criminal Justice Act 2003 itself and in previous decisions of the Court of Appeal.[69] If *Lawson* is to remain the leading authority in this area, it is to be hoped that judges will insist on a strict showing of the substantial probative value required for admission under gateway (e).

6.12 GATEWAY (F): IT IS EVIDENCE TO CORRECT A FALSE IMPRESSION GIVEN BY THE DEFENDANT

This gateway is supplemented by s. 105, which provides:

> (1) For the purposes of section 101(1)(f)—
>   (a) the defendant gives a false impression if he is responsible for the making of an express or implied assertion which is apt to give the court or jury a false or misleading impression about the defendant;
>   (b) evidence to correct such an impression is evidence which has probative value in correcting it.
> (2) A defendant is treated as being responsible for the making of an assertion if—
>   (a) the assertion is made by the defendant in the proceedings (whether or not in evidence given by him),
>   (b) the assertion was made by the defendant—
>   (i) on being questioned under caution, before charge, about the offence with which he is charged, or
>   (ii) on being charged with the offence or officially informed that he might be prosecuted for it,
>   and evidence of the assertion is given in the proceedings,
>   (c) the assertion is made by a witness called by the defendant,
>   (d) the assertion is made by any witness in cross-examination in response to a question asked by the defendant that is intended to elicit it, or is likely to do so, or
>   (e) the assertion was made by any person out of court, and the defendant adduces evidence of it in the proceedings.
> (3) A defendant who would otherwise be treated as responsible for the making of an assertion shall not be so treated if, or to the extent that, he withdraws it or disassociates himself from it.

---

[68] See also *Jarvis* [2008] EWCA Crim 488; P. Mirfield, 'Character and Credibility' [2009] Crim LR 135.
[69] See, e.g., *Hanson and other appeals* [2005] 1 WLR 3169, [13]; *Campbell* [2007] 1 WLR 2798; 6.10.4.

(4) Where it appears to the court that a defendant, by means of his conduct (other than the giving of evidence) in the proceedings, is seeking to give the court or jury an impression about himself that is false or misleading, the court may if it appears just to do so treat the defendant as being responsible for the making of an assertion which is apt to give that impression.

(5) In subsection (4) 'conduct' includes appearance or dress.

(6) Evidence is admissible under section 101(1)(f) only if it goes no further than is necessary to correct the false impression.

(7) Only prosecution evidence is admissible under section 101(1)(f).

We have already seen that at common law, the prosecution was allowed to rebut false evidence of good character adduced by the accused, and we noted briefly the rules which governed such rebuttal at common law (see 5.9). Moreover, under the Criminal Evidence Act 1898, the accused lost his shield against cross-examination about his character if:

> ...he has personally or by his advocate asked questions of the witnesses for the prosecution with a view to establish his own good character, or has given evidence of his own good character...[*Ibid.* at s. 1(3)(ii).]

Gateway (f) and s. 105 lay down a new and broader régime dealing with such assertions by the accused, and the departure from the previous law is considerable. Only the prosecution may adduce evidence under this gateway (s. 105(7)), so a co-accused may not adduce evidence of the accused's bad character simply because the accused has given a false impression; he may do so only if there is an important matter between them and such evidence is independently admissible under gateway (e) (see 6.11). As we have noted in other contexts, there is no longer any distinction between assertions made in cross-examination of the prosecution witnesses and assertions made in the course of evidence given by the accused or his witnesses. But in place of the former test of establishing or giving evidence of his good character, gateway (f) lays down the test of whether the accused has given a false impression. Under s. 105(1)(a) the accused gives a false impression if:

> ...he is responsible for the making of an express or implied assertion which is apt to give the court or jury a false or misleading impression about the defendant.

Section 105(2) provides a number of ways in which the accused can be held to be responsible for an express or implied assertion. The traditional methods of cross-examination of the prosecution witnesses and the adduction of defence evidence are preserved. Unlike the case of gateway (b) (see 6.8), an assertion is deemed to be made as a result of an answer given to a question put in cross-examination, not only if the question was intended to elicit such an answer, but also if the question was likely to elicit that answer (s. 105(2)); which presumably means that, in the opinion of the judge, a witness would reasonably have understood the question as calling on him to give an answer suggestive of the accused's good character. Two additional cases are given in which the accused is to be responsible for the making of an assertion, which go considerably beyond the traditional methods of making an assertion of good character, though both cases seem to be logical and sensible. Both refer to assertions made outside the courtroom which are adduced in evidence at trial. The first deals with an assertion made by the accused outside court, while being questioned by the police or on being charged with the offence, of which evidence is given at trial (s. 105(2)(b)). Generally, evidence of such statements would be adduced by the prosecution as part of its case, but there is no reason why it could not also be adduced by the defence. The second deals with an assertion made by any other person outside court of which evidence is adduced by the defendant at trial (s. 105(2)(e)). In this case, the defendant is simply adopting the statement and using it to his advantage in court. An important safeguard is provided by s. 105(3), which allows the accused to avoid being held to be responsible for the making of a false or misleading assertion if, or to the extent that he withdraws it or disassociates himself from it. This leaves the accused with a clear and non-prejudicial means of extricating himself from the consequences of an unintended or ill-considered assertion; for example, where a defence witness makes an unforeseen and misguided attempt to 'assist' him by means of an implication of good character; or where the accused offered the police a spontaneous protest about his respectability on being arrested. The accused may also correct, without withdrawing entirely, an assertion which, though partially correct, goes too far or contains inaccurate statements about his character. It is suggested that where the accused takes advantage of this subsection, the withdrawal or disassociation should be made in unambiguous terms by his advocate in open court, in the presence of the jury; where the assertion was made out of court, it should be made in writing by his solicitor at the earliest possible time. In the appeal of *Renda* in *Renda and other appeals* [2006] 2 All ER 553, [21], the Court of Appeal held that an accused who wishes to take advantage of s. 105(3) must make a 'specific and positive decision' to dissociate himself from the false assertion. Thus, where the accused persisted in a false assertion during his examination in chief, and a concession that the assertion was false was 'extracted' from him during cross-examination, it was held that he was not entitled to claim that he had dissociated himself from the assertion.

Neither s. 101(1)(f) nor s. 105 states specifically what is meant by an assertion which is apt to give a false or misleading impression. It is the impression which must be false or misleading, not necessarily the assertion. For example, the accused may truthfully state that he is a regular churchgoer; if he has several previous convictions, the impression created by his truthful statement is false and misleading. The definition must certainly include any statement, however broadly or narrowly made, which is calculated to give the jury the impression that the accused is a person of good character; such as 'I'm a respectable family man', 'I am a woman of strict moral principles', or 'I've never been in any kind of trouble with the law'. But it is submitted that any statement from which a reasonable juror would be likely to draw the same conclusion would also qualify. Thus, it was enough to cause the accused to lose his shield under s. 1(3)(ii) of the Criminal Evidence Act 1898, and would presumably be enough to invoke gateway (f), for the accused to state that he is married and has a steady job,[70] or that he is a religious person,[71] that he has abstained from alcohol for a number of years,[72] or that he is a member of a generally respected profession, institution, society, or club, or that he has any other attributes which people generally would think to be commendable. But an important distinction must be made. Very often, some aspects of the accused's work or home life or his activities are relevant to the issue of guilt or innocence. If the accused adduces evidence of such matters because they are relevant factually to his defence, it is submitted that, as long as the jury is not misled, he does not make an assertion for the purposes of gateway (f) even if he has, in other respects, a bad character. For example, if an accused is found in possession of apparent house-breaking implements, and explains his possession of them by giving evidence that he is a builder or a locksmith by trade, it is submitted that he does not thereby give a false impression; though if he goes on to add that he earns his

---

[70] *Baker* (1912) 7 Cr App R 252; *Coulman* (1927) 20 Cr App R 106.

[71] *Ferguson* (1909) 2 Cr App R 250.

[72] *Douglass* (1989) 89 Cr App R 264, though in this case it was significant that the accused intended to induce the jury to view him favourably compared to his co-accused, who had been drunk at the time of the events relevant to the case.

living honestly as a builder or a locksmith, and therefore has no need to steal, the result might be different.[73] Such cases are unlikely to give rise to difficulties.

However, the provisions of s. 105(4) and (5) dealing with the circumstances in which the accused seeks to give the court a false or misleading impression by means of his conduct in court, other than the giving of evidence, may prove to be controversial. It seems clear enough in principle that an accused may make an implied assertion of his good character by means of his appearance or dress, for example if he appears in court wearing a clerical collar or a military or police uniform. But the few cases of this kind decided under the Criminal Evidence Act 1898 were strangely ambivalent. In *Robinson*,[74] the Court of Appeal held that the trial judge had erred in holding that the accused had lost his shield as a result of holding a copy of the Bible in his hands while giving evidence about his respectable family life, but at the same time held that the judge should have warned him about the possible consequences of so doing. The basis for the decision appears to have been that a witness may be sworn on the Bible, and it is, therefore, inconsistent to hold that he asserts his good character if he holds it while giving evidence. With all due respect to the Court, and to the Law Commission, which expressed its agreement with the decision,[75] it is submitted that this case was wrongly decided. Holding a Bible throughout one's evidence sends a very different message to the jury than holding it for a few seconds while taking the oath. One would hope that the case would be decided differently under the Criminal Justice Act 2003. At the same time, it is submitted that judges should approach this matter from a common sense standpoint. Solicitors invariably advise their male clients to get their hair cut and put on a suit and tie for their appearance in court (and, of course, offer corresponding advice to female clients). Even if the accused would never ordinarily dress in that way, and his hair is usually long and unkempt, it is submitted that he does not make an assertion about his character by following his solicitor's advice. Indeed, it might properly be interpreted simply as showing appropriate respect for the court.

The false impression need not relate to the false assertion of good character in the usual sense of that expression. In *Kiernan* [2008] EWCA Crim 972, where the accused stated that he had 'paid his debt to society' in relation to a previous offence without mentioning that he had absconded from prison and remained at large, it was held that he had thereby given a false impression.

Section 105(6) provides that evidence is admissible under gateway (f) only if it goes no further than is necessary to correct the false impression. It will be interesting to see how judges interpret this provision. As we have seen (5.9) at common law and under the Criminal Evidence Act 1898, the accused's character was taken to be indivisible. He could not assert a part of his character, which he considered to be favourable, without having the whole inquired into on rebuttal. But the Law Commission proposed a different approach based on a more specific relevance,[76] and it seems that s. 105(6) is consistent with that approach. On this basis, the starting point must be the substance of the assertion actually made by the accused. If, for example, the assertion is, 'I have no previous convictions', then clearly any evidence of previous convictions is justifiable for the

---

[73] Cf. *Thompson* [1966] 1 WLR 405 (where the accused explained his running away from a police officer by stating that he feared he was being arrested for non-payment of a fine, he was simply rebutting a piece of otherwise incriminating evidence, and not asserting his character; accordingly, the judge erred in compelling him to answer questions about the offence for which he had been fined and about other previous convictions); *Stronach* [1988] Crim LR 48.

[74] [2001] Crim LR 478; and see *Hamilton* [1969] LR 486, in which it was held that the trial judge had erred in giving the accused the option of removing the regimental blazer he was wearing before giving evidence, or losing his shield.

[75] Report 273, para. 13.19, note 6.

[76] Report 274, para. 1.8(6).

purpose of correcting the false impression. But evidence that the accused has been the subject of an anti-social behaviour order, or was expelled from university for cheating during his examinations, should not be admitted. On the other hand, if the assertion is, 'I am a person of unimpeachable morals, and I would never dream of doing anything dishonest', then the evidence admissible may well be considerably broader in its scope because the false impression offered to the jury is broader. Presumably, it is not necessary to be unduly literal, certainly in the case of an implied assertion. If the accused appears in court dressed in a clerical collar, it is submitted that the prosecution could go further than simply proving that he is not an ordained minister. The accused could hardly be heard to complain if the prosecution sought to adduce, not only evidence of previous convictions, but also evidence of other reprehensible behaviour. The substance of the assertion is not simply that the accused is a minister of religion; more importantly, it is that he possesses a character appropriate to a minister of religion.

6.13 GATEWAY (G): DEFENDANT HAS MADE AN ATTACK ON ANOTHER PERSON'S CHARACTER

Gateway (g) is supplemented by s. 106, which provides:

> (1) For the purposes of section 101(1)(g) a defendant makes an attack on another person's character if—
>> (a) he adduces evidence attacking the other person's character,
>> (b) he (or any legal representative appointed under section 38(4) of the Youth Justice and Criminal Evidence Act 1999 (c. 23) to cross-examine a witness in his interests) asks questions in cross-examination that are intended to elicit such evidence, or are likely to do so, or
>> (c) evidence is given of an imputation about the other person made by the defendant—
>>> (i) on being questioned under caution, before charge, about the offence with which he is charged, or
>>> (ii) on being charged with the offence or officially informed that he might be prosecuted for it.
> (2) In subsection (1) 'evidence attacking the other person's character' means evidence to the effect that the other person—
>> (a) has committed an offence (whether a different offence from the one with which the defendant is charged or the same one), or
>> (b) has behaved, or is disposed to behave, in a reprehensible way;
> and 'imputation about the other person' means an assertion to that effect.
> (3) Only prosecution evidence is admissible under section 101(1)(g).

Gateway (g) is the successor of the 'imputation' provision of s. 1(3)(ii) of the Criminal Evidence Act 1898, which provided that the accused lost shield against cross-examination about his character if:

> …the nature or conduct of the defence is such as to involve imputations on the character of the prosecutor, the witnesses for the prosecution, or the deceased victim of the alleged crime.

The word 'imputation' was not defined by the 1898 Act. It was interpreted judicially as meaning any suggestion of a serious wrongful act, fault, or vice,[77] the most obvious cases consisting

---

[77] *Selvey v DPP* [1970] AC 304; *Bishop* [1975] QB 274. The question of what amounted to an imputation was left to be interpreted by judges, hopefully to a reasonable degree in accordance with current *mores*, and much depended on the apparent seriousness of the allegation. In that respect, it can be compared to the likely interpretation of 'reprehensible behaviour' under the Criminal Justice Act 2003; see discussion at 6.3.4.

of alleged misconduct in relation to the offence charged, or its investigation or prosecution; for example, where it was suggested that a witness for the prosecution had actually committed the offence with which the accused was charged, or had fabricated evidence against him, or was committing perjury in giving evidence against him.[78] Conversely, if the suggestion was simply that the witness was honestly mistaken, or if the suggestion made by the defence was not seriously discreditable to the witness, no imputation was made.[79] The word 'imputation' appears again in s. 106 of the Criminal Justice Act 2003, and this time, is given a statutory definition. Making an 'imputation' about another person, for the purposes of the Criminal Justice Act 2003, is the making of an attack on that person's character in the form of an assertion (s. 106(2) and text below). Curiously, the word is employed only in one particular context, namely, in connection with the case in which the accused attacks the character of another outside court, while being questioned by the police, or on being charged with the offence (s. 106(1)(c)). For all practical purposes, an attack on the character of another person under the Criminal Justice Act 2003 will cover much the same ground as did imputations under the Criminal Evidence Act 1898. So it may be that the retention of the word 'imputation' for a limited purpose will not cause any real confusion. But it is certainly arguable that it might have been preferable to avoid the use of a word with such a long history under the previous law.

The key term, for the purposes of the new law, is not 'imputation', but 'attack on another person's character'. The definition of this term falls into two parts. Firstly, s. 106(1) defines an attack on the character of another person as adducing evidence which has that effect. This may occur when the defence calls witnesses to give evidence, or cross-examines prosecution witnesses; or when evidence is given (usually by the prosecution) of an imputation (as defined by s. 106(1)(c)) made by the accused about another person while being questioned or when charged with the offence. An attack on character will be deemed to be made as a result of an answer given to a question put in cross-examination, not only if the question was intended to elicit such an answer, but also if the question was likely to elicit that answer (s. 106(1)(b)); which presumably means that, in the opinion of the judge, the question put can be reasonably understood only as calling for evidence of the bad character of another person. Secondly, s. 106(2) defines evidence attacking the character of another person as meaning evidence that the other person has committed an offence, or has behaved or is disposed to behave in a reprehensible way (as to this, see 6.3.3; 6.3.4). If the evidence is that the other person committed an offence, the offence in question may either be the offence with which the accused is charged, or any other offence. Despite a similarity of language, there is an important difference between this definition of 'evidence attacking the other person's character' under s. 106(2) and the definition of 'bad character' under s. 98 (see 6.3.1). Under the latter section, the definition of 'bad character' excludes misconduct which has to do with the alleged facts of the offence with which the defendant is charged or in connection with the investigation or prosecution of that offence. But the only real importance of an attack on the character of prosecution witnesses is in a case in which that attack is directed to misconduct in connection with the offence, or its investigation or prosecution. If that element is removed, gateway (g) loses any semblance of practical utility. Thus, for the purposes of gateway (g) and s. 106, the attack on the character of another person not only may, but usually will, be directed either to an allegation that the other person committed the offence charged, or of

---

[78] *Hudson* [1912] 2 KB 464; *Clark* [1955] 2 QB 469; *Wright* (1910) 5 Cr App R 131; *Jones* (1923) 17 Cr App R 117.
[79] *McLean* [1978] Crim LR 430.

some misconduct such as fabrication of evidence, depriving the accused of his rights during the investigation, or committing perjury by giving evidence against him at trial, in relation to the investigation or prosecution of the offence. Where such allegations are made, gateway (g) comes into play, and evidence of the accused's bad character becomes admissible.

Unlike s. 1(3)(ii) of the Criminal Evidence Act 1898, which (as amended) specified that the imputation must be against either the prosecutor, the witnesses for the prosecution, or the deceased victim of the alleged crime, s. 101(1)(g) of the Criminal Justice Act 2003 applies to an attack by the accused on the character of any other person. But for the reasons given above, the attacks on character with which the courts will continue to be principally concerned will be those made against the same persons, notably prosecution witnesses such as police officers. Attacks on the character of other persons are likely to be of little, if any relevance. If the accused gives vent to an outburst in which he blames his troubles on the failings of his parents, or offers a gratuitous insult to the Prime Minister or the Archbishop of Canterbury, one would hope that judges will take a commonsense approach to gateway (g) and not allow the prosecution to respond by adducing evidence of the accused's bad character. This is to suggest no more than that the application of gateway (g) should be somehow relevant to the case.

The admission of evidence of bad character in this situation is in effect a thinly veiled form of retaliation against the accused for having the temerity to make an attack on the character of prosecution witnesses. It was one of the more controversial uses of character evidence under the Criminal Evidence Act 1898. The Law Commission (Report 273, paras 4.51, 4.52) noted the depth of feeling aroused in many commentators by the so-called 'tit-for-tat' principle which is said to justify it. Although expressed as a rule of fairness, whose purpose was to let the jury know the nature of the source of the imputations and thereby be enabled to assess their credibility, it often operated in a grossly unfair way, in effect penalizing the accused for presenting his defence, if that defence in any manner suggested wrongful conduct on the part of any prosecution witness.[80] It seemed to have been established as a matter of principle that the accused could assert that he was not guilty, and even do so vigorously, without losing his shield, as long as he did not go further than was necessary to make the assertion. Indeed, in one sense, if that were not the position, it could be argued that the accused should lose his shield merely by pleading not guilty. But in reality, there are many cases in which the defence simply cannot be presented without making an attack on the character of a prosecution witness, and the distinction simply proved to be unrealistic.[81] It was suggested in the 9th edition of this work (para. 6.13) that the Criminal Justice Act 2003 offered a new opportunity to judges to make this troubled area of the law operate more fairly. Gateway (g) is subject to the duty to exclude evidence of bad character on the ground that its admission would have an unacceptably adverse effect on the fairness of the proceedings under s. 101(3): see 6.20; it is submitted that, in the interests of fairness, judges should consider

---

[80] Because s. 1(3)(ii) specified that it was enough if either the 'nature' or the 'conduct' of the defence involved imputations, the shield was lost even if the accused had no other way to present his defence, and regretted the necessity of making the imputations: *Selvey v DPP* [1970] AC 370; *Bishop* [1975] QB 274. This reality could not be avoided by framing questions of the prosecution witnesses in terms of their being 'mistaken' rather than dishonest: *Britzman* [1983] 1 All ER 369; *Tanner* (1977) 66 Cr App R 56; a principle which appears to be preserved by s. 106(1)(b) of the Criminal Justice Act 2003 (text above). In *Wainwright* [1998] Crim LR 665, it seems to have been held that the shield was lost even where the imputation made was not seriously disputed: a particularly outrageous decision. For one general criticism of the rule, see P. Murphy (1998) 2 E & P 71.

[81] The claimed distinction was often charmingly, though unconvincingly, illustrated by contrasting *Rouse* [1904] 1 KB 184 ('liar' held to be merely an emphatic denial of guilt) with *Rappolt* (1911) 6 Cr App R 156 ('such a horrible liar that his brother would not speak to him' held to be an imputation on character).

with particular care whether that duty compels them to exclude evidence tendered under this gateway. It is further submitted that an accused should not be held to have attacked the character of another where he simply asserts that he is not guilty, even where he does so in vigorous terms. It is further submitted that judges should continue to draw a distinction between cases in which the accused attacks the character of another, and cases in which he merely asserts that the other has made an innocent mistake. But there is thus far little to suggest that the courts are inclined to mitigate the prejudicial effect of evidence adduced under gateway (g). Indeed, as we have already noted (see 6.6.1) it has been held that evidence adduced under this gateway may be used for any purpose for which it is relevant, for example as evidence of propensity, in addition to any value it may have on the accused's credibility as the author of an attack on the character of another: see *Highton and other appeals* [2005] 1 WLR 3472. This is consistent with the intention of Parliament.[82] But it is an area that brings the law little credit for fairness. It would be interesting to see the principles underlying gateway (g) subjected to a robust challenge under the fair trial provisions of art. 6 of the European Convention on Human Rights.

6.13.1 Admissibility in rebuttal of good character of person attacked

There is a paucity of authority as to whether, if the accused attacks the character of another person, evidence of that person's good character may be adduced in rebuttal. In *O'Connor (Brendan)* 29 October 1996, unreported, case no. 9606365 Y4, the Court of Appeal permitted such evidence to be given, apparently on the simple ground of its relevance. The accused had attacked the character of a number of police officers, whom he had accused of misconduct and perjury in relation to the charges brought against him. The prosecution were permitted to adduce the fact that the officers had no previous convictions and no adverse disciplinary findings recorded against them. The decision seems correct in principle. This was, of course, a decision under the law before the Criminal Justice Act 2003, but there is no reason to think that the decision should be any different under the present law.

C   SECTION 100: EVIDENCE OF BAD CHARACTER OF PERSONS OTHER THAN ACCUSED

SUMMARY OF MAIN POINTS

- Evidence of the bad character of persons other than the accused is governed exclusively by s. 100 of the Criminal Justice Act 2003.

- Section 100(1) provides:

   In criminal proceedings evidence of the bad character of a person other than the defendant is admissible if and only if—

   (a) it is important explanatory evidence,

---

[82] The Home Office Note accompanying s. 106 (para. 382) made clear that the absence of a limitation on the use of the evidence to the issue of credibility was deliberate. The suggestion apparently made in *Hearne* [2009] EWCA Crim 103, that evidence admitted under gateway (g) is limited to credibility, as under the Criminal Evidence Act 1898, is surely incorrect.

(b) it has substantial probative value in relation to a matter which—

    (i)   is a matter in issue in the proceedings, and

    (ii) is of substantial importance in the context of the case as a whole,

or

(c) all parties to the proceedings agree to the evidence being admissible.

6.14 INTRODUCTION

While the bad character of the accused is the most significant issue relating to this kind of evidence, it is by no means the only such issue. The bad character of witnesses, including the alleged victim of an offence, may also be relevant in some manner either to the issue of guilt or to the issue of the credibility of the witness. At common law, witnesses are subject to impeachment by being cross-examined about their bad character, subject to the power of the judge to restrain excessive cross-examination in the interests of fairness.[83] However, cross-examination with respect to issues relevant only to credibility, which are known as collateral issues, are subject to the so-called rule of finality, discussed in detail at 17.8 *et seq*. The rule of finality provides that, subject to some important exceptions, although a party may cross-examine on collateral issues, he must accept the witness's answers on such matters as final, i.e., he may not adduce extrinsic evidence to contradict those answers. By way of contrast, if the issue which is the subject of the cross-examination is also relevant to a substantive issue in the case, such as the issue of guilt, evidence to contradict the witness's answers may be adduced. As we shall see (17.8.1), the boundaries between evidence relevant to substantive issues and evidence relevant only to credit are not always completely clear. It will be submitted below that, in the light of s. 99 of the Criminal Justice Act 2003, the rule of finality must be taken to have been abrogated insofar as it applies to evidence of bad character: see 6.15.1.[84] The common law rule on impeachment applied to all witnesses, including parties, except the accused in a criminal case. When the Criminal Evidence Act 1898 enabled the accused to give evidence in his defence, it exempted him from the general common law rule, and provided that he could be cross-examined about his previous convictions and bad character only if he lost his shield in the circumstances specified by s. 1(3) of the Act. But these provisions, as we have seen, were repealed and superseded by the Criminal Justice Act 2003. Thus, in criminal cases, the Criminal Justice Act 2003 now governs the admissibility of evidence of the bad character, not only of the accused, but also of witnesses and any other persons. Of the class of persons other than the accused, witnesses, and particularly prosecution witnesses, provide the most important cases in which evidence of bad character must be considered. There are occasionally cases in which the bad character of a person who is neither a defendant nor a witness becomes relevant; for example, where the accused contends that his conduct was intended as an innocent protest against reprehensible conduct of another; or where he contends that a third party committed the offence charged, and seeks to adduce evidence of other offences or

---

[83] *Sweet-Escott* (1971) 55 Cr App R 316; see generally 17.2.

[84] There was already a statutory exception to the rule of finality under s. 6 of the Criminal Procedure Act 1865, which permitted proof that a witness has been convicted of an offence if he denies or fails to admit that fact, or refuses to answer a question about it: see 17.9. But it now appears that evidence of bad character of any kind (e.g., reprehensible behaviour) must also be admissible, despite the rule of finality, even when relevant only to credit.

misconduct in support of that contention. The use of evidence of bad character for the purpose of impeaching a witness has always been confined to attacking the credibility of witnesses on the other side. Section 112(3)(a) specifically preserves the rule that a party may not impeach the credit of his own witness by general evidence of bad character: see Criminal Procedure Act 1865, s. 3; 16.15 *et seq*. Two other matters should also be mentioned.

Firstly, other statutory provisions significantly changed the common law in the case of witnesses who are also complainants in cases of sexual offences. The provisions now in force are of those of s. 41 of the Youth Justice and Criminal Evidence Act 1999, by virtue of which there are serious restrictions on cross-examination about, or the adduction of evidence about the complainant's sexual behaviour. The rules under this section are expressly preserved by s. 112(3)(b) of the Criminal Justice Act 2003. Evidence of sexual behaviour is not evidence of bad character, although given the breadth of the definition of 'bad character' under the Criminal Justice Act 2003, it may in some circumstances qualify as such as 'reprehensible' behaviour, so that there may be some overlap (see 6.27). Be that as it may, evidence of the complainant's sexual behaviour continues to be governed by s. 41 of the 1999 Act. In all other respects, of course, the bad character of the complainant now falls under the provisions of the Criminal Justice Act 2003.

Secondly, as we have seen (6.4.1) evidence that a person has been convicted of an offence is admissible for the purpose of proving that that person committed the offence of which he was convicted by virtue of ss. 73 and 74 of the Police and Criminal Evidence Act 1984. The conviction of another person may be relevant to the guilt of the accused, for example where the accused is charged with handling stolen goods, and the conviction of the thief is admitted for the purpose of proving that the goods in question are stolen goods. The rules under the 1984 Act relating to the proof and admissibility of previous convictions for such purposes are not affected by the Criminal Justice Act 2003: see further 12.17 *et seq*.

The admissibility of evidence of the bad character of persons other than the accused is governed by s. 100 of the Criminal Justice Act 2003, which provides:

> (1) In criminal proceedings evidence of the bad character of a person other than the defendant is admissible if and only if—
>> (a) it is important explanatory evidence,
>> (b) it has substantial probative value in relation to a matter which—
>>> (i) is a matter in issue in the proceedings, and
>>> (ii) is of substantial importance in the context of the case as a whole,
>>   or
>> (c) all parties to the proceedings agree to the evidence being admissible.
> (2) For the purposes of subsection (1)(a) evidence is important explanatory evidence if—
>> (a) without it, the court or jury would find it impossible or difficult properly to understand other evidence in the case, and
>> (b) its value for understanding the case as a whole is substantial.
> (3) In assessing the probative value of evidence for the purposes of subsection (1)(b) the court must have regard to the following factors (and to any others it considers relevant)—
>> (a) the nature and number of the events, or other things, to which the evidence relates;
>> (b) when those events or things are alleged to have happened or existed;
>> (c) where—
>>> (i) the evidence is evidence of a person's misconduct, and
>>> (ii) it is suggested that the evidence has probative value by reason of similarity between that misconduct and other alleged misconduct,

the nature and extent of the similarities and the dissimilarities between each of the alleged instances of misconduct;

(d) where—

  (i)   the evidence is evidence of a person's misconduct,

  (ii) it is suggested that that person is also responsible for the misconduct charged, and

  (iii) the identity of the person responsible for the misconduct charged is disputed, the extent to which the evidence shows or tends to show that the same person was responsible each time.

(4) Except where subsection (1)(c) applies, evidence of the bad character of a person other than the defendant must not be given without leave of the court.

6.15 REQUIREMENT OF LEAVE

Subject to the rule against impeaching one's own witness (above), evidence under s. 100 may be adduced by any party. But s. 100 makes a significant change to the practice at common law. This is the requirement of s. 100(4) that, except where all parties to the proceedings agree to the evidence being admitted, evidence of the bad character other than a person other than the defendant must not be given without leave of the court. At common law, cross-examination of a witness was permitted without leave as to any matter relating to the character of a witness (except, in sexual cases, matters excluded by statute). To that extent, the Act imposes a significant restriction. The perception that references to the bad character of witnesses were being made unnecessarily and excessively in cross-examination under common law principles was one which concerned both the Law Commission and the government.[85] As we have seen (note 83) there was a discretion at common law to restrain improper or excessive cross-examination. But in the case of non-defendants, the government was clearly persuaded that that discretion was either inadequate, or was insufficiently exercised. Although it continues to be a matter for decision by the trial judge, s. 100(4) substitutes a rule of inadmissibility without leave for the common law rule of admissibility subject to discretion, and so emphasizes the need for a stricter judicial scrutiny of the proposed evidence in every case.

But it is important to keep in mind that the definition of bad character under s. 98 of the Act does not include evidence of misconduct which has to do with the facts of the offence charged or the investigation or prosecution of that offence. Accordingly, if the accused's case is that a prosecution witness committed the offence charged, or fabricated evidence against the accused, that does not amount to evidence of the bad character of the witness for the purpose of s. 98.[86] The accused is entitled to make that suggestion, and to adduce any evidence based on the facts of the case or the investigation which supports that suggestion (for example, evidence that the witness was observed committing the offence charged or tampering with evidence), without seeking leave under s. 100(4). On the other hand, if the accused wishes to adduce evidence that the witness has committed other offences or reprehensible conduct, or has a bad reputation, for the purpose of supporting his suggestion (for example, evidence of a previous conviction for a similar offence, or reprehensible conduct which shows a propensity to behave in that way); or for the

---

[85] 'The present law suffers from a number of defects…often exposing witnesses to gratuitous and humiliating exposure of long forgotten misconduct': Law Commission Report No. 273, para. 1.7.

[86] Cf. *Smith* [2007] EWCA Crim 2105, where the evidence consisted of an admission by the co-accused to having committed the offence charged; no question of bad character evidence arose.

purpose of attacking his credibility (for example, a previous conviction for perjury); that would be evidence of the bad character of the witness, which would require leave under s. 100(4).

Leave may be granted only in one of the three circumstances specified in s. 100(1). Nothing more need be said about s. 100(1)(c), the case in which all parties to the proceedings agree, except perhaps that, given the concern to prevent unnecessary references to the bad character of witnesses, it might have been expected that the judge should have the last word in every case; in this case, however, the parties have the last word.

6.15.1 Abrogation of rule of finality as to evidence of bad character

In one respect, the Act seems to allow more liberal proof than the common law. It is submitted that the Act must be taken to have abrogated the common law rule of finality in relation to collateral matters, insofar as it applies to any evidence of bad character admissible by virtue of the Act. As we have noted, the rule of finality provides that, although a party may cross-examine on collateral issues, he must accept the witness's answers on such matters as final, i.e., he may not adduce extrinsic evidence to contradict those answers. But if the issue which is the subject of the cross-examination is also relevant to a substantive issue in the case, such as the issue of guilt, evidence to contradict the witness's answers may be adduced. For a more detailed discussion of the rule and its exceptions, see generally 17.8 *et seq*. There has long been a statutory exception to the rule of finality applicable to previous convictions. Section 6 of the Criminal Procedure Act 1865 provides that if a witness denies that he has been convicted of an offence, fails to admit that fact, or refuses to answer a question about it, the conviction may be proved (see 17.9). This exception is preserved, albeit amended, by virtue of Part 5 of Sch. 36 to the Criminal Justice Act 2003. As amended, s. 6 provides:

> If upon a witness being lawfully questioned as to whether he has been convicted of any [offence][87] he either denies or does not admit the fact, or refuses to answer, it shall be lawful for the cross-examining party to prove such conviction...

The amendment repealed the former opening words of the section: '[A] witness may be [questioned]', a permissive provision which was no longer necessary because both cross-examination and proof of the previous conviction are now permitted, regardless of any answer given by the witness, by virtue of the Criminal Justice Act 2003. This is consistent with the general position under the 2003 Act that there is no longer any distinction between evidence of bad character adduced by way of cross-examination and evidence adduced otherwise. Section 6 does not apply to evidence of bad character other than previous convictions. But there is no basis under the Criminal Justice Act 2003 for treating evidence of previous convictions differently from other kinds of evidence of bad character, i.e., all kinds of evidence of bad character may be adduced either in cross-examination or otherwise. Hence, it is submitted, the same rule must apply also to any kind of evidence of bad character which may be admitted under the Act, for example misconduct in the form of reprehensible behaviour. Section 99 of the Act abolishes all common law rules governing the admissibility of evidence of bad character. The rule of finality of answers on collateral matters is a common law rule, and accordingly, it is submitted, insofar as it previously restricted the proof of collateral matters consisting of evidence of bad character other than previous convictions, it must be taken to be abrogated by the Criminal Justice Act 2003. This means

---

[87] The original enactment referred to questioning about conviction for any felony or misdemeanour, but the distinction between felonies and misdemeanours was abolished by Criminal Law Act 1967, s. 1.

that, if leave is granted under s. 100(4), a party is entitled not only to cross-examine a witness or other person about his or her bad character, but is entitled to prove that bad character to the extent that it is not admitted, even if the only or the primary relevance of the evidence is to the credit of the witness.

6.16 SECTION 100(1)(A): IT IS IMPORTANT EXPLANATORY EVIDENCE

The definition of 'important explanatory evidence' in s. 100(2) is identical to that in s. 102 relating to evidence of the bad character of the accused, and, it is submitted, should be interpreted in much the same way (see 6.9). Evidence of this kind may be admissible under the *res gestae* principle, or as background evidence. For example, if an accused charged with murder claims that he killed the deceased in self-defence or under provocation, or if the accused claims that a pattern of abuse by her spouse led up to the incident during which she killed him, it may be relevant to prove a course of conduct by the deceased, involving violence or other abuse, on a number of occasions or over a period of time. This may help the jury to understand the background against which the killing was committed and so evaluate the defence.

6.17 SECTION 100(1)(B): EVIDENCE HAVING SUBSTANTIAL PROBATIVE VALUE

The test of admissibility in this case goes beyond simple relevance. The judge must be satisfied that the evidence would (on the assumption that it is true: see s. 109) not only be relevant, but would also be likely to have considerable probative value with respect to the issue to which it is relevant. Moreover, that issue must itself be of substantial importance in the context of the case as a whole. Reading s. 100(1)(b)(ii) and s. 112 together, it seems clear that it must be an 'important issue' in the same sense as that expression is used in s. 101(1)(d) in the case of the defendant's bad character. Using the same expression in both sections would have contributed both to conciseness and clarity. The overall concept seems to be that the admission of the evidence must have the clear potential to make a difference in the way in which the jury is likely to view the evidence, or the case as a whole, and, therefore, a clear potential to affect the outcome of the case. In the absence of restriction, it appears that the issue may relate either to the issue of guilt directly or to the issue of the credibility of the witness (which may affect the issue of guilt indirectly).[88] In *S* [2007] 1 WLR 63, the accused, a man of previous good character, paid the complainant, a prostitute, £10 for an act of masturbation. Shortly after the act had been performed, the complainant accused him of sexual assault, and he was charged. The accused alleged that the complainant had demanded more money, had tried to seize a gold chain he was wearing, and had threatened to accuse him of rape if he did not pay more. When he refused to pay more, the complainant made good on her threat. At trial, the accused sought to admit evidence of the complainant's previous convictions for going equipped for theft, burglary, and handling stolen goods. The argument at trial proceeded on the basis that the evidence was relevant to show her propensity for untruthfulness, and the judge rejected it. The Court of Appeal allowed the appeal against conviction, but on the ground that the previous convictions should have been admitted to show, not propensity for untruthfulness (as to which it was probably irrelevant: see *Hanson and other appeals* [2005]

---

[88] This is confirmed by the judgment of the Court of Appeal in the appeal of *Yaxley-Lennon* in *Weir and other appeals* [2006] 1 WLR 1885, [73].

1 WLR 3169, [13]; 6.10.4), but propensity to act in the kind of dishonest way described by the accused. The evidence would have had substantial probative value to the jury in helping them to evaluate the accused's account of what had happened, and depriving the jury of the evidence rendered the conviction unsafe.

It must be relevant for the court to consider, not only the nature and gravity of the allegations of bad character, on which s. 100(3) concentrates (below), but also the relationship of the witness himself to the case as a whole. If he is a key witness on whose evidence the case against the accused effectively stands or falls, his bad character should obviously be viewed in a different light to that of a peripheral witness who gives evidence on a relatively minor issue. In the latter case, even evidence of very bad character might be unlikely to affect the ultimate outcome of the case. The same might be true when, even though the witness's evidence is of great importance, his evidence is not disputed except with respect to relatively minor matters. Evidence of bad character might also be less persuasive where the witness has absolutely no interest in the outcome of a case, and so has no conceivable motive to do anything other than testify truthfully, for example where a prisoner who has just been released from a long prison sentence happens, on the way home, to be an eyewitness to a piece of dangerous driving that results in a death. The few pronouncements in this area thus far by the Court of Appeal appear to be consistent with this general approach, but have not sought to lay down any overarching principles beyond those discussed above in relation to the bad character of the accused. Indeed, in *Renda and other appeals* [2006] 2 All ER 553, which involved cases on the application of s.100, Sir Igor Judge P observed at the outset of the judgment of the Court that to create 'a vast body of so-called "authority", in reality representing no more than observations on a fact-specific decision of the judge in the Crown Court' would be unnecessary and might well be counter-productive (*ibid.* at [3]).[89] It does appear, however, that in the case of persons other than the accused, trial judges are encouraged to take a more robust approach, and to exclude evidence of bad character whenever it is doubtful that it could have substantial probative value, especially where the time of the court might be consumed in 'satellite litigation' over the details of the character itself: see *Bovell; Dowds* [2005] 2 Cr App R 27, [22].[90]

6.18 FACTORS RELEVANT TO PROBATIVE VALUE

Section 100(3) enumerates four factors to which the court should have regard, together with any other apparently relevant factors. Subsection (3)(a) and (b) encompasses basic matters such as the nature, gravity, and extent of any previous offences or other misconduct. A previous conviction may range from the obviously serious and compelling, for example a conviction for perjury a year ago, to the almost inconsequential, for example, a 10-year-old conviction for obtaining a second-hand television set by deception. Both may suggest a propensity to be less than truthful, but the court is entitled to consider the likely impact of the evidence on the credibility of the witness in the eyes of a jury here and now. A number of previous convictions for relatively minor offences, however, may be telling as evidence of persistent dishonesty. If the issue is simply one

---

[89] See, in accordance with this approach, the factually-based judgment of the Court in the appeals of *Akram, Osbourne,* and *Razaq* in that case, in which the court dealt with the merits in terms of the facts of the individual cases without seeking to lay down any broader legal principles. See also *Bovell; Dowds* [2005] 2 Cr App R 27.

[90] Citing *Hanson and other appeals* [2005] 1 WLR 3169, [12]: 'Where past events are disputed the judge must take care not to permit the trial unreasonably to be diverted into an investigation of matters not charged on the indictment'.

of credibility, even previous convictions for serious offences, such as murder, may have little real relevance if they do not necessarily suggest dishonesty; though their prejudicial value to the witness may be substantial. Subsection 3(c) deals with the case in which the relevance of evidence of bad character is based on similar misconduct. This may be the case where the accused claims that the witness's series of previous convictions for strikingly similar offences makes the witness a person more likely to be guilty of the offence charged than the accused, in a case in which other evidence suggests that either might have done so. For example, a divorced father accused of sexual assault of his child may seek to adduce evidence that the child's step-father has a record of similar offences. An accused charged with rape may seek to show that the complainant has on a number of previous occasions made accusations of rape against other men, which subsequently proved to be false. As in the case of similar fact evidence at common law, and when it is adduced under s. 101(d) in the case of the accused, it is appropriate for the court to consider both the similarities and dissimilarities of the misconduct, in order to assess whether it is relevant and has substantial probative value. Subsection (3)(d) is a special case of subsection (3)(c), in which the issue is specifically the identity of the person who committed the offence charged, and the accused alleges that a witness or third party is in fact the guilty party. In this case, the question is the extent to which either the similarity of the various instances of misconduct, or other characteristics of the evidence, show or tend to show that the same person was responsible for all of them, including the offence charged. Section 100(3) makes it clear that the court may take into account any other factors which appear to be relevant.

D   SAFEGUARDS UNDER CRIMINAL JUSTICE ACT 2003

> **SUMMARY OF MAIN POINTS**
>
> - The Criminal Justice Act 2003 provides important safeguards in relation to evidence of bad character. The most important of these is provided by s. 103(1):
>
>   > The court must not admit evidence under subsection (1)(d) or (g) if, on an application by the defendant to exclude it, it appears to the court that the admission of the evidence would have such an adverse effect on the fairness of the proceedings that the court ought not to admit it
>
> - In cases other than gateways (d) and (g) the judge retains the discretion to exclude evidence tendered by the prosecution (but not an accused) under s. 78 of the Police and Criminal Evidence Act 1984.
>
> - Section 107 of the Criminal Justice Act 2003 provides that the judge must stop the case if evidence is contaminated by collusion between witnesses.

6.19 INTRODUCTION

We saw at 5.2 that the introduction of evidence of bad character, particularly the bad character of the accused, necessarily has a massive impact on the course of a criminal trial, and may often produce an irreversible change of course despite even the most scrupulous directions by the judge. Both at common law and under s. 78 of the Police and Criminal Evidence Act 1984, the judicial discretion to exclude evidence in the interests of securing a fair trial for the accused was the safeguard afforded to the accused against the admission of evidence of bad character in circumstances in which its admission might be unfair or unduly prejudicial: see generally 3.7. The protection afforded to persons other than the accused at common law was also discretionary, but a good deal less systematic, and depended on the sense of the judge that a cross-examination might be going too far (see note 83). In the case of the bad character of non-defendants, the Act replaces the common law discretionary rules with a much more cogent rule, by virtue of which evidence of the bad character of any non-defendant can be admitted only with leave of the court, unless all parties to the proceedings agree that it should be admitted: see s. 100(1)(c) and 6.15. Although this may in some cases result in such evidence being somewhat less likely to be admitted than it should be, the rule has the merit of being clear and consistent. The Law Commission had recommended that the same rule should apply to evidence of the bad character of the accused also.[91] Another logical alternative might have been to declare (for the avoidance of doubt) that s. 78 of the Police and Criminal Evidence Act 1984 should apply to the admission of evidence of the accused's bad character. Parliament followed neither course, but instead enacted a number of entirely new discrete provisions, which operate in different ways. Taken together, and if consistently applied by trial judges, they may offer a sufficient safeguard, but in the light of the wide principles of admissibility of evidence of bad character, strict judicial scrutiny of such evidence will be required. The most important of these provisions is s. 101(3), which, employing language to be found in s. 78, creates a judicial duty to exclude evidence of the accused's bad character in some cases, in the circumstances which would justify the exercise of the discretion under s. 78. This duty, however, applies only to certain of the gateways under s. 101, and the Act left open the question of whether the judge may, assuming he reaches the same conclusion as to the impact of the evidence on the fairness of the proceedings, continue to apply the discretion under s. 78 (or, for that matter, the common law discretion) to the cases not covered by the new duty.[92] In addition, s. 107 of the Act provides a new judicial duty to stop the case if evidence of the accused's bad character is admitted which proves to be 'contaminated' and if, because of this, and the importance of the evidence to the case, a conviction would be unsafe. The definition of 'contaminated' in s. 107(5) is vague and imprecise, making it hard to interpret, but its apparent intended meaning restricts it to a narrow range of cases. Certain other more specific provisions, intended to provide of protection in particular cases, are also dealt with below.

6.20 SECTION 101(3): DUTY TO EXCLUDE EVIDENCE IN CERTAIN CASES

Section 101(3) provides:

> The court must not admit evidence under subsection (1)(d) or (g) if, on an application by the defendant to exclude it, it appears to the court that the admission of the evidence would have such an adverse effect on the fairness of the proceedings that the court ought not to admit it.

---

[91] The draft bill attached to the Law Commission's Report No. 273 would have provided that leave of the court should be required to adduce all evidence of bad character, unless all parties agreed or it was adduced by the accused.

[92] It now seems to be established that the discretion under s. 78 does apply in such cases: see *Highton and other appeals* [2005] 1 WLR 3472, [13]–[14]; appeal of *Somanathan* in *Weir and other appeals* [2006] 1 WLR 1885, [44]; 6.20.

This is supplemented by s. 101(4):

On an application to exclude evidence under subsection (3) the court must have regard, in particular, to the length of time between the matters to which that evidence relates and the matters which form the subject of the offence charged.

There are two striking features of s. 101(3). Firstly, the word 'must' indicates that the judge has a duty to exclude the evidence in the circumstances mentioned, if an application is made to him to do so. These are, of course, exactly the same circumstances in which the judge has a discretion to exclude evidence under s. 78 of the Police and Criminal Evidence Act 1984. But under s. 101(3), if persuaded that the admission of the evidence would have such an adverse impact on the fairness of the proceedings, the judge has no choice but to exclude it. Whether this makes much difference in practice is open to question; if the judge has reached the conclusion that the admission of the evidence would have that extreme effect, it would seem to be inconsistent with his duty to secure a fair trial to admit it, and to do so might well necessarily amount to a violation of art. 6 of the European Convention on Human Rights. Nonetheless, the language imposing a duty is to be welcomed, and was expressly emphasized by Rose LJ in *Hanson* [2005] 1 WLR 3169, [10]. Secondly, the duty is confined to cases in which evidence is admitted either under gateway (d) (evidence relevant to an important matter in issue between the defendant and the prosecution) or gateway (g) (where the defendant has made an attack on another person's character). Of course, it is unnecessary to apply the duty to gateways (a) and (b), in which the evidence is admitted by agreement of all the parties, or at the instigation of the accused. Moreover, the fact that it does not apply to gateway (e) mirrors the position with respect to the exclusionary discretion, both at common law and under s. 78, namely that the discretion to exclude applies only to evidence adduced by the prosecution and not to evidence adduced by a co-accused. Although there would have been a case for extending the duty to this gateway (see 3.9) the failure to do is understandable. Less understandable is the failure to extend it to gateway (c) (important explanatory evidence). As we have seen (2.7, 6.9) the admission of evidence as background evidence and under the *res gestae* principle can range over a wide area, and has the potential to allow in evidence which has relatively low probative value but may be highly prejudicial to the accused. It may be that the requirement that the explanatory evidence be 'important' within the meaning of s. 102 is thought to be a sufficient safeguard in this case, as it ought to have the effect of excluding evidence of limited probative value. But it is submitted that no harm could have been done by extending s. 101(3) to this gateway. In the case of gateway (f) (evidence admissible to correct a false impression given by the defendant), a more limited protection is provided by s. 105(6) which restricts the scope of the evidence to that which is necessary to correct the false impression. To this extent, as we have already noted (5.9, 6.12) it appears that this modifies the common law rule by virtue of which the accused's character was held to be indivisible, so that the assertion of any kind of good character opened the whole character up to scrutiny. But there remains some potential for unfairness, and it is submitted that s. 101(3) might usefully have been extended to this gateway also. It seems illogical to restrict the duty to gateways (d) and (g). One illustration of this is the fact that the duty to stop the case when evidence of bad character is found to be contaminated after it has been admitted (6.21) applies to each of the gateways (c)–(g). If contamination were to be found before the evidence is admitted under gateway (c), for example, it would be absurd if the judge had no power to exclude it, but was obliged to admit the evidence and then stop the case.

However, it now appears clear that, in the cases to which the duty to exclude does not apply, the court retains a discretion to exclude evidence of bad character under s. 78 of the Police and Criminal Evidence Act 1984.[93] In *Highton and other appeals* [2005] 1 WLR 3472, [13]–[14], Lord Woolf CJ said:

> The question also arises as to whether reliance can be placed on s.78 of the Police and Criminal Evidence Act 1984 ("PACE"). The application of s.78 does not call directly for decision in this case. We, therefore, do not propose to express any concluded view as to the relevance of s.78. However, it is right that we should say that, without having heard full argument, our inclination is to say that s.78 provides an additional protection to a defendant. In light of this preliminary view of s.78 of PACE, judges may consider that it is a sensible precaution, when making rulings as to the use of evidence of bad character, to apply the provisions of s.78 and exclude evidence where it would be appropriate to do so under s. 78, pending a definitive ruling to the contrary. Adopting this course will avoid any risk of injustice to the defendant. In addition, as s.78 serves a very similar purpose to Art. 6 of the European Convention on Human Rights, following the course we have recommended should avoid any risk of the court failing to comply with Art. 6. To apply s.78 should also be consistent with the result to which the court would come if it complied with its obligations under s.3 of the Human Rights Act 1998 to construe s. 101 and 103 of the 2003 Act in accordance with the Convention.

Although *obiter*, Lord Woolf's observations are, it is submitted, not only sensible, but right in principle. In considering the appeal of *Somanathan* in *Weir and other appeals* [2006] 1 WLR 1885, [44] a later Court of Appeal expressly approved Lord Woolf's approach in a case concerned with gateway (f), to which the duty to exclude under s. 101(3) does not apply. It is submitted that this view now represents the law.

6.20.1 Duty to exclude: matters to be considered

Section 101(3) suggests that the duty to exclude does not arise unless an application is made to exclude the evidence, although if the circumstances were sufficiently compelling, it is submitted that the judge might properly take it upon himself to invite the defence to make the application. The Act itself refers only to one matter to which the court is to have regard in ruling on an application to exclude under s. 101(3). By virtue of s. 101(4) the court must have regard to the length of time separating the matters to which the evidence relates and the offence charged. This is an important matter. Evidence of bad character based solely on events which occurred in the distant past are generally of low probative value, and its admission may well have an adverse impact on the fairness of the trial. Such evidence may consist of spent convictions (see 6.4.3) or may simply ignore compelling evidence of rehabilitation. It is always appropriate for the court to consider the question of time. But it is submitted that this is not the only matter to be considered, and the use of the words 'in particular' in subsection (4) suggests that it is not intended to be exclusive. A variety of other matters may bear on the question of the fairness of the proceedings. Many of these matters were the subject of discussion in cases dealing with evidence of bad character admissible at common law, or under the Criminal Evidence Act 1898. Because s. 101(3) creates a duty rather than a discretionary power to exclude, and because the discretion to exclude (when applicable)

---

[93] As the Act is drafted, the question was not beyond argument. Section 126(2)(a) specifically preserves the application of s. 78 of the Police and Criminal Evidence Act 1984 in relation to the hearsay provisions of Chapter 2 of Part 11 of the Criminal Justice Act 2003, so the omission of any such reference in Chapter 1 of Part 11 cannot be disregarded. On the other hand, s. 112(3)(c) provides: 'Nothing in this Chapter affects the exclusion of evidence...on grounds other than the fact that it is evidence of a person's bad character'.

will be exercised in relation to statutory rules very different to the rules at common law and under the Criminal Evidence Act 1898, there would be little point in cataloguing in detail the various guidelines for the exercise of the discretion promulgated by the courts in older cases. But some salient points may remain useful. The ultimate test in every case is whether the admission of the evidence would have such an adverse effect on the fairness of the proceedings that the court ought not to admit it. It is submitted that it remains true, as Lord Guest put it in *Selvey v DPP*,[94] that 'the guiding star should be fairness to the accused'. Thus, in considering evidence admissible under gateway (d), the court should have regard, not only to the probative value of evidence of other offences or other misconduct on the part of the accused, but also to the likely prejudicial effect of admitting it, in the sense that the jury may easily be swayed by the fact that the accused is a person of bad character, and judge him according to his character rather than according to the evidence in relation to the offence charged.[95] The judge must evaluate the probative value of evidence of bad character with reference, for example, to how far it truly succeeds in showing his propensity to commit an offence of the kind charged, as opposed to simply having a general propensity towards irresponsible behaviour; or how far the similarity of other offences truly connects the accused to the offence charged, as opposed to simply showing that he has a tendency to commit offences generally. The judge should in every case consider whether the evidence of bad character is so prejudicial that it may in practical terms become impossible for the jury to consider the merits of the case dispassionately. In relation to gateway (g), in a case in which the accused is doing no more than denying his guilt, and presenting his defence in the only way open to him, and to do so necessarily involves an attack on the character of another, the judge should again weigh the probative value of the evidence against its likely prejudicial effect, and consider the adverse effect on the fairness of the proceedings.[96] If the accused has no alternative way of presenting his case, the judge may find that it has a considerable impact on the fairness of the trial to admit evidence of bad character. This may be all the more true if a substantial part of the accused's attack is not disputed or appears to be justified. Conversely, where the attack is gratuitous and willful, and the defence case could have been presented equally well without an attack on another's character, the judge may come to a different conclusion. As in the case of the judicial discretion to exclude, each case must be looked at on its own merits, and hard and fast rules are unlikely to be of much value.

6.20.2 Requirement of application to exclude

Finally, it must be noted that strictly, the duty to exclude evidence under s. 101(3) applies only where an application to exclude is made. In the appeal of *Highton* in *Highton and other appeals* [2005] 1 WLR 3472, [23] (in which no application was made) it was held that the duty to exclude could not have arisen, and that the trial judge could not be criticized for failing to act of his own motion. While this view does reflect the wording of the section, a differently constituted court in the appeal of *Somanathan* in *Weir and other appeals* [2006] 1 WLR 1885, [38] (a case in which an application was in fact made) took a slightly more pro-active approach. Kennedy LJ said:

> ...bearing in mind the provisions of art. 6 of the European Convention...we consider it important that a judge should if necessary encourage the making of such an application wherever it appears that the

---

[94] [1970] AC 304, 352; see also *Cook* [1959] 2 QB 340, 347 per Devlin J.

[95] *Noor Mohamed v R* [1949] AC 182, 192 per Lord du Parcq.

[96] *Selvey v DPP* [1970] AC 304; *Britzman* [1983] 1 WLR 350, 355 per Lawton LJ; *Burke* (1985) 82 Cr App R 156 per Ackner LJ; *McLeod* [1994] 1 WLR 1500.

admission of the evidence may have such an adverse effect on the fairness of the proceedings that the court ought not to admit it. As [counsel for the prosecution] accepts, s.101(3) does require the judge to perform a balancing exercise, and that exercise does require the judge to look carefully at the evidence sought to be excluded.

The terms in which Kennedy LJ couches this instruction suggest that the fact that the judge offers encouragement to make the application also serves as notice that he intends to grant it. The judge is to encourage the application if he believes that the circumstances in which the evidence should be excluded exist, in which case, *ex hypothesi*, he should then grant the application. This may render the independent requirement for an application somewhat academic. Nonetheless, it is submitted that, in view of the importance of scrupulously performing the balancing exercise in every case, the approach suggested by Kennedy LJ is to be welcomed and should be followed by trial judges.

6.21 SECTION 107: DUTY TO STOP CASE WHERE EVIDENCE CONTAMINATED

Section 107 of the Act provides:

> (1) If on a defendant's trial before a judge and jury for an offence—
>   (a) evidence of his bad character has been admitted under any of paragraphs (c) to (g) of section 101(1), and
>   (b) the court is satisfied at any time after the close of the case for the prosecution that—
>   (i) the evidence is contaminated, and
>   (ii) the contamination is such that, considering the importance of the evidence to the case against the defendant, his conviction of the offence would be unsafe,
> the court must either direct the jury to acquit the defendant of the offence or, if it considers that there ought to be a retrial, discharge the jury.

(2) Where—
   (a) a jury is directed under subsection (1) to acquit a defendant of an offence, and
   (b) the circumstances are such that, apart from this subsection, the defendant could if acquitted of that offence be found guilty of another offence,
the defendant may not be found guilty of that other offence if the court is satisfied as mentioned in subsection (1)(b) in respect of it.
   (3) If—
      (a) a jury is required to determine under section 4A(2) of the Criminal Procedure (Insanity) Act 1964 (c. 84) whether a person charged on an indictment with an offence did the act or made the omission charged,
      (b) evidence of the person's bad character has been admitted under any of paragraphs (c) to (g) of section 101(1), and
      (c) the court is satisfied at any time after the close of the case for the prosecution that—
         (i) the evidence is contaminated, and
         (ii) the contamination is such that, considering the importance of the evidence to the case against the person, a finding that he did the act or made the omission would be unsafe,
the court must either direct the jury to acquit the defendant of the offence or, if it considers that there ought to be a rehearing, discharge the jury.
   (4) This section does not prejudice any other power a court may have to direct a jury to acquit a person of an offence or to discharge a jury.

(5) For the purposes of this section a person's evidence is contaminated where—

    (a) as a result of an agreement or understanding between the person and one or more others, or

    (b) as a result of the person being aware of anything alleged by one or more others whose evidence may be, or has been, given in the proceedings,

the evidence is false or misleading in any respect, or is different from what it would otherwise have been.

This safeguard applies only to trials on indictment before a judge and jury (s. 107(1)), and not to summary proceedings or proceedings on indictment tried by a judge sitting alone. This is a strange provision. It seems odd that magistrates or a judge sitting alone must continue to hear the case despite finding that the case against the accused has been fatally compromised by contaminated evidence. The duty to 'stop the case' means that, in the circumstances specified in s. 107(1)(a) and (b), the judge must either direct the jury to acquit the accused, or discharge the jury and order a re-trial. Presumably, the judge would choose the first course of action in a case in which, without the contaminated evidence, the case against the accused would not amount to a *prima facie* case; or where the remaining case would be so weak that it would be unfair to require the accused to stand trial again. He would choose the second in a case in which there was a sufficient case against the accused, apart from the contaminated evidence, to justify requiring him to stand trial, but it would be impossible to continue the trial before the present jury because of the prejudice to the accused caused by the admission of the contaminated evidence. If the judge takes the course of directing the jury to acquit, s. 107(2) provides further that the accused may not be convicted of any offences with respect to which the jury would have been entitled to return an alternative verdict and which are also affected in the same way by the contaminated evidence.[97] Section 107(3) applies the same principles to proceedings to determine whether the accused did the act or made the omission charged for the purposes of s. 4(A)(2) of the Criminal Procedure (Insanity) Act 1964.[98]

Section 107(1)(a) provides that the contamination principle may apply in the case of evidence of bad character adduced by virtue of s. 101(1)(c)–(g), i.e., evidence of the bad the character of the accused (but not of any other person) adduced other than by agreement of all the parties or at the instigation of the accused. Section 107(1)(b) requires that (i) after the evidence has been admitted and after the close of the prosecution case, the evidence is found to be contaminated; and (ii) the contamination is such that, considering the importance of the evidence to the case against the accused, his conviction for the offence would be unsafe. If the contamination is obvious before the evidence is admitted, presumably the judge should exclude it pursuant to his duty under s. 101(3) in the case of evidence admitted by virtue of s. 101(1)(d) or (g) or pursuant to his discretionary power to exclude in the case of evidence admitted under s. 101(1)(c), (e), or (f): see 6.20.[99] The definition of contamination is provided by s. 107(5), a remarkably imprecise and confusing piece of drafting for which the Law Commission must bear the blame, as it is taken from clause 13 of the draft bill annexed to the Commission's Report No. 273. The apparent

[97] As to the circumstances in which a jury may return alternative verdicts, see Criminal Law Act 1967, s. 6(3); *Blackstone's Criminal Practice*, 2009 edn, para. D18.41 *et seq.*

[98] See *Blackstone's Criminal Practice*, 2009 edn, para. D12.2 *et seq.*

[99] See *DPP* v *Boardman* [1975] AC 421, 444 per Lord Wilberforce; *DPP* v *Kilbourne* [1973] AC 729, 750; *H* [1995] AC 596, text below.

intended meaning of the subsection is best provided by the Law Commission's own commentary on clause 13:

> By virtue of subsection (5) evidence might be 'contaminated' as a result of: deliberate fabrication of allegations resulting from an agreement between witnesses; concoction of an allegation by one person (no conspiracy); collusion between witnesses to make their evidence sound more credible falling short of concoction of allegations; deliberate alteration of evidence or unconscious alteration of evidence, resulting from having become aware of what the evidence of another will be or has been.[100]

It is difficult to see why Parliament did not simply provide that if it comes to light, after evidence of the bad character of the accused is admitted, that that evidence is for any reason suspect or unreliable (and that the effect of such prejudicial evidence on the jury is unacceptably unfair) the judge must stop the case. As subsection (5) is written, it appears to apply only to cases in which a witness commits perjury either as a result of active collusion with one or more other witnesses, or as a result of his decision to tailor his evidence to correspond with that of others. The risk of collusion between witnesses, particularly in cases involving sexual offences against children, was discussed in a number of leading cases decided on common law principles. There was a considerable divergence of opinion as to whether the risk of collusion was a matter which should affect the admissibility of evidence, including the question of whether it was a factor to be taken into account in exercising the discretion to exclude, or whether it was a question of the weight of the evidence to be left to the jury with the benefit of a direction by the judge to treat the evidence with caution.[101] In *H* [1995] AC 596, the House of Lords resolved the question in favour of the latter view.[102] Parliament took the view that this was unsatisfactory, and has now entrusted the judge with the duty to stop the case, not only where there is collusion, but in the other instances of perjury to which subsection (5) refers. How the judge is to make the determination that the evidence is contaminated in such a way is not specified. Presumably the judge may have regard to the substance of the evidence (for example, a suspicious degree of similarity in the language employed by the witnesses, or a suspicious degree of agreement in details, or where a witness purports to have knowledge of facts of which it is unlikely he could have known) or to the demeanor of the witnesses, or to other circumstantial matters. It may be that, despite the observations of the House of Lords in *H* (see note 101) the judge may sometimes have recourse to a trial-within-a-trial in order to determine the matter. Presumably the defence may apply to the judge to stop the case under s. 107, and if that is the case, it would be strange if they could not also invite the judge to inquire into a possible issue of contamination. Whatever subsection (5) may eventually be interpreted to mean, it is strange that the duty to stop the case should not apply to any case in which evidence of the bad character of the accused is fatally compromised, and the jury is thereby prejudiced. Section 107(4) provides that the section does not prejudice

---

[100] Cf. the Home Office's Explanatory Notes, para. 383: '…contaminated, that is, has been affected by an agreement with other witnesses or by hearing the views or evidence of other witnesses so that it is false or misleading.' It has been suggested that the proper time to assess whether there has been contamination is not at a pre-trial hearing, but at trial, when the substance of the evidence has become clear: *C* [2006] 3 All ER 689.

[101] *Ananthanarayanan* [1994] 1 WLR 788; *Ryder* [1994] 2 All ER 859; *W* [1994] 1 WLR 800. The issue, as dealt with in these cases and in *H* [1995] AC 596 (text), was complicated by considerations relating to the common law requirement for a corroboration warning. This requirement has since been abrogated: Criminal Justice and Public Order Act 1994, s. 32(1); 18.3.3.

[102] The House rejected the suggestion that a trial-within-a-trial should be held to resolve the question of whether collusion existed (see, e.g., per Lord Mustill at 616 *et seq.*) though Lord Mackay left open the possibility that this might be done in a very exceptional case (*ibid.* at 612).

any other power of the court to direct an acquittal or discharge the jury, and it is submitted that the court should have the power to do so whenever it is clear that the trial has gone awry for such a reason. But this is not the present position. In the appeal of *Renda* in *Renda and other appeals* [2006] 2 All ER 553, [27], the Court of Appeal held that the question of contamination is confined to the express terms of s. 107(5) and cannot be extended to other criticisms that may be made of evidence of bad character.

6.22 OTHER SAFEGUARDS

Other safeguards provided by the Criminal Justice Act 2003, some of which have already been referred to, may be dealt with briefly.

6.22.1 Sections 101(d) and 103(3)

Under the latter subsection, an offence of the same description or of the same category may not be used to show propensity as an important matter in issue between the defendant and the prosecution if the length of time since the conviction or any other reason renders it unjust to use the conviction for this purpose. This provision may well be unnecessary. The same result should surely follow from s. 101(3) and (4), which apply to this case.

6.22.2 Sections 101(f) and 105(3) and (6)

Section 105(3) allows the defendant to avoid the admission of evidence of bad character where he withdraws or disassociates himself from a false or misleading assertion about his character. Subsection (6) restricts the admissibility of evidence under gateway (f) to that which is necessary to correct the false impression. See 6.12.

6.22.3 Section 110: court's duty to give reasons for rulings

Section 110 of the Act requires the court to give reasons in open court (in the absence of the jury, if there is one) for any ruling made as to: whether a particular piece of evidence is or is not evidence of a person's bad character; whether or not any such evidence is admissible under s. 100 or s. 101; whether evidence of bad character is to be excluded by virtue of s. 101(3); or whether the case is to be stopped by virtue of s. 107.

6.22.4 Section 111: rules of court; notice

Section 111 of the Act empowers the making of rules of court for the purposes of its bad character provisions. In particular, such rules may (and, in the case of the prosecution, must) provide that a party who wishes to adduce evidence of, or cross-examine a witness about the bad character of a defendant shall serve notice on the defendant in question, such notice to include particulars of the evidence to be adduced, or to be the subject of cross-examination (s. 111(2)). The rules promulgated by virtue of this section are to be found in Part 35 of the Criminal Procedure Rules 2005. The importance of giving notice has been emphasized by the Court of Appeal on a number occasions, including *Bovell; Dowds* [2005] 2 Cr App R 27. In *Urushadze* [2008] EWCA Crim 2498, during a first trial the prosecution did not seek to adduce evidence of the accused's previous convictions. At a later re-trial they not only sought to do so, but sought to do so without having given notice. The Court of Appeal found this conduct unacceptable. The Court held that in such a case, the judge must consider firstly, any reason proffered for the failure to comply with the rules, and secondly, whether any prejudice would be caused to the accused by admitting the evidence. The combination of answers to these questions, particularly of course the second, may in itself justify the judge in excluding the evidence. In *Musone* [2007] 1 WLR 2467, the Court also held that the judge was entitled to exclude evidence of bad character sought to be adduced against the accused under gateway (e) by a co-accused. The evidence consisted of an alleged admission of a murder (an offence of which the accused had been acquitted some 12 years previously). The evidence was adduced without notice, very late in the trial, and amounted to a deliberate ambush of the accused. As we have seen (6.11), the Act itself provides no general power or discretion to exclude evidence of bad character tendered by a co-accused. But it is submitted that the Court's view that the judge may nonetheless do so, in the case of a deliberate breach of the rules having an obvious potential to prejudice the accused, is correct.

But there will be circumstances in which it is impracticable to give notice as provided by the rules, for example where the accused makes an attack on the character of another person or on the defence of a co-accused for the first time while cross-examining a prosecution witness, or while giving evidence at trial. In such cases, the judge must use his discretion to ensure fairness for all parties as far as possible.[103] In some cases, it may be necessary to adjourn the proceedings for a short time to allow for the investigation and preparation of evidence of bad character.

E   OTHER STATUTORY PROVISIONS DEALING WITH BAD CHARACTER

SUMMARY OF MAIN POINTS

- Evidence of an aspect of bad character is admissible where it is an element of an offence charged.
- Section 27(3) of the Theft Act 1968 provides a form of statutory relevance for certain evidence on charges of handling stolen goods.
- Section 41 of the Youth Justice and Criminal Evidence Act 1999 imposes restrictions on the adduction of evidence of, and cross-examination about, the sexual behaviour of complainants in sexual cases. Such evidence may be adduced only as permitted by the section, and after an application for leave.

6.23 CONVICTION OR BAD CHARACTER AS AN ELEMENT OF OFFENCE

In a small number of instances, a previous conviction or the bad character of the accused may be an element of a statutory offence, i.e., the offence can be committed only by a person who has a previous conviction of the kind specified, or a person who is of bad character in the sense specified by the statutory provision which creates the offence. Because of the obvious potential for unfairness inherent in such an enactment, such offences are enacted infrequently, and only for the purpose of redressing a particular evil. By virtue of s. 21 of the Firearms Act 1968 as amended, it is an offence for a person who has been sentenced to imprisonment for a term of three years or

---

[103] For other observations on the exercise of discretion in cases of failure to give notice, see *R (Robinson)* v *Sutton Coldfield Magistrates' Court* [2006] 2 Cr App R 13.

more to have a firearm or ammunition in his possession at any time. On a prosecution for this offence, evidence must be adduced of the fact that the accused was sentenced to such a term of imprisonment on a previous occasion. This fact is an essential element of the offence, and if it is not proved, a conviction is impossible. The offence was created to address the particular problem posed by repeat offenders who engage in violent crime with the aid of firearms. However, only the previous sentence is an element of the crime, and evidence of any other aspect of the accused's bad character can be admitted, if at all, only in accordance with the rules laid down by s. 101 of the Criminal Justice Act 2003. In order to avoid unnecessary prejudice, the accused should enter into a formal admission that he has previously been sentenced to the relevant term of imprisonment, and it is then unnecessary for evidence to be adduced on the subject. If he fails to do so, the prosecution must prove the conviction by producing a certificate of conviction admissible under s. 73 of the Police and Criminal Evidence Act 1984. If this happens, some details of the previous offence will inevitably be made known to the jury, because s. 73(2) of the Act provides that a certificate of conviction on indictment shall contain the 'substance and effect (omitting the formal parts) of the indictment and of the conviction...': see 12.17. But if the accused formally admits the sentence, it is submitted that it would be improper for the jury to be told for what offence he was sentenced, unless that fact is independently admissible under one of the provisions of s. 101 of the Criminal Justice Act 2003. The judge should direct the jury not to speculate about the accused's bad character, and should make it clear that the previous sentence goes only to prove an essential element of the crime, and is not evidence of any other fact: for example, it has no probative value in relation to the allegation that he was in possession of a firearm or ammunition. On a prosecution for driving a motor vehicle on a road while disqualified from holding or obtaining a driving licence, contrary to s. 103 of the Road Traffic Act 1988, proof must be given that the defendant was a person subject to that disqualification on the relevant date. But again, only the fact of the disqualification is an essential element of the offence, and the defendant's bad character must be dealt with in accordance with s. 101 of the Criminal Justice Act 2003. The offence of loitering or soliciting for the purpose of prostitution, contrary to s. 1 of the Street Offences Act 1959, can be committed only by a 'common prostitute'. This term has been defined as referring to any person, male or female, who engages in sexual activity or acts of lewdness with all and sundry: *Morris-Lowe* [1985] 1 WLR 29, which, apart from any previous convictions for offences relating to prostitution, would seem to fit within the definition of 'bad character' under ss. 98 and 112 of the Criminal Justice Act 2003, as being misconduct in the form of reprehensible behaviour (see 6.3.4). If the defendant denies being a prostitute, it would seem that the prosecution must adduce evidence either of previous convictions or conduct consistent with being a common prostitute for the purpose of proving an essential element of the offence. In all other respects, evidence of the bad character of the defendant is admissible only when permitted by s. 101 of the Criminal Justice Act 2003.

6.24 EVIDENCE ADMISSIBLE UNDER S. 27(3) OF THE THEFT ACT 1968

Section 27(3) of the Theft Act 1968 provides:

> Where a person is being proceeded against for handling stolen goods (but not for any offence other than handling stolen goods) then at any stage of the proceedings, if evidence has been given of his having or arranging to have in his possession the goods the subject of the charge, or of his undertaking or assisting in, or arranging to undertake or assist in, their retention, removal, disposal or realisation,

the following evidence shall be admissible for the purpose of proving that he knew or believed the goods to be stolen goods—

(a) evidence that he has had in his possession, or has undertaken or assisted in the retention, removal, disposal or realisation of stolen goods from any theft taking place not earlier than 12 months before the offence charged; and

(b) [subject to notice] evidence that he has within the five years preceding the date of the offence charged been convicted of theft or of handling stolen goods.

This section is unaffected by the Criminal Justice Act 2003, though there may be cases in which its provisions overlap with those of s. 101(1)(d) of the 2003 Act. The only rationale of s. 27(3) is that experience of dealing with stolen goods tends to create an increased awareness of being in their presence on later occasions. Accordingly, the evidence admissible under s. 27(3) is admissible only for the purpose of proving that the accused knew or believed the goods to be stolen, and only after evidence of the applicable *actus reus* has been adduced. The section should be strictly construed, and only the evidence specifically permitted may be adduced. No detailed account of the previous transactions in which the accused was involved, or of his previous convictions, may be given,[104] but it must now be borne in mind that the prosecution may be able to adduce further details if they rely additionally on s. 101(d) of the Criminal Justice Act 2003. And in *Hacker* [1994] 1 WLR 1659, the House of Lords held that where a previous conviction is admissible, s. 73(2) of the Police and Criminal Evidence Act 1984 applies, with the result that the substance and effect of the previous indictment given in the certificate of conviction will be admissible as a necessary part of proof of the conviction (see 12.13). The judge may exclude evidence admissible under s. 27(3) in the exercise of his discretionary power under s. 78 of the Police and Criminal Evidence Act 1984 (see 3.7 *et seq.*) and it has been held that he should do so if the evidence tendered offers 'no more than minimal assistance' to the jury.[105]

6.25 EVIDENCE OF SEXUAL BEHAVIOUR OF COMPLAINANTS

Cases in which an accused charged with a sexual offence wishes to adduce evidence of the complainant's sexual behaviour have occasioned considerable difficulty. Whereas evidence of the complainant's bad character (a separate, but sometimes closely related issue) is now governed by s. 100 of the Criminal Justice Act 2003, as in the case of other non-defendants, the specific question of his or her sexual behaviour is governed by other statutory provisions which are not affected by that Act. It must, therefore, be considered separately. The crucial question is why the sexual behaviour of the complainant is said to be relevant to the defence. There are cases in which some aspect of the complainant's past sexual behaviour is clearly relevant to the substantive issues. For example, in a rape case in which consent is the issue, a history of previous sexual relations between the complainant and the accused may very well be relevant, depending on the time frame during which the relationship continued and the question of whether or not anything occurred to end it. In some cases in which the accused claims that he was not the rapist, or that the complainant has made a false complaint against him, evidence of the complainant's sexual relationship with a third party may be relevant. But at common law, evidence of the complainant's sexual behaviour generally or of her reputation in sexual matters was often adduced,

---

[104] *Bradley* (1979) 79 Cr App R 200; *Wood* [1987] 1 WLR 779.

[105] *Perry* [1984] Crim LR 680; *Knott* [1973] Crim LR 36; *Herron* [1967] 1 QB 107 (decided under the corresponding provision of the Larceny Act 1916 and the common law discretion to exclude).

not because it was relevant to any substantive issue, but purportedly on the issue of the complainant's credibility. In reality, such evidence was a thinly disguised attack on the complainant's character, intended to do no more than portray the complainant in an unfavourable light with a view to making her appear less sympathetic in the eyes of the jury. Such tactics, often referred to as 'putting the victim on trial', tended to deter victims from making complaints of sexual offences or from giving evidence in criminal trials for those offences.[106]

Evidence of the complainant's sexual behaviour is now governed by statutory provisions which attempt to strike a balance between allowing the accused to adduce relevant evidence which legitimately supports his defence on the facts, and evidence whose only purpose would be an attempt to discredit the complainant in the eyes of the jury. Consequently, the common law position is considered only briefly. The first statutory provisions were contained in s. 2 of the Sexual Offences (Amendment) Act 1976. These provisions were limited to cases involving 'rape offences', i.e., rape itself, inchoate offences with respect to rape, and burglary with intent to rape. They had the effect of limiting the circumstances in which the accused should be permitted to cross-examine the complainant about her sexual behaviour with persons other than the accused, and did not affect cases in which the accused adduced evidence of his own relationship with the complainant on the issue of consent. They were replaced by the broader provisions of ss. 41 to 43 of the Youth Justice and Criminal Evidence Act 1999, which apply to proceedings for any sexual offence included in s. 62 of the Act. As amended, this includes any offence under Part 1 of the Sexual Offences Act 2003, i.e., sexual offences generally, a development which seems sensible and is to be welcomed. The provisions of the 1999 Act also address both cases of consent and other issues, and are a good deal more specific than those of the 1976 Act, which caused considerable difficulties of interpretation for the appellate courts.[107]

6.25.1 Restrictions on cross-examination at common law

The distinction between cases in which the accused tenders evidence of sexual behaviour between the complainant and himself, and cases in which he tenders evidence of sexual behaviour between the complainant and others was well recognized at common law. Relevant evidence of voluntary sexual behaviour between the complainant and the accused was admissible on a charge of rape on the substantive issue of whether the complainant consented to the act of sexual intercourse which formed the basis of the charge (*Riley* (1887) 18 QBD 481). In such cases the accused was entitled to cross-examine the complainant with a view to establishing the sexual behaviour in question, and to adduce evidence of his own by giving evidence or calling witnesses. Conversely, relevant evidence of sexual behaviour between the complainant and persons other than the accused was admissible only on the issue of the credit of the complainant, effectively as an impeachment of the complainant based on her alleged bad character in sexual matters. Thus, that evidence was subject to the collateral matters rule (see 17.8), whereby the accused was entitled to cross-examine on the subject but not to adduce evidence of his own to prove the behaviour, even if the complainant denied it in cross-examination (*Holmes* (1871) LR 1 CCR 334). But

---

[106] It was the growing repugnance for such tactics which led to s. 2 of the Sexual Offences (Amendment) Act 1976. See the Report of the Advisory Group on the Law of Rape (Heilbron Committee) (1975) (Cmnd 6325). Many other jurisdictions have adopted similar rules, e.g., American Federal Rule of Evidence 412 (note 114, below); Galvin (1986) 70 Minn L Rev 763.

[107] See, e.g., *Viola* [1982] 1 WLR 1138; *Lawrence* [1997] Crim LR 492; *Barton* (1986) 85 Cr App R 5; and cf. *Funderburk* [1990] 1 WLR 587 (see 17.8); see generally the 7th edn of this work at 17.4.2 *et seq.*

even this kind of evidence was sometimes held to be relevant to the issue of consent, for example if it tended to show that the complainant was promiscuous or was a prostitute (*Bashir* [1969] 1 WLR 1303; *Krausz* (1973) 57 Cr App R 466) or if it brought into question whether a young complainant's extensive knowledge of sexual matters must have been acquired as a result of sexual activity with persons other than the accused (*Walker* [1994] Crim LR 763; cf. *Ahmed* [1994] Crim LR 669). In such cases, the evidence might be admitted on the issue of consent. This was a question of fact to be decided on the facts of each particular case. The result of these rules was that in many cases, there was little if any effective restraint on the exploration of the complainant's sexual character.

6.26 RESTRICTIONS ON EVIDENCE OF SEXUAL BEHAVIOUR UNDER S. 41 OF THE YOUTH JUSTICE AND CRIMINAL EVIDENCE ACT 1999

The common law rules were first modified by s. 2 of the Sexual Offences (Amendment) Act 1976. The restrictions imposed by this Act were significantly narrower than those now imposed by the 1999 Act. In particular, as mentioned above, the 1976 Act applied only to evidence of sexual behaviour between the complainant and persons other than the accused, and did not affect evidence of sexual behaviour between the complainant and the accused; and it applied only to prosecutions for 'rape offences', i.e., rape itself, inchoate offences with respect to rape, and burglary with intent to rape. Section 2 of the 1976 Act was repealed by the Youth Justice and Criminal Evidence Act 1999. Section 41 of the 1999 Act provides:

> (1) If at a trial a person is charged with a sexual offence, then, except with the leave of the court—
>
> (a) no evidence may be adduced, and
>
> (b) no question may be asked in cross-examination,
>
> by or on behalf of any accused at the trial, about any sexual behaviour of the complainant.
>
> (2) The court may give leave in relation to any evidence or question only on an application made by or on behalf of an accused, and may not give such leave unless it is satisfied—
>
> (a) that subsection (3) or (5) applies, and
>
> (b) that a refusal of leave might have the result of rendering unsafe a conclusion of the jury or (as the case may be) the court on any relevant issue in the case.
>
> (3) This subsection applies if the evidence or question relates to a relevant issue in the case and either—
>
> (a) that issue is not an issue of consent; or
>
> (b) it is an issue of consent and the sexual behaviour of the complainant to which the evidence or question relates is alleged to have taken place at or about the same time as the event which is the subject matter of the charge against the accused; or
>
> (c) it is an issue of consent and the sexual behaviour of the complainant to which the evidence or question relates is alleged to have been, in any respect, so similar—
>
> (i)   to any sexual behaviour of the complainant which (according to evidence adduced or to be adduced by or on behalf of the accused) took place as part of the event which is the subject matter of the charge against the accused, or
>
> (ii) to any other sexual behaviour of the complainant which (according to such evidence) took place at or about the same time as that event,
>
> that the similarity cannot reasonably be explained as a coincidence.
>
> (4) For the purposes of subsection (3) no evidence or question shall be regarded as relating to a relevant issue in the case if it appears to the court to be reasonable to assume that the purpose (or main

purpose) for which it would be adduced or asked is to establish or elicit material for impugning the credibility of the complainant as a witness.

    (5) This subsection applies if the evidence or question—

        (a) relates to any evidence adduced by the prosecution about any sexual behaviour of the complainant; and

        (b) in the opinion of the court, would go no further than is necessary to enable the evidence adduced by the prosecution to be rebutted or explained by or on behalf of the accused.[108]

These provisions have the merit of being considerably more specific than those of s. 2 of the Sexual Offences (Amendment) Act 1976. There are two main differences. Firstly, the 1999 Act does not differentiate between evidence of sexual behaviour of the complainant with the accused and of sexual behaviour of the complainant with persons other than the accused. There is a general prohibition against evidence of either kind, but either may be admitted with the leave of the court. On the question of leave, s. 41 focuses on the relevance of the evidence. It remains true to say that in general the complainant's sexual behaviour with the accused is more likely to be relevant to issues of consent, while her sexual behaviour with others is more likely to be relevant in cases of misidentification and false accusations. But this will not hold true in every case. Secondly, ss. 41 to 43 apply not only to rape offences, but to any 'sexual offence'. By s. 42(2), the phrase 'sexual offence' is to be construed in accordance with s. 62 of the Act, which includes any offence under Part 1 of the Sexual Offences Act 2003, i.e., sexual offences generally. Thus, no issue of consent will arise in many cases covered by s. 41. Section 42(1)(c) defines 'sexual behaviour' as meaning any sexual behaviour or experience except that relating to the subject-matter of the offence charged, whether or not it involves the accused or any other person (therefore covering even the auto-erotic behaviour which was not covered by s. 2 of the 1976 Act: *Barnes* [1994] Crim LR 691). Section 42(1)(b) expressly excludes from the definition of consent any issue as to the accused's belief that the complainant consented to the conduct which is the basis of the offence charged.

    The scheme of s. 41 is that no evidence may be adduced and no question may be asked in cross-examination by or on behalf of any accused about any sexual behaviour of the complainant, without leave of the court. Leave may be granted only in accordance with s. 41(3) or (5) and if refusal of leave might render unsafe a conclusion by the jury or court on any relevant issue. Any evidence for which leave is given must be evidence of specific instances of sexual behaviour (s. 41(6)). The Act rightly prohibits the worst excess of the common law, under which the accused sought to introduce evidence of the complainant's reputation for sexual behaviour. There is no prohibition on evidence adduced or questions asked by the prosecution, in which case s. 41(5) provides that leave may be given to permit the accused to explain or rebut the evidence adduced by the prosecution.

    Section 43 provides that applications for leave must be made in private and in the absence of the complainant, and that the court must state specifically its reasons for giving or refusing leave. Rules governing applications for leave under s. 41 are to be found in Part 36 of the Criminal Procedure Rules 2005. The court's powers include the power to give leave as to some evidence sought to be admitted, and to refuse it with respect to other evidence. This might be done where the court feels that some evidence on the issue is required, but that certain evidence tendered

---

[108] Section 41 applies to complaints of sexual offences committed both before and after 1 May 2004 (the date of coming into force of the Sexual Offences Act 2003) despite any express provision or transitional provisions to that effect in the 2003 Act. Thus, it applies also to historic offences charged under the Sexual Offences Act 1956 even if tried after 1 May 2004: *C* [2008] 1 WLR 966.

by the accused is unnecessarily embarrassing to the complainant and may result in unnecessary prejudice in the eyes of the jury.

6.27 SEXUAL BEHAVIOUR AND FALSE ACCUSATIONS

In *Mukadi* [2004] Crim LR 73, the question of what amounts to sexual behaviour was said to be a matter of impression and common sense. But although the definition of 'sexual behaviour' seems straightforward enough, it has given rise to some serious difficulties. The simplest cases are those in which there is specific evidence of overt sexual activity, which pose few problems even in cases where the activity is implied, for example evidence that the complainant has had an abortion. That particular point was raised but not decided in *Kirk and Kirk* [2008] EWCA Crim 434; it is submitted that it must amount to evidence of sexual behaviour. More difficult are the cases identified by Lord Clyde in *A (No. 2)* [2002] 1 AC 45, [128]. Lord Clyde there contrasted the phrase 'sexual behaviour' with the existence of a relationship, acquaintanceship or familiarity, which may not involve any overt activity. It is not always a straightforward matter to make the distinction, especially where the evidence consists, as it often does, only of statements made by the complainant about her relationships or behaviour. In *Winter* [2008] EWCA Crim 3, it was held that a statement made to the accused by the complainant, to the effect that she was having an (impliedly) sexual relationship with a third person, amounted to evidence of sexual behaviour. But in such cases, much will turn on the exact statement made by the complainant, and it submitted that it must be scrutinized with care.

One group of cases which poses particular difficulty is that involving alleged false allegations of sexual offences made by the complainant on previous occasions. In *S* [2003] All ER (D) 408 (Feb.), it was held that an allegation that the complainant had lied about her previous sexual experience by falsely claiming to have been a virgin at the time of the alleged rape was an allegation of sexual behaviour. It appeared that, in fact, she had had sexual intercourse with a person other than the accused earlier on the same day. The falsity of the assertion by the complainant that she was a virgin involved, by necessary implication, the proposition that she had had a sexual experience. Yet this was not evidence of sexual behaviour in the usual sense. It was more in the nature of evidence of a false statement affecting the complainant's credibility. Evidence that the complainant is making a false complaint, or has in the past made false accusations of sexual misconduct against the accused or others, does not, as such, amount to evidence of sexual behaviour. Accordingly, it is not excluded by s. 41. But evidence of false allegations and evidence of sexual behaviour are often closely intertwined. Even if the case seems clear, it would seem advisable to make an application before attempting to adduce or cross-examine about evidence of previous complaints, so that the judge may be satisfied that no allegation of sexual behaviour is involved.[109] As *S* illustrates, the lines may not always be drawn as clearly as might be wished. In *Martin* [2004] 2 Cr App R 22, the defence was that the complainant had maliciously invented a false accusation of sexual assault against the accused because he had rebuffed her invitation to have sexual intercourse on a previous occasion, but it was conceded that some more limited sexual activity had in fact occurred on the previous occasion. It was held that, although the limited

---

[109] *T; H* [2002] 1 WLR 632; the judge should also satisfy himself that there is a reasonable basis of fact for the allegation, i.e., that there is a proper evidential basis for asserting both that the accusation was made, and that it was false. The same rules as to false accusations appear to have applied under the 1976 Act: see *Cox* (1987) 84 Cr App R 132.

sexual activity was not the gravamen of the defence, which was based solely on the allegation that accusation was fabricated, the case fell under s. 41 because evidence of sexual behaviour was involved. The Court of Appeal held that the accused had clearly been entitled to adduce the evidence on the facts of the case, because it was essential to the full and fair presentation of his defence. Nonetheless, the case shows that it is not always possible to segregate the evidential issues into neat categories.

Another complication arising from cases of false complaints is that it is necessary to deal with the interface of s. 41 and s. 100 of the Criminal Justice Act 2003. Making a false accusation against another amounts to misconduct in the form of reprehensible behaviour, and is therefore evidence of bad character for the purpose of ss. 98 and 112 of the Criminal Justice Act 2003 (6.3.4).[110] A false accusation having to do with the instant offence falls outside the definition of bad character for the purpose of s. 98 of the Act (see 6.3.1); (though if the accused makes the allegation, he attacks the character of the complainant, with result that his own bad character becomes admissible by virtue of s. 101(g): see 6.13). But if the accused's allegation is that the complainant has made false accusations against him or others in the past, with a view to suggesting that she has a propensity to make false accusations and that the accusation in the instant case is also false, that evidence clearly amounts to evidence of bad character. An interesting situation would arise if, by analogy to the facts of *Martin*, the allegations of false accusations also contained evidence of the complainant's sexual behaviour. Would the accused be required to seek leave to adduce the evidence under s. 100(4) of the 2003 Act, or under s. 41, or both? It is submitted that the answer must be: both. Even though the evidence of the complainant's sexual behaviour may be closely related to her misconduct in making false allegations, it remains evidence of sexual behaviour and remains subject to s. 41. Similarly, if the accused makes the general allegation that the complainant is a prostitute (in addition to alleging that she was acting as such on the occasion of the alleged offence) he may require leave under both provisions; the general allegation that the complainant is a prostitute probably amounts to an allegation of bad character, but it is also evidence of sexual behaviour.[111]

6.28 INTERPRETATION OF S. 41 AND THE EUROPEAN CONVENTION

The restrictions on cross-examination imposed by s. 41 have the potential to affect the accused's right to a fair trial guaranteed by art. 6 of the European Convention on Human Rights, particularly the right to examine the witnesses against him pursuant to art. 6(3)(d). In *A (No. 2)* [2002] 1 AC 45, the accused was charged with rape and raised the defence of consent. He sought leave under s. 41 to adduce evidence with a view to proving (1) that he had enjoyed a consensual sexual relationship with the complainant until a time within the week of the alleged rape; and (2) that the complainant had had a sexual relationship with a friend of the accused. At a preliminary hearing, the trial judge ruled that he would admit the second category of evidence under s. 41(3)(b), but not the first. The accused appealed against the ruling with leave of the judge on the ground that it violated his right to a fair trial under art. 6. Allowing the appeal the Court of Appeal reversed the judge's ruling on both points. As to the first category, the Court held that the evidence of the accused's own relationship with the complainant might be relevant to the issue

---

[110] See *V* [2006] EWCA Crim 1901.

[111] The fact that the complainant is, or may have been, a prostitute is not in itself a basis for admitting evidence of sexual behaviour: see *White* [2004] All ER (D) 103 (Mar.); 6.31.

of his belief in her consent. The prosecution appealed to the House of Lords. The House held that the accused's right to a fair trial is absolute and fundamental and would be infringed if he were to be denied the admission of relevant evidence whose absence might lead to his conviction. As to s. 41(3)(b) the temporal restriction limited the evidence to that which was 'really contemporaneous' with the event in question. As to s. 41(3)(c) the test was (while taking into account the need to afford due protection to the complainant) whether the evidence was nevertheless so relevant to the issue of consent that to exclude it would endanger the fairness of the trial under art. 6; if so, the evidence should not be excluded.[112] In the light of this decision, the provisions of s. 41 may be summarized as follows.

6.29 GENERAL RESTRICTION: S. 41(1) AND (2)

Any cross-examination of the complainant about any sexual behaviour on her part requires leave, which may be given only if the judge is satisfied that subsection (3) or subsection (5) applies and that unless leave is given any resulting conclusion on the part of the jury or court may be rendered unsafe. The extent of the restriction caused the House of Lords a certain amount of disquiet. Parliament was, in the words of Lord Hope of Craighead, 'entering upon a very sensitive area' (at 81). But the House did not consider that s. 41 in itself infringed the right to a fair trial. As Lord Hope put it (at 81) even though the right to a fair trial is fundamental and absolute, this does not 'give the accused an absolute and unqualified right to put whatever questions he chooses to the witnesses'. Thus, the right of cross-examination is, in principle, subject to modification or restriction as long as this does not infringe the right to a fair trial. Lord Steyn, with whom Lord Hutton agreed, made a distinction between the provision restricting cross-examination as to the complainant's behaviour with persons other than the accused, which he regarded as reasonable in the light of the legitimate goal of protecting the complainant from undue embarrassment and distress, and the restriction on cross-examination as to the sexual history between the accused and the complainant, which 'poses an acute problem of proportionality' (at 61). Lord Clyde was also disturbed by the lack of distinction between the two cases, and pointed out that it had long been recognized that they were distinct and should be treated differently.[113] Thus, s. 41 must be read in such a way as to preserve the accused's right to a fair trial, and if relevant evidence which may affect the outcome of the case is tendered, it should not be excluded.[114]

---

[112] On the facts, the House concluded that it had insufficient facts to permit it to make a judgment on this issue, and accordingly remitted the case to the trial judge to enable an appropriate inquiry to be made. For general comment on s. 41, see D. Birch [2002] Crim LR 531; J. Spencer [2001] CLJ 452; J. McEwan [2001] 5 E & P 257; J. Temkin [2003] Crim LR 217; D. Birch [2003] Crim LR 370; N. Kibble [2005] Crim LR 190.

[113] The House was much influenced by the decision of the Supreme Court of Canada in *Seaboyer* [1991] 2 SCR 577, in which it was held that a blanket exclusion of cross-examination of the complainant was unconstitutional for reasons akin to those applicable under art. 6 of the Convention. The distinction was, of course, long recognized by the common law and by s. 2 of the 1976 Act and cases decided under that Act. See also *Dickie v HM Advocate* (1897) 24 R(J) 82 at 84, per Lord Justice-Clerk McDonald; and generally the Report of the Advisory Group on the Law of Rape (Heilbron Committee) (1975) (Cmnd 6325) paras 100–101.

[114] This is ultimately a test of balance and proportionality, as is always the case in dealing with Convention rights (see generally 1.7). The approach of the American Federal Rules of Evidence in dealing with the analogous rights guaranteed by the Sixth Amendment to the United States Constitution is interesting. Rule 412 provides in pertinent part:

    (a) Evidence generally inadmissible. The following evidence is not admissible in any civil or criminal proceeding involving alleged sexual misconduct except as provided in subdivisions (b) and...:
      (1) Evidence offered to prove that any alleged victim engaged in other sexual behavior.
      (2) Evidence offered to prove any victim's sexual predisposition.

6.30 SECTION 41(3)(a): ISSUES OTHER THAN CONSENT

If the issue is not one of consent, it is likely to involve either the defence of mistaken belief in consent or the defence that the complainant had some improper motive to bring a false charge against the accused; although these defences do not exhaust the possible situations in which this subsection may apply.[115] In *Barton* (1986) 85 Cr App R 5, a case decided under s. 2 of the Sexual Offences (Amendment) Act 1976, the defence on a charge of rape was belief in consent. Section 1(2) of the 1976 Act provided that the presence or absence of reasonable grounds for the accused's belief was a matter to which the jury was to have regard (in conjunction with other matters) in deciding whether or not the accused did believe that there was consent. The accused applied for the admission of evidence of the complainant's sexual conduct with other men, of which he claimed he had known before the incident which led to the charge against him, for the purpose of suggesting that he had reasonable grounds for his belief. The trial judge's refusal to admit the evidence was upheld by the Court of Appeal. The evidence was not so closely related to the incident in question that the judge was obliged to admit it. The test now, on the same facts, under s. 41(3)(a) and the decision in *A*, must be one of relevance. It is submitted that under s. 41(3)(a) such evidence is relevant to the issue of belief, but that the subsection need not be read, even in the light of the decision in *A*, in such a way as to render it necessarily admissible in cases such as *Barton*. It remains a balancing test for the judge. In such cases, the judge will often conclude that the evidence is intended primarily to attack the credibility of the complainant, in which case the evidence should be excluded under s. 43(4). It must be stressed that under s. 41(4), leave may not be granted to adduce any evidence if it is reasonable to assume that the purpose, or main purpose, of adducing it would be to impugn the credibility of the complainant.[116]

6.31 SECTION 41(3)(b) AND (c): ISSUE OF CONSENT, ACTS CLOSELY RELATED BY TIME OR SIMILARITY

Where the issue is one of consent, the evidence must be capable of being linked to the event which forms the subject of the charge either by proximity in time, or by similarity of the sexual

---

(b) Exceptions.
    (1) In a criminal case, the following evidence is admissible, if otherwise admissible under these rules:
        (A) evidence of specific instances of sexual behavior by the alleged victim offered to prove that a person other than the accused was the source of semen, injury, or other physical evidence;
        (B) evidence of specific instances of sexual behavior by the alleged victim with respect to the person accused of the sexual misconduct offered by the accused to prove consent, or by the prosecution; and
        (C) evidence the exclusion of which would violate the constitutional rights of the defendant.

Exception (C) is a residual provision designed to ensure that the judge has ample power to admit evidence where it is necessary to ensure a fair trial.

[115] In some cases an issue arises as to how a young complainant acquired sufficient knowledge of sexual matters to talk about them; if it seems that the knowledge must be the product of previous sexual behaviour then s. 41 is triggered. But it will often appear that there may be other sources such as information imparted by friends: see, e.g., *M* [2005] EWCA Crim 3376.

[116] But the relevance of the evidence must be assessed in relation to all uses that could reasonably be made of it. It does not follow from the fact that evidence has the effect of impugning credibility that impugning credibility is its only purpose, or its main purpose: see *F* [2005] 1 WLR 2848, per Judge LJ at [27]. This case is dealt with further at 6.32.

behaviour of the complainant which formed part of the event or took place at or about the same time. Both matters were considered by the House of Lords in *A*, but the decision did not yield any definitive guidelines. The time restriction under s. 41(3)(b), even with the wording 'at or about', is extremely narrow and it is certainly arguable that it would exclude much evidence which would in fact be relevant to the issue of consent, especially in cases where the accused contended that he had had an ongoing consensual sexual relationship with the complainant and that that relationship had not necessarily ended. In *A*, Lord Hope (at 79) had no hesitation in holding that the most recent sexual conduct relied on by the accused (one week before the event) was too remote to fall within the phrase 'at or about the same time', but held that this question must be one of fact and degree in every case. While this may almost inevitably be true of such phrases (cf. the older cases on the contemporaneity of memory-refreshing documents; 16.3.1) it should not be overlooked that the right of the accused to a fair trial under art. 6 may be infringed by the exclusion of such evidence. It is to be hoped that this may prompt some further reflection on the need for such a strict limitation, and even a possible amendment of the subsection.[117]

The similarity provision of s. 41(3)(c) also caused a good deal of inconclusive heart-searching on the part of the members of the House. The obvious parallel is the common law test for the admission of evidence of extraneous offences. The celebrated test of 'striking similarity' between the facts of the offence charged and the facts of the extraneous cases was laid down by the House of Lords in *Boardman* [1975] AC 421. But after the later decision of the House in *DPP* v *P* [1991] 2 AC 447, the test became the wider one of relevance, and striking similarity was thought to be more properly regarded as simply one specific case of relevance. In seeking to find an appropriate definition of the concept of similarity under s. 41(3)(c) the House was inevitably drawn to consider these decisions. It seems clear that the details must go beyond the commonplace if they are to be relevant. Thus, as Lord Hutton pointed out, evidence of normal affectionate behaviour preceding the act of intercourse would not suffice. But the House saw no need to confine the evidence permitted to cases of bizarre conduct (which was often the case under the extraneous offences rule) because the only necessary effect of the evidence is to render it unreasonable to explain the similarity on the basis of coincidence. Lord Clyde held that evidence falling short of striking similarity could be admitted ('it is only a similarity that is required, not an identity. Moreover the words "in any respect" deserve to be stressed', at 135). Lord Clyde also doubted whether the fact that the sexual behaviour had always taken place with the accused, while a relevant factor, could be decisive in and of itself, as this would seem to open up much if not all of the relationship between the accused and the complainant, which is clearly not the intent of the subsection. It is submitted that this must be correct. In the end, it seems to be established only that the question of similarity is not confined to the test appropriate to the extraneous offences rule, but is a question to be decided on the facts of each case. But this decision must be made in the light of the fact that it may infringe on the accused's right to a fair trial under art. 6. Accordingly,

---

[117] The attention of the House of Lords in *A* was drawn to the Home Office Explanatory Note to the Act, which revealed an expectation that in general, the time period would be construed as being not be more than 24 hours before or after the event. This reveals what appears to be a rather startling naiveté about human relationships on the part of those who draft and enact our statutory law. As Lord Steyn noted, the period would cover invitations to sexual activity made earlier the same evening. But it would not cover many other not unreasonable cases, for example one in which in which an ongoing relationship is undergoing a period of stress, and the question of sexual relationship is genuinely uncertain for a prolonged period.

the primary test must be whether the evidence is relevant and whether its exclusion may result in the accused being wrongly convicted.[118]

In *White* [2004] All ER (D) 103 (Mar.) the accused appealed against his conviction for rape on the ground that he had improperly been refused leave to cross-examine the complainant to the effect that she was a prostitute, and had been working as such on the occasion of the alleged rape. The issue at trial had been consent. The accused alleged that the complainant had asked him for money, which he had refused to pay, and that, after having consensual sexual intercourse with him, she had attempted to take money from his wallet. The Court of Appeal dismissed the appeal, holding that leave had been rightly refused. As the accused did not contend that he had offered to pay to have sex with the complainant, the question of whether or not she was a prostitute, on that or any other occasion, was irrelevant. The complainant had been just as much entitled to withhold her consent as any other woman in the same situation, and the issue was simply whether she had done so.

6.32 SECTION 41(5): REBUTTAL OR EXPLANATION OF EVIDENCE ADDUCED BY PROSECUTION

Under this subsection, the accused may adduce evidence intended to rebut or explain evidence adduced by the prosecution. Thus, if the prosecution places the sexual behaviour of the complainant in question, or adduces medical or forensic evidence which may be disputed, the accused must be free to deal with such evidence, and as long as it does not exceed what is necessary for that purpose, there is no objection if the accused's evidence must also deal with the complainant's sexual behaviour. For example, the prosecution may adduce evidence tending to show that the accused is the source of semen or other biological matter found on the complainant's body, and he may wish to contest that evidence. It is submitted that the accused's right to a fair trial under art. 6 renders this provision necessary. It is one thing to restrict the accused in cross-examination, where he seeks to raise issues not raised by the prosecution; it would be quite another to forbid the accused to challenge or explore issues raised by the prosecution which are said to show his guilt of the offence charged. In *F* [2005] 1 WLR 2848, the accused was charged with specimen charges of rape and gross indecency with his stepdaughter, who was his junior by thirteen years. It was alleged that he had engaged in a persistent course of sexual abuse of the complainant between the ages of 7 and 16. But it was not disputed that between the ages of 18 and 24, the complainant had lived with the accused in a consensual adult sexual relationship which appeared to be a happy one. The prosecution contended that the complainant had been unable to leave the accused because of her fear of him, and because he had 'groomed' her over many years to be subservient to him. The judge permitted the accused to adduce detailed evidence of the adult relationship, but refused leave to adduce photographic and video materials made during the adult relationship, some of which purported to show the complainant in various states of undress, others of which purported to show her masturbating and performing other sexual acts, and all of which appeared to show her relaxed and enjoying herself. The accused was convicted and appealed on the ground that the evidence ought to have been admitted. The appeal was allowed. The Court of Appeal held that, given the prosecution's case of fear, subservience and grooming, the evidence was admissible to rebut the allegations against the accused, and the judge had no discretion to exclude it.

---

[118] For a good example of evidence bearing a striking similarity to evidence the subject of the charge, see *T* [2004] 2 Cr App R 32.

6.33 RECOMMENDED FURTHER READING

Allan, T.R.S., 'Some favourite fallacies about similar facts' (1988) **8** *Legal Studies* 35.

Birch, D., 'Untangling sexual history evidence: a rejoinder to Professor Temkin' [2003] *Criminal Law Review* 370.

Darbyshire, P., 'Previous misconduct and magistrates' courts—some tales from the real world' [1997] *Criminal Law Review* 105.

Kibble, N., 'Judicial perspectives on the operation of s. 41 and the relevance and admissibility of prior sexual history evidence: four scenarios: part 1' [2005] *Criminal Law Review* 190.

Kibble, N., 'Judicial discretion and the admissibility of prior sexual history evidence under section 41 of the Youth Justice and Criminal Evidence Act 1999: sometimes sticking to your guns means shooting yourself in the foot: part 2' [2005] *Criminal Law Review* 263.

Lloyd-Bostock, S., 'The effects on juries of hearing about the defendant's previous criminal record: a simulation study' [2000] *Criminal Law Review* 734.

McEwan, J., 'The rape shield askew?' [2001] **5**(4) *International Journal of Evidence and Proof* 257.

Redmayne, M., 'Myths, relationships and coincidences: the new problems of sexual history' (2003) **7**(2) *International Journal of Evidence and Proof* 75.

Stone, J., 'The rule of exclusion of similar fact evidence: England' (1933) **46** *Harvard Law Review* 954.

Temkin, J., 'Sexual history evidence: beware the backlash' [2003] *Criminal Law Review* 217.

6.34 QUESTIONS FOR DISCUSSION BASED ON *R* v *COKE; LITTLETON* (for case files go to the Online Resource Centre)

1. May the prosecution adduce against Coke evidence of (a) his previous conviction for sexual assault; (b) his previous conviction for attempting to pervert the course of justice?

2. If so, under which gateway(s) would each be adduced?

3. What details would the prosecution have to adduce in each case in addition to the fact of conviction?

4. Is Littleton entitled to adduce either or both of Coke's convictions? If so, under which gateway(s)?

5. Is Coke entitled to:

   (a) Cross-examine Margaret Blackstone suggesting that she consented to have sex with him on the occasion of the alleged rape?

   (b) Cross-examine Margaret about her previous conviction for shoplifting and accuse her of being generally dishonest?

   (c) Adduce evidence that she threatened to accuse Kevin of raping her last year?

   (d) Adduce evidence that she has a reputation for being promiscuous?

6. In each of the above cases, would the prosecution then be entitled to adduce evidence of Coke's bad character, and if so, to what extent?

7. What would be the effect of each of the following in terms of the admission of evidence of Coke's bad character—

   (a) Coke gives evidence that he is honest and in steady employment?

   (b) Coke gives evidence that he saw Littleton indecently assault Angela Blackstone?

(c) Coke gives evidence that D/I Glanvil failed to caution him and intimidated him during his police interview thereby causing to make admissions he would not otherwise have made?

6.35 GENERAL QUESTIONS FOR DISCUSSION

1. Which best describes the character provisions of the 2003 Act—'exclusionary' or 'inclusionary' of bad character evidence?

2. Define 'bad character'.

3. Does the 'gateway' through which evidence of bad character is admitted define the purpose for which the evidence may be used, or does it become admissible for any relevant purpose?

4. Which, arguably, is the widest gateway for the admission of bad character evidence?

5. What is 'reprehensible behaviour'?

6. Jane, an adult, is on trial for theft and has previous convictions for common assault when she was 12 years old. Are these convictions admissible?

7. What may count as 'important explanatory evidence' for the purposes of gateway (c)?

8. Name some offences that demonstrate a 'propensity to be untruthful'. Will offences of dishonesty always be admissible for this purpose?

9. What is the 'tit-for-tat' principle?

10. If an accused asserts that a complainant has a bad reputation for violence and this reputation is not disputed by the prosecution, will the accused's record of previous convictions be admissible?

11. In what circumstances is the bad character of a person, other than the accused, admissible in evidence?

12. In what circumstances may bad character evidence be described as 'contaminated'?

13. A man charged with handling stolen goods was convicted of theft two years ago. Which statutory provisions will assist the prosecution in proving that he knew or believed the goods were stolen?

14. To what extent did s. 41 of the Youth Justice and Criminal Evidence Act 1999 remedy perceived defects in the Sexual Offences (Amendment) Act 1976?

15. How did the House of Lords interpret s. 41(3)(c) in *A (No. 2)*? Did they, in effect, re-write the provision?

7

THE RULE AGAINST HEARSAY I: SCOPE AND WORKING OF THE RULE

SUMMARY OF MAIN POINTS

- Hearsay is evidence consisting of a statement made by a person, other than while giving evidence in the instant case, if the statement is tendered solely for the purpose of proving the truth of any fact stated by that person.

- If the statement is tendered for any other relevant purpose, e.g. to prove that the statement was made; was made on a particular occasion; or in particular circumstances; or to prove the state of mind of the maker, the statement is not hearsay.

- Hearsay within hearsay, or multiple hearsay, occurs when a hearsay statement contains within itself an additional layer of separate hearsay. In criminal cases, this gives rise to enhanced conditions of admissibility.

- If a fact is not intentionally stated, but may be implied from the statement, the evidence is not hearsay if tendered for the implied statement.

- At common law, the Rule against Hearsay states that hearsay is inadmissible unless it falls within an exception to the Rule.

- In civil cases the Rule has been abrogated by the Civil Evidence Act 1995; its hearsay quality now affects the weight, but not the admissibility, of evidence.

- In criminal cases, the Criminal Justice Act 2003 supercedes the common law and provides an exclusive statutory code for the admission of hearsay, though certain common law exceptions to the Rule are preserved.

A   THE RULE AGAINST HEARSAY

7.1 DEFINITION OF HEARSAY

The rule against hearsay is one of the most important and commonly applied rules of the law of evidence, and yet at the same time, the least understood by students, the profession, and the judiciary. Many definitions of hearsay have been advanced. In *Sharp* [1988] 1 WLR 7, Lord Havers adopted that given in the 6th edition of *Cross on Evidence* (p. 38):

> An assertion other than one made by a person[1] while giving oral evidence in the proceedings is inadmissible as evidence of any fact asserted.

In earlier editions of this work, the present author offered the following longer, but perhaps more descriptive alternative:

> Evidence from any witness which consists of what another person stated (whether verbally, in writing, or by any other method of assertion such as a gesture) on any prior occasion, is inadmissible, if its only relevant purpose is to prove that any fact so stated by that person on that prior occasion is true. Such a statement may, however, be admitted for any relevant purpose other than proving the truth of facts stated in it.

Similarly, American Federal Rule of Evidence 801(c) provides that 'hearsay':

> ...is a statement, other than one made by the declarant while testifying at the trial or hearing, offered in evidence to prove the truth of the matter asserted.

It is one of the curiosities of the law of evidence that, despite the fact that the rule against hearsay has been one of the most heavily litigated areas of the law for almost two centuries, and the

---

[1] The rule against hearsay does not apply to evidence consisting of the observed behaviour of animals: *Pieterson* [1995] 1 WLR 293 (police tracker dog). Such evidence is more aptly regarded as real evidence (see 19.19). It may properly be made subject to safeguards of reliability other than the hearsay rule.

subject of significant legislative activity in recent years, no statutory definition of hearsay existed until the Civil Evidence Act 1995 came into effect on 31 January 1997.

Section 1(2) of the Act provides:

> In this Act—
> (a) 'hearsay' means a statement made otherwise than by a person while giving oral evidence in the proceedings which is tendered as evidence of the matters stated; and
> (b) references to hearsay include hearsay of whatever degree.

Section 13 adds that the term 'statement' means 'any representation of fact or opinion, however made'. This definition applies only for the purposes of the Civil Evidence Act 1995, which effectively abolishes the rule against hearsay in civil cases (see 8.30), and has no application to criminal cases. There is no reason why the definition of hearsay should vary as between civil and criminal cases, and it might have been thought not unreasonable to apply the definition given in the 1995 Act to criminal cases.[2] But as this was not done, it was necessary for the Criminal Justice Act 2003, which now governs the admissibility of hearsay evidence in criminal cases, to adopt its own definition. This definition follows the model of the Civil Evidence 1995, but has the rather curious feature that it does not employ the word 'hearsay' itself.[3]

Section 114(1) begins:

> In criminal proceedings a statement not made in oral evidence in the proceedings is admissible as evidence of any matter stated if, but only if...

Section 115(2) and (3) adds:

> (2) A statement is any representation of fact or opinion made by a person by whatever means;...
> (3) A matter stated is one to which this Chapter applies if (and only if) the purpose or one of the purposes of the person making the statement appears to the court to have been—
> (a) to cause another person to believe the matter; or
> (b) to cause another person to act or a machine to operate on the basis that the matter is as stated.

The essence of the two definitions is the same, but s. 115(3) of the Criminal Justice Act 2003 places greater emphasis on the element of deliberate assertion on the part of the maker of the statement to communicate the fact which is the subject of the hearsay. This might have had unintended consequences in relation to cases in which the subject of the hearsay is some fact not specifically stated, but which may be implied from the statement. As we shall see (7.15.1) this kind of case caused difficulties at common law, which Parliament believed it was resolving by enacting the statutory definitions of hearsay. The emphasis on deliberate assertion might have been interpreted as excluding implied statements from the statutory definitions of hearsay, with

---

[2] Certain other definitions in the Civil Evidence Act 1995 were applied also to criminal cases. The definitions of 'document' and 'copy' provided in s. 13 were incorporated into s. 72(1) of the Police and Criminal Evidence Act 1984 and Sch. 2 to the Criminal Justice Act 1988 (see Sch. 1 to the Civil Evidence Act 1995). These definitions are now re-enacted by s. 134 of the Criminal Justice Act 2003.

[3] But the word is used in a separate definition in s. 121(2), which applies only for the purposes of assessing the admissibility of multiple hearsay (see 7.6.3). Under this definition the term 'hearsay statement' means 'a statement not made in oral evidence that is relied on as evidence of a matter stated in it'. This differs significantly from the general definition, in that it omits the phrase 'in the proceedings', thereby excluding from the definition of hearsay any statement made while giving evidence, even when the evidence is given in other proceedings.

the result that implied statements remained inadmissible hearsay at common law. It was not clear that this question of interpretation must necessarily be answered in the same way in relation to the 1995 and 2003 Acts. But it seems that the difficulty has now been resolved by the decision of the Court of Appeal in *Sukadeve Singh* [2006] 1 WLR 1564. The Court held that the statutory law of hearsay under the Criminal Justice Act 2003 replaces the common law of hearsay in its entirety, and that as the statutory definition of hearsay does not include implied statements, such implied statements are no longer inadmissible as hearsay.[4]

7.2 DANGERS OF HEARSAY EVIDENCE

The rule against hearsay originated in centuries-old judicial awareness that the admission of hearsay evidence involves two serious dangers. The first is that the repetition of any statement involves the inherent danger of error or distortion, which increases in proportion to the number of repetitions and the complexity of the statement. The second is that it is virtually impossible to engage in effective cross-examination of a witness who is testifying about a hearsay statement, because the witness did not perceive the events in question. The latter disadvantage is the more serious. As Lord Bridge of Harwich put it in *Blastland* [1986] AC 41, 54:

> The rationale of excluding [hearsay evidence] as inadmissible, rooted as it is in the system of trial by jury, is a recognition of the great difficulty, even more acute for a juror than for a trained judicial mind, of assessing what, if any, weight can properly be given to a statement by a person whom the jury have not seen or heard and which has not been subject to any test of reliability by cross-examination.

However, neither disadvantage is theoretically fatal to the admissibility of hearsay evidence. The judges might have taken the view that hearsay should be admitted, and that the focus of the inquiry should be the factual one of the weight to be accorded to it, which will obviously vary significantly from case to case. In modern times, and especially since it has been the practice for almost all civil cases to be tried by a judge sitting without a jury, this has essentially been the approach adopted in civil cases. The Civil Evidence Act 1968 rendered most hearsay evidence admissible in civil cases, although the rule against hearsay continued formally to apply. The Civil Evidence Act 1995 has taken this approach to its logical conclusion by abrogating the rule against hearsay completely in civil cases. In criminal cases, in which jury trial continues to be employed, the rule continues in force, although the scope of exceptions to it continues to grow. Alternatively, the judges might have required corroboration of hearsay evidence from a non-hearsay source, a solution which is still discussed, and has been adopted in some American jurisdictions: see R. Pattendon (1991) 107 LQR 317. Not all hearsay evidence is unreliable. Documentary hearsay, in particular, frequently emanates from an unimpeachable source and proves to be highly reliable.

---

[4] The issue was whether a statement could be hearsay with respect, not only to matters consciously represented by the maker of the statement, but also with respect to matters which might be inferred or thought to be implied in the statement, but not intended by the maker to be represented. As the Civil Evidence Act 1995 was clearly intended to abrogate the rule against hearsay in civil cases, it would be quite ironic if Parliament must be taken to have done so with regard only to deliberate communications of fact, but not with regard to implied facts. This was not necessarily true of the Criminal Justice Act 2003, because the rule against hearsay remains in force in criminal cases, albeit now in statutory form, and the emphasis on intentionality in the definition of hearsay in this Act is much stronger. See 7.15.1. See also Cross and Tapper, *Evidence*, 11th edn, pp. 625 *et seq.*, 643 *et seq.*

When there is added to these objections, however, the risk of concoction, which Cross described as 'one aspect of the great pathological dread of manufactured evidence which beset English lawyers of the late eighteenth and early nineteenth centuries',[5] one can see why the common law set its face firmly against the admission of hearsay evidence.

7.3 DEVELOPMENT OF EXCEPTIONS AND REFORM OF RULE

Almost as soon as the rule against hearsay had been formulated, the judges recognized the necessity for some exceptions to the rule, and began to create them. Where necessary witnesses were dead, where acts were hopelessly ambiguous without some contemporary explanation by those who performed them, where the only record of family history was local reputation, the evidence, though hardly satisfactory, had at least the merit of being available. In some cases, for example statements and reputation regarding family history and boundaries, it seems that the necessity was directly related to the contemporary popularity of those areas of litigation. Such exceptions had few indicia of reliability. But even bad evidence is preferable to no evidence at all, and, even if it would not satisfy a modern theory of reliability, it did satisfy the then still prevalent theory of best evidence.[6] Some, though by no means all, of the common law exceptions were based on sustainable theories of reliability. There was a general judicial sense that public records were inherently more reliable than other documents, a faith in the spontaneity of *res gestae* statements, and a confidence in the motives of a declarant at the point of death. But there was no systematic attempt to construct categories of exceptions, and no general theory of what might make some hearsay evidence acceptably reliable. Like the law of evidence generally, the hearsay exceptions evolved gradually and as piecemeal solutions to specific problems which confronted the courts from time to time. On the eve of the catalytic decision in *Myers* v *DPP* [1965] AC 1001, it could be said with some justification that the common law exceptions were too few in number, too limited in scope, and too technical in their operation to provide a useful modern basis for the law. Judicial criticisms abounded.[7]

Myers proved to be an important turning point, though not quite in the way that might have been expected. The accused was charged with and convicted of serious offences of dishonesty in relation to motor vehicles. His practice was to buy up wrecked cars together with their log books, to steal other cars, to disguise the stolen vehicles so that they appeared to correspond with the wrecks, and to sell the stolen cars as if they were the wrecks. The crucial pieces of evidence in the prosecution's efforts to prove what the accused had done were microfilmed documents containing the manufacturers' records. These yielded the cylinder- block numbers of the vehicles in question, and as it was proved that the cylinder-block numbers were stamped indelibly on

---

[5] *Evidence*, 5th edn, p. 479. See generally R. Cross, 'The scope of the rule against hearsay' (1956) 72 LQR 91; E. Morgan, 'Hearsay dangers and the application of the hearsay concept' (1948) 62 Harv L Rev 177. And see 1.5.2.

[6] That the rule against hearsay did not depend on the best evidence theory seems clear from the fact that relatively few exceptions developed. Hearsay is not infrequently the best evidence, and, if this had been the test, a number of further exceptions might have been expected to be recognized. Nonetheless, references to this objection to hearsay are to be found as late as the speech of Lord Normand, delivering the advice of the Privy Council in *Teper* v *R* [1952] AC 480, 486.

[7] In *Jones* v *Metcalfe* [1967] 1 WLR 1286, Diplock LJ described hearsay as 'a branch of the law which has little to do with common sense'. In *Myers* v *DPP* [1965] AC 1001, Lord Reid said that it was 'difficult to make any general statement about the law of hearsay evidence which is entirely accurate', and called for a thorough review and reform of the law.

to the engines of the cars at the time of manufacture, they provided excellent evidence of the true identity of the vehicles. On appeal against conviction, it was contended that the micro-filmed documents were hearsay not covered by an exception, and had been wrongly admitted. With great reluctance, the House of Lords felt compelled to accede to the argument, and allowed the appeal.

The actual point for decision in *Myers* presented little difficulty. It was quite apparent that the accused's argument was correct, as the law then stood. The documents in question were plainly not public records, and there was no other applicable exception. The prosecution contended, however, that the House should create an exception to cover business records. As a matter of policy, the argument was compelling, indeed almost overwhelming. The records had been com-piled as a routine matter by workers whose duty was to record the information accurately, and who had no conceivable motive to misrepresent anything. The records had indicia of reliability practically equivalent to that of public records. Cross-examination of the workers would have been futile, even if they could have been made available, because they could not reasonably be expected to have any recollection of such routine details recorded so long before. Moreover, in the absence of an exception, many prosecutions for sophisticated offences of dishonesty were likely to come to the same abrupt end as did *Myers* itself. There was certainly nothing in the his-tory of the rule against hearsay to suggest that the House would be taking too radical a step by creating the exception suggested. Two members of the House, Lords Pearce and Donovan, would have been prepared to do so. But the majority (Lords Reid, Morris of Borth-y-Gest, and Hodson), while recognizing the need for it, held that the era of judicial creation of major exceptions had ended, and that the time had come for Parliament to provide a comprehensive legislative basis for the rule and the exceptions to it. Lord Reid said ([1965] AC at 1022):

> The only satisfactory solution is by legislation following on a wide survey of the field, and I think that such a survey is overdue. A policy of make do and mend is no longer adequate.

In the area of civil cases, the legislative response to *Myers* has been specific, and, on the whole, successful, culminating in the abolition of the hearsay rule in civil cases by the Civil Evidence Act 1995. The response with respect to criminal cases, however, could hardly have been more ironic. It has consisted of a series of piecemeal reforms, beginning with the hastily drafted Criminal Evidence Act 1965, none of which has so far had an air of permanence. It is hardly an exaggeration to say that Parliament reacted to *Myers* by substituting a legislative make do and mend policy for the judicial make do and mend policy which had preceded *Myers*. The majority of the House of Lords in *Myers* certainly achieved their goal of stimulating Parliament to act, but one wonders whether, if their Lordships could have foreseen the course of legislative events, they might not have opted to prolong the era of judicial creation of exceptions for some time.[8]

7.3.1 Civil cases

The Evidence Act 1938 had made early, and very narrow inroads into the rule against hearsay in civil cases. But it was the Civil Evidence Act 1968 which first provided a systematic alternative approach to the subject. Although the Act was sometimes spoken of as creating exceptions to

---

[8] Since *Myers* there has been general agreement that reform of the hearsay rule is now a matter for Parliament rather than the courts. But this view has not gone entirely unchallenged: see, e.g., P. Carter (1993) 109 LQR 573. For an example of post-*Myers* modification of a common law exception to the rule, see *Halpin* [1975] QB 907.

the rule against hearsay, it was in fact a self-contained, comprehensive code, which provided that the hearsay nature of evidence should be primarily a question of weight, rather than admissibility. The Act rendered admissible: (a) statements made, either orally or in a document or otherwise, and whether or not the maker of the statement was called as a witness, as long as direct oral evidence of the facts stated by the maker would have been admissible; (b) statements contained in records compiled by persons acting under a duty from information supplied by a person who had personal knowledge of it; and (c) certain statements produced by computers.[9] The Act called for an elaborate network of procedural safeguards,[10] and made documentary hearsay easier, to some extent, to admit than oral hearsay.[11] Ancillary provisions dealt with matters affecting weight, and evidence admissible to attack or support the credibility of the maker of an admissible hearsay statement.[12] The Civil Evidence Act 1968 was a highly successful piece of legislation. After some years of experience with it, a consensus developed that the continuation of the rule against hearsay itself was probably unnecessary in civil cases, and following a recommendation by the Law Commission,[13] the rule was abolished in civil cases by the Civil Evidence Act 1995, which, with minor exceptions, came into effect on 31 January 1997.

7.3.2 Criminal cases

There can be no doubt that the greater willingness to experiment with the admission of hearsay evidence in civil cases than in criminal is related directly to the fact that in almost all civil cases, the tribunal of fact is a judge sitting alone, whereas in criminal trials on indictment, the tribunal of fact is (almost always) a jury. It has generally been felt to be safer to entrust the proper evaluation of hearsay to the trained judicial mind rather than to the lay minds of jurors, who may have become accustomed in their daily lives to acting uncritically on what they are told by others. In more recent times, however, such truisms have been doubted. Many commentators have suggested that juries are, in fact, quite capable of understanding that hearsay evidence, being untested by cross-examination, should be treated with a certain amount of caution. Indeed, by comparison with some other directions which juries are expected to assimilate under existing law, a direction to treat hearsay evidence with caution would seem to be relatively straightforward.[14] A number of compelling American studies of actual and 'mock' jurors have suggested that

---

[9] The Act also rendered admissible by statute, though without altering their substance, certain common law exceptions, such as admissions. These adopted common law exceptions remained outside the procedural notice provisions which applied to the new statutory law (Civil Evidence Act 1968, s. 9). These same exceptions are in turn adopted by s. 7 of the Civil Evidence Act 1995. See 8.2.

[10] Civil Evidence Act 1968, s. 8, implemented by the former RSC Ord. 38, rr. 21–31 and CCR Ord. 20, rr. 14–26. For the detail of these rules, see the 5th edn of this work at 10.7 *et seq.*

[11] See Civil Evidence Act 1968, s. 2(3).

[12] Civil Evidence Act 1968, ss. 6, 7.

[13] Law Commission Report No. 216 (Cm 2321, 1993). Some limited encroachments had already been made. It had been held that the rule did not apply to essentially inquisitorial, non-adversarial proceedings: see *Humberside County Council* v *R* [1977] 1 WLR 1251; *Commission for Racial Equality, ex parte Cottrell & Rothon* [1980] 1 WLR 1580. The Children (Admissibility of Hearsay Evidence) Order 1993 made pursuant to s. 96 of the Children Act 1989, rendered hearsay evidence admissible if given in connection with the upbringing, maintenance, or welfare of a child. This provision was necessary because of the apparent anomaly that certain kinds of proceedings involving the welfare of children were essentially inquisitorial, while others were adversarial: see *H* v *H (Minors) (Child Abuse: Evidence)* [1990] Fam 86; *Bradford City Metropolitan Council* v *K* [1990] Fam 140. All such situations are now covered by the Civil Evidence Act 1995.

[14] 'Juries are credited with the ability to follow the most technical directions in dismissing evidence from consideration, while at the same time they are of such low-grade intelligence that they cannot, even with the

jurors are quite able to evaluate such evidence responsibly, even in the absence of judicial direction, and may actually tend to accord less weight to hearsay in some circumstances than might a lawyer.[15] It is submitted that these studies carry considerable weight. In the United States, jury trial is guaranteed in both civil and criminal cases by the Sixth and Seventh Amendments to the Constitution, and jury trial is accordingly routine in cases of both kinds. Juries habitually consider hearsay evidence admissible under a broad range of exceptions, and, on the whole, seem to cope with it perfectly adequately.

The Criminal Evidence Act 1965 was no more than a hurried attempt to plug the hole in the dyke created by *Myers* v *DPP* [1965] AC 1001. The Act rendered certain records of a trade or business admissible, which would have solved the immediate problem posed by *Myers*, but went no farther. In practice, the Act gave rise to a number of problems of its own, including the question of what was meant by a 'trade or business', and of what amounted to a 'record'. These problems were never solved satisfactorily. The 1965 Act was replaced by the hearsay provisions of the Police and Criminal Evidence Act 1984, which, in turn, were replaced by those of the Criminal Justice Acts 1988 and 2003. Both the Law Reform Committee and the Criminal Law Revision Committee,[16] have in the past made proposals for reform significantly wider than any provisions yet enacted. The Criminal Justice Act 2003, which was based on (though it did not entirely follow) the recommendations of the Law Commission in its Report No. 245 (*Evidence in Criminal Proceedings: Hearsay and Related Topics*) creates the most comprehensive self-contained body of provisions yet enacted dealing with the admission of hearsay in criminal cases.[17] The Act replaces the hearsay provisions of the Criminal Justice Act 1988 with broadly similar, though extended, provisions allowing the admissibility of hearsay statements made by persons who are not available to give evidence at trial (including for the first time statements made orally) and documentary hearsay contained in business records. The broadest and most radical of its provisions allows the judge to admit hearsay statements generally where it is in the interests of justice to do so, subject to safeguards designed to ensure the reliability of the evidence admitted. Following the example of the Civil Evidence Acts 1968 and 1995, the Act preserves, without altering in substance, a number of common law exceptions. A number of general safeguards are enacted, including a power enabling the judge to stop a jury trial if hearsay evidence important to the case against the accused is admitted, but turns out to be unconvincing. Provision is made for rules of court to require notice of an intention to adduce hearsay evidence. Whether or not the Criminal Justice Act 2003 fulfills the hope expressed by the House of Lords in *Myers* v *DPP* that a simplified

---

assistance of the judge's observations, attach the proper degree of importance to hearsay' (Glanville Williams, *The Proof of Guilt: A Study of the English Criminal Trial*, 3rd edn (1963), p. 207). The Judicial Studies Board has developed a model form of direction to the jury dealing with the treatment of admissible hearsay evidence, which is reproduced in the Law Commission's Report No. 245 (referred to in more detail in the text below) at para. 3.23; and see *Cole* [1990] 1 WLR 866, 869.

[15] Landsman and Rakos, 'A preliminary empirical enquiry concerning the prohibition of hearsay evidence in American courts' 15 Law & Psychol Rev 65; Bull Kovera, Penrod, and Park, 'Jurors' perceptions of hearsay evidence' (1992) 76 Minn L Rev 703; Miene, Park, and Borgida, 'Juror decision making and the evaluation of hearsay evidence' (1992) 76 Minn L Rev 683; see also P. Murphy (1997) 1 E & P No. 2, p. 107; No. 3, p. 105.

[16] Law Reform Committee, *13th Report*, paras 48–52; Criminal Law Revision Committee, *11th Report*, paras 229–48. See also the report of the Roskill Committee on procedure in fraud cases, para. 5.35. See also, as to Law Commission Report No. 245, C. Tapper [1997] Crim LR 771; P. Murphy (1997) 1 E 8 P No. 2, 107; No. 3, 105; and as to the hearsay provisions of the Criminal Justice Act 2003, D. Birch [2004] Crim LR 556.

[17] The Act does not affect the law relating to confessions (Chapter 9) or the effect of the accused's denials and silence when questioned (Chapter 10).

legislative code would one day govern the admissibility of hearsay evidence may be debated. But it certainly illustrates the growing willingness to admit hearsay and to allow fact finders to evalu- ate it as they would other evidence. The hearsay provisions of the Criminal Justice Act 2003 came into effect for the purposes of all trials commencing on or after 4 April 2005.

For all the legislative changes, the rule against hearsay and its exceptions continue to occupy a good deal of space in this book. The remainder of this chapter is devoted to the scope and working of the rule itself. Chapter 8 deals with the statutory exceptions to the rule in civil and criminal cases, including the majority of the common law exceptions preserved by the Civil Evidence Act 1995 and the Criminal Justice Act 2003. Chapter 9 deals with admissions and confessions, the most important of all the preserved common law exceptions. Confessions are now admissible subject to the provisions of s. 76 of the Police and Criminal Evidence Act 1984, although the tests provided by that section in large measure reflect the way in which confessions were dealt with at common law. Chapter 10 deals with the closely related subject of the accused's denials and silence, the latter now subject to separate statutory rules under ss. 34 to 38 of the Youth Justice and Criminal Evidence Act 1994.

7.4 HEARSAY TENDERED BY THE DEFENCE

There is sometimes a tendency in criminal cases to permit limited relaxations of the rule in relation to evidence tendered by the defence, but the practice is contrary to authority and has been deprecated. In *Turner* (1975) 61 Cr App R 67, the trial judge was held to have been correct in refusing to admit evidence to the effect that a person not called as a witness had admitted having committed the offence charged. The person concerned had withdrawn the admission after making it, but this should not have affected the admissibility of what he had said. Only by calling him as a witness (when their difficulties would have included his privilege against self-incrimination) could the defence have properly put the evidence before the court.

7.4.1 Hearsay statements tending to exculpate accused

Turner represents an important kind of case. It is submitted that the law on this subject is in an unsatisfactory condition. Where, for example, a third party makes a statement in which he admits or suggests his guilt of an offence with which an accused is charged, the statement is inadmissible hearsay if tendered to prove that the third party, rather than the accused, committed the offence. It would, in theory, be open to the accused to avoid the hearsay problem by calling the third party as a witness. But, in practice, for obvious reasons he is very likely to become unavailable by the time of trial, and even if he were called, he would be entitled to assert the privilege against self-incrimination.[18] These considerations led in the United States to the view that due process and fairness require that the accused be permitted to adduce the statement of the third party in such circumstances (*Chambers* v *Mississippi* 410 US 284 (1973)). Until recently, it seemed that English law did not accept this principle, even after Parliament enabled confessions made by a co-accused to be adduced for this purpose (Criminal Justice Act 2003, s. 128; and see *Myers* [1998] AC 124; text below, and 9.13).

---

[18] Subject to a ruling that he had waived the privilege by making the statement (see 13.2). But, as the only sanction would be the limited one of being held to be in contempt of court, it would be improbable that such a ruling would induce the witness to answer questions if the offence in question were a serious one.

In *Sparks v R* [1964] AC 964, where the accused was charged with indecently assaulting a girl aged just under four years, who did not give evidence and was presumably incompetent to do so, the Privy Council held that the evidence of the girl's mother to the effect that the girl had told her that the attacker was coloured (the accused being white) had been rightly rejected. Dealing with this point, Lord Morris of Borth-y-Gest, giving the reasons for the committee's advice, said (*ibid.* at 978):

> It was said that 'it was manifestly unjust for the jury to be left throughout the whole trial with the impression that the child could not give any clue to the identity of her assailant'. The cause of justice is, however, best served by adherence to rules which have long been recognized and settled. If the girl had made a remark to her mother (not in the presence of the appellant) to the effect that it was the appellant who had assaulted her and if the girl was not to be a witness at the trial, evidence as to what she had said would be the merest hearsay. In such circumstances it would be the defence who would wish to challenge a contention, if advanced, that it would be 'manifestly unjust' for the jury not to know that the girl had given a clue to the identity of her assailant.

Later, after rejecting a contention that the evidence was admissible under the *res gestae* exception to the hearsay rule (see 8.3; 8.5), Lord Morris pointed out that, if the evidence had been of an incriminating statement which had been admitted for the prosecution as part of a recent complaint, it would not have been evidence of the truth of what the girl had said. He added:

> Their Lordships can see no basis upon which evidence concerning a remark made by her to her mother could be admitted. Even if any basis for its admission could be found the evidence of the making of the remark would not be any evidence of the truth of the remark. Evidence of the making of the remark could not in any event possess a higher probative value than would attach to evidence of the making of a complaint in a case where the complainant gives evidence or to evidence of an accusation made to or in the presence of an accused. Nor can the principle of the matter vary according as to whether a remark is helpful to or hurtful to an accused person.

In *Blastland* [1986] AC 41, the accused was charged with buggery and murder of a boy. The prosecution's case was a strong one, because the accused had admittedly engaged in homosexual acts with the boy shortly before his death, but there was disturbing evidence that one M, a known homosexual, had expressed to various witnesses knowledge of the boy's murder at a very early time and had been visibly distressed by it, and that M had made to the police, and then withdrawn, admissions that he had committed the offences with which the accused was charged. The accused's case was that M, and not he himself, had committed those offences. The trial judge refused to permit the defence to adduce evidence of the statements made by M, on the ground that they were hearsay. On appeal to the House of Lords, Lord Bridge, in a speech with which the other members of the House agreed, upheld the accused's contention that such statements would not be hearsay if tendered to prove M's state of mind. He held, however, that the statements were not admissible because M's state of mind was irrelevant to any issue before the jury. It is impossible to understand this decision without reference to a strange procedural turn of events. The Court of Appeal had certified as being of general public importance two questions of law: the first dealing with the admissibility of confessions of guilt of the offence charged made by persons other than the accused; the second dealing with statements made by a person other than the accused from which the guilt of that person might be inferred. However, the House of Lords granted leave to appeal only with respect to the second of these, with the result that the alleged confessions to the police were not considered. The statements to other witnesses showed no more than that M knew of the murder and indicated no source of that knowledge, so that they could not have assisted the jury in deciding whether the accused committed the offences charged.[19]

An attempt to persuade the European Commission of Human Rights that the decision in *Blastland* infringed the right to a fair trial guaranteed to the accused by art. 6 of the European Convention on Human Rights failed,[20] on the unconvincing reasoning that the accused's right to a fair trial was protected procedurally by the fact that he was entitled (theoretically) to call M as a witness, and to challenge the trial judge's decision to refuse to admit M's statements. Recognizing that this decision might well provide a basis for continuing complaints under art. 6, the Law Commission (Consultation Paper 138, para. 5.39) found that the existing law was open to criticism, and provisionally recommended that evidence of the kind rejected in *Sparks* and *Blastland* should be admissible. No such specific recommendation was contained in the Law Commission's final report (No. 245) and no such specific provision is contained in the Criminal Justice Act 2003.

But it now appears that an exculpatory statement by a person not charged in the proceedings is admissible under one of two provisions of the Criminal Justice Act 2003. In some cases, it may be admissible under s. 116, if the maker of the statement is unavailable to give evidence, perhaps because he can no longer be found or is afraid to give evidence: see 8.15. It is also be admissible by virtue of the judge's general power to admit hearsay evidence in the interests of justice under s. 114(1)(d), though this must obviously depend greatly on the view taken by the judge of the reliability and probative value of the statement and the other matters he is required to consider under s. 114(2), which imposes stringent conditions of admissibility.

It has been said that s. 114(1)(d) is a provision which may in principle be used to admit a hearsay statement of any kind, and this must include exculpatory statements.[21] It has been prayed in aid in a number of cases which suggest that it is now an appropriate vehicle for such statements. In *Finch* [2007] 1 WLR 1645, the accused was charged with the illegal possession of a firearm and ammunition. A co-accused, R, pleaded guilty to the offence and made a statement to the effect that the accused knew nothing about the matter. The defence produced R at court, but he was reluctant to give evidence and defence counsel decided not to call him. Instead, the defence tendered R's statement under s. 114(1)(d).[22] It was held that the statement should not be admitted. R was available and it was undesirable in those circumstances to put his statement, untested by cross-examination, before the jury. Nonetheless, the decision strongly suggests that as a matter of principle such a statement may fall within s. 114(1)(d) and might have been admitted under other circumstances, for example if R had been unavailable. A number of cases suggest that s. 114(1)(d) provides a basis for statements made by third parties to be tendered by

---

[19] Compelling as this reasoning is as an exercise in logic, the history of the case as a whole is, it is submitted, disturbing. Although taken in isolation, the statements made by M showing mere knowledge might be regarded as of doubtful relevance, the totality of the available evidence, including his confessions and distressed state (evidence of the last of which would not be objectionable as hearsay) might well have led the jury to take a different view of the prosecution's case against the accused. While Lord Bridge certainly notes that the prosecution's case was cogent, and that the police evidently had some reason to disbelieve M's confessions, he does not divulge any detail on the subject. Cf. *Williams* [1998] Crim LR 494.

[20] *Blastland* v *United Kingdom* (1987) 10 EHRR 528. As to the application of art. 6 to the admission of hearsay evidence generally, see 7.5.

[21] See *McLean* [2008] 1 Cr App R 11, as explained in *Y* [2008] 1 WLR 1683; *March* [2008] EWCA Crim 1816.

[22] The statement was not admissible as the confession of a co-accused under s. 76A of the Police and Criminal Evidence Act 1984 (see 9.13.2) because R had pleaded guilty and was no longer a co-accused.

the prosecution; these cases are discussed at 8.20. If this is correct, it must surely follow that the defence may also make use of the subsection in an appropriate case.

7.5 HEARSAY AND THE EUROPEAN CONVENTION ON HUMAN RIGHTS

In 1.7, we noted the impact of certain articles of the European Convention on Human Rights on the law of evidence. The text of the relevant portions of those articles may be found there. Article 6 of the Convention guarantees the accused in a criminal case the right to a fair trial. While this right obviously encompasses a wide variety of issues, an important issue is the effect of art. 6.3(d) on the admission of hearsay evidence against an accused in a criminal case. Article 6.3 provides (as far as here pertinent):

> Everyone charged with a criminal offence has the following minimum rights:...
> (d) *to examine or have examined witnesses against him* and to obtain the attendance and examin-ation of witnesses on his behalf under the same conditions as witnesses against him. [Emphasis added.]

The emphasized words draw attention to the second of the two dangers of hearsay evidence referred to at 7.2. This danger exists, of course, in the admission of any hearsay evidence, whether in civil or criminal cases, and in a criminal case, whether adduced on behalf of the prosecu-tion or the defence. It has not prevented the admission of hearsay evidence under a variety of exceptions to the rule against hearsay (see 7.3). But when hearsay is adduced on behalf of the prosecution against the accused in a criminal case, the absence of cross-examination assumes a greater significance.[23] The right of the accused to cross-examine the witnesses against him is an internationally recognized fundamental right, often referred to as the right to confront or to be confronted with the witnesses against him, or, more simply, the right of confrontation. Although more usually associated with the Sixth Amendment to the United States Constitution, which specifically employs the phrase 'confronted with the witnesses against him', the right of con-frontation derives from English common law, on which the Sixth Amendment was based. The wording of art. 6.3(d) of the European Convention articulates the same right without the use of the term confrontation. Curiously, contemporary English law saw little, if any, explicit connec-tion between the right of confrontation and the rule against hearsay until the coming into effect of the Human Rights Act 1998. For the most part, the rules of evidence apply alike to evidence tendered by the prosecution and the defence, and this is true specifically of the rule against hear-say (see 7.4).[24] But art. 6.3(d) of the Convention requires that the admission of hearsay against the accused be scrutinized with a view to ensuring the overall fairness of the trial, and since the com-ing into effect of the Human Rights Act 1998, the courts have been called on to do so in a number of cases. Because the right of confrontation has received relatively little attention in England, it

---

[23] The admission of hearsay evidence under the Civil Evidence Act 1995 has so far proved to be uncontrover-sial in civil cases, and does not in itself infringe art. 6.3(d) of the European Convention, even in civil cases having criminal attributes: see *R (McCann)* v *Crown Court at Manchester* [2003] 1 AC 787, [35]; see 4.15.2. But this is not an absolute rule, and the possibility of a violation of the article cannot be excluded in such cases. In civil cases generally, the possibility of a violation affecting the fairness of the trial seems extremely remote.

[24] There are some exceptions, for example the standard of proof required of the prosecution (see 4.12) and the discretionary powers to exclude admissible prosecution evidence (see 3.7).

is instructive, before turning to the English cases, to consider briefly how it has affected the rule against hearsay in the more developed law of the United States.

7.5.1 The Sixth Amendment

The Sixth Amendment to the United States Constitution provides, so far as pertinent:

> In all criminal prosecutions, the accused shall enjoy the right...; *to be confronted with the witnesses against him*; to have compulsory process for obtaining witnesses in his favor... [Emphasis added.]

The emphasized language deals with the same concerns as those in art. 6.3(d) of the European Convention, and is referred to as 'the right of confrontation'. Because the Constitution is the supreme law of the land, and prevails over any inconsistent statutory or judge-made law, its impact on the use of hearsay evidence against an accused is clear. But the right of confrontation has not been interpreted as a constitutional entrenchment of the rule against hearsay, creating a blanket prohibition on the use of hearsay against the accused.[25] Instead, it has been interpreted by the United States Supreme Court as being the right to cross-examine the witnesses against the accused in open court (*Turner* v *Louisiana* 379 US 466 (1965)). Where the statement concerned is tendered at trial in substitution for the oral evidence of the maker of the statement, the Sixth Amendment requires that the accused be given the opportunity to cross-examine the maker. Unless he has the opportunity to cross-examine, the evidence is inadmissible. This is the case whether the statement is the record of testimony given in a prior hearing, or a statement of any other kind, for example one given to the police. The test is whether it is tendered as hearsay evidence against the accused at trial. In *Crawford* v *Washington* 124 S Ct 1354, 1370 (2004) Scalia J, writing for the majority of the United States Supreme Court, said:

> Admitting statements deemed reliable by a judge is fundamentally at odds with the right of confrontation. To be sure, the [Sixth Amendment's] ultimate goal is to ensure reliability of evidence, but it is a procedural rather than a substantive guarantee. It commands, not that evidence be reliable, but that reliability be assessed in a particular manner; by testing in the crucible of cross-examination.

Accordingly, the Court held that in such cases, the Sixth Amendment requires that hearsay statements tendered against the accused in substitution for the oral evidence of the maker of the statement cannot be admitted unless two conditions are satisfied: firstly, the accused must have been afforded the right to confront the witness at some stage, if not at trial;[26] and secondly, it must be shown that the witness is unavailable to give evidence at trial.[27] Because the trial court had admitted evidence in violation of this principle, the accused's appeal against conviction was allowed.[28]

---

[25] Such an interpretation could not have been excluded as a matter of theory. Experience with the indiscriminate use of hearsay against the accused in seventeenth-century English treason trials, notably that of Sir Walter Raleigh, was the main inspiration for the right of confrontation. See generally P. Heller, *The Sixth Amendment* (1951); R. Patton (1993) 17 S Ill LJ 573; *Mattox* v *United States* 156 US 237 (1895); *Turner* v *Louisiana* 379 US 466 (1965).

[26] For example, at a preliminary hearing: *California* v *Green* 399 US 149 (1970).

[27] In addition to the obvious cases of unavailability, such as death, serious illness, and disappearance, a witness is unavailable if he properly declines to testify in the exercise of a privilege, or persistently refuses to testify despite being ordered by the court to do so; but a witness is not unavailable if he is kept out of the way by the party who wishes to use his statement (Federal Rule of Evidence 804(a)). A witness is also not unavailable if it was within the power of the prosecution to produce him, but they have failed to do so without cause: *Pointer* v *Texas* 380 US 400 (1965); *Barber* v *Page* 390 US 719 (1968).

[28] The Court's judgment makes interesting reading for English lawyers. The Court's finding that the Sixth Amendment guaranteed the right of confrontation to the accused in that form was based on an analysis of what

In other cases hearsay evidence may be admitted as an exception to the rule against hearsay if it bears 'adequate indicia of reliability' (*Ohio* v *Roberts* 448 US 56 (1980)). This rule is intended to address both the dangers of hearsay evidence dealt with at 7.2. The test of reliability need not be applied afresh in each case, but is applied generically to categories of hearsay evidence, which are then accepted as exceptions to the rule against hearsay (though the judge may exclude any particular piece of evidence in any particular case as a matter of discretion).[29]

7.5.2 Article 6(3)(d)

Unlike the United States Supreme Court, the European Court of Human Rights has no power to regulate the operation of criminal procedure, including the rules of evidence, in a State which is bound by the Human Rights Convention.[30] Unlike the Sixth Amendment, art. 6.3(d) is not part of a transcendent constitutional law, and does not directly affect the content of the evidence law of a State which is bound by the Convention. It does, however, guarantee the right to fair trial, thus providing a context within which the rules of evidence must be made and operated, a context which has become more conspicuous in England with the coming into effect of the Human Rights Act 1998. Notwithstanding this, neither the Law Commission's Report (*Evidence in Criminal Proceedings: Hearsay and Related Topics*) (Law Com. No. 245) nor the Criminal Justice Act 2003 made any overt concession to art. 6.3(d), presumably relying on the underlying soundness of as the hearsay rule in criminal cases to comply with the requirements of art. 6.3(d).[31] Such optimism may be justified. Thus far, the English hearsay rules have not been faulted by the European Court or by English courts as being in any way inherently unfair for the purposes of art. 6 of the Convention.[32] Of particular importance in leading to this conclusion are: the overall salutary purpose of a rule against hearsay providing for the admission of hearsay in limited and defined circumstances; the safeguards provided to the accused when hearsay is tendered against him (see generally 8.23 *et seq*.), including (under the present law) the duty of the judge to stop the case where unconvincing hearsay evidence has been admitted, and the discretion to exclude hearsay in the interests of fairness; the procedural protection provided by the right to dispute

English law would have required at the time of adoption of the Bill of Rights. The assumption is that the principles which governed English law at the time would have been adopted by the framers of the Bill of Rights. Both the majority and the minority engaged in a detailed investigation of that question.

[29] If hearsay is of a kind deemed to be sufficiently reliable, then, except in the case of previous testimony and one or two other cases, it is not required that the maker of the statement be unavailable to give evidence at trial (*United States* v *Inadi* 475 US 387 (1986); *Idaho* v *Wright* 497 US 805 (1990); *White* v *Illinois* 502 US 546 (1992). As to the discretionary exclusion of evidence see Federal Rule of Evidence 403, cited at 3.7.

[30] 'The taking of evidence is governed primarily by the rules of domestic law ... it is in principle for the national courts to assess the evidence before them. The ... task [of the European Court of Human Rights] is to ascertain whether the proceedings in their entirety, including the way in which evidence was taken, was fair' (*Saidi* v *France* (1993) 17 EHRR 251, para. 43). 'It has to be recalled at the outset that admissibility of evidence is primarily a matter for regulation by national law' (*Kostovski* v *Netherlands* (1989) 12 EHRR 434). See also *Unterpertinger* v *Austria* (1986) 13 EHRR 175.

[31] The Law Commission abandoned in the face of criticism (Report, para. 5.41) a provisional recommendation (Consultation Paper 1995, No. 138, para. 9.5) that, to comply with art. 6.3(d), an accused should not be convicted on the basis of hearsay evidence unsupported by direct evidence. The Law Commission's final view was that this was unnecessary. But s. 125 of the Criminal Justice Act 2003 allows the judge to stop the case if the evidence against the accused is 'unconvincing': see 8.24.

[32] Though they may have had a close call in *Blastland* v *United Kingdom* (1987) 10 EHRR 528, in which the European Court was understandably disturbed by the rule forbidding the accused to adduce evidence of an admission by a third party of guilt of the offence charged, but was persuaded that the English rule against hearsay, taken as a whole, served a benign purpose. See 7.4.

admissibility and challenge the evidence at trial; the duty of the judge to give the jury a specific and reasoned direction to treat hearsay evidence with caution (see 8.9.1); and the right to appeal on the ground that the wrongful admission of hearsay has made the conviction unsafe. On this view, any finding of unfairness arising from the admission of hearsay can arise only on a case-by-case basis.

The underlying test with respect to the admission of hearsay for the purposes of art. 6.3(d) was well expressed by the European Court of Human Rights in *Lucà* v *Italy* (2003) 36 EHRR 46 at [40] as follows:

> If the defendant has been given an adequate and proper opportunity to challenge the depositions, either when made or at a later stage, their admission in evidence will not in itself contravene art. 6(1) and art. 6(3)(d). The corollary of that, however, is that where a conviction is based solely or to a decisive degree on depositions that have been made by a person whom the accused has had no opportunity to examine or have examined, whether during the investigation or at the trial, the rights of the defence are restricted to an extent that is incompatible with the guarantees provided by art. 6.[33]

In *Gokal*,[34] the Court of Appeal held, taking into account art. 6, that the accused's right to a fair trial was not violated by the admission into evidence of a hearsay statement made by a person who was not called as a witness, as then permitted under ss. 23 to 26 of the Criminal Justice Act 1988. It was held that the accused's rights were adequately safeguarded by s. 26 of the Act which required the judge to have regard, *inter alia*, to the extent to which the accused would be able to controvert the evidence by cross-examination of other witnesses, by giving evidence himself, or by calling other witnesses. The Court conceded that: 'At first blush the use of that evidence in circumstances where it is not possible to examine the witness may seem a breach of art. 6.3(d)' but added that that was not how the European Court had construed the article. The Court of Appeal cited the following passage from an earlier decision of the European Court of Human Rights, *Unterpertinger* v *Austria* (1986) 13 EHRR 175:

> In itself, the reading out of statements in this way cannot be regarded as being inconsistent with art. 6.1 and 3(d) of the Convention, but the use made of them as evidence must nevertheless comply with the rights of the defence, which it is the object and purpose of art. 6 to protect. This is especially so where the person 'charged with a criminal offence', who has the right under art. 6.3(d) to 'examine or have examined' witnesses against him, has not had an opportunity at any stage in the earlier proceedings to question the persons whose statements are read out at the hearing.

The Court of Appeal also referred to a passage from *Kostovski* v *Netherlands* (1989) 12 EHRR 434 (see 1.7) to the effect that the purpose of art. 6 of the Convention was not to regulate the domestic law of evidence, but to ensure overall fairness in the trial process, and concluded ([1997] 2 Cr App R at 280):

> Since the whole basis of the exercise of the discretion conferred by s. 26 is to assess the interests of justice by reference to the risk of unfairness to the accused, our procedures appear to us to accord fully with our treaty obligations.

---

[33] See to the same general effect *Kaste and Mathisen* v *Norway* (2009) 48 EHRR 3; but see also the somewhat strange decision in *Eskelinen* v *Finland* (2007) 45 EHRR 1, which purports to exclude from the right of confrontation a person described as a 'legal expert', even though this person's statement had been read to the trial court as evidence.

[34] [1997] 2 Cr App R 266; cf. *Thomas* [1998] Crim LR 887; and as to civil cases, *Clingham* v *Kensington and Chelsea London Borough Council, The Times,* 20 February 2001.

In *Gokal*, it appeared that the maker of the hearsay statement had deliberately disappeared and was both unwilling and unavailable to return to England to give evidence. Conversely, in *Radak*,[35] the whereabouts of the witness in the United States were known, and it would have been possible to take his evidence on commission. Because the prosecution failed to take advantage of this possibility, it was held that the admission of his hearsay statement at trial had been unfair and that the statement should have been excluded under s. 26 of the 1988 Act.[36] Finding that the same result was called for by art. 6 of the European Convention, the Court of Appeal said that: '...the proper application of the Convention coincides with the proper application of the statute'. In each case, there must be a balance between the needs of the case and the rights of the accused. The court may legitimately take into account the whole picture, including ways in which the fairness of the trial can be safeguarded by means other than cross-examining the maker of the statement, for example the availability of other witnesses who can give evidence about the same facts. Provided that such safeguards are in place, it has hitherto been held to be proper to read hearsay statements to the jury if, for example, the maker of the statement has died (*Al-Khawaja* [2006] 1 WLR 1078) or is too ill to attend court (*Dragic* [1996] 2 Cr App R 232), or even where the witness does not attend court to give evidence because of fear (*Sellick* [2005] 1 WLR 3257). The statutory requirements for the admission of evidence in this way under the Criminal Justice Act 2003 are dealt with in Chapter 8, 8.10 *et seq.*

But the approach taken by English law may have to be revised at least to some extent in light of the decision of the European Court of Human Rights in *Al-Khawaja and Tahery v United Kingdom*, 20 January 2009, application nos 26766/05 and 22228/06. Al-Khawaja (whose case before the domestic courts is noted above) was charged with sexual assault against two patients he was treating as a therapist. One complainant committed suicide before trial (though it was not suggested that her suicide was related to the accused's conduct) and her statement was read at trial. Tahery was charged with wounding with intent by stabbing. The statement of a witness who purported to have seen the stabbing was read to the jury on the basis that he did not give evidence through fear. In both cases the Court noted that the hearsay evidence was 'the sole, or at least the decisive evidence' against the accused. The Court found that there had been a violation of the fair trial provisions of art. 6. The measures put in place by English law, including the directions given by trial judges to the jury emphasizing the care to be taken over statements not subjected to cross-examination, and the accused's right to give evidence, were inadequate to safeguard the fairness of trial in a case where the hearsay statement admitted was the sole or decisive evidence against the accused. The Court's judgment in these cases directly calls into question the decision in *Cole; Keet* [2008] 1 Cr App R 5, in which the Court of Appeal held that the fact that hearsay might be the sole or decisive evidence was not in itself a ground for excluding it, but must be considered together with any other factors bearing on the fairness of the trial. It is submitted that this case must now be treated as having been wrongly decided. The European Court's judgment may well have a much broader effect. Where the hearsay is the sole evidence against the accused, it is submitted that it must be excluded. It may be difficult to say in a particular case whether or not a statement is 'decisive' evidence, but in some cases the conclusion may be hard to resist, for

---

[35] [1999] 1 Cr App R 187; and see *French* (1993) 97 Cr App R 421; *P.S. v Germany* (2003) 36 EHRR 61.

[36] If the accused had been afforded the opportunity to cross-examine the witness on commission, the result would have been consistent with the American position on the right of confrontation (*California v Green* 399 US 149 (1970) and note 25, above).

example where the evidence is that of the alleged victim of the offence.[37] It is submitted that the judge must now consider the importance of the evidence in the context of the case as a whole in that light, in addition to any specific conditions of admissibility imposed by the Criminal Justice Act 2003 and his discretion to exclude the evidence under s. 78 of the Police and Criminal Evidence Act 1984. In cases in which the hearsay is not the sole or decisive evidence, it would appear that the safeguards adopted by English law are not called into question directly, but the judgment may perhaps prompt some review of the law by Parliament or the courts.

B HEARSAY AND NON-HEARSAY STATEMENTS

7.6 HEARSAY AND NON-HEARSAY STATEMENTS: THE TWO QUESTIONS

At the outset of this chapter, we saw that the rule against hearsay excludes evidence of statements made by others on prior occasions if tendered for the purpose of proving that any fact so stated on the prior occasion is true, but not for any other relevant purpose. It is essential to remember that evidence of a statement made on a prior occasion is not necessarily hearsay. It may, depending on the purpose for which it is tendered, be admissible evidence of, e.g., the fact that the statement was made, or that it was made on a certain occasion or in a certain way, or that it had a certain legal effect. Whether the evidence is admissible for one or more of these purposes will depend upon whether any such issue is relevant. If the only relevance of the statement is the proof of the truth of some fact stated, the evidence is hearsay.

Another way of distinguishing hearsay and non-hearsay[38] statements is to note that when a statement is tendered for the (hearsay) purpose of proving the truth of some fact stated in it, it constitutes direct evidence of that fact: to accept the fact as proved, the jury need do no more than accept the evidence; whereas, when a statement is tendered for some other (non-hearsay) purpose, it is circumstantial evidence, because the jury, in addition to accepting the evidence, must draw an inference from it, in order to find the fact proved (see 2.3.1). Consider the following example. A witness offers evidence that, while the claimant was trapped in his car following an accident, he heard the claimant shout out: 'My leg is broken'. If this statement is tendered to prove that the claimant sustained a broken leg in the accident (the truth of the matter stated, hence hearsay), it would be direct evidence of that fact. If the judge believes the claimant's statement, he will find that the claimant sustained a broken leg, and no inference is necessary. Conversely, if the statement is tendered to prove that the claimant was conscious while trapped in the car (non-hearsay, offered for a relevant purpose other than the truth of the matter stated), the evidence is circumstantial. As well as believing that the claimant made the statement, the judge must draw

---

[37] Cases such as *L* [2008] 2 Cr App R 18 may come under particular scrutiny. The accused's wife, who was a competent but not compellable witness against him (see 15.7) declined to give evidence; her witness statement was then read to the jury in lieu of her evidence under s. 114(1)(d): see the discussion at 8.20.

[38] This helpful expression is borrowed from American Federal Rule of Evidence 801. It avoids the confusion latent in describing non-hearsay evidence as 'direct', an ambiguous term which has been used to mean both the opposite of hearsay and the opposite of circumstantial (see 2.3.1, 2.3.2). Because of the discussion of direct and circumstantial evidence in the text, it is preferable to confine 'direct' to the second of those meanings. A good alternative is to substitute the word 'percipient' in the context of the first meaning, and this is done below.

the inference that the claimant was conscious from the fact that he was able to speak. It will be found that the same is true of all the examples of non-hearsay statements given below.

The simplest way to determine whether a statement is hearsay or non-hearsay is to ask two questions:

Question 1: Was the statement made on a 'prior' occasion? This is almost always straightforward. Unless the statement was made in the course of giving oral evidence in the instant proceedings, it was made on a prior occasion.

Question 2: For what purpose or purposes is the evidence tendered? The failure to answer this question correctly is the most common source of error. Another way to ask it is: Why is this evidence said to be relevant? If it is relevant only to prove the truth of the matter stated, the evidence is hearsay for that purpose. But it will be non-hearsay for any other purpose for which it is relevant. If the evidence is admitted, the jury should be directed to consider it only for its non-hearsay purpose.[39] To use a charming example suggested to the author by Professor Cross: if X makes the prior statement, 'This afternoon, I saw pink elephants crossing the lawn', the statement would be hearsay if offered to prove that pink elephants were crossing the lawn, but non-hearsay if offered to prove that X had had too much to drink.

7.6.1 Statement relevant only to prove the fact of the matter asserted

Before analysing hearsay in more detail, let us return for a moment to the claimant trapped in the car with the broken leg. As diagram 1 shows, hearsay evidence is tendered by a witness who did not perceive the facts stated. The claimant (C) perceived that his leg was broken, and there could be no objection to his giving evidence of that fact. A hearsay problem will arise only if C is not called as a witness, and the witness (W) who heard C speak is called instead. W did not perceive that C had a broken leg, and indeed has no knowledge of the fact except for what he heard C say. Because C's statement is a prior statement offered to prove that C suffered a broken leg, the evidence is hearsay coming from W. The diagram illustrates the problem by showing the interposition of W between the person who perceived the event (C) and the evidence presented to the court.

Hearsay diagram 1

Fact: perception   statement   evidence
C broke his leg ⟶ C ⟶ W ⟶ Court

7.6.2 Statement relevant to prove fact other than truth of matter stated

Hearsay diagram 2 illustrates the difference where the evidence of C's statement is tendered to prove that he was conscious while trapped in the car. The purpose of W's evidence is now to prove, not that C's leg was broken (which W did not perceive) but that C was able to speak (which

---

[39] This question arose in a very early reported criminal case: *Adam and Others* Gen 3: 9–19. The Man, the Woman, and the Serpent were charged with conspiracy to eat of the fruit of the Tree of the Knowledge of Good and Evil. When questioned about her part in the offence, the Woman replied: 'The Serpent beguiled me and I did eat'. This statement would be admissible to prove the Woman's state of mind, if relevant to her defence. But it was inadmissible hearsay against the Serpent. The report does not indicate that there was any other evidence against the Serpent, and it is difficult to avoid the conclusion that he was wrongly convicted.

W did perceive). As we have noted, W's evidence is now circumstantial. The judge will be asked to infer, from the fact that the statement was made, that C was conscious. The diagram shows that there is no longer any interposition between the percipient witness and the court. The rule against hearsay has not changed. What has changed is the fact to be proved, and, therefore, the relevance of the evidence.

Hearsay diagram 2

Fact: perception   evidence
C spoke while in the car ————————→ W ————————→ Court

7.6.3 Hearsay within hearsay or multiple hearsay

It will sometimes happen that the maker of a hearsay statement (A) will include in that statement another hearsay statement made to A by B. An example would be where A writes a report, in which he describes events related to him by B, and proceeds to comment on them. This situation, which occurs frequently in documentary hearsay, may be described as hearsay within hearsay or multiple hearsay. It is submitted that, in such cases, the rule should be that both the statement made by A and the included statement made by B can be admitted only if covered by an exception to the rule against hearsay, and that each must be considered separately. A cannot invest B's statement to him with admissibility simply by including it within his own (hearsay) statement. In some cases, B's statement to A will be independently admissible. American Federal Rule of Evidence 805 provides, in this situation, that: 'Hearsay included within hearsay is not excluded under the hearsay rule if each part of the combined statements conforms with an exception to the hearsay rule provided in these rules'. In England, at common law, there is a curious paucity of authority. But in *Compagnie Générale Maritime* v *Diahan Spirit SA* (*The Ymnos*) [1981] 1 Lloyd's Rep 550, it was held that where a statement admissible under the Civil Evidence Act 1968, s. 2(1), contained statements related to the maker of the statement by third parties, the latter were not admissible, unless they constituted admissions by agents of the party against whom they were offered (an exception to the hearsay rule: see 9.1 *et seq.*). This seems to confirm the position suggested above.

There is now at least a partial statutory rule both in civil and criminal cases. In civil cases, hearsay within hearsay is now admissible by virtue of s. 1 of the Civil Evidence Act 1995. The hearsay quality of evidence is no longer a bar to its admission in civil cases (see 8.30). Section 1(2)(b) of the Act further provides that '...references to hearsay include hearsay of whatever degree'.

In criminal cases, s. 121 of the Criminal Justice Act 2003 provides:

> (1) A hearsay statement is not admissible to prove the fact that an earlier hearsay statement was made unless—
>> (a) either of the statements is admissible under section 117, 119 or 120,
>> (b) all parties to the proceedings so agree, or
>> (c) the court is satisfied that the value of the evidence in question, taking into account how reliable the statements appear to be, is so high that the interests of justice require the later statement to be admissible for that purpose.
>
> (2) In this section 'hearsay statement' means a statement not made in oral evidence, that is relied on as evidence of a matter stated in it.

This section lays down a strangely specific and circumscribed rule. There are three cases, and three only, in which A's hearsay statement can be admitted for the purpose of proving B's hearsay statement to A contained in it or referred to in it. Firstly, consistently with general principle, the evidence is admissible if all parties agree. Secondly, the judge is given an overriding power to admit the evidence in the interests of justice, where the statements appear to be reliable and the probative value of the combined evidence would be high. Thirdly, one of the statements must be admissible either because it is a business or similar record (s. 117) or because it is a previous statement made by a witness in the proceedings (ss. 119 and 120) who is accordingly available for cross-examination. Statements made by an unavailable witness admissible under s. 116 and statements admissible by virtue of the common law hearsay exceptions preserved by s. 118 are excluded for this purpose, so that such a statement can be admissible as part of a multiple hearsay package only if the other statement is admissible under s. 117, s. 119, or s. 120.[40] But it should also be noted that, by virtue of s. 121(2), any statement made while giving oral evidence is not a hearsay statement for the purposes of this rule, even though it may have been made in different proceedings and even though the maker of the statement may not be available for cross-examination in the present proceedings. Thus, statements made while giving evidence may always be used for the purpose of proving earlier hearsay statements made in them. The purpose of this rather convoluted structure is to ensure, as far as possible, the reliability of at least one part of the multiple hearsay package. But it is not entirely clear why statements admissible under ss. 116 and 118 are not included. Some statements, for example some made by persons since deceased, may be reliable enough. The section could simply have given the judge a discretion, or confirmed that the judge has a discretion, to exclude evidence which seems too unreliable to admit. It has been held that the provisions of the subsection must be scrupulously followed, and that the judge must give the jury an enhanced direction to treat multiple hearsay with special care: see *Scorah* [2008] EWCA Crim 1786. A direction to treat any hearsay with care is required, the judge drawing particular attention to the fact that the evidence is untested by cross-examination, and the particular need for a strong direction in the case of multiple hearsay seems clear.

However, secondary hearsay may well be of less weight than primary hearsay, especially when the court has no reliable means of inquiring into the reliability of the secondary statements.

Where the statements by B included in A's statement are held to be inadmissible, they must be excluded from the version of A's statement tendered to the court, but A's statement, if otherwise admissible, may be admitted without them.

7.7 THE FIRST QUESTION: WHEN AND HOW MADE?

We must now return to examine the two questions in more detail. Question 1 can be analysed by asking when and how the statement was made.

7.7.1 When

The rule against hearsay applies to all statements made by a person, other than while giving evidence in the actual proceedings in which the suspected hearsay is tendered. Both s. 1(2) of the Civil Evidence Act 1995 and s. 114(1) of the Criminal Justice Act 2003 specify, when defining hearsay, that the definition refers to statements made other than in 'oral evidence in the

---

[40] See, e.g., *Xhabri* [2006] 1 All ER 76.

proceedings', i.e., the proceedings now taking place. Such statements are sometimes referred to as 'out-of-court' statements, but the phrase can be misleading because the rule excludes statements even when made in court in the course of giving evidence in other proceedings.[41] Even where the two proceedings are closely related, a prior sworn statement is hearsay. For example, a deposition taken at old-style committal proceedings was hearsay for the purpose of the trial and could be admitted as evidence at trial only where a statutory exception to the rule against hearsay applied. The same applies where a witness makes a written witness statement, even though it is made expressly subject to the penalty of perjury. The rule against hearsay also applies to prior statements made by the witness himself, repeated by the witness at trial. These statements, however, are the subject of separate rules, which depend on whether the prior statement is consistent or inconsistent with the testimony of the witness at trial, and are considered in chapters 16 and 17.

7.7.2 How

It matters not whether the statement was made orally, in a document, by gesture or by any other medium of communication. At common law, the rule against hearsay applies to statements made or produced by any means, as long as the statement was intended by the maker to communicate information.[42] The definitions of hearsay contained in both the Civil Evidence Act 1995 (ss. 1(2) and 13) and the Criminal Justice Act 2003 (ss. 114(1) and 115(2) and (3)) appear to make it clear that a statement can be hearsay only insofar as it is a representation of a fact or opinion, or (which would seem to amount to the same thing) if the purpose of the maker of the statement was to cause another person to believe the matter stated. Cases in which a fact may be inferred from a statement, but in which it cannot be said that the fact was one which the maker of the statement intended to communicate, caused difficulties at common law. These difficulties have probably been resolved by the statutory definitions of hearsay, although the question is still not entirely free from difficulty. This is considered further at 7.15.1. The principle, however, is simple enough. It is the effect of a statement, not the means by which it is made, which is most significant. The rule against hearsay is designed to prevent a party from proving facts through the mouth of someone who is not before the court to give evidence and to be cross-examined. It is logical that the rule should also prevent attempts to prove the facts through that someone's pen, his camera, his computer, his bodily movements, or any other means of expression.

Section 115(2) of the Criminal Justice Act 2003 specifies that, for the purposes of that Act, the term 'statement' means 'any representation of fact or opinion made by a person by whatever means', and includes 'a representation made in a sketch, photofit, or other pictorial form'.[43]

7.8 THE SECOND QUESTION: FOR WHAT PURPOSE TENDERED?

The source of the statement alone does not determine whether or not it is hearsay. The crucial second question must also be asked and answered. Failure to do so may lead to the wrongful exclusion of perfectly admissible non-hearsay evidence. Such errors are a result of what Cross

---

[41] *Eriswell (Inhabitants)* (1790) 3 TR 707; *Haines v Guthrie* (1884) 13 QBD 818. Statute may render some statements made in evidence in other proceedings admissible as exceptions to the hearsay rule. But the only case in which such statements are exempted from the definition of hearsay is s. 121(2) of the Criminal Justice Act 2003, in the case of multiple hearsay (see 7.6.3).

[42] *Chandrasekera v R* [1937] AC 220: a gesture.

[43] This is a welcome clarification of a matter which had caused some unnecessary confusion at common law: see *Cook* [1987] QB 417; *Smith (Percy)* [1976] Crim LR 511.

called the 'superstitious awe...about having any truck with evidence which involves A's tell-ing the court what B said'.[44] In analysing the second question, the consideration of relevance is always the key. Could the statement be relevant for a purpose other than proving the truth of some fact asserted in it? We shall look at examples of both hearsay and non-hearsay statements. The hearsay statements, which will be examined first, are those cases in which the statement has no relevance except proving the truth of some fact stated. The non-hearsay statements, although probably impossible to classify comprehensively, are relevant for the most part for one or more of the following reasons, and will be examined in those categories:

(a) statements having legal effect or significance;
(b) statements as direct evidence that the statement was made, or was made on a particular occa-sion or in a certain way;
(c) statements as circumstantial evidence of the state of mind of the maker or recipient of the statement;
(d) statements as circumstantial evidence of other relevant facts.

We shall also examine three particularly problematical areas on the borderline between hearsay and non-hearsay—(a) unintended communications, (b) evidence of the absence of records or information where its presence would have been significant, and (c) the relationship between hearsay and real evidence (especially in relation to evidence produced by computers and other mechanical devices).

It must be borne in mind in considering the cases dealt with below that some of the hearsay problems discussed in this chapter would now be avoided by applying one of the modern statu-tory rules provided by the Civil Evidence Act 1995 or the Criminal Justice Act 2003. Detailed dis-cussion of these rules must await Chapter 8. We are presently considering only the common law rule against hearsay, which remains of importance in criminal cases. The problems posed by the older cases can and do recur in analogous situations.

7.9 HEARSAY STATEMENTS

In *Gibson* (1887) 18 QBD 537, in which the accused was charged with wounding, an unidentified woman had said to the prosecutor at the scene, 'The man who threw the stone went in there', indicating a house in which the accused was found. The woman's statement to the prosecutor was not made while giving evidence in the proceedings, and was obviously tendered for the pur-pose of suggesting that the person found in the house was the culprit, i.e., that the fact stated was true. The statement was inadmissible hearsay; evidence of the identity of the accused should have been given by calling the woman. Such cases, in which statements are tendered for the purpose of proving identity, and which plainly cannot be justified as having relevance to any other issue, are a good example of the working of rule at common law.

In *Jones* v *Metcalfe* [1967] 1 WLR 1286, an eyewitness to a road traffic accident took the regis-tration number of a lorry, the bad driving of which was said to have caused a collision between two other vehicles. The eyewitness reported the number to the police. The police interviewed the defendant, and obtained his admission that he had been driving a lorry of that number on the relevant day. He denied, however, that his driving had been such as to cause any accident. By the time the defendant was tried by the magistrates for driving without due care and atten-tion, the eyewitness was unable to remember the number of the lorry. The issue was: could the

[44] [1965] Crim LR 68, 82.

police officer give evidence of the number instead? The difficulty was that the police officer could only say what he had been told by the eyewitness. His evidence was hearsay and inadmissible because it consisted of a statement made by the eyewitness other than while giving evidence at the trial which was clearly relevant only to the issue of identity of the lorry. The conviction was quashed by the Divisional Court, on the ground that there was no evidence upon which the justices were entitled to find that a lorry of the number recorded was that responsible for the accident.

It will be observed that at common law it made no difference that, in *Gibson*, the woman was unable to be called to give evidence at all, whereas in *Jones* v *Metcalfe* the eyewitness was called, and testified about everything except the question of identity. Yet, there is obviously a considerable qualitative difference between evidence in the two cases. The eyewitness in *Jones* v *Metcalfe* afforded evidence of everything except the number, and he would have been able to give evidence even of this, by refreshing his memory from the police officer's note, had he verified it contemporaneously.[45] The artificiality of this position drew comment from all three members of the Divisional Court. In particular, Diplock LJ said (*ibid.* at 1290–1):

> I reluctantly agree. Like [Lord Parker CJ] I have every sympathy with the magistrates because the inference of fact that the appellant was the driver of the lorry at the time of the accident is irresistible as a matter of common sense. But this is a branch of the law which has little to do with common sense. The inference that the appellant was the driver of the lorry was really an inference of what the independent witness said to the police when he gave them the lorry number, and since what he had said to the police would have been inadmissible as hearsay, to infer what he said to the police is inadmissible also. What makes it even more absurd is, as [Lord Parker CJ] pointed out, that if when the independent witness gave the number of the lorry to the police officer, the latter had written it down in his presence, then the police officer's note could have been shown to the independent witness and he could have used it, not to tell the justices what he told the police officer, but to refresh his memory. This case does illustrate . . . the need to reform the law of evidence.

The identity cases are only one example of the working of the rule excluding hearsay statements at common law. In *Attard*,[46] for instance, the prosecution sought to prove the substance of an interview which had taken place between the accused and a police officer, relating to the offence charged. The interview had been conducted through the medium of an interpreter, because the accused, who was Maltese, was unable to speak English. All would have been well, had the interpreter been called to prove the conversation, but the officer purported to give evidence of what had been said between the accused and himself. It was held that his evidence as to what had been said was hearsay. The officer could not give percipient evidence of the substance of what had been said in Maltese by the accused or the interpreter; he was relating what the interpreter had said the conversation had been, with a view to proving what it had in fact been.

7.9.1 Admissions based on hearsay

Where hearsay evidence would be inadmissible to prove the truth of a fact, it would seem to follow, and has been held, that any admission made by a party against his interest, based solely

---

[45] As to refreshing the memory from contemporaneous notes, see 16.3.1.

[46] (1958) 43 Cr App R 90. This decision led to the universal practice of calling the interpreter as a witness in such cases. Cf. *Duffy* [1999] QB 919. And see *R (Saifi)* v *Governor of Brixton Prison and another* [2001] 1 WLR 1134: contrast the case referred to in P. Murphy [1978] Crim LR 474.

upon that hearsay and not upon matters within his own knowledge, should be rejected as having no more evidential value than the hearsay on which it was based.[47] Thus, in *Surujpaul v R*[48] the accused was charged with murder as an accessory before the fact. He made an admission that the murder in question had in fact been committed. It was held that this admission should not have been received in evidence, because the accused had not been present at the murder, had no personal knowledge of the facts which he was purporting to admit and was relying entirely upon what he had been told by another. In *Comptroller of Customs v Western Lectric Co. Ltd* [1966] AC 367, the respondents were charged with making a false declaration on a customs import entry produced to a customs officer, the false declaration relating to the country of origin of certain goods. The articles were entered as having their origin either in Australia or the UK, and if this had been true, they would have been subject to a preferential tariff. Inspection of the goods by a customs officer revealed that the articles were labelled respectively, 'Denmark' and 'Made in USA', and in the light of this, the respondents' agent filed a further entry stating the origin of the goods to be Denmark and the United States. This further entry was subsequently relied on as an admission by the respondents of the true origin of the goods. The Privy Council held that a conviction could not be based upon an admission so clearly made solely in reliance on the hearsay markings of the goods.[49] Lord Hodson, delivering the judgment of their Lordships, observed that:

> If a man admits something of which he knows nothing it is of no real evidential value. The admission made by the respondents' agent was an admission made upon reading the marks and labels on those goods and was of no more evidential value than those marks and labels themselves.

For very similar reasons, in *Marshall*[50] the trial judge accepted a submission of no case to answer where, on a charge of handling stolen goods, the only evidence from which the jury could infer that the goods were stolen was an admission made to the police by the accused that this was the case. This admission was based solely on what the accused had been told by a man who sold him the goods. The decision is an excellent illustration of the extent of the hearsay rule, because although the admission was not evidence that the goods were stolen, it would have been admissible and cogent evidence that the accused knew or believed them to be stolen, i.e., of his state of mind at the time when he received them.

7.10 NON-HEARSAY STATEMENTS

Statements made on prior occasions will be non-hearsay and admissible where they enjoy a relevance independent of the proof of the truth of facts stated therein. It is impossible to categorize definitively the cases in which evidence of prior statements is admissible as non-hearsay evidence. But the most important examples fall into four categories, which may be regarded as typical.

---

[47] For the admissibility of admissions against interest, see 9.1 *et seq.*

[48] [1958] 1 WLR 1050, but see *Chatwood* [1980] 1 WLR 874, *Korniak* [1983] Crim LR 109; and 9.3.

[49] As to which see *Patel v Comptroller of Customs* [1966] AC 356. Where the accused has some personal knowledge of the facts which he admits, his admission may be *prima facie* evidence of the facts admitted even though based solely upon his past experience: see *Chatwood* [1980] 1 WLR 874.

[50] [1977] Crim LR 106, but see also *Korniak* [1983] Crim LR 109.

7.11 STATEMENT HAVING LEGAL EFFECT OR SIGNIFICANCE

A statement may be admitted as non-hearsay evidence if it is tendered for the purpose of proving that making the statement itself gave rise to legal consequences. For example, if P alleges that he entered into an oral contract with D, P may testify as to the words spoken by D which are alleged to constitute D's offer or acceptance, or the consideration which D agreed to accept and provide. In a criminal context, a police officer may give evidence that he heard D1, D2, and D3 have a conversation which amounted to a conspiracy, or that he found a letter written by D1 to D2 containing the terms of a conspiracy. Such statements, known to some American writers as 'verbal acts', have legal effect or significance. There is no relevant issue of the truth or otherwise of any fact stated by the parties. The only issue is what statement was made, and whether the statement was sufficient in law to bring about the claimed legal consequences. On these issues, evidence of the making of the statement is clearly non-hearsay and direct evidence that the legal effect was created.

In some cases, the making of a statement must be proved, not because the statement itself gives rise directly to legal consequences, but because the making of the statement is a necessary preliminary to other steps having legal consequences. In *Chapman* [1969] 2 QB 436, the accused was charged with driving with excess alcohol, following a road traffic accident which had resulted in his being taken to hospital. Under those circumstances, the Road Safety Act 1967 provided that before the accused was required to supply a specimen of breath, the police officer should ascertain from the doctor in charge of the accused that the former had no objection to such specimen being required. The officer gave evidence that he had asked the doctor, who had offered no objection. It was argued on appeal that the doctor should have been called to state that he had had no objection, but the Court of Appeal rejected the suggestion that the officer's evidence was hearsay. The only issue was whether the doctor had or had not in fact given his consent to the sample being required. Whether what the doctor said was true or not was not in issue. The giving of consent created the legal consequence that the accused was required to supply the sample.

7.12 STATEMENT ADMISSIBLE TO PROVE THAT IT WAS MADE OR WAS MADE ON A PARTICULAR OCCASION OR IN A CERTAIN WAY

The fact that a statement was made, was made on a particular occasion or was made in a certain way may itself be an essential element of a claim, charge or defence, and so be a fact in issue in the case. For example, in a claim for defamation, or a prosecution for sedition, the fact that the statement complained of was made, and made on the occasion and in the manner alleged may be proved as part of the case. If the defendant to the claim for defamation raises a defence of privilege, he may give evidence that the form or occasion of the statement were such as entitle him to claim the privilege. Although the tribunal of fact will eventually have to consider also the defamatory or seditious nature of the statements, the first issue is whether they were made, and if so, in what circumstances. Evidence of the statements will be non- hearsay and admissible on that issue. As in the case of statements having legal effect or significance, the statements themselves produce certain legal consequences, which in this instance are in terms of creating or negating a claim, charge, or defence.

The fact that a statement was made, or made on a particular occasion, or in a certain way, may also be circumstantially relevant to other facts. If there is an issue as to whether a person gave notice, or prepared a report, or did so within a specified time, the notice or report will be admissible on that issue. The fact that a person is alleged to have made a statement in fluent English may be relevant to an issue as to his command of the language. The physical characteristics of a written statement may be relevant to an issue of whether or not the statement was made hastily, or under pressure. The appearance or language of a holographic will may be relevant to the issue of whether or not the testator was of sound mind when he made it, or to the issue of whether or not it was forged. A previous statement made by a witness may be relevant to the credibility of the witness, by showing that the witness has previously spoken consistently or inconsistently with his evidence at trial.

7.13 STATEMENT AS CIRCUMSTANTIAL EVIDENCE OF STATE OF MIND

A statement may be non-hearsay, circumstantial evidence of the state of mind of the maker or the recipient of the statement. Since a person's state of mind cannot be proved directly, statements made to or by that person constitute valuable evidence on that issue. The state of a person's mind is affected by statements received, and reflected by statements made, and both may be relevant where the state of mind of that person is in issue. The circumstances in which state of mind is relevant are many and varied. Intent, whether guilty or innocent, knowledge or belief and motive may all be proved by circumstantial evidence of statements made or received by the subject, and for this purpose, such statements are non-hearsay.

7.13.1 Accused tendering evidence of state of mind of others

In *Gilfoyle* [1996] 3 All ER 883, the accused was charged with the murder of his wife. He contended that she had committed suicide. It was held that notes written before her death by the wife, which tended to show that she had considered committing suicide, were admissible to support the accused's defence that she had in fact done so (as were other notes which tended to contradict that fact). The notes were circumstantial evidence of the wife's state of mind at the time. The judgment of the Court of Appeal appears somewhat ambivalent about whether the notes which contradicted suicide were admissible as non-hearsay statements or under the common law exception permitting statements of the contemporaneous state of mind of the maker (see 8.6). However, it is submitted that the better view is that the notes were non-hearsay evidence. The state of mind of others may be relevant to the defence in various situations. For example, in cases where the accused is charged with an offence involving deception, he might be allowed to admit statements made by the alleged victim showing that he was not deceived by or did not rely on the misrepresentations made to him by the accused. Contrast with this kind of case, those in which the accused tenders evidence of hearsay statements made by a third party for the purpose of suggesting that the third party may have committed the offence with which the accused is charged. These cases are discussed at 7.4.1.

7.13.2 Accused tendering evidence of his own state of mind

Because proof of a guilty or an innocent mind is often relevant in criminal cases, the accused may tender statements made to him by others as circumstantial evidence of an innocent state of mind. Such statements are relevant because they tend to establish some knowledge or belief on his part consistent with innocence. A good example was provided by the facts of *Marshall*.[51] In cases involving dishonestly handling stolen goods, the accused may adduce evidence tending to show that he did not know or believe that the goods were stolen at the time he received them. Such evidence will typically consist of evidence that the person who supplied the goods to him told him that they were not stolen, which is circumstantial evidence of the accused's belief of that fact. The same statement would, of course, be inadmissible hearsay if tendered for the (hearsay) purpose of proving that the goods were not in fact stolen.

In *Subramaniam* v *Public Prosecutor* [1956] 1 WLR 965, the accused was charged with unlawful possession of firearms, contrary to certain emergency regulations. It would have been a defence for the accused to show that he had a lawful excuse for the possession, and he sought to give evidence that he had been threatened by terrorists, and possessed the weapons only while in a state of duress induced by the threats made by the terrorists. The accused was prevented from giving this evidence on the ground that it was hearsay—a classic example of error resulting from failure to ask what we have called the second question. On appeal, the Privy Council held that the accused had been entitled to give evidence of what the terrorists had said to him, which was clearly relevant to his claimed state of mind. The statements received by the accused could have affected his mind in relation to his possession of the firearms, and so were circumstantial evidence of the defence of duress.

In *Davis* [1998] Crim LR 659, the accused sought to give evidence about a conversation he had had with his solicitor before an interview with the police, for the purpose of explaining his failure to mention facts on which he later relied for his defence at trial. The trial judge refused to allow the evidence on the ground that anything the solicitor said to the accused was hearsay. The Court of Appeal disagreed. By virtue of s. 34 of the Criminal Justice and Public Order Act 1994 (see 10.5 *et seq.*) an adverse inference might have been drawn against the accused because of his failure to mention the facts in question, and it was therefore relevant for the accused to explain his failure to do so by reference to what he had been told by his solicitor. The evidence would not have been admissible to prove that the facts stated were true, for which purpose it would have been hearsay, but it was non-hearsay and admissible for the purpose of proving the accused's state of mind at the time of the interview and suggesting that no adverse inference should be drawn against him.

7.13.3 Prosecution offering evidence of the state of mind of third party

Where it is relevant for the prosecution to prove the state of mind of a third party, for example, the victim of the offence, statements made to or by the victim may be admissible for that purpose. In most cases, evidence of the state of mind of the victim will be irrelevant, but in some cases it is both relevant and admissible. Such a case might be where it is alleged that the accused robbed the victim by putting him in fear of his life, or raped the victim using threats against her life, or demanded money with menaces designed to put the victim in such a state of mind that he would pay without resistance. It is submitted that in these cases the statements made by the accused, or statements made by the victim indicating his or her state of mind, are relevant and admissible as non-hearsay evidence.

---

[51] [1997] Crim LR 106, and see 7.9.1. See also *Willis* [1960] 1 WLR 55.

A good example is *Ratten* v *R* [1972] AC 378. The accused was charged with the murder of his wife by shooting her. He contended that the gun had discharged accidentally. The Privy Council upheld the admission of the details of a telephone call made by a 'hysterical' woman (the deceased wife, as it must have been) from the accused's home five minutes before she was known to have died, in which she asked the operator to get the police. The admission of this evidence was justified as showing the circumstances which existed at the accused's home, including the state of mind of the wife at that time. This evidence was relevant, because the husband's defence to the charge of murder was one of accident, and the fact that the wife was in a hysterical and terrified state immediately before her death had the specific effect of refuting that defence.[52]

7.13.4 Prosecution tendering statement as evidence of accused's state of mind

The prosecution may wish to tender a statement made by the accused as evidence of a guilty state of mind. In the vast majority of cases, this is done by introducing a confession. Confessions are admissible as an exception to the rule against hearsay, but are subject to distinct and important principles of admissibility governed by s. 76 and s. 78 of the Police and Criminal Evidence Act 1984. These principles are dealt with in Chapter 9. Confessions are hearsay because almost always, the prosecution tender them for the purpose of proving the truth of the facts stated by the accused in the confession, which amount to admissions of his guilt of the offence charged. But there are some cases in which a statement made by the accused may have evidential value on the issue of guilt irrespective of the truth of the facts stated in it. In these cases, the nature of the statement or the circumstances in which it is made suggest a guilty state of mind. The accused may, for example, offer a false explanation of his conduct which is later disproved, which suggests a guilty intent to deceive the police and the court. Or the statement may bear such a close relationship to statements made by other suspects that it suggests a premeditated plan to present a concerted false defence. In these cases, the statement may be admitted for the non-hearsay purpose of proving the accused's state of mind. It is suggested, however, that even in these cases, the statement is still a confession within the meaning of s. 76 of the Police and Criminal Evidence Act 1984 (see 9.5.1) and should not be admitted unless the circumstances in which it was obtained do not require its exclusion under the rules of admissibility laid down by s. 76 or the power to exclude under s. 78 of the Act.

In *Jones* v *Director of Public Prosecutions* [1962] AC 635, the facts of which were given at 6.10.5, the prosecution were able to make use of a false alibi given by the accused, and to show that it bore a striking resemblance to an alibi which he had attempted unsuccessfully to assert in an earlier, unrelated case. The facts suggested that the kind of explanation of his conduct the accused had attempted to advance was one he had invented in response to being accused of a serious offence, and its repetition showed that it was a standard story he was disposed to tell when he was not disposed to tell the truth about his involvement in an offence. However, this inference could be drawn only because of the strikingly similar nature of the two alibis, and it was this similarity which was primarily relevant.

In *Khan* v *R* [1967] 1 AC 454, the accused were charged with the murder of another man on a certain day, and it was alleged that they had been injured in the course of the murder. Each made a statement to the police, independently of the other, giving an identical alibi, according to

---

[52] It was held alternatively that even if the statement made by the wife was hearsay, it was admissible under the *res gestae* principle: see 8.5.

which they had been together at a club and had sustained their injuries in the course of fighting each other there. Neither accused gave evidence at the trial, and they subsequently appealed on the ground that the trial judge had invited the jury to view the statements as evidence against both of them, if satisfied that they were fabrications. This would have been a clearly erroneous direction if the prosecution had tendered the statements as confessions, asserting and relying on their truth, because in such a case a statement is evidence only against the maker, and not against anyone else affected by its contents.[53] If the statements in this case were hearsay and admissible only as confessions, therefore, the trial judge was guilty of a serious misdirection. The Privy Council, upholding the majority view of the Supreme Court of Hong Kong, held that the statements were not hearsay. The trial judge had directed the jury as follows:

> The Crown's case here is not that these statements are true and that what one says ought to be considered as evidence of what actually happened. What the Crown say is that these statements have been shown to be a tissue of lies and that they disclose an attempt to fabricate a joint story. Now . . . if you come to that conclusion then the fabrication of a joint story would be evidence against both. It would be evidence that they had cooperated after the alleged crime.

Holding this direction to be a proper one, Lord Hodson said (*ibid.* at 462):

> Their Lordships agree with Hogan CJ and Rigby AJ in accepting the generality of the proposition maintained by the text writers and to be found in *Subramaniam's* case that a statement is not hearsay and is admissible when it is proposed to establish by the evidence, not the truth of the statement, but the fact that it was made. Not only therefore can the statements of each appellant be used against each appellant individually . . . but they can without any breach of the hearsay rule be used, not for the purpose of establishing the truth of the assertions contained therein, but for the purpose of asking the jury to hold the assertions false and to draw inferences from their falsity.
>
> The statements were relevant as tending to show that the makers were acting in concert and that such action indicated a common guilt.

What was of relevance to the issue was not the truth of any fact actually contained in either statement, but the fact that two statements had been made, apparently independently of each other, but asserting in detail the same innocent account of the matter. If the jury rejected this account, having heard the whole of the evidence, then it was relevant for them to consider the implications of having before them two statements, obviously fabricated as part of a prearranged plan, and to draw inferences about the guilt of the accused.

7.14 STATEMENT AS CIRCUMSTANTIAL EVIDENCE OF OTHER RELEVANT FACTS

By far the most difficult problems in distinguishing between hearsay and non-hearsay evidence are to be found in cases in which the statement is said to be relevant to a fact in issue other than state of mind. Some very close distinctions have been made by the courts, which are by no means beyond criticism. It is necessary, by way of introduction, to appreciate that the courts have been anxious to limit the exclusionary effects of the common law rule against hearsay. It was not until the decision in *Myers v DPP* [1965] AC 1001 (see 7.3) that the true scale of the need for legislative

---

[53] See 9.16.1. The statements could be said to be evidence 'against' the accused only in so far as the jury rejected them as statements of truth. As they were entirely self-serving, they could otherwise have no evidential value in a case where the makers did not give evidence. Where a jury conclude that the accused has deliberately lied in order to seek to exculpate himself, they are entitled to draw adverse inferences from that conclusion.

reform became fully apparent. Before that time, the courts had wrestled valiantly with the common law exceptions to the rule against hearsay, and had attempted to use the concept of circumstantial evidence to circumvent the most restrictive effects of the rule. In many cases, the courts admitted statements as circumstantial evidence of facts, to which the state of mind of the maker of the statement bore no obvious relevance. In such cases, it was difficult to see how the statement could have any relevance to the facts in issue, except on the basis of at least a tacit assumption that some facts stated were true. In many cases, the need for such artificial reasoning has now been removed by statutory reform, under the Civil Evidence Act 1995, the Police and Criminal Evidence Act 1984, and the Criminal Justice Act 2003, but once again, the common law position remains of importance in criminal cases.

7.14.1 Statements as evidence of the existence of a state of affairs

Not all cases where a statement is offered as circumstantial evidence present difficulties. Just as there are cases in which a statement may itself constitute a criminal or tortious act, so a statement may be clear circumstantial evidence that such an act has occurred or is occurring. An excellent illustration is *Woodhouse v Hall*,[54] in which the Divisional Court held that evidence of conversations that allegedly took place between police officers and women working in a massage parlour, in which details of the availability and cost of sexual services were discussed, was admissible as non-hearsay, circumstantial evidence that the premises were being operated as a brothel. The very fact that such statements were made was evidence from which the justices could draw that inference, and there was no question of the statements being used to prove the truth of facts stated.

Delivering the judgment of the Court, Donaldson LJ said (*ibid.* at 42):

> We have been referred to *Ratten v R.*...[1972] AC 378, a Privy Council case, but one which reflects English law. For my part I think it is sufficient to refer to a short passage in the opinion of the Board which was delivered by Lord Wilberforce...: 'The mere fact that evidence of a witness includes evidence as to words spoken by another person who is not called, is no objection to its admissibility. Words spoken are facts just as much as any other action by a human being. If the speaking of words is a relevant fact, a witness may give evidence that they were spoken. A question of hearsay only arises when the words spoken are relied on "testimonially", i.e., as establishing some fact narrated by the words...'
>
> There is no question here of the hearsay rule arising at all. The relevant issue was, did these ladies make these offers? The offers were oral and the police officers were entitled to give evidence of them. The evidence, in my judgment, was wrongly excluded and should have been admitted.[55]

Woodhouse v Hall was, however, distinguished in two subsequent cases, *Harry* (1986) 86 Cr App R 105 and *Kearley* [1992] 2 AC 228. In both cases, police officers arrested accused who were suspected of supplying drugs from certain premises, and thereafter intercepted telephone calls made to those premises by persons apparently interested in buying drugs. The accused were not present when the telephone calls were received. In *Harry*, the accused (H) sought to adduce evidence that the callers had asked for his co-accused (P) in order to suggest that P and not H, was the dealer. In *Kearley*, the prosecution sought to adduce the evidence in order to prove both that K was a dealer and that K's premises were being used for the supply of drugs. In *Harry* the Court of Appeal held that the proposed evidence was hearsay, because it was being offered to prove the truth of facts

---

[54] (1980) 72 Cr App R 39; cf. *Roberts v DPP* [1994] Crim LR 926.
[55] The use made of the statement in *Ratten* as non-hearsay evidence is considered in 7.13.3.

asserted by the callers. In *Kearley* the Court of Appeal ((1990) 93 Cr App R 222) reached a different result, holding (following *Woodhouse* v *Hall*) that because the evidence was admissible to prove the use being made of the premises (which was not in dispute in *Harry*) in addition to the identity of the supplier, it was admissible for the non-hearsay purpose of proving what activities were being carried on in the premises.

This distinction appears less than convincing, and was rejected on appeal in *Kearley* by a majority of the House of Lords (Lords Bridge of Harwich, Ackner, and Oliver of Aylmerton; Lords Griffith and Browne-Wilkinson dissenting) ([1992] 2 AC 228). The majority held that the evidence tendered was arguably irrelevant to prove that K was supplying drugs. At best, it tended to show that the callers believed that drugs were being supplied by K or at his home. Even if relevant, the majority held that the evidence of the calls was hearsay; that the case was distinguishable from *Ratten*, because the telephone call in *Ratten* was relevant to the defence of accident, showing as it did the wife's state of mind at the time of the shooting, and was part of the *res gestae* of the offence; and that the use of the telephone calls in *Kearley* offended against the rule excluding implied hearsay statements laid down in *Wright* v *Doe d Tatham* (1837) 7 Ad & El 313.

Whatever the merits of the decisions in *Kearly* and *Harry*, the issue has now been laid to rest by s. 115(2) and (3) of the Criminal Justice Act 2003 (see 7.1) and the decision of the Court of Appeal in *Sukadeve Singh* [2006] 1 WLR 1564. These subsections adopt a definition of hearsay covering only cases in which a statement is a deliberate representation of the matter stated, in the sense that the maker of the statement intended to cause another person to believe the matter stated. Where the purpose of adducing the evidence is to invite an inference as to a matter thought to be implied in the statement, but it is a matter which the maker did not intend to convey, the statement is not hearsay for the purposes of the Act. This has the effect of reversing the rule in *Wright* v *Doe d Tatham*: see 7.15.1. Thus, the principle stated in *Woodhouse* v *Hall* remains valid, and such statements can be used as non-hearsay evidence to prove the existence of a state of affairs to which they are relevant.

7.14.2 Statements as evidence of identity or origin

An important and vexed question is whether or not the identity or origin of a person or a thing may be proved by the existence of a written piece of identification, for example a ticket or label, or other writing bearing a name or identifying markings. In these cases, it is often permissible to doubt whether the document concerned makes any 'statement' about identity, though the act of attaching a label or any similarly deliberate piece of identification to an object probably amounts to a statement. In reality, these materials have both hearsay and non-hearsay components, and no absolutely satisfactory theoretical resolution of the problem can be achieved.

An excellent illustration of the difficulties is the decision of the Court of Criminal Appeal in *Rice* [1963] 1 QB 857. On a charge of conspiracy, part of the prosecution case against Rice was that he had taken a flight to Manchester on or about a certain date, in the company of a co-accused, Hoather. This was denied. The prosecution produced an airline ticket to Manchester in respect of a date at about the relevant time, affording two seats in the names of Rice and Moore (another co-accused). The prosecution suggested that Hoather flew in place of Moore. The ticket was put to Rice in cross-examination, and, he having denied all knowledge of it, it was exhibited and shown to the jury. On appeal it was argued, understandably, that the ticket could have been tendered for no purpose except that of suggesting to the jury that it was evidence of the fact that Rice had flown to Manchester on the day shown, and that it was accordingly hearsay and had been wrongly admitted. The Court rejected the argument on the basis that the ticket was relevant and admissible circumstantial evidence on the issue of whether Rice had flown to Manchester. The following passages are taken from the judgment of the Court delivered by Winn J (*ibid.* at 872–3):

> The court thinks that it would have been more accurate had the recorder said that the production of the ticket from the place where used tickets would properly be kept was a fact from which the jury might infer that probably two people had flown on the particular flight and that it might or might not seem to them by applying their common knowledge of such matters that the passengers bore the surnames which were written on the ticket.
>
> It is plain that the latter inference was not one to be readily accepted in a case where it was not suggested that [the appellant] Moore, whose name was on the ticket, had actually flown; indeed it is obvious that *pro tanto* the potential inference was excluded. Nevertheless it remained open for partial acceptance in respect of [the appellant] Rice . . .
>
> So far as Rice was concerned the ticket was treated differently and assumed importance from the direction given that the jury might, if they saw fit, regard it as corroboration of Hoather's evidence that Rice flew with him to Manchester and that Rice booked the ticket . . .
>
> The court finds no misdirection in that passage . . .
>
> The court doubts whether the air ticket could constitute admissible evidence that the booking was effected either by Rice or even by any man of that name but it does not think that for relevant purposes the distinction between the booking of the ticket and the use of it was material with regard either to the case against Rice or to his defence.

It is apparent from the above passages that the Court appreciated the difficulty which was eventually conceded by the House of Lords in *Myers* v *DPP* [1965] AC 1001, that a strict application of the rule against hearsay would artificially deprive the courts of much valuable evidence. In many cases, such evidence would now be admissible under s. 117 of the Criminal Justice Act 2003, but the underlying problem remains. The solution adopted by Winn J in *Rice* is that the mere existence of the ticket in that form, including the name 'Rice', was non-hearsay, circumstantial evidence that someone using the name Rice flew to Manchester on the relevant day, and therefore also of the fact that the accused Rice had done so. Of course, this is true only on the assumption that the statement made by the ticket is true. This is no doubt why, in *Myers*, the reasoning in *Rice* found only limited support in the Court of Appeal and the House of Lords.[56]

It is submitted that, because no ideal solution to the problem can be found, the courts are free to balance or choose between the hearsay and non-hearsay components of such pieces of evidence. *Myers* suggests that the hearsay component should prevail, and that it is for the legislature, and not the courts, to formulate new exceptions to the rule against hearsay. The latter proposition is undoubtedly true, and we have noted that Parliament has provided statutory exceptions in response to that decision. It is also true that other cases have stressed the hearsay nature of such evidence of identification, for example those dealing with attempts to prove the origin of goods by reference to stamps or marks purporting to record this.[57] However, nothing in *Myers* prevents

---

[56] See [1965] AC 1001, per Widgery J at 1007–8, Lord Pearce at 1044, Lord Donovan at 1048, all of whom saw *Myers* and *Rice* as involving essentially the same problem. Effectively, the solution adopted in *Rice* makes the ticket into a piece of real evidence, from which the court can draw conclusions by using its senses: see the not dissimilar reasoning of Sir Jocelyn Simon P in *The Statue of Liberty* [1968] 1 WLR 739, and generally 19.22; and see 7.15.3.

[57] See, e.g., *Comptroller of Customs* v *Western Lectric Co. Ltd* [1966] AC 367; *Patel* v *Comptroller of Customs* [1966] AC 356. But contrast *United States* v *Snow* 517 F 2d 441 (9th Cir, 1975) (tag on briefcase seized at airport, which bore the name of the accused, 'Bill Snow', admitted as circumstantial evidence of the accused's possession of

the courts from admitting non-hearsay evidence, and the real question is whether evidence such as the *Rice* ticket may be so described.

The trend is now to favour the non-hearsay, circumstantial nature of such identifying evidence, and this seems consistent with the breadth of the present statutory exceptions permitting the adduction of documentary hearsay evidence of the kinds rejected in the earlier cases. Even as long ago as *Podmore* (1930) 22 Cr App R 36, it was held that the finding of a document partly in the handwriting of the deceased was admissible, non-hearsay, circumstantial evidence that a generally dishonest relationship existed between the deceased and the accused. The precise nature of the relationship was immaterial, and the mere existence of the document at the place where it was found sufficed, without consideration of its detailed contents, as to which a hearsay problem might have arisen. In *Lydon* (1986) 85 Cr App R 221, it was held that two pieces of paper bearing the name 'Sean' (the accused's first name) found near a gun used in the robbery with which the accused was charged, was admissible evidence to link the accused with the gun, in a case where the accused put forward an alibi. The case bears an obvious similarity to *Rice* and the American cases of *Snow* and *Liebermann* referred to in note 57, and it is submitted that it was rightly decided. Although it might be argued that the writing on the paper had a certain hearsay quality, it is not easy to define what statement, if any, it could be said to make (the writing was 'Sean rules' and 'Sean rule, 85'), and the fact that it was found in the place where it was had an obvious circumstantial value in refuting the accused's claimed alibi.

7.14.3 Statements admissible as confirming other evidence

In some older cases, attempts were made to avoid the operation of the rule against hearsay by admitting evidence for the sole purpose of confirming other admissible evidence in the case. Like the identification and origin cases discussed above, there is no doubt that such statements have a hearsay component. Indeed, that component should probably be held to prevail, because it is difficult to discern in these cases how the statements admitted can have the effect of confirming anything unless it is assumed, at least tacitly, that what the makers of the statements said was true. The circumstantial effect of the making of the statement alone is of little force. Happily, the reasoning employed in these cases is now unlikely to be a necessary resort, since statute has supplied a remedy in all reasonably conceivable cases in which the problem is likely to arise. For this reason, these cases are dealt with briefly, and using selective examples.

In *Lloyd* v *Powell Duffryn Steam Coal Co. Ltd* [1914] AC 733 it was sought to show that the plaintiff and her child were dependants of a workman who had been killed, it was alleged, through the fault of the defendant. In order to show this, the plaintiff had to prove that the deceased was the father of her child, and had promised and intended to marry her. The House of Lords held that the plaintiff's evidence of paternity and of the deceased's intentions towards her could be supported by evidence of statements made by the deceased during his lifetime, which were to the effect that he regarded the plaintiff as his fiancée and the child as his. The words were held to be circumstantial evidence that the deceased believed himself to be the father of the child and that he intended to support the plaintiff and the child as his dependants. As the deceased's statements were inadmissible as statements by a person, since deceased, against his interest, they could not be evidence that the child was his, and their admissibility was, therefore, confined to support of what the plaintiff had said. But the distinction is plainly tenuous. It surely cannot be

briefcase); and *United States* v *Liebermann* 637 F 2d 95 (2d Cir, 1980) (entry in hotel registration book, correctly showing the accused's name and address and other particulars, admitted as circumstantial evidence that the accused stayed at the hotel on the relevant night).

realistically maintained that the belief or statement of the deceased could support the evidence of the plaintiff, unless at least some assumption were made that such belief or statement was the truth; the fact that the belief was held, or the statement made, taken alone, assists not at all. The same reasoning, however, was employed in *Re Jenion, Jenion v Wynne* [1952] Ch 454 where, the declarations of a deceased mother being admissible at common law (as an exception to the hearsay rule) for the purpose of proving that her children were illegitimate, the statements of the putative father that the children were his, were held admissible for the purpose, not of proving the illegitimacy, but of supporting the declarations of the mother.

7.15 THREE HEARSAY PROBLEMS

Three areas of particular difficulty were identified at common law with regard to the distinction between hearsay and non-hearsay evidence. These were unintended communications, evidence of the absence of records or information where their presence would have been of significance, and the relationship between hearsay and real evidence, with special reference to evidence produced by computers and other mechanical devices. Although statute has now provided partial solutions to the problems posed, these problems cannot be regarded as having been solved entirely. They must still be examined briefly.

7.15.1 Unintended communications

This problem, an occasionally vexatious one at common law, has been referred to in passing above, at 7.1 and 7.14.1. Although the problem has apparently been solved by statute, the factual context in which it arises can be elusive and difficult to identify. It merits a short discussion. In the context of the rule against hearsay, the phrase unintended or implied communications refers to statements which are not intended to communicate a fact, and which do not express the fact directly, but which nonetheless do suggest the fact by necessary implication. In the classic case of *Wright v Doe d Tatham* (1837) 7 Ad & El 313, the question arose whether, on the issue of the testamentary capacity of a testator, evidence could be admitted of letters written to the testator by businessmen during the relevant period of his life, which were said to be of such a nature that they would have been written only to a person in command of his mental faculties. In deciding this question, the court had two options. It was open to it to regard the evidence as hearsay, because the letters were tendered as being, in effect, statements that the testator was of sound mind, and for the purpose of proving that fact. It was also open to it to admit the letters as circumstantial evidence of the testator's testamentary capacity, because the letters might be seen as no more than a piece of evidence that the testator was, at the time he received them, conducting normal business affairs.

Parke B preferred the former option, and excluded the letters on the ground that they were hearsay if tendered for the purpose of proving the testamentary capacity of the testator.[58] He likened the case to one in which a sea captain, having inspected a vessel, embarked on it with his family, which evidence the learned Baron thought would be inadmissible on the issue of the seaworthiness of the vessel. The principle derived from this and other cases is that a statement which by implication conveys facts which it was not intended to communicate may be hearsay, if tendered for the purpose of proving the truth of those facts. In *Teper v R* [1952] AC 480, the Privy

---

[58] A further objection to the evidence was that the letters represented inadmissible opinion evidence by the authors on the issue of the testator's testamentary capacity.

Council quashed the conviction of the accused on a charge of arson of his shop, where the prosecution had been permitted, in order to contradict the accused's alibi, to adduce evidence that a woman at the scene of the blaze had been heard to shout to a passing motorist (who resembled the accused) 'your place burning down and you going away from the fire'. Although not intended as a statement of identification, the statement in fact offered evidence of identification to the tribunal of fact, and was therefore hearsay when tendered to prove that the person driving away from the scene had been the accused.

This problem has now been resolved by statute, though not as clearly or simply as one might have wished. In civil cases, by virtue of the Civil Evidence Act 1995, evidence is no longer excluded on the ground that it is hearsay (see 8.30). But the definition of hearsay provided by ss. 1(2) and 13 of the Act restricts hearsay to statements which amount to a 'representation' of fact or opinion, which seems to require the element of conscious intent to communicate the matter stated. In criminal cases, s. 115(2) and (3) of the Criminal Evidence Act 2003 are even more clear and provide unambiguously:

> (2) A statement is any representation of fact or opinion made by a person by whatever means;...
> (3) A matter stated is one to which this Chapter applies if (and only if) the purpose or one of the purposes of the person making the statement appears to the court to have been—
>   (a) to cause another person to believe the matter; or
>   (b) to cause another person to act or a machine to operate on the basis that the matter is as stated.

The provisions of both Acts might have been interpreted in either of two ways. The intention seems to be that, for the purposes of the statutes, a statement is hearsay only insofar as it is tendered to prove a matter which the maker of the statement intended to communicate. It is not hearsay with respect to a matter not intended to be communicated by the maker, which may thereafter be inferred from the statement, or may be thought to be implied by it. But there are two possible consequences of this analysis. On the one hand, it could be argued that implied statements fall outside the statutory definitions, and must therefore continue to be dealt with in accordance with the common law rule against hearsay. The statutes simply do not apply to them. At least in the case of the Civil Evidence Act 1995, however, such an interpretation would lead to an absurd result. It was the intent of the Act to abrogate the rule against hearsay in civil cases.[59] It would be odd indeed if the Act had to be interpreted as achieving that goal in the case of deliberate statements of fact, but not in the case of implied facts. An analogous argument could be made in the case of the Criminal Justice Act 2003, but in this case it is not quite so compelling. The rule against hearsay remains in existence in criminal cases. The Act's purpose is to regulate the admission of hearsay evidence in criminal cases in a comprehensive way, but it does not abrogate the rule itself. Moreover, while the definitions of hearsay in both Acts use the term 'representation', the additional definition of the term 'matter stated' in s. 115(3) of the Criminal Justice Act 2003, which does not appear in the 1995 Act, places a far stronger emphasis on the element of intentionality. Nonetheless, it would have been a remarkable result in the case of the 2003 Act also if the intended reform of the hearsay rules required implied statements to continue to be dealt with as a common law hearsay issue. On the other hand, however, it could be argued, in relation to both the 1995 and the 2003 Acts, that the exclusion of implied statements from the definition indicates an intention on the part of Parliament that such cases should no longer

---

[59] Though the 1995 Act preserves certain common law hearsay rules, as does the Criminal Justice Act 2003: Civil Evidence 1995, s. 7(2)–(4); Criminal Justice Act 2003, s. 118(1).

be regarded as hearsay at all. It seems clear that this was in fact the intent of Parliament,[60] and on this basis, *Wright* v *Doe d Tatham* should no longer represent the law. This was confirmed by the Court of Appeal in *Sukadeve Singh* [2006] 1 WLR 1564, in which information stored in the memories of mobile phones used by alleged co-conspirators about the identities and phone numbers of other co-conspirators was held to be non-hearsay and admissible circumstantial evidence, from which the jury was entitled to draw inferences about the participation of those persons in the conspiracy. Under the rule in *Wright* v *Doe d Tatham*, the evidence would have been classified as hearsay in the form of unintended communications, but the Court held, rejecting the contrary argument summarized above, that such evidence was no longer to be regarded as hearsay in view of the definitions contained in s. 115 of the Criminal Justice Act 2003. The change is a welcome one, which removes an unnecessary piece of artificiality from the law.[61]

7.15.2 Absence of record or information

The question posed here is whether a party may adduce evidence of the absence of any record or information of a fact or event, for the purpose of proving that the fact is untrue or the event did not occur, in circumstances where, if the fact were true or the event had occurred, some record or information about it would ordinarily have been compiled and maintained. The concept gives rise to a hearsay problem in the same way as would the adduction of a record to prove that the fact is true or that the event occurred, because in a sense the absence of a record is just as much a statement circumstantially relevant to the issue of the truth of the fact as the presence of a record.

In *Patel* [1981] 3 All ER 94, the accused was charged with assisting the illegal entry into the UK of one Ashraf. In order to prove that Ashraf was not a person entitled to enter the UK, the prosecution called a chief immigration officer, who testified that he had examined Home Office records, which revealed that fact. It was argued on appeal that this evidence was inadmissible, because the Home Office records were inadmissible hearsay and the immigration officer's testimony about the absence of Ashraf's name was likewise hearsay and inadmissible. The Court of Appeal accepted the submission and allowed the appeal. It was conceded that the Home Office records would have been hearsay at common law, in the light of *Myers* v *DPP*, and that they were not admissible under the then applicable Criminal Evidence Act 1965 because that Act applied only to records of a 'trade or business'.[62] This led the Court to venture the strange observation that:

> …an officer responsible for their compilation and custody should have been called to give evidence that the method of compilation and custody is such that if Ashraf's name is not there, he must be an illegal entrant. It is not suggested that [the officer actually called] is such an officer.

---

[60] In *Sukadeve Singh* [2006] 1 WLR 1564, [14] , Rose LJ appears to suggest that this is so clear from ss. 114 and 118 of the Act as to foreclose any ambiguity, but with respect, those sections do not resolve the difficulty in themselves, because both are dependent on the interpretation of the definitions in s. 115. See the discussion in Cross and Tapper, *Evidence*, 11th edn, pp. 625 *et seq.*, 643 *et seq.*

[61] *Wright* has caused dissension in other common law jurisdictions. In the United States, there is a lively division of opinion between jurisdictions, some of which follow and some of which reject the rule laid down in the case. The trend, as exemplified by the Federal Rules of Evidence, is away from *Wright*, though it has some way to go. Federal Rule of Evidence 801(a) defines 'statement' as '(1) an oral or written assertion or (2) non-verbal conduct of a person, if it is intended by the person as an assertion'. The word 'assertion' indicates an intent to communicate.

[62] The same records would now be admissible under s. 117 of the Criminal Justice Act 2003. However, this would not necessarily resolve the problem—see the comments on the later case of *Shone* in the text.

With respect, it is not clear why this would have made any difference, unless the officer called had some actual personal knowledge about Ashraf. Even had such an officer testified about the method of compilation, the conclusion that Ashraf was an illegal entrant could be reached only on the assumption that the absence of his name accurately reflected his status, or in other words that the information suggested by the absence of the record was true. If the court was inclined to treat the evidence as hearsay, rather than as circumstantial evidence, it is submitted that the evidence suggested by the court would not have cured the defect.[63]

However, the Court's observation had an effect on the subsequent Court of Appeal which considered *Shone* (1982) 76 Cr App R 72. The accused was charged with dishonestly handling stolen goods, namely three vehicle springs. The springs were found on the accused's premises and were subsequently identified as having been supplied by the manufacturer to the company from which they were stolen. The prosecution called the stock clerk and parts sales manager of the company. The effect of their testimony was that the receipt, sale, and use of all parts in the company's possession were recorded in the company's records, and that there was no record of the sale or use of the springs in question. From this evidence, the jury were invited to infer that the springs had left the company's premises through theft. The Court dismissed an appeal against conviction based in part on a submission that the evidence of the absence of records was hearsay. The Court noted the comments of the court in *Patel*, and held that the witnesses called by the prosecution had complied with the requirement of testifying about the method of compilation. As the records in *Shone* were, unlike those in *Patel*, admissible by virtue of the Criminal Evidence Act 1965, the court could presumably have held that the evidence of the absence of a record was admissible despite its hearsay character. However, the court took the different view that the absence of record indicating the sale or use of the springs was non-hearsay, circumstantial evidence, from which the jury were entitled to draw the inference that the springs had been stolen.

This question cannot be resolved simply by reference to statutory provisions which render the records themselves admissible. Business and similar records are now admissible both in civil and criminal cases. Section 9(3) of the Civil Evidence Act 1995 provides specifically that the absence of an entry in the records of a business or public authority may be proved in civil proceedings by the affidavit of an officer of the business or authority to which the records belong. But this does not resolve the evidential status of the absence of entry, once proved to exist, which is a separate hearsay issue.[64] In civil cases evidence is no longer excluded on the ground that it is hearsay (Civil Evidence Act 1995, s. 1; 8.30), so it seems clear that the court may simply draw such inference from the absence of entry as appears to be warranted. In criminal cases, there is no provision equivalent to s. 9(3) of the 1995 Act, and even if there were, the hearsay problem would remain. Section 117 of the Criminal Justice Act 2003 provides for the admission of business and similar records, but does not address this issue. It might be possible to infer from s. 115(2) and (3) of the Act (see 7.15.1) that an absence of entry is no longer hearsay because it cannot be regarded as a

---

[63] For a further example of this kind of error, leading to an improper admission of hearsay, see *Muir* (1983) 79 Cr App R 153, in which a district manager was permitted to give evidence that his head office had not re-possessed a video recorder which the accused was charged with stealing, even though the manager had no personal knowledge of the activities of the head office, and was simply repeating what he had been told.

[64] This is clearly recognized in American jurisdictions, which generally espouse two separate hearsay exceptions, one to admit business and similar records for the purpose of proving the existence or occurrence of matters stated in them, and a second to admit, subject to the same conditions, the absence from such a record of a matter which would ordinarily be expected to appear in the record, for the purpose of proving that the matter does not exist or did not occur. See, e.g., Federal Rule of Evidence 803(6) and (7).

statement made with the purpose of causing another person to believe a matter stated. But such a solution is hardly satisfactory; in many cases, an absence of entry is deliberate and intended to communicate information just as much as a positive entry. Moreover, there would be a technical question as to whether the evidence should be regarded as an example of multiple hearsay, and should be admitted only subject to the additional requirements of s. 121 of the Act (see 7.6.3). Until the question is resolved either by statute or judicial decision, the evidential status of the absence of entries in a record remains unclear. It is submitted that the best solution would be to declare the absence of entry to be a piece of non-hearsay evidence from which the finder of fact can draw such inferences as may appear warranted, as is the position in civil cases. To regard such evidence as hearsay seems unnecessarily anachronistic.

7.15.3 Hearsay and real evidence

Real evidence is evidence of a tangible nature from which the tribunal of fact can derive information using its own senses: see generally Part B of Chapter 19. This information results in direct or circumstantial evidence of relevant facts, for example where the court is presented with a photograph or tape-recording, from which direct evidence can be derived or inferences drawn about relevant facts depicted therein. An uncomfortable interface exists between real evidence and the rule against hearsay, particularly where the real evidence is produced by a mechanical device, be that device a clock, an automatic traffic signal, a radar device, or a computer. As technology has produced ever more efficient machines, so the problem has intensified. So far as mechanical devices other than computers are concerned, readings and other information produced by a mechanical device are now admitted at common law as real evidence, provided that the device is shown to have been working properly or to have been accurate on the relevant occasion. The proponent of the evidence is aided in this regard by a presumption that the device was functioning correctly (see 20.14.2).

In *Minors*,[65] a distinction was drawn between cases in which a computer is used essentially as a calculator, making calculations or performing functions without human intervention which can then be printed out, and cases in which statements containing information are produced by human authors using the computer as a tool for writing. It was held that in the former case, there is no hearsay issue, and the printouts of the computer's activity are admissible, essentially as a species of real evidence. This approach seems sensible, and agrees with reasoning of Sir Jocelyn Simon P in *The Statue of Liberty* [1968] 1 WLR 639, in which he held, following common law principles, that the automatic record of the movements of ships produced by a radar set at a shore radio station was admissible to prove what the movement of the ships had been. In *Castle v Cross* [1984] 1 WLR 1372, it was held that the printout of an Intoximeter machine, used to analyse specimens of breath, was non-hearsay and admissible. This decision was confirmed by the House of Lords in *DPP v McKeown* [1997] 1 WLR 295. Conversely, however, where a person makes a statement using a computer as a writing tool, the same hearsay issues arise as in a case where that person makes a statement by any other means. The position in these cases is considered at 8.29. This view is apparently supported by s. 129 of the Criminal Justice Act 2003, dealt with in the same place.

---

[65] [1989] 1 WLR 441, following *Wood* (1982) 76 Cr App R 23; and see *Coventry Justices, ex parte Bullard* (1992) 95 Cr App R 175.

7.16 PRACTICAL CONSIDERATIONS: AVOIDANCE AND EVASION

The rule against hearsay often produces a sense of frustration in practitioners and witnesses because of the exclusion of relevant and cogent evidence. This frustration has led to the widespread use of devices, some legitimate others less so, designed to avoid or evade the rule. The ideal avoidance is, of course, to call percipient evidence of the fact or event to be proved, from a witness who perceived it. But such evidence is not always available. A witness can, of course, be asked to say, answering merely yes or no, whether he had a conversation with someone or looked at some document, but such evidence is usually neither very relevant nor very useful. In practice, devices are habitually tolerated which necessarily involve the tacit assertion by a witness of what he has been told by another, but which give meaning and sequence to his evidence of what he himself saw or did. The classic instance is the evidence of a police officer, beginning with the words, 'acting on information received'. Of course, the jury are bound to realize that there is a connection between what the officer was told, and the inquiries he thereafter made, and in many cases it will inevitably appear that the officer was told something about the accused. But in practice, there can really be little objection; no jury is likely to think that the officer commenced his inquiries through some telepathy or divine revelation, and in many cases if the information seems to have been inaccurate, it may actually assist the defence. Certainly, the jury are unlikely to give any weight at all to a communication whose details are unknown, made by someone about whom they are told nothing.[66]

There are, however, other devices which are less harmless, which have been deprecated by the appellate courts, but which continue to enjoy a surprising degree of liberty in practice. They may be illustrated by the following examples:

(a) On a charge of theft:
     Q. Did you have a conversation with X?
     A. Yes.
     Q. Then what did you do?
     A. As a result of that conversation, I arrested the accused for theft.
(b) On a charge of obtaining by false pretences (taken from *Saunders* [1899] 1 QB 490):
     Q. Did you make inquiries as to whether any trade had been done by the prisoners?
     A. I did.
     Q. Did you as the result of such inquiries find that any had been done?
     A. I did not.

Both passages are technically objectionable because, although neither reveals the exact terms of the conversation or enquiry which took place, each reveals the substance of it by necessary implication. In each case, the first question and answer is undoubtedly admissible, so far as it goes. But at the stage of the second question and answer, it may be that the two diverge. In the first example, the passage may perhaps be justified as a slight extension of the 'acting on information received' sequence, whose dangers are more formidable in theory than in practice; the jury may simply think that the officer should have made further inquiries by questioning the accused.

---

[66] But *quaere* whether the relaxation should be permitted further than really necessary to account for what is subsequently done. Should, for instance, 'as a result of an emergency call' be allowed?

But in the second, the passage is a naked evasion of the rule, in that the witness is being asked, in effect to relate the substance of what he was told, even though the question is framed so as to seem to ask him what he did.

Quite separate problems arise where a witness states that, having spoken to X, he said to the accused, 'X tells me that you have stolen his property. What do you say?' If the accused adopts the truth of what X has said, by admitting his guilt, then all is well: his admission will be evidence against him. But if he denies it, or refuses to answer, the admissibility of the passage can be a difficult matter, which is explored in Chapter 10. It is certain, however, that the witness's assertion of what X said is not evidence against the accused in and of itself.

The lesson to be learnt from these examples is that it is the actual effect and not the form of the question and answer which matters, and that one has to look at the whole passage in order to gauge this, and not just at individual questions and answers. Evidence is not admissible if it in fact consists of hearsay, whether or not a question seems to be framed so as to deal with evidence of what the witness perceived or did. In the analogous context of privilege, the use of such devices was criticized by Lord Devlin in *Glinski v McIver* [1962] AC 726, 780, in the following terms:

> But it was thought...that privilege would be claimed....So the customary devices were employed which are popularly supposed, though I do not understand why, to evade objections of inadmissibility based on hearsay or privilege or the like. The first consists in not asking what was said in a conversation or written in a document but in asking what the conversation or document was about; it is apparently thought that what would be objectionable if fully exposed is permissible if decently veiled....The other device is to ask by means of 'Yes' or 'No' questions what was done. (Just answer 'Yes' or 'No': Did you go to see counsel? Do not tell us what he said but as a result of it did you do something? What did you do?) This device is commonly defended on the ground that counsel is asking only about what was done and not about what was said. But in truth what was done is relevant only because from it there can be inferred something about what was said. Such evidence seems to me to be clearly objectionable. If there is nothing in it, it is irrelevant; if there is something in it, what there is in it is inadmissible.

This deprecation notwithstanding, in practice witnesses continue to be permitted to state that they had conversations with others and that as a result of such conversations, took certain steps or acted in certain ways, and it may be that in most cases, no or little harm can result, while the evidence is made easier for the jury to follow. The judge has ample power to intervene in a case where harm may be done.

7.17 RECOMMENDED FURTHER READING

Cross, R., 'The scope of the rule against hearsay' (1956) **72** *Law Quarterly Review* 91.

Jackson, J.D., 'Hearsay: the sacred cow that won't be slaughtered?' (1998) **4**(2) *International Journal of Evidence and Proof* 107.

Morgan, E., 'Hearsay dangers and the application of the hearsay concept' (1948) **62** *Harvard Law Review* 177.

Murphy, P., 'Hearsay: the road to reform' (1997) **1**(2) *International Journal of Evidence and Proof* 107.

Spencer, J.R., 'Hearsay reform: a bridge not far enough' [1996] *Criminal Law Review* 29.

Tribe, L.H., 'Triangulating hearsay' (1974) **87** *Harvard Law Review* 957.

7.18 QUESTIONS FOR DISCUSSION BASED ON *R v COKE; LITTLETON* (for case files go to the Online Resource Centre)

1. Prepare a list of pieces of prosecution evidence which might be objected to as hearsay. For the purpose of this exercise, do not consider any statement which is or may be a confession. Which of the items you have listed are hearsay? Which could be defended as being tendered for a non-hearsay purpose? (Note: do not consider at this stage whether any of the statements may be admissible, but keep your list to consider this question after studying Chapter 8.)

2. Consider specifically Exhibit GG1 (the material suspected of being in the handwriting of Coke, found in his flat by D/I Glanvil). Is this material objectionable as hearsay if tendered by the prosecution?

7.19 GENERAL QUESTIONS FOR DISCUSSION

1. Define hearsay. Is it, simply, any out-of-court statement?

2. What have been perceived to be the dangers of admitting hearsay evidence?

3. Which article of the European Convention of Human Rights is potentially applicable to hearsay evidence?

4. Which two questions help to determine whether a statement is hearsay?

5. 'This afternoon, I saw pink elephants crossing the lawn'. When would this statement count as inadmissible hearsay?

6. A complainant testifies that, while chasing him, he lost sight of his assailant but that an unidentified woman pointed him to the door of the house where the accused was found. The accused claims that it is mistaken identity. Is the complainant's evidence inadmissible hearsay?

7. What is meant by the expression 'multiple hearsay'?

8. A statement is admitted in evidence to establish the state of mind of the maker of a statement—is it inadmissible hearsay?

9. What was the principle in *Kearley* and does it remain good law?

10. The accused's name is absent from a list of wedding guests. The prosecution wants to adduce the list in order to prove that she was not a guest and obtained a meal by fraud. May it do so?

8

THE RULE AGAINST HEARSAY II: COMMON LAW AND STATUTORY EXCEPTIONS

SUMMARY OF MAIN POINTS

- In criminal cases, the Rule against Hearsay is now statutory. The Criminal Justice Act 2003 provides a self-contained code for the admission of hearsay.

- In civil cases, hearsay is no longer a bar to the admissibility of evidence by virtue of the Civil Evidence Act 1995.

8.1 INTRODUCTION

In Chapter 7, we noted that the exceptions to the rule against hearsay which grew up at common law proved inadequate to deal with demands of modern litigation. Yet statutory reform was slow to come and, until recently, limited in scope. A variety of statutes provided for the admissibility of individual kinds of documentary hearsay. The use of depositions and statements taken out of court before justices of the peace for limited evidential purposes in criminal cases was well recognized, and the Criminal Justice Act 1967 provided for the wider use of witness statements both in committal proceedings and at trial, subject, however, to the absence of objection. In civil cases, the Evidence Act 1938 made some tentative concessions to hearsay. However, these provisions, while useful, were more in the nature of responses to individual needs than systematic attempts to modernize the rules of evidence. They will not be dealt with here.

At length, the decision of the House of Lords in *Myers* v *DPP* [1965] AC 1001, confirmed what many had already sensed, namely that the time had come when the law of evidence must be adapted to fit the needs of litigation in the latter half of the twentieth century. No longer could the courts sensibly be deprived of access to manifestly reliable forms of hearsay evidence, as society's dependence on documentary records and information created by and stored in computers increased. *Myers* made it clear that the courts could or would not take responsibility for such radical changes in the law, and that reform must come from Parliament. The Criminal Evidence Act 1965 was a hastily drafted stop-gap measure which did duty valiantly for 20 years. Yet it was relatively limited in scope, providing only for the admissibility of documentary records of a trade or business, and then only when direct oral evidence of the recorded facts was unavailable for specified reasons. It encountered problems with evidence produced by or stored in machines. More comprehensive reform was advocated by the Law Reform Committee and the Criminal Law Revision Committee.[1]

8.1.1 Civil cases

The Civil Evidence Act 1968 represented a far more radical and thorough-going reform. The fact that jury trial is comparatively rare in civil cases encouraged experimentation with reform. The Act did far more than just provide exceptions to the rule against hearsay. It created a new code of evidence law for civil cases, which rendered much hearsay evidence admissible, not only documentary hearsay contained in records, but also oral and written hearsay statements and statements produced by computers. In many cases, the hearsay evidence was admissible even though the maker of the statement was available as a witness. Section 2 of the Act established a general principle that a statement, whether oral or written or otherwise, should be admissible in civil proceedings as evidence of any fact of which direct oral evidence by the maker of the statement would be admissible, were he to be called as a witness. Where the party tendering the statement proposed also to call the maker as a witness, certain restrictions applied. Section 4 rendered admissible statements contained in documents which were, or formed part of, a record, provided, firstly that the compiler of the record and any person who assisted in transmitting the facts from the supplier of the information to the compiler was acting under a duty to do so; and secondly, that the person who supplied the information contained in the record had, or may reasonably be supposed to have had, personal knowledge of that information. Section 5 provided for the admissibility of statements produced by computers.

The admissibility of evidence under the Act was circumscribed by an elaborate system of procedural safeguards, consisting of the serving of notices of intention to adduce the evidence by the proponent, and counter-notices by the opponent. The Act successfully shifted the focus from the issue of admissibility to that of weight. In cases tried by a judge sitting alone, the professional judgment of the parties' legal advisers proved to be just as effective in keeping out unreliable evidence as any rule of admissibility.[2] The Civil Evidence Act 1968 applied only to statements of fact, but the Civil Evidence Act 1972 extended the operation of the 1968 Act to statements of opinion also (see 11.1.2). In view of the success of these provisions, the Law Commission (Report 216, Cm 2321 (1993)) recommended the total abolition of the rule against hearsay in civil cases. This was achieved by the Civil Evidence Act 1995, which, with a fairly minor exception,[3] came into effect on 31 January 1997. The Civil Procedure Rules 1998 add a much-simplified framework of procedural safeguards where hearsay is admitted.

8.1.2 Criminal cases

Not until the coming into effect of the Police and Criminal Evidence Act 1984, was any broad attempt made to introduce documentary hearsay evidence into criminal cases. That Act made considerably wider provision than the Criminal Evidence Act 1965. Section 68 provided for the

---

[1] Law Reform Committee, 13th Report, paras 48–52; Criminal Law Revision Committee, 11th Report, paras 229–48.

[2] For the detail of the Civil Evidence Act 1968 and the procedural rules as to notice, see the 5th edn of this work at 10.2 *et seq.*

[3] Relating to the admissibility of the 'Ogden' actuarial tables issued by the government's Actuarial Department, and used in personal injury and fatal accident cases.

admissibility of statements contained in records without the restriction of the 1965 Act that they be the records of a trade or business. Their admissibility was subject to conditions analogous to those of s. 4 of the Civil Evidence Act 1968, requiring that the compiler of the record be acting under a duty, and that the supplier of the information have, or reasonably be supposed to have had, personal knowledge of the facts. It also required (in effect) that the supplier of the information be unavailable to give evidence, or that it would be pointless to call him as a witness. This provision was repealed and replaced by ss. 23 and 24 of the Criminal Justice Act 1988. Section 69 of the 1984 Act introduced a much simplified provision corresponding with s. 5 of the Civil Evidence Act 1968, which provided for the admissibility of statements produced by computers.

The Criminal Justice Act 1988 made broader provisions for criminal cases. Section 23 introduced for the first time a general rule that, subject to extensive safeguards, firsthand documentary hearsay should be admissible in criminal cases where, in effect, the maker of the statement is unavailable to give evidence or it would be pointless to call him as a witness. Section 24 expanded the admissibility of documentary hearsay by permitting the admission of documents created or received in the course of a trade, business, occupation, profession, or a paid or unpaid office. The requirement that such documents be, or be part of, a record, was removed, and there was no express requirement that the creator or receiver of the document acted under a duty, though the provision that it must have been created or received in the course of a trade, business, etc. had a similar effect. Nor was there any longer a general requirement that the person who supplied the information be effectively unavailable to give oral evidence. The requirement of personal knowledge on the part of the supplier of the information was, however, preserved. There was no provision for the admissibility of oral hearsay statements. Moreover, the court was given wide powers to exclude hearsay evidence admissible under the Act, especially where the statement was made for the purposes of pending or contemplated criminal proceedings, or a criminal investigation, and had a duty to consider the exercise of those powers.

The Criminal Justice Act 2003 repeals and replaces the hearsay provisions of the Criminal Justice Act 1988 and makes the broadest provision to date for the admissibility of hearsay evidence in criminal cases. Section 114 of the Act provides that hearsay may be admitted in criminal cases only by virtue of the Act, and enumerates four categories of admissible evidence. The first category comprises evidence admissible by virtue of later provisions of the Act itself. This refers principally to ss. 116 and 117, which are essentially expanded versions of ss. 23 and 24 of the 1988 Act. The main expansion is that s. 116, dealing with the admissibility of statements made by persons not available to give evidence, applies to statements made orally; s. 23 of the 1988 Act applied only to statements contained in documents. The second category refers to common law exceptions preserved by s. 118 (see 8.1.3). The third category consists of evidence which all parties agree shall be admitted. The fourth category represents the most radical change in the law. By virtue of s. 114(1)(d) the judge may admit hearsay evidence if satisfied that it is in the interests of justice to do so. This power is clearly potentially very wide, but is circumscribed by s. 114(2) which provides a long list of factors designed to ensure the reliability of any evidence admitted, to which the judge is to have regard before reaching the conclusion that admission is in the interests of justice. The powers to exclude under ss. 25 and 26 of the Criminal Justice Act 1988 are replaced by several discrete safeguards, most notably a new power to stop a jury trial if hearsay evidence important to the case against the accused is admitted, but later determined to be unconvincing, and if any conviction would thereby be rendered unsafe. The only discretionary power to exclude created in relation to hearsay is a novel and ostensibly pointless provision to exclude in the interests of saving time (s. 126(1)) though s. 126(2) expressly preserves the application of

s. 78 of the Police and Criminal Evidence Act 1984 to the hearsay provisions of the Act. The Act also includes a statutory rule dealing with multiple hearsay (s. 121), and provisions for inquiring into the competence of the maker of an admissible hearsay statement (s. 123). The hearsay provisions of the Act apply to all trials commencing on or after 4 April 2005.

8.1.3 Preserved common law exceptions

Both s. 7 of the Civil Evidence Act 1995 and s. 118(1) of the Criminal Justice Act 2003 preserve without altering in substance certain common law exceptions to the rule against hearsay. These exceptions now operate as part of the statutory framework, although they retain their common law character and are applied as before. The Civil Evidence Act 1995 effectively abolishes the rule against hearsay in civil cases, while s. 118(2) of the Criminal Justice Act 2003 abolishes any common law exceptions not preserved by s. 118(1). Thus, all the extant exceptions to the rule against hearsay now technically have statutory effect, though to distinguish the rules preserved, we will refer to them as preserved common law exceptions. The only important common law exceptions which did not survive s. 118(1) of the Criminal Justice Act 2003 are the group comprising statements by persons since deceased, including statements against interest and dying declarations. Although among the common law's most romantic rules, the considerable jurisprudence they generated at common law is now only of historical interest.[4] Statements previously admissible by virtue of these exceptions may now be admissible under s. 116(2)(a) or s. 114(1)(d) of the Criminal Justice Act 2003.

A   PRESERVED COMMON LAW EXCEPTIONS

> **SUMMARY OF MAIN POINTS**
> - Both s. 7(1) of the Civil Evidence Act 1995 and s. 118(1) of the Criminal Justice Act 2003 preserve without altering a number of important common law exceptions to the Rule against Hearsay, including evidence of reputation and facts contained in public records and documents.
> - In particular, s. 118(1) of the Criminal Justice Act 2003 preserves the rules relating to confessions and the group of exceptions known collectively as *res gestae*.

8.2   INTRODUCTION

The common law exceptions preserved by s. 7 of the Civil Evidence Act 1995 and s. 118(1) of the Criminal Justice Act 2003 have, broadly speaking, two characteristics, both more compelling in some exceptions than in others. Without these characteristics, the judges would not have admitted such evidence in the face of the well-recognized dangers inherent in hearsay. The first is a justification. If the exception did not exist, it would be difficult, if possible at all, to prove certain facts. Public documents, for example, contain a multitude of facts which no person who compiles or maintains such records could possibly be expected to remember. Reputation evidence was originally and for a long period the best available substitute for records which simply

---

[4] The law relating to these exceptions can be found in the 8th edn of this work at 7.22 *et seq.*

did not exist. The former exceptions relating to statements by persons since deceased recognized the plain truth that a hearsay statement represented the only way for the court to learn what the maker of the statement had to say. These statements, and statements admitted under the *res gestae* rule, often enabled the court to reconstruct events which occurred long ago, and about which there was no other extant evidence. The second characteristic is some degree of assurance that the evidence being admitted could be regarded as reliable. In the case of public documents, the fact that the documents were created and maintained for public reference by public officials acting under a duty to do so, and who had no motive to fabricate information, provided such an assurance. In the case of the *res gestae* rule, there is the sometimes less than compelling consideration of the spontaneity and contemporaneity of the statement. Reputation evidence depends on the fact that it is an amalgamation of many individual opinions, a form of safety in numbers. As we shall see, statutory exceptions too have their justifications (today, usually the simple desire to make as much relevant evidence available as is reasonably possible) and their elaborate safeguards in search of the elusive factor of reliability. Today, we seek reliability, not only in the case of various kinds of evidence generically, but also in the case of the specific pieces of evidence actually adduced. The ultimate safeguard is the discretion of the judge to ensure the fairness of the trial by excluding technically admissible evidence when it appears necessary to do so.

When evidence is adduced by virtue of any exception to the rule against hearsay, it is adduced as evidence of the truth of the matters stated, i.e., for the purpose for which it would have been excluded but for the exception.

Section 7 of the Civil Evidence Act 1995 provides:

(1) The common law rule effectively preserved by section 9(1) and (2)(a) of the Civil Evidence Act 1968 (admissibility of admissions adverse to a party) is superseded by the provisions of this Act.

(2) The common law rules effectively preserved by section 9(1) and (2)(b) to (d) of the Civil Evidence Act 1968, that is, any rule of law whereby in civil proceedings—

    (a) published works dealing with matters of a public nature (for example, histories, scientific works, dictionaries and maps) are admissible as evidence of facts of a public nature stated in them,

    (b) public documents (for example, public registers, and returns made under public authority with respect to matters of public interest) are admissible as evidence of facts stated in them, or

    (c) records (for example, the records of certain courts, treaties, Crown grants, pardons and commissions) are admissible as evidence of facts stated in them,

shall continue to have effect.

(3) The common law rules effectively preserved by section 9(3) and (4) of the Civil Evidence Act 1968, that is, any rule of law whereby in civil proceedings—

    (a) evidence of person's reputation is admissible for the purpose of proving his good or bad character, or

    (b) evidence of reputation or family tradition is admissible—

        (i) for the purpose of proving or disproving pedigree or the existence of a marriage,[5] or

        (ii) for the purpose of proving or disproving the existence of any public or general right or identifying any person or thing,

shall continue to have effect in so far as they authorize the court to treat such evidence as proving or disproving that matter.

---

[5] By virtue of s. 84(5) of the Civil Partnership Act 2004, this rule applies to proof of a civil partnership as it does to proof of a marriage.

Where any such rule applies, reputation or family tradition shall be treated for the purpose of this Act as a fact and not as a statement or multiplicity of statements about the matter in question.

(4) The words in which a rule of law mentioned in this section is described are intended only to identify the rule and shall not be construed as altering it in any way.

Section 118 of the Criminal Justice Act 2003 provides:

118—(1) The following rules of law are preserved.

Public information etc

1 Any rule of law under which in criminal proceedings—

    (a) Published works dealing with matters of a public nature (such as histories, scientific works, dictionaries and maps) are admissible as evidence of facts of a public nature stated in them,

    (b) public documents (such as public registers, and returns made under public authority with respect to matters of public interest) are admissible as evidence of facts stated in them,

    (c) records (such as the records of certain courts, treaties, Crown grants, pardons and commissions) are admissible as evidence of facts stated in them, or

    (d) evidence relating to a person's age or date or place of birth may be given by a person without personal knowledge of the matter.

Reputation as to character

2 Any rule of law under which in criminal proceedings evidence of a person's reputation is admissible for the purpose of proving his good or bad character.

Note

The rule is preserved only so far as it allows the court to treat such evidence as proving the matter concerned.

Reputation or family tradition

3 Any rule of law under which in criminal proceedings evidence of reputation or family tradition is admissible for the purpose of proving or disproving—

    (a) pedigree or the existence of a marriage,[6]

    (b) the existence of any public or general right, or

    (c) The identity of any person or thing.

Note

The rule is preserved only so far as it allows the court to treat such evidence as proving or disproving the matter concerned.

Res gestae

4 Any rule of law under which in criminal proceedings a statement is admissible as evidence of any matter stated if—

    (a) the statement was made by a person so emotionally overpowered by an event that the possibility of concoction or distortion can be disregarded,

    (b) the statement accompanied an act which can be properly evaluated as evidence only if considered in conjunction with the statement, or

    (c) the statement relates to a physical sensation or a mental state (such as intention or emotion).

---

[6] By virtue of s. 84(5) of the Civil Partnership Act 2004, this rule also applies to proof of a civil partnership as it does to proof of a marriage.

Confessions etc

5 Any rule of law relating to the admissibility of confessions or mixed statements in criminal proceedings.

Admissions by agents etc

6 Any rule of law under which in criminal proceedings—

(a) an admission made by an agent of a defendant is admissible against the defendant as evidence of any matter stated, or

(b) a statement made by a person to whom a defendant refers a person for information is admissible against the defendant as evidence of any matter stated.

Common enterprise

7 Any rule of law under which in criminal proceedings a statement made by a party to a common enterprise is admissible against another party to the enterprise as evidence of any matter stated.

Expert evidence

8 Any rule of law under which in criminal proceedings an expert witness may draw on the body of expertise relevant to his field.

(2) With the exception of the rules preserved by this section, the common law rules governing the admissibility of hearsay evidence in criminal proceedings are abolished.

8.3 THE *RES GESTAE* PRINCIPLE

The actual expression 'res gestae' is probably best ignored, save for the amusement it has afforded to writers and judges. It is a piece of grammatical nonsense, in that if the phrase is to be employed at all, it should certainly appear, not in its plural form, but in the singular '*pars rei gestae*'. It has been unkindly but aptly demystified by Lord Wilberforce, who said that 'the expression "res gestae", like many Latin phrases, is often used to cover situations insufficiently analysed in clear English terms'.[7] We have already encountered the *res gestae* principle in its broader sense, i.e., the principle that events should be seen in the context of their surrounding circumstances and antecedents, and not in a factual vacuum. This indicates that evidence of other facts and events may be adduced to explain and amplify a fact, even if to some degree it is prejudicial to the party against whom it is adduced. Examples of this principle were given at 2.7. We now encounter a specific, but very important application of the *res gestae* principle, in the context of hearsay statements. In many cases, an event is ambiguous or incomplete without evidence of a contemporaneous statement made by a participant in or an observer of the event. The accompanying statement is an integral part of the event or transaction as a whole. Therefore, the statement is in the same position as the other acts or events we saw in the cases in 2.7, and may be admitted in evidence accordingly as an exception to the hearsay rule.[8] This general principle has been applied to a number of discrete factual patterns, and how these are classified is not a matter of critical importance. It is, however, usual to put them in certain categories, and those employed in

---

[7] In *Ratten v R* [1972] AC 378, 388. See generally D. Ormerod [1998] Crim LR 301; W. Nokes (1954) 70 LQR 370; E. Gooderson [1956] CLJ 199, [1957] CLJ 55.

[8] Despite a few *dicta* to the contrary (see, e.g., *Christie* [1914] AC 545, 553 per Lord Atkinson) it is generally accepted that the evidential value of the statement is not simply to explain the accompanying act. The statement is admissible as evidence of the truth of the matter stated in its own right.

this work follow the description of the rule in s. 118(1) of the Criminal Justice Act 2003.[9] What is more significant is to observe the common thread which runs through all these cases, which was well expressed by Grove J in *Howe* v *Malkin* (1878) 40 LT 196: 'Though you cannot give in evidence a declaration *per se*, yet when there is an act accompanied by a statement which is so mixed up with it as to become party of the *res gestae*, evidence of such a statement may be given'. There is no rule that a statement cannot be admitted under the *res gestae* principle where the maker of the statement is available to give evidence, and the statement may have evidential value both as evidence of the truth of the matters stated and to show its consistency with the witness's evidence. In *Fowkes* (1856) *The Times*, 8 March 1856, a witness was allowed to give evidence that, on seeing what he believed to be the face of the accused at the window through which the shot that killed the victim had been fired, he exclaimed 'there's Butcher', 'Butcher' being the name by which the accused was generally known.[10]

8.4 *RES GESTAE*: STATEMENTS ACCOMPANYING AND EXPLAINING RELEVANT ACTS

Where the true significance of a relevant act falls to be proved, the statement of the actor on that subject may be the best evidence of it, provided that the statement is not a calculated justification, and provided that the statement actually relates and refers to the act which it is said to explain. These provisos dictate the conditions under which such cases may be brought within the rule. Firstly, the statement must be contemporaneous with the act; whether it is so is a question of fact and degree in every case, and the test seems to be whether the statement does in reality accompany and explain the act, as opposed to being no more than a subsequent justification of the act, made after reflection. Where the act is a continuing one, however, the statement may be one made during its continuance, as where the stated intentions of a bankrupt in going or remaining abroad are admitted to show his intention vis-à-vis his creditors. His intention may be equivocal at the time of his departure, and may only become apparent by his statements made while abroad.[11] Secondly, the statement must relate to the act. In *Bliss* (1837) 7 Ad & El 550, evidence that, when planting a tree, a tenant of land (since deceased) had said that the tree was being planted on the boundary of his estate, was rejected as evidence of the location of the boundary. Had the tree been planted as a deliberate act of demarcation of the boundary, the case might have been different; but the statement as an observation coincidental to any possible question of the boundary's limits at the time when it was made could not be said to explain the planting of the tree. In cases falling under this head, the statement to be admitted must be that of the actor, who alone could explain his act by direct evidence, and not the (opinion) evidence of someone who witnessed the act.

---

[9] Cf. *Evidence*, 5th edn, para. 576 *et seq.*; Cross and Tapper, *Evidence*, 11th edn, para. 606 *et seq.*

[10] See also *Attorney-General's Reference (No. 1 of 2003)* [2003] Crim LR 547. But the court should also heed the stricture of Lord Ackner in *Andrews* [1987] AC 281, 302, that any practice of using the *res gestae* rule as a device to avoid calling an available witness was to be deprecated. It may be added that this practice would have obvious implications for the fairness of the trial in the light of art. 6 of the European Convention on Human Rights unless there were good reasons for not calling the witness (see 7.5.2).

[11] See, e.g., *Rouch* v *Great Western Railway Co.* (1841) 1 QB 51.

8.5 *RES GESTAE*: STATEMENTS BY PERSONS EMOTIONALLY OVERPOWERED BY EVENTS

The common law recognized that an event might also be explained by some spontaneous state-ment in the nature of an uncalculated outburst in the heat of the moment, made by someone who either played some part in the event in question or who witnessed it. This application of the rule is known in the United States by the graphic name 'the excited utterance rule'. The obvious need in cases of this kind was for a safeguard against concoction to the advantage of the maker of the statement, and this was achieved by a rule requiring strict proof of spontaneity. The rule is one of some antiquity, as may be seen from the decision in *Thompson* v *Trevanion* (1693) Skin 402, which was an action by the plaintiff for an assault on his wife. Holt CJ held 'that what the wife said immediately upon the hurt received, and before that she had time to devise or contrive any thing for her own advantage, might be given in evidence'. The *dictum* struck exactly the right note, in stressing the rationale of the requirement of spontaneity, and it would have been as well if it had been adhered to in the spirit, rather than the letter.

But in the nineteenth century, the concept of spontaneity was carried to absurd lengths for its own sake, rather than for the purpose of ensuring the necessary degree of reliability. The most striking example of this must be the grotesque case of *Bedingfield* (1879) 14 Cox CC 341, in which evidence that the victim of an alleged murder stumbled from a room where she had been alone with the accused, her throat cut by a mortal wound, and exclaimed, 'See what Harry has done!', was rejected by Cockburn CJ, on the ground that the statement was insufficiently spontaneous. The decision in *Bedingfield* was not dictated by earlier authority. Indeed, it was plainly contrary to that in *Foster* (1834) 6 Car & P 325, in which on a charge of manslaughter by the reckless driving of a cabriolet, a statement made by the deceased after the event was admitted to prove the nature of the vehicle which had run him down. The absurdity of the decision in *Bedingfield* was realized, and it has now been overruled.

Commenting on *Bedingfield* in *Ratten* v *R*,[12] Lord Wilberforce observed that 'there could hardly be a case where the words uttered carried more clearly the mark of spontaneity and intense involvement.' The facts of *Ratten* were given in 7.13.3, when we concentrated on the primary ground of the decision of the Privy Council, that the substance of the telephone call made by the wife very shortly before her death at the hands of the accused was not hearsay, because it represented circumstantial evidence of the state of affairs then prevailing at the accused's house, and powerfully contradicted his defence of accident. But as an alternative basis for their decision, the Privy Council held that, even had the evidence of the call been hearsay, it would have been admissible by virtue of the *res gestae* principle. On a strict application of *Bedingfield*, the evidence must have been rejected, but the Privy Council did not view this approach as the correct one. Lord Wilberforce proposed a quite different test ([1972] AC 378, 389):

> The possibility of concoction, or fabrication, where it exists, is on the other hand an entirely valid reason for exclusion, and is probably the real test which judges in fact apply. In their Lordships' opinion this should be recognized and applied directly as the relevant test: the test should not be the uncertain one whether the making of the statement was in some sense part of the event or transac-tion. This may often be difficult to establish: such external matters as the time which elapses between

---

[12] [1972] AC 378, 390. *Bedingfield* had also been doubted elsewhere: see, e.g., *Taylor* (Supreme Court of South Africa) 1961 (3) SA 616. American Federal Rule of Evidence 803(1) and (2) provides a more liberal time element.

the events and the speaking of the words (or vice versa), and differences in location being relevant factors but not, taken by themselves, decisive criteria. As regards statements made after the event it must be for the judge, by preliminary ruling, to satisfy himself that the statement was so clearly made in circumstances of spontaneity or involvement in the event that the possibility of concoction can be disregarded. Conversely, if he considers that the statement was made by way of narrative of a detached prior event so that the speaker was so disengaged from it as to be able to construct or adapt his account, he should exclude it. And the same must in principle be true of statements made before the event. The test should be not the uncertain one, whether the making of the statement should be regarded as part of the event or transaction. This may often be difficult to show. But if the drama, leading up to the climax, has commenced and assumed such intensity and pressure that the utterance can safely be regarded as a true reflection of what was unrolling or actually happening, it ought to be received. The expression '*res gestae*' may conveniently sum up these criteria, but the reality of them must always be kept in mind: it is this that lies behind the best reasoned of the judges' rulings.

In due course, the House of Lords took the opportunity of overruling *Bedingfield* and restating the rule in more contemporary terms. In *Andrews*,[13] the seriously wounded victim of a robbery told police officers that he had been robbed by two men, and gave the name of the accused as one of the two. The victim then became unconscious and was taken to hospital, where he died some two months later. The trial judge permitted the prosecution to adduce evidence of the statement made by the victim naming the accused, and the accused appealed against conviction, contending that the statement was inadmissible hearsay. The Court of Appeal upheld the conviction, and the accused appealed unsuccessfully to the House of Lords.

The statement made by the victim was clearly hearsay, tendered to prove the identity of the accused as one of the two robbers. It was inadmissible as a dying declaration, because there could be no showing that the victim had been under a settled, hopeless expectation of death (see the 8th edition of this work at 7.26). It was therefore admissible, if at all, only under the *res gestae* rule. The House of Lords held that the statement had been rightly admitted under that rule. It was argued for the accused, relying on *Bedingfield*, that the statement was inadmissible because the criminal activity described had ceased by the time it was made, or in other words, that it was not sufficiently contemporaneous. The House held, however, that *Bedingfield* no longer represented the law. It was not so much the passage of time, in and of itself, that mattered, but whether or not the statement was sufficiently spontaneous to eliminate any real risk of concoction. Lord Ackner said ([1987] AC at 300):

My Lords, may I therefore summarize the position which confronts the trial judge when faced in a criminal case with an application under the *res gestae* doctrine to admit evidence of statements, with a view to establishing the truth of some fact thus narrated, such evidence being truly categorized as 'hearsay evidence'. (1) The primary question which the judge must ask himself is: can the possibility of concoction or distortion be disregarded? (2) To answer that question, the judge must first consider the circumstances in which the particular statement was made, in order to satisfy himself that the event was so unusual or startling or dramatic as to dominate the thoughts of the victim, so that his utterance was an instinctive reaction to that event, thus giving no real opportunity for reasoned reflection. In such a situation, the judge would be entitled to conclude that the involvement or the pressure of the event would exclude the possibility of concoction or distortion, providing that the statement was made in conditions of approximate but not exact contemporaneity. (3) In order for the statement to be sufficiently 'spontaneous' it must be so closely associated with the event which has excited the statement that it can be fairly stated that the mind of the declarant was still dominated by the event. Thus, the judge must be satisfied that

---

[13] [1987] AC 281; and see *Mills v R* [1995] 1 WLR 511.

the event which provided the trigger mechanism for the statement was still operative. The fact that the statement was made in answer to a question is but one factor to consider under this heading. (4) Quite apart from the time factor, there may be special features in the case, which relate to the possibility of concoction or distortion...The judge must be satisfied that the circumstances were such that, having regard to the special feature of malice, there was no possibility of any concoction or distortion to the advantage of the maker or the disadvantage of the accused. (5) As to the possibility of error in the facts narrated in the statement, if only the ordinary fallibility of human recollection is relied on, this goes to the weight to be attached to and not to the admissibility of the statement...However, here again, there may be special features that may give rise to the possibility of error. In the instant case there was evidence that the deceased had drunk to excess....In such circumstances the trial judge must consider whether he can exclude the possibility of error.

It seems clear that spontaneity and contemporaneity will remain significant in assessing the reliability of statements tendered under the *res gestae* rule, but will no longer be the sole determining factor, as in *Bedingfield*. In *Andrews* the trial judge found that the statement had been made within a few minutes of the injury being sustained, but held that, even if this had not been the case, he was satisfied that the statement had not been concocted. The House of Lords approved this approach. The new statement of the rule, like the old, permits doubt as to the correctness of the decision in *Nye* (1977) 66 Cr App R 252, in which the driver of a vehicle involved in an accident was assaulted by a passenger in another vehicle. He then sat in his car, recovering from the combined effects of the accident and the assault, and several minutes later identified his assailant to the police. It was held that evidence of this statement had rightly been admitted. But on the facts of this case, which were relatively undramatic and where the victim had both an obvious motive for speaking to his own advantage and ample opportunity to think of what to say, the result is surely questionable.[14] In *Tobi* v *Nicholas* [1988] RTR 343, it was held to be wrong to admit the statement of a driver, made about 20 minutes after an accident in which only vehicle damage was caused. In addition to the obviously considerable lapse of time before the statement was made, it seems improbable that a damage-only accident could be regarded as sufficiently startling or dramatic as to guarantee that a statement made so long afterwards would be the result of the speaker being emotionally overpowered.

American Federal Rule of Evidence 803(2), dealing with 'excited utterances', seems to capture the common law spirit well by providing for the admissibility of '...A statement relating to a startling event or condition made while the declarant was under the stress of excitement caused by the event or condition'. This may allow for extended periods of time, for example where the declarant suffers shock and cannot speak for some time after the event.

8.6 *RES GESTAE*: CONTEMPORANEOUS DECLARATIONS OF THE PHYSICAL OR MENTAL STATE OF THE SPEAKER

Statements narrating the contemporaneous physical or mental state of the speaker, including his intentions, emotions and feelings are admitted as part of the *res gestae*, because of the inherent

---

[14] Cf. *Turnbull* (1985) 80 Cr App R 104, in which a statement by a dying victim with a Scots accent, who had been drinking heavily, that he had been stabbed by 'Ronnie Tommo' was held admissible as evidence of the identity of the accused, Ronald Turnbull, under the *res gestae* rule. The statement was made to various witnesses very shortly after the event, but while the victim was not only severely intoxicated, but dying from wounds that might have affected his ability to speak and understand. The judge was satisfied that there was no concoction. The remaining matters were questions of weight for the jury. Where there is a serious possibility that the speaker has concocted the statement for his own advantage, it should be excluded (*Callender* [1998] Crim LR 337).

likelihood of spontaneity and involvement. The rule permits only a statement of conditions contemporaneous with it, and not of past conditions, though it is submitted that a statement of a condition which arose in the past, but is continuing at the time of the statement, may be admissible.[15] This is a 'present tense' exception. In *Nicholas* (1846) 2 Car & K 246 at 248, the rule was explained by Pollock CB, as follows:

> If a man says to his surgeon, 'I have a pain in the head', or in such a part of the body, that is evidence; but, if he says to his surgeon, 'I have a wound'; and was to add, 'I met John Thomas, who had a sword, and ran me through the body with it', that would be no evidence against John Thomas.

Thus, in *Condé* (1868) 10 Cox CC 547, on a charge of neglect of a child by depriving it of food, the child's complaints of feeling hungry were held to be admissible. The rule permits a statement of what the condition was, but not of its cause, unless the cause is itself admissible by virtue of the *res gestae* principle or some other exception to the hearsay rule. In *Horsford* (1898) *The Times*, 2 June 1898, the deceased had made a statement to a doctor in the terms, 'I have taken poison; [the accused] sent it to me'. On the trial of the accused for murder, the first part of the statement was admitted, but the second rejected. The same result was reached by the United States Supreme Court in the celebrated case of *Shepard* v *United States* 290 US 96 (1933), rejecting under this rule the statement made by the since deceased wife of the accused: 'Dr Shepard has poisoned me.' The wife's statement of the symptoms she was experiencing would, however, be admissible.

The statement must concern only the contemporaneous condition of the speaker. In *Parker* (1960) 45 Cr App R 1, it was held to be wrong to admit evidence that the accused's wife (with whose unlawful wounding the accused was charged) had said to a neighbour, 'He shot me; he said he would'. See also *Bradshaw* (1985) 82 Cr App R 79; *Gilfoyle* [1996] 3 All ER 883.

8.7 PUBLIC INFORMATION EXCEPTIONS

Both s. 7(2) of the Civil Evidence Act 1995 and s. 118(1) of the Criminal Justice Act 2003 preserve a group of public information exceptions, which are of some antiquity and based on the presumptive reliability of sources of information contained in authoritative published works, in public documents created and maintained by public officials for the purpose of public reference, and in other official records. In each case, the exceptions provide for the proof of matters of public interest, or of a public nature. These exceptions are of occasional importance in contemporary practice. The exceptions dealing with facts contained in public documents and references contained in published works are dealt with briefly here. The detailed and rather esoteric statutory and common law rules about records of courts, Crown grants, treaties, pardons, commissions, and the like are too rarely encountered to justify inclusion. As to these rules, reference should be made to the current edition of Phipson, *Evidence*, 16th edn, para. 32–55 *et seq*.

8.7.1 Facts contained in public documents

Statements made in public documents were, at common law, admissible as *prima facie*, though not conclusive, evidence of the facts contained in them.[16] This exception to the rule against

---

[15] Whether a statement was contemporaneous is a question of fact and degree in every case: see *Aveson* v *Lord Kinnaird* (1805) 6 East 188; *Gloster* (1888) 16 Cox CC 471; *Thomson* [1912] 3 KB 19; *Black* (1922) 16 Cr App R 118.

[16] See generally *Irish Society* v *Bishop of Derry* (HL) (1846) 12 Cl & F 641; *Sturla* v *Freccia* (1880) 5 App Cas 623. A certified copy is sufficient proof of such a document.

hearsay is justified by the presumptive reliability of records made by impartial public officials for future reference. The law also took account of the formidable problems which might otherwise arise of proving a multiplicity of facts of public concern or interest, recorded over considerable periods of time, by a variety of public officials, who, even if not dead or unavailable, could not be expected to have any recollection of the matters recorded. The number and types of public documents falling within the rule was, of course, immense and continually growing, but the common law rule diminished considerably in significance because of interventions by statute in favour of the admissibility of specific classes of document. Quite apart from the many specific provisions in particular statutes, the common law rule has in most cases been superseded by the provisions of the Civil Evidence Act 1995 and the Criminal Justice Act 2003. The effect of s. 7(2)(b) of the Civil Evidence Act 1995 is that any statements made in public documents which would formerly have been admissible as evidence of the facts contained in them by virtue of the common law rule, are now admissible for that purpose by virtue of that section. As to proof of public documents in civil proceedings, see s. 9 of the Act and 19.11. Section 118 of the Criminal Justice Act 2003 (perhaps unnecessarily) preserves the common law rule in addition to its broader statutory exceptions.

The safeguard at common law, lay in the circumstances in which the document was compiled. The conditions of admissibility under the rule were: (a) that the document must have been made and preserved for public use and must contain matters of public interest (see *Lilley* v *Pettit* [1946] KB 401);[17] (b) that it must be open to public inspection; (c) that the entry or record sought to be proved must have been made promptly after the events which it purports to record; and (d) that the entry or record sought to be proved must have been made by a person having a duty to inquire into and satisfy himself of the truth of the facts recorded (see *Sturla* v *Freccia* (1880) 5 App Cas 623).

The last of these conditions gave rise to difficulty in modern times, because of the changing nature of public records. The most important part of the common law safeguard was the duty to inquire into the facts, which lay upon a public official charged with compiling a document for public reference. But the whole theory of the safeguard depended upon the premise that records made for public use were in earlier times compiled by local officers, who would habitually either officiate at or have personal knowledge of the events which they recorded, or who could at least reasonably be expected to make any necessary inquiries from those immediately concerned. The classic illustration is that of the vicar who kept records of baptism, marriages, and burials within the parish. In an uncomplicated and localized society, such records might reasonably be trusted on that basis. But in a complex, more diverse and much larger society, the reality is very different, and public officers are now charged with making many records for public use, the contents of which they could not possibly personally know or verify.

This exposed a serious deficiency in the common law rule, when applied to modern records, a deficiency which was clearly and forcibly demonstrated in *Halpin* [1975] QB 907. Halpin and others were charged with conspiracy to defraud a local authority and corruption, arising from the performance of a service contract for the supply and renewal of paving stones for the local authority. It was relevant for the prosecution to prove that, during the period of the conspiracy, the accused and his wife were in effect the sole shareholders and directors of the company which

---

[17] *Ioannou* v *Demetriou* [1952] AC 84. Documents made by persons other than public officials are not covered by the rule (*Re Woodward* [1913] 1 Ch 392—records of Quakers). And even records compiled by a public official will not be admissible under the rule if made for the private reference of the official rather than reference by the public (*Merrick* v *Wakley* (1838) 8 Ad & El 170).

had the contract with the local authority, from which the jury might be invited to infer that the accused was in a position to, and did in fact, exercise control over the transactions which were said to be fraudulent. In order to prove this, the prosecution adduced the contents of the file from the Companies Register containing the annual statutory returns of the company, which were required to be made by the company and submitted to the Registrar by virtue of s. 124 of the Companies Act 1948. Although such returns were required to be made and submitted, there was no statutory provision for the admissibility of the statements contained in them, so that, being hearsay, they could be admitted for the purposes desired by the prosecution only if they were admissible under the public documents rule. It was cogently argued on appeal that the returns were inadmissible because they failed to satisfy the fourth condition, in that the file was not made by a person having a duty to inquire into and satisfy himself of the truth of the facts recorded. To this argument, in the light of authority including *Sturla* v *Freccia* (1880) 5 App Cas 623, there was really no answer, but the Court of Appeal, holding that the common law must, 'move with the times', were content to modify the condition judicially to suit modern conditions. Geoffrey Lane LJ, delivering the judgment of the Court, said ([1957] QB at 915):

> ...the common law should move with the times and should recognize the fact that the official charged with recording matters of public import can no longer in this highly complicated world, as like as not, have personal knowledge of their accuracy.
>
> What has happened now is that the function originally performed by one man has had to be shared between two: the first having the knowledge and the statutory duty to record that knowledge and forward it to the Registrar of Companies, the second having the duty to preserve that document and to show it to members of the public under proper conditions as required.
>
> Where a duty is cast upon a limited company by statute to make accurate returns of company matters to the Registrar of Companies, so that those returns can be filed and inspected by members of the public, the necessary conditions, in the judgment of this court, have been fulfilled for that document to have been admissible.

The terms of the judgment in *Halpin* foreshadowed later statutory provisions leading up to s. 117 of the Criminal Justice Act 2003, by alluding to the two separate requirements of compilation under a duty, and the supply of information by a person having, or who might reasonably be supposed to have personal knowledge of the facts. In criminal cases, it should now be possible to admit public documents under the latter section in almost every case. For this reason, it would be an uneconomic use of space to reproduce here the material contained in the first edition of this work dealing with what documents are public. The distinction between private and public documents should now rarely, if ever, be significant. If necessary, reference should be made to the 1st edition of this work at pp. 150–1.

8.7.2 References in published works

Historical facts of a public (though not of a private or local nature)[18] may be proved by references contained in published historical works. It would seem that it should be established that the work referred to is of an authoritative nature, though this is a matter of which the court may presumably readily take judicial notice, based on the credentials of the author and the reputation of the publishing house. Similarly, references contained in a published map or survey may be admitted for the purpose of showing the location and relative position of States, cities, or any

---

[18] *Read* v *Bishop of Lincoln* [1892] AC 644, 653.

other relevant geographical and topographical features.[19] The meaning of words may be proved by reference to entries in published dictionaries.[20] But some cases have gone considerably further, and have permitted the use of such entries to prove, not only the meaning of a word, but also the uses to which an object described in a dictionary is commonly put.[21] If this is correct, it must surely also be allowable to permit reference to other works generally accepted as authoritative, for example encyclopaedias; and it may well be that in contemporary practice, new life might properly be breathed into this rule by allowing reference to duly authenticated materials available by way of the internet. Scientific and professional tables may be used to prove facts stated therein which are generally accepted for the purposes of reference, for example, the tables used for the purpose of establishing average life expectancies.[22] It is submitted that directories in common use, for example telephone directories, may be admitted for the purpose of proving facts stated in them, such as the number assigned to a certain person or business at the date of the directory. Similarly, it is submitted, the professional standing of a solicitor, barrister, member of the medical profession, or clergyman, might be established by reference to the appropriate register or list in which their present standing is recorded by their professional governing body. Even though such records are maintained by private bodies, the information recorded is maintained for public use and is of an essentially public nature.[23] Curiously, the courts have not permitted reference to almanacs for the purpose of proving facts stated therein, even where such facts seem to be beyond reasonable dispute, such as the time of sunrise or sunset on a particular day at a particular location.[24]

It should be borne in mind that in all the cases mentioned above, there is also the possibility that the court may be persuaded to take judicial notice of the facts in question. Judicial notice is dealt with in detail in Chapter 20. Facts contained in the kinds of works referred to above are likely to be notorious (i.e., beyond reasonable dispute) for the purposes of judicial notice (see 20.5) and the court may refer to any appropriate source for the purpose of informing itself about the propriety of judicial notice (see 20.6). It is submitted that this should provide a solution to those cases in which obviously reliable information, such as the time of sunset or sunrise, is contained

---

[19] *Edmondson* v *Avery, The Times,* 28 and 31 January 1911. As to the use of maps for the purpose of measuring distance, see *Mouflet* v *Cole* (1872) LR 8 Ex 32.

[20] *Peters* (1886) 16 QBD 636, 641 per Lord Coleridge CJ. However, the distinction should be noted between words used in their ordinary meaning, and words used in a technical sense or words in a foreign language, which may require to be proved by expert evidence: see 3.1.

[21] *The Coca Cola Co. of Canada Ltd* v *Pepsi Cola of Canada Ltd* (1942) 59 RPC 127, 133 per Lord Russell of Killowen; *Re Demuth* (1948) 65 RPC 342.

[22] *Rowley* v *L & NW Railway* L R 8 Ex 221. See also *Dickins* v *Randerson* [1901] 1 KB 437 (admissibility of the *British Pharmacopoeia* to prove approved standards for the composition of drugs). One would suppose that directories reliably showing the average price of used cars or the value of stocks and shares at any given time might equally be admissible.

[23] A number of professional lists are admissible by statute for the purpose of proving a person's professional qualifications, or lack thereof: see *Blackstone's Criminal Practice,* 2009 edn, para. F8.18. Cf. American Federal Rule of Evidence 803(17) which creates an exception to the rule against hearsay for: 'Market quotations, tabulations, lists, directories, or other published compilations, generally used and relied upon by the public or by persons in particular occupations'.

[24] *Crush* [1978] Crim LR 357; *Tutton* v *Darke* (1860) 5 H & N 647. There is respectable precedent for the alternative view. Wigmore refers to a celebrated story in which Abraham Lincoln is credited with securing an acquittal in the trial of Cal Armstrong for murder in 1858 by using an almanac to discredit the evidence of the main prosecution witness. The witness gave evidence that he had seen the accused commit the crime charged by moonlight. Lincoln was able to demonstrate that there would have been no moonlight at the relevant time (J. Wigmore, *The Principles of Judicial Proof* (1913), Case Study 339, p. 662 (citing I. N. Arnold, *Life of Abraham Lincoln* (1885) p. 87)).

in authoritative and readily available sources which fall outside the common law exception to the hearsay rule. Even if the source is not itself admissible, the court may nonetheless refer to it, and then take judicial notice of the facts stated. In practice, it is submitted, such information may be used by the court in almost every case, either by way of evidence or judicial notice.

8.8 EVIDENCE OF AGE AND DATE OF BIRTH

Section 118(1) of the Criminal Justice Act 2003 (but not s. 7 of the Civil Evidence Act 1995) purports to preserve a common law rule whereby evidence of a person's age or date or place of birth may be given by a person without personal knowledge of the matter. Curiously, however, it seems doubtful whether any such rule actually exists as such at common law, and, if it does exist, what its scope may be. It has long been the informal practice to permit any witness to testify about his or her own age and date and place of birth. Such evidence is necessarily based on hearsay, and is technically inadmissible in the absence of a specific exception to the hearsay rule which allows it. For obvious reasons, the practice is convenient and usually unobjectionable, though there may be cases in which other evidence of the facts should be required. But the evidence of a witness about the age of another person has no such practical advantages to recommend it, and, unless the witness was present at the birth, is also inadmissible hearsay in the absence of some specific exception to the hearsay rule which allows it. The 5th edition of *Cross on Evidence* (at p. 569) suggests that a somewhat different form of exception should be recognized, though not necessarily that it has been recognized, and refers to a number of cases in which the evidence of persons who were not present at the birth appears to have been admitted for the purpose of confirming the identity of a person as being the person named in a birth certificate.[25] If this is the rule, it is rather narrower than the rule which s. 118(1) purports to preserve. The general rule at common law appears to be that strict proof of age is generally required, i.e., testimony from a witness present at the subject's birth or an authenticated birth certificate (now admissible by statute) coupled in each case with evidence of identification of the person as being one and the same.[26] The authorities referred to by Cross establish at most that the evidence of identification may be provided by a person who was not present at the birth, and it is submitted that the witness must have personal knowledge of the fact that the subject is the same person as the person named in the birth certificate. In cases where strict proof is not required, circumstantial evidence, such as the subject's physical appearance of being a certain age,[27] or evidence of treatment of a person as being of a certain age,[28] may be admissible. In most cases, the accepted existing practice of allowing informal proof of these matters by the subject himself is unobjectionable, and is to be welcomed as saving time and eliminating technical requirements. There will be cases in which it is undesirable; for example, in a case to decide a question of pedigree or inheritance, in which a person has something to gain by misrepresenting his identity or age. But this is not the same as

---

[25] *Weaver* (1873) LR 2 CCR 85; *Wilton & Co.* v *Phillips* (1903) 19 TLR 390; *Re Bulley's Settlement* [1886] WN 80; *Bellis* (1911) 6 Cr App R 283.

[26] See, e.g., *Haines* v *Guthrie* (1884) 13 QBD 819, in which the court required strict proof where a defendant raised the defence of infancy to an action for the price of goods supplied. The court rejected as inadmissible hearsay an affidavit by the alleged infant's since deceased father which had been made for the purpose of another action between different parties. As to the admissibility of birth certificates, see Births and Death Registration Act 1953, s. 34.

[27] *Wallworth* v *Balmer* [1966] 1 WLR 16. There are also certain statutory instances of reliance on appearance, a form of real evidence: see, e.g., Magistrates' Courts Act 1980, s. 150(4).

[28] *Cox* [1898] 1 QB 179. In certain cases, a particular method of proof may be required by statute.

admitting general evidence of age from others who lack personal knowledge, and it is submitted that the evidence of such persons can do no more than confirm identity. It is submitted that the effect of the 'preservation' of this common law rule by s. 118(1) is unclear, and that Parliament should deal with this subject more directly by enacting a comprehensive set of rules governing the proof of age and birth for all purposes.

B   HEARSAY ADMISSIBLE BY STATUTE IN CRIMINAL CASES

SUMMARY OF MAIN POINTS

- Hearsay in criminal cases is governed exclusively by the Criminal Justice Act 2003.

- Section 114(1) of the Act provides that hearsay is admissible if, but only if:

  (a) any provision of this Chapter or any other statutory provision makes it admissible,

  (b) any rule of law preserved by section 118 makes it admissible,

  (c) all parties to the proceedings agree to it being admissible, or

  (d) the court is satisfied that it is in the interests of justice for it to be admissible.

- Certain safeguards are provided, including a duty to stop the case if the evidence is unconvincing, and provisions for the impeachment of the maker of a hearsay statement.

8.9 INTRODUCTION: CRIMINAL JUSTICE ACT 2003, S. 114(1)

The admissibility of hearsay evidence in criminal cases is now governed by the hearsay provisions of the Criminal Justice Act 2003, which are contained in Chapter 2 of Part 11 of the Act. With the exception of s. 132 dealing with rules of court (which came into effect on 29 January 2004) these provisions came into effect on 4 April 2005. The intent of the Act is to provide a complete statutory scheme for the admission of hearsay evidence in criminal proceedings.[29] The common law exceptions to the rule against hearsay, other than those specifically preserved by s. 118(1) of the Act, are abolished by s. 118(2). Nothing in the Act affects the exclusion of evidence of a statement on grounds other than hearsay: s. 114(3).

The basis for the statutory admission of hearsay evidence is provided by s. 114(1) and is limited to four categories.

Section 114(1) provides:

> In criminal proceedings a statement not made in oral evidence in the proceedings is admissible as evidence of any matter stated if, but only if—
>
> (a) any provision of this Chapter or any other statutory provision makes it admissible,
>
> (b) any rule of law preserved by section 118 makes it admissible,

---

[29] In accordance with the definition adopted for the purposes of the Act generally, s. 134(1) defines the term 'criminal proceedings' as meaning criminal proceedings to which the strict rules of evidence reply. The identical definition in s. 112 applying to the bad character provisions of the Act was rightly criticized as unnecessarily confusing in *Bradley* [2005] EWCA Crim 20, [36] by the Court of Appeal, which pointed out that all criminal proceedings are governed by the strict rules of evidence. The hearsay provisions of the Criminal Justice Act 2003 apply also to proceedings under s. 4(A) of the Criminal Procedure (Insanity) Act 1964: *Chal* [2008] 1 Cr App R 247.

> (c) all parties to the proceedings agree to it being admissible, or
> (d) the court is satisfied that it is in the interests of justice for it to be admissible.

Although hearsay is the subject of Chapter 2 of Part 11, it is noteworthy that s. 114 does not use the word 'hearsay' itself. Instead, it offers a definition composed of certain basic terms, which are defined. The definitions of 'statement' and 'matter stated' for the purposes of the hearsay provisions of the Act are contained in s. 115(2) and (3), which provide:

> (2) A statement is any representation of fact or opinion made by a person by whatever means; . . .
> (3) A matter stated is one to which this Chapter applies if (and only if) the purpose or one of the purposes of the person making the statement appears to the court to have been—
>> (a) to cause another person to believe the matter; or
>> (b) to cause another person to act or a machine to operate on the basis that the matter is as
>> stated.

Some of the implications of these subsections for the definition of hearsay as a concept were considered at 7.1 and 7.15.1. The provisions of s. 121 dealing with the additional requirement in the case of multiple hearsay were also considered at 7.6.3.

By virtue of s. 134 of the Act, 'oral evidence' includes:

> . . . evidence which, by reason of any disability, disorder or other impairment, a person called as a witness gives in writing or by signs or by way of any device.[30]

8.9.1 Section 114(1)(b) and (c)

Only two of the four cases in s. 114(1), namely s. 114(1)(a) and (d), are considered in detail here. As to s. 114(1)(b), the rules of law preserved by s. 118 are dealt with elsewhere. The former common law public information and *res gestae* exceptions are dealt with in Part A of this chapter. Those relating to reputation as to character and family tradition, and references by expert witnesses to materials pertaining to their field, are dealt with in Chapter 11: see 11.2 *et seq.*; 11.5. Admissions, confessions, and the common enterprise rule are dealt with in Chapter 9.

Little comment is needed as to s. 114(1)(c), the case in which all parties agree to the admission of the evidence. It is submitted that, unless the scope of the agreement is obvious, the parties should reduce the agreement to writing, so that the court and the jury are left in no doubt as to the nature and extent of the evidence to be admitted. In *Williams* v *VOSA* [2008] EWHC 849 (Admin) it was held that an agreement to admit hearsay need not be in any particular form. If a party fails to object to hearsay being admitted, that fact may be enough to allow the court to infer that the hearsay is admitted by agreement under s. 114(c). Where the hearsay is of little consequence, it may well be agreed to by lack of objection in an informal manner. But it is submitted that an agreement should not automatically be inferred from a failure to object, and that the judge should inquire into the intention of the party concerned before admitting the evidence in any case where it may have significant weight.

8.9.2 Hearsay: direction to jury

In *Grant* v *The State* [2006] 2 WLR 835, the Privy Council, considering a statutory scheme similar to that of the Criminal Justice Act 2003, drew attention to the importance of the direction

---

[30] For the analogous provision applicable to civil cases, see Civil Evidence Act 1995, s. 13: 8.31.

to be given to the jury whenever hearsay evidence is admitted. In particular, the jury must be reminded that the evidence has not been verified by evidence at trial, and has not been tested by cross-examination. The risks of accepting the evidence must be pointed out specifically, and the jury must be told to scrutinize the evidence with great care. It is appropriate to draw their attention to the quality of the evidence generally, including any discrepancies between the hearsay and other evidence given in the case. While a failure to give a proper direction would not necessarily render the trial unfair, it may certainly give rise to concerns under art. 6.3(d) of the European Convention on Human Rights, and there is some risk that a resulting conviction may be regarded as unsafe. Much will depend on how important the hearsay is in the context of the trial as a whole, and on the quality of the other evidence against the accused. In the case of multiple hearsay (see 7.6.3) the judge must give the jury an enhanced direction to treat the evidence with special care, having regard to the fact that it contains at least two levels of hearsay untested by cross-examination: see *Scorah* [2008] EWCA Crim 1786.

8.10 SECTIONS 114(1)(a) AND 116(1): RELEVANT PERSON UNAVAILABLE

Section 116 of the Criminal Justice Act 2003 deals with the admissibility of statements made by unavailable witnesses:

> (1) In criminal proceedings a statement not made in oral evidence in the proceedings is admissible as evidence of any matter stated if—
>> (a) oral evidence given in the proceedings by the person who made the statement would be admissible as evidence of that matter,
>> (b) the person who made the statement (the relevant person) is identified to the court's satisfaction, and
>> (c) any of the five conditions mentioned in subsection (2) is satisfied.
> (2) The conditions are—
>> (a) that the relevant person is dead;
>> (b) that the relevant person is unfit to be a witness because of his bodily or mental condition;
>> (c) that the relevant person is outside the United Kingdom and it is not reasonably practicable to secure his attendance;
>> (d) that the relevant person cannot be found although such steps as it is reasonably practicable to take to find him have been taken;
>> (e) that through fear the relevant person does not give (or does not continue to give) oral evidence in the proceedings, either at all or in connection with the subject matter of the statement, and the court gives leave for the statement to be given in evidence.
> (3) For the purposes of subsection (2)(e) 'fear' is to be widely construed and (for example) includes fear of the death or injury of another person or of financial loss.
> (4) Leave may be given under subsection (2)(e) only if the court considers that the statement ought to be admitted in the interests of justice, having regard—
>> (a) to the statement's contents,
>> (b) to any risk that its admission or exclusion will result in unfairness to any party to the proceedings (and in particular to how difficult it will be to challenge the statement if the relevant person does not give oral evidence),
>> (c) in appropriate cases, to the fact that a direction under section 19 of the Youth Justice and Criminal Evidence Act 1999 (c. 23) (special measures for the giving of evidence by fearful witnesses etc) could be made in relation to the relevant person, and
>> (d) to any other relevant circumstances.

(5) A condition set out in any paragraph of subsection (2) which is in fact satisfied is to be treated as not satisfied if it is shown that the circumstances described in that paragraph are caused—

    (a) by the person in support of whose case it is sought to give the statement in evidence, or

    (b) by a person acting on his behalf,

in order to prevent the relevant person giving oral evidence in the proceedings (whether at all or in connection with the subject matter of the statement).

Section 116(1) permits a hearsay statement to be admitted in criminal proceedings if the evidence of the maker of the statement (called the 'relevant person') about the matter stated would be admissible if he were giving oral evidence (i.e., it is not inadmissible for a reason other than its hearsay quality); if the relevant person is properly identified;[31] and if any one of the five conditions specified in subsection (2) is satisfied. These conditions of admissibility are broadly similar to those of s. 23 of the Criminal Justice Act 1988, which s. 116 replaces, although there are some refinements based on the experience of the courts in applying s. 23. There is also one very important difference. Under s. 23 of the 1988 Act, a statement was admissible only if it was contained in a document. Statements made orally were not admissible under s. 23 or any other provision of the 1988 Act, and were admissible, if at all, only by virtue of one of the common law exceptions. Under s. 116 of the Criminal Justice Act 2003, for the first time, oral statements are admissible by statute under the same circumstances as statements contained in documents, though the problems of identifying the relevant person and of proving the content of the statement may be more acute in the case of oral statements, and they may in some cases tend to carry less weight. Subsection (5) provides that a party cannot rely on any of the conditions under subsection (2) if he or someone acting on his behalf has brought the condition about in order to prevent the relevant person from testifying at trial. Clearly, it would be wrong to allow a party to profit from his own wrongdoing by permitting him to adduce the relevant person's hearsay statement, thereby depriving his opponent of the opportunity to cross-examine or impeach the witness, or to develop further testimony about the matter stated. However, there would be no objection to permitting the opponent to adduce the statement to compensate for the absence of the relevant person's oral evidence, if he wishes to do so.

8.11 SECTION 116(2): CONDITIONS PERTAINING TO UNAVAILABILITY

The conditions laid down by subsection (2) are all concerned with the unavailability of the relevant person to give oral evidence. The concept of unavailability is an old one, which has to do with the right of confrontation (see 7.5). But the modern definition of unavailability extends well beyond the literal sense of the term, that the relevant person is physically unable to attend court, e.g., because of death or disability. These cases are provided for, but a person may also be

---

[31] In relation to business records, it was recognized in cases decided under the Criminal Justice Act 1988 that references to a person who 'makes' a statement may be ambiguous, in a case where A records information supplied by B. This gave rise to a difficulty as to who the 'relevant person' should be, and the issue attracted different views as to the proper interpretation of 'the person who made the statement' for the purposes of s. 24(4) of the 1988 Act: see *Derodra* [2000] 1 Cr App R 41; *Bedi* (1992) 95 Cr App R 21; *Carrington* [1994] Crim L R 438. The Law Commission (Report No. 245, para. 4.39) attributed the ambiguity in the 1998 Act to drafting errors. It appears to have been corrected by s. 117(2)(b) with respect to that section (see 8.17.2), but it is not clarified with respect to s. 116. Although the problem is less likely to arise with respect to s. 116, it cannot be excluded altogether, and a more general clarification would have been preferable.

unavailable in an extended sense if he cannot be found, if it is impracticable to bring him to testify from a place outside the UK, or, most controversially, if he does not give or complete his evidence about a particular matter stated through fear.[32] This last condition renders a hearsay statement admissible only with leave. By virtue of s. 116(1)(c), the conditions under subsection (2) operate disjunctively, i.e., any one standing alone is sufficient. For the purposes of s. 23 of the Criminal Justice Act 1988 it was established that the party seeking to admit the evidence bore the burden of proving that a condition was satisfied. This is in accordance with the general rule, and it is submitted that the same principle should apply in cases under s. 116.[33] As is to be expected, the section exhibits a clear preference for oral evidence in criminal trials.[34]

8.12 CASES (A) AND (B): RELEVANT PERSON DEAD OR UNFIT TO BE WITNESS

Little comment is necessary on these conditions. The question of unfitness, of course, is to be judged with reference to the time at which the relevant person is required to give evidence, not the time when he made the statement.[35] The party seeking to adduce the statement must adduce admissible evidence to show that the relevant person is either dead or unfit to be a witness because of his physical or mental condition.[36] In the latter case, the party should produce appropriate medical evidence. No doubt the condition must be serious enough to suggest that the relevant person is unlikely to recover sufficiently to be fit to be a witness within a reasonable time, if at all, and that nothing would be gained by adjourning the trial for some period of time. Whereas s. 23 of the 1988 Act provided that the maker of the statement must be unfit to 'attend' as a witness, s. 116(2)(b) requires that the relevant person should be unfit to 'be' a witness. The difference in wording suggests that under s. 116(2)(b), the question is not so much whether the relevant person could be brought to court, but whether there would be any point in doing so.

---

[32] Interestingly, s. 116 does not expressly reproduce the additional condition contained in s. 23 of the 1988 Act that the maker of the statement does not give evidence because he is being 'kept out of the way'. In many cases, this may be covered by the condition that he cannot be found, coupled with the provision of subsection (5), but it is not hard to imagine cases which do not fit this condition very well, but in which the relevant person is being prevented from giving evidence. It is also interesting to note that s. 116 does not extend the concept of unavailability as far as American Federal Rule of Evidence 804(a), by virtue of which a person may also be unavailable if his claim to privilege with respect to testifying about the subject-matter of the statement is upheld; or if he persists in refusing to testify about it despite an order of the court to do so; or if he testifies to a lack of memory of the matter stated. In England, it may be that inability to remember the matter stated renders the relevant person unfit to be a witness: see 8.12.

[33] *Minors* [1989] 1 WLR 441. As in analogous cases, the standard or proof varies as to whether the prosecution or the defence bears the burden of proof: see 4.14.

[34] The right of confrontation (see 7.5) requires that oral evidence be insisted on whenever possible. The fear that criminal trials might be reduced to 'paper' trials is one which pervaded the debate not only on the Criminal Justice Act 2003 (see, e.g., Law Commission Report No. 245, para. 1.29) but earlier debates on the same subject, e.g., that on the bill which became the Criminal Justice Act 1988 (see, e.g., D. Wolchover (1988) 138 NLJ 461).

[35] As to the question of capability to make the statement, see s. 123 of the Act, 8.26.

[36] For examples, see generally *Al-Khawaja* [2006] 1 WLR 1078; *D* [2003] QB 90; *Dragic* [1996] 2 Cr App R 232 (the last two being cases under the analogous provisions of the Criminal Justice Act 1988). But as to the consistency of the admission of the evidence with the fair trial provisions of art. 6.3(d) of the European Convention on Human Rights, see 7.5.2.

A person with a serious mental condition may be perfectly well able to attend court but nonetheless be unfit to be a witness.[37]

8.13 CASE (C): RELEVANT PERSON OUTSIDE UNITED KINGDOM AND ATTENDANCE CANNOT BE SECURED

The party seeking to adduce the evidence must prove, not only that the relevant person is outside the UK, but also that it is not reasonably practicable to secure his attendance, i.e., to bring the relevant person to court with a view to his being a witness; whether this is so is a matter on which the opponent is entitled to be heard and which he is entitled to contest.[38] It is not enough simply to aver, or even to prove, that he is outside the UK. What is to be regarded as reasonably practicable in any given case will depend on the circumstances. It is clearly unacceptable simply to take no action. In *Bray*,[39] a case decided under s. 23 of the Criminal Justice Act 1988, the prosecution failed to take any steps to secure the attendance of a proposed witness who was in Korea and whose whereabouts were known to them for some seven months leading up to the time of trial. The Court of Appeal held that the prosecution were not entitled to adduce the statement made by the proposed witness, because they had not satisfied the obligation to take reasonable steps to secure his attendance. It was also held that the court was entitled to consider whether everything reasonable had been done to secure the attendance of the maker of the statement in deciding whether to exercise the discretionary powers under ss. 25 and 26 of the 1988 Act to exclude evidence otherwise admissible under s. 23.[40] In *French*,[41] the Court of Appeal held that it was proper to have regard to the fact that the prosecution's delay in failing to ensure that the trial took place before a foreign witness returned home had been responsible for the fact that the witness was unavailable and unwilling to attend at the time of trial. The mere fact that the relevant person is outside the UK, and is reluctant to attend, does not mean that no reasonable steps can be taken. It may not be possible to compel his attendance by means of legal process, but it may be possible to do so by persuasion and by rendering a certain amount of practical assistance. Although the phrase 'reasonably practicable' seems apt to refer only to the feasibility of the various steps which might be taken to secure the attendance of the relevant person,[42] and should not involve the nature and posture of the case itself, in practice it is likely that the court will take a broader view. It is submitted that the court may properly assess what is reasonably practicable having regard to the circumstances of the particular case before it, including the gravity of the case; the importance of the evidence the relevant person could give in relation to the case as a whole; the degree of ease or difficulty in bringing him to court;[43] his apparent willingness to attend, or lack thereof; the extent to which his evidence is likely to be disputed; and whether or

---

[37] This may include the case in which the relevant person has no recollection of the matter stated, but only if his lack of recollection is attributable to a medical condition: cf. *Setz-Dempsey* (1994) 98 Cr App R 23. It may be necessary for the judge to hold a hearing to determine that question.

[38] *Elliott* [2003] EWCA Crim 1695, [18].

[39] (1988) 88 Cr App R 354; see also *Castillo* [1996] 1 Cr App R 438; *Maloney* [1994] Crim LR 525; *Gonzales de Orango* [1992] Crim LR 180.

[40] These powers are not reproduced in the Criminal Justice Act 2003; see 8.23.

[41] (1993) 97 Cr App R 241; cf. *Radak* [1999] 1 Cr App R 187.

[42] In s. 23 of the Criminal Justice Act 1988, this phrase was used only in relation to efforts to secure attendance. In relation to finding the maker of the statement, 'all reasonable steps' had to be taken.

[43] See, e.g., *Hurst* [1995] 1 Cr App R 82.

not oral evidence of the same facts may be available from another witness.[44] Where the charge is a serious one, and the relevant person would be an important witness, the court may legitimately expect greater efforts to be made to secure the relevant person's attendance than it might where the charge is a less serious one, or in a case in which he could give only relatively peripheral or insubstantial evidence.

8.14 CASE (D): RELEVANT PERSON CANNOT BE FOUND

Much the same observations apply in this case. It is not enough for the person seeking to adduce the evidence to aver, or even to prove that the relevant person cannot be found. It is also necessary to satisfy the court that all reasonably practicable steps have been taken to find him. In today's world, the techniques available for tracing people (even those who make considerable efforts to keep themselves hidden) are relatively advanced, and it may be that it will become more and more difficult to persuade the court that all reasonably practicable steps have been taken. But the court, it is submitted, should follow broadly the same approach as under case (c). Of course, there may be cases in which the relevant person is found to be outside the UK, in which case the test under case (c) must then be applied.

8.15 CASE (E): RELEVANT PERSON NOT GIVING EVIDENCE BECAUSE OF FEAR; REQUIREMENT OF LEAVE

Attempts to intimidate witnesses with a view to persuading them not to give evidence are not new, but have in recent times occasioned greater concern in the light of experience with cases involving terrorism and organized crime. It is obviously necessary that the courts should be able to deal effectively with such situations, and there are now administrative steps which can be taken to offer protection and reassurance to witnesses who feel threatened, with a view to ensuring that they are enabled to give evidence.[45] In addition to pre-trial protective measures, special measures directions for the giving of evidence in court may be made in the case of a vulnerable witness by virtue of s. 17 of the Youth Justice and Criminal Evidence Act 1999 (see generally *Blackstone's Criminal Practice*, 2009 edn, para. D14.97 *et seq.*). These measures include screening the witness from the accused, and having the witness give evidence by means of a video recording or live television link. In certain circumstances governed by the Criminal Evidence (Witness Anonymity) Act 2008, a witness may also give evidence without revealing his identity, though there are significant risks that the trial may be rendered unfair, and the provisions of the Act may attract challenges under art. 6 of the Convention.[46]

[44] Some of these considerations were specifically taken into account in considering the exercise of the court's power to exclude hearsay evidence under s. 25 of the Criminal Justice Act 1988. Although this power to exclude is not reproduced for the purpose of s. 116 of the Criminal Justice Act 2003, they are matters which have the potential to affect the fairness of the trial, and, it is submitted, should continue to play some part in the court's decision as to whether to admit hearsay under s. 116. Similar considerations do affect evidence admissible by virtue of s. 114(1)(d): see s. 114(2); and to some extent evidence admissible under s. 116(2)(e): see s. 116(4).

[45] Such protective measures are more developed in international criminal law: see, e.g., Rome Statute of the International Criminal Court, art. 68; Rules of Procedure and Evidence of the International Criminal Tribunal for the Former Yugoslavia, Rule 75; Rules of Procedure and Evidence of the International Criminal Tribunal for Rwanda, Rule 75. In addition to the measures listed in the text, witnesses may give evidence in closed session (i.e. *in camera*) or with facial or voice distortion, and may be referred to by a pseudonym.

[46] The Act was passed to nullify the decision of the House of Lords in *Davis* [2008] 1 AC 1128, which held that the practice of permitting witnesses to give evidence anonymously was contrary to English law and unfair in terms of art. 6. See also '*Mayers* and other appeals' [2009] Crim LR 272.

However, it is also necessary that the law should make some provision for the admission of other evidence in a case in which, despite the availability of such measures, intimidation has deprived the court of the evidence of a particular witness. A similar provision was contained in s. 23 of the Criminal Justice Act 1988,[47] but there are two important differences between this former provision and s. 116(2)(e). Firstly, under the 1988 Act, where the ground relied on was that the maker of the statement did not give evidence through fear, a statement could be admitted only if it had been made to a police officer or other person charged with the duty of investigating offences or charging offenders. In the absence of restriction, it may be assumed that a statement of any kind may be admitted under s. 116(2)(e). Secondly, evidence can be admitted under s. 116(2)(e) only with the leave of the court. Section 116(4) provides that leave may be granted only where the court considers that the statement ought to be admitted in the interests of justice, and lays down three specific matters to which the court is to have regard in considering that question, in addition to any other relevant matters. The contents of the statement (subsection (4)(a)) may be relevant because they may suggest some degree of unreliability. The risk of unfairness, including considerations of whether the opponent can effectively challenge the statement (subsection (4)(b)), is related to the question of unreliability, and, of course, together the matters referred to in (a) and (b) represent the classic dangers of admitting hearsay evidence. It is, therefore, not surprising that the court is enjoined to consider them. The special measures directions referred to in subsection (4)(c) are designed to allay the fear of the relevant person about giving evidence.[48] Clearly, if that can be done, and the relevant person agrees to give evidence, that would generally be the preferred solution. It is not clear what other matters are to be considered relevant under subsection (4)(d), but it would be surprising if they did not to some extent correspond to those enumerated in s. 114(2) to guide the court in deciding the same question when it arises under s. 114(1)(d). Despite the necessity for these provisions, the court must always have in mind the danger to the fairness of the trial, and must have regard to the extent to which the accused will be able to challenge the evidence contained in the statement by other means (see generally 7.5.2). The suggestion was made in *Sellick*[49] that, where the accused causes a witness to be in a state of fear, with the result that the court admits his hearsay statement, the accused has deprived himself of the right of confrontation, and no question of a violation of the right to a fair trial can arise. It is submitted that this principle must be applied with great caution. The section does not specify that the fear must have been occasioned by or on behalf of the accused (though this will be the usual case) and the evidence linking the accused to the fear may be tenuous. Only in the clearest case of overt threats or intimidation would it seem right to assume that no question of the fairness of the trial could arise. It is submitted that, in general, the court must take the risk of unfairness into consideration, even if it is less likely to be a siginificant factor than, say, in cases where the maker of the statement is dead or too ill to give evidence.

[47] There were no corresponding provisions in the Criminal Justice Act 1965 or the Police and Criminal Evidence Act 1984, though there was a somewhat similar provision in s. 13(3) of the Criminal Justice Act 1925, which was repealed by the Criminal Justice and Public Order Act 1994.

[48] As to special measures directions generally see *Blackstone's Criminal Practice*, 2009 edn, para. D14.97 *et seq.*

[49] [2005] 1 WLR 3257, [37]–[38]; cf. *Arnold* [2004] EWCA Crim 1293 (in which the Court of Appeal warned that such cases do not provide a licence for proof by hearsay); *R (Robinson) v Sutton Coldfield Magistrates' Court* [2006] EWHC 307 (Admin).

8.15.1 Meaning of 'does not give evidence'

The wording of s. 23 of the Criminal Justice Act 1988, that the maker of the statement 'does not give oral evidence through fear…' gave rise to difficulties in cases in which the maker gave some evidence, but did not complete it through fear. For example, the witness might give evidence of some matters, but fail to so with respect to others; he might fail to complete his examination-in-chief; or, having completed his examination-in-chief, he might fail to appear for cross-examination. In *Ashford Magistrates' Court, ex parte Hilden* [1993] QB 555, it was held that the phrase 'does not give oral evidence' must be interpreted as including a case where the witness gave some evidence, but did not complete it. But the court found itself unable to say whether this should apply regardless of the extent of the evidence given, or whether, for example, it should apply only where the witness had not given any significant evidence, or whether some other test should be applied. Section 116(2)(e) resolves the matter by specifying that the relevant person may either not give evidence at all, or may begin to give evidence but not continue, or may not give evidence with respect only to the subject-matter of the statement, while giving evidence of other matters. In any of these cases, the statement becomes admissible, subject to leave.

8.15.2 Nature of fear

The fear need not be of immediate physical harm to the relevant person himself. Section 116(3) provides that 'fear' is to be 'widely construed', and by way of example, mentions a fear on behalf of another, or a fear of financial loss. While it is certainly right that the fear should not be restricted to fear for his own personal safety, it is submitted that it ought to be insisted on, and perhaps should have been made clear in s. 116, that the fear must be that some consequence of a serious nature will result if the relevant person gives evidence. While what is perceived as serious is bound to vary from individual to individual, some objective standard should be adopted, perhaps that the perceived consequence should be such that a person of reasonable firmness might be deterred from giving evidence if he feared that the consequence would be likely to result from his doing so. Thus, if the relevant person feared merely that he might lose a day's business through attending court to give evidence, it is submitted that leave to admit the statement should be refused. Conversely, if the fear arose from a threat to close down his business altogether by means of burning down his premises, or boycotting the business in retaliation for giving evidence, the position would be different. It must be proved that the fear exists at the time when the relevant person is required to give evidence. In *H* [2001] Crim LR 815,[50] a witness made a statement claiming to be afraid of giving evidence some two months before trial. But he continued to reside in the area in which he said he was afraid, and was even arrested there. At trial there was no evidence that the witness continued to be afraid. The Court of Appeal held that the evidence of fear was insufficient to justify the admission of the statement. While the question of time must be viewed in a reasonable way, and any statement of fear must inevitably relate to a time which precedes the trial to some extent, there must be some reasonable basis for assuming that the fear continues until the time of trial. The prosecution had failed to establish such a basis.

---

[50] And see *McCoy* [1999] All ER (D) 1410.

8.15.3 Reasonableness of grounds for fear

As in the case of s. 23 of the Criminal Justice Act 1988, s. 116(2)(e) does not make it a condition of admissibility that the fear be a reasonable one, i.e., that there are reasonable grounds for fearing that the apprehended consequence of giving evidence will in fact ensue. In a number of cases, the courts held that no such language should be read into s. 23,[51] and it is to be anticipated that the same view will be taken of s. 116. However, the reasonableness or otherwise of the fear may be relevant as bearing on the question of whether it is genuine.

8.15.4 Proof of fear

In cases decided under the corresponding provisions of the Criminal Justice Act 1988, the party seeking to adduce the statement was required to prove that the relevant person does not give evidence through fear. This can be a difficult matter either to prove or to refute. If the same rule applies to s. 116(2)(e), the prosecution must show that the conditions required are present by adducing admissible evidence to that effect.[52] In *Neill v North Antrim Magistrates' Court* [1992] 1 WLR 1220, the House of Lords held that the evidence of the mother of two boys, whom the prosecution wished to call to give evidence, to the effect that the boys were afraid, was inadmissible hearsay and could not be used to prove the fear. Some admissible evidence of the boys' fear should have been adduced. In *Belmarsh Magistrates' Court, ex parte Gilligan* [1998] 1 Cr App R 14, it was suggested that the court must receive admissible oral evidence on that subject, but it is not clear why this requirement should apply in all cases. Other evidence may be sufficient. In *Waters* (1997) 161 JP 249, it was held that the judge is entitled to have regard to the demeanour of a witness in deciding whether he is afraid. But while this may be acceptable as a form of real evidence (see 19.19, 19.20) it is unlikely that this would be enough in the absence of some other evidence. The use of a hearsay statement in lieu of the oral evidence of the witness is a serious matter, and the court must be persuaded that the fear is genuine. The ideal way to do this is to call a police officer to deal with the circumstances in which the fear arose. But the practice is to take a further witness statement from the witness, giving details of the fear and its origins. Such a statement by a witness about his fear may be admissible as a *res gestae* statement of present state of mind, a preserved common law exception to the rule against hearsay.[53] But some doubt has been cast on the position by the decision in *Davies* [2007] 2 All ER 1070. In this case, the suggestion was made that the judge might attempt to assess whether a witness is in fear by means of hearing from the witness himself by live link. But the Court was opposed to such a course, because, if the witness has to attend court for this purpose, then to some extent it defeats the purpose of the exercise. Instead, the Court held that the judge should decide the matter on basis of the written statements in lieu of any other evidence; and that the Criminal Justice Act 2003 was intended to change the practice under the Criminal Justice Act 1988 so as to allow this to be done. It is submitted that the decision is not at all satisfactory. It was hardly necessary to make the leap from disapproving

---

[51] *Acton Justices, ex parte McMullen* (1990) 92 Cr App R 98; *Ashford Magistrates' Court, ex parte Hilden* [1993] QB 555; *Ricketts* [1991] Crim LR 915.

[52] Cf. *O'Loughlin* [1988] 3 All ER 431; decided with reference to s. 23(3) of the Criminal Justice Act 1988. The repealed s. 13(3) of the Criminal Justice Act 1925 required that this be proved by the evidence of a 'credible witness'.

[53] *Neill v North Antrim Magistrates' Court* [1992] 1 WLR 1220; *O'Loughlin* [1988] 3 All ER 431. As to the present state of mind exception, see 8.6.

of the use of live link to dispensing with any evidence at all apart from the statements. The possibilities canvassed above in relation to the 1988 Act remain viable. At para. [14] the Court refers to the written statements on which the judge is to rely as 'evidence' of the fear, but they are not admissible evidence of the fear unless admitted under one of the grounds provided by s. 114(1), or the *res gestae* rule. The last possibility may suffice in some cases, though it has the significant drawback of being limited in its scope to the actual feeling of fear as opposed to its cause (see 8.6). To rule the statements admissible on the ground of fear under s. 116(2)(e) is unacceptable, as fear is the very fact to be proved. It would seem, therefore, that they would have to be held admissible in the interests of justice under s. 114(1)(d), but the absence of any opportunity to challenge or refute the evidence should in theory form a significant obstacle under s. 114(2): see 8.20. Moreover, the Court's view that the practice must have changed under the Criminal Justice Act 2003, so as to render less formal proof acceptable, may be debatable. The Court seems to rely heavily on the provision of s. 116(3) that 'fear' should be widely construed (see at [14]); but it is far from obvious what, if anything, that has to do with the proof of the fear.[54]

It appears that the fear need not be attributable to the offence itself, or something said or done subsequently which can be linked to the offence. In *Acton Justices, ex parte McMullen* (1990) 92 Cr App R 98, Watkins LJ suggested that this might be the case. However, in *Martin* [1996] Crim LR 589 this restriction was rejected as not being provided for by the Act, in a case where a witness had been intimidated by the appearance of a silent stranger outside his home. Despite the fact that there was no evidence that the stranger said or did anything, and that he could not be related directly to the offence, it was held that the witness's understandable fear was enough.

8.16 SECTIONS 114(1)(a) AND 117: BUSINESS AND OTHER DOCUMENTS

Section 117 of the Act, replacing in somewhat similar terms s. 24 of the Criminal Justice Act 1988, deals with the admissibility of business and other documents.

Section 117 provides:

> (1) In criminal proceedings a statement contained in a document is admissible as evidence of any matter stated if—
> (a) oral evidence given in the proceedings would be admissible as evidence of that matter,
> (b) the requirements of subsection (2) are satisfied, and
> (c) the requirements of subsection (5) are satisfied, in a case where subsection (4) requires them to be.
> (2) The requirements of this subsection are satisfied if—
> (a) the document or the part containing the statement was created or received by a person in the course of a trade, business, profession or other occupation, or as the holder of a paid or unpaid office,
> (b) the person who supplied the information contained in the statement (the relevant person) had or may reasonably be supposed to have had personal knowledge of the matters dealt with, and
> (c) each person (if any) through whom the information was supplied from the relevant person to the person mentioned in paragraph (a) received the information in the course of a trade, business, profession or other occupation, or as the holder of a paid or unpaid office.

---

[54] But *Davies* is not the only case to advocate this position: see also *Doherty* (2007) 171 JP 79.

(3) The persons mentioned in paragraphs (a) and (b) of subsection (2) may be the same person.

(4) The additional requirements of subsection (5) must be satisfied if the statement—

    (a) was prepared for the purposes of pending or contemplated criminal proceedings, or for a criminal investigation, but

    (b) was not obtained pursuant to a request under section 7 of the Crime (International Co-operation) Act 2003 (c. 32) or an order under paragraph 6 of Schedule 13 to the Criminal Justice Act 1988 (c. 33) (which relate to overseas evidence).

(5) The requirements of this subsection are satisfied if—

    (a) any of the five conditions mentioned in section 116(2) is satisfied (absence of relevant person etc), or

    (b) the relevant person cannot reasonably be expected to have any recollection of the matters dealt with in the statement (having regard to the length of time since he supplied the information and all other circumstances).

(6) A statement is not admissible under this section if the court makes a direction to that effect under subsection (7).

(7) The court may make a direction under this subsection if satisfied that the statement's reliability as evidence for the purpose for which it is tendered is doubtful in view of—

    (a) its contents,

    (b) the source of the information contained in it,

    (c) the way in which or the circumstances in which the information was supplied or received, or

    (d) the way in which or the circumstances in which the document concerned was created or received.

Section 134(1), following s. 13 of the Civil Evidence Act 1995, defines 'document' as 'anything in which information of any description is recorded'.

Section 117(1) requires that (as in the case of s. 116(1)) the evidence should not be inadmissible for a reason other than its hearsay quality; and that the additional conditions laid down by subsection (2) or subsection (4) should be satisfied. These conditions are concerned with the admissibility of documents of this kind as a class.

8.17 SECTION 117(2): GUARANTEES OF RELIABILITY OF BUSINESS DOCUMENTS

The language of s. 117(2) follows that of s. 24 of the Criminal Justice Act 1988. The purpose of the subsection is to guarantee the likely reliability of a class of documents, which may be described generically as business documents; though as s. 117(2)(a) makes clear, the activity in the course of which the document is created or received is not restricted to commercial undertakings, but extends across the entire spectrum of private and public organizations, large or small. The precise nature of the activities of the organization is not really of concern. The guarantee of reliability has three elements.

8.17.1 Subsection (2)(a): reliability deriving from creation or receipt of document

Subsection (2)(a) requires that the document (or the part containing the statement sought to be admitted) should have been created or received in the course of the one of the enumerated activities. This language, reproducing that of s. 24 of the Criminal Justice Act 1988, is the successor to earlier enactments which had required that the document be compiled by a person 'acting under a duty'.[55] The underlying purpose is the same. The existence of a duty to preserve information and record it accurately is a strong indication of reliability. The existence of such a duty is clearly implied, though no longer stated expressly, in s. 117(2)(a). It will be recalled that a very similar consideration was responsible for the admission of public documents as a class at common law: see 8.7.1. Any requirement of proving a duty independently of the course of professional or official activity seems unnecessary. Unless there are exceptional circumstances, a person acting in his professional or official capacity may properly be taken as acting under a duty to preserve information and to create the document honestly and accurately. If such exceptional circumstances exist in the case of a particular document, it may cause the judge to consider whether it should be excluded under subsections (6) and (7): see 8.19. The fact that a document was created in the course of a business activity may be inferred from all the circumstances, including the appearance and contents of the document itself: see *Foxley* [1995] 2 Cr App R 523 (a case under the corresponding provisions of the Criminal Justice Act 1988). On this basis, the subsection seems to provide a substantial guarantee of reliability as far as the creation of a document is concerned. But why it should be thought to be a safeguard that a document is *received* in the course of a trade, business, etc., is less clear.[56] If there is no quality control with respect to the circumstances in which the document is created, there is no real guarantee that the information contained in it (even though accurate as originally supplied) has been incorporated accurately into the document. If the subsection required that the receiver of the document should have verified the contents of the document while acting in the course of a trade or business etc., or stipulated that the document should have been received from a professional, business, or official source, the value of 'receiving' as a guarantee of reliability might be more obvious. But in the last case, the manner of creation of the document could be relied on, and the fact of the document being received would be otiose.

8.17.2 Subsection (2)(b): reliability deriving from personal knowledge of information

The second guarantee of reliability is that the person who supplied the information contained in the document had, or may reasonably be supposed to have had, personal knowledge of the matters dealt with. This is perhaps the strongest guarantee of all, because it relates to the source of the information. The inference of personal knowledge may be drawn from the circumstances surrounding the supply of the information. Section 117(3) provides that the persons mentioned in subsections (2)(a) and (b) may be the same person. In practice, this would seem to mean that the person who supplies the information may himself create the document containing the information: it is hard to imagine how he could be the receiver of the document. Whether one person fulfills both roles or two persons fulfill them, subsection (2)(b) makes it clear that it is the supplier of the information who is the 'relevant person' for the purposes of s. 117. This is a welcome clarification. Under s. 24 of the Criminal Justice Act 1988, a serious ambiguity was exposed in the phrase 'the maker of the statement' for the purposes of s. 24(4), the equivalent of s. 117(4)

---

[55] Police and Criminal Evidence Act 1984, s. 68; and to the same effect, Civil Evidence Act 1968, s. 4. With reference to the former provision, any reference in s. 68 to a person acting under a duty included 'a reference to a person acting in the course of any trade, business, profession or other occupation in which he is engaged or employed or for the purposes of any paid or unpaid office held by him': Sch. 3, para. 6 to the Act.

[56] For an interesting example of documents being received in such a way, see *Clowes* [1992] 3 All ER 440.

and (5) (see 8.18). The effect of the ambiguity was that it was unclear whether the unavailability conditions applicable to the 'maker of the statement' under that subsection applied to the person who supplied the information or the person who created the document, a serious problem where two different people were involved. Grammatically speaking, the more natural sense of the phrase 'the maker of the statement' might have been the person who created the document. But the reality was that, insofar as the admission of the hearsay statement deprived the opponent of the opportunity to cross-examine, the person one would wish to cross-examine would be the supplier of the information, so that it would have been more logical to apply the conditions of admissibility to him. The courts were divided on the issue, but it is submitted that decision in *Derodra*,[57] in which the supplier of the information was held to be the 'maker of the statement', was correct. This view is adopted by s. 117(2)(b).

8.17.3 Section 117(2)(c): reliability deriving from transmission of information

To the extent that intermediaries are concerned in the transmission of information between the relevant person and the creator of the document, the guarantee is the fact that the intermediaries also receive and transmit the information while acting in the course of a trade, business, etc. This is essentially the same duty as in the case of the creator of the document, and does not require separate comment.

8.18 SECTION 117(4): DOCUMENTS PREPARED FOR PURPOSES OF PROCEEDINGS OR INVESTIGATION

Documents prepared for the purposes of pending or contemplated criminal proceedings or a criminal investigation are treated separately by s. 117, as they were by ss. 24(4) and 26 of the Criminal Justice Act 1988. Even though they fit the description of business documents, they form a special class of documents, and are not dealt with under the general provisions of s. 117(2). The typical document of this kind is a prosecution witness statement or other report dealing with the facts of the case. Even though such documents may be signed by the relevant person, they are prepared by the police or prosecuting authorities. They are partisan in nature and so are unlikely to be neutral in tone. They pose a particular problem if offered as hearsay statements as evidence of the matters stated in them. Of course, similar documents prepared by the defence for the purposes of the case are subject to exactly the same observation. Consequently, although these documents qualify as business documents, they are subject to additional conditions of admissibility. The additional conditions of admissibility under s. 117(4) and (5) are significantly less onerous than those under ss. 24(4) and 26 of the 1988 Act. Under the latter provisions, in addition to a requirement that one of the unavailability conditions be fulfilled, such statements were admissible only with leave, and leave could be granted only on the basis of a finding that admission was required in the interests of justice. The provisions of s. 117(5) are considerably more lenient. Subsection (5) requires only that either one of the unavailability conditions of s. 116(2) (above) or a new unavailability condition be fulfilled with respect to the relevant person (the person who supplied the information). The new condition, contained in subsection (5)(b), is that the relevant

---

[57] [2000] 1 Cr App R 41; the opposite view was taken in *Bedi* (1992) 95 Cr App R 21, and *Carrington* [1994] Crim LR 438.

person cannot reasonably be expected to have any recollection of the matters dealt with in the statement (having regard to the length of time since he supplied the information and all other circumstances). This is in fact a quite reasonable condition, which is often fulfilled in relation to business documents. Such documents frequently contain routine and detailed information which no one could reasonably be expected to remember after the passage of some time.

8.19 SECTION 117(6) AND (7): EXCLUSION OF PARTICULAR DOCUMENTS

The conditions of admissibility discussed above relate to business and similar documents as a class. However, subsections (6) and (7) also give the court power to exclude a particular document falling within the class by declaring that it is not admissible because the reliability of the particular document as evidence for the purpose of which it is tendered is doubtful. The grounds for finding that the reliability of a particular document is doubtful are set out in subsection (7) and seem straightforward. Doubts may arise because of the contents of the document itself; or because of the source of the information contained in it; or because of the way in which the information was supplied or received; or because of the way in which the document was created or received. For example, it may appear that the information contained in the document was based on rumour, or on sources whose authenticity cannot be verified, or which are known to have been compromised; the original information may have been lost and reconstructed in a doubtful way for the purpose of creating the document; or, perhaps worst of all, it may appear that the document has been prepared in anticipation of litigation and is deliberately self-serving, or is a forgery, or has been altered or tampered with *ex post facto*.

8.20 SECTION 114(1)(d): ADMISSION OF HEARSAY IN INTERESTS OF JUSTICE

Section 114(1)(d) creates for the first time an explicit power to admit hearsay evidence not covered by a particular exception if the court is satisfied that it is in the interests of justice for it to be admissible. While there had been some measure of agreement that some power of this kind would be useful, the Law Commission felt that it should be of a limited scope.[58] In one sense s. 114(1)(d) is limited; the test that admission must be in the interests of justice is a strong one, and s. 114(2) provides a long list of factors to which the court must have regard before pronouncing itself to be satisfied. But it is also a broad provision in the sense that there is no restriction on the kind of statement which can be admitted in the interests of justice. Despite this, it has been held that the provision is not incompatible with art. 6.3(d) of the European Convention on Human Rights (see 7.5.2). In *Xhabri* [2006] 1 All ER 776, the accused was charged with false imprisonment, rape, threats to kill, and control of prostitution for gain. The prosecution's case was that he controlled the complainant and other young women through violence and threats, including effectively imprisoning them, and compelled them to engage in acts of prostitution. At trial, the prosecution sought to admit evidence of communications said to have been made

---

[58] Report No. 245, para. 6.49. The Home Office Explanatory Note on s. 114 (para. 396) states: 'The intention...is that the court should be able to admit an out-of-court statement which does not fall within any of the other categories of admissibility, where it is cogent and reliable'. But this hardly seems to be an adequate statement of the test laid down by s. 114(1)(d) and (2).

by phone, directly or indirectly, between the complainant and her parents, a neighbour, and a police officer. The evidence was admitted under s. 114(1)(d), and the accused was convicted. On appeal, he argued that the evidence had been wrongly admitted, and that s. 114(1)(d) itself was incompatible with art. 6.3(d). Dismissing the appeal, the Court of Appeal saw no incompatibility. Given the safeguards available to the trial judge, including the power to exclude the evidence having regard to the factors mentioned in s. 114(2), the basic requirements of art. 6.3(d) were satisfied. Further, given that the complainant had been available for cross-examination and the accused had in fact been able to challenge most, if not all, of the evidence against him, the trial had not been unfair.

However, subsequent cases have not afforded the defence such clear protection. A number of cases have been decided under s. 114(1)(d) which seem to justify the worst fears expressed, in past editions of this work and by other commentators, about the wide scope for admitting hearsay of kinds which, until very recently, it would have been regarded as contrary to principle to admit in criminal cases. Indeed, taken together with *Hayter*[59] and its progeny in the realm of confessions, they could be seen as reflecting an emerging view in the Court of Appeal and House of Lords that (1) the Criminal Justice Act 2003 lays down a code of admissibility rather than inadmissibility; (2) all four cases of admissibility under s. 114(1) are of equal stature, none being subordinate to any other; and (3) that being the case, any kind of hearsay statement is admissible under s. 114(1)(d), subject only to s. 114(2). If that is correct, it would seem to render s. 114(1)(a), (b), and (c) essentially otiose. Section 114(1)(d) becomes an all-purpose tool for opening the door to hearsay generally, subject to exclusion on the facts of particular cases. It is a weapon of first resort, rather than a weapon of last resort as might have been expected on a reading of s. 114(1) as a whole. It will be suggested below that this approach is flawed and dangerous in relation to the fairness of criminal proceedings.

The following cases will serve as an illustration of recent developments. In *L* [2008] 2 Cr App R 18, a wife was a competent but not compellable witness against her husband, and refused to give evidence for the prosecution. The prosecution applied for and were given leave to adduce her witness statement, which had been made voluntarily, in lieu of her evidence under s. 114(1)(d). The police had not cautioned the wife that she was not compellable to give evidence before she made her statement, and it was held that they were under no obligation to do so (although it was conceded that there may be occasions when some warning may be advisable).[60] The accused was deprived of any real opportunity to cross-examine a possibly decisive witness against him. In *Y* [2008] 1 Cr App R 34, the Court held that, in principle, a hearsay statement made by a person not charged in the proceedings can be adduced under s. 114(1)(d), even if it tends to incriminate the accused. The fact that the statement tends to incriminate the accused does not automatically preclude its admissibility, though this is an important factor to be taken into account in deciding to exclude it pursuant to s. 114(2). Nor is the statement rendered inadmissible because it may amount to an admission of some guilt by the person who made it. It was argued that the admission of the evidence was improper because the statement amounted to a confession, and s. 118(1) preserves the rules governing confessions, which were not followed. But

---

[59] [2005] 1 WLR 605; see 9.16.1.

[60] This case provides a striking contrast with the position laid down by the United States Supreme Court in *Crawford* v *Washington* 124 S Ct 1354, 1370 (2004) by virtue of which the same evidence would not only have been inadmissible but would have constituted a serious violation of the accused's constitutional right to confront the witnesses against him: see 7.5.1. See also *B and S* [2008] EWCA Crim 365, in which it was held that a statement under caution made by an accused may be admitted against another accused under s. 114(1)(d).

the Court held that this did not affect the position. If the statement is a confession it is admissible separately under s. 114(b) as a preserved exception, but because the four cases of admissibility enumerated in s. 114(1) stand separately and are of equal stature, none being subordinated to another, it is also admissible under s. 114(1)(d).

A case in which the result differed, though on the facts rather than as a matter of principle, is *T (AB)* [2007] 1 Cr App R 43. The complainant alleged sexual abuse by three of her relations, including her step-grandfather, who made a statement admitting the abuse, but died before trial. The prosecution applied to adduce his statement under s. 114(1)(d). It was held that in principle, there was no objection to evidence of a statement made by a person who had been charged being admitted under s. 114(1)(d). But in this case, it was not alleged that the three relations had acted together; indeed, there was no question of joint enterprise, and the three allegations were unrelated to each other except insofar as the same victim was involved in each. It was held that the statement should not be admitted. Had there been a connection between the three allegations, it seems that the statement would have been admitted subject to considerations under s. 114(2). A case where there was such a connection is *McLean* [2008] 1 Cr App R 11, in which a joint enterprise was alleged. In this case, it was held that an accused was entitled to adduce a hearsay statement made by his co-accused under s. 114(1)(d), and that the statement thereupon became evidence in the case generally. The Court in *Y* (above) explained *McLean* as holding that in principle any kind of statement might be admitted under s. 114(1)(d).

As might be expected, the courts have shown some reluctance to permit hearsay statements to be adduced under s. 114(1)(d) where the maker of the statement is available and could be produced to give evidence, or where the evidence appears to be suspect or unreliable. In *Marsh* [2008] EWCA Crim 1816, [25], the Court observed that judges should be slow to admit in those circumstances (*ibid.* at [25]). An accused charged with importing cocaine sought to admit a hearsay statement made in prison by a person not on trial, R, to a person serving a life sentence for murder, B, to the effect that R was 'setting the accused up' for the charge. The Court held that although the statement was in principle admissible, the trial judge had been right to exclude the evidence because its reliability depended on the veracity of R, which could not be tested; and because its reliability was obviously open to considerable question. A further factor was that the defence had other evidence available to present in lieu of R's statement, so that exclusion was not fatal to the accused's line of defence. Hughes LJ said:

> The test applied to an application by the defendant defending himself on a serious charge may quite properly be less exacting than that which could be applied to an application made by the Crown. Quite often that may well be the case. But the interests of justice which are the governing feature of section 114(1)(d) are not wholly synonymous with the interests of the defendant. They mean the public interest in arriving at the right conclusion in the case, including of course the acquittal of anyone about whose guilt there is proper doubt. We are influenced in this case by the amount of other evidence available to Marsh of the involvement of R. [*Ibid.* at [24].]

In *Finch* [2007] 1 WLR 1645, the accused was charged with the illegal possession of a firearm and ammunition. A former co-accused, R, had pleaded guilty to the offence and made a statement to the effect that the accused knew nothing about the matter. The defence produced R at court, but he was reluctant to give evidence and defence counsel decided not to call him. Instead, the defence tendered R's statement under s. 114(1)(d).[61] It was held that the statement was admissible

---

[61] The statement was not admissible as the confession of a co-accused under s. 76A of the Police and Criminal Evidence Act 1984 (see 9.13.2) because R had pleaded guilty and was no longer a co-accused.

in principle, but should not be admitted in the circumstances of the case. R was available to give evidence and it was undesirable in those circumstances to put his statement, untested by cross-examination, before the jury.

Every case involving s. 114(1)(d) requires the judge to consider the range of factors enumerated by s. 114(2) before admitting the evidence (see 8.20.1). Furthermore, it is submitted that the courts must take account of views of the European Court of Human Rights as to the possible impact of hearsay on the fairness of proceedings, particularly where the hearsay is the sole or decisive evidence against the accused (see 7.5.2). But it would seem that these considerations now represent the last and only refuge against the general admission of hearsay of all kinds. The way in which the law is developing suggests that the position may soon be that any hearsay statement can be admitted under s. 114(1)(d), which permits the party adducing the evidence to circumvent the conditions of admissibility under other provisions of the Criminal Justice Act 2003 and, most worryingly, those pertaining to confessions under s. 76 and s. 76A of the Police and Criminal Evidence Act 1984. From there it is an easy next step simply to abolish the Rule against Hearsay altogether, as has been done in civil cases, subject to certain safeguards. It is submitted that this abrogation of the right of confrontation would not satisfy the fair trial provisions of art. 6 of the Convention. It is also submitted that the wisdom of two centuries of jurisprudence should not be set aside so lightly. It is an approach which is flawed and dangerous.

8.20.1 Section 114(2): matters to be considered

Section 114(2) provides a list of nine matters to which the court is to have regard in considering whether it is in the interests of justice for a hearsay statement to be admitted under s. 114(1)(d). The subsection provides:

> In deciding whether a statement not made in oral evidence should be admitted under subsection (1)(d), the court must have regard to the following factors (and to any others it considers relevant)—
> (a) how much probative value the statement has (assuming it to be true) in relation to a matter in issue in the proceedings, or how valuable it is for the understanding of other evidence in the case;
> (b) what other evidence has been, or can be, given on the matter or evidence mentioned in paragraph (a);
> (c) how important the matter or evidence mentioned in paragraph (a) is in the context of the case as a whole;
> (d) the circumstances in which the statement was made;
> (e) how reliable the maker of the statement appears to be;
> (f) how reliable the evidence of the making of the statement appears to be;
> (g) whether oral evidence of the matter stated can be given and, if not, why it cannot;
> (h) the amount of difficulty involved in challenging the statement;
> (i) the extent to which that difficulty would be likely to prejudice the party facing it.

The list is expressed not to be exhaustive; the court must also have regard to any other matters it considers relevant, though the list is quite comprehensive and certainly seems to cover all the considerations which would usually arise. The matters to be considered are self-explanatory. Understandably, they focus on the quality of the evidence itself (its reliability and probative value); how important it is in the context of the case as a whole; whether the facts to which the evidence is relevant could be proved by means of other evidence; and the degree of the difficulty posed to opposing parties by the admission of the evidence in terms of challenging it or dealing with it generally.[62] These are all considerations of fairness which arise from the classical dangers of hearsay evidence, and we have seen that consideration of some of these factors is required for other purposes, when evaluating the issue of fairness under s. 116(4)(b) and when evaluating reliability under s. 117(6) and (7). Some indication of how the subsection works can be gleaned from the cases discussed at 8.20. The judge must have regard to all the factors when evaluating evidence tendered under s. 114(1)(d). But in considering the matters enumerated by s. 114(2) he may make an overall judgment. Indeed, from a practical point of view it is difficult to see how it could be otherwise; the various factors overlap and affect each other to a considerable degree. Hence, the judge must take all the matters into account, but it is not necessary to make individual findings with respect to each: see *Taylor* [2006] 2 Cr App R 222.

8.21 SECTIONS 119, 120, AND 122: PREVIOUS STATEMENTS BY WITNESSES

These sections are concerned with cases in which previous statements made by witnesses who give oral evidence in the proceedings are adduced for certain purposes because they are either consistent or inconsistent with the oral evidence of the witness. Although such statements do involve hearsay considerations, they are also subject to special rules, which are considered in detail under the headings of examination-in-chief and cross-examination: see generally 16.7 *et seq.*; 17.7. In essence, the effect of ss. 119 and 120 is to reverse the common law rules that such statements were not admissible as evidence of the matters stated, but only for certain lesser purposes. In civil cases, the common law rule was reversed by the Civil Evidence Act 1995. It had been widely advocated that the rule, which was in many ways inconvenient and difficult for juries to understand, should be reversed in criminal cases also. This has now been done.

8.22 SECTION 133: PROOF OF STATEMENTS IN DOCUMENTS

By section 133 of the Act:

> Where a statement in a document is admissible in evidence in criminal proceedings, the statement may be proved by producing either—
> (a) the document, or
> (b) (whether or not the document exists) a copy of the document or of the material part of it, authenticated in whatever way the court may approve.

This section corresponds to s. 8 of the Civil Evidence Act 1995, and replaces an almost identical provision contained in s. 27 of the Criminal Justice Act 1988. By virtue of both sections, the strict common law requirement that the original document be produced when the document is admitted as (non-hearsay) evidence of its own contents (the 'best evidence rule') is dispensed with when a document is to be proved only for the purpose of admitting a hearsay statement

---

[62] The accompanying Home Office Note (para. 398) states that the list: '…is intended to focus attention on whether the circumstances surrounding the making of the out of court statement indicate that it can be treated as reliable enough to admit it as evidence, despite the fact that it will not be subject to cross-examination', which, once again, seemingly fails to capture the depth of the subsection.

contained in it. (For the best evidence rule, see 19.1, 19.2.) This provision applies to any form of admissible documentary hearsay.

By s. 134(1) of the Act:

> 'copy', in relation to a document, means anything on to which information recorded in the document has been copied, by whatever means, and whether directly or indirectly...

8.23 SAFEGUARDS IN RELATION TO ADMISSION OF HEARSAY EVIDENCE

The Criminal Justice Act 1988 contained two specific powers to exclude hearsay evidence. Section 25 of the Act empowered the judge to exclude hearsay generally if he considered that, although technically admissible, it ought not to be admitted. Section 26 restricted the admissibility of hearsay statements contained in documents prepared for the purposes of pending or contemplated criminal proceedings or a criminal investigation.[63] The Criminal Justice Act 2003 repeals these powers and replaces them with very different safeguards, the main features of which are a wholly new power to stop the case where the case against the accused depends on 'unconvincing' hearsay evidence, and a new weak and essentially pointless power to exclude hearsay evidence if admitting it would result in an undue waste of time. Section 126(2)(a) expressly preserves the discretionary power to exclude evidence under s. 78 of the Police and Criminal Evidence Act 1984 (see 3.7) in relation to hearsay evidence admissible under Chapter 2 of Part 11; and s. 126(2)(b) preserves any other exclusionary powers of the court to exclude evidence. The preservation of the power to exclude under s. 78 is likely to be the most valuable safeguard, though it must be recalled that it applies only to evidence tendered by the prosecution (see 3.9). The power to stop the case, by its own terms, is likely to be of limited utility.

8.24 SECTION 125: DUTY TO STOP CASE WHERE EVIDENCE UNCONVINCING

Section 125 of the Act provides:

> (1) If on a defendant's trial before a judge and jury for an offence the court is satisfied at any time after the close of the case for the prosecution that—
>> (a) the case against the defendant is based wholly or partly on a statement not made in oral evidence in the proceedings, and
>> (b) the evidence provided by the statement is so unconvincing that, considering its importance to the case against the defendant, his conviction of the offence would be unsafe,
>
> the court must either direct the jury to acquit the defendant of the offence or, if it considers that there ought to be a retrial, discharge the jury.

(2) Where—
  (a) a jury is directed under subsection (1) to acquit a defendant of an offence, and
  (b) the circumstances are such that, apart from this subsection, the defendant could if acquitted of that offence be found guilty of another offence,

the defendant may not be found guilty of that other offence if the court is satisfied as mentioned in subsection (1) in respect of it.

---

[63] For the principles applicable to the exercise of these powers, see the 8th edn of this work, 10.11 *et seq.*

(3) If—
     (a) a jury is required to determine under section 4A(2) of the Criminal Procedure (Insanity) Act 1964 (c. 84) whether a person charged on an indictment with an offence did the act or made the omission charged, and
     (b) the court is satisfied as mentioned in subsection (1) above at any time after the close of the case for the prosecution that—
          (i) the case against the defendant is based wholly or partly on a statement not made in oral evidence in the proceedings, and
          (ii) the evidence provided by the statement is so unconvincing that, considering its importance to the case against the person, a finding that he did the act or made the omission would be unsafe,

the court must either direct the jury to acquit the defendant of the offence or, if it considers that there ought to be a rehearing, discharge the jury.

(4) This section does not prejudice any other power a court may have to direct a jury to acquit a person of an offence or to discharge a jury.

This provision is essentially the same as the power under s. 107 of the Act to stop the trial where contaminated evidence of bad character has been admitted (see 6.21). As in the case of s. 107, the power under s. 125 applies only to trials on indictment before a judge and jury (s. 125(1)), and not to summary proceedings or proceedings on indictment tried by a judge sitting alone. Clearly, there may be cases in which a judge or magistrates might prefer not to continue with a trial when unconvincing evidence of such importance has been adduced, and it is submitted that they have ample power to acquit or order a re-trial in such a case apart from s. 125. The duty to 'stop the case' means that, in the circumstances specified in s. 125(1)(a) and (b), the judge must either direct the jury to acquit the accused, or discharge the jury and order a re-trial. The judge would choose the first course of action in what will presumably be the most usual case, i.e., the case in which the case against the accused, including the unconvincing hearsay evidence, is so weak that it would be pointless or unfair to require the accused to stand trial again. He would choose the second in a case in which there might be a *prima facie* case against the accused apart from the unconvincing hearsay evidence, so that a re-trial is justified. It would, of course, be impossible to continue the trial before the present jury because of the prejudice to the accused caused by the admission of the unconvincing evidence. The Act offers no definition of 'unconvincing'. Given that s. 125(1)(a) envisages that a conviction may be unsafe if the evidence is sufficiently important to the case against the accused, it is submitted that it must mean that the evidence is so unreliable or lacking in probative value that it would be not be safe to base a conviction on it either wholly or substantially. If so, where a judge stops the case on this basis, he is likely to take the view that the evidence should be excluded at the re-trial (though that must be a matter for the judge who presides at the re-trial). But presumably, in many cases, there will be no reason why the judge could not form the view that the evidence is unconvincing at the stage when he is asked to admit it, rather than after it has been admitted; in which case he could avoid s. 125 simply by excluding the evidence under s. 78 of the Police and Criminal Evidence Act 1984. If the judge takes the course of directing the jury to acquit, s. 125(2) provides further that the accused may not be not be convicted of any offences with respect to which the jury would have been entitled to return an alternative verdict and which are also affected in the same way by the unconvincing evidence.[64] Section 125(3) applies the same principles to proceedings to determine whether the

---

[64] As to the circumstances in which a jury may return alternative verdicts, see Criminal Law Act 1967, s. 6(3); *Blackstone's Criminal Practice*, 2009 edn, para. D18.41 *et seq.*

accused did the act or made the omission charged for the purposes of s. 4(A)(2) of the Criminal Procedure (Insanity) Act 1964.[65] Section 125(4) preserves any other powers of the court in a trial on indictment to direct an acquittal or discharge the jury.

8.25 SECTION 126(1): EXCLUSIONARY DISCRETION

Section 126(1) of the Act provides:

> In criminal proceedings the court may refuse to admit a statement as evidence of a matter stated if—
> (a) the statement was made other than in oral evidence in the proceedings, and
> (b) the court is satisfied that the case for excluding the statement, taking account of the danger that to admit it would result in undue waste of time, substantially outweighs the case for admitting it, taking account of the value of the evidence.

This is an essentially pointless provision, which itself represents an undue waste of time. Unlike s. 78 of the Police and Criminal Evidence Act 1984, s. 126(1) applies to evidence adduced by any party, and is not restricted to evidence adduced by the prosecution. There was clearly a case for giving the court the power to exclude certain kinds of hearsay evidence when tendered by any party, for example evidence which appears to be seriously flawed or unreliable, or evidence which might be effectively beyond challenge by an opponent, or the admission of which might for any reason be so unfair that it ought to be excluded. But if some such power to exclude was to be provided in relation to hearsay evidence generally, it would surely have been preferable to give the court power to exclude on some more substantial ground.[66] Given the strong test that the case for exclusion (under which the probative value of the evidence is displaced by nothing more tangible than the danger of undue waste of time) must substantially outweigh the case for admission, if evidence falls to be excluded by virtue of s. 126(1), it would seem that it must have virtually no probative value whatsoever. If so, it was hardly necessary to give the court a specific statutory ground for excluding it. The discretion may perhaps be employed to exclude evidence where other (and perhaps more cogent) evidence of the same facts has been given, or is available.

8.26 SECTION 123: INQUIRY INTO CAPABILITY OF MAKER OF STATEMENT

Section 123 of the Act provides:

> (1) Nothing in section 116, 119 or 120 makes a statement admissible as evidence if it was made by a person who did not have the required capability at the time when he made the statement.
> (2) Nothing in section 117 makes a statement admissible as evidence if any person who, in order for the requirements of section 117(2) to be satisfied, must at any time have supplied or received the information concerned or created or received the document or part concerned—
> (a) did not have the required capability at that time, or

---

[65] See *Blackstone's Criminal Practice*, 2009 edn, para. D12.2 *et seq.*

[66] A model which might well have been followed is that of American Federal Rule of Evidence 403, which includes the concern of s. 126 without making it the central issue. This rule provides: 'Although relevant, evidence may be excluded if its probative value is substantially outweighed by the danger of unfair prejudice, confusion of the issues, or misleading the jury, or by considerations of undue delay, waste of time, or needless presentation of cumulative evidence'.

> (b) cannot be identified but cannot reasonably be assumed to have had the required capability at that time.
>
> (3) For the purposes of this section a person has the required capability if he is capable of—
>   (a) understanding questions put to him about the matters stated, and
>   (b) giving answers to such questions which can be understood.

(4) Where by reason of this section there is an issue as to whether a person had the required capability when he made a statement—
    (a) proceedings held for the determination of the issue must take place in the absence of the jury (if there is one);
    (b) in determining the issue the court may receive expert evidence and evidence from any person to whom the statement in question was made;
    (c) the burden of proof on the issue lies on the party seeking to adduce the statement, and the standard of proof is the balance of probabilities.

The court must be satisfied that the maker of a hearsay statement admissible under ss. 116, 119, and 120, or the person who supplied the information or created or received a document for the purposes of s. 117(2), had the required capability to do so. If there is an issue as to that matter, s. 123(4) requires the court to inquire into it. The inquiry must be held in the absence of the jury, if there is one. The burden of proof in the inquiry lies on the party who seeks to adduce the statement and may be satisfied on the balance of probability. The court may receive evidence from any person to whom the statement was made, and, if appropriate, from an expert witness. By virtue of s. 123(3) a person has the required capability if he is capable of understanding questions put to him about the matters stated, and of giving answers to those questions which can be understood. Although s. 123 does not use the word 'competent', this test is in fact the same as the general test for the competence of witnesses under s. 53(3) of the Youth Justice and Criminal Evidence Act 1999: as to this see 15.3. But under s. 123, the competence of the person in question must be determined with reference to the time at which the statement was made, or, in the case of s. 117(2) the time at which the information was supplied or the document was created or received. This is true even if (in the case of statements admissible under s. 119 or s. 120) the maker of the statement also gives evidence as a witness at trial. In order for the maker of the statement to have become a witness, of course, the court must have been further satisfied of his competence to give evidence at the time of trial.

8.27 SECTION 124: IMPEACHMENT OF MAKER OF HEARSAY STATEMENT

Where a hearsay statement is admitted and the maker of the statement does not give evidence at trial, it is, of course, impossible for the opponent to cross-examine him. This is, as we have seen, the main objection to the admission of hearsay evidence. In order to compensate for this disadvantage, s. 124 of the Act enables the opponent to adduce certain evidence affecting the credit of the maker of the statement for the purpose of attacking his credibility. The admission of this evidence simulates those weapons which would have been available for the same purpose in the hands of a cross-examiner. For example, evidence may be adduced of other statements made by the maker of the statement which has been admitted which are inconsistent with it, or of any facts which may give rise to a suspicion of bias or partiality on his part.

This section is dealt with further in the context of attacking the credit of witnesses generally: see 17.13.

8.28 SECTION 132: RULES OF COURT

Section 132 of the Act provides for rules of court to be made dealing with the admission of hearsay evidence in criminal cases. These rules deal with the notice to be given by a party who wishes to adduce such evidence, so that the opposing parties may be prepared to deal with it. The rules made pursuant to this section are contained in Part 34 of the Criminal Procedure Rules 2005.

8.29 HEARSAY STATEMENTS PRODUCED BY COMPUTERS

We saw at 7.15.3 that, where a computer or other mechanical device is used to perform calculations or other automatic functions without human intervention, no hearsay issue arises, and the printouts of the machine's functions are admissible as real evidence (*Minors* [1989] 1 WLR 441; *DPP v McKeown* [1997] 1 WLR 295). But where a person makes a statement using a computer as a writing tool, the same hearsay issues arise as in a case where that person makes a statement by any other means. In civil cases, hearsay computer records were first made admissible by s. 5 of the Civil Evidence Act 1968. But there is now no hearsay objection to the admission of records produced by computers in civil cases, because the rule against hearsay has been abolished in civil cases by the Civil Evidence Act 1995 which, accordingly, repealed s. 5 of the 1968 Act.

In criminal cases, hearsay statements produced by computers were formerly governed by s. 69 of the Police and Criminal Evidence Act 1984, which laid down the conditions under which they could be admitted. But the House of Lords in *Governor of Brixton Prison, ex parte Levin* [1997] AC 741 and *Shephard* [1993] AC 380 made it clear that s. 69 operated only to impose conditions on the admissibility of computer records, relating to proof of the proper functioning of the computer, and did not confer admissibility on them. As there was no common law basis for the admission of hearsay records produced by computers (as opposed to the non-hearsay records discussed above) it followed that they could be admitted in criminal cases only when they were admissible under s. 23 or s. 24 of the Criminal Justice Act 1988. On the recommendation of the Law Commission (No. 245, para. 13.23) s. 69 was repealed with effect from 14 April 2000, without replacement, by s. 60 of the Youth Justice and Criminal Evidence Act 1999. The Law Commission felt that the restrictions imposed by s. 69 were unnecessary and worked badly. The result is that hearsay statements produced by computers remained admissible under s. 23 or s. 24 and no conditions pertaining to the working of the computer were imposed.

The admissibility provisions of ss. 23 and 24 of the Criminal Justice Act 1988 were not entirely apposite to the particular case of computer records, and this was shown by the manner in which the courts sometimes struggled to fit them within the existing statutory framework. A good example is *Governor of Brixton Prison, ex parte Levin* [1997] AC 741. The United States government sought the extradition of the applicant to face charges involving his unauthorized access to a computer belonging to Citibank in Parsipanny, New Jersey, whereby he was alleged fraudulently to have effected the transfer of sums of money from the accounts of Citibank customers into bank accounts which he controlled. He argued that the computer printouts tendered to prove the transfers of funds were hearsay, and had been improperly admitted at the extradition proceedings under s. 69 of the Police and Criminal Evidence Act 1984. The House rejected this argument. Lord Hoffmann said (*ibid.* at 746):

> The printouts are tendered to prove the transfers of funds which they record. They do not assert that such transfers took place. They record the transfers themselves, created by the interaction between whoever purported to request the transfers and the computer program in Parsipanny. The evidential status of the printouts is no different from that of a photocopy of a forged cheque.
>
> If the printouts were hearsay, s. 69 would not make them admissible. They might be admissible under s. 23 or 24 of the Criminal Justice Act 1988.

The evidence adduced in *Levin* was plainly evidence which should be admissible. But the appellant's argument that it was hearsay appears to be correct. Lord Hoffmann's analogy to the photocopy of the forged cheque is hardly convincing. A better analogy would be to a handwritten report of the fund transfers, which would be hearsay, and could only have been admissible under s. 23 or 24 of the 1988 Act. It is difficult to see how the printouts could be said to 'record the transfers themselves', yet not to 'assert that such transfers took place'. The law in this respect was in a position akin to that of hearsay generally before *Myers v DPP* [1965] AC 1001 (see 7.3) drew attention to the urgency of the need for simplification and reform. Given the increasingly widespread use of computer records of all kinds as evidence, it was to be hoped that the situation would be remedied swiftly. Parliament apparently intended to accomplish this through s. 129 of the Criminal Justice Act 2003, which provides:

> (1) Where a representation of any fact—
>   (a) is made otherwise than by a person, but
>   (b) depends for its accuracy on information supplied (directly or indirectly) by a person,
> the representation is not admissible in criminal proceedings as evidence of the fact unless it is proved that the information was accurate.[67]

The definition of the phrase 'matter stated' in s. 115(3) of the Act (see 7.1) appears to confirm that a representation of fact 'made' by a computer is hearsay, because the computer produces the statement as a result of the input of information by a person who intends to cause the computer to operate on the basis that the information is correct. It is submitted that s. 129, like s. 69 of the 1984 Act, does not render such a statement admissible, but imposes conditions on its admissibility. The difference is that under s. 129, the conditions pertain to the accuracy of the information rather than the working of the computer. In a sense, therefore, the statement is one made jointly by the person and the computer. This is a modest improvement, but it seems that the statement must be admissible, if at all, under the statutory admissibility rules, and if this is true, s. 129 essentially provides only a revised version of the position under s. 23 of the 1988 Act and s. 69 of the 1984 Act. If this analysis is correct, and the Home Office Explanatory Note to s. 129 (para. 432) in no way contradicts it, the ultimate hearsay problem as to computer-generated evidence has still not been resolved. This seems highly unsatisfactory, given that it would be relatively simple to do so by statute.

---

[67] Section 129(2) provides that this does not effect the presumption that a mechanical device has been properly set or calibrated; see 20.14.2.

C   HEARSAY ADMISSIBLE BY STATUTE IN CIVIL CASES

SUMMARY OF MAIN POINTS

- The Rule against Hearsay was abrogated in civil cases by the Civil Evidence Act 1995. Its hearsay quality may affect the weight of evidence, but not its admissibility.
- Provision is made for the impeachment of the maker of a hearsay statement.

8.30 EVIDENCE ADMISSIBLE BY VIRTUE OF THE CIVIL EVIDENCE ACT 1995

The Civil Evidence Act 1995 achieved the abolition of the rule against hearsay in civil cases. This means that hearsay statements are generally admissible in civil proceedings as evidence of the truth of any relevant matter stated in them, regardless of any other evidential value they may have.[68]

In common with other statutes which have provided for the admissibility of hearsay evidence, the 1995 Act does not cure any defect of evidence other than its hearsay quality. Section 14 specifically provides that nothing in the Act affects the exclusion of evidence on a ground other than hearsay: 'whether the evidence falls to be excluded in pursuance of any enactment or rule of law, for failure to comply with rules of court or an order of the court, or otherwise'. The Act is silent on the question of any judicial discretion to exclude evidence. But as we saw at 3.6, the judge's powers to control and regulate the evidence admitted in civil cases under r. 32.1 of the Civil Procedure Rules 1998 correspond to a general discretionary power and may be used at least as broadly as those available in criminal cases under s. 78 of the Police and Criminal Evidence Act 1984 (see 3.7).

Section 5(1) of the Act excludes hearsay evidence contained in statements made by those who would be regarded as incompetent as witnesses. The section provides:

> (1) Hearsay evidence shall not be admitted in civil proceedings if or to the extent that it is shown to consist of, or to be proved by means of, a statement made by a person who at the time he made the statement was not competent as a witness.

For this purpose 'not competent as a witness' means suffering from such mental or physical infirmity, or lack of understanding, as would render a person incompetent as a witness in civil proceedings; but a child shall be treated as competent as a witness if he satisfies the requirements of s. 96(2)(a) and (b) of the Children Act 1989 (conditions for reception of unsworn evidence of child).[69]

---

[68] For example, as previous consistent or inconsistent statements; though, in these cases, s. 6 of the Act preserves the common law rules of admissibility while widening their evidential value: see 16.7 *et seq.*, 17.7.

[69] As to the competence of children and persons suffering from mental disability, see 15.12, 15.13. As to persons with physical disabilities related to hearing and speech, their evidence by means of writing or signs is included in the definition of 'oral evidence' by s. 13, so they are presumably to be regarded as competent, as they are at common law. A party seeking to exclude evidence under s. 5(1) has the burden of proving that the maker of

8.31 ABOLITION OF THE RULE AGAINST HEARSAY IN CIVIL PROCEEDINGS

Subsections (1) and (2) of s. 1 of the Civil Evidence Act 1995 provide:

> (1) In civil proceedings evidence shall not be excluded on the ground that it is hearsay.
> (2) In this Act—
>   (a) 'hearsay' means a statement made otherwise than by a person while giving oral evidence in the proceedings which is tendered as evidence of the matters stated; and
>   (b) references to hearsay include hearsay of whatever degree.

Section 13 provides, *inter alia*:

> 'statement' means any representation of fact or opinion, however made.
>
> 'oral evidence' includes evidence which, by reason of a defect of speech or hearing, a person called as a witness gives in writing or by signs.

The automatic admission of hearsay evidence in civil cases under the Civil Evidence Act 1995 does not of itself violate the fair trial provisions of art. 6 of the European Convention on Human Rights. The test is always whether or not basic procedural fairness is afforded to the parties: see 1.7; 7.5.

The definition of hearsay provided by s. 1(2) was the first statutory definition of hearsay to be enacted. It corresponds well with the accepted definitions adopted at common law (see 7.1). It should be noted that, unlike the Civil Evidence Act 1968, the 1995 Act does not distinguish between different levels of hearsay, thereby avoiding the complexities of the hearsay-within-hearsay cases under the 1968 Act and at common law (see 7.6.3). However, the presence of multiple hearsay may adversely affect the weight of a statement (Civil Evidence Act 1995, s. 4(2)(c)). By virtue of the definition of 'statement' in s. 13, the Act applies alike to statements of fact and statements of opinion.

In evaluating multiple hearsay, it may be important to have regard to the original statement, i. e., the source of the facts or opinion in question. Section 13 defines 'original statement' as follows:

> 'the original statement', in relation to hearsay evidence, means the underlying statement (if any) by—
>   (a) in the case of evidence of fact, a person having personal knowledge of that fact, or
>   (b) in the case of evidence of opinion, the person whose opinion it is.

8.32 MEANING OF 'CIVIL PROCEEDINGS'

Section 11 of the Civil Evidence Act 1995 provides:

> In this Act 'civil proceedings' means civil proceedings, before any tribunal, in relation to which the strict rules of evidence apply, whether as a matter of law or by agreement of the parties.
>   References to 'the court' and 'rules of court' shall be construed accordingly.

The Civil Evidence Acts 1938 and 1968 did not apply to civil proceedings in the magistrates' courts, though there were some specific provisions, such as rules made pursuant to s. 96 of the

the statement was incompetent: *JC v CC* [2001] EWCA Civ 1625. Compare the provision in criminal cases under s. 123 of the Criminal Justice Act 2003: 8.26.

Children Act 1989, which did. Section 11 of the 1995 Act is wide enough to cover any proceedings in magistrates' courts. Of course, the Act has no application to criminal proceedings in any court.

8.33 PROCEDURAL SAFEGUARDS

Section 2 of the Civil Evidence Act 1995 provides:

(1) A party proposing to adduce hearsay evidence in civil proceedings shall, subject to the following provisions of this section, give to the other party or parties to the proceedings—
    (a) such notice (if any) of that fact, and
    (b) on request, such particulars of or relating to the evidence,
as is reasonable and practicable in the circumstances for the purpose of enabling him or them to deal with any matters arising from its being hearsay.

(2) Provision may be made by rules of court—
    (a) specifying classes of proceedings or evidence in relation to which subsection (1) does not apply, and
    (b) as to the manner in which (including the time within which) the duties imposed by that subsection are to be complied with in the cases where it does apply.
(3) Subsection (1) may also be excluded by agreement of the parties; and compliance with the duty to give notice may in any case be waived by the person to whom notice is required to be given.
(4) A failure to comply with subsection (1), or with rules under subsection (2)(b), does not affect the admissibility of the evidence but may be taken into account by the court—
    (a) in considering the exercise of its powers with respect to the course of the proceedings and costs, and
    (b) as a matter adversely affecting the weight to be given to the evidence in accordance with section 4.

Rule 33.2 of the Civil Procedure Rules 1998 provides that the service of a witness statement is a sufficient notice of the intention to adduce hearsay evidence contained in it, whether or not it is proposed to call the maker of the witness statement to give evidence. But where it is not proposed to call the maker to give evidence, the other parties must be informed of that fact and of the reason why he will not be called. These matters may affect the weight of the evidence (see s. 4(2) of the Act). Where the hearsay evidence is contained in a document other than a witness statement, for example, in business records, r. 33.2 requires the service of a separate notice identifying the hearsay evidence, stating that the party adducing it proposes to rely on it at trial, and giving the reason why the maker of the hearsay statement will not be called as a witness. These rules do not apply to evidence to be adduced at hearings other than trials, for example, interim applications (r. 33.3). The structure of the rules is considerably simpler than that laid down by s. 8 of the Civil Evidence Act 1968, which required a progression of notice by the proponent, and counter-notice by an opponent who wished to require production of the maker of a statement for cross-examination.[70] Under s. 2 of the 1995 Act, the form and content of the notice are straightforward, and there is no system of counter-notice. But s. 3 of the Act provides:

Rules of court may provide that where a party to civil proceedings adduces hearsay evidence of a statement made by a person and does not call that person as a witness, any other party to the proceedings

---

[70] See the fifth edn of this work at 10.7 *et seq.*

may, with the leave of the court, call that person as a witness and cross-examine him on the statement as if he had been called by the first-mentioned party and as if the hearsay statement were his evidence in chief.

Rule 33.4 of the Civil Procedure Rules 1998 provides a procedure which gives effect to this section.

Evidence may also be admissible other than by virtue of the Act, though, unlike the Civil Evidence Act 1968, it is difficult to think of evidence which would not be admissible under the Civil Evidence Act 1995. With respect to any such evidence, it is provided in s. 1(3) and (4) that:

> (3) Nothing in this Act affects the admissibility of evidence admissible apart from this section.
>
> (4) The provisions of sections 2 to 6 (safeguards and supplementary provisions relating to hearsay evidence) do not apply in relation to hearsay evidence admissible apart from this section, notwithstanding that it may also be admissible by virtue of this section.

Further provision for the making of rules for carrying the provisions of the Act into effect, and for the application of the Act to arbitration proceedings is made by s. 12. For the applicable rules, see *Blackstone's Civil Practice*, 2009 edn, ch. 51.

8.34 WEIGHT

Section 4 of the Civil Evidence Act 1995 provides:

> (1) In estimating the weight (if any) to be given to hearsay evidence in civil proceedings the court shall have regard to any circumstances from which any inference can reasonably be drawn as to the reliability or otherwise of the evidence.
> (2) Regard may be had, in particular, to the following—
>   (a) whether it would have been reasonable and practicable for the party by whom the evidence was adduced to have produced the maker of the original statement as a witness;
>   (b) whether the original statement was made contemporaneously with the occurrence or existence of the matters stated;
>   (c) whether the evidence involves multiple hearsay;
>   (d) whether any person involved had any motive to conceal or misrepresent matters;
>   (e) whether the original statement was an edited account, or was made in collaboration with another or for a particular purpose;
>   (f) whether the circumstances in which the evidence is adduced as hearsay are such as to suggest an attempt to prevent proper evaluation of its weight.

In common with earlier statutes, the Act lays down specific matters to be taken into account in assessing the weight of the evidence admitted. As weight, rather than admissibility is now the focus, the provision is understandable. But it may be observed that s. 4(2) suggests factors which any experienced judge would automatically take into account. The list of factors is not intended to be exhaustive. Section 4(2)(a) is a welcome indication that live oral evidence is to be preferred, and that it will be unwise to use the Act to protect potential witnesses from having to undergo cross-examination. Ordinarily, the weight of a hearsay statement must be considerably less where it is clear that the maker could have been called as a witness without undue difficulty.

8.35 OTHER PROVISIONS

8.35.1 Use of copies

Section 8 of the Civil Evidence Act 1995 provides:

> (1) Where a statement contained in a document is admissible as evidence in civil proceedings, it may be proved—
>   (a) by production of that document, or
>   (b) whether or not that document is still in existence, by the production of a copy of that document or of the material part of it,
> authenticated in such manner as the court may approve.
> (2) It is immaterial for this purpose how many removes there are between a copy and the original.

Section 13 provides, inter alia:

> 'document' means anything in which information of any description is recorded, and 'copy', in relation to a document, means anything onto which information recorded in the document has been copied, by whatever means and whether directly or indirectly.

These provisions are the same as those now applicable in criminal cases: see Criminal Justice Act 2003, s. 133 (see 8.22).

8.35.2 Previous statements of persons called as witnesses

Section 6 makes provision for cases in which a previous statement made by a person called as a witness may be admitted. These statements raise other issues, and are dealt with in the appropriate places in this book: see 16.7; 17.7. For the corresponding provision in criminal cases, see 8.21.

8.35.3 Impeachment of maker of admissible hearsay statement

Where a hearsay statement is admissible by virtue of the Act, s. 5(2) provides that certain evidence may be adduced to attack or support the credibility of the maker, akin to the evidence which might have been adduced had the maker been called as a witness. This evidence is subject to other rules, and is considered at 17.13. Rule 33.5 of the Civil Procedure Rules 1998 provides a procedure which gives effect to this subsection. For the corresponding provision in criminal cases, see 8.27.

8.35.4 Preservation of common law exceptions

Continuing provisions contained in s. 9 of the Civil Evidence Act 1968, s. 7(2) of the Civil Evidence Act 1995 preserves without altering in substance certain common law exceptions to the rule against hearsay relating to admissions, public records, published works, and evidence of reputation and family tradition. As to these rules, see 8.2 *et seq.* For the rules governing admissions, which are said to be 'superseded' by the Act, see 9.1.

8.35.5 Records of business and public authority

Section 9 makes provision for the authentication of records of businesses and public authorities. The details of this section may be found at 19.11.

8.36 RECOMMENDED FURTHER READING

Birch, D., 'Criminal Justice Act 2003 Hearsay: same old story, same old song?' [2004] *Criminal Law Review* 556.

Murphy, P., 'Practising safe hearsay: surrender may be inevitable, but shouldn't we take precautions?' (1997) 1(3) *International Journal of Evidence and Proof* 105.

Taylor, G., 'Two English hearsay heresies' (2005) 9(2) *International Journal of Evidence and Proof* 105.

Wilde, D., 'Hearsay in criminal cases: *res gestae* and dying declarations: *R v Bedingfield* revisited' (2000) 4(2) *International Journal of Evidence and Proof* 107.

Zuckerman, A.A.S., 'The futility of hearsay' [1996] *Criminal Law Review* 4.

 ## 8.37 QUESTIONS FOR DISCUSSION BASED ON *R* v *COKE; LITTLETON* AND *BLACKSTONE* v *COKE* (for case files go to the Online Resource Centre)

8.37.1 *Coke; Littleton*

1. Referring to the list you prepared after studying Chapter 7 (see 7.18), consider whether each item of evidence listed which you concluded is hearsay may be admissible under the Criminal Justice Act 2003.

2. Assume that Dr Espinasse accomplished his work using a computer, and that the results of his work are available as a printout of the data produced by the computer. Is the printout admissible, and if so, for what purpose? What foundation would have to be laid for it to be admissible?

3. If you had to prove Angela Blackstone's age at the date of the alleged assault, how would you do it?

8.37.2 *Blackstone* v *Coke*

1. Discuss the admissibility of the proof of evidence supplied by Anthony Hennecky. If admitted, what weight would it have? What steps would Coke have to take to have it admitted?

2. Discuss the admissibility of the medical records kept by the hospital concerning the birth of Margaret's son. How could they be authenticated?

8.38 GENERAL QUESTIONS FOR DISCUSSION

1. What statements are included in *res gestae*?

2. What are the 'public information exceptions' preserved by s. 118 of the Criminal Justice Act 2003?

3. In what circumstances may the statement of a person who is dead be admitted in evidence in a criminal trial? And in a civil trial?

4. An important prosecution witness in a murder trial has emigrated to Australia and has stated that she is too busy to return to testify. What would the prosecutor have to establish in order to make her witness statement admissible in evidence?

5. If a witness has an irrational fear of testifying, will their written statement be admissible under s. 116 of the Criminal Justice Act 2003?

6. Under which provision of the Criminal Justice Act 2003 would a bank's internal reports on lost and stolen credit cards be admissible?

7. If the prosecution wants to adduce the witness statement of a person who is unavailable to give evidence at trial, which provision of the Criminal Justice Act 2003 will it rely on and what conditions must be met?

8. When is leave of court required to admit statements under ss. 116 and 117 of the Criminal Justice Act 2003?

9. A woman refuses to give evidence at the trial of her husband for the rape of their 19-year-old daughter. Under which provision of the Criminal Justice Act 2003 may it be possible for her witness statement, which was adverse to his interests, to be admitted?

10. What safeguards apply to the admission of hearsay evidence in civil trials?

9

THE RULE AGAINST HEARSAY III: ADMISSIONS AND CONFESSIONS

A ADMISSIONS

SUMMARY OF MAIN POINTS

- An admission is a statement in any form adverse to the interests of the person who made it.

- Admissions are admissible at common law as an exception to the Rule against Hearsay provided they are made freely and voluntarily.

- Section 7(1) of the Civil Evidence 1995 supercedes the common law but preserves the admissibility of admissions, which must now be regarded as non-hearsay in civil cases.

- In certain circumstances a party may be bound by admissions made by his agent (including his legal representatives) if the agent has either an express or an implied power to make admissions on behalf of the party.

- Admissions must be distinguished from a separate common law rule whereby acts and declarations of co-conspirators, or those acting pursuant to a joint enterprise, made in the course of and in furtherance of the common design, may be admitted against all the accused as evidence of the common design.

Admissions and confessions are the most important common law exceptions to the rule against hearsay. 'Confession' is the name given to an admission made by the accused in a criminal case. Although subject to the overriding consideration that they should have been made freely and voluntarily (a condition on which the common law insisted rigorously as a reaction to the common practice of obtaining confessions by torture, which persisted in the continental civil law systems until the late eighteenth or early nineteenth centuries) admissions and confessions are regarded as among the most reliable and cogent kinds of evidence. The underlying justification for this view is that a party would not voluntarily make a statement adverse to his case unless it were true. The general practice in the United States is now to regard admissions and confessions as a form of non-hearsay evidence, and many rules now declare that they enjoy that status (see, e.g., Federal Rule of Evidence 801(d)(2)). In England, no such express transformation has occurred, but the basis of admissibility has been modified by statute, and in civil cases, the position is in effect the same. The relevant provisions are set out at 8.2. Section 7(1) of the Civil Evidence Act 1995 declares that the common law rule relating to admissions, which had previously been 'preserved' by the Civil Evidence Act 1968, is 'superseded' by the provisions of the 1995 Act. The effect of this provision must be that admissions, rather than being admissible by virtue of an exception to the rule against hearsay, are now admissible because the hearsay quality of evidence is no longer a bar to admissibility in civil proceedings (see 8.30). But the question of the scope of admissions may continue to raise questions, especially in the case of admissions made other than by a party personally, and the common law rules may occasionally prove useful, at least by way of analogy. Section 118(1) of the Criminal Justice Act 2003 preserves any rule of law relating to the admissibility of admissions made by agents in criminal proceedings. Section 118(1) also preserves any rules of law relating to the admissibility of confessions or mixed statements in criminal proceedings. The admissibility of confessions when tendered by the prosecution is now governed by s. 76 of the Police and Criminal Evidence Act 1984, but the principles developed at common law remain valuable as a source of guidance in the application of that section. Mixed statements are still governed, at least to some extent, by common law rules. Section 128 of the Criminal Justice Act 2003, by inserting a new s. 76A into the Police and Criminal Evidence Act 1984, introduces a test for admissibility of confessions when tendered by a co-accused which is (apart from the standard of proof) the same as that laid down by s. 76. Admissions are dealt with in this part of this chapter; confessions and mixed statements are dealt with in Part B.

9.1 PRINCIPLES OF ADMISSIBILITY

The admissions dealt with in this chapter are properly referred to as informal admissions. This term serves to distinguish them from formal admissions,[1] which are concessions made *inter partes* for the purpose of the proceedings, have the effect of establishing the facts formally admitted without the need for recourse to evidence, and which cannot be withdrawn without leave.

Informal admissions are statements made by a party (or by some person by whose admission a party is bound as a matter of law) from which the court would be entitled to, but is not bound to find facts or draw inferences adverse to the case of that party. An informal admission is, therefore, merely one piece of evidence to which the court may have regard when considering the facts to which it relates. Its weight will depend upon the circumstances in which it is made, and the clarity or ambiguity of the contents of the statement. Evidence may be given to explain away or contradict the admission, or to show that because of the circumstances in which it was made, no or little weight should be attached to it. An admission may be inferred from a statement in any form, whether oral, in writing or by some conduct which can only be interpreted as an acknowledgement of a weakness or defect in a party's case, such as evidence of a conspiracy between a relative of the party and a solicitor's clerk to suborn false witnesses at the trial,[2] the deliberate destruction of evidence, or failing to submit to a test which would establish paternity.[3]

Section 9 of the Civil Evidence Act 1968 provided that admissions in civil cases should be admissible by virtue of that section, in any circumstances in which they would have been admissible at common law, i.e., the section preserved and adopted the common law rule without altering its substance. However, this section has now been replaced by s. 7(1) of the Civil Evidence Act 1995, which provides:

> The common law rule effectively preserved by section 9(1) and (2)(a) of the Civil Evidence Act 1968 (admissibility of admissions adverse to a party) is superseded by the provisions of this Act.

The apparent intent of this provision is that admissions should be admissible without reference to the rule against hearsay, which the Act abolishes altogether in civil proceedings. This being so, the difficulty which has long arisen in criminal cases over 'mixed' statements (which are partially unfavourable and partially favourable to the maker) will not occur in a civil case: the whole of such a statement will be of evidential value. Moreover, there is no reason why an admission should not be evidence in the case generally, in contrast to the common law rule applicable to criminal cases that a confession is evidence against the accused who makes it, but not against any other person implicated by it. However, there is a question whether statements by persons who lack authority to bind a party by their statements should be admissible, for example, a statement made by an agent, purportedly on behalf of a party, but made in excess of the agent's authority. It

---

[1] See Chapter 20, Part A; and see the subject of judicial confessions, dealt with in 14.2.2. Certain admissions may also have effect as estoppels by conduct or *per rem judicatam*.

[2] *Moriarty v London, Chatham & Dover Railway Co.* (1870) LR 5 QB 314. And see *Li Shu-Ling v R* [1989] AC 270, in which the Privy Council upheld the admissibility as a confession of a videotaped re-enactment of the killing of the victim, with whose murder the accused was charged, made by the accused at the request of police officers. The accused did not dispute that he killed the victim, but told the police that it was an accident, and he was fully cautioned before agreeing to participate in the re-enactment. But see also *Timothy v State* [2000] 1 WLR 485.

[3] *Re H (A Minor) (Blood Tests: Parental Rights)* [1996] 4 All ER 28; *Re CB (A Minor) (Blood Tests)* [1994] 2 FLR 762; *Re L (An Infant)* [1968] P 119.

is submitted that there is now no reason why such statements should not be admissible, but that their weight should be regarded as more akin to that of ordinary hearsay statements, rather than the usually much greater weight accorded to admissions. The common law rules on this subject are given below in deference to this uncertainty, and because they are sometimes of importance in criminal cases.

Because an informal admission is no more than a piece of evidence relevant to the determination of the truth or probability of certain facts, and because consequently its effect and weight (if any) are questions of fact, the proper interpretation of the statement is of great importance. It is, therefore, a fundamental principle that the whole of a statement said to contain an admission adverse to the case of the maker should be looked at by the court. It would be quite wrong to isolate, and perhaps take out of context, some part of a statement which appears on the face of it to constitute an admission. The statement read as a whole may have a quite different effect, which may modify or altogether nullify the appearance of an adverse admission. The evidential value of statements partly favourable and partly adverse to the maker has given rise to considerable problems in criminal cases, in which self-serving statements are inadmissible to prove the truth of any relevant facts stated therein. This is considered further in 9.17. But in civil cases, there is now no reason why those parts of the statement favourable to the maker should not be admissible to prove the truth of the facts stated, in the same way as those parts which are adverse. Be this as it may, the whole statement must be put before the court.[4]

The important rules at common law concern the circumstances in which a party may be bound by admissions (a) made by other persons or (b) made while acting in a different capacity and (c) the extent of the facts which may be proved by adverse admission. These matters will now be considered.

9.2 WHAT ADMISSIONS MAY BIND A PARTY

When an admission is admissible against a party, that party is often said to be bound by the admission. The simplest kind of binding admission is where a party himself makes a statement in his personal capacity. But in law, a party may in certain circumstances be bound by admissions which he did not make personally, or which he made while acting in another capacity. An example of the former is a statement made on his behalf by a party's duly authorized agent, for example his solicitor. An example of the latter is an admission made by the party while representing a person subject to disability, such as a minor, or while representing an estate or an organization. In these cases, the admission is imputed to the party as a matter of law, and may be admissible against him in his personal capacity.

9.2.1 Parties in other capacities

Wherever a party litigates in his personal capacity, either as claimant or defendant or otherwise, any admission made by him on another occasion may be proved against him, even though it may have been made by him in a representative or other capacity, such as in proceedings in which he represented a person under disability,[5] or acted on behalf of beneficiaries or dependants.

---

[4] In criminal cases, statements may sometimes be edited, so as to exclude matters which are inadmissible and prejudicial, for example revelations of bad character. See 9.15.2.

[5] *Stanton v Percival* (1855) 5 HL Cas 257.

At common law, however, the converse proposition does not hold good. There is no justification, in the absence of some other relationship of privity, for holding that a party to proceedings in which he is necessarily represented by another, should be prejudiced by any admission made by that representative elsewhere in his personal capacity. Thus, in *Legge* v *Edmonds* (1855) 25 LJ Ch 125, where the issue was the legitimacy or illegitimacy of a child of the plaintiff, who was suing as administratix of her husband's estate, admissions made by the plaintiff tending to show that she had committed adultery were held to be inadmissible, although in any proceedings involving the plaintiff in her personal capacity, they would clearly have been admissible on the same issue. As representative proceedings refer in reality only to civil cases, it seems probable that the common law has now been wholly superseded by statute though, as suggested above, the weight of admissions admitted in such circumstances may not always be very great. The position of private prosecutors in criminal cases may, however, prompt some academic speculation.

9.2.2 Other parties

At common law, it is a cardinal rule that an admission or a confession is admissible against the party who makes it, or who is bound by it, but not against any other party who may be implicated it. This rule is of considerable importance in criminal cases, and will be discussed in detail in relation to confessions at 9.16.[6] The rule has the logical, though curious consequence that if A and B are jointly charged with the offence of conspiracy, which cannot be committed by one person acting alone, and if the only evidence available to the prosecution is A's admission that he and B were guilty of the conspiracy, A may be convicted, but B must be acquitted because there is no admissible evidence against him.[7] Before the Civil Evidence Act 1968, the same result often obtained in divorce cases, in which A might be granted a divorce on the ground of Mrs A's admission of adultery with B, while B had to be dismissed from the suit for lack of evidence against him.[8] But now, it would seem that, because the common law rules about admissions have been superseded by the Civil Evidence Act 1995, with the result that admissions are now admissible without regard to hearsay considerations, an admission made by defendant A may be admissible also against co-defendant B.[9] The weight of the admission as against B may be far less than against A, at least in the absence of other evidence supporting it. In criminal cases, by way of contrast, an admission is admissible only against the party who makes it, or is bound by it.

---

[6] Although some inroad into this principle appears to have been made by the decision of the House of Lords in *Hayter* [2005] 1 WLR 605, it will be submitted that it remains a fundamental principle of the law relating to confessions: see 9.16.

[7] See, e.g., *Shannon* v *DPP* [1975] AC 717. As to conspiracy, see also Criminal Law Act 1977, s. 5(8) and (9).

[8] See, e.g., *Rutherford* v *Richardson* [1923] AC 1, 5 per Viscount Birkenhead.

[9] In the United States, as we have seen, Federal Rule 801(d)(2) specifically declares admissions to be non-hearsay. But there has been little enthusiasm for the logical consequence that admissions should be evidence in the case generally. A strong court in *O'Neal* v *Morgan* 637 F 2d 846 (2d Cir, 1980) held that an admission made by A was admissible also against co-defendant B to the extent that B failed to rebut the facts admitted, but the decision has found little support. In criminal cases in the United States, the rule that a confession is evidence against the maker only is not only a rule of evidence, but also raises issues of the right to confront the witnesses (see 7.5), given that a co-accused has no right to compel the accused who made the statement to submit to cross-examination. The rule is, therefore strictly insisted on.

9.2.3 Declarations in furtherance of common design contrasted

The common law rule about admissions must be carefully distinguished from a very different rule, with which it is sometimes confused, namely: if A and B are jointly charged and the prosecution allege a common design, the acts and declarations of A and B in furtherance of the common design, even though made by one in the absence of the other, are admissible evidence against both to prove the existence and carrying out of the common design.[10] This rule is specifically preserved by s. 118(1) of the Criminal Justice Act 2003 (see 8.2) but not by s. 7 of the Civil Evidence Act 1995. These acts and declarations are distinguishable from admissions because they are a part of the planning or implementation of the joint purpose. Where it is sought to admit the acts and declarations of one conspirator as evidence against another, it must be shown that the other was an accomplice with the first conspirator in a common offence or series of offences, and that the acts and declarations relate to such offence or offences. In *Gray* [1995] 2 Cr App R 100, it was alleged that a number of individuals had operated a 'network' for the purpose of committing offences of insider trading. The evidence against them consisted largely of telephone conversations between them, which were alleged to have been the means of disseminating information which enabled the offences to be committed. But the actual offences were committed by the individuals acting alone, so that, although it could be said in a general sense that there had been a conspiracy, the unlawful agreement did not relate to any offence committed jointly. The Court of Appeal held that, in these circumstances, the better view was that the common design rule had no application, with the result that the judge had misdirected the jury in inviting them to regard the acts and declarations of each conspirator as evidence against the others as well as himself. The Court left open the possibility that the rule could be stated more widely, but made it clear that, at a minimum, the prosecution would be obliged to identify some agreement to which the evidence was said to relate. As this had not been done in the instant case, the appeal had to be allowed in any event. It is submitted, however, that this principle should not be applied too rigidly. There are many varieties of conspiracy, and the participation of a conspirator may be important to the success of a conspiracy, even though he does not participate in each overt act which forms part of it.

The common design rule has been beset by serious misconceptions. It is sometimes said, quite wrongly, that it applies only to cases of conspiracy. While the rule clearly does apply to cases of conspiracy, it is by no means limited to cases where conspiracy is charged as such, but extends to all cases where an agreement to engage in a common design is implicit in the charge. This principle is correctly stated in *Jones* [1997] 2 Cr App R 119. Thus, whether a number of accused are charged with conspiracy, or with a number of substantive offences committed pursuant to a conspiracy, should not affect the principle, and it is submitted that *dicta* in some cases such as *Dawson* [1960] 1 WLR 163, 170, to the effect that charges of conspiracy may work injustice by rendering admissible evidence which would be inadmissible on equivalent substantive charges, are ill-founded.

---

[10] The rule is one of some antiquity at common law, and admits, for example, the individual speeches, placards, and printed leaflets of various accused, made for the purposes of the common design, as evidence against each of them: see, e.g., *Duffield* (1851) 5 Cox CC 404. The existence of the conspiracy or joint enterprise is a condition precedent to the admissibility of the statements, and therefore cannot be proved by evidence of the statements proposed to be admitted, without more (*Jones* [1997] 2 Cr App R 119; *Whittaker* [1914] 3 KB 1283). But the court may consider the statements together with other evidence, in determining whether or not the conspiracy or joint enterprise has been shown to exist: *Donat* (1985) 82 Cr App R 173.

However, it is also submitted that this misconception flows from another and more fundamental misconception, namely that declarations in furtherance of a common design are hearsay in character, and therefore are admitted by virtue of the exception in favour of admissions. The rule has been justified variously as an example of implied agency, a variation of the *res gestae* principle, or an exception to the hearsay rule *sui generis* which arises from the special nature of conspiracy cases, all of which flow from a basic supposition that such evidence is a form of hearsay. In the opinion of the present author, these views are incorrect. In fact, it is submitted, such declarations are non-hearsay evidence of the common design. If A and B combine together to rob a bank, and while A waits in the getaway car, B enters the bank and says to the cashier, 'I've got a gun; give me the money', it is absurd to suggest that A can object to a witness relating B's words on the ground of hearsay. Words can amount to conduct, and B's words are just as much direct evidence of the carrying out of the common design as would be the fact that B actually produced a gun and silently threatened the cashier with it.[11]

Of course, once the common design has come to an end, evidence of any declarations *made subsequently* by individual accused would be hearsay, and admissible only by virtue of an exception, if at all. Thus, if the design is ended by the arrest of the accused, and A makes admissions to the police implicating both himself and B, what he says can be treated as evidence only against himself and not against B. And even during the continuance of the common design, declarations which are in no way in furtherance of it, and therefore have no value as non-hearsay evidence, may equally be hearsay. In *Blake and Tye* (1844) 6 QB 126, where Tye made entries in two books which tended to incriminate both himself and Blake in a conspiracy to evade customs duty, the entries in one book, which were part of the mechanics of the conspiracy, were admissible against both Tye and Blake as being declarations in furtherance of it. However, those in the second book, which were pure matters of record made for Tye's personal convenience and unrelated to the carrying out of the common design, were admissible against Tye as an admission, but inadmissible hearsay against Blake. This case was distinguished in *Devonport* [1996] 1 Cr App R 221, on the ground that a note made by the accused of the prospective division of the proceeds of the planned offences among the conspirators should be regarded as being in furtherance of the conspiracy, rather than merely an *ex post facto* memorial of it. Like Tye's second book, the note had been made primarily for the accused's personal convenience, but it was held that it was nonetheless useful in implementing an ongoing conspiracy. Accordingly, it was held that the declarations contained in the record were admissible as evidence of the common design.

9.2.4 Witnesses in other proceedings

At common law there was some controversy over the position of a person who was a party in two successive legal actions. What view should be taken of evidence which such a person had relied on in the first action but which could be taken as an admission on an issue in the second action? It was clear that, in general, unless the same witness would give the same evidence in the second action, it was not possible to use in the second action evidence given only in the first without

---

[11] The declarations may also have legal effect as constituting the unlawful agreement. In any event, it is submitted, they are non-hearsay and admissible: see generally 7.11. That these declarations are non-hearsay is the view generally taken in the United States: see Federal Rule of Evidence 801(d)(2), though it is right to add that the same rule deals with admissions, which it also declares to be non-hearsay.

violating the rule against hearsay.[12] However, in some cases, the courts permitted reliance upon admissions contained in affidavits of witnesses previously relied upon by a party.[13] No doubt such evidence is now admissible under the Civil Evidence Act 1995. In criminal cases, while it is theoretically possible that recourse might be had to the common law rules, it is difficult to dispute the view of Cross[14] that it is highly improbable that a criminal court would permit the use against an accused of admissions contained in affidavits made by third parties, even where the accused had relied upon them in some earlier proceedings.

9.2.5 Agents

Admissions made by an agent acting within the scope of his authority are admissible against his principal. The agent acts within his authority, for this purpose, not only when he is authorized to make such admissions expressly, but also when he is authorized to represent the principal for any purpose and the admissions are made in the proper course of that representation. It is, therefore, unlikely that admissions made by an agent relating to transactions prior to the commencement of the agency will be admissible, but there is no reason why the agent should not be given express authority to deal with them. Similarly, it is unlikely that a servant of the principal should be able to make admissions which may be received against his employer, but it is a question of fact whether he has received any proper authority. In civil cases, statements made by agents or employees may now be admitted under the Civil Evidence Act 1995, thus removing a number of difficult questions which arose at common law concerning the scope of the agency.[15]

Before the admission made by the agent can be received, it must be proved both that the agency existed and that the agent was authorized to make a statement relating to the matter in question. The agency may be proved by direct evidence, or in a civil case presumably by the hearsay statement of the agent. But there seems to be no reason why the court should not infer the existence and scope of the agency from the facts before it, for example where a person, in response to a request to see someone able to deal authoritatively with a certain matter, comes forward and purports to deal with the inquirer.[16] An analogous rule appears to be preserved by s. 118(1) of the Criminal Justice Act 2003.

Admissions by agents are statements made by the agent to third parties, and not those contained in statements made by the agent to the principal. Thus, although the directors of a company may make admissions admissible against the company during the course of proper dealings on the company's behalf with third parties, their statements made, for example, to a meeting of the shareholders, cannot be received as admissions against the company.[17]

---

[12] See generally *British Thomson-Houston Co. Ltd* v *British Insulated & Helsby Cables Ltd* [1924] 2 Ch 160. The rule was confused by the possibility of using such admissions to prove knowledge or agency, and by the possibility of estoppel.

[13] *Evans* v *Merthyr Tydfil Urban District Council* [1899] 1 Ch 241.

[14] *Evidence*, 5th edn, pp. 523–4.

[15] See, e.g., *Burr* v *Ware Rural District Council* [1939] 2 All ER 688.

[16] *Edwards* v *Brookes (Milk) Ltd* [1963] 1 WLR 795. But see also *Evans* [1981] Crim LR 699 which suggests that at least in a criminal case, the existence of the agency must be proved directly. The best evidence of this would-be evidence that the accused asked another to provide information on his behalf: see, e.g., *Mallory* (1884) 13 QBD 33.

[17] *Re Devala Provident Gold Mining Co.* (1883) 22 ChD 593. Though they might, if relevant, be received as admissions against the directors personally.

It is worth commenting specifically upon two particular instances of the many conceivable forms of agency which may give rise to admissions, namely those of legal representatives and spouses of parties.

9.2.5.1 Legal representatives

In civil cases, a solicitor has an implied authority, arising from his general instructions, to make statements on behalf of his client. If such statements subsequently prove to be adverse to the client's case, they may become admissible as informal admissions. Such statements may be made in court or in chambers, or in correspondence or documents written in connection with the subject-matter of the proceedings.[18] But an admission made by the solicitor to a person other than an adverse party to the proceedings, or outside his proper conduct of the proceedings, or by way of fraud on his client, cannot be received. The position here, too, may now be different under the Civil Evidence Act 1995. In criminal cases, statements which later prove adverse will be admissible as informal admissions only where they are made upon the express instructions of the client, and not where they are made only upon the basis of a solicitor's general instructions.[19] By s. 11(5) of the Criminal Justice Act 1967 a notice of alibi given pursuant to that section by a solicitor was deemed to have been given with the authority of the accused, unless the contrary was proved. No corresponding provision is contained in s. 5 of the Criminal Procedure and Investigations Act 1996, which has replaced s. 11 of the 1967 Act, but it is submitted that the courts should apply the same principle.

Counsel may likewise make admissions, which may later be admitted against his client, although his authority is narrower than that of the solicitor, in that he must have been acting within the terms of his brief or instructions in relation to the matter in question. Statements made in court or in chambers by counsel, or assented to by signing an endorsement on his opponent's brief, may be relied upon by the court as admissions. However, admissions made in such ways will be admissible only for the purposes of the proceedings in which they are made, and admissions made in interlocutory proceedings will, it seems, not bind the client on the hearing of the main suit, at least where there is no estoppel and the other side would not be prejudiced by the rejection of the admission.[20] In criminal cases also, statements made by counsel in open court may be admitted against the accused, because of counsel's general authority to speak on his client's behalf and on the basis of his instructions. In *Turner* (1975) 61 Cr App R 67, an admission of an offence made by counsel in the course of mitigation of *another offence*, was held to be admissible on the prosecution of the accused for the offence so admitted. But statements made by counsel in the course of mitigation of the offence of which the accused has been convicted, after a plea of not guilty, should not be construed as an admission of *that offence*, because counsel has a duty to accept the verdict of guilty, and address the court in mitigation of sentence, notwithstanding that the verdict contradicts his instructions on the issue of guilt (*Wu Chun-Piu* v *R* [1996] 1 WLR 1113). Whether this should apply where the accused addresses the court personally in mitigation is an interesting question.

---

[18] An admission by letter that the client has no defence may be proved with a view to obtaining immediate judgment: *Ellis* v *Allen* [1914] 1 Ch 904. This does not of course apply to without-prejudice communications: see 14.21.

[19] See, e.g., *Downer* (1880) 14 Cox CC 486.

[20] *H. Clark (Doncaster) Ltd* v *Wilkinson* [1965] Ch. 694. Whether this ought to be the position seems, to say the least, open to question. See also *Langdale* v *Danby* [1982] 1 WLR 112.

Another interesting question is whether admissions made by an advocate appointed by the court to cross-examine a witness under s. 38 of the Youth Justice and Criminal Evidence Act 1999 are binding on the accused.[21] Section 38(5) provides that an advocate appointed for this purpose 'shall not be responsible to the accused'. But it must presumably be necessary for the advocate to take instructions from the accused in some circumstances. And, as in the case of any advocate, the nature of the cross-examination and any exchanges with the judge on questions of admissibility may betray facts which the jury may find to be adverse to the accused's case. If the general rule applies, it is clearly possible in theory for an appointed advocate to make admissions which are binding on the accused. The position here may have to be clarified in due course.

9.2.5.2 Spouses

The common law does not impute any *agency* capable of permitting evidence of admissions against the 'principal', merely because of the relationship of husband and wife. There may on the facts of a given case be evidence that one spouse gave sufficient authority to the other, for example to conduct his business, but in the absence of such evidence, admissions made by one spouse will not be evidence against the other.[22] The same principle applies to other relationships, for example that of parent and child.[23]

9.3 WHAT MAY BE PROVED BY ADMISSION

Informal admissions may be received on matters of fact or law, or on both together. So far as matters of fact are concerned, we have seen[24] that admissions should be founded upon the personal knowledge of the maker of the statement, and will be rejected as evidence of the facts admitted where the admission is based upon pure hearsay as to which the maker has no personal knowledge. But where the maker of the statement is speaking about matters perceived by him, his admission may be *prima facie* evidence of the facts admitted, even where further evidence, such as expert evidence, ought to be tendered in order to prove the facts more specifically. Thus, in *Chatwood*,[25] the admission of an experienced drug user was admitted as *prima facie* evidence that the substance with which he injected himself was a dangerous drug. There would seem to be no conflict between this decision and those in such cases as *Comptroller of Customs* v *Western Lectric Co. Ltd* (see note 24) because in the *Chatwood* case, the identity of the drug was in any event a matter to be proved by evidence of opinion, and although expert opinion might be of more value, that of an experienced user was by no means to be disregarded, and was evidence upon which the jury was entitled to act. And there have been instances where facts within the peculiar competence of the accused have been proved by his own admission, even though necessarily based

---

[21] This will occur where an otherwise unrepresented accused is precluded from cross-examining a witness in person by virtue of s. 34, 35, or 36 of the Act (as to which see 17.4 *et seq.*) and does not arrange for his own legal representation for this purpose. This situation also gives rise to related questions of legal professional privilege (see 14.9).

[22] An example of specific authorization given by one spouse to the other is *Mallory* (1884) 13 QBD 33, in which the accused told the police that his wife would supply them with a list showing the origin of goods suspected of being stolen. It was held that the list supplied by the wife at the accused's request was admissible against him. Presumably the same rule applies to civil partners under the Civil Partnership Act 2004.

[23] *G (A)* v *G (T)* [1970] 2 QB 643.

[24] 7.9.1; *Comptroller of Customs* v *Western Lectric Co. Ltd* [1966] AC 367; *Marshall* [1977] Crim LR 106.

[25] [1980] 1 WLR 874. See also *Korniak* [1983] Crim LR 109; *Hulbert* (1979) 69 Cr App R 243.

upon hearsay, as for example his age.[26] The explanation of these decisions seems to be one of convenience and the unlikelihood of injustice to the accused. The weight of admissions of fact is, as we have seen, a question of fact depending upon the circumstances and terms of the statement. In cases where the maker of the statement may have some interest to serve in making it, the court will scrutinize the admission with care, as it will if there appears to be any doubt about the reliability of the statement, having regard to the maker's state of mind at the time.

Admissions of matters of law, though admissible, are usually of little weight, being founded on (generally uninformed) opinion. Indeed, an admission on a question of foreign law, for instance the validity of a marriage celebrated abroad, where the prosecution is for bigamy, will be rejected altogether.[27] But admissions of the validity of English marriages are admissible,[28] and the cases show a variety of other matters of law which have been established by admission, including the existence of a nuisance.[29] There is no objection to the reception of an admission of law which seems even to conclude the very point which the jury have to decide, for example an admission that the accused stole the property, the subject of the indictment, though the weight of such admission must still be considered: there may be cases where the accused's apparently clear admission is nullified by evidence that he did not understand the legal nature of theft, and intended only to admit a perhaps innocent taking of the property. But such admissions, particularly when dealing with non-technical and common offences, are often of very great weight, and may in fact conclude the case against the accused in themselves. There is, of course, an obvious danger in acting on an admission of a matter of law where the matter is a technical one or may be open to debate, and there will be cases where the only safe course is to reject the admission altogether, as was done in *Philp* (1830) 1 Mood CC 263, where the accused's admission of the prosecutor's title to property (obviously a technical question) met precisely that fate.

B CONFESSIONS

SUMMARY OF MAIN POINTS

- A confession is the name given to an admission made by an accused in a criminal case. The admissibility of confessions is governed by special rules.

- Confessions are now admissible by statute by virtue of s. 76(1) of the Police and Criminal Evidence Act 1984, preserved by s. 114(1)(b) of the Criminal Justice Act 2003.

- A confession must be excluded in the following circumstances under s. 76(2) of the Police and Criminal Evidence Act 1984:

    If, in any proceedings where the prosecution proposes to give in evidence a confession made by an accused person, it is represented to the court that the confession was or may have been obtained—
    (a) by oppression of the person who made it; or

---

[26] *Walker* (1844) 1 Cox CC 99; *Turner* [1910] 1 KB 346.
[27] *Naguib* [1917] 1 KB 359.
[28] *Flaherty* (1847) 2 Car & K 782; though the admission would not of itself justify a conviction for bigamy.
[29] *Neville* (1791) 1 Peake 91.

(b) in consequence of anything said or done which was likely, in the circumstances existing at the time, to render unreliable any confession which might be made by him in consequence thereof,

the court shall not allow the confession to be given in evidence against him except in so far as the prosecution proves to the court beyond reasonable doubt that the confession (notwithstanding that it may be true) was not obtained as aforesaid.

- By virtue of s. 76A of the Police and Criminal Evidence Act 1984, almost exactly the same test applies where a co-accused wishes to adduce an accused's confession.

- The judge may also exclude a confession in the exercise of his discretion under s. 78 of the Police and Criminal Evidence Act 1984. This discretion may be exercised for various reasons, including failure to allow the accused access to legal advice, or any serious breach of Code of Practice C.

- It is a cardinal rule of common law that a confession is evidence only against the accused who made it and not against any other accused. But some inroads have been made on this rule in recent cases.

- Where the accused makes a 'mixed' statement, which is partly incriminating and partly exculpatory, the jury must look at the statement as a whole to determine its significance. The exculpatory parts may be given less weight than the incriminating parts.

9.4 ADMISSIBILITY OF CONFESSIONS: INTRODUCTION, POSITION AT COMMON LAW

An adverse admission relevant to the issue of guilt in a criminal case is known at common law as a confession, and the same terminology is employed by the Police and Criminal Evidence Act 1984. As indicated above, confessions represent the most important and most frequently encountered exception to the rule against hearsay in criminal cases. Fundamental changes in the law pertaining to confessions were introduced by the Police and Criminal Evidence Act 1984. To understand these changes, it is necessary to understand the principles of admissibility developed at common law to govern the admissibility of confessions. This introduction will summarize the most important aspects of the common law rules. We will then proceed to examine the new statutory definition and rules of admissibility of confessions.

While the common law recognized that a confession might be both reliable and cogent as evidence of guilt, and indeed saw no objection to a conviction in cases where a confession was the only evidence against the accused,[30] the law also recognized that a confession could be regarded as reliable only when given freely and voluntarily. If coerced or forced, the reliability of the confession might be fatally compromised, and the integrity of the system of administration of justice itself made to suffer. The exclusion of evidence obtained by torture, force, or other coercive methods was the means of protection of the accused developed by the judges during the eighteenth and nineteenth centuries, when the memory of an age when such methods were

---

[30] See, e.g., *Baldry* (1852) 1 Den 430; though some American jurisdictions require corroboration of a confession in such a case, a safeguard which is not without its advocates in England (see R. Pattenden (1991) 107 LQR 317).

commonplace (as they still were in Continental Europe) still lingered. Its significance may be gauged by the fact that in English law, the rule that a confession obtained by oppression or in circumstances likely to render it unreliable must be excluded, is the only instance of the mandatory exclusion of illegally or unfairly obtained evidence.[31]

9.4.1 Admissibility at common law

The classic statement of the common law rule as to admissibility of confessions was that of Lord Sumner in *Ibrahim v R* [1914] AC 599 at 609:

> It has long been established... that no statement by an accused is admissible in evidence against him unless it is shown by the prosecution to have been a voluntary statement, in the sense that it has not been obtained from him either by fear of prejudice or hope of advantage exercised[32] or held out by a person in authority.

In common parlance, 'voluntary' meant simply 'of one's own free will'.[33]

The test of voluntariness, as defined by Lord Sumner, was supplemented by Lord Parker CJ in *Callis v Gunn* [1964] 1 QB 495, 501, when he added the requirement that a confession must not have been obtained in 'an oppressive manner'. Whether Lord Parker CJ intended to add to the legal requirements for admissibility is open to some doubt, as his observation was, strictly speaking, *obiter*—the case involved the admissibility of fingerprint evidence. But when the Judges' Rules appeared in revised form in 1964, the introduction stated that the Rules did not affect the principle, which was 'overriding and applicable in all cases', that:

> ...it is a fundamental condition of the admissibility in evidence against any person, equally of any oral answer given by that person to a question put by a police officer and of any statement made by that person, that it shall have been voluntary, in the sense that it has not been obtained from him by fear of prejudice or hope of advantage, exercised or held out by a person in authority, *or by oppression*. [Emphasis added.]

Whether the requirement of oppression in fact added anything to that of voluntariness is open to doubt. Oppression was defined judicially only once before the coming into force of the Police and Criminal Evidence Act 1984, by Sachs J in *Priestly*:[34]

> ...to my mind, this word, in the context of the principles under consideration imports something which tends to sap, and has sapped, that free will which must exist before a confession is voluntary... Whether or not there is oppression in an individual case depends upon many elements. I am not going into all of them. They include such things as the length of time of any individual period of questioning, the length of time intervening between periods of questioning, whether the accused person had been given proper refreshment or not, and the characteristics of the person who makes the statement.

---

[31] See *Sang* [1980] AC 402 and 3.10. The trial judge may take the method of obtaining other kinds of evidence into account in deciding whether to exercise his general discretion to exclude legally admissible evidence: see Police and Criminal Evidence Act 1984, s. 78(1) and 3.11, 3.12. In the United States, the 'exclusionary rule' applies to any evidence illegally obtained. In India, any confession made to a police officer is inadmissible unless confirmed before a magistrate (Indian Evidence Act 1872, s. 25).

[32] In *DPP v Ping Lin* [1976] AC 574, 597–8, Lord Hailsham of St Marylebone pointed out that the word 'exercised' in this passage is probably a reporter's mis-rendering of 'excited'.

[33] See *Rennie* [1982] 1 WLR 64, per Lord Lane CJ at 70.

[34] (1965) 51 Cr App R 1; and see Lord MacDermott extra-judicially (1968) 21 *Current Legal Problems* 10. See also now *Fulling* [1987] QB 426; *Burut v Public Prosecutor* [1995] 2 AC 579; and 9.7.

What may be oppressive as regards a child, an invalid or an old man or somebody inexperienced in the ways of this world may turn out not to be oppressive when one finds that the accused person is of a tough character and an experienced man of the world.

The definition suggests little distinction between voluntariness and an absence of oppression.

Lord Sumner's phrases 'fear of prejudice' and 'hope of advantage' are habitually spoken of as 'threats' and 'inducements' respectively. While this is a useful form of shorthand, it gave rise to some problems in the application of the rules of admissibility at common law. In particular, the suggestion of some deliberate act in the words 'threats' and 'inducements' for a time led the courts to concentrate on the mind of the questioner, rather than on the mind of the suspect. As the problem may recur, despite the apparently clear wording of the 1984 Act, it is worth pursuing briefly. In *Isequilla* [1975] 1 WLR 716 at 721–2, the Court of Appeal concluded that:

> ... under the existing law the exclusion of a confession as a matter of law because it is not voluntary is always related to some conduct on the part of authority which is improper or unjustified. Included in the phrase 'improper or unjustified' of course must be the offering of an inducement, because it is improper in this context for those in authority to try to induce a suspect to make a confession.

This view of the law would have left the accused without recourse in a case where, without any improper intent and perhaps even without realizing it, the questioner created some fear of prejudice or hope of advantage in the mind of the suspect. In such a case, the resulting confession might well be involuntary, but under the *Isequilla* rule, would nonetheless be admissible. In *DPP v Ping Lin* [1976] AC 574, the House of Lords was called upon to decide whether it was the state of mind of the questioner or that of the suspect which was to control the question of voluntariness. The House firmly held that it was the latter that governed the question of whether or not the confession was voluntary, and that should therefore also control the question of admissibility. Lord Salmon (*ibid.* at 606) said:

> In the context of the question raised by this appeal, it is difficult to understand the relevance of the references to impropriety in some of the cases to which we have been referred. No doubt, for anyone to obtain a confession or statement in breach of the established rule is *ex hypothesi* improper. Indeed, it is impossible to imagine how the rule could be breached with propriety. It would seem, therefore, that the references to impropriety add nothing...

In my opinion, the intention of a person in authority who makes a threat or a promise or offers any inducement prior to an accused making a confession or statement is irrelevant. So is the fact that the threat is gentle or the promise or inducement slight save in so far as this may throw any light on the vital question—was the confession or statement procured by the express or implicit threat, promise or inducement.

9.4.2 Persons in authority

At common law the rules of admissibility applied only where the fear of prejudice or hope of advantage was excited or held out, or the oppression created by a 'person in authority'. There was much case law bearing on the question of what persons were or were not persons in authority.[35] It was, however, settled that a person in authority must have, or reasonably be thought by the suspect to have, some influence over his arrest, detention, or prosecution, or in other words, be

---

[35] See, e.g., *Deokinanan v R* [1969] 1 AC 20; *Wilson* [1967] 2 QB 406, and generally the 1st edn of this work, pp. 160–2.

a person from whom a threat or inducement might appear credible. The limitation of the rule in this way was not of great importance, since the vast majority of confessions are made to police officers and others who are undoubtedly persons in authority, and it has now been abolished expressly by the Police and Criminal Evidence Act 1984. But it remains germane to consider it in the light of the common law rule that the fear of prejudice or hope of advantage must have been generated by the person in authority, with the consequence that self-generated fears and hopes would not destroy the voluntariness of the confession.[36] We shall see that the result should be different under the new statutory rules, even though the confession is made to a person who would previously have been a person in authority.

9.4.3 Discretion

In addition to the rules governing admissibility, at common law the trial judge had power to exclude a confession, in the exercise of his discretion, where it had been obtained by means of or following a breach of the Judges' Rules. The Judges' Rules were rules of conduct and procedure for the guidance of police officers and others concerned in the arrest, detention, and interrogation of suspects. They were first promulgated by the judges of the then King's Bench Division in 1912, and subsequently revised from time to time. The Rules were not rules of law, and did not affect the legal principles of admissibility of confessions. However, in *May* (1952) 36 Cr App R 91, 93, Lord Goddard CJ held that the trial judge might refuse to admit a statement if a breach of the rules occurred. But the main importance of the Rules always lay in the fact that a breach of the rules might provide evidence that the resulting confession was not voluntary. The Rules are superseded by Codes of Practice introduced pursuant to the Police and Criminal Evidence Act 1984, and the effect of the Codes on the exclusionary rules is discussed at 9.12 *et seq*.

9.5 ADMISSIBILITY OF CONFESSIONS BY STATUTE

9.5.1 Definition of 'confession'

At common law, a confession was the name given to an adverse admission by the accused relevant to the issue of guilt in a criminal case. Section 82(1) of the Police and Criminal Evidence Act 1984 now provides the following statutory definition:

> 'confession' includes any statement wholly or partly adverse to the person who made it, whether made to a person in authority or not and whether made in words or otherwise.

A confession, like any other admission, may be made orally, in writing, by conduct, or in any way from which a proper inference may be drawn adverse to the maker. Usually, confessions are made to police officers or other investigators as a result of interrogation, but they may equally be made to the victim of an offence, a friend or relative, or any other person. The law regarding confessions is now the same in all cases, and it no longer matters whether the person to whom the confession is made is a person in authority. It must be proved that the confession was made by the person against whom it is tendered. In the usual case of a confession made during interview, which will have been tape-recorded, this is unlikely to be disputed. Before the advent of the practice of tape-recording interviews, it was not uncommon for there to be a dispute as to whether or

---

[36] See *Rennie* [1982] 1 WLR 64; see 9.8.1.

not the accused had made a verbal confession imputed to him, and there may be cases of doubt even in contemporary practice relating to verbal and written statements. In *Mawdesley v Chief Constable of the Cheshire Constabulary; Yorke v DPP* [2004] 1 WLR 1035, it was held to be a proper inference that a person had made a statement by completing a form requiring information as to the identity of the driver of a vehicle sent to him under s. 172 of the Road Traffic Act 1988, in circumstances in which the requested details had been written on the form by hand (in one case, allegedly by the defendant's agent) but the signature space had been left blank. The fact that the forms had been completed after being sent out, together with the detailed information provided, was circumstantial evidence that the persons to whom the forms had been sent had provided the information requested. Thus, despite the absence of signature, the forms were capable of amounting to confessions 'made' by the defendants for the purposes of s. 82(1) of the Police and Criminal Evidence Act 1984.[37]

9.5.1.1 Meaning of 'adverse to the person who made it'

Although in common parlance, the word 'confession' connotes a full admission of guilt, it has no such meaning in law, either at common law or under the statutory definition. As long as any part of a statement is adverse to the maker, in that it has some relevance to the issue of guilt, it will be deemed a confession for the purpose of the law of evidence. Even an indirect admission will suffice, if some adverse inference can properly be drawn. In *Sat-Bhambra* (1988) 88 Cr App R 55, however, the Court of Appeal, *obiter*, doubted whether a statement, which was wholly self-serving and exculpatory when made, could later be regarded as a confession if it transpired that it was in conflict with a defence actually put forward at trial, and so had ceased to be exculpatory. Similarly *obiter* doubts were expressed by the Court of Appeal in *Jelen* (1989) 90 Cr App R 456 about what the Court called 'potentially incriminating remarks' made by the accused.[38]

A very different view was taken by a later Court of Appeal in *Z* [2003] 2 Cr App R 12. The accused had spoken with police officers in a confidential setting intended to discuss the violent activities of X, on which the accused later relied at trial to establish a defence of duress to a charge of aggravated burglary. The steps which would have been required under Code of Practice C in the case of an interview were not taken: the accused was not cautioned, and the meeting was not tape-recorded, though the officers made some notes of what had been said. Because of the way in which the accused presented his defence of duress, the prosecution applied to cross-examine him about the meeting. The issue on appeal turned on whether or not what the accused had said amounted to a 'confession' for the purpose of s. 82(1). If so, the prosecution had failed to prove that it had been obtained in circumstances which would render it admissible under s. 76 of the Act (see 9.5.2, below), and it should not have been referred to. The trial judge, following *Sat-Bhambra*, held that, because the conversation with the officers was intended to assist his defence at the time when it took place, it could not be said to be 'adverse' to him, and so could not amount to a confession. Accordingly, he permitted the cross-examination. The Court of Appeal allowed the appeal against conviction. It was held that the true test was whether the statement made by the accused was 'adverse' to him at the time when it was tendered as evidence. The Court referred to *Saunders v United Kingdom* (1996) 23 EHRR 313, in which the European Court of Human Rights, applying art. 6 of the Convention, took the view that a statement exculpatory when made, but

---

[37] Though the lack of signature did not satisfy the requirements of s. 12 of the Road Traffic Offenders Act 1988 so as to enable the forms to be used as proof of identity by virtue of that section.

[38] See to the same effect *Park* [1994] Crim LR 285.

later tendered as a confession, was in fact a confession, and was subject to the same treatment flowing from the right of silence and fairness to the accused as any other confession. Declining to follow *Sat-Bhambra*, Rix LJ said ([2003] 2 Cr App R at [37]):

> In our judgment, the [Human Rights Act 1998] and in particular its s.3(1), which provides that: 'So far as it is possible to do so, primary legislation and subordinate legislation must be read and given effect to in a way which is compatible with the Convention rights', require us to reconsider this issue. The discussion in *Sat-Bhambra* already indicates that two views are possible as to what amounts to an 'adverse' (or, more generally, an incriminating) statement and *Saunders* shows that the ECtHR has adopted for itself the view expressed by the Supreme Courts of Canada and the USA rather than that of our courts. The definition of 'confession' is an inclusive one and clearly intended to be a broad one. The question in any event arises: *at what time is* the judgment, whether a statement is or is not a confession, whether it is or is not adverse, to be made? *Sat-Bhambra* indicates that the decision is to be made at the time of the statement; but *prima facie* one would have thought that the test is to be made at the time when it is sought to give the statement in evidence. That is, to our mind, confirmed by the underlying rationale of s. 76 ... Section 76 goes back to an earlier time when the concern was that an accused, who has a right of silence, may be prevailed upon both to surrender his right and to make unreliable statements by reason of either 'oppression' or: 'anything said or done ... likely ... to render unreliable' what he says (s. 76(2)). In such circumstances the prosecution bear the criminal burden of proving that the confession was *not* obtained in such circumstances. If therefore an accused is driven to make adverse statements by reason of oppression, why should he lose the protection of s. 76(2) just because, although he may have sought to exculpate himself, in fact he damned himself? We therefore think that the confidential statement was, at the time it had to be considered, a confession. [Emphasis in original.]

It is submitted that this view is correct. If the prosecution intends to make use of a statement in a way which will damage the accused's case, it is difficult to avoid the conclusion that the statement is 'adverse' to the accused. To put it another way, if the prosecution intends to use the statement as a confession, it should be the use made of it rather than its contents that governs whether or not it is treated as a confession. The accused should, accordingly, be entitled to the protection of the rules governing the admissibility of confessions under s. 76. The additional protection of the general discretionary power to exclude under s. 78 is available in the case of all confessions, and it should be no answer to say that the availability of s. 78 necessarily makes it fair to dispense with s. 76.

But the opposite view has prevailed. The prosecution in *Z* succeeded in a further appeal to the House of Lords, *sub nom. Hasan* [2005] AC 467. Reversing the Court of Appeal, and upholding the earlier decision in *Sat-Bhambra*, the House held that a confession did not fall within s. 76 unless it was inculpatory at the time when it was made; that the decision in *Saunders* v *United Kingdom* offered no assistance, because the court in that case had not been concerned to interpret s. 76 and was dealing with statements of a different kind; and that, although the accused was not entitled to the protection of s. 76 no violation of the fair trial provisions of art. 6 was involved because the judge retained the power to exclude the statement under s. 78 if he considered that its admission would have an unacceptably unfair effect on the trial. Lord Steyn said:

> ... it is wholly implausible that the draftsman [of s.82(1)] would have made the express reference only to wholly or partly adverse statements if he also had in mind covering under the definition of "confession" wholly exculpatory statements. There is no support in the preceding case law for such a view ... Neither the 11th Report of the Criminal Law Revision Committee (Cmnd 4991) nor any other external aid to PACE give any assistance to such an argument. The plain meaning of the statute is against such a strange interpretation. And it is inconceivable, on policy grounds, that the legislature would have introduced such a fundamental change in the law by leaving the question whether an exculpatory statement is a confession to depend on developments at trial.

There is nothing in the statutory context which compels a strained interpretation of section 82(1). After all, as has been pointed out, section 78 is wide enough to permit the court to exclude wholly exculpatory statements which were obtained by oppression, e.g. to fabricate a false exculpatory account to the detriment of the defendant. In these circumstances, the House ought now to affirm the interpretation suggested in *Sat-Bhambra*...

Properly construed, section 76(1), read with section 82(1), requires the court to interpret a statement in the light of the circumstances when it was made. A purely exculpatory statement (e.g. "I was not there") is not within the scope of section 76(1). It is not a confession within the meaning of s. 76. The safeguards of section 76 are not applicable. But the safeguards of section 78 are available. [*Ibid.* at [56]–[58].]

9.5.2 Statutory basis of admissibility

At common law, confessions were admissible as an exception to the rule against hearsay, to prove the truth of the matters admitted. This is still the case, but their admissibility is now provided for expressly by statute. Section 76(1) of the Police and Criminal Evidence Act 1984 provides that:

> In any proceedings a confession made by an accused person may be given in evidence against him in so far as it is relevant to any matter in issue in the proceedings and is not excluded by the court in pursuance of this section.

'Proceedings' means criminal proceedings, including courts martial: s. 82(1). This subsection governs the admissibility of confessions in all such proceedings.[39] However, it applies only to confessions tendered by the prosecution.[40]

The law relating to the admissibility of confessions, including s. 76(1), is expressly preserved without substantive change by s. 118(1) of the Criminal Justice Act 2003. In common with the other preserved exceptions, confessions are now formally admissible by virtue of s. 114(1)(b) of the Act, which provides that the preserved exceptions constitute one of the four exclusive grounds of admissibility of hearsay in criminal cases (see 8.2). But this formal change has led to unexpected consequences. In *Y* [2008] 1 WLR 1683, it was held that the fact that s. 118(1) of the Criminal Justice Act 2003 preserves the rules relating to confessions, and so permits a statement which qualifies as an admission to be admitted under s. 114(1)(b) of the Act, does not prevent it from being admitted alternatively under s. 114(1)(d) in the interests of justice. All four grounds of admissibility of hearsay under s. 114(1) are equal and independent, and none is subordinated to any other. Logical as this may appear, it may well result in serious injustice. As we shall see (9.6; 9.13) confessions (whether adduced by the prosecution or a co-accused) are subject to mandatory or discretionary exclusion in certain cases under ss. 76(2) and 78 of the Police and Criminal Evidence Act 1984, designed to ensure that any confession admitted is made voluntarily and in fair circumstances. It would be very unfortunate if these rules, which have stood the test of time at common law and under s. 76(1), and which Parliament evidently intended to preserve, were to swept away by the simple procedural device of employing a different ground of admissibility. It was argued at 8.20 that this approach is flawed and dangerous in relation to hearsay of all kinds. But the argument has particular resonance in relation to confessions. It is true that s. 114(1)(d) is itself subject to stringent conditions of admissibility under s. 114(2), but these conditions fail to address the issue of voluntariness and fairness of confessions, and are more appropriate to other

---

[39] But magistrates inquiring into an offence as examining justices have no power to exclude a confession; this must be left to the trial court: see 3.2.4.

[40] As to the position where a confession is tendered by a co-accused, see 9.13. The position is now governed by statute. The test for admissibility is the same, except with respect to the standard of proof: see Criminal Justice Act 2003, s. 128, inserting s. 76A into the Police and Criminal Evidence Act 1984; 9.13.2.

kinds of hearsay statement (see 8.20.1). It is submitted that, insofar as *Y* holds that confessions are now admissible under s. 114(1)(d) without consideration of the grounds of exclusion under s. 76(2) of the Police and Criminal Evidence Act 1984, the case confuses the formal transfer of statutory basis under s. 118(1) with a substantive change in the law, and was wrongly decided. There is an obvious potential for injustice to the accused if scrutiny is to be diverted from the requirements for the admissibility of confessions.

9.6 EXCLUSION OF CONFESSIONS: BURDEN AND STANDARD OF PROOF

9.6.1 Grounds for exclusion of confessions

The grounds on which a confession may be excluded are laid down by s. 76(2) and (3) as follows:

> (2) If, in any proceedings where the prosecution proposes to give in evidence a confession made by an accused person, it is represented to the court that the confession was or may have been obtained—
>   (a) by oppression of the person who made it; or
>   (b) in consequence of anything said or done which was likely, in the circumstances existing at the time, to render unreliable any confession which might be made by him in consequence thereof,
> the court shall not allow the confession to be given in evidence against him except in so far as the prosecution proves to the court beyond reasonable doubt that the confession (notwithstanding that it may be true) was not obtained as aforesaid.
> (3) In any proceedings where the prosecution proposes to give in evidence a confession made by an accused person, the court may of its own motion require the prosecution, as a condition of allowing it to do so, to prove that the confession was not obtained as mentioned in subsection (2) above.

It should be noted that exclusion of the confession is mandatory unless the prosecution prove that it was not obtained in either of the ways mentioned in subsection (2)—the court is given no discretion in this respect. Moreover, the court, in its role as protector of the right of the accused to a fair trial, may of its own motion require the prosecution to demonstrate the admissibility of the confession, even where no objection is made by the defence. As to the procedure to be adopted, see 3.2.

Another important point made clear by subsection (2) and often overlooked at common law, is that the test of admissibility is not whether the confession appears to be true, but the manner in which it was obtained. True or false, the confession must be excluded unless the prosecution prove that it was not obtained in either of the proscribed ways. Whether or not the confession is true is a matter for the jury, which can arise only if it is first determined that it is admissible.

There must, as at common law, be a causal connection between the oppression or the circumstances and the making of the confession. This is made clear by the words 'by oppression' and 'in consequence of anything said or done'. It is not enough that the court conclude that oppression or circumstances may have existed. The court must also conclude that the confession may in fact have been made as a result. This, as Lord Salmon observed in *DPP v Ping Lin* [1976] AC 574 (see 9.4.1) is and will continue to be the 'vital question', and the question which will almost always require the evidence of the accused himself on the *voir dire* in support of his application to exclude a confession.

9.6.2 Burden and standard of proof

Following the rule at common law, the burden lies on the prosecution to prove the admissibility of a confession, if this is disputed by the accused or if so ordered by the court of its own motion. The standard of proof is that beyond reasonable doubt, which was always recognized as the required standard at common law on the issue of admissibility of a confession, whatever the vagaries of the standard of proof on other secondary issues (see 4.14). It follows that the judge must exclude a confession if he concludes that it may have been obtained in either of the proscribed ways; he need not conclude that it was so obtained.[41]

9.7 EXCLUSION OF CONFESSIONS: STATEMENTS OBTAINED BY OPPRESSION

Despite the paucity of definition of the term 'oppression' at common law, the Police and Criminal Evidence Act 1984 offers no complete statutory definition of the circumstances under which a confession may have to be excluded by virtue of s. 76(2)(a). There is a partial definition in s. 76(8), which provides:

> In this section 'oppression' includes torture, inhuman or degrading treatment, and the use or threat of violence (whether or not amounting to torture).[42]

The subsection leaves much to construction by the courts. In *Fulling* [1987] QB 426, the accused was arrested and detained in a cell at the police station for questioning. The accused alleged that during interrogation, a police officer advised her that her boyfriend had, for about three years past, been having an affair with another woman, C, who had already been arrested, and was in the next cell. After she had confirmed this state of affairs by talking to C, the accused agreed to a statement being taken from her. Her case was that she was bitterly distressed, that she had to get out of the cells, and that making a statement was the only way to achieve this. However, it was not alleged that the police had offered her bail in return for a statement. The trial judge admitted the statement over the accused's objection that it had been obtained by oppression. It was not contended that there were other circumstances that rendered any confession she might have made unreliable. The accused was convicted, and appealed to the Court of Appeal against her conviction. Dismissing the appeal, the Court held that the alleged conduct of the police could not have amounted to oppression. As at common law, the issue arose as to whether it was necessary that 'oppression' should involve impropriety on the part of the officers. The Court held, in effect, that such impropriety must be looked for. Although this may appear to be a step back from the common law position as stated in *Ping Lin*, it may be justified on the basis that at

---

[41] But where the confession is tendered by a co-accused, the standard of proof is the balance of probability: see Police and Criminal Evidence Act 1984, s. 76A inserted by Criminal Justice Act 2003, s. 128: 9.13.2.

[42] See now also the decision of the House of Lords in *A and others* v *Secretary of State for the Home Department (No. 2)* [2006] 2 AC 221 (3.10) holding that any evidence obtained by means of torture is inadmissible under English law. For the purpose of this decision, and of s. 76, this would obviously include torture as an offence under the Criminal Justice Act 1988, s. 134, but need not be limited to such cases. See also art. 3 of the European Convention on Human Rights (1.7); *Republic of Ireland* v *United Kingdom* (1978) 2 EHRR 25. For an example of clearly oppressive conduct, see *Burut* v *Public Prosecutor* [1995] 2 AC 579 (hooding and manacling of suspects under interrogation).

common law there was but a single test of admissibility. Under the Act there are two very different tests. The Court seems to acknowledge (*obiter*, but clearly rightly) that there would be no such requirement under s. 76(2)(b). Lord Lane CJ observed that the question was one of statutory construction. He referred to the common law authorities, including *Priestly*, *Prager*, and *Ping Lin*. Lord Lane then pointed out that in the Police and Criminal Evidence Act 1984, Parliament had deliberately provided two distinct grounds for the exclusion of confessions. He continued ([1987] QB at 432):

> Paragraph (b) [of s. 76(2)] is wider than the old formulation, namely that the confession must be shown to be voluntary in the sense that it was not obtained by fear of prejudice or hope of advantage, excited or held out by a person in authority. It is wide enough to cover some of the circumstances which under the earlier rule were embraced by what seems to us to be the artificially wide definition of oppression approved in *Prager*.
>
> This in turn leads us to believe that 'oppression' in s. 76(2)(a) should be given its ordinary dictionary meaning. The *Oxford English Dictionary* as its third definition of the word runs as follows: 'Exercise of authority or power in a burdensome, harsh or wrongful manner; unjust or cruel treatment of subjects, inferiors etc.; the imposition of unreasonable or unjust burdens.' One of the quotations given under that paragraph runs as follows: 'There is not a word in our language which expresses more detestable wickedness than oppression.'
>
> We find it hard to envisage any circumstances in which such oppression would not entail some impropriety on the part of the interrogator. We do not think that the judge was wrong in using that test.

The Court of Appeal indicates, not unreasonably, that where an accused relies on the kind of treatment described in *Priestly* and *Prager*, which falls short of 'oppression' as defined in s. 76(8) and in *Fulling*, the proper ground of objection is s. 76(2)(b) and not s. 76(2)(a).

Article 3 of the European Convention on Human Rights guarantees the fundamental right not to be subjected to torture or to inhuman or degrading treatment or punishment. By virtue of the Human Rights Act 1998 this right is now part of the domestic law of the UK. The text of the article was given and the implications of this change were discussed at 1.7. Although the jurisprudence of the European Court of Human Rights[43] is that the Convention is designed, not to dictate the rules of evidence of a State which is party to it, but to ensure overall fairness for the accused in the trial process, in this case the two would seem to go hand in hand. It is to be hoped that, if an English court were to find that an accused had been compelled to make a confession by means which violated art. 3, that confession would inevitably be excluded by virtue of s. 76(2)(a) of the Police and Criminal Evidence Act 1984. For that reason, it may be said that the English law with respect to the admission of confessions is in accord with art. 3 of the Convention. Other issues arise with respect to the discretionary exclusion of confessions where there has been a possible breach of art. 6 of the Convention. These are discussed at 9.12.5.

There is obviously a fertile field for factual distinction in considering what degree of misconduct is required to amount to oppression. For example, mere loss of patience or use of bad language by a police officer has been held not to amount to oppression (*Emmerson* (1990) 92 Cr App R 284); whereas a course of 'hectoring and bullying' which, in the opinion of the court, could hardly have been worse in the absence of physical violence, was held to amount to oppression (*Paris* (1992) 97 Cr App R 99). No doubt each of these cases was rightly decided on its own facts,

---

[43] *Kostovski* v *Netherlands* (1989) 12 EHRR 434; *Saidi* v *France* (1993) 17 EHRR 251; and see *Republic of Ireland* v *United Kingdom* (1978) 2 EHRR 25.

but neither assists in laying down a general principle more specifically than did the court in *Fulling*. But it has been held that the judge is entitled to take into account, in deciding whether or not there has been oppression, the personal attributes of the accused. A hardened, professional criminal may be interrogated a good deal more severely than a frail or elderly suspect of previous good character, without the risk of the interrogation becoming oppressive. In *Seelig*[44] the Court of Appeal held that the trial judge had been correct in taking account of the fact that the accused, a merchant banker, was 'experienced', 'intelligent', and 'sophisticated' in assessing the effect of the questioning to which he had been subjected. This approach is consistent with the approach to oppression taken at common law, and with the approach to the issue of unreliability dealt with in 9.8.

9.8 EXCLUSION OF CONFESSIONS: UNRELIABLE CONFESSIONS

The second ground for exclusion is potentially very wide, and represents a welcome extension of the common law rules. The reference to 'circumstances', the use of the word 'reliable' rather than 'voluntary' and of the phrase 'anything said or done', appear to give the court a broad mandate to inquire thoroughly into the circumstances in which the confession was made.[45] In contrast to the extreme treatment which, according to the Court of Appeal in *Fulling* [1987] QB 426, must characterize 'oppression', unreliable circumstances may comprehend the multitude of factors adumbrated by Sachs J in *Priestly* (1965) 51 Cr App R 1, including the length of and between periods of questioning, the availability of refreshments, whether or not the suspect was kept in isolation, and so on, all of which may go to make up a composite picture. If it is reliability, rather than extremes of conduct, that counts, then the effect of all the circumstances on the individual suspect should be considered. Exclusion of a confession may not require anything extreme, particularly where the suspect is vulnerable because of youth, age, sickness, or simply being overawed by a first experience of detention. In the context of s. 76(2)(b), it is too soon to discard the words of Lord Parker CJ in *Smith* [1959] 2 QB 35 at 37, when he observed that the court would be 'at pains to hold that even the most gentle...threats or slight inducements will taint a confession', or those of Lord Reid in *Commissioners of Customs and Excise* v *Harz* [1967] 1 AC 760 at 820:

> It is true that many of the so-called inducements have been so vague that no reasonable man would have been influenced by them, but one must remember that not all accused are reasonable men or women: they may be very ignorant and terrified by the predicament in which they find themselves. So it may have been right to err on the safe side.

Although invoked under the old common law rule, the principle stated by Lord Reid may usefully be applied to s. 76(2)(b).

The court is no longer confined to considerations of voluntariness as developed by the cases. Although at common law it was said that the categories of threats and inducements which might render a confession involuntary were never closed,[46] so that the court could consider any kind of threat or inducement that might be alleged, the court was nonetheless able to exclude only where there was a fear of prejudice or hope of advantage excited or held out by a person in authority. If a threat of detention or promise of bail was made, a threat of further charges or a promise

---

[44] [1992] 1 WLR 148; *Smith* [1994] 1 WLR 1396.
[45] See *Barry* (1992) 95 Cr App R 384; *Wahab* [2003] 1 Cr App R 15.
[46] See *Middleton* [1975] QB 191, 197 per Edmund Davies LJ.

of reduced charges, a threat to charge the wife or a promise not to charge the husband, the law worked well enough. But it did not provide for cases in which some personal circumstance, perhaps unknown to the police officers and irrelevant to the charge, acted as its own inducement to confess. Under the Act, the court may consider circumstances entirely unconnected with the police officers (which may lead courts to exclude more readily than was the case when some implication of wrongful conduct was almost inevitable). The test is not whether anyone did something wrong, but whether the court feels confident that a jury should be permitted to act on the confession.[47]

The Act contains no definition of 'reliable' or 'unreliable', probably because none is required. Obviously, the court is not to usurp the function of the jury in determining the weight to be accorded to the confession. It is submitted that the role of the court is to consider whether the circumstances, considered as a whole, disclose any reason to doubt that it would be safe to leave the confession to the jury for their consideration. It is to be noted that the Act requires only that that which was said or done may have been likely, in the light of the circumstances, to render any confession which might have been made in consequence thereof, unreliable. The court is not required to find, and should not attempt to find that the confession actually made is, or even that it may, in fact, be unreliable; this is a question of weight for the jury. If what was said or done is such that *any* confession that might have been made in consequence thereof is likely to be unreliable, then the confession actually made in consequence thereof must be excluded: see *Re Proulx* [2001] 1 All ER 57, [46] per Mance LJ.

The Act clarified a specific and recurring problem under the common law voluntariness test by confirming the decision of the House of Lords in *DPP* v *Ping Lin* [1976] AC 574 (see 9.4.1) that the intent of the police officers or other persons to whom the confession is made, is irrelevant, except as evidence that the confession may have been obtained in such a way that it must be excluded. There is no need to show or suggest any wrongful conduct, whether deliberate or inadvertent, on the part of the officers, unless the sole ground of the application to exclude is deliberate oppression such as that consisting of the conduct specified in s. 76(8) (see *Fulling* [1987] QB 426, and 9.7).

9.8.1 Self-generated fears; accused's mental state

In *Rennie* [1982] 1 WLR 64, it had been held at common law that a self-generated fear conceived by the accused that members of his family might be implicated in the investigation of the offence was insufficient to justify the exclusion of the resulting confession, because it had not been 'obtained by anything said or done by a person in authority' (per Lord Lane CJ at 69). In the light of the wording of s. 76(2)(b), it appeared arguable that this decision need not be followed when considering the statutory issue of unreliability, because what was said or done by the accused might have the effect of rendering unreliable any confession which the accused might have made. However, it has been held that what is said or done by the accused himself cannot suffice to render a confession unreliable, for the purposes of s. 76(2)(b). In *Goldenberg* (1988) 88 Cr App R 285, for example, the accused alleged that he was interviewed while in custody, and that, being a heroin addict, he was prepared to do or say anything to gain his release from custody, so that any

---

[47] See, e.g., *Effik* (1992) 95 Cr App R 427. The accused cannot argue that a confession should be excluded because he made it after receiving questionable advice from his solicitor; as long as the accused made the decision to provide a statement, the court will not inquire into the wisdom of the advice given by the solicitor: *Wahab* [2003] 1 Cr App R 15.

confession he might have made would have been unreliable. The Court of Appeal held that what was said or done by the accused, and the state of mind of the accused, were not within the scope of this provision, and could not be considered. This suggests the unsatisfactory position that, if the police know that an accused is addicted to drugs, and deliberately (albeit lawfully) detain him with the result that he makes a statement, s. 76(2)(b) could be relied upon, whereas if the police officers are ignorant of his condition, the accused has no remedy. An unsuccessful attempt was made to argue an analogous point in *Crampton* (1990) 92 Cr App R 369. It is worth stressing again that, unlike the ground of oppression, the ground of unreliability does not depend logically on any factors external to the accused.

The illogicality of the position taken in *Goldenberg* is illustrated, it is submitted, by the fact that the Court of Appeal has been prepared, in other cases, to hold that trial judges should take into account the mental state of certain suspects in considering questions of unreliability. Thus, in *Everett*[48] the Court held that the circumstances to be considered 'obviously' included the mental state, as later ascertained from a doctor, of a 42-year-old accused with a mental age of eight, who had made confessions to indecent assault of a child. The Court held, quashing the conviction, that the confession ought to have been excluded. And in *Effik* (1992) 95 Cr App R 427, the Court of Appeal spoke with approval of the view of the trial judge that he would have excluded a confession made by an accused who was addicted to heroin, if the confession had been made while he was experiencing acute withdrawal symptoms. In *Walker* [1998] Crim LR 211, the Court of Appeal seems to have accepted that the fact that an accused had ingested cocaine before making a confession was a circumstance relevant to the question of whether any confession he might have made might be unreliable. This approach is virtually impossible to reconcile with that taken in *Goldenberg*, and seems greatly preferable to that taken in *Goldenberg*.

9.8.2 Confession not caused by oppression or circumstances

As at common law, there may be cases where the oppression or circumstances pass away before the confession is made, so that there is no causal connection between the former and the latter, and in such a case, the confession may be received. An example is *Smith* [1959] 2 QB 35. The first confession made by the accused, a serving soldier, was rejected because it was made to his regimental sergeant-major (a person in authority) who had threatened to keep a number of soldiers on parade until a confession was forthcoming from one of them. However, when that treatment had ended, the accused made further oral and written confessions to regular investigating officers, who presented no fear of prejudice or hope of advantage. These latter confessions were admitted. In *Prouse v DPP* [1999] All ER (D) 748, it was held that where the accused was at first improperly denied access to legal advice, but that impropriety was corrected before the accused made his confession, it could not be said that the confession was caused by the denial of legal advice and the confession was properly admitted. In *Roberts* [1997] 1 Cr App R 217, it was held that an accused is not entitled to have a confession excluded because of a breach of the Code of Practice applicable to another suspect. There would be no causal link between the breach and the confession made by the accused in such a case. But both at common law, and under the Police and Criminal Evidence Act 1984, it has been held that a confession, which itself is properly obtained, may be excluded as tainted by an earlier irregularity if there is an appropriate causal link.[49]

---

[48] [1988] Crim LR 826; see also *Re Proulx* [2001] 1 All ER 57; *Harvey* [1988] Crim LR 241.

[49] See, e.g., *Wood* [1994] Crim LR 222 (several breaches of Code during initial interview with mentally handicapped suspect tainted later confession obtained properly); *Glaves* [1993] Crim LR 685 (impression given to a

9.9 EVIDENCE YIELDED BY INADMISSIBLE CONFESSIONS

Confessions may be useful to the prosecution for more reasons than one. We have so far considered the admissibility of the confession as evidence of the truth of the facts admitted, as an exception to the rule against hearsay. But a confession may also yield other admissible evidence, the discovery of which is made possible or facilitated by what is said in the confession, as where the accused in his confession tells the police where to find the stolen goods or the body of his victim. If the confession is admissible, no difficulty arises, for the prosecution are then entitled to adduce evidence, not only of the confession itself but also of the evidence discovered as a result. But if the confession is excluded at trial, does other evidence discovered as a result of it become 'tainted' as being 'the fruit of the poisonous tree', and must it therefore be excluded also? In fact, this question contains two distinct sub-questions. Firstly, may the prosecution adduce the discovered evidence without reference to the confession? Secondly, may the prosecution adduce evidence that the other evidence was discovered because of a confession made by the accused?

At common law, it was held that the discovered evidence might be admitted, even though the confession was excluded, provided that the discovered evidence was capable of being 'fully and satisfactorily proved' without any reference to the confession.[50] It was suggested at one time that that part of the confession necessary to explain the discovery of the other evidence might be admitted for that limited purpose, while the remainder of the confession was excluded, but this unsatisfactory approach was ultimately rejected.[51] In some cases, the discovered evidence was held to be so intimately connected with the inadmissible confession that the former could not be adduced. In *Barker* [1941] 2 KB 381, confessions made by the accused were excluded because of inducements made to him by officers of the Inland Revenue. The prosecution sought, nonetheless, to adduce evidence of books produced by the accused, which were said to contain evidence of fraud. However, as it appeared that the books were part and parcel of the confession, and had been produced as part of and for the purpose of explaining the confession, it was held that they, too, must be rejected.

By s. 76(4), (5), and (6) of the Police and Criminal Evidence Act 1984:

> (4) The fact that a confession is wholly or partly excluded in pursuance of this section shall not affect the admissibility in evidence—
>
> (a) of any facts discovered as a result of the confession...
>
> (5) Evidence that a fact to which this subsection applies was discovered as a result of a statement made by an accused person shall not be admissible unless evidence of how it was discovered is given by him or on his behalf.
>
> (6) Subsection (5) above applies—
>
> (a) to any fact discovered as a result of a confession which is wholly excluded in pursuance of this section; and

juvenile, who had no access to legal advice, that he was obliged to answer questions, tainted later confession obtained after caution by other officers); see also *Ismail* [1990] Crim LR 109; P. Mirfield [1996] Crim LR 554.

[50] *Warickshall* (1783) 1 Leach 263. But see also the opinion of the Privy Council in *Timothy v State* [2000] 1 WLR 485, decided under the law of Trinidad and Tobago. Where a confession is excluded, generally it must not be referred to by the prosecution in the presence of the jury for any purpose: *Treacy* [1944] 2 All ER 229. But see *Rowson* [1986] QB 174; Police and Criminal Evidence Act 1984, s. 76(4)(b); 9.13.

[51] *Gould* (1840) 9 Car & P 364; *Berriman* (1854) 6 Cox CC 388.

> (b) to any fact discovered as a result of a confession which is partly so excluded, if the fact is
> discovered as a result of the excluded part of the confession.

Subsection (4) deals with the first of the two sub-questions posed above. The subsection does not appear to alter the common law rule that an excluded confession, or part, may not be referred to in the presence of the jury for any purpose. It does, however, provide that the discovered evidence shall be admissible, notwithstanding that the confession is excluded. It is unclear what, if anything, Parliament intended to happen in future in situations such as that in *Barker*. It is submitted that, where the discovered evidence cannot be adduced without necessarily referring to the confession, it must be excluded. The discovered evidence may appear strange to a jury because of the absence of evidence as to how it was discovered, but where, for example, evidence is discovered because of some inadmissible hearsay communication to the police, the same problem occurs. It is usually not a serious one, and can if necessary be mitigated by a direction to the jury against speculation about the source of the discovered evidence.

Subsections (5) and (6) answer our second sub-question by providing that evidence that the discovered evidence was discovered because of an excluded confession may be introduced only by the defence. Once introduced, however, the prosecution may presumably investigate the matter further, in accordance with the usual rule of evidence that to introduce a subject which might have been excluded opens up the whole to scrutiny. The defence should consider long and hard before opening the door.

9.10 EXCLUDED CONFESSIONS AS RELEVANT NON-HEARSAY EVIDENCE

By s. 76(4) of the Police and Criminal Evidence Act 1984:

> (4) The fact that a confession is wholly or partly excluded in pursuance of this section shall not
> affect the admissibility in evidence—
>
>   ...
>
>   (b) where the confession is relevant as showing that the accused speaks, writes or expresses
>   himself in a particular way, of so much of the confession as is necessary to show that he
>   does so.

We saw in 7.10 that a statement may be admissible as non-hearsay evidence, if relevant for a purpose other than proving the truth of facts stated therein. A statement (whether or not it is a confession) may be relevant as showing, inter alia, the way in which the maker expresses himself, including his command or lack of command of the English language, his use of idiom, his grammatical ability, his vocabulary, and his style of writing. A classic instance was *Voisin*,[52] in which the accused's eccentric mis-spelling of the phrase 'bloody Belgian' was used to connect him with the crime; a form of highly specific identification evidence. Frequently, these matters are canvassed in the course of an application to exclude a confession, in order to suggest that the accused could or could not have made, or is or is not likely to have made the alleged confession. But since the subsection is dealing with confessions that have already been excluded, it is clear that the intended relevance lies elsewhere. An example would be where the accused alleges that

---

[52] [1918] 1 KB 531; for a more recent application of much the same principle, see *Nottle* [2004] EWCA Crim 599.

he cannot speak English, and his ability to speak English is relevant to an issue in the case, for example his ability to complete an allegedly fraudulent loan application; or where an accused charged with a sophisticated offence of bank fraud claims to be virtually illiterate. In such cases, the prosecution would be entitled to make use of the confession under s. 76(4)(b).

9.11 CONFESSIONS BY THE MENTALLY HANDICAPPED AND THOSE OTHERWISE IMPAIRED

By s. 77 of the Police and Criminal Evidence Act 1984, as amended:

> (1) Without prejudice to the general duty of the court at a trial on indictment with a jury to direct the jury on any matter on which it appears to the court appropriate to do so, where at such a trial—
>> (a) the case against the accused depends wholly or substantially on a confession by him; and
>> (b) the court is satisfied—
>>> (i) that he is mentally handicapped; and
>>> (ii) that the confession was not made in the presence of an independent person,[53]
> the court shall warn the jury that there is a special need for caution before convicting the accused in reliance on the confession, and shall explain that the need arises because of the circumstances mentioned in paragraphs (a) and (b) above.

Section 77(2) makes provision for a magistrates' court conducting a summary trial to treat such cases as requiring special caution. Section 77(3) defines a person as mentally handicapped when 'he is in a state of arrested or incomplete development of mind which includes significant impairment of intelligence and social functioning'. The same subsection defines an 'independent person' as excluding a police officer or a person employed for or engaged on police purposes. The direction called for by the section is mandatory in all such cases, even where the judge considers that no question of unreliability arises. The weight of the confession, if admitted, is of course a question of fact for the jury.

There have been some cases which suggest that, in the circumstances envisaged by s. 77(1), it may be appropriate to exclude the confession altogether. In *MacKenzie*[54] the Court of Appeal went so far as to say that in a case in which the prosecution relied wholly on confessions, the accused suffered from a significant degree of mental handicap, and the confessions were so unconvincing that it would be unsafe to ask a jury to convict on the basis of them, the judge should not only exclude the confessions, but also withdraw the case from the jury—as would seem to be inevitable in the circumstances postulated by the Court. In this case, not only were the confessions unsupported by other evidence, but their credibility was undermined by other confessions made by the accused to offences which the prosecution did not believe he had committed. In such a case, it would seem that s. 76(2)(b) surely dictates the exclusion of the confessions, but it also seems clear that this would not be true in all cases where the accused happens to suffer from some degree of mental handicap, and that the direction called for by s. 77(1) would often suffice.

Section 77 is itself of fairly limited application, and leaves unresolved the problem of how to approach cases in which a suspect being interrogated is permanently or temporarily impaired

---

[53] Code of Practice C requires the presence of an 'appropriate adult' during an interview of a person who is mentally disordered or vulnerable (see para. 1.7(b) and note 1D), a requirement which is not identical to that of an 'independent person'.

[54] (1992) 96 Cr App R 98. See also *Aspinall* [1999] 2 Cr App R 115; *Moss* (1990) 91 Cr App R 371; *Lamont* [1989] Crim LR 813; cf. *Law-Thompson* [1997] Crim LR 674.

by reason of mental illness or the effect of alcohol or drugs (legal or otherwise). It would seem that in such circumstances there is an obvious potential for any confession that might be made to be unreliable. Such cases do not fall within s. 77 and they must be considered under the usual exclusionary rules of s. 76(2)(a) or (b). There is a curious paucity of authority. In *Miller* [1986] 1 WLR 1191, the accused was a paranoid schizophrenic, who was charged with the murder of his girlfriend. He made a series of long, rambling confessions, in which he stated, inter alia, that he had stabbed the girlfriend repeatedly in response to voices inside his head, and because 'arbitrised humans and small molecular people' were screaming at him. The trial took place before the coming into effect of the Police and Criminal Evidence Act 1984, though it was in force at the date of hearing of the appeal against conviction, and the judgment of the Court of Appeal delivered by Watkins LJ shows that the Court at least considered ss. 76 and 78 of the Act. This procedural history is unfortunate, in that at common law, the argument for the accused could be mounted only on the bases: (1) that questioning of a person in the accused's mental state was almost necessarily oppressive; and (2) that in any event, the judge should have exercised his discretion to exclude the confession, having regard to all the circumstances. Predictably, the argument on oppression failed, as it would no doubt fail under the new law in the light of *Fulling* [1987] QB 426 (see 9.7) because there was nothing in the circumstances to correspond with the meaning of the term. As to discretion, the Court felt unable to criticize the trial judge, who had had the advantage of hearing psychiatric evidence called for the defence, and had concluded that there was no reason not to let the confession go to the jury. And indeed, it is true that, leaving aside the nonsensical motivations, the accused made the clearest possible admission of having deliberately killed the girlfriend with a knife.

It is submitted that the proper test now is that laid down by s. 76(2)(b). It may be that on the facts of *Miller* the same result would be arrived at. But there will be cases where illness or impairment will dictate exclusion on the ground that any confession made would, in the circumstances, have been likely to be unreliable. This would include cases in which the impairment was caused by the voluntary consumption of alcohol or drugs.[55] In such cases, the defence would be entitled to raise arguments not available in *Miller*.

If a confession made by a person suffering from a recognizable mental disorder is admitted, expert evidence may be admitted to assist the jury in assessing its weight (*Ward* [1993] 1 WLR 619). In *Blackburn* [2005] 2 Cr App R 30, the Court of Appeal held that expert evidence was admissible on the subject of 'coerced compliant confession', a phenomenon affecting young and otherwise vulnerable suspects, who may be compelled by fatigue and loss of control over their surroundings to confess with a view to ending an interrogation, even in the absence of any personality disorder.

9.12 THE CODES OF PRACTICE AND THE DISCRETIONARY EXCLUSION OF CONFESSIONS

Pursuant to s. 66 of the Police and Criminal Evidence Act 1984, there have been promulgated Codes of Practice dealing comprehensively with almost every conceivable facet of the relationship between investigating police officers and suspects. The Codes provide rules of practice, rather than of law, but are admissible in evidence by virtue of s. 67(11) of the Act. Codes of Practice C, which governs the detention, treatment, questioning, and identification of suspects by police

---

[55] See 9.8.1; *Walker* [1998] Crim LR 211; *Effik* (1992) 95 Cr App R 427; *Harvey* [1988] Crim LR 241.

officers, and E, dealing with the tape recording of statements are, for obvious reasons, of greatest significance when a court has to inquire into how a confession came to be made.[56] The Codes of Practice have an immediate impact on the fairness of the trial, in the sense that the court may have to consider whether any breach of the Codes renders it unfair to admit against the accused evidence obtained in consequence of the breach. It is now well established that the judge has the discretionary power, at common law and under s. 78 of the Police and Criminal Evidence Act 1984, to exclude evidence on this ground. The most important example of this power is the discretionary exclusion of confessions obtained in breach of Code of Practice C. Because the right to a fair trial is guaranteed by art. 6 of the European Convention on Human Rights, this article must now also be considered when application to exclude a confession on this ground is made.

9.12.1 Discretionary exclusion of confessions prior to Codes of Practice

Code of Practice C was designed to supplant the Judges' Rules, which, since they were first formulated in 1912, were the rules of practice recognized by the courts for the conduct of police officers and other professional investigators in relation to detention, arrest, search, and interrogation. The relationship between breaches of the Judges' Rules and the admissibility of confessions that resulted from or followed such breaches was never satisfactorily defined. The Rules were rules of practice only, and not rules of law. Their preamble made it clear that they did not affect the overriding principle that confessions must have been voluntary and obtained in the absence of oppression. But it went on to add:

Within that principle the following rules are put forward as a guide to police officers conducting investigations. Non-conformity with these rules may render answers and statements liable to be excluded from evidence in subsequent criminal proceedings.

In *May*[57] Lord Goddard CJ said:

The test of the admissibility of a statement is whether it is a voluntary statement. There are certain rules known as the Judges' Rules which are not rules of law but rules of practice drawn up for the guidance of police officers; and if a statement has been made in circumstances not in accordance with the Rules, in law that statement is not made inadmissible if it is a voluntary statement, although in its discretion the court can always refuse to admit it if the court thinks there has been a breach of the Rules.

In practice, the courts proved reluctant to exclude a confession on account of a 'technical breach' of the Rules, in other words in cases where the breach had no effect on the voluntariness of the statement, either because the breach was a relatively minor one, or because the breach was not closely related to the making of the confession. The Rules were generally regarded as an aid to the determination of whether the confession had been made voluntarily, rather than as a basis for exclusion in their own right. This was clearly indicated by the decision of the Court of Appeal in *Prager* [1972] 1 WLR 260. The accused, who was charged with serious offences contrary to the Official Secrets Acts, was interrogated without caution in breach of Rule 2 of the Judges' Rules. The decision not to caution was taken deliberately and in advance of the interrogation by the interrogating officers, a decision said to be justified by the serious nature of the case and

---

[56] The contents of the Codes are too voluminous to be reproduced in this work. For the complete text, see *Blackstone's Criminal Practice*, 2009 edn, appendix 2.

[57] (1952) 36 Cr App R 91, 93. The discretion referred to by Lord Goddard CJ was expressly re-affirmed by the House of Lords in *Sang* [1980] AC 402, even though the House held that there was no general common law discretion to exclude other evidence obtained illegally or unfairly.

the possibility of damage to the national interest. The trial judge, Lord Widgery CJ, held that the resulting confession was voluntary and declined to consider separately whether or not it should be excluded on discretionary grounds because of the breach of Rule 2. On appeal, it was argued that this approach was impermissible. However, Edmund Davies LJ, in dismissing the appeal, said (*ibid.* at 265–6):

> [Counsel] submitted before us that it was imperative that Lord Widgery CJ decide first whether Rule 2 had or had not been breached, for, if it had been, the confession should not have been admitted unless there emerged 'some compelling reason why the breach should have been overlooked'. He cited no authority for that proposition, which, he claimed, involved a point of law of very great importance. This 'complete lack of authority' (to use [counsel's] phrase) is not surprising, for in our judgment, the proposition advanced involves no point of law and is manifestly unsound. Its acceptance would exalt the Judges' Rules into rules of law. That they do not purport to be, and there is abundant authority for saying that they are nothing of the kind. Their non-observance may, and at times does, lead to the exclusion of an alleged confession; but ultimately all turns on the judge's decision whether, breach or no breach, it has been shown to have been made voluntarily. In the present case, Lord Widgery CJ was, without deciding the point, prepared to assume in the accused's favour that there had been a breach of Rule 2, and then proceeded to consider whether its voluntary nature had nevertheless been established. In our judgment, no valid criticism of that approach can be made. On the contrary, it appears to us entirely sound.

9.12.2 Discretionary exclusion of confessions for breach of Codes of Practice

Logically enough, it appears that the courts will treat the Codes of Practice in the same way as they formerly treated the Judges' Rules, i.e., as rules of practice, breach of which may, but will not necessarily lead to the exclusion of a confession obtained thereby. Section 67(11) of the Police and Criminal Evidence Act 1984 provides expressly that the provisions of the Codes shall be admissible in evidence, and may be taken into account by the court to the extent relevant. In the context of the exclusion of confessions, the provisions of the Codes may clearly be relevant whenever the court considers whether a confession should be excluded on the ground of oppression (see 9.7) or unreliability (see 9.8) or in the exercise of discretion under s. 78 of the Act (see 3.7).

As under the Judges' Rules, the magnitude of the breach, the gravity of the charge, the practicability of successfully investigating the case while scrupulously observing the provisions of the Codes, and any element of deliberation on the part of the investigating officers, may all be taken into account. Each case must depend on its own facts. However, the accused is entitled to have a judicial decision on the merits of his application to exclude, without reference to any possibility that he would be entitled to seek to remedy the situation by giving evidence at trial: *Keenan* [1990] 2 QB 54. In the same case, the Court stressed that the Act and the Codes must be taken seriously, and that trial judges should not be slow to exclude, where 'substantial' breaches are shown to have occurred. Thus, in a case where a necessary caution has been omitted, or where the interview has not been properly recorded, or where an appropriate adult has not been provided for a person under disability, the breach may well affect the reliability of the confession or the fairness of the procedure by means of which it is obtained, and in such a case the court may well exclude the resulting confession: see, e.g., *Weekes* (1993) 97 Cr App R 222 (failure to record interview and failure to ensure presence of appropriate adult); *Weedersteyn* [1995] 1 Cr App R 405 (failure to caution and misleading accused as to nature of interview); *Coelho* [2008] EWCA Crim 627 (failure to allow a suspect to check and sign a record of what he has said, and to provide a record additionally in the original language in which his statements were made, if other than English). Conversely, there are many cases in which the alleged breach of a Code is technical, or in which it seems clear that the breach could not have led to any risk of unfairness. In *Ridehalgh v DPP* [2005] RTR 353, where there was a failure to administer the proper caution, an incriminating statement made by the defendant was nonetheless properly admitted in a case where the defendant was himself a police officer, who was well aware of his rights, and who repeated the statement at a later time while under caution. And in *Dunn* (1990) 91 Cr App R 150, where the breach was admittedly not a technical one, in that the interviewing officer had failed to observe provisions designed to prevent fabrication of the interview record, it was held that it was not improper to admit a statement made by the accused because his solicitor's clerk had been present throughout and was able to safeguard his rights. The most common examples of alleged breaches are of failures to comply with the requirements of Code C in interviews, including the administration of cautions.

9.12.3 What amounts to an interview

Before the adoption of the Codes of Practice, the questioning of suspects was a relatively informal affair, oral answers given by the suspect being recorded in the notebooks of the interviewing officers, or included in a written statement under caution. The resulting inevitable disputes about what had been said consumed vast amounts of time during trials, with officers often being cross-examined in considerable detail about their notes. This practice was highly unsatisfactory, and was in due course replaced by the present procedures under Codes C and E. In contemporary practice, the questioning of a suspect designed to obtain an admission of his involvement in an offence must, with narrow exceptions, be conducted under caution[58] and at a police station, and must be tape-recorded. Any such questioning is known as an interview. Most applications to exclude confessions because of breaches of Code C are based on alleged failures to follow the appropriate procedure for the conduct of interviews. In some cases, police officers are reluctant to compromise a promising investigation by taking the formal step of taking a suspect into custody, which might cause the suspect to give less information than he might if allowed to remain at liberty, and after which the secrecy of the investigation might be at an end. In other cases, officers sometimes overlook that a conversation with a suspect is, in fact, an interview. The following provisions of Code C dealing with the conduct of interviews (here cited in part) are of particular importance in the context of applications to exclude confessions:[59]

> Para. 11.1A: an interview is the questioning of a person regarding their involvement or suspected involvement in a criminal offence or offences which...must be carried out under caution.[60]
>
> Para. 10.1: a person whom there are grounds to suspect of an offence...must be cautioned before any questions about an offence, or further questions if the answers provide the grounds for suspicion, are put to them if either the suspect's answers or silence...may be given in evidence to a court in a prosecution.

---

[58] The wording of the caution is, 'You do not have to say anything. But it may harm your defence if you do not mention when questioned something which you later rely on in court. Anything you do say may be given in evidence': Code of Practice C, para. 10.5.

[59] They are, of course, by no means the only important provisions. The physical circumstances of a suspect's detention may also be highly relevant, and are provided for in detail in sections 8 and 9 of the Code. Provisions supplementing the statutory right to legal advice are provided in section 6.

[60] The obligation to caution applies to all police officers and to others professionally involved with the investigation of offences, for example investigators of HM Revenue & Customs. A senior prison officer may have an obligation to caution a suspect if he has powers of arrest in relation to offences committed within the precincts of the prison: *Devani* [2008] 1 Cr App R 4.

Para. 11.11: unless it is impracticable the suspect shall be given the opportunity to read the interview record and to sign it as correct or to indicate how they consider it inaccurate.

Para. 11.13: a written record shall be made of any comments made by a suspect, including unsolicited comments, which are outside the context of an interview but which might be relevant to an offence. Any such record must be timed and signed by the maker. When practicable the suspect shall be given the opportunity to read that record and to sign it as correct or to indicate how they consider it inaccurate.[61]

Despite these apparently clear provisions, there remains some room for doubt in particular cases as to whether a series of questions or answers amounts to an interview. In *Cox* [1993] 1 WLR 188, the Court of Appeal suggested that the word 'interview' should not be construed strictly, as if it were a statutory provision, but rather that the courts should judge each situation on its merits, having regard to what might be fair. An example of the kind of problem which could arise is *Matthews* (1989) 91 Cr App R 43, where the accused asked that a conversation with an officer be kept 'off the record'—the exact antithesis of what is envisaged by the Codes. It was held that the resulting confession had been rightly admitted, even though the officer had failed to show the accused any note of what had been said. But in *Okafor*[62] it was held that a confession should have been excluded where customs officers deliberately failed to caution the accused, so as to avoid the possibility that he might realize that drugs had been detected in his luggage. And in *Christou* [1992] QB 979, it was held to be improper for police officers to adopt a disguise to enable them to ask questions without having to observe the provisions of the Codes. Some forms of questioning may take place without triggering the interview provisions of Code C. For example, where officers arrive at an address to search the premises, they may question a suspect for the preliminary purpose of being directed to parts of the building, or to a particular vehicle or items under the suspect's control (see para. 10(1) of Code C); but if the questioning then proceeds further in such a way as to suggest that he is being questioned about his involvement in an offence, the questioning, however brief, amounts to an interview and may be excluded, particularly if para. 11.13 is not complied with.

9.12.4 Denial of access to legal advice: domestic provisions

An important case which is linked to, but goes beyond the Code of Practice, is the denial of access to legal advice. Section 58 of the Police and Criminal Evidence Act 1984 provides that any person who has been arrested and is being held in custody at a police station is entitled, at his request, to consult a solicitor privately at any time. Access to legal advice may be be delayed only in a narrow range of circumstances and for the shortest time compatible with achieving certain overriding objectives: see section 6 of Code C. If a denial of the right to legal advice right causes the accused to make a confession, serious issues arise.

In *Walsh* (1989) 91 Cr App R 161, the Court of Appeal, dealing with a case in which it was conceded that the accused had improperly been denied access to legal advice, observed (at 163);

To our minds it follows that if there are significant and substantial breaches of section 58 or the provisions of the Code, then *prima facie* at least the standards of fairness set by Parliament have not

---

[61] This provision applies to words spoken as comment or in answer to questions about an offence. They are not apt to apply to words alleged to constitute the *actus reus* of the offence itself. Thus where the defendant was charged with threatening, abusive, or insulting words and behaviour, it was not necessary for him to be given the opportunity of signing the record of those words as spoken: *DPP v Lawrence* [2008] 1 Cr App R 10.

[62] [1994] 3 All ER 741. See also *Weerdersteyn* [1995] 1 Cr App R 405.

been met. So far as a defendant is concerned, it seems to us also to follow that to admit evidence against him which has been obtained in circumstances where these standards have not been met, cannot but have an adverse effect on the fairness of the proceedings. This does not mean, of course, that in every case of a significant or substantial breach of section 58 or the Code of Practice the evidence concerned will automatically be excluded. Section 78 does not so provide. The task of the court is not merely to consider whether there would be an adverse effect on the fairness of the proceedings, but such an adverse effect that justice requires the evidence to be excluded.

Similar observations were made in *Delaney* (1988) 88 Cr App R 338 and *Parris* (1988) 89 Cr App R 68.

In *Alladice* (1988) 87 Cr App R 380, where it was also shown that the police officers, through a misunderstanding, had denied the accused access to legal advice to which he was entitled, the appeal was nonetheless dismissed, because the accused admitted in evidence that he had understood his legal rights, and the caution, and that he had been able to cope with the interviews. Conversely, in *Samuel*[63] the accused was charged with burglaries and robbery. He was denied access to a solicitor even after he had confessed to and had been charged with the burglaries. On being further detained and questioned without access to legal advice, the accused made a further confession to robbery. The confessions were admitted at trial, and the accused was convicted. The Court of Appeal allowed the appeal and quashed the conviction. It was not argued that the conduct of the police was oppressive, an argument which after *Fulling* must have failed, or that any confession made was likely to be unreliable, but that the judge should have exercised his discretion to exclude the confession because of the flagrant breaches of the Code of Practice indulged in to obtain it. The Court of Appeal agreed, and held that the right to legal advice was fundamental, and that the prosecution had not discharged the heavy burden of justifying refusal of access to a solicitor merely by general allegations that other suspects might be alerted or evidence destroyed. Under s. 78 of the Police and Criminal Evidence Act 1984 this had such an adverse effect on the fairness of the proceedings that the judge ought to have excluded the confession.

In the narrow range of cases in which it is proper to delay access to legal advice for a time, a failure to provide access to legal advice will not necessarily prevent the admission of a confession made during the period of delay. This includes confessions made during 'safety interviews', i.e., interviews permitted before legal advice is provided, under Sch. 8 to the Terrorism Act 2000, or in other cases when a senior police officer has reasonable grounds for believing that the delay involved in providing legal advice may result in loss of life, serious injury, or serious damage to property. There is no ground for excluding such confessions as a matter of principle, but the judge must take the absence of legal advice into account when considering whether to exclude a confession in the exercise of his discretion under s. 78: *Ibrahim and others* [2008] 4 All ER 208; see also para. 6.6 and annex C to Code C.

9.12.5 Denial of access to legal advice: art. 6 of the European Convention

This approach may no longer be sufficient in the light of art. 6 of the European Convention on Human Rights. As we have seen, art. 6 does not purport to regulate the content of the law of

---

[63] [1988] QB 615. See also *Canale* [1990] 2 All ER 187; *Absolam* (1988) 88 Cr App R 232; but see also *Roberts* [1997] 1 Cr App R 217; contrast *Kwabena Poku* [1978] Crim LR 488.

States bound by the Convention,[64] but requires that the accused be given a fair trial. However, the right to receive legal advice is a fundamental right expressly guaranteed by the article:

> 3. Everyone charged with a criminal offence has the following minimum rights:...
>   (c) to defend himself in person or through legal assistance of his own choosing or, if he has not sufficient means to pay for legal assistance, to be given it free when the interests of justice so require...

As a matter of English law, the right to legal advice is expressly provided by s. 58 of the Police and Criminal Evidence Act 1984.[65] But s. 58 has not resulted in the automatic exclusion of confessions obtained when the accused has been deprived of that advice. As shown by the cases of *Alladice* (1988) 87 Cr App R 30 and *Samuel* [1988] QB 615 discussed above, the question of exclusion has turned on the particular circumstances of each case, and cases such as *Alladice* have suggested that the courts can hold that the right to legal advice is effectively dispensed with if, in the judgment of the court, the accused seemed to cope without it. But art. 6 may require that this view be reconsidered. The jurisprudence of the European Court of Human Rights has taken a strong view, which could be interpreted as holding that a refusal of access to legal advice is incompatible with the right to a fair trial: see *Murray* v *United Kingdom* (1996) 22 EHRR 29. For this purpose, the right to legal advice and representation applies to various stages of criminal proceedings, especially, the right to be legally represented at trial. But it is surely no less important at the stage where the accused is to be interviewed, and a possible result is that he may make a confession.

In *Murray*, the accused was detained for 48 hours before being allowed access to a solicitor, and at his trial the judge, sitting in Northern Ireland, drew an adverse inference against him because of his failure to answer police questions, as permitted by provisions in effect in Northern Ireland akin to those of ss. 34 to 38 of the Criminal Justice and Public Order Act 1994. Noting that art. 6 did not expressly enshrine the right of silence, the European Court of Human Rights held that the fact that an adverse admission might be drawn from the accused's silence did not in itself violate the accused's right to a fair trial under art. 6, but that it might do so in conjunction with other factors, of which the denial of access to legal advice was an example. On the facts, the denial of access to a solicitor, which influenced the accused's decision to remain silent, violated art. 6. In the proceedings before the European Commission of Human Rights, the majority said (*ibid.* at paras 47–8):

> The Commission recalls that the Convention does not expressly guarantee the right of an accused to communicate *freely* with his defence counsel for the preparation of his defence or otherwise, *or for the defence counsel to be present during pre-trial examinations*. Article 6(3)(c), which reflects a specific aspect of the general concept of a fair trial set out in paragraph 1 of the same article, confers the right on an accused to defend himself through legal assistance. The Commission recalls that the Convention is intended to guarantee rights which are not theoretical or illusory but rights that are practical and effective; this is of particular relevance to the rights of the defence given the prominent place held in a democratic society by the right to a fair trial. *Restrictions on an accused's access to his lawyer and the refusal to allow the lawyer to attend during examinations of his client may influence the material position of the defence at the trial and*

---

[64] *Kostovski* v *Netherlands* (1989) 12 EHRR 434; *Saidi* v *France* (1993) 17 EHRR 251; *Republic of Ireland* v *United Kingdom* (1978) 2 EHRR 25; *Murray* v *United Kingdom* (1996) 22 EHRR 29; cf. *Funke* v *France* (1993) 16 EHRR 297.

[65] The right is entirely statutory as it relates to police interviews. There is no common law right to legal advice at that time (*Chief Constable of the Royal Ulster Constabulary, ex parte Begley* [1997] 1 WLR 1475). Contrast *Mohammed* v *State* [1999] 2 AC 111 decided under the Constitution of Trinidad and Tobago.

therefore also the outcome of the proceedings. The Court and the Commission have accordingly considered that guarantees of art. 6 normally extend to an accused the right to assistance and support by a lawyer throughout the proceedings. [Emphasis added, footnotes omitted.]

The Court, having referred to the Commission's Report, concluded (*ibid.* at para. 66):

> Under such conditions [i.e., that inferences could be drawn from silence and failure to give evidence] the concept of fairness enshrined in art. 6 requires that the accused has the benefit of the assistance of a lawyer already at the initial stages of a police interrogation. To deny access to a lawyer for the first 48 hours of police questioning, in a situation where the rights of the defence may well be irretrievably prejudiced is—whatever the justification for such denial—incompatible with the rights of the accused under art. 6.

Consistently with these principles, in *Magee* v *United Kingdom* (2001) 31 EHRR 35, it was held that the denial of access to a solicitor for 48 hours, during which time the accused made damaging admissions, violated his rights under the Convention. But each case must be considered on its own facts. In *Brennan* v *United Kingdom* (2002) 34 EHRR 18, *Magee* was distinguished. In *Brennan*, it was held that, where the accused was denied access to a solicitor for the lesser period of 24 hours and where his admissions were made only after that period, there had been no breach of art. 6. The Court also held that no violation of art. 6 was involved in the questioning of the accused in the absence of his solicitor where the interviews were not recorded. The ground of this holding was that the accused had the opportunity to contest the interviews in the course of an adversarial proceeding, which satisfied the test of fairness under art. 6. It is submitted that this reasoning is not entirely convincing. In the absence of his solicitor, the accused might be at a substantial disadvantage vis-à-vis the interviewing officers, and that disadvantage might well prejudice his ability to contest the interviews effectively at trial. The Court did find, however, that art. 6. had been violated by the presence of a police officer during the accused's consultations with his solicitor, and this would seem clearly to be right.

9.12.5.1 Vulnerable suspects

In *Aspinall* [1999] 2 Cr App R 115, the appellant, who had been provisionally diagnosed as suffering from schizophrenia, and who required constant medication, was detained at a police station for about 13 hours before being interviewed. He agreed to be interviewed without the assistance of a solicitor, having expressed a desire to leave the police station to return home to his family. No appropriate adult was provided for the appellant. The trial judge refused to exclude the resulting confession in the exercise of his discretion, and the appellant was convicted. The Court of Appeal found that he had been in a very vulnerable position and that the absence of both a solicitor and an appropriate adult should have led the judge to exclude the confession. Delivering the judgment of the Court, Bracewell J said (*ibid.* at 122–3):

> The right to access to legal advice is a fundamental right under art. 6 of the European Convention on Human Rights and *Murray* v *United Kingdom* (1996) 22 EHRR 29 sets out that delaying access to legal advice, whatever the justification, is incompatible with the right to a fair trial. In the judgment of this court, even greater importance must be attached to legal advice for a vulnerable person such as the appellant....
>
>   A vulnerable person may not be able to judge what is in his best interests, and that is the essential reason why Parliament enacted safeguards in the Police and Criminal Evidence Act 1984. In our judgment the exercise of discretion by the recorder was fundamentally flawed in his ruling under s. 78. It is not

every breach which will lead to exclusion of evidence, but in this appeal we have concluded that the breaches were so fundamental that the interview should have been excluded under s. 78.

It is submitted that this approach is correct. Suspects may, of course, be vulnerable for many different reasons, by no means all of which are connected to mental illness. While there may be cases in which it can be said with confidence that a particular suspect was not disadvantaged by a denial of access to legal advice, such cases should be rare and scrutinized with great care. Even where an accused states that he understands his rights, and is apparently knowledgeable and sophisticated, it cannot be taken for granted that he understands all the legal issues involved in the matter in which he is suspected. It is to be hoped that future courts, even if they follow the policy thus far adopted of treating art. 6 as merely one factor to be considered in the exercise of the s. 78 power, will nonetheless accept that it should only be in highly unusual circumstances that it could be held that a denial of legal advice did not result in unfairness. The result of this should be that confessions obtained in such circumstances should be excluded. It is further submitted that this view is confirmed by s. 58 of the Youth Justice and Criminal Evidence Act 1999, which prohibits the drawing of adverse inferences against the accused under ss. 34 and 36 to 38 of the Criminal Justice and Public Order Act 1994 (10.5 and 10.5.1) because of his failure to mention relevant facts, where he was at an authorized place of detention but was not permitted to consult a solicitor before being questioned. Section 58 was enacted with the intention of bringing the law into line with *Murray* v *United Kingdom*.

9.12.6 Discretionary exclusion of confessions for other causes

The discretion to exclude is not confined to cases in which there has been a breach of the Codes of Practice. It may extend to cases in which there has been an unfair subterfuge or deception of the accused, including those of the kind considered at 3.12. In *Kirk* [2000] 1 WLR 567, it was held to be unfair for the police to question a suspect about an offence for which he had not been arrested, and more serious than the one for which he had been arrested. The suspect did not know the true object of the questions being put to him. The Court of Appeal held that fairness demanded at a minimum, that he should have been told the true nature of the police inquiry. It appears that there is a growing trend to exclude confessions under s. 78 in cases where there is manifest unfairness independent of any clear breach of the Code. Such a case is *Mason*.[66] The accused was charged with arson of a car belonging to his former girlfriend's father. On their own admission, police officers 'set about conning' the accused and his solicitor by falsely representing to both that they had incriminating evidence against the accused, consisting of his finger prints on a fragment of glass from the bottle that had contained the inflammable liquid used in the arson. This evidence did not in fact exist. In response to this misinformation, the accused made a statement admitting his guilt, and was convicted at his trial. Allowing the appeal against conviction, the Court of Appeal held that the trial judge had erred in not exercising his discretion to exclude the confession under s. 78. Even though the accused's confession, in response to what he may have perceived to be a hopeless situation, may in fact have been reliable, and though it was made without oppression and with the knowledge of the accused's solicitor, the deception (a kind which the Court of Appeal hoped would never occur again) had such an adverse effect on the fairness of the proceedings that it should have been excluded. On the other hand, there is a difference between lying to the accused and simply failing to disclose all the evidence known to the

---

[66] [1988] 1 WLR 139. See also *H* [1987] Crim LR 47; *DPP* v *Marshall* [1988] 3 All ER 683.

police at the time of an interview; the latter is unobjectionable.[67] It may be unfair to an accused to question him when, even if he has not been actively misled, he is under a misunderstanding of the nature of the interview and does not realize that he is suspected of criminal activity: see for example *Smith*,[68] where the accused was interviewed by a bank manager and believed that the purpose of the discussion was simply to obtain information about the effect of certain transactions on the financial market.

9.13 USE OF CONFESSIONS BY CO-ACCUSED

9.13.1 Position before Criminal Justice Act 2003, s. 128

The rules of admissibility of confessions are designed to deal with the usual case in which a confession is tendered against the accused by the prosecution. But in some cases, a co-accused may wish to make use of a confession made by the accused, either because it supports the co-accused's case in some way, or because he wishes to cross-examine the accused on the statement to show some inconsistency between the confession and the accused's evidence at trial. Where the confession has been admitted at the instance of the prosecution, less difficulty arises. The confession is evidence against the accused, and may be used as such at least for the purpose of impeachment. But, before s. 128 of the Criminal Justice Act 2003 (see 9.13.2), where the prosecution elect not to use the confession, or where the judge has excluded the confession when tendered by the prosecution, considerable difficulties arose. Section 76 of the Police and Criminal Evidence Act 1984 (as originally enacted) applies only where the confession is tendered by the prosecution. Clearly, the co-accused should be entitled to present his case as fully as possible, and is not subject to the same rules as the prosecution (including the exercise of discretion). To the extent that the confession tends to exculpate the co-accused, the position is not unlike that in which a third party has made an exculpatory statement (see 7.4.1). The co-accused faces the same difficulty in both cases, namely, that he cannot compel the maker of the statement to give evidence. But at the same time, the position of the accused who made the statement should also be considered, especially where the judge has ruled that the confession is inadmissible under s. 76.

The classical common law rule, laid down in *Treacy* [1944] 2 All ER 229, was that, where a confession was excluded, it was inadmissible for any purpose. This included any purpose for which it might be tendered by a co-accused. But in *Rowson* [1986] QB 174, the Court of Appeal held that the fact that a confession had been excluded when tendered by the prosecution did not prevent a co-accused from cross-examining the maker of the statement for the purpose of showing inconsistency with his evidence at trial, subject to a showing of relevance. However, the Court held that, because the confession was hearsay, its use was limited to the credit of the maker as a witness, and the co-accused could not rely on it for the purposes of proving any facts admitted. This decision was approved by the Privy Council in *Lui Mei Lin* v *R* [1989] AC 288.

These decisions prompted further argument on the question of whether the co-accused is entitled to use the confession for the purpose of proving facts admitted in it where those facts are relevant to his defence, e.g., because they tend to exculpate the co-accused. On this point, a direct conflict of authority developed in the Court of Appeal.[69] This conflict was, up to a point, resolved

---

[67] *Farrell* [2004] EWCA Crim 597.

[68] [1994] 1 WLR 1396; see also *De Silva* [2003] 2 Cr App R 74 (where the accused acted in a guilty manner, believing that he was cooperating with Customs officers in facilitating the arrest of others after he had participated in a 'cooperation interview').

[69] *Beckford* [1991] Crim LR 833; *Campbell* [1993] Crim LR 448; Hirst [1998] CLJ 146.

by the House of Lords in *Myers* [1998] AC 124. A and B were jointly charged with the murder of a taxi driver, the alleged motive being robbery. A made confessions which amounted to an admission that she had stabbed the victim, although she denied any intent to kill. Because of apparent breaches of the Code of Practice, the prosecution did not attempt to have these confessions admitted in evidence. B contended that he was entitled to cross-examine about the confessions and adduce them in evidence in so far as they were relevant to his case. The trial judge, taking the view that he had no discretion to prevent B from doing so, allowed this. On appeal by A against conviction, the House of Lords held that B had been entitled to make use of the confessions. After a thorough review of the authorities (including *Blastland* [1986] AC 41 (see 7.4.1)), on the issue of admissions made by non-accused third parties, Lord Slynn of Hadley said ([1998] AC 124 at 137):

> A confession may be relevant both as to credibility and as to the facts in issue and it does not cease to be admissible because it is so. Indeed so long as it is relevant to establish his defence or to undermine the prosecution case against him a defendant should in my view be allowed to cross-examine a co-defendant as to his confession which goes to the facts in issue rather than only to the credibility of the maker of the statement. He should not less be allowed to cross-examine the person to whom a statement is made as to the terms of the confession even though, since the co-defendant has not given evidence, the question of credibility has not arisen.
>
> In *Rowson* and *Lui Mei Lin* v *R* the Court of Appeal and the Privy Council respectively stressed that the judge must tell the jury that weight should not be placed on such statement in considering the prosecution case against the maker of the statement; it was considered that the jury would be able to understand the difference and give effect to the judge's direction. On the other hand for a jury to make this distinction may not always be easy as has been fully recognized by the trial judge in the present case, by Lord Lane CJ in *O'Boyle* (1990) 92 Cr App R 202 and by academic commentators. But even allowing for a risk of prejudice to the maker of the statement in the mind of the jury, the authorities to which reference has been made make it plain that a defendant must be allowed to cross-examine a co-defendant as to, and in appropriate circumstances to introduce, relevant evidence of a previous confession made by the co-defendant.[70]

It follows from this decision that a co-accused may not only cross-examine the maker of the statement, but may also cross-examine a police officer to whom the confession was made, if the maker does not give evidence, and that the judge has no discretion to prevent this.

9.13.2 Criminal Justice Act 2003, s. 128: admissibility of confession tendered by co-accused

Parliament has now provided a test for the admissibility of confessions when tendered by a co-accused in almost the same terms as the test under s. 76 applicable to confessions tendered by the prosecution. Section 128, which came into effect on 4 April 2005, provides:

> (1) In the Police and Criminal Evidence Act 1984 (c. 60) the following section is inserted after section 76—
>
> **"76A Confessions may be given in evidence for co-accused**
>   (1) In any proceedings a confession made by an accused person may be given in evidence for another person charged in the same proceedings (a co-accused) in so far as it is relevant to any matter in issue in the proceedings and is not excluded by the court in pursuance of this section.

---

[70] See also *Corelli* [2001] Crim LR 913.

(2) If, in any proceedings where a co-accused proposes to give in evidence a confession made by an accused person, it is represented to the court that the confession was or may have been obtained—

    (a) by oppression of the person who made it; or

    (b) in consequence of anything said or done which was likely, in the circumstances existing at the time, to render unreliable any confession which might be made by him in consequence thereof,

the court shall not allow the confession to be given in evidence for the co-accused except in so far as it is proved to the court on the balance of probabilities that the confession (notwithstanding that it may be true) was not so obtained.

(3) Before allowing a confession made by an accused person to be given in evidence for a co-accused in any proceedings, the court may of its own motion require the fact that the confession was not obtained as mentioned in subsection (2) above to be proved in the proceedings on the balance of probabilities.

(4) The fact that a confession is wholly or partly excluded in pursuance of this section shall not affect the admissibility in evidence—

    (a) of any facts discovered as a result of the confession; or

    (b) where the confession is relevant as showing that the accused speaks, writes or expresses himself in a particular way, of so much of the confession as is necessary to show that he does so.

(5) Evidence that a fact to which this subsection applies was discovered as a result of a statement made by an accused person shall not be admissible unless evidence of how it was discovered is given by him or on his behalf.

(6) Subsection (5) above applies—

    (a) to any fact discovered as a result of a confession which is wholly excluded in pursuance of this section; and

    (b) to any fact discovered as a result of a confession which is partly so excluded, if the fact is discovered as a result of the excluded part of the confession.

(7) In this section 'oppression' includes torture, inhuman or degrading treatment, and the use or threat of violence (whether or not amounting to torture)."

(2) Subject to subsection (1), nothing in this Chapter makes a confession by a defendant admissible if it would not be admissible under section 76 of the Police and Criminal Evidence Act 1984 (c. 60).

(3) In subsection (2) "confession" has the meaning given by section 82 of that Act.

For the purposes of s. 76A, 'accused person' means a person charged with an offence and before the court. In *Finch* [2007] 1 WLR 1645 it was held that a person who had pleaded guilty to the offence was no longer an accused, and his confession could not be admitted under s. 76A. It was admissible, if at all, under s. 114(1)(d) of the Criminal Justice Act 2003 (see 8.20). The spectre of confessions being admitted under s. 114(1)(d) when they might be admitted under s. 76A in the light of *Y* [2008] 1 WLR 1683 raises serious issues as to the protection to be afforded to the accused. Comment was made on this point in relation to confessions adduced by the prosecution (see 9.5.2) and need not be repeated. See also 8.20.

The difference between s. 76 and s. 76A lies in the standard of proof, which, consistently with the general rule in the case of the defence (see 4.13) is the balance of probability. But the co-accused has the burden of proving admissibility, and, as in the case of s. 76, the court may require proof of its own motion (s. 76(3)). These provisions raise the interesting possibility that, as the confession, once admitted, becomes evidence in the case against its maker, the prosecution may occasionally benefit from the tendering of the confession by a co-accused in circumstances in which they cannot, or have not, succeeded in having the confession admitted themselves. The possibility cannot be altogether discounted that the judge may not be persuaded by the prosecution beyond reasonable doubt that a confession is admissible under s. 76, but may later be persuaded by a co-accused that it is admissible on the balance of probability under s. 76A. In such a case, the protection afforded to the maker of the confession by s. 76 is weakened. Moreover, the discretion to exclude evidence under s. 78 of the Police and Criminal Evidence Act 1984 does not apply to evidence tendered by the defence (see 3.9), and s. 76A provides no additional exclusionary power. At the same time, it is hard to see how the co-accused could realistically prove the admissibility of the confession without some degree of cooperation by the prosecution, as the evidence of police officers is generally indispensable to that proof. Putting all these factors together, it is surely not mere paranoia to imagine that the prosecution may occasionally be tempted to consider an unholy alliance with a co-accused with a view to having the confession admitted more easily by the latter. It is submitted that judges should be vigilant to prevent the possibility of unfairness to the maker of the confession which could arise if s. 76A is abused in such a way for the purpose of easing the prosecution's task under s. 76 and s. 78. The risk that this will happen is mitigated by the fact that the prosecution must present its case first, and if the prosecution wish to make use of the confession, it would raise obvious suspicions if they did not seek to admit it as part of their case. But, on the face of it, this would not prevent the co-accused from seeking to have the confession admitted at a later stage. Certainly, if the prosecution sought to admit it, and were unsuccessful, this would not prevent the co-accused from seeking to admit it later in the trial. It is submitted, nonetheless, that the judge ought to inquire into the circumstances in order to ensure fairness for the accused who made the confession. There may be some cases in which the co-accused has an interest in admitting the confession, while the prosecution does not. But the most obvious example of that was the case before s. 76A was enacted (such as *Myers*) in which the prosecution had abandoned the possibility of admitting the confession only because it seemed to be clearly inadmissible under s. 76. The House of Lords in *Myers* expressly left open the question of whether a confession could be admitted on behalf of a co-accused in circumstances in which the prosecution could not admit it because the conditions imposed by s. 76 were not satisfied.[71] Section 76A has substantially resolved that matter by requiring proof of the same conditions of admissibility in both cases. It would seem, therefore, that only in an unusual case would a co-accused have an interest in seeking the admission of a confession which the prosecution does not wish to have admitted. But there may be such cases, for example where the prosecution takes the view that, while the confession incriminates the maker to some extent, it puts the case against the co-accused in a way the prosecution rejects; or where the prosecution simply takes the view that, although the confession is incriminating, it would, for some reason, be unfair to the maker to admit it.

Section 76(A) provides the test for admissibility, but does not define the purposes for which a confession may be admitted. By virtue of s. 76A(1), the confession must be relevant to a matter in issue in the proceedings. It is submitted that, in the absence of restriction, any relevant matter suffices for this purpose. In *Lawless*,[72] the Court of Appeal suggested that the principle of admissibility in *Myers* applied only in the case in which the confession made by accused A and tendered by co-accused B established that A alone was guilty of the offence charged, and that B must be

---

[71] [1998] AC at 138 per Lord Slynn of Hadley, 146 per Lord Hope of Craighead.
[72] [2003] EWCA Crim 271; cf. *Iqbal* [2003] EWCA Crim 989.

not guilty. It is submitted that this decision is inconsistent with s. 76A, which permits the admission of the confession for any relevant purpose subject to proof of the conditions laid down by the section.

9.14 PRACTICE: USE OF EVIDENCE GIVEN BY ACCUSED ON *VOIR DIRE*

We saw in 3.2 that where the admissibility of a confession is disputed, the trial judge should inquire into the circumstances in which it was obtained by means of proceedings in the absence of the jury, known as a 'trial within a trial' or proceedings on the *voir dire*. The accused is entitled to give evidence on the *voir dire* on the limited issue of the admissibility of the confession.[73] If he does so, the question arises whether the prosecution may make use of any answers given by the accused in evidence at that stage (in the absence of the jury) which may tend to incriminate him as to the offence charged, or shed light on the truth of any facts admitted in the confession. These questions were considered by the Privy Council in *Wong Kam Ming* v *R*.[74] It was held that the prosecution are not entitled to adduce as part of their case before the jury incriminating evidence given by the accused in the trial within a trial, but that if the confession is admitted into evidence and the accused gives evidence again in front of the jury, he may be cross-examined about any inconsistencies between his evidence before the jury and his evidence on the *voir dire*. The Privy Council further held that the accused may not be asked during his evidence in the trial within a trial whether or not his confession is true. The Privy Council's opinion on this last point is consistent with the later enacted s. 76(2) of the Police and Criminal Evidence Act 1984, which makes the question of whether or not the confession is true inadmissible on the issue of whether it should be admitted (on which issue it is also, it is submitted, usually, though not invariably, irrelevant).

While it is, in one sense, strange that the prosecution should be deprived of the opportunity to adduce apparently relevant and cogent evidence of guilt, the decision may be justified by the importance of according the accused the freedom to give evidence fully and frankly on the issue of whether the confession should be admitted. The decision in *Wong Kam Ming* v *R* with respect to the prohibition against using evidence given by the accused on the *voir dire* was confirmed by the House of Lords in *Brophy* [1982] AC 476.

9.15 PRACTICE: USE OF CONFESSIONS

9.15.1 Against the maker

A confession, proved as an exception to the rule against hearsay, is admissible as evidence of the truth of the matters adverse to the accused contained therein, if relevant to any matter in issue: s. 76(1) and (7) of the Police and Criminal Evidence Act 1984. It may, if the jury think it right, be relied upon to convict, even in the absence of other evidence. As Erle J said in *Baldry* (1852) 1 Den 430, a 'confession...well proved...is the best evidence that can be produced'. Because the

---

[73] The failure of the accused to give evidence on the *voir dire* may be taken into account by the judge in deciding whether the accused has been prejudiced by a breach of the Code (*Oni* [1992] Crim LR 183).

[74] [1980] AC 247, effectively overruling the decision of the Court of Criminal Appeal in *Hammond* [1941] 3 All ER 318.

weight of a confession is a question of fact, the Court of Appeal will rarely interfere with a conviction based upon such evidence, even where it is unsupported by other evidence.[75] However, where the terms of the confession are such that no reasonable jury could safely draw the necessary inference of guilt from it, the conviction may be quashed as being unsafe and unsatisfactory; this may occur where the accused's words are wholly ambiguous, as where he merely says in answer to an allegation: 'All right', which may amount to no more than an acknowledgement that it has been made, or as in *Schofield* (1917) 12 Cr App R 191: 'Just my luck', which may indicate no more than an expression of dismay at being wrongly suspected. The confession should, it is submitted, be clear and compelling before a jury are invited to act on it, unsupported, to convict, but if it is so, then it must be left to them on that basis.

A recurring problem has been how to direct the jury in a case where the judge has admitted a confession following an unsuccessful challenge by the defence under s. 76 suggesting oppression or unreliability. The challenge will have been heard on the *voir dire* in the absence of the jury, and the practice is not to inform the jury of the judge's decision because of the danger that the jury may be disposed to give too much weight to the judge's opinion in favour of the reliability of the confession.[76] But the defence is entitled to raise exactly the same issues again in the presence of the jury after the confession has been admitted, because they are relevant to the question of what weight the jury should accord to the confession. In most cases, it was formerly the practice for the judge to direct the jury that they should decide whether or not the confession was true, and that, if they were satisfied that it was true, they were entitled to rely on it notwithstanding any evidence about the way in which it was obtained. Though to some extent logical, this direction created a tension between the legal protections offered to the accused under s. 76(2) and the free use of the confession as a question of fact. In *Mushtaq* [2005] 1 WLR 1513, the majority of the House of Lords held that the direction was incorrect and should no longer be given. The basis for this holding was that the direction permitted the jury to make a decision not only incompatible with s. 76(2), but also incompatible with the accused's right not to incriminate himself, a right which is necessarily infringed if the jury act on a confession obtained by oppression or in circumstances which may have rendered it unreliable. This in turn is inconsistent with the accused's right to a fair trial under art. 6 of the European Convention on Human Rights. It seems to follow from this that the jury must be directed to disregard the confession if they find that it was, or may have been, obtained in a manner which could have led to its exclusion under s. 76, and the majority in *Mushtaq* endorsed this view. The position is far from ideal. It seems that the jury must go over the same ground as the judge with the possibility of inconsistent findings, albeit ultimately for a different purpose.[77] Moreover, it is a difficult exercise for the jury to disregard a confession which they believe to be true. But it is difficult to suggest a logical alternative.

---

[75] But see the observations of Cave J in *Thompson* [1893] 2 QB 12, 18. And, as mentioned earlier, some authorities, particularly in the United States, advocate a requirement for corroboration, at least where the confession is the only evidence against the accused.

[76] *Mitchell v The Queen* [1998] AC 695; *Thompson v R* [1998] AC 811.

[77] The House unanimously upheld the decision of the Court of Appeal that the jury is not a 'public authority' for the purposes of s. 6(3) of the Human Rights Act 1998, and that, accordingly, it is not necessary for them to assess the admissibility of the confession independently of the judge so as to scrutinize the fairness of the trial. Thus, the division of functions as to questions of law and questions of fact between judge and jury is not affected by the Act.

9.15.2 Editing of confessions

Confessions are subject to the rule regarding admissions generally that the whole statement must be put before the court, to be looked at as a whole and in context. This means that where a statement is partly adverse to, and partly favourable to, the accused, he is entitled to have both parts placed before the jury, although this may cause problems of evidential value which are considered in 9.17. But there are occasions when confessions should be placed before the jury in an 'edited' form, in order to prevent the jury from being exposed to prejudicial and inadmissible material. When a confession is made, it is important that it should be recorded in the accused's words, exactly as it is made. Frequently, confessions contain some allusion to the accused's bad character. Clearly, the jury are entitled to hear what the accused said to the police officer, but any probative value in the allusion to his previous convictions is usually more than outweighed by the prejudicial effect which the answer might have in the minds of the jury. The answer should, therefore, be edited to omit the offending passage, provided that this can be done without doing a fatal degree of violence to the sense (in which case the judge may have to exclude altogether). If this is not done, and the inadmissible and prejudicial part is given in evidence, the conviction will almost certainly be quashed.[78] This principle applies equally to tape-recorded interviews, and transcripts thereof, and any admissible written or oral statement made by the accused. Edited copies of the transcript or statement should be produced for the use of the jury or the bench, with no marks of editing. Where a statement, as originally made, contains references to offences with which the accused is not charged, a fresh statement should be made in which all such references are omitted (*Consolidated Criminal Practice Direction*, para. III.24.4) and it is submitted that this practice might be followed in other cases in which there is a clear risk of prejudice.

The court has no power to order the editing out of otherwise admissible evidence contained in an accused's statement, for the purpose of avoiding the risk of injustice to a co-accused, at least without the consent of the prosecution and the accused who made the statement. In *Lobban* v *R*[79] the co-accused, R, made a statement which was partly incriminating and partly exculpatory to himself, but which also implicated L in the offence charged. The prosecution tendered the statement in evidence as a confession by R, relying on the incriminating parts as against R. R wished to rely on the exculpatory parts of his statement. The entire statement was, therefore, admissible. L applied for an order that the statement be edited to omit the parts which tended to incriminate him, and which were not admissible against him. It was held that L was not entitled to have the statement edited in his own interests, given that the other parties were entitled to the benefit of the full evidential value of the statement. In the absence of agreement between all parties, the statement must be placed before the jury in its original form. It is submitted, however, that this principle applies only where the material objected to is admissible at the instance of the other parties. If, for example, R's statement referred to L's previous character, and evidence of L's

---

[78] However, the rule is one of practice, rather than law. If the accused makes an incriminating reply to an allegation put to him, it is probably admissible in strict law, even though it would tend to expose some aspect of his character; and in *Turner* v *Underwood* [1948] 2 KB 284, such a reply which revealed a matter of bad character was held to have been properly admitted as a matter of law. But the Court emphasized that as a matter of almost invariable practice, it should be excluded, at least in jury cases. (*Turner* v *Underwood* was an appeal from a magistrates' court.) In *Knight* (1946) 31 Cr App R 52, a conviction on indictment was quashed because of a failure to edit out details of previous convictions, and it is submitted that this must be correct in almost every case.

[79] [1995] 1 WLR 877; see also *Jefferson* [1994] 1 All ER 270.

character were inadmissible, it seems clear that the material must be edited out, just as in the case of the maker of the statement himself.

9.16 CONFESSIONS IMPLICATING CO-ACCUSED

9.16.1 General rule: confession admissible only against maker

At common law, it is a fundamental principle of the use of admissions and confessions that an admission or confession is evidence against the maker of the confession only, and not against any other person implicated by it. This is a rule applicable to statements made in all circumstances by way of admission, including a plea of guilty in the face of the court. It is sometimes said that the co-accused may make the statement evidence against him if he is present when it is made, and does not dissent from it, or adopts it as his own. However, this is an apparent exception only, in that if, on the whole of the evidence, the jury think that the co-accused has adopted what was said, then it is in reality his own confession and no longer merely that of the maker of the statement. The rule has no exception at common law; a confession is inadmissible hearsay against all but the maker of it. This is, of course, in stark contrast to the position when an accused gives evidence from the witness-box in the course of the trial, when, like any other evidence, what he says is evidence in the case for all purposes, whether or not it implicates the co-accused. In civil cases, the effect of the Civil Evidence Act 1995 is to make admissions evidence in the case generally and, in this respect, civil and criminal cases must be sharply distinguished.

An excellent example of the rule is *Spinks* [1982] 1 All ER 587. The accused was charged with doing an act, namely concealing a knife, with intent to impede the apprehension or prosecution of another, F, who had committed the arrestable offence of wounding. At the accused's trial, there was no evidence that F had committed a wounding except F's own confession to the police, which had not, of course, been made in the accused's presence. The trial judge refused to withdraw the case from the jury. The accused did not give evidence, and was convicted. On appeal, the Court of Appeal re-affirmed that F's confession, though evidence against F, was not evidence against the accused that F had committed a wounding. Russell J said:

> In the judgment of this court the offence with which the appellant was charged and the means of establishing it do not provide any exception to the universal rule which excludes out of court admissions being used to provide evidence against a co-accused, whether indicted jointly or separately....
>
> In his summing up the recorder left the jury with the clear impression that they could, if they wished, rely on [F's] admissions to prove the wounding, not only against him but against the appellant. In so doing there was a plain misdirection and for the reasons we have indicated we have come to the conclusion that this appeal must be allowed and the conviction quashed.

A disturbing and, it is submitted, incorrect inroad was made into the common law principle of admissibility by a majority of the House of Lords in *Hayter*.[80] The prosecution alleged that A murdered C, having been procured to do so by Mrs C, and that B was a middleman, who recruited A to commit the murder. The only evidence against A was a confession which he was alleged to have made to his girlfriend, which incriminated both himself and B. The case against B depended entirely on the guilt of A. At the close of the prosecution case, B made a submission of no case to answer, arguing that the only evidence tendered against him was A's confession,

---

[80] [2005] 1 WLR 605; Lords Steyn, Bingham, and Brown; Lords Rodger and Carswell dissenting. See also *McLean* [2008] 1 Cr App R 11 (8.20).

which was inadmissible against him. The judge rejected the submission and left the case to the jury. The judge directed the jury that the confession was evidence only against A, but that if they came to the conclusion that A was guilty, they could make use of the fact of A's conviction as evidence against B. The latter direction was based on s. 74 of the Police and Criminal Evidence Act 1984, which provides that the conviction of a person other than the accused is admissible to prove, where relevant to do so, that the person convicted committed the offence of which he was convicted, whether or not other evidence of his having committed that offence is given.[81] Both A and B were convicted. B appealed against conviction on the grounds that A's conviction was based entirely on his own confession, and, therefore, it followed that A's confession had (in effect) wrongly been used as evidence against B; and that the judge erred in rejecting B's submission of no case to answer because at that stage, A had not been convicted, and there was no admissible evidence against B. The majority of the House of Lords dismissed the first ground of appeal on the basis that, even though s. 74 of the Police and Criminal Evidence Act 1984 usually applied where a person other than the accused was convicted in earlier proceedings, it was capable of being applied to the conviction of a co-accused in a joint trial, and there was no objection to the jury using their own conviction of A as evidence against B that A had murdered C.[82] Of more immediate concern to our present discussion is the fact that the second ground of appeal was also dismissed. Lord Steyn held that the judge's ruling on B's application for a finding of no case to answer was merely a conditional one. With the agreement of Lords Bingham and Brown, he held that to make such a conditional ruling leaving the case against B to the jury on the basis of A's confession involved only a 'modest adjustment' to the rule against hearsay ([2005] 1 WLR at [25]) and that to decline to do so would be to ignore 'the dynamics of a criminal trial by a judge and jury' (*ibid.* at [28]).[83] Lords Rodger and Carswell dissented in strong terms.

Lord Rodger pointed out that if A and B had been tried separately, A's confession would not have been admissible against B, and no distinction between the parts incriminating to A and those incriminating to B could be made. If the prosecution had decided to try A first, and, if he was convicted, then to rely on his conviction as evidence against B, they would have been entitled to do so, but that had not been done in this case. On the question of the use of A's confession, Lord Rodger said (*ibid.* at [51]):

> . . . in reality, on the Crown's approach, what the jury are being asked to do is to use their conclusions on the evidence against A in the case of B. That is tantamount to using the evidence itself, which is admissible against A, as evidence against B, against whom it is inadmissible.

Lord Rodger added that the course taken by the judge in this case 'simply obliterates the rule [against hearsay] as it applies to statements of co-defendants in a joint trial' (*ibid.* at [51]).

---

[81] Section 74(2) further provides that the person convicted shall be taken as having committed the offence of which he was convicted unless the contrary is proved. Section 74 is dealt with further at 12.7 *et seq.*

[82] This holding is understandable, though it is by no means free of difficulty. It seems unrealistic to expect a jury to treat the cases of A and B completely separately in such circumstances, and the risk of unfairness to B is heightened, by comparison with other uses of s. 74. Moreover, there is no opportunity for either A or B to seek to show that A did not commit the offence, which is expressly envisaged by s. 74(2). This would seem to raise issues of fairness under art. 6 of the European Convention on Human Rights. It is also submitted that, technically, A has not been convicted of an offence until the jury return a verdict to that effect, and it must be improper for them to deliberate on B's case using the 'conviction' of A as evidence against B until that has been done. Another way of looking at it is that no evidence of A's conviction was admitted and presented to the jury before they retired to consider their verdict.

[83] Lord Steyn appealed to some academic sources, including Cross and Tapper, *Evidence*, 10th edn at p. 79 to support his proposition.

Lord Carswell cited with approval the statement at 8.15.3 of the 8th edition of this work (9.16.1 in this edition) that there are no exceptions at common law to the rule that a confession is admissible only against the maker, and not against any other person implicated by it (*ibid.* at [71]). He concluded on this point:

> I agree with the view expressed by Lord Rodger of Earlsferry [47] that this would turn inadmissible into admissible evidence. Such alchemy should not form part of the criminal law. Nor is it desirable that juries should be given directions which require them to draw such difficult distinctions and which are bound to cause confusion in their minds and misunderstanding. [*Ibid.* at [73].]

It is submitted that, whatever the merits of the use of s. 74 of the Police and Criminal Evidence Act 1984 (a subject dealt with further in Chapter 12) the decision of the majority of the House of Lords in this case on the hearsay question was wrong and contrary to principle, and ought to be reconsidered. The common law rule that confessions are admissible only against the maker is not only a rule of evidence, but affects the right of the accused to confront the witnesses against him (see 7.5) and its breach may well raise issues of fairness under art. 6 of the European Convention on Human Rights. With all respect to Lord Steyn, the use made of A's confession was not simply a 'modest adjustment' to the rule against hearsay. It effectively reverses the common law rule, and amounts to a new common law exception to the rule against hearsay. Lord Rodger (at [57]) made the interesting and important point that, since *Myers* v *DPP* [1965] AC 1001, it has generally been accepted that modifications to the rule against hearsay should be made by Parliament rather than the courts, even the House of Lords: see 7.3. Indeed, it is difficult to see how the decision of the majority of the House of Lords in *Hayter* can be reconciled with the provisions of ss. 114(1) and 118(2) of the Criminal Justice Act 2003, by virtue of which all common law exceptions to the rule against hearsay not preserved by s. 118(1) are abolished, and hearsay evidence in criminal cases is admissible exclusively in the cases enumerated by s. 114(1).

Hayter was distinguished by the Privy Council in *Persad* v *State of Trinidad and Tobago* [2008] 1 Cr App R 9, a case in which, although the accused were jointly charged with robbery and with several sexual offences said to have been committed against the same victim during the robbery, no issue of joint enterprise between the accused was left to the jury with respect to the sexual offences, which the prosecution accepted were individual offences. Because it was clear that only one of the accused could have committed each offence, the Privy Council held that it would not be proper to admit a statement made by one accused against the other in the way permitted in *Hayter* in an attempt to bolster its case against the other on one of the sexual offences. Welcome though this distinction is, it fails to mitigate the decision of the majority of the House of Lords in *Hayter*, which when considered with other recent cases in which hearsay statements made by co-accused and third parties (see 9.5.2. and 8.20) constitutes a radical and serious assault on the traditional protections afforded to the accused against hearsay generally and confessions in particular.

9.16.2 Confession admissible only against maker: practice; direction to jury

The traditional rule is not always easy to administer in practice. Confessions by one accused implicating another are one of the hazards of joint trial, which must be accepted. The mere fact that the situation arises is no ground, in itself, for separate trials. Where accused are jointly charged they should ordinarily be tried together. In *Lake*[84] the accused and two others were charged with

---

[84] (1976) 64 Cr App R 172; and see the observations of the Court of Appeal in *Josephs* (1977) 65 Cr App R 253. Cf. *Christou* [1997] AC 117.

conspiracy to burgle. Both co-accused made statements to the police which implicated Lake very seriously in the offence. Despite the risk of prejudice arising from the volume of inadmissible material against Lake, the Court of Appeal declined to interfere with the decision of the trial judge to refuse an application for separate trial. But the Court of Appeal recognized that there would be exceptional cases, where the probative value of a confession is very considerable against the maker, while the prejudicial effect is equally considerable against the co-accused, where such an order may be necessary. Sometimes, the problem can be solved, or at least minimized, by editing. But, for the reasons given in 9.15.2, this course is not always appropriate.

What is vital, in any case where A's statement implicates B, is that the judge should direct the jury that the statement is evidence against A only and not against B. How far juries succeed in this exercise in mental gymnastics is a legitimate question, but they are frequently assisted by the observation that it is clearly unfair to hold against B a statement made in his absence by A, who may have his own reasons for implicating B, and to which B had no chance of replying. Be that as it may, the absence of a clear direction on the point will be fatal to B's conviction.[85] The statement cannot be evidence against B for any purpose. In *Dibble* (1908) 1 Cr App R 155, this applied even where A offered to give evidence for the prosecution against B, was treated as hostile and cross-examined on his statement. A's statement implicated B, but was evidence going only to A's credit, and the failure of the trial judge to direct the jury not to regard it as evidence against B was fatal to B's conviction.

Of course, if a co-accused elects to make use of the accused's confession in support of his own case, as permitted by the decision of the House of Lords in *Myers* [1998] AC 124 (see 9.13) then he must accept that the contents of the confession become evidence at his instance. Accordingly, he must accept that the jury may consider any parts of the confession which are adverse to his own case, as well as those which assist him. Only by remaining silent about the confession can the co-accused ensure that it does not become evidence against him.

9.17 PARTLY ADVERSE ('MIXED') STATEMENTS

It happens frequently that an accused will make a written or oral statement which, while partly adverse to his case, also contains exculpatory or self-serving passages. Such statements are known as 'mixed' statements.[86] We have already seen that the whole of the statement must in general go to the jury, and that the weight of the statement as a confession is a matter of fact for the jury. The latter proposition involves the further conclusion that it is for the jury to say whether the statement tendered amounts to a confession at all. Unless it does, the jury will not act on it as evidence against the accused. But the undoubtedly proper admission of entire statements also involves a problem of evidential value in criminal cases, in that self-serving statements are not evidence of the truth of the facts contained in them, whereas confessions are so.[87]

In *Storey* (1968) 52 Cr App R 334, the accused was charged with possession of cannabis. The prosecution succeeded in establishing a *prima facie* case against her, and she did not give evidence. The accused then sought to rely for her defence on a statement she had made to the police

---

[85] *Gunewardene* [1951] 2 KB 600; cf. *Lobban v R* [1995] 1 WLR 877.

[86] A statement is mixed if, instead of being wholly exculpatory, it contains an admission of fact significant to any issue in the case and capable of adding weight to the prosecution case: *Papworth and Doyle* [2008] 1 Cr App R 36.

[87] In civil cases, the Civil Evidence Act 1995 renders self-serving statements admissible as evidence of the truth of the facts stated in them, so that, except in relation to weight, the problem is avoided.

which was exculpatory in content. The trial judge, however, summed up to the jury on the basis that the statement was inadmissible to prove the truth of any facts stated therein. On appeal against conviction, the Court of Appeal held that the summing up was proper. Had the accused given evidence on oath to the same effect, the jury could have considered her evidence, but not her prior statement, as evidence of the truth of the facts stated.

No assistance can be derived from the fact that s. 82(1) of the Police and Criminal Evidence Act 1984 defines a 'confession' as 'any statement *wholly or partly adverse to the person who made it'*. Although s. 76(1) renders a confession, thus defined, admissible, it also specifies that it shall be admissible 'against' the accused who made it. No legislative intent to render exculpatory passages admissible in favour of the accused, for the purpose of proving the truth of facts stated therein, can therefore be inferred.[88]

However, the rule stated in *Storey* was known to cause formidable problems in cases where the prosecution tender a mixed statement as a confession, and rely on it as evidence against the accused. In such a case, as we have seen (9.15.2), the entire statement should generally be placed before the jury. The jury must consider the exculpatory parts of the statement in order to form a view as to whether the statement, taken as a whole, amounts to a confession, and, if so, what weight should be accorded to it. Applying the principle in *Storey*, this leads to the logical, but unduly confusing result that the exculpatory parts of the statement are admissible to refute the prosecution's contention that the statement is a confession, but inadmissible as evidence of the facts stated in those parts. The different evidential effects of adverse and exculpatory passages within the same statement produced substantial problems for juries, and it is doubtful whether juries were completely faithful to the directions they received from judges. In *Donaldson* (1976) 64 Cr App R 59 at 65, James LJ said:

> In our view there is a clear distinction to be made between statements of admission adduced by the Crown as part of the case against the defendant and statements entirely of a self-serving nature made and sought to be relied upon by a defendant. When the Crown adduce a statement relied upon as an admission it is for the jury to consider the whole statement including any passages that contain qualifications or explanations favourable to the defendant, that bear upon the passages relied upon by the prosecution as an admission, and it is for the jury to decide whether the statement viewed as a whole constitutes an admission. To this extent, the statement may be said to be evidence of the facts stated therein...
>
> When the Crown adduce evidence in the form of a statement by the defendant which is not relied on as an admission of the offence charged, such a statement is evidence in the trial, in that it is evidence that the defendant made the statement and of his reaction, which is part of the general picture which the jury have to consider, but it is not evidence of the facts stated.

This 'clear distinction' was no doubt clear enough to the Court of Appeal, but it was just as clear that some other approach must be devised if juries were to be enabled to look properly at the whole of a statement made by an accused and offered in evidence as a confession. It is true that the exculpatory passages may also have relevance for purposes other than to prove the truth of facts stated, for example to show the accused's reaction when taxed with the offence, as 'part of the general picture'. Moreover, the accused is entitled to have the jury read passages which negate or present in a different light passages which might otherwise appear incriminating.[89] But

---

[88] On the contrary, it is plain that Parliament did not intend to render exculpatory material admissible, since a clause having exactly that effect (clause 73(4)) appeared in the bill brought from the House of Commons on 17 May 1984, but was subsequently deleted and does not appear in the Act. See also J.C. Smith [1995] Crim LR 280.

[89] *McGregor* [1968] 1 QB 371; *Pearce* (1979) 69 Cr App R 365.

in many cases, the subtlety of the distinction must have been lost on juries, who most probably viewed the statement as a whole and assessed its value accordingly.

In *Duncan* (1981) 73 Cr App R 359, a differently constituted Court of Appeal proposed a fresh approach, after a review of the authorities. The accused was charged with murder, and made a statement, part of which appeared to be a confession of guilt as charged and part of which appeared to suggest the defence of provocation. Lord Lane CJ said:

> The issue between the parties here is the extent to which confessions are properly to be regarded as evidence of the truth of the facts which they state. Both parties are agreed that if a statement is adduced as an admission against interest, the whole of the statement must be admitted. Any other course would obviously be unfair.
>
> It is contended on behalf of the Crown that this rule does not, however, make the contents of the statement evidence of the facts contained therein except in so far as those statements are admissions against interest. [Counsel for the appellant] on the other hand...contends that the whole statement is evidence of the truth of the facts contained therein. He, however, concedes that the judge is entitled to explain to the jury, if indeed it needs explanation, that the weight to be given to those parts of the statement which contain admissions against interest may be very different from the weight to be given to the parts which are self-exculpatory.
>
> One is bound to observe that if the contentions of the Crown are correct, the judge would be faced with a very difficult task in trying to explain to the jury the difference between those parts of a 'mixed' statement (if we may call it such) which were truly confessions and those parts which were self-exculpatory. It is doubtful if the result would be readily intelligible.... Judges should not be obliged to give meaningless or unintelligible directions to juries.

The learned Lord Chief Justice then reviewed the authorities, and concluded:

> Where a 'mixed' statement is under consideration by the jury in a case where the accused has not given evidence, it seems to us that the simplest, and therefore the method most likely to produce a just result, is for the jury to be told that the whole statement, both the incriminating parts and the excuses or explanations, must be considered by them in deciding where the truth lies. It is, to say the least, not helpful to try to explain to the jury that the exculpatory parts of a statement are something less than evidence of the facts they state. Equally, where appropriate, as it usually will be, the judge may, and should, point out that the incriminating parts are likely to be true (otherwise why say them?), whereas the excuses do not have the same weight.

It is submitted that this approach is to be preferred to that called for by earlier cases. As the whole statement is admitted in evidence because it is relied on by the prosecution as a confession, the jury must decide whether, taken as a whole, it is a confession. The theoretical objection that the exculpatory parts are not evidence of the truth of the facts stated therein may be overcome by the fact that the jury have to take the statement as a whole, and give such weight to it as they think fit. It has always been recognized that the exculpatory passages may be relied on by the defence for the purpose of rebutting the contention that the statement is a confession, and no real extension of this principle is called for by the approach taken in *Duncan*. No real repudiation of the rule against self-serving statements is involved, since the statement is adduced by the prosecution, and the jury is being directed to do no more than to subject prosecution evidence to proper scrutiny.[90] The situation is obviously very different from that in *Storey*, in which the defence sought to rely on a self-serving statement to establish a defence. The principles laid down in *Duncan* were approved by the House of Lords in *Sharp* [1988] 1 WLR 7. The House confirmed

---

[90] See the observations of the House of Lords in *Aziz* [1996] AC 41, 50; *Western v DPP* [1997] 1 Cr App R 474.

that the entire statement is evidence in the case, though it is appropriate for the judge to direct the jury that the exculpatory portions may carry less weight than the inculpatory portions.[91]

There is some question as to whether a mixed statement which is not relied on by the prosecution at all can be regarded as having any evidential value to the defence. In *Aziz* [1996] AC 41, 50, the House of Lords appears to have considered that it cannot. Strictly, in such circumstances, the statement can have no value as a confession because it has not been adduced as such, and the self-serving, exculpatory parts of the statement ought to be inadmissible. But it is submitted that the better view is that a statement which is truly mixed should be regarded as being evidence in the case generally, whether or not the prosecution rely on it. In such a case, the accused has the option of remaining silent about it. But to the extent that he seeks to rely on the statement, the accused must accept that it is at least partly incriminating. It seems unsatisfactory that the prosecution should be able to control the accused's right to adduce the statement in such circumstances. The suggested approach would be consistent with the decisions of the Court of Appeal in *Garrod* [1997] Crim LR 445 and the Divisional Court in *Western v DPP* [1997] 1 Cr App R 474, but these decisions may be irreconcilable with *Aziz*, and probably do not represent the present state of the law. It should be noted that the court is entitled to exclude a statement made by the accused which is deliberately self-serving, especially one made after consultation with a solicitor, which may be designed to 'infiltrate' the prosecution case. Although as a general rule the jury should be told what the accused says in answer to the charge (unless it consists of an inadmissible confession), the prosecution do not have to permit the accused to make use of a set piece. However, each case must be considered on its own facts, and a statement cannot be excluded merely because the accused had spoken with a solicitor before making it.[92]

9.18 RECOMMENDED FURTHER READING

Cape, E., 'The rise (and fall?) of a criminal defence profession' [2004] *Criminal Law Review* 401.

Choo, A.L.-T. and Nash, S., 'What's the matter with section 78?' [1999] *Criminal Law Review* 929.

Dennis, I., 'Miscarriages of justice and the law of confessions: evidentiary issues and solutions' [1993] *Public Law* 291. Royal Commission on Criminal Procedure (Phillips Commission) Report (Cmnd 8092, 1981).

Hartshorne, J., 'Defensive use of a co-accused's confession and the Criminal Justice Act 2003' (2004) 8(3) *International Journal of Evidence and Proof* 165.

Hirst, M., 'Confessions as proof of innocence' (1998) **57**(1) *Cambridge Law Journal* 146.

9.19 QUESTIONS FOR DISCUSSION BASED ON *R v COKE; LITTLETON*
(for case files go to the Online Resource Centre)

9.19.1 *Coke; Littleton*

1. What arguments should be made for and against the admissibility of:

    (a) Coke's alleged reply to D/I Glanvil on being arrested at his flat; and

    (b) his answers during interview at the police station?

---

[91] It now seems to be established that exculpatory passages in a statement made by an accused may suffice to raise an issue such as self-defence, so as to require the prosecution to rebut it beyond reasonable doubt: *Hamand* (1985) 82 Cr App R 65; and see 4.8.3.

[92] *Newsome* (1980) 71 Cr App R 325; *McCarthy* (1980) 71 Cr App R 142; *Pearce* (1979) 69 Cr App R 365.

2. What factors will affect the weight of this evidence, if admitted?

3. What steps should be taken at trial to decide the admissibility of this evidence?

4. How should the judge direct the jury as to how to regard Coke's answers during interview in considering the guilt or innocence of Littleton?

9.19.2 *Blackstone* v *Coke*

1. May Coke adduce as an admission:

   (a) Margaret's refusal to undergo a blood test? Does it matter that this refusal was communicated by her solicitors?

   (b) The contents of Margaret's letter to Henneky?

2. May Coke adduce as an admission Henneky's statement that he had sexual intercourse with Margaret at a time consistent with the conception of her child?

9.20 GENERAL QUESTIONS FOR DISCUSSION

1. Define 'an informal admission'?

2. Where a solicitor makes an informal admission in a letter to an opponent, in the course of civil proceedings, will it be admissible in evidence?

3. Is there any difference between an admission and a confession?

4. How and where is 'confession' defined in statute?

5. Which statutory provision governs the admissibility of a confession?

6. A suspect was refused access to legal advice at the police station unlawfully. However, he was experienced in police interviews and stated that he 'knew his rights'. Would you expect his confession to be excluded?

7. Where a confession is excluded at trial, will evidence discovered as a result of the confession also be rendered inadmissible?

8. If a confession is obtained in breach of the Police and Criminal Evidence Act 1984 Codes of Practice must it be excluded from evidence?

9. Will a confession that also implicates a co-accused be admissible against the co-accused?

10. What are 'mixed' statements and how will a jury be directed to deal with them?

10

THE RULE AGAINST HEARSAY IV:
THE ACCUSED'S DENIALS AND SILENCE

SUMMARY OF MAIN POINTS

- Where a party is confronted with an offence and denies it, the denial is generally of no probative value as evidence against him; but is often admitted as part of the general picture or to show his reaction when confronted with the offence. If the accused denies the offence on a false basis, that fact may provide relevant evidence against him.

- At common law in civil cases, a party's silence when confronted with an allegation may be taken as an admission by him that the allegation is or may be true.

- At common law in criminal cases, the accused is entitled to remain silent when questioned about an offence, without any adverse inference being drawn against him. This principle is subject to an apparent exception where the questioner and the accused were on 'even terms' when the questioning took place.

- By virtue of ss. 34 to 38 of the Criminal Justice and Public Order Act 1994 (as amended) an adverse inference may be drawn against the accused in certain circumstances if he either:

    - fails to mention when questioned or charged a fact on which he later relies for his defence; or

    - fails to account for certain objects, substances, or marks on his person or clothing or in his possession; or

    - fails to account for his presence at the scene of and at about the time of an offence

- The accused may not be convicted wholly or substantially by reason of such an adverse inference, and the jury must be directed carefully as to the matters to consider before drawing any inference.

- Sections 34 to 38 do not affect the right to silence, but merely provide that an inference may be drawn against the accused in certain circumstances if he exercises the right.

10.1 INTRODUCTION

The rules applicable to confessions are not necessarily applicable to all statements made by a suspect when confronted with his suspected involvement in an offence, because not all such statements are even partly inculpatory. Two situations are of particular importance: those in which the accused denies the allegations put to him, and those in which he remains silent in the face of the allegations. Both present difficulties, but the latter raised many problems at common law, and must now be considered in the light of ss. 34 to 38 of the Criminal Justice and Public Order Act 1994.

The accused's silence is difficult, less from the point of view of the law of evidence than from that of the policy underlying the conduct of criminal prosecutions.[1] In civil cases, failure to respond to an allegation, in circumstances in which an innocent party might reasonably have been expected to refute it, has long been accepted as a form of admission, from which the court is entitled to draw an adverse inference against the party accused.[2] But in civil cases, the parties are regarded as being on equal terms, and the law extends no special protection to them. In criminal cases, however, the policy has traditionally been to afford the accused a considerable measure of protection, one of the cornerstones of which has been the so-called right of silence or privilege against self-incrimination.

The right of silence has two aspects: the right not to be compelled to give evidence, and the right not to make incriminating statements when confronted with an alleged offence.[3] The former will be dealt with in Chapter 15, when considering the position of the accused as a witness. The latter is the subject of much of this chapter.

This right or privilege is not derived from the law of evidence, but from constitutional considerations based on a repugnance to methods of compelling confessions and other incriminating evidence which were commonplace in earlier times. In the United States, the right is enshrined in the Constitution by the Fifth Amendment, which provides, so far as here pertinent:

> ...nor shall [any person] be compelled in any criminal case to be a witness against himself, nor be deprived of life, liberty or property, without due process of law.[4]

---

[1] For an interesting analysis of the extent of the right of silence in Australia see Williams (1994) 110 LQR 629.

[2] See, e.g., *Wiedemann v Walpole* [1891] 2 QB 534, per Lord Esher MR at 537–8; *Bessela v Stern* (1877) 2 CPD 265.

[3] In *Director of Serious Fraud Office, ex parte Smith* [1993] AC 1, Lord Mustill identified six apparently discrete rights, but, broadly speaking, it is submitted they can be reduced to the two stated in the text.

[4] This provision has been interpreted by the United States Supreme Court as being restricted to prohibiting compelled confessions and testimony by the accused. It does not prevent the prosecution from obtaining by compulsion incriminating evidence from the accused, or from thereafter adducing such evidence, for example, specimens of blood (*Schmerber v California* 384 US 757 (1966)).

In England, the right to silence can depend only on statute and the common law. The right not to be compelled to give evidence was of no significance until the passing of the Criminal Evidence Act 1898, because, before that time, the accused was not competent to give evidence in his defence. When the 1898 Act empowered the accused to give evidence, it was expressly provided by s. 1(a) that the accused should give evidence only 'on his own application', i.e., that he was not to be compellable. This is still the law, although the efficacy of this protection has been significantly reduced by s. 35 of the Criminal Justice and Public Order Act 1994, which permits the drawing of an adverse inference from the accused's failure to give evidence or answer a particular question. The Act also repeals the protection of s. 1(b) of the 1898 Act against adverse comment on such a failure by the prosecution. This is dealt with at 15.5.

The right not to be compelled to make an incriminating statement has never been specifically recognized by statute, although s. 76 of the Police and Criminal Evidence Act 1984 now renders confessions obtained in circumstances of compulsion inadmissible (see 9.7). It is, however, well-recognized at common law, and was enshrined in the Judges' Rules and the Codes of Practice through the practice of cautioning a suspect before he is interrogated or charged. At common law, no adverse inference can be drawn against the accused by reason of his failure to answer questions, although this principle must be stated with some reservation. Where the accused can be said to be 'on even terms' with the interrogator, or where the accused's purported silence is more in the nature of an admission by conduct (for example, where, in response to an allegation, he attacks his accuser or runs away) some cases have held that it is proper to draw an adverse inference. Conversely, if the accused remains silent in an interview under caution, no such inference can be drawn. This is dealt with more fully in 10.3.

Sections 34, 36, and 37 of the Criminal Justice and Public Order Act 1994 have significantly weakened this aspect of the right to silence by providing that adverse inferences may be drawn against the accused in certain circumstances from his failure to mention certain facts, to account for his possession of certain objects, substances or marks, or to account for his presence at certain places.[5] A revised version of the caution has been promulgated to reflect these changes. These provisions are dealt with at 10.5 *et seq*. The effect of the new law is that the accused's silence may now, in many cases, be used as evidence against him as if it were a confession.[6] It is hard not to regard this as a retrograde step. Apologists for ss. 34 to 38 have pointed out, not without justification, that they are restricted in their scope, and that many cases will still fall to be decided under the common law principles. The extent to which this is true may be doubted. But it is true at least to the extent that it remains necessary to consider the common law rules first, before proceeding to examine the new statutory provisions.

10.2 THE ACCUSED'S DENIALS

The main difficulty in relation to denials is that, assuming that the accused's reaction to the charge is not in any way inculpatory, the statements made by the accused have no evidential

---

[5] There were already some procedural provisions which obliged the accused to divulge aspects of his defence before trial, for example, notice of alibi (Criminal Justice Act 1967, s. 11) and notice of intended expert evidence (Police and Criminal Evidence Act 1984, s. 81) (see 11.6). As to fraud cases, see Criminal Justice Act 1987, s. 2. These disclosure requirements have since been greatly widened by the Criminal Procedure and Investigations Act 1996, which contains substantial requirements for the pre-trial disclosure of details of the defence.

[6] As to the possible application of the rules relating to confessions, and the application of judicial discretion, in such circumstances, see 10.5.4 and 10.5.5.

value in proving his guilt, and the allegations denied by the accused are thinly disguised hearsay. Therefore, if a police officer gives evidence of an interview with the accused, in which the officer recited allegations, and the accused consistently denied those allegations, the prosecution's case is not advanced, but the jury is exposed to inadmissible (hearsay) evidence of mere allegations. The practice of adducing evidence of such an interview is often said to be justified as showing the accused's reaction when charged with the offence, but, given that the accused has not made any kind of confession, it is difficult to see why this should be relevant to the prosecution's case. In some cases, where the accused's denials are consistent with his defence at trial, the evidence may tend to assist the defence, but in other cases, the repetition of detailed allegations (which has no evidential value) may be prejudicial to the accused. This may be contrasted with the position where the accused expressly or implicitly accepts allegations made to him, in which case he makes a confession, which is of legitimate evidential value to the prosecution.

This is not to say that denials can never have any evidential value. For example, where the accused makes denials on a false basis, thereby lying to the officer, the exposure of this fact is obviously relevant, and is also admissible. But in such a case, the reality is that the accused is giving a false explanation, which is rather different from a denial, and is certainly suggestive of guilt unless explained away.

There is clear authority that, as a matter of practice, statements made in the accused's presence should be excluded if, in the opinion of the judge, there is no material on which the jury could properly find that the accused accepted the truth of what was being put to him, and accordingly adopted the allegations by way of confession. If the jury may properly draw that conclusion, then it must be left to them as a question of fact. In *Norton* [1910] 2 KB 496, the Court of Criminal Appeal quashed a conviction in a case where the accused was charged with unlawful sexual intercourse with a young girl who was not called as a witness, and the prosecution were permitted to adduce hearsay allegations made to the accused by the girl. Despite her repeated charges, the accused had consistently denied any wrongdoing. Delivering the judgment of the Court, Pickford J held that the statements made by the girl could not be evidence of the facts stated (they were hearsay). He continued:

> If the answer given amount to an admission of the statements or some part of them, they or that part become relevant as showing what facts are admitted; if the answer be not such an admission, the statements are irrelevant to the matter under consideration and should be disregarded. This seems to us to be correctly and shortly stated in *Taylor on Evidence*, s. 814, p. 574: 'The statements only become evidence when by such acceptance he makes them his own statements'.
>
> No objection was taken in this case to the admission of the statements in evidence, but as the prisoner may be tried again on an indictment on which that question may arise, we think it well to state in what cases such statements can be given in evidence. We think that the contents of such statements should not be given in evidence unless the judge is satisfied that there is evidence fit to be submitted to the jury that the prisoner by his answer to them, whether given by word or conduct, acknowledged the truth of the whole or part of them. If there be no such evidence, then the contents of the statement should be excluded; if there be such evidence, then they should be admitted, and the question whether the prisoner's answer, by words or conduct, did or did not in fact amount to an acknowledgement of them left to the jury.

The soundness of this approach was accepted by the House of Lords in *Christie* [1914] AC 545. The accused was charged with indecent assault on a small boy. The boy was called to give evidence unsworn, but although he described the assault, he did not speak to the fact that shortly afterwards, he had identified the accused to his mother and a police officer. The mother and the officer were called to give evidence of the identification, and the evidence was that when confronted in this way, the accused said, 'I am innocent'—an account which he maintained from first to last. One of the matters canvassed on appeal was that the boy's statement should have been excluded in view of the reaction of the accused to it. The House quashed the conviction because of a misdirection on corroboration, but the argument mentioned drew some sympathy. Lord Reading said (*ibid.* at 565):

> In general, such evidence can have little or no value in its direct bearing on the case unless the accused, upon hearing the statement, by conduct and demeanour, or by the answer made by him, or in certain circumstances by the refraining from an answer, acknowledged the truth of the statement either in whole or in part, or did or said something from which the jury could infer such an acknowledgement, for if he acknowledged its truth, he accepted it as his own statement of the facts.

Lord Moulton referred to the rule of exclusion, in the absence of some evidence of acceptance by the accused, as 'a practice of a very salutary nature', and indicated that the hearsay statement could have no evidential value unless somehow adopted.[7]

As a matter of practice, it will be apparent that in many cases there will be no risk of prejudice simply because there is other, direct evidence of the nature of the prosecution's allegations, and for the jury to hear it repeated with a denial can do no real harm; indeed, the evidence of consistency with the defence offered at trial may actually assist the accused. But where there is no such direct evidence, the risk is very great. Even where this risk is not present, if the allegations are numerous or very grave, there is some danger that the jury may unconsciously adopt them as fact. In all such cases, and where there is any possibility of prejudice, it is submitted that such hearsay evidence is better excluded.[8]

10.3 THE ACCUSED'S SILENCE AT COMMON LAW

At common law, a person is entitled not to answer questions put to him about his possible involvement in a criminal offence, and his refusal or failure to answer such questions may not be made the subject of any adverse inference by the prosecution.[9] Despite distinctions attempted in some cases between pre- and post-caution questioning, this right derives from the law; the caution does not create the right to remain silent, but merely serves to remind the suspect of that right. This general rule appears to be subject to an exception where the interrogator and the suspect are speaking 'on even terms'. The extent of this exception has never been clearly defined. Moreover, an adverse inference may be drawn where the accused exhibits a guilty reaction such as violence or flight in response to an allegation; even though he may, in a sense, remain silent, his actions constitute a confession just as surely as any words.

In *Hall v R* [1971] 1 WLR 298, the accused was charged with possession of a controlled drug. The evidence against him was that, the drug having been found on premises which he occupied jointly with others, but not in his room, he was told by an officer that another accused had said that the drug belonged to him, and that the accused made no reply to this allegation.

---

[7] *Ibid.* at 559–60. See also per Lord Atkinson at 553–4.

[8] For an instance of extreme prejudice, see *Taylor* [1978] Crim LR 92.

[9] There is at least one *dictum* which suggests the contrary, namely that of Pickford J in *Norton* [1910] 2 KB 496 at 499: 'Such answer may, of course, be given either by words or by conduct, e.g., by remaining silent on an occasion which demanded an answer'. However, it is unsupported by authority, and is *obiter*.

The Privy Council held that the accused's conviction could not be sustained. Lord Diplock said (*ibid.* at 301):

> It is a clear and widely known principle of the common law...that a person is entitled to refrain from answering a question put to him for the purpose of discovering whether he has committed a criminal offence. *A fortiori* he is under no obligation to comment when he is informed that someone else has accused him of an offence. It may be that in very exceptional circumstances an inference may be drawn from a failure to give an explanation or a disclaimer, but in their Lordships' view silence alone on being informed by a police officer that someone else has made an accusation against him cannot give rise to an inference that the person to whom this information is communicated accepts the truth of the accusation....
>
> The caution merely serves to remind the accused of a right which he already possesses at common law. The fact that in a particular case he has not been reminded of it is no ground for inferring that his silence was not in exercise of that right, but was an acknowledgement of the truth of the accusation.

10.3.1 The 'even terms' principle: development; meaning of 'even terms'

Lord Diplock's reference to 'very exceptional circumstances', in which silence might be held to constitute some form of admission, may have been based on what Cave J had said in *Mitchell* (1892) 17 Cox CC 503 at 508, although *Mitchell* may not have been cited in argument in *Hall*. It is important to put the *dictum* of Cave J into context. The accused in *Mitchell* was charged with procuring a miscarriage by unlawful means, and so causing the death of the woman concerned. A statement made by the deceased woman was held not to be admissible as a dying declaration. The taking of her deposition by a magistrate had to be stopped when the deceased became too ill to continue, and before the accused's solicitor had had any opportunity to cross-examine her; it was accordingly inadmissible in evidence, as it might have been by statute if completed. It was sought to admit what there was of the deposition as a statement made in the presence of the accused. Cave J rejected the attempt, holding that the accused, who was legally represented, could not reasonably have been expected to make any reply in the circumstances. Against that background, the learned judge said:

> Now the whole admissibility of statement of this kind rests upon the consideration that if a charge is made against a person in that person's presence, it is reasonable to expect that he or she will immediately deny it, and that the absence of such a denial is some evidence of an admission on the part of the person charged, and of the truth of the charge. Undoubtedly, when persons are speaking on even terms and a charge is made, and the person charged says nothing, and expresses no indignation, and does nothing to repel the charge, that is some evidence to show that he admits the charge to be true.

The important emphases in this *dictum* are firstly, the circumstance that the accused and his accuser should have been 'on even terms', and secondly, that it must have been reasonable to expect some reaction, in the way of indignation or refutation of the charge. In such a context, the principle seems unobjectionable, especially where the accused is confronted not by a police officer but by the victim or some other person.[10] But it fits uneasily in more modern times into the context of a formal interview between accused and police officer, where more mature consideration

---

[10] See, e.g., *Bessela v Stern* (1877) 2 CPD 265.

has supervened upon the heat of the moment. It is tempting to add that the *dictum* seems to fit especially uneasily where the accused has been cautioned, but remembering the words of Lord Diplock in *Hall*, that the caution is a reminder, not a creator, of the right of silence, perhaps this should not, of itself, matter.[11]

Nonetheless, in *Chandler* [1976] 1 WLR 585, the Court of Appeal applied the *dictum* to just such a case. The 'even terms' were said to result from the fact that the accused was in the company of his solicitor when interviewed. But even on the basis that this may produce even terms within the meaning of the *dictum*, it is difficult to see why the accused might reasonably have been expected to seek to rebut the charge. Indeed, the facts of *Mitchell*, and the decision of Cave J on those facts, are so obviously different from those of *Chandler* as to suggest exactly the opposite. Lawton LJ said:

> Some comment on the defendant's lack of frankness before he was cautioned was justified provided the jury's attention was directed to the right issue, which was whether in the circumstances the defendant's silence amounted to an acceptance by him of what the detective sergeant had said. If he accepted what had been said, then the next question should have been whether guilt could reasonably be inferred from what he had accepted. To suggest, as the judge did, that the defendant's silence could indicate guilt was to short-circuit the intellectual process which has to be followed.

With respect, the intellectual process advocated by Lawton LJ seems to be just as suspect as that advocated by the trial judge. It was apparently pointed out in argument to the Court of Appeal that no distinction could properly be drawn between pre- and post-caution interrogation, if the right of silence was to prevail, and the words of Lord Diplock in *Hall* were drawn to the Court's attention. But these were stigmatized by Lawton LJ as seeming 'to conflict with *Christie* and with earlier cases and authorities'. A passage from the speech of Lord Atkinson in *Christie* [1914] AC 545, 554, was cited to lend weight to this proposition. But the House of Lords in *Christie* was not concerned with such a situation, because the accused in that case did rebut the charge, and the passage cited bears no obvious relation to the facts which the Privy Council had to consider in *Hall*. If *Chandler* was rightly decided, it would seem to follow that, even at common law, a solicitor who is present when his client is interviewed can no longer safely advise his client to exercise his right of silence. This is, of course, even more clearly the case under the Criminal Justice and Public Order Act 1994: see *Condron* [1997] 1 WLR 827; 10.5.

Some support for *Chandler* is sometimes claimed in the decision of the Privy Council in *Parkes* v *R* [1976] 1 WLR 1251, in which the advice was delivered by Lord Diplock. *Parkes* was decided after *Chandler*, but the latter case appears not to have been cited. The accused was charged with the murder of a girl. The girl's mother found her bleeding very shortly after the infliction of the wound, and saw the accused nearby holding a knife. The mother twice accused the accused of stabbing her daughter, and to these accusations he made no reply, but when the mother said that she intended to detain him until the police arrived, the accused attempted to stab her with the knife. Lord Diplock based himself upon the *dictum* of Cave J in *Mitchell*, and held that the trial judge had been 'perfectly entitled to instruct the jury that the accused's reactions to the accusations, including his silence, were matters which they could take into account along with other evidence in deciding whether the accused in fact committed the act with which he was charged'. It is submitted that this must be correct. It was precisely the sort of case which Cave J presumably had in mind. One might perhaps go further, and say that this was not really a case about

---

[11] In any case, the new form of caution, designed to correspond with the provisions of the Criminal Justice and Public Order Act 1994, reminds suspects of the consequences of exercising the right of silence. See 9.12.3.

silence at all. The silence was merely a relatively small part of an obviously guilty reaction to the mother's accusation which included the attempt to stab her. His action in attacking the mother could be considered as an admission by conduct that there was truth in her accusations. *Parkes* could hardly be further away from *Chandler* on the facts.

The fact remains that the facts of *Mitchell*, and of cases such as *Parkes*, where the accused is confronted, not by a police officer, but by the victim or some concerned person, are quite different from those of a contemporary police interview, and it may not be safe to attempt the comparison. If there is validity in the 'even terms' principle in the context of an interview (bearing in mind the exhaustive procedural requirements for interviews contained in Codes of Practice C and E) it must surely depend on the facts of each case. The concept of even terms seems to hinge on whether the natural advantage of the interrogator over the suspect has been neutralized by the surrounding circumstances. It is submitted that the mere fact that the accused is legally represented is not enough to produce this result in all cases. Nor can it be assumed that police officer always has an advantage which must be neutralized. Indeed, in *Chandler*, Lawton LJ said:

> We do not accept that a police officer always has an advantage over someone he is questioning. Everything depends upon the circumstances. A young detective questioning a local dignitary in the course of an inquiry into alleged local government corruption may be very much at a disadvantage. This kind of situation may be contrasted with that of a tearful housewife accused of shoplifting or of a parent being questioned about the suspected wrongdoing of his son.

Similarly, the experience, or lack thereof, of a solicitor or his clerk, the physical and mental condition of the suspect, the suspect's status, intelligence, and sophistication, and the information available to the suspect and his solicitor about the alleged offence, may be relevant factors. See *Seelig* [1992] 1 WLR 148; *Smith* [1994] 1 WLR 1396; 9.7.

10.3.2 Modern statement of 'even terms' rule

In *Collins and Keep* [2004] 2 Cr App R 11, the accused were charged with kidnapping and having a firearm with intent to commit that offence. Shortly after the incident in question, C and a co-accused, B, were stopped and questioned by a police officer. When asked what they were doing, B in the presence and hearing of C, lied to the officer about their activities. C took no steps to correct the lie. The trial judge directed the jury that they were entitled to consider C's silence as joining in the lie told by B, and that if they did so, they could consider it as evidence of guilt and as evidence supporting the evidence of the victim of the offence. C was convicted and appealed against his conviction. Allowing the appeal, the Court of Appeal held that the jury were entitled to consider whether his reaction to the question put by the officer and B's reply could amount to an adoption of the lie. But it was necessary for the judge to direct the jury that they must first consider whether the exchange called for a reaction from C, and if so, then to consider whether by his reaction C had in fact adopted the lie. In the present case, there was no evidence as to C's reaction, and because C and the officer were not on even terms, it must be assumed that C may simply have been exercising his right to silence. Moreover, the judge had failed to direct the jury properly on the matter.[12] The Court took the opportunity to re-state the common law rule in the

---

[12] The Court rejected a further argument that using the accused's silence against him violated his right to a fair trial under art. 6 of the European Convention on Human Rights, holding, following *Condron v United Kingdom* (2001) 31 EHRR 1 (10.5.1) that, provided that the judge gave a balanced direction to the jury, no such unfairness arose.

light of the earlier authorities. Having considered *Christie*, *Hall*, *Parkes*, and *Chandler*, Thomas LJ continued:

> From the authorities to which we have referred, it is clear that where an allegation is made against the accused in his presence:
>
> (i)   It is for the jury to determine whether a statement made in the presence of the accused calls for some response;
>
> (ii) If it does, and if no response is made, the statement can only be evidence against the accused if by his reaction to it, he accepts that statement as true; although that is a question for the jury to determine, mere silence cannot of itself amount to an acknowledgement of the truth of an allegation;
>
> (iii) A distinction is made in the authorities between cases where the defendant is on equal terms with those making the accusation (in which case silence may be used against him) and those where the defendant is at a disadvantage (in which case silence cannot be used against him).
>
> The issue in the present case did not concern an accusation made against the appellant, but an untruthful statement made by a companion in answer to a question from the police addressed to both the appellant and his companion. However, we consider that similar principles are applicable where circumstances arise where an important question is asked in the presence of an accused and an answer given and the issue arises as to whether he has joined in the answer; we consider therefore that a jury was entitled to consider whether his reaction to that question and answer could amount to his adoption of that answer, provided that the jury were directed first to consider the question as to whether in all the circumstances, the question called for some response from the defendant and secondly, whether by his reaction the defendant adopted the answer made. [[2004] 2 Cr App R 11, [34], [35].]

The appellant had raised the issue that he had not been cautioned or arrested, and that he had been deprived of the protections of ss. 34, 35, and 37 of the Criminal Justice and Public Order Act 1994; that he would have been entitled to remain silent on being arrested and interviewed; and that accordingly, his silence could not be regarded as joining in a lie. The prosecution argued, and the Court accepted that the common law rules had survived the Act in circumstances such as those in the instant case. Thus, in a case to which the Act does not apply, the common law right of silence is preserved, but subject to the principle that silence may be used against the accused when he is on even terms with his accuser.

10.4 DISSATISFACTION WITH THE COMMON LAW RULE

A number of courts felt that the common law rule often worked unduly favourably to the accused. Such frustrations no doubt underlie judgments such as that of Lawton LJ in *Chandler* [1976] 1 WLR 585, and are, to some extent, understandable. The rule is salutary in many cases, for example, where the accused and his advisers do not even know, at the time of the interview, with what offences he may be charged, or where the offences are complicated or technical, or where it is genuinely uncertain what defence, if any, the accused may have. In these cases, it is unwise and premature for the accused to make any statement. In other cases, however, silence is less reasonable. Where the accused asserts at trial a defence of alibi, or self-defence, the facts of which must have been known to him from the outset, his silence impedes investigation of his defence, and one clear inference which could be drawn from his silence when interviewed is that the defence was invented after the fact. Similarly, the accused's failure to give an innocent explanation for his presence at the scene of a crime, or his possession of apparently incriminating articles, which explanation must have existed at the time, provides an obvious commonsense basis for questioning his veracity when he offers it as a defence at trial.

In *Gilbert*,[13] the Court of Appeal held it to be error to invite the jury by implication to draw an adverse inference against an accused who failed, during interview and after caution, to make any reference to a defence of self-defence later raised at trial. However, the Court did so with manifest reluctance, and dismissed the appeal by applying the proviso to s. 2 of the Criminal Appeal Act 1968. Lord Dilhorne said (*ibid.* at 244):

> We regard the present position as unsatisfactory. In our view it may not be a misdirection to say simply 'this defence was first put forward at this trial', or words to that effect, but if more is said, it may give rise to an inference that a jury is being invited to disregard the defence put forward because the accused exercised his right of silence, in which case a conviction will be placed in jeopardy. It is not within our competence sitting in this court to change the law. . . . A right of silence is one thing. No accused can be compelled to speak before, or for that matter, at his trial. But it is another thing to say that if he chooses to exercise his right of silence, that must not be the subject of any comment adverse to the accused. . . . Our task is to apply the law as it now is; and in the light of the authorities to which we have referred, in our opinion the judge in asking the jury to consider whether it was remarkable that, when making his statement, the accused said nothing about self-defence, fell into error and misdirected them.

10.5 STATUTORY PROVISIONS: GENERAL PRINCIPLES

The dissatisfaction with the common law rules led to the enactment of ss. 34 to 38 of the Criminal Justice and Public Order Act 1994.[14] During debate on the Bill, these sections provoked considerable controversy because they were correctly perceived as altering fundamental rights of the accused in the process of criminal prosecution. Similar legislation had been proposed for England before this particular bill was introduced, and had been implemented in Northern Ireland, resulting in some degree of judicial experience with the new rules.[15] Sections 34, 36, and 37 were amended by s. 58 of the Youth Justice and Criminal Evidence Act 1999, to bring the law into compliance with art. 6(3) of the European Convention on Human Rights, which requires that the accused be given access to legal advice (*Murray* v *United Kingdom* (1996) 22 EHRR 29; 9.12.5). As thus amended, these provisions and their impact on the right of silence do not in themselves violate the fair trial provisions of art. 6 of the European Convention on Human Rights, subject, however, to some important qualifications regarding the directions to be given to the jury about the circumstances in which they may draw an adverse inference against the accused (*Condron* v *United Kingdom* [2000] Crim LR 679). This is dealt with further at 10.5.1, 10.5.2.

---

[13] (1977) 66 Cr App R 237 and see *Alladice* (1988) 87 Cr App R 380 per Lord Lane CJ; *Sullivan* (1966) 51 Cr App R 102. For an interesting (though unsuccessful) argument that the so-called doctrine of recent possession in relation to handling stolen goods amounted to an infringement of the right of silence, see *Raviraj* (1986) 85 Cr App R 93.

[14] These sections are the subject of an important amendment by s. 58 of the Youth Justice and Criminal Evidence Act 1999 (see below). Section 35 of the Act, which applies to the accused's failure to give evidence at trial is dealt with at 15.6. The remaining sections are dealt with below.

[15] Criminal Evidence (Northern Ireland) Order 1988. For the background to the debate, see the 11th Report of the Criminal Law Revision Committee, *Evidence* (Cmnd 4991, 1972) and the report of the Royal Commission on Criminal Justice (Cm 2263, 1993). The corresponding provisions in Northern Ireland had been held not to infringe the accused's right to a fair trial under art. 6 of the European Convention on Human Rights (*Murray* v *United Kingdom* (1996) 22 EHRR 29; R. Munday [1996] Crim LR 370; R. Pattendon [1995] Crim LR 602. But see 10.5.1.

Sections 34, 35, 36, and 37 contain the substance of the law. Each of these sections permits the court to draw 'such inferences as appear proper' against the accused in certain circumstances. The circumstances differ as between the three sections. In the cases of ss. 34, 36, and 37, the adverse inference may be drawn either by a jury or bench of magistrates in deciding whether or not the accused is guilty of the offence charged, or whether there is a case to answer (see ss. 34(2), 36(2), 37(2)).[16] Whether it is proper to draw any inference, and, if so, what inference is proper, must depend on the facts of each particular case.

10.5.1 The European Convention and directions to be given to jury

In *Cowan* [1996] QB 373, the Court of Appeal laid down important principles relating to the treatment, under s. 35 of the Act, of cases in which the accused declines to give evidence. This subject is dealt with generally at 15.6, but the principles stated by the Court are now applied by analogy to cases arising under ss. 34, 36, and 37. The principles correspond with the Judicial Studies Board's specimen jury direction for s. 35 cases, which the Court approved. They may be summarized as follows:

> (a) The jury must receive a proper direction on the burden and standard of proof, i.e., the prosecution must prove the guilt of the accused so that the jury feel sure of guilt or beyond reasonable doubt).
>
> (b) The judge must make it clear that the accused continues to be entitled not to give evidence.
>
> (c) The judge must explain that, pursuant to s. 38(3) of the Act, the accused's failure to give evidence cannot be sufficient in itself to prove his guilt.
>
> (d) The judge must make it clear that the jury must be satisfied that the prosecution has established a case to answer, based on the prosecution's evidence, before any inference against the accused may be drawn from the accused's failure to give evidence. (But see the comment on this principle at 15.6.4.)
>
> (e) If the jury conclude, having regard to any explanation advanced to explain the accused's silence or the absence of explanation, that the accused's silence can only sensibly be attributed to the accused's having no answer to the case against him, or no answer likely to stand up to cross-examination, they may draw an adverse inference against him.

In *Condron* [1997] 1 WLR 827, in a case concerned with s. 34, the Court of Appeal held it to be desirable that the jury should be directed in accordance with the principles laid down in *Cowan*. Of course, this requires some adjustments in wording to make the direction consistent with s. 34 rather than s. 35.[17] In *Condron* (also considered at 10.6.4) the accused argued that no inference should have been drawn against them because of their failure to state facts when questioned on which they later relied for their defence, because their solicitor had decided not to permit them

---

[16] Section 39 empowers the Secretary of State to extend the provisions of ss. 34 to 38, with appropriate modifications, to proceedings in military tribunals, including courts martial.

[17] Thus, references to 'not giving evidence' would be replaced by 'not answering questions' or 'failing to mention facts'. In principle (e), the appropriate reference would be to the accused's answer standing up to 'questioning' or 'investigation', rather than 'cross-examination': *Betts and Hall* [2001] 2 Cr App R 257. In *Doldur* [2000] Crim LR 178, the Court of Appeal suggested that in cases based on s. 34, it was unnecessary to direct the jury in accordance with principle (d) because, while the existence of a case to answer has a logical relationship with the question of whether or not the accused chooses to give evidence, it does not necessarily have one with the question of whether he answered questions during the investigation. This seems reasonable, but it would be contrary to *Condron*, and its consistency with the European Convention cases (text below) has been questioned: *Milford* [2001] Crim LR 330.

to be interviewed. The accused were charged with offences of supplying heroin. They were both heroin addicts, and the solicitor believed (albeit apparently in the face of medical advice to the contrary) that they were not fit to be interviewed because they were experiencing withdrawal symptoms. The Court held that the fact that the accused had relied on their solicitor's advice was not in itself a reason for holding that an inference should not be drawn. Nonetheless, the jury must be directed in terms of the *Cowan* principles, and in particular must be directed in relation to paragraph (e) to consider the reason put forward by the accused for remaining silent. If the jury had been satisfied that the accused's reliance on the advice of their solicitor was in fact the reason for their failure to mention the facts, they would been entitled to conclude that the accused were not trying to protect a hopeless story against police questioning, but were acting reasonably; the jury might then have felt that it would be wrong to draw an adverse inference.[18] Because the judge had failed to direct the jury adequately on this point, the appeal would have been allowed if the evidence against the accused had not been overwhelming. In subsequent proceedings before the European Court of Human Rights (*Condron* v *United Kingdom* [2001] 31 EHRR 1) it was argued that the operation of s. 34 (and, therefore, presumably also of ss. 35 to 38) was incompatible with the fair trial provisions of art. 6 of the European Convention on Human Rights (see 1.7). The Court held that the provisions of s. 34 did not of themselves violate art. 6. The Convention did not require an absolute right of silence, and because English law allowed the jury a choice of whether or not to draw an adverse inference, and the accused could seek to persuade them not to do so in adversarial proceedings, the basic standard of fairness was present. It was also held, however, that that article would be violated if an adverse inference were to be drawn against the accused when they had a good explanation for their silence, which would include acting on legal advice. Thus, the direction under principle (e) propounded in *Cowan* is vital and must always be given. Failure to do so may violate art. 6. The result of the holding in the European Court of Human Rights in *Condron* is in fact, it is submitted, that a full *Cowan* direction is now not merely desirable, as stated by the Court of Appeal in *Condron*, but mandatory in every case. The European Court conceded that in some instances, when the circumstances of a particular case may be said to 'call out for an explanation', it may be proper to draw an adverse inference from the accused's failure to provide one, and this does not violate art. 6. But even in these circumstances, a trial court should proceed 'with particular caution' before holding the accused's silence against him. This decision was followed in *Beckles* v *United Kingdom* (2003) 36 EHRR 13, in which the trial judge gave the jury a wholly inadequate direction regarding the accused's reason for failing to mention facts, which again was legal advice, and regarding the imperative of not drawing an adverse inference against the accused except in terms of principle (e).[19]

Further guidelines were laid down by the Court of Appeal in *Petkar; Farquhar* [2004] 1 Cr App R 22, [51]. Rix LJ said:

> In the light of the current model JSB direction, it might be said that, in addition to or else in amplification or clarification of the statutory conditions emphasized in *Argent* and the five essentials

---

[18] The jury must be directed to consider whether the reason given by the accused for failing to mention facts is a genuine reason, not whether his decision was a good one. Unless the jury are sure that the only reason for the accused's failure to mention facts is that he had no answer to the case against him likely to stand up to investigation (principle (e)), they should not draw an adverse inference against him: *Betts and Hall* [2001] 2 Cr App R 257.

[19] It appears that the judge also actively misdirected the jury by telling them that there was no evidence of what advice the accused had been given by his solicitor, whereas in fact there was such evidence.

emphasized in *Cowan* and *Condron*, the following matters should be set before a jury in a well-crafted and careful direction.

(i)   The facts which the accused failed to mention but which are relied on in his defence should be identified: see para.2 of the model direction and *Chenia* [[2003] 2 Cr App R 83] at paras. 87/89, where Clarke L.J. said that this requirement must be approached in a common-sense way.

(ii)   The inferences (or conclusions, as they are called in the direction) which it is suggested might be drawn from failure to mention such facts should be identified, to the extent that they may go beyond the standard inference of late fabrication: see para.2 of the model direction.

(iii)   The jury should be told that, if an inference is drawn, they should not convict 'wholly or mainly on the strength of it': see para.2 of the model direction and *Murray v United Kingdom* (1996) 22 E.H.R.R. 29 at 60, para.47. The first of those alternatives ('wholly') is a clear way of putting the need for the prosecution to be able to prove a case to answer, otherwise than by means of any inference drawn. The second alternative ('or mainly') buttresses that need.

(iv)   The jury should be told that an inference should be drawn 'only if you think it is a fair and proper conclusion': para.3 of the model direction. This is not stated in the statute, but is perhaps inherent in that part of it emphasized in Lord Bingham's sixth condition. In *R. v McGarry* [1999] 1 Cr App R 377 at 383G this court glossed that condition as requiring a jury 'not arbitrarily to draw adverse inferences'.

(v)   An inference should be drawn 'only if...the only sensible explanation for his failure is that he had no answer or none that would stand up to scrutiny: para.3 of the model direction, reflecting Lord Taylor's fifth essential in *Cowan*. In other words the inference canvassed should only be drawn if there is no other sensible explanation for the failure. That is analogous to the essence of a direction on lies.

(vi)   An inference should only be drawn if, apart from the defendant's failure to mention facts later relied on in his defence, the prosecution case is 'so strong that it clearly calls for an answer by him': para.3 of the model direction. This is a striking way to put the need, reflected in Lord Taylor's third and fourth essentials in *Cowan*, for a case to answer. A note, note 16, to the JSB guideline explains that it reflects 'a cautious approach'.

(vii)   The jury should be reminded of the evidence on the basis of which the jury are invited not to draw any conclusion from the defendant's silence: see para.4 of the model direction and *R. v Gill* [2001] 1 Cr App R 160 at paras 30/31. This goes with point (iv) above, because it is only after a jury has considered the defendant's explanation for his failure that they can conclude that there is no other sensible explanation for it.

(viii) A special direction should be given where the explanation for silence of which evidence has been given is that the defendant was advised by his solicitor to remain silent: see para.5 of the model direction.

Both *Petkar* and the earlier decision of the Court of Appeal in *Chenia* [2003] 2 Cr App R 6 indicate that an appeal against conviction on the ground of a misdirection, or a failure to direct the jury fully about the issue of inferences to be drawn will not necessarily succeed if the trial was substantially fair, and the evidence against the accused was overwhelming.

In *McGarry* [1999] 1 WLR 1500, the Court of Appeal held that, where the judge forms the view that there is no evidence on which the jury could properly conclude that the accused failed to mention a fact relied on in his defence, and accordingly rules that no adverse inference can be drawn against the accused under s. 34, it is mandatory that the judge give the jury a positive direction that no adverse inference should be drawn. Because of the potential for prejudice to the accused, it is not sufficient that the jury should be left without guidance on the matter. Because the trial judge had not only failed to give the required direction, but had given the jury a direction from which they were likely to infer that they could draw an adverse inference, the conviction was quashed.

10.5.2 The European Convention and access to legal advice

We have seen previously (9.12.5) that the denial of access to legal advice, other than within reasonable limits and for good reason, during the stage of interrogation constitutes a violation of art. 6(3) of the European Convention. The facts of the leading case of *Murray v United Kingdom* (1996) 22 EHRR 29 and the decision of the European Court of Human Rights in that case were explored there, and need not be repeated. As a result of the decision in *Murray*, Parliament appreciated that the statutory provisions of English law which permit an adverse inference to be drawn against an accused in derogation from the right of silence were not compatible with art. 6(3) without some further provision to guarantee access to legal advice. Consequently, ss. 34, 36, and 37 were amended by s. 58 of the Youth Justice and Criminal Evidence Act 1999, so as to provide that an adverse inference may not be drawn unless before the time of the failure to mention facts (to take the example of s. 34) the accused has been permitted an opportunity to consult a solicitor. As thus amended, the sections appear to be compatible with art. 6(3). The amendment was achieved by adding new subsections (s. 34(2A), s. 36(4A), and s. 37(3A)) which are almost identical and which have the same effect.

Section 34(2A) provides:

> Where the accused was at an authorised place of detention at the time of the failure, subsections (1) and (2) above do not apply if he had not been allowed an opportunity to consult a solicitor prior to being questioned, charged or informed as mentioned in subsection (1) above.

Sections 36(4A) and 37(3A) provide:

> Where the accused was at an authorised place of detention at the time of the failure or refusal subsections (1) and (2) above do not apply if he had not been allowed an opportunity to consult a solicitor prior to the request being made.

A new s. 38(2A) provides that in each of the above provisions, an 'authorised place of detention' means a police station or any other place prescribed by order of the Secretary of State.

10.5.3 Conviction, etc. not to be based solely on inference

Section 38(3) provides that a conviction, or a decision that the accused has a case to answer, may not be based solely on an inference permitted by any of ss. 34(2), 35(2), 36(2), and 37(2).[20] Section 38(4) provides that a judge shall not refuse to grant an accused's application to dismiss the charge, based solely on such an inference, but in this case, the restriction does not apply to inferences drawn under s. 35(2).[21] These subsections offer some degree of protection by requiring the prosecution to have some other evidence against the accused with which to sustain the charge.

---

[20] The jury must be so directed: see *Petkar; Farquhar* [2004] 1 Cr App R 22, [51]: 10.5.1.
[21] As to s. 35(2) see 15.6.

10.5.4 Preservation of other rules of evidence

Section 38(5) provides:

> Nothing in sections 34, 35, 36 or 37 prejudices the operation of a provision of any enactment which provides (in whatever words) that any answer or evidence given by a person in specified circumstances shall not be admissible in evidence against him or some other person in any proceedings or class of proceedings (however described, and whether civil or criminal). In this subsection, the reference to giving evidence is a reference to giving evidence in any manner, whether by furnishing information, making discovery, producing documents or otherwise.

This subsection is designed to ensure that the rules of evidence generally shall apply to inferences drawn under any of the sections from the accused's silence, in the same way as they would apply to any answer or evidence which he might have given. Thus, any inference drawn should not infringe any privilege to which the accused is entitled (for example, where it may relate to advice given to the accused by his legal advisers) and must not relate to any inadmissible revelation of bad character.

The most intriguing question is whether any such inferences must be drawn only subject to the rules governing confessions.[22] It may be arguable that, if the accused was silent in circumstances in which, had he made a confession, such confession would have to be excluded on the ground of oppression or unreliability (see Police and Criminal Evidence Act 1984, s. 76(2), and 9.5 *et seq.*) no inference should be permitted to be drawn from his silence. There are two difficulties in the way of such an argument.

The first is that it would have to be shown that the circumstances were such as to cause the accused to remain silent when he might otherwise have made a statement consistent with his innocence. This seems by no means insuperable. For example, an inexperienced accused, who is wrongly denied access to legal advice, or is subjected to a highly intimidating interrogation, may be too frightened or uncertain to venture his explanation, even though he knows it to be true. See *Argent* [1997] 2 Cr App R 27; 10.6.3.

The second difficulty is more substantial. Section 82(1) of the Police and Criminal Evidence Act, 1984, defines a confession as: 'any *statement* wholly or partly adverse to the person who made it' (emphasis added). It is doubtful whether the accused's failure to say anything could properly be construed as being a 'statement'. The point may not be beyond argument because s. 82(1) adds that a confession may be made 'in words or otherwise'. But the natural meaning of this language is that a confession may be made by other means of assertion, such as gestures. The argument proposed, if accepted, might also have the unfortunate logical consequence that silence must be regarded as a confession for all purposes, which is clearly not the intent of s. 82(1) and does not correspond with the present position at common law or the provisions of the 1994 Act.

10.5.5 Judicial discretion

The solution to the problem posed above may reside in s. 38(6), which provides:

> Nothing in sections 34, 35, 36 or 37 prejudices any power of a court, in any proceedings, to exclude evidence (whether by preventing questions being put or otherwise) at its discretion.

---

[22] See generally 9.5 *et seq.*

The judge may, in the exercise of his usual discretion to exclude admissible prosecution evidence so as to ensure a fair trial for the accused, exclude evidence in the form of an inference which might otherwise be drawn under ss. 34 to 37.[23] If the accused is treated in an oppressive way, or in any case where the drawing of the inference would be unfair in the light of all the circumstances (for example, where the accused refuses to make a statement about technical or complicated offences, or at a time when he is unsure with what offences he might be charged), it would be appropriate for the judge to direct the jury to draw no inference from the accused's silence. As at common law, there is, no doubt, no discretion to restrain comment by co-accused.

10.6 ACCUSED'S FAILURE TO MENTION FACTS WHEN QUESTIONED OR CHARGED

Section 34 deals with the accused's failure to mention certain facts on being questioned about or charged with (or officially informed that he may be prosecuted for) an offence. Section 34(2) provides that 'such inferences from the failure as appear proper' may be drawn for any of the purposes listed above in 10.5. The text of the new s. 34(2A) is given at 10.5.2.

Section 34(1) and (5) provide as follows:

> (1) Where, in any proceedings against a person for an offence, evidence is given that the accused—
>> (a) at any time before he was charged with the offence, on being questioned under caution by a constable trying to discover whether or by whom the offence had been committed, failed to mention any fact relied on in his defence in those proceedings; or
>> (b) on being charged with the offence or officially informed that he might be prosecuted for it, failed to mention any such fact,
>
> being a fact which in the circumstances existing at the time the accused could reasonably have been expected to mention when so questioned, charged or informed, as the case may be, subsection (2) below applies.
>
> (5) This section does not—
>> (a) prejudice the admissibility in evidence of the silence or other reaction of the accused in the face of anything said in his presence relating to the conduct in respect of which he is charged, in so far as evidence thereof would be admissible apart from this section; or
>> (b) preclude the drawing of any inference from any such silence or other reaction of the accused which could properly be drawn apart from this section.

The power to permit an inference to be drawn under s. 34 arises only where the accused fails to mention a *fact* which he could reasonably have been expected to mention. In *Nikolson* [1999] Crim LR 62, it was held that the accused's failure to mention a theory or speculation about the case, or to offer an opinion about it, as opposed to a fact, was also outside the scope of s. 34(1)(a) and no adverse inference could be drawn from it. Moreover, if it is claimed that the accused failed to mention facts on being questioned, it must be shown that he was in fact questioned. Thus, where no questioning occurred because the accused refused to leave his cell for the purpose of being interviewed, no inference should have been drawn against him for failing to mention facts at that stage: *Johnson* (2005) *The Times*, 5 May 2005; though a subsequent failure to mention facts when charged might give raise to an inference. And if the accused is questioned, an inference may not be drawn if he mentions the relevant facts, even though he does so other than in direct

---

[23] See generally the Police and Criminal Evidence Act 1984, s. 78; 3.7 *et seq.*

response to the questions put to him. In *Knight* [2004] 1 Cr App R 9, the accused was charged with indecently assaulting a young girl. At the police interview which followed his arrest, his solicitor read out a prepared statement, which exactly corresponded with the accused's defence at trial. But the accused declined to answer questions. At trial the judge permitted the jury to draw an adverse inference from this failure. The accused's appeal against conviction was allowed. Laws LJ said (*ibid.* at [10]):

> ...it seems to us there was no proper space for any adverse inference to be drawn by the jury in this case, where the defendant gave his full account in a pre-prepared statement from which he did not depart in the witness box. Unless s. 34(1)(a) was enacted distinctly to promote not only the giving, but also the testing, of a suspect's account, there is no sensible difference between the events which happened in this case and the disclosure of a suspect's account in response to police questions rather than in a pre-prepared statement. The suspect has mentioned *all* the facts on which he later relies in his defence. The fact that he has not mentioned them specifically in response to police questions must be immaterial unless the questioning process itself is intended by the subsection to secure results over and above the disclosure of the suspect's account; and such results could only consist in the presumed benefits of having the account cross-examined to.
>
> We have come to the clear conclusion that the aim of s. 34(1)(a) does not distinctly include police cross-examination of a suspect upon his account over and above the disclosure of that account. Had that been intended, it seems to us that Parliament would have used significantly different language. [Emphasis in original.] Sections 34(1) (a) and (b) operate independently, and may come into play in the same case. In *Dervish* [2002] 2 Cr App R 105, the Court of Appeal held that where the trial judge excluded evidence of interviews between the accused and the investigating police officers because of breaches of Code of Practice C, and accordingly no question could arise of any failure to mention facts during the interviews, it was still open to the jury to draw an adverse inference against the accused by reason of his failure to mention those facts at the stage when he was charged.

10.6.1 Accused being questioned under caution

Code of Practice C requires a police officer to caution the accused before questioning him, once there are grounds to suspect him of an offence. A new form of caution was introduced to explain the effect of s. 34, so as to put the accused on notice of the possible consequences of his failure to mention relevant facts. This also ensures that the questioning should take place in the context of a formal interview, and should result in a taped record of what facts the accused did or did not mention (see 9.12.3). Even so, there will be cases in which the accused will, at trial, assert that he did mention facts to the officers which were not recorded. The judge must resolve such factual issues before deciding what inferences, if any, can be permitted. Section 34(3) provides that evidence of the accused's failure to mention a fact which forms part of his defence may be given even before evidence of the fact itself, unless the court otherwise directs. Section 34(4) provides that the section applies to persons other than police officers charged with the duty of investigating offences, for example Customs and Excise officers.

10.6.2 Fact relied on in the accused's defence

The issue here is one of relevance. The strongest inference which can be drawn from the accused's silence on being questioned or charged arises where he fails to mention a fact which he later offers as part of his defence, in which case the relevance of the fact and of the failure to mention it is obvious. Where a fact does not form part of the defence, it may in many cases be irrelevant, and it is obviously wrong to draw any inference against the accused for not having mentioned it: see *Turner* [2004] 1 All ER 1025. In *Moshaid* [1998] Crim LR 420, the appellant, on the advice of his solicitor, did not answer questions when interviewed. At trial he did not give evidence and did not call witnesses. On appeal against conviction, it was held that no inference could be drawn against the appellant. Because there were no facts on which the appellant relied for his defence at trial, it was not a case to which s. 34 applied. Because the trial judge failed to make that fact clear to the jury, and indeed gave the jury the contrary impression, the conviction was quashed. But, although *Moshaid* was clearly rightly decided on the facts, it is submitted that the principle stated must be applied with some caution.[24] In this case, it appears that the accused simply put the prosecution to proof of their case and did not present any positive line of defence.

However, it would be possible for an accused to develop evidence for his defence by cross-examining prosecution witnesses, or by adducing documentary hearsay evidence, even though he does not give evidence or call witnesses. In these cases, it would seem that an adverse inference under s. 34 would be proper. This was accepted by the House of Lords in *Webber* [2004] 1 WLR 404, in which the accused did not give evidence, but in which his counsel put to a witness in cross-examination a number of positive factual suggestions about relevant and important matters, which the witness did not accept, and thereafter adopted in his closing speech evidence given by a co-accused. The judge directed the jury that they were entitled to draw an adverse inference against the accused because of his failure to mention the facts put in cross-examination and adopted in the closing speech. He appealed against his conviction on the ground that the judge had erred in so doing. The House of Lords dismissed the appeal. Delivering the unanimous opinion of the House, Lord Bingham of Cornhill said:

> Since the object of s. 34 is to bring the law back into line with common sense, we think it clear that 'fact' should be given a broad and not a narrow or pedantic meaning. The word covers any alleged fact which is in issue and is put forward as part of the defence case: if the defendant advances at trial any pure fact or exculpatory explanation or account which, if it were true, he could reasonably have been expected to advance earlier, s. 34 is potentially applicable...
>
>   We consider that a defendant relies on a fact or matter in his defence not only when he gives or adduces evidence of it but also when counsel, acting on his instructions, puts a specific and positive case to prosecution witnesses, as opposed to asking questions intended to probe or test the prosecution case. This is so whether or not the prosecution witness accepts the suggestion put. Two considerations in particular lead us to that conclusion. (1) While it is of course true that questions put by counsel are not evidence and do not become so unless accepted by a witness, the effect of specific, positive suggestions put by counsel on behalf of a defendant is to plant in the jury's mind the defendant's version of events. This may be so even if the witness rejects the suggestion, since the jury may for whatever reason distrust the witness's evidence...(2) Since subsection 2(c) of s. 34 permits the court to draw proper inferences when determining whether there is a case to answer, the section may apply at a stage of the trial when the defendant has had no opportunity to give or adduce evidence, and when it will not be known (perhaps not even decided) whether the defendant will give or call evidence or not. But the court is likely to know, from questions put to prosecution witnesses, what (if any) positive case the defendant advances.

Thus, it may be assumed that an inference may be proper whenever the accused in any way advances a fact which he has not mentioned as part of a positive case, and not only when he does so by giving or adducing evidence. As Lord Bingham points out, the effect on the mind of the

---

[24] A later Court of Appeal in *Chenia* [2003] 2 Cr App R 6, [25], declined to follow *Moshaid*.

jury is the same, by whatever means the fact may be advanced, and there is no reason why the accused's failure to mention the fact in question should not be the subject of an inference.

An intriguing question is whether the jury should be invited to draw an adverse inference where the accused fails to mention a fact which constitutes his entire defence. In such a case, the jury cannot logically reach the point of drawing an inference against him without in effect concluding that he is guilty of the offence charged. In *Mountford* [1999] Crim LR 575, the accused was seen to throw packets, later discovered to contain drugs, out of a window of the premises in which he was arrested, in an apparent attempt to escape detection. He failed when questioned to mention the fact that another person, W, and not he himself was dealing drugs on the premises, and that he was present only as a customer. The trial judge directed the jury that they were entitled to draw an adverse inference against the accused for his failure to mention that fact when questioned. But that fact was also the accused's entire defence. The Court of Appeal held that the trial judge had erred. Assuming that the jury remain faithful to principle (e) and draw an adverse inference only if sure that the accused failed to mention the fact because he had no answer to the charge capable of holding up to investigation, it seems to follow that they could not evaluate whether or not to draw the adverse inference without at the same time deciding the question of M's guilt. They could not reject the accused's reason for failing to mention the fact without concluding that the fact was untrue. In such circumstances, the Court held, they should not be invited to consider the inference. The decision in *Mountford* has the merit of simplifying the jury's task. If the issue the jury would have to decide under s. 34 is identical with the issue of guilt itself, what is the point of complicating matters by making them consider the merits of drawing a particular inference? But *Mountford* was doubted in *Daly*.[25] The accused was charged with robbery. He had been filmed in the act of theft by a security camera, and offered to plead guilty to the lesser charge of theft, an offer the prosecution rejected. He did not make any separate admission of theft. At his trial, he admitted theft, but not robbery, and that was his defence. It was held that nothing in s. 34 provided that the section did not apply to facts on which the entire defence was based, and that the jury had been entitled to draw an adverse inference against him. The fact that theft was an element of the offence charged was, in the Court's view, irrelevant. However, the appeal was allowed because the judge failed to direct the jury in proper terms to consider the accused's reason for remaining silent. This was important because the accused did not know the strength of the prosecution's case against him, and this might have provided him with a plausible reason not to admit theft. It is submitted that *Mountford* is to be preferred, if for no other reason, because it seems to make matters simpler for the jury.

10.6.3 Fact which the accused could reasonably have been expected to mention

This will be a question of fact in each case.[26] As we have already seen, there are some cases where the facts relied on for a defence must have been known to the accused at the time of being questioned or charged, for example, alibi or self-defence. In these cases, where the accused later offers such a defence at trial, the accused's failure to mention the facts may obviously give rise to the inference that the defence has been invented. This, of course, will also depend on the extent of

---

[25] [2002] 2 Cr App R 201; and see *Gowland-Wynn* [2002] 1 Cr App R 569. Conversely, the decision in *Gill* [2001] 1 Cr App R 160 supports *Mountford*.

[26] See *Haw Tua Tau v Public Prosecutor* [1982] AC 136, 153 per Lord Diplock, a case which turned on similar legislation in Singapore.

the information given to the accused by the police. Facts such as the date and place of the offence, and the actual offence of which the accused is suspected, will bear on the reasonableness or otherwise of the accused's failure to offer an alibi or other specific exculpatory explanation. The accused's mental state, level of intelligence, articulateness, command of English, level of sophistication or experience, or his existing knowledge of the facts surrounding the offence, may also be relevant in some cases.[27] In *Argent* [1997] 2 Cr App R 247, the Court of Appeal held that such matters should be taken into consideration, and that the reference in s. 34(1) to 'circumstances existing at the time' should not be construed restrictively in determining whether or not it was reasonable for the accused to fail to mention the facts in question.

Even in cases where it may not be unreasonable for the accused to say nothing on being questioned initially, for example, because he has been injured or shocked, or asks for legal advice, it would appear far less reasonable for him to fail to mention the facts before or when being charged, especially as he will, by then, have had the opportunity to seek legal advice. However, in cases where the defence is complicated, technical, or legitimately uncertain, it may, even at that relatively late stage, be unclear what facts might be relevant, and in these cases, what inference should be drawn may be less clear. In cases of doubt, the judge may exercise his discretion to forbid the inference under s. 38(6) (see 10.5.4).

10.6.4 Accused remaining silent as result of legal advice

The fact that an accused has been advised by a solicitor not to disclose information does not, in itself, prevent an adverse inference from being drawn, though the jury may take into account the advice given by the solicitor in deciding whether it is reasonable to draw an adverse inference against the accused. For this purpose, it will often be necessary, to give substance to his argument, for the accused to give evidence about the exact advice given, and to call his solicitor as a witness, as opposed to merely giving evidence that he acted on the solicitor's advice. But if he does so, it appears that he must waive the legal professional privilege in relation to his communications with the solicitor.[28] As we have seen (10.5.1) in *Condron*,[29] a solicitor refused to allow his clients to be interviewed about a suspected offence of supplying heroin, because he believed that they were unfit to be interviewed while suffering from symptoms of withdrawal from the drug, even though doctors called to examine the accused thought otherwise. At trial, the accused relied on facts which they could have told the police at the time of the interview. It was held that whether or not it was reasonable to draw an adverse inference against the accused was a matter for the jury. The fact that the solicitor had advised them not to be interviewed was a matter to be considered, but ordinarily the bare assertion of that fact would be insufficient to prevent an inference from being drawn. If the accused and the solicitor did give evidence, they could be cross-examined about any other possible motives for the advice, for example, the hope of gaining some tactical advantage.

In *Beckles* [2005] 1 All ER 705, the Court of Appeal held that the judge must direct the jury to consider both the genuineness and the reasonableness of the accused's reliance on his solicitor's advice. It seems that this must be correct. It should be of particular importance to consider whether the reliance on legal advice was simply a cover for the fact that the accused had no

---

[27] Clearly it is wrong to permit the jury to draw any adverse inference without proof that the accused knew at the relevant time the fact he failed to mention: *B (MT)* [2000] Crim LR 181.

[28] *Bowden* [1999] 1 WLR 823. As to waiver of privilege see 13.2.

[29] [1997] 1 WLR 827; *Roble* [1997] Crim LR 449.

account of the facts to give which would withstand scrutiny. In this situation, the fact that the accused is entitled to act on legal advice is not the real reason for his doing so: see the observations of Auld LJ in *Hoare* [2005] 1 WLR 1804. Nonetheless, the way in which the question of reasonableness has been dealt with is, it is submitted, open to question. In *Knight* [2004] 1 Cr App R 9, the Court of Appeal observed, *per curiam*,[30] that the fact that the accused receives legal advice not to disclose certain facts does not confer on him any immunity from having an adverse inference drawn from his failure to mention facts on which he later relies, if he could reasonably have been expected to mention them. Laws LJ re-stated the view of the earlier Court in *Howell* [2003] EWCA Crim 1, [24], in which he had himself given the judgment of the Court, in the following terms:

> ...the public interest that adheres in reasonable disclosure by a suspected person of what he has to say when faced with a set of facts which accuse him, is thwarted if currency is given to the belief that if a suspect remains silent on legal advice he may systematically avoid adverse comment at his trial. And it may encourage solicitors to advise silence for other than good objective reasons. We do not consider...that once it is shown that the advice (of whatever quality) has genuinely been relied on as the reason for the suspect's remaining silent, adverse comment is thereby disallowed. The premise of such a position is that in such circumstances it is in principle not reasonable to expect the suspect to mention the facts in question. We do not believe that is so. What is reasonable depends on all the circumstances...There must always be soundly based objective reasons for silence, sufficiently cogent and telling to weigh in the balance against the clear public interest in an account being given by the suspect to the police. Solicitors bearing the important responsibility of giving advice to suspects at police stations must always have that in mind.

It is far from clear what such 'soundly based objective reasons' may be. The Court was constrained to depart from *dicta* in some earlier cases which suggested that more weight should be given to legal advice, certainly where it was not demonstrably groundless.[31] If the accused can no longer safely rely on the advice of his solicitor, it may be that solicitors can no longer advise clients to remain silent except in cases in which the accused himself ought to realize that it is reasonable for him to do so, for example where he is too unwell to concentrate on or answer the questions being asked, or where the charge is uncertain or highly technical, and where any defence is likely to be legal rather than factual. In any other kind of case, there is at least a substantial risk that legal advice will avail the accused nothing. With all due respect to the Court of Appeal, it is not clear how the decision in *Howell* and the observations in *Knight* can be reconciled with the opinion of the European Court of Human Rights in *Condron* v *United Kingdom* [2001] 21 EHRR 1 (see 10.5.1) that art. 6 of the Convention may be violated if s. 34 is applied in a case where the accused has a genuine and reasonable explanation for remaining silent. The proposition which seems to be emerging from the decisions of the Court of Appeal, that it is in general unreasonable for an accused to rely on legal advice to remain silent, seems to run contrary to that principle. It would, of course, frustrate the working of the Act if solicitors could give routine advice to suspects to remain silent, and thus immunize them against the drawing of adverse inferences at trial. But it is submitted that more weight should be given not only to the professional opinion of solicitors, but also to the effect likely to be produced on suspects by being given legal advice. It would surely

[30] The Appeal was allowed on another ground: see 10.6.
[31] See, e.g., *Betts and Hall* [2001] 2 Cr App R 257; and *Argent* [1997] 2 Cr App R 27, in which Lord Bingham CJ seems to imply that acting on legal advice might be regarded as a reasonable reason for failing to mention a fact other than in rare cases.

be only rarely that a suspect, already in a stressful situation being detained at a police station and interrogated by police officers, would consider accumulating the additional stress of rejecting his solicitor's advice. It may be that this area is ripe for a mature, reflective decision by the House of Lords.

10.6.5 Other inferences

Section 34(5) preserves the admissibility of any other inference which might be drawn from the accused's silence or other reaction to being confronted with the offence. Thus, in cases in which it is legitimate for an inference to be drawn at common law, for example, when the accused is confronted by someone other than a police officer, with whom he is on even terms, or when a reaction such as violence or flight suggests guilt, or when the accused offers a false denial, an appropriate inference may be drawn. As to these cases, see 10.2 and 10.3. Ironically, the scope of the inference may perhaps be wider in such cases than under s. 34.

10.7 ACCUSED'S FAILURE TO ACCOUNT FOR OBJECTS, SUBSTANCES, OR MARKS

Section 36 deals with the failure or refusal of the accused to account, on his arrest, for the presence of objects, substances or marks in certain circumstances. Section 36(2) permits the drawing of 'such inferences from the failure or refusal as appear proper' for any of the purposes listed in 10.5. The text of the new s. 36(4A) is given at 10.5.2. Section 36(1) and (4) to (6) provide as follows:

(1) Where—
    (a) a person is arrested by a constable, and there is—
        (i) on his person; or
        (ii) in or on his clothing or footwear; or
        (iii) otherwise in his possession; or
        (iv) in any place in which he is at the time of his arrest,
        (v) any object, substance or mark, or there is any mark on any such object; and
    (b) that or another constable investigating the case reasonably believes that the presence of the object, substance or mark may be attributable to the participation of the person arrested in the commission of an offence specified by the constable; and
    (c) the constable informs the person arrested that he so believes, and requests him to account for the presence of the object, substance or mark; and
    (d) the person fails or refuses to do so,
then if, in any proceedings against the person for the offence so specified, evidence of those matters is given, subsection (2) below applies.

(4) Subsections (1) and (2) above do not apply unless the accused was told in ordinary language by the constable when making the request mentioned in subsection (1)(c) above what the effect of this section would be if he failed or refused to comply with the request.

(5) This section applies in relation to officers of customs and excise as it applies in relation to constables.

(6) This section does not preclude the drawing of any inference from a failure or refusal of the accused to account for the presence of an object, substance or mark or from the condition of clothing or footwear which could properly be drawn apart from this section.

Section 36(3) provides that subsections (1) and (2) apply to the condition of clothing or footwear (e.g., being torn or scuffed) as they apply to substances or marks thereon.

10.7.1 Accused being arrested

The section applies only to the time when the accused is arrested, which is, in some ways, a curious restriction, as suspicious circumstances may have existed at a time before the arrest. The accused may have had time to discard some suspicious object or article of clothing before being arrested. On the other hand, the restriction may reduce factual disputes about the nature or condition of the accused's clothes or possessions, as the police officers will be able to make a record of them after the accused has been arrested.

10.7.2 Accused to be told effect of section in ordinary language

This is the equivalent of the caution requirement under s. 34, and is designed to make the accused aware of the possible consequences of failing to give an explanation.

10.7.3 What inferences are proper

The question of what inferences may be proper will depend on the facts of each case, and the inference may carry more weight in some cases than others. For example, where the accused is arrested wearing blood-stained clothing in a murder case, or in possession of apparent house-breaking implements in a burglary case, his failure to explain them at the time may have clear implications. On the other hand, less obviously incriminating items, such as computer software programs in a fraud or copyright case, may seem less necessary to explain. As in the case of s. 34, it would seem that much will depend on the level of the accused's understanding of the offence of which he is suspected, the amount of information he is given by the officers, his intelligence, mental state, experience, and sophistication, and the more or less technical or complicated nature of the charges: see 10.5.

10.7.4 Other inferences

Like s. 34(5), s. 36(6) permits the drawing of any other inferences which can properly be drawn apart from the section. The possession of incriminating objects or articles of clothing is, in itself, circumstantial evidence against the accused, which does not depend on the accused's silence about them. But where the accused fails to explain them, or gives some false explanation which is later disproved, the weight of the evidence is obviously all the greater. In most cases, it is doubtful whether this subsection adds anything, but it may be of assistance where the prosecution can prove possession of such items at a relevant time other than the time of arrest.

10.8 ACCUSED'S FAILURE TO ACCOUNT FOR PRESENCE AT SCENE OF OFFENCE

Section 37 deals with the failure or refusal of the accused to account for his presence at a place at which an offence for which he was arrested was allegedly committed. Section 37(2) permits the drawing of 'such inferences from the failure or refusal as appear proper' for any of the purposes listed in 10.5. The text of the new s. 37(3A) is given at 10.5.2. Section 37(1) and (3) to (5) provide as follows:

> (1) Where—
>   (a) a person arrested by a constable was found by him at a place at or about the time the offence for which he was arrested is alleged to have been committed; and

(b) he or another constable investigating the offence reasonably believes that the presence of the person at that place and at that time may be attributable to his participation in the commission of the offence; and

(c) the constable informs the person that he so believes, and requests him to account for that presence; and

(d) the person fails or refuses to do so,

then if, in any proceedings against the person for the offence, evidence of those matters is given, subsection (2) below applies.

(3) Subsections (1) and (2) do not apply unless the accused was told in ordinary language by the constable when making the request mentioned in subsection (1)(c) above what the effect of this section would be if he failed or refused to comply with the request.

(4) This section applies in relation to officers of customs and excise as it applies in relation to constables.

(5) This section does not preclude the drawing of any inference from a failure or refusal of the accused to account for his presence at a place which could properly be drawn apart from this section.

This section is very similar to s. 36, but relates to the accused's suspicious presence at the scene of the offence, rather than the possession of incriminating objects or articles of clothing. The element of time is rather more widely drawn, so as to include the possibility that the accused may be arrested some time after the offence has been committed, for example, because the arrival of the police has been delayed or the accused has been hiding. For the same reasons as in s. 36, the effect of the section must be explained to the accused in ordinary language. And again, the section does not prevent any other proper inferences from being drawn apart from the section; the presence of the accused at the scene of the offence, at or near the time when it was committed, is circumstantial evidence against him regardless of his silence, but his failure to explain it, or his giving of a false explanation which is later disproved, increases the weight of the evidence.

10.9 RECOMMENDED FURTHER READING

Bucke, T., Street, R., and Brown, D., Home Office Research Study No. 199, 'The right of silence: the impact of the CJPOA 1994' (2000) www.homeoffice.gov.uk/rds/pdfs/hors199.pdf.

Choo, A.L.-T., 'Prepared statements, legal advice and the right to silence: *R v Knight*' (2004) 8(1) *International Journal of Evidence and Proof* 62.

Cooper, S., 'Legal advice and pre-trial silence—unreasonable developments' (2006) 10(1) *International Journal of Evidence and Proof* 60.

Greer, S., 'The right to silence: a review of the current debate' (1990) 53 *Modern Law Review* 709.

Jackson, J.D., 'Silence and proof: extending the boundaries of criminal proceedings in the United Kingdom' (2001) 5(3) *International Journal of Evidence and Proof* 145.

Stannard, J.E., 'A presumption and four burdens' (2000) 51(4) *Northern Ireland Legal Quarterly* 560.

 ## 10.10 QUESTIONS FOR DISCUSSION BASED ON *R* v *COKE; LITTLETON* AND *BLACKSTONE* v *COKE* (for case files go to the Online Resource Centre)

10.10.1 *Coke; Littleton*

1. Should the jury be invited to draw an inference from Littleton's failure to answer questions in interview? Does the fact that he was legally represented affect your answer? Does the fact that he volunteered a prepared statement affect your answer?

2. Should Littleton's reply on being confronted by Angela Blackstone and the police officers in the street be admitted, and if so, for what purpose? If he had remained silent, could this be used as evidence against him? What if, instead, he attempted to run away?

3. If Coke had remained completely silent on being questioned at his flat before his arrest, could this silence be used as evidence against him?

4. If Coke had given no explanation for the handwritten notes found at his flat (exhibit GG1) could the jury be invited to draw any inference? If he had said that they belonged to a named person, what would the position be?

10.10.2 *Blackstone v Coke*

If Margaret Blackstone wrote to Coke, on learning that she was pregnant, and Coke failed to answer the letter, what use might Margaret make of that fact?

10.11 GENERAL QUESTIONS FOR DISCUSSION

1. What was the common law position in relation to an accused's silence?

2. Which statutory provisions altered the law?

3. What principles were enunciated in *Cowan*?

4. Can adverse inferences be drawn from a suspect's silence at the police station if she has been refused legal advice?

5. Is the potential for a jury to draw an adverse inference contrary to the presumption of innocence?

6. Can an accused by convicted solely on the basis of an adverse inference from silence?

7. A suspect makes no comment in his police interview and declines to give evidence at trial or call witnesses. May an adverse inference be drawn if he puts forward a case through his advocate's cross-examination of prosecution witnesses?

8. May a jury ever draw an adverse inference when an accused asserts that he remained silent on his solicitor's advice?

11

OPINION EVIDENCE

SUMMARY OF MAIN POINTS

- At common law the opinion of a witness is inadmissible to prove the matter believed or inferred.

- This rule is subject to three exceptions:

  (1) evidence of general reputation is admissible to prove character; marriage or pedigree; or certain matters of public concern;

  (2) the opinion of an expert witness within his area of expertise is admissible to assist the court to determine a specialized question which the court might be unable to determine unaided;

  (3) the opinion of any witness is admissible as a way of conveying facts he perceives, being facts within the competence of members of the public generally which do not call for specialized knowledge.

11.1 ADMISSIBILITY OF OPINION EVIDENCE: GENERAL RULE

The general rule of common law was that the opinions, beliefs, and inferences of a witness were inadmissible to prove the truth of the matters believed or inferred if such matters were in issue or relevant to facts in issue in the case. Apart from the question of the relevance and reliability of opinion evidence, it was held that such evidence usurped the function of the court to form an opinion on the facts in issue on the basis of the facts proved by the evidence placed before it.

This did not, of course, prevent the admission of such evidence for other purposes, notably for the purpose of proving what the state of mind of the holder of an opinion was, at a certain time, if relevant to do so. Thus, in *Sheen v Bumpstead* (1863) 2 Hurl & C 193 the belief of a party who represented that a trader was solvent was held admissible on the question, not whether the trader was solvent, but whether the representation was made in good faith. And the belief of an accused charged with handling stolen goods will be admitted to show that he knew or believed, or did not know or believe, that the goods were stolen, but will be inadmissible to prove that the goods were in fact stolen.[1]

The same rule applied to evidence of general reputation and public opinion, which are no more than extended forms of opinion evidence. Such evidence will be inadmissible to prove the truth of the matters generally reputed or believed to be true, but will be admissible to prove what the general reputation of a matter, or the state of public opinion on that matter, in fact was at a given time, if relevant to do so.[2]

The common law rule that opinion evidence is inadmissible to prove the truth of the matter believed is subject to three important exceptions, but otherwise remains in full effect. The exceptions are:

(a) General reputation is admissible to prove the good or bad character of a person; pedigree or the existence of a marriage; and certain matters of public concern, which would otherwise be impossible or very difficult to prove.

(b) Expert opinion evidence is admissible to prove matters of specialized knowledge, on which the court would be unable properly to reach a conclusion unaided.

(c) Non-expert opinion evidence may be received on matters within the competence and experience of lay persons generally.

11.2 GENERAL REPUTATION: PRINCIPLES OF ADMISSIBILITY

We have already observed that the common law succeeded in overcoming its objections to certain kinds of hearsay evidence in cases where, unless such evidence were admitted, no evidence would be available. One kind of evidence permitted in certain cases was evidence of general reputation. At the time when the rule evolved, matters of public concern and family history were often difficult to prove, either because of the difficulty of physically marshalling the necessary volume of evidence, or because relevant witnesses might be dead or unavailable. Happily, the increasing availability and reliability of public records has rendered the task progressively easier, but resort is still had to the common law in some circumstances.

At common law, evidence of general reputation may be admitted in the circumstances set out in 11.2.1 to 11.2.4. Section 9 of the Civil Evidence Act 1968 preserved the common law rule about general reputation (including family tradition, a variant of reputation used to prove or disprove marriage or pedigree) in civil cases without changing its nature or effect. The Act gave the rule statutory recognition, but the rule itself continued to operate substantively as it had at common law.

The Civil Evidence Act 1995 continues this approach by providing, in s. 7(3) and (4):

> (3) The common law rules effectively preserved by section 9(3) and (4) of the Civil Evidence Act 1968, that is, any rule of law whereby in civil proceedings—
>
> (a) evidence of a person's reputation is admissible for the purpose of proving his good or bad character, or

---

[1] Cf. *Marshall* [1977] Crim LR 106.
[2] See 11.2.4.

(b) evidence of reputation or family tradition is admissible—
    (i) for the purpose of proving or disproving pedigree or the existence of a marriage, or
    (ii) for the purpose of proving or disproving the existence of any public or general right or
        of identifying any person or thing,
shall continue to have effect in so far as they authorise the court to treat such evidence as proving or
disproving that matter.

Where any such rule applies, reputation or family tradition shall be treated for the purposes of
this Act as a fact and not as a statement or multiplicity of statements about the matter in question.

(4) The words in which a rule of law mentioned in this section is described are intended only to
identify the rule and shall not be construed as altering it in any way.

The last sentence of subsection (3) is of interest. The same provision was formerly made by s. 9(3) of the Civil Evidence Act 1968. By nature, evidence of general reputation consists of an accumulation of statements about a matter, garnered over some period of time. When a witness gives evidence of a person's reputation, he is repeating what he has heard about that person. Hence, it was inevitable that, at common law, reputation should be regarded as hearsay and should be admissible only pursuant to an exception. But the subsection appears to reclassify reputation conceptually. Hearsay consists, by definition, of a statement, or statements. This is inherent in the common law definition of hearsay, and is stated expressly in the definition of hearsay provided by s. 1(2) of the Civil Evidence Act 1995 (see 7.1). By declaring that reputation is not to be regarded as a statement or a multiplicity of statements, but as a 'fact', s. 7(3) removes reputation from the category of hearsay. As the Civil Evidence Act 1995 abolishes the rule against hearsay in civil cases, it might have been thought that this redefinition was no longer necessary. Certainly, it can do no harm. But some reservation about the concept is legitimate.

The reliability of reputation as evidence is more questionable today than might have been the case a century ago. In an age in which most people lived in the same community throughout their lives, a person's reputation in his community carried significant weight. In an age of almost universal social mobility, its weight must decline. Artificial communities, such as a profession, a university, or a club, must be substituted for a geographical community, to give reputation continuing validity as evidence. Such evidence is, in any event, of limited contemporary importance in civil cases. So far as matters of pedigree and public concern are concerned, more reliable evidence in the form of records is now generally available. By far the most important contemporary use of reputation is as evidence of a person's good or bad character. This is of primary importance in criminal cases, to which the Civil Evidence Act 1995 does not apply. It is submitted that no attempt should be made to reclassify reputation as a 'fact' at common law, i.e., for the purposes of criminal cases. To do so might be to invest such evidence in the minds of juries with a cogency which it by no means always deserves.

The corresponding statutory provision applicable to criminal cases avoids this risk. Section 118(1) of the Criminal Justice Act 2003 preserves in criminal cases the rules of law relating to reputation for the purpose of proving the same matters as those listed in s. 7(3)(b) of the Civil Evidence Act 1995. In each case, the provision is accompanied by a note, which states:

The rule is preserved only so far as it allows the court to treat such evidence as proving the matter concerned.

The effect of the note is unclear. It is not apparent for what other purpose the rules in question could be applied. But the Criminal Justice Act 2003 omits the provision of s. 7(3) of the

Civil Evidence 1995 that reputation shall be treated as a fact rather than as a multiplicity of statements.

11.2.1 To establish matters of pedigree or the existence of a marriage

The contemporary importance of the rule lies in the proof of such questions of some antiquity, as matters of more recent marriage and descent are, increasingly, capable of proof by official records.

11.2.2 To identify a reference to a person or thing, or to prove the existence of a public or general right

The question of identification of a reference here is one of identification of a reference in the mind of the public generally. Thus, in an action for defamation, it is necessary to show that the matter complained of referred to the claimant. This may be proved by evidence that the matter was taken, by the public generally, as referring to the claimant, for which purpose evidence, e.g., that the claimant was publicly jeered at after publication, may be admitted to prove the reference.[3] And in the rather strange case of *Re Steel, Wappett v Robinson* [1903] 1 Ch 135, the extent of a devise of land in a will was proved by evidence that certain fields were known locally as 'customary freeholds', and so corresponded with the words of the devise of 'my freehold lands and hereditaments at Morland Field', although the fields in question were, in fact, privileged copyholds.

11.2.3 To prove good or bad character

In *Rowton* (1865) Le & Ca 520, it was held that character should be equated with the general reputation of a person in his locality, so that at common law such evidence was not only admissible, but was the only admissible evidence for this purpose. In modern times, it is generally accepted that 'character' is a wider concept than one of reputation, and indeed the use of evidence of reputation has been criticized as tending to show, not the actual character but merely the generally accepted character of a person.[4] Nonetheless, such evidence is certainly admissible whenever it is relevant to prove character, and is of considerable importance where the accused in a criminal case seeks to establish his good character. It should be noted that reputation only provides a method of proving character, and cannot be admissible unless the character itself is admissible.[5] Sections 99(2) and 118(1) of the Criminal Justice Act 2003 preserve reputation as a method of proving bad character: see 6.4.

11.2.4 To prove the state of public opinion on a matter

Public opinion may be relevant in cases involving passing off, trademarks, and the like, where it may be necessary to show the effect of representations about or the promotion of a product. Frequently, this may be proved by evidence of reputation based on a survey of public opinion, if shown to be prepared by reliable methods and to be based on accurate and representative

---

[3] See, e.g., *Cook v Ward* (1830) 6 Bing 409.

[4] As to the definition of bad character for the purposes of the Criminal Justice Act 2003, see s. 98 of the Act; 6.3.1 *et seq.*

[5] As to the cases in which character evidence is admissible, see generally Chapters 5 and 6.

sources of information: *Customglass Boats Ltd* v *Salthouse Bros Ltd* [1976] RPC 589. Such a survey may be used by an expert as a basis for an expert opinion as to the present or likely future state of public opinion on such an issue: *Sodastream Ltd* v *Thorn Cascade Ltd* [1982] RPC 459; *Lego Systems A/S* v *Lego M. Lemelstrich Ltd* [1983] FSR 155, 173–82.

11.3 EXPERT OPINION EVIDENCE: COMPETENCE, ADMISSIBILITY, AND WEIGHT

11.3.1 Competence of expert witnesses

It is an ancient rule of the common law that on a subject requiring special knowledge and competence, evidence is admissible from witnesses who have acquired, by study or practice, the necessary expertise on the subject. Such witnesses are known as 'experts'. The evidence is justified by the fact that the court would be unable, unaided, to draw proper inferences and form proper opinions from such specialised facts as might be proved, and even perhaps to judge what facts have been satisfactorily proved. As long ago as the mid-sixteenth century, Saunders J was able to express pride in the readiness of the law to accept guidance from suitably qualified experts. In *Buckley* v *Rice Thomas* (1554) Plowd 118, 124, he said:

> ...if matters arise in our law which concern other sciences or faculties, we commonly apply for the aid of that science or faculty which it concerns. Which is an honourable and commendable thing in our law. For thereby it appears that we do not despise all other sciences but our own, but we approve of them and encourage them as things worthy of commendation.

In *Folkes* v *Chadd* (1782) 3 Doug KB 157, Lord Mansfield confirmed that the opinion of scientific men upon proven facts may be given by 'men of science within their own science'.

Qualification to give expert evidence is technically a matter of competence, and the court should investigate the credentials of a proposed witness before permitting him to give expert evidence. No doubt a witness who lacks any apparent qualification should not be heard, but if the witness has some claim to expertise, the modern practice is to receive his evidence, though its weight may be open to serious adverse comment if the apparent expertise is not translated into reality. The court is concerned with actual expertise, not with the means by which that expertise is acquired. Paper qualifications by themselves may not be a guarantee of actual skills relevant to the questions before the court, and expertise gained by substantial relevant experience certainly renders an expert witness competent, and may invest his evidence with considerable weight. In *Silverlock*[6] a solicitor, who had made a study of handwriting, was allowed to give evidence as an expert, notwithstanding his lack of formal qualification on the subject, because of his demonstrable actual skill. However, a statute may impose more specific requirements: see, e.g., s. 1 of the

---

[6] [1894] 2 QB 766. Cf. *Oakley* (1979) 70 Cr App R 7; *Murphy* [1980] QB 434, and American Federal Rule of Evidence 702: 'If scientific, technical or other specialised knowledge will assist the trier of fact to understand the evidence or to determine a fact in issue, a witness qualified as an expert *by knowledge, skill, experience, training or education* may testify thereto in the form of an opinion or otherwise.' Thus, police officers experienced in investigating road traffic accidents may give an opinion about how an accident occurred, see, e.g., *Oakley* (1979) 70 Cr App R 7, a prosecution for causing death by dangerous driving. The competence of experts can generally be determined by reference to their credentials and the facts of the case, but in an unusual case, it may be necessary to hold a hearing on the *voir dire*: see *G* [2004] 2 Cr App R 368. The Law Commission has recently proposed a more stringent test of admissibility: see Law Com Consultation Paper No. 190 (2009).

Criminal Procedure (Insanity and Unfitness to Plead) Act 1991, dealing with the qualification of certain medical practitioners.

An expert witness, if competent, is, like any other witness, also compellable. In *Harmony Shipping Co. SA v Saudi Europe Line Ltd* [1979] 1 WLR 1380, a handwriting expert, having been consulted on behalf of the plaintiffs, was later consulted by solicitors for the defendants. After giving them his opinion on certain documents relevant to the action, the expert realized that he had inadvertently advised both sides and, in accordance with his professional rules, declined to accept further instructions from the defendants. The defendants served on him a *subpoena ad testificandum*, which he sought to have set aside. The Court of Appeal held that he was compellable to give evidence for the defendants, and that there was no contractual relationship between the expert and the plaintiff which would (even if enforceable, which must be doubtful[7]) bind the expert not to appear for the defendants. Of course, some of the communications passing between the expert and the plaintiffs would be protected by legal professional privilege, subject to any waiver by the plaintiffs.[8]

11.3.2 Independence and objectivity

It is essential that an expert be independent, that is to say that although he may have been identified, retained, and remunerated by one of the parties, the court must be satisfied that he will give his opinion in an objective and balanced manner appropriate to scientific discourse, and that he will place his duty to assist the court above any duty of loyalty to the party who has retained him. If an expert has a conflict of interest of any kind, he may be disqualified from acting as an expert in the case. Even if he is not disqualified, it is unlikely that his evidence will command weight: see generally *Toth v Jarman* [2006] 4 All ER 1276. In *Liverpool Roman Catholic Diocese Trustees Inc.* v *Goldberg (No. 2)* [2001] 4 All ER 950, it was held that Queen's Counsel should not act as an expert witness on behalf of a member of his chambers who was the defendant in an action for professional negligence, especially where the witness had admitted to an understandable degree of personal sympathy for the party on whose behalf he was retained. This decision has been criticized as applying the wrong test, one more appropriate for assessing apparent bias in a tribunal: see *R (Factortame Ltd)* v *Secretary of State for Labour, Local Government and the Regions (No. 8)* [2003] QB 381, per Lord Phillips of Worth Matravers MR at [70]. But it is submitted that the earlier decision is well reasoned and should be followed. There are many similar circumstances in which the independence of an expert witness may be called into question, for example where he is related to a party, or is an employee of a corporate party, or even perhaps where he has given evidence for the same party or for other claimants or defendants in similar cases on previous occasions.[9] Even if the court were to admit the evidence of an expert witness in such circumstances, its weight would obviously be seriously compromised, and it would be an error of

---

[7] As Lord Denning MR pointed out at 1386, such a contract would probably be held to be contrary to public policy. Indeed, if the decision in the case had been otherwise, one party might, by instructing every reputable expert, effectively deprive his opponent of expert advice, and create 'property' in expert witnesses.

[8] This would apply to confidential communications between a party, or his legal advisers, and the expert. But not to documents or other tangible evidence on which the expert bases his opinion, or to the opinion itself. See *King* [1983] 1 WLR 411; and 14.11, 14.12.

[9] There have been many *dicta* against the employment of experts in such situations, see, e.g., *Vernon v Bosley (No. 1)* [1997] 1 All ER 577, 600 per Evans LJ; *National Justice Compania Naviera SA* v *Prudential Assurance Co. Ltd* [1993] 2 Lloyd's Rep 68; *Whitehouse v Jordan* [1981] 1 WLR 246, per Lord Wilberforce.

judgment on the part of a party's legal advisers to seek to rely on such evidence. The requirement of independence is driven home by the provisions of r. 35.3 of the Civil Procedure Rules 1998:

> (1) It is the duty of an expert to help the court on the matters within his expertise.
> (2) This function overrides any obligation to the person from whom he has received instructions or by whom he is paid.[10]

There have been several judicial pronouncements elaborating on the principles stated in this rule. In *Meadow* v *General Medical Council* [2007] 1 All ER 1, the Court of Appeal offered a number of observations on the duties of experts. Sir Anthony Clarke MR drew attention to the *Protocol for Instruction of Experts to give Evidence in Civil Claims* (Civil Justice Council, June 2005) and cited with approval the following paragraph (para. 4.1):

> Experts always owe a duty to exercise reasonable skill and care to those instructing them, and to comply with any relevant professional code of ethics. However, when they are instructed to give or prepare evidence for the purposes of civil proceedings in England and Wales they have an overriding duty to help the court on matters within their expertise (CPR 35.3). This duty overrides any obligation to the person instructing or paying them. Experts must not serve the exclusive interests of those who retain them.[11]

The requirement of objectivity suggests that the expert should avoid assuming the role of an advocate, and must be candid in revealing: the extent to which any questions that may be raised fall outside his sphere of expertise; the extent to which any opinion he expresses is controversial; any materials which may contradict his opinion; and the extent to which the data provided to him restrict his ability to render more than a provisional opinion. The expert should also cooperate in limiting as far as possible the ambit of disagreement between the experts on different sides of the case: see, e.g., *Harris* [2006] 1 Cr App R 55.[12]

This does not mean, however, that an expert witness should not express an opinion favourable to one party and against another as strongly as he feels it appropriate to do so. The function of the expert is to assist the court in reaching the correct conclusion on the facts, and if he considers, after an objective scientific review of the facts, that those facts favour the party on whose behalf he is retained, he should say so. No breach of the obligation to be independent is involved in the forceful expression of a scientifically defensible opinion; indeed, the expert has a positive duty to the court to render it.

11.3.3 Admissibility and weight of expert evidence

Expert opinion evidence may be contradicted and cross-examined to, like any other evidence, and the attack may include cross-examination going to credit. The position of an expert is that he must be regarded as any other independent witness, and although he enjoys such weight as may follow from his peculiar ability to assist the court, it will be a misdirection to direct the jury that

---

[10] Rule 35.10(2) requires the expert to state in his report that he understands his duty to the court and that he has complied with it. See to similar effect Pt 33 of the Criminal Procedure Rules 2005.

[11] See also the guidance offered by Creswell J in *National Justice Compania Naviera SA* v *Prudential Assurance Co. Ltd* [1993] 2 Lloyd's Rep 68 at 81.

[12] Drawing on the guidance of Creswell J (see previous note). As to the specific expectations of experts in cases involving the welfare of children, see the observations of Wall J in *In Re AB (Child Abuse: Expert Witnesses)* [1995] 1 FLR 181, also referred to in *Harris*; and those of Thorpe LJ in *Meadow* at [226]–[245].

his evidence should be accepted unless the witness himself betrays reasons for rejecting it.[13] The tribunal of fact must obviously retain control over the findings of fact, which are its ultimate reponsibility. This does not mean that expert evidence of a categorical nature, which is effectively unchallenged, may be disregarded capriciously in favour of unaided lay opinion, and it would be equally wrong to invite the jury to take this course[14] or to content themselves with unaided observation on a matter calling for expert evidence.[15] But there will be occasions where the tribunal of fact will be driven to reject evidence, and occasions where the tribunal will have to choose between conflicting opinions from experts dealing with the same matters. And there are some cases in which lay evidence may be preferable to expert evidence. For example, the percipient evidence of an attesting witness to a disputed will, who can testify directly about the events surrounding the signing of the will, may be quite legitimately preferable on the issue of whether the will is genuine to the opinion of a handwriting expert, who has no personal knowledge of those events and can only attempt to reconstruct them in a scientific manner.[16]

In civil cases, the admissibility of expert evidence is now circumscribed by the Civil Procedure Rules 1998, which effectively supersede the right of the parties at common law to present expert evidence as they see fit. The new rules are based on the perceptions contained in the Woolf report that the free admission of expert evidence in civil cases was a serious evil which promoted an industry of highly paid experts who tended to render opinions in accordance with the needs of the parties by whom they were retained, and the cost of which helped to restrict access to justice.[17] There was obviously some force in these criticisms. The field of expert evidence had been growing apace, as had the fees charged by some experts. But it may be that the criticisms go too far, and place too little reliance on the ability of trial judges to make it clear when expert evidence is likely to be helpful and when it is not, and to make appropriate orders for costs. Judges cannot be experts on specialized matters of all kinds, and there are many cases in which recourse to informed opinion is both necessary and salutary if cases are to be rightly decided. The proposition that expert witnesses should strive for objectivity and have a duty to assist the court had been expressed judicially before the enactment of the new rules,[18] and it may be argued that there were remedies for failure to follow these principles other than restricting access to competent and professional expert assistance.

The admission of expert evidence in civil cases is now governed by the following provisions of r. 35 of the Civil Procedure Rules 1998. Rule 35.1 provides that expert evidence shall be restricted to that which is reasonably required to resolve the proceedings. Rule 35.3 provides that it is the duty of an expert to help the court on the matters within his expertise, and that duty overrides any obligation to the person from whom he has received instructions, or by whom he

---

[13] *Lanfear* [1968] 2 QB 77.

[14] *Anderson* v *R* [1972] AC 100.

[15] *Tilley* [1961] 1 WLR 1309. In at least one case, the Court of Appeal has overturned a verdict of guilty where unchallenged and uncontradicted expert evidence clearly suggested that such a verdict could not be sustained: see *Matheson* [1958] 1 WLR 474. This suggests that expert evidence is not only admissible in cases involving issues beyond the expertise of the tribunal of fact, but also that it may be determinative of such issues if uncontroverted. Cf. *Sanders* (1991) 93 Cr App R 245. So too in civil cases, a judge should prefer the uncontradicted opinion of an expert to lay evidence on a matter on which expert evidence is appropriate: *Re B (A Minor)* [2000] 1 WLR 790; *Re M (Child: Residence)* [2002] 2 FLR 1059.

[16] *Fuller* v *Strum* (2000) *The Times*, 14 February 2001, reversed on other grounds [2002] 1 WLR 1097. See also 11.7.3.

[17] *Access to Justice. Final Report*, p. 137 *et seq*. The same views had been expressed judicially on various occasions, see, e.g., *Liddell* v *Middleton* [1996] PIQR 36, deploring the use of accident reconstruction experts.

[18] See the cases referred to in note 9.

is paid. This is complemented by r. 35.10, which provides, inter alia, that expert reports must be addressed to the court rather than any party retaining the expert, and must contain a statement that the expert understands and has complied with his duty to the court, and that the facts and opinions stated are true and correct. Rule 35.4 provides:

> (1) No party may call an expert or put in evidence an expert's report without the court's permission.
> (2) When a party applies for permission under this rule, he must identify—
>> (a) the field in which he wishes to rely on expert evidence; and
>> (b) where practicable the expert in that field on whose evidence he wishes to rely.
> (3) If permission is granted under this rule it shall be in relation only to the expert named or the field identified under paragraph (2).

11.4 FUNCTION OF EXPERT EVIDENCE

11.4.1 Opinions on an ultimate issue

The function of an expert witness is to assist the court by giving evidence of his opinion on the matters of specialized knowledge on which his assistance is sought. At common law, this was held to mean that the expert might not be asked his opinion on the 'ultimate question', or in other words he might not be asked directly his opinion on an issue in the case. The reason was that he would thereby usurp the function of the court. Thus, the witness might describe to the court the mental condition of the accused, but might not be asked whether the accused was insane if that was the issue which the court had to decide.[19] It has not been decided whether the rule precluding expert testimony on an ultimate issue remains in effect at common law, though it has often been assumed that experts need no longer be so confined.[20] Certainly, in civil cases it would seem to matter little whether or not an expert witness expresses in so many words to a judge who is the tribunal of fact what is obviously the necessary conclusion of his testimony on a relevant issue, and this has now been provided for by statute (see below). In criminal cases, it may be that the trial judge should retain the power to stop the expert short of doing the jury's work for them. This seems to have been the experience in the United States. For some time, the Federal Rules of Evidence permitted experts to testify freely on ultimate issues, both in civil and criminal cases. However, because it appeared that such testimony might be accorded undue weight by juries in criminal cases, particularly in those involving questions of the accused's mental state, the relevant rule was modified to restore the common law position in part. Federal Rule of Evidence 704 now provides:

(a) Except as provided in subdivision (b), testimony in the form of an opinion or inference otherwise admissible is not objectionable because it embraces an ultimate issue to be decided by the trier of fact.

(b) No expert witness testifying with respect to the mental state or condition of an accused in a criminal case may state an opinion or inference as to whether the accused did or did not have the mental state or condition constituting the element of the crime charged or of a defense thereto. Such ultimate issues are matters for the trier of fact alone.

---

[19] *Daniel M'Naghten's Case* (1843) 10 Cl & F 200.

[20] See, e.g., the 11th Report of the Criminal Law Revision Committee (Cm 4991), para. 268 *et seq*; *Stockwell* (1993) 97 Cr App R 260, 265 per Lord Taylor of Gosforth CJ.

It is submitted that the English common law should now permit expressions of opinion by experts on ultimate issues, subject to the power of the judge in a jury trial to limit testimony in any case where there is a danger of the jury according the testimony undue weight, cases involving such defences as insanity, diminished responsibility, or automatism being examples of cases where this may be desirable. This was the view of the Criminal Law Revision Committee in its 11th Report (Cmnd 4991, para. 270) and of Lord Parker CJ, judicially, in *DPP v A & BC Chewing Gum Ltd* [1968] 1 QB 159, 164.

In civil cases, the common law position has been abrogated, sensibly, by s. 3 of the Civil Evidence Act 1972, which provides:

> (1) Subject to any rules of court...where a person is called as a witness in any civil proceedings, his opinion on any relevant matter on which he is qualified to give expert evidence, shall be admissible in evidence...
> (3) In this section 'relevant matter' includes an issue in the proceedings in question.

In *Re M and R (Minors) (Sexual Abuse: Video Evidence)*,[21] the Court of Appeal held, in a case concerned with alleged child abuse, that a suitably qualified expert witness might express an opinion about the credibility of a child whose evidence had been admitted by way of videotaped interview. Butler-Sloss LJ held that such an opinion was admissible by virtue of s. 3 of the Civil Evidence Act 1972. It is submitted, with respect, that this analysis is inaccurate. The ultimate issue in such a case is not whether the child's evidence is credible, but whether the alleged abuse occurred (though obviously, the question of the child's credibility is of great importance in resolving the ultimate issue).[22] Nonetheless, the court's decision can be defended on another basis. Although in general, expert evidence is not admissible on the issue of credibility, which is a matter of valid lay opinion (see 11.4.2), it is within the province of psychiatrists and psychologists to form an opinion about credibility, because their diagnoses and recommendations for treatment or therapy are often based on the factual accounts given to them by their patients and clients. The fact that such an expert witness believed what he was told is a fact which is essential to explain the formation of his opinion, and can be admitted on that basis without considering the ultimate issue rule.[23] In this respect, expert psychiatric and psychological expert witnesses and perhaps sometimes other medical expert witnesses are in a position different from that of other experts.

11.4.2 Subjects of valid lay opinion

Also of great importance is the rule that expert opinion evidence will not be admitted if it relates only to a question on which the lay opinion of the tribunal of fact is equally valid. This is to state no more than the obvious proposition that expert evidence is confined to those matters on which it is necessary in order to assist the court to determine the issues. Thus, where the

---

[21] [1996] 4 All ER 239, differing from *Re N (A Minor) (Sexual Abuse: Video Evidence)* [1997] 1 WLR 153. As to the practice of presenting the evidence of children by means of videotaped interviews, see generally 16.17.2, and the observations of the court in *Re N*.

[22] See, e.g., Children Act 1989, s. 31(2), and the statement of the ultimate issue, and the burden and standard of proof on that issue, by the House of Lords in *Re H (Minors) (Sexual Abuse: Standard of Proof)* [1996] AC 563, considered at 4.15, 4.16.

[23] And, in a criminal case, without violating the rule against hearsay (see 11.6), though there may often be grounds for a judge to exclude such evidence in a criminal case in the exercise of his discretion. It is one thing to allow an expert to offer an opinion as to credibility to a judge; it is quite another to allow him to offer it to a jury.

question is one of the intent of an accused, in a case where there is no question of mental illness, the evidence of psychiatrists will not assist the jury to determine that issue, the matter being one within the jury's experience of everyday affairs.[24] And it has been said, with reference to an issue of provocation, that psychiatric evidence 'has not yet become a satisfactory substitute for the common sense of juries or magistrates on matters within their experience of life'.[25] The reaction of the accused to certain provoking circumstances, and the reasonableness of that reaction, have been held to be issues determinable without expert assistance.[26]

On the other hand, defences which fall outside the ordinary experience of jurors, such as insanity and diminished responsibility, are proper subjects of expert medical evidence, and although the jury are not bound to accept such evidence, and must look at all evidence in the case including any conflict in the medical evidence,[27] they should act on the evidence before them. Similarly, the defence of automatism is one outside the normal experience of juries, and is a proper subject of expert evidence. In *Smith* [1979] 1 WLR 1445, the Court of Appeal upheld the admission of expert evidence tending to show that the evidence of the accused consistent with his defence of automatism, that he had killed in his sleep, was scientifically impossible.

11.4.3 Credibility

Expert evidence is not admissible on the issue of the credibility of a witness save in exceptional circumstances.[28] In the case of *Lowery* v *R* [1974] AC 85, which is generally thought to turn upon its own facts, two accused were charged with the murder of a girl, in circumstances from which it was likely that one or other of them, or possibly both, must have been guilty of the murder. There was no motive for the murder except the sadistic pleasure of committing it. In order to show that his co-accused was the more likely of the two to have committed the murder, one accused called evidence from a psychiatrist, tending to show that the co-accused had a character and disposition which rendered him likely to behave in the way alleged, certainly more so than the accused. The co-accused contended on appeal that the evidence had been wrongly admitted. Although on the face of it, the evidence was open to considerable question, because it was an attempt to adduce expert opinion evidence on the very subject which the jury had to decide and which seemed to be a matter within their competence, the Privy Council dismissed the appeal. It was held that on the specific issue before the jury, which required a decision as to the veracity of the two accused, the evidence was relevant and admissible and assisted the jury, if they accepted it, to resolve that question. The decision is probably best regarded as applying only to such specific circumstances, and not as any general exception to the usual rule. In *Turner* [1975] QB 834, the Court of Appeal, in holding that the trial judge had been correct in rejecting the expert evidence of a psychiatrist, the effect of which was to suggest that the accused's evidence as to how he came to kill his girlfriend was credible in the light of his mental state at the time, specifically treated *Lowery* as having been decided on 'its special facts'. The Court added:

> We do not consider that it is an authority for the proposition that in all cases psychologists and psychiatrists can be called to prove the probability of the accused's veracity. If any such rule was applied

[24] *Wood* [1990] Crim LR 264; *Chard* (1971) 56 Cr App R 268.

[25] *Turner* (CA) [1975] QB 834, per Lawton LJ at 843. *Gilfoyle* [2001] 2 Cr App R 57 (see 11.4.3).

[26] But where a mental abnormality may have affected a state of mind such as intent, the position is different: see 11.7.2.

[27] *Walton* v *R* [1978] AC 788; *Kiszko* (1978) 68 Cr App R 62. And see *Toner* (1991) 93 Cr App R 382.

[28] But see also *Re M and R (Minors) (Sexual Abuse: Video Evidence)* [1996] 4 All ER 239; *Browning* [1995] Crim LR 227; 11.4.1 and text below.

in our courts trial by psychiatrists would be likely to take the place of trial by jury and magistrates. We do not find that prospect attractive and the law does not at present provide for it.[29]

In *Rimmer* [1983] Crim LR 250, a case not dissimilar to *Lowery*, the Court of Appeal upheld the decision of the trial judge to exclude expert evidence which appeared to affect only veracity, apparently on the ground that such evidence would do no more than explore collateral issues which would be likely to confuse rather than assist the jury. B had cross-examined R with a view to showing that R had suffered from mental illness, and had killed the victim in a typical fit of uncontrollable temper. It was held that R was not entitled to call expert medical evidence with a view to showing that he had never been mentally ill. But while it is true that the cross-examination was relevant to veracity, it seems that it also went directly to the issue the jury had to decide, i.e., whether R or B had committed the murder, and it is submitted that the decision may not be correct.

But the courts have proved willing to depart from the general rule in cases where the expert evidence clearly assists the court in evaluating credibility by reference to matters which fall outside ordinary experience and can be understood only with expert assistance. We have already referred to the decision of the Court of Appeal in *Re M and R (Minors) (Sexual Abuse: Video Evidence)* [1996] 4 All ER 239 (see 11.4.1), which may be regarded as an exception to the traditional rule, even though, as we saw, the reasoning of the Court is by no means free from difficulty. The *ratio decidendi* of the case is actually quite narrow, i.e., that in a case involving the welfare of children, an expert may express an opinion about the credibility of a child whose evidence has been admitted by way of videotaped interview. But it may be that there is some scope for applying the principle to other cases involving the credibility of children, and perhaps other witnesses with special characteristics. In *H (JR) (Childhood Amnesia)* [2006] 1 Cr App R 10, the Court of Appeal agreed to hear evidence from a psychologist who was an expert in the field of memory formation and development. The accused had been convicted of offences of indecent assault on his daughter said to have been committed when she was four or five years of age. The complainant claimed to have a clear and detailed memory of events in her life from a very early time, and her recollection of these events had provided crucial evidence leading to the conviction of the accused. The expert's opinion was that, in the light of scientific knowledge of memory development in young children, there was reason to question the accuracy of the complainant's statements. The Court of Appeal held that, if the jury had had access to this evidence, it was possible that they would have taken a different view of the case. The Court concluded accordingly that the convictions were unsafe, and the appeal was allowed. The Court stressed (at [48]) that it would be only in exceptional cases that such evidence would be admitted. In general, the principle reflected by *Turner* was sound. But in some cases, it is proper to offer the jury the assistance of expert evidence on an issue of credibility when there are factors outside their normal experience to consider.

A disturbing and, it is submitted, incorrect use of expert evidence occurred in *Somanathan* in *Weir and other appeals* [2006] 1 WLR 1885. The accused, a Tamil Hindu priest, was convicted of raping a female member of his congregation. The prosecution were permitted to call a professor of Hinduism as an expert witness, who was asked to state 'how difficult' it would be for a Tamil

---

[29] See also *Henry* [2006] 1 Cr App R 6 (held, applying *Turner*, that expert evidence which went no farther than showing that the accused had a low IQ, and did not show that he suffered from mental illness or was mentally defective, was not admissible to support the credibility of the accused's evidence that he lacked the intention to commit solicitation and conspiracy to murder).

woman living in England to make a complaint of rape against a priest, given the community background and the person against whom the allegation was made. He answered that it would be a 'mind-boggling thing to do', that it would be an 'extraordinary act', and would require a 'tremendous amount of courage' (*ibid.* at 16). The accused contended on appeal that the evidence should not have been admitted because it essentially permitted the witness to express an opinion about the credibility of the complainant's allegations and evidence. In a short passage, devoid of either analysis or authority, the Court summarily rejected the argument. Kennedy LJ said:

> [Counsel] did not ask the witness to express a view about the truth or falsehood of the allegation, and he did not purport to do so, but the jury was entitled to know from an expert whether or not within the Hindu community an allegation of this kind was unusual. [*Ibid.* at [49].]

With respect, whether or not the allegation was unusual (and whether or not it required courage, etc.) was irrelevant to the case except insofar as it tended to confirm the credibility of the complainant. Thus, the only basis on which the court might have sought to defend the admissibility of the evidence was that the jury would be unable to assess the complainant's credibility without expert assistance. This would involve the proposition that the reluctance of a Hindu woman to accuse a priest of rape is a concept beyond the ordinary experience of most jurors, and so justifies a departure from the general rule expounded in *Turner*. This does not seem an especially difficult concept with which to grapple, and it is submitted that the common sense of the jurors would have been more than adequate to the task. It is certainly a far cry from infant memory development. It is to be hoped that the decision will not be followed.

It should be noted, to avoid confusion, that a specific common law rule of evidence permits the calling of medical evidence to show that any witness (including an accused who gives evidence) suffers from a disease, defect, or abnormality of mind such as to affect the reliability of his evidence (see *Toohey* v *Commissioner of Police of the Metropolis* [1965] AC 595 and 17.12). This, however, relates to the state of mind of the witness at the time of testifying at trial, and not to his state of mind at the time when the offence was committed.

11.4.4 Subject-matter of evidence lacking scientific validity

The court should reject claimed expert evidence on a subject whose scientific validity cannot be demonstrated, even though the expert may be very well qualified personally to express an opinion on it. The fact that a party may have retained the best available psychic to reconstruct the facts of the case does not mean that the psychic's evidence should be received. In the vast majority of cases, expert witnesses give evidence about subjects such as medicine or engineering which are universally recognized as a valid subject of scientific study. But it would be possible for an expert to offer to give evidence in a field whose scientific validity is not universally recognized. This need not necessarily be because the subject is in fact invalid. It may simply be that it has not yet developed to the extent necessary for recognition by the scientific community, that the requisite research has not yet been completed. The field of fingerprint evidence provides a good example. When first introduced as a method of detection in the nineteenth century, it was regarded with considerable scepticism and was rejected by the courts. But in due course, as the technology developed and its reliability was demonstrated, it reached a level of scientific validity which was acceptable as a basis for expert evidence. In other areas, for example that of polygraph tests, the courts have still not been persuaded that there is a sufficient level of scientific acceptance, and it may be that evidence of the results of such tests will never be regarded as a proper subject of expert evidence. Moreover, even within a scientifically recognized field, an expert may offer to give evidence about a theory or to make use of a methodology which is not recognized or is controversial, for example where he purports to provide a link between a substance ingested or inhaled by a person and the subsequent onset of cancer in that person. The law must have a test for determining what subjects and what methods are proper subjects of expert evidence, but for obvious reasons is to some extent in the hands of the community of experts in formulating such a test.

In *Gilfoyle* [2001] 2 Cr App R 57 a husband was charged with the murder of his wife. He asserted that she had committed suicide. On an application to the Court of Appeal to hear fresh evidence, the Court refused to receive evidence of a so-called 'psychological autopsy' for the purpose of resolving this question. The ostensible goal of this evidence, offered by a distinguished expert psychological witness, was to provide the court with a scientific reconstruction of the wife's mental state during the relevant period, and so to assist the court in determining whether it was likely that she might have committed suicide. Observing (with respect, rather glibly) that whether a person appeared to have been happy was not a matter which required assessment by experts, the Court held that psychological autopsies were not recognized as having any real scientific basis and so should not form the subject of expert evidence. The expert had never previously attempted a psychological autopsy (though this would not in itself have prevented the reception of this evidence); there was no literature or body of knowledge or experiments by reference to which the Court could test the methodology or the expert's particular application of it; but the Court did judge the expert's work negatively as being based mainly on information received from the accused and his family. In view of the relative paucity of authority in English law and the relatively substantial authority on this point in the United States, the Court placed some reliance on the decision of the United States Supreme Court in *Frye* v *US* 293 F 1013 (1923) which had laid down the test that the scientific validity of the subject or the expert's methodology must be 'generally accepted by the scientific community'. The Court held that this accorded with the test in English law. This may not have been a particularly apt choice of authority, inasmuch as a more recent Supreme Court in *Daubert* v *Merrell Dow Pharmaceuticals Inc.* 509 US 579 (1993) held that *Frye* should no longer be followed.[30] The Court in *Daubert*, reflecting a widely felt dissatisfaction with *Frye* (on a number of grounds, including the ground that *Frye* hands over the judicial responsibility for ruling on the admissibility of evidence to a vaguely-defined community of scientists) substituted a much wider test. The essential elements of the *Daubert* test, though expressed at much greater length in the opinion of the Court, are that the evidence must be relevant; that it must be reliable (based on a number of factors including but not limited to general scientific acceptance); and that there must be no reason to suppose that the evidence would mislead the jury or make the case unnecessarily complicated for them. An amendment to Federal Rule of Evidence 702, the expressed intent of which is to make that rule conform to *Daubert*, defines the component of reliability as meaning that '(1) the testimony is based upon sufficient facts or data, (2) the testimony is the product of reliable principles and methods, and (3) the witness has

---

[30] See also *Kumho Tire Co.* v *Carmichael* 119 S Ct 1167 (1999) extending the rule in *Daubert* to all expert evidence and not just evidence in traditionally scientific fields. It should be said that, in addition to reflecting general dissatisfaction with the *Frye* test, the Court in *Daubert* overruled the case on the technical ground that *Frye* had been decided on common law principles before the coming into effect of the Federal Rules of Evidence, and was not authoritative under those rules now used in the federal courts. This means that State courts need not necessarily follow *Daubert* for the purposes of State rules of evidence, and some State jurisdictions have chosen to continue to follow *Frye*, though the clear majority view is now against the older case.

applied the methods reliably to the facts of the case'.[31] The practical result of *Daubert* has been that the courts now tend to engage in a thorough pre-trial review of any expert evidence proposed to be tendered by the parties, and hearings on the issue of admissibility are now common. It is submitted that, while *Gilfoyle* is correct in insisting that the courts must scrutinize proposed expert evidence with some care, the question of what standards English courts will apply may not yet have been finally decided. *Frye* involves a number of difficulties, not the least of which is that it tends to exclude potentially useful techniques and methods about whose validity there may in fact be little real doubt. Given the length of time inevitably involved in the scientific publication and peer review process, the courts may deprive themselves of valuable work which is in the process of being validated. At the time of writing, the Law Commission has proposed a more stringent approach to the scientific reliability of expert evidence: see Consultation Paper No. 190 (2009).

11.4.5 Matters of law

Expert evidence is not admissible to prove the law of England. The law is a matter for the court with the assistance of argument from counsel, and any attempt to use expert evidence to establish the state of the law would usurp the function of the court.[32] However, the proof of foreign law is a question of fact, which can and should be proved by expert evidence (see 11.7.6).

11.5 MATERIALS USED BY EXPERT IN FORMING OPINION

One area which causes problems is the relationship of expert testimony to the primary or underlying data on which an expert opinion may be based, in whole or in part. An expert bases his opinion on many matters derived from his general knowledge, training and education, and his professional experience, including experience of other cases, research conducted for the purpose of the case in which he is retained, and authoritative works in the field.[33] Much of the material available to the expert from experience and research is material which would be inadmissible as evidence in its own right because it is hearsay. The question is, therefore, to what extent an expert can deal with such material in explaining his opinion.

At common law, an expert cannot, by using underlying facts as the basis of his opinion, make those facts evidence in the case, unless fortuitously he happens to have personal knowledge of the transactions concerned.[34] Therefore, either the expert or other witnesses, as appropriate,

---

[31] The *Daubert* Court did not intend to lay down a definitive list of factors relevant to reliability, but among others referred to whether the expert's theory is subjective or based on objectively verifiable criteria; whether his work has been published and subjected to peer review; the effect of any apparent rates of error in the work; whether the work was performed subject to proper controls; and (as in *Frye*) the extent to which the methodology has been accepted in the scientific community.

[32] *Liverpool Roman Catholic Diocese Trustees Inc.* v *Goldberg (No. 2)* [2001] 4 All ER 950; *Clarke* v *Marlborough Fine Art (London) Ltd* [2002] EWHC 11 (Ch); *Midland Bank Trust Co. Ltd* v *Hett Stubbs and Kemp (A Firm)* [1979] Ch 384.

[33] At common law, such a work is hearsay. But both in civil cases, by virtue of s. 7(2)(a) of the Civil Evidence Act 1995, and s. 118(1) of the Criminal Justice Act 2003, published works dealing with matters of a public nature, for example histories, scientific works, dictionaries, and maps, are admissible as evidence of facts of a public nature stated in them: see 8.7.2. It is submitted that, to the extent they are admitted for the purpose of explaining the expert's position, they may equally be held admissible as non-hearsay evidence, which might make their contents admissible without reference to the public nature of the facts. Cf. American Federal Rule of Evidence 803(18), which permits an expert to read passages from an authoritative work into the record, including any opinion expressed in the work, as an exception to the hearsay rule, without limitation on the nature of the facts.

[34] *English Exporters (London) Ltd* v *Eldonwall Ltd* [1973] Ch 415.

must prove by direct, competent evidence all the facts necessary to establish the elements of the charge, claim, or defence. The strictness of this requirement has been relaxed to some extent by statute. In civil cases, by virtue of the Civil Evidence Act 1995, evidence is no longer inadmissible by virtue of its hearsay quality, and there is accordingly no reason why material on which the expert bases his opinion should be either excluded or given limited evidential effect on this basis. The judge may decide, however, to accord little weight to such material other than as a basis for the expert's opinion. In criminal cases, as we shall see (11.6.2), s. 127 of the Criminal Justice Act 2003 permits the expert to base his opinion on statements of fact made by others for the purpose of the proceedings, subject to certain conditions. To the extent that he does so, the statements become evidence of the matters stated in them: s. 127(3). Even where s. 127 does not apply, the expert may obviously make use of any material relevant to his field of expertise. The function of the expert is to give his opinion on independently established facts. This does not mean, however, that the expert cannot base his opinion on other material, which may well be hearsay and inadmissible, and which is not a part of the factual background of the case which the other witnesses are to prove.[35]

The question of the evidential value of such material at common law is more difficult. In *Bradshaw* (1985) 82 Cr App R 79, the Court of Appeal held it to be proper for a judge to direct the jury that the evidence of an expert psychiatrist lacked weight, where his opinion about the accused's mental state at the time of the offence was based entirely on what the accused had told him (which the court held to be inadmissible hearsay). The Court seems to have been influenced in part by the fact that the defence was one of diminished responsibility, on which the accused bore the burden of proof. But it seems to have overlooked that psychiatric diagnosis is frequently based on interviews with the patient (see 11.4.1, 11.4.2), and that statements of symptoms by the patient, if contemporaneous, are admissible under a preserved common law exception to the hearsay rule (see 8.6).

In *Abadom*,[36] the accused was charged with robbery. The prosecution relied on the fact that the accused had broken a window during the robbery, and that fragments of glass adhering to and embedded in a pair of shoes taken from his home subsequently had come from the broken window. An expert witness gave evidence that glass taken from the window and the glass taken from the accused's shoes had an identical refractive index. The witness further testified that he had consulted statistics compiled by the Home Office Central Research Establishment, which revealed that the refractive index referred to occurred only in 4 per cent of all glass samples investigated by the Establishment. He then gave it as his opinion that there was a very strong likelihood that the glass found on the shoes had come from the broken window. The accused was convicted and appealed on the ground that the evidence of the statistics was hearsay and inadmissible. Dismissing the appeal, the Court of Appeal held that since the necessary primary facts as to the source of the glass samples had been proved by other competent evidence, the expert had been entitled to make use of statistical material in forming his opinion, in the same way as other work, including unpublished work in the field. Furthermore, the expert should refer to that material during his testimony, so that the court may weigh the cogency and probative value of the opinion. Reliance by an expert on the work of others did not infringe the rule against hearsay. It was conceded that if the same statistical information had been contained in an authoritative

---

[35] See also R. Pattendon [1982] Crim LR 85. Cf. American Federal Rule of Evidence 703: 'The facts or data in the particular case upon which an expert bases an opinion or inference may be those perceived or made known to the expert at or before the hearing. If of a type reasonably relied upon by experts in the particular field in forming opinions or inferences upon the subject, the facts or data need not be admissible in evidence'.

[36] [1983] 1 WLR 126. See also *Hodges* [2003] 2 Cr App R 247.

reference work, the expert might have relied upon it, and the Court saw no reason to preclude reference to unpublished data known to the expert.

While *Abadom* provides a more practical approach to the matter, it does not wholly resolve the question of the evidential status of the material on which the expert bases his opinion. In that case, the material relied upon by the expert was clearly reliable and was proved by other evidence. In such cases, it would seem unnecessarily artificial to direct the jury to regard such material only as forming the basis of the expert's opinion and not as evidence of any facts stated, when the expert has clearly proceeded on the basis that those facts are true and there is no reason to suppose otherwise. It may be that a distinction can be drawn between officially compiled data and publications of an academic kind, on the one hand, and statements of facts related specifically to a case such as those uncovered during an investigation, on the other. As to the former, there is support for the view taken in *Abadom*. In *H* v *Schering Chemicals Ltd*,[37] an action in which it was alleged that the defendants had negligently manufactured and marketed a drug, a question arose as to the admissibility of documents consisting of summaries of the results of research into the drug, and published articles and letters about the drug taken from medical journals. Bingham J held that, although the documents in question were hearsay and were not admissible under the Civil Evidence Act 1968 or otherwise in their own right, the plaintiffs were entitled to have their expert witnesses refer to them, and the court would thereupon consider them for the limited purpose of assessing the weight of that expert evidence. The learned judge also observed that where an expert refers to the results of research published by a reputable authority in a reputable journal, the court will ordinarily regard those results as supporting any inferences fairly to be drawn from them, unless and until some different approach is shown to be correct. (The evidence would now be admissible in a civil case under the Civil Evidence Act 1995.)

It is submitted that in the case of facts uncovered by the investigation, the present position is less clear. In a case to which s. 127 of the Criminal Justice Act 2003 does not apply, it may be that such materials are evidence of the facts stated only if they would be independently admissible under s. 116 or s. 117 of the Act. If that is correct, the jury must be directed that any material referred to by the expert is admissible only for the purpose of forming the basis of his opinion. But there is clearly a more compelling reason, in the case of factual material not covered by s. 127, for hesitating to make it evidence in the case generally. The potential for a party to admit a great deal of dubious material in the guise of the basis for an expert opinion is very real.

Section 118(1) of the Criminal Justice Act 2003 preserves:

> Any rule of law under which in criminal proceedings an expert witness may draw on the body of expertise relevant to his field.

But, except in cases covered by s. 127, it is by no means clear what that rule is, or what its effect is. *Abadom* cannot safely be taken as laying down a rule of general application, and some further clarification would be welcome as to the evidential value of this kind of material.

11.6 FORM OF EXPERT EVIDENCE: EXPERT REPORTS

11.6.1 Civil cases

The invariable contemporary practice is for the expert to prepare a written statement of his evidence. Such statements are known as expert reports. They tend to save time, narrow the issues

---

[37] [1983] 1 WLR 143. See also *Seyfang* v *G.D. Searle & Co.* [1973] QB 148; *Turner* [1975] QB 834.

in advance of trial, and make expert evidence more comprehensible and more readily accessible. Expert reports are a form of hearsay. They were first rendered admissible in civil cases by ss. 1 and 2(1) and (2) of the Civil Evidence Act 1972, which brought them under the umbrella of Part I of the Civil Evidence Act 1968, but subject to different rules of notice and disclosure from other statements of opinion, and statements of fact.[38] The Civil Evidence Act 1995 repealed Part I of the 1968 Act, and, in consequence, also repealed ss. 1 and 2(1) and (2) of the 1972 Act. The Civil Evidence Act 1995 abolishes the rule against hearsay in civil cases, and s. 1(2)(a) defines hearsay as follows:

'hearsay' means a statement made otherwise than by a person while giving oral evidence in the proceedings which is tendered as evidence of the matters stated.

Section 13 of the Act defines 'statement' as meaning 'any representation of fact or opinion, however made'. Thus, expert reports are now admissible by virtue of s. 1 of the Civil Evidence Act 1995, subject to the other provisions of the Act, as far as applicable.[39]

Moreover, the practice in relation to expert evidence has undergone fundamental changes as a result of the trenchant criticisms made by Lord Woolf (*Access to Justice. Final Report*, p. 137 *et seq.*) of the perceived abuses of the contentious and prolonged expert evidence which had become common in civil cases, and the consequent enactment of new provisions in the Civil Procedure Rules 1998. Rule 35.5 provides that expert evidence is now to be given by way of written report in all cases unless the court otherwise directs. For cases on the fast track, the court will not direct that oral expert evidence be given unless the interests of justice so require. Wherever possible, the evidence should be given by a single expert, and even where experts are retained by each side, they are to meet and, if possible, cooperate in producing a joint report (r. 35.12).[40] The contents of the report are regulated by r. 35.10, and r. 35.11 provides that once an expert's report has been disclosed, it may be used as evidence at trial by any party. This would accord with the rule of admissibility established by the Civil Evidence Act 1995.

11.6.2 Criminal cases

Until the coming into effect of the Criminal Justice Act 1988, there was no provision for the admissibility of expert reports in criminal cases. The hearsay provisions of the Criminal Evidence Act 1965 and the Police and Criminal Evidence Act 1984 applied only to statements of fact. However, s. 30 of the Criminal Justice Act 1988, provides:

(1) An expert report shall be admissible as evidence in criminal proceedings, whether or not the person making it attends to give oral evidence in those proceedings.
(2) If it is proposed that the person making the report shall not give oral evidence, the report shall only be admissible with the leave of the court.
(3) For the purpose of determining whether to give leave the court shall have regard—
    (a) to the contents of the report;

---

[38] See Civil Evidence Act 1972, s. 2(3); and the former RSC, Ord. 38, rr. 36–44. Statements of fact or opinion other than expert reports were governed by s. 8 of the Civil Evidence Act 1968 and RSC, Ord. 38, rr. 21–31.

[39] See generally 8.30 *et seq.*

[40] The purpose of this is to limit the area of disagreement between the experts and eliminate the need for evidence on undisputed subjects. Where a party's expert changes his opinion after a meeting of experts, that party will not be permitted to discard the expert and select another unless there is a compelling reason: see *Stallwood v David and another* [2007] 1 All ER 206.

> (b) to the reasons why it is proposed that the person making the report shall not give oral evidence;
> (c) to any risk, having regard in particular to whether it is likely to be possible to controvert statements in the report if the person making it does not attend to give oral evidence in the proceedings, that its admission or exclusion will result in unfairness to the accused, or, if there is more than one, to any of them; and
> (d) to any other circumstances that appear to the court to be relevant.
>
> (4) An expert report, when admitted, shall be evidence of any fact or opinion of which the person making it could have given oral evidence.
>
> (5) In this section 'expert report' means a written report by a person dealing wholly or mainly with matters on which he is (or would if living be) qualified to give expert evidence.

The most important point to note is that, while expert reports are now generally admissible in criminal proceedings, they are admissible only with the leave of the court, where it is not proposed to call the expert to give oral evidence. It is to be hoped that the courts will continue to exercise caution in the application of this new provision. An expert report may contain matters of fact as well as opinion, and may be extremely cogent. Subsection (4) makes admissible relevant findings of fact by the expert, such as facts which he has investigated in the course of forming his opinion.[41]

The rule enacted by s. 30 seems sensible and entirely appropriate in cases in which it is proposed that the expert should give oral evidence. The admission of his report in addition to his oral evidence will generally assist the jury in understanding both his evidence in chief and cross-examination. It is also obviously appropriate where there is no dispute about the expert evidence, for example where the evidence concerns analysis of a specimen of blood or of a suspected substance, which is effectively agreed. In such cases, the expert's attendance is unlikely to be required. His witness statement could in any event be read to the jury in the absence of objection, and the only practical change under the new rule is the helpful one that, unlike the witness statement, the expert report is admissible evidence in its own right, so that there is no reason why the jury should not take the report with them when they retire to consider their verdict. But in cases where the expert evidence is seriously disputed, for example evidence of a handwriting expert in a forgery case, it is submitted that only in very rare cases, for example where the expert has died before trial, should such reports be admitted if it is not proposed to call the expert to give oral evidence. Subsection (3)(c) makes clear that an important concern in such a case is the possibility that the opponent may be deprived of the opportunity to controvert the evidence. It should be borne in mind that juries often find expert evidence compelling, and when that evidence is reduced to writing and introduced into the jury room, its effect may be increased substantially.

Section 127 of the Criminal Justice Act 2003 enables an expert witness in criminal proceedings to base his opinion on a statement prepared by another person for the purposes of the proceedings subject to a number of conditions. The section provides:

> (1) This section applies if—
> (a) a statement has been prepared for the purposes of criminal proceedings,
> (b) the person who prepared the statement had or may reasonably be supposed to have had personal knowledge of the matters stated,

---

[41] For observations about the proper content of expert reports in criminal cases, see *B(T)* [2006] 2 Cr App R 3, [174]–[178]; *Harris* [2006] 1 Cr App R 5.

    (c) notice is given under the appropriate rules that another person (the expert) will in evidence
        given in the proceedings orally or under section 9 of the Criminal Justice Act 1967 (c. 80) base
        an opinion or inference on the statement, and
    (d) the notice gives the name of the person who prepared the statement and the nature of the
        matters stated.

  (2) In evidence given in the proceedings the expert may base an opinion or inference on the
statement.

  (3) If evidence based on the statement is given under subsection (2) the statement is to be treated as
evidence of what it states.

  (4) This section does not apply if the court, on an application by a party to the proceedings, orders that
it is not in the interests of justice that it should apply.

  (5) The matters to be considered by the court in deciding whether to make an order under subsection (4) include—

    (a) the expense of calling as a witness the person who prepared the statement;
    (b) whether relevant evidence could be given by that person which could not be given by the
        expert;
    (c) whether that person can reasonably be expected to remember the matters stated well enough
        to give oral evidence of them.

  (6) Subsections (1) to (5) apply to a statement prepared for the purposes of a criminal investigation as
they apply to a statement prepared for the purposes of criminal proceedings, and in such a case references
to the proceedings are to criminal proceedings arising from the investigation.

The section recognizes that an expert will not always personally investigate the facts as to
which his opinion is sought. He may rely on an investigation conducted by others, or an account
of the facts prepared by others, and may base his opinion on, or draw an inference from a statement made by whoever made the investigation or provided an account of the facts: s. 127(2).
The statement itself is hearsay if tendered to prove any matter stated in it in its own right, and
would be independently admissible, if at all, subject to the conditions in s. 117(5) of the Act: see
s. 117(4); 8.18. Section 127(1)(b) requires that the person who made the statement had, or may
reasonably be supposed to have had personal knowledge of the matters stated. This a guarantee
of the reliability and the accuracy of the statement akin to that required in the case of business
records generally: see s. 117(2)(b). If the expert bases an opinion on the facts stated, then by virtue
of s. 127(3), the statement is to be treated as evidence of those facts, so that essentially, s. 127(3)
creates an additional statutory exception to the rule against hearsay. Section 127(4) gives the
court power to order that the section should not apply in a particular case if it would not be in
the interests of justice for it to apply. Subsection (5) enumerates three matters to which the court
is to have regard before reaching this conclusion, all of which are concerned with the question
of whether the maker of the statement should be called for the purpose of giving evidence about
the facts in question. These matters are self-explanatory. They appear to require the court to take
a pragmatic view as to whether it would be worth calling the maker of the statement as a witness.
The question of whether the maker of the statement could reasonably be expected to remember
the facts well enough to give evidence about them is of interest. In the ordinary case, if the statement has been made for the purpose of the proceedings, one would expect that he would be able
to remember. But there may be cases where the statement consists of material such as detailed
financial records or technical data, where the maker of the statement could plausibly say that he
checked the data at the time of making the statement, and is satisfied that it is accurate, but no
longer has any recollection of the details. In such a case, it would be pointless to call him. There

may also be cases in which considerable time has elapsed between the making of the statement and the time of trial. Subsection (6) provides that the statement may have been made for the purposes of a criminal investigation, which may precede the commencement of proceedings by some time. Section 127(1)(c) and (d) require that notice be given of the intention to ask the expert to base an opinion on the statement, such notice to identify the maker of the statement and the matters stated. Rules in connection with notice of expert evidence are contained in Part 24 of the Criminal Procedure Rules 2005.

11.6.3 Pre-trial disclosure of expert evidence

Pre-trial disclosure of proposed expert evidence is essential to the smooth running of a trial. A party taken by surprise by expert evidence, which is often highly technical and detailed in nature, would have no adequate opportunity to prepare to meet it, and an adjournment with the accompanying waste of time and costs would be inevitable. (For judicial observations on this point, see the cases mentioned in note 9.) For this reason, rules of court now provide both in civil and criminal cases that the pre-trial disclosure of the evidence on which a party intends to rely is a condition of the evidence being admitted. Failure to disclose, subject to the court's discretionary powers, will result in exclusion of the evidence, and, very likely, in an order for costs.

11.6.3.1 Civil cases

In civil cases, the statutory basis for the rules is s. 2 of the Civil Evidence Act 1972, as amended by the Civil Evidence Act 1995. Rule 35.13 of the Civil Procedure Rules 1998 provides that a party who fails to disclose an expert report may not use that report or call the expert to give oral evidence without the court's permission. The full disclosure of expert reports is actually an inevitable consequence of the approach to expert evidence taken by the rules, given the emphasis on using joint experts and agreeing the contents of expert reports, reference to which was made at 11.1.2 and 11.3. Even when the parties retain their own separate experts, the contents of the reports cannot be agreed, and oral evidence is required, the rule of disclosure applies.[42] For the text of the rules, see *Blackstone's Civil Practice*, 2009 edn, appendix 1, Part 35.

11.6.3.2 Criminal cases

In criminal cases, provision for rules of court was made for the first time by s. 81 of the Police and Criminal Evidence Act 1984. This section, too, empowered the rules to provide that failure to disclose expert evidence on which a party proposed to rely would result in the exclusion of the evidence, subject to the court's discretion. The rules which now govern the disclosure of expert evidence in criminal cases are those in Part 24 of the Criminal Procedure Rules 2005. For the text of the rules, see *Blackstone's Criminal Practice*, 2009 edn, appendix 1, Part 24.[43]

---

[42] In cases decided under the former RSC, Ord. 38, rr. 36–44, it was held that the disclosure rules apply equally to parties qualified as experts who give evidence on their own behalf, and to 'in-house' experts giving evidence on behalf of their employers (*Shell Pensions Trust Ltd* v *Pell Frischmann and Partners* [1986] 2 All ER 911; cf. *Comfort Hotels Ltd* v *Wembley Stadium Ltd* [1988] 1 WLR 872).

[43] See also *Disclosure—Expert's Evidence and Unused Material: Guidance Booklet for Experts*, February 2006, produced by the Attorney General for the guidance of prosecution experts.

11.6.4 Privilege

It should be noted that consultations between a party, his legal advisers, and an expert are in principle privileged.[44] But if it is intended to call the expert as a witness, waiver of the privilege is the price of doing so. The Civil Procedure Rules 1998 do not alter this position, but because of the emphasis on joint experts and expert reports, the circumstances in which it will be feasible to maintain any privilege are greatly reduced. For example, r. 35.10 requires an expert report to disclose any oral or written instructions on the basis of which the report was written. The instructions are not privileged in that situation, although r. 35.10(4) provides some protection against the compelled disclosure of other documents which may be privileged and against examination of the witness intended to reveal privileged information, unless the court is satisfied that the instructions as stated in the report are incomplete or inaccurate. It is unlikely that a party would recover the costs of instructing an expert who has not been approved by the court under r. 35.4. Nonetheless, there will be cases in which it is prudent for a party to obtain a privileged opinion from an expert whom it is not intended to call in the event of a trial, for example, where it is uncertain whether the evidence justifies commencing a claim, or where the highly technical nature of the evidence requires the services of an expert to explain the nature of the case to a party or his legal advisers with a view to evaluating the case.[45]

11.7 COMMON SUBJECTS OF EXPERT EVIDENCE

Although there is a considerable number of subjects upon which expert opinion evidence may be admitted, the following are of common occurrence in practice, and merit some individual mention.

11.7.1 Scientific and technical matters

The range of scientific and technological evidence is obviously vast, and is continually expanding. Among the most common kinds of scientific witnesses are doctors, who may give evidence in personal injury cases, disputes over disability, or medical negligence cases; engineers, who may give evidence in construction cases and cases of accidents involving mechanical devices from cars to gas stoves; and accountants who may give evidence in a wide variety of commercial cases, as well as dealing with life expectancy issues in wrongful death cases. There are, of course, experts who specialize in every area of these disciplines, and experts who develop areas of specialization of their own in existing areas such as applied economics, often used in the calculation of damage awards, and new areas such as information technology. The particular field of forensic science ranges over a very wide range of matters—of particular though not exclusive significance in criminal cases—matters such as the presence and age of fingerprints and blood stains; the analysis of DNA samples; the examination of weapons and ammunition; the identification of drugs, poisons and chemicals, fibres and paint; the comparison of specimens of handwriting; the authenticity

---

[44] See generally 14.10; *Causton v Mann Egerton (Johnsons) Ltd* [1974] 1 WLR 162; but see also as to cases involving the welfare of children *Re L (A Minor) (Police Investigation: Privilege)* [1997] AC 16; 14.13.

[45] Disclosure of an expert report does not necessarily waive privilege in earlier versions of the report (*Jackson v Marley Davenport Ltd* [2004] 1 WLR 2926) though on the facts, two or more versions may be so inter-connected that disclosure of the final report does require disclosure of earlier versions: for the applicable principles, see 13.2.1.

of audio and video recordings; and analysis of samples of drugs, blood and other bodily fluids, and tissue.

11.7.2 Mental state or condition

Expert evidence is frequently admissible on the issue of the condition or state of mind of the accused in a criminal case. In some cases, for example, where a defence such as insanity or diminished responsibility is raised, the issue cannot be decided without competent psychiatric evidence, and the same is true of related defences such as insane automatism, which involve mental illness.[46] As we have seen (11.4.2) expert evidence is generally not admissible on questions such as intent, which are matters within the competence of the tribunal of fact, applying its experience of everyday life, but even on an issue of intent, expert evidence will be admissible where the accused's ability to form the required intent is alleged to have been affected by some condition of mind which requires expert explanation.[47] It has been held that expert evidence cannot be admitted on the issue of whether the accused was provoked, which is an issue generally within the competence of a jury, but *quaere*, in the light of *DPP v Camplin* [1978] AC 705, whether the jury should not have the advantage of expert evidence in cases in which the accused's likely reaction to provocation might have been affected by some mental condition. The expert evidence of psychiatrists, psychologists, and other professionals with relevant expertise is frequently used to assist the court in dealing with questions relating to the welfare of children. This, too, involves evidence of state of mind, but in a much broader sense than the kinds of evidence adduced in criminal cases. In *Blackburn* [2005] 2 Cr App R 440, expert evidence was held to be admissible to show that a confession made by the accused was unreliable because of the phenomenon of coerced compliant confessions (see 9.11).

11.7.3 Specimens of handwriting

In cases such as forgery where it is necessary to establish whether a document, or part of a document, is in the handwriting of a particular person, an expert may scientifically compare the questioned document with a known specimen of that person's handwriting.[48] Section 8 of the Criminal Procedure Act 1865 provides:

> Comparison of a disputed writing with any writing proved to the satisfaction of the court to be genuine shall be permitted to be made by witnesses; and such writings, and the evidence of witnesses respecting the same, may be submitted to the court and jury as evidence of the genuineness or otherwise of the writing in dispute.

The phrase 'proved to the satisfaction of the court' has given rise to difficulties in ascertaining the applicable standard of proof in such cases: see *Ewing* [1983] QB 1039; *Angeli* [1979] 1

---

[46] *Smith* [1979] 1 WLR 1445; *Dix* (1981) 74 Cr App R 306; *Byrne* [1960] 2 QB 396. And see the unusual case of *Chan-Fook* [1994] 1 WLR 689, where the prosecution relied on an alleged psychiatric injury to establish assault occasioning actual bodily harm.

[47] *Toner* (1991) 93 Cr App R 382 (hypoglycaemic state); contrast *Gilfoyle* [2001] 2 Cr App R 57 (see 11.4.3); *Chard* (1971) 56 Cr App R 268; *Masih* [1986] Crim LR 395. And see *Huckerby* [2004] EWCA Crim 3251, in which expert evidence that the accused suffered from post-traumatic stress disorder was admitted for the purpose of enabling the jury to assess whether it was likely that he had panicked and acted in a manner in which he might otherwise not have acted.

[48] In *Lockheed-Arabia v Owen* [1993] QB 780, it was held proper for the expert to use a copy of the questioned document, where the original had been lost, though the weight of the expert's evidence may not be as great in such a case.

WLR 26. This is dealt with at 4.14. A lay witness who is personally familiar with the handwriting of the person concerned may give evidence about the authenticity of the document, but, in the absence of any evidence personal familiarity, the evidence must be given by an expert, based on a scientific comparison.

11.7.4 Art, literature, learning, etc.

Expert evidence on these subjects may be adduced where matters concerning specialised fields fall to be proved. There may be various uses of it, but one which tends to occur frequently is in relation to the defence of 'public good' under s. 4 of the Obscene Publications Act 1959, as amended. The defence provides that a person shall not be convicted of an offence under s. 2 in relation to an obscene article, 'if it is proved that publication of the article in question is justified as being for the public good on the ground that it is in the interests of science, literature, art or learning, or of other objects of general concern'. The phrase 'other objects of general concern' is restricted to the specific matters alluded to in s. 4 and does not permit of a wider interpretation, for instance the relief of sexual tension in the context of the general pyschiatric health of the community.[49]

Expert evidence is admissible to prove or disprove the defence under s. 4 which is clearly a matter upon which the jury will require guidance, in order to arrive at a proper opinion. However, the defence will only arise on the assumption that the jury consider the article to be obscene, which is a question of fact for them, and upon which expert evidence is not admissible.[50]

11.7.5 Professional and trade practices and standards

Evidence from members of a profession or trade, either generally or in a particular field of reference or a particular geographical area, will be admissible as expert opinion evidence to show the practice of the profession or trade, or the standard expected of reasonably competent members thereof. Such evidence is relevant to establish customary terms of contracts of various sorts, the existence of trade practices, the reasonableness of covenants in restraint of trade, and perhaps most importantly, the standard of professional competence reasonably expected of a person against whom negligence is alleged in the exercise of his profession.

11.7.6 Foreign law

Questions of foreign law, which for this purpose means the law prevailing in any jurisdiction other than England and Wales, are questions of fact, and should, where relevant, be proved by evidence, like any other question of fact.[51] It is obviously desirable, and has always been the practice, that foreign law should be proved by expert evidence from a witness who has knowledge or

---

[49] *DPP* v *Jordan* [1977] AC 699.

[50] *Attorney-General's Reference (No. 3 of 1977)* [1978] 1 WLR 1123. In an exceptional case, a jury may be assisted by expert evidence on the likely effect of material on special classes of reader, e.g, children, in their task of deciding whether the material would be likely to deprave or corrupt: *DPP* v *A & BC Chewing Gum Ltd* [1968] 1 QB 159. See also *Skirving* [1985] QB 819, in which an expert was permitted to give evidence for the prosecution as to the methods and effects of ingesting cocaine (a matter said to be outside the competence of people generally) in order to assist the jury in deciding whether a book dealing with those matters had a tendency to deprave and corrupt. The issue of whether the book in fact had that tendency was, however, a question of fact within the sole province of the jury.

[51] Notwithstanding this, such questions are a matter for the judge. The judge may have to decide between conflicting opinions: *Re Duke of Wellington, Glentanar* v *Wellington* [1947] Ch 506; affirmed (CA) [1948] Ch 118. As to

experience of the law concerned. Moreover, the court should resist the temptation of delving into foreign law books or reports, and accept the expert evidence offered to it, certainly in any case where there is no dispute between the experts (*Bumper Development Corporation* v *Commissioner of Police of the Metropolis* [1991] 1 WLR 1362). In relation to civil proceedings, s. 4(1) of the Civil Evidence Act 1972 now provides that:

> It is hereby declared that in civil proceedings a person who is suitably qualified to do so on account of his knowledge or experience is competent to give expert evidence as to the law of any country or territory outside [England and Wales] irrespective of whether he has acted or is entitled to act as a legal practitioner there.

The form of the section as a declaration suggests that it is intended to confirm what was thought to be the position at common law, and the common law authorities broadly support this view.[52]

Section 4(2), designed to avoid the embarrassing prospect of different decisions by English courts on identical points of foreign law, provides for proof of such points by reference to reported decisions of superior courts in England in which they have previously been decided. Such evidence, of which notice must be given, may be contradicted, for example by evidence that the foreign law in question has changed, or simply that the point was wrongly decided in the earlier case. Moreover, a proviso to s. 4(2) provides that the provision does not apply where there are conflicting earlier decisions on the same point of law. But, if no such countervailing evidence is adduced, the earlier decision will be sufficient to prove the point of foreign law concerned.[53] There is older authority to the effect that at common law, a point of foreign law must be proved in each case by new expert evidence, notwithstanding that it may already have been decided in an earlier English case case: *M'Cormick* v *Garnett* (1854) 5 De GM & G 278. This may be the position in criminal cases. But it is submitted that the judge could properly take judicial notice of the earlier decision. It would remain open to a party, as it would under s. 4(2), to show that there are conflicting English decisions on the point, that the foreign law has changed since the earlier decision, or that the foreign law must be applied differently on the facts of the instant case.

11.8 NON-EXPERT OPINION EVIDENCE: PRINCIPLES OF ADMISSIBILITY

As was observed at the outset of this chapter, opinion evidence was rejected at common law as evidence of the truth of the matters believed, at least partly because it tended to usurp the function of the court. Nowhere is this defect more apparent than in relation to the opinion of persons not qualified as experts on matters directly in issue in the proceedings. But by s. 3(2) of the Civil Evidence Act 1972:

> It is hereby declared that where a person is called as a witness in any civil proceedings, a statement opinion by him on any relevant matter on which he is not qualified to give expert evidence, if

---

the law of other parts of Her Majesty's dominions see the Evidence (Colonial Statutes) Act 1907, s. 1; the Colonial Laws Validity Act 1865, s. 6; and the British Law Ascertainment Act 1859.

[52] See *Baron de Bode's Case* (1845) 8 QB 208; *Vander Donckt* v *Thellusson* (1849) 8 CB 812; *Re Dost Aly Khan's Goods* (1880) 6 PD 6; *Ajami* v *Comptroller of Customs* [1954] 1 WLR 1405; *Brailey* v *Rhodesia Consolidated Ltd* [1912] 2 Ch 95. Qualification to practise in the jurisdiction was required at common law (*Bristow* v *Sequeville* (1850) 5 Ex 275) but it was no bar that the expert had not actually done so (*Barford* v *Barford* [1918] P 140).

[53] *Phoenix Marine Inc.* v *China Ocean Shipping Co.* [1999] 1 Lloyd's Rep 682; see also r. 33.7 of the Civil Procedure Rules 1998.

made as a way of conveying relevant facts personally perceived by him, is admissible as evidence of what he perceived.

It is an open question whether this declaration accurately represents the state of the common law, and therefore whether it may apply in effect to criminal cases also.[54] It is submitted that this is and should be the case. The admissibility of such opinion evidence is confined to matters within the general competence and experience of people generally, which they are able and accustomed to appreciate by a process of observation of commonplace facts, and which require no process of conscious deduction. They are in reality matters of perception, perceived directly by the witness while using his ordinary senses, so that while in an abstract sense it may be said that the witness is expressing an opinion, he is in fact merely using natural language to convey facts which he perceived, and which would otherwise be difficult, if not impossible, to relate. The American Federal Rule of Evidence 701 expresses the same idea in the following language:

> *Opinion testimony by lay witnesses.* If the witness is not testifying as an expert, his testimony in the form of opinions or inferences is limited to those opinions or inferences which are (a) rationally based on the perception of the witness and (b) helpful to a clear understanding of his testimony or the determination of a fact in issue.

There can be no final rule on where the line of admissibility may be drawn. In any case tried without a jury, the matter is likely to be resolved by the judge taking a realistic view of what the witness is trying to say. The following cases are examples only of the use of non-expert opinion evidence.

11.8.1 Identity and resemblance

A witness may state that a person, thing or document is the same as, or bears a resemblance to, one that he has seen on a previous occasion. The matter is one of perception, and there would be formidable difficulties of proof in very many cases if this were not permitted.[55] Both the identifying witness and any other person who witnessed a previous identification, may give evidence of what transpired on that occasion.[56] This is subject, in criminal cases, to the safeguards required in the interests of preventing potentially misleading or incorrect evidence being given of identification, and to the various administrative requirements for the proper treatment of evidence of identification.[57] But in general, a witness may give evidence of matters within this category, and may be referred to any photograph or other exhibit necessary to enable him to explain what he perceived.

---

[54] The point apparently passed unnoticed in *Rasool* v *West Midland Passenger Transport Executive* [1974] 3 All ER 638, where a statement made by the defendants' witness (admissible otherwise under s. 2 of the Civil Evidence Act 1968) contained the words: 'The bus driver was in no way to blame for the accident'. This statement was no doubt thought to be justified by the fact that the witness was merely seeking to explain what she had seen, but the decision is hardly satisfactory.

[55] See, e.g., *Fryer* v *Gathercole* (1849) 4 Ex 262 per Pollock CB. The rule also applies to identification by handwriting (*Doe d Mudd* v *Suckermore* (1836) 5 Ad & El 703) or the sound of a voice (*Robb* (1991) 93 Cr App R 161) with which the witness is personally familiar.

[56] *Osbourne* [1973] QB 678.

[57] *Turnbull* [1977] QB 224. See generally 16.12.

11.8.2 Mental or physical condition

The rule applies to observable conditions, insofar as expert evidence is not required of them. The condition of the witness himself is admissible as well as that of others, and he may state his reaction to events or circumstances, or his reasons for his acts, provided that he does not infringe the rule against previous consistent statements. He may not, however, state his opinion of the intentions of others,[58] which must be objectionable as inadmissible opinion or hearsay, or both. Wherever the condition of a person must be proved with more precision than a lay person can provide, so that the court must have expert evidence of it, the opinion of a witness other than an expert is inadmissible. A good illustration is *Davies* [1962] 1 WLR 1111, where it was held that, although a lay witness could state that a person had been drinking, which was a matter of general competence, he might not state that that person was unfit to drive through drink, which was a matter of expert medical evidence.[59] For the same reason, a lay witness may not be called to prove the sanity of another[60] although his evidence is apparently admissible on the issue of his own sanity.[61]

11.8.3 Age, speed, value

These matters are usually assumed to be within ordinary human experience, although opinion evidence can obviously prove them only to a reasonable approximation.[62] The weight of such evidence will depend, *inter alia*, on the apparent experience of the witness, e.g., as a driver or passenger if his evidence relates to speed. It would seem that evidence of value should be admissible only in respect of objects in common use and not where the object is, for example, an antique or otherwise of special value, upon which expert evidence would be required.[63]

11.9 RECOMMENDED FURTHER READING

Blom-Cooper, L., 'Experts and assessors: past, present and future' (2002) **21** *Civil Justice Quarterly* 341.

Dwyer, D., 'The causes and manifestations of bias in civil expert evidence' (2007) **26** *Civil Justice Quarterly* 425.

Edis, A., 'Privilege and immunity: problems of expert evidence' (2007) **26** *Civil Justice Quarterly* 40.

Jackson, J.D., 'The ultimate issue rule: one rule too many?' [1984] *Criminal Law Review* 75.

Roberts, A., 'Drawing on expertise: legal decision-making and the reception of expert evidence' [2008] *Criminal Law Review* 443.

Spencer, J.R., 'The neutral expert: an implausible bogey' [1991] *Criminal Law Review* 106.

---

[58] *Townsend v Moore* [1905] P 66.

[59] On the same point see *Tagg* [2002] 1 Cr App R 22, in which on a charge of being drunk on an aircraft, members of the cabin crew who had observed the defendant were permitted to state the opinion that he was drunk.

[60] *Neville* (1837) Craw & D Abr Cas 96; *Greenslade v Dare* (1855) 20 Beav 284.

[61] *Hunter v Edney* (1885) 10 PD 93.

[62] No one is liable to be convicted of speeding on the uncorroborated evidence of opinion of one witness as to speed: Road Traffic Regulation Act 1984, s. 89(2).

[63] *Beckett* (1913) 8 Cr App R 204.

11.10 QUESTIONS FOR DISCUSSION BASED ON *R v COKE; LITTLETON* AND *BLACKSTONE v COKE* (for case files go to the Online Resource Centre)

11.10.1 *Coke; Littleton*

1. Discuss the relevance and admissibility of the expert testimony to be given by (a) Mr Hale; (b) Dr Vesey; (c) Dr Espinasse. What steps should (a) the prosecution and (b) Coke's solicitors take before trial with respect to this evidence?

2. Frame a series of questions designed to adduce the evidence in chief of Mr Hale. How would you make use of the chart which he has prepared?

3. Assume that you act for Coke, and that your handwriting expert has advised you that Mr Hale's conclusion can be attacked, because a leading work on the scientific examination of documents suggests that he had insufficient known samples of Coke's handwriting to enable a valid comparison to be made. How would you cross-examine Mr Hale, and what use might be made of the leading work?

11.10.2 *Blackstone v Coke*

Discuss the principles applicable to the evidence of Mr Hale, Dr Vesey, and Dr Espinasse, on the assumption that the claimant proposes to call each to give evidence at trial. What steps should each side take?

11.11 GENERAL QUESTIONS FOR DISCUSSION

1. What is the general rule regarding the admissibility of opinion evidence?

2. For opinion evidence to be admitted it is always necessary for the witness to have identifiable paper qualifications in his field of expertise. Is this correct?

3. Which provisions of the Civil and Criminal Procedure Rules, respectively, are relevant to an expert witness's independence and objectivity?

4. What is the function of the expert witness in a trial?

5. Can an expert witness give evidence on the 'ultimate issue' in a case?

6. Is expert evidence admissible on the issue of the credibility of a witness?

7. What issues should a judge consider if a party wishes to adduce expert evidence of a novel nature?

8. How are expert reports admitted in evidence in civil and criminal proceedings?

9. In what circumstances may an expert witness provide an opinion based on someone else's statement?

10. What is non-expert opinion evidence?

12

PREVIOUS JUDGMENTS AS EVIDENCE

12.1 INTRODUCTION

There are at least two theoretical objections to the use of previous judgments to prove the truth of facts upon which they were based. The first is that such evidence would be mere evidence of the opinion of the previous court, by which strangers (i.e., those who were not parties) to the judgment are not bound, and should not be prejudiced. The second is that a judgment so used is, in effect, hearsay. For these reasons, the common law adopted the position, albeit not without some hesitation, that previous judgments should not be admissible as evidence of the truth of the facts on which they are based, as against strangers to the judgment.

However, the position was by no means as simple as that. Although a judgment was inadmissible for the purpose of proving the truth of facts on which it was based, it was admissible to prove, if relevant to do so, the existence and formal details of the judgment itself, its content, or its legal effect. Moreover, even if it were sought to use the judgment for the purpose of proving the truth of facts on which it was based, the position was different in a case where the parties to the instant proceedings had also been the parties to the previous proceedings. In that case, the common law's sensible policy of preventing repetitious and oppressive litigation, was best served by treating as binding the final judgment of a court of competent jurisdiction, as a definitive finding of the facts in issue as between those parties. A judgment could, therefore, be relied upon if the issues were re-opened in subsequent proceedings between the same parties or those claiming through them. Persons claiming through a party to previous proceedings are known for this purpose as that party's 'privies'. Privity may arise in various relationships, for example 'in estate', between lessor and lessee, vendor and purchaser; 'in blood', between ancestor and heir; or 'in law', between testator and executor. In these and other cases of privity the privy stands, as it were, in the shoes of the party with respect to the instant proceedings.

In considering the evidential value of previous judgments, therefore, the following cases must be distinguished:

(a) Judgments as evidence of their own existence, content and legal effect.
(b) Judgments as evidence of the truth of facts on which they are based, as between the parties to the proceedings in which the judgment was given, and their privies.
(c) Judgments as evidence of the truth of facts on which they are based, as between strangers to the proceedings in which the judgment was given, or as between parties to the proceedings (or their privies) and strangers.

For our purposes, it is necessary to consider only the first and third of these subjects. Judgments as evidence of their own existence, content and legal effect constitute a compact topic which presents few difficulties. It is dealt with in Part A of this chapter. Judgments as evidence of the truth of the facts on which they are based is a much larger and more difficult subject, one which has come a long way since the celebrated rule in *Hollington v Hewthorn* (now largely abrogated by statute in both civil and criminal cases) and which is of great practical importance. It is dealt with in Part B of this chapter. The subject of judgments as evidence of the truth of the facts as between parties is also of great importance in practice. But it has become a subject which has little relationship in modern practice to the law of evidence. In civil cases, it takes the form of estoppel *per rem judicatam* and issue estoppel, which are now areas of substantive law of considerable complexity and sophistication; indeed, specialized areas in their own right. In criminal cases, it comprises the subject of pleas in bar, which fulfil functions not dissimilar to that of the *res judicata* doctrine, and are now generally thought of as procedural matters. For this reason, although a summary of these subjects was provided in earlier editions of this work, the time has come to recognize that they fall outside the scope of a general work on evidence.[1]

A JUDGMENTS AS EVIDENCE OF THEIR EXISTENCE, CONTENT, AND LEGAL EFFECT

SUMMARY OF MAIN POINTS

- At common law a judgment given in previous litigation is conclusive evidence of its own existence, content, and legal effect. But it is not admissible as evidence of the facts on which it is based except as between parties to that litigation.

---

[1] In relation to estoppel *per rem judicatam* and issue estoppel, reference should be made to the current edition of *Spencer Bower and Turner, The Doctrine of Res Judicata*, or to the section on the subject in *Halsbury's Laws of England*. In relation to pleas in bar, see *Blackstone's Criminal Practice*, 2009 edn, para. D12.19 *et seq.*

- At common law there is also a rule that a previous verdict may not be contradicted in subsequent
  litigation. This does not necessarily prevent evidence given in the previous trial from being given
  again in a later trial.

12.2 JUDGMENTS CONCLUSIVE EVIDENCE OF THEIR OWN EXISTENCE, CONTENT, AND LEGAL EFFECT

Judgments of courts of competent jurisdiction are public records, and so presumed to be faithfully made and recorded. Thus, at common law, all such judgments were not only evidence, but conclusive evidence of their own existence, content and legal effect, both against parties or their privies, and against strangers; even though, as we have seen, they were not even admissible evidence of any facts on which the judgment was based. The common law rule was adopted, without changing its nature or scope, by s. 9 of the Civil Evidence Act 1968. It is provided in s. 7(2) and (4) of the Civil Evidence Act 1995 that:

> (2) The common law rules effectively preserved by section 9(1) and (2)(b) to (d) of the Civil Evidence Act 1968, that is, any rule of law whereby in civil proceedings—
>
> ...
>
>   (c) records (for example, the records of certain courts, treaties, Crown grants, pardons and commissions) are admissible as evidence of facts stated in them, shall continue to have effect.
>
> (4) The words in which a rule of law mentioned in this section is described are intended only to identify the rule and shall not be construed as altering it in any way.

The same rule is preserved in criminal cases by s. 118(1) of the Criminal Justice Act 2003.

Thus, in an action for malicious prosecution, the record of the verdict of the jury acquitting the plaintiff was conclusive evidence of the fact that the defendant had prosecuted the plaintiff unsuccessfully, but was inadmissible to prove either the plaintiff's innocence of the offence charged or malice on the part of the defendant (*Purcell* v *M'Namara* (1808) 1 Camp 199). Similarly, where an action was brought against a master in respect of the negligence of his servant and a verdict was entered for the plaintiff, in a subsequent action by the master against the servant the first judgment was conclusive of the amount of damages awarded against the master, but was inadmissible to prove that the servant had been negligent (*Green* v *New River Co.* (1792) 4 TR 590).

12.2.1 Rule against contradiction of previous judgment or verdict

It follows from the conclusive nature of the content and legal effect of the judgment, that a witness cannot be heard to give evidence which has the effect of contradicting it. Thus, although the judgment is inadmissible to prove the truth of any facts on which it was based, it is admissible for the purpose of contradicting a witness who seeks to give evidence conflicting with its formal parts. This principle is known as the rule against contradiction of previous judgments or verdicts. In *Watson* v *Little* (1860) 5 Hurl & N 572 a witness gave evidence that a son was born to her on a certain day, being five days after her marriage. Evidence was received to contradict her in the form of an affiliation order made by justices, since deceased, reciting that they had found on the evidence of the witness that the child had been born on a day prior to her marriage. This evidence, though admissible to contradict the witness, was not evidence that the child was illegitimate.

And in a trial for handling stolen goods, the evidence of a witness that he stole the goods in question may apparently be contradicted by evidence of the witness's acquittal on that charge (*M'Cue* (1831) Jebb 120).[2]

In *Sambasivam* v *Public Prosecutor, Federation of Malaya* [1950] AC 458, the accused was charged with two offences, possessing a firearm and possessing ammunition, contrary to certain emergency regulations of the Federated Malay States. Under the emergency regulations the case was tried by a judge and two assessors. At his trial, the accused was acquitted of possessing the ammunition, and on the charge of possessing the firearm, the court being unable to agree, there was a new trial with different assessors. In the course of the new trial, the prosecution sought to rely upon a confession, allegedly made by the accused, to both offences. No warning was given to the assessors that there would be a reference to the ammunition charge. The Privy Council quashed the conviction on the new trial. The prosecution were not entitled to introduce the reference to the charge on which the accused had been acquitted without making it plain that the accused was not guilty of that charge, which had obvious consequences affecting the reliability of the confession as a whole. The Judicial Committee said (*ibid.* at 479):

> The effect of a verdict of acquittal pronounced by a competent court on a lawful charge and after a lawful trial is not completely stated by saying that the person acquitted cannot be tried again for the same offence. To that it must be added that the verdict is binding and conclusive in all subsequent proceedings between the parties to the adjudication. The maxim *Res judicata pro veritate accipitur* is no less applicable to criminal than to civil proceedings.[3]

But the rule against contradiction of previous verdicts does not necessarily preclude the prosecution from tendering in a subsequent case evidence previously tendered in a case in which the accused was acquitted. In *Z* [2000] 2 AC 483, it was held that the fact that the accused had been tried and acquitted in respect of certain previous conduct did not of itself prevent the court from admitting evidence of that previous conduct in a later case under the similar fact rule.[4] The accused was charged with rape. He had been tried for other alleged rapes on four previous occasions, and had been convicted in respect of one of the alleged offences and acquitted in respect of the others. The prosecution sought to call the complainants in the three cases in which the accused had been acquitted to give evidence of a striking similarity between the accused's conduct in those cases and his alleged conduct in the instant case. The accused contended that the evidence was inadmissible because, in the light of his acquittals, the admission of the evidence exposed him to double jeopardy and violated the rule against the contradiction of previous verdicts. The House, correctly it is submitted, rejected the argument that the admission of the evidence infringed the rule against double jeopardy, because there was no question of the accused being tried again for an offence of which he had been acquitted; the only issue was whether evidence adduced in the previous trial could be adduced again in the instant case. But the House also rejected the argument that the admission of the evidence violated the rule against the contradiction of previous

---

[2] Though in criminal cases this principle must now be viewed in the light of *Z* [2000] 2 AC 483 (below).

[3] It was argued in *DPP* v *Humphrys* [1977] AC 1 that this decision was authority for the proposition that the doctrine of issue estoppel was applicable to criminal cases in the same way as to civil cases, but the House of Lords rejected the argument. There is a difference between seeking to contradict an acquittal and re-opening an issue in the previous case.

[4] I.e., as relevant evidence of bad character. At the time of the decision in *Z*, evidence of similar facts was admissible at common law. Such evidence is now admissible by virtue of gateway (d) under s. 101(1) of the Criminal Justice Act 2003: see 6.3.3; 6.10. See also *McAllister* [2009] 1 Cr App R 10.

verdicts, and this decision is far less satisfactory. Lord Hutton, in an opinion with which the other members of the House agreed, considered *Sambasivam* and concluded (at 504):

> My Lords, I consider, with great respect, that in *Sambasivam's* case it was right to set aside the conviction, and that the proper ground for doing so was for the reason given by Lord Pearce in *Connelly* v *Director of Public Prosecutions* [1964] AC 1254, 1362, 1364, namely, that a man should not be prosecuted a second time where the two offences were in fact founded on one and the same incident and that a man ought not to be tried for a second offence which was manifestly inconsistent on the facts with a previous acquittal. The carrying of the revolver and the carrying of the ammunition constituted one and the same incident, and the appellant having been acquitted of having possession of the ammunition the allegation of carrying the revolver (in which some of the ammunition was loaded) was manifestly inconsistent with the previous acquittal. But I consider that provided that a defendant is not placed in double jeopardy in the way described by Lord Pearce, evidence which is relevant on a subsequent prosecution is not inadmissible because it shows or tends to show that the defendant was, in fact, guilty of an offence of which he had earlier been acquitted.

Thus, while the previous verdict cannot be re-opened for the purpose of convicting the accused of the offence in that case, evidence tending to cast doubt on the previous acquittal is admissible if relevant to the present case, even though that evidence suggests that the accused ought to have been convicted in the previous trial. This holding involved overruling the decision in *G (An Infant)* v *Coltart* [1967] 1 QB 432, which had suggested that evidence should not be admissible in such circumstances. The decision in *Sambasivam* survives because the two offences were inextricably intertwined—the ammunition could not be separated from the revolver. But on this basis, it may be that the decision in *Sambasivam* owes more to the double jeopardy principle than the rule against contradiction of previous verdicts: if he were to be convicted of carrying the revolver, he must necessarily be convicted of possessing the ammunition. It is not clear that the House in *Z* fully recognized this distinction. Although the reasoning of the House in *Z* is consistent with the double jeopardy principle—there was no question of the accused being re-tried for or convicted of the previous charge—it may not be entirely consistent with the rule against contradiction of previous verdicts. The latter arises from the formal validity of the previous verdict, not from the principle of preventing a second prosecution. It is submitted, however, that the decision in *Z* can to some extent be reconciled with *Sambasivam*, if the true effect of an acquittal is borne in mind. In *Terry* [2005] QB 996, the Court of Appeal pointed out that an acquittal is not conclusive evidence of innocence. This seems self-evident. Given that, to obtain a conviction, the prosecution must prove the guilt of the accused beyond reasonable doubt, a verdict of not guilty does not necessarily indicate anything more than the existence of a reasonable doubt as to guilt. Nor does it generally follow from an acquittal (though it may do so in a particular case) that all the issues in the case must have been resolved in favour of the accused. Thus, in *Z*, it might be argued that the jury did not necessarily reject the evidence of the complainants in whose cases they decided to acquit the accused. Nonetheless, the reconciliation not altogether satisfactory, and some further elucidation of the continuing effect of the rule against contradiction of previous verdicts in criminal cases seems necessary.

12.3 JUDGMENTS *IN REM* AND *IN PERSONAM*

The position as to the effect of a judgment is somewhat more complicated where the judgment in question is a judgment '*in rem*'. A judgment *in rem* may be defined as one which has the effect of declaring the status of a person or thing for all legal purposes and hence as against all the world, as opposed to a judgment ('*in personam*') which has effect merely to establish the rights and obligations, in respect of the subject-matter of the proceedings, of the parties and their privies.

Whether a judgment is one *in rem* is a matter of law, to be decided having regard to the jurisdiction of the court to utter such a judgment, and to the nature and form of the judgment itself. The most obvious example is a decree of divorce or nullity of marriage, which has the effect of declaring the personal status of the parties in addition to deciding their rights and obligations as litigants vis-à-vis each other.[5] Similarly, a grant of probate is declaratory of the status of the executor to whom it is granted, as may be seen from the rather striking facts of *Allen* v *Dundas* (1789) 3 TR 125. The defendant owed a debt to the deceased, which after the death, he paid to the deceased's executor. Subsequently, the plaintiff succeeded in having the will set aside in his own favour, on the ground that it had been forged. The plaintiff sought to recover the debt (which had not been accounted for by the original executor) from the defendant. It was held that the plaintiff could not be heard to challenge the original executorship as that status subsisted until the will was set aside. Accordingly, the defendant, who had paid the debt to a person who at the material time had the status of executor, had discharged the debt properly and was not liable further. Other examples of judgments *in rem* are adjudications in bankruptcy,[6] adjudications of the General Medical and Dental Councils striking off a practitioner,[7] and judgments of a prize court condemning a ship and her cargo on the ground that the cargo did not enjoy neutral status.[8] A noteworthy 'exception', in the sense that the judgment appears on the face of it to have a declaratory effect, is that of judgments affecting legitimacy or illegitimacy. Thus, an affiliation order affected only the parties to the proceedings in which it was pronounced,[9] and by s. 45(5) of the Matrimonial Causes Act 1973 a declaration of legitimacy shall not prejudice any person who has not been given notice of or made a party to the proceedings and who is not the privy of a person who has so been given notice or made a party.

B JUDGMENTS AS EVIDENCE OF THE FACTS ON WHICH THEY WERE BASED: STRANGERS

SUMMARY OF MAIN POINTS

- The rule that a previous judgment is not admissible as evidence of the facts on which it is based except as between parties to that litigation is known as the rule in *Hollington* v *Hewthorn*.

- The rule has been abrogated by ss. 11–13 of the Civil Evidence Act 1968 with respect to (1) previous convictions relevant to civil proceedings; (2) findings of adultery and paternity relevant to civil proceedings; and (3) previous convictions relevant to defamation proceedings; except in

---

[5] See, e.g., *Salvesen* v *Administrator of Austrian Property* [1927] AC 641. In the case of older divorce cases, the reference is to a decree absolute, and not to a decree *nisi*, which could be set aside on cause being shown, and which did not alter the status of the parties: *Travers* v *Holley* [1953] P 246.

[6] See Insolvency Rules 1986 (S.I. 1986 No. 1925), r. 12.20(2). It is submitted that the different wording of the provision in the 1986 Rules does not alter the position established under the Bankruptcy Act 1914.

[7] *Hill* v *Clifford* [1907] 2 Ch 236.

[8] *Geyer* v *Aguilar* (1798) 7 TR 681.

[9] *Anderson* v *Collinson* [1901] 2 KB 107. Affiliation proceedings have been abolished (Family Law Reform Act 1987, s. 17) but this does not affect the principle stated in the text.

the last case (in which the evidence of conviction is conclusive) a party may seek to prove that the conviction or finding was erroneous. In cases not covered by ss. 11–13 the Rule continues in effect.

* The rule has been abrogated in criminal cases by s. 74 of the Police and Criminal Evidence Act 1984 with respect to the previous conviction or acquittal of any person. Section 73 of the Act provides for proof of the conviction or acquittal. A person convicted of an offence is taken to have committed the offence unless the contrary is proved; the compatibility of this rule with art. 6 of the Convention is unclear.

12.4 GENERALLY

At common law there was until relatively recently no fixed view of the admissibility of a judgment as evidence of the facts upon which it was based, for or against strangers to the judgment (i.e., those not parties to the suit in which it was pronounced). There was some authority either way, and it was certainly possible to find examples of cases where, with obviously convenient results, the courts overcame the apparent stumbling blocks of hearsay and inadmissible opinion (see 12.1) and allowed reliance on previous judgments. Thus, in *Re Crippen* [1911] P 108, a husband, who was subsequently executed for the murder of his wife, made a will, and the executrix thereby appointed sought to administer the estate of the murdered wife. Application was made to vest the wife's estate elsewhere, on the ground that the husband's estate should not be permitted to benefit from his crime and for this purpose it was necessary to prove that he had murdered his wife. It was argued that the conviction of the husband was not admissible for that purpose. But the court held that, where there was an issue of rights accruing as a result of crime, the conviction was admissible as *prima facie* evidence of the commission of such crime. And in *Partington v Partington and Atkinson* [1925] P 34 a finding of adultery against a husband made in a suit in which the husband was co-respondent, and to which the wife was not a party, was held to be admissible for the wife, in a subsequent suit brought by her against the husband, as *prima facie* evidence of his adultery.

It seems from these cases that there was a limited recognition of previous judgments as evidence of facts on which they were based but that, unlike the position when only the formal existence or effect of the judgment is relied on, the evidence could be only *prima facie*, and was certainly not conclusive. The question was further complicated by confusion in some authorities between this question, and the question of the operation of judgments *in rem*, and questions of other exceptional rules of evidence concerned with such matters as custom and public rights, which might sometimes be established by judgments.

12.5 THE RULE IN *HOLLINGTON* v *HEWTHORN*

At length, the tide turned against the admissibility of judgments for or against strangers to prove the facts on which the judgment was based, and the rule was authoritatively laid down by the Court of Appeal in *Hollington v F. Hewthorn & Co. Ltd* [1943] KB 587. In an action for negligence by the plaintiff against an individual defendant and his employer, arising from a road traffic accident, it was held that the conviction of the individual defendant of the offence of driving without due care and attention was not admissible to prove that the individual defendant had been negligent. Despite the superficial attraction of the close similarity of issues in the different proceedings, and of the argument that the plaintiff, although not a party to the prosecution, could hardly be prejudiced by the admission of the conviction, the evidence was rejected for three reasons: that the opinion of the previous tribunal was irrelevant; that findings of fact by the justices, especially in an uncontested case, might be qualitatively different from those which should prevail in a contested action in the High Court; and that it would be extremely difficult, if possible at all, to identify the facts upon which the conviction was based. The obvious inconvenience, and to some extent the artificiality of the rule eventually provoked a limited statutory intervention.

12.6 REVERSAL OF THE RULE IN *HOLLINGTON* v *HEWTHORN* IN CIVIL CASES

The first statutory inroad on the rule in *Hollington* v *Hewthorn* was made in civil cases. In civil cases in which several different claimants or defendants may be entitled to recover or may be liable for the consequences of the same wrongful civil act, procedural provisions permit joinder of all necessary parties and consolidation of claims. This means that closely related civil claims can usually be adjudicated together and that the need for reliance upon previous judgments given in civil proceedings can often be avoided. However, problems may still arise with previous criminal convictions and findings of adultery or paternity. Three kinds of case are principally concerned:

(a) Where the claimant wishes to prove the conviction of the defendant of a criminal offence, relevant to the claim or to an issue in civil proceedings.

(b) Where a party to a claim for defamation wishes to prove that the claimant has been convicted of a criminal offence, where the commission or otherwise of such offence is relevant to the claim.

(c) Where a party to civil proceedings (e.g., divorce) wishes to rely upon a finding of adultery or paternity made against another in previous proceedings relevant to his claim or an issue in the instant proceedings.

In these kinds of case, Parliament decided that the convenience of permitting proof to be made in the manner described above outweighs even the cogent reservations expressed in *Hollington* v *Hewthorn*, and by ss. 11 to 13 of the Civil Evidence Act 1968 made previous judgments admissible, but in these kinds of case only. The Police and Criminal Evidence Act 1984, ss. 74 and 75 has now made for criminal cases provision similar to s. 11 of the 1968 Act. This is considered in 12.13 *et seq*. In cases not covered by these statutory provisions, the rule in *Hollington* v *Hewthorn* continues to apply.[10]

12.6.1 Convictions relevant to civil proceedings

Section 11 of the Civil Evidence Act 1968, provides as follows:

> (1) In any civil proceedings the fact that a person has been convicted of an offence by or before any court in the United Kingdom or by a court-martial there or elsewhere[11] shall...be admissible in evidence for the purpose of proving, where to do so is relevant to any issue in those proceedings, that he

---

[10] See *Three Rivers District Council* v *Bank of England (No. 3)* [2003] AC 1; *Secretary of State for Trade and Industry* v *Bairstow* [2004] Ch 1; *D* [1996] QB 283; *Land Securities plc* v *Westminster City Council* [1993] 1 WLR 286. But certain administrative findings have been admitted as *prima facie* evidence (only) of the facts found: see *Hill* v *Clifford* [1907] 2 Ch 236 (finding of professional misconduct by the General Medical Council); *Faulder* v *Silk* (1811) 3 Camp 126 (findings of inquisition in lunacy); cf. *Conlon* v *Simms* [2008] 1 WLR 484.

[11] A conviction by a foreign court may not be used under this section, or under s. 13 (see s. 13(3)); *Union Carbide Corporation* v *Naturin Ltd* [1987] FSR 538. This is because of the possible difficulty in evaluating the basis

committed that offence, whether he was so convicted upon a plea of guilty or otherwise and whether or not he is a party to the civil proceedings; but no conviction other than a subsisting one shall be admissible in evidence by virtue of this section.

(2) In any civil proceedings in which by virtue of this section a person is proved to have been convicted of an offence by or before any court in the United Kingdom or by a court-martial there or elsewhere—

    (a) he shall be taken to have committed that offence unless the contrary is proved; and

    (b) without prejudice to the reception of any other admissible evidence for the purpose of identifying the facts on which the conviction was based, the contents of any document which is admissible as evidence of the conviction, and the contents of the information, complaint, indictment or charge-sheet on which the person in question was convicted, shall be admissible in evidence for that purpose.

So far as s. 11(1) is concerned, the following points should be noted:

(a) The section has no application to a conviction by a court outside the UK, other than a court-martial.

(b) It is irrelevant whether or not the person convicted is a party to the civil proceedings, for example the servant or agent of the defendant for whose acts the defendant is vicariously liable; it is also irrelevant whether or not the criminal proceedings were contested.

(c) A 'subsisting' conviction means one which has not been quashed on appeal, and will include a conviction substituted by an appellate court for the original conviction. But the mere fact that an appeal is pending against a conviction does not mean that the conviction is not 'subsisting' for the purpose of s. 1; in such a case, any civil proceedings to which the conviction is said to be relevant should be adjourned, if necessary, pending the outcome of the appeal.[12]

The construction of s. 11(2)(a) has given rise to some difference of opinion. It is generally accepted that where a conviction is proved by virtue of s. 11, it has the effect of reversing the burden of proof, so that the party seeking to assert that the person convicted did not commit the offence bears the burden of proving that fact on the balance of probabilities. This should mean that proof must be made that the person convicted did not commit the offence, as opposed to proof that there was some technical defect in the conviction, such as the wrongful admission of evidence or a misdirection to the jury, even if the defect led to the conviction being unsafe, or that the trial was an abuse of process: see *Raja* v *van Hoogstraten* [2005] EWHC 1642 (Ch). Where the commission of the offence is an issue central to the claim or defence, the burden of proof on the party seeking to disprove it will be the legal burden. Thus in *Wauchope* v *Mordecai* [1970] 1 WLR 317, the plaintiff had been knocked off his bicycle when the defendant opened the door of a car as the plaintiff was passing. The defendant was later convicted of the offence of opening the door so as to cause injury or danger. By an oversight, the trial judge was not referred to s. 11 and found for the defendant, basing his decision on the failure of the plaintiff to discharge the legal burden

and quality of the decision of a foreign court. While a British court-martial may convene outside the UK, it is applying the military law of the UK.

[12] *Re Raphael, Raphael* v *d'Antin* [1973] 1 WLR 998. Section 11(5) of the Act, as amended, provides that s. 14 of the Powers of Criminal Courts (Sentencing) Act 2000, under which convictions which lead to a discharge are to be disregarded for certain purposes, does not affect the operation of s. 11. Convictions which are spent under the Rehabilitation of Offenders Act 1974 may also be used for the purpose of s. 11 to the extent that justice cannot otherwise be done: *Thomas* v *Commissioner of Police of the Metropolis* [1997] QB 813; as to this see 6.4.3.

of proof. The Court of Appeal allowed the plaintiff's appeal. The burden lay on the defendant to prove that he had not opened the door negligently, and if the judge had considered s. 11, he must have found that that burden had not been discharged.

The decision in *Wauchope v Mordecai* left open, however, the question of the weight which should be attached to the conviction as evidence of the commission of the offence. In *Taylor v Taylor* [1970] 1 WLR 1148, a wife petitioned for divorce on the ground of her husband's adultery. The adultery complained of was incestuous, in that it had been committed with the daughter of the family. The husband had been convicted of the relevant incest, and his application for leave to appeal against conviction was refused. The wife tendered evidence of the conviction in the divorce proceedings under s. 11, and the husband sought to prove that he had not committed the offence. The trial judge found, on the basis of the depositions used at the trial and on the basis of oral evidence taken before him, which the Court of Appeal found to be unsatisfactory, that the husband had discharged the burden on him and had proved that he had not committed incest. The Court of Appeal allowed an appeal by the wife. In the words of Davies LJ 'it is obvious that, when a man has been convicted by twelve of his fellow countrymen and countrywomen at a criminal trial, the verdict of the jury is a matter which is entitled to very great weight when the convicted person is seeking, in the words of the statute, to prove the contrary' ([1970] 1 WLR at 1152). The trial judge should, accordingly, have obtained a transcript, or otherwise satisfied himself with regard to the evidence and details of the criminal trial and thus embarked upon a full and searching investigation of the husband's case, to see whether the burden of proof was discharged. There was not sufficient evidence upon which his conclusion could have been based.[13]

The Court of Appeal in *Taylor v Taylor* was referred to the decision at first instance of Paull J in *Stupple v Royal Insurance Co. Ltd* [1971] 1 QB 50, which had not then reached the Court of Appeal. That case involved a claim and counterclaim in respect of sums of money, said to be the proceeds of a robbery, of which Stupple had been convicted. The issue, in effect, was whether his conviction was correct. Paull J asked himself the question, what his view would have been if he had sat as a juryman on the criminal trial. Though this approach won some support in *Taylor v Taylor*, it won none from the differently constituted Court of Appeal that heard the *Stupple* case. But the Court upheld the judge's view that the conviction, and its affirmation by the Court of Criminal Appeal, were: 'from a practical point of view…conclusive'.[14] The Court of Appeal was, however, unable to agree on the precise effect of s. 11(2)(a) in terms of weight. Lord Denning MR thought that the evidence went further than merely shifting the burden of proof, and was 'a weighty piece of evidence in itself'. The conviction 'itself tells in the scale in the civil action'. Conversely Buckley LJ said: 'In my judgment, proof of conviction under this section gives rise to

---

[13] The limits of the means by which a party may discharge the burden of disproving a conviction cannot be said to be settled. In *Stupple v Royal Insurance Co. Ltd* [1971] 1 QB 50, Lord Denning MR conceived of a broad range of weapons, by calling fresh evidence, discrediting evidence given at the trial, and even by explaining a plea of guilty or a failure to appeal, to rebut the obvious inference. But it seems, as Paull J held at first instance, that the court is not entitled to consider, as if it were a criminal appellate court, the circumstances of the conduct of the trial; it must confine itself to the evidence and papers, and the formal record. Cf. *D* [1996] QB 283. But the transcript of the trial, including the summing-up, would be admissible in the light of the Civil Evidence Act 1995; cf. *Brinks Ltd v Abu-Saleh (No. 2)* [1995] 1 WLR 1487 (a decision under the Civil Evidence Act 1968).

[14] Lord Denning MR subsequently said (in *McIlkenny v Chief Constable of the West Midlands Police* [1980] QB 283) that evidence adduced to disprove a conviction must be decisive. This was doubted in the 1st edn of this work, and judicially by Lord Diplock on appeal in the same case, *sub nom. Hunter v Chief Constable of the West Midlands Police* [1982] AC 529, 544. Lord Diplock held that the usual civil standard of proof applied. He conceded, though, that disproof would be an 'uphill task'.

the statutory presumption laid down in s. 11(2)(a), which, like any other presumption, will give way to evidence establishing the contrary on the balance of probability, without itself affording any evidential weight to be taken into account in determining whether that onus has been discharged' ([1971] 1 QB 50 at 76). The third member of the court, Winn LJ expressed no opinion on the point. It is submitted that the intention and wording of the section are alike better served by the view of Lord Denning MR.

12.6.2 Effect of acquittals

Although there is little authority on the point, it appears that the rule in *Hollington* v *Hewthorn* applies to acquittals, with the result that an acquittal in criminal proceedings cannot be used in later civil proceedings as evidence that the person acquitted was innocent of the offence charged.[15] The decision of the Court of Appeal in *Terry* [2005] QB 996 confirms the principle that a verdict of not guilty cannot be assumed to mean more than that the jury or court did not find the guilt of the accused proved beyond reasonable doubt. This is not the same thing as a finding of innocence, and it does not follow that the same allegations could not be proved on the balance of probability in civil proceedings.

12.6.3 Findings of adultery and paternity relevant to civil proceedings

Section 12 of the Civil Evidence Act 1968, as amended, provides:

> (1) In any civil proceedings—
>   (a) the fact that a person has been found guilty of adultery in any matrimonial proceedings; and
>   (b) the fact that a person has been found to be the father of a child in relevant proceedings before any court in England and Wales or adjudged to be the father of a child in affiliation proceedings[16] before any court in the United Kingdom,
> shall...be admissible in evidence for the purpose of proving, where to do so is relevant to any issue in those civil proceedings, that he committed the adultery to which the finding relates or, as the case may be, is (or was) the father of that child, whether or not he offered any defence to the allegation of adultery or paternity and whether or not he is a party to the civil proceedings; but no finding or adjudication other than a subsisting one shall be admissible in evidence by virtue of this section.
>   (2) In any civil proceedings in which by virtue of this section a person is proved to have been found guilty of adultery as mentioned in subsection (1)(a) above or to have been found or adjudged to be the father of a child as mentioned in subsection (1)(b) above—
>   (a) he shall be taken to have committed the adultery to which the finding relates or, as the case may be, to be (or have been) the father of that child, unless the contrary is proved; and
>   (b) [provides for the admissibility of evidence to show the facts on which the finding or adjudication was based].

It will be observed that the section follows closely the provisions of s. 11, and it would appear that the law relating to s. 11, as set out above, will apply with any necessary modifications to this section also. Certainly, it has been held that the effect of the section is to reverse the

---

[15] See *Loughans* v *Odhams Press* [1963] 1 QB 299.

[16] Affiliation proceedings were abolished by s. 17 of the Family Law Reform Act 1987, but orders made while the Affiliation Proceedings Act 1957 was still in force, continue to be covered by s. 12 of the Civil Evidence Act 1968. See also Family Law Reform Act 1987, Sch. 3, para. 6.

burden of proof and to require the party seeking to disprove the finding or adjudication to do so, on a balance of probabilities.[17] The expression 'matrimonial proceedings' does not include matrimonial proceedings in a magistrates' court, and is confined to proceedings in England and Wales (s. 12(5)).

12.6.4 Convictions relevant to defamation actions

Section 13 of the Civil Evidence Act 1968, as amended by the Defamation Act 1996, provides:

> (1) In an action for libel or slander in which the question whether the [claimant] did or did not commit a criminal offence is relevant to an issue arising in the action, proof that at the time when that issue falls to be determined, he stands convicted of that offence shall be conclusive evidence that he committed that offence; and his conviction thereof shall be admissible in evidence accordingly.

The operation of s. 13 differs greatly from that of s. 11, in that the conviction is conclusive evidence of the commission of the offence. The reason for this wording of the section is to prevent the abuse of defamation proceedings for the purpose of attempting to re-open convictions even when they may have been affirmed on appeal, and also to protect those concerned in writing or publishing justifiable material, relying upon the conviction for the truth of what they write or publish. It must, therefore, follow that particulars of claim, which do no more than complain of a statement, accurate in itself, which asserts and fairly comments upon the fact that the claimant has committed an offence of which he has been lawfully convicted, are insufficient to establish a claim; though where the statement complained of also alleges matter not covered by s. 13, it may be right to leave the whole statement of case intact.[18]

As originally enacted, s. 13 applied to convictions of any person, insofar as relevant to a defamation action. But s. 12 of the Defamation Act 1996 amended s. 13 to restrict the conclusiveness to convictions of the claimant, or, if there is more than one claimant, convictions of any of them (see s. 13(2A)), to that effect, added by the 1996 Act). This makes the intent of the section more precise. It follows that a relevant conviction of a party other than a claimant in a defamation action will be governed by s. 11 of the Civil Evidence Act 1968, as in any other civil action.

By s. 13(3), a person stands convicted of an offence only if there is against him a subsisting conviction of the offence by or before a court in the UK or a court martial there or elsewhere (see 12.6.1).

12.6.5 Sections 11–13: general considerations

Where any document is admissible to identify the facts upon which a conviction, finding or adjudication is based, a certified or authenticated copy of such document shall be admissible in evidence, and shall be taken to be a true copy, unless the contrary is shown (ss. 11(4), 12(4), 13(4)).

By Practice Direction 16, para. 8.1, supplementing part 16 of the Civil Procedure Rules 1998, a claimant who wishes to rely on evidence pursuant to s. 11 or s. 12 must plead his intention, specifying the fact relied upon, and must indicate the issue in the case to which it is relevant. The rule does not apply to evidence admissible under s. 13, presumably because the evidence is not

---

[17] *Sutton v Sutton* [1970] 1 WLR 183. For the use of transcripts of previous matrimonial proceedings, see *Practice Direction (Finding of Adultery: Subsequent Proof)* [1969] 1 WLR 1192.

[18] *Levene v Roxhan* [1970] 1 WLR 1322.

open to challenge except to deny that there is a subsisting conviction. There would appear to be no reason why such evidence should not be pleaded, in view of its effect in law.

12.7 REVERSAL OF THE RULE IN *HOLLINGTON* v *HEWTHORN* IN CRIMINAL CASES

The Police and Criminal Evidence Act 1984, introduced provisions similar to those of s. 11 of the Civil Evidence Act 1968, applicable to criminal proceedings. Section 73 of the Act provides:

> (1) Where in any proceedings the fact that a person has in the United Kingdom been convicted or acquitted of an offence otherwise than by a Service court is admissible in evidence, it may be proved by producing a certificate of conviction or, as the case may be, of acquittal relating to that offence, and proving that the person named in the certificate as having been convicted or acquitted of the offence is the person whose conviction or acquittal of the offence is to be proved.
>
> (2) For the purposes of this section a certificate of conviction or of acquittal—
>
> > (a) shall, as regards a conviction or acquittal on indictment, consist of a certificate, signed by the clerk of the court where the conviction or acquittal took place, giving the substance and effect (omitting the formal parts) of the indictment and of the conviction or acquittal; and
> >
> > (b) shall, as regards a conviction or acquittal on a summary trial, consist of a copy of the conviction or of the dismissal of the information, signed by the clerk of the court where the conviction or acquittal took place or by the clerk of the court, if any, to which a memorandum of the conviction or acquittal was sent; ...
>
> (4) The method of proving a conviction or acquittal authorized by this section shall be in addition to and not to the exclusion of any other authorized manner of proving a conviction or acquittal.

This section governs the proof of the conviction or acquittal itself. Section 73 does not deal with the circumstances in which a conviction is admissible, but merely provides a method of proving a conviction when it is admissible. Proof of the fact that the person convicted did in fact commit the offence charged is dealt with by s. 74, and it is this section which reverses the rule in *Hollington* v *Hewthorn*. Proof of the facts underlying the charge is provided for by s. 75 (see 12.12). But in the case of a conviction on indictment, the mere proof of the conviction itself under s. 73 will inevitably reveal more than the bare fact of conviction, because of the provision of s. 73(2)(a) that the certificate of conviction shall give the substance and effect of the indictment. Section 73 may, of course, be used for the purpose of proving a previous conviction as an element of evidence of bad character, when permitted by s. 100 or s. 101 of the Criminal Justice Act 2003 (see Chapter 6).

The party adducing evidence of the conviction must be prepared to adduce evidence sufficient to prove that the person whose conviction or acquittal is to be proved is the person named in the certificate, if this is not admitted. Whether this has been proved is a question of fact for the jury.[19] For the purpose of s. 6 of the Criminal Procedure Act 1865, which permits proof of a conviction when denied by a witness (see 17.9) it was held that the evidence of identity need only be such that the court can properly draw the inference that it has been established, and need not be conclusive.[20] But in *Pattinson* v *DPP* [2006] 2 All ER 317, it was held that, where the prosecution wishes to rely on a conviction of the accused as evidence against him in criminal proceedings, the identity of the person named in the certificate must be proved beyond reasonable doubt. There

---

[19] *Burns* [2006] 2 Cr App R 16; *Lewendon* [2006] 2 Cr App R 19; *Pattinson* v *DPP* (see text below).
[20] *Martin* v *White* [1910] 1 KB 665.

is no prescribed method of proof, but obvious methods include the evidence of a person present in court at the time of conviction (for example, the investigating officer) or fingerprint identification. The mere fact that the personal details of the person convicted correspond with those of the accused will be sufficient to amount to a *prima facie* case, and if the accused does not dispute the matter by giving evidence, an inference might be drawn against him under s. 35 of the Criminal Justice and Public Order Act Act 1994 (15.6).

Section 74 of the 1984 Act makes convictions admissible for the purpose of proving that the person convicted of an offence committed that offence. Section 75(4) limits this to subsisting convictions. A subsisting conviction is one which results from a verdict of guilty which has not been quashed on appeal, or on a plea of guilty which has not been withdrawn (even if the person convicted has not yet been sentenced) (see *Robertson* [1987] QB 920; 12.9). Although the Act is silent on the point, it would seem safe to assume that a conviction quashed on appeal or the subject of a free pardon would not be subsisting, but that the mere fact that an appeal is pending would not affect the subsistence of the conviction; cf. *Re Raphael, Raphael v d'Antin* [1973] 1 WLR 998 and see 12.6.1. For the purpose of criminal proceedings, we must distinguish two different types of case: those in which a conviction of a person other than the accused is relevant; and those in which a conviction of the accused is relevant. These cases are provided for separately by s. 74.

12.8 PERSONS OTHER THAN THE ACCUSED

As to these persons, s. 74 as amended provides:

> (1) In any proceedings the fact that a person other than the accused has been convicted of an offence by or before any court in the United Kingdom or by a Service court outside the United Kingdom shall be admissible in evidence for the purpose of proving that that person committed that offence, where evidence of his having done so is admissible, whether or not any other evidence of his having committed that offence is given.
>
> (2) In any proceedings in which by virtue of this section a person other than the accused is proved to have been convicted of an offence by or before any court in the United Kingdom or by a Service court outside the United Kingdom, he shall be taken to have committed that offence unless the contrary is proved.

As with s. 11 of the Civil Evidence Act 1968 in civil cases, these provisions have the effect of abrogating the rule in *Hollington* v *Hewthorn*, so that not only is the conviction admissible evidence to prove that the person convicted committed the offence, but that person is also taken to have committed the offence unless the contrary is proved. Disproof of the commission of offences in criminal cases is considered in 12.11.

This section sounded the death-knell for at least one of the best-known rules of criminal evidence, namely that which provided that on a charge of handling stolen goods, the conviction of the thief should not be admissible for the purpose of proving that the goods were stolen. The conviction of the thief is now admissible for this very purpose, and establishes the fact unless the contrary is proved.[21] Similarly, in a prosecution for assisting an offender, contrary to s. 4 of the Criminal Law Act 1967, the conviction of the principal offender is admissible to prove that the person assisted had committed an arrestable offence. In certain cases, however, these

---

[21] Cf. *Pigram* [1995] Crim LR 808.

provisions may equally be useful to the defence. There could now surely be no objection to an accused adducing evidence of the fact that another was convicted of the offence with which the accused is now charged, if such conviction suggests that the accused must be innocent of the offence charged. If the evidence as a whole is equally consistent with the guilt of both, the point may be more difficult, though it is not hard to imagine circumstances in which the conviction of the other might still be relevant.

But the conviction of a third party cannot be admitted under s. 74(1) unless it is relevant to some issue in the present case. In *Hasson* [1997] Crim LR 579, where the accused was charged with being involved in the supply of drugs, it was held that evidence of the drug-related convictions of six men with whom the accused had a social relationship was wrongly admitted, where there was no allegation that the accused had supplied the men with drugs, or that their meetings had anything to do with the supply of drugs. And in *Mahmood* [1997] 1 Cr App R 414, it was held to be wrong to admit evidence that one of three men charged with a rape had pleaded guilty to the charge, where there was uncertainty as to the basis of the plea. The prosecution's case was that the victim of the rape had been too drunk to consent competently to sexual intercourse. There was a real danger that the jury might conclude that the man who had pleaded guilty had done so because he had known that the victim was too drunk to consent (which might not have been the reason for the plea) and that the jury might, therefore, assume that the same was true of the other two accused. If so, the defence of the other two accused would be seriously compromised. In such cases, and bearing in mind the observations made in the cases of *O'Connor* (1987) 85 Cr App R 298 and *Robertson* [1987] QB 920 discussed below, it would also seem proper for the court to exercise its discretion to exclude this kind of evidence in cases where its relevance is unclear, or there is a real danger that the jury may be misled.

12.9 SCOPE OF S. 74(1) GENERALLY

An important issue under s. 74(1) is whether or not it is restricted to proof of convictions of others as a necessary condition precedent to the prosecution of the accused (as in the handling stolen goods and assisting offenders cases mentioned above), or whether it permits evidence of the conviction to prove underlying facts in any relevant case.

In *O'Connor* (1987) 85 Cr App R 298, the accused and the co-accused, B, were charged with conspiracy to defraud two insurance companies by falsely reporting and claiming that a vehicle had been stolen. B pleaded guilty to the charge, and the accused was subsequently tried for it. The prosecution were permitted to adduce evidence of the conviction of B, based on his plea of guilty, in order to prove the existence of the conspiracy. This evidence went beyond any formal necessity, because although it takes two to conspire, the jury would have been entitled to convict the accused without evidence that B had been convicted. On appeal, it was argued that s. 74(1) should be confined to cases in which it was necessary to prove a conviction as a condition precedent to the conviction of the accused, and that the trial judge should in any event have excluded the evidence in the exercise of his discretion under s. 78 of the Police and Criminal Evidence Act 1984, on the ground that it would have such an adverse effect on the fairness of the proceedings that it ought not to be admitted. The Court of Appeal declined to decide the scope of s. 74(1), holding that the trial judge had been wrong not to exercise his discretion to exclude. However, the Court dismissed the appeal by applying the proviso to s. 2(1) of the Criminal Appeal Act 1968, because the evidence was otherwise overwhelming. The Court based its decision on the fact that s. 74(1) permitted the relevant count of the indictment to which B had pleaded guilty to be adduced to identify the facts underlying the charge, and that count revealed that B and the accused were both named and were the only alleged conspirators. This, the Court felt, was likely to impel the jury towards the conclusion that if B had admitted the conspiracy with the accused as charged, and if B could not conspire alone, then it would follow that the accused conspired with B. No doubt the prosecution also foresaw and intended this result, and it is not clear that this would be impermissible, as s. 74(1) is drafted.

Soon afterwards, the Court of Appeal considered two further appeals involving s. 74(1): *Robertson; Golder* [1987] QB 920. The appeal of *Robertson* permitted some distinction of *O'Connor*. The accused was charged with conspiring with two others, P and L, to commit burglary. P and L had previously pleaded guilty to individual counts of burglary, and the accused did not dispute that these burglaries had occurred. However, the accused had not been charged jointly with P and L, and consequently his name did not appear on the relevant counts. The prosecution were permitted to adduce evidence of the convictions of P and L as evidence of a conspiracy between P and L, there being other evidence suggesting that the accused had been a party to that conspiracy. The Court of Appeal upheld the admission of the evidence.

Unlike the Court in *O'Connor*,[22] the *Robertson* Court was inclined to think that s. 74(1) was not restricted to cases of necessity for proving a condition precedent. Lord Lane CJ pointed out that the section provides that evidence of a conviction shall be admissible for the purpose of proving that the person convicted committed the offence 'where to do so is relevant to *any issue in those proceedings*' (emphasis added). It was argued for the accused that there was no such issue, because the commission of the burglaries by P and L was not disputed by the accused. Of this, Lord Lane CJ said (*ibid.* at 311):

> We think the time has come to attempt to provide some guidance for courts who have the task of applying section 74. The word 'issue' in relation to a trial is apt to cover not only an issue which is an essential ingredient in the offence charged, for instance in a handling case the fact that the goods were stolen (that is the restricted meaning) but also less fundamental issues, for instance evidential issues arising during the course of the proceedings (that is the extended meaning). Section 74 by using the words 'any issue in those proceedings' does not seek to limit the word 'issue' to the restricted meaning indicated above...
>
> So far as the present case is concerned, there was certainly an issue. Indeed, it was probably an issue in the restricted sense, namely the issue of whether there was a conspiracy between Poole and Long (of which their joint conviction of burglary was the clearest evidence). It was that conspiracy to which the prosecution sought to prove the appellant was a party. It is true that the appellant was prepared to accept that there had been a series of burglaries at Comet's premises during the material times, but that would not preclude the prosecution from relying on s. 74 as the words of subsection (1) of that section make clear.

The Court also held that there was no reason for the judge to exclude the evidence in his discretion on the facts presented, distinguishing *O'Connor* for the reasons mentioned above. At the same time, Lord Lane added (*ibid.* at 312):

> It only remains to add this. Section 74 is a provision which should be sparingly used. There will be occasions where, although the evidence may be technically admissible, its effect is likely to be so

---

[22] Lord Lane CJ was a member of both courts. He delivered the judgment of the court in *Robertson*. Taylor J delivered the judgment in *O'Connor*. See also R. Munday [1990] Crim LR 236; *Lunnon* (1988) 88 Cr App R 71; *Turner* [1991] Crim LR 57; *Humphreys* [1993] Crim LR 288.

> slight that it will be wiser not to adduce it.... Secondly, where the evidence is admitted, the judge should be careful, as [the trial judge] was here, to explain to the jury the effect of the evidence and its limitations.

It is submitted that Lord Lane CJ may have erred in regarding the issue as a 'restricted' one, since the convictions of P and L of the burglaries were not necessary in law to support a conviction of the accused of conspiring with them to commit burglary. His Lordship's statement raises some doubt as to whether the case can be regarded as clear authority for the proposition that s. 74 permits the use of convictions as evidence on 'extended' issues. It is submitted, however, that this was the intent of the Court, and that, seen in this light, *Robertson* was rightly decided, and should be followed.[23]

It is submitted that the observations of Lord Lane CJ in *Robertson* regarding the use of s. 74 should be scrupulously heeded. Care must be taken not to suggest to the jury that the fact of the conviction of another automatically points to the guilt of the accused, and the judge should direct the jury clearly to that effect. The danger is particularly acute in cases where it is suggested that the accused and the person convicted committed an offence such as conspiracy or affray jointly. The true evidential value of the evidence is only to establish the commission of an offence by the person convicted. But there is a real risk that the admission of the conviction may lead the jury to conclude that the accused participated in the offence, even though the evidence cannot have that effect as a matter of law. It is, therefore, important for the judge to insist that the prosecution identify the precise purpose for which the conviction is said to be relevant, and confine it to that purpose. The dangers are increased by the fact that, because s. 73(1) of the Act permits proof of the conviction by means of a certificate, it will generally be unnecessary for the prosecution to call the person convicted as a witness, and the accused will have no opportunity to cross-examine him.[24] It would be possible to argue that this violates the accused's right to a fair trial guaranteed by art. 6 of the European Convention on Human Rights (see 1.7 and 7.5). Certainly, it would appear appropriate for the court to take art. 6 into account in assessing the admissibility of evidence tendered under s. 74(1) or in deciding whether or not to exclude such evidence in the exercise of its discretion.

12.9.1 Use of s. 74 in same proceedings

A radical extension of the application of s. 74 was approved by the majority of the House of Lords in *Hayter*.[25] The prosecution alleged that A murdered C, having been procured to do so by Mrs C, and that B was a middleman, who recruited A to commit the murder. The only evidence against A was a confession which he was alleged to have made to his girlfriend, which incriminated both himself and B. The case against B depended entirely on the guilt of A. At the close of

---

[23] In the accompanying appeal of *Golder*, it was argued that the word 'conviction' as used in s. 74 imported that the person found guilty should also have been sentenced, and accordingly that an unsentenced person had not been 'convicted' within the meaning of the subsection. Rejecting this argument, the Court held that a 'conviction' imported only a finding of guilt, which subsisted unless and until a plea of guilty was withdrawn or the verdict of a jury quashed on appeal. Whether or not sentencing had taken place was irrelevant.

[24] See *Kempster* [1989] 1 WLR 1125; *Mahmood* [1997] 1 Cr App R 414. Cf. *Curry* [1988] Crim LR 527; *Lunnon* (1988) 88 Cr App R 71. The Court in *Curry* also said that s. 74 should be used sparingly. It is submitted that judges should also bear in mind their discretion to exclude. There are many cases in which it is almost inevitable that the accused will be tainted unfairly by association with the person convicted.

[25] [2005] 1 WLR 605; Lords Steyn, Bingham, and Brown; Lords Rodger and Carswell dissenting.

the prosecution case, B made a submission of no case to answer, arguing that the only evidence tendered against him was A's confession, which was inadmissible against him. The judge rejected the submission and left the case to the jury. The judge directed the jury that the confession was evidence only against A, but that if they came to the conclusion that A was guilty, they could make use of the fact of A's conviction as evidence against B. The latter direction was based on s. 74 of the Police and Criminal Evidence Act 1984. Both A and B were convicted. B appealed against conviction on the grounds that A's conviction was based entirely on his own confession, and, therefore, it followed that A's confession had (in effect) wrongly been used as evidence against B;[26] and that the judge had erred by inviting the jury to use A's conviction as evidence against B; and that he had further erred in rejecting B's submission of no case to answer because at that stage, A had not been convicted, and there was no admissible evidence against B. The majority of the House of Lords dismissed the appeal based on s. 74 on the basis that, even though the section usually applied where a person other than the accused was convicted in earlier proceedings, it was capable of being applied to the conviction of a co-accused in the same proceedings, and there was no objection to the jury using their own conviction of A as evidence against B that A had murdered C. This decision, though apparently convenient, gives rise to significant difficulties. On a practical level, as Lord Carswell, dissenting, pointed out (at [73]) it seems unrealistic to expect a jury to treat the cases of A and B completely separately in such circumstances, and the risk of unfairness to B is heightened, by comparison with other uses of s. 74. But there are more substantive difficulties which, with respect, make the majority's decision very hard to defend, if it can be defended at all. The use of s. 74 permitted by the judge deprived B of the opportunity to seek to show that A did not commit the offence independently of the trial itself (an opportunity which is expressly envisaged by s. 74(2)). This would seem to violate s. 74(2) by effectively making the conviction conclusive evidence of that fact, rather than presumptive evidence as the subsection provides. It surely raises issues of fairness under art. 6 of the European Convention on Human Rights. There is also a technical issue about the admissibility of the claimed evidence of A's 'conviction' under s. 74. A was not in fact 'convicted' of an offence until the jury returned a verdict to that effect, and there was, therefore, no conviction which could be used as evidence against B until that stage was reached. It must have been improper for the jury to deliberate on B's case using the 'conviction' of A as evidence against B. Section 74 permits the admission in evidence of a conviction, but not the use of a jury's prospective intention to convict. Given the rule that all the evidence in the case must be adduced before the jury retire to consider their verdict, the problem could not have been solved, even if it were appropriate procedurally, by the judge taking a verdict in A's case and then sending them out again to deliberate further on B's case. Finally, it seems clear that B's application for a finding of no case to answer ought to have succeeded on any view of the matter. On any view, there was no evidence against him at the close of the prosecution's case, and this lack could not be remedied except by a verdict of guilty against A, which was then simply one future possibility. It is submitted that the decision of the majority in *Hayter* may cause many more problems than it was thought to solve. Such problems as the prosecution had could have been solved simply enough by applying for separate trials and trying A before B. If A were convicted in the first trial, there could be no objection to the admission of his conviction in B's trial, and no question of a finding of no case to answer could arise.

---

[26] This hearsay issue as to the admissibility of confessions against persons other than the maker is dealt with at 9.16.

12.10 THE ACCUSED

As to the accused, s. 74 (as amended) provides:

> (3) In any proceedings where evidence is admissible of the fact that the accused has committed an offence, if the accused is proved to have been convicted of the offence—
> (a) by or before any court in the United Kingdom; or
> (b) by a Service court outside the United Kingdom,
> he shall be taken to have committed that offence unless the contrary is proved.

The section permits the proof of a conviction to stand as evidence that the accused did commit an offence relevant and properly admissible, such as one relied upon by the prosecution as evidence of bad character under s. 101 of the Criminal Evidence Act 2003. By rendering the conviction admissible evidence of this fact, and by placing the burden of disproving commission of the offence on the accused, Parliament simplified the task of jurors in cases where the accused denies commission of such offences, despite a conviction, and laid to rest the doubts expressed in *Shepherd* (1980) 71 Cr App R 120, as to the admissibility of the fact of conviction in such cases: see 6.3.3. Section 74(3) also provides a means of proof in cases where the commission of a previous offence is itself a fact in issue in the case, or where the commission of an offence is expressly made admissible by statute, for example under s. 27(3) of the Theft Act 1968.

12.11 DISPROOF OF CONVICTIONS: ART. 6 OF THE CONVENTION

As in the case of s. 11 of the Civil Evidence Act 1968, s. 74 provides that a party who contests the correctness of the conviction shall bear the burden of proving (on the balance of probabilities; see 4.13) that the person convicted did not commit the offence. In the light of the decision of the House of Lords in *Lambert* [2002] 2 AC 545, it is now arguable that, to the extent that the section imposes the legal burden of proof on the accused in a criminal case, it is incompatible with art. 6 of the European Convention on Human Rights, and must be read as if it imposes only an evidential burden (see 4.8 *et seq.*). In *Lambert* the House of Lords expressed a strong view that ordinarily the accused should bear no more than an evidential burden, and that any imposition of the legal burden of proof must be evaluated according to a test of proportionality. The issue in *Lambert* was, of course, somewhat different from that presented under s. 74, because the case was concerned with the burden of proof in relation to statutory defences open to the accused, not with the proof or disproof of previous convictions. It is submitted that, where the accused seeks to prove as part of his defence that a person did not commit an offence of which he was convicted, the same basic principle must apply, namely the principle of fairness under art. 6. But it seems that the principle must be applied rather differently. The test of proportionality adopted by the House of Lords in relation to particular statutory defences requires the court to have regard to the policy factors in favour of imposing the burden of proof, for example the seriousness or prevalence of the offence, and those militating against it, for example the possibility of dealing with such offences without affecting the burden of proof, and to weigh these factors in the light of the principle of fairness to the accused. This test could not really be applied to s. 74 because the question is one which does not depend on particular defences and, realistically, should not vary from case to case. Rather it is one which should be decided on a once-and-for-all basis as a discrete issue: namely, what is the correct burden of proof under s. 74 in any case in which it is invoked, in the light of art. 6?

It is submitted that the courts could fairly take the view that the strong public policy in upholding the principle of finality of litigation and in upholding previous decisions of courts of the UK fully justifies the imposition of the legal burden in this instance. As Davies LJ observed in *Taylor* v *Taylor* [1970] 1 WLR 1148 (see 12.6.1) the decision of a jury is not to be set aside lightly, particularly as the person convicted had the right to defend himself, the right to be presumed innocent until the case against him was proved beyond reasonable doubt, and the right to challenge the conviction on appeal. Given this, it does not seem unreasonable to impose the legal burden of proof on this issue on the party who wishes to have such a decision, in effect, set aside. On the other hand, it must be said that to revert to imposing the legal burden of proof on the prosecution would be no more than to revert to the rule in *Hollington* v *Hewthorn* under which the law worked tolerably well for most of its history. Nonetheless, given the convenience of the rule established by s. 74 and the fact that it would only be in rare cases that the court would entertain enough doubt about a previous conviction to go so far as to set it aside, it seems that there is little risk of injustice to the accused, and consequently little risk of unfairness in the trial process.

Assuming that the accused is to bear the legal burden of proof, the question of the weight to be attached to the previous conviction arises in much the same way as it does in civil cases (see 12.6.1). As with the corresponding provision of s. 11 of the Civil Evidence Act 1968, the section fails to address the question of the weight to be attached to the conviction, once proved. The arguments advanced in this as yet unresolved controversy in *Taylor* v *Taylor* [1970] 1 WLR 1148, *Stupple* v *Royal Insurance Co. Ltd* [1971] 1 QB 50, and *Hunter* v *Chief Constable of the West Midlands Police* [1982] AC 529 were fully rehearsed in 12.6.1 and need not be repeated. But it may be that the courts will feel that less weight should be accorded to a conviction in a criminal case, and that the approach of Buckley LJ in *Stupple* should be preferred to that of Lord Denning MR. If so, this will not be because the weight to be accorded to the verdict or finding of a previous criminal court should be less in a later criminal court than in a later civil court, but because of the proper reluctance of criminal courts to put any fact of consequence to the issue of guilt effectively beyond disproof by the accused. It would seem wrong to direct the jury that the commission of the previous offence, or the proof of the previous conviction, carry any especial weight in themselves.

12.12 PROOF OF UNDERLYING FACTS

Section 75 of the Police and Criminal Evidence Act 1984, provides as follows for the proof of the facts on which a conviction was based:

> (1) Where evidence that a person has been convicted of an offence is admissible by virtue of s. 74 above, then without prejudice to the reception of any other admissible evidence for the purpose of identifying the facts on which the conviction was based—
> (a) the contents of any document which is admissible as evidence of the conviction; and
> (b) the contents of the information, complaint, indictment or charge-sheet on which the person in question was convicted,
> shall be admissible in evidence for that purpose.

Section 75(2) provides for the admissibility of properly authenticated copies of the documents admissible as proof by virtue of s. 75(1). The phrase 'the contents of any document which is admissible as evidence of the conviction' includes the contents of a certificate of conviction, which by virtue of s. 73(1) is, together with proof of the identity of the person who was convicted as the person now before the court, evidence of the conviction.

For the reason given above, it is to be assumed that this section is not intended to affect the rules governing the admissibility of the underlying facts of a previous offence. The detail of the facts which could be proved by means of evidence admissible under s. 75(1) would in all probability be insufficient to provide the detail necessary for proof of previous convictions as evidence of extraneous acts, in which cases the calling of witnesses to the previous offences will still be necessary. But it will suffice for cases where the commission of the previous offence is a fact in issue or is relevant to guilt for a purpose unconnected with the detail of the offence, for example where proof of the theft of stolen goods is needed but the exact circumstances of the theft are irrelevant. Frequently, the documents made admissible by this section may assist the court in determining whether the previous conviction is relevant or admissible, or perhaps whether it would have such an adverse effect on the fairness of the proceedings that it should be excluded as a matter of discretion.

12.13 SECTIONS 73–75: GENERAL CONSIDERATIONS

Because of the difficulty of proving the effect and facts of foreign convictions, the Act limits its provisions to convictions of courts in the UK and of service courts elsewhere, as do the corresponding provisions of the Civil Evidence Act 1968 (see 12.6).

The Act does not require notice to be given of an intention to adduce evidence of previous convictions under s. 74. But s. 111 of the Criminal Justice Act 2003 calls for rules of court to be made which provide for notice of intention to adduce evidence of bad character under s. 100 and s. 101 of the Act. These rules are contained in Part 35 of the Criminal Procedure Rules 2005 and cover all cases in which convictions are tendered as evidence of bad character.

By s. 73(1) of the Act, the conviction itself may be proved by a combination of two matters; firstly, a certificate of conviction as defined in the subsection; secondly, proof that the person named in the certificate is the person now before the court and alleged to be the person named therein: see 12.7.

Section 74(4) provides that nothing in the section is intended to prejudice the admissibility of any conviction admissible apart from the section, or any enactment which makes a conviction conclusive evidence of any fact.

12.14 RECOMMENDED FURTHER READING

McGourlay, C., 'Is criminal practice impervious to logic? *R v Hayter*' (2006) **10**(2) *International Journal of Evidence and Proof* 128.

Munday, R., 'Proof of guilt by association under section 74 of the Police and Criminal Evidence Act 1984' [1990] *Criminal Law Review* 236.

Roberts, P., 'Acquitted misconduct evidence and double jeopardy principles, from *Sambisavam* to *Z*' [2000] *Criminal Law Review* 952.

Samuels, A., 'Issues arising from joint charge of co-defendants' (2005) **169** *Justice of the Peace* 555.

Tapper, C., 'Fair's fair?' (2008) **12**(1) *International Journal of Evidence and Proof* 53.

12.15 QUESTIONS FOR DISCUSSION BASED ON *R* v *COKE; LITTLETON* AND *BLACKSTONE* v *COKE* (for case files go to the Online Resource Centre)

12.15.1 *Coke; Littleton*

1. If Littleton pleads guilty to indecent assault of Angela Blackstone, may the prosecution adduce evidence of his plea against Coke on the charge of raping Margaret? If Coke pleads guilty, could the prosecution use his plea against Littleton?

2. If the judge admits evidence of Coke's previous convictions as evidence of bad character, how would you prove the convictions? How would you prove the underlying facts?

12.15.2 *Blackstone* v *Coke*

1. If Coke is convicted at his criminal trial of raping Margaret, what use may Margaret make of that conviction as evidence in her claim against Coke?

2. Would Coke be entitled to seek to prove that, despite the conviction, he was not guilty of the rape? What proof would be required for this?

3. How would Margaret go about proving the conviction and the facts on which it was based?

4. What difference, if any, would it make if, at the time of trial in the civil action, Coke's conviction was the subject of a pending appeal to the Court of Appeal, Criminal Division?

5. If Coke is acquitted of the charge of raping Margaret, would Margaret be entitled to maintain her allegation of rape in her civil claim?

12.16 GENERAL QUESTIONS FOR DISCUSSION

1. May a witness give evidence that contradicts a previous judgment?

2. Does this preclude the prosecution from tendering evidence of previous acquittals where they concern relevant evidence of bad character?

3. What are judgments *in rem* and *in personam*?

4. Zac was convicted of murdering his wife. A playwright is writing a play based on the facts of the case. Zac wants to bring an action for libel against her as he claims that he was not guilty. May he do so?

5. What is the rule in *Hollington* v *Hewthorn* and how was it affected by enactment of the Civil Evidence Act 1968?

6. What is the effect of a certificate of conviction or acquittal in criminal law?

7. In relation to a charge of handling stolen goods, can the prosecution prove that the goods were stolen by adducing evidence of the conviction of the person who stole the goods? That is, when will the previous conviction of somebody other than an accused be admissible?

8. What was the significance of the decision in *Hayter*?

13

PUBLIC INTEREST IMMUNITY AND PRIVILEGE I: PUBLIC INTEREST IMMUNITY

A   PUBLIC INTEREST IMMUNITY AND PRIVILEGE CONTRASTED

SUMMARY OF MAIN POINTS

- The general policy favouring disclosure of all potentially relevant material may yield to competing policies: (1) entitling and sometimes compelling governmental and other bodies to withhold information in the public interest; or (2) entitling private parties to withhold privileged information.

- Public interest immunity and privilege are subject to different rules. Of interest are the approaches taken with respect to waiver of the right to withhold; and the use of secondary evidence if the original is immune from production.

13.1 GENERAL PRINCIPLES

One of the major principles recognized by the law in the conduct of litigation is that of disclosure of evidence. By this expression is meant that the parties should disclose to each other, for the purposes of the proceedings,[1] any and all evidence, relevant to the issues in those proceedings, which is or has been in their possession, custody, and power. The object of the principle is simply that all such relevant evidence in the case should be available to be inspected by all parties, and that the parties should be free to place before the court any evidence which will assist it in determining the truth and in doing justice between the parties. The idea of inspection of evidence in the possession of another party is primarily of importance in the field of documentary and real evidence, and most of the battles in the field of public interest immunity and privilege have been fought in relation to such evidence. But the principle of disclosure and its object of enabling the parties to place before the court all relevant and admissible evidence, applies to evidence in whatever form, and the rules of privilege in particular are of considerable significance in relation to certain kinds of oral evidence.

The principle has as a necessary corollary the rule that no party should be entitled to frustrate or hinder the doing of justice in any proceedings by withholding from his opponent or from the court evidence which is relevant and admissible for that purpose. But this cannot be an absolute rule. It may be overridden by some important public interest that certain evidence should not be disclosed to a party because of the likelihood of danger to the national interest or of impairment of the working of some aspect of the public service. In such a case, as Lord Reid pointed out in *Conway* v *Rimmer* [1968] AC 910, 940, the public interest in the doing of justice as between the parties to litigation has to be balanced against a different but equally demanding public interest:

> It is universally recognized that here there are two kinds of public interest which may clash. There is the public interest that harm shall not be done to the nation or the public service by disclosure of certain documents, and there is the public interest that the administration of justice shall not be frustrated by the withholding of documents which must be produced if justice is to be done. There are many cases where the nature of the injury which would or might be done to the nation or the public service is of so grave a character that no other interest, public or private, can be allowed to prevail over it.

The result of such considerations may be that facts of undoubted relevance to proceedings, which may indeed sometimes be potentially conclusive of such proceedings, will not be permitted to be proved. Such facts are said to be excluded by public policy. This exclusion applies in criminal cases, as well as civil.

The law also recognizes some private interests as prevailing over the general rule of disclosure of evidence. Although most private interests must bow to the requirement of a fair and open trial, some are important enough to override it. Certain rules may prevent evidence from being given, for example the rule that no person should be compelled to divulge what has passed between him and his legal advisers in the course of seeking and giving legal advice. Evidence which enjoys protection for a reason of this kind is said to be privileged. Privilege is dealt with in detail in the next chapter, but is referred to here to the extent necessary to compare and contrast it with public interest immunity. Again, evidence of undoubted relevance, and sometimes potentially conclusive evidence, may be withheld, and the interests of other parties are affected

---

[1] The court will not countenance the abuse of its process which results from the improper use of evidence ordered to be disclosed, i.e., the use of such evidence for purposes other than the proper conduct of the instant proceedings: *Riddick* v *Thames Board Mills Ltd* [1977] QB 881; *Church of Scientology* v *DHSS* (CA) [1979] 1 WLR 723; *Home Office* v *Harman* [1983] 1 AC 280; Criminal Procedure and Investigations Act 1996, s. 17; Civil Procedure Rules 1998, r. 31.22; Criminal Procedure Rules 2005, Part 26; *Taylor* v *Director of the Serious Fraud Office* [1999] 2 AC 177.

accordingly. Where a privilege is claimed and upheld, no adverse inference may be drawn by the tribunal of fact against the person claiming the privilege, based upon that party's refusal to give or disclose the privileged evidence.[2] The privileges recognized by English law are few and limited. The privileges against self-incrimination and compelled disclosure of confidential communications between lawyer and client are recognized generally in common law jurisdictions, including England. But in other respects, English law maintains an illiberal attitude to confidential communications. Parliament, it is true, created in deference to art. 10 of the European Convention on Human Rights (see 1.7) a limited privilege for journalists with respect to their sources of information (Contempt of Court Act 1981, s. 10: see 14.20). But it also abolished entirely the privilege against compelled matrimonial communications (Police and Criminal Evidence Act 1984, s. 80(9)). The law has failed to accord recognition to other privileges which American common law has generally upheld, for example the privileges against compelled disclosure of confidential communications between doctor or psychotherapist and patient, or priest and penitent.

The fact that evidence which is relevant[3] and otherwise admissible may be excluded by public policy or privilege, lends to the groups of rules an appearance of similarity which is misleading. The rules and their operation are quite distinct, and any superficial identity of result is more than outweighed by substantial and far-reaching differences.[4] A private privilege is a right to withhold information for the purpose of protecting the private interests of the party who exercises the privilege, and no other considerations, including that of motive, are relevant. On the other hand, public interest immunity exists for the benefit of some defined public interest, of which all concerned should, in theory, regard themselves as the guardians. In *Makanjuola* v *Commissioner of Police of the Metropolis* [1992] 3 All ER 617, 623, Bingham LJ said:

> Where a litigant asserts that documents are immune from production or disclosure on public interest grounds he is not (if the claim is well founded) claiming a right but observing a duty. Public interest immunity is not a trump card vouchsafed to certain privileged players to play when and as they wish. It is an exclusionary rule, imposed on parties in certain circumstances, even where it is to their disadvantage in the litigation.

Although *Makanjuola* was overruled by the House of Lords in *Chief Constable of Midlands Police, ex parte Wiley* [1995] 1 AC 274, Lord Woolf described this passage as 'a very clear statement as to the nature of public interest immunity', and, while he doubted some of the further observations of Bingham LJ in *Makanjuola*, Lord Woolf endorsed the above passage 'unhesitatingly'. Lord Woolf went on to add ([1995] 1 AC 274, 298) that a decision to withhold and a decision to disclose documents for which public interest immunity was claimed are not conflicting decisions of public policy, but simply different aspects of public policy. In the event of a decision to disclose, the aspect of public policy which favours the availability of information for use in litigation outweighs the aspect of public policy which favours the withholding of information to protect the working of the public service. It is submitted that, by way of contrast, in cases involving private privilege, there is no countervailing policy of disclosure; the policy is in favour of granting

---

[2] *Wentworth* v *Lloyd* (1864) 10 HL Cas 589.

[3] If evidence is not relevant then no question of public policy or privilege will arise: *Cheltenham Justices, ex parte Secretary of State for Trade* [1977] 1 WLR 95.

[4] The distinction is not assisted by the use of the misleading term 'Crown privilege' to describe some aspects of public policy. For criticism of this usage, see *Rogers* v *Home Secretary* [1973] AC 388, per Lord Reid at 400 and Lord Pearson at 406.

a party the right to withhold, and disclosure may be ordered only on some specific ground, for example that the privilege has been waived, or that it is been exercised in furtherance of some crime or fraud. As to the duty of ministers to uphold claims for public interest immunity, see the reforms advocated by the Scott Report (*Report of the Inquiry into the Export of Defence Equipment and Dual-use Goods to Iraq and Related Prosecutions* (House of Commons Papers, Session 1995–96, 115)); see Forsyth [1997] CLJ 51.

The main practical differences between public interest immunity and privileges reside in the areas of waiver and the use of secondary evidence (see 13.2 and 13.3).

13.2 POSSIBILITY OF WAIVER

13.2.1 Meaning and effect of waiver

Private privilege has always been a rule against compulsion, and has never prevented the voluntary disclosure or giving of privileged evidence by a person entitled to insist on the privilege. A person who voluntarily discloses in such circumstances is said to waive his privilege. Privilege may, according to the circumstances in which it arises, apply to evidence in the possession of, or capable of being given by, a party to proceedings, or any witness in the proceedings. The privilege is personal to that party or witness, and he alone can waive it.[5] Conversely, the onus of asserting the privilege also rests on the party or witness entitled to it, and evidence disclosed or given other than under unlawful compulsion will be admissible for all purposes, even though privilege might with advice or diligence have been asserted in respect of it.[6] Waiver may occur in a variety of ways, most commonly by volunteering information while giving evidence or producing documents to an opponent for inspection and copying without objection.[7] A party necessarily waives a privilege by instituting proceedings in which he relies on privileged information as part of his case, for example where he sues his solicitor for professional negligence.[8]

When a privilege is waived, the result is that the evidence may be given by any party, and is treated like any other evidence in the case. A party may not waive privilege with respect to part of a communication, which he regards as favourable and wishes to adduce in evidence, and claim to maintain the privilege with respect to other parts which he would prefer to withhold, unless the different parts are clearly and readily severable and deal with quite different subjects. In *Great Atlantic Insurance Co.* v *Home Insurance Co.* [1981] 1 WLR 529, the Court of Appeal held that by reading into the record two paragraphs of a memorandum received by the plaintiffs from their American attorneys, the whole of which was clearly privileged, counsel for the plaintiffs had waived any privilege in the whole document, since both the part read and the parts withheld dealt with the same subject-matter. Templeman LJ referred to *Churton* v *Frewen* (1865) 2 Drew & Sm 390, in which the court refused disclosure of a privileged report which contained extracts

---

[5] It seems to follow, and has been held, that a party cannot in general found an appeal on the upholding or rejection of a privilege attaching to his witness: *Kinglake* (1870) 22 LT 335.

[6] See *Re L (A Minor) (Police Investigation: Privilege)* [1997] AC 16; *Noel* [1914] 3 KB 848. But disclosure of materials for a specific purpose for the purposes of litigation does not amount to a waiver for purposes extraneous to the litigation (*Bourns Inc.* v *Raychem Corporation* [1999] 3 All ER 154); and waiver may be made expressly for a limited purpose, preserving privilege for all other purposes: *B* v *Auckland District Law Society* [2004] 4 All ER 269 (PC).

[7] But not simply by mentioning a document in a pleading or witness statement, without more: *Rubin* v *Expandable Ltd* [2008] 1 WLR 1099; see Civil Procedure Rules 1998, r. 31.14.

[8] See generally *Kershaw* v *Whelan* [1996] 1 WLR 358; *Bowden* [1999] 1 WLR 823. Though privilege may be maintained in communications unrelated to the litigation: see *Paragon Finance plc* v *Freshfields* [1999] 1 WLR 1183.

from and references to documents and records kept in a public registry, these latter not being privileged. Although this was a case in which it was sought to obtain disclosure of, rather than withhold a part, the reasoning is equally applicable to both situations. The court said (*ibid.* at 394) that:

> ...it would be very dangerous, and trench very much upon the principle which protects the report itself, if that were permitted; for it would be hardly possible to seal up and effectually protect from inspection those parts which constitute the report, and which it is admitted there is no right to see. Such a report would most probably (indeed, from its nature, almost necessarily) be not merely a collection of extracts from and copies of ancient records, with a distinct and separate report referring to them; but the extracts and copies would be so interspersed with...observations and comments...as to render it quite impossible to separate the different portions.

For this reason, it is incumbent on a party to consider carefully before making use of any part of a privileged document or other communication; the remainder should be scrutinized with great care. It is to be noted that in *Great Atlantic*, the plaintiffs did not intend any waiver. Indeed, counsel had mistakenly thought that he had read the whole document into the record. But it is actual disclosure, and not intent, which governs whether a waiver has occurred. It may be, and often is, wholly inadvertent.[9]

On the other hand, although the waiver operates with respect to the entirety of the communication, it does not extend beyond the transaction dealt with in the communication and cannot be used to defeat privilege in unrelated communications. What is unrelated must be decided by the court as a question of fact in each case.[10]

13.2.2 Waiver of public interest immunity

An objection made on the ground of public interest immunity may be made by any person, and in many cases a governmental entity makes the objection, even though not a party to the case, by means of intervention. The court may even take the point of its own motion. Because of the nature of the public interest objection, it has been doubted whether it can ever be waived, though the better view would seem to be that it depends on the nature of the document. In *Rogers* v *Home Secretary*[11] Lord Simon said:

> It is true that the public interest which demands that evidence be withheld has to be weighed against the public interest in the administration of justice that courts should have the fullest possible access to all relevant material...; but once the former public interest is held to outweigh the latter, the evidence cannot in any circumstances be admitted. It is not a privilege which may be waived—by the Crown...or by anyone else.

However, in *Alfred Crompton Amusement Machines Ltd* v *Customs and Excise Commissioners (No. 2)* [1974] AC 405, 434 Lord Cross indicated that if a person or party (such as an informer) for whose

---

[9] But see on this point Newbold (1991) 107 LQR 99.

[10] See, e.g., *Fulham Leisure Holdings Ltd* v *Nicholson Graham & Jones (A Firm)* [2006] 2 All ER 599; *Paragon Finance plc* v *Freshfields* [1999] 1 WLR 1183; *General Accident Fire and Life Assurance Corp. Ltd* v *Tanter* [1984] 1 WLR 100.

[11] [1973] AC 388, 407. In *Air Canada* v *Secretary of State for Trade* [1983] 2 AC 394 at 436, Lord Fraser, apparently *obiter*, seemed to agree with Lord Simon's view that waiver is precluded in all cases. But there seem to be cases in which the government does not make an arguable case for non-disclosure, which may be an informal way of reaching the same result.

benefit the objection was made volunteered to testify or disclose the evidence, then a waiver could be permitted.

The Court of Appeal in *Hehir* v *Commissioner of Police of the Metropolis* [1982] 1 WLR 715 (overruled on other grounds by *Chief Constable of West Midlands Police, ex parte Wiley* [1995] 1 AC 274) was faced with this conflict of authority. The plaintiff was arrested and charged with a minor offence under the Vagrancy Act 1824, which was subsequently dismissed. He filed suit against the Commissioner, claiming damages for alleged false imprisonment and malicious prosecution on the part of the police officers involved. The plaintiff had made a statement for the purposes of a police inquiry conducted under s. 49 of the Police Act 1964. At that time, all such statements were automatically protected from disclosure because of the need for candid, confidential statements to be made by police officers and others.[12] At trial, counsel for the Commissioner sought to cross-examine the plaintiff on his statement, and the plaintiff objected. A two-judge Court of Appeal, on an interlocutory appeal, reluctantly upheld the plaintiff's objection. Since the whole of the material compiled during the s. 49 inquiry was subject to immunity from disclosure in the public interest, so as to encourage future candour, the Commissioner was not entitled to waive the immunity as to any part, even for the purpose of cross-examining the plaintiff. Lawton and Brightman LJJ were unanimous in holding that waiver could not be permitted on the facts presented, though Brightman LJ left open for future decision the question whether public policy immunity might not in certain circumstances be waived.

Lord Denning MR said on more than one occasion that waiver might be permitted in certain cases. In *Campbell* v *Tameside MBC*[13] he indicated disapproval of the decision in *Hehir* and added:

> I know that in the days of the old Crown Privilege it was often said that it could not be waived. That is still correct when the documents are in the vital category spoken of by Lord Reid in *Conway* v *Rimmer* [1968] AC 910 at 940. This category includes all those documents which must be kept top secret because the disclosure of them would be injurious to national defence or to diplomatic relations or the detection of crime (as the names of informers). But not where the documents come within Lord Reid's lower category. This category includes documents which are kept confidential in order that subordinates should be frank and candid in their reports, or for any other good reason. In those cases, the privilege can be waived by the maker and recipients of the confidential document.

It is submitted that Lord Denning's *obiter dicta* should be followed as a sensible way of balancing competing interests. Not every document capable of attracting public policy immunity must necessarily be withheld in every case. And there is increasing support for the proposition that some distinction should be drawn between 'higher' and 'lower' level documents, i.e., between those documents whose disclosure would involve some risk to national security or the efficient detection of crime, and those requiring confidentiality for some lesser purpose, such as promoting candour among those who write or contribute information to them. There has been some support for the view expressed by Lord Denning in *Campbell* (above) that, in the case of lower-level documents, immunity may be waived by the maker or recipient of the document. See also Lord Denning's observations in *Neilson* v *Laugharne* [1981] QB 736, 747; *Alfred Crompton*

---

[12] See *Neilson* v *Laugharne* [1981] QB 736, since overruled by *Chief Constable of West Midlands Police, ex parte Wiley* [1995] 1 AC 274.

[13] [1982] QB 1065, where Lord Denning MR was plainly speaking *obiter*, as he was on the same subject in *Neilson* v *Laugharne* [1981] QB 736, 747. See also Lord Denning's remarks dissenting in the Court of Appeal in *Burmah Oil Co. Ltd* v *Bank of England* [1979] 1 WLR 473, 487.

Amusement Machines Ltd v *Customs and Excise Commissioners (No. 2)* [1974] AC 405, 434 per Lord Cross. In *Governor of Brixton Prison, ex parte Osman* [1991] 1 WLR 281, it was held that, while a prior disclosure in other proceedings of documents subject to immunity did not in and of itself constitute a waiver in the instant proceedings, it was nonetheless a factor to be considered in balancing the interests of the government and the litigant seeking disclosure, and *dicta* in this case suggest that public interest immunity can be waived. And in *Horseferry Road Magistrates' Court, ex parte Bennett (No. 2)* [1994] 1 All ER 289, the Court laid down the procedure to be followed for voluntary disclosure by the Crown of sensitive public documents in criminal cases, which suggests that, at least in criminal cases, the principle may now be firmly established.

In *Chief Constable of West Midlands Police, ex parte Wiley* [1995] 1 AC 274, 298, Lord Woolf made the following observation about the *dictum* of Lord Simon of Glaisdale in *Rogers* v *Home Secretary* (quoted above) which, it is submitted, aptly summarizes the real issue with respect to waiver in the context of claims for public policy immunity:

> It will be observed from that passage that when Lord Simon said that the privilege was one which could not be waived, he was referring to the situation after it had been determined that the public interest against disclosure outweighed that of disclosure in the interests of the administration of justice. When that is the determination which has been made, it is inevitable that the preservation of the document should follow so as to protect what has been held to be the dominant public interest. It is, however, unhelpful to talk of 'waiver' in the different situations where the balancing of the conflicting public interests has not yet been carried out or where it has been carried out and the result requires disclosure. Although it is the practice to talk of conflicting public interests this can be misleading. The conflict is more accurately described as being between two different *aspects* of the public interest. If it is decided that the aspect of the public interest which reflects the requirements of the administration of justice outweighs the aspect of the interest which is against disclosure, then it is the public interest which requires disclosure.

13.3 USE OF SECONDARY EVIDENCE

Where facts are excluded by public interest immunity, not only are the documents which are the immediate subject of the exclusion affected, but the result is that the contents of such documents cannot be proved in evidence by secondary means. This excludes copies of such documents, oral evidence of their contents and even their use by a witness to refresh his memory.[14] In the case of private privilege, however, a different rule applies at common law. A privilege attaches only to an original document or communication, and secondary evidence of the contents is admissible to prove the contents of the document or communication (*Calcraft* v *Guest* [1889] 1 QB 759). If an opponent was able to obtain evidence such as a copy of a privileged document, or to give oral evidence of its contents, this evidence was not precluded by the rule of privilege. As will appear below, however, considerable difficulty was encountered in reconciling this rule with another rule, whereby a party was entitled to apply for an injunction to secure the return of privileged documents which had been disclosed inadvertently, or which had been obtained by some improper action by an opponent, and to restrain the use of evidence based on the documents (*Lord Ashburton* v *Pape* [1913] 2 Ch 469). Despite the introduction of r. 31.20 of the Civil

---

[14] See *Gain* v *Gain* [1961] 1 WLR 1469. Any course which expressly or by necessary implication involves the revelation of the contents seems to be prohibited.

Procedure Rules 1998 (below) to deal with such cases, the common law position may continue to be important in some situations, and may be relevant in deciding how the new rule is to be applied.

In *Calcraft* v *Guest* [1889] 1 QB 759, the defendant was held to be entitled to put in evidence copies of proofs of evidence of witnesses of the plaintiff's predecessor in title, relating to a previous action, the originals of these documents (which were plainly privileged under the legal professional privilege rule) having been returned to the plaintiff. The privilege attached only to the original, and did not inhibit the proof of the contents by other means, even though the plaintiff could not be compelled to produce the original or to disclose it to the defendant. In *Rumping* v *DPP* [1964] AC 814, the House of Lords held that a letter written by the accused to his wife, which amounted to a confession to the murder with which he was charged, could be put in evidence by the prosecution, it having been handed over to the police by a person to whom it had been entrusted for posting. The letter would have been privileged, had it reached the wife's hands, as a matrimonial communication, and the decision illustrates an even wider rule than that in *Calcraft* v *Guest*, namely that privilege attaching to the original can be lost by its actual disclosure, even where no waiver is intended.

The rule in *Calcraft* v *Guest* was complicated, however, by the later decision of the Court of Appeal in *Lord Ashburton* v *Pape* [1913] 2 Ch 469. The plaintiff, Lord Ashburton, opposed the discharge of the defendant, Pape, from bankruptcy. Pape, by a trick, succeeded in obtaining from a clerk employed by Lord Ashburton's solicitors, a number of documents, which he caused to be copied. Lord Ashburton applied successfully for an injunction requiring Pape to hand over all the original documents in his possession, and restraining him from making use of the copies or any information contained in them, except for the purpose of the bankruptcy proceedings and subject to the directions of the Bankruptcy Court. On appeal, the Court of Appeal held that Lord Ashburton was entitled to the injunction, including an order restraining use of the copies without the limitation expressed in the judgment at first instance. All the members of the Court agreed that equitable relief was available to restrain the use of copies of documents, possession of which had been wrongfully obtained (see the judgments of Cozens-Hardy MR, *ibid.* at 472, Kennedy LJ at 473–4, and Swinfen Eady LJ at 475).

It was argued for the defendant that *Calcraft* v *Guest* was authority for the proposition that the defendant was entitled to make use of the copies in the bankruptcy proceedings, if for no other purpose, and despite the fact that Lord Ashburton might be entitled to the return of the originals. However, the Court of Appeal found a clear ground of distinction between the two cases. Cozens-Hardy MR said (*ibid.* at 473):

> The rule of evidence as explained in *Calcraft* v *Guest*...merely amounts to this, that if a litigant wants to prove a particular document which by reason of privilege or some circumstances he cannot furnish by the production of the original, he may produce a copy as secondary evidence although that copy has been obtained by improper means.... The court in such an action is not really trying the circumstances under which the document was produced. That is not an issue in the case... But that does not seem to me to have any bearing upon a case where the whole subject-matter of the action is the right to retain the originals or copies of certain documents which are privileged.

Swinfen Eady LJ said (*ibid.* at 477):

> The fact...that a document, whether original or copy, is admissible in evidence is no answer to the demand of the lawful owner for the delivery up of the document, and no answer to an application by the lawful owner of confidential information to restrain it from being published or copied.

In *Goddard* v *Nationwide Building Society* [1987] QB 670, the Court of Appeal was faced with the task of attempting the reconciliation between these cases, and did so by holding that *Lord Ashburton* v *Pape* continued to permit injunctive relief. A solicitor acting for the plaintiffs in the purchase of a house also acted for the defendant building society, from which the plaintiffs obtained a mortgage to finance the purchase. The plaintiffs sued the defendant for alleged negligence on the part of its surveyor. The defendant obtained and proposed to make use of an attendance note made by the solicitor, dealing with a conversation he had had with the plaintiffs. The plaintiffs contended that the note was privileged, and applied for an injunction restraining the defendant from using it. The judge at first instance refused the application, but the plaintiffs succeeded on appeal.

May LJ said ([1987] QB at 683):

> I confess that I do not find the decision in *Lord Ashburton* v *Pape* logically satisfactory, depending as it does on the order in which applications are made in litigation. Nonetheless, I think that it and *Calcraft* v *Guest* are good authority for the following proposition. If a litigant has in his possession copies of documents to which legal professional privilege attaches, he may nonetheless use such copies as secondary evidence in his litigation: however, if he has not yet used the documents in that way, the mere fact that he intends to do so is no answer to a claim against him by the person in whom the privilege is vested for delivery up of the copies or to restrain him from disclosing or making any use of any information contained in them.

Despite this effort to reconcile the two principles, there was much uncertainty as to the result in such cases, and in the end the matter seemed to resolve itself into the procedural one of whether or not the party entitled to the return of the documents applied for relief in time to prevent their use as evidence by his opponent. The relevance of the manner in which the documents were obtained by the opponent, if any, was also never satisfactorily resolved.[15] In civil cases,[16] the procedural complication has apparently been simplified by r. 31.20 of the Civil Procedure Rules 1998, which provides:

> Restriction on use of a privileged document inspection of which has been inadvertently allowed.
> Where a party inadvertently allows a privileged document to be inspected, the party who has inspected the document may use it or its contents only with the permission of the court.

This rule obviates the need for the party seeking the return of the document to apply for injunctive relief merely to prevent an opponent from adducing the document in evidence, although there may be cases in which a party would still apply for an order restoring the document to his possession, either to prevent any wider disclosure or to limit the opponent's access to the intellectual property in the document (which is often the most damaging result of an inadvertent disclosure, and which cannot be altogether cured by any order made by the court). It is submitted that the court may, either on the application of a party or of its own motion, order the return of a document to which r. 31.20 applies in the course of the proceedings, without requiring the party

---

[15] See *Goddard* v *Nationwide Building Society* [1987] QB 670; *Guinness Peat Properties Ltd* v *Fitzroy Robinson Partnership* [1987] 2 All ER 716; *English and American Insurance Co. Ltd* v *Herbert Smith & Co.* (1987) 137 NLJ 148. The problem was complicated by the rule that general equitable principles might prevent the grant of injunctive relief to a party guilty of inordinate delay.

[16] In criminal cases, an injunction cannot be granted to restrain the use of evidence by the Crown in a public prosecution (*Butler* v *Board of Trade* [1971] Ch 680).

entitled to commence separate proceedings for that purpose.[17] There is no doubt that r. 31.20 provides a welcome step forward in civil cases.

However, some questions remain to be answered. Rule 31.19(8) makes clear that the new disclosure rules do not affect the rules of law which require or permit a document to be withheld from disclosure or inspection on the ground of public interest immunity. Nor do the new rules affect the question of whether a particular document is or is not privileged. Most importantly, the courts must decide what r. 31.20 means by 'inadvertent', and on what basis permission to use an inadvertently disclosed document should be given or refused. The most obvious case of inadvertence is failing to comply with the requirement of r. 31.19(3) that a party must state in writing any right or duty he has to withhold a document, and if necessary, apply to the court under r. 31.19(5) to decide whether or not the claim to withhold the document is correct. In the absence of such a statement, the other parties may inspect the document and, technically, any privilege in it has been waived. The wording of r. 31.20 clearly suggests that this is the kind of inadvertence to which it is intended to apply. But equally, an inadvertent disclosure, in the general sense of that phrase, may be made by sending the document to an opponent or allowing an opponent to come into possession of it in other circumstances.[18]

Whether or not the court should take into account the manner in which the document was obtained in deciding whether to give or refuse permission to use the document must also be resolved. As we have seen (3.10.2) the general rule of English law is that the manner in which a document is obtained does not render the document inadmissible if it is relevant and admissible apart from that question. But in *ITC Distributors Ltd* v *Video Exchange Ltd* [1982] Ch 436, Warner J refused to allow the defendant to make use of documents which he had obtained by a trick, after the plaintiffs and their solicitors had brought them into court for the purposes of the trial, in circumstances which constituted a serious contempt of court. Warner J did not make it clear whether the basis for his decision was the exercise of his discretion or a matter of public policy in preventing such abuses of the court's procedure. In *Goddard* v *Nationwide Building Society* [1987] QB 670, 684, Nourse LJ held that the latter was the true basis. This was consistent with the view taken by Nourse LJ in *Goddard* that the grant of injunctive relief did not depend on whether or not the conduct of the party who obtained the document was innocent or improper, because the only issue was whether or not the party claiming the return of the document was entitled to have it. But it is less consistent with the view taken by Slade LJ in *Guinness Peat Properties Ltd* v *Fitzroy Robinson Partnership* [1987] 2 All ER 716 that the general common law rule (that a party was entitled to make use of secondary evidence of privileged documents) would apply unless it was appropriate to grant injunctive relief because the document had been obtained by 'fraud' or 'obvious mistake'.[19] An interesting question is whether or not a document obtained by fraud or a trick has been 'inadvertently disclosed' for the purposes of r. 31.20. It is submitted that the

---

[17] See Part 25 of the Civil Procedure Rules 1998. This position also seems to have been reached eventually under the old procedural rules: see *Goddard* v *Nationwide Building Society* [1987] QB 670, 684 per Nourse LJ, doubting the view of Warner J in *ITC Film Distributors Ltd* v *Video Exchange Ltd* [1982] Ch 436 that no relief could be granted unless applied for in separate proceedings. Nourse LJ held that, at most, the issue of a *pro forma* writ (claim form) would be all that was required.

[18] And see *English and American Insurance Co. Ltd* v *Herbert Smith & Co.* (1987) 137 NLJ 148, where the error was made by counsel's clerk. This decision contains interesting and still pertinent observations about the duty of solicitors who come into possession of documents in such circumstances.

[19] As to 'obvious mistake', see *Al Fayed* v *Commissioner of Police for the Metropolis* (2002) *The Times*, 17 June 2002; *English and American Insurance Co. Ltd* v *Herbert Smith & Co.* (1987) 137 NLJ 148. For an example of 'fraud' in this context, see *ISTIL Group* v *Zahoor* [2003] 2 All ER 252.

general equitable principles which govern the grant of injunctions need not be applied strictly now that the court has a specific power to rule on the use of documents obtained in such circumstances. How far the manner in which the document has been obtained should affect the result, and whether the general rule as to evidence illegally or unfairly obtained will be adhered to, remains to be seen.

The lesson to be learned is that privilege must be jealously guarded: it ceases to exist if waived or lost, and is rendered impotent by copying unless prompt action can be taken to restrain the copier. The lesson was learned the hard way in *Tompkins* (1977) 67 Cr App R 181, where, the accused having given certain evidence in chief, he was asked to look during cross-examination at a note which he had earlier written to his counsel which contradicted his evidence. The contents of the note were not read out, but on seeing it, the accused admitted that he had not told the truth in chief and altered his evidence. He was subsequently convicted. The Court of Appeal held that the prosecution had been entitled to make use of the note as a previous inconsistent statement. Although originally privileged, as a communication between client and legal adviser, its loss entitled the prosecution to make use of it, once it was in their hands. Ormrod LJ observed, perhaps a little unkindly, that it would require 'a remarkable exercise in moral philosophy' to conclude that perjury should not be exposed where such means came to hand. And in *Cottrill* [1997] Crim LR 56, it was held, applying *Tomkins*, that the prosecution were entitled to cross-examine the accused about a statement he had made in writing to his solicitors, even though the solicitors had sent the statement to the prosecution without the accused's knowledge or consent.

B   PUBLIC INTEREST IMMUNITY

SUMMARY OF MAIN POINTS

- Where an application for public interest immunity is made in civil cases, the court should inspect the documents in question and then balance the public interest in withholding the information against the public interest in making them available for the purposes of the litigation.

- In criminal cases the court must regard as the most important factor the accused's right to a fair trial, and must also consider the public interest in withholding information. The general rule is that there must be disclosure of any unused material which may weaken the prosecution case or strengthen the defence. If any withholding occurs, everything possible must be done to protect the rights of the accused; in some cases it may be wrong to allow the case against him to continue.

- In addition to 'affairs of state' in the strict sense, public interest immunity may attach to the materials of a wide range of governmental and quasi-government bodies acting in the public service.

- Public interest immunity attaches to the identity of persons who supply information for the detection of crime. This may extend to the identity of premises used for surveillance and the occupiers of such premises, and to methods of surveillance and intelligence gathering.

- No immunity or privilege attaches to material simply because it is created and used confidentially, though the courts will respect confidentiality in non-privileged professional relationships as far as possible.

13.4 APPLICATIONS TO WITHOLD MATERIAL SUBJECT TO PUBLIC INTEREST IMMUNITY

13.4.1 Civil cases

In civil cases, the Crown or other interested organization is entitled to object to the disclosure of documents for which it claims public interest immunity. If the Crown or the organization is not a party to the claim, it may intervene for the purpose of preventing disclosure. Rule 31.19 of the Civil Procedure Rules 1998 permits any person to apply for an order that he is entitled to withhold a document on the ground of public interest immunity. The application must be supported by evidence. In cases decided before the coming into effect of this rule, the practice was for the evidence to be in the form of an affidavit or certificate given on behalf of the Crown by the relevant minister or a senior subordinate,[20] or by an officer of corresponding rank in the organization. The court retains the power to regulate the method of proof, and may require further evidence, but no doubt it will usually accept an affidavit or certificate as before. The affidavit or certificate should disclose with particularity the identity and nature of the documents. It should explain the nature of the objection to disclosure, and state that the maker has personally examined the documents before coming to the conclusion that they should be withheld in the public interest.[21] The court may require that the documents in question be produced for its inspection (r. 31.19(6)) and this will, no doubt, be the usual procedure. Rule 31.1(6) permits representations to the court to be made by any person, so that, if the initial application is made by a person other than the Crown or an affected organization, the views of the Crown or the organization may be taken into consideration.

13.4.2 Criminal cases

In criminal cases also, it had been held that the court must be the final arbiter of the question of whether or not documents should be withheld on the ground of public interest immunity.[22] In *Davis* [1993] 1 WLR 613, the Court of Appeal laid down detailed guidelines as to the procedure to be followed in such cases. In essence, the Court held that the duty of the prosecution in general is to make voluntary disclosure of all relevant materials. Where they consider that material should be withheld on the ground of public interest immunity, the prosecution should notify the defence that an application to withhold will be made, and indicate the general nature of the evidence in question. The defence will then be entitled to be heard on the application. In rare cases, where even these steps would jeopardize the need for confidentiality, an application may be made *ex parte* and, in a very rare case, even without informing the defence that this step is to

---

[20] *Alfred Crompton Amusement Machines Ltd* v *Commissioners of Customs & Excise (No. 2)* [1972] 2 QB 102 (Court of Appeal; the point was not considered in the House of Lords).

[21] See *Re Grosvenor Hotel, London (No. 2)* [1965] Ch 1210, per Lord Denning MR at 1244. The certificate is not conclusive except in very limited cases, such as matters affecting national security (*Balfour* v *Foreign and Commonwealth Office* [1994] 1 WLR 681; see 13.6). Rule 31.19 does not affect the substantive law governing whether or not evidence is subject to public interest immunity: see r. 31.19(8).

[22] *Ward* [1993] 1 WLR 619. In trials on indictment, the court means the Crown Court—the transferring magistrates should not attempt to make such a decision (*DPP, ex parte Warby* [1994] Crim LR 281). As to the practice where the case is to be tried summarily, see *H* [2004] 2 AC 134, [43] *et seq.*; *Bromley Magistrates' Court, ex parte Smith* [1995] 1 WLR 944; *South Worcestershire Justices, ex parte Lilley* [1995] 1 WLR 1595; *Stipendiary Magistrate for Norfolk, ex parte Taylor* (1997) 161 JP 773.

be taken.[23] Any ruling made by the court on such an application would not be final, but could be reviewed by the judge throughout the trial. If circumstances changed, or if the original ruling appeared to be wrong, the judge could make a new ruling, offering the prosecution the choice between making disclosure and abandoning the case.

The Criminal Procedure and Investigations Act 1996, which introduced new rules regarding the pre-trial disclosure of evidence in criminal cases (now amended by ss. 32 to 39 of the Criminal Justice Act 2003), made provision for the treatment of 'sensitive' materials, a category which includes, but is wider than, documents subject to public interest immunity. These provisions are supported by Part 25 of the Criminal Procedure Rules 2005 which, broadly speaking, correspond to the guidelines laid down in *Davis*.[24] Section 3(6) of the Act provides:

> Material must not be disclosed under this section to the extent that the court, on an application by the prosecutor, concludes that it is not in the public interest to disclose it and orders accordingly.

Rule 25(2) and (3) of the Rules require that, in general, notice of an application should be served on the court and the defence, but by r. 25(4) and (5) this procedure need not be followed where to do so would necessarily give away the nature of the materials sought to be withheld. In these cases, the application may be made *ex parte* and, if necessary, without informing the defence that it is being made.

Sections 14 and 15 of the Act provide that, if a ruling is made that the materials should not be disclosed, the court must keep the question of whether or not it is necessary to withhold the evidence under review throughout the trial. In cases tried on indictment, s. 15 imposes this duty on the court irrespective of whether or not the accused applies for review of the court's original decision, though the accused may do so at any time during the case. In cases tried summarily, s. 14 requires a review only where requested by the defendant. In either case, if the court forms the opinion that disclosure should be made because the public interest now requires disclosure, it must order accordingly and so inform the prosecution. The prosecutor must then either comply with the court's order or abandon the case.

13.4.3 Withholding evidence and the European Convention

The withholding of evidence, especially evidence which might assist the defence, is a serious step and one which should be taken only where a strong public interest in withholding it clearly outweighs the general obligation of disclosure. Moreover, this decision must be made by the trial judge. This rule raises obvious issues of fairness under art. 6 of the European Convention on Human Rights. The appellants in *Davis* (above) petitioned the European Court of Human Rights for relief following their conviction and the dismissal of their appeal by the Court of Appeal. The Court held (*Rowe and Davis* v *United Kingdom* (2000) 30 EHRR 1) that the right to a fair trial guaranteed by art. 6 of the Convention in general requires that the prosecution disclose all relevant evidence in their possession to the accused, whether the evidence is favourable to the prosecution or to the defence. There may, however, be exceptional cases in which overriding competing interests such as national security, protection of the identity of informers,

---

[23] The hearing of *ex parte* applications should be strictly confined to cases in which it is necessary; all other applications, including those made by the defence, should be heard *inter partes*: see *Templar* [2003] EWCA Crim 3186; *Smith* [1998] 2 Cr App 1; and see *Rowe and Davis* v *United Kingdom*, text below.

[24] For further details as to the practice in such cases, see *Blackstone's Criminal Practice*, 2009 edn, para. D9.26 *et seq.*

or protection of methods of investigation, may justify the withholding of some evidence. But such withholding must be confined to that which is strictly necessary, and any prejudice to the accused must be remedied by procedural means. In the instant case, at the trial the material in question had been withheld both from the defence and the trial judge (who had the duty to rule on whether it should be disclosed or withheld). The material had further been withheld until the time of the Appeal, when it was disclosed on an *ex parte* basis to the Court of Appeal. In these circumstances, there had been a clear violation of art. 6, because neither at the trial nor at the appellate stage were the accused able to contest the withholding of the material in any effective way. The Court did not clearly indicate its opinion of the procedural sufficiency of the provisions of the Criminal Procedure and Investigations Act 1996 and the rules made pursuant to that Act governing disclosure (text and note 21 above). As a result of this decision, another Court of Appeal subsequently allowed a further appeal by the appellants against conviction.[25] It is of some interest that the trial in *Davis* took place in 1990, some years before the introduction of the rules made under the 1996 Act, and some years before the coming into effect of the Human Rights Act 1998.

As in relation to other aspects of the law of evidence, the European Court of Human Rights is concerned to protect the underlying fairness of the trial and not to regulate the detailed rules of evidence of a Convention State. The Court will, therefore, be concerned primarily with whether the procedural safeguards offered by domestic law are adequate to protect the right of the accused to a fair trial in the context of decisions on applications to withhold material.[26] The Court will consider whether the State has provided the accused with an essentially adversarial process and with equality of arms appropriate to the nature of the proceedings. It will be less concerned with the specific outcome of those applications. Thus in *Jasper* v *United Kingdom*,[27] where, although the application was made *ex parte*, the accused was given as much information as possible, and was allowed to make representations based on his limited knowledge of the materials, the Court held that no violation of art. 6 of the Convention had occurred. The materials the prosecution sought to withhold were not, in fact, placed before the jury. But in *Edwards* v *United Kingdom* (2003) 15 BHRC 189, where the judge was the tribunal of fact on an issue of entrapment, it was held that a violation of art. 6 occurred when an *ex parte* application was made, the accused was not informed, and he was given no opportunity to make representations. There had been no opportunity for the accused to play a role in an adversarial proceeding relating to the evidence in question, and they had been disclosed to the tribunal of fact. However, the procedural fairness required by art. 6 may be satisfied by full access to an appellate review of the case.[28]

In *H* [2004] 2 AC 134, the House of Lords considered public interest immunity applications further in the light of these decisions, and gave detailed guidance about the approach to be taken

---

[25] *The Independent*, 18 July 2000.

[26] *Dowset* v *United Kingdom* (2003) 38 EHRR 845; and see generally 1.7.2.

[27] (2000) 30 EHRR 441; the decision was made by a narrow majority of the Court. See also *Fitt* v *United Kingdom* (2000) EHRR 480; contrast *Atlan* v *United Kingdom* (2001) 34 EHRR 833.

[28] In *Botmeh* [2002] 1 WLR 531, it was suggested that in proceedings before the Court of Appeal, any *ex parte* application is improper because of the role of the court in providing a fair procedural review of the proceedings at first instance. The Court declined to lay down any such rule, holding that such an application is not *per se* unfair. It may be, however, that *ex parte* applications in the Court of Appeal should be even harder to justify than at first instance.

by judges when considering public interest immunity applications. The essential points, in the order in which they should be dealt with, are as follows:

> (1) Identify whether the material sought to be withheld may weaken the prosecution case or strengthen the defence case: (a) if it would not, it may be withheld; (b) if it would, the 'golden rule' is that it must be disclosed subject to considering further—
>
> (2) Ask whether there is a real risk of serious prejudice to an important and identified public interest: (a) if no, then no public interest immunity attaches and it must be disclosed; (b) if yes, consider further—
>
> (3) Ask whether the accused's interests can be protected without disclosure, or whether disclosure can be ordered in such a way as to afford adequate protection both to the public interest and to the accused; (a) if no, it may be necessary to stop the case; (b) if yes, consider further—
>
> (4) If limited disclosure is possible, the prosecution may be invited to prepare formal admissions of fact, summaries or extracts, or redacted versions of the documents in question;
>
> (5) Keep in mind throughout the question of whether this represents the minimum withholding necessary to protect the public interest; if not, it may be necessary to order further disclosure;
>
> (6) If the possibility of unfairness to the accused remains, or if the prosecution is unable to comply, it will be necessary to stop the case;
>
> (7) The question of disclosure must be kept under review as the trial proceeds; if circumstances change, a further decision may be necessary.

In summary, the House held that the court must always give full weight to the duty to the prosecution to disclose all relevant evidence which may tend to undermine the prosecution's case or to strengthen the defence. Any derogation from the disclosure should be the minimum necessary to uphold the public interest. Applications on an *ex parte* basis should be made only where strictly necessary.[29] Delivering the opinion of the House, Lord Bingham of Cornhill said: (*ibid.* at [14]):

> Fairness ordinarily requires that any material held by the prosecution which weakens its case or strengthens that of the defendant, if not relied on as part of its formal case against the defendant, should be disclosed to the defence. Bitter experience has shown that miscarriages of justice may occur where such material is withheld from disclosure. The golden rule is that full disclosure of such material should be made.

At para. [37] Lord Bingham added:

> Throughout his or her consideration of any disclosure issue the trial judge must bear constantly in mind the overriding principles referred to in this opinion. In applying them, the judge should involve the defence to the maximum extent possible without disclosing that which the general interest requires to be protected but taking full account of the specific defence which is relied on. There will be very few cases indeed in which some measure of disclosure to the defence will not be possible, even if this is confined to the fact that an *ex parte* application is to be made. If even that information is withheld and if the material to be withheld is of significant help to the defendant, there must be a very serious question whether the prosecution should proceed, since special counsel, even if appointed, cannot then receive any instructions from the defence at all.

---

[29] For observations on the dangers inherent in *ex parte* meetings between the judge and prosecuting counsel, see *Templar* [2003] EWCA Crim 3186. See also *Smith* [1998] 2 Cr App R 1, in which it was emphasized that a record should be made of all such meetings by a court reporter.

13.4.3.1 Appointment of special counsel

The possibility of appointing special counsel to inspect and advise on applications to withhold material on the basis of public interest immunity has been canvassed in a number of cases. In *Edwards v United Kingdom* it was suggested that this would be the proper course to take in any case where the judge must act as the tribunal of fact on an issue such as entrapment, which might effectively determine the outcome of the case. There may be cases in which it would be useful to have an independent third party inspect the materials in such a case, and a suggestion to that effect was made by Sir Robin Auld in his *Review of the Criminal Courts of England and Wales* (2001), paras 193–7. In *H* it was argued to the House of Lords that, in any case where neither the accused nor his legal representative is present during a hearing of an application to withhold, the decision in *Edwards* requires the appointment of special counsel. The House declined to lay down any such rule, but made it clear that in exceptional circumstances it may be necessary to do so to protect the interests of the accused.[30] The House seems to have had a clear preference for other measures, such as providing the defence with an edited version of the material from which sensitive matters have been expunged (*ibid.* at [36]) and so enabling the defence to make some representations. If the goal is, as it should be, to achieve an adversarial process, this view is certainly correct. Special counsel can never represent the views of the defence as effectively as the defence advocate. But there will be cases, where the defence can be given little or no information, where the defence advocate is powerless to assist the accused, and in such cases, special counsel is better than no counsel. Having referred to the various drawbacks of appointing special counsel, Lord Bingham said (*ibid.* at [22]):

> None of these problems should deter the court from appointing special counsel where the interests of justice are shown to require it. But the need must be shown. Such an appointment will always be exceptional, never automatic; a course of last and never first resort. It should not be ordered unless and until the trial judge is satisfied that no other course will adequately meet the overriding requirement of fairness to the defendant.

13.5 THE NATIONAL INTEREST: THE 'AFFAIRS OF STATE' CASES

Until the decision in *Rogers v Home Secretary* [1973] AC 388, the expression 'Crown Privilege' was employed to denote the cases in which evidence might be excluded on the ground that an important public interest outweighed the interest of the court and the parties in having access to all relevant evidence. The term was misleading for three reasons, and should no longer be used. Firstly, the Crown need not be the party raising the objection, and need not be, and often is not a party to the case. Secondly, the rule now applies to information in the possession of organs of local, as well as central, government and does not have to relate to matters of high national concern, such as affairs of state. Thirdly, for the reasons given above, it is not a privilege in the true sense of that word. The phrase 'public interest immunity' or some variation thereof is now generally substituted as a name for the rule.

However, the old term 'Crown Privilege' serves to call to mind that much of the law relating to public interest immunity was developed by the courts in cases concerned with the highest

---

[30] As to the practical difficulties of the appointment and work of special counsel, see para. [22] of the opinion. As to the propriety of special counsel being appointed by the Attorney General (who also supervises the work of the Director of Public Prosecutions) see paras [45]–[46].

affairs of state, such as national security, state secrets in time of war and matters of great diplomatic importance. The obviously high public interest in conserving the confidentiality of evidence touching on such matters had important consequences in the rules of evidence which the courts developed. Thus, it was at one time held that the court could not question a certificate given by the competent minister which stated that evidence must be withheld in the national interest. The supposed rule that public interest immunity cannot be waived, which has still not finally been confirmed or rejected (see 13.2) derives from the same concern. The public interest in the administration of justice could not compete with such clearly higher public interests. In *Asiatic Petroleum Co. Ltd* v *Anglo-Persian Oil Co. Ltd* [1916] 1 KB 822, the Court refused to permit disclosure of documents which would have revealed details of military plans during the First World War. And in the celebrated case of *Duncan* v *Cammell Laird & Co. Ltd*[31] the plaintiff in an action for damages for personal injury, which arose from his work on the submarine *Thetis*, was refused discovery of the plans and specifications of the submarine for similar reasons of policy. In this case, the First Lord of the Admiralty, on behalf of the government, ordered the defendants to object to the disclosure of the requested documents.

If public interest immunity was originally confined to such high affairs of state, it is certain that it is no longer so confined, and lesser areas of public interest have been identified, some of which must give way to the public interest in the administration of justice which requires disclosure.[32] The law of public interest immunity now develops in three well-established categories, which are dealt with in detail below. These are: (a) governmental and administrative matters (a vast area in which the 'affairs of state' cases are now included); (b) cases involving information given for the detection of crime and other necessary public purposes; and (c) cases involving other confidential information.[33]

The public policy referred to in connection with public interest immunity is that of the UK. The law does not recognize 'foreign state privilege'.[34]

It remains to add one more observation about the 'affairs of state' cases. There is still a school of thought that certain documents of high importance should never be disclosed in litigation. An objection to disclosure of documents relating to such matters should almost always be allowed, even on a class basis. Such documents relate to the workings of inner government, the formulation of national policy and similarly high matters. They were dealt with by Lord Reid in his speech in *Conway* v *Rimmer* [1968] AC 910, 952, as follows:

> I do not doubt that there are certain classes of documents which ought not to be disclosed whatever their content may be. Virtually everyone agrees that cabinet minutes and the like ought not to be disclosed until such time as they are only of historical interest.

---

[31] [1942] AC 624. Until a later House of Lords in *Conway* v *Rimmer* [1968] AC 910, departed from it, *Duncan* v *Cammell Laird & Co. Ltd* was the leading authority. None of the strictures cast on it in *Conway* v *Rimmer* appear to cast doubt on the correctness of the decision in *Duncan* on its own facts.

[32] See, e.g., *Campbell* v *Tameside MBC* [1982] QB 1065.

[33] The better view is probably that public policy develops within these categories, rather than that new categories can be recognized by the courts. In *Fender* v *St John-Mildmay* [1938] AC 1, Lord Atkin at 10 and Lord Thankerton at 23 saw any extension of the categories as a matter for Parliament, not the courts. The contrary view of Lord Hailsham of St Marylebone expressed in *D* v *NSPCC* [1978] AC 171 at 230, that the courts may extend the categories as conditions change, has not received universal agreement. However, given the scope for expanding the existing categories, the point may be only of academic interest.

[34] See *Buttes Gas and Oil Co.* v *Hammer (No. 3)* [1981] QB 223. The decision of the House of Lords on the substantive issues ([1982] AC 888) rendered the disclosure issue moot, and it was not considered by the House.

The most important reason for this was that:

> ...such disclosure would create or fan ill-informed or captious public or political criticism. The business of government is difficult enough as it is, and no government could contemplate with equanimity the inner workings of the government machine being exposed to the gaze of those ready to criticize without adequate knowledge of the background and perhaps with some axe to grind.

In Lord Reid's view, this would apply to:

> ...all documents concerned with policy making within departments including, it may be, minutes and the like by quite junior officials and correspondence with outside bodies.

And significantly, Lord Reid added:

> Further it may be that deliberations about a particular case require protection as much as deliberations about policy.

Lord Reid's sentiments were echoed in respect of documents such as cabinet minutes, dispatches from ambassadors and communications between departmental heads, by the other members of the House.[35] For similar reasons the conduct of military affairs,[36] the government's activities in the administration of colonies,[37] the good relations of the UK with foreign powers,[38] and other similar affairs of state in the strictest sense, have generally been protected against disclosure.[39] And there remain cases in which, for all practical purposes, disclosure will never be made, e.g., matters affecting national security (*Balfour* v *Foreign and Commonwealth Office* [1994] 1 WLR 681).

However, as the House of Lords in *Conway* v *Rimmer* was expressly abrogating the rule in the older cases, including *Duncan* v *Cammell Laird & Co. Ltd*, that the minister's certificate could not be questioned by the court, it would seem that no class of documents should be excluded automatically. In *Burmah Oil Co. Ltd* v *Bank of England* [1980] AC 1090, 1134, a case in which the House of Lords considered memoranda of meetings attended by government ministers and other documents which would have revealed the inner workings of high-level government, Lord Keith of Kinkel restated the position in, it is submitted, a more satisfactory way:

> In my opinion, it would be going too far to lay down that no document in any particular one of the categories mentioned [by the House of Lords in *Conway* v *Rimmer*] should never in any circumstances be ordered to be produced, and indeed I did not understand counsel for the Attorney-General to pitch his submission that high before this House...the nature of the litigation and the apparent importance to it of the documents in question may in extreme cases demand production even of the most sensitive communications at the highest level. Such a case might fortunately be unlikely to arise in this country, but in circumstances such as those of *Sankey* v *Whitlam* (1978) 142 CLR 1 or *Nixon* v *United States* 418 US 683 (1974)...I do not doubt that the principles there expounded would fall to be applied. There can be discerned in modern times a trend towards more open governmental methods than were prevalent in the past. No doubt it is for Parliament and not for courts of law to say how far that trend should go. The courts

---

[35] See the speeches of Lord Hodson at 973 and Lord Pearce at 987, and *Shearson Lehman Bros Inc.* v *Maclaine Watson & Co. Ltd (No. 2)* [1988] 1 All ER 116 (considerations of diplomatic concern and international comity surrounding possible disclosure of documents of the International Tin Council).

[36] *Beatson* v *Skene* (1860) 5 Hurl & N 838; *HMS Bellerophon* (1874) 44 LJ Adm 5.

[37] *Hennessy* v *Wright (No. 2)* (1888) 21 QBD 509.

[38] *Governor of Brixton Prison, ex parte Soblen* [1963] 2 QB 243, 273–4. See also *Buttes Gas & Oil Co.* v *Hammer (No. 3)* [1981] 1 QB 223.

[39] See the list of examples given in Phipson, *Evidence*, 16th edn, para. 25–25 *et seq*. However, many of the older cases might have been decided differently if they had been heard after *Conway* v *Rimmer*.

are, however, concerned with the consideration that it is in the public interest that justice should be done and should be publicly recognized as having been done. This may demand, though no doubt only in a very limited number of cases, that the inner workings of government should be exposed to public gaze, and there may be some who would regard this as likely to lead, not to captious or ill-informed criticism, but to criticism calculated to improve the nature of that working as affecting the individual citizen.

Lord Scarman in the same case (*ibid.* at 1144) thought that it would be inconsistent with *Conway* v *Rimmer* to hold that the court should not be permitted to consider the issue of disclosure solely because of the apparently 'high level' nature of the documents.

In *Air Canada* v *Secretary of State for Trade* [1983] 2 AC 394, 432, Lord Fraser of Tullybelton said, referring to the passage from Lord Reid's speech in *Conway* v *Rimmer* quoted above:

> The latter observation was strictly speaking *obiter* in *Conway* v *Rimmer*, where the documents in question were reports on a probationer police constable by his superiors.
>
>   I do not think that even Cabinet minutes are completely immune from disclosure in a case where, for example, the issue in a litigation involves serious misconduct by a Cabinet minister. Such cases have occurred in Australia (see *Sankey* v *Whitlam*)…and in the United States (see *Nixon* v *United States*)…but fortunately not in the United Kingdom: see also the New Zealand case of *Environmental Defence Society Inc.* v *South Pacific Aluminium Ltd (No. 2)* [1981] 1 NZLR 153. But, while Cabinet documents do not have complete immunity, they are entitled to a high degree of protection against disclosure.

No doubt the occasion would be rare when such documents would in fact be disclosed, but the point made by Lord Fraser, and by Lords Keith and Scarman in *Burmah Oil*, appears well taken. The documents which Lord Fraser was considering were such that they did 'not quite enjoy the status of Cabinet minutes, but they approach that level in that they may disclose the reasons for Cabinet decisions and the process by which the decisions were reached'. The case turned on other issues, but Lord Fraser was content to assume that normally, such documents should not be disclosed until they have become of purely historical interest.

If this be right, then the 'affairs of state' cases do not form a separate category, and differ from other cases involving governmental and administrative matters only in degree, that is to say, that the high probability that disclosure will be refused depends upon the facts of the case, the nature of the evidence itself, and not upon a rule of law.

With this in mind, we must now answer two important questions about the operation of public interest immunity in modern law. These questions are:

(a) Are the courts able or entitled to question the assertion by the minister that documents should be withheld on the ground of public policy?

(b) If the answer to question (a) be yes, by what criterion should the minister's claim be judged?

13.6 MAY THE COURT QUESTION THE CLAIM TO WITHHOLD?

In both civil and criminal cases, there is now no doubt that the court must have the final say in whether documents may be withheld on the ground of public interest immunity.

13.6.1 Civil cases

The point of departure from the rules laid down in the 'affairs of state' cases was the decision of the House of Lords in *Conway* v *Rimmer* [1968] AC 910. The appellant had been a probationer police officer in the Cheshire Constabulary, but had been dismissed as unlikely to become an efficient police officer. During his term of service, he had been charged with, but acquitted of, theft, the allegation being that he had stolen a torch belonging to a colleague. Being dissatisfied with his treatment, he brought an action for malicious prosecution against the chief constable. At the stage of discovery, the Home Secretary claimed that certain reports, relating to the appellant's qualities as a probationer officer and to the decision to prosecute him, should be withheld on the ground of public interest. The reports were undoubtedly relevant to the action, and an interesting facet of the case was that the chief constable had no objection to their disclosure. The ground advanced by the Home Secretary was simply that the production of the documents would be 'injurious to the public interest'. With this encouragement, the House of Lords abrogated the rule developed in the older 'affairs of state' cases, and held that the courts may review and consider the claim made by the government, and were not obliged to accept it as final. The House ordered the documents in question to be produced for their inspection, and it appearing that no real harm to the administration of the Cheshire Constabulary was likely to result, but that the documents would be useful to the plaintiff in his action, their disclosure was ordered.

On the question whether the court had any power to question the view of the minister, the House acknowledged, as it had to, that the minister was far better placed than the court to assess what was in the public interest. This consideration had led an earlier House of Lords, in *Duncan v Cammell Laird & Co. Ltd* [1942] AC 624, to hold that the minister's certificate should be conclusive and binding on the court, so that the trial judge had no power to admit or order disclosure of documents protected, in effect, by executive decision. For a variety of reasons, the later House in *Conway v Rimmer* had no compunction about departing from the decision in *Duncan*. The exhaustive review of the authorities undertaken by Lords Reid and Morris of Borth-y-Gest shows that the conclusion reached in *Duncan v Cammell Laird & Co. Ltd* was founded in part on an erroneous belief that the law of Scotland regarded ministerial objections as conclusive, and on the related reasoning that in such a respect the law of England ought not to differ from that of Scotland. Given the correctness of the first proposition, the second would surely also be correct, but as Lord Morris was able to show, the first was incorrect. This suggested that the House need not show undue concern in refusing to follow *Duncan v Cammell Laird & Co. Ltd*.

Undoubtedly the most cogent reason for the decision in *Conway v Rimmer* was the dissatisfaction felt almost universally with the former rule, because of the ease with which it could be used to provide a blanket immunity from production for documents of no more than marginal importance to any identifiable national interest. After *Duncan v Cammell Laird & Co. Ltd* there had been a number of cases which had given rise to a strongly expressed judicial disquiet. In *Broome v Broome*[40] the minister objected to the admission in divorce proceedings of documents relating to efforts by a Service welfare organization to reconcile the parties, on the ground that its disclosure might 'prejudice the morale of the armed forces'. The Court, scathing in its impotence, commented on the lack of discernible public interest in the matter and remarked that the matter was one which properly fell under the head of private privilege and no more. In *Ellis v Home Office* [1953] 2 QB 135, Devlin J, faced with an objection from the Home Office to the disclosure of reports by doctors and prison officers on the mental condition of a prisoner and dealing with his assault on a fellow prisoner, who sought damages against the Home Office, referred to an 'uneasy feeling' that justice had not been done and more than an uneasy feeling that justice had not been seen to be done.

---

[40] [1955] P 190. Much the same thing happened in *Gain v Gain* [1961] 1 WLR 1469 in respect of a medical report of a naval surgeon commander.

Weighing these frustrations of the courts against the undoubtedly greater competence of the minister in assessing the dictates of public interest, Lord Reid reached the following conclusion:[41]

> I would therefore propose that the House ought now to decide that courts have and are entitled to exercise a power and duty to hold a balance between the public interest, as expressed by a minister, to withhold certain documents or other evidence, and the public interest in ensuring the proper administration of justice. That does not mean that a court would reject a minister's view: full weight must be given to it in every case, and if the minister's reasons are of a character which judicial experience is not competent to weigh, then the minister's view must prevail. But experience has shown that reasons given for withholding whole classes of documents are often not of that character.

Lord Pearce said:[42]

> It is conceded that under the existing practice there can be no weighing of injustice in particular cases against the general public disadvantage of disclosure and its effect on candour. But it is argued that a judge, who is the only person who can properly weigh the former, is incapable of properly weighing the latter. I do not understand why he cannot do so, especially if the ministry gives some specific details of the type of document in question and some specific reasons why it is undesirable to allow production. It is a judge's constant task to weigh human behaviour and the points that tell for or against candour. He knows full well that in general a report will be less inhibited if it will never see the light of public scrutiny, and that in some cases and on some subjects this may be wholly desirable. He also knows that on many subjects this fact has little if any important effect. Against this he can consider whether the documents in question are of much or little weight in the litigation, whether their absence will result in a complete or partial denial of justice to one or other of the parties or perhaps to both, and what is the importance of the particular litigation to the parties and the public. All these are matters which should be considered if the court is to decide where the public interest lies.

13.6.2 Criminal cases

As we have seen (13.4) the position in criminal cases is now governed by the provisions of the Criminal Procedure and Investigations Act 1996 and the related rules. These provisions and the decisions in *H* [2004] 2 AC 134, *Ward* [1993] 1 WLR 619, and *Davis* [1993] 1 WLR 613, make it clear that the court must decide on the claim to withhold in all cases. Failure to do so will be a violation of the accused's right to a fair trial under art. 6 of the European Convention on Human Rights (*Rowe and Davis* v *United Kingdom* (2000) 30 EHRR 1, 13.4.3).

In rare cases such as those involving national security or other affairs of state at the highest level, it may be that, notwithstanding this, the court cannot claim the power to question the minister's certificate, which will accordingly be conclusive (see *Balfour* v *Foreign and Commonwealth Office* [1994] 1 WLR 681). With this exception, and especially in criminal cases, the court may and should scrutinize all claims to withhold, and the documents in question must be produced to the court for its inspection.

---

[41] [1968] AC 910, 952. This conclusion had been contended for in untested decisions of the Court of Appeal: see *Re Grosvenor Hotel, London (No. 2)* [1965] Ch 1210.

[42] [1968] AC 910, 987. The 'candour' argument in favour of withholding documents has never recovered from the blows dealt to it in *Conway* v *Rimmer*, and is demonstrably less valid than the similar, but distinct, argument in relation to informers; but see 13.7.1.

13.7 BY WHAT CRITERIA SHOULD THE CLAIM TO WITHHOLD BE JUDGED?

As the speech of Lord Reid in *Conway* v *Rimmer* [1968] AC 910 makes clear, the process of weighing the competing claims to withhold and to compel disclosure is one of balancing the interests of all parties. There is authority that the court's scrutiny of a claim to withhold should be especially vigorous in criminal cases: see, e.g., *Governor of Brixton Prison, ex parte Osman* [1991] 1 WLR 281, a point which is strengthened by art. 6 of the European Convention on Human Rights and the decision in *Rowe and Davis* v *United Kingdom*. In a civil case, the party claiming that the documents should be disclosed must show that production of the documents is necessary for the purpose of fairly disposing of the case. In addition, the courts have been troubled by the question of whether, and if so under what circumstances, the court should privately inspect the documents in order to make its determination.

13.7.1 'Class' versus 'contents' claims

A class claim is a claim to withhold all documents falling within a specifically described class, for example minutes of Cabinet meetings. In this kind of claim, the actual contents of the documents are irrelevant, and the claim is based on an invariable need for confidentiality of documents of the kind described in the claim. The courts have regarded class claims relatively unfavourably, because of the possibility of a blanket attempt to protect documents, many of which may be of a purely routine nature.

A contents claim is based on the contents of an individual document, and is more favourably regarded because of the more specific justification provided to the court. In *Conway* v *Rimmer*,[43] Lord Reid said that in the case of a contents claim, the court would comparatively rarely be disposed to dissent from the view taken by the government, because the responsible minister must usually be more competent than the court to assess the possible harm to the public interest that might result from disclosure. In the case of a class claim, it is more practicable for the court to form a judgment as to the cogency of the minister's claim.

For this reason and in the light of the Scott Report, the Lord Chancellor announced (Hansard HL, 18 December 1996, cols 1507–17) that in future, the government would not attempt to justify withholding documents on a class (as opposed to contents) basis, but would rely on the specific damage likely to be done to the public interest by the disclosure of particular documents. The relevant minister would be required to give reasons for the objection to disclosure based on the foreseeable damage, rather than simply relying on the nature of the document. This apparent abandonment of the class-based approach is likely to assist the balancing process, and it is to be hoped that non-governmental organizations will follow suit. Nonetheless, it is possible that certain very high-level documents, for example minutes of Cabinet meetings, may continue to be protected from disclosure as a class, albeit for reasons other than those usually advanced in the past. In this respect, it remains worth noting some of the more recent judicial observations on the subject.

The main justification for class claims was once the need to promote candour in those who wrote reports. It was suggested that, if it became known that confidential reports might be disclosed for the purposes of private litigation, the elements of frankness and candour in their

---

[43] [1968] AC 910, 943. See also the speech of Lord Upjohn, *ibid.* at 933.

preparation might be lost. However, in more recent cases, the courts declined to hold that responsible public servants would forbear to be candid merely because of the possibility of some future disclosure. In *Science Research Council* v *Nassé* [1980] AC 1028, 1070, Lord Salmon rejected the argument entirely. In the same case, Lord Fraser (*ibid.* at 1081) thought that the concern to prevent disclosure was not a matter of public policy at all, but a private interest of the individuals who prepared the documents, which must yield to the public interest in favour of disclosure. Subsequent cases appear to have held specifically that possible loss of candour is not, *per se*, a sufficient ground to support a class claim.[44] But the powerful dissent of Lord Wilberforce in *Burmah Oil Co. Ltd* v *Bank of England* [1980] AC 1090, 1112, should not be lightly dismissed. Speaking of the candour argument, Lord Wilberforce said:

> It seems now rather fashionable to decry this, but if as a ground it may at one time have been exaggerated, it has now, in my opinion, received an excessive dose of cold water. I am certainly not prepared, against the view of the Minister, to discount the need, in the formation of such very controversial policy as that with which we are here involved, for frank and uninhibited advice from the Bank to the government, from and between civil servants and between Ministers.

In *Chief Constable of West Midlands Police, ex parte Wiley* [1995] 1 AC 274, 305, Lord Woolf said: 'The recognition of a new class-based public interest immunity requires clear and compelling evidence that it is necessary'. The House of Lords, overruling a number of earlier decisions of the Court of Appeal to the contrary, held that, in the absence of any clear and compelling evidence that it was necessary, there was no justification for imposing a general class immunity on all documents generated by an investigation into a complaint against the police under Part IX of the Police and Criminal Evidence Act 1984. But specific grounds might exist for excluding a subclass of documents within that class, or for a contents-based claim in relation to particular documents, and there is no reason why such grounds should not be relied on and provide a basis for exclusion in a particular case. (For an example, see *Taylor* v *Anderton* [1995] 1 WLR 447.)

13.7.2 Civil cases: necessity for fairly disposing of the case

Before the balancing test can be applied, a party seeking disclosure of documents which may be subject to public interest immunity must show that he has a legitimate interest in seeking disclosure. Under the Civil Procedure Rules 1998, standard disclosure is to be made of documents on which a party relies and those which adversely affect his case, or support or adversely affect the case of another party (r. 31.6). However, in cases involving documents subject to public interest immunity, it is more likely that an order for disclosure will be sought against the Crown or an organization which is not a party to the case. In these circumstances, r. 31.17(3) provides that an order for disclosure may be made only where:

(a)   the documents of which disclosure is sought are likely to support the case of the applicant or adversely affect the case of one of the other parties to the proceedings; and

(b)   disclosure is necessary in order to dispose fairly of the claim or to save costs.

The language of r. 31.17(3)(b) reproduces that of the former RSC, Ord. 24, r. 13(1), under which some significant cases on this point were decided. Rule 31.17(3)(a) adds the requirement that the

---

[44] See, e.g., *Campbell* v *Tameside MBC* [1982] QB 1065, per Ackner LJ at 1077; *Williams* v *Home Office* [1981] 1 All ER 1151.

evidence be likely to assist the applicant either by supporting his case or adversely affecting the case of another party. In the cases decided under RSC, Ord. 24, r. 13(1), it had been held that the benefit to the applicant's case was an aspect of the necessity of disclosure, so that the court would not hold that disclosure was necessary unless the applicant showed why the documents would help his case. There was a two-part test. First, the applicant had to show that the documents were likely to be necessary because they would assist his case. Second, he had to show that they were necessary for the purpose of fairly disposing of the case, in the sense that without them, his chances of success would be significantly less. The language of the new rule, clarifying the meaning of the first part of the test, may lead to a less confusing analysis, though it is submitted that the two-part test remains.

In *Air Canada v Secretary of State for Trade (No. 2)*,[45] a number of airlines sued the Secretary of State, alleging that he had acted *ultra vires* and unlawfully in directing the British Airports Authority to increase landing charges at Heathrow airport in an allegedly discriminatory manner. The government successfully objected to the requested production of communications between ministers, and memoranda prepared for the use of ministers, which related to the formulation of government policy as to the Authority and the limitation of public sector borrowing. The House of Lords found that the documents were not likely to be 'necessary' for the purposes of Ord. 24, r. 13(1) and on that ground refused to inspect them. The judge at first instance, Bingham J, had agreed to inspect the documents on the ground that they were likely to affect the outcome of the case 'one way or the other'. Both the Court of Appeal and the House of Lords held that this approach was incorrect. The test was not whether the documents would be in any way helpful, but whether they would help the party seeking disclosure.

In *Science Research Council v Nassé* [1980] AC 1028, 1071, Lord Salmon posed the question of what 'necessary' in the present context means. He answered the question in the following way:

> It, of course, includes the case where the party applying for an order for discovery and inspection of certain documents could not possibly succeed in the proceedings unless he obtained the order; but it is not confined to such cases. Suppose, for example, a man had a very slim chance of success without inspection of documents, but a very strong chance of success with inspection, surely the proceedings could not be regarded as being fairly disposed of, were he to be denied inspection.

In *Campbell v Tameside MBC* [1982] QB 1065, the plaintiff was a schoolteacher who had been attacked in the classroom by an unruly pupil and seriously injured. She sought preliminary discovery[46] of reports maintained by the local education authority, which were believed to contain material which might reveal whether the authority had known of the pupil's propensity for violence, which was such that he should have been placed in a special school. The Court of Appeal agreed with the conclusion of the judge at first instance that there was 'a real risk of the plaintiff being the victim of a denial of justice if the documents were not disclosed', and so found that they were 'necessary'. The procedure for disclosure before proceedings start is expressly designed to assist plaintiffs in cases where insufficient evidence to justify commencement of a claim is

---

[45] [1983] 2 AC 394; see also, *Burmah Oil Co. Ltd v Bank of England* [1980] AC 1090; *Conway v Rimmer* [1968] AC 910.

[46] The procedure formerly known as preliminary discovery under RSC, Ord. 24, r. 7A(1), is now known as disclosure before proceedings start, and is governed by r. 31.16 of the Civil Procedure Rules 1998. Its purpose remains the same.

available without disclosure of documents in the possession of a proposed defendant. Such cases therefore fit aptly within Lord Salmon's definition of 'necessary'.

13.7.3 Civil cases: balancing competing interests

If the documents sought appear 'necessary for disposing fairly of the case', then the court must balance the public interest in the administration of justice, which requires disclosure of necessary evidence, against any asserted public interest in withholding the documents. The balancing process is well described in the quotation from the speech of Lord Reid in *Conway* v *Rimmer* ([1968] AC 910, 952) set forth in 13.6. Lord Reid added that the test was to be whether the withholding of the documents was 'really necessary for the proper functioning of the public service'.[47]

In *Campbell* v *Tameside MBC* [1982] QB 1065, 1075–6, Ackner LJ stated a number of 'basic principles' relating to the balancing process, among which are:

> 1. The exclusion of relevant evidence always calls for clear justification. All relevant documents, whether or not confidential, are subject to disclosure unless upon some recognized ground, including the public interest, their non-disclosure is permissible.
>
> 2. Since it has been accepted in this court that the documents for which the respondent seeks discovery are relevant to the contemplated litigation, there is a heavy burden upon the appellants [a local education authority] to justify withholding them from disclosure...
>
> 5. The proper approach where there is a question of public interest immunity is a weighing, on balance, of the two public interests, that of the nation or the public service in non-disclosure and that of justice in the production of the documents. Both in the 'class' objection and the 'contents' objection the courts retain the residual power to inspect and to order disclosure...
>
> 6. A judge conducting the balancing exercise needs to know whether the documents in question are of much or little weight in the litigation, whether their absence will result in a complete or partial denial of justice to one or other of the parties or perhaps to both, and what is the importance of the particular litigation to the parties and the public. All these are matters which should be considered if the court is to decide where the public interest lies.

It is submitted that the emphasis in the judgment of Ackner LJ in favour of disclosure, and the burden of justification falling upon the entity seeking non-disclosure is to be welcomed. The more routine or 'low level' the documents, the more jealously should any claim to withhold be scrutinized. This principle comports not only with the principles laid down by Lord Reid in *Conway* v *Rimmer* and the *Air Canada* case, but also with the spirit of the Rules of Court and the public interest in the free availability of relevant evidence.

13.7.4 Criminal cases: balancing the competing interests

The balance of competing interests is also to be sought in criminal cases, but in a different way, having regard to the penal nature of the proceedings and the need to afford a greater protection to the accused than is afforded to the parties in civil cases. Article 6 of the European Convention on Human Rights requires that the accused be granted a fair trial. The House of Lords in *H* [2004] 2 AC 134 (discussed at 13.4.3) has made clear that the principle of fairness requires that full disclosure should be the golden rule, and a clear showing of harm to the public interest must be shown to justify withholding any material which might weaken the prosecution case or strengthen that

---

[47] See also *Air Canada* v *Secretary of State for Trade (No. 2)* [1983] 2 AC 394.

of the accused. Any derogation from the rule of disclosure must be the minimum necessary to protect the public interest. While it may be possible to continue to speak of a balancing process in criminal cases, the phrase must be understood in this light.

13.7.5 Should the court inspect the documents?

The question of whether the court should privately inspect the documents as part of the balancing process has caused some division of opinion in civil cases.[48] Since *Conway* v *Rimmer* [1968] AC 910, it has rarely been doubted that the court has power to do so, but the wisdom of exercising that power has been challenged, on the basis that the court cannot assess the possible harm to the public interest as competently as the minister seeking to withhold. In this regard, there was again a distinction between class claims and contents claims, the court being much less reluctant to inspect in the former than in the latter. So too, the court will be more ready to inspect in the case of lower level documents, such as the chief constable's reports in *Conway* v *Rimmer* itself, and the local education authority's documents in *Campbell* v *Tameside MBC* [1982] QB 1065.

Both in *Burmah Oil Co. Ltd* v *Bank of England* [1980] AC 1090 and *Air Canada* v *Secretary of State for Trade* [1983] 2 AC 394 the House of Lords accepted that the court should inspect the documents, once it was shown that they were likely to be necessary for fairly disposing of the case, and it is submitted that this is plainly correct. In *Burmah Oil*, Lord Edmund Davies observed ([1980] AC 1090, 1129) that a judge may well feel that he cannot profitably embark on a balancing exercise without himself seeing the documents in question, and cited in support the *dicta* of Lord Reid and Lord Upjohn in *Conway* v *Rimmer* [1968] AC 910, 953 and 995 respectively. This *dictum* was cited and followed by Ackner LJ in *Campbell* v *Thameside MBC* [1982] QB 1065, 1076 and is surely both sensible and correct. In *Wallace Smith Trust Co. Ltd* v *Deloitte Haskins and Sells*,[49] where the judge had failed to inspect the documents for the purpose of making a determination under the former RSC, Ord. 24, r. 13 (see 13.7.2), the Court of Appeal set aside the judge's findings that the documents did not attract public interest immunity but were not necessary for the fair disposal of the action, and referred the matter back to the judge for him to inspect the documents and make a fresh determination.

No doubt there may be cases in which a contents claim is made for a document of high public interest, in an 'affairs of state' case or some comparable situation, where the court is in no position to question the minister's grounds of objection, in which inspection would be both fruitless and undesirable. The court has power to act accordingly. But it is submitted that in general, even in the case of the high level documents which the court was called upon to consider in the *Burmah Oil* and *Air Canada* cases, inspection should be the usual procedure. This would be in accordance with the spirit of the principles laid down in *Conway* v *Rimmer*, which form the basis of the present law. It should not be overlooked that the right to a fair trial under art. 6 of the European Convention on Human Rights applies to civil cases as well as criminal.

It has already been noted that, in criminal cases, the court must always inspect the documents, and that the prosecution must disclose them to the court for this purpose: see 13.4.2.

---

[48] In *Conway* v *Rimmer*, the House rejected the argument that inspection by the court without reference to the parties was contrary to the rules of natural justice, whether or not the Crown is a party. Lord Morris, more cautious, held that there was a power to inspect which should be exercised sparingly. To the same effect are the observations of Lord Wilberforce in *Burmah Oil Co. Ltd* v *Bank of England* [1980] AC 1090, 1116–17.

[49] [1997] 1 WLR 257; see also *Evans* v *Chief Constable of Surrey* [1988] QB 588.

13.8 GOVERNMENTAL AND ADMINISTRATIVE MATTERS

Nothing in the authorities on affairs of state limits the area of governmental activity to the comparatively dramatic circumstances of the wartime cases, or to the lofty foreign-policy cases. Government policy is nowadays formulated and carried out in relation to a wide and ever-increasing sphere of activity, and the principles laid down in *Conway* v *Rimmer* [1968] AC 910 apply over the whole spectrum. They apply to local as well as national government. It is no doubt true to say that the more mundane and essentially administrative the subject, the less likely it is that a class of documents will satisfy the test propounded by Lord Reid, or that the contents of any given document will be of sufficient delicacy and gravity to warrant its exclusion; but each case will be examined on its merits. The illustrations that follow are those areas in which the courts have been called upon most frequently to weigh the competing interests, and which seem to be the most critical in practice.

13.8.1 Economic and fiscal policy

A good illustration in modern times is that of documents relating to the government's economic policy. It was at one time doubted whether economic as opposed to political content would suffice to give rise to a claim based on public interest immunity at all. Thus, in *Smith* v *East India Co.* (1841) 1 Ph 50, in what was essentially a commercial action, despite the fact that the company played a vital role in the political government of India, documents passing between the court of directors and the British government Commissioners for India were held to be the subject of public interest immunity, but solely by virtue of their political content. But as it became more and more clear that it is an important function of government to regulate if not to participate in economic and commercial activity, the mood changed. In *M. Isaacs & Sons Ltd* v *Cook*,[50] it was held that communications passing between the Prime Minister of Australia and the Australian High Commissioner in London, which were said to contain matter defamatory of the plaintiff, were to be withheld on the ground of public policy, even though the contents of such communications were plainly commercial in character, and had little political significance outside the commercial sphere.

In *Burmah Oil Co. Ltd* v *Bank of England*[51] the company sought a declaration against the Bank that a sale by the company to the Bank of certain stock at a price required by the government, pursuant to an agreement made in 1975, was inequitable and unfair, and claimed an order for the transfer back of the stock at the 1975 price. The company had, at the time of the agreement, been in dire financial straits because of an international oil crisis, and the agreement had been designed to 'rescue' the company, under the very close control of the government working through the Bank. The company sought discovery of all relevant documents. The Crown (which was not a party to the suit), intervened and objected to the production of some 62 documents, which for this purpose were divided into three categories. Categories A and B both related to the formulation of government economic policy, at ministerial level and at a lower level.[52] The majority of the Court of Appeal[53] were in favour of upholding the objection taken by the Crown.

---

[50] [1925] 2 KB 391. In a case of a commercial nature, there is no doubt that the court will scrutinize a claim based on public policy with great care: see, e.g., *Robinson* v *State of South Australia (No. 2)* [1931] AC 704, 715–16.

[51] [1979] 1 WLR 473; affirmed [1980] AC 1090.

[52] Category C was classified as 'confidential'. As to this, see 13.10.

[53] Bridge and Templeman LJJ (upholding Foster J at first instance).

Lord Denning MR, dissenting, did not accept that the 'rescue' operation was a matter of policy. He said ([1979] 1 WLR at 486):

> Now I can understand that privilege in regard to high questions of state policy, such as those dealing with foreign affairs or the defence or security of the realm. But I do not think it should be extended to commercial transactions undertaken by the government or the Bank of England. This rescue operation of Burmah was *par excellence* a commercial transaction. Such as those which the City of London has undertaken many a time in recent years.

The House of Lords upheld the majority of the Court of Appeal. Lord Wilberforce saw no need to inspect the documents, in view of the clear and detailed certificate of the minister. The other Lords, having inspected the documents, held that none of them contained matter of such evidential value as to make an order for their disclosure necessary to dispose fairly of the case. Lord Scarman ([1980] AC at 1144) described the documents as '…"high level". They are concerned with the formulation of policy. They are part of the inner working of the government machine.'

Although Burmah's application was unsuccessful for the reasons stated, the case makes it clear that the formulation of policy in any area may be the basis of an objection to disclosure based on public-policy immunity. The court is no longer limited to consideration of what would formerly have been regarded as political in the sense of the highest affairs of state.

13.8.2 Other home affairs

Other functions of central government are now to be treated in the same way. We have seen that the courts have considered claims to public interest immunity based on the government's policy as to the British Airports Authority (*Air Canada* v *Secretary of State for Trade* [1983] 2 AC 394). In *Williams* v *Home Office* [1981] 1 All ER 1151, McNeill J considered, and in part overruled, an objection to the disclosure of communications between, and memoranda relating to meetings between, ministers and highly placed officials concerning a so-called prison 'control unit', based on the fact that such documents were intimately involved with the formulation of government policy. The plaintiff was a prisoner who claimed damages against the Home Office for alleged false imprisonment and *ultra vires* conduct in placing him in such a unit.

Documents relating to different kinds of inquiries and internal investigations involving police officers have provided a particularly fertile field for public interest immunity disputes. Indeed, the seminal case of *Conway* v *Rimmer* [1968] AC 910 (see 13.6.1) was concerned with such an issue. Immunity on a class basis formerly attached to documents created by the police and sent to the Director of Public Prosecutions for the purposes of a criminal investigation,[54] subject to the balancing exercise described above. But there was no class immunity for documents relating to the investigation of complaints against police officers under Part IX of the Police and Criminal Evidence Act 1984,[55] or to written complaints against officers which result in such an investigation (*Ex parte Coventry Newspapers* [1993] QB 278) or to statements made during the

---

[54] *Evans* v *Chief Constable of Surrey* [1988] QB 588; and see *Horseferry Magistrates' Court, ex parte Bennett (No. 2)* [1994] 1 All ER 289 (documents exchanged internationally between police forces for purposes of investigation). *Wallace Smith Trust Co. Ltd* v *Deloitte Hoskins and Sells* [1997] 1 WLR 257 (tapes and transcripts of interviews conducted by Serious Fraud Office).

[55] *Chief Constable of West Midlands Police, ex parte Wiley* [1995] 1 AC 274, overruling *Neilson* v *Laugharne* [1981] QB 736 and other contrary decisions of the Court of Appeal. Section 49 of the Police Act 1964 was repealed by the Police and Criminal Evidence Act 1984, and the older cases dealing with complaints against the police under s. 49 must be read in the light of the decision in *Ex parte Wiley*. See also *Peach* v *Commissioner of Police for the Metropolis* [1986] QB 1064; *Conerney* v *Jacklin* [1985] Crim LR 234.

course of grievance procedures brought by police officers against a police force alleging racial or sexual discrimination (*Commissioner of Police of the Metropolis* v *Locker* [1993] ICR 440). However, in all these cases, a claim for immunity may be entertained on a contents basis: *Taylor* v *Anderton* [1995] 1 WLR 447.

To a limited extent, public interest immunity may attach to evidence given or statements made in connection with the performance of a statutory duty, or an official inquiry, where the effective accomplishment of the purpose involved might otherwise be compromised by a refusal to cooperate.[56]

13.8.3 Local governmental, statutory, and other bodies

Since much of the burden of government now devolves upon local government and a variety of statutory bodies, the same rules are now to be applied to documents in the custody of these entities. We have seen, for example, that in *Campbell* v *Tameside MBC* [1982] QB 1065 the court considered an application for public interest immunity pertaining to the records of a local education authority.

The application of the rules to entities under the level of central government was emphatically affirmed by the House of Lords in *D* v *NSPCC* [1978] AC 171, in which it was argued, *inter alia*, that the Society could not maintain a claim of public interest immunity because it was not an organ of central government. The Society, a voluntary body incorporated by royal charter, had power under the Children and Young Persons Act 1969 to bring care proceedings in a juvenile court, although it was under no duty to do so. The Society sought help from members of the public in supplying it with information about children who might be ill-treated, and offered a guarantee of confidentiality to informants. Someone informed the Society that the plaintiff's daughter had been ill-treated, information which proved to be without foundation. The plaintiff brought an action for damages for negligence on the part of the Society, alleging that it had exercised insufficient care in investigating the complaint before sending an inspector to her home to see the child. The plaintiff sought discovery of, *inter alia*, the identity of the informant and the Society claimed that the identity ought to be withheld on the ground of public policy.

The Court of Appeal by a majority[57] held that the plaintiff was entitled to discovery of the identity, Scarman LJ and Sir John Pennycuick holding specifically that public interest immunity was confined to matters of central government. The House of Lords reversed the ruling. The decision turned primarily on the analogy of the immunity accorded to police informers (see 13.9) but the House also disposed of the contention that the Society could not claim public interest immunity because it was not an organ of central government. Lord Simon of Glaisdale, in the course of a careful refutation of any such requirement, observed ([1978] AC at 235–6):

> ... 'the State', cannot on any sensible political theory be restricted to the Crown and the departments of central government (which are, indeed, part of the Crown in constitutional law). The state is the whole organization of the body politic for supreme civil rule and government—the whole political organization which is the basis of civil government. As such it certainly extends to local—and, as I think, also statutory bodies in so far as they are exercising autonomous rule.

---

[56] *Lonrho Ltd* v *Shell Petroleum Co. Ltd* [1980] 1 WLR 627; *Re Barlow Clowes Gilt Managers Ltd* [1992] Ch 208; *Hamilton* v *Naviede* [1995] 2 AC 75.

[57] Scarman LJ and Sir John Pennycuick, Lord Denning MR dissenting.

> …There is a recurrent transfer of functions between central, local and statutory authorities. For example, near the heart of the issue before your Lordships, the Crown as *parens patriae* had traditionally a general jurisdiction over children; a residue is now exercised in the High Court, but the bulk has been devolved by statute on local authorities.

Although *D* v *NSPCC* was a case involving a voluntary body, it represents a fairly fruitful field of inquiry for the courts in relation to public-policy immunity. Matters concerning the welfare of children provide not only a substantial field of litigation, but also a wide variety of documentation compiled by those concerned with child welfare, some of it adverse to one or both parents, and almost all of it clearly relevant to the litigation. The reports made by local authority social workers dealing with the welfare of children have been sought by parents for the purposes of litigation of issues of custody, wardship, and adoption. Such reports are confidential and contain a good deal of confidential material, yet they may represent a significant source of potential evidence. The courts have generally held such reports to be protected from disclosure, on the ground that there is an important public policy in keeping confidential the workings of social services departments and similar bodies.[58]

In *City of Birmingham District Council, ex parte O* [1982] 1 WLR 679, a majority of the Court of Appeal[59] went so far as to hold that the social services committee of a local authority and the authority's social services department, to which the authority, as required by statute, had delegated its social services functions, were entitled to withhold from a councillor its files relating to prospective adoptive parents. The councillor was not a member of the social services committee, but was concerned about the suitability of the proposed adoptive parents. She alleged, and the Court of Appeal appear to have accepted, that access to the files would assist her in properly discharging her duties as a councillor. However, the Court held that the need for confidentiality in such a sensitive area must prevail.

It may probably now be stated as a general principle that the confidentiality of documents pertaining to the welfare of children will be respected, unless there are powerful reasons for disclosure, for example because the documents are important to the defence in a criminal case.[60] Thus, in *Re D (Minors) (Conciliation: Disclosure of Information)* [1993] Fam 231, it was held that documents concerned with an attempted conciliation should be disclosed only where it was necessary in the public interest. And in *Brown* v *Matthews* [1990] Ch 662, the Court held that disclosure of confidential reports made by court-appointed welfare officers may be ordered if necessary in the best interests of the child.

Documents on the court's file which relate to the welfare of a child are specifically protected from disclosure by r. 4.23 of the Family Proceedings Rules 1991, which gives effect to the rule developed in wardship cases referred to above. It has been held that this rule applies to reports

---

[58] See, e.g., *Official Solicitor* v *K* [1965] AC 201; *Re D (Infants)* [1970] 1 WLR 599. It should be noted, however, that it was not the practice to allow discovery in wardship cases, and it is difficult to tell how far these cases turn on that point, rather than public interest immunity. See also *Re D (Minors) (Wardship: Disclosure)* [1994] 1 FLR 346; *Hampshire County Council, ex parte K* [1990] 2 QB 71; Family Proceedings Rules 1991, r. 4.23; *Re M (Minors)* [1987] 1 FLR 46; *Gaskin* v *Liverpool City Council* [1980] 1 WLR 1549.

[59] Lord Denning MR and Sir Sebag Shaw, Donaldson LJ dissenting. Donaldson LJ dissented primarily on the ground that, in his opinion, the authority had no right to keep its documents from an elected representative, even if she was not a member of the social services committee. The decision of the majority turned in part on the contrary proposition: cf. *Lancashire County Council Police Committee, ex parte Hook* [1980] QB 603.

[60] See, e.g., *K (TD)* (1992) 97 Cr App R 342 (record of a therapeutic interview with the child victim of an alleged sexual offence).

written by the guardian *ad litem*, and information obtained for the purposes of that report, and to statements made by the parents to the guardian or a social worker.[61] But it may be that statements made by the parents to a social worker are vulnerable to disclosure if not filed in court. This may include disclosure to police officers of matters concerning injuries to a child which may form the basis of a later criminal prosecution.

This was the view of the majority (Butler-Sloss LJ and Sir Roger Parker) in *Re G (A Minor) (Social Worker: Disclosure)*,[62] in which it was held that a local authority was entitled to disclose to the police incriminating statements made to a social worker by the parents. The majority based their view on the fact that the police were part of an inter-agency team, whose purpose was the investigation of matters affecting the child's welfare, and that, unlike a guardian, whose functions are specific and related to proceedings before the court, a social worker has wider duties towards the child, which are not confined to the court proceedings. Auld LJ, dissenting, held that any such statements made by the parents to a social worker, once reduced to writing, were in no way different from documents filed with the court containing statements made by the parents to the guardian, and accordingly, were protected by r. 4.23. He pointed out that the statements would be likely eventually to form part of the court's file, and could find no ground on which to distinguish them from other documents intended to be filed. In view of the important and frequently recurring nature of this question, *Re G* is unlikely to be the last word on the subject.

It is submitted that, while the view of the majority has the merit of furthering investigations into possible acts of child abuse and criminal prosecutions, when justified, it also has the potential to lead parents and others to be rather less frank in future, and to increase their suspicion of the motives of the local authority and its social workers.

13.9 INFORMATION GIVEN FOR THE DETECTION OF CRIME, ETC.

13.9.1 Protection of informers

It has long been a rule of English law that in any public prosecution, or information for fraud against the revenue laws, or in any civil proceedings arising from either of these, no question may be asked and no evidence may be given which would tend to reveal the identity of any person who has given information leading to the institution of the prosecution or information or the nature of that information. There is said to be an overriding public interest in preserving the anonymity of informants, because of the obvious likelihood of sources of information drying up otherwise. A public prosecution is, in modern law, likely to include any case brought by or after investigation by the police, or any executive body having police powers for any purpose, and indeed the police informer is the classic example of the species. But the rule should,

---

[61] *Oxfordshire County Council v P* [1995] Fam 161; *Cleveland County Council v F* [1995] 1 WLR 785; *Oxfordshire County Council v M* [1994] Fam 151; these decisions were disapproved by the majority in *Re G (A Minor) (Social Worker: Disclosure)* [1996] 1 WLR 1407, 1414. The court may, of course, give leave for disclosure of any document in its files for good reason, see, e.g., *Re L (A Minor) (Police Investigation: Privilege)* [1997] AC 16.

[62] [1996] 1 WLR 1407. Such information would potentially be subject to the privilege against self-incrimination, but voluntary disclosure of it would amount to a waiver of the privilege: see *Re L (A Minor) (Police Investigation: Privilege)* [1997] AC 16. In *Re G*, Auld LJ, dissenting, said that the parent's statements would enjoy the lesser protection against self-incrimination provided by s. 98 of the Children Act 1989. Butler-Sloss LJ took the view that the section is confined by its own terms to statements made while giving evidence. Both views were *obiter*, but it is submitted that the view of Butler-Sloss LJ is clearly more consistent with the plain wording of the section, and is to be preferred. Auld LJ may have overlooked the fact that, if s. 98 does not apply, the ordinary privilege against self-incrimination does. See generally 14.2 *et seq*.

it is submitted, and might now well be held to, apply also to private prosecutions, there being no obvious ground of public policy for distinguishing private from public prosecutions for this purpose. The rule prevents any question, direct or indirect, which would tend to reveal the identity of an informant or the channel of information.

In *Marks v Beyfus* (1890) 25 QBD 494, the modern rule was stated by Lord Esher MR. The plaintiff, who had brought an action alleging a conspiracy to prosecute maliciously, sought to elicit from the Director of Public Prosecutions the name of his informant. The refusal of the Director to answer was upheld. But Lord Esher did recognize that there must be one exceptional case (*ibid.* at 498):

> ...if upon the trial of a prisoner the judge should be of opinion that the disclosure of the name of the informant is necessary or right in order to show the prisoner's innocence, then one public policy is in conflict with another public policy, and that which says that an innocent man is not to be condemned when his innocence can be proved is the policy that must prevail.

It is for the accused to show that there is a good reason to depart from the usual rule of immunity, and, as Lord Esher indicated, that reason must be connected with necessity in presenting the defence. One case in which the accused was able to do this was *Agar* (1989) 90 Cr App R 318. The accused alleged that the police had induced an informer to go to a house, at which the police had allegedly 'planted' a quantity of drugs. It was held that the accused had been entitled to cross-examine with a view to showing what the communications between the police and the informer had been, so that his defence could be fully presented. But necessity is a stringent requirement. It will not suffice that the accused would find it convenient to have the information, or that it would make the presentation of the defence easier. The judge must find that, without it, there is a risk of injustice because the defence cannot be presented fully and fairly. Much will turn on whether the informant acted simply as an informant, in which case his identity is usually unlikely to be necessary to the presentation of the defence, or whether (as in *Agar*) it is alleged that the informant went beyond the supplying of information, and participated in the events constituting or surrounding the offence charged. In *Turner* [1995] 1 WLR 264, 268, Lord Taylor of Gosforth CJ said that even the latter circumstance would not automatically make disclosure of the identity of the informant necessary to the presentation of the defence, but the judge should take the informant's role into account in considering that question.

Despite the *dicta* of Lord Esher MR in *Marks v Beyfus*, and later *dicta* in cases such as *Governor of Brixton Prison, ex parte Osman* [1991] 1 WLR 281, which can be read in such a way as to suggest that there is a rule of automatic disclosure in cases where disclosure appears necessary to the defence, it would be wrong to suppose that the informer rule departs from the usual practice in public interest immunity cases of balancing the rights of the accused against the public interest (as to which see 13.7.4).

In *Keane* [1994] 1 WLR 746, Lord Taylor of Gosforth CJ said:

> We prefer to say that the outcome [in earlier cases] results from performing the balancing exercise, not from dispensing with it.

However, Lord Taylor added:

> If the disputed material may prove the defendant's innocence or avoid a miscarriage of justice, then the balance comes down resoundingly in favour of disclosing it.

This seems to indicate that, in almost every conceivable case, the result called for by Lord Esher MR in *Marks v Beyfus* would still be reached on the balancing test as described by Lord Taylor. It is submitted, therefore, that, not only is Lord Taylor's approach consistent with the earlier *dicta* of Lord Esher MR, but that the same principle should apply to all cases in which public interest immunity is claimed against the accused in criminal proceedings.

In *Savage v Chief Constable of Hampshire* [1997] 1 WLR 1061, it was held that, where the informer wishes to reveal his identity, this is a matter which may be taken into account, but is not conclusive on the question of whether his identity should be disclosed. There may be other factors to be considered, for example, the safety of others involved in ongoing investigations and the continuing efficacy of those investigations, and the extent to which other suspects may be enabled to avoid detection.

13.9.2 Protection of occupiers of premises used for surveillance

A modern extension of the informer rule was recognized by the Court of Appeal in *Rankine* [1986] QB 861. The accused was charged with supplying a controlled drug. The prosecution case was based on the observation of two police officers, who were watching from an observation post as the accused apparently sold cannabis on ten different occasions in the course of an hour. The accused appealed against his conviction on the ground that the trial judge had erred in ruling that the officers were entitled to withhold the identity and the location of the observation post. The Court of Appeal dismissed the appeal on the ground that any revelation of the identity of persons who permit property to be used for surveillance carries with it the likelihood that the observation post will lose its utility in future, as well as the risk of reprisals. The case was, therefore, directly analogous to the case of the informer, and disclosure should be ordered only in the same circumstances.[63]

After reviewing the earlier cases dealing with informers, including *Marks v Beyfus*, Mann J said ([1986] QB at 867):

> In our judgment the reasons which give rise to the rule that an informer is not to be identified apply with equal force to the identification of the owner or occupier of premises used for surveillance and to the identification of the premises themselves. The cases are indistinguishable, and the same rule must apply to each. That being so, the only question could be whether the judge in the instant case was correct in not exercising the duty exceptionally to admit in order to avoid a miscarriage of justice. Counsel for the appellant accepted that, if the rule in regard to informers applied, the performance of the duty could not be criticized. We agree.
>
> For those reasons this appeal is dismissed.

To invoke the protection offered to occupiers of premises it is not necessary that any actual threat be made to the occupier. It is sufficient if the occupier is in fear of some adverse consequences (*Blake v DPP* (1992) 97 Cr App R 169).

---

[63] But the *ratio* of the decision has been held to be the need to protect the occupier of the premises, and not merely to protect the secrecy of methods of surveillance. The latter may be protected only as a matter of distinct public policy, and on the basis of evidence given by senior police officers who are independent of the investigation which led to the particular charges being brought. Thus, it was wrong to deny an accused who alleged that he had been 'fitted up' cross-examination of police witnesses about the detail of the surveillance activities themselves: *Brown* (1987) 87 Cr App R 52. Clearly, however, there will be cases in which the methods of surveillance and the identity of the occupier cannot be separated, and in such cases, it is submitted that *Rankine* should be followed.

In *Johnson*,[64] Watkins LJ held that the prosecution should provide evidence of the attitude of the occupiers of the premises to the use of the premises, and to any possible subsequent disclosure of that information. The court may also consider evidence of any difficulty which may be encountered in the particular area of the observation, in obtaining the cooperation of members of the public.

13.9.3 Cases other than detection of crime by police

The police informer supplying information about crime is, of course, not the only source of information upon which public bodies may act and indeed depend for their ability to act. The identity of informers on matters involving possible frauds against the revenue laws has long been protected, and in a modern context this application of the rule was confirmed in *Alfred Crompton Amusement Machines Ltd v Commissioners of Customs & Excise (No. 2)* [1974] AC 405 where the commissioners had obtained information from customers of the company and others, relevant to assessments of the company's liability for purchase tax, which were the subject of an intended arbitration. It was held that the commissioners were entitled to withhold documents which would reveal the sources of their information, because if it became known that sources of information could not be kept secret, the working of the legislation under which the commissioners' powers were exercised in relation to the tax would be harmed by a lack of information. Lord Cross of Chelsea, with whom the other members of the House, on this point, agreed, said:[65]

> Here...one can well see that the third parties who have supplied this information to the commissioners because of the existence of their statutory powers would very much resent its disclosure by the commissioners to the appellants and that it is not at all fanciful...to say that the knowledge that the commissioners cannot keep such information secret may be harmful to the efficient working of the Act. In a case where the considerations for and against disclosure appear to be fairly evenly balanced the courts should I think, uphold a claim to privilege on the ground of public interest and trust to the head of the department concerned to do whatever he can to mitigate the ill effects of non-disclosure.

The obvious importance of a free supply of information to the working of various public bodies has been responsible for the extension of the informant rule to situations beyond, but analogous to, the original example of the detection of crime. In *Rogers v Home Secretary* [1973] AC 388, the Gaming Board refused applications by Rogers for certificates of consent to the grant to him of licences under the Gaming Act 1968 to operate certain gaming establishments. The refusal followed a letter to the Board from the Assistant Chief Constable of Sussex concerning Rogers. In some unexplained way, Rogers obtained a copy of the letter, and laid an information against the Assistant Chief Constable, alleging criminal libel. The proceedings resulted from the issue by Rogers of witness summonses against the Chief Constable of Sussex and the secretary of the Board, to attend at the magistrates' court and produce documents, including copies of the letter.

---

[64] [1988] 1 WLR 1377. See also *Hewitt* (1991) 95 Cr App R 81; *Grimes* [1994] Crim LR 213.

[65] [1974] AC at 434. The remarks contained in the last sentence cited from the speech of Lord Cross on the 'burden of proof' point, should be read in conjunction with those of Lord Reid in *Conway v Rimmer* [1968] AC 910, 952; see 13.6. And as to the protection by liquidators of information supplied to them in confidence to assist the process of compulsory liquidation, see *Re Barlow Clowes Gilt Managers Ltd* [1992] Ch 208.

The House of Lords held that the witness summonses should be set aside. Lord Reid said (*ibid.* at 401):

> I do not think that 'the public service' should be construed narrowly. Here the question is whether the withholding of this class of documents is really necessary to enable the board adequately to perform its statutory duties. If it is, then we are enabling the will of Parliament to be carried out.
>
> There are very unusual features about this case. The board require the fullest information they can get in order to identify and exclude persons of dubious character and reputation from the privilege of obtaining a licence to conduct a gaming establishment. There is no obligation on anyone to give any information to the board. No doubt many law-abiding citizens would tell what they know even if there was some risk of their identity becoming known, although many perfectly honourable people do not want to be thought to be mixed up in such affairs. But it is obvious that the best source of information about dubious characters must often be persons of dubious character themselves. It has long been recognized that the identity of police informers must in the public interest be kept secret and the same considerations must apply to those who volunteer information to the board. Indeed, it is in evidence that many refuse to speak unless assured of absolute secrecy.

Rogers was a not inconsiderable extension of the rule as expounded in *Marks* v *Beyfus*, because not only did it involve applying the rule to administrative rather than judicial proceedings but it extended the rule to cover information which need not involve criminal or dishonest conduct at all, but could be general observations on character or reputation, based perhaps in part on opinion. It seems, therefore, that the doctrine may have been extended to cover information given secretly for the benefit of the suppression of undesirable behaviour generally, or the promotion of any necessary vigilance over the conduct of public affairs, if those objects are at least partly dependent on the free flow of information.

This impression is supported by the (*obiter*) remarks of Lord Widgery CJ on the subject of evidence and correspondence given and supplied to inspectors who carried out a statutory investigation into the affairs of a company.[66] It is convincingly confirmed by the decision of the House of Lords in *D* v *NSPCC* [1978] AC 171, the facts of which were stated in 13.8.3. The House was perfectly prepared to draw an analogy between information supplied to the police, and that supplied to the Society for the purpose of enabling it to carry out its duties and to take decisions whether to exercise its powers to institute care proceedings. Lord Simon of Glaisdale said (*ibid.* at 241):

> I have already cited long-standing and approved authority to the effect that sources of police information are not subject to forensic investigation. This is because liability to general disclosure would cause those sources of information to dry up, so that police protection of the community would be impaired. Exactly the same argument applies in the instant case if for 'police' you read 'NSPCC' and for 'community' you read 'that part of the community which consists of children who may be in peril'. There can be no material distinction between police and/or local authorities on the one hand and the appellants on the other as regards protection of children. It follows that, on the strictest analogical approach and as a matter of legal rule, the appellants are bound to refuse to disclose their sources of information.

Lord Diplock, having observed engagingly (*ibid.* at 218–19):

> My Lords, in [*Rogers* v *Home Secretary*] this House did not hesitate to extend to persons from whom the Gaming Board received information for the purposes of the exercise of their statutory functions under the Gaming Act 1968 immunity from disclosure of their identity analogous to that which the law had previously accorded to police informers. Your Lordships' sense of values might well be open to reproach

---

[66] *Cheltenham Justices, ex parte Secretary of State for Trade* [1977] 1 WLR 95, 100. See also *Hasselblad (GB) Ltd* v *Orbinson* [1985] 1 All ER 173 and the cases referred to in note 56.

if this House were to treat the confidentiality of information given to those who are authorized by statute to institute proceedings for the protection of neglected or ill-treated children as entitled to less favourable treatment in a court of law than information given to the Gaming Board...

saw the same analogy as Lord Simon:

> The anonymity of those who tell the police of their suspicions of neglect or ill-treatment of a child would be preserved without any extension of the existing law. To draw a distinction in this respect between information given to the police and that passed on directly to a local authority or to the NSPCC would seem much too irrational a consequence to have been within the contemplation of Parliament when enacting the Children and Young Persons Act 1969.

It is true that the neglect and ill-treatment of children may well amount to a criminal offence, but the information passed to the Society is not given primarily for this purpose, but in order to enable suitable steps to be taken on behalf of any children found to be neglected or ill-treated. It would appear that the way is now open for further extensions of the informant rule in suitable cases, along the lines which have been suggested.

One such extension was apparently made by Sir Robert Megarry V-C in *Buckley* v *Law Society* [1984] 3 All ER 313, when he held that the Society's duty under the Solicitors Act 1974 to intervene in the practice of a solicitor suspected of dishonesty, a power exercised in the public interest, entitled the Society to refuse to disclose the identity of persons who had supplied information about solicitors suspected of dishonesty.

13.10 CONFIDENTIALITY

Where A supplies to B documents or information under some promise, express or implied, of confidentiality, the question whether B may subsequently be compelled to disclose or produce such documents or information has given rise to considerable debate. Attempts to avoid disclosure may be, and have been, asserted in two guises. Firstly, it may be said that confidential information is in itself a separate ground of private privilege, which attaches to documents and information in certain circumstances and is subject to the usual rules of private privilege. As to this, it now seems to be established that, except: (a) in cases to which legal professional privilege or the limited, statutory 'journalistic' privilege applies; and (b) in cases where confidential information is imparted in the course of bona fide 'without-prejudice' negotiations (in which cases the material is privileged irrespective of any question of confidentiality as such), no privilege arises in respect of material imparted in confidence.[67]

Secondly, it may be said that imparting confidential information may involve questions of public policy, and may enable an objection to be taken upon that basis. This argument has met with rather more success. It is true that it cannot be in every case that the mere fact of confidentiality will outweigh the public interest in disclosure for the purposes of litigation, but in certain cases it may as part of the overall picture have that effect. In *Alfred Crompton Amusement Machines Ltd* v *Commissioners of Customs & Excise (No. 2)* [1974] AC 405, the House of Lords considered, and rejected, the argument for the commissioners that the fact of receipt of information from customers of the company relating to the company's liability for purchase tax, in circumstances

---

[67] *Chantrey Martin & Co.* v *Martin* [1953] 2 QB 286. The separate privilege point was briefly revived by Lord Denning MR in the Court of Appeal in the *Alfred Crompton* case [1972] 2 QB 102, 134, once again tapping the stream of Equity.

obviously intended to be confidential, of itself entitled the commissioners (and indeed bound them) to withhold that information on the ground of public policy. But Lord Cross of Chelsea said (*ibid.* at 433–4):

> 'Confidentiality' is not a separate head of privilege, but it may be a very material consideration to bear in mind when privilege is claimed on the ground of public interest. What the court has to do is to weigh on the one hand the considerations which suggest that it is in the public interest that the documents in question should be disclosed and on the other hand those which suggest that it is in the public interest that they should not be disclosed and to balance one against the other.

This approach has been approved and followed in subsequent decisions.[68] Although the circumstances in which confidential information is imparted vary considerably from case to case, it is no doubt true, as Browne LJ observed in *Science Research Council v Nassé*[69] that 'the courts should and will do all they can to uphold the moral and social duty not to break confidences'. But unless there is some compelling public interest in the confidence, it will not prevail over the public interest in disclosure.

A misleading impression is sometimes given by references in the context of confidentiality to such cases as *Rogers, Alfred Crompton,* and *D v NSPCC.* Although it is true that the information given in those cases was given in confidence, and though that issue was discussed, the real ground of decision in each was that the information was necessary for the efficient running of some part of the public service, be it the collection of tax, the management of gaming establishments, or the protection of neglected children, and that disclosure would be likely to result, not only in a breach of confidence, but in information not being given in future. Balancing the public interests, as Lord Cross of Chelsea proposed, led accordingly to a decision against disclosure, but to see such a decision as giving effect to confidentiality *per se* would be to miss the point. (See also the comparable cases referred to in note 64.)

The law relating to confidential reports was much discussed in the Court of Appeal and the House of Lords in *Science Research Council v Nassé* [1979] QB 144 (CA); [1980] AC 1028 (HL). These two appeals, which were heard together, concerned employees who alleged that refusal of promotion by their employers was motivated by unlawful discrimination. They wanted discovery of confidential reports by their employers concerning both themselves and the other employees who were considered for promotion at the same time.

The employers in each case did not object to disclosure of the reports relating to the applicants, but did object to discovery of those dealing with the rivals. Both the Court of Appeal and the House of Lords accepted Lord Cross of Chelsea's treatment of confidentiality as the correct one. It was argued for the applicants that the reports were necessary for disposing fairly of the case, and that once it was shown that they were relevant, no element of confidentiality could protect them from disclosure. The argument was rejected, and although much of the decision turned on the particular practice of discovery in industrial tribunals, both the Court of Appeal and the House of Lords were prepared to view the case in a wider context.

---

[68] See, e.g., *D v NSPCC* [1978] AC 171; *Science Research Council v Nassé* [1980] AC 1028; *Lonrho plc v Fayed (No. 4)* [1994] QB 749; *Taylor v Director of the Serious Fraud Office* [1999] 2 AC 177; *Woolgar v Chief Constable of Sussex Police* [2000] 1 WLR 25; and see the cases referred to in note 56. The view was not entirely new: see, e.g., *Wheeler v Le Marchant* (1881) 17 ChD 675, per Sir George Jessel MR at 681.

[69] [1979] QB 144, 179, affirmed by the House of Lords [1980] AC 1028.

In the House of Lords, it was held, while upholding the actual decision of the Court of Appeal, that the tribunal should inspect the documents in order to determine whether discovery was necessary for disposing fairly of the case. While reiterating that confidentiality itself would be insufficient to create public interest immunity, the House also rejected the notion that confidentiality should be ignored once the relevance of the documents was established. The true position was clearly stated by Lord Edmund Davies, who may have had in mind the observation of Browne LJ in the Court of Appeal on the duty of the courts to uphold the 'moral and social duty not to break confidences' ([1980] AC 1028, 1074):

> Learned counsel for the appellants went so far as to submit that the confidential nature of the documents here in question is totally irrelevant to the matter of discovery, and that the tribunal or court should therefore wholly ignore the protests of third parties against the disclosure of information furnished by them in the belief that neither it nor its sources would ever be revealed…But for myself I am wholly unable to spell out from the absence of [statutory provision] the conclusion that confidentiality is an irrelevance. It is true that it cannot of *itself* ensure protection from disclosure [his Lordship referred to the *Alfred Crompton* case and *D v NSPCC*], but confidentiality may nevertheless properly play a potent part in the way in which a tribunal or court exercises its discretion in the matter of discovery.
>
> There was ample evidence supporting the view expressed by the Court of Appeal that the disclosure to inspection of confidential reports could well create upsets and unrest which would have a general deleterious effect. And a court, mindful of that risk, may understandably—and properly—think it right to scrutinize with particular care a request for their inspection. That is not to say, however, that the fear of possible unrest should deter the court from ordering discovery where the demands of justice clearly require it, but it serves to counsel caution in such cases.

There is developing a general doctrine that materials or information disclosed in confidence for official purposes may not be used for other, extraneous purposes unless the interests of justice require it. Thus, in *Taylor v Director of the Serious Fraud Office*,[70] it was held that confidential materials disclosed to the defence for the purposes of a criminal trial could not be used as the basis of a claim for defamation arising from the contents of those materials. Both in criminal and civil cases, the House of Lords held, there is an implied undertaking on the part of the recipient of confidential materials to use them only for the purpose for which they are disclosed.[71]

13.11 RECOMMENDED FURTHER READING

Allen, T.R.S., 'Public interest immunity and ministers' responsibilities' [1993] *Criminal Law Review* 660.

Brown, S., 'Public interest immunity' [1994] *Public Law* 579.

Forsyth, C., 'Public interest immunity: recent and future developments' (1997) **56**(1) *Cambridge Law Journal* 51.

Scott, Sir R., 'The acceptable and unacceptable use of public interest immunity' [1996] *Public Law* 427.

Taylor, C., 'What next for public interest immunity?' (2005) **69**(1) *Journal of Criminal Law* 75.

Van Harten, G., 'Weaknesses of adjudication in the face of secret evidence: adjudication in the face of secret evidence' (2009) **13**(1) *International Journal of Evidence and Proof* 1.

---

[70] [1999] 2 AC 177, overruling *Mahon v Rahn* [1998] QB 424. See also *Woolgar v Chief Constable of Sussex Police* [2000] 1 WLR 25; though there is also authority that if the materials are read out in open court, they cease to be confidential (*Bunn v British Broadcasting Corporation* [1998] 3 All ER 552); *Semble* this would still not justify their use for other purposes.

[71] As to the disclosure and treatment of confidential material in criminal cases, see the Criminal Procedure and Investigations Act 1996, s. 17 and Part 26 of the Criminal Procedure Rules 2005.

**13.12 QUESTIONS FOR DISCUSSION BASED ON *BLACKSTONE*
v *COKE* (for case files go to the Online Resource Centre)**

1. May the local authority successfully object to Coke's application for production of their files, made with a view to showing that Margaret may have given the authority a different account of how she became pregnant?

2. May Margaret make use of a copy of the letter of 20 February Yr—0, the original of which was inadvertently sent to her solicitors? Had Margaret's solicitors refused to return the original, what should Coke's solicitors have done?

13.13 GENERAL QUESTIONS FOR DISCUSSION

1. If a party claims public interest immunity, from what is the party claiming immunity?

2. Can public interest immunity ever be waived?

3. Which three categories of material may be excluded by public interest immunity?

4. Will material concerned with 'affairs of state' always be excluded?

5. Are the courts in both civil and criminal proceedings able to question a claim to withhold material on the basis of public interest immunity?

6. If yes, by what criterion should the minister's claim be judged?

7. What are 'class' and 'contents' claims?

8. Is the requirement to balance competing interests in criminal proceedings of a different nature from that in civil proceedings?

9. Is the identity of police informers always protected by public interest immunity?

10. Is 'confidentiality' a separate head of privilege?

14

PUBLIC INTEREST IMMUNITY AND PRIVILEGE II: PRIVILEGE

SUMMARY OF MAIN POINTS

- A privilege is a rule of law which permits a witness to refuse to answer a question, or a party to refuse to produce certain materials.

- The privileges recognized by English law are:

  (a) the privilege against self-incrimination;

  (b) legal professional privilege (and litigation privilege);

  (c) the privilege for sources of information contained in publications; and

  (d) the privilege not to disclose without prejudice communications.

- There is no privilege for materials simply because they are created or used confidentially, though the courts will respect confidentiality as far as it can.

- No comment may be made about the fact that a witness or party rightly claims a privilege.

14.1 PRIVILEGE GENERALLY

The distinctions between public interest immunity and private privilege were dealt with in Part A of Chapter 13. The circumstances under which, and the extent to which a private privilege may be waived were dealt with at 13.2.1. These matters need not be repeated here. This chapter is concerned with the detailed rules of law applicable to those private privileges which the law recognizes.

The privileges recognized by English law are few and limited. The privilege against self-incrimination and legal professional privilege have long been recognized at common law. However, by virtue of ss. 34 to 38 of the Criminal Justice and Public Order Act 1994, in certain situations the privilege against self-incrimination no longer prevents the drawing of adverse inferences against the accused in criminal cases if he chooses to exercise the privilege in relation to the offence charged, and despite affirmation of its continued existence by the Court of Appeal, the privilege is now of much reduced significance in that context.[1] It has also recently been the subject of attack in its application to attempts to resist disclosure of evidence in civil cases, in which strong judicial hints have been dropped that it should be greatly modified, if not abolished altogether.[2] Legal professional privilege has been the object of sustained attack in its application to prevent the disclosure of confidential communications involving the welfare of children.[3] The suggestion has been made that it is inappropriate to non-adversarial proceedings generally[4] and that its application to non-litigious areas of legal practice should be re-examined.[5] But the House

---

[1] *Cowan* [1996] QB 373; 10.5 *et seq.*, 15.6; 14.2.

[2] See *AT&T Istel Ltd* v *Tully* [1993] AC 45, per Lord Templeman at 53, Lord Griffiths at 57. The first step towards removing the privilege in this area may already have been taken: see *C plc* v *P* [2006] Ch 549; 14.8.

[3] *Re L (A Minor) (Police Investigation: Privilege)* [1997] AC 16; 14.11; cf. *Re G (A Minor) (Social Worker: Disclosure)* [1996] 1 WLR 1407.

[4] *Three Rivers District Council and others* v *Governor and Company of the Bank of England (No. 5)* [2003] QB 1556, [2], a view apparently based (incorrectly, it is submitted) on the decision of the House of Lords in *Re L (A Minor) (Police Investigation: Privilege)* [1997] AC 16: 14.13.

[5] *Three Rivers District Council and others* v *Governor and Company of the Bank of England (No. 6)* [2004] QB 916, [39].

of Lords has generally supported the existence of the privilege, not only as a rule of the common law, but also as a fundamental right supported by the European Convention.[6]

These two privileges are generally recognized in common law jurisdictions, so that in this respect, at least pending further incursions by Parliament or the courts, England is in step with the general approach. But in other respects, English law has a distinctly illiberal attitude to the matter of protecting confidential communications from compelled disclosure at the instance of an opponent. Parliament, it is true, created, fairly recently, for the first time, a limited privilege for journalists with respect to their sources of information (Contempt of Court Act 1981, s. 10: see 14.19 *et seq.*, a concession to art. 10 of the European Convention on Human Rights). But it has also abolished entirely the privilege against compelled matrimonial communications (Police and Criminal Evidence Act 1984, s. 80(9)). Without prejudice communications between the parties are privileged for most purposes (see 14.21). But English law does not recognize other privileges recognized and accorded some importance by American common law, for example the privileges between spouses,[7] ministers of religion and those who consult them,[8] medical advisers and their patients[9] or, for that matter, professionals of any kind other than lawyers and their clients.[10] In these cases, those involved in the relationship must rely on the reluctance of the courts to compel disclosure of confidential communications when it can be avoided. The courts have in general expressed a willingness to protect confidential information to the extent possible, but if disclosure is deemed to be necessary to the case, confidentiality will give way to the needs of litigation.[11]

Where and to the extent a privilege applies in his favour, a party cannot be compelled to disclose the information concerned, and no adverse inference may be drawn against him by virtue of his exercise of the privilege. Indeed, no comment must be made about the fact that the privilege is exercised.[12] However, as indicated above, these principles no longer apply to the privilege against self-incrimination of the accused in a criminal case in relation to the offence charged.

14.1.1 Non-privileged but confidential information

As a matter of law, information imparted otherwise than in the context of a recognized privilege cannot be protected against compelled disclosure, notwithstanding that it may have been imparted with a desire for, or a mistaken assumption of confidentiality on the part of all those concerned.[13] Thus, confidential communications to one's psychotherapist, doctor, minister of religion, probation officer, social worker, accountant, or spouse must ultimately be disclosed if disclosure is sought. However, in practice, it is not in every case that the courts permit this rule to operate to its full effect. The courts recognize the public interest in the free exercise of confidential relationships, and will not lightly compel answers which may result in the damaging of an individual relationship, or of the standing of a professional man or his profession generally.

---

[6] *Derby Magistrates' Court, ex parte B* [1996] AC 487; *R (On application of Morgan Grenfell & Co. Ltd) v Special Commissioner of Income Tax* [2003] 1 AC 563: 14.9.

[7] Civil Evidence Act 1968, s. 16(3); Police and Criminal Evidence Act 1980, s. 80(9): 14.18.

[8] *Wheeler v Le Marchant* (1881) 17 ChD 675, 681; cf. *Hay* (1860) 2 F & F 4, *Broad v Pitt* (1828) 3 C & P 518.

[9] *Duchess of Kingston's Case* (1776) 20 St Tr 355; *Gibbons* (1823) 1 C & P 97; *Hunter v Mann* [1974] QB 767.

[10] *Chantrey Martin & Co. v Martin* [1953] 2 QB 286 (accountants).

[11] See 14.1.1.

[12] *Wentworth v Lloyd* (1864) 10 HL Cas 589. In order to claim a privilege a witness must first be sworn and then make the claim specifically: *Boyle v Wiseman* (1855) 1 Exch 647; *Thomas v Newton* (1827) 2 C & P 60 though, as witnesses are generally unrepresented, the judge will sometimes warn the witness of a possible privilege.

[13] As to the relevance of confidentiality in the context of public interest immunity, see 13.10.

In particular, the courts will not compel breaches of confidence when no good purpose would be served thereby.[14] Thus in *Broad v Pitt* (1828) 3 C & P 518, Best CJ declared that he would never compel a clergyman to disclose communications made to him by a prisoner, though he would probably qualify that declaration today in the light of later authority (below). In *Elleray* [2003] 2 Cr App R 165, it was suggested that the prosecution should hesitate to make use of a (non-privileged) admission to a further offence made by an accused to a probation officer during an interview for the purpose of a pre-sentence report, and should consider carefully whether or not it is in the public interest to do so. But if the prosecution chose to make use of the admission, the court's only power to exclude it would be the discretionary power under s. 78 of the Police and Criminal Evidence Act 1984 (see 3.7).

The law on this subject was developed in part by important cases involving proceedings for contempt of court against journalists, and although Parliament has now provided a limited privilege for those responsible for publications with respect to their sources of information, these cases remain useful as indicating the approach the courts will take towards non-privileged confidential communications generally.[15] In *Attorney-General v Mulholland* [1963] 2 QB 477, 492, Donovan LJ said:

> While the journalist has no privilege entitling him as of right to refuse to disclose the source, so I think the interrogator has no absolute right to require such disclosure. In the first place the question has to be relevant to be admissible at all: in the second place it ought to be one the answer to which will serve a useful purpose in relation to the proceedings in hand—I prefer that expression to the term 'necessary'. Both these matters are for the consideration and, if need be, the decision of the judge. And over and above these two requirements, there may be other considerations, impossible to define in advance, but arising out of the infinite variety of fact and circumstance which a court encounters, which may lead a judge to conclude that more harm than good would result from compelling a disclosure or punishing a refusal to answer.

These words are all the more striking for having been delivered in the course of a case in which Donovan LJ, like the other members of the Court of Appeal, found unhesitatingly that two journalists had been guilty of a grave contempt in refusing to answer questions properly put to them at a public inquiry dealing with matters of high national security. In another case arising from the same inquiry, *Attorney-General v Clough* [1963] 1 QB 773, 792 Lord Parker CJ said that: '...it still...would remain open to this court to say in the special circumstances of any particular case that public policy did demand that the journalist should be immune'.

The effect of these views was summarized by Lord Denning MR in *Mulholland* in the following terms:[16]

> Take the clergyman, the banker or the medical man. None of these is entitled to refuse to answer when directed by a judge. Let me not be mistaken. The judge will respect the confidences which each member of these honourable professions receives in the course of it, and will not direct him to answer

---

[14] The court will balance the interests of the parties to the confidential communication in maintaining confidentiality against those of the parties to the litigation in having an order for disclosure. The matter appears to be essentially discretionary.

[15] See Contempt of Court Act 1981, s. 10. The present position of journalists and others responsible for publications, including the important cases of *British Steel Corporation v Granada Television Ltd* [1981] AC 1096 and *Secretary of State for Defence v Guardian Newspapers Ltd* [1985] AC 339, is considered at 14.19. See also *Umoh* (1986) 84 Cr App R 138.

[16] [1963] 2 QB 477, 489. See also *Senior v Holdworth, ex parte Independent Television News Ltd* [1976] QB 23.

unless not only is it relevant but also it is a proper and, indeed, necessary question in the course of justice to be put and answered. A judge is the person entrusted, on behalf of the community, to weigh these conflicting interests.

In *K (TD)* (1992) 97 C App R 342, it was held that the confidential record of a therapeutic interview with the child victim of an alleged sexual offence may be ordered to be disclosed if there is a strong need for disclosure for the purposes of defending a criminal case. The confidentiality of such a record would generally be respected, but no privilege attached to it.[17] And it appears that a professional adviser such as a psychiatrist may divulge confidential information to a local authority if that information raises a concern about child abuse: *Re B (Children: Patient Confidentiality)* [2003] 2 FLR 813.

A   PRIVILEGE AGAINST SELF-INCRIMINATION

SUMMARY OF MAIN POINTS

- No person is bound to answer a question, if in the opinion of the judge it would tend to expose him to a criminal charge, penalty, or criminal forfeiture.

- The judge must be satisfied (1) that the answer would tend to expose the witness to the charge; and (2) that the risk is not merely remote or insubstantial.

- Some statutory provisions remove the privilege and compel answers to certain questions. This does not of itself violate right to a fair trial. As a result of fair trial concerns, such provisions typically add that the answers shall not be used against the accused in a later criminal prosecution. If not, the judge should consider excluding the evidence as a matter of discretion.

- Currently, the privilege against self-incrimination applies to the disclosure of evidence in civil cases, but there is growing judicial criticism of its application in this context.

- A privilege exists in civil cases by virtue of s. 14(1) of the Civil Evidence Act 1968 to refuse to answer when the answer might incriminate a spouse or civil partner. It is uncertain whether a privilege exists at common law (in relation to criminal cases).

14.2 THE NEED FOR THE PRIVILEGE AGAINST SELF-INCRIMINATION

In order to appreciate the need for privilege against self-incrimination, it is important to understand that a person who, in the course of giving evidence in judicial or quasi-judicial proceedings, gives an answer which may be construed as an admission of some offence or wrongdoing, is liable to have that answer used as evidence against him in subsequent proceedings in respect

---

[17] Guidance as to disclosure of confidential materials to the police by local authorities in care cases was given in *Borough Council v A and others (Chief Constable Intervening)* [2007] 1 All ER 293. See also *Morrow v DPP* [1994] Crim LR 58 (documents dealing with abortions); *Re D (Minors) (Conciliation: Disclosure of Information)* [1993] Fam 231 (attempts at conciliation); *Brown v Matthews* [1990] Ch 662 (court welfare officers' reports), but see also *Re G (A Minor) (Social Worker: Disclosure)* [1996] 1 WLR 1407; 13.8.3.

of the offence or wrongdoing. An answer which may be used in this way is sometimes described as a 'judicial confession'.

14.2.1 With respect to offence charged

The most obvious kind of judicial confession is an admission by the accused that he committed the offence charged (including a plea of guilty). This is relatively straightforward. The accused is entitled not to make any statement with respect to allegations made against him, and if tried for an offence, he is entitled not to give evidence.[18] In the circumstances specified, and subject to the limitations imposed by ss. 34 to 38 of the Criminal Justice and Public Order Act 1994, an adverse inference may be drawn against him if he avails himself of these rights.[19] But if the accused volunteers an incriminating statement, it may be admitted in evidence against him subject to the rules governing the admissibility of confessions,[20] and if he elects to give evidence, he may be cross-examined with a view to showing his guilt of the offence charged.

14.2.2 With respect to offences not yet charged

What is more material for present purposes is putting to a witness any question, the truthful answer to which will or may incriminate him in respect of some offence with which he is *not* then charged. The answer itself may lead to his being charged, or, if the charge is already contemplated, may provide evidence against him to support it. In this case, too, the rule is that an answer given on oath will be admissible in the subsequent proceedings as a judicial confession. Thus in *Chapman* (1912) 29 TLR 117, when the accused was before examining justices charged with unlawful carnal knowledge of a girl aged between 13 and 16, he admitted that he had had carnal knowledge of the girl while she was under 13, and that admission was received on a subsequent indictment for that offence. The precise nature of the proceedings is immaterial, provided that they are of a judicial or quasi-judicial kind, at which evidence is lawfully taken under oath. Thus, in addition to any civil or criminal proceedings, answers given at a coroner's inquest[21] or at a military tribunal of inquiry[22] will, equally, be admissible subsequently.

14.3 SCOPE OF THE PRIVILEGE

No witness is bound to answer any question if the answer thereto would, in the opinion of the judge, have a tendency to expose the witness to any criminal charge, penalty or, in a criminal case, forfeiture which the judge regards as reasonably likely to be preferred or sued for. If the witness is wrongly compelled to answer such a question, his answer may not be admitted as evidence against him in a later prosecution.

---

[18] Criminal Evidence Act 1898, s. 1(a), repealed and replaced by s. 80(4) of the Police and Criminal Evidence Act 1984 as amended by the Youth Justice and Criminal Evidence Act 1999; *Cowan* [1996] QB 373; 15.4.

[19] Chapter 10; 15.6. As we saw in Chapter 10, this is now subject to the requirement that the jury be directed in accordance with the principles laid down in *Cowan* [1996] QB 373, in compliance with art. 6 of the Convention; see *Condron* v *United Kingdom* [2000] Crim LR 679; 10.5.1.

[20] See 9.4 *et seq.*

[21] The importance of evidence given at inquests has diminished with the powers of the court, which is no longer able to take depositions or to return verdicts implicating named persons in an offence. See Criminal Law Act 1977, s. 56.

[22] *Colpus* [1917] 1 KB 574.

In practice, it is the exposure to possible criminal charges which is of importance. The rare and unimportant cases of liability to penalties and forfeiture seem to have had their origin in what are now remote and old rules of practice that Equity would not, by discovery or interrogatories, aid either common informers or proceedings for forfeiture. The courts now have wide powers to give relief from forfeiture, and that part of the privilege has been abolished except in relation to criminal proceedings by s. 16(1)(a) of the Civil Evidence Act 1968. There is no privilege with regard to questions the answer to which would tend to expose the witness to the risk of civil proceedings, even at the suit of the Crown[23] except in the rare instance of proceedings for a penalty. It was at one time thought that the common law privilege included the right to refuse to answer a question tending to show that the witness had committed adultery. The view was never supported by any basis more substantial than that the ecclesiastical courts had some power, purely notional in modern history, to impose forfeiture on lay offenders. Although the privilege was asserted as recently as 1891 by Bowen LJ in *Redfern v Redfern* [1891] P 139, it was demolished beyond recall as 'fanciful' by a more secularly inclined Court of Appeal in *Blunt v Park Lane Hotel Ltd* [1942] 2 KB 253. There was, indeed, a statutory privilege to the like effect, by virtue of s. 3 of the Evidence Further Amendment Act 1869, but it applied only to 'proceedings instituted in consequence of adultery' and was abolished for all purposes by s. 16(5) of the Civil Evidence Act 1968.[24]

Where the privilege applies, it permits the witness to refuse to answer, not only questions which may be incriminating directly, but also questions the answers to which are clearly capable of use in providing evidence against him. Thus, in *Slaney* (1832) 5 Car & P 213, a witness in a prosecution for criminal libel, by advertisement in newspapers, stated in evidence that he knew who had written to a newspaper with an advertisement. He was permitted to refuse to answer a further question about the identity of this person, on the ground that the information could have enabled evidence of his own possible complicity to be obtained.

A corporation, being a legal person, may claim the privilege against self-incrimination, but when this occurs, the privilege is that of the corporation, and the privilege of the corporation does not extend to the incrimination of its officers; though the officers are entitled to claim individual privileges on their own behalf (*Rio Tinto Zinc Corporation v Westinghouse Electric Corporation* [1978] AC 547, 637–8; *Sociedade Nacional de Combustiveis de Angola UEE v Lundqvist* [1991] 2 QB 310 per Beldam J at 336).

14.4 TEST TO BE APPLIED

There is a judicial function of some importance of deciding whether the privilege should be allowed, or whether a witness must be compelled to answer an incriminating question.[25] The judge must satisfy himself of two matters. First, by taking evidence in the absence of the jury and, if necessary, *in camera*, that the answer to the question would tend to expose the witness to a criminal charge. This is a process of legal inquiry, in the sense that the judge must look at the elements of the apprehended charge, and see whether the witness's fears are justified as a matter of law. Second, that the institution of the proceedings is not just 'a remote or insubstantial risk'

---

[23] Witnesses Act 1806.

[24] So a witness may be asked for further information directly about his commission of adultery: *Nast v Nast and Walker* [1972] Fam 142.

[25] The judge must weigh the reality of the danger of prosecution, and cannot simply defer to the opinion of, e.g., a party's solicitor: *R (CPS) v Bolton Magistrates' Court* [2004] 1 WLR 835.

but that there is a 'real and appreciable' danger to the witness, having regard to the ordinary operation of the law.[26]

This second requirement is sometimes far from easy. There are obvious cases where there would be clear evidence of a serious offence which in the ordinary way could not be overlooked. There are equally clear cases where no danger is involved, as in *Blunt* v *Park Lane Hotel Ltd* [1942] 2 KB 253, where the Court of Appeal saw not the remotest prospect of a witness being exposed, in 1942, to an ecclesiastical forfeiture in respect of her adultery, and *Boyes* (1861) 1 B & S 311, 330, where although the accused's possession of a royal pardon under the Great Seal would have been no answer to a prosecution by impeachment, it was unthinkable that such proceedings would be instituted against him. It was said in this last case that, once it appears that a witness is at risk, 'great latitude should be allowed to him in judging for himself of the effect of any particular question'. But this does not deprive the judge of the duty to rule on the privilege, and he must do so on the basis of what appear to be the practical realities of the situation.

It may be right to disallow the claim to privilege where the witness has already jeopardized himself by making a similar statement to the police, or is for some other reason already in peril.[27] The judge can also take into account the apparent rarity of certain prosecutions, the trivial nature of the offence, or the lapse of time since its commission, in assessing the likelihood of proceedings. In *Rank Film Distributors Ltd* v *Video Information Centre* [1982] AC 380, 445, Lord Fraser took into account the remoteness of the possibility of a prosecution under s. 56 of the Copyright Act 1956. Copyright infringement is regarded as essentially a civil matter, and the protection of the rights of those affected was far more significant than consideration of the improbable scenario of a criminal prosecution. But these matters must be weighed with great care.[28] The rarity of prosecutions seems to have influenced the argument in such cases as *Rio Tinto Zinc Corporation* v *Westinghouse Electric Corporation* [1978] AC 547, where it was contended that because the European Commission had failed to impose fines (under art. 81 (formerly 85) of the EC Treaty) in respect of a cartel, of which it had knowledge, companies thought to be implicated in establishing or operating the cartel could be required to produce documents which might have the effect of incriminating them. Both the Court of Appeal and the House of Lords held that the argument was fallacious. Although there might be cases where such an inference could safely be drawn, in the present circumstances it was likely that production would increase the prospect of proceedings, by offering evidence upon which the Commission might be disposed, at last, to act. It would seem, therefore, that the judge should take into account an increase in the danger to the witness, which would result from making available evidence whose previous absence may have inhibited the institution of proceedings. Some limited forbearance on the part of an authority empowered to commence proceedings cannot necessarily be equated with inaction or unconcern.

Where a witness is wrongly compelled to answer a question in breach of the privilege against self-incrimination, his answer will be inadmissible in subsequent proceedings against him.[29]

---

[26] *Rio Tinto Zinc Corporation* v *Westinghouse Electric Corporation* [1978] AC 547, per Lord Denning MR at 574; *Renworth Ltd* v *Stephansen* [1996] 3 All ER 244; *Tate Access Floors Inc.* v *Boswell* [1991] Ch 512.

[27] *Khan* v *Khan* [1982] 1 WLR 513; *Brebner* v *Perry* [1961] SASR 177.

[28] *Triplex Safety Glass Co. Ltd* v *Lancegaye Safety Glass (1934) Ltd* [1939] 2 KB 935.

[29] *Garbett* (1847) 1 Den 236.

14.5 EXPOSURE TO PROSECUTION UNDER FOREIGN LAW

Curiously, it was never finally decided at common law to what extent, if at all, the privilege may be claimed in response to a question which might have the effect of exposing the witness to some charge or penalty under the law of another country. The better view was probably that there was no such privilege, unless the provisions of the relevant foreign law (a question of fact) were admitted on the pleadings, which suggests that it was felt to be inappropriate for the judge to attempt to assess the likelihood of proceedings being commenced in another jurisdiction.[30] There is clearly much force in this, as the judge must otherwise try to weigh, not only the substantive law but also the practice of the foreign court or prosecuting authority in order to assess whether the risk is real and appreciable.

In civil cases, the question is now governed by statute, and it may be that the common law would follow the same approach, were the matter to arise in a criminal case. By s. 14(1) of the Civil Evidence Act 1968:

> The right of a person in any legal proceedings other than criminal proceedings to refuse to answer any question or produce any document or thing if to do so would tend to expose that person to proceedings for an offence or for the recovery of a penalty—
> (a) shall apply only as regards criminal offences under the law of any part of the United Kingdom and penalties provided for by such law.

It should be noted that, since the European Communities Act 1972, the law of what is now the European Union has been a part of the law of England. Accordingly, in the *Westinghouse* case, it was not disputed in the House of Lords that fines which the European Commission could impose under art. 81 (formerly 85), and which were recoverable by proceedings under English law, were, 'a penalty provided for by such law', within the meaning of the subsection.

While the subsection does extend the privilege to charges and penalties which may arise under law which is technically foreign, for instance the law of Scotland, it limits the sphere of operation territorially to that which an English judge is plainly competent to assess.

14.6 INCRIMINATION OF SPOUSES

It has never been decided definitively in England whether the common law recognizes a privilege to refuse to answer questions which would tend to expose the spouse of the witness to some charge or penalty. If there is such a common law privilege against spouse-incrimination, it seems that it does not extend to members of the family other than the spouse.[31] Considerable light is shed on this question in an article by D. Lusty (2004) UNSW Law J 1, which suggests that the existence of a common law spousal privilege is implicit in the common law rules relating to the competence and compellability of the spouse; that the privilege has a lineage quite distinct from the privilege against self-incrimination; that its existence was recognized at the latest by the time of Coke; and that the continued existence of the privilege can be derived from a proper reading of the speeches of the House of Lords in *Hoskyn v Commission of Police for the Metropolis* [1979]

---

[30] *United States of America v McRae* (1868) LR 3 Ch App 79; *King of the Two Sicilies v Willcox* (1851) 1 Sim NS 301; *Re Atherton* [1912] 2 KB 251; cf. *Arab Monetary Fund v Hashim* [1989] 1 WLR 565.

[31] *All Saints, Worcester (Inhabitants)* (1817) 6 M & S 194, per Bayley J at 201; presumably a civil partner would be covered.

AC 474 dealing with the modern competence and compellability rules (see 15.8). Although it is certainly possible to contest this last conclusion as following inevitably from *Hoskyn*, Lusty's analysis of the history of the competence rules provides a compelling basis for concluding that a spouse-incrimination privilege was at one time thought to exist, and that there is no reason to suppose that it has been abrogated. His reasoning was sufficient to persuade the Supreme Court of Queensland to declare the existence of the privilege as a matter of English common law in *Callanan* v *B* [2004] QCA 478. It is submitted that this view is correct, and should be followed in England when the occasion arises.

The existing authority in England is meagre and unsatisfactory. There are *dicta* to the effect that there is no privilege not to incriminate a spouse in the course of giving evidence in criminal proceedings: see *Rio Tinto Zinc Corporation* v *Westinghouse Electric Corporation* [1978] AC 547, 637, per Lord Diplock; *Pitt* [1983] QB 25. The Court of Appeal in *Pitt* held that, where the spouse is a competent witness, she should be treated like any other witness in the case, and it has since apparently been assumed from this that it would be anomalous if she were to enjoy a privilege not to incriminate the accused. But the assumption made in these cases is an over-simplification of the issue, and rests on the failure to distinguish between incriminating the accused *as to the offence charged*, and incriminating the accused *as to other offences*. The spouse of the accused is a competent witness in a criminal case (see 15.7). But the spouse is compellable as a witness only if called by the accused, or in the small number of specified offences, by the prosecution or a co-accused. If she is called voluntarily on behalf of the accused, there would clearly be a waiver of any privilege against self-incrimination as to the offence charged, as in the case where the accused gives evidence himself. But this does not logically mean that the privilege could not be claimed as to offences with which the accused is *not* charged,[32] particularly if the evidence of the spouse would be the only basis on which he might later be charged with those offences. If she is compelled to give evidence by the prosecution or a co-accused, a similar, though not identical, observation holds true. There is no waiver by the spouse in this case, but it would certainly seem anomalous for the spouse to enjoy a privilege not to incriminate the accused as to the offence charged. Again, however, the same is not necessarily true of offences with which the accused is not then charged. Nonetheless, it must be conceded that there is a distinct and as yet open question as to whether the common law privilege should extend to testimony given in criminal proceedings. This does not mean that the privilege should not be recognized in other circumstances. This is now the position by statute in civil cases, and there is surely no logical reason why the position at common law in criminal cases should differ.

Section 14(1) of the Civil Evidence Act 1968 provides:

> The right of a person in any legal proceedings other than criminal proceedings to refuse to answer any question or produce any document or thing if to do so would tend to expose that person to proceedings for an offence or for the recovery of a penalty—...
>> (b) shall include a like right to refuse to answer any question or produce any document or thing if to do so would tend to expose the husband or wife of that person to proceedings for any such criminal offence or for the recovery of any such penalty.[33]

---

[32] Evidence of offences with which the accused is not charged is often irrelevant and inadmissible in criminal cases. (See generally Chapters 5 and 6.) Such evidence is admissible as evidence of bad character when permitted by s. 101 of the Criminal Justice Act 2003: see Part B of Chapter 6.

[33] By virtue of s. 84 of and Sch. 27 to the Civil Partnership Act 2004, this provision applies to civil partners as it does to spouses.

Section 14(2) applies the same immunity to statutory rights not to give self-incriminating answers in proceedings under statutory powers of inspection and investigation (as to which see 14.7). Section 14(3) provides that where, by statute, a witness is compellable to answer even incriminating questions, such compulsion applies to answers which would incriminate the spouse as well as those which would incriminate the witness himself. And s. 14(4) provides that any statutory provision that answers given by a witness shall not be admissible against him in any given proceedings, shall be construed as providing also that such answers shall not be admissible in such proceedings against the spouse of the witness. These provisions refer to the statutory powers to investigate and obtain evidence in which the common law privilege against self-incrimination is replaced or modified. However, subsections (2) to (4) of s. 14 apply only to statutory provisions enacted before the Civil Evidence Act 1968 itself (s. 14(5)). The most important statutory provisions of this kind were enacted after the 1968 Act, and accordingly are not subject to s. 14(2) to (4). In cases not covered by s. 14(2) to (4) any privilege against incriminating the spouse would have to be provided for specifically in the wording of the statute which creates the power of investigation. These provisions should be read together with those of s. 18(2) that references to the husband or wife of a person in the Act or in any amendment made by the Act do not include references to a person who is no longer married to that person. Section 84(4) of the Civil Partnership Act 2004 makes the same provision in the case of civil partnership.

14.7 STATUTORY DEROGATIONS FROM THE PRIVILEGE: THE EUROPEAN CONVENTION

A number of statutes confer broad investigative powers on duly appointed inspectors for the purpose of inquiring into apparent breaches of the law, for example, the commission of corporate or securities offences. These powers typically include the right to interview under oath persons who may be able to assist in their inquiries, and to require those interviewed to answer incriminating questions and to produce potentially incriminating documents. To this extent, these statutory provisions override the privilege against self-incrimination. But an alternative protection can be conferred by a provision restricting the use of incriminating answers given in any subsequent criminal proceedings against the person interviewed, and any such provision prevails over the common law privilege in such cases, even if the protection offered is more limited. Until the coming into effect of the Human Rights Act 1998 (see 1.7 and below) the only rule was that whether or not there was any restriction on the admissibility of answers given and documents produced in such circumstances in subsequent criminal proceedings against the person interviewed, and what degree of protection was conferred, depended on the wording or apparent intention of the statute. Some statutes provide that answers must be given to questions on certain matters dealt with by the statute, but provide a specific degree of protection against the subsequent use of the answers given against the person who gives them. In this situation, the provisions of the statute prevail over the common law privilege against self-incrimination, and the witness is entitled only to the protection afforded by the statute. The object of such provisions is to ensure that information is given for a purpose deemed important by Parliament, or to induce cooperation by persons who would otherwise withhold their cooperation through fear that what they might say might be used against them subsequently as evidence. Many such provisions deal with the question expressly[34] but where they do not, the general rule seems to be that answers will

---

[34] See, e.g., Theft Act 1968, s. 31; Supreme Court Act 1981, s. 72; Children Act 1989, s. 98; Criminal Justice Act 1987, s. 2; Fraud Act 2006, s. 13, and see *Kensington International Ltd* v *Republic of Congo* [2008] 1 WLR 1145;

be admissible in subsequent proceedings, unless the witness was by the statute under compulsion to answer even incriminating questions. Some such statutory provisions have been construed as rendering answers admissible by necessary implication.[35] However, even where a statute provides for admissibility in subsequent proceedings, answers will be excluded if the questions put fall outside the scope of the statute and thus outside the power of the questioner.[36]

14.7.1 Statutory derogations and the European Convention on Human Rights

The law stated above must now be considered in the light of the fair trial provisions of art. 6 of the European Convention on Human Rights (see 1.7). The privilege against self-incrimination is not provided for expressly in the Convention, but the jurisprudence of the European Court of Human Rights makes it clear that if the accused is deprived of the privilege it will normally, though not inevitably, involve a breach of the fair trial provisions of art. 6.[37] In *O'Halloran* v *United Kingdom* (2007) 47 EHRR 397, a case involving a failure to comply with s. 172 of the Road Traffic Act 1988 by providing information about the person driving a vehicle on a given occasion, the Court held that a direct compulsion to provide information in derogation of the privilege against self-incrimination did not automatically violate the fair trial provisions of art. 6. It was held that an overall assessment of the effect of the statutory provisions must be made on a case-by-case basis, taking into account: the nature of the compulsion to provide information and the severity of the penalty for failing to comply; whether or not the compulsion is part of a regulatory scheme which, taken as a whole, serves a benign purpose; whether or not the use of any information provided is restricted to that which is strictly necessary for the working of the regulatory scheme and does not render a person criminally liable for extraneous matters; and, as always, the availability of safeguards such as judicial discretion to exclude evidence which guarantee the overall fairness of the trial. Each case must be considered on its own merits.

In cases where the statute provides that any answers given or documents produced are inadmissible in later criminal proceedings, no problem will arise.[38] But in other cases, art. 6 must be considered. In *Saunders* v *United Kingdom* (1997) 23 EHRR 313, the Court held that where an accused was deprived completely of the benefits of the privilege by virtue of statutory provisions which purported to remove the privilege and require the accused to provide information, art. 6 was violated. But English law did not immediately conform to this principle. In *Staines* [1997] 2 Cr App R 426, the appellants argued that the trial judge should have excluded, as a matter of discretion, evidence consisting of answers given to inspectors under s. 177 of the Financial Services

Director of Serious Fraud Office, ex parte Smith [1993] AC 1. See also Civil Evidence Act 1968, s. 14 (4); *London and County Securities Ltd* v *Nicholson* [1980] 1 WLR 948; *Sociedade Nacional de Combustiveis de Angola UEE* v *Lundqvist* [1991] 2 QB 310; *Re G (A Minor) (Social Worker: Disclosure)* [1996] 1 WLR 1407.

[35] Banking Act 1987, s. 42 (*Bank of England* v *Riley* [1992] Ch 475); Companies Act 1985, s. 434 (*Re London United Investments plc* [1992] Ch 578); and see *Bishopsgate Investment Management Ltd* v *Maxwell* [1993] Ch 1; *Kansal* [1993] QB 244.

[36] *Commissioners of Customs & Excise* v *Harz* [1967] 1 AC 760; *Karak Rubber Co. Ltd* v *Burden* [1971] 1 WLR 1748.

[37] *IJL, GMR and AKP* v *United Kingdom* [2001] Crim LR 133; *Funke* v *France* (1993) 16 EHRR 297; *Saunders* v *United Kingdom* (1997) 23 EHRR 313; *Kansal* v *United Kingdom* (2004) 39 EHRR 31. Cf. *JB* v *Switzerland* [2001] Crim LR 748.

[38] It seems that it must clearly appear that this is the case. In *JB* v *Switzerland* [2001] Crim LR 748, the applicant refused to produce documents to the Swiss tax authorities although he was subject to disciplinary fines for refusing to do so. It was held that proceedings to enforce these fines were criminal in nature where the possibility could not be excluded that any documents the applicant might have produced would be used against him in later criminal proceedings.

Act 1986, which empowered the inspectors to require answers to be given under oath, and made the answers admissible in evidence in subsequent proceedings against the person interviewed. The appellants pointed out that the European Court of Human Rights had held, in *Saunders*, that such a procedure violated art. 6. But the Court of Appeal bluntly replied[39] that, while, pursuant to the UK's treaty obligations, the Court was bound to consider the Convention and the jurisprudence of the European Court of Human Rights, any such decision holding that the English practice was unfair could not prevail over an unambiguous English statutory provision which Parliament must be taken to have deemed to be fair.

This position, which, as the Court itself was constrained to admit ([1997] 2 Cr App R at 443) resulted in an unsatisfactory and inevitable conflict between English law and the jurisprudence of the European Court of Human Rights, had to be abandoned by Parliament in the light of the incorporation of the European Convention into the law of the UK by the Human Rights Act 1998. To give effect to art. 6, as interpreted in *Saunders v United Kingdom*, s. 59 of and Sch. 3 to the Youth Justice and Criminal Evidence Act 1999 make important amendments to some, but by no means all of the statutory provisions which offended the principle laid down in *Saunders* by inserting into each an essentially identical subsection, of which the new s. 434(5A) of the Companies Act 1985 may be given as an example:[40]

> However, in criminal proceedings in which [the person who gave the answers] is charged with an offence...—
>   (a) no evidence relating to the answer may be adduced, and
>   (b) no question relating to it may be asked,
> by or on behalf of the prosecution, unless evidence relating to it is adduced, or a question relating to it asked, in the proceedings by or on behalf of that person.

In cases to which s. 59 of the 1999 Act does not apply, the courts must now apply the domestic English rules as modified by the jurisprudence of the European Court. It is submitted that the test should be essentially a threefold one. Firstly, the court must construe the wording of the statute to ascertain whether or not it does have the effect of derogating from the privilege against self-incrimination, and to ascertain what alternative provisions the statute makes by way of offering the accused some protection against the use of his answers and any documents he produces in subsequent criminal proceedings. Secondly, the court must then look at these provisions in the light of art. 6 to see whether any unfairness to the accused results from them. Thirdly, the court must balance the potential unfairness to the accused against the importance of the public policy underlying the statutory derogation. But the enthusiasm of the courts for the principles laid down in *Saunders v United Kingdom* has so far proved fickle, and there are signs that they may be tending to revert to the common law position in cases to which s. 59 does not apply, as expressed in *Staines*. In *R (Hertfordshire County Council), ex parte Green Environmental Industries Ltd and another* [2000] AC 412, s. 71(2) of the Environmental Protection Act 1990 conferred power on officials to require a person or organization to supply information relevant to the enforcement of

---

[39] Following the judgment of the Court of Appeal in *Saunders* itself [1996] 1 Cr App R 463, 477 per Lord Taylor of Gosforth CJ.

[40] The statutes affected are the Insurance Companies Act 1982, the Companies Act 1985, the Insolvency Act 1986, the Company Directors Disqualification Act 1986, the Building Societies Act 1986, the Financial Services Act 1986, the Banking Act 1987, the Companies Act 1989, the Friendly Societies Act 1992; and see the new s. 2(8AA) of the Criminal Justice Act 1987 (answers given in response to the Director of the Serious Fraud Office).

that Act. Although it was a case to which s. 59 of the 1999 Act did not apply, the company argued that, because the purpose of the 1990 Act was to implement European environmental standards, it must have been intended that art. 6 apply, and that the compulsion to supply information was unfair. The House of Lords disagreed, holding that art. 6 and the cases decided by the European Court of Human Rights dealt with the fairness of the trial, not with regulatory matters, and that, since s. 59 of the 1999 Act did not apply, the matter was simply one of statutory construction. The decision is hardly satisfactory. The company's argument that the 1990 Act implemented European standards, while creative, was unnecessary and missed the point. The principles laid down in *Saunders* do not apply only to selected cases in which Parliament has made an express amendment, but require the courts in all cases to balance the policy involved in compelling certain information for the purpose of enforcing the law with the rights of the accused. The House pointed out that the trial judge has a discretion to exclude evidence so obtained in later criminal proceedings, but this is surely not a satisfactory way of safeguarding such a basic right to a fair trial.

There have, however, been other cases in which the courts have held that some particular policy justifies qualifying or restricting the impact of art. 6 on provisions for compulsory disclosure, but in which the need for a balancing test has received greater attention.[41] It appears that the court should consider, for the purposes of the balancing test, both the gravity of the offences involved and the extent of the sanction to which the accused was liable if he failed to answer questions or produce documents. Thus, in *Heaney and McGuinness v Ireland* [2001] Crim LR 481, an Irish statute, the Offences against the State Act 1939, s. 52, made it an offence punishable by imprisonment for a person detained on suspicion of terrorist offences to refuse to account fully to the police for his movements and actions during certain periods of time. It was held that the fact that the accused faced substantial terms of imprisonment for serious offences if convicted meant that, although the privilege against self-incrimination is not absolute, the degree of compulsion involved in the provisions of s. 52, together with the sanction of imprisonment under that section violated art. 6. Conversely, in *Brown v Stott* [2003] 1 AC 681, it was held not to violate art. 6 to permit the prosecution to adduce evidence of an answer compelled under s. 172 of the Road Traffic Act 1988, to the effect that the defendant was the driver of a motor vehicle at the relevant time. The State had a strong interest in prosecuting and deterring serious driving offences, and the penalty for non-compliance with s. 172 was moderate and non-custodial.[42]

In *Saunders* the majority of the members of the European Court of Human Rights drew a distinction between cases in which the statute compels the accused to answer questions, and cases in which the statute compels the production of documents or other potentially incriminating evidence. The majority held that the privilege against self-incrimination applied to the former, but not the latter. This view was against the view taken in the seminal case of *Funke v France* (1993) 16 EHRR 297,[43] but was justified by the observation that documents and other items of physical

---

[41] *Kearns* [2002] 1 WLR 2815 (policy in favour of investigating the affairs of bankrupts justified such a provision in Insolvency Act 1986, s. 354(a)); *Allen (No. 2)* [2001] 4 All ER 768 (similar policy in relation to enforcement of tax laws justified provision in Taxes Management Act 1970, s. 20(1)); *R (Bright) v Central Criminal Court* [2001] 1 WLR 662 (no violation of art. 6 in making an order for production of incriminating documents pursuant to s. 9 of the Police and Criminal Evidence Act 1984, subject to statutory safeguards).

[42] See, to similar effect, *Maudesley v Chief Constable of Cheshire Constabulary* [2004] 1 WLR 1035.

[43] Though not against the view generally taken at common law. Thus, English law has never extended the privilege to evidence such as blood or urine samples taken from a defendant in excess alcohol cases. The jurisprudence

evidence have an existence independent of any decision of the accused to reveal information. It appears that English law favours this position. In *Attorney-General's Reference (No. 7 of 2000)* [2001] 1 WLR 1879, it was held that no violation of art. 6 was involved in the use of documents disclosed by a bankrupt under the compulsory provisions of s. 291 of the Insolvency Act 1986 in his subsequent prosecution for contributing to his bankruptcy by gambling. Because the documents disclosed by the accused could just as well have been discovered by other means, including a search warrant, they constituted evidence independent of the accused.[44] But in *Shannon v United Kingdom* (2006) 42 EHRR 31, it was held that where the accused was the target of a criminal investigation and had even been charged, a coercive demand that he attend an interview without any guarantee that answers he was compelled to give would not be used against him in the criminal proceedings resulted in a clear violation of the fair trial provision of art. 6 (*ibid.* at [38]).

14.8 APPLICATION OF PRIVILEGE TO DISCLOSURE OF EVIDENCE IN CIVIL CASES

Somewhat analogous problems arise in relation to the disclosure of evidence in civil cases. In principle, it would seem that a party should be able to invoke the privilege, within the framework of the principles dealt with above, to avoid having to disclose potentially incriminating evidence in response to a court order such as a search order or freezing injunction made against him in civil proceedings.[45] This result was conceded, albeit with reluctance, by the House of Lords in *Rank Film Distributors Ltd* v *Video Information Centre* [1982] AC 380. In the not uncommon circumstances of that case, compliance with the order, which had been obtained by the plaintiffs, might have provided evidence against the defendants relevant in a later criminal prosecution under s. 21 of the Copyright Act 1956. The actual result in this case would now be affected by statute,[46] but the principle remains sound, as the power to make such orders is not restricted to cases involving intellectual property rights.[47] Nonetheless, there has recently been much strong judicial feeling that the privilege against self-incrimination should not be used to avoid disclosure of information properly sought in civil proceedings. The main arguments in favour of this view are that the privilege against self-incrimination applies only to statements or documents made by the party claiming it, and not to free-standing evidential material, which is the usual target of a search order; that it is clear that the privilege would not prevent seizure of the latter material pursuant to a search warrant in a criminal case, so that there is an apparently pointless difference between civil and criminal proceedings; and that, in the event of a later criminal prosecution of the party concerned, the trial judge may exclude the evidence under s. 78 of the Police and Criminal Evidence Act 1984 if there are concerns about the fairness of the

---

of the United States Supreme Court in relation to the Fourth Amendment prohibition on unreasonable search and seizure is in accord: see, e.g., *Schmerber v California* 384 US 757 (1966). See also the interesting analysis by Easton [1991] Crim LR 18.

[44] *Hundal; Dhaliwal* [2004] 2 Cr App R 19; *Kearns* [2002] 1 WLR 2815; cf. *C plc v P* [2006] Ch 549, 14.8.

[45] An order made in *ex parte* proceedings to permit premises to be searched, with a view to finding tangible evidence, e.g., of copyright infringement—a remedy much used in actions involving intellectual property rights or to prevent the dispersal of evidence and assets pending trial. The 'additional damages' which may be awarded in copyright actions are not a 'penalty' (*Rank Film Distributors Ltd v Video Information Centre* [1982] AC 380); *Tate Access Floors Inc.* v *Boswell* [1991] Ch 512.

[46] See Supreme Court Act 1981, s. 72. See also *Universal City Studios Inc.* v *Hubbard* [1983] Ch 241.

[47] See, e.g., *Emanuel v Emanuel* [1982] 1 WLR 669, in which the order was made in aid of the power of the Family Division of the High Court to make orders for ancillary relief.

proceedings. There have been a number of expressions of concern over the apparently anomalous state of the law on this point. In *AT&T Istel v Tully* [1993] AC 45, 53, Lord Templeman said:

> I regard the privilege against self-incrimination...exercisable in civil proceedings as an archaic and unjustifiable survival from the past when the court directs the production of relevant documents and requires the defendant to specify his dealings with the plaintiff's property or money.

Lord Griffiths (at 57) said that the law was in need of 'radical re-appraisal'. But in this case, the judge at first instance had specifically protected the defendants' position by making his order for disclosure subject to the order that the material so disclosed should not be used for the purposes of a criminal prosecution. The Crown Prosecution Service (CPS) had been invited, but had declined, to intervene to contest this order. Although it seems clear that the CPS (which was not a party to the case) could not be bound by such an order,[48] the House appears to have thought that the judge in a subsequent criminal case would have sufficient power to protect the rights of the defendant. The House clearly thought also that any abrogation of the privilege in such cases could be made only by statute.[49] It is submitted that this is the correct approach. While the statutory derogation cases dealt with at 14.7 show that it is open to Parliament to modify the operation of the privilege, and even remove it in some cases, they also show that there are fair trial concerns under art. 6 of the European Convention that must be addressed in the form of some alternative protection. Thus, any reform of the law should be undertaken with care, especially in relation to cases such as *AT & T Istel v Tully*, in which there is an obvious danger of a subsequent prosecution for fraud. This is certainly reflected in the statutory provisions enacted since the decision of the European Court of Human Rights in *Saunders v United Kingdom*, dealt with above.

But despite these seemingly cogent considerations, a bold judicial step towards the 'radical re-appraisal' called for by Lord Griffiths was taken by Evans-Lombe J in his remarkably radical judgment in *C plc v P* [2006] Ch 549. A search order made against P under s. 7 of the Civil Procedure Act 1997, for the purpose of finding materials relevant to an action for breach of confidence and copyright infringement, led to the unanticipated discovery on computers under P's control of a number of images of children, possession of which would be a criminal offence. P had invoked his privilege against self-incrimination before the search in relation to whatever might be found, but had then permitted the search to proceed. It was common ground that P's invocation of the privilege did not pertain specifically to the images, of which P in fact denied all knowledge. In accordance with the terms of the search order, the independent computer specialist appointed to take charge of the computers, who was obliged to hold the materials on a confidential basis, applied to the court for directions as to what to do with the materials, i.e. whether they should be handed over to the police. It was held that, at least on the facts of this case, the common law privilege against self-incrimination should not operate to prevent such free-standing evidence, which had not been created by P, from being handed over to the police. The learned judge began his careful and thorough judgment by holding that P had not waived his privilege by allowing the search to proceed. He had specifically made his claim to privilege and the court's order had specified that any materials found be held in confidence, and in these circumstances, P's obedience to the court's order did not amount to a waiver (judgment, paras [15]–[23]). However, while the privilege against self- incrimination would apply to a statement or document made by P under

---

[48] Cf. *Re O (Restraint Order: Disclosure of Assets)* [1991] 2 QB 520.

[49] 'It is...deeply embedded in English law and can only be removed or moderated by Parliament...': *ibid.* at 57, per Lord Griffiths.

compulsion (such as a court order) it did not apply to free-standing evidence not created by P, which could have been seized pursuant to a search warrant in criminal proceedings. Moreover, the common law privilege against self-incrimination is not an absolute right, but one from which derogations can be made by statute, and free-standing evidence obtained by compulsion in such cases can be used against an accused in a criminal case without necessarily infringing the fair trial provisions of art. 6 of the European Convention on Human Rights (*ibid.* at [24]–[42]).[50] A balance must be struck between the right to a fair trial and the right of society at large to be protected against criminal conduct, a right which the court is also enjoined to enforce under arts 2 and 8 of the Convention.[51] As a result, there is a difference as between the operation of the privilege in the setting of criminal cases and the European Convention ('European PSI') and in the context of civil proceedings in England ('domestic PSI'). In the absence of authority, Evans-Lombe J would resolve the issue in favour of the approach of European PSI. At para. [56] he said:

> It seems to me that the public's right under arts 2, 3 and 8 to be protected from the effect of criminal activity when balanced against P's right to domestic PSI, which would otherwise operate to prevent me from directing that the offending materials be passed to the police, requires me to modify P's right so as to enable the material to be so transferred. I am reinforced in arriving at that conclusion to know that it will be open to P to apply to the trial judge, at any prosecution of him for the offence of possession of such material, to exclude it as evidence under section 78 of the 1984 Act. I am further reinforced in arriving at that conclusion by the following considerations: (i) the current anomaly between the scope of the privilege in civil proceedings and the scope of the privilege in criminal proceedings would disappear...(ii) it puts an end to what appears to be an irrational difference between the scope of domestic PSI and European PSI as recognised to form part of the rights comprised in art. 6 by convention jurisprudence; (iii) it would remove or certainly reduce the anomalies in the application of domestic PSI presently imposed on disclosure in civil proceedings of which complaint has been made in such cases as *AT&T Istel* v *Tully*...(iv) the potential offence revealed by the offending material is serious enough, having regard to the inhuman treatment of children which its production must have involved.

There was, of course, no absence of authority.[52] But brushing aside, not only this fact, but the clear view of the House of Lords in *AT&T Istel* v *Tully* that reform in this area should be statutory, Evans-Lombe J declined to follow earlier authority, basing himself on the principle laid down by the House of Lords in *Kay and others* v *Lambeth London Borough Council* [2006] AC 465 that in an exceptional case, an English court may depart from the rules of domestic precedent where it is clear that an earlier decision cannot stand in the light of the Human Rights Act 1998 (see 1.7.2.1). Consequently, it was ordered that the materials be handed over to the police.

---

[50] *Hundal; Dhaliwal* [2004] 2 Cr App R 307; *Attorney-General's Reference (No. 7 of 2000)* [2001] 1 WLR 1879; *Kearns* [2002] 1 WLR 2815; *Saunders* v *United Kingdom* (1997) 23 EHRR 313; and see generally 14.7, above.

[51] See, e.g., *Osman* v *United Kingdom* [1999] 1 FLR 193; though, with respect, this principle must be stated with more caution than is shown by the learned judge. It has rightly been invoked in connection with specific and tangible issues, for example, the protection of witnesses who have been intimidated (see 8.15) but it is submitted that it would be dangerous to allow an amorphous concept such as protecting 'society' to erode the right to a fair trial. Clearly, almost any incursion into the right to a fair trial could be justified by a sufficiently broad reading of art. 2. This is not what the Court in *Osman* intended; its decision refers specifically to the protection of 'an *individual* whose life is at risk from the criminal acts of another individual' (*ibid.* at para. 115, emphasis added) and it envisages a duty to protect arising 'in certain well-defined circumstances' (*ibid.*).

[52] In addition to *AT&T Istel* v *Tully*, the common law right to the privilege had been re-asserted in relation to disclosure by the Court of Appeal in *Den Norske Bank ASA* v *Antonatos* [1999] QB 271, and by Arden J in *Memory Corporation plc* v *Sidhu* [2000] 1 All ER 434, though a general sense of frustration throughout the judiciary with the working of the law is apparent.

On appeal from this decision, however, the Court of Appeal took a far more conservative approach (*C plc* v *P (Attorney-General intervening)* [2008] Ch 1). Upholding the actual order made in the court below, the majority, Longmore LJ and Sir Martin Nourse, held that the privilege against self-incrimination does not attach to materials having existence independent of the person claiming the privilege, a much narrower ground, and one corresponding with the rule in cases of legal professional privilege (see 14.12). Lawrence Collins LJ, dissenting, would have held that it was unnecessary even to reach this point because the materials themselves were not capable of attracting the privilege. The majority also held that Evans-Lombe J's reliance on *Kay and others* v *Lambeth London Borough Council* was misplaced; the principle stated in that case could not be used to abrogate an important individual right which would otherwise exist under English law. At the time of writing, leave has been granted to appeal to the House of Lords. It remains to be seen whether the House will take this opportunity of putting the law in this area on a new basis.

B   LEGAL PROFESSIONAL PRIVILEGE

SUMMARY OF MAIN POINTS

- There are two forms of legal privilege:

  (a) legal professional privilege for communications between lawyer and client in the course of providing legal advice;

  (b) litigation privilege for communications between lawyer and third parties where the dominant purpose of the communication is that of litigation.

- Legal professional privilege is absolute and potentially permanent, i.e., it does not end even with the death of the client and continues indefinitely unless waived.

- There is no privilege for evidential material, i.e., pieces of evidence which were generated neither in the course of the lawyer–client relationship nor within the scope of the litigation privilege.

- The litigation privilege does not apply to essentially non-adversarial care proceedings brought under the Children Act 1989.

- Legal privilege does not apply where a claimed communication between lawyer and client is in furtherance of a crime or fraud.

14.9 THE TWO KINDS OF LEGAL PROFESSIONAL PRIVILEGE; THE PRIVILEGE A FUNDAMENTAL RIGHT

At common law, communications passing between lawyer and client and materials prepared for the purposes of litigation are privileged. The term 'legal professional privilege', which is not entirely satisfactory, is used to describe two distinct rules. The first is the rule that communications between lawyer and client, made in the course of seeking and giving advice within the normal scope of legal practice, are privileged in all cases, at the instance of the client. The second is the rule that communications passing between a client or his legal adviser and third parties in contemplation of actual litigation are privileged, provided that use for the purpose of litigation is at least the dominant purpose of the communication; in this case too, the privilege is that of the client. In both cases, it is immaterial whether the communication is with advisers or third parties in England or elsewhere, or whether the contemplated litigation may take place in England or elsewhere.[53]

Legal professional privilege is a fundamental right. In *Derby Magistrates' Court, ex parte B* [1996] AC 487, the facts of which are considered at 14.16, Lord Taylor of Gosforth CJ reviewed the historical origins of legal professional privilege, and summarized its importance in the following striking passage:[54]

> The principle which runs through all these cases, and the many other cases which were cited, is that a man must be able to consult his lawyer in confidence, since otherwise he might hold back half the truth. The client must be sure that what he tells his lawyer in confidence will never be revealed without his consent. Legal professional privilege is thus much more than an ordinary rule of evidence, limited in its application to the facts of a particular case. It is a fundamental condition on which the administration of justice as a whole rests.

Lord Taylor concluded his speech by saying:

> But it is not for the sake of the applicant alone that the privilege must be upheld. It is in the wider interests of all those hereafter who might otherwise be deterred from telling the whole truth to their solicitors. For this reason I am of the opinion that no exception should be allowed to the absolute nature of legal professional privilege, once established.

In *R (On application of Morgan Grenfell & Co. Ltd)* v *Special Commissioner of Income Tax* [2003] 1 AC 563, the House of Lords took the opportunity to state again the rule that legal professional privilege is a basic right, and that any statutory attempt to derogate from it must be made in express language or by necessary implication. Morgan Grenfell had devised and marketed a tax avoidance scheme which depended on the validity of certain tax deductions claimed by the company and its clients. The validity of the deductions was the subject of a dispute between the company and the Inland Revenue. The scheme had been designed in reliance on legal advice given to the company by its solicitors and counsel. The inspector of taxes sought disclosure of the opinions given by the solicitor and counsel on which the validity of the scheme rested under s. 20(1) of the Taxes Management Act 1970 as amended, under which he claimed to be entitled to disclosure of any documents relevant to any tax liability of the taxpayer or the amount thereof. Morgan Grenfell objected to the disclosure on the ground that the documents were the subject of legal professional privilege. The House of Lords upheld their objection. Lord Hoffmann said (at 5):

> Two of the principles relevant to construction are not in dispute. First, Legal Professional Privilege is a fundamental human right long established in the common law. It is a necessary corollary of the right of any person to obtain skilled advice about the law. Such advice cannot be effectively obtained unless the client is able to put all the facts before the advisor without fear that they may afterwards be

---

[53] *Re Duncan, Garfield* v *Fay* [1968] P 306. As to the privilege in investigative proceedings before the Commission of the European Communities, see *AM & S (Europe) Ltd* v *Commission of the European Communities* (case 155/79) [1983] QB 878.

[54] *Ibid.* at 507. As to the origins of the privilege, see *Berd* v *Lovelace* (1577) Cary 62; *Dennis* v *Codrington* (1579) Cary 100; *Wilson* v *Rastall* (1792) 4 TR 753; *Greenhough* v *Gaskell* (1833) Coop Brough 96; *Bolton* v *Liverpool Corporation* (1833) 1 My & K 88.

disclosed and used to his prejudice. The cases establishing this principle are collected in the speech of Lord Taylor of Gosforth CJ in *R v Derby Magistrates' Court, ex parte B* [1996] AC 487. It has been held by the European Court of Human Rights to be part of the right of privacy guaranteed by art. 8 of the European Convention for the Protection of Human Rights and Fundamental Freedoms... (see *Campbell v UK* (1992) 15 EHRR 137; *Foxley v UK* (2000) 8 BHRC 571) and held by the Court of Justice of the European Communities to be a part of Community law (see *AM & S Europe Ltd v EC Commission*, Case No. 155/79 [1983] 1 All ER 705.[55]

Secondly, the courts will ordinarily construe general words in a statute, although literally capable of having some startling or unreasonable consequence, such as overriding fundamental human rights, as not having been intended to do so. An intention to override such rights must be expressly stated or appear by necessary implication. The speeches of Lord Steyn and myself in *R v Secretary of State for the Home Department, ex parte Simms* [2000] 2 AC 115 contain some discussion of this principle and its constitutional justification in the context of human rights. But the wider principle itself is hardly new. It can be traced back at least to *Stradling v Morgan* (1560) 1 Plowd 199.

It is submitted that this case, together with the *Derby Magistrates' Court* case, establish beyond doubt that legal professional privilege is a fundamental right, both under English law and under the Convention, and that any attempt to derogate from it must be strictly construed.

14.9.1 Legal professional privilege and procedural rules

Both the Civil Procedure Rules 1998 and the Criminal Procedure Rules 2005 begin with a declaration of the overriding objective of dealing with cases justly. In the pursuit of that objective, both provide that the parties have an obligation to assist the court in achieving it, and that this includes cooperating in the disclosure of evidence and the identification of the issues which will be put before the court.[56] If a party is required to disclose evidential material or information which may reveal the strategy formulated by his legal advisers, this sets up a conflict between that party's obligations under the rules, on the one hand, and his right to assert legal professional or litigation privilege, on the other. Thus far the courts have insisted that the privilege, as a fundamental right, must prevail over purely procedural subordinate legislation, and it is submitted that this must be correct. Subordinate legislation such as a rule of court is not intended to, and could not in any event, have the effect of abrogating a fundamental right recognized by the law.[57]

In *General Mediterranean Holdings SA v Patel*[58] Toulson J struck a strong blow for legal professional privilege, holding that r. 48.7(3) of the Civil Procedure Rules 1998 was '*ultra vires* and unenforceable' insofar as it purports to give power to require the disclosure of documents subject to legal professional privilege. The rule provides that, on an application for a wasted costs order, the court may order disclosure of privileged documents at first to the court and then potentially

---

[55] Although the House found it unnecessary to rely on the Convention in this case, Lord Hoffmann is clear that the privilege is enshrined by art. 8. The House doubted, without overruling, the view of the Court of Appeal in *Parry-Jones v Law Society* [1969] 1 Ch 1 that a solicitor is under an obligation to obey any rules of the Law Society requiring disclosure of his client's files to an accountant appointed by the Society.

[56] See Civil Procedure Rules 1998, r. 1; Criminal Procedure Rules 1005, rr. 1 and 3.

[57] Of course a statutory provision would be a different matter. Section 6C(1) of the Criminal Procedure and Investigations Act 1996, inserted by s. 34 of the Criminal Justice Act 2003, is not yet in effect. That section would require disclosure of the detail of a defence case, and would permit an adverse inference to be drawn against the accused if he fails to comply. If brought into effect the effect of this provision will have to be considered separately to see whether it is sufficient to overcome the privilege.

[58] [2000] 1 WLR 272; see also *Paragon Finance plc v Freshfields* [1999] 1 WLR 1183; *Ridehalgh v Horsefield* [1994] Ch 205.

to the other side. But Toulson J held that the privilege must prevail over such a rule in the absence of a clear statutory provision to the contrary. Paragraph 4 of Sch. 1 to the Civil Procedure Act 1997 provides:

> Civil Procedure Rules may modify the rule of evidence as they apply to proceedings in any court within the scope of the rules.

The learned judge considered this insufficiently specific to have the effect of abrogating such a well-recognized common law privilege. He also considered that privileged communications were on the face of it, also protected under art. 8 of the European Convention on Human Rights (see 1.7) and that it would be wrong to invade this right unless it was clearly necessary to do so. In the light of this, Toulson J held that it would have been inappropriate to order disclosure under r. 48.7(3) for the purposes of a wasted costs order.

Toulson J's decision is strongly supported by several other cases, in which it has been held that general words, especially those of an essentially procedural provision, cannot by a sidewind abrogate a fundamental right.[59] In *R (Kelly)* v *Warley Magistrates' Court* [2008] 1 WLR 2001, it was held that a district judge was not entitled to require the defence in a criminal case to disclose before trial the identity of the witnesses intended to be called at trial. The district judge had relied on rr. 3.5 and 3.10 of the Criminal Procedure Rules 2005.[60] Laws LJ held that litigation privilege attached to the identity of the witnesses proposed to be called in adversarial litigation, whether civil or criminal, whether or not it is the result of legal advice being given (*ibid.* at [20]). He added that this was part of a litigant's 'historic right not to disclose his case until he presents it' (*ibid.*). With respect, this is to state the matter too widely. There is no reason in general why rules of court should not require disclosure of the anticipated issues, and both the Civil Procedure Rules 1998 and the Criminal Procedure Rules 2005 do so. But Laws LJ is clearly right in any case where to require disclosure based only on such authority would violate legal privilege. He said:

> Such a right [i.e. legal professional or litigation privilege] may only be intruded upon by force of subordinate legislation if the statute providing the subordinate instrument's *vires* makes it plain by express words or necessary implication that such an authority was intended to be conveyed. [*Ibid.* at [25].]

Later, he continued:

> In my judgment a power to require disclosure of privileged material may only be characterised as doing no more than regulatory practice and procedure if it forms part of a code (I mean only a series or group of provisions—'code' is not a term of art) having that purpose. If such a power is open-ended, not coloured and confined by moderate procedural sanctions for breach, it is likely to be regarded by the courts as an attempt to infringe privilege as such; and that will be unlawful unless strictly authorised by express provision or necessary implication.
>
> I have referred to 'moderate' procedural sanctions. 'Proportionate' might be a better term. In my judgment this is an important condition to be met if a rule is to be treated as no more than a procedural regulation. In principle such a rule must provide for no more than might reasonably be required for the

---

[59] 'Fundamental rights cannot be overriden by general words': *R* v *Secretary of State for the Home Department, ex parte Simms* [2000] 2 AC 115, 131. And see *Bowman* v *Fels (Bar Council intervening)* [2005] 1 WLR 3083, [87], holding that provisions of the Proceeds of Crime Act 2002, dealing with offences of money laundering, were not specific enough to overcome legal professional privilege.

[60] The latter rule on its face authorizes the court to require this information as part of its court management powers, but it is not obvious why the identity of the witnesses (as opposed, say, to the number of witnesses) would assist the court in this respect. The most obvious use of the rule is to give the prosecution time to check whether the witnesses are persons of bad character.

proper working of such a regulation. If it goes further, it will not be categorised as procedural only. It will be liable to be treated as purporting to change the general law of evidence. Unconditional orders for disclosure of privileged information plainly exceed this boundary. So, I think, would a rule which absolutely prohibited a party—with no discretion in the trial court—from calling a witness whose identity he had not disclosed in advance. [*Ibid.* at [32]–[33].]

14.10 COMMUNICATIONS BETWEEN LAWYER AND CLIENT: SCOPE OF PRIVILEGE

All communications passing between a legal adviser and his client, in the course of seeking and giving legal advice within the proper scope of the professional work of the legal adviser, are privileged at the instance of the client (not of the adviser). It is irrelevant in this case whether or not the advice is immediately connected with litigation then in contemplation, though it is probably true to say that all legal advice is concerned with a possible ultimate resort to litigation, even if (as is almost always the case) the advice is directed to avoiding it wherever possible.

14.10.1 Meaning of 'legal advice'

The test is whether the communication was made for the purposes of the giving and receiving of legal advice, and for this purpose, it matters not that the communication may be broadly worded, or that it does not in so many words refer to the giving or receiving of advice, as long as it is reasonably inferable that it was made pursuant to the professional relationship of lawyer and client. Moreover, the communication may be one made in the course of continuing instructions, and is not confined to the situation where a lawyer is retained in regard to a specific matter.[61] But if it clearly appears that a communication is not directly related to the giving of legal advice, then that communication should not be regarded as privileged. Thus, in *Manchester Crown Court, ex parte Rogers*[62] it was relevant for the prosecution to prove the time at which the appellant had visited the office of his solicitor. It was held that notes of the time of an appointment or visit made in the solicitor's attendance note, or on a time sheet or fee record, could not, as such, be regarded as pertaining to the giving of legal advice, and were accordingly not privileged.

But the scope of a lawyer's work is something which changes and evolves over time, and, in a complex society, lawyers may be called on to give advice and perform functions which appear to diverge from traditional ideas of what amounts to giving legal advice. This is a question of increasing concern now that many lawyers are also qualified in fields such as accounting, tax advice, and financial consultancy, which are not fields of legal practice as such, and many firms of solicitors offer a broad range of services. In *Three Rivers District Council and others* v *Governor and Company of the Bank of England (No. 6)* [2005] 1 AC 610 at [58], Lord Rodger observed:

> Especially in the 19th century, many solicitors or attorneys acted as 'men of business'. They not only gave legal advice and assistance but carried on business, for instance, as patent agents, as agents for

---

[61] *Balabel* v *Air India* [1988] Ch 317; *Greenhough* v *Gaskell* (1833) Coop Brough 96. As to the position of copies of privileged documents see now *Sumitomo Corp.* v *Credit Lyonnais Rouse Ltd* [2002] 1 WLR 479, overruling on certain points *Dubai Bank Ltd* v *Galadari* [1990] Ch 98, 4.9; *Board of Inland Revenue, ex parte Goldberg* [1989] QB 267; 13.3. As to the relationship between the police and the Director of Public Prosecutions see *Goodridge* v *Chief Constable of Hampshire* [1999] 1 WLR 1558.

[62] [1999] 1 WLR 832; *R (Miller Gardner Solicitors)* v *Minshull Street Crown Court* [2002] EWCA 3077 (Admin) (no privilege for dates of telephone calls between solicitor and client); *Ainsworth* v *Wilding* [1900] 2 Ch 315.

colonial companies, as deposit agents for colonial banks, and as stewards or factors running estates. They would also lend money to their clients, sometimes in relation to the purchase of property. Until fairly recently, Scottish solicitors had succeeded in keeping for themselves all the work of selling houses that estate agents were doing in England. Given the varied functions performed by lawyers, it is scarcely surprising that questions frequently arose as to the capacity in which the lawyer or firm was acting in a particular transaction...Lawyers today may be instructed in situations in which they would not have been instructed in the past or which did not even exist in the past...In relation to legal advice privilege what matters today remains the same as what mattered in the past: whether the lawyers are being asked *qua* lawyers to provide legal advice.

The *Three Rivers District Council* litigation brought this issue into sharp focus. It raised the relatively narrow question of whether communications passing between solicitors and clients for the purpose of preparing 'presentational materials' for the purpose of the Bingham inquiry into the collapse of BCCI attracted legal professional privilege as being communications for the purpose of legal advice. In *Three Rivers District Council and others* v *Governor and Company of the Bank of England (No. 6)*, both the Court of Appeal and the House of Lords considered the legal advice privilege in some depth. The Court of Appeal ([2004] QB 916), recognized that the work of solicitors in modern times had expanded beyond the traditional fields of legal representation into areas which are not exclusively legal in nature, but held that only those aspects of the work specifically and strictly connected with the giving and receiving of legal advice attract privilege. The Court held that the preparation of the presentational materials did not fall within this definition. But the House of Lords ([2005] 1 AC 610) allowed an appeal from this decision, holding that the preparation of such materials was a form of advocacy and so fell squarely within the definition of legal advice. In so holding, the House took the opportunity to offer a somewhat broader approach. While the privilege must be restricted to legal advice, that phrase must be understood as encompassing advice as to what action a client should take and how best to take that action, in the light of the legal advice given. As long as the work is undertaken within a 'legal context', privilege should attach. At para. [38], in a passage with which the other members of the House concurred, Lord Scott said:

> In *Balabel* v *Air India* [1988] Ch. 317 Taylor LJ said, at p.330, that for the purpose of attracting legal advice privilege
>
>> 'legal advice is not confined to telling the client the law; it must include advice as to what should prudently and sensibly be done in the relevant legal context.'
>
> I would venture to draw attention to Taylor LJ's reference to "the relevant legal context". That there must be a "relevant legal context" in order for the advice to attract legal professional privilege should not be in doubt. Taylor LJ said, at p.331, that
>
>> 'to extend privilege without limit to all solicitor and client communication within the ordinary business of a solicitor and referable to that relationship [would be] too wide.'
>
> This remark is, in my respectful opinion, plainly correct. If a solicitor becomes the client's "man of business" and some solicitors do, responsible for advising the client on all matters of business, including investment policy, finance policy and other business matters, the advice may lack a relevant legal context. There is, in my opinion, no way of avoiding difficulty in deciding in marginal cases whether the seeking of advice from or the giving of advice by lawyers does or does not take place in a relevant legal context so as to attract legal advice privilege. In case of doubt the judge called upon to make the decision should ask whether the advice relates to the rights, obligations or remedies of the client either under private law or under public law. If it does not, then, in my opinion, legal advice privilege would not apply...The criterion must, in my opinion, be an objective one.

It is submitted that, as *Three Rivers (No. 6)* makes all too clear, the present law creates unnecessary artificiality and places unnecessary difficulties in the way of both solicitors and clients who practice under modern business conditions. It would be possible to modify the privilege to cover advice in other fields when that advice is necessarily based at least in part on legal considerations. It may even be that the time has come to recognize a privilege between certain other professionals, such as chartered accountants, financial advisers, and their clients, though in the present climate, it seems that such an initiative would have to come from Parliament; the inclination of the courts at present is to restrict rather than expand the scope of privileges.

14.10.2 Legal advisers and clients

The privilege applies to solicitor and counsel alike, and so covers any advice given orally or in writing and any instructions given for the purposes of such advice. It is submitted that the privilege must also apply in the case of advocates appointed by the court to cross-examine witnesses whom the accused is precluded from cross-examining in person by virtue of s. 38 of the Youth Justice and Criminal Evidence Act 1999. Section 38(5) provides that such an advocate 'shall not be responsible to the accused', but presumably the advocate will need instructions, which suggests that confidential communications must take place. The position of special counsel, who may be appointed in various situations, notably in relation to applications to withhold material on the ground of public interest immunity (see 13.4.3.1), will also have to be considered in due course. To the extent that special counsel takes instructions from the accused or his representatives, issues of privilege are bound to arise. The privilege applies also to advice sought of and given by salaried legal advisers, and it has been suggested, though not decided, that it may extend to the so-called 'McKenzie friend' who may appear to advise a layman in the presentation of a case, or to argue before a tribunal to which restrictions on rights of audience do not apply.[63] As we have seen, the law concedes little recognition to other confidential communications. Although statute has provided limited areas of privilege for those responsible for publications (Contempt of Court Act 1981, s. 10) no other confidential relationship enjoys the breadth of privilege accorded to that between lawyer and client.[64] Lawyers depend on assistance from a range of assistants, such as legal secretaries, clerks, and pupils. It is submitted that no breach of confidentiality and no loss or privilege is involved when they are present during interviews, or see, or are involved in preparing or transmitting communications with the client.

Similarly, where the client depends on assistance from others in conducting his legal affairs, the presence of those assisting him will not destroy confidentiality or result in loss of the privilege.[65] This principle is of crucial importance in the case of a corporate client, which can, of course, act only through its directors, officers, or employees. There is an issue as to who may communicate with the company's legal advisers within the scope of the legal advice privilege. If communications are made to or by, or divulged to, officers and employees not entitled to act on behalf of the company, the communication may no longer be regarded as confidential, and the privilege may be lost in consequence. Thus, it must be possible to identify with some certainty

---

[63] *M. & W. Grazebrook Ltd* v *Wallens* [1973] ICR 256. In the case of a layman in such a position, the privilege may extend only to the conduct of the case itself.

[64] As to patent agents and those in other professions who are not lawyers, but whose advice frequently comprehends legal issues, the position is somewhat unclear: Copyright, Designs and Patents Act 1988, s. 280; Trade Marks Act 1994, s. 87; *Wilden Pump Engineering Co.* v *Fusfield* [1985] FSR 159; Miller [1978] EIPR 206; cf. the now repealed s. 15 of the Civil Evidence Act 1968.

[65] See, e.g., *Wright* v *Sullivan* [2006] 1 WLR 172.

who the entitled employees are. There are essentially two possible solutions to the problem. The narrower of the two suggests that there must be a 'control group' of employees who are specifically authorized to deal with the legal advisers, and that all communications must be made to and by members of the group. This view was espoused by the Court of Appeal in *Three Rivers District Council and others* v *Governor and Company of the Bank of England (No. 5)* [2003] QB 1556. It has the merit of offering certainty. But its lack of flexibility can lead to inconvenience, both because litigation of any complexity may demand that the lawyers have access to a broad range of corporate personnel without undue formality, and because the control group must be continually revised to take account of staff turnover. In *Three Rivers District Council and others* v *Governor and Company of the Bank of England (No. 6)* [2005] 1 AC 610, the House of Lords hinted strongly that, if the question were to come before them, they would be likely to prefer the more flexible test of communication with any employees with whom communication is reasonably required in the context of the litigation, which dispenses with a requirement of a formal control group in favour of what may be termed a 'need to know' approach.[66] As the question was not directly raised, the House did not decide it. The decision of the Court of Appeal probably represents the present law, but it may well be that this will change in due course, and it is submitted that the provisional view of the House of Lords would be better suited to modern conditions of practice.

14.10.3 Communication during period of professional relationship

The communications, if they are to be the subject of privilege, must not only have been made within the proper scope of the adviser's work, but also during the continuance of the lawyer–client relationship, i.e., during the currency of the lawyer's professional retainer on behalf of the client. This will, of course, include any communications necessary to bring the relationship into existence, such as an initial consultation or instructions. But no communication is privileged merely because one party to it is a lawyer, and where no professional relationship comes into being, no privilege can arise. In *Minter* v *Priest* [1930] AC 558, where the defendant refused to act as a solicitor in a transaction relating to land, and was alleged to have defamed the plaintiff in the course of giving his reasons for so refusing, it was held that the relationship of solicitor and client had not been established, and that the communication, not being made for the purpose of establishing the relationship, was not privileged. But if a communication is made within the period of the professional relationship, the privilege attaching to it is not destroyed by the subsequent ending of the relationship (see 14.16).

On the other hand, in any case where the relationship of lawyer and client clearly does exist, the privilege is not inhibited by the fact that the lawyer is advising professionally a body of persons of which he happens also to be a member or by which he is employed, for example a tenants' association, voluntary organization, board of trustees, or a corporation.[67]

14.11 COMMUNICATIONS WITH THIRD PARTIES: SCOPE OF PRIVILEGE

Communications made between a party (or his legal adviser on his behalf) and a third party are privileged at the instance of the party if, but only if, they are made for the specific purpose of

---

[66] *Ibid.* at [47] per Lord Scott, citing the decision of the US Supreme Court in *Upjohn Co.* v *US* 449 US 383 (1981) in which that test was strongly advocated.
[67] *O'Rourke* v *Darbishire* [1920] AC 581.

pending or contemplated litigation. This part of the rule is apt to cover communications with witnesses and their proofs of evidence, and is particularly important in relation to communications with potential expert witnesses, from whom it may be desired to obtain an opinion, but who are not legal advisers. Nothing in the provisions of r. 35.13 of the Civil Procedure Rules 1998 or Part 24 of the Criminal Procedure Rules 2005, which impose certain obligations of disclosure of expert reports as a condition of calling the expert evidence concerned, affects the operation of the privilege; but a party may have to elect whether to disclose a report and call evidence of its contents, or to stand on the privilege, use the report for advisory and preparation purposes only and not adduce it as evidence: see 11.6.[68]

The requirement that the communication be made for the purposes of pending or contemplated litigation is one which limits very considerably the material which is so privileged, and represents an important distinction between this and the case of communications between client and legal adviser. In *Wheeler* v *Le Marchant* (1881) 17 ChD 675, the defendant was obliged to produce reports made to his solicitor by a surveyor, because although the reports related to the subject-matter of the litigation, they had been made at a time when no litigation was contemplated by the defendant.

There was at one time considerable uncertainty about whether the communication must have been made solely for the purposes of pending or contemplated litigation, whether it must have been a major, but need not have been the only purpose, or whether litigation need have been no more than one of a number of possible purposes. The debate which raged on this topic in the older cases, many of which seem very unsatisfactory,[69] was resolved by the House of Lords in *Waugh* v *British Railways Board* [1980] AC 521. The plaintiff's husband, who was employed by the defendants, was killed in a collision between two trains, and she brought an action under the Fatal Accidents Act 1976 in respect of his death. The Board denied negligence and alleged contributory negligence on the part of the deceased. The plaintiff sought discovery of an internal report, prepared by the Board for submission to the railway inspectorate and the ministry. The report was also a valuable, and probably the best, source of evidence of the causes of the accident, containing as it did the statements of witnesses and a technical account of the collision. But the report was also designed, according to its heading, 'for the information of the Board's solicitor: this form is to be used by every person reporting an occurrence when litigation by or against the BRB is anticipated. It is . . . to be sent to the solicitor for the purpose of enabling him to advise the BRB in regard thereto'. The Board claimed that it was a privileged document. The House of Lords held that the public interest in the due administration of justice strongly required the disclosure of such a cogent piece of evidence, and that this requirement could be defeated only where preparation for the purposes of litigation was shown to be 'at least the dominant purpose' for which it was prepared. The fact that the report purported on the face of it to have been made for such a purpose, since litigation was clearly foreseeable after such an event, was not conclusive in itself of the dominant purpose of the document, and the court was entitled to look behind

---

[68] But if, after disclosure, an opponent calls the expert, a party can protect privilege in items which are independently privileged, notwithstanding that they may have been disclosed to the expert: see *R* [1994] 1 WLR 758.

[69] See, e.g., *Jones* v *Great Central Railway Co.* [1910] AC 4; *Seabrook* v *British Transport Commission* [1959] 1 WLR 509; *Walsham* v *Stainton* (1863) 2 H & M 1; *Chadwick* v *Bowman* (1886) 16 QBD 561; *Anderson* v *Bank of British Columbia* (1876) 2 ChD 644; *Southall and Vauxhall Water Co.* v *Quick* (1878) 23 QBD 315.

the claim made for itself by the document by its own wording.[70] On the facts of the case, the House of Lords held that the report had other major purposes in relation to the safe running of the railways, and that submission to the solicitor was not shown to be the dominant purpose of preparation; the report must accordingly be disclosed.[71]

14.12 NO PRIVILEGE FOR EVIDENTIAL MATERIAL

Neither the lawyer nor the client can claim privilege with respect to original items of evidence, whether tangible items, such as the murder weapon in a criminal case, or documents relevant to a civil case. These cannot be defined as communications between lawyer and client, or as materials prepared for the purposes of litigation, and, consequently, have no immunity from seizure or disclosure.

By what might perhaps be described as an evidential application of the maxim, '*Nemo dat quod non habet*', it is clear law that a client who could himself maintain no privilege in respect of such materials cannot better his position merely by handing them over to his solicitor. Thus, in *Peterborough Justices, ex parte Hicks* [1977] 1 WLR 1371, where the client was not entitled to prevent the seizure by the police of a document, such seizure being properly made by virtue of a warrant under the Forgery Act 1913, his solicitors were in no better position to resist seizure of the document when in their hands, even though the client had placed it there in connection with the preparation of his defence. The privilege covers communications made for the purposes of giving and receiving legal advice, not pre-existing documents or objects which have become relevant evidence, and which are, as such, subject to the normal rules of disclosure and seizure.

In the apparently anomalous *Frank Truman Export Ltd* v *Commissioner of Police of the Metropolis* [1977] QB 952, Swanwick J held that pre-existing documents, which might have held some evidential value against the plaintiff as evidence of fraud, were privileged in the hands of the plaintiff's solicitor to whom they had been delivered for his consideration and advice in relation to likely criminal charges based on the apparent fraud. If this decision were correct, it would mean that by placing incriminating material in the hands of a solicitor at the crucial moment, a person may protect such material from an otherwise likely exposure by search warrant.[72] It is to be hoped that the decision in the *Truman* case has effectively been overruled by the subsequent decision of the Court of Appeal in *King* [1983] 1 WLR 411, in which the holding referred to above was 'doubted'. The accused, who was charged with conspiracy to defraud, sent certain papers to his solicitors, for transmission to a handwriting expert for his examination. The expert was not called as a witness by the defence, but at trial the prosecution served him with a *subpoena duces tecum* to produce the documents sent to him. The prosecution did not seek to elicit evidence of the instructions given to the expert by the accused's solicitors, and wished only to establish what documents had been provided to him. The trial judge overruled a defence objection that the expert should not produce the documents because legal professional privilege attached to them.

---

[70] The question must be resolved on the whole of the evidence. The dominant purpose must be that of the party commissioning the report, rather than that of its author: *Re Highgate Traders Ltd* [1984] BCLC 151.

[71] See also *Re Sarah C. Getty Trust* [1985] QB 956. In *Sumitomo Corp.* v *Credit Lyonnais Rouse* [2002] 1 WLR 479, it was held that the test was whether the documents had 'really' been generated for the purposes of litigation, which, with respect, hardly seems very helpful.

[72] This result did not follow on the facts of the case, because the plaintiff's solicitor had voluntarily permitted the police to take the documents in question away, and on the issue whether an injunction would be granted against the police, this was conclusive: cf. *Butler* v *Board of Trade* [1971] Ch 680.

The Court of Appeal held that the trial judge had been correct in his ruling. Pointing out that the observation of Swanwick J in *Truman* was 'not necessary for his decision', the Court held that the case provided no authority for any such rule. As the documents were not brought into being for the purpose of the solicitor–client relationship, and were therefore not privileged in the accused's hands, no privilege could attach to them in the hands of his solicitor, or those of the expert. Of course, the instructions given to the expert and his opinion rendered to the accused and his solicitors would have been privileged communications.

14.12.1 Legal work product

Although there is no privilege for evidential documents as such, there is some authority that the methods used by a party's solicitor in selecting, handling or arranging documents may be privileged, on the ground that to reveal them would be to betray something of the legal advice the solicitor is providing to that party.[73] This concept has not, thus far, been refined into anything approaching a doctrine in England, but it bears some resemblance to the American doctrine of protection of the lawyer's 'work product', that is to say, of the intellectual processes which underlie the lawyer's conduct of a case or transaction, the formation of strategy and creative approaches to the case or transaction, and the physical manifestations of those processes which may be revealed by the documents in his files. Even though the documents themselves may not always be privileged, it is submitted that there is some basis for protecting work product as defined above. In *Sumitomo Corp.* v *Credit Lyonnais Rouse Ltd* [2002] 1 WLR 479, it was held that certain documents belonging to a party, to which no privilege attached, could not be invested with privilege by the process of translating them from Japanese into English for possible use in litigation. The process of translation was no more capable of doing this than would be the process of making copies of them. But it was further argued that, because the documents had been arranged in order of priority for the purposes of translation, and because they had in that sense been the subject of a process of selection or arrangement by legal advisers, they were protected under the work product rule. This argument was rejected. It was held that the work product doctrine applied only to the selection and arrangement of third party documents and not to the selection and arrangement of a party's own documents (overruling on this point *Dubai Bank Ltd* v *Galadari (No. 7)* [1992] 1 WLR 106). The test in such cases is whether disclosure of the selection or arrangement would 'betray the advice' given to the party by his legal advisers. Clearly, this is an area of the law which continues to require elaboration.

14.13 CASES INVOLVING THE WELFARE OF CHILDREN

Cases involving the welfare of children, although they may be nominally adversarial in form, are circumscribed by the duty imposed on the court by s. 1(1) of the Children Act 1989 to treat the welfare of the child as paramount. Under the general common law rules described above, legal professional privilege attached to the reports of experts, including those of medical practitioners and other professionals retained by the parties, as in other types of litigation. But the result was that, by withholding those reports thought to be adverse to his case, a party might deprive the court of important information bearing on the child's welfare. In *Essex County Council* v *R* [1994] Fam 167, Thorpe J took the bold step of holding that, in the light of the duty imposed on

---

[73] *Ventouris* v *Mountain* [1991] 1 WLR 607; *Lyell* v *Kennedy (No. 3)* [1884] 27 ChD 1.

the court by the 1989 Act, legal advisers in cases brought under the Act had a positive duty to disclose reports which might contain statements adverse to their clients.[74] The holding in this case amounted to the judicial creation of a limited new exception to the operation of legal professional privilege. Predictably, the view taken by Thorpe J did not escape criticism, and, indeed, the opposite view was taken on similar facts by Douglas Brown J in *Barking and Dagenham London Borough Council v O* [1993] Fam 295.

The opportunity to decide between these conflicting decisions was presented to the Court of Appeal in *Oxfordshire County Council v M* [1994] Fam 151. The local authority had commenced care proceedings under s. 31 of the Act, and the court of first instance had given permission to the parties to disclose to psychiatrists retained in the action all the reports then held by the court, on the condition that the reports later to be written by the psychiatrists should in turn be disclosed to the court and all parties. The mother appealed against the imposition of this condition of disclosure. The court, having considered the cases referred to above, unanimously preferred the view of Thorpe J in *Essex County Council v R*, and dismissed the mother's appeal. Steyn LJ held that the legislative intent of the 1989 Act would be defeated if parties were entitled to suppress unfavourable reports. Care proceedings did not have an 'essentially adversarial character', and considerations of legal professional privilege were outweighed by the statutory paramountcy of the welfare of the child. Both the judgment of Sir Stephen Brown P in the *Oxfordshire County Council* case and that of Thorpe J in the *Essex County Council* case, suggest that the principle applies to all 'children cases', i.e., any case, which, however it may arise, involves the welfare of a child, and is not confined to care proceedings.

The development of the law was taken to its logical conclusion by the House of Lords in *Re L (A Minor) (Police Investigation: Privilege)* [1997] AC 16. A child whose parents were drug addicts was admitted to a hospital after ingesting methadone. The mother's original explanation was that the ingestion had happened accidentally, and the police decided to press no charges. The local authority applied for a care order under Part IV of the Children Act 1989, and the court gave leave to the mother for the disclosure to a medical expert of court papers relating to the circumstances in which the child had swallowed the methadone. The expert prepared a report which contradicted the mother's account and, on application by the police, the judge authorized the disclosure of the report to them, with a view to possible criminal prosecution. The mother appealed on the ground that the disclosure violated her legal professional privilege in communicating confidentially with an expert.[75]

The majority of the House of Lords (Lords Jauncey of Tullichettle, Lloyd of Berwick, and Steyn) held that, while legal professional privilege in the form of communications between lawyer and client was absolute (as indicated by the then recent decision of a differently constituted House in *Derby Magistrates' Court, ex parte B* [1996] AC 487), the form of the privilege applying to confidential communications with third parties for the purposes of litigation had no application to proceedings brought under the Children Act 1989 (and inferentially to any other proceedings affecting the welfare of children). After referring to the passages from the

---

[74] Thorpe J expressed himself to be adopting *obiter dicta* of Johnson J in *Re A (Minors: Disclosure of Material)* [1991] 2 FLR 473. See also the learned judge's extra-judicial observations on this subject in an address to the American Inns of Court Foundation [1993] Fam Law 681.

[75] The mother also asserted the privilege against self-incrimination, but this failed on the basis that the mother had waived this privilege by initiating the disclosure of the documents, filing the report, and disclosing it to other parties.

speech of Lord Taylor of Gosforth in *Derby Magistrates' Court* quoted at 14.7, Lord Jauncey of Tullichettle said (at 24):

> It is clear from the reasoning of the Lord Chief Justice and of the other members of the committee that the reference to legal professional privilege was in the context of the relationship between solicitor and client. Indeed, there was no occasion to consider whether and in what other circumstances absolute legal professional privilege might apply. Notwithstanding this, [counsel for the mother] maintained that the absolute nature of the privilege attaching to the solicitor–client relationship extended equally to all other forms of legal professional privilege.
>
> My lords, I reject this contention. There is, as [counsel for the police and local authority] pointed out, a clear distinction between the privilege attaching to communications between solicitor and client and that attaching to reports by third parties prepared on the instructions of a client for the purposes of litigation. In the former case the privilege attaches to all communications whether related to litigation or not, but in the latter case it attaches only to documents or other written communications prepared with a view to litigation: *Waugh v British Railways Board* [1980] AC 521, 533B, 537G, 544B.
>
> There is this further distinction that whereas a solicitor could not without his client's consent be compelled to express an opinion on the factual or legal merits of the case, a third party who has provided a report to a client can be subpoenaed to give evidence by the other side and cannot decline to answer questions as to his factual findings and opinion thereon. There is no property in the opinion of an expert witness: *Harmony Shipping Co. SA v Saudi Europe Line Ltd* [1979] 1 WLR 1380, 1386G, per Lord Denning MR.

Lord Jauncey then went on to hold that third party legal professional privilege, while applicable to adversarial proceedings, had no application to the essentially non-adversarial cases brought under the 1989 Act, concluding (at 27):

> I would add that if litigation privilege were to apply to Dr France's report it could have the effect of subordinating the welfare of the child to the interests of the mother in preserving its confidentiality. This would appear to frustrate the primary object of the [Children Act 1989].[76]

It is submitted that this unabashed piece of judicial legislation was completely unnecessary on the facts of the case. In view of the fact that the mother had initiated the disclosure of the court papers, had instructed the expert, and had complied with the court's order to file and disclose the report, it is surely plain that she had waived any privilege that might have existed in the report.[77] If Lord Jauncey's sweeping observations about litigation privilege are correct, and it is defeated on the theory that there is no property in an expert witness, it is difficult to see in what circumstances the privilege could ever apply in any form of litigation. The true test, it is submitted, is not whether a witness could be subpoenaed, but whether the report was prepared in confidence and substantially for the purposes of litigation. There was an arguable basis for holding that this was not true on the facts of the case. If, as the majority of the House clearly felt, the mother's factual position was unmeritorious, it would not have been difficult to find against her

---

[76] It was also argued that, not only could the mother not prevent the disclosure of the report, but that she was actually under a positive duty to disclose it. This had been suggested by Thorpe J in *Essex County Council v R* [1994] Fam 167, 168–9, and by Wall J in *Re DH (A Minor) (Child Abuse)* [1994] 1 FLR 679, 704. As to this argument, Lord Jauncey held that it was unnecessary to decide the point, but: 'It may well be that this further development of the practice in cases where the welfare of children is involved is to be welcomed'. If this happens, presumably the privilege against self-incrimination will also have gone in cases involving children.

[77] Which is the exact ground on which the House found against the mother on the issue of the privilege against self-incrimination.

in the circumstances. It is submitted that, while the Children Act 1989 does impose an important responsibility on judges to secure the welfare of children, and while proceedings under that Act should be essentially non-adversarial, the statute does not appear to authorize them to disregard basic rights of the parties. Adversarial or not,[78] such cases are a form of litigation.

Lord Nicholls of Birkenhead, in a speech with which Lord Mustill concurred, presented the opposite view in language, which, it is submitted, should have been irrefutable.[79] He said:

> I do not believe the Children Act 1989 was intended to abrogate legal professional privilege in family proceedings, or that it has done so. Legal professional privilege is deeply embedded in English law. This was confirmed recently by your lordships' House in *Derby Magistrates' Court, ex parte B* [1996] AC 487. The privilege against non-disclosure prevails even where the privileged material might assist the defence of a person charged with murder.
>
> Clear words, therefore, or a compelling context are needed before Parliament can be taken to have intended that the privilege should be ousted in favour of another interest. The Children Act 1989 contains neither. There is no express abrogation of the privilege. Nor do the provisions in the Act, designed to promote the welfare of children, carry with them an implication that in future parents who become involved in court proceedings are not to have the normal freedom to consult lawyers and potential witnesses, and to do so confidentially.

Later in his speech, Lord Nicholls added:

> I can see no reason why parties to family proceedings should not be as much entitled to a fair hearing...as are parties to other court proceedings....
>
> Parents and other parties should be entitled to such a hearing notwithstanding the special role of judges in family proceedings. If this is not to be, Parliament should say so expressly.

It seems, therefore, that cases involving the welfare of children must now be regarded as an exception to that limb of the common law rule of privilege which applies to expert reports and communications with experts. Although reports made by doctors, psychiatrists, psychologists, and other professionals working with children, will be the kinds of documents most often involved, it would seem that the exception would be wide enough to apply to any similar information which might assist the court in carrying out its statutory duty. However, as the House made clear, the exception applies only to such third-party reports. The privilege attaching to communications between legal advisers and their clients in such cases remains unaffected by the decision.

The last word may not yet have been spoken on this controversial subject. The mother petitioned the European Court of Human Rights for relief (*L v United Kingdom* [2000] 2 FLR 322), but predictably failed because she had been free to adduce evidence other than the report in question, so that she was not deprived of the right to a fair trial (which is the only concern of the European Court: see 1.7).[80] But it is submitted that the decision of the House of Lords in *R (On application*

---

[78] The proposition that such proceedings are necessarily or completely 'non-adversarial' was challenged by Lord Nicholls, dissenting. Lord Nicholls felt that they presented 'some adversarial features and some inquisitorial features'. In the light of the action taken by the local authority and the police, it would be interesting to hear the mother's opinion on whether the proceedings were adversarial. It would hardly be surprising if she felt that they were.

[79] Lords Nicholls and Mustill had been members of the appellate committee which decided *Derby Magistrates' Court*.

[80] The mother also lost on the self-incrimination point because it was held that the procedure advocated by the House of Lords was not coercive; because she was not in fact prosecuted for any offence; and because (following the majority view in *Saunders v United Kingdom* (1997) 23 EHRR 313 (see 14.7.1)) the privilege did not apply to documents obtained from the mother as opposed to statements made by her.

of Morgan Grenfell & Co. Ltd) v *Special Commissioner of Income Tax* [2002] 3 All ER 1 (see 14.9) may at least require a further consideration of the whole question of the privilege in relation to cases involving the welfare of children. In that case, it was held that legal professional privilege is a fundamental right under English law and under the Convention, and that any statutory derogation from it must be made in express language or by necessary implication. The rule in *Re L (A Minor)* is a judicial creation. The Children Act 1989 contains no such express or necessarily implied derogation, and it is submitted that the decision may well violate art. 8 of the Convention, as well as being incorrect as a matter of English law.

14.14 COMMUNICATIONS IN FURTHERANCE OF CRIME OR FRAUD

No privilege will arise where the relationship of lawyer and client is in reality a front for the commission or furtherance of some fraudulent or dishonest act. It may be that the lawyer is an accomplice of the client, but the rule applies equally where the lawyer is made the innocent tool of the fraud. In *Jones* (1846) 1 Den 166, the client deviously inserted a forged will into a bundle of documents relating to title, which he had delivered to an attorney, in the hope that the attorney would find and act on the forgery. It was held that the client had no privilege in respect of that matter. The rule applies to any fraud or dishonesty which the client seeks to further under cover of legal advice, where the advice is intended by the client to assist or guide him in his dishonest designs.[81] It extends similarly to tortious acts involving deceit or conspiracy, which are later made the subject of civil actions, but not to other civil wrongs which cannot fairly be said to involve fraud or dishonesty. There must be at least a *prima facie* appearance of fraud or dishonesty before the judge questions an apparent case of legal professional privilege.[82] But this may appear from the allegedly privileged documents themselves (*Governor of Pentonville Prison, ex parte Osman* [1990] 1 WLR 277, 309–10).

Despite sometimes conflicting authority in earlier cases,[83] it is now settled that the criminal intent may be that of a person who is not directly involved in the lawyer–client relationship. In *Central Criminal Court, ex parte Francis and Francis*,[84] the House of Lords, by a majority, held that where a relative of the client intended to use premises being purchased by the client for the purpose of laundering the proceeds of drug trafficking, the documents relating to the purchase in the possession of the solicitor (who was innocent of the scheme) were not privileged. And in *Leeds Magistrates' Court, ex parte Dumbleton* [1993] Crim LR 866, it was held that a document which had been forged by a solicitor did not enjoy privilege as having been 'made in connection with legal proceedings' within the meaning of the Police and Criminal Evidence Act 1984, s. 10(1).

There is an undeveloped doctrine in civil cases that the privilege may also be lost where the conduct of the party seeking to rely on it has been 'iniquitous', for example where that conduct is intended to unfairly prejudice the party's creditors (*Barclays Bank plc* v *Eustice* [1995] 1 WLR 1238) or where a search order was obtained using information gathered by means of a deliberate

---

[81] *Cox* (1884) 14 QBD 153.

[82] *Crescent Farm (Sidcup) Sports Ltd* v *Sterling Offices Ltd* [1972] Ch 553. And see *Dubai Aluminium Co. Ltd* v *Al-Alawi* [1999] 1 WLR 1964; *Barclays Bank plc* v *Eustice* [1995] 1 WLR 1238; *Williams* v *Quebrada Railway, Land & Copper Co.* [1895] 2 Ch 751; *O'Rourke* v *Darbishire* [1920] AC 581.

[83] See, e.g., *Banque Keyser Ullmann SA* v *Skandia (UK) Insurance Co. Ltd* [1986] 1 Lloyd's Rep 336; *Snaresbrook Crown Court, ex parte DPP* [1988] QB 532.

[84] [1989] AC 346; see also *R (Hallinan Blackburn Gittings & Nott (A Firm))* v *Crown Court at Middlesex Guildhall* [2005] 1 WLR 766.

breach of the Data Protection Act 1984 (*Dubai Aluminium Co. Ltd* v *Al-Alawi* [1999] 1 WLR 1964).[85] This seems to go beyond the established rule that the privilege is defeated by its misuse for the purposes of crime or fraud in the classical sense, and seeks to extend the rule to other acts which may simply attract the disapproval of the court as being generally opprobrious.[86] It is submitted that such cases must now be read in the light of *R (On application of Morgan Grenfell & Co. Ltd)* v *Special Commissioner of Income Tax* [2002] 3 All ER 1 (see 14.9). Although there can be no doubt that loss of the privilege through its misuse for the purposes of crime or fraud would not be a violation of art. 6 or art. 8 of the Convention, it is not clear that the same can be said of non-fraudulent conduct of which a court simply disapproves. It is submitted that such a proposed rule would have to be defined using a far greater degree of precision.

14.15 THE DILEMMA OF JOINT CLIENTS

If two or more clients jointly retain the professional services of a solicitor then it may be difficult to determine how the privilege should operate in subsequent litigation between the clients. A typical instance is that of the family solicitor who receives confidences from both husband and wife while helping them towards reconciliation or over some family arrangement. In later divorce proceedings, one party may wish to inquire about admissions made by the other to the solicitor. The rule appears to be a simple enough one, namely that matters arising in the course of and within the scope of a joint retainer must be disclosed to any of the joint clients. But if the solicitor acts or advises any one client outside the scope of the joint retainer, the usual privilege will attach. All that can be said within the ambit of the present work is that the task of distinguishing these areas is usually more difficult than that of stating the rule.[87]

14.16 DURATION OF LEGAL PROFESSIONAL PRIVILEGE

In theory, legal professional privilege does not necessarily come to an end. It may subsist for many years. It may pass from the original holder to a successor in title or interest, though there is obviously some risk that a waiver may occur during that process.[88] But there was some authority that the privilege is only coextensive with the interest of the holder (the client) in preserving it and that, where the holder can derive no further benefit from the exercise of the privilege, it may be defeated by the interest of another person with an immediate need for access to the information contained in the privileged communication. Until the case of *Ataou* [1988] QB 798, the authority to this effect was somewhat sparse.[89]

In *Ataou* [1988] QB 798, a firm of solicitors initially acted for two accused, A and B. A made a statement to the solicitors, which was undoubtedly privileged when made, the effect of which

---

[85] See *Blackstone's Civil Practice*, 2009 edn, para. 48.50.

[86] See, e.g., *C* v *C (Privilege: Criminal Communications)* [2002] Fam 42, a case involving a threat to 'rip [another person's] throat out', which could have been decided on the much simpler ground that such a communication is not one which would attract the privilege in the first place.

[87] See, e.g., *Harris* v *Harris* [1931] P 10.

[88] For example, the personal representative of a deceased client (*Molloy* [1997] 2 Cr App R 283); and see *Crescent Farm (Sidcup) Sports Ltd* v *Sterling Offices Ltd* [1972] Ch 553.

[89] See *Barton* [1973] 1 WLR 115; Cross, *Evidence*, 7th edn, p. 436 (cf. 5th edn, p. 286) referring to the New Zealand case of *Craig* [1975] 1 NZLR 597, in which the accused was prosecuted for perjury with respect to her testimony as a witness for the plaintiff in an earlier civil action, and the question was whether the solicitor who had acted for the plaintiff could give evidence about the proof of evidence he had taken from her.

was to exculpate B. Subsequently, A pleaded guilty and gave evidence for the prosecution against B. B wished to make use of the statement for the purpose of cross-examining A. It was argued that the statement was privileged when made and remained privileged at trial. The trial judge refused to allow B to make use of the statement. B was convicted. The Court of Appeal allowed his appeal. It was held that because A had no further recognizable interest in maintaining the privilege, the interest and need of B in exposing A's inconsistency in cross-examination should prevail, and that B was entitled to make use of the document. A had, by pleading guilty and giving evidence against B for his own advantage, and thereby contradicting his statement, clearly forfeited any interest in the privilege. French J, delivering the judgment of the Court, said:

> Basing ourselves on the principle which attracted Cooke J in *Craig*,[90] amended for the purposes of the issues raised in this appeal, we would set out the principle as follows. When a communication was originally privileged and in criminal proceedings privilege is claimed against the defendant by the client concerned or his solicitor, it should be for the defendant to show on the balance of probabilities that the claim cannot be sustained. That might be done by demonstrating that there is no ground on which the client could any longer reasonably be regarded as having a recognizable interest in asserting the privilege. The judge must then decide whether the legitimate interest of the defendant in seeking to breach the privilege outweighs that of the client in seeking to maintain it.

Applying that test, the Court found that the trial judge had not carried out the balancing process correctly.

But in *Derby Magistrates' Court, ex parte B* [1996] AC 487, the House of Lords overruled *Ataou* and *Barton* and held that legal professional privilege as between lawyer and client is absolute and permanent. The appellant applied for judicial review of the decision of a magistrate to issue summonses, directed to the appellant and his solicitor, requiring them to produce notes of attendance and proofs of evidence relating to a charge of murder which had been brought against the appellant, and of which he had been acquitted. The appellant's step-father was subsequently charged with the murder, and sought to prove that the appellant had admitted the offence to his solicitor.[91] The magistrate had sought to balance the competing interests, as required by *Ataou*, and had concluded that the clear interest of the step-father in being able to challenge the appellant's evidence, and the fact that the appellant could not be retried for the murder, dictated disclosure of the information. But the House held that the appellant was absolutely entitled to maintain his privilege. Extracts from the speech of Lord Taylor, indicating the absolute nature of the privilege were given at 14.9. Dealing with the argument that the balancing test propounded in *Ataou* was appropriate to protect the competing interests, especially in the case of criminal proceedings, Lord Nicholls of Birkenhead said (at 511–12):

> There are real difficulties here. In exercising this discretion the court would be faced with an essentially impossible task. One man's meat is another man's poison. How does one equate exposure to a comparatively minor civil claim or criminal charge against prejudicing a defence to a serious criminal charge? How does one balance a client's risk of loss of reputation, or exposure to public opprobrium, against prejudicing another person's possible defence to a murder charge? But the difficulties go much

---

[90] See previous note.

[91] Under the present law, such statements by the appellant would not be evidence of the facts stated, and so could not be used to exculpate the step-father directly unless the judge was prepared to admit them under s. 114(1)(d) of the Criminal Justice Act 2003: see 7.4.1; 8.20. But they could be used as previous inconsistent statements to cross-examine the appellant if he gave evidence against the step-father, as it was envisaged he would: see 17.7 *et seq*.

further. Could disclosure also be sought by the prosecution, on the ground that there is a public interest in the guilty being convicted? If not, why not?...This highlights the impossibility of the exercise.

It is submitted that, although the firm restatement by the House of the importance of the privilege is welcome, it is not quite as clear as Lord Nicholls suggests that the balancing test could not be performed. Indeed, it would seem that, in the present case, the magistrate had done so well. Certainly, in a criminal case, it is desirable that all evidence which may assist the defence should be made available. On the other hand, it is submitted that the House is correct in emphasizing the central role played by the privilege in all forms of litigation. Any reversion to the position in *Ataou* must now be a matter for Parliament.

For reasons of practicality, the privilege will sometimes end because the client has no alternative but to waive it in order to establish a claim or defence, or to prove some important fact contained in a privileged communication. For example, if the client sues his legal adviser for professional negligence because of the latter's handling of a matter, it would be impossible for the client to maintain any privilege in communications relating to the matter in question, although privilege might be maintained with respect to any separate matters which are irrelevant to the case. In *Bowden* [1999] 1 WLR 823, the accused gave evidence that he had not mentioned certain facts to the police when he was interviewed on the advice of his solicitor. He also elicited, by counsel, in cross-examination of a police officer, a statement made to the police by his solicitor at that time. The accused's purpose was to persuade the jury not to draw an adverse inference against him because of his failure to mention the facts, under s. 34 of the Criminal Justice and Public Order Act 1994 (see 10.6). It was held that the accused had waived all legal professional privilege in communications with his solicitor at the time of the interview, insofar as they related to the reasons why the accused had withheld the facts. Had he merely stated that he had acted on his solicitor's advice without divulging more (which would probably not have been an effective strategy) the privilege would not have been lost, but where the details of the solicitor's advice were made known to the jury, the prosecution were entitled to ask questions designed to probe whether the reasons asserted were genuine or were the only reasons why the accused failed to mention the relevant facts. In those circumstances, the accused must be taken to have waived the privilege.

14.17 SEARCH WARRANTS

In *Sallinen v Finland*,[92] the European Court of Human Rights held that provisions permitting the search and seizure of privileged materials must be based on specific and detailed rules, which minimize the impact of the procedure on the right to private life. This includes any search of a lawyer's office or the seizure of any privileged materials. The Police and Criminal Evidence Act 1984 offers protection to 'items subject to legal privilege' against seizure pursuant to a search warrant issued under s. 8 of the Act. Although the seizure of items of evidence is only one aspect of the claiming of privilege, it is one which is of great importance in criminal cases, in which the police sometimes claim to be entitled to seize items of possible evidential significance from the accused or his solicitors, pursuant to a search warrant. This causes considerable difficulties if material is on the premises to be searched which is in fact privileged, because if material is voluntarily handed over, the privilege may be lost, while if it is wrongly withheld, charges of

---

[92] (2007) 44 EHRR 18; see also *R (Malik) v Manchester Crown Court* [2008] 4 All ER 403.

obstruction may follow. Hopefully, a clear exclusion of certain material will assist. Section 10 defines 'items subject to legal privilege' as follows:

(1) Subject to subsection (2) below, in this Act 'items subject to legal privilege' means—
    (a) communications between a professional legal adviser and his client or any person representing his client made in connection with the giving of legal advice to the client;
    (b) communications between a professional legal adviser and his client or any person representing his client or between such an adviser or his client or any such representative and any other person made in connection with or in contemplation of legal proceedings and for the purposes of such proceedings; and
    (c) items enclosed with or referred to in such communications and made—
        (i) in connection with the giving of legal advice; or
        (ii) in connection with or in contemplation of legal proceedings and for the purposes of such proceedings,
when they are in the possession of a person who is entitled to possession of them.

(2) Items held with the intention of furthering a criminal purpose are not items subject to legal privilege.[93]

The statutory definition follows closely the common law position as to legal professional privilege, and it has been said judicially that the section was intended to reflect the common law (*Central Criminal Court, ex parte Francis and Francis* [1989] AC 346). The Act excludes such items from the general power provided by s. 8 to seize items which are 'likely to be relevant evidence' pursuant to a search warrant, and therefore provides a proper ground for a legal adviser or third party assisting an accused to withhold such items in the event of a search. It is essential to appreciate that items subject to legal privilege are excluded absolutely from seizure, and are not subject to the 'special procedure' established by Sch. 1 to the Act. Items which are apparently subject to legal privilege should, even if in fact not so privileged, be dealt with, not by the magistrates under s. 8 of the Act, but on an application to a circuit judge *inter partes* (*Guildhall Magistrates' Court, ex parte Primlaks Holdings Co. (Panama) Inc.* [1990] 1 QB 261). For more detailed treatment of the subject of search warrants, see the current edition of *Blackstone's Criminal Practice*.

C   OTHER PRIVILEGES

SUMMARY OF MAIN POINTS

- By virtue of s. 10 of the Contempt of Court Act 1981 a person may not be compelled to disclose the source of information contained in a publication for which he is responsible unless disclosure is necessary in the interests of justice or national security or the prevention of disorder or crime.

- In civil cases, a party may make without prejudice communications in a good faith effort to settle to compromise a case, or to resolve a dispute in relation to which litigation is contemplated. Such communications may not be referred to in court on the issue of liability or *quantum*, and are to that extent privileged.

---

[93] As to the construction of s. 10(2), see *Central Criminal Court, ex parte Francis and Francis* [1989] AC 346; *Snaresbrook Crown Court, ex parte DPP* [1988] QB 532; cf. *R (Hallinan Blackburn Gittings & Nott (A Firm)) v Crown Court at Middlesex Guildhall* [2005] 1 WLR 766.

14.18 MATRIMONIAL COMMUNICATIONS

The privilege against compelled disclosure of communications between spouses made during the marriage (matrimonial communications) has now been abolished in all cases. Contrary to popular belief, the privilege recognized in English law was not a common law privilege, but was created by statute to take account of the competence accorded to parties and their spouses by statute during the nineteenth century (see 15.4). It was enacted originally by s. 3 of the Evidence Amendment Act 1853 and reaffirmed in s. 1(d) of the Criminal Evidence Act 1898 to deal with the new competence of the accused and the accused's spouse in criminal cases. As the competence of the spouse as a prosecution witness became broader, similar privilege provisions continued to be enacted, for example in s. 39 of the Sexual Offences Act 1956 and s. 30 of the Theft Act 1968.

Contrary to the feeling in other parts of the common law world, but in accordance with the illiberal attitude of English law towards privileges, the privilege against compelled disclosure of matrimonial communications came to be thought of as anachronistic. It was abolished 'except in relation to criminal proceedings' by s. 16(3) of the Civil Evidence Act 1968. Section 16(4) likewise abolished a related privilege against compelled evidence of the occurrence or non-occurrence of marital intercourse, which existed pursuant to s. 43(1) of the Matrimonial Causes Act 1965. The Police and Criminal Evidence Act 1984, s. 80, created sweeping new rules governing the competence and compellability of the spouse in criminal cases. Until this time, Parliament was no doubt reluctant to abolish a privilege claimable in a criminal case, especially as the House of Lords had previously held that the witness spouse should not be a compellable prosecution witness.[94] But the new provisions provided the opportunity to do so, and both privileges referred to above were abolished by s. 80(9) of the Act.

14.19 SOURCES OF INFORMATION CONTAINED IN PUBLICATIONS: COMMON LAW

As observed in 13.10 and 14.1.1, the law has accorded relatively little formal recognition to the claims of confidential relationships to enjoy privilege. An aspect of professional confidence which troubled the courts on a number of occasions is that existing between persons responsible for publications and their sources of information.[95] At common law, no privilege existed for confidential communications passing between the two, and journalists were sometimes held to be guilty of contempt of court for refusing to disclose the identity of the source. This situation led to some disquiet. It was mitigated hardly at all by the obscure 'newspaper rule', which to a very limited degree protected newspapers and journalists from having to disclose their sources in answer to interrogatories or by pre-trial discovery. The rule applied to libel actions only, and offered protection only during the discovery stage. It was too limited, uncertain, and anachronistic to afford any real protection.[96] The protection realistically available was limited to the reluctance

---

[94] See *Hoskyn* v *Commissioner of Police of the Metropolis* [1979] AC 474; and as to the competence and compellability of the spouse, 15.7. See also Civil Partnership Act 2004, s. 84.

[95] See, e.g., *Attorney-General* v *Mulholland* [1963] 2 QB 477; *Attorney-General* v *Clough* [1963] 1 QB 773; 13.10.

[96] See generally the former RSC, Ord. 82, r. 6; *Hennessy* v *Wright (No. 2)* (1888) 24 QBD 445n; *Hope* v *Brash* [1897] 2 QB 188. For a modern acknowledgement that the rule was inadequate to support a general theory of immunity, see the speech of Lord Fraser of Tullybelton in *British Steel Corporation* v *Granada Television Ltd* [1981] AC 1096, 1197–9.

of the courts to compel the disclosure of sources, unless some compelling reason of public policy demanded it: this we considered in 13.10.

A valiant but unsuccessful attempt was made to assert a general journalistic immunity based on public policy in *British Steel Corporation* v *Granada Television Ltd* [1981] AC 1096. The impact of the arguments made in support of the immunity was, unfortunately, greatly reduced by the fact that, of all the judges who considered the case in its speedy passage to the House of Lords, only Lord Salmon, dissenting in the House, had any doubt that Granada had acted in a manner which would in any event have disqualified them from relief. During a national steel workers' strike in 1980, an unknown executive of BSC 'leaked' some 250 confidential documents belonging to BSC, which had the potential to embarrass the corporation in the light of its public posture about the strike. Granada promised the executive that his identity would be kept confidential, and used the documents in a current affairs programme on which the chairman of BSC appeared. Later, the documents were returned to BSC in a mutilated form, apparently to protect the identity of the executive. BSC commenced proceedings to compel Granada to disclose the name of the source, on the ground that it was relevant to their proceedings for breach of copyright and other wrongs which Granada conceded they had committed. Precedent for such relief was to be found in *Norwich Pharmacal Co.* v *Customs and Excise Commissioners* [1974] AC 133.

At first instance, Sir Robert Megarry V-C declined to find that the press was entitled to any special immunity, and indeed felt that if anything, the authorities pointed the other way. The Court of Appeal proved somewhat more open to the idea. Lord Denning MR held that in general, the press would not be compelled to disclose sources, while emphasising that this did not mean that any privilege existed, merely that the courts would usually forbear to compel. Lord Denning also held that the court's forbearance would be lost if the press acted 'irresponsibly', a phrase which, as Lord Salmon pointed out in the House of Lords, is difficult to define. Lord Denning felt that Granada had behaved 'irresponsibly' in the context of the case at hand.

Watkins LJ shared Lord Denning's view as to the merits of Granada's conduct, but his judgment is nonetheless a remarkably strong assertion of public policy immunity in the context of press sources. He said ([1981] AC at 1138–9):

> It is, I believe, well founded on ample legal authority that newspapers and television and broadcasting authorities and their servants are in principle immune from disclosing their confidential sources of information. This principle has been applied in a number of cases before courts and tribunals, some of which have achieved public prominence. The public can be said to approve of it. It is in their interest to do so. It is, therefore, a public-interest immunity.

Watkins LJ added that no question of privilege was involved, but asserted that the importance of a free press amply justified a general immunity from disclosure of sources. Unfortunately, his Lordship cited no authority in support of his proposition, which for the reasons stated in the judgment of Sir Robert Megarry V-C and at 13.10, appears not to have found support at common law. It may be that Watkins LJ intended only to describe the practice of the courts not to compel in the absence of some compelling reason.

In the House of Lords, Granada's conduct once more proved the undoing of the immunity argument. Only Lord Salmon, who considered Granada to have performed a public service, dissented. The other Lords agreed that, although the courts had an inherent wish to respect journalistic confidences, no public interest immunity existed which would override the public policy of making relevant evidence available to the court and to litigants. Since BSC undoubtedly had a meritorious cause of action, they were entitled to disclosure. Lord Wilberforce disavowed the apparently contrary assertions in the judgments of the Court of Appeal. He said ([1981] AC 1170–1):

> All these authorities (and there is none the other way before this case) came down firmly against immunity for the press or for journalists. To contend that, in principle, journalists enjoy immunity from the obligation to disclose, which may however be withheld in exceptional cases, is, in my opinion a complete reversal of the rule so strongly affirmed...
>
> The only support for reversal is to be found, at least by implication, in some passages in the judgments of the Court of Appeal in the present case. But these must be read in the light of their decision, on the whole matter, that disclosure should be ordered. I do not think that Lord Denning MR should be understood as departing from his judgment in *Attorney-General* v *Mulholland* [1963] 2 QB 477 and from every reported case. Such a reversal would place journalists (how defined?) in a favoured and unique position as compared with priest-confessors, doctors, bankers and other recipients of confidential information and would assimilate them to the police in relation to informers. I can find nothing to encourage such a departure even with the qualifications sought to be introduced to the general principle asserted.

14.20 CONTEMPT OF COURT ACT 1981, S. 10

In the light of art. 10 of the European Convention on Human Rights (see 1.7), Parliament chose to introduce the reversal referred to by Lord Wilberforce and took the most remarkable step of introducing a new statutory privilege. Although earlier cases were argued on the basis of public interest immunity, the wording of the section is in effect apt to create a privilege which will always operate, except in defined circumstances. Section 10 of the Contempt of Court Act 1981 provides:

> No court may require a person to disclose, nor is any person guilty of contempt of court for refusing to disclose, the source of information contained in a publication for which he is responsible, unless it be established to the satisfaction of the court that disclosure is necessary in the interests of justice or national security or for the prevention of disorder or crime.

14.20.1 Scope of s. 10

For the purposes of s. 10 of the Contempt of Court Act 1981, 'publication' includes 'any speech, writing, broadcast or other communication in whatever form, which is addressed to the public at large or any section of the public': see ss. 2(1) and 19. The section does not define the phrase 'for which he is responsible', but it is submitted that the category of responsible persons must include the journalist or reporter, the owner and publisher of a newspaper or periodical, and those involved in a managerial or production capacity with a television or radio broadcast. The privilege applies both before and after publication of the materials concerned (*X Ltd* v *Morgan-Grampian (Publishers) Ltd* [1991] 1 AC 1, per Lord Bridge of Harwich).

In *Secretary of State for Defence* v *Guardian Newspapers Ltd* [1985] AC 339, a copy of a government memorandum, classified secret, was 'leaked' to the *Guardian* newspaper. The memorandum related to the handling of publicity over the installation of nuclear weapons at a Royal Air Force base, and had been circulated to the Prime Minister, senior Cabinet ministers and the Cabinet secretary. The *Guardian* published the memorandum, and the Crown subsequently claimed its return in order to attempt to identify the informant. The *Guardian* asserted that it was entitled to withhold its copy of the memorandum by virtue of s. 10. The House of Lords, in an interlocutory appeal, was unanimous in holding that s. 10 should be of 'wide and general application', and that accordingly, it was sufficient to attract the protection of s. 10 if the order for disclosure might, not necessarily would, have the effect of forcing the disclosure of a source of information. The House also held unanimously that the prohibition on disclosure must prevail unless one of the four specifically enumerated exceptions applied, and that the onus of establishing that an exception applied lay on the party seeking disclosure, and might be discharged by proof on a balance of probabilities.[97] The facts of the case, however, produced substantial disagreement. The judge at first instance, Scott J, and the Court of Appeal, held that the Crown had proved that disclosure was necessary in the interests of national security. In the House of Lords, the majority, Lords Diplock, Roskill, and Bridge agreed with the courts below, but there was powerful dissent by Lords Scarman and Fraser.[98]

In relation to the main point of law decided by the House, Lord Fraser said (*ibid.* at 356):

> The application of [s. 10] is, in my opinion, not limited to the case where a publisher of information is required in terms to disclose the source of information or to do something which will certainly disclose it, and refuses to do so. The provision extends also to a case such as the present, where the publisher is called on, and refuses, to do something which may or may not lead to disclosure of the source. The wider construction of the section which appealed to Griffiths LJ appears to me to be correct (see [1984] Ch. 156 at 166).

The majority of the House also held that the expression 'the interests of justice', as used in s. 10, referred to the administration of justice in the course of legal proceedings in a court, tribunal, or other judicial body, rather than to any abstract concept of justice. Lord Bridge in *X Ltd* v *Morgan-Grampian (Publishers) Ltd* [1991] 1 AC 1 took a different view, namely that it referred to the more concrete rights to enforce legal rights and prevent harm.[99]

In *Re an Inquiry under the Company Securities (Insider Dealing) Act 1985* [1988] AC 660, inspectors were appointed to hold an inquiry into the apparent leakage of information about take-over bids from the Office of Fair Trading, the Department of Trade and Industry, and the Monopolies and Mergers Commission. It was conceded that the inspectors were carrying out a criminal investigation, because the information had been used in connection with statutory offences of insider dealing. The question arose of whether a journalist could be compelled to disclose the source of information, on the basis of which he had written and published articles on the subject of insider dealing, and which suggested that the source would be likely to possess information useful to the investigation. The inspectors contended that the disclosure was 'necessary in the interests of the prevention of . . . crime' and therefore that the journalist was not entitled to the protection of s. 10. The House held that the expression 'for the prevention of crime' need not refer to any definite, identifiable crime, but may refer to crime in general. Therefore, once it was conceded that the inspectors were engaged in an investigation into criminal activities, the information was capable of being necessary for that purpose, even though no specific offence had yet been identified. The purpose could be the prevention of any crime that might otherwise be committed in the future. It

---

[97] In view of the possible consequences of disclosure, it seems arguable that the standard should be higher: see 4.15.2.

[98] To those raised on conventional concepts of judicial functions, the prospect of the Lords dividing over the facts, in the face of unanimous factual agreement by the judge at first instance and the Court of Appeal, is not uninteresting. But as their Lordships observed, the appeal was interlocutory in form, and the evidence left much to be desired.

[99] See 14.20.3. This divergence of opinion may have been resolved by *Ashworth Hospital Authority* v *MGN* [2002] 1 WLR 2033 (see 14.20.4).

is submitted that this is sensible. It would generally be difficult, if possible at all, to identify with precision a crime which has not yet been committed.

14.20.2 Meaning of 'necessary'

The House of Lords in *Re an Inquiry under the Company Securities (Insider Dealing) Act 1985* [1988] AC 660 also considered the meaning of the word 'necessary'. The holding on this question, when compared with that in *Secretary of State for Defence* v *Guardian Newspapers Ltd* [1985] AC 339, is less felicitous. It was readily apparent that it would be useful for the inspectors to obtain the information, because it would facilitate the investigation. However, it could not be said that the investigation could not be continued without it. Some background is necessary to an understanding of the decision of the House.

In *Secretary of State* v *Guardian Newspapers Ltd* Lord Diplock had said ([1985] AC 339 at 350):

> Again, the section uses the word 'necessary' by itself, instead of using the common statutory phrase 'necessary or expedient', to describe what must be established to the satisfaction of the court—which latter phrase gives to the judge a margin of discretion; expediency, however great, is not enough; s. 10 requires actual necessity to be established; and whether it has or not is a question of fact that the judge has to find in favour of necessity as a condition precedent to his having any jurisdiction to order disclosure of sources of information.

This part of Lord Diplock's speech had been considered and applied by the Court of Appeal in *Maxwell* v *Pressdram Ltd* [1987] 1 WLR 298.[100] The plaintiff, a well-known public figure, sued the defendants, the publishers and editor of an equally well-known satirical magazine, *Private Eye*, for alleged libel. The defendants indicated, in the course of opposing successfully an application for an injunction to restrain publication, that they intended to justify their allegations against the plaintiff. Before trial, however, they learned that the journalistic sources on whom they relied to establish the defence of justification would not give evidence. Despite this, they did not abandon that defence until the trial had commenced. The plaintiff contended that the trial judge should compel disclosure of the sources. It was argued that this was 'necessary' in the interests of justice, in order to allow the jury to assess whether the conduct of the defendants had been disgraceful and, if so, whether the plaintiff should be awarded aggravated or exemplary damages. The judge refused the plaintiff's application. On appeal, the Court of Appeal, with some reluctance, upheld the judge's decision. Parker LJ, having read a passage from the speech of Lord Diplock in *Secretary of State for Defence* v *Guardian Newspapers Ltd* ([1985] AC 339, 349) said ([1987] 1 WLR at 310):

> The public interest which s. 10 of the 1981 Act serves is therefore the preservation of sources of information and ensuring that they come forward.
>
> There is recognized in the passage that I have read a competing public interest, namely that a court of law should have before it information which is relevant to the determination of any issue which falls for determination in proceedings before it. That requirement, however, is clearly not one which would be sufficient to override in general the public interest which s. 10 seeks to serve, and it is for that reason that the section provides that there shall be no disclosure unless it is established to the satisfaction of the court that disclosure is *necessary* in the interests of justice....

---

[100] Like *Secretary of State for Defence* v *Guardian Newspapers Ltd*, this was an interlocutory appeal, and was, indeed, heard as a matter of urgency during the trial of the action. It is certainly not the most fortuitous of circumstances that the law relating to s. 10 has been largely formed by such cases, as the tribunals concerned themselves recognized.

> It cannot therefore be sufficient merely to say that the information which it is sought to obtain within the exceptions of s. 10 is information which is relevant to the determination of an issue before the court. Were that so, it would always be possible to obtain an order for disclosure, because unless the information was relevant it would not be admissible, and if it was merely admissible and that was sufficient, an order could always be made.
>
> One must clearly go further and decide in each particular case whether a situation has been created which makes necessary in the interests of justice that the source should be revealed. [Emphasis in original.]

While the Court recognized that it would certainly be relevant for the plaintiff to adduce evidence of the defendants' sources, it was not prepared to hold that the trial judge, who was best placed to decide the question of necessity, and who proposed to deal with the refusal to disclose by a strong direction to the jury, had erred.

But the members of the House of Lords in the *Inquiry* case took a somewhat different view, and held that the true meaning of 'necessary' lay somewhere between 'indispensable' and 'useful' or 'expedient'. It means, said Lord Griffiths (*ibid.* at 65) 'really needed'. With respect, it may be doubted whether this definition does any more than reduce somewhat the standard enacted by Parliament. In the result, the House held it to be 'necessary' within the meaning of s. 10 that the journalist be compelled to reveal his source of information. Lord Griffiths said (*ibid.* at 64):

> What then is meant by the words 'necessary...for the prevention of...crime' in s. 10? I do not think that much light is thrown upon this question by an elaborate discussion of the meaning of the word 'necessary'. 'Necessary' is a word in common usage in everyday speech with which everyone is familiar. Like all words, it will take colour from its context; for example, most people would regard it as 'necessary' to do everything possible to prevent a catastrophe but would not regard it as 'necessary' to do everything possible to prevent some minor inconvenience. Furthermore, whether a particular measure is necessary, although described as a question of fact for the purpose of s. 10, involves the exercise of a judgment on the established facts.

14.20.3 Necessity for preventing residual damage

It appears to be established that it may be necessary in some cases to order disclosure to prevent residual damage which might continue after the publication of materials supplied by an unknown source has occurred. Such damage may occur in various ways, but it is usually related to the potential for the further disclosure of confidential information. This may be so especially where it appears that the source must have had access to privileged information, though this alone will not always justify disclosure (see *Saunders v Punch Ltd* [1998] 1 WLR 986). In the typical case, an employer may seek disclosure of the identity of an employee who has leaked confidential and damaging information to the press, for the purpose of dismissing him and preventing similar damage from occurring in future. In *X Ltd v Morgan-Grampian (Publishers) Ltd* [1991] 1 AC 1, Lord Bridge of Harwich said (*ibid.* at 43):

> It is, in my opinion, 'in the interests of justice', in the sense in which this phrase is used in s. 10, that persons should be enabled to exercise important legal rights and to protect themselves from serious legal wrongs whether or not resort to legal proceedings in a court of law will be necessary to attain these objectives. Thus, to take a very obvious example, if an employer of a large staff is suffering grave damage from the activities of an unidentified disloyal servant, it is undoubtedly in the interests of justice that he should be able to identify him in order to terminate his contract of employment.

The damage suffered, and likely to be suffered by the company in this case, resulted from the disclosure by an employee of confidential information which had an adverse affect on the company's financial status. Lord Bridge described it as follows (at 44–5):

> The importance to the plaintiffs of obtaining disclosure lies in the threat of severe damage to their business, and consequentially to the livelihood of their employees, which would arise from disclosure of the information contained in their corporate plan while their refinancing negotiations are still continuing.

14.20.4 Overall test to be applied

In *Goodwin* v *United Kingdom* (1996) 22 EHRR 123, the European Court of Human Rights considered a petition for relief arising from the case of *X Ltd* v *Morgan-Grampian*, but unlike the House of Lords reached the conclusion that disclosure should not have been ordered.[101] It is difficult to think of another area of law which has produced such a large measure of judicial disagreement, and it is somewhat ironic that s. 10, having been passed to give effect to art. 10 of the Convention, has been interpreted in some ways against the spirit of art. 10. But in *Ashworth Hospital Authority* v *MGN Ltd* [2001] 1 WLR 515, the Court of Appeal attempted to lay down an overall test for the application of s. 10 having regard, not only to art. 10 of the Convention, but also to the incorporation of the Convention rights into the law of the UK by the Human Rights Act 1998, a factor in the decision which makes it particularly important. The Court held that the interpretation of s. 10 should accord with the interpretation of art. 10 of the Convention in the jurisprudence of the European Court of Human Rights. The court should apply the same test of necessity as would be applied by the European Court of Human Rights in construing art. 10(2). The term 'interests of justice' refers to the necessity of allowing parties to enforce concrete interests or rights, rather than to justice in any abstract sense or in the sense of the administration of justice. This includes the various matters enumerated in art. 10(2) as justifying restrictions on the freedom of expression guaranteed by art. 10(1).[102] With this in mind, the court should judge the claim for compelled disclosure by considering whether or not it is necessary to achieve the interests of justice in the sense defined above, and whether or not, even if it is 'necessary', the court should exercise its discretion to give overriding effect to the freedom of expression. In considering the exercise of discretion, a number of other matters may arise, for example the conduct of the party seeking disclosure and the possibility that that party could have obtained the necessary information by means which do not involve compelling disclosure.[103] The Court of Appeal found that disclosure was necessary and proportionate on the facts of the case, which were that a source had leaked to the defendant newspaper publisher details of private medical records of a notorious person detained in a secure hospital administered by the claimant authority. The claimant, having adduced evidence as to the considerable importance of maintaining the confidentiality of such records, sought disclosure of the identity of the source (who, it was suspected, was one of its employees) from the defendant for the purpose of dismissing him (though not of taking

---

[101] Despite attempts to explain this on other grounds in *Camelot Group plc* v *Centaur Communications Ltd* [1999] QB 124, it is hard to resist the conclusion that English courts have much less regard for journalistic privilege than do European courts, including the European Court of Human Rights.

[102] The Court chose on this point to prefer the view of Lord Bridge in *X* v *Morgan-Grampian (Publishers) Ltd* [1991] 1 AC 1, 43, to that of Lord Diplock in *Secretary of State for Defence* v *Guardian Newspapers Ltd* [1985] AC 339, 350; see 14.20.

[103] See, e.g., *John* v *Express Newspapers plc* [2000] 1 WLR 1931; *Saunders* v *Punch Ltd* [1998] 1 WLR 986.

other proceedings against him). It was held that there was a high public interest in granting the disclosure, and that the restriction on the journalistic privilege was limited and reasonable. The House of Lords affirmed the decision of the Court of Appeal ([2002] 1 WLR 2033). Lord Woolf, with whom the other members of the House agreed, said (*ibid.* at [61]–[62]):

> Any disclosure of a journalist's sources has a chilling effect on the freedom of the press. The Court, when making an order for disclosure in exercise of the *Norwich Pharmacal* jurisdiction must have this well in mind…The fact is that information which should be placed in the public domain is frequently made available to the press by individuals who would lack the courage to provide the information if they thought there was a risk of their identity being disclosed. The fact that journalists' sources can be reasonably confident that their identity will not be disclosed makes a significant contribution to the ability of the press to perform their role in society of making information available to the public. It is for this reason that it is well established now that the courts will normally protect journalists' sources from identification. However, this protection is not unqualified. Both s. 10 and art. 10 recognize this. This leads to the difficult issue at the heart of this appeal, namely whether the disclosure ordered was necessary and not disproportionate. The requirements of necessity and proportionality are here separate concepts which substantially cover the same area. In his submissions [counsel] relied correctly on the decision of the European Court in *Goodwin* v *UK* (1996) 1 BHRC 81. I find no difficulty in accepting the approach that the European Court emphasized (at 95–96 (para. 40)) that: (i) 'as a matter of general principle, the necessity for any restriction of freedom of expression must be convincingly established' and (ii) 'limitations on the confidentiality of journalistic sources call for the most careful scrutiny by the Court'. Furthermore, I would also adopt [counsel's] contention that any restriction on the otherwise unqualified right to freedom of expression must meet two further requirements. First, the exercise of the jurisdiction because of art. 10(2) should meet a 'pressing social need' and secondly the restriction should be proportionate to a legitimate aim which is being pursued.

Having considered the facts, Lord Woolf agreed with the Court of Appeal that the disclosure sought was necessary in the light of the importance of maintaining the confidentiality of medical records of patients in secure institutions, and proportionate in the light of the limited and apparently justifiable use which the claimant proposed to make of the information disclosed.

14.20.5 Search warrants

In our discussion of legal professional privilege, we saw that the seizure of items of potential evidential significance represents an important aspect of the claiming of privilege in criminal cases, and that the Police and Criminal Evidence Act 1984 provides protection against the seizure, pursuant to search warrant, of items subject to that privilege (see 14.17).

The Act does not exempt other confidential materials from seizure, but in the case of two kinds of materials, provides that access may be gained to them only by order of a circuit judge, and not pursuant to a search warrant issued by a justice of the peace under s. 8 of the Act. These two categories of materials are known respectively as 'excluded material' and 'special procedure material'. Schedule 1 to the Act provides a procedure for making application to a circuit judge for access to excluded and special procedure material, and specifies the conditions which must be satisfied before an order for access may be made. It is not proposed to explore the detail of these provisions here.

Excluded material and special material are defined by the Act (see ss. 11 to 14) at some length. For our purposes, it will suffice to note that both consist of materials brought into being or acquired pursuant to some relationship of confidence, including journalistic materials, personal medical, psychiatric and counselling records, and business communications. In relation to both excluded material and special procedure material, a person holds material in confidence if he does so under either an express or implied undertaking or obligation. The further detail of these provisions is outside the scope of this work. As in the case of items subject to legal privilege, it is to be hoped that these specific provisions will clarify situations in which confidential materials may in future be withheld in the event of a search pursuant only to a search warrant, and in the absence of any order by a circuit judge. For more detailed treatment of the subject of search warrants, see the current edition of *Blackstone's Criminal Practice*.

14.21 WITHOUT-PREJUDICE NEGOTIATIONS

Because of the obvious public interest in the proper compromise of civil litigation whenever this can be achieved, the law offers a measure of protection to communications designed to arrive at this result. The danger of making or responding to any offer in settlement of litigation is that the gesture may later be construed as some admission of liability, or lack of merit in the case. For this reason, communications with an opponent may be made 'without prejudice'. The effect of this is that they may not, at trial, be referred to on the issue of liability or *quantum*. Such communications are privileged at common law.[104] The importance of inducing the parties to settle claims and potential claims at the earliest possible stage is a central feature of the Woolf Report, which led to the Civil Procedure Rules 1998. Part 36 of the Rules lays down an elaborate scheme for the making of offers and payments into court, which involves penalties in terms of costs and interest for parties who fail to accept an offer or payment which the court later determines should have been accepted. The detail of these rules is outside the scope of the present work (see *Blackstone's Civil Practice*, 2009 edn, ch. 64). However, the common law rules as to without prejudice communications are unaffected by the rules, because a significant period of negotiation may be required before the parties are in a position to make an offer or payment into court. If a case is to be settled, information and ideas about settlement must be exchanged, and the privilege is essential to prevent communications made in a spirit of compromise from being used later as an admission of weakness.

In *Rush & Tompkins Ltd* v *Greater London Council* [1989] AC 1280, Lord Griffiths said (at 1299):

> The rule applies to exclude all negotiations genuinely aimed at settlement whether oral or in writing from being given in evidence. A competent solicitor will always head any negotiating correspondence 'without prejudice' to make clear beyond doubt that in the event of the negotiations being unsuccessful they are not to be referred to at the subsequent trial. However, the application of the rule is not dependent upon the use of the phrase 'without prejudice' and if it is clear from the surrounding circumstances that the parties were seeking to compromise the action, evidence of the content of those negotiations will, as a general rule, not be admissible at the trial and cannot be used to establish an admission or partial admission.

Thus, the privilege attaching to without-prejudice correspondence covers all *bona fide* offers of settlement or compromise of litigation, and efforts to resolve a dispute which it is contemplated may lead to litigation, whether or not any litigation has been commenced: see *Barnetson* v *Framlington Company and another* [2007] 1 WLR 2443. The words 'without prejudice' need not

---

[104] Thus, it is improper to ask the court to draw an adverse inference against a party from any reluctance on the part of that party to disclose without prejudice communications: see *Reed Executive plc* v *Reed Business Information Ltd* [2004] 1 WLR 3026.

actually appear on a letter designed to have the effect described, but the practice of using them by way of heading is both usual and desirable.[105] Conversely, the mere insertion of the words will not assist a letter which is not a *bona fide* approach within the scope of the rule.[106] Once negotiations have commenced, the rule obviously protects not only offers of settlement, but also responses by way of acceptance or counter-offer, or indeed letters which merely initiate settlement negotiations, even if they do not contain an actual offer to settle: *South Shropshire District Council v Amos* [1986] 1 WLR 1271.[107]

In *Rush & Tompkins v Greater London Council* [1989] AC 1280, the plaintiff brought an action against two defendants, D1 and D2. In due course, the plaintiff settled with D1. D2 sought disclosure of the without-prejudice negotiations between the plaintiff and D1, which would admittedly be relevant to the action between the plaintiff and D2. The Court of Appeal held that D2 was entitled to discovery of the material sought, on the ground that the privilege created in the without-prejudice correspondence ended once a final and binding settlement was achieved, because its purpose had been attained. However, the House of Lords reversed the decision of the Court of Appeal, and restored the order of the judge at first instance, who had upheld that plaintiff's claim of privilege. Lord Griffiths, in a speech with which the other members of the House agreed, said that he could not accept the view of the Court of Appeal that, once the negotiations were successful, the privilege in the without-prejudice correspondence had served its purpose, and must be discarded. On the contrary, the privilege should continue, whether or not the negotiations were successful, in the interest of protecting *bona fide* negotiations from being inhibited by the fear of future disclosure, and this had long been the accepted practice. It was argued that a distinction should be made between admissibility and discoverability, i.e., that, even if the correspondence would not be admissible at trial, it had a separate value to D2, if disclosed, in that it would provide information about the view formed by other parties about the merits and potential settlement value of the case. However, Lord Griffiths observed (at 1305) that, even if this were true, it did 'not outweigh the damage that would be done to the conduct of settlement negotiations if solicitors thought that what was said and written between them would become common currency available to all other parties to the litigation'.

Although without-prejudice negotiations are usually carried on by correspondence, there is nothing to preclude their conduct by other means, such as oral attempts at settlement by the parties or their advisers. In particular, in matrimonial cases, negotiations may have taken place through the good offices of a mediator or counsellor and such informal procedures are becoming more common in other civil cases. Where this occurs, and offers and suggestions are relayed to the parties via a third party, it has been held that the substance of the negotiations is privileged as if they were made in correspondence. Thus, in *McTaggart v McTaggart*[108] where an interview between the spouses had been arranged by a probation officer on a 'without-prejudice' basis, either spouse was entitled to object to evidence of what had been said being received at trial. However, the privilege is that of the parties, so that the probation officer is not entitled to object, and where the privilege had been waived by the parties, the judge was bound to admit the

---

[105] *South Shropshire District Council v Amos* [1986] 1 WLR 1271.

[106] *Buckingham County Council v Moran* [1990] Ch 623. Moreover, the court will not countenance abuse of the without prejudice privilege, for example including improper communications such as threats under cover of an offer to settle: see *Unilever plc v Procter & Gamble Co.* [2000] 1 WLR 2436.

[107] As to the difficulties of distinguishing without-prejudice and open correspondence see *Cheddar Valley Engineering Ltd v Chaddlewood Homes Ltd* [1992] 1 WLR 820.

[108] [1949] P 94. See the judgment of Cohen LJ at 96.

evidence. In *Mole* v *Mole*[109] it was held that the principle applies equally where one party only is interviewed by the probation officer with a view to reconciliation, and that where any person acting in the same capacity arranges an interview which is in fact intended to be without prejudice, the same result obtains. However, it must be noted that without-prejudice negotiations can only be conducted where the parties or those acting on their behalf engage in discussions with a view to settlement. Where, therefore, a care worker spoke to the respondent to affiliation proceedings with a view to possible adoption of the child, and was not acting as the agent of either party, the respondent's admissions to the worker of paternity were not privileged, and were admitted on the issue of paternity.[110]

Although without-prejudice correspondence is not admissible at trial on the issue of liability or willingness to settle, it may be admissible on other issues, for example on the question of costs where delay or unreasonable refusal to settle may be material.[111] And because an agreement to compromise litigation is one made for good consideration and fully enforceable, without-prejudice correspondence is admissible to show that an agreement was reached and what the terms of such agreement were in any subsequent proceedings with reference to it.

The former RSC, Ord. 22, r. 14, first gave effect to the suggestion made by Cairns LJ in *Calderbank* v *Calderbank*[112] to the effect that in cases where a payment into court could not be made,[113] a letter might be written suggesting a settlement, and mentioning the possibility of its being shown to the judge on the issue of costs. Such letters became known in the Family Division of the High Court as '*Calderbank* letters'. The idea was so obviously sensible that it was endorsed as a proper and valuable procedure in other cases by Megarry V-C in *Computer Machinery Co. Ltd* v *Drescher* [1983] 1 WLR 1379, and by the Court of Appeal in *Cutts* v *Head* [1984] Ch 290. This procedure is now governed by Part 36 of the Civil Procedure Rules 1998.

There is no procedure akin to without prejudice communications in criminal cases. Thus, in *Hayes* [2004] 1 Cr App R 557, the accused's solicitors wrote a letter to the prosecution indicating that the accused was prepared to enter a plea of guilty to a lesser charge. The letter was consistent with the account given by the accused to the police when interviewed, but markedly inconsistent with the evidence he gave in his defence at trial. It was held that the trial judge had rightly allowed the prosecution to cross-examine the accused about the contents of the letter, so as to demonstrate his lack of credibility. It should be said, however, that the Court of Appeal's judgment focused exclusively on the issue of whether it had been unfair in the circumstances of the case to allow the cross-examination. In view of the fact that the accused had clearly changed his story, it seems fairly obvious that it was not. But it is to be regretted that the Court did not consider the policy underlying the without prejudice principle, on which the accused's counsel addressed them. There may be cases in which the policy dictates a different result, and it is submitted that

---

[109] [1951] P 21. The rule would also apply to communications made between the parties themselves for the same purpose; see *Theodoropoulas* v *Theodoropoulas* [1964] P 311. The suggestion in *Bostock* v *Bostock* [1950] P 154 that the rule does not apply to meetings between the parties and their solicitors can hardly be correct.

[110] *Nottingham Justices, ex parte Bostock* [1970] 1 WLR 1117. In the case of industrial conciliators, Parliament has provided for a statutory privilege in the Employment Tribunals Act 1996, s. 18(7).

[111] See, e.g., *Family Housing Association (Manchester) Ltd* v *Michael Hyde and Partners* [1993] 1 WLR 354. But not on an application for security for costs: *Simaan General Contracting Co.* v *Pilkington Glass Ltd* [1987] 1 All ER 345. These cases were decided under the former RSC, Ord. 22, r. 14, but there is no reason to doubt that the same principle applies under Part 36 of the Civil Procedure Rules 1998.

[112] [1976] Fam 93, 105–6; see also *McDonnell* v *McDonnell* [1977] 1 WLR 34, 38.

[113] As to the cases in which payment into court or offers may be made, and the effect of this procedure, see Part 36 of the Civil Procedure Rules 1998.

it would not be unreasonable to afford the parties some protection where good faith negotiations are conducted with a view to a plea of guilty. What would happen, for example, if the prosecution, having represented to the accused that a plea to a lesser charge was acceptable, changed its mind at the time of trial? It may be that the accused's position would be sufficiently protected by s. 78 of the Police and Criminal Evidence Act 1984 and the fair trial provision of art. 6 of the European Convention, but some further statement of principle would be welcome.

14.22 RECOMMENDED FURTHER READING

Dennis, I., 'Instrumental protection, human right or functional necessity? Reassessing the privilege against self-incrimination' (1995) **54**(2) *Cambridge Law Journal* 342.

Loughrey, J., 'Legal advice privilege and the corporate client' (2005) **9**(5) *International Journal of Evidence and Proof* 183.

Menlowe, M.A., 'Bentham, self-incrimination and the law of evidence' (1988) **104** *Law Quarterly Review* 286.

Redmayne, M., 'Rethinking the privilege against self-incrimination' (2007) **27**(2) *Oxford Journal of Legal Studies* 209.

Zuckerman, A.A.S., 'Legal professional privilege: the cost of absolutism' (1996) **112** *Law Quarterly Review* 535.

 ## 14.23 QUESTIONS FOR DISCUSSION BASED ON *R* v *COKE; LITTLETON* AND *BLACKSTONE* v *COKE* (for case files go to the Online Resource Centre)

14.23.1 *Coke; Littleton*

1. Assume that Coke's solicitors, on his instructions, send samples of his handwriting to a handwriting expert for comparison with Exhibit GG1; having obtained copies from the expert, may the prosecution adduce these samples at trial if Coke objects?

2. Would the position differ if these samples were seized by the police, acting under a valid search warrant, from the offices of Coke's solicitors?

3. Can Littleton assert privilege in the communications with his solicitor which resulted in the volunteering of a prepared statement and the refusal to answer questions in interview? Does the position change if he claims that the jury should not be permitted to draw an adverse inference against him because he relied on legal advice?

4. If Coke and Littleton testify in their defence at trial, may they assert the privilege against self-incrimination in cross-examination with respect to the offences charged against them?

14.23.2 *Blackstone* v *Coke*

May Coke assert any privilege to prevent Fr Wigmore from being compelled to testify about any confession Coke may have made to him?

14.24 GENERAL QUESTIONS FOR DISCUSSION

1. What two-stage test will a judge apply to determine whether the privilege against self-incrimination should be allowed?

2. Does privilege against self-incrimination extend to not being required to incriminate a spouse or 'civil partner'?

3. May an accused rely on the privilege against self-incrimination where a statute requires the production of documents?

4. Indecent images of children are found during the search of Brian's premises pursuant to an order made by a civil court. Will Brian's claim for privilege against self-incrimination prevent the images being handed over to the police?

5. What are the two types of legal professional privilege?

6. Where private communications between a solicitor and his client would reveal that the client had committed a criminal offence, those communications are not, in the public interest, protected by legal professional privilege. Is this correct?

7. Do communications with a priest enjoy a privileged status?

8. Are the following solicitors' letters privileged:

   (a) A letter to a client advising on the completion of the sale of a property?

   (b) A letter that provides financial advice about investing the sale proceeds?

   (c) A letter inviting the client to a corporate hospitality event run by the firm?

9. A law student on placement at a solicitors' firm takes a client's instructions. Will her notes on the solicitor's file be privileged?

10. Are communications between a solicitor and an expert witness always privileged?

11. A client sends her solicitor a parcel. It contains a letter of instructions wrapped around the knife that the client says she used to wound her husband. Are the contents of the parcel privileged?

12. A solicitor is instructed to write a letter marked 'without prejudice' to a creditor to the effect that if they do not withdraw proceedings their client will write to the newspapers about an extra-marital affair. Will the letter be admissible in evidence at a subsequent trial?

15

WITNESSES: COMPETENCE AND COMPELLABILITY; OATHS AND AFFIRMATIONS

A   COMPETENCE AND COMPELLABILITY

SUMMARY OF MAIN POINTS

- The general rule of English law is that all witnesses are both competent (able to give evidence) and compellable (liable to be required to give evidence subject to sanction for contempt).

- In criminal cases this rule is given statutory form by s. 53 of the Youth Justice and Criminal Evidence Act 1999. Section 53(3) provides that a witness is not competent if he is unable to understand questions put to him and give answers to them which can be understood.

- Children and persons under mental disability are subject to the above general rule of competence, but children under 14 must give evidence unsworn. A person over 14 must give evidence unsworn only if he lacks an appreciation of the solemnity of the occasion and the particular responsibility involved in taking an oath in court.

- The accused in a criminal case is not competent as a prosecution witness. He is competent, but not compellable, to give evidence in his own defence and may not be called except on his own application. If the accused fails to give evidence, an adverse inference may be drawn against him in certain circumstances.

- The spouse or civil partner of the accused is (1) competent and compellable as a witness for the accused; (2) competent but, except in the case of certain specified offences, not compellable for the prosecution or a co-accused.

15.1 GENERAL RULE

The most fundamental questions relating to witnesses are those of competence and compellability. These questions are not related to any particular evidence which a witness might give, or to any privilege to which he might be entitled. Rather they deal with the basic questions of whether a particular witness can be heard to give evidence at all (competence) and whether a witness has a legal obligation to give evidence if called upon to do so, which the court can enforce (compellability).[1] A witness is said to be competent if the court may lawfully receive his evidence, and compellable if the court may require him to give evidence over his objection. The proper time for making objections as to the competence of a witness is before the witness has begun to give evidence, unless his incompetence emerges for the first time at a later stage, in which case the objection should be made at that time.[2]

The general rule of English law has always been that all witnesses are both competent and compellable.[3] This is a rule of obvious convenience if it is assumed that the court is to be given access to as much relevant and admissible evidence as possible. But at common law, the general rule was subject to a number of exceptions whose scope in fact deprived the courts of a great deal of relevant and cogent evidence, and whose existence is perhaps the most striking example

---

[1] In appropriate cases, particularly where the witness is a party or has some interest in the outcome of the proceedings, a refusal to give evidence will lead to the drawing of adverse inferences against him. And see Criminal Procedure and Public Order Act 1994, s. 35 (see 15.6). This may be a more consequential sanction than being held in contempt of court, which is also likely; see Supreme Court Act 1981, s. 45(4); Magistrates' Courts Act 1980, s. 97(4).

[2] *Yacoob* (1981) 72 Cr App R 313; *Bartlett* v *Smith* (1843) 11 M & W 483; *Jacobs* v *Layborn* (1843) 11 M & W 685; *Whitehead* (1866) LR 1 CCR 33. The judge may and should keep the question of competence under review if it appears doubtful at first, and if necessary, should rule a witness to be incompetent as soon as it becomes clear that this is the case: see 15.3.

[3] It is sometimes said that there is 'no property in a witness', meaning that any party can call and compel any witness. The rule applies to all witnesses, including experts (*Harmony Shipping Co. SA* v *Saudi Europe Line Ltd* [1979] 1 WLR 1380; *King* [1983] 1 WLR 411; 11.3.1).

of the exclusionary nature of the common law rules of evidence. Fortunately, these exceptions now survive only in vestigial form, and it is necessary to consider them only to the extent necessary to understand the present law. The only cases which have continued to cause difficulty in modern times are those of the competence in criminal cases of the accused, the spouse of the accused, children of tender years, and persons suffering from mental disabilities. In the case of the accused's spouse, the issue of compellability has also proved elusive. These difficulties were the subject of a series of leading cases and statutory reforms, which gradually extended the competence of these witnesses and the compellability of the spouse of the accused. The statutory reforms were often tentative and, in the case of children, sometimes confusing. New and much simpler rules governing competence and compellability were introduced by ss. 53 to 57 of the Youth Justice and Criminal Evidence Act 1999. Section 53 declares that all persons are competent to give evidence in criminal proceedings, regardless of their age, provided that they can understand questions put to them as witnesses and give answers which can be understood. In cases of doubt, the court can resolve the issue, if necessary with the aid of expert evidence. A witness who is under the age of 14, or who lacks the appreciation of the solemnity of the occasion and of the particular responsibility of telling the truth involved in taking the oath, must give evidence unsworn, even if competent, though in the case of a competent witness over the age of 14, it is presumed that he has the necessary appreciation. The accused and his spouse or (by amendment) civil partner are competent on the same basis as any other witness. But the Act maintains the rule that the accused is not compellable to give evidence, and maintains (with certain exceptions) the rule that his spouse or civil partner is compellable only when called by the accused. This simplification of the law in a field which has no obvious need for complexity had been suggested by many commentators, including previous editions of this work, and is to be welcomed.

15.2 COMMON LAW EXCEPTIONS

The exceptions to the general rule of competence which grew up at common law were remarkable in their breadth and scope. The amount of relevant evidence they denied to the courts, which must have made many claims and defences literally impossible to prove, cannot be explained on any basis which seems rational today. They resulted from two fears, which as we saw earlier in this book (see 1.5.2) had a major influence on the development of the law of evidence as a whole. The first was the fear of manufactured evidence and perjury resulting from interest in the outcome of the case. This fear led to the wholesale rejection of the evidence of the parties and their spouses in all cases (though curiously not to the rejection of that of other relatives). A court would also refuse to hear the evidence of any witness who might have some specific ascertainable interest in the outcome of the case. The second fear was that of certain witnesses *per se*, based simply on personal characteristics which suggested that they could not take the oath (a cornerstone of competence at common law) or would not be likely to tell the truth even if they could take the oath. The doubt about the witness's belief in God and in the spiritual consequences of lying under oath was at least as significant in these cases as the concern about the actual likelihood of perjury or unreliable evidence. This fear led to the incompetence of children of tender years, persons subject to mental disability, those convicted of 'infamous crimes', and witnesses who were neither Christians nor Jews (who could not be sworn on either the Old or New Testaments).

Mercifully, subject to vestigial remainders, these incompetences are now long gone, whittled away and finally removed by statute during the nineteenth century. The competence of the accused, the spouse of the accused, children, and persons subject to mental disability are still governed by special rules, dealt with below. But these rules exist for reasons of practicality, and are not concerned with any general theory of self-interest or intent to exclude entire classes of evidence. The evidence of non-Christians was held to be competent as early as *Omychund v Barker* (1745) 1 Atk 21, as long as the witness held a belief in a 'Governor of the Universe', and even atheists were declared to be competent by the Evidence Further Amendment Act 1869, although the precise beliefs or absence of belief of the witness continued to be investigated long into modern times for the purpose of deciding on what book he should be sworn, or whether he was entitled to the (now automatic) right to affirm instead of being sworn. The incompetence of those convicted of infamous crimes was modified in 1828 to make the incompetence coextensive with their sentence only, and was abolished altogether by the Evidence Act 1843. The same Act abolished incompetence stemming only from interest in the outcome of the case. It is worth noting that the weight of the evidence of witnesses who have previous convictions, or who have an interest in the outcome of the case, may be attacked by cross-examination as to their credit (see Chapter 17, Part B) but this affects only the weight of their evidence.[4]

15.3 STATUTORY GENERAL RULE OF COMPETENCE IN CRIMINAL PROCEEDINGS

The common law rule of general competence has proved adequate for civil cases, now that the most extravagant exceptions have been abrogated. But in criminal cases, the position was complicated by the survival of a number of significant common law rules relating to the accused, the accused's spouse, and children of tender years, and later attempts to regulate these rules by statute. These rules will be dealt with in more detail below. The Youth Justice and Criminal Evidence Act 1999 lays down a general statutory rule of competence in criminal cases, together with special provisions for the accused and his spouse. These provisions are contained in ss. 53 to 57 of the Act itself, and new subsections inserted by the Act into the existing s. 80 of the Police and Criminal Evidence Act 1984. The 1999 Act also maintains the importance of the principle that evidence should in general be given under oath (or affirmation, see 15.15) but requires unsworn evidence to be given in the case of certain child witnesses and witnesses who are deemed to be incapable of taking the oath.

Section 53(1) of the Act provides:

> At every stage in criminal proceedings all persons are (whatever their age) competent to give evidence.

Under the corresponding provision of s. 1(a) of the Criminal Evidence Act 1898 (which is replaced by the 1999 Act) it was held that the expression, 'at every stage of the proceedings', meant that the accused is entitled to give evidence not only before the jury at trial, but at committal proceedings, on the *voir dire*, and in mitigation of sentence.[5] No doubt the same will apply

---

[4] Any attempted cross-examination of a witness as to credit based on religious belief or the absence thereof would undoubtedly be disallowed by a judge in modern times, now that a witness may affirm and his affirmation is enough to attract the penalty of perjury (see 15.15.2) and even if not disallowed, would be a forensic disaster. Some jurisdictions, sensibly, have a specific rule prohibiting it: see, e.g., American Rule of Evidence 610. Though in *Mehrban* [2002] 1 Cr App R 561, the Court of Appeal held that it was not improper, within reasonable bounds and subject to leave of the judge, to cross-examine a witness who would ordinarily be expected to be sworn on the Koran about his choice to affirm instead of being sworn—a distinct though obviously related subject.

[5] *Rhodes* [1899] 1 QB 77; *Wheeler* [1917] 1 KB 283; and see 15.5.2.

to the accused and any other witness under s. 53(1) of the 1999 Act. The position of the accused, who continues to be incompetent as a witness for the prosecution and non-compellable as a witness for the defence, is dealt with by s. 53(4) and by the new s. 80(4) of the Police and Criminal Evidence Act 1984. The position of the spouse of the accused is dealt with by the new s. 80(2) to (4) of the 1984 Act. These provisions are dealt with below.

Section 53(2) of the 1999 Act provides that the general rule of competence is subject to the test laid down by s. 53(3). The latter subsection provides:

> A person is not competent to give evidence in criminal proceedings if it appears to the court that he is not a person who is able to—
> (a) understand questions put to him as a witness, and
> (b) give answers to them which can be understood.

The words 'as a witness' in s. 53(3)(a) are important. They convey the sense that the person's ability must be to deal with questions put to him in court, which implies a degree of understanding sufficient to enable him to provide answers in basic English with the seriousness and detail necessary in court proceedings: see *McPherson* [2006] 1 Cr App R 459. There may be cases in which the competence of the witness in this respect is at first unclear. The judge should keep the question under review if it appears doubtful, for example in the case of a child or a person subject to mental disability, and if necessary, should rule the witness to be incompetent as soon as it becomes clear that this is the case. This may necessitate withdrawing the case from the jury if the evidence of the witness is crucial, or if the accused would be prejudiced and the conviction might be unsafe: *Powell* [2006] 1 Cr App R 31.

The procedure for determining whether or not a witness is competent is laid down by s. 54 of the Act. This section provides that the issue of competence may be raised by a party or by the court of its own motion (s. 54(1)).[6] The burden of proof lies on the party seeking to call the witness to satisfy the court on a balance of probabilities that the witness is competent to give evidence (s. 54(2)). In the case of a prosecution witness, the use of the civil standard of proof for this purpose changes the rule at common law, according to which the standard of proof required was that beyond reasonable doubt (*Yacoob* (1981) 72 Cr App R 313). The civil standard applied at common law to issues of the competence of defence witnesses (see further on this subject 4.14). The determination of the issue must take place in the absence of the jury (s. 54(4)). This, too, represents a change of the traditional common law rule, which generally permitted the jury to hear the proceedings (*Reynolds* [1950] 1 KB 606), though more recently the trend had been to exclude the jury, which is not technically concerned with issues of law such as competence. This was true especially in cases where psychiatric evidence had to be called on the issue of competence (*Deakin* [1994] 4 All ER 769) and in the case of child witnesses (*Hampshire* [1996] QB 1). Any questioning of the witness must be undertaken by the court in the presence of the parties (s. 54(6)).

15.3.1 Sworn and unsworn evidence

Even if it is determined that a witness is competent to give evidence, there may be a further question of whether the witness may give evidence under oath or should be permitted to give

---

[6] Section 54(3) provides that, in determining the question of competence, the court shall treat the witness as having the benefit of any protected witness direction which the court has given, or proposes to give, under s. 19 of the Act. As to protected witness directions, see 16.17.

evidence unsworn. The general rule is that all evidence should be given under oath, though there have always been limited exceptions (see 15.17).[7] The use of unsworn evidence to avoid issues surrounding problems of understanding was introduced in the case of children of tender years by s. 38(1) of the Children and Young Persons Act 1933, which provided that if a child called as a witness in criminal proceedings did not understand the nature of an oath, his evidence could be received unsworn, 'if, in the opinion of the court, he is possessed of sufficient intelligence to justify the reception of the evidence, and understands the duty of speaking the truth'. Before this provision came into effect, a child was held to be incompetent if he was unable to understand the nature of the oath, in addition to the importance of speaking the truth. Although s. 38(1) caused some problems with respect to the relationship of sworn and unsworn evidence given by children,[8] it represented a huge improvement of the common law rule of incompetence. A similar rule permitting unsworn evidence by children in civil cases was introduced by s. 96 of the Children Act 1989. Section 52 of the Criminal Justice Act 1991 repealed s. 38(1) of the 1933 Act, and provided that the evidence of witnesses under the age of 14 must be given unsworn. Section 55 of the Youth Justice and Criminal Evidence Act 1999 in turn repeals s. 52 of the 1991 Act, but continues the same rule, subject to a condition of having an appreciation of the solemnity of the occasion and the particular responsibility of telling the truth in sworn testimony. Section 55 also applies the same rule to witnesses over 14, who may give evidence unsworn if they do not have the necessary appreciation, though the witness is presumed to have the necessary appreciation if he is competent within the meaning of s. 53(3): see further 15.11.3.

Subsections (2), (3), and (8) of s. 55 are as follows:

> (2) The witness may not be sworn for [the purpose of giving evidence] unless—
>   (a) he has attained the age of 14, and
>   (b) he has a sufficient appreciation of the solemnity of the occasion and of the particular responsibility to tell the truth which is involved in taking an oath.
> (3) The witness shall, if he is able to give intelligible testimony, be presumed to have a sufficient appreciation of those matters if no evidence tending to show the contrary is adduced (by any party).
> (8) For the purposes of this section a person is able to give intelligible testimony if he is able to—
>   (a) understand questions put to him as a witness, and
>   (b) give answers to them which can be understood.

The remaining subsections of s. 55 make provision for the determination of the question of whether or not a witness should give evidence under oath in the same manner as the determination of competence under s. 53. The hearing is to be conducted in the absence of the jury (s. 55(5)) with expert evidence if necessary (s. 55(6)) and any questioning of the witness is to be done by the court in the presence of the parties (s. 55(7)). The one difference is the issue of the burden of proof. Because of the presumption that a competent witness also possesses the appreciation necessary to take the oath, the burden of proof rests on the party calling the witness only if evidence is adduced by any party tending to show that the witness should not take the oath (s. 55(4)). As under s. 53, the standard of proof in such a case is the balance of probabilities.

---

[7] References to an oath include an affirmation, which the witness is entitled to make if he objects to taking an oath (Oaths Act 1978, s. 5; 15.15.2).

[8] These problems related mainly to complications deriving from the requirements of corroboration, which no longer exist. See generally Chapter 18, and the 1st edn of this work, para. 12.8.

Subsections (2) and (4) of s. 56 provide that the evidence of a competent witness who does not have the appreciation required by s. 55 shall be given and received by the court unsworn.[9] Section 56(5) provides that a conviction shall not be taken to be unsafe for the purposes of an appeal merely because it appears to the Court of Appeal that the trial judge may have been wrong in permitting the witness to give evidence unsworn. Section 57 creates an offence akin to perjury of wilfully giving false unsworn evidence.[10]

The weight of unsworn evidence, given the circumstances which must be found to exist before it is permitted, will in general be less than that of sworn evidence, though not as much so as is often assumed.[11] It is perhaps regrettable that the Act does not call for any direction to be given to the jury about it, and it is submitted that, even if he does not comment on the question of weight, the trial judge should at least explain to the jury the basis on which the witness has given unsworn evidence. It is not necessary to resurrect formal corroboration warnings, which have been abolished generally and with particular reference to children (see 18.3.3) and modern authority tends to the view that there is no need to treat the evidence of children with undue suspicion.[12] But given that there must have been a finding that the witness (whether child or adult) lacks an appreciation of the solemnity of the occasion or of the responsibility involved in taking an oath, some comment by the judge may well be found to be appropriate.

15.4 PARTIES TO THE PROCEEDINGS GENERALLY

The abolition of incompetence through interest in 1843 paved the way for abolishing the incompetence of the parties themselves. In civil proceedings, the abolition was effected by the Evidence Act 1851, with the exception of proceedings instituted in consequence of adultery and actions for breach of promise of marriage, in which cases the incompetence survived until the Evidence Further Amendment Act 1869. The result of the abolition was that the parties became competent witnesses in every case, and, following the general rule, compellable. This is the position in the present law, and it has the logical consequence that a party to civil proceedings may both give evidence himself and, if he thinks it wise, subpoena any other party to give evidence also.

The position of the accused in criminal cases was complicated by a variety of historical considerations. Although it was, on the face of it, desirable that he should be competent in the same way as a party to civil proceedings, the consequence of his being thereby rendered compellable gave rise to much heart-searching. Dark references abounded in the nineteenth century to the inquisitorial practices of Star Chamber and the evil of the accused being compelled to provide evidence against himself by being forced into the witness-box. In the United States, the Fifth Amendment to the Federal Constitution, itself inspired by the same historical considerations, offered the accused the right not to incriminate himself, a right which necessarily included the right not to be compelled to give evidence at his trial. There were also technical problems of reconciling the

---

[9] Including evidence in the form of a deposition when otherwise permitted (s. 56(3)).

[10] As did s. 38(2) of the Children and Young Persons Act 1933, which survived the Criminal Justice Act 1991, but which was repealed by the 1999 Act. The offence created by s. 57 is summary and carries a maximum penalty, in the case of an adult, of imprisonment not exceeding six months and a fine not exceeding £1,000. This almost nominal sanction is hardly satisfactory and is anomalous when compared to those available for perjury (see sentencing guidelines, *Blackstone's Criminal Practice*, 2009 edn, para. B14.4).

[11] As to the divergence between the likely public view of the oath, contrasted with the perhaps undue emphasis placed on it even today by the law, see the observations of the Court of Appeal in *Hayes* [1977] 1 WLR 234, 236–7; 15.11.1.

[12] See, e.g., *Z* [1990] 2 QB 355, per Lord Lane CJ.

idea of a compellable accused with the burden and standard of proof in criminal cases. In the end, the matter was resolved by compromise, in a series of statutory provisions culminating in the Criminal Evidence Act 1898. The compromise was, in essence, that the accused was rendered competent only for the defence, and was expressly made non-compellable.[13] This unique deviation from the traditional rules rendered necessary a series of supplementary provisions dealing with evidence given by the accused.

One of these was originally the rule enacted by s. 1(b) that the prosecution might not comment on the failure of the accused to give evidence. This rule has now been abolished by the Criminal Justice and Public Order Act 1994, because s. 35 of the Act permits inferences to be drawn against the accused because of that failure in certain circumstances.[14] This is dealt with at 15.6. The Act also provided that, if the accused elected to give evidence, although he could be asked any question tending to criminate him or any co-accused in the offence charged, he could not be cross-examined about his character or about any offences not charged, except in the limited circumstances prescribed by the Act.[15] The accused is, unless otherwise ordered, to give his evidence from the witness-box.[16] This provision reflects the fact that if the accused elects to give evidence, his evidence is evidence in the case for all purposes, even if it has the effect of incriminating him or a co-accused,[17] and he is to be regarded in the same way as any other witness called for the prosecution or the defence. The accused must give evidence on oath in the same way as other witnesses. His common law right to make an unsworn statement from the dock was abolished by s. 72 of the Criminal Justice Act 1982: see 15.17.

15.5 THE ACCUSED IN A CRIMINAL CASE

15.5.1 For the prosecution

The accused was first rendered competent as a witness by s. 1 of the Criminal Evidence Act 1898. The part of this section which had this effect was repealed by the Youth Justice and Criminal Evidence Act 1999, because it is otiose in the light of the general statutory rule of competence enacted by s. 53 of that Act. The accused is now a competent witness at every stage of criminal proceedings by virtue of s. 53. However, the Criminal Evidence Act 1898 left untouched a common law rule that the accused is not competent as a witness for the prosecution, and any

---

[13] Criminal Evidence Act 1898, s. 1 and proviso (a). The rule applies to all criminal cases, with the unimportant exception, under the Evidence Act 1877, of prosecutions for public nuisance in which the accused is both competent and compellable.

[14] Section 1(b) did not prevent comment on this subject by the judge, or by a co-accused, although it was held that such comments should be made in a balanced way, and without suggesting that the accused's failure to testify meant that he was guilty. See generally *Rhodes* [1899] 1 QB 77; *Mutch* [1973] 1 All ER 178; *Sparrow* [1973] 1 WLR 488, *Martinez-Tobon* [1994] 1 WLR 388; *Bathurst* [1968] 2 QB 99, 107.

[15] Criminal Evidence Act 1898, s. 1, provisos (2) and (3). These provisions are repealed and replaced by the Criminal Justice Act 2003: see 6.1. If the accused elects to give evidence, then his evidence is evidence for all purposes in the case, including being evidence against co-accused. He will be treated in the same way as any other witness, subject to the other provisions of s. 1 (*Hilton* [1972] 1 QB 421; *Rudd* (1948) 32 Cr App R 138).

[16] Criminal Evidence Act 1898, s. 1(4). This rule need not be followed if the accused is too infirm, or proves to be too violent, unruly or disruptive, to go into the witness-box. But subject to this, he must be permitted to do so, or the appearance of injustice may require the conviction to be quashed (see *Farnham Justices, ex parte Gibson* [1991] RTR 309).

[17] Criminal Evidence Act 1898, s. 1(2), which now applies subject to the bad character provisions of the Criminal Justice Act 2003 (see Part 5 of Sch. 36 to the 2003 Act); *Rudd* (1948) 32 Cr App R 138.

violation of this rule must result in a conviction obtained thereby being reversed.[18] This rule is specifically preserved by s. 53(4) and (5) of the Youth Justice and Criminal Evidence Act 1999, as follows:

> (4) A person charged in criminal proceedings is not competent to give evidence in the proceedings for the prosecution (whether he is the only person, or is one of two or more persons, charged in the proceedings).
>
> (5) In subsection (4) the reference to a person charged in criminal proceedings does not include a person who is not, or is no longer, liable to be convicted of any offence in the proceedings (whether as a result of pleading guilty or for any other reason).

It follows that if the prosecution wish to call a person charged in the proceedings who has neither been acquitted of nor pleaded guilty to all the charges against him, they must first either offer no evidence against him (or enter a *nolle prosequi*) or accept his pleas of guilty to some of the charges and elect not to proceed on the others. In all these cases, the former accused is no longer a person charged in the proceedings, and becomes both competent and compellable for the prosecution.[19] It is, of course, not unusual for an accused person to 'turn Queen's evidence' in this way. Though he becomes a competent prosecution witness, the credibility of his evidence may not be very great, as it will usually have been offered in return for the hope of leniency.[20]

15.5.2 For the defence

As we have seen, the accused is competent as a defence witness at every stage of the proceedings by virtue of s. 53 of the Youth Justice and Criminal Evidence Act 1999, as he was under s. 1 of the Criminal Evidence Act 1898. If he elects to give evidence, the accused's evidence must be treated by the jury in the same way as any other evidence in the case. He must, if competent to do so give evidence under oath;[21] he may be cross-examined to show his own guilt and that of any other accused, subject only to the rules of the Criminal Justice Act 2003 as to bad character.[22] For this reason, although it is theoretically possible for an accused to be called voluntarily by a co-accused, having declined to give evidence on his own behalf, it is hard to imagine a situation in which this would occur.

The provision making the accused competent 'at every stage of the proceedings' was held under the Criminal Evidence Act 1898 to include the right to give evidence, not only before the jury at trial, but also at committal proceedings,[23] on the *voir dire*, and during the course of mitigation of sentence. In *Wheeler* [1917] 1 KB 283, it was argued that the accused was not liable to be convicted of perjury in respect of evidence he had given during mitigation, because a conviction for perjury was possible only where the accused had been 'lawfully sworn', and that as the issue

---

[18] *Grant* [1944] 2 All ER 311; though such a violation did not necessarily invalidate committal proceedings (*Sharrock* [1948] 1 All ER 145), *sed quaere*; *Palmer* (1993) 99 Cr App R 83; *Gooderson* (1952) 11 CLJ 209.

[19] *Boal* [1965] 1 QB 402, 411. As to the unsatisfactory position where the trial of one accused is postponed, see *Richardson* (1967) 51 Cr App R 381.

[20] As to the practice on the timing of sentencing such persons so as to lessen the damage to their credibility, see generally *Blackstone's Criminal Practice*, 2009 edn, para. D12.71; *Payne* [1950] 1 All ER 102; *Weekes* (1980) 74 Cr App R 161; *Chan Wai-Keung* [1995] 1 WLR 251; *Coffey* (1976) 74 Cr App R 168. The witness's previous convictions must be disclosed to the jury by the prosecution at the outset of his evidence (*Taylor* [1999] 2 Cr App R 163).

[21] Criminal Justice Act 1982, s. 72, as amended; Youth Justice and Criminal Evidence Act 1999, s. 55; 15.3.1.

[22] Criminal Evidence Act 1898, s. 1(2) as amended; *Paul* [1920] 2 KB 183; *Rudd* (1948) 32 Cr App R 138; *Hilton* [1972] 1 QB 421; *Rowland* [1910] 1 KB 458.

[23] *Rhodes* [1899] 1 QB 77.

of guilt had been determined, the accused had ceased to be a competent witness. The argument failed. Mitigation of sentence is a stage of the proceedings, and the accused is competent to give evidence at that stage. There is no reason to believe that this position is any different under s. 53 of the Youth Justice and Criminal Evidence Act 1999.

Even though competent as a defence witness, the accused is never compellable.

The following part of s. 1 of the Criminal Evidence Act 1898 remains in force, as amended:

> (1) A person charged in criminal proceedings shall not be called as a witness in the proceedings except upon his own application.

This is reinforced by the new s. 80(4) of the Criminal Evidence Act 1984 (as amended) which provides that even though the spouse or civil partner of the accused may be a compellable witness in certain circumstances, that is never the case if the spouse or partner is also charged in the proceedings. The right of the accused not to give evidence is, therefore, absolute.[24]

15.6 INFERENCES FROM ACCUSED'S FAILURE TO GIVE EVIDENCE

Although the accused is not a compellable witness, it has long been recognized that his right not to give evidence is effectively meaningless if inferences adverse to him can be drawn from his exercise of that right. It was for that reason that s. 1(b) of the Criminal Evidence Act 1898 provided that the prosecution should not be permitted to comment on the accused's failure to give evidence. However, s. 35 of the Criminal Justice and Public Order Act 1994 repealed s. 1(b). Section 35 does not alter the rule that the accused is competent but not compellable (which is specifically preserved by s. 35(4)), but provides that, in certain circumstances, the accused may be called on to testify, and that adverse inferences may be drawn against him if he fails to do so, or refuses to answer a particular question put to him.

Section 35 (as amended) provides:

> (1) At the trial of any person for an offence, subsections (2) and (3) below apply unless—
> (a) the accused's guilt is not in issue; or
> (b) it appears to the court that the physical or mental condition of the accused makes it undesirable for him to give evidence;
> but subsection (2) below does not apply if, at the conclusion of the evidence for the prosecution, his legal representative informs the court that the accused will give evidence or, where he is unrepresented, the court ascertains from him that he will give evidence.
> (2) Where this subsection applies, the court shall, at the conclusion of the evidence for the prosecution, satisfy itself (in the case of proceedings on indictment with a jury, in the presence of the jury) that the accused is aware that the stage has been reached at which evidence can be given for the defence and that he can, if he wishes, give evidence and that, if he chooses not to give evidence, or having been sworn, without good cause refuses to answer any question, it will be permissible for the court or jury to draw such inferences as appear proper from his failure to give evidence or his refusal, without good cause, to answer any question.
> (3) Where this subsection applies, the court or jury, in determining whether the accused is guilty of the offence charged, may draw such inferences as appear proper from the failure of the accused to give evidence or his refusal, without good cause, to answer any question.

---

[24] Though failure to do so carries the risk of an adverse inference under s. 35 of the Criminal Procedure and Public Order Act 1994 (15.6).

(4) This section does not render the accused compellable to give evidence on his own behalf, and he shall accordingly not be guilty of contempt of court by reason of a failure to do so.

(5) For the purposes of this section a person who, having been sworn, refuses to answer any question shall be taken to do so without good cause unless—

    (a) he is entitled to refuse to answer the question by virtue of any enactment, whenever passed or made, or on the ground of privilege; or

    (b) the court in the exercise of its general discretion excuses him from answering it.[25]

The provisions of s. 35 do not in themselves violate the fair trial provisions of art. 6 of the European Convention on Human Rights (see 1.7). The accused has the right to contest the propriety of the drawing of an adverse inference in adversarial proceedings, which satisfies the minimum procedural standards required by art. 6 as interpreted in the jurisprudence of the European Court of Human Rights. But the jury must be directed in accordance with the principles laid down by the Court of Appeal in *Cowan* [1996] QB 373 (set out at 15.6.4). It is submitted that this follows from the decision of the European Court in *Condron v United Kingdom*.[26] Of particular importance is the principle that the jury must be directed that they should draw an adverse inference against the accused only if they conclude that the accused's failure to give evidence can be sensibly attributed only to his having no answer, or no answer likely to stand up to cross-examination, to the case against him. If the trial judge permits the drawing of an adverse inference when it is not proper to do so, or fails to direct the jury clearly on that subject, it may well be that a violation of art. 6 occurs.

15.6.1 Accused being called on to give evidence

By virtue of s. 35(1) and (2) of the Criminal Justice and Public Order Act 1994, unless the accused or his legal adviser informs the court that he intends to give evidence, the court must, at the close of the prosecution case, ensure that the accused is informed of his right to give evidence, and of the possible consequences of his failure to do so, or to answer a particular question put to him. In a trial on indictment, this must be done in the presence of the jury, as this may affect the weight which the jury may attach to the accused's failure to testify. In *Cowan* [1996] QB 373, one ground of appeal was that the form of words prescribed for the judge to make the inquiry called for by s. 35(2) violated the accused's legal professional privilege by requiring the divulging of confidential information.[27] Rejecting this ground of appeal, Lord Taylor of Gosforth CJ said ([1996] QB 373):

    Section 35(2), as already observed, places a mandatory requirement on the court to satisfy itself (in the case of proceedings on indictment, in the presence of the jury) of the matters set out there. The only

---

[25] Section 6 of the Domestic Violence Crime and Victims Act 2004 provides a specific application of s. 35 to cases under s. 5 of that Act: for details, see *Blackstone's Criminal Practice*, 2009 edn, paras B1.59, F19.20.

[26] [2000] Crim LR 679; see also *Beckles v United Kingdom* (2003) 36 EHRR 13; as to the principles established by these cases; these matters are discussed in detail at 10.5.1.

[27] According to the judgment of the court, delivered by Lord Taylor of Gosforth CJ, this ground of appeal was not developed in argument by counsel. It is superficially plausible. But the judge may not inquire into the reasons for the accused's decision to give or not to give evidence, and while the question may violate the privilege in a technical sense, it can do no real harm. Indeed, if the judge were to receive the answer 'No', he might well have a duty to ensure that the accused was being properly represented. The form of words prescribed (now to be found in the *Consolidated Criminal Practice Direction*, para. IV, 44.3) is: 'Have you advised your client that the stage is now being reached at which he may give evidence, and, if he chooses not to do so, or, having been sworn, without good cause refuses to answer any question, the jury may draw such inferences as appear proper from his failure to do so?' (*ibid.* at para. 3).

way the court can do that is to ask either the defendant or his counsel. To bypass counsel and address the defendant directly in the presence of the jury would, we apprehend, give the appearance of greater pressure on the defendant and a more inquisitorial role for the judge than simply to inquire of counsel whether the statutory position has been explained to his client. The subject matter of the inquiry does not concern anything confidential.

15.6.2 Condition of accused making it undesirable for him to give evidence

The meaning of s. 35(1)(b) of the Criminal Justice and Public Order Act 1994 was considered by the Court of Appeal in *Friend* [1997] 1 WLR 1433. The accused, who was 15 years of age, was charged with murder. The judge accepted psychological evidence that he had a mental age of about 9 and that his comprehension and powers of expression were limited, but declined to rule that the accused's mental condition made it undesirable for him to give evidence for the purposes of s. 35(1)(b), in which case it would have been improper for the jury to draw an adverse inference against him. The accused did not give evidence, and was convicted. As s. 35 then stood, it applied only to accused persons over 14 years of age.[28] It was argued on appeal that, as the accused's mental age was below the age of 14, the judge should have refused to allow an adverse inference to be drawn. The Court held that the age of 14 referred to the actual age of the person accused, not his mental age, and that accordingly he was not immune from the operation of s. 35. Although the exact point decided in *Friend* would no longer be arguable in the light of the amendment to s. 35(1), it remains of interest that the Court could find no reason to hold that it might be undesirable for the accused to give evidence (a separate point which does not depend on the amendment). Otton LJ said (*ibid.* at 1441–3):

> In the present case the issue was never raised as to whether he was unfit to plead. It can thus be safely inferred that those representing him at least felt that he crossed the threshold of fitness in that he was of sufficient intellect to comprehend the course of proceedings on the trial, so as to make a proper defence and to know that he might challenge jurors and comprehend the details of the evidence...
>
> The language of this part of the section is simple and clear. It is for the judge in a given case to determine whether or not it is undesirable for the defendant to give evidence. A physical condition might include a risk of an epileptic attack; a mental condition, latent schizophrenia where the experience of giving evidence might trigger a florid state. If it appears to the judge on the *voir dire* that such a physical or mental condition of the defendant makes it undesirable for him to give evidence he will so rule.

It is to be hoped that the courts will not equate the extreme conditions necessary to make an accused unfit to plead with the issue of whether his condition makes it undesirable for him to give evidence. The willingness to consider other conditions is welcome. It is submitted that there must be some cases in which an accused with a low mental age, or some other condition, cannot fairly be expected to give evidence, even if he does understand enough to enable him to understand the nature of the proceedings and the charge against him.

In *Anwoir* [2008] 4 All ER 582, the trial judge, having originally ruled that the accused's medical condition made it undesirable for him to give evidence, considered the matter afresh and reversed his ruling. He thereafter permitted the jury to draw an adverse inference against the accused because of his failure to give evidence. The defence applied to put before the jury the accused's medical records dealing with his condition, as relevant to the question of whether an adverse inference should be drawn against him, but the judge refused to permit this. The Court of Appeal held that the judge's rulings had been unfair and the accused's appeal was allowed.

---

[28] A restriction subsequently removed by s. 35 of the Crime and Disorder Act 1998.

In principle, there was no objection to the judge reconsidering the question of whether the accused's condition made it undesirable for him to give evidence, but such reconsideration must be based on sound reasons, and the defence must be permitted to adduce relevant evidence dealing with the question of whether an inference should be drawn if the accused decided not to give evidence.

15.6.3 Inferences which may be drawn

Section 35(3) of the Criminal Justice and Public Order Act 1994 permits the court or jury, in determining the issue of guilt, to draw 'such inferences as appear proper' from the accused's failure to testify or to answer a particular question 'without good cause'. Section 35(5) provides that the accused's refusal to answer a question is to be taken to have been 'without good cause', unless either he is entitled not to answer by virtue of any statutory right or privilege, or he is excused by the judge in the exercise of his discretion. This protects the accused from having to answer, for example, a question which would violate legal professional privilege, or which the judge regards as unfair. It is submitted that, if the accused is wrongly called on to answer such a question, and an adverse inference is thereafter drawn against him because of his refusal to do so, any resulting conviction would have to be quashed.

Section 38(5) expressly preserves the operation of statutory provisions which restrict the admissibility of evidence or answers given by the accused.[29] Section 38(6) expressly preserves the power of the judge to exercise his general discretion to exclude evidence, under s. 78 of the Police and Criminal Evidence Act 1984.[30] Section 38(3) provides that a conviction, transfer for trial, or finding that the accused has a case to answer may not be based solely on an inference drawn under s. 35.[31] In relation to inferences drawn under s. 35, this provision is of some interest, because a submission of no case to answer at trial is made at the close of the prosecution case, and a question arises whether, before deciding whether or not to leave the case to the jury, the judge is entitled to insist on knowing whether the accused intends to give evidence. The use of the word 'solely' suggests that the judge may take the accused's decision into account, but that, if the case is otherwise insufficient, he must disregard it. If the case is left to the jury, the judge must also direct them that any inference drawn under s. 35 is insufficient to warrant a conviction in and of itself, though it must be weighed together with the other evidence against the accused.

15.6.4 Approach of court to s. 35

In *Cowan* [1996] QB 373, the Court of Appeal considered three separate appeals against conviction (*Cowan*, *Gayle*, and *Ricciardi*), based on what the appellants claimed were misdirections and failures to direct in accordance with the law under s. 35. The Court of Appeal laid down important principles governing the way in which judges should deal with such cases. These principles correspond with the Judicial Studies Board's specimen jury direction for s. 35 cases, which the court approved.[32] They may be summarized as follows:

---

[29] See 14.7.

[30] See 3.7 *et seq.*

[31] These general provisions of s. 38 also apply to inferences drawn under ss. 34, 36, and 37 of the Act: see 10.5.2.

[32] The Court of Appeal pointed out, in fairness to the trial judges concerned, that in the case of the two appellants whose appeals were allowed, the trials took place before the specimen direction was available. As we have seen (15.6) it must now be considered mandatory for the judge to direct the jury in accordance with these principles in the light of art. 6 of the European Convention on Human Rights.

(a) The jury must receive a proper direction on the burden and standard of proof, i.e., the prosecution must prove the guilt of the accused so that the jury feel sure of guilt.

(b) The judge must make it clear that the accused continues to be entitled not to give evidence.

(c) The judge must explain that, pursuant to s. 38(3) of the Act, the accused's failure to give evidence cannot be sufficient in itself to prove his guilt.

(d) The judge must make it clear that the jury must be satisfied that the prosecution have established a case to answer, based on the prosecution's evidence, before any inference against the accused may be drawn from the accused's failure to give evidence.

(e) If the jury conclude, having regard to any explanation advanced to explain the accused's silence or the absence of explanation, that the accused's silence can only sensibly be attributed to the accused's having no answer to the case against him, or no answer likely to stand up to cross-examination, they may draw an adverse inference against him.

In the case of *Cowan*, the judge failed to tell the jury that they could not infer guilt solely from silence, and, in a case involving significant conflicts of evidence, failed to direct them that the condition for drawing an inference was that stated in the fifth principle. In the case of *Gayle*, the judge failed to tell the jury that the accused had the right not to give evidence, a failure compounded by a passage in which he appeared to imply that the right of silence no longer existed. The judge also failed to direct the jury in accordance with the fifth principle. Accordingly, these two appeals were allowed. In the case of *Ricciardi*, the judge directed the jury in accordance with the specimen direction, and the above principles, and the appeal was accordingly dismissed.

Some comment is called for on the fourth principle. Lord Taylor CJ's formulation of the fourth principle was as follows. The word 'therefore' seems to relate back to the third principle, with which his lordship had just dealt.

> Therefore, the jury must be satisfied that the prosecution have established a case to answer before drawing any inferences from silence. Of course, the judge must have thought so or the question whether the defendant was to give evidence would not have arisen. But the jury may not believe the witnesses whose evidence the judge considered sufficient to raise a *prima facie* case. It must therefore be made clear to them that they must find there to be a case to answer on the prosecution evidence before drawing an adverse inference from the defendant's silence.

This formulation is evidently based on the wording of the following passage from the specimen direction (emphasis added):

> What proper inferences can you draw from the defendant's decision not to give evidence before you? *If you conclude that there is a case for him to answer,* you may think that the defendant would have gone into the witness box to give you an explanation for or an answer to the case against him. If the only sensible explanation for his decision not to give evidence is that he has no answer to the case against him, or none that could have stood up to cross-examination, then it would be open to you to hold against him his failure to give evidence. It is for you to decide whether it is fair to do so.

It is submitted that, for several reasons, it is highly undesirable for the jury to be asked to consider whether there is a case to answer. Firstly, the third principle does not require the jury to find that there is a *prima facie* case. It merely requires them to look for some other evidence which they accept (a quasi-corroborative principle) before concluding that they are sure of guilt. Secondly, whether or not there is a *prima facie* case is a question of mixed law and fact, which, accordingly, is a matter for the judge. It is not appropriate to ask a jury to make a decision which is partially one of law. As Lord Taylor himself points out, if there is not a *prima facie* case, the judge should withdraw the case from the jury, and no question will arise of the accused giving evidence. Thirdly, the question of whether or not there is a *prima facie* case is entirely distinct from the question whether or not the jury believe the prosecution's witnesses. The jury's view of the credibility of the witnesses obviously affects their verdict, but it does not affect the existence of a *prima facie* case, which is based on the proposition that there is evidence which, *if believed*, would justify a conviction. Fourthly, it is by no means always an easy task to decide whether there is a case to answer. Given the difficulties which sometimes attend even the usual direction about the burden of proof on the issue of guilt, it seems to be inviting unnecessary problems to invite a jury to undertake this more difficult exercise. In summary, this seems an unfortunate idea, which, when applied to this or any other evidential situation, must make the task of the jury more difficult, and blur the boundaries between questions of law and fact. Nothing in s. 35 requires such a direction, and a simple direction to look for some other credible evidence, in accordance with the third principle, would surely suffice. If the jury must find that there is a *prima facie* case, why should they not be directed so to find as a matter of law? To do so would still leave them free to evaluate the evidence, including any inference they might draw.

15.7 THE SPOUSE (OR CIVIL PARTNER) OF THE ACCUSED

In the discussion that follows, it should be noted that by virtue of s. 84(1) of the Civil Partnership Act 2004 the statutory provisions relating to the competence and compellability of the spouse of the accused under s. 80 of the Police and Criminal Evidence Act 1984 (as amended) now apply to a civil partner of the accused as they do to a spouse. We have seen that in civil cases, the spouses of parties have long been both competent and compellable. But as with the parties themselves, very different considerations prevailed in criminal cases. The position at common law was far from satisfactory. On the one hand, there had always been felt a sense of natural repugnance at the thought of spouses giving evidence against each other[33] and of apprehension at the obvious dangers of perjured and exaggerated evidence. Coupled with these factors was the compelling influence of the legal fiction that husband and wife were one person in law, a fiction which died only with reluctance towards the end of the nineteenth century.[34] But on the other hand, despite these powerful inducements to incompetence, it had been recognized as early as the seventeenth century, that the enforcement of the law demanded some degree of deviation from the strict rule. The precise limits of the deviation were never certain. However, as we shall see, it came to be recognized that an accused's spouse might be a competent witness for the prosecution in some instances.

Two preliminary points should be made. The first is that in *Pitt* [1983] QB 25, a case decided before the coming into effect of the Police and Criminal Evidence Act 1984, it was held that where a wife was a competent, but not compellable witness for the prosecution against her husband, the choice open to the wife to testify or not to testify existed up to the moment she entered the witness-box, and was unaffected by the fact that she might previously have made a witness statement, or even given evidence at the committal proceedings. Once she is sworn, of course,

---

[33] Such feeling of repugnance as has manifested itself in recent times has been directed generally to the idea of compelling spouses, rather than rendering them competent. But even as to this, repugnance has largely receded. See, e.g., the powerful dissenting speech of Lord Edmund Davies in *Hoskyn* v *Commissioner of Police of the Metropolis* [1979] AC 474, 501; Police and Criminal Evidence Act 1984, s. 80; 15.8.

[34] '...it hath been resolved by the justices, that a wife cannot be produced either against or for her husband, *quia sunt duae animae in carne una*; and it might be a cause of implacable discord and dissention between the husband and the wife, and a means of great inconvenience', Co Litt 6b.

she becomes an ordinary witness and must answer any proper questions put to her on behalf of any party, and may be treated as a hostile witness if appropriate.

The second is that by virtue of s. 80A of the Police and Criminal Evidence Act 1984, the failure of the spouse of the accused to give evidence shall not be made the subject of any comment by the prosecution. This prohibition affects only the prosecution, and does not restrict comment by a co-accused, or, within proper and reasonable bounds, by the judge. And, in the light of the inferences which may now be drawn from the accused's failure to testify (see 15.6), it now appears rather anomalous.[35]

15.7.1 Meaning of 'spouse'

In English law, the term 'spouse', for the purpose of the rules governing the competence and compellability of the accused's spouse, means a person who is lawfully married to the accused at the time when he or she is called to give evidence.[36] A person is regarded as lawfully married only if the marriage is one recognized as valid under English law. Thus, the definition excludes persons whose marriage is void (but not voidable) in law; those married pursuant to foreign law in circumstances in which the marriage is not recognized under English law; those in relationships other than legal marriage such as common law marriages, cohabitation, or other informal relationships, even if permanent or of long duration; and homosexual relationships between men or women. In *Khan*,[37] a woman married to an accused who had another living wife, whom he had married in a potentially polygamous Muslim ceremony, was held not to be the accused's spouse for the purpose of the rules of competence and compellability. The case was decided on the basis of the law in effect before the Police and Criminal Evidence Act 1980, which introduced statutory rules on the subject, but there is no reason to doubt that it also represented the law under that Act and now represents the law under the amendments made by the Youth Justice and Criminal Evidence Act 1999.

In *Pearce* [2002] 1 WLR 1553, an unsuccessful attempt was made to argue that the right to respect for private and family life enshrined in art. 8(1) of the European Convention on Human Rights required English law to regard a common law wife as a non-compellable witness. The argument was based on the principles laid down by the European Court of Human Rights in *X, Y and Z v United Kingdom*,[38] in which it was held that the right recognized by art. 8(1) is not confined to relationships based on legal marriage, and that a court is entitled to consider the right as it applies to other relationships, taking into account factors such as the duration and apparent level of commitment of the relationship, the existence of children of the relationship, and any other attributes which might reasonably indicate its familial nature. In *Pearce* it was argued, plausibly it is submitted, that the same policy considerations apply in cases of familial relationships outside marriage as apply to those based on marriage, and that any legal distinction must violate art. 8(1). But the Court of Appeal disagreed, preferring to hold that, given that restrictions on compellability have the effect of depriving the court of relevant and potentially cogent evidence, a State Party was entitled to confine such restrictions to cases of legal marriage as defined by its own law.

---

[35] A violation of this rule will no longer lead to automatic reversal on appeal (*Whitton* [1998] Crim LR 492; see also *Naudeer* [1984] 3 All ER 1036). Section 80A replaces s. 80(8), as originally enacted, and s. 80(8) replaced s. 1(b) of the Criminal Evidence Act 1898.

[36] As to the position of former spouses of the accused, i.e., persons who are no longer married to the accused when called to give evidence, see 15.10.

[37] (1986) 84 Cr App R 44; and see Private International Law (Miscellaneous Provisions) Act 1995, ss. 5 to 8.

[38] (1997) 24 EHRR 143; and see *Fitzpatrick v Sterling Housing Association Ltd* [2001] 1 AC 27.

This was, in the opinion of the Court, 'in accordance with the law and necessary in a democratic society' for a purpose such as the prevention of crime, within the meaning of art. 8(2) of the Convention. No doubt the same rule would apply in cases of other non-marital relationships. The effect of this rule has been mitigated to some extent by s. 84(1) of the Civil Partnership Act 2004 which, as already noted, applies the provisions of s. 80 of the Police and Criminal Evidence Act 1984 (as amended) to civil partners under the Act. It is certainly arguable, however, that the law on this subject to a considerable extent lags behind the prevailing societal attitudes to familial relationships, and it is to be hoped that it may be reconsidered in due course.

15.8 COMPETENCE AND COMPELLABILITY OF SPOUSE AT COMMON LAW

It is helpful to an understanding of the provisions of the newer statutory rules to consider briefly the state of the law which preceded them. At common law, the spouse of the accused was generally incompetent as a prosecution witness. Permitting one spouse to testify against the other in breach of this principle resulted in a reversal of any conviction so obtained on appeal.[39] The rule grew up partly as a result of the legal fiction of the unity of husband and wife, and partly because of the policy of the law in preserving and upholding the integrity of the matrimonial relationship.[40] Even at common law some exceptions were recognized, but the extent of the exceptions was never finally decided. Common law commentators generally agreed that the spouse was competent on a charge of high treason, in which case public policy requiring conviction in the interests of the State overrode that requiring the preservation of the matrimonial relationship. But as to more mundane offences there were few clear rules. It was established that the spouse was a competent witness as to offences of violence committed against the spouse, because in such cases the spouse against whom the offence is committed is often the only available witness and without his or her testimony, the offence might go unpunished.[41] But there was no real agreement on the question of what offences were to be regarded as offences of violence against the spouse for this purpose.[42] There was also some suggestion that the spouse might be competent in the case of offences against minor members of the family, for the same reasons of policy, but this was never settled at common law and was left to the intervention of statute, the Criminal Evidence Act 1898, s. 4(1).

The common law position as to compellability of the spouse as a prosecution witness was also settled very late and with significant dissent. The House of Lords had held in *Leach v R* [1912] AC 305 that where the spouse was competent by virtue of the Criminal Evidence Act 1898, the spouse was nonetheless not compellable. But in *Lapworth* [1931] 1 KB 117, the Court of Criminal Appeal refused to follow that authority in deciding the corresponding question of compellability in a case where the spouse was competent at common law, holding that if the spouse was competent, then like any other witness at common law (except the accused) the spouse was also compellable. In this confused and inconsistent state the law remained until the House of Lords

---

[39] See *Deacon* [1973] 1 WLR 696; *Mount* (1934) 24 Cr App R 135.

[40] The question of the competence of a spouse must be carefully distinguished from that of the privilege of a spouse not to divulge during testimony communications made by the other spouse during the marriage. This privilege was abolished in civil cases by s. 16(3) of the Civil Evidence Act 1968 and in criminal cases by s. 80(9) of the Police and Criminal Evidence Act 1984. See 14.18.

[41] *Lord Audley's Case* (1632) 3 St Tr 402.

[42] See, e.g., *Yeo* [1951] 1 All ER 864n; *Verolla* [1963] 1 QB 285.

(Lords Wilberforce, Dilhorne, Salmon, and Keith of Kinkel, Lord Edmund Davies dissenting) resolved the matter by holding in *Hoskyn v Commissioner of Police of the Metropolis* [1979] AC 474 that even where the spouse was competent, by virtue of whatever common law or statutory rule, he or she was nonetheless never compellable as a prosecution witness. Both the reasoning of the majority of the House and that expressed in the powerful dissenting speech of Lord Edmund Davies had an important influence on the eventual statutory resolution of the law in s. 80 of the Police and Criminal Evidence Act 1984. Lord Salmon (*ibid.* at 495) pointed out that the competence of the wife, in the case of an offence of violence committed against her by her husband, was allowed by the common law for the wife's protection, and should not be forced upon her where she was reluctant, on mature reflection, to testify against him because of forgiveness and reconciliation, and had no fear of further violence. Such compulsion could in some cases destroy the marriage. On the other hand, Lord Edmund Davies[43] pointed out that some offences are too grave to be compromised simply because the wife changes her mind about testifying, and that being compellable is a useful protection for a wife witness who is basically disposed to testify, but is subject to intimidation or coercion if she does so voluntarily.

15.9 COMPETENCE AND COMPELLABILITY OF SPOUSE BY STATUTE

The Criminal Evidence Act 1898, s. 1(c) rendered the spouse a competent witness for the defence of the accused spouse generally, but provided that she could be called only on the accused's application, i.e., not on behalf of a co-accused without the accused's consent. The Act did not settle the question of her compellability on behalf of the accused. Section 4(1) of the Act also made the spouse competent both for the prosecution and the defence in a limited number of cases, the most important of which were offences of violence and sexual offences against children and young persons, in which case the consent of the accused to her being called was dispensed with. Later statutes, notably the Sexual Offences Act 1956, gradually extended the same rule to other offences, the broadest provision of all being that of s. 30(2) and (3) of the Theft Act 1968, which rendered the spouse competent as a witness for or against the accused, 'as if they were not married', as to any offence against the spouse or the spouse's property. By this time, the general common law rule of incompetence of the spouse was beginning to be regarded as no more than an inconvenient anachronism, and policy issues concerned with making the evidence of spouses available, especially in cases of domestic violence and sexual offences against children, were becoming more important considerations.

In due course, and particularly in the light of the strong divisions of opinion in the House of Lords in *Hoskyn*, Parliament for the first time provided a systematic treatment of the subject of the competence and compellability of the spouse by s. 80 of the Police and Criminal Evidence Act 1984. The originally enacted provisions of this section have in turn been replaced by new s. 80(2) to (4), inserted by the Youth Justice and Criminal Evidence Act 1999, and it is unnecessary to consider them further.[44] The question of the spouse's competence as a witness is now easily dealt

---

[43] [1979] AC at 499. See also the 11th Report of the Criminal Law Revision Committee (Cmnd 4991, 1972), para. 149.

[44] Though it should be noted that, in consequence of the comprehensive new statutory scheme, the earlier piecemeal statutory provisions, Criminal Evidence Act 1898, s. 1(c) and (d), Sexual Offences Act 1956, s. 39, and Theft Act 1968, s. 30(3), were repealed by the 1984 Act. For the text of the original provisions of s. 80 of the 1984 Act, see the 7th edn of this work at 15.9.

with. In accordance with the general rule under ss. 53 to 57 of the Youth Justice and Criminal Evidence Act 1999, the spouse of the accused is now a competent witness in criminal proceedings, and it is no longer necessary to consider competence in terms of the spouse being called as a witness for the prosecution or for the defence. However, for the reasons of policy discussed above in relation to the older law, the Act contains more specific rules as to the compellability of the spouse. The new subsections (which now apply also, as noted above, to civil partners under the Civil Partnership Act 2004) provide as follows:

(2) In any proceedings the wife or husband of a person charged in the proceedings shall, subject to subsection (4) below, be compellable to give evidence on behalf of that person.

(2A) In any proceedings the wife or husband of a person charged in the proceedings shall, subject to subsection (4) below, be compellable—

(a) to give evidence on behalf of any other person charged in the proceedings but only in respect of any specified offence with which that other person is charged; or

(b) to give evidence for the prosecution but only in respect of any specified offence with which any person is charged in the proceedings.

(3) In relation to the wife or husband of a person charged in any proceedings, an offence is a specified offence for the purposes of subsection (2A) above if—

(a) it involves an assault on, or injury or a threat of injury to, the wife or husband or a person who was at the material time under the age of 16;

(b) it is a sexual offence alleged to have been committed in respect of a person who was at the material time under that age; or

(c) it consists of attempting or conspiring to commit, or of aiding, abetting, counselling, procuring or inciting the commission of, an offence falling within paragraph (a) or (b) above.

(4) No person who is charged in any proceedings shall be compellable by virtue of subsection (2) or (2A) above to give evidence in the proceedings.

(4A) References in this section to a person charged in any proceedings do not include a person who is not, or is no longer, liable to be convicted of any offence in the proceedings (whether as a result of pleading guilty or for any other reason).

The effect of these provisions may be summarized as follows. The accused's spouse, although always competent, is generally compellable only on behalf of the accused spouse. She is compellable on behalf of the prosecution or any other accused only in the cases specified in subsection (3), which reflects the kind of case which gave rise to particular concern at common law, and prompted the earlier common law and statutory rules referred to at 15.8. Subsections (4) and (4A) maintain the rule that, if the spouse is also charged in the proceedings, she is to be treated as an accused and, in accordance with the usual rule, is not compellable as long as she remains a person charged (see 15.5). The language 'charged in the proceedings' is a welcome improvement on 'jointly charged', which was used in the originally enacted s. 80, and which produced the artificial and inconvenient result that where A was charged with criminal damage and B with assault occasioning actual bodily harm in the same indictment, A was entitled to compel B's spouse to give evidence on his behalf because A and B were not jointly charged with any offence: *Woolgar* [1991] Crim LR 545. Under the new provisions, the fact that A and B were charged with different offences in the proceedings would not prevent the rules as to compellability from applying.

If the spouse or civil partner refuses to give evidence in a case in which she is not compellable, there is no bar to adducing her witness statement under s. 114(1)(d) of the Criminal Justice Act 2003 (see 8.20)—a subject dealt with in more detail at 7.5.2: see *L* [2008] 2 Cr App R 18. The same case holds that the police have no obligation to caution the spouse or partner that she is not compellable as a witness, or that the statement may be used if she declines to give evidence, before taking the statement; though the Court conceded that to so may be advisable in some cases.

15.10 FORMER SPOUSES: THE RULE IN *MONROE* v *TWISTLETON*

The common law incompetence of the spouse of a party survived the termination of the marriage in respect of matters which occurred during the marriage. This rule, which applied to both civil and criminal cases, was known as the rule in *Monroe* v *Twistleton* (1802) Peake Add Cas 219. In that case, it was held that the plaintiff was not entitled to call the divorced wife of the defendant for the purpose of proving a contract which he alleged he had made with the defendant during the marriage; she was not a competent witness on that issue. Similarly, in *O'Connor* v *Marjoribanks* (1842) 4 Man & G 435, it was held that personal representatives of a deceased who were suing in respect of the alleged conversion of part of the estate were not entitled to call the deceased's widow for the purpose of proving the instructions the deceased had given for the disposal of the estate during the marriage. The rule did not prevent a former spouse from giving evidence about matters which occurred after the termination of the marriage, though whether he or she was incompetent with respect to matters which occurred before the marriage appears never to have been decided. The reason for the termination of the marriage was in general irrelevant, but there was one logical, though curious exception. Where the marriage was terminated by a decree of nullity, the outcome depended on whether the ground of the decree was one which rendered the marriage voidable at the instance of the petitioner, or one which rendered the supposed 'marriage' void *ab initio*. In the former case, the parties were validly married until the pronouncement of the decree, and the spouse was incompetent with respect to events during the marriage in accordance with the usual rule.[45] But the pronouncement of a decree declaring the 'marriage' to have been void *ab initio* meant that there never had been a lawful marriage, and that the 'former spouse' had never in fact been a spouse at all. That being the case, no question of incompetence could arise, let alone survive.[46] As long as the marriage subsisted, the fact that the parties were not cohabiting was irrelevant to the question; they were married, and any consequential incompetence was not affected. This was the case whether the parties were living apart pursuant to a separation agreement, or without any agreement, or pursuant to a decree of judicial separation or a non-cohabitation order granted by a court.[47]

Given the fact that the spouses of the parties were made competent for almost all purposes in civil cases by virtue of s. 1 of the Evidence Amendment Act 1853, it is a legitimate question why the position of former spouses and the rule in *Monroe* v *Twistleton* should still be considered. But it is a curiosity of the law of evidence that the rule has never been specifically reversed in civil cases. In s. 1 of the 1853 Act, the words used to describe those rendered competent were the 'husband' and 'wife' of the parties. If the rule in *Monroe* v *Twistleton* survives, therefore, it must be because those words do not include former husbands and wives. This would produce the preposterous result that while existing spouses are competent and compellable, former spouses are not. For this reason alone, it has generally been assumed that the 1853 Act had the effect of abrogating the rule in civil cases. But this convenient assumption is difficult to reconcile with the decision

---

[45] *Algar* [1954] 1 QB 279.
[46] *Wells* v *Fisher* (1831) 1 Mood & R 99.
[47] *Moss* v *Moss* [1963] 2 QB 799.

of a strong Court of Appeal in *Shenton* v *Tyler* [1939] Ch 620. In that case, the Court held after a thorough review of the authorities that the identical words in s. 3 of the Act, which dealt with matrimonial privilege, were not capable of extending to widows and widowers. The fact remains that the rule in *Monroe* v *Twistleton* is plainly anachronistic in contemporary practice, and its reversal is long overdue.

In criminal cases, the rule has been abolished. At common law, it applied equally to criminal cases. In *Algar* [1954] 1 QB 279, the accused was charged with the forgery of his wife's signature on cheques drawn on her bank account during 1947 and 1948. In 1949, the marriage was annulled because of the accused's impotence, a ground which rendered the marriage voidable only. The former wife was called at the accused's trial in 1953. The Court of Criminal Appeal quashed the conviction, holding, following *Monroe* v *Twistleton*, that she remained incompetent with respect to the matters alleged in the indictment.

However, in keeping with the statutory provisions introduced by s. 80 of the Police and Criminal Evidence Act 1984, the rule in *Monroe* v *Twistleton* was abolished in criminal cases. Section 80(5) of the Act, as amended, now provides:

> In any proceedings a person who has been but is no longer married to the accused shall be compellable to give evidence as if that person and the accused had never been married.

The reference in s. 80(5) to competence was deleted by the Youth Justice and Criminal Evidence Act 1999. It was otiose in the light of the fact that former spouses, like all other witnesses, are competent under the provisions of ss. 53 to 57 of the 1999 Act (see 15.3).

Section 84(4) of the Civil Partnership Act 2004 provides that references in statutory provisions to civil partners do not include former civil partners.

15.11 CHILDREN OF TENDER YEARS

As we saw at 15.3, under the Youth Justice and Criminal Evidence Act 1999, s. 53(1) the general rule is that all witnesses are competent at every stage of criminal proceedings regardless of their age. Consequently, a finding of incompetence can no longer be based on age alone: *McPherson* [2006] 1 Cr App R 459. This relatively simple rule is the culmination of a period of about two centuries of uncertainty, during which common law rules which erred greatly on the side of incompetence were succeeded by statutory provisions which were tentative and often confusing. The modern practice is opposed to the suspicion which attached to the evidence of children at common law.[48] In deference to this, the rules requiring corroboration of their evidence have been abolished (Chapter 18) and they are now competent on the same basis as adults. Time will tell whether these developments are necessarily as desirable as Parliament has assumed. The age of a witness continues to be relevant, because a child's ability to satisfy the test of competence under s. 53(3) will clearly be affected by his age. Moreover, by virtue of s. 55(2) of the Act, children under 14 must give evidence in criminal proceedings unsworn, and those over 14 may be required to do so if they lack the appreciation of the solemnity of the occasion and the particular responsibility to tell the truth involved in taking an oath. It should be borne in mind also that, under ss. 24 and 27 of the Youth Justice and Criminal Evidence Act 1999, the evidence of children in criminal proceedings may be required to be given by live television link or by means of a

---

[48] See, e.g., *Z* [1990] 2 QB 355, per Lord Lane CJ; *DPP* v *M* [1998] QB 913; Criminal Justice Act 1988, s. 34.

videotaped interview. Witnesses in criminal proceedings who are under the age of 17 are eligible for assistance under s. 16, and in certain sexual cases will be in need of special protection under s. 21. In these cases, it is highly likely that one of these methods of taking their evidence will be ordered by virtue of a special measures direction. This subject is dealt with in more detail at 16.17 *et seq.* Whether or not this will complicate, or perhaps in some cases, facilitate a realistic assessment of the competence of a child witness, or his ability or inability to be sworn, remains to be seen.

15.11.1 Common law

At common law, the competence of a child of tender years depended on the opinion of the judge, who had a duty to inquire into the matter by asking questions of the child in open court, in the presence of the jury.[49] This duty was mandatory, in the sense that the judge was not entitled to rely on the views of the parties, or even the fact that the examining justices had found the child to be competent.[50]

It is clear that, in older authorities, the test for determining whether or not the child understood the duty to tell the truth in a court of law hinged on whether or not the child understood the divine sanction of the oath.[51] The questions put by the judge were directed to this subject, and it was not unknown for cases to be adjourned so that the child could receive some appropriate religious instruction before giving evidence. In *Brasier*,[52] the court held that the competence of children depended on 'the sense and reason they entertain of the danger and impiety of falsehood, which is to be collected from their answers to questions propounded to them by the court'.

However, in *Hayes* [1977] 1 WLR 234,[53] the Court of Appeal put the matter on a rather more pragmatic and secular basis. The accused was charged with acts of gross indecency against three boys, and the trial judge permitted the oldest boy, who was 12 years of age at the time of trial, to give evidence on oath, despite the fact that his answers gave rise to considerable doubt as to whether he believed in God or the divine sanction of the oath. The accused was convicted, and applied for leave to appeal on the ground that the boy should have been held to be incompetent. In effect, the case raised the question whether the older view, as expressed in such cases as *Brasier*, should continue to represent the law. The Court said ([1977] 1 WLR at 236–7):

> The court is not convinced that [trying to ascertain belief in God] is really the essence of the court's duty in the difficult situation where the court has to determine whether a young person can or cannot properly be permitted to take an oath before giving evidence. It is unrealistic not to recognize that, in the present state of society, amongst the adult population the divine sanction of an oath is probably not generally recognized. The important consideration, we think, when a judge has to decide whether a child should properly be sworn, is whether the child has a sufficient appreciation of the solemnity of

---

[49] *Khan* (1981) 73 Cr App R 190; *Reynolds* [1950] 1 KB 606; and see *N* (1992) 95 Cr App R 256.

[50] *Surgenor* [1940] 2 All ER 249.

[51] This was true, not only of children, but of other witnesses such as atheists and 'infidels'. The ability to take the oath was at one time regarded as the only safeguard of truthfulness in a witness.

[52] (1779) 1 Leach 199, 1 East PC 443. The child witness in the case is variously reported as having been 'five' and 'under seven'; cf. *Wallwork* (1958) 42 Cr App R 153.

[53] Children under 14 must now give evidence unsworn in criminal cases (Youth Justice and Criminal Evidence Act 1999, s. 55(2) see 15.3.1). When *Hayes* was decided, the judge had to decide whether the child should give evidence sworn or unsworn, depending on the child's answers to the questions. Cf. the not dissimilar approach taken in *Hampshire* [1996] QB 1.

the occasion and the added responsibility to tell the truth, which is involved in taking an oath, over and above the duty to tell the truth which is an ordinary duty of normal social conduct.

At common law, there was no set age at which a child ceased to be 'of tender years'. In *Wallwork* (1958) 42 Cr App R 153, Lord Goddard CJ deprecated the calling of a 5-year-old girl, in an unsuccessful attempt to have her give evidence of alleged acts of incest by her father, and hoped that it would not occur again. As a result of this, some feeling arose that there might be a minimum age of 6, and it was not unusual for 8 to be taken as a desirable minimum in practice. In *Hayes*, the Court of Appeal said that 'the watershed dividing children who are normally considered old enough to take the oath and children normally considered too young to take the oath probably falls between eight and ten'. But the reported cases reveal a considerable divergence of opinion, and perhaps the best way of expressing the matter is that the younger the child, the more the court should approach the issue of competence with caution, and subject the child's answers to a critical scrutiny. Ultimately, it seems that, at common law, competence should depend on the individual characteristics of the child in question, rather that on any standard minimum age.[54] As the Court in *Hayes* put it ([1977] 1 WLR at 237):

...we think it right also to approach the matter on the footing that this is very much a matter within the discretion of the trial judge and we think that this court, although having jurisdiction to interfere if clearly satisfied that the trial judge's discretion was wrongly exercised, should hesitate long before doing so. The judge sees and hears the boy or girl, which means very much more than the bare written word.

15.11.2 Statutory provisions prior to the Youth Justice and Criminal Evidence Act 1999: criminal cases

Before the decision in *Hayes*, frustration with the requirement of religious belief had led to an important statutory change in criminal cases. The Children and Young Persons Act 1933, s. 38(1), provided:

Where, in any proceedings against any person for any offence, any child of tender years called as a witness does not in the opinion of the court understand the nature of an oath, his evidence may be received, though not given on oath, if, in the opinion of the court, he is possessed of sufficient intelligence to justify the reception of the evidence, and he understands the duty of speaking the truth.

The section did not offer any definition of the expression 'tender years'. By a proviso, it was provided that the accused should not be liable to be convicted of the offence charged unless any evidence given unsworn was corroborated by 'some other material evidence in support thereof implicating him'. And, because a witness cannot be convicted of perjury unless he has been 'lawfully sworn', a new offence akin to perjury was created by s. 38(2).[55]

Although this provision represented some improvement on the common law position, it left trial judges to decide often difficult questions of whether a child should give evidence sworn or unsworn. These questions, difficult enough in themselves, were further complicated by issues of

---

[54] A selection of older decisions with respect to children of different ages is given in an earlier edition of Phipson, *Evidence*, 14th edn, para. 9–09. But there is no longer any purpose in compiling statistics on the subject. See also J. Spencer and R. Flin, *The Evidence of Children*, ch. 4. Cf. *Morgan* [1978] 1 WLR 735.

[55] See now the Youth Justice and Criminal Evidence Act 1999, s. 57. Of course, if the child were under the age of 10, he could not be convicted of any offence. However, this is no bar to the admission of the child's evidence (*N* (1992) 95 Cr App R 256).

corroboration, for which sworn evidence was required.[56] A more radical change was, therefore, made by s. 52(1) of the Criminal Justice Act 1991, which inserted into the Criminal Justice Act 1988 the following new s. 33A:

> (1) A child's evidence in criminal proceedings shall be given unsworn.
> (2) A deposition of a child's unsworn evidence may be taken for the purposes of criminal proceedings as if that evidence had been given on oath.
> (3) In this section 'child' means a person under 14 years of age.

By making unsworn evidence mandatory, the section absolved the court of the duty to make the choice demanded by s. 38(1) of the 1933 Act. It also provided the first statutory definition of a 'child' for purposes related to the assessment of competence. But s. 52(1) was not, strictly speaking, a provision dealing with competence. Requiring children to give evidence unsworn is not the same as declaring what children are to be regarded as competent to give evidence, unless it be assumed that the question of competence applies only to sworn testimony, and is irrelevant to unsworn testimony. A provision governing competence was added by s. 33A(2A) of the Criminal Justice Act 1988, which was inserted by the Criminal Justice and Public Order Act 1994, Sch. 9, para. 33:

> A child's evidence shall be received unless it appears to the court that the child is incapable of giving intelligible testimony.[57]

15.11.3 The Youth Justice and Criminal Evidence Act 1999

The provisions of ss. 53 to 57 of the Youth Justice and Criminal Evidence Act 1999 were discussed at 15.3. Although child witnesses are now to be treated in the same way as adult witnesses for the purposes of determining competence, the age and maturity of a child witness remain relevant in two respects.

Firstly, if an issue arises under ss. 53(3) and 54 as to whether the child is able to understand questions put to him as a witness and to give answers to them which can be understood, the child's age will have some bearing on the decision of that question. The age of the child is not the determining factor; the question is whether the child satisfies the test laid down by s. 53(3). But the same was true for the purposes of the common law test of competence: see the authorities mentioned at 15.11.1, and under earlier statutory provisions. In *DPP v M* [1998] QB 913, it was held that a child was capable of giving 'intelligible testimony' for the purposes of s. 33A of the Criminal Justice Act 1988, whatever his age, if the child was able to understand the questions and answer them coherently and comprehensibly—essentially the same test as under s. 53(3). It would be surprising if the courts did not take more or less the same age ranges as a rule of thumb in applying s. 53(3) as the courts did in classifying a child as one 'of tender years' at common law. As a matter of practicality, if not of law, some very young children will necessarily be found to

---

[56] See, e.g., *DPP v Hester* [1973] AC 296; *DPP v Kilbourne* [1973] AC 729. The corroboration problem was allayed by s. 34 of the Criminal Justice Act 1988, which removed any requirement for a corroboration warning simply because a witness was a child, but the dilemma of the oath remained.

[57] The competence provision of the Criminal Justice Act 1991, was s. 52(2), which repealed s. 38(1) of the 1933 Act, and further provided: 'and accordingly the power of the court in any criminal proceedings to determine that a particular person is not competent to give evidence shall apply to children of tender years as it applies to other persons'. The subsection was much criticized: see, e.g., J. Spencer and R. Flin, *The Evidence of Children*, 2nd edn (1993), pp. 62 *et seq.*; D. Birch [1992] Crim LR 262; and it was repealed by the Criminal Justice and Public Order Act 1994 in favour of the new s. 33A(2A) set out in the text.

be incompetent. And there may be other cases of a borderline nature, in which the court will be disposed to exercise its discretionary power to exclude the evidence of a young child.

Secondly, by virtue of s. 55(2) and s. 56, a child under the age of 14 must give evidence unsworn, and a person over that age must do so if he is found to lack the appreciation of the solemnity of the occasion and the particular responsibility to tell the truth involved in taking an oath. Under the law in effect before the coming into force of the Youth Justice and Criminal Evidence Act 1999, it was held that evidence given before trial by a child under 14, in a form permitted in the case of a child under 14, was admissible notwithstanding that the child had reached the age of 14 by the time of trial.[58] If the same principle applies under the 1999 Act, unsworn evidence given by the witness in a deposition or a videotaped interview while under that age would be admissible even if the child had turned 14 by the time of trial, but the court would then have to evaluate afresh the question of whether any further evidence should be sworn or unsworn.

The procedure for determining these questions, which is governed by ss. 54 and 55 of the Act, was described at 15.3. These sections confirm the view of the Court of Appeal in *Hampshire* [1996] QB 1 that an inquiry into the competence of a child must be conducted in the absence of the jury, and that the judge need not inquire in every case into the competence of a child, though he retains the power to do so. But a slight modification of the latter point would be appropriate. *Hampshire* was decided under s. 52(2) of the Criminal Justice Act 1991 (see note 55). Because s. 54(1) of the Youth Justice and Criminal Evidence Act 1999 expressly contemplates that the court may question the child's competence of its own motion, it is submitted that the court should always conduct at least some minimum scrutiny of a child witness. And a full inquiry must be held if any party raises the issue. The decision in *G v DPP* [1998] QB 919, in which it was held that expert evidence was not appropriate in deciding the question of the competence of a child witness, is expressly reversed by ss. 54(5) and 55(6) of the Youth Justice and Criminal Evidence Act 1999. But it is submitted that the use of such evidence should be confined to cases in which the mental or emotional condition of the child, apart from his age, appears to present a problem of competence or his ability to be sworn. It may be that the court will derive some assistance from being able to view a videotaped interview of the child's proposed evidence.

15.11.4 Statutory provisions: civil cases

Section 38 of the Children and Young Persons Act 1938 applied only to criminal cases. In civil cases, the common law principles continued to apply until the enactment of s. 96 of the Children Act 1989. This section effectively adopted the position taken by the 1938 Act, and the common law position as stated in *Hayes* [1977] 1 WLR 234 (see 15.11.1). It provides that in civil proceedings, if a child, in the opinion of the court, does not understand the nature of an oath, his evidence may be heard if, in the court's opinion, he understands that it is his duty to speak the truth, and has sufficient understanding to justify his evidence being heard.[59]

---

[58] *Day* [1997] 1 Cr App R 181; *Sharman* [1998] 1 Cr App R 406.

[59] For the purpose of this section, a child is a person under the age of 18 (see s. 105 of the Act). Section 5(1) of the Civil Evidence Act 1995 adopts the test laid down by s. 96 of the Children Act 1989 for the purposes of competence in relation to hearsay statements admissible by virtue of the 1995 Act.

15.11.5 Wards of court

If competent, children generally, like other witnesses generally, are also compellable, though, for obvious reasons, factors other than compellability are usually involved in any decision to call a child as a witness. A child who is a ward of court is in a somewhat different position, and may not be interviewed with a view to his becoming a witness without leave of the court.[60] The same principle should apply where it is sought to call a ward as a witness in a civil case. However, no leave is required to call a ward as a witness in a criminal case, whether for the prosecution or the defence.[61] In cases where leave is required, it is unlikely that it would be refused if the ward is competent and could give relevant evidence, unless there is such a real and serious danger of harm accruing to the ward as to outweigh these considerations.

15.12 PERSONS OF DEFECTIVE INTELLECT

There was, at common law, an undeveloped view that 'lunacy' was a bar to competence. The view probably resulted both from the dangers of unreliability and from doubtful capacity to appreciate the nature of an oath. It is, of course, a fairly modern tendency in the law to seek to recognize and accommodate the more sophisticated diagnosis and treatment of mental illness, and the law has not always kept pace with the consequences of the obsolescence of the generic classification of mental patients under the heading of lunacy.[62] At common law the inability of a person suffering from mental disability to be sworn was perhaps the most significant factor in the incompetence of such a person. In the light of the corresponding decision of the Court of Appeal dealing with children of tender years, *Hayes* [1977] 1 WLR 234 (see 15.11.1) it might reasonably have been assumed that the ability to understand the importance of speaking the truth would outweigh the ability to understand the theological implications of taking an oath. This did not prevent a contrary ruling by the trial judge in *Bellamy* (1985) 82 Cr App R 222. The victim of an alleged rape suffered from a mental disability, and her competence as a witness fell to be investigated at trial. The trial judge, properly, examined the complainant and heard evidence from a social worker on the subject. Having done so, he found that the complainant was capable of understanding the duty to speak the truth, and of testifying, but that she lacked sufficient belief in or knowledge of God to take the oath. The judge ordered her to affirm. On appeal against conviction, it was argued for the accused that the witness should have been required to take the oath, and that this breach of the rule requiring sworn evidence should lead to the conviction being quashed. The Court of Appeal agreed with the first proposition, and the second would have followed, except that the court found itself able to dismiss the appeal by applying the proviso to s. 2 of the Criminal Appeal Act 1968, since on the whole of the evidence, the result of the trial must have been the same. It was held, by analogy to *Hayes*, that no inquiry need be made into the religious belief of the witness.

Under the rules of competence in criminal proceedings laid down by ss. 53 to 57 of the Youth Justice and Criminal Evidence Act 1999, persons suffering from a degree of mental disability do

---

[60] *Consolidated Criminal Practice Direction*, para. I. 5; *Re R (A Minor) (Wardship: Criminal Proceedings)* [1991] Fam 56; but see also *Re R (Minors)* [1990] 2 All ER 633.

[61] *Re R (A Minor) (Wardship: Criminal Proceedings)* [1991] Fam 56; *Re K (Minors) (Wardship: Criminal Proceedings)* [1988] Fam 1.

[62] As witness the continued existence of the M'Naghten Rules; see 4.8.1.

not form any separate category, but are subject to the same test as other witnesses. If found to be capable of understanding the questions put to him as a witness, and of giving answers to them which can be understood, the witness is competent as a matter of law. Clearly, it would often be appropriate in such cases for the judge to hear expert evidence as permitted by s. 54(5) of the Act. If the witness is found to be competent, there may be a further question, under s. 55, as to whether he has the appreciation of the solemnity of the occasion or the particular responsibility involved in taking the oath, necessary to enable him to be sworn.

The court will take a pragmatic view. The question is whether the proposed witness is, at the time of being called, capable of giving proper evidence. If his lack of capacity is a temporary one, his evidence may be receivable after a suitable adjournment, as may be the case with a witness who arrives at court drunk. At common law, the courts leaned in favour of competence, particularly if the evidence may be important.[63] If the witness is declared to be competent, he may give evidence on any relevant issue,[64] and is subject to the normal rules of evidence.

Section 5(1) of the Civil Evidence Act 1995 provides that if the maker of a hearsay statement admissible by virtue of the Act was not competent at the time when he made the statement, the statement will be inadmissible. The section does not supply any new test of competence, but relies on the position at common law described above. Section 5(1) provides:

> Hearsay evidence shall not be admitted in civil proceedings if or to the extent that it is shown to consist of, or to be proved by means of, a statement made by a person who at the time he made the statement was not competent as a witness.
>
> For this purpose 'not competent as a witness' means suffering from such mental or physical infirmity, or lack of understanding, as would render a person incompetent as a witness in civil proceedings;...[65]

Section 123 of the Criminal Justice Act 2003 makes equivalent provision for the court to assess the capability of the maker of a hearsay statement admissible by virtue of the hearsay provisions of that Act, including the capability of a person who creates or receives a business record. The language of this provision differs from that of s. 5 of the Civil Evidence Act 1995, and is more akin to the language of the competence provisions of s. 53(3) of the Youth Justice and Criminal Evidence Act 1994. As to this, see 8.26.

15.13 JUDGES AND JURORS

The practice of calling judges or jurors to give evidence of matters arising during the performance of their duties as such has obvious drawbacks. Nonetheless, there are occasions when their evidence may be relevant to an understanding of what occurred during earlier proceedings, and there is, therefore, a question as to when they may be competent or compellable to testify.

15.13.1 Judges

Judges (whatever their personal status) are competent, but not compellable to give evidence (in later proceedings) of matters of which they become aware relating to and arising out of the

---

[63] Cf. *Hill* (1851) 2 Den 254, where an inmate of an asylum, whose 'only delusion' (sic) was that spirits occasionally talked to him, was permitted to give evidence in a prosecution for manslaughter. Contrast the position in the case of witnesses with physical speech and hearing impediments (Civil Evidence Act 1995, s. 13; Criminal Justice Act 2003, s. 134(1); *Ruston* (1786) 1 Leach 408).

[64] Including, it seems, that of his own sanity: *Hunter* v *Edney* (1885) 10 PD 93.

[65] A witness is not incompetent merely because a speech or hearing impediment compels him to testify by means of writing or signs (see, e.g., Civil Evidence Act 1995, s. 13; Criminal Justice Act 2003, s. 134(1).

performance of their judicial functions. This question, as to which there was previously little and rather unsatisfactory authority, was resolved by the Court of Appeal in *Warren v Warren*.[66] The issue was whether a solicitor had acted unreasonably, and was therefore liable to a wasted costs order, in subpoenaing a district judge to give evidence in matrimonial proceedings in which he had acted judicially. In the light of the sparse nature of the authorities, the Court held that the solicitor could not be criticized for the course he had taken, and took the opportunity of restating the law. It had been suggested in earlier cases that there was a distinction between judges of the superior and inferior courts with respect to compellability. But Lord Woolf MR, in a judgment with which Butler-Sloss and Saville LJJ agreed said ([1997] QB at 497):

> Although there is a clear constitutional distinction between High Court and other judges and the High Court and other courts, it does not follow that this provides a reason for distinguishing between judges so far as compellability to give evidence is concerned. If there was such a distinction in the past between judges of superior and other courts as to the compellability to give evidence (which is by no means clearly established) then it was difficult to understand the principle on which it was then based and even more difficult to justify it today. There has been a vast change in the extent of the jurisdiction of courts which are not generally regarded as superior courts since the nineteenth century when the relevant judicial comments were made. District judges exercise both a High Court jurisdiction and a county court jurisdiction. The circuit judge's jurisdiction has been extended beyond recognition. In matrimonial matters in particular there is a unified approach to jurisdiction.

Lord Woolf went on to hold that the policy reasons underlying the rule that judges should not be compellable continued to be valid. He added (at 497):

> It is also important to remember that the judge will remain competent to give evidence, and if a situation arises where his evidence is vital, the judge should be able to be relied on not to allow the fact that he cannot be compelled to give evidence to stand in the way of his doing so.

The only policy reason identified by the court as underlying the rule against compellability was that stated by Cleasby B in *Duke of Buccleuch v Metropolitan Board of Works* (1872) LR 5 HL 418, 433, to the effect that there were 'grave objections' to the conduct of judges 'being made the subject of cross-examination and comment (to which hardly any limit could be put)'. However, this would presumably be true (subject to judicial discretion to restrain improper cross-examination and comment) even if a judge gives evidence voluntarily, and there is reason to question whether the rule is really necessary in contemporary practice. There can be no doubt that the courts would express in strong terms their preference for other evidence, when available, so that the practice of judges giving evidence would be one of last resort in any case.

A separate question is whether a judge could give evidence as a witness of fact in a trial over which he is presiding. It is submitted that the answer is clearly in the negative, because the judicial and testimonial functions are incompatible, even if the judge is sitting with a jury. If the judge discovers that he has relevant evidence to give, the only proper course would be to excuse himself from acting further as a judge in that case, discharge the jury, and give evidence at the retrial. American Federal Rule of Evidence 605 so provides expressly.

With respect to any matter not related to a judicial function, a judge is in the same position as any other witness. Thus, to use an example which arose in argument in *Warren v Warren*, if a judge

---

[66] [1999] QB 488. *Duke of Buccleuch v Metropolitan Board of Works* (1872) LR 5 HL 418; *Gazard* (1838) 8 Car & P 595; *McC v Mullan* [1985] AC 528; *Sirros v Moore* [1975] QB 118. As to arbitrators and members of tribunals, see *Ward v Shell Mex and BP Ltd* [1952] 1 KB 280, and as to the rule in magistrates' courts, *McC v Mullan*; *McKinley v McKinley* [1960] 1 WLR 120.

witnessed a murder in his courtroom, he would be a competent and compellable witness at the trial of the person accused of the murder, just as if he had witnessed it on the street.

15.13.2 Jurors

Jurors are not competent to give evidence of discussions in which they were involved, relating to the thought processes which led to the verdict in a case in which they acted as such, or even of the jury's intent or understanding in relation to the verdict returned.[67] However, there is no objection to an inquiry into any irregularity or misconduct on the part of jurors, or improper external pressure brought to bear on them, which may have affected the verdict, and it seems that a juror would be both competent and compellable to testify about such matters. In *Young*[68] some members of the jury in a murder case, after consuming a certain amount of alcoholic drink in the hotel in which they were staying, consulted a ouija board, and purportedly made contact with the deceased who confirmed that the accused had murdered him. The Court of Appeal held that it had power to investigate the matter, since the misconduct had occurred outside the jury's deliberations, and having done so, allowed the appeal against conviction.

The principles stated above were strongly reaffirmed by the House of Lords in *Mirza; Connor and Rollock* [2004] 1 AC 1118. Both cases before the House concerned serious problems involving the jury which had occurred at trial. In the first case (*Mirza*) a juror sent two notes to the judge during the trial indicating the possibility of racial bias against the accused because of his reliance on an interpreter. The prosecution and the defence made a joint submission to the jury that the matter was irrelevant and should be ignored, and the judge directed the jury to similar effect. In the second case, a juror sent a letter after the trial had concluded, in which it was alleged that the jury had improperly considered the cases of the two accused together in order to save time. The House held that it is the duty of the judge to whatever he can to correct such problems where they occur during the trial.[69] In *Mirza*, the judge, with the assistance of counsel, had taken measures to correct the problem when it arose. If he had considered those measures to be insufficient, the judge had the power to discharge the jury. In *Connor and Rollock*, the problem surfaced only after trial, when the judge was *functus officio*. In this situation, the difficulties are in a sense more acute. But the House held that the same rule applied to both cases, namely that, while steps can and must be taken to correct any problem arising during trial, no steps can be taken to question the jury's verdict after the trial based on alleged irregularities in the jury's deliberation process. The House pointed out that the rule requiring that the confidentiality of jury deliberations has a long history at common law.[70] The rule is based on the strong public policy concern of enabling juries to confer fully and frankly without the fear that details of their

---

[67] *Thompson* [1962] 1 All ER 65; *Miah* [1997] 2 Cr App R 12; *Ellis v Deheer* [1922] 2 KB 113. Section 8 of the Contempt of Court Act 1981 makes it an offence to disclose or obtain information about what occurred in the jury room without leave of the court. See *Mickleburgh* [1995] 1 Cr App R 297; *McCluskey* (1993) 98 Cr App R 216. Cf. American Federal Rule of Evidence 606.

[68] [1995] QB 324. Cf. *Box* [1964] 1 QB 430, and generally *Blackstone's Criminal Practice*, 2009 edn, para. D18.27 *et seq*. In addition to the obvious procedural irregularity in *Young*, it seems clear that the evidence of the statement made by the deceased was hearsay. *Quaere*, whether it could now be admitted by virtue of s. 116(2)(a) of the Criminal Justice Act 2003.

[69] See, e.g., per Lord Hope of Craighead at [112].

[70] *Varse v Delaval* (1785) 1 TR 11; *Ellis v Deheer* [1922] 2 KB 113; *Quereshi* [2002] 1 WLR 518. The rule derives exclusively from common law. It is not based on the prohibition on divulging jury deliberations under s. 8 of the Contempt of Court Act 1981: it would be absurd to suppose that a court could be in contempt of itself (per Lord Slynn of Hadley in *Mirza* at [57], disapproving *dicta* to the contrary in *Young* (text above)). As to the necessity for

deliberations might later be revealed: it must be maintained. The House (Lord Steyn dissenting as to the case of *Mirza*), though clearly troubled by the disturbing course of both cases, held that this policy must prevail, and that no inquiry as to what had occurred in the jury room could be permitted. Lord Steyn's willingness to intervene on the facts of *Mirza* is of interest. At para. [4] he said:

> The philosophy became firmly established that there is a positive duty on judges, when things have gone seriously wrong in the criminal justice system, to do everything possible to put it right. In the world of today enlightened public opinion would accept nothing less. It would be contrary to the spirit of these developments to say that in one area, namely the deliberations of the jury, injustice can be tolerated as the price for protecting the jury system.

In Lord Steyn's view, while the confidentiality of the jury's deliberations remains of great importance, it must occasionally yield to considerations of justice and fairness to the accused. Lord Steyn took that view that his position is supported by the decision of the European Court of Human Rights in *Remli v France* (1996) 22 EHRR 253, in which it was held that an inquiry as to an apparent problem regarding the impartiality of a jury (again involving an issue of racial bias) might be required in the interests of fairness.[71] It is submitted that this view has much to commend it. Indeed, in cases such as *Mirza*, it might be argued plausibly that no violation of the secrecy of the jury room is needed to correct the apparent injustice. It would be sufficient for an appellate court to be satisfied that the judge erred in not discharging the jury and that the verdict is unsafe for that reason. While the exercise of the power to discharge the jury resides in the sound discretion of the trial judge, it is not beyond question on appeal in a case where there is reason to think that the alternative measures taken by the judge were not sufficiently effective to remove the risk of injustice or unfairness. In cases where the alleged irregularity comes to light only after the trial, it is submitted that the time may have come to permit some inquiry in cases in which an appellate court is satisfied that it is in the interests of justice to permit it. An alternative solution would be for the appellate court to order a retrial without an inquiry if satisfied that the interests of justice so required. It must be conceded that, where no problem has surfaced during the trial, this should be done only in exceptional circumstances. The presumption in favour of the impartiality of the jury is a strong one,[72] and the courts must be aware of the risk that a disgruntled juror may seek to impugn a verdict after it has been given simply because of resentment or second thoughts. It seems that any initiative for change in this area would have to come from Parliament. The other members of the House were of the opinion that the rule of secrecy must be strictly maintained in all cases.[73]

---

preserving the impartiality of juries as an attribute of a fair trial, and the implications under art. 6 of the European Convention, see *Gregory v United Kingdom* (1997) 25 EHRR 577, [44].

[71] Though Lord Hope of Craighead (at [111]) pointed out that in *Remli*, the problem regarding the juror had surfaced during trial, so that the case does not necessarily provide guidance in cases where the problem comes to light only after the trial.

[72] See *Rojas v Berllaque (Attorney-General for Gibraltar Intervening)* [2004] 1 WLR 201.

[73] Lord Hope of Craighead (at [123]) tentatively said that he might be prepared to countenance an exception in circumstances in which the jury had, e.g., decided the case by the toss of a coin, in which case it could be said that the jury had not deliberated at all. It is submitted that this view could be supported without violating the general rule by analogy to the circumstances of *Young* (text above); the coin and the ouija board fulfil essentially the same function in such a case, and both could be viewed as an extrinsic influence on the jury, into which an inquiry has traditionally been permitted. For academic comment on the rule, see M. Zander (2000) 150 NLJ 723; J. Spencer [2002] CLJ 291.

15.14 MISCELLANEOUS EXCEPTIONS TO THE RULE OF COMPELLABILITY

Apart from the accused and the accused's spouse in criminal cases, the general rule is that all competent witnesses are compellable to give evidence. There are a number of comparatively unimportant further exceptions, which are noted here, primarily for the sake of completeness.

The Sovereign and foreign heads of state, though competent, are not compellable. By virtue of various statutory provisions, certain persons who are accredited diplomats or officers of international organizations, enjoy a greater or lesser degree of immunity from compellability, according to their accredited status as such.[74]

By s. 6 of the Bankers' Books Evidence Act 1879:

> A banker or officer of a bank shall not in any legal proceeding to which the bank is not a party, be compellable to produce any banker's book the contents of which can be proved under this Act, or to appear as a witness to prove the matters, transactions, and accounts therein recorded, unless by order of a judge made for special cause.

The purpose of the provision is to protect banks and their officers from the onerous requirements which might otherwise follow from the frequent recourse of the courts to evidence contained in bankers' books. The Act provides sufficient modes of proof of entries in such books, and a procedure for obtaining orders for their discovery and inspection. These are dealt with in 19.10.

B   OATHS AND AFFIRMATIONS

SUMMARY OF MAIN POINTS

- With a few exceptions (including children under 14) evidence must be given on oath or affirmation.
- An oath may be taken in such lawful manner as the witness considers binding; if no objection is made by the witness and it appears to the court to be binding on him, the oath is binding once taken.
- Any witness who objects to being sworn must be permitted to affirm.
- Giving false evidence after being sworn or affirming may result in a prosecution for perjury.

15.15 THE REQUIREMENT OF SWORN EVIDENCE

We saw in the preceding section of this chapter that the ability to take the oath was, at common law, a central and probably the central element of competence as a witness. It was, historically, and is today a fundamental rule that evidence given to the court for any purpose shall be sworn, though more modern times have countenanced exceptional cases, which would not have been

---

[74] Diplomatic Privileges Act 1964: Consular Relations Act 1968; International Organisations Act 1968; Diplomatic and Other Privileges Act 1971; State Immunity Act 1978, s. 20; International Organisations Act 1981.

admitted in earlier days. Evidence is sworn if the witness is first required to take a lawful oath or affirmation, which carries with it the sanction of the law against false evidence.[75]

Evidence given unsworn is, unless given in one of the cases recognized as exceptional, a nullity, and any conviction or judgment based on it will be set aside on appeal. In *Marsham, ex parte Pethick Lawrence* [1912] KB 362, where the magistrates' court, by error, conducted a case on the basis of unsworn evidence and thereafter re-heard the case in the proper manner on the same day, an appeal was brought on the ground that the accused had stood in jeopardy twice because of the procedure adopted by the court. The appeal failed. The first hearing, based on unsworn evidence, had been a nullity, and the accused had not then stood in jeopardy. And in *Birch v Somerville* (1852) 2 ICLR 253, where the Lord Lieutenant of Ireland was permitted (irregularly) to give evidence 'on my honour as a peer', it was held that, but for acquiescence at the time, the irregularity would have been sufficient ground for an order for a new trial.

Witnesses may be sworn either by taking the oath in a lawful form, or by affirming. The rules relating to both were formerly complex, but have happily been simplified and rationalized by the Oaths Act 1978. Both possibilities may now be considered shortly.

15.15.1 Oaths

By s. 1(1) of the Oaths Act 1978, any oath may be administered and taken by the witness holding the book in his uplifted hand, and repeating the words of the oath prescribed by law.[76] Section 1(2) goes on to provide that the oath shall be administered in this manner, unless the witness voluntarily objects thereto, or is physically incapable of taking the oath in the prescribed way. This is a significant provision, in that it places the onus on the witness to notify the court of any objections which he may have to being sworn in the prescribed manner, except in the case of physical incapacity. An oath is valid if it appears to the court to be binding on the conscience of the witness, and if the witness so considers it (*Kemble* [1990] 1 WLR 1111). Formerly, the witness was asked his religion, and if, being neither a Christian nor a Jew, it was inappropriate to swear him on the New or Old Testament, the court embarked of its own motion upon an inquiry to find a suitable book, or determine whether the witness should affirm. If no objection is made, it now follows from s. 1 that the witness has been lawfully sworn.

The Act does, however, provide fully for proper objections by witnesses, and clearly it is right that a witness should be sworn in a manner which he regards as binding, wherever this may be done without undue delay or inconvenience. By s. 1(3) of the Act: 'In the case of a person who is neither a Christian nor a Jew, the oath shall be administered in any lawful manner'.

---

[75] Witnesses should be sworn before beginning their evidence. If this step is omitted through inadvertence, the witness should be sworn and begin his evidence again. Where a video recording of an interview with a child is admitted under s. 27 of the Youth Justice and Criminal Evidence Act 1999, and the child is aged 14 or more, the oath must be administered before cross-examination: *Simmonds* [1996] Crim LR 816, a decision under the earlier provision of s. 32A of the Criminal Justice Act 1988, but no doubt applicable to the 1999 Act also.

[76] The forms of oath were at one time diverse. In 1927, the judges of the King's Bench Division approved by resolution the following form for all civil and criminal proceedings in the courts over which they presided, and it has now passed into universal usage: 'I swear by Almighty God that the evidence I shall give shall be the truth, the whole truth and nothing but the truth'. The phrase 'Almighty God' may be replaced by a description of the Deity appropriate to the beliefs of a particular witness. By virtue of s. 28(1) of the Children and Young Persons Act 1963, as amended, where a witness is between the ages of 14 and 17, the phrase 'swear by Almighty God' is replaced by 'promise'.

The 'lawful manners' referred to are various,[77] and have grown up haphazardly over a period of time. Adherents of non-Christian religions (other than Jews) are permitted to be sworn upon a book regarded in their religion as holy,[78] although the appropriateness of holy books has been judged, not always accurately, by the court's own view of the dictates of witnesses' beliefs. There are special forms of oath appropriate to Quakers and Moravians. The ancient practice of swearing by kissing the Testament is permitted, and the Scots practice of swearing by the uplifted hand is specifically preserved as a lawful form by s. 3 of the Act.

15.15.2 Affirmations

By the Oaths Act 1978, s. 5:

> (1) Any person who objects to being sworn shall be permitted to make his solemn affirmation instead of taking the oath.[79]
> (4) A solemn affirmation shall be of the same force and effect as an oath.

The section has the welcome result that any witness may choose to affirm, as a voluntary alternative to being sworn. Previously, the judge was required to be satisfied after inquiry, either that the witness had no religious belief, or that being sworn would be contrary to his religious belief, although the letter of the law was frequently ignored in practice.

In addition to those who object to being sworn, a person may be permitted to affirm if 'it is not reasonably practicable without inconvenience or delay to administer an oath in the manner appropriate to his religious belief' (s. 5(2)). This provision is designed to cater for oaths of an unusual nature which might find the court administration unprepared and ill-equipped. It happens that witnesses occasionally insist upon some form of unusual oath, for the purpose of embarrassing the court, or of seeking to avoid giving evidence, and in order to meet this possibility, s. 5(2) is made enforceable by s. 5(3): 'A person who may be permitted under subsection (2)...to make his solemn affirmation may also be required to do so.'

15.16 EFFECT OF OATHS AND AFFIRMATIONS

In *Hayes*[80] the Court of Appeal observed that it would be unrealistic to suppose that in contemporary society, the divine sanction of an oath was generally recognized. The case was concerned with child witnesses, but the observation was directed also to adults and it can hardly be denied that more temporal sanctions probably have more effect in ensuring, so far as it can be ensured, that witnesses are under some influence to speak the truth. The courts will not investigate the intricacies of a particular religious belief, if it appears that the oath was administered without objection and in due form (*Kemble* [1990] 1 WLR 1111).

The Oaths Act 1978 recognizes the trend by implication, by providing that the formal taking of the oath in court is to be the binding and effective act, for legal purposes, rather than the belief or conscience which may or may not lie behind the oath in the case of any individual witness. In

---

[77] A fascinating compendium may be found in Phipson, *Evidence*, 16th edn, para. 9–26 *et seq.*

[78] See, e.g., *Morgan* (1764) 1 Leach 54.

[79] The form of affirmation, which was provided by the Oaths Act 1888, s. 2 (now the Oaths Act 1978, s. 6(1)), is as follows: 'I [full name] do solemnly, sincerely, and truly declare and affirm that the evidence I shall give shall be the truth, the whole truth and nothing but the truth.'

[80] [1977] 1 WLR 234; *Bellamy* (1985) 82 Cr App R 222; 15.11.1, 15.12.

other words, a witness is not to be permitted to escape the consequences of having been sworn simply by claiming subsequently that the oath was not such as to bind him, having regard to his beliefs.

Section 4 of the Act provides:

> (1) In any case in which an oath may lawfully be and has been administered to any person, if it has been administered in a form and manner other than that prescribed by law, he is bound by it if it has been administered in such form and with such ceremonies as he may have declared to be binding.
>
> (2) Where an oath has been duly administered and taken, the fact that the person to whom it was administered had, at the time of taking it, no religious belief, shall not for any purpose affect the validity of the oath.

The real sanction against false evidence given on oath is, of course, prosecution for perjury. By s. 1 of the Perjury Act 1911, perjury in a judicial proceeding is committed: '[i]f any person lawfully sworn as a witness...in a judicial proceeding wilfully makes a statement material in that proceeding, which he knows to be false or does not believe to be true'.[81] The importance of the lawful swearing of witnesses is clearly apparent, because this offence, providing the sanction, cannot be committed otherwise. But it would be sufficient if the oath were taken in the circumstances envisaged by s. 4 of the Oaths Act 1978, and because, by s. 5(4) of the 1978 Act, an affirmation is 'of the same force and effect as an oath', false evidence on affirmation falls within the scope of perjury.

15.17 EXCEPTIONS TO THE REQUIREMENT OF SWORN EVIDENCE

There are some exceptions to the rule requiring sworn testimony. These are described briefly below. Until comparatively recently, there also existed an exception or apparent exception, in the form of the unsworn statement from the dock in a criminal case. This occupied a substantial amount of space in the 1st edition of this work, but the abolition by statute of this venerable piece of legal history now requires nothing more than a short requiem. The exceptions are as follows:

(a) The evidence of witnesses under 14 years of age must be given unsworn in criminal cases: see Youth and Criminal Justice Act 1999, s. 55; this provision also applies to any witness who lacks the appreciation of the solemnity of the occasion or the particular responsibility to tell the truth involved in taking an oath; the evidence of children may be admitted unsworn in civil cases: see s. 96 of the Children Act 1989; 15.11.3, 15.11.4.

(b) The evidence of a witness called merely to produce a document may be received unsworn, provided that the document can be identified, or its identity is not in dispute.[82]

(c) Where a judge or counsel is asked to explain some aspect of a case in which he has been judicially or professionally engaged, he may appear and speak unsworn from his proper place in court.[83]

---

[81] As to the law concerning perjury generally, see *Blackstone's Criminal Practice*, 2009 edn, para. B14.1 *et seq.*

[82] *Perry* v *Gibson* (1834) 1 Ad & El 48.

[83] See, e.g., *Hickman* v *Berens* [1895] 2 Ch 638. The practice is one of last resort, for obvious reasons of avoiding embarrassment. But see *Warren* v *Warren* [1997] QB 488; 15.13.1. The practice of the Court of Appeal, Criminal Division, is now to prefer evidence from counsel on affidavit, where necessary, dealing with his conduct of a case at trial.

(d) On licensing applications, evidence may be received unsworn, although the court may refuse to accept unsworn evidence, if the application is opposed.[84]

(e) In extradition cases, a statement made abroad, usually in the country seeking extradition of the accused, may be admitted in evidence even if not made under oath and subject to the penalty of perjury, provided that it was made in circumstances of sufficient gravity and formal solemnity for the witness to appreciate fully the importance of telling the truth: see *Governor of Pentonville Prison, ex parte Passingham* [1983] 2 AC 464.

(f) The strict rules of evidence do not apply to civil cases on the small claims track, and the court is not obliged to require witnesses to be sworn: see Civil Procedure Rules 1998, r. 27.8(4).

Unsworn statements made from the dock by the accused in a criminal case were traditionally regarded as an exception to the requirement of sworn evidence, although this is rather misleading because such statements were not really 'evidence' in the true sense. The right of an accused to make an unsworn statement grew up in the course of the nineteenth century, in order to compensate for his inability to give evidence in his defence (before 1898), and for his inability, in cases of felony, to be represented by counsel (before 1836).[85] The rule evolved that the accused might put his case to the jury in his own words without being liable to cross-examination, and it seems to have been analogous to counsel's closing speech, rather than to the giving of evidence. But it came to be perceived as an unnecessary encumbrance on modern criminal procedure, a protection no longer needed by the accused. It died of old age, complicated by statutory abolition: Criminal Justice Act 1982, s. 72.[86] The accused is now subject to the same general rule as other witnesses, and must give evidence under oath, but the section permits an unrepresented accused to make a speech to the jury, and to address the court in mitigation.

15.18 RECOMMENDED FURTHER READING

Creighton, P., 'Spouse competence and compellability' [1990] *Criminal Law Review* 34.

Munday, R., 'Sham marriages and spousal compellability' (2001) 65(4) *Journal of Criminal Law* 336.

Spencer, J.R., 'Spouses as witnesses: back to Brighton Rock?' (2003) 62(2) *Cambridge Law Journal* 250.

Spencer, J. and Flin, R., *The Evidence of Children: the Law and Psychology*, 2nd edn (London: Blackstone Press, 1993).

Taylor, G., 'The Accused Persons Evidence Act 1882 of South Australia: a model for British criminal law?' (2002) 31(4) *Common Law World Review* 332.

 ## 15.19 QUESTIONS FOR DISCUSSION BASED ON *R* v *COKE; LITTLETON* (for case files go to the Online Resource Centre)

1. In what circumstances might Coke and Littleton be competent witnesses (a) for the prosecution; (b) in their own defence; (c) for each other? Would they be compellable in any such case?

---

[84] *Sharman* [1898] 1 QB 578.

[85] The accused was from an early date entitled to counsel in cases of misdemeanour, and in cases of treason, after 1695 (see also 1.5.3 and note 23 of Chapter 1).

[86] A similar concept exists in international criminal law. For example, rule 84 *bis* of the Rules of Procedure and Evidence of the International Criminal Tribunal for the Former Yugoslavia permits the accused to make such a statement, albeit immediately after opening statements rather than at the end of the case. Article 67(1)(h) of the statute of the International Criminal Court gives the accused the right to make such a statement in his defence without specifying the time at which it is to be made.

2. In what circumstances may Littleton's wife be a competent witness (a) for the prosecution; (b) for her husband; (c) for Coke? Will she be compellable in any such case?

3. Is Angela Blackstone a competent witness?

15.20 GENERAL QUESTIONS FOR DISCUSSION

1. What is the general rule of English law regarding competence and compellability of witnesses?

2. To be competent to give evidence in criminal proceedings a person must be able to do which two things?

3. Can a 12-year-old give sworn evidence?

4. Is the accused ever competent to give evidence for the prosecution?

5. The jury send a note to the judge in a case in which the accused did not give evidence. They disbelieve all the prosecution witnesses but want to draw an adverse inference from the accused's silence at trial and convict him on that basis. How should they be directed?

6. Can an accused's spouse be compelled to give evidence for the prosecution in a trial:

   (a) For shoplifting?

   (b) For the sexual assault of a 15-year-old neighbour?

   (c) For affray, in the course of which the spouse was injured?

7. When will a person with 'learning difficulties' be competent to give sworn evidence?

8. A man wins an action for libel but is believed to have lied on oath. What may be the consequences?

16

EXAMINATION IN CHIEF

A   INTRODUCTION

SUMMARY OF MAIN POINTS

- Evidence in chief is the procedure of adducing the evidence of one's own witness. In criminal cases witnesses other than experts and the officer in charge of the case are excluded from court before giving evidence.

- Leading questions are not permitted during examination in chief.

- Previous statements by the witness, including memory-refreshing documents, are generally inadmissible in chief. There are a number of exceptions to this rule, dealt with in Parts B and C of this chapter. At common law these statements, if admitted, were admitted only for a limited purpose appropriate to the statement concerned and not as evidence of the truth of any facts stated in them.

- In civil cases this distinction is no longer relevant because of the abrogation of the Rule against Hearsay by the Civil Evidence Act 1995.

- In criminal cases, ss. 119 and 120 of the Criminal Justice Act 2003 now provide that when such statements are admitted they are admissible as evidence of any facts stated in them of which oral evidence by the witness would be admissible.

16.1 NATURE AND CONDUCT OF EXAMINATION IN CHIEF

Examination in chief is the process whereby a party, who has called a witness to give evidence on his behalf, elicits from that witness evidence relevant to the issues and favourable to the examiner's case. The examination can be conducted safely only on the basis of a signed proof of evidence or witness statement supplied by the witness, dealing with the matters on which he can speak, but of course the examination need not be confined to the contents of the proof, and may range over any matters relevant to the issues which transpire to be within the competence of the witness. In a criminal case, examination in chief of the prosecution witnesses is conducted on the basis of, but is not restricted to, the contents of the deposition or witness statement of the witness. As we shall see in Part D of this chapter, the practice in relation to examination in chief has changed significantly in recent times. In civil cases, it is now usual for the direct examination of a witness to consist of the presentation of his written witness statement, after which he is tendered for cross-examination. In both civil and criminal cases there are statutory provisions for evidence to be given by live video link, and in criminal cases, the evidence of children and other witnesses may be given by way of video-recorded evidence or a video-recorded statement. The issues of law in relation to evidence in chief are almost exclusively concerned with the admissibility and use of previous statements made by the witness himself, a distinct kind of hearsay statement. At common law, such statements were subject to special rules, some of which continue to apply. But the admissibility of previous statements by a witness has been simplified greatly by statute, with the result that they are now often admissible as evidence of the matters stated in them. Documents used by a witness to refresh his memory constitute a special class, closely related to, though not identical to previous statements made by a witness, and must still be considered separately. These matters are dealt with in Parts A and B of this chapter. We must

also consider the position of witnesses who prove to be unfavourable or hostile to the party calling them. The treatment of such witnesses during examination in chief is also subject to special
rules, which include the use of previous statements by the witness inconsistent with his evidence.
These rules are dealt with in Part C of this chapter. A general introduction to the law on these
subjects is given at 16.2. Before proceeding to this, we will deal briefly with three preliminary
matters which are important to examination in chief generally.

16.1.1 Exclusion of witnesses from court before testifying

With the exception of the parties themselves, and of expert witnesses, who are never excluded
from court, the judge may require that a witness withdraw from court until called to give evidence. In criminal cases, this is the general rule for all witnesses, although the police officer in
charge of the case is usually permitted to remain in court, at least until the start of police evidence, in the absence of any specific objection to his presence. In civil cases, the witnesses are
usually present, unless specifically ordered to withdraw upon the application of any party. The
matter is one for the discretion of the judge, and no question of natural justice is involved. If a
witness deliberately remains in court after being ordered to leave, his evidence may not be admitted, but a judge has no discretion to exclude evidence on the sole ground that the witness has
been present in court before giving evidence.[1]

16.1.2 Leading questions

It is important that evidence in chief should be given in the words of the witness, not those of
the examiner, and consequently leading questions are not permitted.[2] A leading question is one
which puts words into the witness's mouth, or suggests directly the answer which the examiner
expects of him.[3] It is, however, permissible to lead the witness on the following matters:

(a)   On preliminary matters, preparatory to questions about the facts in issue. It is usual, for
      example to lead the witness's name and address.[4]
(b)   On any matters which are not in dispute.
(c)   Where a witness is called to deal with some fact already in evidence, he may be asked directly
      about that fact.
(d)   Where leave has been granted to treat the witness as hostile: see Part C of this chapter.
(e)   By agreement between all concerned. It is common and good practice for an advocate to
      indicate to his opponent over what area the opponent may lead a given witness without
      objection.

16.1.3 Identification of witnesses

Strictly, every witness called is required to identify himself to the court by giving his name and
address. At common law, in a case where disclosure of the name and address of the witness

---

[1] See generally *Moore v Registrar of Lambeth County Court* [1969] 1 WLR 141; *Briggs* (1930) 22 Cr App R 68;
Tomlinson v Tomlinson [1980] 1 WLR 323.

[2] Evidence elicited in chief by leading questions is not inadmissible, but its weight is often very slight: *Moor v
Moor* [1954] 1 WLR 927.

[3] The avoidance of leading questions is not an easy technique to acquire. For practical hints, see Murphy and
Barnard, *Evidence & Advocacy*, 5th edn, pp. 169 *et seq.*

[4] Unless the address is in itself relevant, e.g., to the question of jurisdiction. And see *Socialist Worker Printers &
Publishers Ltd, ex parte Attorney-General* [1975] QB 637.

might endanger the witness, or where it is necessary to the proper administration of justice, the judge has power to allow the details to be written down.[5] In practice, for security reasons, witnesses are no longer called on to give their address unless it is relevant to an issue in the case. Witness statements in criminal cases now require the witness only to say that he resides at 'an address known to police'. Police officers should identify themselves by name and badge number and state to which police station or unit they are attached. In the case of undercover officers, or in any case in which the officer's security might be endangered, this information may be provided to the judge without being given in evidence. There are statutory provisions to prevent the publication of personal details of complainants in cases of rape offences, and of children and young persons in proceedings of any kind.[6]

16.2 PREVIOUS STATEMENTS BY WITNESS AND MEMORY-REFRESHING DOCUMENTS: OUTLINE

16.2.1 Position at common law

The definition of hearsay both at common law and by statute (see 7.1) includes a statement made on a previous occasion by a witness who gives evidence in the proceedings, if the statement is tendered as evidence of the matters stated. But at common law, such statements are subject to special rules, which vary according to whether or not the statement is consistent or inconsistent with the evidence given by the witness in the proceedings. If the statement is inconsistent with the evidence given by the witness in the proceedings, its primary use lies in discrediting the witness by showing the inconsistency of the various accounts of the matters stated he has given. This is a particularly effective form of impeachment. It is also technically a non-hearsay use of the statement, because it is tendered not to prove the truth of the matters stated, but for the purpose of showing the inconsistency of the witness. For obvious reasons, previous inconsistent statements are more often employed during cross-examination for the purpose of attacking the credibility of a witness called by the opponent. This subject is dealt with at 17.7. But they are sometimes used during examination in chief in the case of one's own witness if that witness proves to be hostile. The practice with respect to attacking the credit of witnesses in this way has long been regulated to some degree by statute, ss. 3, 4 and 5 of the Criminal Procedure Act 1865. But these provisions did not alter the rule at common law as to the limited admissibility of previous inconsistent statements. At common law, they were admissible only for the non-hearsay purpose of attacking the credit of the witness, and were not admissible for the hearsay purpose of proving the truth of the matters stated in them. For example, if the witness gave evidence that the traffic light was green in the claimant's favour when he entered the intersection, but was then impeached by reference to a previous statement (even one given under oath) to the effect that the light was red, the previous statement was admissible to prove that the witness had contradicted himself and was unreliable as a witness, but it was not evidence that the light was red when the claimant entered the intersection. This rule of course required that the jury receive a direction to that effect, a direction which was inevitably confusing and difficult to follow.

---

[5] *Evesham Justices, ex parte McDonagh* [1988] QB 553; *Socialist Worker Printers & Publishers Ltd, ex parte Attorney-General* [1975] QB 637.

[6] See the Sexual Offences (Amendment) Act 1993, s. 1; Youth Justice and Criminal Evidence Act 1999, s. 46; Contempt of Court Act 1981, s. 11; Children and Young Persons Act 1933, s. 39, as amended. There is no longer any provision for anonymity of the accused in cases of rape offences; see Criminal Justice Act 1988, s. 158 repealing s. 6 of the Sexual Offences (Amendment) Act 1976.

Statements consistent with the evidence given by the witness in the proceedings presented a different problem. In general, they lack the non-hearsay relevance of previous inconsistent statements. If tendered during evidence in chief in addition to the evidence of the witness, they are simply cumulative and self-serving, and have the undesirable effect of needlessly supporting the credibility of the witness before anyone has attacked it. For example, if a witness gives evidence that the light was green in the claimant's favour when he entered the intersection, and adds that he has been saying exactly the same thing to anyone willing to listen ever since the accident happened, the latter statement has no real evidential value. At common law, therefore, previous consistent statements are generally inadmissible. But there are certain specific cases in which a previous statement made by a witness enjoys an additional relevance, and in these cases, they may be admissible at common law. The cases identified at common law as bringing about such additional relevance are:[7]

(a)   where the statement is admissible under the *res gestae* principle as an exception to the rule against hearsay, for the purpose of explaining and supplementing evidence of events of which it is an integral part (see 8.3 *et seq.*);
(b)   where a wholly or partially exculpatory statement is made by the accused in a criminal case in response to questions put to him about the offence (see 9.17);
(c)   where the statement is tendered for the purpose of rebutting an allegation of recent fabrication;
(d)   where the statement is admissible as a recent complaint in a sexual case for the purpose of confirming the complainant's evidence; and
(e)   where the statement is one identifying the accused in a criminal case as the person who committed the offence charged.

In these cases, previous consistent statements are admitted at common law for a specific and limited purpose. With the probable exception of statements of identification (whose status at common law was controversial) each of them involved giving the same kind of difficult and confusing direction to the jury as was required in the case of previous inconsistent statements, namely that the statement was evidence only for the limited purpose for which it was admitted, and was not (hearsay) evidence of the truth of the matters stated in it.

A separate though closely related problem arose in connection with documents used by a witness for the purpose of refreshing his memory while giving his evidence in chief. At common law, both in civil and criminal cases, a witness is permitted to refresh his memory by referring to a document which he made or verified contemporaneously with the events in question. This class of document is somewhat wider than the class of previous statements made by the witness, because it includes documents which the witness did not make personally (though he must have verified the document, in the sense of verifying the accuracy of the matters stated in it at or shortly after the time of its making). The classic example is the police officer's note book, which contains notes made by the officer throughout his inquiries during or shortly after the events recorded. Such a document, of course, could not be adduced in evidence by the party calling the witness. It was inadmissible hearsay if tendered as evidence of the matters stated in it, and

---

[7] It cannot be pretended that in all these cases, the claimed relevance is as clear as might have been wished. In the case of recent complaints, the exception owes more to the survival of an anachronistic historical rule of procedure. In the case of statements of identification, it owes more to the practical realities of securing a reliable identification, for which purpose the rule is salutary.

could become evidence only when inspected and cross-examined on by the opponent. Indeed, even then, the document could not be adduced by the party calling the witness unless the cross-examination strayed into areas of the statement not used by the witness to refresh his memory. And even in this case, the common law rule was that the document was evidence only of its consistency or inconsistency with the evidence of the witness, and was, therefore, evidence only of his credibility. The jury had to be directed that the statement was not evidence of the truth of any matters stated in it.

In each of these cases, the common law rules of admissibility, though logical in terms of the rule against hearsay, were artificial and inconvenient, particularly because they were very difficult for juries to follow. Fortunately, they have been simplified to a large extent by statute. It will be convenient to examine these statutory provisions in full now. They will be considered individually in greater detail when discussing the various kinds of statement to which they relate later in this chapter, and, in the case of previous inconsistent statements when used in cross-examination, in Chapter 17. These provisions render previous statements admissible, subject to various conditions, as evidence of the matters stated in them, as well as evidence for the particular purpose for which they are adduced. This is a particularly welcome reform. The Criminal Justice Act 2003 also defines the kinds of document and other material which may be used by a witness to refresh his memory; introduces a new statutory rule of admissibility in cases of statements of past recollection recorded (an extended kind of memory-refreshing document once removed); and replaces the common law rules dealing with recent complaints and statements of identification with new statutory rules of admissibility.

16.2.2 Statutory provisions in civil cases

Section 6 of the Civil Evidence Act 1995 provides:

(1) Subject as follows, the provisions of this Act as to hearsay evidence in civil proceedings apply equally (but with any necessary modifications) in relation to a previous statement made by a person called as a witness in the proceedings.

(2) A party who has called or intends to call a person as a witness in civil proceedings may not in those proceedings adduce evidence of a previous statement made by that person, except—
   (a) with the leave of the court, or
   (b) for the purpose of rebutting a suggestion that his evidence has been fabricated.
This shall not be construed as preventing a witness statement (that is, a written statement of oral evidence which a party to the proceedings intends to lead) from being adopted by a witness in giving evidence or treated as his evidence.

(3) Where in the case of civil proceedings section 3, 4 or 5 of the Criminal Procedure Act 1865 applies, which make provision as to—
   (a) how far a witness may be discredited by the party producing him,
   (b) the proof of contradictory statements made by a witness, and
   (c) cross-examination as to previous statements in writing,
this Act does not authorize the adducing of evidence of a previous inconsistent or contradictory statement otherwise than in accordance with those sections.
This is without prejudice to any provision made by rules of court under section 3 above (power to call witness for cross-examination on hearsay statement).

(4) Nothing in this Act affects any of the rules of law as to the circumstances in which, where a person called as a witness in civil proceedings is cross-examined on a document used by him to refresh his memory, that document may be made evidence in the proceedings.

(5) Nothing in this section shall be construed as preventing a statement of any description referred to above from being admissible by virtue of section 1 as evidence of the matters stated.

As we have seen (8.30) the Civil Evidence Act 1995 provides that hearsay is no longer a bar to the admissibility of evidence in civil proceedings. The rules of admissibility of previous statements made by witnesses were, therefore, not only inconvenient but anachronistic in civil cases. Nonetheless, out of deference to the fact that previous consistent statements and documents used to refresh the memory are of limited relevance and may lack weight in circumstances other than the exceptional instances recognized at common law, s. 6 does not affect the rules governing the use of those statements. Section 6(2) provides that such a statement may not be admitted without leave, except in the case where it is admitted for the purpose of rebutting an allegation of recent fabrication (see 16.10). Subsections (3) and (4) expressly preserve the rules relating to previous inconsistent statements and documents used to refresh the memory. Thus, these cases must still be considered separately. But the section provides that when those statements are admitted, they are admissible as evidence of the truth of the matters stated in them in addition to the more limited purpose for which they were admissible at common law. At the same time, it must be borne in mind that because most evidence in chief is now given by way of written witness statements in civil cases, the rules under which previous statements made by the witness are admitted are applied with far greater flexibility than was formerly the case. As s. 6(1) and (5) recognize, hearsay is no longer a bar to admissibility, and the latter provides that any statement may be admitted as evidence of the matters stated by virtue of s. 1 of the Act. Moreover, r. 32.1 of the Civil Procedure Rules 1998 gives the court considerable power to regulate the kind of evidence to be presented in civil cases (see 3.6) and it is submitted that, at least as a matter of practice, the judge can make whatever use he feels appropriate of any such statements having regard to their relevance and apparent probative value in the circumstances of a particular case.

16.2.3 Statutory provisions in criminal cases

Sections 119 and 120 of the Criminal Justice Act 2003 provide:

119 Inconsistent statements

(1) If in criminal proceedings a person gives oral evidence and—

(a) he admits making a previous inconsistent statement, or

(b) a previous inconsistent statement made by him is proved by virtue of section 3, 4 or 5 of the Criminal Procedure Act 1865 (c. 18),

the statement is admissible as evidence of any matter stated of which oral evidence by him would be admissible.

(2) If in criminal proceedings evidence of an inconsistent statement by any person is given under section 124(2)(c), the statement is admissible as evidence of any matter stated in it of which oral evidence by that person would be admissible.

120 Other previous statements of witnesses

(1) This section applies where a person (the witness) is called to give evidence in criminal proceedings.

(2) If a previous statement by the witness is admitted as evidence to rebut a suggestion that his oral evidence has been fabricated, that statement is admissible as evidence of any matter stated of which oral evidence by the witness would be admissible.

(3) A statement made by the witness in a document—

    (a) which is used by him to refresh his memory while giving evidence,

    (b) on which he is cross-examined and

    (c) which as a consequence is received in evidence in the proceedings,

is admissible as evidence of any matter stated of which oral evidence by him would be admissible.

(4) A previous statement by the witness is admissible as evidence of any matter stated of which oral evidence by him would be admissible, if—

    (a) any of the following three conditions is satisfied, and

    (b) while giving evidence the witness indicates that to the best of his belief he made the statement, and that to the best of his belief it states the truth.

(5) The first condition is that the statement identifies or describes a person, object or place.

(6) The second condition is that the statement was made by the witness when the matters stated were fresh in his memory but he does not remember them, and cannot reasonably be expected to remember them, well enough to give oral evidence of them in the proceedings.

(7) The third condition is that—

    (a) the witness claims to be a person against whom an offence has been committed,

    (b) the offence is one to which the proceedings relate,

    (c) the statement consists of a complaint made by the witness (whether to a person in authority or not) about conduct which would, if proved, constitute the offence or part of the offence,

    (d) the complaint was made as soon as could reasonably be expected after the alleged conduct,

    (e) the complaint was not made as a result of a threat or a promise, and

    (f) before the statement is adduced the witness gives oral evidence in connection with its subject matter.

(8) For the purposes of subsection (7) the fact that the complaint was elicited (for example, by a leading question) is irrelevant unless a threat or a promise was involved.

Section 119 deals with previous inconsistent statements.[8] Section 120 deals with documents used to refresh the memory and with admissible previous consistent statements. Section 120(3) is concerned with documents used to refresh the memory. It should be read with s. 139, which defines the kinds of document and other material which may be used to refresh memory in criminal proceedings, and is to be found at 16.3.2. Section 120(2) deals with rebuttal of allegations of recent fabrication. In both cases, the Act follows the model of s. 6 of the Civil Evidence Act 1995 in providing that the statements may admitted as evidence of the truth of the matters stated in addition to the more limited use made of them at common law, but does not (except for s. 139) affect the circumstances in which they are generally used. Section 120(4) creates the wholly new rule of admissibility of statements containing recorded recollection, and the reformed rules of admissibility in cases of statements of identification and recent complaints, and in these cases, the section radically alters the common law practice.

Documents admitted pursuant to ss. 119 and 120 are subject to s. 122, which provides:

(1) This section applies if on a trial before a judge and jury for an offence—

    (a) a statement made in a document is admitted in evidence under section 119 or 120, and

    (b) the document or a copy of it is produced as an exhibit.

(2) The exhibit must not accompany the jury when they retire to consider their verdict unless—

    (a) the court considers it appropriate, or

    (b) all the parties to the proceedings agree that it should accompany the jury.

---

[8] Section 119(2) refers to the impeachment of a maker of a hearsay statement admissible by virtue of the Act who does not give evidence in the proceedings. This is dealt with at 17.13.

The purpose of the provision is to the prevent the jury from being placed in a better position vis-à-vis the previous statement than they would be vis-à-vis the evidence of the witness. When the jury retire to consider their verdict, they are not provided with a transcript of the evidence given by the witnesses (though they may have as exhibits documents which have been admitted as evidence in their own right, and are not part of the evidence of the witnesses). If they wish, they may ask to be reminded of parts of the evidence given by the witnesses, but they have no permanent record of it. If statements admitted by virtue of s. 119 or s. 120 were routinely provided to the jury as exhibits, they would enjoy a favoured position relative to the rest of the evidence. They are, therefore, generally not to accompany the jury when they retire, and the jury must be content with listening to the documents read and referred to during the course of evidence: see *Hulme* [2007] 1 Cr App R 334. But there may be cases in which, perhaps because of the complexity of the statement or its particular significance, the judge considers or all parties agree that the general rule should not be followed, and in such cases the exhibits may accompany the jury.[9]

B   REFRESHING THE MEMORY

SUMMARY OF MAIN POINTS

- At common law any witness may refresh his recollection while giving evidence, with leave of the court, using any document made or verified by him at or near the time of the events about which he is giving evidence.

- In civil cases the judge has a broad discretion to regulate the working of the rule and draw any conclusions he wishes if the witness is dependent on documents.

- In criminal cases, s. 139(1) of the Criminal Justice Act 2003 now provides:

  A person giving oral evidence in criminal proceedings about any matter may, at any stage in the course of doing so, refresh his memory of it from a document made or verified by him at an earlier time if—

  (a) he states in his oral evidence that the document records his recollection of the matter at that earlier time, and
  (b) his recollection of the matter is likely to have been significantly better at that time than it is at the time of his oral evidence.

- Both at common law and by statute, a document used to refresh the memory is not admissible in chief, but may be made admissible in certain circumstances as a result of cross-examination. If admitted it is now admissible in both civil and criminal cases as evidence of any fact stated in it of which oral evidence by the witness would be admissible.

- In addition, s. 120(4) and (6) of the Criminal Justice Act 2003 create a new rule of admissibility of statements of past recollection recorded (see 16.2.3).

---

[9] This was sometimes done in cases dealt with under common law principles when the authenticity of the document came into question, and its appearance might assist the jury in resolving that issue: see *Sekhon* (1986) 85 Cr App R 19; *Bass* [1953] 1 QB 680. But this was not the general rule unless all parties agreed: see, e.g., *Fenlon* (1980) 71 Cr App R 307.

16.3 INTRODUCTION

All too often, a considerable time elapses between the occurrence of events relevant to proceedings, and the trial of the proceedings themselves. It would be unrealistic to expect that a witness will always be able to give accurate and reliable evidence about events unless he is able to refresh his memory by looking at some note or document. This is true particularly of witnesses such as police officers, who have to give evidence in many different cases. On the other hand, a document cannot refresh the memory accurately unless its own accuracy can be vouched for, a factor which in effect dictates the making of the document as soon as possible after the events with which it deals. The common law rule is that any witness may, with the permission of the judge, refresh his memory by reference to a document which he made or verified contemporaneously with the events with which the document deals. The rule has now been given statutory form in criminal cases by s. 139 of the Criminal Justice Act 2003 (see 16.3.2). In civil cases, although the common law rule continues to apply in principle, the judge has ample power to allow the witness to refer to any document which appears to be reliable for the purpose. If it appears that the witness has little or no independent recollection of the events, the weight of his evidence will suffer regardless of whether or not he is permitted to refer to a document, and because hearsay is no longer a bar to admissibility in civil cases, there would be little point in refusing the witness permission to refer to a document which may well be admissible in its own right. It is submitted that, in all cases, the court should bear in mind that no witness can remember everything, and evidence should be a test of honesty and reliability rather than a test of memory.[10] For these reasons, the position at common law is stated briefly below.[11]

16.3.1 Common law rule

The common law applies only where the witness seeks permission to refresh his memory while giving evidence. There is no objection to a witness refreshing his memory from any proper source before giving evidence.[12] And it appears that the judge may permit a witness to pause in his testimony for the purpose of refreshing his memory outside the presence of the court, though for obvious reasons, that course should be taken only when necessary to enable the witness to give evidence.[13] The witness must ask permission of the judge before being shown a memory-refreshing document, and the judge must satisfy himself that the use of the particular document is proper. The opponent is entitled to cross-examine the witness on this subject. If the witness did not make the document himself, he must have verified it, that is to say, he must have satisfied himself at or near the time it was made that the matters stated in it were accurate.[14] A good example is where two or more police officers jointly observe an event, and one then makes a note which the other signs or acknowledges at the time; signing, while desirable as evidence, is not

---

[10] See the observations to that effect in *Richardson* [1971] 2 QB 484; and *Bass* [1953] 1 QB 680.

[11] For fuller treatment, see the 8th edn of this work at para. 16.2 *et seq.*

[12] *Richardson* [1971] 2 QB 484; though it is not proper to encourage discussion between witnesses outside court or to show a witness a statement made by another witness: *Shaw* [2002] EWCA Crim 3004; *Skinner* (1993) 99 Cr App R 212. For observations as to the professional duty of advocates to advise the opponent that witnesses have looked at their statements outside court, see *Worley v Bentley* [1976] 2 All ER 449; *Westwell* [1976] 2 All ER 812.

[13] *Da Silva* [1990] 1 WLR 31; *South Ribble Magistrates' Court, ex parte Cochrane* [1996] 2 Cr Apr R 544.

[14] *Anderson v Whalley* (1852) 3 Car & K 54.

strictly required.[15] It is sufficient to amount to a verification if the witness has the document read to him contemporaneously and thereupon confirms its accuracy.[16] To be contemporaneous, the document must have been made or verified either at the time of the events recorded, or, more usually, at the first practicable opportunity thereafter. The question of whether the document was made at the first practicable opportunity is one of fact, and must be judged by reference to the facts of each case. While the length of time which elapsed between the events and the making or verification of the document is obviously a significant factor, the practicability of making or veri-fying the document is ultimately decisive, and this may depend on other factors.[17] The original rule was that the witness must refresh his memory from the original document,[18] but in modern practice, the witness may use a copy of the document, a witness statement made on the basis of the original,[19] or a fuller note of the events made on the basis of the original.[20]

16.3.2 Criminal Evidence Act 2003, s. 139

The question of what materials may be referred to in criminal cases is now governed by s. 139 of the Criminal Justice Act 2003, which provides:

> (1) A person giving oral evidence in criminal proceedings about any matter may, at any stage in the course of doing so, refresh his memory of it from a document made or verified by him at an earlier time if—
>> (a) he states in his oral evidence that the document records his recollection of the matter at that earlier time, and
>> (b) his recollection of the matter is likely to have been significantly better at that time than it is at the time of his oral evidence.
> (2) Where—
>> (a) a person giving oral evidence in criminal proceedings about any matter has previously given an oral account, of which a sound recording was made, and he states in that evidence that the account represented his recollection of the matter at that time,
>> (b) his recollection of the matter is likely to have been significantly better at the time of the previous account than it is at the time of his oral evidence, and
>> (c) a transcript has been made of the sound recording,
> he may, at any stage in the course of giving his evidence, refresh his memory of the matter from that transcript.

Section 139(a) removes the need for inquiry by the judge, provided that the witness can testify to the matters required by s. 139(1)(a) and (b). If the witness so testifies, he is entitled to refresh his memory from the document. The fact required by subsection (1)(b) is virtually axiomatic. There is no longer a requirement that the document should have been made or verified contem-poraneously; the witness need only state that it was made or verified at an earlier time, which is also axiomatic. Thus, the witness could refresh his memory using his witness statement, which may have been made quite some time after the event. But there may still be cases in which the

---

[15] See the observations of the Court of Criminal Appeal in *Bass* [1953] 1 QB 680.
[16] *Kelsey* (1981) 74 Cr App R 213.
[17] *Richardson* [1971] 2 QB 484; *Langton* (1876) 2 QBD 296; *Fotheringham* [1975] Crim LR 710.
[18] *Harvey* (1869) 11 Cox CC 546.
[19] *Cheng* (1976) 63 Cr App R 20.
[20] *Attorney-General's Reference (No. 3 of 1979)* (1979) 69 Cr App R 411; and see the case of a dyslexic witness having the statement read to him, *Gordon* [2002] EWCA Crim 1.

lapse of time is significant. The conditions imposed by subsection (1)(a) and (b) grow less com-pelling with time, and if the document is made soon before trial, it may be that the judge would be entitled to conclude that the requirements could not be satisfied. This may be true especially where the witness has been assisted in making the document by a police officer or a solicitor, in which case (without implying any impropriety) there may be reason to doubt that the document accurately records the witness's memory of the events. Section 139(2) applies an analogous rule to a recorded statement made by the witness which has been transcribed, in which case he may refer to the transcript. This separate provision is necessary because s. 140 of the Act, which applies to s. 139, defines 'document' as: 'anything in which information of any description is recorded, but not including any recording of sounds or moving images'. For practical reasons it would not be desirable to allow the witness to listen to the original recording in court; it may include inad-missible material which the jury should not hear.

16.4 ADMISSIBILITY OF MEMORY-REFRESHING DOCUMENTS

16.4.1 Admissibility in chief

Reference by a witness to a contemporaneous document may have one of two results. The first, termed 'present recollection revived', is that the document will succeed in refreshing the mem-ory of the witness, enabling him to give oral evidence about the facts. The second, termed 'past recollection recorded', is that the document will be unsuccessful, so that the witness can, at best, say that the document was accurate when made, and that the events were fresh in his mind at that time. This may occur, for example, when the document is a record of routine transactions, and is one of many similar documents made by the witness, perhaps a considerable time in the past. In many cases, there is no reason to distrust the record, even though the witness may no longer have any personal memory of the facts, as long as he can vouch for the reliability of the record. But American writers, from Wigmore on, have generally advocated dealing with these two results in different ways. In the case of present recollection revived, they would require the witness to give evidence from his refreshed memory, and accord the document no evidential value. This corres-ponds with the view of English law. In the case of past recollection recorded, however, they would permit the witness to read the relevant parts of the document by way of an exception to the rule against hearsay (though the document itself would not be admitted as an exhibit).[21] On the face of it, this differs from the English approach, but the difference may be more apparent than real because, in practice, it is not unusual for judges to relax the strict rule, and permit a witness to read from the document under the guise of giving evidence from a refreshed memory. Such evi-dence is, of course, open to obvious comment, and may have relatively little weight.

English law has perceived no need for such subtleties. At least since *Maugham* v *Hubbard* (1828) 8 B & C 14, it has been established that even in the case of past recollection recorded, which Cross termed 'reconstruction' of the events (*Evidence*, 5th edn, p. 233), the witness is treated as having personal knowledge of the events recorded in the document, provided that he can state that the

---

[21] Federal Rule of Evidence 803(5) creates the following exception to the hearsay rule: 'Recorded recollection. A memorandum or record concerning a matter about which a witness once had knowledge but now has insuffi-cient recollection to enable the witness to testify fully and accurately, shown to have been made or adopted by the witness when the matter was fresh in the witness's memory and to reflect that knowledge correctly. If admit-ted, the memorandum or record may be read into evidence but may not itself be received as an exhibit unless offered by an adverse party'.

document was made contemporaneously and was accurate when made. In *Maugham* v *Hubbard*, a witness was shown an acknowledgement of a payment, signed by him, and thereupon testified that, although he had no recollection of having been paid the sum stated in it, he had no doubt that such was the case. This evidence was held to be sufficient to prove the payment, even though the acknowledgement was unstamped and therefore could not be sufficient without the parole evidence of the witness that the payment had in fact been made. Thus, at common law, whether the case is one of present recollection revived or of past recollection recorded, the witness may give evidence, having looked at the document; but the document itself is hearsay, and will not be admissible in chief as evidence of the facts stated in it.

16.4.2 Admissibility as result of inspection and cross-examination

The opposing party is entitled to inspect a document used by a witness, either before testifying or while in the witness-box, for the purpose of refreshing his memory.[22] The opposing party may further cross-examine the witness with regard to any part of the document used by the witness to refresh his memory, without making the document evidence for the party calling the witness.[23] If, however, cross-examination takes place on other parts of the document, the rule is that the party calling the witness is entitled to put the document in evidence as part of his case.[24] The reason for this is that matters falling outside the use of the document as a memory refresher have been raised, the document has a new relevance and the jury are entitled to see the subject-matter of the cross-examination; whereas cross-examination restricted to the portions referred to by the witness amounts to no more than questioning on his oral evidence. At common law, where a memory-refreshing document is put in evidence, it is not evidence of the facts stated; it is evidence only of the consistency of the witness, and goes only to his credit. In *Virgo* (1978) 67 Cr App R 323, the conviction was quashed where the trial judge directed the jury, by necessary implication, that the diary of a prosecution witness, used by the witness to refresh his memory, could be regarded as evidence of the truth of the facts stated in it. The witness had been cross-examined extensively on the document in a way which clearly justified its being put in evidence. But the jury should have been directed to regard the document as relevant only in assessing the weight to be accorded to the evidence of the witness which could be affected by its consistency or otherwise with the document.

But this position has now been modified by statute in both civil and criminal cases. The relevant provisions were given at 16.2.2 and 16.2.3. By virtue of s. 6(1) of the Civil Evidence Act 1995, the rule that hearsay is no longer a bar to admissibility in civil cases applies equally to previous statements made by a witness. Although subsection (1) does not mention statements verified by the witness, it is submitted that they too are covered by virtue of s. 6(5). The effect is to render the statements admissible as evidence of any matters stated which would be admissible apart from the hearsay rule. But s. 6(4) preserves the common law rule as to the circumstances in which

---

[22] *Burgess* v *Bennett* (1872) 20 WR 720; *Owen* v *Edwards* (1983) 77 Cr App R 191. The inspection must be confined to matters relevant to the case, though it need not be confined to the parts used by the witness to refresh his memory.

[23] This should not be confused with the rule that calling in cross-examination for a document in the possession of the opponent (not one used as a memory refresher) involves putting the document in evidence if called upon to do so. See 17.15; cf. *Senat* v *Senat* [1965] P 172 with *Stroud* v *Stroud* [1963] 1 WLR 1080; and see *Britton* [1987] 1 WLR 539.

[24] *Gregory* v *Tavernor* (1833) 6 Car & P 280; *Senat* v *Senat* [1965] P 172; *Owen* v *Edwards* (1983) 77 Cr App R 191.

a document used to refresh the memory may be made evidence in the proceedings, so that the document becomes evidence only in those circumstances, subject only to the flexible approach to statements of any kind in civil proceedings (see s. 6(5)). Similarly, s. 120(3) of the Criminal Justice Act 2003 provides that a statement used by a witness to refresh his memory is admissible of any matter stated of which oral evidence by him would be admissible, but only where he is cross-examined on the document and it is as a consequence received in evidence in the proceedings. Thus, the effect of both sections is that a document used to refresh the memory is not admissible in chief, but may be made evidence by virtue of the course of cross-examination (as at common law), and if admitted, is admissible as evidence of all matters stated which are admissible apart from the hearsay rule.

16.5 ADMISSIBILITY OF STATEMENTS OF PAST RECOLLECTION RECORDED

Although neither s. 6 of the Civil Evidence Act nor s. 120(3) of the Criminal Evidence Act 2003 alters the rule that documents used to refresh the memory are not admissible in chief, s. 120(4) and (6) of the Criminal Justice Act 2003 create a new rule of admissibility for statements of past recollection recorded in criminal proceedings. This provision is set out at 16.2.3. If the conditions required by subsections (4) and (6) are fulfilled, the statement is evidence of any matter stated of which oral evidence by the maker would be admissible. Section 120(4)(b) requires that the witness be able to testify that he made the statement, and that to the best of his belief it states the truth. Section 120(6) requires that the witness testify that he made the statement when the matters stated were fresh in his memory, but that he does not remember them, and cannot reasonably be expected to remember them well enough to give oral evidence of them in the proceedings. The new provision closely resembles Federal Rule of Evidence 803(5) (see note 21). It is useful in the case where the statement is contained in a document which was made a considerable time before the witness is asked to give evidence about the matters stated, or which contains routine and detailed facts, or complicated data. There may be no reason to doubt the accuracy of the document when made, but it would clearly be unreasonable to expect the witness to remember its contents. It is not necessary that the witness have no memory at all of the matters stated; it is enough that his memory is not and cannot reasonably be expected to be enough to enable him to give evidence of them. The statement need not have been made in a document. Nothing in subsection (4) precludes the use of a statement made orally, though it seems logical that it would have to have been recorded in some form in order to be used at trial. It is essential that the witness is called to give evidence in the proceedings. Section 120(1) makes clear that this is a necessary condition of admissibility. There is no power to admit such a statement where the maker does not give evidence.

The section applies only to criminal proceedings. In civil cases, such a statement would have to be admitted by virtue of the general rule admitting hearsay in civil cases under s. 1 and s. 6(5) of the Civil Evidence Act 1995 and, assuming that the maker of the statement is called or is to be called as a witness, could be admitted only with leave pursuant to s. 6(2).

16.6 REFRESHING MEMORY OF WITNESS BY HYPNOSIS

There is little authority in English law on the practice of using hypnosis to refresh the memory of a witness before trial. Experience in the United States suggests that hypnosis may be effective as an investigative tool, for example, to obtain information from a rape victim who suffers from some degree of traumatic amnesia, but that the use of hypnotically refreshed testimony at trial can be dangerous because of the considerable danger of suggestion, and the possibility of creating 'memory', rather than refreshing memory. Nonetheless, there is a growing trend to accept hypnotically refreshed testimony subject to stringent safeguards.[25]

Similar safeguards in the form of guidelines were drafted by the Home Office in 1987, for use in England, primarily for investigative purposes. These require, in essence, that the memory of the witness before being hypnotized must be accurately recorded, that the entire hypnotic session should be videotaped and transcribed for use as an exhibit at trial, and that the witness should make a further statement, incorporating any further facts revealed by the hypnosis. The police must disclose to the Crown Prosecution Service that hypnosis has taken place during the investigation. In *Browning* [1995] Crim LR 227, the Court of Appeal allowed an appeal against a conviction for murder, where the existence of a videotape of the hypnosis of a key witness, whose memory proved to be unreliable, was withheld from the defence. Lord Taylor of Gosforth CJ held that this had deprived the defence of an important opportunity to challenge the witness's evidence, and constituted a material irregularity. The Lord Chief Justice also emphasized that hypnosis should be used with extreme caution, and only in accordance with the Home Office guidelines.

C   PREVIOUS CONSISTENT STATEMENTS

SUMMARY OF MAIN POINTS

- Previous statements by the witness are generally inadmissible in chief. There are exceptions to this rule, namely:

  (a) statements admissible under the *res gestae* principle;

  (b) answers given by the accused when taxed with an offence which are wholly or partially exculpatory;

  (c) statements admissible to rebut an allegation of recent fabrication;

  (d) statements admissible as 'recent complaints';

  (e) statements identifying the accused as the person who committed an offence.

- At common law these statements, if admitted, were admitted only for a limited purpose appropriate to the statement concerned and not as evidence of the truth of any facts stated in them.

- In civil cases this distinction is no longer relevant because of the abrogation of the Rule against Hearsay by the Civil Evidence Act 1995.

- In criminal cases, ss. 119 and 120 of the Criminal Justice Act 2003 now provide that when such statements are admitted they are admissible as evidence of any facts stated in them of which oral evidence by the witness would be admissible.

---

[25] See, e.g., *Rock v Arkansas* 483 US 44 (1987); *United States v Valdez* 722 F 2d 1196 (5th Cir, 1984).

16.7 PREVIOUS CONSISTENT STATEMENTS: GENERAL RULE

At common law, a witness may not give evidence that he has, on a previous occasion, made a statement consistent with his present evidence. Variously called the rule against previous consistent statements and the rule against self-serving statements, the rule is soundly based on the proposition that such a statement can have no improving effect on the evidence of the witness given on oath in court. Such statements are also objectionable as hearsay. At common law, they are excluded, subject to certain exceptions, both as evidence of consistency and as evidence of the truth of the facts stated. Thus, in *Roberts* [1942] 1 All ER 187, where the accused was charged with murder, he was not permitted to state in evidence that two days after the killing, he had told his father that his defence would be one of accident, as it indeed was at the trial. The rule applies to statements in any form, including what might be termed indirect statements by conduct. In *Corke v Corke and Cook* [1958] P 93, a suit for divorce, the wife and co-respondent, who had been found together in compromising circumstances but had denied adultery, were not permitted to give evidence that they had telephoned a doctor to ask for a medical examination (which did not take place), with a view to confirming their denial of adultery. We must now consider the exceptions to the rule, which were listed at 16.2.

16.8 STATEMENTS ADMISSIBLE UNDER THE *RES GESTAE* RULE

The *res gestae* rule is one of the preserved common law exceptions to the rule against hearsay (see 8.1), and in effect allows evidence, otherwise objectionable as hearsay, to be given, where a statement is an integral part of the transaction to which it relates, and so ought to be given in evidence to invest the evidence of the transaction with a completeness, in the absence of which the evidence might be ambiguous or misleading. A typical case is of a spontaneous statement made contemporaneously with the transaction by a participant or bystander. Therefore, the rule operates to admit what are in reality previous consistent statements, although they are also often given in evidence by other witnesses, who heard them being made. The *res gestae* rule is considered in detail in 8.3 *et seq.*

16.9 WHOLLY OR PARTLY EXCULPATORY STATEMENTS MADE BY THE ACCUSED WHEN QUESTIONED ABOUT THE OFFENCE

Statements made by the accused concerning the offence charged in response to questioning occupy, in their own right, the entirety of Chapters 9 and 10. The accused may admit the offence charged; but conversely, he may deny it in a manner consistent with his defence at trial, in which case the statement which he makes is self-serving within the meaning of the present rule. Very frequently, he makes a statement which the jury may regard as partly incriminating and partly self-serving. It seems that, with the exception of statements of a self-serving nature made with the express intention of ensuring their inclusion in the evidence given for the prosecution, by way of 'infiltration' of the prosecution case, the jury ought to hear whatever the accused may say about the allegation made against him, in order to determine whether the statement, read as a whole, amounts to a confession. It is true that the evidential value of a self-serving statement is materially less than that of a confession of guilt or an adverse admission, but the accused's prior statements are admitted in evidence, both for the above reason and as evidence of his reaction when charged with the offence and, if he gives evidence to the same effect, as evidence of consistency. See generally 9.17, 10.2.

16.10 REBUTTAL OF ALLEGATION OF RECENT FABRICATION

Although this rule is one which arises in re-examination, rather than examination in chief, it is convenient to deal with it here because it is an exception to the rule against previous consistent statements. The exception is that where, in cross-examination, it is suggested that the witness has fabricated his evidence within some ascertainable period of time, he may rebut the suggestion by showing that before that time, he had made a statement consistent with his evidence. The relevance of the previous statement in such circumstances is clear.

Where, therefore, a witness gave evidence that a will had been forged, and it was suggested to him that he had invented his evidence out of enmity towards the accused, the witness was permitted to prove that he had made the same statement to a third person, at a time before the cause of the enmity arose.[26] And in *Oyesiku* (1971) 56 Cr App R 240, where it was put to the accused's wife that she had prepared her evidence in collusion with her husband, she was likewise allowed to prove that, after the accused's arrest and before she had any opportunity to speak to him, she had given his solicitor a statement to the same effect.

16.10.1 Necessity for specific allegation

The suggestion to be rebutted must, however, be specifically one of recent fabrication. A general cross-examination designed to show that the evidence is unreliable, or even untruthful, will not let in a previous consistent statement, even where the witness is impeached by reference to a previous inconsistent statement (*Beattie* (1989) 89 Cr App R 302, 306). In *Fox v General Medical Council* [1960] 1 WLR 1017, a doctor was charged with infamous conduct, in relation to his adulterous association with a woman patient, who subsequently committed suicide. The Privy Council upheld the decision of the General Medical Council that the evidence of a friend of the doctor, stating that the doctor had, after the patient's death, made to him a statement consistent with his case, was not admissible merely because the doctor's evidence was challenged as being generally untrue. Lord Radcliffe stated the rule in the following terms:

> If in cross-examination a witness's account of some incident or set of facts is challenged as being a recent invention, thus presenting a clear issue as to whether at some previous time he said or thought what he has been saying at the trial, he may support himself by evidence of earlier statements by him to the same effect. Plainly the rule that sets up the exception cannot be formulated with any great precision, since its application will depend on the nature of the challenge offered by the course of cross-examination and the relative cogency of the evidence tendered to repel it.

Lord Radcliffe then considered the nature of the cross-examination which had taken place, and concluded that it was directed to showing the general untruthfulness of the doctor's evidence and that his answers were consistent with either view of the case. His Lordship went on:

> Could it have made any contribution to the [Disciplinary Committee's] judgment on the veracity of his whole account for them to know that in such a situation he had told the old friend substantially

---

[26] *Flanagan* v *Fahy* [1918] 2 IR 361. Cf. *Coll* (1889) 24 LR Ir 522 in which the witness was asked why no reference had appeared in his statement to the accused, when he had implicated the accused in his evidence. He was allowed, having admitted that the statement made no such reference, to explain the inconsistency in terms of an omission, and to point out that an earlier statement made by him had referred to the accused. See also *Benjamin* (1913) 8 Cr App R 146.

the same story as to his innocence of the matters charged as he was now telling at the hearing? Their Lordships do not think that it could. In their view, the challenge to the appellant's evidence that was raised by the cross-examination was not of the order that could be affected by proof of statements made by him of that kind at that date. No tribunal that was not otherwise prepared to accept the appellant's general story could have been led to do so by hearing what he had told [the friend] on April 15. So regarded, the evidence rejected is no more than the previous assertion of the defence story told at the trial, which Humphreys J pointed out in *Roberts* is clearly inadmissible.

It seems that it must be possible for the court to detect a specific time at or after which it is suggested that the fabrication took place. This and this alone lends relevance to a statement made before that time, tending to negative the suggestion.[27]

16.10.2 Evidential value of statement

At common law, a statement admitted by virtue of this exception was admissible only for the limited purpose of rebutting the allegation of recent fabrication, and not as evidence of the truth of the matters stated. Statute has altered this position both in civil and criminal cases. The relevant provisions were given at 16.2.2 and 16.2.3. Under s. 6(2) of the Civil Evidence Act 1995, a statement offered to rebut an allegation of recent fabrication is admissible without leave, and by virtue of s. 6(1) of the Act is admissible as evidence of the truth of the matters stated, as well as for the more limited purpose of rebutting the allegation. The same provision is made for criminal proceedings by s. 120(2) of the Criminal Justice Act 2003.

16.11 RECENT COMPLAINTS

16.11.1 Introduction

At common law, a 'recent complaint' made by the complainant on a charge of rape was admissible for limited purposes as an exception to the rule against previous consistent statements. The rule was extended to apply to other sexual offences, but not to offences of any other kind. The rule was widely held to be anachronistic in modern times, and it might have been expected that it would be abolished. The common law rule itself has now presumably been abrogated by the Criminal Justice Act 2003,[28] but it has been replaced by a similar and wider rule applicable to offences of any kind, and one which permits the complaint to be admitted as evidence of the truth of the matters stated. This rule is enacted by s. 120(4) and (7) of the Act: see 16.2.3. Because some of the principles developed in the cases dealing with the common law rule may yet prove to be instructive in the interpretation of the new rule, they will be described briefly below.[29]

---

[27] There are signs that the courts may be moving towards relaxing the strictness of this requirement in favour of a more general power to admit a previous statement when it is necessary to correct a false impression created by cross-examination: see *Ali* [2004] 1 Cr App R 39. But in *Trewin* [2008] EWCA Crim 14, the Court of Appeal insisted that s. 120 of the Criminal Justice Act 2003 does not alter the rules as to admissibility of a statement tendered in rebuttal of allegations of recent fabrication, and the only change relates to the evidential value of the statement if admitted.

[28] The rule is not one of the common law exceptions preserved by s. 118(1) of the Act and so may be taken to have been abolished by virtue of the exclusive regime established by s. 114(1) for the admissibility of hearsay evidence. It would also be otiose in the light of the new rule under s. 120(4) and (7). But the rule is not abolished in express terms.

[29] For fuller treatment, see the 8th edn of this work at para. 16.14 *et seq.*

It must be confessed that, if ever there was some reasoned basis for the ancient recent complaint exception, it has become well hidden in the mists of time. Bracton tells us somewhat enigmatically that a woman who complains of rape should 'go to the next town and there make discovery to some credible persons of the injury she has suffered'.[30] The reason for this may lie in the suspicion which fell at common law on a woman who failed to complain within a short time of an outrage done to her, but almost certainly Oliver Wendell Holmes J is correct in his unkind stigmatization of the recent complaint as 'a perverted survival of the ancient requirement that a woman should make hue and cry as a preliminary to an appeal of rape' (*Commonwealth* v *Cleary* (1898) 172 Mass 175). Whatever its origin, the rule survived uneasily as a rule of evidence in modern law, even though any requirement for a complaint as a prerequisite to conviction had long since perished. The rule was that in sexual cases, evidence might be given by the complainant and by any person to whom the complaint was made, of a complaint made voluntarily, and at the first opportunity reasonably afforded. The complaint was admissible only for either of two purposes: (a) to confirm the evidence of the complainant relating to the offence; and/or (b) to rebut or disprove consent on the part of the complainant, if consent was an issue in the case.

16.11.2 Common law rule in sexual cases

The common law rule applied, in its developed form, to all sexual offences, but not to offences of any other kind.[31] The complaint had to be 'recent'. Whether the complaint was 'recent' depended on much the same factors as the 'first reasonable opportunity' test in the case of documents used to refresh the memory (see 16.3.1). The complaint must have been made when the first reasonable opportunity presented itself. The length of time elapsing between the alleged offence and the complaint was significant, but not decisive.[32] The availability of a person to whom the complaint could be made was taken into account, and the courts would consider the complainant's natural inclination to wait for the chance to confide in a relative or friend, and not necessarily the first person encountered after the offence was committed.[33] The complaint must also have been 'spontaneous', in the sense of having been volunteered by the complainant rather than dragged out of her by leading or threatening questions, or force. But the mere fact that the complaint was induced by a question would not be enough to exclude it.[34] When giving evidence, the complainant was permitted not only to state that she had made the complaint, but also to state the substance of the complaint.[35] If admissible, the complaint was not evidence of the truth of the matters stated, but was admitted only for either or both of two more limited purposes, namely (a) confirming the evidence of the complainant; and/or (b) disproving consent if consent was an issue in the case. Consequently, if the complainant did not give evidence, and consent was

---

[30] *De Corona*, bk 3, fol. 147; expounded in *Blackstone's Commentaries*, bk 4, ch. 15, 211. Blackstone points out that there was, in effect, a statute of limitations in rape cases in early times, which ran in the absence of a recent complaint and at one time had statutory force, though by Blackstone's time it had long since been abrogated.

[31] *Lillyman* [1896] 2 QB 167; *Osborne* [1905] 1 KB 551. These cases effectively supersede older authority which suggested that the rule could apply more widely, e.g., *Wink* (1834) 6 Car & P 397 (robbery); *Berry* v *Berry and Carpenter* (1898) 78 LT 688 (charge of cruelty in a divorce case). Some older cases do not distinguish adequately between the recent complaint rule and the dying declaration and *res gestae* rules, with which it sometimes overlaps. But the rule did apply to offences against males as well as females: *Camalleri* [1922] 2 KB 122.

[32] *Birks* [2003] 2 Cr App R 7; *Cummings* [1948] 1 All ER 551.

[33] *Valentine* [1996] 2 Cr App R 213.

[34] *Osborne* [1905] 1 KB 551, 556 per Ridley J.

[35] *Lillyman* [1896] 2 QB 167.

not an issue, the complaint was inadmissible.[36] If it was tendered to confirm the evidence of the complainant, the evidence must in fact be capable of having that effect, and in all cases the jury must be carefully directed about the purposes for which the evidence was admissible.[37] Moreover, the judge must point out to the jury the various consistencies and inconsistencies between the complainant's evidence and the complaint.[38] The Privy Council held in *White* v *R*[39] that, unless the person to whom the complaint was made was also called as a witness the evidence had no probative value either on the issue of confirmation of the complainant's evidence or on that of consent, because evidence from an independent source was required.

16.11.3 Statutory rule: Criminal Justice Act 2003, s. 120(4) and (7)

A new rule, which does not use the title 'recent complaint', but derives from the common law rule, was created by s. 120(4) and (7) of the Criminal Justice Act 2003. These provisions were given at 16.2.3. Provided that the conditions imposed by subsections (4) and (7) are fulfilled the complaint is admitted as evidence of the truth of the matters stated. Subsection (4)(b) requires that the witness be able to testify that he made the statement, and that to the best of his belief it states the truth. Subsection (7) reproduces the main features of the common law rule, but with the notable difference that it applies to offences of any kind, and is no longer restricted to sexual cases. The common law requirements of recency and spontaneity are given statutory form. Subsection (7)(d) continues the requirement that the complaint should have been made as soon after the alleged conduct as could reasonably be expected, and it may be anticipated that the common law authorities referred to above will continue to be of assistance to the judge in assessing whether or not that requirement has been met. Subsection (7)(e), read with subsection (8) seems to be consistent with the common law position that the complaint must have been spontaneous. But this concept is made more specific. Unless a threat or promise of some kind has been made, the fact that the complaint was elicited by questions, including leading questions, will not prevent it from being admitted. It is irrelevant to whom the complaint was made. The reference to 'a person in authority' in subsection (7)(c) is to a police officer or other person charged with investigating or prosecuting offences. The same expression was used at common law in relation to the law relating to confessions (see 9.4.2). The complainant must, of course, give evidence (s. 120(1)) and the complaint is not admissible until he has 'given oral evidence in connection with its subject matter' (subsection (7)(f)). It is not clear whether this means that the complainant must have completed his evidence, or whether the complaint can be admitted after his examination in chief, or during his examination in chief after he has given evidence about the commission of the offence. It is submitted that this last possibility is the most natural interpretation of the subsection, and the most useful in practice. It would surely be inconvenient and artificial if the complainant could not be asked about the complaint at that stage. In *O* [2006] 2 Cr App R 27, the Court of Appeal held that s. 120(7) creates free-standing criteria of admissibility which are to be interpreted in their own right, and not as a codification of the common law rules. The Court

---

[36] *Wallwork* (1958) 42 Cr App R 153.

[37] *S* [2004] 3 All ER 9; *White* v *R* [1999] 1 AC 210.

[38] *Spooner* [2004] EWCA Crim 1320.

[39] [1999] 1 AC 210; *sed quaere*. See also *Islam* [1999] 1 Cr Apr R 22; *Churchill* [1999] Crim LR 664. At common law the evidence of the complainant required corroboration (see 18.3.2) and the complaint could not provide corroboration because it was not from an independent source. But that did not prevent the complaint from being admitted. The requirement of corroboration was abrogated by statute (see 18.3.3) and it is not easy to see how the decision in *White* can be reconciled with earlier authority.

also held that there is no objection, subject to any considerations of unfairness to the accused, to the admission of multiple complaints made on different occasions.

This provision has no application to civil cases. An equivalent statement could be admitted in civil proceedings only with leave by virtue of s. 6(2) of the Act, subject to the judge's general powers to admit hearsay evidence under s. 1 and s. 6(5) of the Act.

16.12 STATEMENTS OF IDENTIFICATION

Evidence of the visual identification of the accused as the person who committed an offence has long been recognized as one of the most troubling areas of criminal law and practice. The possibilities of mistaken identification are many, and can be attributed to such various factors as the time available to make the identification, the quality of the light, and the trauma caused to a victim of the offence by its very commission. These matters have been addressed by the courts, and have resulted in specific rules dealing with the treatment of identification evidence and the direction to be given to juries to assist them in evaluating it. These rules are dealt with below (see 16.12.2). But there is also a theoretical objection to the admissibility of previous statements of visual identification of the accused when consistent with the evidence of the identifying witness at trial to the same effect. In practice, such a statement often consists of a statement made to a police officer supervising an identification parade. But it may also be made to any other person, and there may be occasions when it might be admissible under the new statutory complaint rule under s. 120(4) and (7) of the Criminal Justice Act 2003. Previous statements of identification were recognized as an exception to the rule against previous consistent statements at common law, for very sound reasons of practice: the sooner a witness is given the opportunity to identify a suspect, the more reliable the identification is likely to be, which (if the witness identifies someone other than the accused) may redound to the benefit of the suspect as well as the prosecution. But the theoretical basis for the exception was more tenuous, and was never satisfactorily resolved. In particular, the question of whether the statement was admissible as evidence that the accused was the person who committed the offence, or merely as evidence confirming the evidence of the identifying witness at trial was never properly settled.[40] Fortunately, s. 120(4) and (5) of the Criminal Justice Act 2003 have resolved this issue, and it is unnecessary to pursue it.[41]

16.12.1 Admissibility of statements of identification

The provisions of s. 120(4) and (5) were given at 16.2. Provided that the conditions imposed by subsections (4) and (5) are fulfilled the statement is admitted as evidence of the truth of the matters stated, i.e. (in the typical case), that the person identified committed the offence. Subsection (4)(b) requires that the witness be able to testify that he made the statement, and that to the best of his belief it states the truth. Subsection (5) requires only that the statement be one identifying a person, object or place (so that the statements admissible are not confined to statements identifying an accused or suspect). Before the coming into force of the Act, there was some uncertainty as to the position where a witness collaborates with the police in preparing a photofit picture by supplying a statement of identification. Both the photofit and the statement of identification which produced it might have been regarded as hearsay. This suggestion was rejected

---

[40] See, e.g., *Osbourne* [1973] 1 QB 678; *Christie* [1914] AC 545; *Burke and Kelly* (1847) 2 Cox CC 295.
[41] This issue is discussed in depth in the 8th edn of this work at para. 16.13.1.

in *Smith* [1976] Crim LR 511. But it was pursued again in *Cook* [1987] QB 417, this time with the support of the additional argument that they might violate the rule against previous consistent statements, where the witness gave evidence at trial. The Court of Appeal rejected the argument that a photofit was a 'statement' for the purposes of the rule against hearsay and held it to be a kind of evidence *sui generis* which was admissible.[42] It is submitted that s. 115(2) of the Criminal Justice Act, read together with s. 120(4) and (5), has provided a statutory solution to the problem. Section 115(2) defines 'statement' for the purposes of the Act as including 'a representation made in a sketch, photofit or other pictorial form'. Thus, material of this kind is hearsay if tendered to prove the matters stated, i.e., the identification of the accused. But it would be admissible as a statement of identification subject to the conditions imposed by s. 120(4) and (5).

16.12.2 Treatment of identification evidence

Admissibility is only the first facet of evidence of identification, and has probably given rise to less concern than the vexed question of the weight and reliability of such evidence. Periodically, cases where some miscarriage of justice appears to have occurred because of mistaken evidence of identification reopen the problems of trying to ensure the detection of faulty evidence in a field more open to error than most. In *Turnbull*[43] a five-member Court of Appeal considered four separate appeals against conviction, and laid down guidelines for the treatment of cases which depend wholly or substantially on the correctness of one or more identifications of the accused. The guidelines were said to 'involve only changes of practice, not law', but the Court also empha-sized that failure to follow them is likely to lead to a conviction being quashed, and will do so where the failure results in the conviction being regarded by the Court of Appeal as unsafe. The guidelines may be summarized as follows:

(a) The judge should always warn the jury of the special need for caution before convicting the accused in reliance upon the correctness of identification evidence, drawing their attention to the possibilities of error.

(b) The judge should invite the attention of the jury to examine closely the circumstances in which the identification was made; the conditions under which and the length of time for which the observation took place. Was the accused known to the witness, or was there any particular reason why the witness might be expected to remember the accused? How soon after the event did the witness give a description to the police?

(c) The judge should remind the jury specifically of any weaknesses which have appeared in the iden-tification evidence.

(d) If the prosecution have reason to believe that there is any material discrepancy between the description of the accused given at first to the police, and his actual appearance, or in any case where the defence so request, they should supply the defence with particulars of the description first supplied to the police.

(e) Where the quality of identification evidence is good, the jury may safely be left to assess it, and may convict on that basis. Conversely, where the quality of the evidence is poor, the judge should withdraw the case from the jury, and direct an acquittal, unless there is other evidence which goes

[42] The Court described as a 'step in the right direction' a suggestion made in the 1st edn of this work (at 130) that the witness might be permitted to refresh his memory using the photofit (via a commentary by D. Birch [1982] Crim LR 748): see [1987] QB at 424–5. But the Court found admissibility preferable.

[43] [1977] QB 224, Lord Widgery CJ, Roskill and Lawton LJJ, Cusack and May JJ. As to the conditions under which evidence of identification or recognition of the accused may be given based on viewing a film or photo-graph of the crime scene, see *Attorney-General's Reference (No. 2 of 2002)* [2003] 1 Cr App R 21.

to support the correctness of the identification. The judge should tell the jury what evidence there is which may support the identification. In particular, he must direct them that the fact that the accused elects not to give evidence cannot of itself support it, although he may, of course, point out that the identification evidence is uncontradicted by evidence from the accused. Where the accused puts forward an alibi, a defence which is of course crucial to the correctness of identification evidence, the jury may regard its falsity as supporting the identification, but should only do so if they think that the false alibi was put forward for the purpose of deceiving them, and not, for example, out of stupidity or panic.

Although a number of courts have considered these guidelines since *Turnbull*, there has been little need to elaborate on them. It has been pointed out that *Turnbull* is not to be interpreted inflexibly, and is concerned with the dangers of 'fleeting glance' identifications and the like, so that not every minor issue of identification need call for the full-blown *Turnbull* treatment (*Oakwell*[44]). However, in *Weeder* (1980) 71 Cr App R 228, the Court pointed out helpfully that the quality of identification evidence can be poor even though given by a number of witnesses, if they have only the opportunity of a fleeting glance or an observation made in difficult conditions. Consequently, if the judge leaves such evidence to the jury, he should direct them specifically that even a number of honest witnesses can be mistaken. In *Breslin* (1984) 80 Cr App R 226, it was held that such a direction should be given in every case where it is appropriate. It is submitted that all identification cases must be treated within the guidelines, even if in some cases the warnings may be phrased less strongly than in others.[45]

In *Shand* v *R* [1996] 1 WLR 67, the Privy Council held that, save in wholly exceptional circumstances, a *Turnbull* direction must be given also in 'recognition cases', i.e., cases in which a witness states that he identified the accused as a person known to him. In *Shand*, not only did the witness give evidence to that effect, but the accused's defence was, not that the witness was mistaken in her identification, but that she was deliberately lying in identifying him. But for the fact that the evidence against the accused was otherwise overwhelming, the appeal would have been allowed, because of the judge's failure to give a *Turnbull* direction. If this be correct, it shows that the circumstances in which it will be safe not to give the direction will be rare indeed.

In addition to the guidelines laid down in *Turnbull* for the treatment of evidence actually before the court, Code of Practice D lays down detailed rules for the guidance of the police, covering the conduct of identification procedures and the use of photographs for the purpose of identifying suspects. The detailed provisions of these rules are outside the scope of the present work (see generally *Blackstone's Criminal Practice*, 2009 edn, appendix 2).[46]

Following the report of Lord Devlin's Committee on Evidence of Identification, the Attorney General, in a written answer to the House of Commons,[47] stated that the Director of Public

---

[44] [1978] 1 WLR 32; see also *Keane* (1977) 65 Cr App R 247; *Reid* v *R* [1990] 1 AC 363; *Scott* v *R* [1989] AC 1242.

[45] Provided that a full *Turnbull* direction is given, it is not necessary to give a further direction to the specific effect that the jury should not convict based on identification evidence alone: see *Ley* [2007] 1 Cr App R 25.

[46] The holding of a properly constituted identification procedure pursuant to para. 2.3 of Code D is in general mandatory where identification may be in issue. But the failure to do so does not necessarily violate art. 6 of the European Convention on Human Rights: *Forbes* [2001] 1 AC 473. As to the use of photographs and videotapes in the identification of suspects, see generally *Lamb* (1980) 71 Cr App R 198; *Fowden* [1982] Crim LR 588; *Dodson* [1984] 1 WLR 971; *Libling* [1978] Crim LR 344.

[47] Although the answer related strictly only to cases of which the Director had the conduct, the hope was expressed that other prosecuting authorities would follow his lead, and this seems to have been the case. Hansard

Prosecutions would attach very considerable importance to the proper working of the rules when deciding whether or not to institute proceedings. Moreover, in any committal proceedings or subsequent trial, the prosecutor would not invite a witness to make a 'dock identification' where the witness had not previously identified the accused at an identification parade. This statement of principle was of great importance, and led directly to the contemporary practices surrounding the holding of properly constituted identification parades in accordance with Code of Practice D. The practice of dock identification is dangerous because of the risk that the presence of the suspect in the dock may in itself encourage the witness to believe in the accuracy of the identification.[48] It is uncertain to what extent these considerations apply in summary proceedings, particularly road traffic cases, in which the holding of a formal identification parade may be an uneconomic use of resources. There is no reason to assume that the dangers of identification are any less in summary cases, however, and there are *dicta* to the effect that the courts should adopt similar standards.[49]

D UNFAVOURABLE AND HOSTILE WITNESSES

SUMMARY OF MAIN POINTS

- A hostile witness is one who evinces an intention not to give evidence honestly, or who sets out to be uncooperative or to sabotage the case of the party calling him. Whether or not a witness may be treated as hostile is a matter for the judge.

- The fact that a witness fails to come up to proof does not make him hostile.

- The fact that a witness is hostile does not prevent a party from calling other admissible evidence.

- A hostile witness may be cross-examined and impeached by the party calling him with leave of the court, by reference to his previous statement, in the circumstances laid down by s. 3 of the Criminal Procedure Act 1865.

- At common law a previous inconsistent statement admitted for this purpose was admitted only for the limited purpose of contradicting the witness, and not as evidence of the truth of any facts stated in it.

- In civil cases this distinction is no longer relevant because of the abrogation of the Rule against Hearsay by the Civil Evidence Act 1995.

HC, Written Answers, 27 May 1976, cols 287–9. As the Director is now the head of the Crown Prosecution Service, the distinction is no longer significant.

[48] This principle may be departed from where it is impracticable to hold a proper identification parade, for example because the accused is of very unusual physical appearance (*Hunter* [1969] Crim LR 262) or refuses to attend a parade or to take part (*John* [1973] Crim LR 113); cf. Code of Practice D, para. 2.14. And in *Creamer* (1984) 80 Cr App R 248, the court allowed identification evidence to be given where the witness had not picked out the accused on the parade because she felt intimidated, but stated that she had in fact recognized him at the time of the parade, and identified him in a different situation later. The appellate courts have in the past quashed convictions where the method of obtaining identification evidence was irregular and unsafe (*Cartwright* (1914) 10 Cr App R 219); but see *Forbes* [2001] 1 AC 473; *Quinn* [1995] 1 Cr App R 480.

[49] *North Yorkshire Trading Standards Dept* v *Williams* (1994) 159 JP 383; but cf. *Barnes* v *Chief Constable of Durham* [1997] 2 Cr App R 505, per Popplewell J.

- In criminal cases, ss. 119 and 120 of the Criminal Justice Act 2003 now provide that when such a statement is admitted it is admissible as evidence of any facts stated in it of which oral evidence by the witness would be admissible.

16.13 MEANING OF 'HOSTILE'

Witnesses who 'fail to come up to proof', in other words who are unfavourable in their evidence to the party calling them, or less favourable than might have been expected, are one of the hazards of litigation. It by no means follows that a witness in this position is dishonest, or motivated by malice towards the party calling him. It may be that his knowledge or recollection are not as great as was supposed, or as was once the case. The tenor of what he is able to say may have been misunderstood or exaggerated in the course of taking his proof of evidence. It may, however, be that the witness is dishonest, uncooperative, or malicious, and he may actually set out to sabotage the case of the party calling him. In such a case, the witness is said to be hostile. Given that a party may not, generally, in evidence in chief put leading questions to his own witness, or in effect cross-examine him, what is that party entitled to do in order to repair any damage caused to his case? The answer involves consideration of two possible remedies, which are: (a) the acceptance of the evidence, combined with calling other admissible evidence in favour of the party's case; and (b) direct discrediting of the witness by reference to previous statements made by him inconsistent with his evidence.

16.14 USE OF OTHER EVIDENCE

Any party to litigation is entitled to call all the admissible evidence at his disposal which may assist him in proving his case. This principle is not affected by the fact that part of that evidence turns out to be unfavourable or insufficiently favourable. Consequently, the mere fact that a witness proves unfavourable does not prevent the calling of any other available evidence dealing with the matters which the witness was supposed to prove.[50] Indeed, if the rule were otherwise, the quantity of evidence which could be called would depend upon the accidental factor of whether the unfavourable witness was called first or last.

Within the category of other available evidence must now be counted, in civil cases, hearsay statements made by the witness himself, which may be admissible with leave by virtue of s. 6(2) of the Civil Evidence Act 1995 (see 16.2.2). It is submitted that tendering such statements is appropriate to cases where a witness is unfavourable, or insufficiently favourable because of his inability properly to deal with the matters put to him as a result of failing recollection caused by age, illness, or the lapse of time. Hearsay evidence would no doubt be an inappropriate subject of leave (and would anyway be devoid of weight) where it was sought to bolster up an inherently unreliable or reluctant witness. But the use of hearsay evidence to supplement unfavourable

---

[50] *Ewer* v *Ambrose* (1825) 3 B & C 746, where the defendant had the misfortune to call a witness who proved the exact opposite of the proposition which he had been called to support. But where a witness insists that he cannot remember anything, or is unable or unwilling to assist, the judge may rule that he should not be called, and may hold a trial within a trial to determine whether this would be the proper course (*Honeyghon* [1999] Crim LR 221).

evidence in proper cases was recognized even before the Civil Evidence Acts 1968 and 1995. In *Harvey* v *Smith-Wood* [1964] 2 QB 171, an elderly witness was called for the plaintiff on the trial of her action in March 1963. The witness was unable to deal, to the plaintiff's satisfaction, with certain crucial events, which had occurred in January 1951, by reason of his own age and the considerable lapse of time. Lawton J 'with some regret' acceded to an application to admit in evidence a written statement made by the witness in 1956, dealing with those events, under s. 1(1) of the Evidence Act 1938.[51] The regret expressed was 'because it seems to me that it is an unfortunate situation if counsel can call a witness and, when that witness does not come up to proof, counsel should be allowed to produce some earlier document which shows that on some other occasion the witness made a different statement'. Lawton J went on to say that counsel should hesitate to adopt such a course 'except in very special circumstances'. It is submitted, with respect, that the reservations alluded to by Lawton J may more happily be applied to questions of weight, than to those of admissibility.[52]

16.15 DIRECT DISCREDITING BY IMPEACHMENT

English law regards it as embarrassing and undesirable that a party should be permitted to impeach directly the evidence of a witness whom he has tendered to the court as a witness of truth. It is clear that he may do so only where the witness is not simply unfavourable, but is 'hostile' in the sense that he displays some hostile *animus* towards the party calling him, and evinces no desire to give evidence fairly or to tell the truth. Hostility may stem from malice, bribery, intimidation, or a mere indisposition to cooperate. It is interesting to note that not all common law jurisdictions find the 'voucher rule', whereby a party cannot impeach his own witness, necessary or even desirable. A majority of American jurisdictions now permit a party to impeach a witness he has called, on the ground that a party is not responsible to the court for the testimony merely because that party has called the witness in the hope of supporting his case. These jurisdictions provide accordingly that a witness may be impeached by any party, including the party calling him: see, e.g., Federal Rule of Evidence 607.

The position at common law was never developed to any satisfactory extent, beyond the principle stated above. The judge always enjoys a residual power to put any question which he thinks necessary in the interests of justice, even though such questioning may take the form of cross-examination.[53] But the real problem was whether a party could ever impeach a hostile witness called by him, by putting to the witness a statement previously made by him inconsistent with his evidence. There were *dicta* that this course was permissible, based mainly upon policy considerations of preventing bribery and other dishonest acts of interference with the administration of justice.[54] But it was left to Parliament to lay down a general rule to that effect, and the need grew in urgency with the growth of the practice of taking proofs of evidence in all forms of litigation.

---

[51] This section differed in important respects from the Civil Evidence Acts 1968 and 1995, but it is necessary only to refer to the fact that, under the 1938 Act, the statement was admissible without leave on the facts of *Harvey* v *Smith-Wood*.

[52] This view had received judicial support previously, e.g., in *Bearman's Ltd* v *Metropolitan Police District Receiver* [1961] 1 WLR 634, per Devlin LJ at 655. This case was cited to Lawton J and must have been in his mind, as he had himself appeared as counsel on that occasion, though the case turned mainly on a different point.

[53] *Bastin* v *Carew* (1824) Ry & M 127.

[54] *Melhuish* v *Collier* (1850) 15 QB 878, per Erle CJ at 890 is an example.

The provision now in force is s. 3 of the Criminal Procedure Act 1865 which provides:

> A party producing a witness shall not be allowed to impeach his credit by general evidence of bad character; but he may, in case the witness shall in the opinion of the judge prove adverse, contradict him by other evidence, or, by leave of the judge, prove that he has made at other times a statement inconsistent with his present testimony; but before such last-mentioned proof can be given the circumstances of the supposed statement, sufficient to designate the particular occasion, must be mentioned to the witness, and he must be asked whether or not he has made such statement.

The construction of this inelegantly worded enactment has caused great difficulty. It is clear enough that the section applies alike to civil and criminal proceedings, and that proof of a previous inconsistent statement requires leave of the judge.[55] But what is the meaning of 'adverse' which the judge is required to assess? It is unfortunate that the draftsmen of the 1865 Act did not heed the comments made in *Greenough* v *Eccles*[56] when there fell to be construed the identically worded s. 22 of the Common Law Procedure Act 1854. The Court held that the word 'adverse' must be construed to mean 'hostile', on the somewhat desperate reasoning that, if the word signified no more than 'unfavourable', it was hard to see how the judge should be able to form any opinion on that matter; whereas hostility could be demonstrated to him by reference to the previous statement and the demeanour of the witness.

An application must be made in every case in which it is sought to treat a witness as hostile, and the judge must be shown the statement proposed to be proved.[57] In a criminal case, it is the duty of prosecuting counsel to show the statement to the judge in any case where the witness is clearly hostile, and to ask for leave to cross-examine the witness as hostile.[58] The treatment of a hostile witness must be confined to the courses permitted by the section, that is to say contradiction by other evidence (as might be done with an unfavourable witness) and (with leave) proof of a previous inconsistent statement, subject to the preliminary questions required by the section to establish authorship of such a statement. It is not permissible to attack the credit of a party's own witness by general evidence of bad character.

It seems that the Act has not, however, removed the power of the judge at common law to allow any question to be put which seems to him to be necessary in the interests of justice. In *Thompson* (1976) 64 Cr App R 96, the victim of an alleged offence of incest was called for the prosecution, but refused to give evidence. The trial judge permitted her to be treated as hostile. It was argued on appeal that this course was not open, at least insofar as the proof of her previous statement was concerned, because the witness having given no evidence, there was no 'present testimony' with which the previous statement could be said to be 'inconsistent', under s. 3. This

---

[55] This is a question of pure discretion for the trial judge. The requirement of leave cannot be circumvented by reliance on s. 4 of the Act (see 17.7.1) which has been held not to apply to one's own hostile witnesses: *Booth* (1981) 74 Cr App R 123.

[56] (1859) 5 CB NS 786 per Williams and Willes JJ. The section reduced Cockburn CJ to the anguished cry: 'The solution by my learned brothers is a solution of a difficulty, otherwise incapable of any solution, but I am not satisfied therewith, and without actually dissenting from their judgment, I do not altogether assent to it'. (As reported in 28 LJ CP 160, 164.) The section also causes problems over the words, 'contradict him by other evidence', which at common law, might have been done in the case even of a merely unfavourable witness; the phrase is generally assumed to restate this right, which involves reading into the section the parenthesis, 'as he might have done heretofore, and also [to prove etc.]'. This is a drastic piece of construction, but it is difficult to make sense of the section otherwise.

[57] Even where the witness is a party called by his opponent, there must be a ruling on hostility; *Price* v *Manning* (1889) 42 ChD 372.

[58] *Fraser* (1956) 40 Cr App R 160. Where a witness turned hostile at committal proceedings, the prosecution were entitled to wait until the trial before treating him as such: *Mann* (1972) 56 Cr App R 750.

attractive argument failed. The Court of Appeal held that, whatever the position might be under the statute, the judge retained a power at common law to satisfy the interests of justice by requiring the witness to answer any question directed to that end.

16.15.1 Evidential effect of statement used for impeachment

At common law, a statement admitted to impeach a witness by virtue of s. 3 of the Criminal Procedure Act 1865 was admissible only for the limited purpose of attacking the credit of the witness, and was not admissible for the purpose of proving the truth of the matters stated.[59] Although s. 6(3) of the Civil Evidence Act 1995 does not alter the practice relating to such statements under s. 3 of the 1865 Act, they are now admissible in civil proceedings as evidence of the truth of the matter stated, as well as for the purpose of impeachment, by virtue of s. 1, s. 6(1), and s. 6(5) of the Act. Section 119(1) of the Criminal Justice Act 2003 has the same effect in criminal cases: see 6.2.3. In *Gibbons* [2008] EWCA Crim 1574 the Court of Appeal considered and rejected an argument that the judge should be cautious about finding a witness to be hostile because of the consequence that a hearsay statement may become admissible for the truth of its contents under s. 119(1). In this particular case reliance on s. 119(1) was unnecessary because the witness accepted the truth of the witness statement. But even if that had not been the case, the Court found that there were sufficient safeguards in the judge's discretion to exclude, which applied to s. 119(1) as to other evidence tendered by the prosecution: on this point see also *Coates* [2008] 1 Cr App R 52. In addition, the general rule is that jury should not take with them on retirement a statement admitted under s. 119(1); unless there are special circumstance it suffices if the statement is read to them in court (so that the statement enjoys no advantage compared to live evidence: see *Hulme* [2007] 1 Cr App R 334 and s. 122 of the Act (see 16.2.3)).

E   PRESENTATION OF EVIDENCE BY NON-TRADITIONAL MEANS

> **SUMMARY OF MAIN POINTS**
>
> - In contemporary practice, evidence in chief is often given other than by means of traditional examination of the witness in the courtroom.
>
> - In criminal cases the evidence of children and other vulnerable witnesses is given by means of a pre-recorded video interview. Evidence in chief may also be given by means of a live television link. A variety of other 'special measures' may be applied to live evidence in the courtroom to reduce the trauma of giving evidence.
>
> - In civil cases it is usual to allow the witness statement made by the witness to stand as his evidence in chief. Evidence may also be given by video link or other means approved by the court.

16.16   INTRODUCTION

In recent times, both Parliament and the courts have indicated a willingness to permit testimony to be given outside the traditional courtroom setting in some limited circumstances. For the most

---

[59] *Harris* (1927) 20 Cr App R 144, 147; *White* (1922) 17 Cr App R 60, 64; *Golder* [1960] 1 WLR 1169.

part, this is a reaction to concerns expressed for many years regarding the exposure of children to the ordeal of giving evidence, particularly in cases in which they are the victims of physical or sexual abuse.[60] Section 32 of the Criminal Justice Act 1988 introduced provisions for the evidence of children to be given through a live television link in certain cases. Section 54 of the Criminal Justice Act 1991 introduced provisions for the admissibility of a videotaped interview of a child witness in certain cases, in lieu of the child being examined in chief in court. This was achieved by inserting a new s. 32A into the Criminal Justice Act 1988. These provisions were replaced in extended form by those of Part II, Chapter 1 of the Youth Justice and Criminal Evidence Act 1999, to cover any vulnerable or intimidated witness (including children). By virtue of ss. 16 to 19 of the 1999 Act, 'special measures directions' may be made in the case of such witnesses, and these measures may include directions for evidence to be given by means of a live link (s. 24) or by means of a video-recorded interview of the witness (ss. 27 to 28). In the case of child witnesses, s. 21 of the Act provides that the measure must provide for the evidence in chief of the child to be given by means of a video-recorded interview, and for any evidence not so given (for example, in cross-examination) to be given by means of a live link. Where the child is in need of special protection under s. 21(1)(b) (because the offence is one of the sexual offences specified by s. 35) the measure must provide for cross-examination and re-examination of the witness also to be given in the form of a video recording. In civil cases also, r. 32.3 of the Civil Procedure Rules 1998 now permits the court to allow any witness to give evidence by way of a video link or any other means. This express provision avoids the uncertainty faced by the courts in trying to make this option available under the former RSC, Ord. 38, as illustrated by the case of *Garcin* v *Amerindo Investment Advisers Ltd* [1991] 1 WLR 1140.

It is obvious that these methods of adducing evidence raise some fundamental issues of fairness. While they do have the effect of reducing the trauma of vulnerable witnesses to some extent, there is also an extremely significant effect on the right of the accused to conduct his case fully and fairly. It is right to say that the Act provides some safeguards for the accused, but it inevitably detracts from the immediacy of 'live' testimony in the courtroom, which provides the jury with the best opportunity to test the credibility of the witness. If the defendant is to be afforded a full and fair defence, it would seem that the accused must rely on the vigilance of the courts, and their willingness to use their discretionary powers to prevent unfairness. The traditional methods of testing the evidence of children and other witnesses deemed to be vulnerable in a courtroom setting have to some extent been deprived of their efficacy. The implications of the provisions of s. 21 of the Act dealing with special measures for witnesses in need of special protection, in the light of the fairness requirements of art. 6 of the European Convention on Human Rights, were considered by the House of Lords in *R (On application by D)* v *Camberwell Green Youth Court* [2005] 1 WLR 393. It was argued that such special measures infringed the defendant's right to a fair trial. But the House took the view that the measures did not violate the article. Parliament had enacted the provisions of the 1999 Act, and the courts were given flexible powers to ensure a fair trial, including the right to exclude evidence and to require evidence to be given in court. The court was entitled to avail itself of the benefits of modern technology in order to afford protection to vulnerable witnesses. Both Lord Rodger of Earlsferry (at [13]–[14]) and Baroness Hale (at [49]) emphasized that art. 6 does not require face-to-face confrontation in court as an element of fairness. Lord Rodger took the view that art. 6 does not go so far as the Sixth Amendment

---

[60] See generally J. Spencer and R. Flin, *The Evidence of Children*, 2nd edn (London: Blackstone, 1993); J. Spencer [1987] Crim LR 76.

to the United States Constitution in its interpretation of the right of confrontation (see 7.5.1). Accordingly, such provisions did not infringe the right to a fair trial.[61]

The courts have, on occasion, experimented with less drastic measures, such as the use of a screen which prevents the accused from seeing the witness, while permitting the judge, the jury, and counsel to do so (see, e.g., *X* (1989) 91 Cr App R 36). Some of these measures are adopted and given statutory force by the Youth Justice and Criminal Evidence Act 1999. Thus, a special measures direction made for the benefit of a vulnerable or intimidated witness may provide for screening the witness from the accused (but not from the judge or court, the jury, and the legal representatives) during his evidence (s. 23); the exclusion of specified persons (with the same exceptions) from court during the evidence of a witness in proceedings relating to sexual offences, or where the witness might be intimidated by a person other than the accused (s. 25); and the removal of wigs and gowns by the judge and the advocates during the witness's evidence (s. 26).

Less controversially, in civil cases r. 32.5 of the Civil Procedure Rules 1998, replacing the former RSC, Ord. 38, r. 2A, now permits the court to direct that witness statements exchanged by the parties shall serve as the evidence in chief of the witnesses concerned. This reflects the fact that, in actions tried by a judge without a jury, the judge can glean the evidence in chief just as well from a written statement as from a live witness. The witness is, of course, subject to cross-examination, and the witness statement must be confined to matters which are admissible in evidence.

16.17 CRIMINAL CASES

The presentation of evidence in chief other than by means of evidence given in the courtroom is now governed in criminal cases by Part II, Chapter 1 of the Youth Justice and Criminal Evidence Act 1999. The Act creates a new category of vulnerable and intimidated witnesses who may be eligible for 'assistance' in giving evidence. This assistance is provided in the form of 'special measures directions'. Some of these directions, such as those noted above involving the screening of witnesses, exclusion of persons from the courtroom, and the removal of wigs and gowns, are essentially administrative. But others, including the presentation of evidence in ways intended to protect the witness from fear or intimidation either from external sources or from the nature of the trial process itself, have a substantive effect on the law of evidence. The full provisions of the Act are outside the scope of this work: see *Blackstone's Criminal Practice*, 2009 edn, para. D14.97 *et seq*. But it is pertinent to note the most important provisions which govern the presentation of evidence.

A witness is eligible for assistance if he falls within s. 16 or s. 17 of the Act. The cases under s. 16 are those in which the witness is a 'child witness', i.e., one who is under the age of 17 at the time of the hearing,[62] or suffers from mental disorder or a significant impairment of intelligence and social functioning. The cases under s. 17 are those in which the court is satisfied that the

---

[61] Cf. the decision of the European Court of Human Rights in *SN v Sweden* (2004) 39 EHRR 304.

[62] In general, a special measures direction applicable to a witness who is eligible solely on the ground of age ceases to have effect when the witness attains the age of 17, unless he has already begun to give evidence in the proceedings (s. 21(8)). However, s. 21(9) provides that where a special measures direction provides for the evidence of the witness to be given by video recording, the measure may provide that it continue to have effect even after the witness attains the age of 17. For the practice under s. 54 of the Criminal Justice Act 1991 in this situation, see *Day* [1997] 1 Cr App R 181.

quality of evidence given by the witness is likely to be diminished by reason of fear or distress in connection with testifying in the proceedings. Where the witness is the complainant in respect of a sexual offence, s. 17(4) provides that the witness is eligible for assistance unless the witness informs the court that he does not wish to receive assistance. In addition, where the witness is eligible on the ground of age (whether or not he is also otherwise eligible) s. 21(1)(b) provides that he is to be regarded as 'in need of special protection' if any of the offences involved in the proceedings is a sexual offence or an offence of kidnapping or certain assaults specified by s. 35(3) of the Act.[63] A special measures direction made for the assistance of such witnesses may include a provision for the giving of evidence by means of a live link, or by means of a video-recorded interview.[64]

16.17.1 Evidence given by live link

By virtue of s. 24(1) of the Youth Justice and Criminal Evidence Act 1999, a special measures direction may provide for the witness to give evidence by means of a live link. Where this direction is given, the witness may not give evidence in any other way without the permission of the court (s. 24(2)). Section 24(8) defines the phrase 'live link' as meaning:

> ...a live television link or other arrangement whereby a witness, while absent from the courtroom or other place where the proceedings are being held, is able to see and hear a person there and to be seen and heard by [the judge or justices, jury, legal representatives, and interpreter or other person appointed to assist the witness].

Subsection (3) adds that the court may give permission for the witness to give evidence in another way if satisfied that it would be in the interests of justice to do so, either of its own motion, or on an application by a party to the proceedings based on a material change of circumstances since the direction was given.

16.17.2 Evidence given by video recording

Section 27(1) of the Youth Justice and Criminal Evidence Act 1999 provides that a special measures direction may provide for the evidence in chief of a witness to be given by means of a video-recorded interview of the witness.[65] As in the case of evidence given by live link, once the court has made a special measures direction that a witness should give evidence by means of a video recording, the witness may not give evidence in chief in any other manner unless the court so

---

[63] This provision also may continue in certain circumstances where the witness was under 17 at the time when a video recording of his evidence was made but has subsequently attained that age: see s. 22.

[64] All special measures directions are subject to the availability of the appropriate facilities and technological support for such measures in the area (see s. 18). Given the rapid spread of technological capability, this limitation should not inhibit the use of such directions for long. See also *D (DPP)* v *Redbridge Youth Court* [2001] 4 All ER 416.

[65] Although a video recording lacks the immediacy of courtroom evidence, it does create a permanent record of the evidence. Under the corresponding provisions of s. 32A of the Criminal Justice Act 1988, it was held that, subject to the judge's power to refuse permission if it would result in unfairness to the accused, it is permissible to replay the recording for the benefit of the court (*Rawlings* [1995] 1 WLR 178) and to make use of a transcript of the recording with a warning that it is the recording itself, and not the transcript, which is evidence in the case (*Welstead* [1996] 1 Cr App R 59). There would seem to be no reason why these decisions should not continue to be followed.

orders on the ground that it would be in the interests of justice (see s. 27(5)(b) and (7)). Because of the obvious potential for prejudice to the accused which may result from the evidence in chief of a prosecution witness being given in this form, the court is given power to exclude the whole or any part of the recording in certain circumstances. Section 27(2) and (3) provide that the court may take this step if it would be in the interests of justice to do so, and in considering this matter, the court must ask itself whether the prejudice to the accused would be outweighed by the desirability of admitting the recording. Most importantly, however, s. 27(5)(a) requires that the party tendering the recording must call the witness to give evidence unless the special measures direction provides for cross-examination to be given otherwise than by evidence in court, or the parties agree that he need not be called. And by virtue of s. 27(4) the court may refuse to admit the recording if it appears that the witness will not be available for cross examination, unless the parties agree that he need not be made available for that purpose.

In *D* [2003] QB 90, an elderly witness who suffered from Alzheimer's Disease had made a videotaped recording before trial setting forth his knowledge of the facts. By the time of trial, the witness was effectively unavailable to give evidence because of his medical condition. An application was made to the trial judge to admit the video recording as a hearsay statement under s. 23 of the Criminal Justice Act 1988. There was at that time no other provision under which it could have been admitted. Although, strictly, no question of the competence of the witness arose under s. 23 (though it might have affected the judge's discretion to exclude under s. 26 of the Act) the judge nonetheless considered the matter, applying the test provided by s. 53 of the Youth Justice and Criminal Evidence Act 1999, which was not yet in effect (see 15.1). It was not apparent that the witness had been suffering from any disability when the recording was made. The judge then admitted the evidence. The accused challenged the resulting conviction on the ground that the admission of the evidence violated his right to a fair trial under art. 6 of the European Convention on Human Rights (see 1.7). Although there was an obvious disadvantage to the accused, who was unable effectively to challenge the evidence, the Court of Appeal held that no violation of art. 6 had been involved. The matter is one for the judgment of the trial judge, who must have regard to the question of fairness. It is submitted that clearly, in such circumstances, the judge should hesitate to admit such evidence and, if it is admitted, a strong direction should be given to the jury to treat the evidence with the greatest possible care.

Section 21(3) makes special provision for the evidence of child witnesses:

> (3) The primary rule in the case of a child witness is that the court must give a special measures direction in relation to the witness which complies with the following requirements—
>> (a) it must provide for any relevant recording to be admitted under s. 27 ...; and
>> (b) it must provide for any evidence given by the witness in the proceedings which is not given by means of a video recording (whether in chief or otherwise) to be given by means of a live link in accordance with s. 24.

This primary rule must be applied subject to the court's power to exclude under s. 27(2) and (unless the child is in need of special protection) does not apply if the court is not satisfied that to do so would be likely to maximize the quality of the witness's evidence (see s. 21(4)). In *Powell* [2006] 1 Cr App R 468, the evidence in chief of a child under 4 years of age was properly given by way of video recording, but on cross-examination it appeared that the child was incompetent as a witness because of a lack of ability to answer questions put to her as a witness. It was held that the judge was obliged to re-visit the question of competence, to declare that the witness was incompetent, and to withdraw the case from the jury.

A video recording made for the purposes of being used in evidence should comply with the guidelines provided in the Home Office paper, *Achieving Best Evidence: Guidance for Vulnerable or Intimidated Witnesses, including Children*. The guidelines, which concern the conduct of the video-taped interview, are designed to reduce the trauma of the process for the witness; to make the evidence clear and unambiguous; and to prevent inadmissible evidence and evidence elicited by means of leading questions from being included. Such interviews are now routinely conducted by specially trained police officers and are often referred to as 'A.B.E. interviews'. A failure to comply in all respects with the guidelines does not render the evidence contained in the video recording inadmissible unless it would be contrary to the interests of justice to admit it: *G v DPP* [1998] QB 919. The test was said in *K* [2006] 2 Cr App R 175 to be whether a jury, properly directed, could (though not necessarily would) find that the witness had given a credible and accurate account of the facts. In case of doubt the judge is entitled to exercise his discretion to exclude evidence, bearing in mind that any inadmissible portions may be edited out, as long as this can be done without undue violence to the evidence as a whole.

A very radical and significant extension of the law is made by s. 28 of the Act. Under s. 32(A) of the Criminal Justice Act 1988, only the evidence in chief of a child witness could be given by means of a video recording. But by virtue of s. 28 of the 1999 Act, where a special measures direction provides for the evidence in chief of a witness to be given by way of video recording, the direction may also provide for any cross-examination and re-examination of the witness to be given in the same manner. This provision does not apply where the accused is entitled to cross-examine the witness in person, as opposed to having the cross-examination conducted by his advocate.[66] Any cross-examination by the accused in person must take place in the court-room (even if the witness is giving evidence by a live link). In fact, the accused may not be present during the making of the recording, but he must be able to see and hear the examination of the witness and communicate with his legal advisers. The judge or magistrates and the legal representatives must be able to see and hear the examination and to communicate with any persons in whose presence the recording is being made (s. 28(2)). Of course, the accused would not be present during an interview with a witness which is made with a view to its admission as evidence in chief, and the purpose of the use of video recordings would be frustrated if the accused were entitled to be present in person at any stage of the interview. By s. 21(6) of the Act, where a child witness is in need of special protection, a special measures direction which (in accordance with the primary rule) provides for evidence in chief to be given by video recording, must also provide that any cross-examination and re-examination of the witness shall be given in the same manner.

16.17.3 General provisions

Section 31 of the Act makes important general provisions regarding the status of evidence admitted under the provisions discussed above. The main provisions of this section are as follows:

---

[66] There are significant restrictions on the right of the accused to cross-examine certain witnesses in person, most recently enacted by ss. 34 to 37 of the Youth Justice and Criminal Evidence Act 1999: see 17.4. It is very likely that the accused will not be able to cross-examine in person a witness eligible for assistance under the Act.

> (1) Subsections (2) to (4) apply to a statement made by a witness in criminal proceedings which, in accordance with a special measures direction, is not made by the witness in direct oral testimony in court but forms part of the witness's evidence in those proceedings.
>
> (2) The statement shall be treated as if made by the witness in direct oral testimony in court; and accordingly—
>
>> (a) it is admissible evidence of any fact of which such testimony from the witness would be admissible;
>>
>> (b) it is not capable of corroborating any other evidence given by the witness.
>
> (3) Subsection (2) applies to a statement admitted under section 27 or 28 which is not made by the witness on oath even though it would have been required to be made on oath if made by the witness in direct oral testimony in court.
>
> (4) In estimating the weight (if any) to be attached to the statement, the court must have regard to all the circumstances from which an inference can reasonably be drawn (as to the accuracy of the statement or otherwise).
>
> (5) Nothing in this Chapter (apart from subsection (3)) affects the operation of any rule of law relating to evidence in criminal proceedings.

Subsection (6) renders a witness liable for perjury, or an offence akin to perjury, for any false evidence given by the means prescribed by a special measures direction. The purpose of these provisions is to ensure that only admissible evidence is given. This is particularly crucial in the case of an interview with a child witness made with a view to its admission as evidence in chief. Such an interview is likely to be conducted by a lay person sympathetic to the child, and is likely to contain a good deal of inadmissible material, for example hearsay statements, and may feature the liberal use of leading questions. It is submitted that the court must be scrupulous in analysing the admissibility of the evidence before allowing it to be presented to the jury. The rules of evidence in criminal cases preserved by s. 31(5) must, it is submitted, include the court's powers, at common law and under s. 78 of the Police and Criminal Evidence Act 1984, to exclude any prosecution evidence in the interests of fairness to the accused, which now coexist with the specific powers to exclude evidence referred to above.

16.17.4 Criminal Justice Act 2003, s. 137

A further provision is made for evidence to be adduced by means of video link by s. 137 of the Criminal Justice Act 2003. This section applies to persons (other than the accused: see s. 137(3)(a)) who claim to have witnessed the offence or events closely connected with the offence and who give evidence in the proceedings (s. 137(1)(a) and (b)). Where such a person has previously given a videotaped account of what he witnessed at a time when the events were fresh in his memory, the court may give a direction that the recording should be admitted as his evidence in chief (s. 137(1)(b)–(g)). If or to the extent that the witness states that the statements made by him in the recording are true, they are to be treated as if he had given evidence of them (s. 137(2)) even though there is no requirement that the recording should have been made under oath (s. 137(5)). Subsection (3)(b) lays down the test for making the direction, namely (i) that the witness's recollection of events is likely to have been significantly better at the time of the recording than at the time of his testimony; and (ii) that it would be in the interests of justice to make the direction having regard to four self-explanatory factors enumerated in subsection (4) relating to the likely accuracy of the matters stated, the quality of the recording, and the witness's own views. Section 138 of the Act contains supplementary provisions. The only one of these that requires comment is s. 138(3), which provides that, if the court considers admitting part but not all of the recording, it must consider the risk of prejudice to the accused, and whether it would be in the interests of justice to admit only part of it.

16.18 CIVIL CASES

As we have noted, r. 32.3 of the Civil Procedure Rules 1998 now makes it possible for evidence to be given in civil cases by means of video link or any other means. In contrast to the complex rules in criminal proceedings, in civil proceedings there is no restriction on the kinds of witness to whom, or evidence to which, this rule applies. But in criminal cases, Parliament had to take into account the need to safeguard, at least to some extent, the particular rights of the accused, and to ensure that the evidence can be evaluated by a jury. In a civil case, if the rule is invoked without sufficient cause, or in an attempt to diminish the effectiveness of cross-examination for tactical reasons, the judge has ample power to treat the evidence of the witness as being of little weight and to draw an adverse inference against the party seeking to present evidence in such a manner. The question of when the use of non-traditional methods of presenting evidence in civil cases might be improper was explored with a remarkable degree of judicial disagreement in *Polanski v Condé Nast Publications Ltd* [2005] 1 WLR 637. The claimant sought leave to give evidence by video link from France pursuant to r. 32.3 of the Civil Procedure Rules 1998 in the course of an action for libel against the defendant publishers. The claimant, a celebrated film director, had for many years lived in France as a fugitive from justice in the United States, where he was wanted in connection with criminal proceedings. He claimed that if he came to England, he would be arrested and extradited to the United States, whereas if he remained in France, no such action would be taken against him. The judge at first instance found his application to be proper and granted it. The Court of Appeal, by a majority, reversed the judge on the ground that the application was essentially an abuse of the process of the court, especially in the context of an action for libel, which the Court felt to be a form of voluntary litigation which the claimant could have avoided. The House of Lords, by a majority of three to two,[67] reversed the decision of the Court of Appeal. It was held that the video-link procedure should be open to all litigants equally. There was no rule that a fugitive was not entitled to initiate or defend proceedings, and in so doing he was entitled to avail himself of the procedures of the courts. It is not entirely clear what lesson is to be learned from this case, except perhaps that the court will not enter into moral judgments against litigants unconnected with the case at hand.

The main innovation in civil cases, however, has been the general practice of exchanging witness statements and having the witness statements stand as the evidence in chief of the witnesses. This practice was introduced in cases in the High Court by the former RSC, Ord. 38, r. 2A, but now applies to all civil cases by virtue of r. 32 of the Civil Procedure Rules 1998. Rule 32.4(1) defines a witness statement as:

> ...a written statement signed by a person which contains the evidence which that person would be allowed to give orally.

This definition reflects a requirement that the contents of witness statements be confined to material which is admissible in evidence, although this is less crucial than in criminal cases

---

[67] Lords Nicholls, Hope, and Baroness Hale; Lords Slynn and Carswell dissenting.

because of the admissibility of hearsay evidence in civil cases. Nonetheless, there will be occasions on which a witness statement cannot be permitted to stand as evidence in chief without the removal of some inadmissible material.

Rule 32.4(2) provides that the court will order the parties to serve on each other any witness statement of the oral evidence on which they intend to rely in relation to any issues of fact to be decided at the trial, and r. 32.4(3) adds that the court may give directions as to the order in which the witness statements are to be served.[68] Failure to serve a witness statement within the time prescribed by the court will result in the party being unable to call the witness in question to give oral evidence without the court's permission (r. 32.10). By virtue of r. 32.5, where a witness statement is served and the party doing so wishes to rely on the evidence of the witness, he must call the witness to give oral evidence, unless the court orders otherwise, or he is content to adduce the statement as hearsay evidence, in which case the witness statement is sufficient notice of that intention.[69] The same rule provides that where the witness gives oral evidence, his witness statement shall stand as his evidence in chief unless the court otherwise orders, though he may be permitted to amplify his evidence if necessary and to deal with any matters which have arisen since his witness statement was served (r. 32.5(2) and (3)). Where a party serves a witness statement but does not call the witness to give evidence or use the statement as hearsay evidence, any other party may use the statement as hearsay evidence (r. 32.5(5)).[70] Where the witness is called to give oral evidence, r. 32.11 permits all other parties to cross-examine the witness about any part of his witness statement, even where that part was not referred to in his evidence in chief, though in general this would follow from the fact that the witness statement will have been ordered to stand as the witness's evidence in chief.

Under the former RSC, Ord. 38, r. 2A, some reservations were expressed about the desirability of reducing all evidence in chief to a series of written statements. In *Mercer v Chief Constable of the Lancashire Constabulary* [1991] 1 WLR 367, the Court of Appeal held that each case should be approached individually, that it was undesirable to give uniform directions in all cases, and that evidence of opinion was more appropriately given by way of the exchange of written statements than evidence of fact. However, under the old procedure, the exchange of witness statements, and the extent to which they should stand as evidence in chief, depended on specific directions given by the court in each case, whereas under r. 32.4 the exchange is to take place automatically, with the court having the power to give directions as to the order of service, and there is a general rule that witness statements shall stand as evidence in chief. Nonetheless, there may be cases in which the crucial or strongly contested nature of certain evidence will make it inappropriate for the witness statement to stand as evidence in chief, and in which the traditional process of oral evidence will assist the judge more in assessing the weight of the evidence. In such cases, it is submitted that the judge should not hesitate to order that the evidence in chief be given by means of oral evidence.

---

[68] Where a party intends to rely on the evidence of a witness but is unable to obtain a signed witness statement, he may serve a witness summary of the intended evidence under r. 32.9, which will then be treated in the same manner as a witness statement.

[69] Notice of intention to adduce hearsay evidence as required by s. 2(1)(a) of the Civil Evidence Act 1995 is dealt with separately by rr. 33.2 to 33.4: see 8.33.

[70] This rule reverses the practice under the old procedure: see, e.g., *Black & Decker Inc. v Flymo Ltd* [1991] 1 WLR 753; *Prudential Assurance Co. Ltd v Fountain Page Ltd* [1991] 1 WLR 756.

16.19 RECOMMENDED FURTHER READING

Bromby, M., MacMillan, M., and McKellar, P., 'An examination of criminal jury directions in relation to eyewitness identification in Commonwealth jurisdictions' (2007) **36**(4) *Common Law World Review* 303.

Burton, M., Evans, R., and Sanders, A., 'Vulnerable and intimidated witnesses and the adversarial process in England and Wales' (2007) **11**(1) *International Journal of Evidence and Proof* 1.

Lewis, P., 'Delayed complaints in childhood sexual abuse prosecutions—a comparative evaluation of admissibility determinations and judicial warnings' (2006) **10**(2) *International Journal of Evidence and Proof* 104.

Newark, M, 'The hostile witness and the adversary system' [1986] *Criminal Law Review* 441.

Pattenden, R., 'The hostile witness' (1992) **56** *Journal of Criminal Law* 414.

Roberts, P., Cooper, M., and Judge, S., 'Monitoring success, accounting for failure: the outcome of prosecutors' applications for special measures directions under the Youth Justice and Criminal Evidence Act 1999' (2005) **9**(4) *International Journal of Evidence and Proof* 269.

16.20 QUESTIONS FOR DISCUSSION BASED ON *R* v *COKE; LITTLETON* AND *BLACKSTONE* v *COKE* (for case files go to the Online Resource Centre)

16.20.1 *Coke; Littleton*

1. Devise a series of questions to take Margaret Blackstone through her evidence in chief, without leading her.

2. If D/I Glanvil and D/S Bracton apply to refresh their memories from their notebooks, what must the judge take into account before permitting this?

3. Under what circumstances may the officers' notebooks be put in evidence? What evidential value would they have?

4. May Angela Blackstone, her mother, or the officers give evidence of the identification of Littleton in the street? What considerations apply generally to the evidence of identification of Littleton?

5. May evidence be given of the accounts given to their mother by Margaret and Angela of what had happened at Coke's flat? If so, what evidence may be given, and to what effect?

6. If at trial, Margaret refuses to give evidence, or asserts that she consented to the act of intercourse, what should counsel for the prosecution do?

7. How should the evidence in chief of Angela Blackstone be presented?

16.20.2 *Blackstone* v *Coke*

Consider questions 3, 4, 5, and 7 above in the context of *Blackstone* v *Coke*.

16.21 GENERAL QUESTIONS FOR DISCUSSION

1. An advocate asks their witness: 'The man you saw steal from your shop was wearing a red hat, wasn't he?' Is there anything wrong with that question? In what circumstances could he ask that question during examination in chief?

2. In civil proceedings, in what circumstances may a witness be permitted to refer to a previous statement to refresh his memory?

3. Is it correct that, in criminal proceedings, a witness may only refresh his memory from a document made or verified contemporaneously with the events about which he is testifying?

4. In general, may a witness give evidence about a statement that she made on a previous occasion?

5. What if a witness is cross-examined to the effect that they are lying and the earlier statement would demonstrate that their evidence is truthful?

6. A witness only catches a 'fleeting glance' of the suspect. How should the jury be directed?

7. What is a 'hostile witness'?

8. How may an advocate respond if their witness gives unfavourable evidence but is not actively hostile to their party's case?

9. A witness is scared to give evidence in court. What practical steps might a prosecutor take to allay their fears?

10. In what way does the procedure for examination in chief in civil proceedings differ from that in criminal proceedings?

17

CROSS-EXAMINATION AND BEYOND

17.1 INTRODUCTION

Consideration of the course of evidence, following the discussion of examination in chief in the last chapter, must take into account both cross-examination by the party against whom a witness is called, and re-examination by the party calling the witness, where necessary in the light of cross-examination. But it will also be convenient to deal, in this chapter, with two subjects falling outside what might be termed the routine course of evidence. These are evidence called in rebuttal, and witnesses called by the judge of his own motion. These topics will each be examined in the sections which follow, and, as with examination in chief, we shall be concerned with their evidential rather than procedural aspects, although some comment on the latter will be helpful, and will be made where the practice of calling witnesses bears upon the evidential questions which arise.

A CROSS-EXAMINATION: GENERAL PRINCIPLES

SUMMARY OF MAIN POINTS

- Cross-examination is the process of challenging the evidence of a witness called on behalf of another party. Any witness who has taken the oath becomes liable to cross-examination by any other party.

- In general the rules of evidence apply to cross-examination as to examination in chief, though cross-examination is subject to a few specific rules.

- Leading questions are permitted in cross-examination.

- Cross-examination may be directed to substantive issues and/or the credit of the witness.

- Advocates are under a duty to put their case to the witness in cross-examination. Failure to cross-examine may be regarded as an admission of the truth of the evidence given by the witness.

- Sections 34–40 of the Youth Justice and Criminal Evidence Act 1999 impose restrictions on cross-examination by an accused in person where the witness is a child or a complainant in a sexual case, or in any case where the judge makes certain findings about the quality of the evidence and the interests of justice. The accused must then be given the opportunity to instruct an advocate and, if he declines to do so, the court must consider whether to appoint an advocate to cross-examine for him.

17.2 LIABILITY TO CROSS-EXAMINATION

Cross-examination is the process whereby a party seeks: (a) to test the veracity and accuracy of evidence in chief given by a witness called for another party; and (b) to elicit from that witness any relevant facts which may be favourable to the case for the cross-examiner. Cross-examination designed solely to discredit the witness and to destroy or reduce his credibility, is sometimes known as 'impeachment' and is perfectly permissible in its own right.

A witness who has been sworn is compellable to answer any proper question put in cross-examination, whether directed to an issue in the case (i.e., to the substance of his evidence) or to his credit as a witness. With the exception of the accused in a criminal case, whose position is governed by s. 101 of the Criminal Justice Act 2003: Part B of Chapter 6, a witness may be compelled to answer even questions directed to showing his bad character, for the purpose of impugning his credit as a witness; though such cross-examination now requires leave and is subject to the provisions of s. 100 of the Criminal Justice Act 2003: see 6.15 *et seq*. There are statutory restrictions on cross-examination of the complainant in a sexual case with respect to his or her sexual behaviour. These are dealt with at 6.25 *et seq*. The credit of a witness depends upon the view which the tribunal of the fact ultimately takes of: (a) his knowledge of the facts; (b) his impartiality; (c) his truthfulness; and (d) his respect for his oath or affirmation. These qualities may, therefore, be attacked to the extent necessary to dissuade the tribunal from relying on the witness's evidence, but counsel has a duty not to exceed what is required, and the judge may restrain unnecessary cross-examination, even where some basis for the questions can be found as a matter of law.[1]

Any witness who has been sworn on behalf of any party is liable to be cross-examined on behalf of any other party to the proceedings. The liability does not depend upon whether the witness has given evidence adverse to the case of the cross-examining party, because it is perfectly proper for cross-examination to take place for the purpose of eliciting facts favourable to the cross-examiner's case, irrespective of the nature of the witness's evidence in chief.[2] The right to cross-examine exists even where the witness has given no evidence in chief, either because counsel calling him decides, once he has been sworn, not to ask any questions of him,[3] or because, as frequently happens in the case of witnesses who exactly corroborate witnesses already called, he is sworn solely for the purpose of being tendered for cross-examination. The latter practice is common in the case of police officers whose evidence in chief will be identical, any one of whom can give the relevant evidence in chief, but all of whom may be required for cross-examination by the defence. In a criminal case involving more than one accused, the accused should cross-examine prosecution witnesses in the order in which they appear on the indictment.[4] The same order should be followed for the cross-examination of defence witnesses, and in this case, the prosecution should cross-examine after cross-examination by all accused.

Cross-examination is, like any other questioning, subject to the rules of evidence, one of which is that the answers elicited must be directly relevant to an issue in the case, or indirectly so, as in the case of questions going to credit. Where it appears that a witness is unable to give relevant evidence, it would seem that no question of cross-examination can arise, and the same result obtains where examination in chief is stopped by the judge for any reason properly within his power, before any relevant question has been put.[5]

It seems that where a witness, who has given evidence in chief, becomes unavailable to be cross-examined, his evidence in chief remains admissible, but is unlikely to carry very much

---

[1] *Sweet-Escott* (1971) 55 Cr App R 316. It is not unfair, *per se*, for the judge to impose some time limit on cross-examination in the interests of the proper management of the trial, especially when it tends towards prolixity, but clearly this should be considered with great care to prevent unfairness from arising: *B* [2005] EWCA Crim 805. Courts have also held various methods of cross-examination unfair; see, e.g., the now forbidden practice of cross-examining the accused on his application for legal aid: *Stubbs* [1982] 1 All ER 424. Though improper restraint or interruptions by the judge may be a ground of appeal (see, e.g., *Sharp* [1994] QB 261).

[2] This is not true in many American jurisdictions. Cross-examination may be restricted to matters dealt with in chief, plus issues affecting credibility. To elicit other matters, a party must recall the witness as his own and examine in chief. See, e.g., Federal Rule of Evidence 611. Because of the obvious potential for inconvenience and waste of time, however, many judges interpret this rule liberally.

[3] *Brooke* (1819) 2 Stark 472. If a witness gives no evidence in chief then there can be no cross-examination concerning his credit because it cannot be relevant: *Hobbs v C.T. Tinling & Co. Ltd* [1929] 2 KB 1. But issues of credibility may arise during cross-examination.

[4] *Barber* (1844) 1 Car & Kir 434.

[5] *Creevy v Carr* (1835) 7 Car & P 64.

weight.[6] A most difficult problem faced the trial judge in *Stretton* (1986) 86 Cr App R 7. The complainant in a case of attempted rape gave evidence in chief, and was cross-examined on behalf of the accused for a period of three and a half hours over two separate days, restricted sessions being necessary because of her medical condition, but cross-examination had not been concluded. After this, she became too ill for further cross-examination. The accused asked the judge to rule that the trial could not continue, since they had been deprived of the opportunity to conclude the cross-examination of the complainant. The judge permitted the trial to proceed, and warned the jury to bear in mind the fact that the complainant had not been fully cross-examined. The accused were convicted. On appeal, the Court of Appeal held that the judge had exercised his discretion correctly, in view of the length of the cross-examination that had been possible and in view of the clear warning he had given to the jury. It is not difficult to sympathize with the trial judge, in a case where there was evidently some doubt whether the complainant would be able to testify in a subsequent trial, so that discharging the jury might have been the equivalent of directing a verdict of not guilty. There will be cases where the facts dictate a different exercise of discretion. Such a case was *Lawless* (1993) 98 Cr App R 342, in which a prosecution witness on whose evidence the whole case against the accused rested suffered a heart attack at the end of his examination in chief, and could not be cross-examined. In such a case, the only fair course must be to direct the jury to return a verdict of not guilty. The unavailability of a witness for cross-examination, or complete cross-examination is a matter which has the potential to affect the accused's right to a fair trial under art. 6 of the European Convention on Human Rights (see 1.7). The decision in *D* [2003] QB 90 (the facts of which were discussed at 16.17.2) indicates that, provided that the judge exercises his legal and discretionary powers to allow the evidence to stand or the trial to continue after full consideration of all the circumstances, and with due regard to the question of fairness to the accused, no violation of art. 6 is involved. It is submitted that a strong warning to the jury to treat the evidence with caution is appropriate in any such case. In an extreme case, in which the accused is deprived of all opportunity to challenge crucial evidence by means of cross-examination, it may be the judge would be obliged to exclude the evidence or, if evidence has been given, to discharge the jury. Each case must be considered on its own facts.

If the witness's absence from the witness-box is temporary, for instance because of illness, it is obviously desirable that an adjournment should be granted, wherever this can be done without undue inconvenience or delay, in order to allow cross-examination to take place. However, if a witness absconds with a view to avoiding cross-examination, an obvious inference is to be drawn by the tribunal of fact, which would be justified in rejecting the witness's evidence altogether.[7]

If a witness gives evidence unsworn (see 15.3 and 15.18), he is liable to cross-examination, except, apparently, where a witness is called only to produce a document whose identity is otherwise proved, and where a judge or counsel speaks from his place in court about a case in which he has been judicially or professionally engaged.

17.3 EFFECT OF OMISSION TO CROSS-EXAMINE

Failure to cross-examine a witness who has given relevant evidence for the other side is held technically to amount to an acceptance of the witness's evidence in chief. It is, therefore, not

---

[6] For example, where the witness dies after giving evidence in chief: see *Doolin* (1832) Jebb 123 (in which the witness fainted and was 'supposed by many to be dead').

[7] *Shea* v *Green* (1866) 2 TLR 533.

open to a party to impugn in a closing speech, or otherwise, the unchallenged evidence of a witness called by his opponent, or even to seek to explain to the tribunal of fact the reason for the failure to cross-examine. In *Bircham*,[8] for example, counsel for the accused was not permitted to suggest to the jury that the co-accused and a witness for the prosecution were the perpetrators of the offence charged, where that allegation had not been put to either in cross-examination. Accordingly, it is an advocate's duty, in every case: (a) to challenge every part of a witness's evidence which runs contrary to his own instructions; (b) to put to the witness, in terms, any allegation against him which must be made in the proper conduct of the case; and (c) to put to the witness counsel's own case, in so far as the witness is apparently able to assist with relevant matters, or would be so able, given the truth of counsel's case.[9] The duty is, of course, not to be interpreted as a licence to introduce irrelevant matters, and is to be carried out with due regard to the undoubted discretion of counsel to omit reference to matters of an apparently trivial or minor significance in the context of the case as a whole. In contemporary practice the duty to cross-examine appropriately is linked to the 'overriding objective' of dealing with cases justly under both the Civil Procedure Rules 1998 and the Criminal Procedure Rules 2005. In pursuit of this objective the parties have an obligation to assist the court to identify the 'real issues' in the case at an early stage.[10] In at least one case, the duty to put one's case to the witness in cross-examination has been said to be a part of the duty to assist the court in identifying the issues: see *Malcolm v DPP* [2007] 1 WLR 1230, [32]–[33] (dealt with further at 17.17). This certainly seems logical, although in most proceedings, the real issues should have be made clear before the trial begins. *Malcolm* involved a summary trial in the magistrates' court in which the issues still often emerge for the first time during trial.

The second consequence of failure to cross-examine is a tactical one, but no less important for that. Where a party's case has not been put to witnesses called for the other side, who might reasonably have been expected to be able to deal with it, that party himself will probably be asked in cross-examination why he is giving evidence about matters which were never put in cross-examination on his behalf. The implication of the question is that the party is fabricating evidence in the witness-box, because if he had ever mentioned the matters in question to his legal advisers, then they would have been put on his behalf at the proper time. The point is one much beloved of prosecuting counsel in criminal cases, though quite what weight juries attach to it, if they follow it at all, is unclear. However, there is some risk that the accused's credit as a witness may be affected by failure to cross-examine fully on his behalf. If counsel has, by inadvertence, omitted to put some part of the case which should have been put, it is accordingly his duty, at the first possible moment, to mention that fact to the judge and apply for any necessary witness to be recalled for that purpose. The judge has a discretion in every case whether or not to allow any witness to be recalled for further cross-examination,[11] and will ordinarily permit this if it can be done without undue inconvenience, delay, or injustice to another party.

---

[8] [1972] Crim LR 430; *Wood Green Crown Court, ex parte Taylor* [1995] Crim LR 879. The rule has been held not to apply to trials in magistrates' courts (*O'Connell v Adams* [1973] RTR 150): *sed quaere*. In *Wilkinson v DPP* [2003] EWHC 865 (Admin), it was held that a district judge was entitled to reject the evidence of the defendant, and to convict on that basis, even though the prosecutor failed to cross-examine the defendant.

[9] This duty extends to putting the case to a co-accused and his witnesses, as well as to the prosecutor and his witnesses: *Fenlon* (1980) 71 Cr App R 307; *Browne v Dunn* (1893) 6 R 67, 70 per Lord Herschell LC.

[10] Civil Procedure Rules 1998, rr. 1.1, 1.3, 1.4; Criminal Procedure Rules 2005, rr. 1.1, 1.2, 3.2.

[11] *Cannan* [1998] Crim LR 284. In *Wilson* [1977] Crim LR 553, the Court of Appeal refused to interfere with the discretion of the trial judge, who had allowed the accused to be recalled for the purpose of being cross-examined as to his previous convictions, where such course was proper, but had been inadvertently omitted. The Court

17.4 LIMITATIONS ON CROSS-EXAMINATION
BY ACCUSED IN PERSON

The Criminal Justice Act 1991 introduced for the first time a specific prohibition on cross-examination conducted by the accused in person, as opposed to his counsel or solicitor, in certain cases. Section 55(7) of the Act inserted into the Criminal Justice Act 1988 a new s. 34A. This subsection precluded cross-examination by the accused in person of certain child witnesses and witnesses who were complainants of or who witnessed any of the offences specified by s. 32(2) of the 1988 Act. These offences were essentially offences of violence and various sexual offences, and were also the offences with respect to which the Act permitted evidence to be given by way of a live television link or by means of a video-recorded interview (see 16.17). The purpose of this provision was to prevent intimidation of the witness by the accused in circumstances in which it is likely that the witness will find a personal confrontation with the accused to be a traumatic experience, and in which the witness's evidence is, therefore, likely to be adversely affected. Nothing in the section prevented or in any way limited cross-examination of any witness on behalf of the accused by his counsel or solicitor.

This provision was repealed and replaced by the broader provisions of ss. 34 to 40 of the Youth Justice and Criminal Evidence Act 1999. Section 34 imposes a general prohibition on cross-examination by an accused in person of the complainant in any case involving a sexual offence. Section 35 essentially re-enacts s. 34A of the 1988 Act, and imposes a prohibition against cross-examination by the accused in person of child witnesses and witnesses who are complainants to or who witnessed a sexual offence, various offences against children, or offences involving assault, the causing of injury, or threat of injury. But s. 36 contains a new and radical provision which gives the court a discretion, in cases not covered by s. 34 or s. 35, to prohibit cross-examination by the accused in person in any case, either of its own motion or on the application of the prosecution. This power may be exercised in any case where it appears to the court that the quality of the evidence given by the witness on cross-examination is likely to be diminished by the cross-examination in person, is likely to be improved if such cross-examination were prohibited, and that it would not be contrary to the interests of justice to do so. Where the court prohibits cross-examination by virtue of any of these sections, s. 38 provides that it must invite the accused to obtain legal representation for the purpose of conducting the cross-examination. If he fails to do so, the court must, if satisfied that it would be in the interests of justice to do so, appoint an advocate to conduct the cross-examination on behalf of the accused. Section 40 provides for the costs of this representation.[12] Section 39 requires the judge to give the jury such warning (if any) as he may consider necessary to ensure that the accused is not prejudiced by his inability to cross-examine a witness in person, or by the fact that any cross-examination was conducted by an advocate appointed by the court. Despite the language of the section, it is submitted that such a direction should, in practice, always be given.

had some doubts, but inadvertence is a fact of life, especially in a complicated case, and should not be allowed to prevent a fair trial, if it can be avoided.

[12] These provisions arguably amount to a technical violation of art. 6 of the European Convention on Human Rights (see 1.7) which gives the accused the rights 'to defend himself in person or through legal assistance of his own choosing' (art. 6.3(c)) and 'to examine or have examined witnesses against him' (art. 6.3(d)). But it is hard to imagine any court holding that they render the trial unfair, if only because the accused, even if unwillingly, will be the beneficiary of what ought to be a more competent cross-examination. But see the comment on s. 38(5) of the Act, text below.

17.4.1 General prohibitions: ss. 34 and 35

Sections 34 and 35 of the Youth Justice and Criminal Evidence Act 1999 (as amended) provide as follows:

> 34. No person charged with a sexual offence may in any criminal proceedings cross-examine in person a witness who is the complainant, either—
>
> > (a) in connection with that offence, or
> >
> > (b) in connection with any other offence (of whatever nature) with which that person is charged in the proceedings.
>
> 35.—(1) No person charged with an offence to which this section applies may in any criminal proceedings cross-examine in person a protected witness, either—
>
> > (a) in connection with that offence, or
> >
> > (b) in connection with any other offence (of whatever nature) with which that person is charged in the proceedings.
>
> (2) For the purposes of subsection (1) a 'protected witness' is a witness who—
>
> > (a) either is the complainant or is alleged to have been a witness to the commission of the offence to which this section applies, and
> >
> > (b) either is a child or falls to be cross-examined after giving evidence in chief (whether wholly or in part)—
> >
> > > (i) means of a video recording made (for the purposes of section 27) at a time when the witness was a child, or
> > >
> > > (ii) in any other way at any such time.
>
> (3) The offences to which this section applies are—
>
> > (a) any offence under—
> >
> > > (i)   the Sexual Offences Act 1956,
> > >
> > > (ii) the Indecency with Children Act 1960,
> > >
> > > (iii) the Sexual Offences Act 1967,
> > >
> > > (iv) section 54 of the Criminal Law Act 1977,
> > >
> > > (v)   the Protection of Children Act 1978,
> > >
> > > (vi) Part 1 of the Sexual Offences Act 2003.
> >
> > (b) kidnapping, false imprisonment or an offence under section 1 or 2 of the Child Abduction Act 1984;
> >
> > (c) any offence under section 1 of the Children and Young Persons Act 1933;
> >
> > (d) any offence (not within any of the preceding paragraphs) which involves an assault on, or injury or a threat of injury to, any person.
>
> (4) In this section 'child' means—
>
> > (a) where the offence falls within subsection (3)(a), a person under the age of 17; or
> >
> > (b) where the offence falls within subsection (3)(b), (c) or (d), a person under the age of 14.
>
> (5) For the purposes of this section 'witness' includes a witness who is charged with an offence in the proceedings.

By virtue of s. 34(b), it is not possible to sever cross-examination as to a sexual offence from cross-examination as to a non-sexual offence with which the accused may be charged in the same proceedings. The effect of cross-examination in person on the witness would be the same in relation to the latter kind of offence as it would in relation to the former. Moreover, any other rule would be a procedural nightmare. It would generally be very difficult, if not impossible, to identify which parts of the cross-examination relate to which offence, given that the offences are sufficiently closely related to be tried together in the same proceedings. The same rule applies in cases falling under s. 35 by virtue of s. 35(1)(b). Under s. 35(5), the category of 'witness' includes a co-accused. In cases of sexual offences and offences of violence, it is by no means unknown for one accused to be in a highly intimidating position with respect to another, and the subsection takes account of this by protecting the accused in the same manner as any other witness.

17.4.2 Prohibition in particular cases: s. 36

Section 36(1) and (2) of the Youth Justice and Criminal Evidence Act 1999 provide:

> (1) This section applies where, in a case where neither of sections 34 and 35 operates to prevent an accused in any criminal proceedings from cross-examining a witness in person—
>> (a) the prosecutor makes an application for the court to give a direction under this section in relation to the witness, or
>> (b) the court of its own motion raises the issue whether such a direction should be given.
> (2) If it appears to the court—
>> (a) that the quality of evidence given by the witness on cross-examination—
>>> (i) is likely to be diminished if the cross-examination (or further cross-examination) is conducted by the accused in person, and
>>> (ii) would be likely to be improved if a direction were given under this section, and
>> (b) that it would not be contrary to the interests of justice to give such a direction, the court may give a direction prohibiting the accused from cross-examining (or further cross-examining) the witness in person.

Section 36(3) provides a list of the matters to which the court must have regard in exercising its discretion under the section. They include any views expressed by the witness himself, the prior relationship, if any, between the accused and the witness, any behaviour on the part of the accused during the proceedings, the nature of the questions likely to be asked in cross-examination, and whether or not there is or may be a special measures direction with respect to the witness under s. 19 of the Act (see 16.18).[13] In contrast to s. 35, the term 'witness' for the purposes of s. 36 does not include a co-accused, so that there can be no discretionary prohibition on one accused cross-examining another in person (s. 36(4)). Section 37 makes provision for any direction given under s. 36 to be discharged if it appears to be in the interests of justice to do so. The court may do this either of its own motion, or on the application of any party on the ground that there has been a material change of circumstances since the direction was made. Section 37(5), which authorizes the making of rules of court governing applications for s. 36 directions, appears to envisage that in some cases, the court will receive evidence, including expert evidence, in connection with the application.

17.4.3 Cross-examination on behalf of accused

Sections 38(1) to (5) of the Youth Justice and Criminal Evidence Act 1999 provide as follows:

> (1) This section applies where an accused is prevented from cross-examining a witness in person by virtue of section 34, 35 or 36.
> (2) Where it appears to the court that this section applies, it must—
>> (a) invite the accused to arrange for a legal representative to act for him for the purpose of cross-examining the witness; and

---

[13] The accused must be given the opportunity to make representations about the matters dealt with by s. 36(3): *R (Hillman)* v *Richmond Magistrates' Court* [2003] EWHC 2580 (Admin).

(b) require the accused to notify the court, by the end of such period as it may specify, whether a legal representative is to act for him for that purpose.

(3) If by the end of the period mentioned in subsection (2)(b) either—

(a) the accused has notified the court that no legal representative is to act for him for the purpose of cross-examining the witness, or

(b) no notification has been received by the court and it appears to the court that no legal representative is to so act,

the court must consider whether it is necessary in the interests of justice for the witness to be cross-examined by a legal representative appointed to represent the interests of the accused.

(4) If the court decides that it is necessary in the interests of justice for the witness to be so cross-examined, the court must appoint a qualified legal representative (chosen by the court) to cross-examine the witness in the interests of the accused.

(5) A person so appointed shall not be responsible to the accused.

Although some provision for legal representation is clearly necessary, and although the court cannot compel an accused to accept representation as his own, as opposed to appointing an advocate despite the accused's unwillingness to accept one, s. 38(5) is troubling and may represent the one area of the new statutory scheme which may cause problems in terms of art. 6 of the European Convention on Human Rights. The meaning of the phrase 'shall not be responsible to the accused' is unclear. This concern is aggravated by the wording of s. 39(1)(b), according to which the judge must consider whether to give the jury a direction to prevent the accused from being prejudiced by 'the fact that the cross-examination was carried out by [an appointed advocate] and not by a person acting as the accused's own legal representative'. Section 38(5) presumably does not mean that the appointed advocate is not obliged to represent the best interests of the accused in conducting the cross-examination. In very many cases, the complainant is the crucial witness against the accused, and a full and searching cross-examination is vital to the defence. It is submitted that the cross-examination must be conducted having regard to the actual defence put forward by the accused, and not having regard to what defence the court thinks the accused is putting forward, or ought to put forward. If this be correct, the appointed advocate cannot shrink from putting to the witness the questions which the accused would have put in person, even if they are forceful or distressing to the witness, as long as the questioning conforms to the law of evidence and the rules of professional ethics and conduct. This would seem to follow from the wording of s. 38(4) that the advocate must cross-examine the witness 'in the interests of the accused'. Like any other advocate, the appointed advocate must use his or her professional judgment as to the propriety of the cross-examination, and must not ask questions calculated merely to intimidate the witness. But this duty exists irrespective of the provisions of s. 38(5), and the court has ample powers to restrain improper cross-examination in any case. If this subsection means that the court may dictate to the appointed advocate the nature or scope of the cross-examination, or deny the accused the benefit of a full and fair cross-examination, it is submitted that it certainly violates art. 6. Such a violation would go well beyond the technical violation involved in depriving the accused of a choice of the manner of his representation for the purposes of the cross-examination, and would amount to unfairly depriving the accused of the right to present his defence. It is submitted that an appointed advocate should owe the same duty to the accused as an advocate chosen by the accused.

The subsection also raises the question of legal professional privilege as it applies to an appointed advocate. It is difficult to see how the appointed advocate could carry out his or her duties properly without taking instructions from the accused to ascertain the nature of the defence and the facts on which the accused relies to support the defence.[14] It is submitted that, despite s. 38(5), any communications between the accused and the appointed advocate must be subject to legal professional privilege, and that the appointed advocate must be responsible to the accused at least to the extent of maintaining the privilege.

17.5 APPLICATION OF THE RULES OF EVIDENCE TO CROSS-EXAMINATION

17.5.1 General rule: rules of evidence apply to cross-examination

The rules of evidence apply to matters elicited in cross-examination, as they do to matters elicited in chief. There is no licence to elicit evidence which is inadmissible merely because it arises in the course of cross-examination. Thus, in *Thomson* [1912] 3 KB 19, where the accused was charged with using an instrument on a woman (who had died) with intent to procure her miscarriage, the accused's counsel was held to have been rightly prevented from asking a prosecution witness in cross-examination whether the deceased woman had not told her that she intended to procure her own miscarriage, and later, that she had in fact done so. The evidence was hearsay at any stage of the examination of the witness.

Recent decisions have suggested a degree of departure from this long-standing rule in criminal cases involving more than one accused, where a piece of evidence, though inadmissible in the hands of the prosecution against one accused, is relevant to the defence of a co-accused. In cases involving a single accused, it appears well established that the prosecution may not refer for any purpose to any evidence excluded by the judge.[15] But in *Rowson* [1986] QB 174, in which R and K were jointly charged with causing grievous bodily harm to W, K had made a statement to the police in which he admitted having struck W on the head with a piece of wood. At trial, the judge excluded this evidence, on the ground of a breach of the Judges' Rules, as he was entitled to do as a matter of discretion. This meant that the prosecution were not entitled to make use of K's statement for any purpose. However, K gave evidence and contradicted the statement by testifying that he could not recall whether or not he had had a piece of wood. Counsel for R applied to the judge for leave to cross-examine K about his statement. The trial judge, who apparently regarded the point as one of first impression, permitted counsel for R to ask K whether he had ever made a statement to the effect that he had struck W with a piece of wood, but required counsel to be bound by the answers of K, whose evidence was that he had made the statement, but that it had been untrue. The judge refused to permit counsel to put the statement to K to contradict him (as would be the usual practice with a previous inconsistent statement: see 17.7.1; 17.7.2). R appealed, contending that this, too, should have been permitted. The Court of Appeal held that R's argument was correct. Distinguishing *Treacy* on the ground that it was a case involving a single

---

[14] Section 38(6)(b) authorizes the making of rules to ensure that the appointed advocate is provided with 'evidence or other material relating to the proceedings'. Indeed, it is to be hoped that the advocate would have access to the indictment or charge, the witness statements, any documentary or other exhibits, and perhaps a transcript of the most vital evidence given before his or her appointment. But it will surely still be desirable for the advocate to take instructions.

[15] See *Treacy* [1944] 2 All ER 229; *Re P* [1989] Crim LR 897; though counsel is, obviously, free to use any information yielded by such evidence for the purpose of framing questions for cross-examination, as long as it is not revealed to the jury that the information came from a piece of evidence which has been excluded: *Rice* [1963] 1 QB 857. And see Police and Criminal Evidence Act 1984, s. 76(4), and 9.10, 9.13.

accused, the Court held that it would be wrong to fetter a co-accused merely because evidence has been excluded vis-à-vis the prosecution. The Court certified that a point of law of general public importance was involved, but the House of Lords refused leave to appeal. This case was followed in *Lui Mei Lin* v *R* [1989] AC 288.

In *Myers* [1998] AC 124, the House of Lords held that an accused in a joint trial should be permitted to use voluntary statements made by co-accused to cross-examine those co-accused and persons to whom the statements were made, even though the statements tended to incriminate the makers and were not adduced in evidence by the prosecution. This case is considered fully at 9.13.[16] It seems to follow that, at least in the case of evidence of this kind, the fact that evidence is not adduced (and may be inadmissible if tendered) by the prosecution is not necessarily a bar to its use in cross-examination by an accused. The House laid stress on the fact that the statements were relevant both to the substance of the accused's defence and to the credibility of the makers. A further factor is that the discretion to exclude evidence at common law and under s. 78 of the Police and Criminal Evidence Act 1984 applies only to evidence tendered by the prosecution and not to evidence tendered by one accused against another.[17] To this extent, *Rowson* and *Myers* may be said to represent an exception to the rule that cross-examination must conform to the rules of evidence generally. But it is probably more accurate to say that the rules of evidence in criminal cases must to some extent differ as between the prosecution and the defence, and the extent of this difference is still being explored. The courts may well give further guidance on this subject in due course.

17.5.2 'Opening the door'

It should be noted that the course taken in cross-examination may, of itself, render admissible evidence which would have been inadmissible from the witness in chief, and then the witness may deal with the evidence in cross-examination and re-examination. The point is that cross-examination may legitimately raise further issues, and therefore render admissible evidence which could not previously have been given. Where this occurs, it is sometimes said that the previous examination 'opens the door' to the new matter. We saw in the last chapter that, where a witness is cross-examined upon the contents of a document from which he has refreshed his memory, if the cross-examination strays beyond those parts of the document actually used for that purpose, then the document becomes evidence where it certainly was not before, and may be referred to and asked about accordingly. Much the same will occur where a document is admitted in chief for the purpose, say, of identifying handwriting contained in it, and in cross-examination its contents are referred to. The contents are then made evidence by reason of the cross-examination. And where a witness is asked for the first time in cross-examination about acts done by him, or words spoken between him and a party to the proceedings, such acts and words thereupon become evidence, and may be dealt with accordingly. In the case of the words spoken the witness would be permitted, in cross-examination or re-examination, to state the whole of the conversation put to him.

---

[16] Confessions are now admissible at the instance of a co-accused subject to conditions of admissibility almost identical to those required of the prosecution: see Police and Criminal Evidence Act 1984, s. 76A, inserted by Criminal Justice Act 2003, s. 128: see 9.13.2.

[17] The Court in *Rowson* relied heavily on the decision to this effect in *Murdoch* v *Taylor* [1965] AC 574, though this case turned on the specific instance of cross-examination as to character where one accused has given evidence against another, a course expressly permitted by s. 1(3) of the Criminal Evidence Act 1898 as amended.

B CROSS-EXAMINATION AS TO CREDIT

SUMMARY OF MAIN POINTS

- Cross-examination as to credit is always permitted.

- Where questions are put which are relevant solely to matters affecting credit and not to the substantive issues in the case, the answers given by the witness are said to be 'collateral'. Answers on collateral matters must be accepted in the sense that no extrinsic evidence may be adduced to contradict them. There are limited exceptions to this rule, most importantly evidence of bad character.

- A witness may be cross-examined about any previous statement he has made inconsistent with his evidence.

- At common law a previous inconsistent statement could be used only for the purpose of showing the inconsistency, and not to prove the truth of any fact stated in it.

- In civil cases the distinction is no longer relevant because of the abrogation of the Rule against Hearsay.

- In criminal cases, by statute, the statement can now be used also as evidence of the truth of any fact stated of which oral evidence by the witness would be admissible.

- Relevant medical evidence may be adduced on the question of the reliability of a witness.

- Evidence may be given that a witness has a reputation for untruthfulness.

- Section 5(2) of the Civil Evidence Act 1995 and s. 124 of the Criminal Justice Act 2003 make provision for evidence to be adduced attacking the credit of the makers of admissible hearsay statements, where it is not possible to cross-examine them.

17.6 IMPEACHMENT; MEANING OF 'COLLATERAL'

Cross-examination as to credit, or impeachment, is cross-examination designed to attack the credibility of the witness in the eyes of the jury. It may consist of exploration of the facts of the case using a previous statement made by the witness inconsistent with the witness's evidence at trial, or it may involve matters extraneous to the actual facts of the case, for example, evidence of bad character or medical or other evidence, the effect of which is to suggest that the witness should not be believed on oath. Matters which affect only the credit of the witness, and are not otherwise relevant to the case, are said to be 'collateral'. There is an important rule that, while it is perfectly permissible to conduct a cross-examination solely on the issue of credit, the cross-examiner may not thereafter introduce further evidence of his own to contradict answers given by the witness during that cross-examination, if the further evidence would be relevant only to collateral issues. However, it is not always easy to distinguish collateral issues from issues which may have some other relevance, and the rule as to collateral issues itself has a number of important exceptions. These matters are dealt with below.

17.7 PREVIOUS INCONSISTENT STATEMENTS

We saw in 16.14 *et seq.* that previous statements made by a hostile witness inconsistent with his evidence may be used for the purpose of impeaching the witness. The same weapon is available in the case of witnesses called for the other side, who are expected and assumed to be hostile. At common law, it was open to a cross-examiner to ask a witness about any previous inconsistent statements he may have made, but the rule was circumscribed by the requirements[18] that, if the statement put was in writing, the witness must be shown the document before he could be asked whether he had said something different on another occasion (which removed the element of surprise); and that if the statement was proved, having been denied by the witness, it must be made evidence as part of the cross-examiner's case (which inhibited the use of statements in many cases). The use of previous inconsistent statements in cross-examination is now governed by s. 4 and s. 5 of the Criminal Procedure Act 1865, which complement the provision of s. 3 dealing with the use of such statements against a party's own hostile witnesses.[19]

17.7.1 Criminal Procedure Act 1865, s. 4

Section 4 provides:

> If a witness upon cross-examination as to a former statement made by him relative to the subject-matter of the indictment or proceeding and inconsistent with his present testimony, does not distinctly admit that he has made such statement, proof may be given that he did in fact make it; but before such proof can be given the circumstances of the supposed statement, sufficient to designate the particular occasion, must be mentioned to the witness, and he must be asked whether or not he has made such statement.

The section is not expressed to apply exclusively to oral or written statements, and it may be assumed that s. 4 is intended to apply to both written and oral statements.[20] It is implicit in the section that the cross-examiner is entitled to ask the witness about the former statement, and the draftsman evidently considered that he was building upon that rule of common law. The right to prove the making of any statement which is not 'distinctly admitted' covers both outright denials and ambivalent or evasive answers as to whether the witness made the previous statement. It also precludes the objection that the proof of the previous statement, if denied, might offend against the rule of common law that answers in cross-examination which go only to collateral matters must be accepted as final.[21]

The section applies alike to statements made previously on oath, for example, a deposition made in committal proceedings, and those made previously unsworn in any circumstances, for example on being interviewed by the police.[22] The question whether such statement is 'relative

---

[18] Said to derive from *Queen Caroline's Case* (1820) 2 Brod & Bing 287, which itself is hardly compelling authority, but may well have reflected the contemporary position at common law.

[19] Like s. 3, s. 4 and s. 5 apply to civil and criminal proceedings alike, and succeed provisions of the Common Law Procedure Act 1854.

[20] The statement to this effect in the 5th edn of this work was expressly approved by the House of Lords in *Derby Magistrates' Court, ex parte B* [1996] 1 AC 487, 498–9.

[21] See 17.8.

[22] *Hart* (1957) 42 Cr App R 47: *O'Neill* [1969] Crim LR 260. In the latter, an accused who gave evidence exculpating a co-accused was rightly cross-examined on his oral statement to the police, in which he had said the opposite of his evidence.

to the subject-matter of the indictment or proceeding' is essentially one of relevance and is a matter for the judge, and not for the judgment of the cross-examiner, or the opinion of the witness.[23] There are some cases in which this can be difficult to decide, as is shown by the decision of the Court of Appeal in *Funderburk* [1990] 1 WLR 587, where the Court held that a matter which appeared to be strictly collateral (a previous inconsistent statement) was one relative to the subject-matter of the indictment. This case is discussed in more detail at 17.8.1.

The words following the semi-colon in s. 4 correspond to those in s. 3, and require a fair and proper foundation to be laid before the statement may be proved.

17.7.2 Criminal Procedure Act 1865, s. 5

Section 5 of the Act provides:

> A witness may be cross-examined as to previous statements made by him in writing, or reduced into writing, relative to the subject-matter of the indictment or proceeding, without such writing being shown to him; but if it is intended to contradict such witness by the writing, his attention must, before such contradictory proof can be given, be called to those parts of the writing which are to be used for the purpose of so contradicting him: Provided always, that it shall be competent for the judge, at any time during the trial, to require the production of the writing for his inspection, and he may thereupon make such use of it for the purposes of the trial as he may think fit.

The section envisages two stages in the use of previous inconsistent statements made in, or reduced into, writing. The first part of the section permits the cross-examiner rather more scope for surprise than did the common law rule, as applied in *Queen Caroline's Case* (1820) 2 Brod & Bing 287, and indeed was intended to abrogate the requirement of showing the witness the document before any questions were asked. The cross-examiner may show the document to the witness and ask questions while it is in the hands of the witness. But the use made of the statement must, in order to remain within the first part of the section, fall short of 'contradiction' of the witness. This seems to mean that the cross-examiner may ask the witness, first whether he has ever made a statement on another occasion inconsistent with his evidence, and second (showing him the document) whether, on seeing the statement, he wishes to adhere to the evidence he has given. If the answer is that the witness is prepared to alter his evidence materially, the damage to his credit is done. If he sticks to his evidence, the cross-examiner must choose whether to accept that answer, or whether to enter the second stage. If he chooses the latter course, he will proceed to contradict the witness by the document, in other words put to him that it is the document (identifying it to him) that is a true account, rather than the witness's evidence. At this point, but not before—another significant departure from the common law rule—the document may be proved to contradict the witness, and must then be put in evidence, having of course been made relevant by the second stage of cross-examination.

17.7.3 Evidential value of previous inconsistent statement

At common law, where a previous inconsistent statement was used for the purpose of cross-examination as to credit, it was evidence only of the inconsistency of the witness, and was not admissible as evidence of any matters stated. Statute has now altered this rule, both in civil and criminal cases. The relevant provisions are given at 16.2.2 and 16.2.3. In civil cases, s. 6(3) of

---

[23] *Bashir* [1969] 1 WLR 1303, per Veale J at 1306.

the Civil Evidence Act 1995 preserves the circumstances under which a statement may become evidence by virtue of s. 4 or s. 5 of the Criminal Procedure Act 1865, but where the statement becomes evidence, it is now admissible as evidence of the matters stated as well as of inconsistency by virtue of s. 1 and s. 6(1) of the Act. Section 119(1) of the Criminal Justice Act 2003 has the same effect in criminal cases.

17.8 GENERAL RULE OF FINALITY OF ANSWERS ON COLLATERAL ISSUES

Because cross-examination may be directed to matters going solely to the credit or the character of the witness, and because cross-examination may elicit evidence which was not elicited in chief, and even evidence that would not have been admissible in chief, it may result in some proliferation of the issues aired before the court. If this were wholly unrestrained, the time and attention of the court might be devoted, in a measure disproportionate to their importance, to a series of facts not directly relevant to the issues between the parties in the proceedings. There is, therefore, a sensible rule, that a cross-examiner must accept as final answers given in response to questions dealing with 'collateral' matters. Acceptance as final means only that the cross-examiner cannot seek to contradict the answer by calling further evidence in rebuttal on his own behalf, and not that he himself cannot continue to challenge it in cross-examination, or is obliged to admit its truth. Whether or not a matter is collateral depends on whether it has any relevance to the proceedings other than its relevance to the credit of a witness. If the sole relevance of the matter is to the credit of a witness, the matter is collateral. If, on the other hand, the matter is relevant to a fact in issue in the case, i.e., if it is relevant to some issue which the court must decide to determine liability, it is not collateral. Where the matter is relevant both to a fact in issue and to the credit of the witness, it is not collateral. But as we shall see, the distinction between relevance to the facts in issue and relevance to credit is sometimes blurred; there are some close cases, and the rule is by no means always easy to apply. One old but still helpful statement of the rule was given by Pollock CB in *Attorney-General* v *Hitchcock* (1847) 1 Ex 91, in which he said that an answer given by a witness in cross-examination is not collateral if the same answer would have been admissible if given by the witness in examination in chief. Because a witness is not permitted to deal with his own credibility in chief, if his answer would have been admissible at that stage, it cannot be collateral. This simple observation often sheds considerable light on difficult questions of what is collateral and what is not.

17.8.1 Application of general rule

In *Burke* (1858) 8 Cox CC 44, an Irish witness, giving evidence through an interpreter, asserted that he was unable to speak English. He denied in cross-examination having spoken English to two persons in court. It was held not to be permissible to call evidence in rebuttal to the effect that the witness had spoken in English, because the cross-examination was designed solely to attack the veracity of the witness. But the position would be quite different if the witness's command of the language had been relevant, e.g., to his alleged authorship of some material document, or his ability to make an alleged confession or adverse admission and so had gone to an issue in the case. In *Marsh* (1985) 83 Cr App R 165, it was held that where a witness denied in cross-examination that he had threatened the accused, and the accused relied as part of his defence on a belief that the witness intended to attack him, the matter was not collateral. The threat was relevant to the accused's defence, and the accused should have been permitted to adduce evidence to contradict the witness's answer.

These cases seem clear enough. But occasionally, the distinction between material and collateral matters proves difficult and can produce serious ambiguity. One such case was *Funderburk* [1990] 1 WLR 587. The accused was charged with three offences of unlawful sexual intercourse with a girl under 13. His defence was that the girl had fabricated her story. Her account of one of the alleged incidents clearly suggested that the accused had caused her to lose her virginity. The issues arose of (a) whether the accused was entitled to cross-examine the complainant about a statement she had made to a defence witness concerning previous acts of sexual intercourse with other men, and (b) whether, if she denied that conversation, the accused would be entitled to call the witness to contradict her. The trial judge ruled against the accused on both issues, but the Court of Appeal held that, in so doing, he had erred. It seems clear that the cross-examination should have been allowed, because it would have affected the complainant's credibility. But if it were a matter of credibility only, the matter would have been collateral and the accused would not have been entitled to call the witness. The Court of Appeal held that the issue of the complainant's previous inconsistent statement was not only a collateral matter of credit, but was also 'relative to the subject-matter of the indictment', and accordingly fell within the scope of s. 4 of the Criminal Procedure Act 1865 (see 17.7.1). The circumstances in which the complainant had lost her virginity were relevant directly to the guilt of the accused. The evidence had some potential to show that the complainant's story was untrue, not only because there was reason to believe that she might be an untruthful witness, but also because it tended to show that the accused might not have had sexual intercourse with her. On this basis, it was held that the evidence was not collateral, though the distinction is certainly a narrow one.

In *Nagrecha* [1997] 2 Cr App R 401, the Court of Appeal allowed an appeal against conviction in a case where the trial judge had refused to allow the accused to adduce evidence that the complainant in a case of indecent assault had made previous complaints of a similar nature against other men. The alleged assault had occurred in a restaurant when only the complainant and the accused were present. The complainant had denied in cross-examination that she had made previous complaints. Evidence was available to contradict her, though only in one instance was there evidence which clearly suggested that the previous complaints had been false, and this would have been a highly contentious issue. The Court of Appeal held that the evidence would have gone to the issue of whether any assault had occurred at all, and not merely to the issue of the complainant's credibility. Accordingly, it should have been admitted. But it is submitted that the decision in *Nagrecha* is also an extremely close one. While the evidence would have tended to discredit the complainant, it did not shed light directly on what had happened at the restaurant, a point which would justify some distinction of *Funderburk*. *Funderburk* and *Nagrecha* considered together support the view that a more liberal approach to the collateral answers rule is developing in criminal cases.[24] Both decisions depend greatly on the statement made in successive editions of *Cross* and *Cross and Tapper*[25] that in sexual cases where the evidence of the complainant

---

[24] *Cross and Tapper on Evidence*, 11th edn, p. 392 *et seq*. The observation to this effect in the 8th edn of the work was approved by the Court in *Nagrecha*. From a practical point of view, this approach would be consistent with the bias and partiality cases such as *Busby* (1982) 75 Cr App R 79 (17.10). But as Lord Hutton observed in relation to a different issue: 'Issues of consent and issues of credibility may well run so close to each other as almost to coincide. A very sharp knife may be required to separate what may be admitted from what may not': *A (No. 2)* [2002] 1 AC 45, [138].

[25] *Evidence*, 6th edn, p. 295; cf. 11th edn, p. 358.

and the accused are at odds, the distinction between evidence going to the substantive issue and evidence going only to credit is reduced 'to vanishing point', an idea which found favour with both courts. But it is submitted that the distinction is one which can be made. The decision in *Funderburk* appears more in accord with principle than that in *Nagrecha* as the law stands now. But it is hard to deny that the prospect of the jury being left in ignorance of previous accusations in the circumstances of *Nagrecha* is disquieting, and it may be that the time has come to consider a specific reform of the law.

17.8.2 Exceptions to the rule of finality

There are certain common law and statutory rules which constitute exceptions to the rule of finality on collateral matters. These rules provide that, in certain cases, evidence may be adduced to contradict denials made in cross-examination, or generally to deal with the question of the credibility of a witness or the maker of an admissible hearsay statement. These exceptions are important in practice. They are:

(a) if a witness denies that he has been convicted of a criminal offence, evidence may be adduced to prove that he was so convicted;

(b) evidence may be adduced to show that a witness has a bias or partiality against a party to the case;

(c) evidence may be adduced of the reputation of a witness for untruthfulness;

(d) medical evidence may be adduced to show that a witness is unreliable;

(e) evidence may be adduced to challenge the credibility of the maker of an admissible hearsay statement, such evidence being akin to that which might have been adduced if the maker of the statement had been called to give evidence.

17.9 PROOF OF PREVIOUS CONVICTIONS

By s. 6 of the Criminal Procedure Act 1865 (as amended):

> If upon a witness being lawfully questioned as to whether he has been convicted of any [offence] he either denies or does not admit the fact, or refuses to answer, it shall be lawful for the cross-examining party to prove such conviction...[26]

This provision must, of course, be read in conjunction with the bad character provisions of the Criminal Justice Act 2003, which are dealt with in Chapter 6. In other words, s. 6 must be read as meaning that the conviction can be proved in all cases in which it is admissible and in which the questioning of the witness on the subject was proper. It is questionable whether s. 6 is now as useful a provision as it once was. It would appear that the rule of finality of collateral issues no longer applies to evidence of bad character generally. The Criminal Justice Act 2003 has abrogated the distinction which prevailed in earlier law, by virtue of the common law and the Criminal Evidence Act 1898, between evidence of bad character adduced as part of the case in chief and bad character elicited by way of cross-examination. It would seem, therefore, that in

---

[26] The original wording referred to 'any felony or misdemeanour'; but by s. 1 of the Criminal Law Act 1967 the distinction between felonies and misdemeanours was abolished, and the practice in all cases was assimilated to that relating to misdemeanours, all special rules in relation to felonies being abrogated. *Quaere*, whether the section applies to purely summary offences, whose status at common law was unclear.

any case in which evidence of bad character is admissible, that evidence may be adduced regardless of whether the witness is cross-examined about it. If the witness is not questioned about the offence, and s. 6 does not apply, it would seem that the previous conviction could nonetheless be proved under s. 73 of the Police and Criminal Evidence Act 1984 (see 12.7). Moreover, evidence of bad character under the Criminal Justice Act 2003 is not limited to evidence of previous convictions. For these reasons, it may be that the rule should now be stated as being that evidence of bad character generally, and not merely evidence of previous convictions is an exception to the rule of finality. (As to this, see also 6.15.1.) The Criminal Justice Act 2003 does not in general distinguish between the relevance of evidence of bad character to the issue of guilt and its relevance to credit, and it would seem that little purpose would be served by seeking to preserve the rule of finality in relation to evidence of bad character.

In *Forbes* [1999] 2 Cr App R 501, the accused refused to continue giving evidence after the judge had ruled that the prosecution were entitled to cross-examine him as to his bad character because he had made a false assertion of good character and because he had made imputations on the character of the prosecution witnesses. It was held that, in these circumstances, the prosecution were entitled to prove the accused's previous convictions. It is submitted that this decision was correct. The only course which the judge could reasonably take would be to assume that the accused would deny, or at least would not be prepared to admit, the previous convictions, and to deal with the situation accordingly. In these circumstances the prosecution would be entitled to prove the previous convictions.

17.10 PROOF OF BIAS OR PARTIALITY

Any fact tending to suggest bias or partiality on the part of a witness may be cross-examined to, and may be proved in rebuttal, if denied. Although essentially collateral, bias and partiality often involve attempts on the part of the witness to affect the outcome of the case, and therefore go beyond a mere issue of credit as a witness. In *Mendy*[27] it was said that the rule of finality is not absolute, and that it is wrong to keep matters from the jury, which may suggest some attempt to interfere with the course of the trial in order to favour some bias or partiality. In that case the accused's husband, who was to be called as a witness on her behalf, was waiting outside court (according to the usual practice in criminal cases) until his turn to give evidence. He denied later, in cross-examination, that while outside court he had spoken to a man who had been seen in the public gallery taking notes of other evidence. The implication was that the witness was prepared to inform himself illicitly of what was going on in court, prior to his being called, for the purpose of tailoring his evidence to the advantage of his wife. The prosecution were allowed to rebut the denial.

17.10.1 What may amount to bias and partiality

There are many ways in which bias or partiality may be manifested. In *Shaw* (1888) 16 Cox CC 503, a prosecution witness, who denied in cross-examination that he had quarrelled with the accused and had threatened to take revenge on him, was allowed to be contradicted. In *Phillips* (1936) 26 Cr App R 17, the accused was charged with incest with his daughter. He alleged that the daughter, and another daughter called to give evidence for the prosecution, had been 'schooled'

---

[27] (1976) 64 Cr App R 4. And see *Attorney-General* v *Hitchcock* (1847) 1 Ex 91, per Pollock CB at 100.

in their evidence by their mother, and that the charge was a fabrication. In addition to this, it was suggested that the daughters had given similarly schooled evidence at a previous summary trial, at which the accused had been bound over in respect of an alleged indecent assault on the same daughter. The girls denied in cross-examination that they were giving false evidence, and further denied having made admissions that their evidence at the summary trial had been schooled. It was held that the trial judge had erred in refusing to permit the accused to call rebutting evidence from persons to whom the admissions were said to have been made. The Court of Criminal Appeal held that such evidence went 'to the very foundation of the appellant's answer to the charge', and not just to a question of credit.[28]

In *Busby* (1982) 75 Cr App R 79, it was held that where it was alleged that police officers had threatened a defence witness, in order to seek to deter him from testifying on behalf of the accused, the officers' denial of that allegation was not a collateral issue, and that the witness had been wrongly prevented from giving evidence of the alleged threat. If true, the evidence would have shown that the officers had attempted to influence the outcome of the trial against the accused. Referring to *Phillips* and *Mendy*, the Court held that the evidence was clearly admissible. It is interesting to note that the Court did not refer to, and may not have been referred to, the old case of *Harris* v *Tippett* (1811) 2 Camp 637, in which the decision was contrary to that in *Busby*, and which must presumably now be treated as overruled. It is submitted, however, that this development is to be welcomed, and that *Busby* is plainly to be preferred. In *Funderburk* [1990] 1 WLR 587 (and see 17.8) it was suggested that *Busby* represented a novel departure, and was effectively a new exception to the rule of finality. But it is submitted that it fits aptly within the bias and partiality exception. In *Edwards* [1991] 1 WLR 207 the issue was whether the accused had been entitled to cross-examine police officers with a view to showing that the officers had given evidence in other trials, in which there had been reason to believe that their evidence had been dishonest, and which ended in verdicts of not guilty. The Court of Appeal held that, while a previous verdict of not guilty did not in itself cast doubt on the veracity of particular witnesses, the fact that there was independent evidence of lack of veracity made the history of the other trials relevant and admissible. But because the issue was one of the officers' credibility in the instant trial, it was collateral, so that the accused had been entitled to cross-examine about it, but had to accept the answers as final. It is submitted that this case was correctly distinguished from *Busby*, in that *Busby* involved a direct interference by the officers with potential evidence in the instant case, rather than an attack on their credibility by reference to their conduct in other cases.[29]

Bias or partiality may, in some circumstances, arise simply from the relationship between a witness and the party on whose behalf he is called, although there must be some positive evidence, over and above the fact of the relationship itself, which suggests actual bias or partiality. In *Thomas* v *David*[30] in an action on a promissory note, a witness called for the plaintiff denied

---

[28] The phrasing of the judgment is not, with respect, entirely happy. The foundation of the defence was that the charge was untrue, not that the girls were not to be believed because they had admitted fabricating evidence before. Nor is the court's view that the rebutting evidence could be treated as evidence of the truth of the facts stated, free from difficulty. However, the decision is clearly right on the facts.

[29] Cross-examination about conduct in other cases, such as that in *Edwards*, should be admitted only where it can be shown that the previous acquittal must have been based on the jury's disbelief of the officer's evidence, and not simply, e.g., acceptance of the defence put forward in that case (*Twitchell* [2000] 1 Cr App R 373; *Y* [1992] Crim LR 436; *Hui Chi-ming* v *R* [1992] 1 AC 34). See *Thorne* (1977) 66 Cr App R 6; and the interesting application of *Edwards* in *D* [1996] QB 283. Such cross-examination should be based on a conviction, a finding in a civil action, or a finding in a disciplinary proceeding against the officer: *Twitchell* (above).

[30] (1836) 7 Car & P 350. The decision has not escaped criticism: see, e.g., *Cargill* (CCA) [1913] 2 KB 271.

a suggestion made to her in cross-examination that she was the mistress of the plaintiff, her employer. The defendant's case was that he was not the maker of the note, in effect that it was a forgery. Coleridge J held that the relationship was relevant to the facts in issue, and that the witness might be contradicted. After further evidence, a verdict was entered for the defendant. Coleridge J said:

> Is it not material to the issue whether the principal witness who comes to support the plaintiff's case is his kept mistress? If the question had been whether the witness had walked the streets as a common prostitute, I think that that would have been collateral to the issue, and that, had the witness denied such a charge, she could not have been contradicted; but here, the question is, whether the witness had contracted such a relationship with the plaintiff, as might induce her the more readily to conspire with him to support a forgery.

Similarly, efforts by a party to present or support a false or exaggerated claim are not collateral. For example, the plaintiff may have been heard to admit that he suffered injuries in a manner inconsistent with his cause of action against the defendant in respect of those injuries,[31] or there may be evidence that the plaintiff has suborned false witnesses.[32] These matters go beyond the question of credit, and are actually admissible in their own right as admissions by conduct (see 8.1). If, therefore, such matters are put to a party called as a witness and are denied, they may be proved in rebuttal because they are relevant to the facts in issue.

17.10.2 Actual bias or partiality to be proved

But the exception seems to apply only where there is alleged in cross-examination actual bias or partiality. The mere fact that a witness is alleged to have admitted some fact consistent with bias or partiality, for example that he has been offered a bribe in connection with his evidence in the case, will not suffice to defeat the finality rule, unless it is suggested that he in fact accepted the bribe, i.e., that he is actually biased or partial.[33] The fact that a witness has spoken of being offered a bribe may drastically affect his credit, but is nonetheless collateral to the issues in the case; a suggestion that he in fact accepted a bribe may point to some actual falsity in his evidence which is directly relevant to the outcome of the case. In *Phillips*, the suggestion that the girls had admitted having given schooled evidence on a previous occasion, was secondary to the accused's actual line of defence, which was that their evidence at the instant trial was false and schooled, and it was to this point that the cross-examination was ultimately directed.

In *Attorney-General* v *Hitchcock* (1847) 1 Ex 91, the accused, a maltster, was charged with using a cistern in breach of certain statutory requirements. His counsel asked a prosecution witness in cross-examination whether he had not previously said that he had been offered £20 by officers of the Crown, if he would testify that the cistern had been so used. The witness denied the allegation. The question was whether the defence were entitled to call a witness of their own to state that the prosecution witness had said this. It was held that they could not. Pollock CB said (*ibid.* at 101) that the reason was:

> ...that it is totally irrelevant to the matter in issue, that some person should have thought fit to offer a bribe to the witness to give an untrue account of a transaction, and it is of no importance

---

[31] Cf. *Moriarty* v *London, Chatham & Dover Railway Co.* (1870) LR 5 QB 314.
[32] Cf. *Melhuish* v *Collier* (1850) 15 QB 878.
[33] *Attorney-General* v *Hitchcock* (1847) 1 Ex 91; and see *Masters* [2004] All ER (D) 92 (Jul.).

whatever, if that bribe was not accepted. It is no disparagement to a man that a bribe is offered to him: it may be a disparagement to the person who makes the offer. If, therefore, the witness is asked the fact, and denies it, or if he is asked whether he said so and so, and denies it, he cannot be contradicted as to what he has said. *Lord Stafford's* case[34] was totally different. There the witness himself had been implicated in offering a bribe to some other person. That immediately affected him, as proving that he had acted the part of a suborner for the purpose of perverting the truth.

A similar point arose more recently in *TM* [2004] EWCA Crim 2085. The accused was charged with a number of sexual offences. The allegations were made against him initially in the course of interviews conducted by private investigators inquiring into an alleged affair between the accused and a married woman for the purpose of matrimonial proceedings. The accused alleged that the husband of the married woman had offered the witnesses a financial reward for making allegations against him. He sought to adduce evidence from a witness who had refused to supply information to the investigators, and was then told that money was available for the right information. The issue was whether this evidence dealt only with a collateral issue. It was held that the issue was not solely collateral, and that the accused should have been permitted to adduce the evidence. Judged by reference to the classical approach to the rule, it is arguable that the case was wrongly decided. The witness had not accepted a bribe, and had not supplied information against the accused. But it is certainly in keeping with the modern trend to take a more liberal approach. It is submitted that the decision can be defended on the basis that there was a specific suggestion by the defence that witnesses (albeit not the witness proposed to be called) had been induced to supply false information by the offer of financial reward. It would seem questionable, to say the least, to keep that information from the jury. Moreover, more modern considerations of the accused's right to a fair trial certainly point in the same direction, and may make it appropriate to err on the side of admitting such evidence in a doubtful case, at least when the evidence is tendered by the accused.

17.11 EVIDENCE OF REPUTATION FOR UNTRUTHFULNESS

A witness may be called to state his opinion that a witness called on the other side should not be believed, or that the witness has a reputation for untruthfulness. This form of evidence is little used, and almost devoid of modern authority, but did arise in *Richardson*,[35] in which the Court of Appeal held that a witness may be asked about the reputation of the impugned witness for truthfulness. In the case under appeal the trial judge had permitted evidence of reputation to be given but refused to allow a further question to be put in the form, 'From your personal knowledge of Mrs C, would you believe her on her oath?' It was held that this question should have been allowed also, and that the witness may state his own opinion in addition to his evidence of general reputation, provided always that his evidence is based upon his own personal knowledge. However, the Court of Appeal added that a witness called for this purpose cannot give the reasons underlying his opinion in chief. The inadmissibility of reasons in evidence in chief is an old rule, which at one time applied strictly to any evidence of opinion. It has ceased to have effect, so far as expert opinion evidence is concerned (see 11.6). But it is submitted that in the present context, it is of some value in preventing a multiplicity of side issues from arising, which the court

---

[34] (1680) 7 St Tr 1293, 1400.
[35] [1969] 1 QB 299. Older authority includes *Mawson v Hartsink* (1802) 4 Esp 102; *Watson* (1817) 2 Stark 116; *Brown* (1867) 10 Cox CC 453.

could not hope to investigate satisfactorily. There is no power to prevent the witness being asked for his reasons in cross-examination, although the course would ordinarily be a perilous one. In *Beard* [1998] Crim LR 585, it was held that evidence may be given in rebuttal of evidence of reputation for untruthfulness, but only where the credibility of the witness has been attacked by reputation evidence given in the course of the trial. The mere fact that the witness's credibility has been impugned in other circumstances, such as in the course of an interview with the police, will not open the door to evidence designed to support his credibility. In the same case it was doubted whether a party (as opposed to a witness called by a party) may give evidence of reputation for untruthfulness. It may perhaps be added that, even if this were to be allowed, the evidence would probably be of little weight.

The position of a witness in a criminal case with respect to his bad character is governed by separate rules. Where the witness gives evidence, any evidence as to his character, including evidence of reputation for untruthfulness, may be given only when permitted by s. 100 or s. 101 of the Criminal Justice Act 2003. These rules are discussed in detail in Chapter 6.

17.12 MEDICAL EVIDENCE AFFECTING RELIABILITY

Medical evidence may be called to show that a witness suffers from some disease, defect or abnormality of the mind, such as to affect the reliability of his evidence. The rule is akin to, but more specialized than that just discussed concerning reputation and opinion. The modern rule is to be gleaned from *Toohey* v *Commissioner of Police of the Metropolis* [1965] AC 595. Toohey and two others were charged with assault with intent to rob. Their defence was that the alleged victim had been drinking and was behaving very strangely, and that while they were taking him home, he had become hysterical and had imagined that he was going to be robbed. A police surgeon gave evidence for the defence and said that when he examined the alleged victim there were no signs of injury on him, that he smelt of alcohol, and that throughout the examination he was weeping and hysterical. The appeal turned on the question whether the trial judge was correct in refusing to allow the doctor to be asked his opinion of the part played by alcohol in the victim's hysteria, and whether he was more prone to hysteria than a normal person. The House of Lords held that the further questions should have been permitted, firstly because they sought to elicit matters of direct relevance to the defence, and secondly, because the evidence was admissible for the purpose of questioning the victim's reliability as a witness. The second of these reasons involved overruling the decision of the Court of Criminal Appeal in *Gunewardene* [1951] 2 KB 600, in which it had been held that the most that could be asked of a medical witness was whether, from his knowledge, he would believe the impugned witness on his oath; and that no reasons might be given in chief. This equated a doctor with a witness called to deal with general reputation or to give a lay opinion based upon personal knowledge. Lord Pearce reviewed the older authorities, concluding that 'the older cases are concerned with lying as an aspect of bad character, and are of little help in establishing any principle that will deal with modern scientific knowledge of mental disease and its effect on the reliability of a witness'. Later in his speech with which the other members of the House concurred, Lord Pearce observed (*ibid*. at 608):

> Human evidence shares the frailties of those who give it. It is subject to many cross-currents such as partiality, prejudice, self-interest and above all, imagination and inaccuracy. Those are matters with which the jury, helped by cross-examination and common sense, must do their best. But when a witness through physical (in which I include mental) disease or abnormality is not capable of giving a true or reliable account to the jury, it must surely be allowed for medical science to reveal this vital hidden fact to them.

Lord Pearce concluded (*ibid.* at 609):

> *Gunewardene's* case was, in my opinion, wrongly decided. Medical evidence is admissible to show that a witness suffers from some disease or defect or abnormality of mind that affects the reliability of his evidence. Such evidence is not confined to a general opinion of the unreliability of the witness but may give all the matters necessary to show, not only the foundation of and reasons for the diagnosis, but also the extent to which the credibility of the witness is affected.

The evidence given by the psychiatrist need not consist of evidence of serious mental disorder. Provided that the evidence shows that there is some 'deviation from the norm' which has a history pre-dating the witness's being called to give evidence, and that there is reason to believe that the witness's condition affects the reliability of his evidence, the evidence is admissible. One test is whether or not, if the witness were making a confession, it would have to be excluded from evidence pursuant to s. 76(2)(b) of the Police and Criminal Evidence Act 1984 (see 9.8.1): *O'Brien* [2000] Crim LR 676.

The court will generally not admit expert opinion on the issue of credibility unless it provides a medical explanation for the alleged unreliability of the witness (see 11.4.2). But if such an opinion is tendered, the jury may be left to evaluate it. The fact that the expert has not examined the witness will affect the weight of the evidence, but will not necessarily result in its exclusion: see *MacKenney* [2004] 2 Cr App R 32.[36]

Evidence is permitted to rebut medical evidence of the unreliability of a witness. However, the rebuttal evidence must be strictly confined to that which is required to meet the specific challenge made to the witness's reliability. Consistently with the principles discussed above, the right to call rebuttal evidence may not be regarded as a licence to support the credibility or reliability of the witness generally, in terms which fall outside the scope of the challenge offered by the medical evidence.[37]

17.13 EVIDENCE AFFECTING CREDIT OF MAKER OF ADMISSIBLE HEARSAY STATEMENT

The Civil Evidence Act 1995 and the Criminal Justice Act 1988 make provision for certain evidence to be given on collateral issues, for the purpose of attacking the credit of the makers of admissible hearsay statements. The purpose of such evidence is to offset the disadvantage suffered by a party against whom the hearsay is offered. The major objection to the admission of hearsay evidence is that it cannot effectively be cross-examined to, and in particular, it is difficult, if it is possible at all, to impugn effectively the credibility of the maker of a hearsay statement, who is not called as a witness.

17.13.1 Civil cases

Section 5(2) of the Civil Evidence Act 1995, provides:

> Where in civil proceedings evidence is adduced and the maker of the original statement, or of any statement relied on to prove another statement, is not called as a witness—
>   (a) evidence which if he had been so called would be admissible for the purpose of attacking or
>   supporting his credibility as a witness is admissible for that purpose in the proceedings; and

---

[36] Reversing, after a reference by the Criminal Cases Review Commission, *MacKenney* (1981) 72 Cr App R 78.
[37] *Robinson* [1994] 3 All ER 346; cf. *Beard* [1998] Crim LR 585.

(b) evidence tending to prove that, whether before or after he made the statement, he made any other statement inconsistent with it is admissible for the purpose of showing that he had contradicted himself.

Provided that evidence may not be given of any matter of which, if he had been called as a witness and had denied that matter in cross-examination, evidence could not have been adduced by the cross-examining party.

The section simulates the cross-examiner's weapons of cross-examination as to credit, and the use of previous inconsistent statements. The effect is to adopt the common law rules on cross-examination as to credit, including the rule that answers on collateral issues must be accepted as final (see 17.8 *et seq.*), and the admissibility of statements which, in the case of a witness, could have been put in cross-examination under ss. 4 and 5 of the Criminal Procedure Act 1865 (see 17.7 *et seq.*). It is submitted that, in the latter case, s. 5(2) must be read together with s. 6(3) of the Act (see 16.2.2). If this is done, it would seem that, once statements are admitted under s. 4 or s. 5 of the 1865 Act, they are admissible as evidence of any relevant matter stated in them, as well as matters affecting the credibility of the maker of the statement. This is clearly the position in relation to previous statements made by a witness, and it would seem anomalous if the position were different where the maker is not called as a witness.

In the absence of the maker of the statement, the weapons provided by s. 5(2) may sometimes be less effective than in a case where cross-examination is possible. However, this is by no means always the case. The weight to be attached to an admissible hearsay statement will often be less than that attached to oral evidence to begin with, and any significant attack on the maker's credibility may reduce that weight to little or nothing. Moreover, the party tendering the statement may have no opportunity to restore the credibility of the maker by explaining away apparent inconsistencies or ambiguities in his statement.

17.13.2 Criminal cases

Section 124 of the Criminal Justice Act 2003 makes similar provision for the impeachment of the maker of an admissible hearsay statement in criminal cases. The section provides:

(1) This section applies if in criminal proceedings—
   (a) a statement not made in oral evidence in the proceedings is admitted as evidence of a matter stated, and
   (b) the maker of the statement does not give oral evidence in connection with the subject matter of the statement.
(2) In such a case—
   (a) any evidence which (if he had given such evidence) would have been admissible as relevant to his credibility as a witness is so admissible in the proceedings;
   (b) evidence may with the court's leave be given of any matter which (if he had given such evidence) could have been put to him in cross-examination as relevant to his credibility as a witness but of which evidence could not have been adduced by the cross-examining party;
   (c) evidence tending to prove that he made (at whatever time) any other statement inconsistent with the statement admitted as evidence is admissible for the purpose of showing that he contradicted himself.
   (3) If as a result of evidence admitted under this section an allegation is made against the maker of a statement, the court may permit a party to lead additional evidence of such description as the court may specify for the purposes of denying or answering the allegation.

(4) In the case of a statement in a document which is admitted as evidence under section 117 each person who, in order for the statement to be admissible, must have supplied or received the information concerned or created or received the document or part concerned is to be treated as the maker of the statement for the purposes of subsections (1) to (3) above.

The section applies to the maker of any hearsay statement admitted in criminal proceedings who does not give evidence in the proceedings. This includes, where the hearsay statement is admitted under s. 117 of the Act, any person who created or received the document in circumstances such as to render it admissible; any such person is to be treated as the maker of the statement: s. 124(4). Subsection (2) permits a party to adduce (a) any evidence which would have been admissible as relevant to the maker's credibility; (b) (with leave) evidence of any matters about which he could have been cross-examined but which would have been subject to the rule of finality of collateral matters; and (c) any previous inconsistent statement made by him. Subsection (3) permits such additional evidence as the court may permit for the purpose of rehabilitating the credit of the maker of the statement with respect to any allegation made against him in evidence admitted under subsection (2). Section 124 contains no provision to the effect that evidence admitted by virtue of the section is admissible as evidence of any matter stated, but s. 119(2) provides that where a previous inconsistent statement is admitted by virtue of s. 124(2)(c), it is admissible as evidence of any matter stated in it of which oral evidence by the maker of the statement would be admissible. In the absence of any other provision, however, evidence admitted by virtue of subsections (a) and (b) is admissible only the issue of the credit of the maker of the statement, as at common law.

C   CROSS-EXAMINATION ON DOCUMENTS

SUMMARY OF MAIN POINTS

- The use of an otherwise inadmissible document in cross-examination does not make it admissible.
- But if the cross-examiner calls for a document in the possession of an opponent and inspects it, he is bound to put the document in evidence as part of his case. In the context of modern pre-trial disclosure obligations, this rule is now rarely applied.

17.14 DOCUMENTS GENERALLY

We have already dealt with the rules relating to the use of previous written statements inconsistent with the present testimony of a witness (see 16.14 and 17.7) and cross-examination on documents used to refresh the memory (see 16.4.2). We must now look at the use in cross-examination of documents which do not fall into those categories, but stand or fall in their own right as pieces of evidence, according to the normal rules of admissibility. Such documents are obviously of an almost infinitely various nature, and may be either in the possession of the cross-examiner or of the opponent of the cross-examiner.

A document in the possession of the cross-examiner is either admissible in itself, in which case it may be put in evidence and cross-examined upon in its own right, or inadmissible (usually on the ground of hearsay) in itself. We have seen that evidence cannot be made admissible just because it is used in cross-examination if it was inadmissible in chief, as in *Treacy* [1944] 2 All ER 229, where it was held improper to cross-examine upon the contents of a document which had been held to be inadmissible.[38] The most that can be done with an inadmissible document, therefore, is to ask the witness to look at the document and, without describing the nature or contents of the document to the court, to invite him to consider whether he wishes to give any further or different evidence.[39] If a witness, on being shown a document, asserts or admits that its contents are true, then those contents which he so adopts become part of his evidence. But the contents of an inadmissible document cannot be made evidence unless they are so adopted. In *Gillespie* (1967) 51 Cr App R 172, the accused were convicted of offences of dishonesty in account-ing to their employers for sums of money less than those which, according to the documenta-tion prepared by sales staff, had been received from customers. The conviction was quashed, on the ground that the accused had been asked in cross-examination to read aloud the documents prepared by member of the sales staff, who had not been called to give evidence. What the pros-ecution had done was to purport to make admissible the contents of documents which were inadmissible hearsay, merely by putting them to the accused, when the accused did not in any way adopt or acknowledge the truth of those contents. Similarly, in *Cooper* (1985) 82 Cr App R 74, it was held to be improper for the judge to permit the prosecution, on a charge involving drugs offences, to admit against the accused letters written by his wife, which contained passages that could well have been taken as referring to transactions involving drugs, in the absence of a show-ing that the accused knew of the contents of the letters and in some way adopted them.

17.15 DOCUMENTS IN THE POSSESSION OF AN OPPONENT

Documents in the possession of the opponent of the cross-examiner are subject to a special rule. At common law, if the cross-examiner calls for and inspects in court a document in the possession of his opponent or his opponent's witness, then the cross-examiner is bound to put the docu-ment in evidence as part of the cross-examiner's case. Thus in *Stroud* v *Stroud*[40] in the course of a defended suit for divorce, counsel for the husband cross-examined a doctor called on behalf of the wife, and called for and inspected in court certain medical reports prepared by other doctors concerning the wife, which the witness had with him. It was held that counsel for the wife was entitled to insist upon the reports being put in as part of the husband's case; and counsel for the husband having elected to put in some of them, counsel for the wife was entitled to have the remainder put in also. The rule is a curious one, and it is to be noted that it comes into operation even if the cross-examination has not been concerned with the contents of the documents. The rule developed in the absence of a general process of discovery at common law, and it was argued before Wrangham J in *Stroud* v *Stroud* that the modern principle of disclosure of all relevant,

[38] To similar effect is *Windass* (1988) 89 Cr App R 258. But see now also *Myers* [1998] AC 124; *Rowson* [1986] QB 174, discussed at 9.13; 17.5.1. Of course, the contents of an inadmissible document may be extremely useful in providing information from which questions in cross-examination may be framed. It is perfectly proper to make use of the contents for the purpose of framing the most effective questions, provided that the existence and contents of the document are not revealed to the court: *Rice* [1963] 1 QB 857.

[39] See *Yousry* (1914) 11 Cr App R 13.

[40] [1963] 1 WLR 1080. Contrast carefully the rule applying to documents used to refresh the memory, which is quite distinct: *Senat* v *Senat* [1965] P 172; see 16.4.2. As to the practice of cross-examination using police custody records, see *Hackney* (1982) 74 Cr App R 194. This practice is of increasing significance since the coming into effect of the Police and Criminal Evidence Act 1984 and Code of Practice C.

non-privileged documents, had rendered the rule obsolete. The learned judge accepted that in the case of documents which had not, but ought to have been disclosed on discovery, the cross-examiner would be entitled to inspect them in court without being compelled to put them in evidence, as he would have been before the start of the trial. But although the importance of the rule has undoubtedly diminished since the advent of a general principle of disclosure, Wrangham J pointed out that the rule may still be of significance in cases where there is no, or limited, disclosure, particularly in criminal cases: and indeed, it would seem still to apply to such cases.

D   BEYOND CROSS-EXAMINATION

SUMMARY OF MAIN POINTS

- Re-examination is examination by the party calling a witness to clarify points made in cross-examination. It must be confined to matters raised in cross-examination. Leading questions are not permitted.

- Evidence must generally be presented during a party's case. Exceptionally a party may be permitted to re-open his case to call evidence in rebuttal.

- At common law, the traditional test for permitting evidence in rebuttal was that a party must have been unable to foresee that the evidence would be required. But in contemporary practice, it is permitted in any case in which the judge considers it appropriate in the interests of justice and no prejudice is caused.

- The judge has a limited power to call a witness whom neither party proposes to call. This power must be used sparingly and with great caution.

17.16 RE-EXAMINATION

Very little need be said about re-examination. It is the process whereby a party calling a witness may seek to explain or clarify any points that arose in cross-examination and appear to be unfavourable to his case. Re-examination is, therefore, possible only where there has been cross-examination and is limited to matters raised in cross-examination: it is not an opportunity to adduce further evidence in chief. But cross-examination opens the door to re-examination on any matters raised for the first time in cross-examination. Thus, in *Prince* v *Samo* (1838) 7 Ad & El 627, where a witness for the plaintiff was cross-examined about part of a hearsay statement, which would have been wholly inadmissible in chief, the plaintiff was entitled to re-examine on any matter arising from the portion of the statement referred to in cross-examination, but was not entitled to elicit any other portion. The re-examiner may deal with all matters relevant to those raised in cross-examination, even if not dealt with expressly by the cross-examiner.

   A witness is entitled to explain any apparent contradiction or ambiguity in his evidence or damage to his credit arising from cross-examination, and this may involve reference to facts which have not previously been given in evidence, if they are properly relevant in order to deal with the points put in cross-examination. Where, therefore, a witness was asked in cross-examination why his evidence was that the accused was one of a number of persons who attacked a deceased, when he had made a statement in which he did not refer to the accused at all, he was allowed to be asked in re-examination whether he had made an earlier statement, in which he had referred to the accused.[41] In this case, the re-examination was directed to re-establishing the credit of the witness but the principle is the same where it is sought to clear up some question of fact. Evidence admitted in re-examination can, therefore, be powerful and dangerous. The effect of cross-examination in opening the door to further evidence must be carefully considered before it is embarked upon. If, for example, it is suggested in cross-examination of a police officer that the officer followed the accused because of a determination to be vindictive against him, the officer may be re-examined to elicit his true reasons for following him. The resulting evidence, which would have been wholly inadmissible in chief, is potentially devastating.

Leading questions are not permitted in re-examination, for the same reason as in the case of examination in chief (see 16.1.2).

17.17 EVIDENCE IN REBUTTAL

The general rule of practice, in both criminal and civil cases, is that every party must call all the evidence on which he proposes to rely during the presentation of his case, and before closing his case; see, e.g., *Kane* (1977) 65 Cr App R 270. This involves the proposition that the parties should foresee, during their preparations for trial, what the issues will be, and what evidence is available and necessary in order to deal with those issues. The definition of the issues in a civil case by exchange of statements of case and witness statements, and in a criminal case (to a far more limited extent) by service of the prosecution statements and the settling of an indictment,[42] is designed to enable this to be done wherever possible.

It must, however, be recognized that in some cases, it will not be possible to foresee every piece of evidence which may be required, because proceedings have a habit of taking courses which occasion surprise and sometimes embarrassment to one or more of the parties. It has long been the rule that the judge may permit evidence to be called by a party who has been taken by surprise by some development at the trial, in order to 'rebut' evidence given against him by the other side, after that party's case has been formally closed. In a case tried with a jury, no evidence may be given after the retirement of the jury. In a criminal case, any breach of this rule will lead to the conviction being quashed (*Owen* [1952] 2 QB 362); even where the evidence is apparently irrelevant (*Wilson* (1957) 41 Cr App R 226); and even where the defence purport to consent to the evidence being given (*Corless* (1972) 56 Cr App R 341).[43] In non-jury trials there is somewhat more flexibility, though it would only be in the most exceptional circumstances that evidence would be admitted after the court has retired to consider its decision or has begun to render its decision.[44] Such a case was *Malcolm* v *DPP* [2007] 1 WLR 1230, in which it was held to be proper to permit the prosecution to adduce additional evidence even after the magistrates

---

[41] *Coll* (1889) 24 LR Ir 522.

[42] As to the prosecution's duty in this regard, see the observations of the Court of Appeal in *Sansom* [1991] 2 QB 130. As to the requirements of disclosure by the defence, see Criminal Procedure and Investigations Act 1996, ss. 5, 11 as amended.

[43] Though the Court of Criminal Appeal has approved the admission of evidence for the defence where a witness arrived at court during the summing-up (and so was not being recalled) and the judge summed up his evidence subsequently: *Sanderson* [1953] 1 WLR 392.

[44] As to the position in magistrates' courts, see *Cook* v *DPP* [2001] Crim LR 321; *Webb* v *Leadbetter* [1966] 1 WLR 245.

had returned to court and had begun to announce their decision. The defence had raised for the first time in its closing speech the issue of non-compliance with the requirement for a warning under s. 7(7) of the Road Traffic Act 1988, an issue crucial to the outcome of the case. No cross-examination had been directed to the issue and the prosecution, believing that the point was not at issue, were taken completely by surprise. When the magistrates indicated that they accepted the defence's position, the prosecution sought and were granted leave to adduce evidence on that issue. The decision was upheld on appeal. The Divisional Court said:

> Criminal proceedings are no longer to be treated as a game in which each move is final and any omission by the prosecution leads to its failure. It is the duty of the defence to make its defence . . . That duty is implicit in rule 3.3 of the Criminal Procedure Rules 2005, which requires the parties actively to assist the exercise by the court of its case management powers, the exercise of which requires early identification of the *real* issues. [*Ibid.* at [31], emphasis in original.]

It is submitted that the decision is correct. Even leaving aside the provisions of the rules, the conduct of the defence was unacceptable (see 17.3) and had an obvious potential to result in injustice. But in less extreme circumstances, the circumstances in which the court's discretion should be exercised have not always been so clear.

The discretion should not be exercised in order to aid a careless or inadvertent party, who has simply failed to take the trouble to prepare his case adequately (*Pilcher* (1974) 60 Cr App R 1). And it would be carelessness or inadvertence to fail to foresee that the other side will bring evidence designed to contradict and disprove one's case. The test was originally that laid down by Tindal CJ in *Frost*,[45] in fairly narrow terms:

> The Crown . . . cannot afterwards support their case by calling fresh witnesses, because they are met by certain evidence that contradicts it. They stand or fall by the evidence they have given . . . but if any matter arises *ex improviso* which no human ingenuity can foresee . . . there seems to me no reason why the matter which so arose *ex improviso* may not be answered by contrary evidence on the part of the Crown.

More recently, it has been felt that the test propounded by Tindal CJ is unduly narrow, and ought to be restated to allow the trial judge more discretion to further the interests of justice,[46] and it is pertinent to note that the competence of the accused as a witness since 1898, coupled with his right in most cases (until recently) to withhold his defence until trial, has made the task of prosecution more difficult. It may be, although *Frost* has not been overruled, that the test is now one of reasonable foreseeability, and that if the course of the trial takes a party into uncharted waters, which could not have been anticipated before trial on a sensible and alert view of the case, further evidence ought to be permitted to deal with the matters which have occasioned surprise.[47] Certainly, it would seem wrong for the court to be deprived of relevant evidence in such circumstances, which might be the case on the basis of an unbending interpretation of the words, 'which no human ingenuity can foresee'. There are cases in which relevant evidence becomes available unexpectedly for the first time at a late stage of the proceeding (see, e.g., *Doran* (1972) 56 Cr App R 492[48]).

---

[45] (1840) 9 Car & P 129 as reported in 4 St Tr NS 85 at 386.

[46] See, e.g., *Crippen* [1911] 1 KB 149 *Cook* v *DPP* [2001] Crim LR 321.

[47] Cf. *Owen* [1952] 2 QB 362, per Lord Goddard CJ at 366; *Milliken* (1969) 53 Cr App R 330, 333; *Hutchinson* (1985) 82 Cr App R 51, per Watkins LJ at 59.

[48] And see *Scott* (1984) 79 Cr App R 49.

But even on the basis of the more liberal test, there is no ground for permitting the late intro-duction of evidence which was both available and foreseeably necessary before a party's case was closed and ought to have been adduced as a proper and necessary part of the prosecution case. In *Day*,[49] a conviction was quashed where the prosecution were permitted to call a handwriting expert, not only after the close of their own case, but after the accused had given evidence, and where it was obvious from the outset that the evidence might well be required. Conversely, in *Cunningham* [1985] Crim LR 374, it was held proper to permit the prosecution to call in rebuttal two police officers, who had not given evidence as part of the prosecution case in chief, where the defence based their attack on a confession on alleged conduct by those officers, which was explored in cross-examination of a third officer, and where the defence did not request a 'trial within a trial'. Although it was reasonably foreseeable that the two officers would have to be called if there was an issue as to the admissibility of the confession, the defence, by not asking for a hearing on the *voir dire* during the prosecution case, and by deferring their attack on it until after the close of the prosecution case, had given the prosecution insufficient opportunity to deal with the issue. It is submitted that this result would not follow in all similar cases; it was effectively conceded that the prosecution was not 'surprised' within the normal meaning of that term, but on the other hand, it is true to say that the prosecution had little reason to call the two officers as part of their case.

The court should readily give leave for a party's case to be re-opened for the introduction of formal evidence, which cannot be the subject of reasonable dispute, which has been inadvert-ently omitted (see, e.g., *Palastanga* v *Solman* [1962] Crim LR 334: proof of regulation by HMSO copy). The same is true even of evidence of substantial import, such as evidence proving part of an identification, where the omission is simply due to a reasonable misunderstanding as to whether the facts dealt with by the omitted evidence were in dispute (*Francis* [1990] 1 WLR 1264).

In civil cases, evidence in rebuttal has been permitted in cases where evidence has been given, or issues raised, which could not have been foreseen on the statements of case and which have accordingly taken a party by surprise; or where a party has been misled about the true nature of the claim or defence. But in a civil action, the judge may equally decline to entertain any unasserted issue, and will usually do so if the departure from the asserted issues is a serious one, going to the very nature of the claim or defence. This consideration indeed reflects the true objection to evidence in rebuttal, which is that the contrary case will already have been presented, to an end and in a way which does not correspond with the actuality, and the preju-dice which can arise if a party is allowed to alter his case, after the case against him has been presented, is obvious.

Evidence in rebuttal is not permissible of collateral matters except in certain cases (see 17.8 *et seq.*) or where it would simply be confirmatory of the party's case as already put.[50]

17.18 JUDGE'S POWER TO CALL WITNESSES

Ordinarily, the working of the adversarial system of litigation requires that the judge should not interfere with the decision of the parties to call or not to call a particular witness or to tender or not to tender a particular piece of evidence. In a civil case, where the judge has the duty of find-ing the facts, as well as that of presiding over the conduct of the trial, he is entitled to draw any

---

[49] [1940] 1 All ER 402; and see *Pilcher* (1974) 60 Cr App R 1.
[50] *Jacobs* v *Tarleton* (1848) 11 QB 421.

proper inferences about the strength or weakness of a party's case from that party's failure to call what appears to be relevant and available evidence. Accordingly, the traditional rule in civil cases was that the judge would not call a witness over the objection of the parties, except in the (criminal) setting of proceedings for contempt of court.[51] The court's powers to achieve the overriding objective under r. 32.1 of the Civil Procedure Rules 1998 appear not to extend to ordering a party to call a witness,[52] but the editors of *Blackstone's Civil Practice* (2009 edn, at para. 47.52) appear to leave open the possibility that the power does extend to giving directions which make it clear which witnesses the judge believes should be called, and in what order. Whether this would permit the judge to call a witness himself if the parties failed to do so after having received such a direction, is unclear. In a criminal case, however, somewhat different considerations apply, because of the high standard of proof required of the prosecution, the needs of the jury, and the judge's specific duty to ensure a fair trial for the accused.

It has long been recognized that the judge has power, in a criminal trial, to call of his own motion any witness who has not been called either for the prosecution or the defence, if in his opinion it is necessary to do so in the interests of justice.[53] The power must be exercised with great care, bearing in mind that it is the duty of the prosecution to call all the witnesses who can give relevant evidence, unless they appear to be incapable of belief, even where they may give evidence inconsistent with the prosecution case. If the prosecution fail to call a witness who on the face of it ought to be called, it is open to the judge to invite the prosecution to call him.[54] If neither side calls a witness, the judge should assume that there is a good reason for such a course, especially where neither side makes any application to him in the matter. It has often been said that the judge's power to call a witness should be exercised rarely and sparingly.[55] Like any other evidence, the witness must be called before the retirement of the jury, and there is no doubt that it must be even rarer than suggested above that he should be called after the defence case has been closed. In *Cleghorn* [1967] 2 QB 584, a conviction was quashed where, on a charge of rape, the trial judge called a witness who had not been called by either side. The witness was called after the defence case had been closed, and the case thereafter assumed a different aspect. Although no rule applicable to all cases can be laid down, it has been helpfully suggested[56] that the calling of witnesses by the judge should generally be confined to cases where analogously to the case of *Frost*,[57] a matter has arisen '*ex improviso*, which no human ingenuity can foresee'. One proper use of the power is a case where the judge concludes that the prosecution are wrongly declining to call a witness who ought to be called in the interests of a fair trial. It is not always an answer to say that the defence can call the witness, because they should be in a position to cross-examine and not be obliged to call him as their witness in chief.[58] It may also be proper for

[51] *Re Enoch and Zaretzky, Bock and Co.'s Arbitration* [1910] 1 KB 327; *Yianni v Yianni* [1966] 1 WLR 120.
[52] *Society of Lloyd's v Jaffray* (2000) *The Times*, 3 August 2000.
[53] *Chapman* (1838) 8 Car & P 558; *Roberts* (1984) 80 Cr App R 89.
[54] *Oliva* [1965] 1 WLR 1028.
[55] See, e.g., *Edwards* (1848) 3 Cox CC 82; *Cleghorn* [1967] 2 QB 584.
[56] In *Harris* [1927] 2 KB 587.
[57] (1840) 9 Car & P 129 as reported in 4 St Tr NS 85 at 386. See 17.17.
[58] Cf. *Tregear* [1967] 2 QB 574. The prosecution's duty must be exercised so as to further the cause of justice, which must involve consideration of the consequences of the defence calling a witness in chief. But if the evidence of a witness would form part of the defence case then the prosecution are not obliged to call him, particularly if doing so would merely confuse the jury: *Nugent* [1977] 1 WLR 789.

the judge to call a witness who seems hostile to both sides, but whose evidence may nonetheless be relevant.

A witness called by the judge may be cross-examined by either side only with leave,[59] although if his evidence affects adversely the case for either side, it is inconceivable that leave should be refused.

17.19 RECOMMENDED FURTHER READING

Hoyano, L.C.H., 'The child witness review: much ado about too little' [2007] *Criminal Law Review* 849.

Hunter, J., 'Battling a Good Story: Cross-examining the Failure of the Law of Evidence' in Roberts, P. and Redmayne, M., *Innovations in Evidence and Proof* (Oxford: Hart Publishing, 2007) pp. 261–91.

Newark, M., 'Opening up the collateral issue rule' (1992) **43** *Northern Ireland Legal Quarterly* 166.

O'Brian, W.E., 'The right of confrontation: US and European perspectives' (2005) **121** *Law Quarterly Review* 481.

Pattenden, R., 'Evidence of previous malpractice by police witnesses and *R v Edwards*' [1992] *Criminal Law Review* 549.

Stone, M., 'Instant lie detection? Demeanour and credibility in criminal trials' [1991] *Criminal Law Review* 821.

17.20 QUESTIONS FOR DISCUSSION BASED ON *R v COKE; LITTLETON* AND *BLACKSTONE v COKE* (for case files go to the Online Resource Centre)

17.20.1 *Coke; Littleton*

1. May counsel for Coke cross-examine Margaret Blackstone as to:

   (a) The fact that she consented to have sexual intercourse with Coke on 8 July Yr—1?

   (b) The fact that she had led him to believe on other occasions that she was prepared to have sexual intercourse with him?

   (c) The fact that Margaret is promiscuous?

   (d) The fact that Margaret has had sexual intercourse with Coke's mate, Kevin?

   (e) The fact that Margaret threatened to accuse Kevin of raping her?

   (f) The fact that Margaret has a previous conviction for theft?

2. In relation to any of these matters on which cross-examination is possible, would the defence be entitled to call evidence in rebuttal if Margaret denies them in cross-examination?

3. If Margaret's evidence in chief varies materially from the contents of her statement to the police, what steps may Coke's counsel take? What results will any such course have, and what must counsel bear in mind before embarking on it?

4. If Margaret has a known history of lying, what evidence might be called on behalf of Coke to deal with this?

---

[59] *Coulson v Disborough* [1894] 2 QB 316.

17.20.2 *Blackstone* v *Coke*

1. Consider question 3 above in the context of *Blackstone* v *Coke*.

2. If Coke is permitted to adduce the hearsay statement of Anthony Henneky, what steps might Margaret take to discredit it?

17.21 GENERAL QUESTIONS FOR DISCUSSION

1. What is the purpose of cross-examination?

2. What is the effect of an omission to cross-examine?

3. A man is charged with offences of rape and theft arising from the same set of circumstances. May he cross-examine the complainant in person regarding the theft?

4. May a co-accused be cross-examined about a confession that has not been adduced in evidence by the prosecution because it was obtained unfairly?

5. A prosecution witness contradicts her witness statement when she testifies. How might she be cross-examined?

6. What is a collateral issue?

7. What is 'opening the door'?

8. In the course of a rape trial the complainant is cross-examined to the effect that she has previously made false complaints of rape. Is it likely that her answers will be final?

9. A police officer is asked in cross-examination if he has threatened a defence witness. Is his answer final?

10. What is the purpose of re-examination?

18

CORROBORATION AND SUSPECT WITNESS WARNINGS

SUMMARY OF MAIN POINTS

- There is no general requirement for corroboration in English law; in the absence of a specific rule to the contrary a conviction or judgment may be based on the evidence of a single witness.

- There are a few cases in which statute requires corroboration of certain facts before there can be a conviction.

- At one time there was a rule of practice requiring the judge to direct the jury to exercise caution before convicting in the absence of corroboration; this rule applied to the evidence of accomplices of the accused, the evidence of children, and the evidence of complainants in sexual cases. The rule has now been abolished.

- But the judge should give the jury a warning to approach evidence with caution (a 'suspect witness warning') if the witness may be unreliable, or appears to have a purpose of his own to serve (e.g., accomplices and co-accused) or if the judge thinks it appropriate in any case.

18.1 INTRODUCTION

Until recently, requirements for corroboration played an important part in the law of evidence in criminal cases. But, as a result of statutory changes, and the decision of the Court of Appeal in *Makanjuola* [1995] 1 WLR 1348, almost nothing remains of this once major common law rule. However, there does remain a practice of giving suitable directions to juries about the evidence of witnesses who, for any reason, are suspect, i.e., when the evidence of a witness should be regarded with suspicion, either because of some personal characteristic of the witness or because of the nature of the evidence. For this reason it remains desirable to deal briefly with the corroboration rule, and the new practice of suspect witness warnings. For a detailed treatment of the corroboration rules in their final state, see the 4th edition of this work, Chapter 15.

18.2 MEANING AND FUNCTION OF CORROBORATION

The word 'corroboration' means support or confirmation. In relation to the law of evidence, it refers to any rule of law or practice which requires that certain kinds of evidence be confirmed or supported by other, independent evidence, in order to be sufficient to sustain a given result, such as conviction of a criminal offence.[1]

From the point of view of weight, it is obvious that evidence is likely to appear more persuasive to the tribunal of fact when it is corroborated than when it is not. But the question of weight is not the issue with which the law has been mainly concerned. There has long been a question of whether certain kinds of evidence, for example, the evidence of young children or accomplices in the crime charged, should be sufficient for a conviction in the absence of corroboration, or whether the jury should at least be warned of the danger of convicting on the basis of such evidence, if uncorroborated. The desirability of corroboration in these cases arises from the perception that certain kinds of evidence are inherently suspect, either because of the nature of the witness himself (e.g., a young child or a person under mental disability) or because of the likelihood that the witness may have some purpose of his own to serve in giving evidence against the accused (as with, for example, an accomplice). If the evidence of such a witness is corroborated by other evidence which comes from a source independent of the witness, for example, a fingerprint or a confession made by the accused, its reliability is clearly enhanced.

In practice, issues of corroboration played a crucial role only in criminal cases tried on indictment. Although the rules which developed applied technically to summary trials (and occasionally to civil matters, for example affiliation proceedings,[2] and the evidence of claimants to the property of deceased persons[3]) it is very difficult to investigate, for the purpose of appeal, what, if any, attention the court may have paid to corroboration requirements when the tribunals of law and fact are the same. This proved possible in some cases, in which the court's approach became clear from a judgment or case stated for appeal. But the law developed almost exclusively by reference to criminal jury trials, in which it is possible to assess precisely whether or not the judge's summing-up dealt accurately with any issues of corroboration.

---

[1] 'There is nothing technical in the idea of corroboration. When in the ordinary affairs of life one is doubtful whether or not to believe a particular statement, one naturally looks to see whether it fits in with other statements or circumstances relating to the particular matter; the better it fits in, the more one is inclined to believe it' (*DPP* v *Kilbourne* [1973] AC 729, 750 per Lord Reid). But the law of corroboration was in some respects highly technical. For example, evidence was not capable of being corroborative unless it both emanated from a source independent of the evidence to be corroborated, and implicated the accused in the commission of the offence.

[2] Affiliation proceedings, which required the complainant's evidence to be corroborated as a matter of law, were abolished by the Family Law Reform Act 1987, s. 17, and proceedings to establish paternity are no longer subject to any requirement for corroboration.

[3] See *Re Hodgson, Beckett* v *Ramsdale* (1885) 31 ChD 177; *Re Cummins, Cummins* v *Thompson* [1972] Ch 62. The requirement for corroboration in these cases (which are tried without a jury) is one of practice only, and is not invariably insisted on. But it is unaffected by any statutory provisions to date, and appears to survive.

18.3 NO GENERAL REQUIREMENT FOR CORROBORATION AT COMMON LAW

In contrast to some other legal systems, the common law never had any general requirement of corroboration. Both in civil and criminal cases, the general rule is that any judgment or conviction may be based on the uncorroborated evidence of a single witness or on uncorroborated evidence of any other kind.

The general rule, however, became subject to two groups of exceptions:

18.3.1 Corroboration required as a matter of law

This group consists of cases in which statute requires certain evidence to be corroborated as a matter of law. The effect of this is that if no other evidence capable of corroborating that evidence exists, no conviction or judgment can be based on it, and any conviction or judgment so obtained must be set aside on appeal. This group still exists, and is considered in more detail at 18.4.

18.3.2 Corroboration to be looked for as a matter of practice

This group consisted of cases developed judicially. Although corroboration was not required as a matter of law, the judge must as a matter of practice direct the jury (or the court must warn itself) of the danger of convicting on the basis of certain uncorroborated evidence. Despite the use of the term 'matter of practice', the requirement for a warning was mandatory, and its absence was a ground of appeal. However, if the warning was properly given, the jury was entitled to convict even in the absence of corroboration. Originally, this requirement was confined to three specific kinds of evidence: namely, that of accomplices of the accused, that of children of tender years, and that of complainants in sexual cases.[4] But, in more recent times, it was suggested, and apparently accepted, that there might be other cases in which corroboration should be looked for, where the evidence of a particular witness is for any reason suspect, for example, because the witness appears to have some improper motive or purpose of his own to serve in giving evidence against the accused.[5] Such a rule was finally rejected in *Makanjuola* [1995] 1 WLR 1348, though some appropriate warning should be given in such cases (see 18.5).

18.3.3 Statutory erosion of corroboration requirements

For almost a century, these exceptions were of great importance, reflecting the view of the courts (and to a lesser extent, Parliament) that there was some merit in looking for corroboration of some categories of suspect evidence. More recently, however, the trend has been to revert to a position more consistent with the general common law rule, and both groups of exceptions have now been whittled away by statute almost to the point of extinction.

This development was probably due less to a retreat from the view that certain kinds of evidence are inherently suspect, than to the fact that the rules regarding corroboration became

---

[4] *Baskerville* [1916] 2 KB 658; *Davies* v *DPP* [1954] AC 378. The requirement for a corroboration warning solely because evidence falls into these categories has been abolished by statute: see 18.3.3. The essence of a full corroboration warning was that it would be dangerous to convict on the uncorroborated evidence of the witness concerned. But the judge was also obliged to identify for the jury those pieces of evidence which were capable of being corroborative and the issues to which they were relevant.

[5] See *Spencer* [1987] AC 128; *Beck* [1982] 1 WLR 461; *Prater* [1960] 2 QB 464; 18.4.

rather technical, and were widely regarded as confusing and unnecessarily restrictive.[6] Many convictions were overturned because of the failure of the trial judge to comply with the technical requirements of the rule in summing up to the jury. For example, it was at one time held that the evidence of the complaining witness in a rape case required a corroboration warning even in a case where the accused did not dispute the witness's evidence that she had been raped, and the only issue was one of identification. Such inflexibility was unnecessary, led to absurd results, and produced understandable judicial frustration. At the same time, the courts were experimenting, apparently successfully, with less technical directions to juries which simply instructed them to exercise caution in evaluating suspect kinds of evidence, but without the technicalities of a full corroboration warning.[7] The present view is that such less technical directions are adequate, and can be applied to any evidence which seems to merit them, and need not be confined to any particular categories.

In the case of the first group, which consists of statutory rules, it is possible to state definitively to what cases the corroboration requirement continues to apply. Thus, a number of requirements for corroboration as a matter of law in sexual cases were abolished by the Criminal Justice and Public Order Act 1994, s. 33. But those cases not affected by the Act (e.g., speeding) remain.

The second group no longer exists as such. The effect of s. 34(2) of the Criminal Justice Act 1988 and s. 32(1) of the Criminal Justice and Public Order Act 1994 was to abolish any requirement for a corroboration warning solely because a witness may fall into one of the categories identified in *Baskerville*. After these provisions, the only question which remained was whether or not a corroboration warning might be required in a case where a witness is suspect, whether or not he falls within one of the common law categories, for example, the witness with a purpose of his own to serve by giving evidence. This question was answered in the negative by the Court of Appeal in *Makanjuola* [1995] 1 WLR 1348, insofar as a technical corroboration warning was concerned, but the Court did recognize the desirability of a direction to the jury to treat evidence with caution in certain cases (a suspect witness warning). This is dealt with more fully at 18.5.

18.4 CORROBORATION REQUIRED AS A MATTER OF LAW

We have already noted that the exceptions within this category are statutory cases, and that the absence of evidence capable of amounting to the necessary corroboration will be fatal to the conviction or judgment. It must also follow that if the jury reject all the evidence capable of amounting to such corroboration, no conviction is possible, and the jury should be directed in those terms. The terms and extent of the corroboration required in each case are provided for by the statute itself, and except as so provided no further corroboration is necessary as a matter of law.

The number of cases in this category has been subject to steady erosion. The unsworn evidence of children, permitted by s. 38(1) of the Children and Young Persons Act 1933 was originally made subject to the express statutory proviso that an accused might not be convicted of a

---

[6] See, for example, the comments made by the courts in *Cheema* [1994] 1 WLR 147; *Chance* [1988] QB 932; and those of the Law Commission Report on Corroboration of Evidence in Criminal Trials (Law Com. No. 202, Cm 1620) adopted by the Royal Commission on Criminal Justice (Cm 2263, 1993). Evidence was not capable of being corroborative unless it was independent of the evidence which required corroboration, and implicated the accused in the commission of the offence: *Baskerville* [1916] 2 KB 658, 667.

[7] For example, cases involving evidence of visual identification of the accused, which has long been considered a suspect kind of evidence, but which never became a specific category of evidence requiring a corroboration warning. See 16.12.2.

criminal offence on the basis of such evidence, unless it was 'corroborated by some other material evidence in support thereof implicating him'.[8] This requirement was abrogated by s. 34(1) of the Criminal Justice Act 1988. Both provisions have since been repealed, and ss. 53 to 56 of the Youth Justice and Criminal Evidence Act 1999 contain no requirement of corroboration. Requirements for corroboration in relation to a number of sexual offences were repealed by the Criminal Justice and Public Order Act 1994, s. 33. Affiliation proceedings, in which corroboration of the evidence of the complainant was also required as a matter of law by the Affiliation Proceedings Act 1957, were abolished by s. 17 of the Family Law Reform Act 1987, and no new corresponding provision for cases involving the issue of paternity has been introduced. A requirement of corroboration in cases of corrupt and illegal practices at elections, contained successively in s. 147(5) of the Representation of the People Act 1949, and s. 168(5) of the Representation of the People Act 1983, has likewise been abolished.

The principal cases which remain are as follows:

18.4.1 Treason

In a prosecution for High Treason by compassing the death or restraint of the Sovereign or the heirs of the Sovereign, it is provided by s. 1 of the Treason Act 1795 that there should be no conviction without 'the oaths of two lawful and credible witnesses'. The use of the word 'credible' must presumably be taken to import that the jury must accept the evidence of both or all such witnesses, and be prepared to act on the evidence of each taken individually.

18.4.2 Perjury

Perjury was the one exception known to the common law, in which the evidence of one witness was insufficient for a conviction. However, the position is now governed by s. 13 of the Perjury Act 1911, which provides that a person shall not be convicted of any offence against the Act, or of any other statutory offence of perjury or subornation of perjury, 'solely upon the evidence of one witness as to the falsity of any statement alleged to be false'. It will be observed that the statute prescribes the element of the offence for which corroboration is required, that is to say the falsity of the statement, and no requirement is imposed in respect of other elements of the offence. The corroborative evidence must, therefore, be directed to that issue (*Rider* (1986) 83 Cr App R 207).

18.4.3 Speeding

Under s. 89 of the Road Traffic Regulation Act 1984 a person charged with an offence of exceeding the speed limit 'shall not be liable to be convicted solely on the evidence of one witness to the effect that in the opinion of the witness the person prosecuted was driving the vehicle at a speed exceeding a specified limit'. The purpose of this provision is to provide a safeguard against the possible unreliability of such evidence of opinion, because of the likelihood of error in relating an impression of the speed of a vehicle to a precise speed limit. The corroboration must go to the observation of the witness.[9] However, the evidence of the reading of a speedometer or other

---

[8] At common law, even the sworn evidence of a child of tender years required a corroboration warning, though such sworn evidence fell into the category of corroboration looked for as a matter of practice, so that conviction on the uncorroborated sworn evidence of a child was possible. The common law requirement, also, was abrogated in relation to trials on indictment by the Criminal Justice Act 1988, s. 34(2).

[9] *Brighty* v *Pearson* [1938] 4 All ER 127.

measuring device is evidence of fact, so that readings of such instruments are not within the section, and indeed may themselves be corroborative of opinion evidence of observation.[10]

18.4.4 Quasi-corroborative rule applying to certain inferences

Sections 34 to 37 of the Criminal Justice and Public Order Act 1994 permit certain inferences to be drawn against the accused.[11] Section 34 provides that, in certain circumstances, the court may draw 'such inferences as appear proper' from the accused's failure, on being questioned under caution, or charged with an offence, to mention facts on which he subsequently relies for his defence at trial and which he could reasonably have been expected to mention at the time. Section 35 provides that 'such inferences as appear proper' may be drawn from the accused's failure to give evidence, or refusal to answer a particular question without good cause. Sections 36 and 37 make similar provision for the accused's failure, when arrested, to account for certain objects, marks or substances on his person or in his possession, or his presence at the scene of the offence charged.

Section 38(3) of the Act provides:

> A person shall not have the proceedings against him transferred to the Crown Court for trial, have a case to answer or be convicted of an offence solely on an inference drawn from such a failure or refusal as is mentioned in section 34(2), 35(3), 36(2) or 37(2).[12]

This rule does not impose a requirement for corroboration, but does impose a requirement for additional evidence against the accused. Moreover, it imposes the requirement as a matter of law. No conviction may be sustained solely on the basis of an inference drawn under any of ss. 34 to 37. For this reason, the rule may be described as a quasi-corroborative rule of law. The difference between this rule and rules requiring corroboration is that, in this rule, the other evidence need not technically be capable of constituting corroboration. Any admissible evidence against the accused will suffice to satisfy the requirement.

18.5 DEVELOPMENT OF SUSPECT WITNESS WARNINGS

The suggestion that the jury should be warned to exercise caution in evaluating the evidence of certain witnesses who did not fall within the categories identified in *Baskerville* [1916] 2 KB 658 goes back at least as far as *Prater* [1960] 2 QB 464, 466, in which Edmund Davies J expressed the view that such a warning would be desirable 'in cases where a person may be regarded as having some purpose of his own to serve'. The warning referred to by Edmund Davies J in that case was, however, a corroboration warning, and perhaps because the courts were reluctant to extend the requirement to a category which was difficult to define precisely, there was a good deal of ambivalence as to whether the suggestion made in *Prater* should be followed.[13]

---

[10] *Nicholas v Penny* [1950] 2 KB 466; *Swain v Gillett* [1974] RTR 446.

[11] These provisions are considered in detail at 10.6, 10.7, 10.8, 15.6.

[12] Section 38(4) provides that an application for dismissal of a charge shall not be based solely on such an inference (except that inferences under s. 35(2), which can arise only at trial, cannot apply in this instance). As to the direction to be given to the jury in cases under s. 35 of the Act, see *Cowan* [1996] QB 373; 15.6.4. See also the particular inferences permitted under s. 6 of the Domestic Violence, Crime and Victims Act 2004: *Blackstone's Criminal Practice*, 2009 edn, paras B1.59; F19.20.

[13] In *Stannard* [1965] 2 QB 1, 14, Winn J described what had been said in *Prater* as: 'if it be a rule...no more than a rule of practice'; and see *Whitaker* (1976) 63 Cr App R 193. But support was lent by Lord Hailsham of

The only case in which the requirement for a full corroboration direction was whole-heartedly adopted and applied seems to have been *Bagshaw* [1984] 1 WLR 477, in which the trial judge failed to give the jury a corroboration warning with respect to the evidence of patients at Rampton Hospital (an institution for criminal offenders suffering from severe mental illness), who alleged that they had been assaulted by nurses at the hospital. The Court of Appeal quashed the conviction, holding that, although no new category of witness was to be created, the witnesses in question fulfilled the criteria for a corroboration warning, and that the full warning should have been given. However, this decision was in conflict with the earlier decision of the Court of Appeal in *Beck*.[14] *Beck* was a case in which the witnesses had a purpose of their own to serve by giving evidence, but did not fit into any of the common law categories, and were not patients. Ackner LJ said ([1982] 1 WLR at 469):

> While we in no way wish to detract from the obligation upon a judge to advise a jury to proceed with caution when there is material to suggest that a witness's evidence may be tainted by an improper motive, and the strength of that advice must vary according to the facts of the case, we cannot accept that there is any obligation to give the accomplice warning with all that entails, when it is common ground that there is no basis for suggesting that the witness is a participant or in any way involved in the crime the subject matter of the trial.

In *Spencer* [1987] AC 128, another case arising from alleged assaults on patients at Rampton Hospital, in which the direction to the jury had been the same as that in *Bagshaw*, the House of Lords expressly overruled *Bagshaw* and approved *Beck*. The point of law certified was:

> In a case where the evidence for the Crown is solely that of a witness who is not in one of the accepted categories of suspect witnesses, but who, by reason of his particular mental condition and criminal connection, fulfilled the same criteria, must the judge warn the jury that it is dangerous to convict on his uncorroborated evidence?

In dealing with this question, Lord Ackner said ([1987] AC at 142):

> I would amend the question by substituting for the words 'the same criteria', 'analogous criteria'. I would then answer the question in the affirmative, adding, for the sake of clarity, that while it may often be convenient to use the words 'danger' or 'dangerous', the use of such words is not essential to an adequate warning, so long as the jury are made fully aware of the dangers of convicting on such evidence. Again, for the sake of clarity, I would further add that *Beck* was rightly decided and that in a case which does not fall into the three established categories and where there exists potential corroborative material, the extent to which the trial judge should make reference to that material depends upon the facts of each case. The overriding rule is that he must put the defence fairly and adequately.

Despite this decision, the position remained somewhat unclear in the light of the statutory abolition of the corroboration rules in the cases of the three common law categories. Neither the Criminal Justice Act 1988 nor the Criminal Justice and Public Order Act 1994 addressed the question of suspect witnesses generally. This was an unfortunate omission, because it left in conflict the clear legislative intent to abolish requirements for corroboration and the clear mandate of the House of Lords in *Spencer* that there would be cases where a warning was required. The narrower

---

St Marylebone in *DPP* v *Kilbourne* [1973] AC 729, 740; and in *Jones; Jenkins* [2004] 1 Cr App R 5, [39], Auld LJ said that 'the *law* since *R* v *Prater*…has been that some such warning should be given' (emphasis added).

[14] [1982] 1 WLR 461. Because of a procedural quirk, the point regarding the absence of a warning was argued only briefly in *Bagshaw*, and the court was not referred to *Beck*. In *Spencer* [1987] AC 128, the House of Lords described *Bagshaw* as having been decided *per incuriam*.

question which remained was whether, given that some warning is required in the case of any suspect witness, that warning should be a full corroboration warning, or something less.

Some indication of the likely answer to this question was to be found in the willingness of the courts to approve less formal warnings, even in cases in which a corroboration requirement would by no means have been unreasonable. For example, the potential inaccuracy of evidence of visual identification was a frequently recurring source of serious reservations about the evidence of identifying witnesses. In *Turnbull*[15] a five-member Court of Appeal held that, where the quality of evidence of identification is poor, and the case against the accused depends wholly or substantially on such evidence, the trial judge should withdraw the case from the jury and direct an acquittal 'unless there is other evidence which goes to support the correctness of the identification'. Lord Widgery CJ continued (at 230):

> This may be corroboration in the sense lawyers use that word; but it need not be so if its effect is to make the jury sure that there has been no mistaken identification.

The judge should point out to the jury evidence capable of supporting the identification, and also any evidence which the jury might mistakenly think to be so capable, for example the defendant's decision not to give evidence.[16]

The Court's decision to require evidence which merely 'supports', rather than (in the technical sense) corroborates the evidence of identification, was very significant. It demonstrated a judicial confidence that even serious reservations about prosecution evidence can be explained to a jury by means of a straightforward direction, and that the jury can then be left to evaluate the evidence without the complexity of a corroboration warning. However, it is submitted that an important part of the overall *Turnbull* approach is the role of the judge in taking cases of substantial doubt away from the jury, and it may not be out of place to ask whether the form of the direction should differ in cases other than identification cases, in which the judge may have no basis for withdrawing the case from them. Nonetheless, the identification cases became a significant barometer of the likely approach of the courts in other kinds of case.

18.5.1 Form and content of suspect witness warning

The Court of Appeal resolved the question of content and form of a suspect witness warning in *Makanjuola* [1995] 1 WLR 1348. The issue in two consolidated appeals involved the evidence of complaining witnesses in cases of sexual assault. At common law, this was one of three categories requiring a corroboration warning, but the common law requirement had been abrogated by s. 32(1) of the Criminal Justice Act 1988, and accordingly the trial judge gave no corroboration warning. It was argued on appeal that the danger posed by witnesses in the three common law categories still existed, and that, despite the statutory intervention, trial judges should continue to give a corroboration warning in such cases as a matter of discretion. The Court of Appeal rejected this argument in strong terms. The judgment of the Court, delivered by Lord Taylor of Gosforth CJ, is phrased in terms applicable to suspect witnesses generally, and undoubtedly represents the law in all such cases, even if technically *obiter* in relation to witnesses other than complainants in sexual cases. Lord Taylor summarized the law in a series of eight propositions,

---

[15] [1977] QB 224; see 16.12.2.

[16] Today, Lord Widgery CJ would have to choose a different example; see Criminal Justice and Public Order Act 1994, s. 35; 15.6.

the most important of which are as follows (*ibid.* at 1351):

> (2) It is a matter for the judge's discretion what, if any, warning he considers appropriate in respect of such a witness as indeed in respect of any other witness in whatever type of case. Whether he chooses to give a warning and in what terms will depend on the circumstances of the case, the issues raised and the content and quality of the witness's evidence. (3) In some cases, it may be appropriate for the judge to warn the jury to exercise caution before acting upon the unsupported evidence of a witness. This will not be so simply because the witness is a complainant of a sexual offence nor will it necessarily be so because a witness is alleged to be an accomplice. There will need to be an evidential basis for suggesting that the evidence of the witness may be unreliable. An evidential basis does not include mere suggestion by cross-examining counsel. (4) If any question arises as to whether the judge should give a special warning in respect of a witness, it is desirable that the question be resolved by discussion with counsel in the absence of the jury before final speeches. (5) Where the judge does decide to give some warning in respect of a witness, it will be appropriate to do so as part of the judge's review of the evidence and his comments as to how the jury should evaluate it rather than as a set-piece legal direction. (6) Where some warning is required, it will be for the judge to decide the strength and terms of the warning. It does not have to be invested with the whole florid regime of the old corroboration rules. . . . (8) Finally, this court will be disinclined to interfere with a trial judge's exercise of his discretion save in a case where that exercise is unreasonable in the *Wednesbury* sense (see *Associated Provincial Picture Houses Ltd* v *Wednesbury Corporation* [1948] 1 KB 223).

The approach taken in *Makanjuola* is consistent with that recommended by the Royal Commission on Criminal Justice (Cm 2263, 1993):

> It may still be necessary for the judge . . . to warn the jury of the dangers of accepting evidence from particular witnesses. We agree, however, with the Law Commission that the approach should be, not that the same warning should be applied inflexibly to every case, but that, if a warning is required, the judge should tailor it to the particular circumstances of the case.

18.6 CASES IN WHICH SUSPECT WITNESS WARNING REQUIRED

The result of the development of the law outlined above may be summarized as follows. Unlike the cases in which corroboration warnings were required at common law, the cases in which suspect witness warnings are required do not constitute closed categories and remain flexible. Instead of rules requiring set warnings in a cases falling within a fixed category, a new general principle has emerged by virtue of which a judge should give a suspect warning in any case in which it may seem to be necessary, having regard to the overriding dictate of fairness. But it is only natural that attention should be focused to some extent on the cases in which corroboration warnings were previously mandatory. The corroboration rules reflected kinds of evidence which should be approached with caution, and the abolition of those rules in no way altered that practical reality. The case which has caused the most concern is that of accomplices and co-accused, including the case in which they put forward a 'cut-throat defence'.

18.6.1 Evidence of accomplices and co-accused

At common law, the rule requiring a corroboration warning in the case of accomplices applied only where the accomplice gave evidence as a prosecution witness. An accused giving evidence on his own behalf was not an 'accomplice' for the purposes of the corroboration rule.[17] But there was some authority that the judge could give the jury a general warning to treat the evidence of an accused given on his own behalf with caution to the extent that he had an interest to serve in giving evidence in a manner adverse to a co-accused.[18] Such a warning should, however, hold the balance fairly between the two accused. This warning was not required to be in terms of a full corroboration warning, because the evidence did not require corroboration, but should be tailored to fit the facts of the individual case.[19] In the light of *Makanjuola*, the form and content of the warning should correspond only to those appropriate to a suspect witness warning, and should accordingly remain flexible. But where a 'cut-throat' defence is involved, i.e., the various accused either seek to attribute responsibility for the offence charged to each other directly (a 'mirror image' cut-throat defence), or present cases adverse to each other more generally, it has been held that the judge should at least warn the jury that each has an interest of his own to serve. In *Jones; Jenkins* [2004] 1 Cr App R 5, Auld LJ held that the duty to warn in cases involving witnesses with an interest of their own to serve had been required since the decision in *Prater* (see 18.5). He said:

> We see no reason to depart from the approach of this Court in *R v Knowledon and Knowleden* (1983) 77 Cr App R 94, and confirmed by it in *Cheema* that a judge, in exercising his discretion as to what to say to the jury should at least warn them, where one defendant has given evidence adverse to another, to examine the evidence of each with care because each has or may have an interest of his own to serve . . .
>
> [Counsel] suggested that a judge, when dealing with the case against and defence of each co-defendant, might consider four points to put to the jury—points that would not offend any sense of justice and certainly would not cast the judge in the light of one who has formed an adverse view against either or both co-defendants. First, the jury should consider the case for and against each defendant separately. Secondly, the jury should decide the case on all the evidence, including the evidence of each defendant's co-defendant. Thirdly, when considering the evidence of co-defendants, the jury should bear in mind that he or she may have an interest to serve, or, as it is often put, an axe to grind. Fourthly, the jury should assess the evidence of co-defendants in the same way as that of the evidence of any other witness in the case. That seems to us to be a useful—and suitably focused—approach when judges are faced with this particular problem, and we commend it. [*Ibid.* at [41], [47].]

The Court held that the judge should consider such a warning even in a mirror-image case in which each accused has given evidence against the other.[20] In such a case, however, the warning must be given carefully so as to ensure fairness to all accused. There may be a particular need for a warning when one accused has failed to make any statement on being interviewed, and is not tied to any particular account of the facts before trial. The judge's failure to give a warning in such circumstances will not necessarily result in a conviction being overturned on appeal if it must have been obvious to the jury that each accused had his own interests to serve arising from the nature or conduct of the defence.[21] Of course, accomplices continue to give evidence for the prosecution after pleading guilty and often have an interest in giving evidence against the remaining accused in order to attract or justify a lenient sentence. Even though the common law corroboration rule no longer applies, a warning to treat such evidence with caution should be given.[22]

---

[17] *Barnes* [1940] 2 All ER 229.
[18] *Loveridge* (1982) 76 Cr App R 125; *Knowlden* (1981) 77 Cr App R 94.
[19] *Cheema* [1994] 1 WLR 147.
[20] Differing from *dicta* in *Burrows* [2000] Crim LR 48, which the Court found to have turned on its own facts.
[21] *Petkar* [2004] 1 Cr App R 270.
[22] See *Ashgar* [1995] 1 Cr App R 223; *Chan Wai-Keung v R* [1995] 1 WLR 251.

18.6.2 Evidence of witness tainted by improper motive

It has been recognized since the decision in *Prater* [1960] 2 QB 464 (see 18.5) that the judge has the power to warn the jury to treat with caution the evidence of any witness whose evidence may be tainted by an improper motive, even if the witness is not at risk of being convicted of any offence in the proceedings. The witness may be biased or partial, or may have an interest of his own to serve in seeing a particular accused convicted, for example a witness who may have something to gain from civil proceedings to be brought in the event of a conviction, or the spouse of an accomplice who is called as a witness on his behalf.[23] In *Benedetto v R*,[24] the Privy Council emphasized the self-evident need for a suspect witness warning in a case in which a fellow prisoner testifies to a confession allegedly made by the accused while in prison awaiting trial. The jury must be warned of the self-interest the witness may have in providing such evidence against the accused.

18.7 SUSPECT WITNESS WARNINGS AND CONFIRMING EVIDENCE

Despite the demise of the technical rules of corroboration, it remains an important part of a suspect witness warning to draw the attention of the jury to the existence or absence of evidence capable of confirming the evidence of the witness. Under the corroboration rule, it was required that any such evidence be independent of the evidence requiring corroboration, and so confirmation could not be found, for example, in an admissible previous consistent statement made by the witness, such as recent complaint. Even though the technical rule no longer applies, this is still a sound rule in terms of common sense. If a witness's evidence is suspect, it makes no sense to say that he himself can offer confirmation of it. But there are many kinds of independent evidence which can do so, for example physical evidence such as fingerprints; admissions by the accused; inferences which can properly be drawn from the accused's silence when questioned on even terms (see 10.3.1 *et seq.*) or from his failure to answer questions during interview or account for various matters of evidence, or his failure to give evidence, in circumstances when such inferences are permissible under ss. 34 to 37 of the Criminal Justice and Public Order Act 1994 (see 10.5 *et seq.*; 15.6); evidence of his refusal to undergo tests which might have established innocence;[25] or of his commission of other offences or reprehensible conduct which may be admissible under s. 101 of the Criminal Justice Act 2003 (see Part B of Chapter 6).[26]

18.7.1 The accused's lies: *Lucas* directions

The extent to which lies told by the accused out of court in relation to the offence charged could amount to corroboration was a source of some difficulty at common law. In *Credland v Knowler* (1951) 35 Cr App R 48, the accused at first denied having left his home to accompany some children to a place where it was alleged he indecently assaulted them. Later, he admitted that this account was false, and that he had been with the children, though he continued to deny assaulting them. It was held that his false denial was capable of amounting to the corroboration

---

[23] See, e.g., *Allen* [1965] 2 QB 295.
[24] [2003] 1 WLR 1545; see also *Pringle v R* [2003] UKPC 9.
[25] *McVeigh v Beattie* [1988] Fam 69; *Turner v Blunden* [1986] Fam 120; *Smith* (1985) 81 Cr App R 286; Police and Criminal Evidence Act 1984, s. 62(10).
[26] Cf. *Hartley* [1941] 1 KB 5; *Mitchell* (1952) 36 Cr App R 79.

which the evidence of the children at that time required. But it was recognized in later cases that a lie told by the accused should not necessarily be regarded as amounting to corroboration. This should depend on the circumstances surrounding the telling of the lie. The test was nicely expressed by Lord Lane CJ in *Lucas* [1981] QB 720, 724 as follows:

> To be capable of amounting to corroboration the lie told out-of-court must first of all be deliberate. Secondly, it must relate to a material issue. Thirdly, the motive for the lie must be the realization of guilt and a fear of the truth. The jury should in appropriate cases be reminded that people sometimes lie, for example, in an attempt to bolster up a just cause, or out of shame or out of a wish to conceal disgraceful behaviour from their family. Fourthly, the statement must be clearly shown to be a lie by evidence, other than that of an accomplice who is to be corroborated, that is to say by admission or by evidence from an independent witness.

These principles apply continue to apply with equal force despite the fact that the technical corroboration requirement no longer applies; and it is now established that the jury should be given a '*Lucas* direction' in any case where it is sought to use the accused's lies as evidence of guilt, including the situation in which they are used as confirming evidence for the purpose of a suspect witness warning.[27]

18.7.2 Evidence given by accused

At common law a difficult and sometimes elusive distinction was drawn for the purposes of the corroboration rules between evidence of facts given by the accused (which was capable of corroborating other evidence against him) and the fact that the jury might choose to disbelieve his evidence (which could not amount to corroboration).[28] In the former case, the corroboration comes from the substance of the facts themselves rather than simply from the jury's opinion about the accused's evidence. It is submitted that this distinction is often hard to make, because the jury may driven to certain factual conclusions as a consequence of rejecting evidence given by an accused. Indeed, in *Lucas* (above) Lord Lane CJ would have disagreed with *Chapman* (see note 28) to the extent that that case suggested that a lie told by the accused while giving evidence could never provide corroboration, and advocated the same considerations in deciding that question as he applied to lies told by the accused outside court. It is, of course, sometimes hard to say that an accused has told a lie during his evidence until the jury decide not to believe what he says. But it is submitted that the distinction, if sometimes hard to make, is nonetheless sound. A statement made in evidence which can be shown to be a plain lie by reference to other evidence is distinct from a mere opinion formed by the jury as to the accused's overall credibility. There are, for example, cases in which the accused is exposed during cross-examination and made to admit that he lied during examination in chief. It is submitted that the rule should be followed in relation to suspect witness warnings, and that, while the judge may refer to facts which have emerged from the accused's evidence, he should not refer to the jury's possible rejection of that evidence as providing confirmation of other evidence unless it can clearly be shown to be false. There appears to be no direct authority on this point as yet.

---

[27] *Burge* [1996] 1 Cr App R 163, 173 per Kennedy LJ; *Goodway* [1993] 4 All ER 894; and see *Middleton* [2001] Crim LR 251.

[28] *Tumahole Bereng* v *R* [1949] AC 253, 270 per Lord MacDermott; *Chapman* [1973] QB 774, 780 per Roskill LJ; *Dossi* (1918) 13 Cr App R 158; *Corfield* v *Hodgson* [1966] 1 WLR 590.

18.7.3 Independent evidence

It is submitted that the common law rule that evidence must be independent of the evidence to be corroborated in order to be capable of providing corroboration is also a sound one, and should be followed in relation to suspect witness warnings. An area of difficulty here has been the question of whether the observed fact that a complainant was in distress at or shortly after the time of an offence allegedly committed against her by the accused can amount to evidence of confirmation. The authorities suggest that the evidence of distress, if witnessed independently, can amount to confirmation if but only if the jury are satisfied that it was genuine and can exclude the possibility that it was feigned.[29] The jury must be warned of the very real danger that distress may be simulated.[30] Clearly, the evidence of distress must be given by a person other than the complainant.

18.7.4 Turning full circle?

It is hard not to see a paradox (albeit a by no means undesirable one) in the re-emergence in a different guise of many of the principles developed at common law in relation to the corroboration rules. In a sense, the wheel has turned almost full circle, and corroboration has re-invented itself in a more contemporary posture. The courts have already come a long way, at least as a matter of practice, from the strict rejection of any semblance of corroboration rules in *Makanjuola*. There is now a significant resemblance between corroboration warnings and suspect witness warnings in the substance of the matters dealt with in the direction to the jury. The difference lies in the absence of a strict legal requirement, although the dictates of practice are in many ways not as different as might be supposed. This is, it is submitted, simply a reflection of the realities of practice.

It is surely legitimate to reflect that the rules requiring corroboration warnings were abolished primarily because they had been allowed to become too technical, and not because they were inapposite. The argument made in *Makanjuola*, that some warning should be retained, though flying in the face of the clear legislative intent, has an obvious appeal. The accumulated judicial wisdom of more than a century did not evaporate overnight. There will inevitably be prosecution witnesses whose evidence is suspect. At the same time, the flexibility of the new rule has much to commend it, especially with respect to the power of the judge to tailor the warning in any given case to the evidence in question. It is submitted that judges should not hesitate to give a warning in a case where the evidence seems suspect, even though the warning may in most cases be confined to a general note of caution.

18.8 RECOMMENDED FURTHER READING

Birch, D.J., 'Corroboration: goodbye to all that?' [1995] *Criminal Law Review* 524.

Dein, J., 'Non tape recorded cell confession evidence—on trial' [2002] *Criminal Law Review* 630.

Hartshorne, J., 'Corroboration and care warnings after *Makanjuola*' (1998) 2(1) *International Journal of Evidence and Proof* 1.

---

[29] *Chauhan* (1981) 73 Cr App R 323; *Redpath* [1962] 46 Cr App R 319.
[30] *Romeo* [2004] 1 Cr App R 30.

Lewis, P., 'A comparative examination of corroboration and caution warnings in prosecutions of sexual offences' [2006] *Criminal Law Review* 889.

Mirfield, P., 'An alternative future for corroboration warnings' (1991) **107** *Law Quarterly Review* 450.

Pattenden, R., 'Should confessions be corroborated?' (1991) **107** *Law Quarterly Review* 317.

18.9 QUESTIONS FOR DISCUSSION BASED ON *R v COKE; LITTLETON* (for case files go to the Online Resource Centre)

What should the judge take into account in deciding whether to warn the jury in the following circumstances? What form of warning would be appropriate in each case?

(a) Littleton pleads guilty, and gives evidence for the prosecution against Coke.

(b) With respect to the evidence of Margaret and Angela Blackstone as prosecution witnesses.

(c) The jury concludes that Coke lied to the police with respect to the sample of handwriting Exhibit GG1.

(d) With respect to the evidence of Angela if Littleton's defence is one of mistaken identification.

18.10 GENERAL QUESTIONS FOR DISCUSSION

1. What is meant by the term 'corroboration'?

2. For which offences is corroboration still required as a matter of law?

3. How should a judge direct the jury if there is a 'cut-throat' defence?

4. Where evidence of identification is poor, a judge will withdraw from the jury a case that depends wholly or substantially on identification, unless that evidence is corroborated. Is this statement correct?

5. In a recent case, defence counsel asserted that evidence of 'cell confessions' by a man accused of murdering his lover were made up by 'unscrupulous criminals' in order to claim a reward. How would the trial judge direct the jury to deal the evidence of those witnesses?

6. What is a *Lucas* direction and what four features should it contain?

19

DOCUMENTARY AND REAL EVIDENCE

A DOCUMENTARY EVIDENCE

SUMMARY OF MAIN POINTS

- Primary evidence of a document usually means the original document (or in the case of counterparts, all originals); a certified copy of an enrolled document; and an admission of the content of the document are also treated as primary evidence; secondary evidence is any other evidence of the content, such as a copy or oral evidence of the content.

- The primary evidence (or best evidence) rule requires primary evidence for the purpose of proving the content of the document; for other purposes secondary evidence may be used.

- Secondary evidence may be used to prove the content in exceptional cases, i.e., if another party fails to produce the original; if a stranger to the litigation lawfully refuses to produce it; if the original has been lost or destroyed; or if the original is impossible to produce.

- Special rules apply to the proof of due execution of a document.

19.1 DOCUMENTARY EVIDENCE GENERALLY

Thus far, this part of this book has considered the principles of adducing evidence by calling witnesses to testify on oath. Evidence may also be given by the production to the court of documents that are admissible in evidence, as evidence of their own contents. An important distinction must be drawn between documents whose contents are admissible in their own right as direct evidence, and documents which contain admissible hearsay, which are admissible, if at all, only to the extent of the hearsay statements contained in them. For example, a lease or a written contract will be admissible in its own right as direct evidence of the existence and terms of the lease or contract, whereas a statement admissible by virtue of the Civil Evidence Act 1995 will be admissible only for the purpose of adducing the admissible statements contained in the record, which may be only peripherally related to the primary purpose of the document. Another way of expressing the distinction is to say that the contents of the lease constitute direct evidence of the lease itself; whereas the contents of the record constitute only evidence of other facts contained in statements made in the record. The admissibility of hearsay contained in documents was considered in Chapter 8. Documents used as direct evidence of their own contents must also be distinguished from documents used to refresh to recollection of a witness who is giving oral evidence, and documents used solely for the purpose of demonstrating the consistency or inconsistency of a witness, which are for any other purpose hearsay. As we have seen, these documents are not admissible unless made so by the conduct of cross-examination, and even then are evidence of the facts stated only by virtue of statute.[1] This chapter will deal with documents the contents of which are admissible as direct evidence in their own right.

It is worth observing at the outset that documentary evidence is subject to the rules of evidence generally. The admissibility of a private document is subject to the same rules, subject only to statutory modification, as is that of oral evidence. A document may, therefore, be objected to on the ground that its contents are inadmissible, for example, because they are hearsay and do not fall within any recognized exception to the rule against hearsay, or because the contents would reveal details of an accused's character, or violate a privilege.[2] But there are three specific rules of evidence which apply to documents adduced as evidence of their own contents, namely:

(a)   the primary evidence rule, otherwise known as the best evidence rule, as to the proof of the contents of a document;

---

[1] See 16.2.2, 16.2.3, 17.7; *Virgo* (1978) 67 Cr App R 323; Civil Evidence Act 1995, s. 6.
[2] See, e.g., *Myers* v *DPP* [1965] AC 1001; 7.3.

(b) the rule as to proof of due execution of certain documents; and

(c) the parol evidence rule, restricting the admissibility of extrinsic evidence to contradict or vary the terms of a document.

The third of these rules is of contemporary importance only in relation to contracts, and is outside the scope of the present work.[3] The first two rules are dealt with below.

19.2 MEANING OF THE TERM 'DOCUMENT'

The question of what exactly may constitute a 'document' is far from easy to answer, and appears not to be capable of being answered uniformly for all purposes. It is clear that the prime characteristic of a document is that it should contain and convey information. It seems also that the word implies writing or other inscription, though in modern times, the storing of information in diagrammatic form or in a computer, or the audio or video-recording of information is probably equally acceptable for many purposes. The form of a document, and the materials of which it is composed, are of limited contemporary importance. In *Daye* [1908] 2 KB 333, Darling J pointed out that paper itself had been preceded by parchment, stone, marble, clay, and metal. He went on to say that an object may be regarded as a document, whatever its material, 'provided it is writing or printing and capable of being evidence'. In more recent times, a tape-recording of a conversation was held to be a document which, if referred to in a party's statement of case, must be produced for inspection on notice (*Grant* v *Southwestern & County Properties Ltd* [1975] Ch 185). And the majority view of the Court of Appeal in *Senior* v *Holdsworth, ex parte Independent Television News Ltd*[4] discredited the older view that film (and presumably videotape) were not to be regarded as documents.

The courts have been disposed to recognize successive technological developments in the storage and reproduction of information, by treating as documents for most purposes anything which is the functional equivalent of the traditional paper document. Happily, however, the courts have at the same time exhibited a reluctance to burden the new documents with the restrictive rule requiring proof by primary evidence. For example, in *Kajala* v *Noble* (1982) 75 Cr App R 149, it was held that that rule was 'limited and confined to written documents in the strict sense of the term, and has no relevance to tapes or films'. No doubt the very different realities of producing copies of the new technological documents abundantly justifies a departure from a rule conceived in an age when the only form of copying was handwritten reproduction. This does not indicate that film, tape, videotape, microfilm, microfiche, and the like are not to be regarded as documents for general purposes.

For the purposes of the Civil Evidence Act 1995, s. 13 of the Act defines 'document' and 'copy' as follows:

'document' means anything in which information of any description is recorded, and 'copy' in relation to a document, means anything onto which information recorded in the document has been copied, by whatever means and whether directly or indirectly.

These definitions are also to be found in r. 31.4 of the Civil Procedure Rules 1998. The same definitions are adopted for criminal proceedings by s. 134(1) of the Criminal Justice Act 2003.

---

[3] See generally *Cross and Tapper*, 11th edn, p. 726 *et seq.*; Phipson, *Evidence*, 16th edn, para. 42–11 *et seq.*

[4] [1976] QB 23. For the older view, see *Glyn* v *Western Feature Film Co.* (1915) 85 LJ Ch 261.

19.3 PROOF OF CONTENTS: THE PRIMARY EVIDENCE RULE

It is an ancient rule of the common law that a party who wishes to rely on the contents of a private document as direct evidence, must adduce 'primary' (as opposed to 'secondary') evidence of the contents of that document.[5] The meaning of these terms is considered below. It may be observed that the usual meaning of the term 'primary evidence' is the production of the original document. Various reasons have been advanced for the rule. It is certainly the last outpost of the 'best-evidence' rule, discussed in 1.5. In *Garton v Hunter* [1969] 2 QB 37, 44, Lord Denning MR referred to an earlier decision in which indirect evidence that a hereditament was let at a rack rent was held to be inadmissible, on the ground that it was not the best evidence of that fact (*Robinson Brothers (Brewers) Ltd v Houghton and Chester-le-Street Assessment Committee* [1937] 2 KB 445, 468–9 per Scott LJ). Disapproving this decision, Lord Denning said:

> It is plain that Scott LJ had in mind the old rule that a party must produce the best evidence that the nature of the case will allow, and that any less good evidence is to be excluded. That old rule has gone by the board long ago. The only remaining instance of it that I know is that if an original document is available in one's hands, one must produce it. One cannot give secondary evidence by producing a copy.

Indeed, the rule requiring primary evidence is frequently referred to as the best evidence rule. Its purpose is to give effect to the terms of the document with as much accuracy and certainty as possible. The rule arose in an age where the only method of producing copies was by handwriting, and the possibilities of fraud or error were legion. The process of reproducing complicated texts, especially those written in copperplate and in the wide pages required for scrolls and deeds, no doubt often in bad light, which was a feature of legal and business practice well into the nineteenth century, made the primary evidence rule a practical necessity. Today, of course, technology allows the production of any number of indistinguishable duplicates at the push of a button on a computer keyboard. Copies which are almost indistinguishable from the original are also easy to produce. The very distinction between originals and copies has become almost meaningless except in the case of handwritten documents, and consequently the dangers of fraud and error which influenced the formation of the common law rule have greatly, though not altogether, receded. Indeed, except in the case of handwritten documents, and in cases involving fraud, forgery, and *ex post facto* alteration, the primary evidence rule might well be abrogated or at least modified to suit modern conditions. Some writers[6] take the view that this has in effect been done by statutory provisions allowing statements contained in documents to be proved by non-primary evidence, and the simplified rules for the production and inspection of documents under the Civil Procedure Rules 1998. But these statutory provisions (Civil Evidence Act 1995, s. 8, Criminal Justice Act 2003, s. 133) apply strictly only to the proof of statements contained in documents (as hearsay evidence) rather than to the proof of the contents of a document as direct evidence, and, even though the 1995 Act abolishes the rules against hearsay in civil cases, these cases remain distinct. It would seem contrary to principle to hold that these provisions abolish the primary evidence rule by a side wind, and that view is also apparently contradicted by the specific rule enacted by s. 71 of the Police and Criminal Evidence Act 1984 (see 19.3.3) which does operate to relax the rule in criminal cases slightly. Moreover, the existence of some separate rule remains salutary in cases in which there is reason to suspect that the original, or one of several

---

[5] For statutory provisions governing the proof of various public and judicial documents see *Blackstone's Criminal Practice*, 2009 edn, para. F8.8 *et seq.*

[6] See, in particular, Cross and Tapper, *Evidence*, 11th edn, p. 713 *et seq.*

counterpart originals, is different in some material way from other counterparts, or copies, or from the recollection of witnesses. This may suggest some forgery or *ex post facto* alteration which may affect the construction of the document and the rights and obligations of the parties. In the event of a conflict, some rule of resolution must be adopted, and a preference for the original remains a logical and workable one.

Nonetheless, there are signs that this ancient rule may soon be largely a matter of history, certainly in civil cases. In *Springsteen v Flute International Ltd*,[7] the Court of Appeal took the view that the best evidence rule should now be regarded as a matter primarily of weight rather than admissibility. If a party could readily produce the original and there is no good reason why it is not produced, a court might continue to take the view that secondary evidence should not be admitted, but on the basis that its weight, compared to that of the original, is slight. On the other hand, if there is a good reason for a party's failure or inability to produce the original, secondary evidence should be admitted for whatever weight it enjoys. In cases falling between these two extremes, the court must make a judgment as to what weight, if any, should be attached to the secondary evidence tendered. This seems to be a sensible approach in cases where the original has no features which make its production effectively indispensable, and serves as a reminder that, as a matter of weight, the original will continue to be unrivalled. A party would be ill-advised to neglect this consideration.

19.3.1 Proof of contents

The rule requiring primary evidence applies to all cases in which a party seeks to rely upon the contents of a document as direct evidence, or as evidence proving the document itself. In *Augustien v Challis* (1847) 1 Ex 279, the plaintiff sued a sheriff for negligence in withdrawing a writ of *fieri facias* (a method of executing on a judgment) in the plaintiff's favour. The sheriff's defence was that another creditor, the debtor's landlord, was entitled to receive rent from the debtor, and that this entitlement enjoyed priority over the judgment debt to the plaintiff. Proof of the priority depended upon proof that the rent was indeed due to the debtor's landlord under the terms of the lease. Since the existence and terms of the lease were to be proved, the rule required the production of the original lease as primary evidence. The landlord failed to produce the lease, and his evidence that rent was due under the lease was held to be inadmissible secondary evidence. And in *MacDonnell v Evans* (1852) 11 CB 930, the court disallowed a question sought to be put to a witness for the plaintiff in cross-examination, the object of which was to elicit the reaction of the witness to a letter written to him accusing him of forgery. Since the existence and terms of the letter were to be proved, the contents of the letter should have been proved by primary evidence, and the question was disallowed because this had not been done.

19.3.2 Proof of matters other than contents

Conversely, where there is no intent to prove the contents of the document as direct evidence, and the document is used for some other purpose only, the rule requiring primary evidence does not apply. If, for example, a party wishes to prove that the relationship of landlord and tenant existed and no more, and is not concerned to prove the terms of the lease, there is no need to adduce primary evidence of the lease. Secondary evidence, such as the oral evidence of one of the parties, may be adduced to prove the relationship: *Holy Trinity, Kingston-upon-Hull (Inhabitants)*

---

[7] [2001] EMLR 654; see also *Post Office Counters Ltd v Mahida* [2003] EWCA Civ 1583.

(1827) 7 B & C 611. Similarly, a document may be identified by a copy, if no reliance is placed on its contents as evidence: *Boyle* v *Wiseman* (1855) 11 Ex 360. A nice example is the American case of *United States* v *Sliker* 751 F 2d 477 (2d Cir, 1984) in which the accused was charged with bank robbery. The prosecution offered evidence that the money deposited in the bank was insured by the Federal Deposit Insurance Corporation (FDIC) but did not produce the original policy of insurance. The accused objected that the evidence did not satisfy the best evidence rule. However, the only relevance of the evidence was that the existence of such insurance with the FDIC gave the federal trial court jurisdiction to try the case, which would otherwise have been tried in a State court. The prosecution did not rely on the terms of the insurance policy, which were irrelevant to the case, but were content to show that a policy existed. Accordingly, it was held that the evidence had been rightly admitted.

In *Elworthy* (1867) LR 1 CCR 103, however, a solicitor was prosecuted for perjury, it being alleged that he had wilfully and falsely denied having prepared a draft of a statutory declaration. The prosecution adduced secondary evidence to show, firstly that the draft in fact existed and was in the possession of the accused, and secondly that certain alterations had been made to its contents. The accused's conviction was quashed on appeal. Although the secondary evidence was perfectly proper for the first purpose, it was inadmissible for the second, because the prosecution then wished not merely to prove the existence and location of the document, but to rely upon its contents as direct evidence of the alleged forgery. For this purpose, primary evidence was required.

19.3.3 Rule restricted to documents in usual sense of term

The primary evidence rule applies only to documents in the usual sense of that term, i.e. written material. The courts have declined to extend it to 'documents' consisting of film, tape, and the like. There is little reason to burden these categories with a restrictive and formalistic rule conceived in the days before technology had begun to spawn new forms of storing information which give a new meaning to the term 'original'.

In *Kajala* v *Noble* (1982) 75 Cr App R 149, a prosecution witness, by viewing a BBC news film, identified the accused as a member of a group of persons who had caused a serious public disturbance. The original film was retained by the BBC, and at trial the prosecution relied on a video-cassette, which the court was satisfied was an authentic copy of the original film. On appeal against conviction, it was argued for the accused that since the prosecution had relied upon the contents of the film, and since the film should be regarded as a document, primary evidence should have been required. The Court declined to extend the rule beyond 'written documents in the strict sense of the term' and held that it had no application to tapes or films. And in *Taylor* v *Chief Constable of Cheshire* [1986] 1 WLR 1479, where a video-recording, which was said to show the accused committing an offence of theft, was mistakenly erased before trial, it was held to be proper for police officers who had viewed the recording to give oral evidence of its contents. Ralph Gibson LJ said (*ibid.* at 1486):

> For my part I can see no effective distinction so far as concerns admissibility between a direct view of the action of an alleged shoplifter by a security officer and a view of those activities by the officer on the video display unit of a camera, or a view of those activities on a recording of what the camera recorded. He who saw may describe what he saw because, as Ackner LJ said in *Kajala* v *Noble* (1982) 75 Cr App R 149, '... it is relevant evidence provided that that which is seen on the camera or recording is connected by sufficient evidence to the alleged actions of the accused at the time and place in question'.

The Police and Criminal Evidence Act 1984, s. 71, provides the following specific relaxation of the rule in criminal cases:

> In any proceedings the contents of a document may (whether or not the document is still in existence) be proved by the production of a microfilm copy of that document or of the material part of it, authenticated in such manner as the court may approve.

As we have seen, the rule requiring primary evidence does not apply to documents admitted because they contain admissible hearsay statements and not as direct evidence in their own right. Rather, express statutory provisions have been made for proof of such documents: see Civil Evidence Act 1995, s. 8; Criminal Justice Act 2003, s. 133.

19.4 KINDS OF PRIMARY EVIDENCE

The following kinds of evidence of the contents of documents are primary, within the meaning of the rule discussed above.

19.4.1 The original

This is of course the most obvious and most satisfactory kind of primary evidence. It is usually possible to identify the original document with certainty, but difficult cases do arise. If a deed is executed by various parties in a number of duplicates, each such duplicate is 'the original' and all must be produced.[8] But counterparts of a document such as a lease, one signed by the lessor only and the other by the lessee only, are each 'the original', so far as the party signing is concerned.[9] In the case of counterparts, therefore, because any counterpart is the original as against the party signing it, if one signatory refuses to produce the counterpart held by him, any other signatory may rely on that signed by the refusing party, which will be sufficient evidence of the contents of the document.

These principles result, of course, from the fact that duplicates and counterparts of the kind mentioned are not in any sense copies, but together represent the deed executed by the parties. Whether a document is a counterpart or a duplicate is essentially a question of intent, rather than of the means by which the document is generated. Ideally, a document intended to be a counterpart should be produced to look like an original, but it is the originality of the execution of the document by signature or other means that really matters. Even if produced by means such as a photocopier, a document can be the original or a counterpart original, if executed as such by the necessary parties. However, if a document is executed and then photocopied, it is likely to be regarded as a copy, unless there is clear evidence that it was nonetheless intended to have effect as an original or a counterpart. Duplicates are traditionally produced by one and the same impression, for example where successive carbons are created by one signature.

19.4.2 Copies of enrolled documents

Where the original private document is one which is, by law, required to be enrolled in a court or other public office, the copy officially issued by such court or office is treated as the original.

---

[8] *Forbes* v *Samuel* [1913] 3 KB 706.
[9] *Roe d West* v *Davis* (1806) 7 East 363. For an interesting definition of 'duplicate' and 'original', see American Federal Rule of Evidence 1001(3) and (4).

Thus, the probate copy of a will is conclusive evidence of the words of the will. However, the court is entitled to look at the original enrolled will when considering any question of construction of the will, for example to look at erasures apparent in the original but not in the probate copy.[10]

19.4.3 Admissions as to contents

A party may adduce as primary evidence of the contents of a private document an admission made by his opponent as to what the contents of the document are or were. The rule applies both to formal and informal admissions, and to oral as well as written admissions. In *Slatterie* v *Pooley* (1840) 6 M & W 664, the plaintiff sued on a covenant, which had the effect of creating an indemnity in respect of certain debts. The debts covered by the indemnity were contained in the schedule to a deed, which was inadmissible in evidence. The inclusion of the debt in the schedule was allowed to be proved by an oral admission, which was binding on the defendant, to that effect.

19.5 ADMISSIBILITY OF SECONDARY EVIDENCE

A party who wishes to rely upon the contents of a document must, as we have seen, adduce primary evidence of the contents. Only in the exceptional cases enumerated below will secondary (i.e., non-primary) evidence be admissible. However, if secondary evidence is admissible, it may be adduced in any form in which it may be available, whether by production of a copy, of a copy of a copy, by oral evidence of the contents or in any other form. It is often said that 'there are no degrees of secondary evidence'. The phrase appears to have been coined by Lord Abinger CB in *Doe d Gilbert* v *Ross* (1840) 7 M & W 102. Thus, the court will not (except as to weight) discriminate between the quality of copies of a document (*Lafone* v *Griffin* (1909) 25 TLR 308), and may admit (subject to the same observation as to weight) oral evidence of the contents of the document, even if a copy is available (*Brown* v *Woodman* (1834) 6 C & P 206). There are some exceptions in the cases of probated wills, judicial documents, public documents, and bankers' books (see generally *Blackstone's Criminal Practice*, 2009 edn, para. F8.8 *et seq.*). The secondary evidence must be authenticated by foundational evidence that the alleged copy is in fact a true copy of the original.[11]

Secondary evidence is admissible to prove the contents of a document in the following exceptional cases:

(a) if a party fails to disclose or produce the original;
(b) if a non-party to proceedings refuses to produce the original;
(c) if the original is lost;
(d) if it is impossible to produce the original;
(e) if the document is or forms part of a bankers' book.

It should be emphasized that the exceptions to the rule requiring primary evidence are designed to provide relief in a case where a party is genuinely unable to produce the original through no fault of that party. If the proponent of the document has the original in his possession or it is within his power to obtain and produce it, he may not rely on the exceptions, even

---

[10] *Re Battie-Wrightson, Cecil* v *Battie-Wrightson* [1920] 2 Ch 330.
[11] *Collins* (1960) 44 Cr App R 170. As to the practice in tendering copies, see *Wayte* (1982) 76 Cr App R 110.

where his failure to produce the original is innocent, in the sense that it is not a deliberate concealment.[12]

19.6 PARTY FAILING TO DISCLOSE OR PRODUCE ORIGINAL

Clearly, a party should not be permitted to take advantage of the primary evidence rule improperly by refusing or failing to disclose or produce an original document which is in his possession, custody or control. At common law, if a party fails to produce the original after notice has been given that its production is required, the result is that, not only may the opponent prove the contents of the document by secondary evidence, but also that the party who has failed to produce may not rely on the original even if it is inconsistent with the secondary evidence.[13] The giving of notice does not compel production of the original, but merely sets the stage for the use of secondary evidence if the original is not produced. Consequently, unlike a *subpoena duces tecum*, a notice to produce may be employed even in the case of the accused in a criminal case, because there is no violation of the accused's right not to give evidence.

In civil cases, under the procedure in effect prior to the Civil Procedure Rules 1998, a party was entitled to serve on his opponent notice to produce documents in the opponent's possession and to admit the contents of those in his own possession. But under the former RSC, Ord. 27, r. 4(3), this was generally unnecessary in the case of documents which were disclosed in a list of documents, in respect of which service of the list itself operated as a notice served by the opponent to produce the listed documents. The procedure has now been further simplified by the disclosure rules of the Civil Procedure Rules 1998. Disclosure of documents as required by Part 31 of the Rules is the standard procedure, and operates as conferring on the opponent the right to inspect the disclosed documents and to have copies of them made (rr. 31.3 and 31.15). Improper failure to disclose or permit inspection of documents will result in a party being unable to make use of the document in evidence without the court's permission (r. 31.21). Consequently, the opponent will be able to prove the contents of the document by secondary evidence.[14] Moreover, r. 32.19(1) provides that a party shall be deemed to admit the authenticity of a document disclosed to him under Part 31 of the Rules unless he serves notice that he requires the document to be proved at trial within the time limit prescribed by r. 32.19(2). But it is submitted that if notice is served and the document is one subject to the primary evidence rule, the proponent of the document must prove the document by primary evidence, unless an exception to the rule applies; and because a notice to produce does not operate in itself to compel production, a party who wishes to ensure production of the original must serve a summons requiring its production under r. 34(2).

19.7 LAWFUL REFUSAL OF NON-PARTY TO PRODUCE

If a document is in the possession or custody of a person who is not a party to the proceedings, its contents may be proved by secondary evidence in any case where the non-party is lawfully entitled to refuse to produce it, for example because it is privileged in his hands, or he is beyond the jurisdiction of the court. If, however, the refusal is unlawful, secondary evidence will not be

---

[12] *Wayte* (1982) 76 Cr App R 110; *Governor of Pentonville Prison, ex parte Osman* [1990] 1 WLR 277, 308.

[13] *Doe d Thompson v Hodgson* (1840) 12 Ad & El 135.

[14] But, of course, this will not apply where the refusal to permit inspection is lawful because the document is privileged or must be withheld on the ground of public policy. As to this, see rr. 31.19 and 31.20; and 13.4.

admissible, because production of the original may be compelled. Refusal to produce by the non-party in such a case may be punishable by proceedings for contempt or by making him liable in respect of any resulting loss.[15] Rule 31.17 of the Civil Procedure Rules 1998 now gives the court in civil cases the express power to make orders for disclosure of documents against persons who are not parties to the proceedings, if the party seeking the order proves that the documents in question are likely to support his case or adversely affect the case of any other party, and that the order is necessary in order to dispose fairly of the case or to save costs. This order will lead to the inspection of any documents disclosed. This procedure should be employed wherever possible, but there will be cases in which a party cannot gain access to such documents, for example, because they are privileged in the non-party's hands, or because the disclosure makes clear that the non-party no longer has possession or control of the documents. In these latter cases, the proponent of the evidence is entitled to prove the contents of the documents by secondary evidence.

An excellent example of the proper working of this exception is *Nowaz* [1976] 1 WLR 830, where documents which the prosecution wished to prove were protected by diplomatic immunity, so that production of the originals could not be compelled. It was held that the prosecution were entitled to give secondary evidence of the contents of the documents by calling a police officer to testify. In *Kajala* v *Noble* (1982) 75 Cr App R 149 (see 19.3.3), it appears to have been assumed that the policy of the BBC in insisting on retaining the originals of their films precluded production of the original, so as to render the video-cassette copy admissible as secondary evidence. It does not appear to have been argued that the original might not have been beyond compulsion. It is right to say that the case was not decided on this basis, because the Court felt that the rule requiring primary evidence should not be applied to films. However, the argument proposed might have strengthened the accused's position on the merits at least to some extent.

19.8 ORIGINAL LOST

Where the original document cannot be found or identified after due search, its contents may be proved by secondary evidence. It is for the party seeking to rely on the document to show that all reasonable steps by way of search have been taken: *Brewster* v *Sewell* (1820) 3 B & Ald 296.

19.9 PRODUCTION OF ORIGINAL IMPOSSIBLE

Secondary evidence will be admissible where the actual production of the original is impossible, for example where the document takes the form of an inscription on a tombstone or a wall. In *Owner* v *Bee Hive Spinning Co. Ltd* [1914] 1 KB 105, the same principle was applied to a notice giving particulars of mealtimes in a factory, which by statute was obliged to remain affixed to the wall of a particular place, and so was 'legally impossible' to produce.

It is interesting to compare, in this respect, the question of production of public documents. Although such documents would rarely, if ever, be impossible to produce, the production of the original would almost always be a matter of very great inconvenience and difficulty. Such a difficulty faced Alderson B in *Mortimer* v *M'Callan* (1840) 6 M & W 58, where it was suggested that the original books of the Bank of England ought to be produced for the purpose of proving their contents. It was held that the resulting inconvenience amounted to impossibility of production. The proof of most public documents of this kind is now governed by statute, and it may be noted

---

[15] *Llanfaethly (Inhabitants)* (1853) 2 El & Bl 940.

that in many cases, the production of a certified or sealed copy will suffice (Evidence Act 1845, s. 1), and that in the absence of any specific provision, a public document produced from proper custody may be proved by a certified or examined copy (Evidence Act 1851, s. 14).

19.10 BANKERS' BOOKS

Bankers' books are relevant to a considerable variety of cases. With the exception of the books of the Bank of England, they are private documents, and so in theory should be proved by primary evidence. Because of the obvious inconvenience of the rule to banks, whose records of customers' accounts are often required in litigation, special provisions were enacted by the Bankers' Books Evidence Act 1879. By s. 3 of the Act:

> Subject to the provisions of this Act, a copy of an entry in a banker's book shall in all legal proceedings be received as *prima facie* evidence of such entry, and of the matters, transactions, and accounts therein recorded.

The provision is subject to two conditions set forth in subsequent sections:

> 4. A copy of an entry in a banker's book shall not be received in evidence under this Act unless it be first proved that the book was at the time of the making of the entry one of the ordinary books of the bank, and that the entry was made in the usual and ordinary course of business, and that the book is in the custody or control of the bank.
> Such proof may be given by a partner or officer of the bank, and may be given orally or by an affidavit sworn before any commissioner or person authorized to take affidavits.
> 5. A copy of an entry in a banker's book shall not be received in evidence under this Act unless it be further proved that the copy has been examined with the original entry and is correct.
> Such proof shall be given by some person who has examined the copy with the original entry, and may be given either orally or by an affidavit sworn before any commissioner or person authorized to take affidavits.

Section 6 provides that where the contents of a banker's book may be proved under the Act, a banker or officer of the bank shall not be compellable to produce the original or to appear as a witness to prove the contents 'unless by order of a judge made for special cause'.

A most important provision for the conduct of many kinds of litigation, in particular prosecutions for offences of dishonesty, is contained in s. 7 of the Act, which provides:

> On the application of any party to a legal proceeding a court or judge may order that such party be at liberty to inspect and take copies of any entries in a banker's book for any of the purposes of such proceedings. An order under this section may be made either with or without summoning the bank or any other party, and shall be served on the bank three clear days before the same is to be obeyed, unless the court or judge otherwise directs.

19.10.1 Meaning of 'bankers' book'

By s. 9 of the Act as originally enacted, expressions relating to 'bankers' books' included 'ledgers, day books, cash books, account books, and all other books used in the ordinary business of the bank'. In *Barker* v *Wilson* [1980] 1 WLR 884, it was argued that records kept on microfilm were not 'bankers' books' for the purposes of s. 9. The Divisional Court, however, saw no reason why the rules enacted for the bankers of 1879 should cease to apply merely because the bankers of 1980 enjoyed greater technological advantages in maintaining their records, and held that microfilm records fell within the terms of s. 9. Recognizing the wisdom of the principle expressed in *Barker v Wilson*, Parliament, by Sch. 6 to the Banking Act 1979, substituted an amended s. 9, which provides by its second subsection that:

> Expressions in this Act relating to 'bankers' books' include ledgers, day books, cash books, account books and other records used in the ordinary business of the bank, whether those records are in written form or are kept on microfilm, magnetic tape or any other form of mechanical or electronic data retrieval mechanism.

Regardless of the manner in which bankers' books are compiled and maintained, the Act permits the use of secondary evidence only in the case of documents that fall within the definition given in the revised s. 9. In *Dadson*,[16] the accused was charged with various offences arising from the alleged misuse of his cheque card. At trial, copies of letters from the bank's correspondence file, written to the accused by the bank, were admitted in evidence in reliance on s. 9. Quashing the conviction, the Court of Appeal held that the correspondence did not constitute 'bankers' books'. It simply fell outside the statutory definition. Moreover, the file in which the letters were maintained was not one of the ordinary books of the bank and the letters were not entries made in the ordinary course of banking business. The copies, had, therefore, been wrongly admitted and in view of the stress laid upon them in the summing-up of the trial judge as evidence that the accused knew that he had no overdraft facility, the appeal was allowed. In *Williams v Williams* [1988] QB 161, the Court of Appeal held that paid cheques and accompanying paying-in slips, which were retained by a bank after the conclusion of the transactions to which they related, but were merely stored without being sorted or organized, were not part of a banker's book, within the meaning of the Act, so that no order could be made under s. 7 with respect to them. There were, of course, records of the transactions concerned in the books of the bank (including computerized records) on which the bank would have relied to prove any such transaction, and which would fall within s. 7, but the cheques and paying-in slips were not a part of such records.

The amended s. 9 also provides that the expressions 'bank' and 'banker' refer to any institution authorized under the Banking Act 1987 or a municipal bank, any building society, the National Savings Bank, and to the Post Office in the exercise of its powers to provide banking services.

19.10.2 Books of banks outside jurisdiction

In *Grossman*,[17] the question arose whether the court had jurisdiction to make an order under the Act directed to the London head office of a bank, but actually designed to have effect in relation to the books of a related bank established under the laws of a foreign jurisdiction. The Commissioners of Inland Revenue sought and were granted an order for the inspection of bankers' books, which it was thought might provide evidence useful in the prosecution of the accused for alleged fraud against the Revenue. The bank account in question was held at Savings and Investment Bank in Douglas, Isle of Man, a company established under Manx law. This bank had no place of business in England, but was licensed to operate as a bank under Manx law and

---

[16] (1983) 77 Cr App R 91; and see *Re Howglen Ltd* [2001] 1 All ER 376.

[17] (1981) 73 Cr App R 302. This case was followed and applied in *Mackinnon v Donaldson, Lufkin and Jenrette Securities Corp.* [1986] Ch 482, in which it was held that such an order directed to a New York bank, a non-party, and purporting to apply to records of transactions in the United States kept under the laws of New York, which provided for a duty of confidentiality to customers there (and enforceable only by subpoena in New York), would be a violation of the sovereignty of the United States.

collected cheques through the medium of Barclays Bank in the Isle of Man. An application was made to the Deemster in the Isle of Man for an order for inspection under the corresponding provisions of the Manx Bankers' Books Evidence Act 1935, but this application was refused, since the Manx Act applied only to proceedings within the Isle of Man. In order to avoid this problem, the Commissioners sought an order against Barclays Bank in London, and not the Douglas branch of Barclays. The order was granted at first instance. Although Barclays took a 'neutral stance' in the matter, Savings and Investment Bank challenged the order, and prevailed in the Court of Appeal. Lord Denning MR pointed out that the Manx banks were subject to a separate legal system, and were separate entities from Barclays of London. It would not be right to compel them to open their books in support of proceedings in England and Wales. Shaw and Oliver LJJ agreed, the latter holding that, while such an order might be made in appropriate circumstances, a very strong showing would be required, no doubt to overcome the natural hesitancy of any court in making an order directed to a foreign jurisdiction. It is submitted that such an order might be appropriate, notwithstanding the difference in jurisdictions, where two banks have a more direct connection than did Barclays and Savings and Investment Bank in this case, though obvious problems of enforcement arise if no books are physically kept within the jurisdiction.

19.10.3 Orders under s. 7 not to be made lightly

The s. 7 provision is a drastic one, applying to civil and criminal proceedings alike and for a great variety of purposes. It has rightly been held that it is a substantial interference with liberty, which should be countenanced only after serious consideration: *Williams* v *Summerfield* [1972] 2 QB 513. This case appears to be the first reported decision dealing with the application of the Act to a criminal case. It had been thought well established that in civil cases the matter should be resolved primarily by discovery, and that matters not discoverable should not be revealed by a side wind, by means of an application under the Act.[18] In *Williams* v *Summerfield*, Lord Widgery CJ recognized that the discovery approach could not be applied to criminal cases. The Lord Chief Justice indicated that magistrates faced with an application for an order under the Act should approach such applications in the same way as an application for a search warrant, the grant of which is, the Lord Chief Justice said, 'a very serious interference with the liberty of the subject, and a step which would be taken only after the most mature, careful consideration of all the facts of the case'. In some cases, magistrates might decline to exercise their jurisdiction, on the ground that the case was one more suitable for the High Court. Another court has echoed, more recently, Lord Widgery CJ's further observation that the order for inspection should be granted to strengthen an existing case, and not to create a case which does not already exist, i.e., only when the application for an order is not, effectively, a fishing expedition: *Nottingham Justices, ex parte Lynn* [1984] Crim LR 554.

The serious nature of the order is amply demonstrated by the fact that it may be applied for on an *ex parte* basis, without notice to the person affected, and may be made against a person who is not a party to the case.[19] In *Grossman* (1981) 71 Cr App R 302, 309, the facts of which have been

---

[18] See generally *Waterhouse* v *Barker* [1942] 2 KB 759; *Bono* (1913) 29 TLR 635. Cf. *Douglas* v *Pindling* [1996] AC 890.

[19] See, e.g., *Andover Justices, ex parte Rhodes* [1980] Crim LR 644 and the observations of the Court of Appeal in *DB Deniz Nakliyati TAS* v *Yugopetrol* [1992] 1 WLR 437. Conversely, of course, an order under s. 7 is unnecessary where both the bank and the customer agree to the production of records and the customer waives confidentiality: *Wheatley* v *Commissioner of Police of the British Virgin Islands* [2006] 1 WLR 1683 (construing the equivalent legislation in the territory).

dealt with above, Oliver LJ made the following observation about the making of orders under such circumstances:

> I am bound to say that I think the practice of making orders *ex parte* in respect of the accounts of persons who are genuinely third parties unconnected with the proceedings (save that they may perhaps be in possession of some evidence) is a most undesirable one. The Act provides no machinery for going back to the judge once the order has been made; so that the party affected, if he wishes to object, must apply (as in this case) to be joined and then appeal to this Court. That strikes me as a profoundly unsatisfactory situation; and speaking for myself, I would like to see it become a regular practice that in cases where third parties are involved the order should either not be made until the account owner has been informed and given an opportunity to be heard or should be made in the form of an order *nisi*, allowing a period for the person affected to come before the court and show cause why the order should not be effective.

In an age in which the obtaining of evidence for fighting terrorism and organized crime, and for tracking and recovering the proceeds of crime, is given high priority, the suggestions made by Oliver LJ for the protection of third parties have not been adopted. Moreover, the Crown Court is now empowered to make orders for the production of banking and other records pursuant to the even wider powers created by s. 345 of the Proceeds of Crime Act 2002 in proceedings involving the proceeds of crime and money laundering, upon proof of the matters enumerated in that section. The practice under the Act is outside the scope of this work: see generally *Blackstone's Criminal Practice*, 2009 edn, para. D8.16 *et seq.*

19.11 PROOF OF BUSINESS AND PUBLIC AUTHORITY RECORDS

The Civil Evidence Act 1995 introduced special rules for the proof of the records of a business or public authority. These documents are admissible by virtue of the Act, and are of considerable importance in many forms of litigation. In most cases, there is no doubt of their authenticity, but the section gives the judge ample power to require further proof if doubt should arise.[20] Section 9 of the Act provides:

> (1) A document which is shown to form part of the records of a business or public authority may be received in evidence in civil proceedings without further proof.

> (2) A document shall be taken to form part of the records of a business or public authority if there is produced to the court a certificate to that effect signed by an officer of the business or authority to which the records belong.
> For this purpose—
>> (a) a document purporting to be a certificate signed by an officer of a business or public authority shall be deemed to have been duly given by such officer and signed by him; and
>> (b) a certificate shall be treated as signed by a person if it purports to bear a facsimile of his signature.
> (3) The absence of an entry in the records of a business or public authority may be proved in civil proceedings by affidavit of an officer of the business or authority to which the record belongs.

---

[20] The provisions of s. 9 follow broadly the practice in many American jurisdictions. In many cases, American rules of evidence provide for the authentication of business records by affidavit or deposition of the custodian of records or other qualified witness (see, e.g., Federal Rules of Evidence 803(6), 902(11) and (12)).

(4) In this section—

'records' means records in whatever form;

'business' includes any activity regularly carried on over a period of time, whether for profit or not, by any body (whether corporate or not) or by an individual;

'officer' includes any person occupying a responsible position in relation to the relevant activities of the business or public authority or in relation to its records; and

'public authority' includes any public or statutory undertaking, any government department and any person holding office under Her Majesty.

(5) The court may, having regard to the circumstances of the case, direct that all or any of the above provisions of this section do not apply in relation to a particular document or record, or description of documents or records.

19.12 PRESENTATION OF DOCUMENTARY EVIDENCE IN COMPLEX CASES

By s. 31 of the Criminal Justice Act 1988, it is provided that Crown Court rules may make provision, for the purpose of helping juries in trials on indictment to understand complicated issues of fact or technical terms:

(a) as to the furnishing of evidence in any form, notwithstanding the existence of admissible material from which the evidence to be given in that form would be derived; and

(b) as to the furnishing of glossaries for such purposes as may be specified...

Presentation of evidence in such forms, or with glossaries, may be made only where required or permitted by the court. It is submitted that this is a very useful provision, which should result in a more imaginative presentation of evidence to juries in complex document cases, or cases which involve substantial expert evidence. A schedule, summary, chart, calculation or other visual representation of the facts contained in the underlying evidence may take the place of the underlying evidence in the courtroom. While such methods have been used by agreement in the past, their recognition in this section is to be welcomed and should, if well used, make complex evidence far easier for jurors to understand.

The section is presumably intended to provide that the underlying, original evidence from which the evidence as presented is derived, must be admissible when judged by the rules of evidence, including the best evidence rule, where appropriate, though it does not say so as clearly as might have been desired. What is intended is not that inadmissible evidence shall be received, but that admissible evidence which may be complicated or voluminous shall be summarized or presented to the jury in a more intelligible way. It is submitted also that the party tendering such evidence should bear the burden of proving that any underlying materials are admissible, and should make available for inspection by the opponent, a reasonable time before trial, not only the original evidence, but a description of the method by which the derivation was made.

No rules have yet been promulgated. When they are, it might be of benefit to bear in mind the provisions of the American Federal Rule of Evidence 1006, which has an analogous purpose. This rule provides:

Summaries. The contents of voluminous writings, recordings or photographs which cannot conveniently be examined in court may be presented in the form of a chart, summary or calculation. The originals, or duplicates, shall be made available for examination or copying or both, by other parties at a reasonable time and place. The court may order that they be produced in court.

19.13 PROOF OF DUE EXECUTION

In the case of public documents, the mere production of an admissible copy is generally sufficient to satisfy any requirement of proof of due execution of the document, in accordance with the maxim, *Omnia praesumuntur rite et solemniter esse acta*. The presumption is, of course, rebuttable, although not without difficulty. In the case of private documents, due execution must be proved by evidence, except where the document is more than 20 years old and comes from proper custody, in which case there arises a presumption of due execution and so of formal validity.

Due execution is proved by evidence of the signature of the person by whom the document purports to be signed and by evidence of attestation, if required for the document in question. Due execution may be admitted in criminal proceedings by virtue of s. 10 of the Criminal Justice Act 1967, and in civil proceedings, in which the admission may be deemed to have been made by virtue of r. 32.19 of the Civil Procedure Rules 1998 (see 19.6). Even at common law, proof of due execution is dispensed with where an opponent refuses to produce a document after notice to do so.[21]

The means of proof of due execution, where required, are: (a) evidence of handwriting; (b) evidence of attestation; and (c) by an applicable presumption.

19.14 EVIDENCE OF HANDWRITING

There is an obvious relevance in evidence which proves the authenticity of the handwriting of the person purporting to be the signer or executer of the document. Handwriting may be proved in any of the following ways.

19.14.1 Direct evidence

The evidence of the signer himself or of a witness who perceived the execution of the document is admissible and sufficient evidence of due execution. The proof of signature by such means will suffice to identify the signer, as well as to establish the name signed, unless the evidence reveals circumstances which call for further investigation, for example where the signature is not distinctive and the name signed is a common one.[22]

19.14.2 Opinion

Non-expert witnesses who are familiar with the signature of the purported signer, or who have on other occasions received documents bearing the purported signature or made in the purported handwriting of the purported signer, may state their opinion that the document is signed by the person by whom it purports to be signed. The weight of such evidence may, of course, vary very considerably according to the circumstances of the case including the degree of the witness's familiarity with the handwriting. See *Doe d Mudd* v *Suckermore* (1836) 5 Ad & El 703; 11.7.3.

---

[21] *Cooke* v *Tanswell* (1818) 8 Taunt 450.
[22] *Jones* v *Jones* (1841) 9 M & W 75.

19.14.3 Comparison

The comparison of disputed writings with known writings by scientific means is a well-established subject of expert opinion evidence. The basis for such evidence is contained in s. 8 of the Criminal Procedure Act 1865, which applied to criminal proceedings a provision which had been available in civil cases since the enactment of the Common Law Procedure Act 1854. The section provides that:

> Comparison of a disputed writing with any writing proved to the satisfaction of the judge to be genuine shall be permitted to be made by witnesses; and such writings, and the evidence of witnesses respecting the same, may be submitted to the court and jury as evidence of the genuineness or otherwise of the writing in dispute.

The phrase 'to the satisfaction of the judge' leaves unresolved the question of the standard to which the 'genuineness' of the writing to be compared with the disputed writing must be proved. It was at one time thought that even in a criminal case, the standard of proof required on such a secondary issue was no higher than the preponderance of probabilities: see *Angeli* [1979] 1 WLR 26. However, in *Ewing* [1983] QB 1039, it was held that the standard required in a criminal case was proof beyond reasonable doubt. These cases have given rise to difficulties in respect of the standard of proof, which are discussed in detail in 4.14.

Possibly because s. 8 predates the general recognition of the scientific study and comparison of handwriting, it is not expressly provided that the comparison should be made by a witness qualified as an expert. Nonetheless, it is unlikely that the evidence would command real weight if made by a lay witness, unless giving evidence of his opinion based on personal familiarity. Scientific comparison of samples of handwriting is a matter for experts. The jury may, and inevitably will where it is relevant to do so, compare the appearance of various documents produced to them, but they should not be invited to make a comparison of handwriting without the help of expert evidence. In *Tilley* [1961] 1 WLR 1309 the prosecution obtained in the course of cross-examination samples of the handwriting of the accused, with a view to comparing the samples with handwriting on a receipt said to be in respect of a car which the accused were charged with stealing. No expert was called concerning the handwriting, and the point was not pursued by the prosecution. However, the conviction was quashed on appeal because the jury were supplied with photographs and a magnifying glass, and were invited by the comments of the judge in summing-up, to form their own unaided comparison of handwriting. It follows, therefore, that where the jury are not being invited to make any such comparison, but have in their possession documents which may lead them to seek to do so, they should be warned specifically against such a course. This done, the jury may of course make other proper use of the documents placed before them in evidence.[23]

The ultimate question of whether the handwriting on the known specimen is also that on the disputed writing, or the document whose due execution is to be proved, is of course a question of fact for the jury or other tribunal of fact. At one time it would have been held that the handwriting expert should, technically, limit his evidence to a statement of the comparison made by him, and his resulting opinion should technically be confined to relevant similarities or differences.[24]

---

[23] *O'Sullivan* [1969] 1 WLR 497.
[24] *Wakeford* v *Bishop of Lincoln* as reported in 90 LJ PC 174.

Nonetheless, the modern practice is for the witness to be permitted to state his opinion about authorship, and in civil cases this would seem to follow from the provisions of s. 3(1) and (3) of the Civil Evidence Act 1972.[25]

19.15 EVIDENCE OF ATTESTATION

Due execution of documents which require attestation may be proved by the evidence of the attesting witnesses, or one of them. At one time, a document requiring attestation could be proved to have been duly executed only in this way, but it was provided by s. 3 of the Evidence Act 1938 that in both civil and criminal cases, it might be proved as if no attesting witness were alive. This means that either of the other methods of proof suggested in this section may be employed, although the most satisfactory way will be to prove the handwriting of an attesting witness, where possible. The older rule still applies to wills, and these must be proved by evidence of attestation, unless it is shown that all the attesting witnesses are dead, insane, beyond the jurisdiction, or unable to be traced. However, the practice is not to insist on the strict application of the rule where probate is granted in common form.

An attesting witness is called as the witness of the court and may be cross-examined by any party, including the party seeking to prove the document.[26] If an attesting witness proves hostile or unreliable, then he may be contradicted by other evidence by any party.[27] An attesting witness may not claim legal professional privilege.[28]

19.16 PRESUMPTIONS

It is presumed:

(a) That a document which is proved or purports to be more than 20 years old, and which is produced from proper custody, was duly executed.[29] 'Proper custody' means only that the document is shown to have been kept in a place in which one might reasonably and naturally have expected to find it, or in the care of a person who might reasonably and naturally be expected to have possession of it, having regard to the nature of the document and the circumstances of the case.[30]

(b) That a document was executed on the date which it bears.[31]

(c) That in the case of a deed other than a will, any alterations thereto were made before execution, but in the case of a will, conversely, that any alterations were made after execution.[32]

---

[25] For the scope of expert opinion evidence generally, including the expression of opinions on ultimate issues, see 11.4.1.

[26] *Oakes* v *Uzzell* [1932] P 19.

[27] *Bowman* v *Hodgson* (1867) LR 1 P & D 362.

[28] *In the Estate of Fuld (No. 2), Hartley* v *Fuld* [1965] P 405.

[29] See Evidence Act 1938, s. 4. Cf. American Federal Rule of Evidence 803(16) which uses the same time period to define an 'ancient document' admissible as an exception to the rule against hearsay.

[30] *Meath (Bishop)* v *Marquis of Winchester* (1836) 3 Bing NC 183.

[31] *Anderson* v *Weston* (1840) 6 Bing NC 296.

[32] *Doe d Tatum* v *Catomore* (1851) 16 QB 745.

B REAL EVIDENCE

SUMMARY OF MAIN POINTS

- Real evidence is evidence from which the tribunal of fact can draw conclusions from its own perception.
- Real evidence may consist of material objects; the appearance of persons or animals; the demeanour of witnesses; views of the *locus in quo*; and video or audio tapes, film, photographs, etc.

19.17 NATURE OF REAL EVIDENCE

Real evidence is the name usually given to quite diverse forms of evidence which have in common the characteristic that the tribunal of fact is invited to observe and draw conclusions from its observation of things, persons, places, or circumstances. Real evidence may, therefore, rank among the most cogent kinds of evidence, but also among the most difficult to assess in terms of weight, at least before the event. The forms of real evidence in common use are the following.

19.18 MATERIAL OBJECTS

The court may look at and draw any proper conclusions from its visual observation of any relevant material object produced before it. The material object may itself be the subject-matter of the case, as where the court looks at the fit of a suit of which the quality is disputed. It may be an object ancillary to the issue but nonetheless relevant to it, as for example where the court looks at an object alleged to be an offensive weapon, by reason of having been adapted for causing injury to the person. The best evidence rule does not apply to tangible objects, and no objection can be made to the introduction of secondary evidence, such as photographs or films of them[33] though failure to produce such an object may affect the weight of the evidence.

The tribunal of fact is entitled to act on conclusions drawn from its own perception, even where this conflicts with other evidence given about the object, although in a case where the true nature or characteristics of the object cannot be assessed by mere visual observations, without the assistance of expert evidence, the jury must be warned not to rely upon unaided visual opinion. This would be the case in looking at objects bearing examples of handwriting, comparisons of which should not be made without assistance[34] although the jury may obviously make use of their observation for any purpose short of comparison. And it has been held to be wrong to direct a jury to feel entirely free to form their own view about the presence and age of blood stains on an object, in the face of categoric scientific evidence on that subject.[35] If expert evidence called on behalf of the parties differs in its conclusions about the object, and the tribunal of fact has, therefore, to choose what evidence to accept, it may, no doubt, use its powers of observation in making such choice.

---

[33] *Armory* v *Delamirie* (1722) 1 Str 505; *Francis* (1874) LR2 CCR 128; *Hocking* v *Ahlquist Bros Ltd* [1944] KB 120.
[34] See 11.7.3; 19.14.3.
[35] *Anderson* v *R* [1972] AC 100.

19.19 APPEARANCE OF PERSONS OR ANIMALS

The physical characteristics of a person or animal may be observed for any relevant purpose. Thus, the height or other personal features may be ascertained by observation, and the nature and extent of any injuries examined. The court may also take into account any characteristics apparent to it on observing the person or animal, even if not intended to be conveyed, such as a tendency to left-handedness, defects in hearing or vision, or the propensity of an animal to be ferocious.

19.20 DEMEANOUR OF WITNESSES

In considering the credit of a witness and the weight to be given to his evidence, the court may consider not only what is said, but the way in which it is said. This includes the attitude of the witness to the court, his general demeanour, his apparent frankness, evasiveness, or other reaction to questioning (particularly hostile interrogation during cross-examination) and his apparent power or lack of power of recollection.

19.21 VIEWS

A view is an inspection, out of court, of the *locus in quo*, or other place relevant to the case, or of some object, person or animal which cannot conveniently be brought to court.[36] The view may involve any appropriate test or demonstration, as if made in court. A view can be a difficult event to control. It is important that all interested parties,[37] their legal representatives, and the tribunal of fact should, as far as can be arranged, have the same sight and opportunity to observe. They must also be protected against exposure to extraneous and irrelevant matters. With a jury, the problems are particularly acute, and it is essential that each member of the jury should attend and be enabled to form an individual impression. Where one member of the jury, who lived close to the *locus in quo*, was 'deputed' to view it and 'report back' to the others, who accordingly had no such opportunity, the conviction was quashed.[38] It is equally essential, if the view is attended by witnesses in order to explain relevant matters or to give some demonstration, that the witness should speak or demonstrate only at the direction of the judge, in the presence of all concerned, and for the purpose only of the necessary demonstration or explanation.[39] In a matter tried by a judge alone, the same rules should be followed, although the dangers to be guarded against are less acute, and the extent of the view may be widened. In the Ocean Island case[40] Sir Robert Megarry V-C personally visited and spent a considerable time on the island and drew numerous conclusions from his lengthy and detailed observation of its characteristics; though the litigation was, on any basis, exceptional.

---

[36] The view must take place before the summing-up: *Lawrence* [1968] 1 WLR 341; cf. *Nixon* [1968] 1 WLR 577.

[37] Especially the accused (*Ely Justices, ex parte Burgess* (1992) 157 JP 484).

[38] *Gurney* [1976] Crim LR 567. See also Juries Act 1974, s. 14. The conviction was also quashed in *Hunter* [1985] 1 WLR 613, where the judge permitted all involved in the trial to go on a view, but felt it unnecessary to attend himself.

[39] *Karamat* v *R* [1956] AC 256. See also *Martin* (1872) LR 1 CCR 378.

[40] *Tito* v *Waddell (No. 2)* [1977] Ch 106.

19.22 TAPES, PHOTOGRAPHS, FILM, ETC.

Although in modern law visual and audio recordings may be regarded as documents, at least for some purposes (see 19.2) they have a further, important potential to supply matter of evidential value, because of the possibility of direct perception. A tape or film may yield detail and nuances over and above the mere text of the matters recorded therein. Some detail of the circumstances of the recording, some visible characteristic, some inflexion of the voice may put a different complexion on the recorded matter, as compared with a mere transcript of the words spoken or the things done. The sound or accent of a voice, the physical appearance of a thing or person, may resolve some ambiguity or clothe with meaning some unexplained passage in the text. The recordings are, therefore, to that extent real evidence and often have an effect similar to a view or the production of a material object. To the extent that recordings are admissible as real evidence, it is no objection to admissibility that the evidence is meant to, and does in fact, convey information because it is offered for direct observation by the court, and not as a species of hearsay.

Thus, in *The Statue of Liberty* [1968] 1 WLR 739, Sir Jocelyn Simon P admitted in evidence a record made on cinematograph film of the radar echoes, recorded mechanically without human intervention, of the vessels involved in a collision. The recording was the equivalent of a photograph or series of photographs, from which the court could, by observation, gain information about the courses of the vessels at material times. This decision represents an uncomfortable interface between the common law hearsay rule and the potential of modern technology. Clearly, Sir Jocelyn Simon P's categorization of the evidence tendered as real evidence cannot disguise the fact that the information produced by the radar device was tendered with a view to showing that the facts stated by the record of the radar echoes were, in fact, true. At common law, there would be a powerful argument for excluding such evidence as hearsay. At the time when *The Statue of Liberty* was decided, the Civil Evidence Act 1968 was not yet in force, and the Evidence Act 1938 did not assist the admissibility of the evidence. It would seem that the evidence would now be admissible under the Civil Evidence Act 1995. As to criminal cases, see generally 7.15.3; 8.29. Whatever the ultimate impact of these technological problems on the rule against hearsay, the reasoning of Sir Jocelyn Simon P has been employed in a number of subsequent cases. In *Wood* (1982) 76 Cr App R 23, it was held that where a computer was used only as a calculator, the information used to program the computer being within the personal knowledge of persons available as witnesses, the print-out which represented the result of the computer's calculations was not hearsay, but was admissible at common law as a piece of real evidence. This case was followed in *Minors* [1989] 1 WLR 441. And in *Castle* v *Cross*,[41] it was held that a police officer was entitled to give evidence of the reading of an 'Intoximeter 3000' device, which was admitted to be efficient to the required degree, and where there was no suggestion that the machine was not working properly. The reading was admitted as a piece of real evidence.

The court must, before admitting recordings as evidence, be satisfied that the evidence which may be yielded is relevant and that the recording produced is authentic and original.[42] The

---

[41] [1984] 1 WLR 1372. Cf. *DPP* v *McKeown* [1997] 1 WLR 295; *Shephard* [1993] AC 380; *Gaimster* v *Marlow* [1984] QB 218; *Cracknell* v *Willis* [1988] AC 450; *Spiby* (1990) 91 Cr App R 186. See generally, on the subject of evidence by computers, C. Tapper, *Computer Law*, 3rd edn, p. 226; J.C. Smith [1981] Crim LR 387; 8.29.

[42] *Maqsud Ali* [1966] 1 QB 688. A tape recording is a 'document' for the purposes of the Criminal Justice Act 2003 so that statements made therein may be proved by copies, pursuant to s. 133. But the copy must be authenticated. And when it consists of statements made during an interview, see Code of Practice E and Home Office

requirement of proof of originality is met by evidence sufficient to raise a *prima facie* case, in that the provenance and history of the recording up to the moment of production in court, are properly accounted for.[43] If there is any real possibility that the recording might have been interfered with, and is not original, it should be excluded.[44] Moreover, it may be that where a recording is of such poor quality that it would be wrong to expect the jury to form a fair assessment of the contents, it should be excluded.[45]

The above principles apply to the use of films produced by hidden, automatic security or CCTV cameras installed in banks and elsewhere for the purpose of recording robberies and other incidents. The jury are entitled to consider the film as identification evidence of the persons recorded on it, subject to the foundational requirements stated above. See, e.g., *Dodson* [1984] 1 WLR 971; and see *Taylor v Chief Constable of Cheshire* [1986] 1 WLR 1479.[46]

19.23 RECOMMENDED FURTHER READING

Elliott, D.W., 'Video tape evidence: the risk of over-persuasion' [1998] *Criminal Law Review* 159.

Ormerod, D., 'A prejudicial view?' [2000] *Criminal Law Review* 452.

Pattenden, R., 'Admissibility in criminal proceedings of third party and real evidence obtained by methods prohibited by UNCAT' (2006) **10**(1) *International Journal of Evidence and Proof* 1.

Pattenden, R., 'Authenticating "things" in English law: principles for adducing tangible evidence in common law jury trials' (2008) **12**(4) *International Journal of Evidence and Proof* 273.

Phipson, S., 'Real evidence' (1920) **29** *Yale Law Journal* 705.

 ## 19.24 QUESTIONS FOR DISCUSSION BASED ON *R v COKE; LITTLETON* AND *BLACKSTONE v COKE* (for case files go to the Online Resource Centre)

19.24.1 *Coke; Littleton*

1. By what evidence should the content of the writing found in Coke's flat (exhibit GG1) be proved?

2. By what evidence should it be proved, if possible, that the writing on exhibit GG1 is that of Coke?

3. What direction, if any, should the jury be given about their use of exhibits GG1 and GG4?

19.24.2 *Blackstone v Coke*

Review the letter sent to Coke by his solicitors dated 20 February Yr—1. If Margaret Blackstone's solicitors obtain this letter and wish to cross-examine Coke on it at trial, how should the letter be proved? (Ignore questions of privilege.)

Circular 76/1988: *Blackstone's Criminal Practice*, 2009 edn, para. F8.40 and appendix 2, *Consolidated Criminal Practice Direction*, para. IV. 43; *Rampling* [1987] Crim LR 823.

[43] *Robson* [1972] 1 WLR 651. For a detailed treatment of this matter, see 4.10 and 4.14.

[44] *Stevenson* [1971] 1 WLR 1.

[45] *Robson* [1972] 1 WLR 651.

[46] See also *Attorney-General's Reference (No. 2 of 2002)* [2003] 1 Cr App R 21. As to the practicalities of making tapes and transcripts thereof available to the jury see *Emmerson* (1990) 92 Cr App R 284, 287; *Riaz* (1991) 94 Cr App R 339; *Aitken* (1991) 94 Cr App R 85; *Tonge* [1993] Crim LR 876.

19.25 GENERAL QUESTIONS FOR DISCUSSION

1. What is a 'document' in civil and criminal proceedings? Would a film, for example, count as a document?

2. To what extent does the 'primary evidence rule' still apply to both criminal and civil proceedings?

3. What is the legal position if it is impossible to produce the original of a document or it is lost?

4. Would a bank's file of correspondence, containing account information, amount to a 'banker's book'?

5. Can the prosecution call an accused's mother to confirm that, in her opinion, an incriminating note was in her son's handwriting? What other ways may be used to prove that it was his handwriting?

6. What is 'real evidence'? For example, are the contents of a tape-recording of a 999 emergency telephone call real evidence?

7. Apart from considering the content of what a witness says in evidence, in what other important way may a court assess the witness?

8. What is the purpose of visiting the *locus in quo*?

20

PROOF WITHOUT EVIDENCE

20.1 WHEN EVIDENCE MAY NOT BE REQUIRED

There are some circumstances in which a court will, or may, find facts in issue or relevant facts established without requiring proof by means of evidence. This chapter will examine these convenient techniques, which often permit considerable savings of judicial time and of costs. The cases to be considered are those in which:

(a) facts are formally admitted for the purpose of the proceedings;
(b) notorious or readily demonstrable facts are noticed judicially by the court; and
(c) facts are presumed in favour of the party asserting them.

Only presumptions have been considered previously in this book (see 4.4) and then only briefly for their effect on the burden of proof.

A   FORMAL ADMISSIONS

> ### SUMMARY OF MAIN POINTS
>
> - Formal admissions may be made in both civil and criminal cases for the purposes of the proceedings.
> - Facts formally admitted are taken to be proved without the need for evidence unless a party is permitted to withdraw the admission.

Proof may be dispensed with altogether where a fact is formally admitted for the purposes of the proceedings, and so ceases to be in dispute between the parties. Before the coming into force of s. 10 of the Criminal Justice Act 1967 formal admissions were possible only in civil cases, but now may be made also in criminal cases.

20.2 CIVIL CASES

In civil cases, formal admissions may be made of the whole of the opponent's case, or of any facts relevant to it, and if the facts admitted justify it, the opponent is entitled to judgment based on the admissions alone. Admissions may be made in a party's statement of case, or simply by letter. The procedure in such cases is governed by Part 14 of the Civil Procedure Rules 1998. By virtue of r. 14.1(1) a party may formally admit the whole or part of another party's case. This may be done by letter or in a statement of case (r. 14.1(2)). Rule 14.1(5) allows the court to permit the party making the admission to withdraw or amend it. A party may also make an admission in his pleading, or by omitting to deal with an allegation in his pleading: see r. 16.5(1), (5). There would seem to be no reason why a party could not also, as at common law, make such an admission orally during the course of proceedings.[1] Under r. 32.18, a party may serve notice on an opponent requiring the opponent to admit any facts specified in the notice. Any facts so admitted will be taken as established without further proof. If a party unreasonably refuses to admit facts which are shown at trial to be readily provable, it may be that the court can reflect this in a suitable order for the costs occasioned by the needless presentation of evidence. However, the facts admitted are admitted only for the purposes of the instant litigation, and, subject to any later cause of action or issue estoppel affecting the parties or their privies, the admission may not be used for any other purpose (r. 32.18(3)). The same rule provides that admissions made pursuant to a notice may be used only by the party who served the notice, but this appears rather unrealistic where there are multiple parties, because, since the abolition of the rule against hearsay, the evidence in civil cases is usually admissible in the case generally, and because it would be easy enough for other parties to serve identical notices and receive identical responses. Rule 32.18(4) permits a party to withdraw an admission on such terms as the court thinks fit, in a case, for example, in which further evidence comes to light which makes the admission inappropriate.[2] Care must be taken,

---

[1] *Urquhar v Butterfield* (1887) 37 ChD 357. As to the propriety of permitting the admission to be withdrawn where it is made in interim proceedings, see *H. Clark (Doncaster) v Wilkinson* [1965] Ch 694.

[2] But it must not be forgotten that a party may also rely on statements made by an opponent at any time as an informal admission (see 9.1 *et seq*). Informal admissions may also be made in correspondence or by statements of

when relying on formal admissions for judgment, that no further facts are necessary to prove the case. Admissions must be strictly confined to their terms, and any facts not admitted, on which a party must rely having regard to the burden of proof, must be proved by evidence.

20.3 CRIMINAL CASES

By s. 10 of the Criminal Justice Act 1967:

> (1) Subject to the provisions of this section, any fact of which oral evidence may be given in any criminal proceedings may be admitted for the purpose of those proceedings by or on behalf of the prosecutor or accused, and the admission by any party of any such fact under this section shall as against that party be conclusive evidence in those proceedings of the fact admitted.
>
> (2) An admission under this section—
>
> (a) may be made before or at the proceedings;
>
> (b) if made otherwise than in court, shall be in writing;
>
> (c) if made in writing by an individual, shall purport to be signed by the person making it and, if so made by a body corporate, shall purport to be signed by a director or manager, or the secretary or clerk, or some other similar officer of the body corporate;
>
> (d) if made on behalf of an accused who is an individual, shall be made by his counsel or solicitor;
>
> (e) if made at any stage before the trial by an accused who is an individual, must be approved by his counsel or solicitor (whether at the time it was made or subsequently) before or at the proceedings in question.
>
> (3) An admission under this section for the purpose of proceedings relating to any matter shall be treated as an admission for the purpose of any subsequent criminal proceedings relating to that matter (including any appeal or retrial).
>
> (4) An admission under this section may with the leave of the court be withdrawn in the proceedings for the purpose of which it is made or any subsequent criminal proceedings relating to the same matter.

This section provides a self-contained code for formal admissions in criminal cases. This practice had not been possible in criminal cases before the enactment of this section. As in civil cases, a formal admission is conclusive of the facts admitted unless withdrawn with the leave of the court under s. 10(4). There is no objection in principle to a formal admission of all the facts alleged by the prosecution, though it may not always be advisable for the court to accept this because it may be difficult for the jury to distinguish between the facts admitted and any other facts relied on by the defence.[3] Although a formal admission may be made orally in court by counsel or solicitor, this must be done in such a way as to enable it to be recorded accurately, and it should then be reduced to writing.[4] While it is possible for leave to be given to withdraw a formal admission after it has been made, leave will generally be given only where a party shows that the admission was made only by reason of a mistake on his part or on the part of his solicitors or counsel: see *Kolton* [2000] Crim LR 761.

---

case, even when altered by withdrawal or amendment, though the weight of such admissions will not be great if the amendment or withdrawal was occasioned by persuasive new evidence.

[3] *Lewis* [1971] Crim LR 414. And the wording of s. 10(1) prevents the court from accepting an admission as to any fact or opinion, of which oral evidence would be inadmissible in criminal proceedings, for example inadmissible hearsay (*Coulson* [1997] Crim LR 886).

[4] *Lennard* [1973] 1 WLR 483; as to summary proceedings, see Criminal Procedure Rules 2005, r. 37.4.

Two general matters merit observation, with respect to both civil and criminal proceedings. The first is that formal admissions must be distinguished carefully from the informal admissions and confessions dealt with in Chapter 9. The latter are merely pieces of evidence tendered among others as constituting evidence against a party supplied by his own acts and words, and may be rejected by the court as inadmissible or of negligible weight, or be made the subject of evidence to contradict or discredit them; they are in no sense formal admissions and are most certainly not conclusive. The second is that in both civil and criminal cases, it is the duty of legal advisers to consider what formal admissions, if any, can and should properly be made on behalf of their clients for the purposes of any proceedings in which they are engaged. Of course, care must be taken not to make unjustified admissions, but failure to admit facts which are not really disputed wastes time and costs, and the latter may be visited on the client. As we have seen, this duty is now reflected in the rules of procedure.

B JUDICIAL NOTICE

SUMMARY OF MAIN POINTS

- A judge may take judicial notice of any fact which is either notorious or readily demonstrable by reference to proper sources. In the latter case the judge may refer to such sources and receive evidence on the subject before deciding whether to take judicial notice.

- In addition, statute provides for judicial notice of numerous public records, seals, etc.

- A fact judicially noticed may be taken as proved without evidence.

- Judicial notice is not the same as the judge's personal knowledge. A tribunal of fact may not substitute any personal knowledge they happen to have for the evidence, but may use that personal knowledge in evaluating the evidence.

By a rule applicable both to civil and criminal cases generally, no evidence is required of a fact of which the court will take judicial notice, that is to say a fact of which the court will acknowledge the truth without the necessity for proof. Facts which will be judicially noticed are those which are notorious, or which are readily demonstrable by reference to proper sources.[5] If the fact is not one which will be judicially noticed, it must be proved by evidence. There are obviously very many facts which will be judicially noticed, and the process is capable of saving a great deal of time which would otherwise be spent in calling the substantial volumes of evidence often curiously necessary to prove the most self-evident facts. As Cross demonstrated,[6] the process of judicial notice is carried on habitually in almost every case which comes before the courts, often without being recognized as such, because of numerous tacit assumptions; the relevance of the accused's possession of a jemmy to a charge of burglary against him is based on an assumption of fact, or generalization (see 1.4) that a jemmy is frequently employed for the purposes of burglary.

---

[5] *Commonwealth Shipping Representative* v *Peninsular and Oriental Branch Service* [1923] AC 191, 212 per Lord Sumner.

[6] *Evidence*, 5th edn, pp. 161–2; cf. Cross and Tapper, *Evidence*, 11th edn, pp. 82 *et seq.* See also Nokes (1958) 74 LQR 59.

We must look, however, principally at judicial notice in the sense of conscious application of the judicial mind to the facts concerned. This in turn involves consideration of (a) notice of notorious facts, (b) notice after reference to sources. In addition there are some cases where judicial notice is to be taken by statute, of statutes, certain official documents, seals and their authenticating or official devices; these need not be considered specifically here. For details, see *Blackstone's Criminal Practice*, 2009 edn, para. F1.5.

20.4 EFFECT OF JUDICIAL NOTICE

Judicial notice differs from formal admissions in that the fact judicially noticed is established, not by concession of a party but at the behest of one party and, if necessary over the objection of the opponent. In a civil case, this is hardly significant, since if the judge is prepared to notice a fact judicially, he would no doubt reach the same conclusion if evidence of the same fact were to be adduced. In a criminal case, however, a problem arises as to how the jury should be directed as to the noticed fact, once the judge has noticed it judicially. The jury, as the tribunal of fact, must of course be directed as to the effect of the judicial notice.

In the United States, a distinction is made between criminal and civil cases as to the direction to be given (juries being commonly used in both kinds of case). This is well illustrated by Federal Rule of Evidence 201(g) which provides:

> Instructing jury. In a civil action or proceeding, the court shall instruct the jury to accept as conclusive any fact judicially noticed. In a criminal case, the court shall instruct the jury that it may, but is not required to accept as conclusive any fact judicially noticed.

This distinction is attributable principally to the constitutional rule that in a criminal case, no directed verdict can be returned against the accused: *Ross* v *United States* 374 F2d 97 (8th Cir, 1967). Directing the jury to accept a judicially noticed fact is regarded as the equivalent of a direction to find proved a part of the prosecution case, and therefore of a partial directed verdict against the accused. In England, it appears to be accepted that, where a fact is judicially noticed, the jury must be directed to accept such fact as proved. For example, in *Simpson* [1983] 1 WLR 1494, the Court of Appeal held that, since a flick-knife is an article within the meaning of s. 1(4) of the Prevention of Crime Act 1953 and is therefore an offensive weapon *per se*, the judge should take judicial notice that a flick-knife is an offensive weapon, and direct the jury accordingly. But, it seems that the question of whether or not a flick-knife is an offensive weapon remains one of fact, and not one of law, and it has been argued powerfully that like any other question of fact it is one which should be decided by the jury.[7]

The American position, therefore, has a certain obvious degree of appeal. That position tends to preserve the role of the jury as the tribunal of fact, and thereby serves an important constitutional interest. However, the English rule also has attractions. Perhaps the most important of these is the need for uniformity in areas which are not subject to reasonable dispute, and which are therefore proper areas for judicial notice. Although the American rule is founded primarily on constitutional considerations, it may be that the point made by Federal Rule of Evidence 201(g) is not beyond argument in England.

---

[7] See *Gibson* v *Wales* [1983] 1 WLR 393; *Williamson* (1977) 67 Cr App R 35; cf. *Hynde* [1998] 1 WLR 1222; *Houghton* v *Chief Constable of Greater Manchester* (1986) 84 Cr App R 319; *Dhindsa* [2005] EWCA Crim 1198 For fuller discussion of this issue see *Blackstone's Criminal Practice*, 2009 edn, para. B12.140 *et seq.*

20.5 NOTORIOUS FACTS

Matters of common knowledge, which are too notorious to be capable of serious dispute or debate will be judicially noticed without reference to any source. There are so many instances in the decided cases, and so many more potential subjects of such notice that any attempt at compilation would be pointless, but it would seem that Cross's category of tacit notice would probably fall under this head. The flavour of the subject will be sufficiently apparent by reference to a few examples, and those most beloved of textbook writers include the facts that a fortnight is too short a period for human gestation,[8] that cats are normally kept for domestic purposes,[9] that criminals have unhappy lives,[10] that the streets of London are full of traffic,[11] that goldfinches are British wild birds,[12] and that the advancement of learning is among the purposes for which the University of Oxford exists.[13] The imagination will readily supply a fund of similarly notorious facts in circumstances of all kinds. The examples given also serve to illustrate how useful judicial notice can be in facilitating the proof of facts which are apparently self-evident, but which, paradoxically, it would be difficult and inconvenient to prove by admissible evidence.

20.6 NOTICE AFTER REFERENCE

This type of notice, while undoubtedly well established, creates one or two problems of a kind which are by no means purely theoretical, in that it explores very keenly the dividing line between the taking of judicial notice and the reception of evidence. The actual differences between the two processes are clear. Judicial notice involves a finding of fact by the judge, after which the jury (if there is one) should be directed on the basis that the fact is established. It involves the proposition that no evidence should be admissible to contradict directly the fact judicially noticed. Judicial notice creates a precedent in law, at any rate coterminous with the existence of the fact or circumstances noticed; judicial notice that camels are domestic animals may be taken as a universal truth affecting camels generally,[14] whereas the status of a particular foreign sovereign may be noticeable only until the next *coup d'état*, and must be established anew by reference in each case. But the taking of evidence has none of these characteristics. Matters sought to be established by evidence, on the other hand, are questions of fact for the jury. Save in the rare case of legally conclusive evidence, evidence may always be contradicted and explained by contrary evidence. Facts found based on evidence are found only for the purposes of the proceedings in which the evidence is tendered, and (except in cases where an estoppel is created) not for the purposes of any other proceedings. Despite these distinctions, however, the two processes operate in very much the same way where the judge makes reference to sources for the purpose of informing himself, and thereafter takes judicial notice.

---

[8] *Luffe* (1807) 8 East 193. But not, curiously, that 360 days is too long: see *Preston-Jones v Preston-Jones* [1951] AC 391.

[9] *Nye v Niblett* [1918] 1 KB 23.

[10] *Burns v Edman* [1970] 2 QB 541.

[11] *Dennis v A.J. White & Co.* [1916] 2 KB 1, 6.

[12] *Hughes v DPP* (2003) 167 JP 589.

[13] *Oxford Poor Rate Case* (1857) 8 El & Bl 184; at the present author's university, this decision was generally regarded as a common law exception rendered necessary by some apparent difficulty of proving such a proposition by evidence.

[14] *McQuaker v Goddard* [1940] 1 KB 687; see 20.7.

It seems clear that the judge should take judicial notice, whether or not he refers to any source, only of facts which appear to him, in the light of his information, to be either sufficiently notorious or to be readily demonstrable. In *Brune v Thompson* (1842) 2 QB 789, it was held that judicial notice could not be taken that part of the Tower of London lay within the City of London, it being equally notorious that part of it lay in the county of Middlesex. It is for the party inviting judicial notice to provide any necessary source of reference, and the judge may refuse to notice any fact for which a proper reference is not provided, a course adopted by Lord Ellenborough in *Van Omeron v Dowick* (1809) 2 Camp 42, when declining to notice a royal proclamation in the absence of the official *Gazette* containing it. It is obviously desirable that all those facts which in reality require evidence should be left to be proved by evidence, and that this necessary step should not be avoided improperly by the taking of judicial notice.

Judicial notice after reference is taken of the following matters, which are briefly stated here:[15]

(a) Of the existence and contents of public statutes and of the law of England (including the law of the European Union); of the procedure and privileges of both Houses of Parliament; and of the jurisdiction and rules of each division of the High Court.[16]

(b) Of customs which have been settled by judicial decision, or certified to and recorded in any division of the High Court, such as those of the City of London certified by the Recorder of London. Recent customs must have been recognized more than once by judicial decision, but there is no other requirement concerning frequency of recognition, and the courts incline against requiring proof by evidence over and over of apparently well-established customs.[17]

(c) Of professional practice, for example that of the Ordnance Survey[18] or of conveyancers[19] in interpreting references on maps or conveyancing documents.

(d) Of political matters and affairs of state, or the view of the government on such matters including the status and recognition of foreign governments. The practice in such cases is to obtain and act upon the certificate of the Secretary of State, which is for this purpose a source from which the facts contained in it are readily demonstrable, and authoritatively stated.[20]

(e) Readily demonstrable public facts, for example historical or geographical facts, or the meaning of words in common usage. For these purposes, reference may be made to apparently objective and authoritative public works, such as histories, maps, and dictionaries, see, e.g., *Read v Bishop of Lincoln* [1892] AC 644.

The matters referred to in (d) and (e) above pose a particular problem of demarcation as between evidence and judicial notice, because there is a specific rule of evidence that facts of public concern, stated in public documents, may be proved by evidence of the contents of those

---

[15] The detail of these matters is comprehensively set out, together with the relevant authorities, in Phipson, *Evidence*, 16th edn, paras 3–07 *et seq.*

[16] See, as to public Acts of Parliament, Interpretation Act 1978, s. 3. But there is no rule permitting judicial notice of foreign law (*Ofori (No. 2)* (1993) 99 Cr App R 223); as to the technically foreign law of other parts of the UK see *Re Nesbitt* (1844) 14 LJ MC 30.

[17] *Brandao v Barnett* (1846) 12 C1 & F 787; *George v Davies* [1911] 2 KB 445.

[18] *Davey v Harrow Corporation* [1958] 1 QB 60 at 69; see also *Heather v P-E Consulting Group Ltd* [1973] 1 Ch 189 (accounting practices).

[19] *Re Rosher* (1884) 26 ChD 801.

[20] The court regards itself as incompetent to judge such matters, and will defer to the view of the responsible minister on behalf of the government: *Duff Development Co. Ltd v Government of Kelantan* [1924] AC 797; *The Parlement Belge* (1880) 5 PD 197; *Mighell v Sultan of Johore* [1894] 1 QB 149.

documents. This rule has common law origins, but now enjoys statutory authority.[21] So far as the matters in (e) are concerned, it may be that the use of such works before taking judicial notice must be confined to what Phipson[22] calls 'refreshing the memory of the judge', in the sense that only notorious or readily demonstrable facts so ascertained may be noticed, any others being a proper subject for evidence. The matters in (d) are more easily reconciled. In practice a certificate of the Secretary of State is invariably regarded as conclusive evidence of the truth of any statement it makes concerning foreign affairs, the status of foreign sovereigns and governments, relations with or between foreign powers and so on. Whether its contents are regarded as matters of conclusive evidence or of judicial notice makes little real difference, despite the varying pronouncements on the subject.[23]

There is no such easy solution, however, to two far more formidable and practically significant problems. These arise: where the court takes judicial notice after receiving evidence on the fact noticed; and where the process of judicial notice is bound up with personal knowledge on the part of the judge.

20.7 JUDICIAL NOTICE AFTER EVIDENCE

There seems to be no doubt that a judge may inform himself by hearing evidence, as well as by reference to works, on matters which he is invited to notice judicially. The *locus classicus* is *McQuaker* v *Goddard* [1940] 1 KB 687. Branson J, faced with the problem of deciding whether a camel was a wild or domestic animal for the purpose of the common law rules governing liability for animals, not only heard a great deal of conflicting expert evidence about the behaviour of camels, but himself consulted books on the subject. Having done so, the learned judge took judicial notice of the fact that the camel was a domestic animal. Both the trial judge, and Clauson LJ in the Court of Appeal, which upheld the decision, made it clear that the process was one of judicial notice, and that the evidence was directed only at assisting the judge to come to his view. Although it may be conducive to the peace of mind of camels and their owners to have a view of them embedded in precedent, it is by no means easy to see how a fact could properly be described as either 'notorious' or 'readily demonstrable', while attracting such a difference of expert opinion, and if the same process could be applied to any such case, the function of a tribunal of fact in assessing evidence might be seriously eroded. The fact that a judge (or jury) forms a view of evidence given in one case cannot generally assist another tribunal of fact in a subsequent case. But it is submitted that this use of judicial notice is proper, provided that it is restricted to the notice of constant facts (such as the nature of camels) which are not dependent upon the facts of any given case.

20.8 PERSONAL KNOWLEDGE

The question of the extent to which a judge may make use of any personal knowledge which he may have of the facts canvassed before him, is an unresolved one. It seems clear that any person involved in a case as a member of a tribunal of fact may not act on his personal knowledge of the particular facts of a case, in the sense of supplementing the evidence from fortuitous

---

[21] Civil Evidence Act 1995, s. 7(2); Criminal Justice Act 2003, s. 118(1); see generally 8.7.2.

[22] *Evidence*, 16th edn, para. 3–24.

[23] In *Duff Development Co. Ltd* v *Government of Kelantan* [1924] AC 797, Lords Finlay and Sumner seem to contradict each other on the point, see 813 and 824.

personal knowledge.[24] But in a more general sense, it has been held that, 'properly and within reasonable limits', a judge may apply such general knowledge as he may have of the subject-matter to the process of understanding and evaluating the evidence.[25] Outside those limits, a judge should exclude from his mind such personal knowledge as he has, and it would seem wrong for him either to act evidentially on such knowledge, or to use that knowledge in the process of judicial notice.

Magistrates and jurors are entitled to make use of such local or general knowledge as they may have, not as a substitute for evidence, but to assist them in evaluating the evidence. In *Blick* (1966) 50 Cr App R 280, a juror passed a note to the trial judge, indicating that he was possessed of local knowledge which tended to contradict an alibi offered by the accused. The judge permitted the prosecution to adduce evidence tending to disprove the alibi. The Court of Appeal upheld the judge's decision. There was no question of the juror substituting his knowledge for the evidence, because the prosecution adduced evidence on the issue of the alibi. All that happened was that the local knowledge of the juror, which would in any event have been put to good and proper use in the jury room, became known to the court. In *Ingram* v *Percival* [1969] 1 QB 548 (DC) it was held that justices had acted properly in making use of their local knowledge of tidal conditions. But in *Wetherall* v *Harrison* [1976] QB 773(DC) while holding that the Bench had been entitled to take into account the professional knowledge of one of their number in evaluating medical evidence called for the prosecution, and to draw on their own wartime experience of inoculations, the Divisional Court stressed that such knowledge might be drawn on only to evaluate evidence given, and not used as evidence in itself. So far as justices (and jurors) are concerned, the court accepted that they must be free to draw on such knowledge, if only because they are not trained judicially to exclude extraneous matters from their minds, but the rule is anyway one of common sense given that one has local benches and juries.

In a sense, this use of personal knowledge may be said to be a form of judicial notice, but it is obvious from the above observations that it is qualitatively very different from true judicial notice, and it is probably best regarded as one means open to the judge of testing the weight of the evidence before him. Certainly, both principle and authority would suggest that judicial notice cannot extend to facts which happen to be within the personal knowledge of each individual judge or magistrate. Fortuitous personal knowledge does not necessarily make a fact either notorious or readily demonstrable; to extend the rule in such a way would introduce a highly subjective element, which seems diametrically opposed to the objective principle inherent in judicial notice. This is not to say that a judge or magistrate can or should ignore his personal knowledge and experience, merely that there must be a judicial exercise of the mind to keep the available information in its proper place.[26]

---

[24] If a member of the tribunal of fact has such particular knowledge then he should be sworn and give evidence but play no further part judicially in the case: *R (Giants' Causeway etc. Tramway Co.)* v *Antrim Justices* [1895] 2 IR 603; cf. *Antrim Justices* [1901] 2 IR 133. See also 15.13.

[25] *Paul* v *DPP* (1989) 90 Cr App R 173; *Chesson* v *Jordan* [1981] Crim LR 333; but cf. *Reynolds* v *Llanelly Associated Tinplate Co. Ltd* [1948] 1 All ER 140 (trial judge wrong to make use of personal knowledge in evaluating prospects of a workman with certain skills and of certain age). Cf. *Mullen* v *Hackney London Borough Council* [1997] 1 WLR 1103 (a judge may properly apply factual knowledge gained in the course of earlier proceedings in the case before him).

[26] See *Paul* v *DPP* (1989) 90 Cr App R 173. Where a tribunal sits as a specialist body, for example an industrial tribunal, it may make much freer use of its expertise, and act on its own view: *Dugdale* v *Kraft Foods Ltd* [1976] 1 WLR 1288; but the rule appears to extend only to such specialist bodies carrying out a specialist statutory function.

C PRESUMPTIONS

SUMMARY OF MAIN POINTS

- A presumption is a rule of law which provides that on proof of fact A (the primary fact) fact B (the presumed fact) shall also be taken to be proved unless the presumption is rebutted. As to what is required to rebut a presumption, see 4.4.

- The most common presumptions are the presumption of legitimacy; the presumption of marriage; the presumption of death; and the presumption of regularity.

Presumptions have already been considered in relation to their effect on the burden of proof (see 4.4). We also saw at that time that, as in the case of judicial notice, American courts, while permitting the use of presumptions against the accused in a criminal case, do not permit the judge to instruct the jury that they must (as opposed to may) find proved the presumed fact on proof of the primary fact. We must now consider the detailed operation of presumptions in general, bearing in mind always the requirements for rebuttal which flow from the effect produced by the presumption upon the burden of proof. We shall also consider the more important individual presumptions to which these principles apply.

20.9 NATURE OF PRESUMPTIONS

A presumption is a rule of law by virtue of which, where a party proves one fact (the primary fact) a second fact (the presumed fact) will also be taken to have been proved, in the absence of evidence to the contrary. A party who adduces evidence sufficient to overcome the effect of the presumption is said to rebut the presumption. The theoretical basis for recognizing presumptions is that the presumed fact would, in the usual course of events, flow naturally from the existence of the primary fact, so that there is such a strong rational connection between the two that it is unnecessary to require evidence of the presumed fact in the absence of unusual circumstances. Where a presumption operates to establish the presumed fact, the judge will, in a civil case, find the presumed fact proved or, in a criminal case, direct the jury to find the presumed fact proved. No evidence is then required to establish the presumed fact. Where a presumption is of the 'persuasive' kind, the opponent may rebut the presumption only by disproving the presumed fact to the appropriate standard of proof. If it is of the 'evidential' kind, the opponent may rebut the presumption by introducing evidence against the presumed fact sufficient to amount to a *prima facie* case, whereupon the presumed fact will be decided according to the applicable rules as to the burden and standard of proof, as any other fact in the case.

It would be comforting to suppose that presumed facts have some common feature, but the recognized presumptions are in fact diverse, and beyond some form of rational connection between the primary and presumed facts (the cogency of which is also rather variable) no common feature of significance can be discerned. Indeed, presumptions have defied attempts at classification, and for present purposes, it will simply be accepted that the law recognizes a number of different presumptions which have distinct characteristics, and which therefore must be examined individually.

20.10 RULES IMPROPERLY DESCRIBED AS PRESUMPTIONS

As we have seen, a presumption requires two things: (a) that a certain primary fact shall be proved; and (b) that on proof of the primary fact, a presumed fact shall thereupon be taken to have been proved, in the absence of evidence to the contrary. If these requirements were universally insisted upon by the courts and by writers, there would be a great deal less confusion about presumptions than there in fact is. A rule of law that has the two requirements set forth above may properly be termed a true presumption. Unfortunately, the term 'presumption' is also frequently applied to rules of law which are in reality quite distinct from presumptions, and for the purpose of distinguishing these false presumptions, true presumptions are then unnecessarily referred to as 'rebuttable presumptions of law'. The three most commonly encountered false presumptions are as follows:

(a)   Rules of law which provide that some fact shall be taken in all cases to be true, without proof of any primary fact, until the contrary is proved. Into this category fall the 'presumptions' of innocence and sanity. These are really no more than expressions of the incidence of the burden of proof in such cases. In one sense, any fact may be said to be true unless somebody proves the contrary, but in reality, such facts fall to be proved in accordance with the normal rules of evidence, including the burden of proof; this is dealt with in Chapter 4.

(b)   Rules of law which preclude the assertion of some necessary fact, without which cases of a certain sort cannot be maintained. Such are the rules that a child under the age of 10 cannot be guilty of a criminal offence, and the former rule in criminal cases that a boy under 14 is incapable of sexual intercourse.[27] It is now almost universally agreed that such rules are rules of substantive law, and have nothing to do with the rules of evidence. Though sometimes termed 'irrebuttable' or 'conclusive' presumptions, they are clearly not presumptions at all. An irrebuttable presumption is a contradiction in terms.[28]

(c)   Inferences of fact, which a tribunal of fact may, but need not, draw, are sometimes known as 'presumptions of fact'. The phrase fully justifies Phipson's stricture that, 'in reality it is no more than a slightly grandiose term for the ordinary process of judicial reasoning about facts'.[29] The phrase expresses the relationship between certain kinds of frequently

---

[27] This rule was abolished by the Sexual Offences Act 1993, s. 1. In civil cases, there is no presumption that a boy under the age of 14 cannot have sexual intercourse, and such an issue will be decided on the whole of the evidence: see *L v K* [1985] Fam 144. The issue in this case was the ability to father a child, not to achieve penetration, which, as Ewbank J pointed out, may be unnecessary to conception because of the phenomenon of *fecundatio ab extra*. But it is submitted that the decision would plainly be correct in either case.

[28] Nonetheless, this terminology continues to be used. A good example is provided by ss. 75 and 76 of the Sexual Offences Act 2003. Section 75 of the Act creates an 'evidential presumption' that the complainant in the case of certain sexual offences did not consent to the conduct said to constitute the offence (and that the accused is not to be taken as reasonably believing that the complainant consented) if the act was committed in circumstances in which the complainant was subjected to violence, put in fear, asleep or unconscious, subject to disability, or stupefied or overpowered by the administration of any substance. In such a case, the accused must adduce sufficient evidence to raise the issue, in order to rebut the presumption. Section 76 creates a 'conclusive presumption' as to the same matters where he intentionally deceived the complainant as to the nature or purpose of the act he committed, or induced the complainant to consent by impersonating a person known to the complainant. In the case of s. 76, it is a rule of law that consent so obtained is no consent, and the accused cannot claim to have a reasonable belief in consent. It would be more precise if the Act simply said so.

[29] *Evidence*, 16th edn, para. 6–17. For a description of the role of inferences in judicial reasoning about facts, see 1.4.

encountered circumstantial evidence, and facts in issue or relevant facts in the case. Where an accused is found in possession of recently stolen goods, or is caught in the act of destroying some item of evidence, then obviously it is open to a jury to draw the inference that he knew or believed the goods to be stolen, or that the evidence was unfavourable to him, as the case may be. To speak of a presumption is unnecessary and misleading, because the jury are not in any circumstances bound to draw that inference, even if no evidence is called for the defence. Much of the difficulty arises from inexact usage, both judicial and extra-judicial. For example, the House of Lords in *DPP v Smith* [1961] AC 290 elevated into a principle of law, effectively into a true presumption, the fairly obvious proposition of common sense that a man apparently in normal control of his faculties should be taken to have intended the natural and probable consequences of his act. In the course of his speech, with which the other Lords agreed, Viscount Kilmuir went so far as to say that it did not matter whether one called it a presumption of law or of fact. By s. 8 of the Criminal Justice Act 1967, Parliament put the matter back where it belonged in the area of fact for the jury. The section is worth citing in full, because it expresses very well how such inferences operate:

> A court or jury, in determining whether a person has committed an offence—
> (a) shall not be bound in law to infer that he intended or foresaw a result of his actions by reason only of its being a natural and probable consequence of those actions; but
> (b) shall decide whether he did intend or foresee that result by reference to all the evidence, drawing such inferences from the evidence as appear proper in the circumstances.

Thus reduced into real terms, the misuse of the word 'presumption', lacking as it does any legal force in this context, is exposed. None of this makes it any less likely that a jury will act on such evidence in appropriate cases.

We shall now turn to the most important true presumptions. It is not proposed to consider the presumptions arising from possession of or title to land, testamentary presumptions, or the maxim *res ipsa loquitur*, for which reference should be made elsewhere in works dealing with the substantive law. The law relating to the statutory presumptions arising under s. 11 and s. 12 of the Civil Evidence Act 1968 and s. 74 of the Police and Criminal Evidence Act 1984 is dealt with at 12.6, 12.7 *et seq.* and that relating to certain presumptions about the due execution of documents at 19.16.

20.11 PRESUMPTION OF LEGITIMACY

It will be presumed that a child is the legitimate child of a husband and wife, and accordingly that access took place between them resulting in conception of the child, on proof of the following primary facts: (a) that the child was born to the wife; (b) that it was born during lawful wedlock or within the normal period of gestation after wedlock has ended; and (c) that the husband was alive at the date of conception.

This presumption is hedged about with historical considerations, principally the concern of the common law not to permit proceedings to bastardize children and so subject them to the once considerable stigma of illegitimacy. The presumption itself remains useful, although its force was weakened by the provision of s. 48(1) of the Matrimonial Causes Act 1973 that the evidence of a husband or wife is admissible in any proceedings to prove that intercourse did or did not take place between them during any period. Furthermore, both spouses are now compellable to give evidence of these matters: Civil Evidence Act 1968, s. 16(4); Police and Criminal Evidence Act 1984, s. 80(9). See 14.18.

Proof of the primary facts must be properly made. The mere fact of voluntary separation during the marriage[30] or the mere fact that divorce proceedings have been commenced or a decree nisi granted,[31] or even that at the time of the birth the mother has remarried following decree absolute[32] will not affect the operation of the presumption, if they are so proved. However, where the separation is by virtue of a court order, not only will the presumption cease to apply, but there will arise a contrary presumption of illegitimacy based on the assumed absence of sexual intercourse between husband and wife in such circumstances, though this presumption may be rebutted by evidence that sexual intercourse did in fact take place between them during the period of ordered separation: *Hetherington* v *Hetherington* (1887) 12 PD 112. Accordingly, where the child is born more than nine months after the making of the order for separation, the child will be presumed to be illegitimate.

At common law, there was originally a rule of law precluding proceedings to bastardize a child if, at the time of conception, the husband was 'within the four seas', so that lawful access could have taken place. This rule of law was abrogated, but left in its wake considerable uncertainty as to what evidence was required to rebut the presumption of legitimacy. Because of the once considerable stigma attaching to illegitimacy, there was some feeling that the presumption should be rebuttable only by evidence that proved illegitimacy beyond reasonable doubt, and despite the gradual erosion of rules which applied that standard to issues of status and conduct in family law cases generally, the position was left unresolved by the decisions of the House of Lords in *Preston-Jones* v *Preston-Jones* [1951] AC 391 and *Blyth* v *Blyth* [1966] AC 643. Eventually, the matter was resolved by statute, s. 26 of the Family Law Reform Act 1969, which provides that:

> Any presumption of law as to the legitimacy or illegitimacy of any person may in any civil proceedings be rebutted by evidence which shows that it is more probable than not that that person is illegitimate or legitimate, as the case may be, and it shall not be necessary to prove that fact beyond reasonable doubt in order to rebut the presumption.

The presumption is unlikely to arise in a criminal case, but it is submitted that, if this should occur, the standard of proof on rebuttal would vary according to whether the rebuttal was being attempted by the prosecution or the defence. Only in the former case would a standard beyond reasonable doubt be required.[33]

In civil cases, the section has laid to rest a number of older authorities which explored the kinds of evidence which might be admissible to rebut the presumption. Any relevant and admissible evidence, whether in the form of evidence of sexual intercourse between the wife and a man other than the husband, the impotence or absence of the husband at the time of conception, evidence derived from blood tests or any other such evidence, may be introduced. Furthermore, it has been held that even relatively slight evidence may be sufficient to rebut the presumption.

---

[30] *Ettenfield* v *Ettenfield* [1940] P 96.

[31] *Knowles* v *Knowles* [1962] P 161.

[32] *Maturin* v *Attorney-General* [1938] 2 All ER 214; *Re Overbury, Sheppard* v *Matthews* [1955] Ch 122.

[33] As to the meaning of 'more probable than not' in this section, see *Serio* v *Serio* (1983) 4 FLR 756; *W* v *K* (1987) 151 JP 589, which, however, must be read together with the speech of Lord Reid in *S* v *S* [1972] AC 24, 41, referred to in the text.

In *S* v *S* Lord Reid said, referring to s. 26:[34]

> That means that the presumption of legitimacy now merely determines the onus of proof. Once evidence has been led it must be weighed without using the presumption as a make-weight in the scale for legitimacy. So even weak evidence against legitimacy must prevail if there is not other evidence to counterbalance it. The presumption will only come in at that stage in the very rare case of the evidence being so evenly balanced that the court is unable to reach a decision on it. I cannot recollect ever having seen or heard of a case of any kind where the court could not reach a decision on the evidence before it.

It is submitted that this statement of the effect of s. 26 is not entirely satisfactory. The implication of Lord Reid's words is that the presumption is only evidential, so that when evidence sufficient to constitute a *prima facie* against the presumed fact is adduced, the presumption disappears, leaving the issue to be determined without it. Yet the section appears to call for disproof of the presumed fact to the usual standard of proof in a civil case, which is consistent with Parliament's intention that the presumption should be persuasive, even though disproof need not be made to the criminal standard of proof. This also seems to be the clear import of the observations of Lord Lloyd of Berwick, dissenting, in *Re H (Minors) (Sexual Abuse: Standard of Proof)* [1996] AC 563 (see 4.16), in the course of which he stated that the presumption can now be rebutted on the balance of probabilities. Although Lord Lloyd was dissenting, and was referring to s. 26, *obiter*, as an 'indirect pointer' as to the appropriate standard of proof on the different issue of the proof of allegations of child abuse for the purposes of the Children Act 1989, his remarks on the construction of s. 26 hardly seem controversial, and it is submitted that they are correct. Evidence which may be adduced for the purpose of rebutting the presumption may include evidence of the lack of relevant sexual intercourse between the spouses (*Banbury Peerage Case* (1811) 1 Sim & St 153); evidence of the husband's impotence (*Legge* v *Edmonds* (1855) 25 LJ Ch 125); an admission of paternity by a third party (*King's Lynn Justices, ex parte M* [1988] 2 FLR 79); and forensic evidence such as blood or DNA testing or a refusal to submit to such tests (*F* v *Child Support Agency* [1999] 2 FLR 244).[35]

20.12 PRESUMPTION OF MARRIAGE

It will be presumed that a man and woman are or were validly married on proof of either of the alternative primary facts: (a) that they went through a ceremony of marriage; or (b) that they have cohabited together. The presumption extends to include the necessary presumption of formal capacity to marry.

In *Piers* v *Piers* (1849) 2 HL Cas 331, where the marriage had been celebrated in a private house and there was no evidence that the necessary special licence had been obtained, the presumption was held nevertheless to apply. And where cohabitation is shown, the presumption is not rebutted merely because it is shown that such cohabitation preceded any ceremony between

---

[34] [1972] AC 24, 41. That the point made in the text about Lord Reid's speech in this case is not entirely academic is shown by the decision of Rees J in *T (H)* v *T (E)* [1971] 1 WLR 429, a case which demonstrates how critical questions of the presumption and the burden of proof can be in a close case.

[35] Given the almost conclusive nature of a properly conducted DNA test in the light of contemporary scientific advances, it has been suggested that the refusal to submit to such a test may now be enough in itself to outweigh the presumption: *Secretary of State for Work and Pensions* v *Jones* (2003) *The Times*, 13 August 2003; *sed quaere*.

the parties[36] or even by evidence that the marriage, if celebrated, took place under a system of law which required registration of it, and that no entry appeared in the relevant register.[37]

The effect is that the presumption is a strong one, although its importance has naturally declined somewhat in modern times with the advent of the more systematic keeping of records such as registers of marriage, the contents of which are admissible in evidence. The presumption may not be employed to prove the validity of an alleged existing marriage in a prosecution for bigamy; in such a case, the existing valid marriage must be proved by direct evidence that the accused was a party to a ceremony which resulted in a valid marriage, though apart from the identity of the accused, this may be proved by production of a certified copy of the entry in the relevant register.[38]

It is clear that strong evidence is needed to rebut the presumption. In *Piers* v *Piers*, Lord Cottenham LC, citing with approval words from older authority said:[39] 'The presumption of law is not lightly to be repelled. It is not to be broken in upon or shaken by a mere balance of probability. The evidence for the purpose of repelling it must be strong, distinct, satisfactory and conclusive.' The word 'conclusive' has been rightly criticized as begging the issue, but it is true that strong evidence is necessary. In *Mahadervan* v *Mahadervan* [1964] P 233, the Divisional Court held that the presumption might be rebutted only by evidence which satisfied the court beyond any reasonable doubt that the marriage was not a valid one, though today it might well be held that the ordinary civil standard of proof applies (see 4.16). The evidence must nonetheless be cogent. Evidence of incapacity[40] or of a valid prior marriage[41] will suffice, but not where the prior marriage is of doubtful validity.[42]

In *Mahadervan* v *Mahadervan*, it was argued that the presumption did not apply in favour of a foreign marriage, at least where such marriage, if proved, would invalidate an English one celebrated subsequently. Of this argument, Sir Jocelyn Simon P said ([1964] P 233, 247):

> To accept it would give expression to a legal chauvinism that has no place in any rational system of private international law. Our courts in my view apply exactly the same weight of presumption in favour of a foreign marriage as of an English one, and the nationality of any later marriage brought into question is quite immaterial.

20.13 PRESUMPTION OF DEATH

A person will be presumed to have died on proof of the following primary facts: (a) that there is no acceptable evidence that the subject has been alive at some time during a continuous period of seven years or more; (b) that there are persons likely to have heard of him, had he been alive, who have not heard of him during that period; and (c) that all due inquiries have been made with a view to locating the subject, without success.[43]

The existence of a person likely to have heard of the subject appears to be a necessary requirement, and was so treated by Sachs J in his judgment in the leading modern case of *Chard* v *Chard*

---

[36] *Hill* v *Hill* [1959] 1 WLR 127.

[37] *Re Taplin, Watson* v *Tate* [1937] 3 All ER 105.

[38] *Kay* (1887) 16 Cox CC 292; in *Shaw* (1943) 60 TLR 344, where evidence was given of a ceremony and the accused did not give evidence, the Court of Criminal Appeal held the evidence to be sufficient. The prior marriage may sometimes be proved by admission by the accused; but see 9.3.

[39] 2 HL Cas 331, 362, citing *Morris* v *Davis* (1837) 5 Cl & F 163, 265 per Lord Lyndhurst.

[40] *Tweney* v *Tweney* [1946] P 180.

[41] *Gatty* v *Attorney-General* [1951] P 444.

[42] *Taylor* v *Taylor* [1967] P 25.

[43] *Chard* v *Chard* [1956] P 259, per Sachs J at 272.

[1956] P 259. The learned judge refused to presume a wife to be dead, even though there was no evidence that she had been alive since 1918. The issue was whether she was alive in 1933 (when she would have been aged 43) in which year the husband had gone through a ceremony of marriage with the petitioner, who now sought a decree of nullity based on its bigamous character. The husband had spent most of the intervening period in prison, and there was no reason to suppose that he was likely to have heard of his first wife between 1918 and 1933. Since there was no person likely to have heard of the first wife during this time, Sachs J held that the presumption of death could not apply, and granted the decree. There is some authority for saying that the absence of a person likely to have heard may be remedied by the making of all reasonable inquiries,[44] but the better view seems to be that the two primary facts are separate, and that each is necessary. What amounts to the making of reasonable inquiries, and what amounts to the absence of acceptable evidence that the subject is alive during the period, are questions of fact in every case.

The presumption is only that the subject died at some time during the period; his death on any particular day will not be presumed, and must be proved by evidence if in issue. In *Re Phené's Trusts* (1870) LR 5 Ch App 139, the court, while prepared to presume that a nephew of the testator was dead in 1868, he having last been heard of as a deserter from the United States Navy in 1860, would not presume that he survived the testator, who had died in January 1861. Indeed, strictly, the presumption is only that the subject is dead at the date of trial, although in a number of decisions it appears to have been applied retrospectively. In *Chipchase v Chipchase* [1939] P 391 the wife married H1 in 1915, and having heard nothing of him after 1916 went through a ceremony of marriage with H2 in 1928. When the wife applied for a maintenance order against H2 in 1939, it was successfully objected that the 1928 marriage was not shown to be valid, there being no evidence that H1 was dead in that year. The Divisional Court remitted the case to the magistrates to consider whether there was any evidence to rebut the presumption of death, although strictly the presumption should have been only that H1 was dead at the date of the trial in 1939, and not in 1928. More significantly, the same more liberal view has been taken in cases of succession,[45] so as to permit the distribution of property along the lines dictated by a presumption that the testator died within a given period before the trial, and it may be said with some caution that this view is likely to be adopted in the future.

The period of seven years is, however, strictly insisted upon, and though the rule is essentially arbitrary, a period of six years and 364 days is not enough. Nor is there any presumption that the subject died from any particular cause, died childless or died celibate. These are all matters which must be proved by admissible evidence, including any circumstantial evidence from which they may be inferred.[46] It should be remembered that, leaving aside the presumption, it is always open to the court to infer death (or that someone is alive) as a question of fact, as it is to make any other proper inferences from the evidence.[47] Thus, if the primary facts required to trigger the presumption of death are not proved, the court is free to infer either death or continuing life from the available evidence as seems proper. But any factual inference that a person is alive must yield to the presumption of death where the primary facts required to trigger the presumption are proved.

---

[44] *Doe d France* v *Andrews* (1850) 15 QB 756, per Alderson B.

[45] *Re Aldersey, Gibson* v *Hall* [1905] 2 Ch 181; though a contrary view was taken in other cases, e.g., *Re Rhodes, Rhodes* v *Rhodes* (1887) 36 ChD 586.

[46] *Re Jackson, Jackson* v *Ward* [1907] 2 Ch 354.

[47] As in *Re Watkins, Watkins* v *Watkins* [1953] 1 WLR 1323, where despite the absence of inquiries, which precluded reliance on the presumption, the court inferred death from the circumstantial evidence, including a very long absence.

The following statutory provisions should be noted in connection with presumptions of death:

(a) By s. 184 of the Law of Property Act 1925, if *commorientes* die after 1925, and it is to be decided who died first, it shall be presumed that they died in order of seniority, and consequently that the younger was the survivor.[48] This rule does not apply to cases where A is proved to have died at a certain time, and B has not been heard of for seven years or more prior to A's death, when the presumption is that A survived B.

(b) By s. 19(3) of the Matrimonial Causes Act 1973, on a petition for presumption of death and dissolution of marriage:

> In any proceedings under this section the fact that for a period of seven years or more the other party to the marriage has been continually absent from the petitioner and the petitioner has no reason to believe that the other party has been living within that time shall be evidence that the other party is dead until the contrary is proved. For the purpose of assessing whether or not the petitioner has had reason to believe that the other party has been living, only events during the period of seven years are relevant.[49]

(c) By the proviso to s. 57 of the Offences against the Person Act 1861 (which defines the offence of bigamy):

> Provided, that nothing in this section contained shall extend to...any person marrying a second time whose husband or wife shall have been continually absent from such person for the space of seven years then last past, and shall not have been known by such person to be living within that time.

Despite sometimes inconsistent authority, it seems to have been established that the accused bears an evidential burden of raising by evidence the issue of absence for seven years, whereupon the prosecution must prove beyond reasonable doubt (in discharge of their legal burden of proof) that he did know the spouse to be living during that period of time.[50]

20.14 PRESUMPTION OF REGULARITY

The 'presumption of regularity', often expressed in the Latin tag, *Omnia praesumuntur rite et solemniter esse acta*, really embodies three separate presumptions, which may be described as follows:

20.14.1 Regularity of official acts

On proof of the primary fact that some official or public act has been performed or that a person acted in an official or public capacity, it is presumed that the act done complied with any necessary formalities, or that the person so acting was properly appointed for the purpose, as the case may be. This presumption applies to judicial acts in the sense that it is presumed that a person presiding over an inferior court or a tribunal, was validly appointed to do so.[51] It applies to a great

---

[48] The rule does not apply to all cases. See, in respect of spouses, one of whom dies intestate, the modification introduced by the Intestates' Estates Act 1952, s. 1(4). See also the Cestui que Vie Act 1666.

[49] *Thompson* v *Thompson* [1956] P 414, per Sachs J at 425.

[50] *Curgerwen* (1865) LR 1 CCR 1. It is submitted that this must now be the case in the light of the decision of the House of Lords in *Lambert* [2002] 2 AC 545; see 4.9.

[51] *Roberts* (1878) 14 Cox CC 101. But there is no presumption that the court or tribunal had jurisdiction in any particular matter: *Christopher Brown Ltd* v *Genossenschaft Oesterreichischer Waldbesitzer Holzwirtschaftsbetriebe Registrierte Genossenschaft mbH* [1954] 1 QB 8, per Devlin J at 13.

variety of other official acts, such as those performed by constables or justices of the peace,[52] and even to acts of divine service performed in a building, which were presumed to have been performed after due consecration.[53] In *R v Inland Revenue Commissioners, ex parte T.C. Coombs & Co.* [1991] 2 AC 283, it was held to be properly presumed that an inspector of taxes and a general commissioner of taxes had acted within their respective spheres of authority, and in good faith, in serving and approving a notice under the Taxes Management Act 1970, s. 20, requiring a firm of stockbrokers to deliver up information relevant to the tax liability of a former employee.

There has been some doubt whether or not the presumption of regularity can be used by the prosecution to establish an essential element of a criminal offence, if that element is disputed by the defence at trial.[54] In *Dillon* [1982] AC 484, the accused, a police officer, was charged in Jamaica with the offence of negligently permitting two prisoners, lawfully in his custody, to escape. The prosecution proved that the accused had permitted the escape of the prisoners, in circumstances from which negligence could be inferred, but adduced no evidence of any authority to hold the prisoners in custody, an issue on which the prosecution bore the burden of proof. The accused submitted to the trial magistrate that there was no case to answer. The magistrate held that the prosecution were entitled to rely on a presumption that such authority existed and rejected the submission. He then convicted the accused without making any factual finding as to the lawfulness of the custody. The Court of Appeal of Jamaica upheld the conviction. The Privy Council held that the accused had been wrongly convicted, because the prosecution were not entitled to rely on a presumption to establish facts central to an offence. Delivering the advice of the Privy Council, Lord Fraser of Tullybelton described this principle as 'well established'. It appears that the Privy Council was swayed in particular by the nature of the offence charged, including the fact that the prisoners themselves might have committed an offence by escaping, and if prosecuted for this offence, it would be wrong that they should be called upon to prove their innocence by proving that no lawful authority for their detention existed. A further consideration was the ease with which the prosecution could be expected to be able to prove the authority, compared with the difficulty the accused might encounter in trying to prove the opposite. But it is submitted that the principle is a sound one, and Lord Fraser did not suggest that its application was limited to any particular case.

There is authority that a party who contends that the presumption should not apply in a particular case must challenge the operation of the presumption by adducing at least some evidence to suggest that it may be rebutted successfully on the facts before the court.[55]

20.14.2 Mechanical devices

On proof of the primary fact that a mechanical instrument is usually in order and working correctly, it will be presumed that it was so working and in order when used on a relevant occasion. Automatic traffic signals are a good example[56] and numerous other devices, for example the speedometer of a police vehicle proved to have been recently checked for accuracy, are treated in the same way. However, there must be evidence of usually correct operation. As to the admissibility

---

[52] *Berryman v Wise* (1791) 4 TR 366; *Gordon* (1789) 1 Leach 515.
[53] *Cresswell* (1873) 1 QBD 446.
[54] *Scott v Baker* [1969] 1 QB 659.
[55] *Campbell v Wallsend Slipway & Engineering Co. Ltd* [1978] ICR 1015.
[56] *Tingle Jacobs & Co. v Kennedy* [1964] 1 WLR 638n; see also *Kelly Communications Ltd v DPP* (2003) 167 JP 73 (public weighbridge). So too with breath-test devices, chronometers, radar equipment, and many other instances.

of evidence of the results of a breath test in excess alcohol cases, where there is a question about the reliability of the testing device, see *Cracknell* v *Willis* [1988] AC 450; *Newton* v *Woods* [1987] RTR 41. See also 8.29.

20.14.3 Efficacy of transactions

On proof that necessary business transactions have been carried out, which require to be effected in a certain order, it will be presumed that they were effected in that order.[57]

20.15 CONFLICTING PRESUMPTIONS

Complex questions may arise when two conflicting presumptions act upon the same fact. Such problems arise principally in relation to the validity of successive marriages, on which may depend questions of legitimacy and of the power of the court to grant matrimonial relief. They also seem to arise in cases where it is uncertain whether a person is dead or alive. However, the conflict is usually illusory as a legal problem in these latter cases, because although the law recognizes certain presumptions of death, continuing life is merely an inference which the tribunal of fact may draw from the absence of evidence of death. The inference in favour of continuing life may or may not be able to be drawn, depending upon whether a presumption of death operates on the facts of the case, and if so, upon whether there is evidence to rebut that presumption.

In *Willshire* (1881) 6 QBD 366, the accused was convicted of bigamy, in that he had married W2 in 1868, during the lifetime of W1, to whom he had been married in 1864. In 1879, the accused married W3 and during W3's lifetime in 1880, married W4 and was again charged with bigamy. The accused's conviction was quashed because of the failure of the trial judge to leave to the jury the issue of whether W1 was alive at the time of the marriage to W3. If she was, then the marriage to W3 would have been invalid, and since the charge of bigamy in marrying W4 depended on proof that W3 was the accused's spouse at the time of the marriage to W4, the accused would have been entitled to a somewhat unmeritorious acquittal.

With the exception of Lord Coleridge CJ, all the members of the Court (Lindley, Hawkins, Lopes, and Bowen JJ) dealt with the issue presented as one simply of the burden of proof in a criminal case. Since the accused had raised the issue of whether W1 was still alive at the time of the marriage to W3, that issue should have been left to the jury and the prosecution had to rebut the accused's allegation beyond reasonable doubt. Lord Coleridge CJ, while dealing with the case as one concerned with the burden of proof, also suggested that the facts gave rise to conflicting presumptions, arising from the presumed validity of the marriages to W1 and W3 respectively. (Lord Coleridge CJ also thought that there was a presumption that W1 was still alive in 1879, because there was no evidence to show that she had died since 1864, but for the reasons stated above, this was actually no more than one possible inference from the facts. The jury could have inferred from the facts that W1 was alive in 1879, if the evidence appeared to warrant such an inference.) Lord Coleridge suggests that where there are conflicting presumptions, the presumptions cancel each other out, leaving the presumed facts to be decided on the whole of the evidence.

In criminal cases, this may be a convenient way of analysing the position, and because the prosecution will always bear the burden of proving the accused's guilt, little harm can result from it. However, in a civil case, cancellation out of conflicting presumptions may do no more than

---

[57] *Eaglehill Ltd* v *J Needham (Builders) Ltd* [1973] AC 992.

deny effect to one of the presumptions. In *Gatty* v *Attorney-General*[58] the petitioner in a legitimacy suit had been born in 1901. His parents had gone through a ceremony of marriage in 1897, after his father had obtained a decree of divorce in the State of North Dakota earlier in the same year. For various reasons of law, there was some doubt as to whether the North Dakota decree was valid. It was held that because of the presumption that the father's first marriage was valid, the petitioner must prove all the facts necessary to show that the North Dakota decree was valid. In such a case, to speak of conflicting presumptions as to the respective validity of the father's first and second marriages would tend to deny the effect of the first in time. Therefore, if there is no evidence tending to cast doubt on the validity of an earlier marriage or to show that the earlier marriage was terminated by death or dissolution, evidence of the earlier marriage should overcome the presumption of validity of the later.

In *Taylor* v *Taylor* [1965] 1 All ER 872, Cairns J had before him a case of great factual complexity. In essence, the petitioner sought a decree of divorce with respect to her marriage to the respondent, which was contracted in 1942. Whether this marriage was valid depended upon the validity of the petitioner's earlier marriage contracted in 1928. Cairns J found as a fact that there was no decisive evidence that the 1928 marriage was invalid, and that a doubtful earlier marriage was insufficient to overcome the presumption of validity of the later marriage. Although the learned judge expressed himself to be following *Gatty*, and rejecting an argument that the conflicting presumptions cancelled each other out, his decision effectively denied the potency of the presumption in favour of the earlier marriage. The petitioner bore the burden of proving the validity of the second marriage, which must have been invalid if the earlier marriage were both valid and undissolved. If the evidence failed to establish the status of the earlier marriage decisively, the presumption in favour of the earlier marriage should probably have been held to overcome the presumption in favour of the validity of the later marriage.

It is submitted that, at least in a civil case, the facts should be analysed to see whether the party who bears the burden of proof has overcome any presumption earlier in time to an apparently conflicting presumption on which that party intends to rely. While it may be possible to question his application of the principle to the complex facts before him, Cairns J was surely correct in *Taylor* in holding that where the conflicting presumptions relate to two different events (here, the two marriages) the validity of the former must be tested first, in which case no 'cancellation' is required, and the validity of the second will depend on the validity of the first. If a case can exist in which two presumptions conflict in relation to the same fact, it would seem that such presumptions must cancel each other out. However, excluding the case of an issue of whether a person is alive or dead (to which only one presumption can apply) it is difficult to envisage a case in which this would occur.

20.16 RECOMMENDED FURTHER READING

Borkowski, A., 'The presumption of marriage' [2002] *Child and Family Law Quarterly* 251.

Bridge, N., 'Presumptions and burdens' (1949) **12** *Modern Law Review* 273.

Denning, A.T., 'Presumptions and burdens' (1945) **61** *Law Quarterly Review* 379.

Duff, R.A., 'Strict Liability, Legal Presumptions, and the Presumption of Innocence' in A.P. Simester (ed.), *Appraising Strict Liability* (Oxford: Oxford University Press, 2005) 138–41.

Maher, G., 'Judicial notice and statute law' (2001) **117** *Law Quarterly Review* 71.

---

[58] [1951] P 444. See also *MacDarmaid* v *Attorney-General* [1950] P 218; *Russell* v *Attorney-General* [1949] P 391.

Nokes, G.D., 'The limits of judicial notice' (1958) **74** *Law Quarterly Review* 59.

Probert, R., 'When are we married? Void, non-existent and presumed marriages' (2002) **22** *Legal Studies* 398.

 20.17 QUESTIONS FOR DISCUSSION BASED ON *R v COKE; LITTLETON* AND *BLACKSTONE v COKE* (for case files go to the Online Resource Centre)

The following questions apply to both *Coke; Littleton* and *Blackstone* v *Coke*.

1. Prepare a list of facts which might properly be admitted formally for the purpose of the proceedings. Explain why those facts should be admitted.

2. What procedural steps should be taken to put the formal admissions before the court? What effect will the formal admissions have at trial?

3. Are there any matters which the judge may notice judicially? How should these matters be presented to the judge for this purpose, and what effect will the facts judicially noticed have at trial?

The following question applies only to *Blackstone* v *Coke*, but assume that the evidence in the earlier criminal case is also available for consideration.

4. Assume hypothetically that Parliament has passed the following statutory provision, which is applicable to these cases:

   Where the paternity of any child is disputed, and a male person over the age of fourteen years admits, orally or in writing or otherwise, that he had sexual intercourse with the mother of the child at or near the time of conception, such male person shall be presumed to be the father of the child unless he proves the contrary.

   Discuss the effect of this presumption on the issues to be resolved at the trial, having regard to the statements made both by Henry Coke and Anthony Henneky.

20.18 GENERAL QUESTIONS FOR DISCUSSION

1. What is the difference between a formal and an informal admission?

2. What is the purpose of making a formal admission?

3. Once a formal admission is made in civil proceedings will it become admissible in other civil proceedings?

4. If it was necessary, how would you seek to establish in court that it takes about an hour to drive from Wolverhampton to Birmingham?

5. A man has not been seen for seven years, can he be presumed to be dead?

6. If the man's spouse remarries, will she have a defence to bigamy?

7. A married couple appears to have died in a car crash simultaneously, which statutory presumption applies to give effect to their wills?

8. Oz is charged with driving without due care and it is alleged that, amongst other things, he drove through traffic lights on red. Must the prosecution prove that the traffic lights were in proper working order?

INDEX